I0890422

# Ellicott's COMMENTARY ON THE WHOLE BIBLE

A VERSE BY VERSE EXPLANATION

EDITED BY
CHARLES JOHN ELLICOTT

VOLUME VII

Acts — Galatians

WIPF & STOCK · Eugene, Oregon

Wipf and Stock Publishers
199 W 8th Ave, Suite 3
Eugene, OR 97401

Ellicott's Commentary on the Whole Bible Volume VII
Acts to Galatians
By Ellicott, Charles J.
ISBN 13: 978-1-4982-0142-1
Publication date 3/30/2015
Previously published by Cassell, 1897

This is a reprint of the 1959 Zondervan edition. Originally
published in 1897 by Cassell as A Bible Commentary for English Readers.

## The Acts of the Apostles

BY

THE VERY REV. E. H. PLUMPTRE, D.D

## The Epistle to the Romans

BY

THE REV. W. SANDAY, M.A., D.D.

## The First Epistle to the Corinthians

BY

THE REV. T. TEIGNMOUTH SHORE, M.A.

*Canon of Worcester and Chaplain-in-Ordinary to the King.*

## The Second Epistle to the Corinthians

BY

THE VERY REV. E. H. PLUMPTRE, D.D.

## The Epistle to the Galatians

BY

THE REV. W. SANDAY, M.A., D.D.

# CONTENTS

# THE ACTS OF THE APOSTLES

# INTRODUCTION

TO

# THE ACTS OF THE APOSTLES

I. **The Author.**—The opening words of the Acts, addressed, like the Gospel of St. Luke, to Theophilus, and referring to a former book, as containing a history of the life and teaching of the Lord Jesus, such as we find in that Gospel, are, at least, *primâ facie* evidence of identity of authorship. The internal evidence of style,* yet more, perhaps, that of character and tendency as shown in the contents of the book, confirm this conclusion. A tradition, going back to the second century, falls in with what has thus been inferred from the book itself. The words of Stephen, "Lay not this sin to their charge," are quoted in the Epistle of the Churches of Lyons and Vienne to those of Asia and Phrygia (A.D. 177), given by Eusebius (*Hist.* v. 2). Irenæus and Clement of Alexandria quote from it, the latter citing St. Paul's speech at Athens (*Strom.* v. 2); as also does Tertullian (*De Jejun.* c. 10). The Muratorian Fragment (see Vol. I., p. xiii.) dwells on its being largely the work of an eye-witness, as seen in its omission of the martyrdom of St. Peter, and St. Paul's journey to Spain. Eusebius (*Hist.* iii. 4) ascribes both books to him, in the same terms; and Jerome (*De Vir. Illust.* c. viii.) almost repeats the words of the Fragment: "Luke wrote his Gospel from what he had heard, but the Acts of the Apostles from what he saw." It will be enough, therefore, as far as the authorship of this book is concerned, to refer for all that is known or conjectured as to the writer to the *Introduction to St. Luke.* There also will be found all that it is necessary to say as to Theophilus as representing the first readers of the Acts.

II. **The Title.**—It does not follow that the present title was prefixed to the book by the writer himself. For him, probably, it would only present itself as the "second treatise," or "book," which came as a natural sequel to the first. It was not strange, however, especially when the books of the New Testament came to be collected together in a volume, and the "former treatise" took its place side by side with the other Gospels, and was thus parted from its companion, that a distinct title should be given to it. In the title itself the Greek MSS. present considerable variations—"Acts of the Apostles," "Acts of all the Apostles," "Acts of the Holy Apostles," sometimes with the addition of the author's name, "Written by Luke the Evangelist," "Written by the Holy and Illustrious Luke, Apostle and Evangelist." The word "Acts" seems to have been in common use in the first and second centuries after Christ for what we should call "Memoirs" or "Biographies," and appears conspicuously in the apocryphal literature of the New Testament, as in the Acts of Pilate, the Acts of Peter and Paul, of Philip, of Matthew, of Bartholomew.

* Not fewer than fifty words are common to the two books, and are not found elsewhere in the New Testament. Many of these are noticed in the Notes.

III. **The Scope of the Book.**—It is obvious that the title, whether by the author or by a transcriber, does but imperfectly describe its real nature. It is in no sense a history of the Apostles as a body. The names of the Eleven meet us but once (chap. i. 13). They are mentioned collectively in chaps. ii. 37, 42, 43; iv. 33—37; v. 2, 12, 18, 29; vi. 6; viii. 1, 14, 18; ix. 27; xi. 1; xv. 2, 4, 6, 22, 23, 33. St. John appears only in chap. iii. 1; iv. 13; viii. 14. Nothing is told us of the individual work of any other. Looking to the contents of the book, it would be better described, if we were to retain the present form at all, as the "Acts of Peter and of Paul," the former Apostle occupying a prominent place in chaps. i.—v., x.—xii., xv., the latter being the central figure in chaps. vii. 58, ix., xi. 25—30, xiii.—xxvii. From another point of view a yet more appropriate title would be (using the term in its familiar literary sense) that of the *Origines Ecclesiæ*—the history of the growth and development of the Church of Christ, and of the mission work of that Church among the Gentiles. The starting-point and the close of the book are in this respect significant. It begins at Jerusalem; it ends at Rome. When it opens, circumcision is required, as well as baptism, of every disciple; the Church of Christ is outwardly but a Jewish sect of some hundred and twenty persons (chap. i. 15). When it ends, every barrier between Jew and Gentile has been broken down, and the Church has become catholic and all-embracing. To trace the stages of that expansion both locally and as affecting the teaching of the Church is the dominant purpose of the book. The "acts" of those who were not concerned in it at all, or played but a subordinate part in it, are, we may venture to say, deliberately passed over. Some principle of selection is clearly involved in the structure of such a book as that now before us, and even without going beyond the four corners of the book itself, we may safely affirm that the main purpose of the writer was to inform a Gentile convert of Rome how the gospel had been brought to him, and how it had gained the width and freedom with which it was actually presented.

IV. **Its Relation to the Gospel of St. Luke.**—The view thus taken is strengthened by the fact that it presents the Acts of the Apostles as the natural sequel to the Gospel which we have seen sufficient reason to assign to the same writer. For there also, as it has been shown (Vol. I., p. 241), we trace the same principle of selection. It is more than any of the other three a Gospel for the Gentiles, bringing out the universality of the kingdom of God, recording parables and incidents which others had not recorded, because they bore witness that the love of God flowed out beyond the limits of the chosen people on robbers and harlots, on Samaritans and Gentiles. It remained for one who had led his catechumen convert to think thus of the Christ during His ministry on earth, to show that the unseen guidance given by the Christ in Heaven, through the working of the Holy Spirit, was leading it on in the same direction, that, though there had been expansion and development, there had been no interruption of continuity. I have ventured to say (Vol. I., p. 242) that the Gospel of St. Luke might be described as emphatically "the Gospel of the Saintly Life." The natural sequel to such a Gospel was a record of the work of the Holy Ghost, the Sanctifier. Looking to the prominence given to the work of the Spirit, from the Day of Pentecost onwards, as guiding both the Church collectively and its individual members, it would hardly be over-bold to say that the book might well be called "the Gospel of the Holy Spirit." At every stage His action is emphatically recognised. Jesus, after His resurrection, had, "through the Holy Ghost, given commandment to the Apostles whom He had chosen" (chap. i. 2). They are to be "baptised with the Holy Ghost" (chap. i. 5), are to "receive power after the Holy Ghost is come upon them" (chap. i. 8). The Holy Ghost had spoken through the mouth of David (chap. i. 16). Then comes the great wonder of the Day of Pentecost, when all the disciples were "filled with the Holy Ghost" (chap. ii. 4), and spake with tongues, and the prophecy, "I will pour out My Spirit upon all flesh" (chap. ii. 17), is quoted as on the verge of fulfilment. Jesus has "received from the Father the promise of the Holy Ghost" (chap. ii. 33). Once again all were "filled with the Holy Ghost, and spake the word with boldness" (chap. iv. 31). The sin of Ananias is a "lie unto the Holy Ghost" (chap. v. 3). He and his wife have "tempted the Spirit of the Lord" (chap. v. 9). The "Holy Ghost, whom God hath given to them that obey Him," is a witness that the Christ is exalted at the right hand of God (chap. v. 32). The seven who are chosen in chap. vi. are "full of the Holy Ghost, and of wisdom" (chap. vi. 3). Stephen is pre-eminently "full of faith and of the Holy Ghost" (chap. vi. 5). His leading charge against priests and scribes is that they "do always resist the Holy Ghost" (chap. vii. 51). His vision of the Son of Man standing at the right hand of God is closely connected with his being at the moment "filled with the Holy Ghost" (chap. vii. 55). Peter and John go down to Samaria that those who had been baptised by Philip "might receive the Holy Ghost" (chap. viii. 15—17): and the sin of Simon the sorcerer is that he thinks that that gift of God can be purchased with money (chap. viii. 18—20). It is the Spirit that impels Philip to join himself to the Ethiopian eunuch (chap. viii. 29), and carries him away after his baptism (chap. viii. 39). Ananias is to lay his hands on Saul of Tarsus, that he "may be filled with the Holy Ghost" (chap. ix. 17). The churches of Judæa and Galilee and Samaria in their interval of rest are "walking in the fear of the Lord and the comfort of the Holy Ghost" (chap. ix. 31). The admission of the Gentiles is attested when "the gift of the Holy Ghost" is poured out on Cornelius and his friends (chap. x. 44—47), and Peter dwells on that attestation in his address to the Church of Jerusalem (chaps. xi. 15—17; xv. 8). Barnabas, when he is sent to carry on that work among the Gentiles at Antioch, is described, as Stephen had been, as "full of the Holy Ghost and of faith" (chap. xi. 24). It is the Holy Ghost who "separates Barnabas and Saul for the work of the ministry," and they are sent forth by Him (chap. xiii. 2—4). Saul, roused to indignation by the subtlety of Elymas, is "filled with the Holy Ghost" (chap. xiii. 9). It is He who guides the decision of the council assembled at Jerusalem (chap. xv. 28), and directs the footsteps of Paul and his companions in their mission journey (chap. xvi. 6, 7). The twelve disciples at Ephesus, baptised before with the baptism of John, "receive the Holy Ghost" when Paul lays his hands on them (chap. xix. 6). He it was who witnessed in every city that bonds and imprisonment awaited the Apostle in Jerusalem (chaps. xx. 23; xxi. 11). It was the Holy Ghost who had made the elders of Ephesus overseers of the Church of God (chap. xx. 28). Well-nigh the last words of the book are those which "the Holy Ghost had spoken by Esaias," and which St. Paul, in the power of the same Spirit, applies to the Jews of his own time (chap. xxviii. 25).

V. **Its Relation to the Controversies of the Time.**—I have thought it right to go through this somewhat full induction because it presents an aspect of the book which has hardly been adequately recognised in the critical inquiries to which it has been subjected. But subject to this, as the dominant idea of the Acts of the Apostles, I see nothing to hinder us from recognising other tendencies and motives, partly as inferred from the book itself, partly as in themselves probable, looking to the circumstances under which it must have been written. An educated convert like Theophilus could hardly have been ignorant of the controversy between St. Paul and the Judaisers, which is so prominent in the Epistle to the Galatians and the Second Epistle to the Corinthians. He would know that the Judaising teachers in the Galatian Church had spoken of the Apostle as a time-server seeking to please men (Gal. i. 10); as having no authority but that which he derived from the Church of Jerusalem (Gal. i. 1, 12, 17, 22); that they used the name of James in support of their exaggerated rigour, and worked upon the mind even of Peter, so as to lead him to, at least, a temporary inconsistency (Gal. ii. 11—13); that others of the same school had appeared at Corinth, boasting of their "letters of commendation" (2 Cor. iii. 1); taunting the Apostle with his "bodily presence weak, and speech contemptible" (2 Cor. x. 10); speaking of him as a "fool" and madman (2 Cor. xi. 16); arrogating to themselves something like an ultra-apostolic authority (2 Cor. xi. 4); boasting that they were Hebrews and ministers of Christ (2 Cor. xi. 22). The language of Rom. xiv. shows that disputes analogous in their nature had sprung up at Rome even before St. Paul's arrival; differences as to days and meats (Rom. xiv. 2—6); connected with the very question of eating "things sacrificed to idols," which had given occasion to one of the canons of the Council of Jerusalem (chap. xv. 20, 29) proposed by James, the bishop of that Church, and which had been discussed fully in the Epistle which St. Paul addressed to the Church of Corinth, at a time when its numbers were largely made up of Roman Christians (1 Cor. viii.—x.). These facts were patent to any one who had any knowledge of St. Paul's work. If Theophilus were, as is probable, an Italian, probably even a Roman, convert (see *Introduction to St. Luke's Gospel*, Vol. I., p. 241), they would be forced upon his notice.

There are, however, other materials for estimating the attitude of the Judaising party towards St. Paul, and the language they habitually used in reference to him. I do not assume that the Pseudo-Clementine *Homilies*, *Recognitions*, and *Epistles* are of an earlier date than the second century, but it is a legitimate inference that they represent the traditions of the party from which they emanated, and they help us to fill up the outline which has been already sketched. In them, accordingly, we find James, the bishop of Jerusalem, as the centre of all church authority, the "lord and bishop of the holy Church" (*Epist. of Peter*, c. i.), the "archbishop" (*Recogn.* c. i. 73). Peter complains that "some among the Gentiles have rejected his preaching, which is according to the Law, and have followed the lawless and insane preaching of the man who is his enemy" (*ibid.* c. 2. Comp. Gal. iv. 16). He complains that he has been misrepresented as agreeing with that "enemy" (*ibid.*). James declares that circumcision is an essential condition of discipleship (*ibid.* c. 4). Under cover of the legendary disputes between Peter and Simon the Sorcerer, the personal discipleship of the former is contrasted with that of one who has only heard the doctrine of Jesus through a vision or a dream (*Hom. Clem.* xvii., c. 14. Comp. chaps. ix. 3, 17; xviii. 9; xxii. 18; xxiii. 11; 2 Cor. xii. 1), and it is suggested that one who trusts in those visions and revelations may have been deceived by a demon (*ibid.* xvii., c. 16). Barnabas is named with praise (*ibid.* i., c. 9), but the name of Paul is systematically ignored. The opposition to Peter at Antioch, of which we read in Gal. ii. 11—14, is represented as the work of the sorcerer (*Recogn.* x., c. 54). Almost the only direct reference to the Apostle of the Gentiles is an allusion to the "enemy" who had received a commission from Caiaphas to go to Damascus and make havoc of the faithful (*Recogn.* i., c. 71), and the fact that the "enemy" afterwards preached the faith which he had once destroyed is kept out of sight. With the strange confusion of chronology characteristic of this apocryphal literature, the "enemy" is represented as entering the Temple, disputing with James, attacking him with violence and throwing him down the Temple stairs, so that he lay there as dead (*Recogn.* i., c. 70).

Representations such as these might be met in two different ways. St. Paul, in the manly indignation of his spirit against such misrepresentations, met them, as in the Epistle to the Galatians, by asserting his entire independence of the Church at Jerusalem (Gal. i. 1—12), by showing that they had learnt from him, not he from them, the fulness and freedom of the gospel which he preached (Gal. ii. 2); that the chief leaders of that Church had given to him and Barnabas the right hand of fellowship in their work among the Gentiles (Gal. ii. 9); that he had not given way by subjection, no, not for an hour, to the Judaising Pharisee section of the Church (Gal. ii. 4, 5); that he had not shrunk from rebuking, with the general approval of the Church at Antioch, the inconsistency of Peter and of Barnabas (Gal. ii. 11—14). He meets them also, as in 2 Cor. xi. 13—27, by challenging a comparison between his own life and that of his antagonists. St. Luke thought it wise, in writing to a Gentile convert, to lay stress on the fact that the history of the Church of Jerusalem, truly stated, was against the policy and the claims of the Judaisers, that the Apostle of the Gentiles in his turn had shown every disposition to conciliate the feelings of the Jews. With this view, he records the fact that charges like those which were brought against St. Paul had been brought also against the martyr Stephen (chap. vi. 14); that the Apostle had been admitted into the Church of Christ by a disciple devout according to the Law (chaps. ix. 10; xxii. 12); that he had been received, after the first natural suspicion had been removed by the testimony of Barnabas, by the Apostles at Jerusalem (chap. ix. 27); that it had been given to Peter to be, perhaps, the first to act on the essential principle of St. Paul's gospel, and to throw open the doors of the Church to the uncircumcised Gentiles (chaps. x.; xi. 1—13); that he and the Church of Jerusalem had sent Barnabas to carry on that work at Antioch (chap. xi. 22); that St. Paul had always addressed himself to the Jews whenever there were any to listen to his preaching (chaps. xiii. 5, 14; xiv. 1; xvii. 2, 17; xviii. 4; xix. 8); that he had lost no opportunity of renewing his friendly intercourse with the Church of Jerusalem (chaps. xv. 2; xviii. 22; xxi. 15); and that James, the bishop of that Church, had throughout received him as a beloved brother (chap. xv. 4, 25, 26); that he had shown his willingness to conciliate the Jewish section of the Church by circumcising Timotheus (chap. xvi. 3), and by his taking on himself the vow of a Nazarite (chaps. xviii. 18; xxi. 26); and, lastly, that the Council of Jerusalem had solemnly formulated a *concordat* by which the freedom of the Gentiles was secured (chap. xv. 23—29).

A principle of selection such as this is naturally open to the charge that has been pressed by unfriendly critics, that it tends to lead the writer to exaggerate the harmony between the two parties whom it seeks to reconcile; and stress has been laid on the omission of the dispute between Paul and Peter at Antioch (Gal. ii. 14), as showing that with this view he slurred over what was an important fact in the history which he undertakes to write. It may fairly be urged, however, on the other side, that there is absolutely no evidence that he was acquainted with that fact. As far as we can gather from his narrative, he was not at Antioch at the time. It was an incident on which St. Paul would naturally be reticent, unless forced to allude to it, as in writing to the Galatians, in vindicating his own independence. And even if he did know it, was this passing, momentary difference of sufficient importance to find a place in a brief compendium of the history of St. Paul's work? Would the writer of a school history of England during the last fifty years feel bound, in tracing the action of the Conservative or Liberal party as a whole, to notice a single passage at arms, in which sharp words were spoken, in debate in cabinet or Parliament, between two of its leaders? Would a writer of English Church History during the same period think it an indispensable duty to record such a difference as that which showed itself between Bishop Thirlwall and Bishop Selwyn in the Pan-Anglican Conference of 1867? That he did not shrink from recording a personal dispute when important consequences were involved is shown by his treatment of the quarrel between Paul and Barnabas (chap. xv. 37—40).

**VI. Its Evidential Value.**—(1) *In relation to the Gospels.* Had the Acts of the Apostles presented itself as an entirely independent book, its evidence as to the main facts of the Gospel history would obviously have been of the highest value. It assumes those facts throughout as well known. The main work of the Apostles is to bear witness of the resurrection (chap. i. 32). Jesus of Nazareth had been "approved of God by miracles, and wonders, and signs" (chap. ii. 22). Against Him "Herod and Pontius Pilate had been gathered together" (chap. iv. 27). God had "anointed Him with the Holy Ghost and with power;" and He "went about doing good, and healing all that were oppressed of the devil, beginning from Galilee, after the baptism which John preached" (chap. x. 37, 38). It is obvious, however, that it does *not* present itself as independent. It looks back to a former book, and that former book is the Gospel according to St. Luke. "It was natural," it has been said, "that the writer should thus take for granted what he had thus himself recorded. You cannot, in such a case, cite the second volume to bear witness to the veracity of the first." Admitting this, however—as in all fairness it must be admitted—the Acts present evidence, as has been already pointed out (Vol. I., p. xxxi.), of another kind. If they are shown, by the numerous coincidences which they present with the writings of St. Paul (see *infra*), by their occasional use of the first personal pronoun (chaps. xvi. 10—15; xx. 5; xxi. 17; xxvii. 1; xxviii. 16), by their stopping at St. Paul's imprisonment at Rome, instead of going on to the close of his work and life, to be, on any fair estimate of circumstantial evidence, the work of a contemporary, and to have been written before St. Paul's death, in A.D. 65 or 66, then it follows that the Gospel from the pen of the same author must have been of even earlier date. The reference to the "many" who had "taken in hand" to set forth a narrative of the gospel (Luke i. 1) connects itself with the quotation from "the words of the Lord Jesus" in chap. xx. 35, as showing that there was not only a widely diffused oral tradition of the facts of the Gospel history (such as that implied in 1 Cor. xi. 23—25; xv. 3—7), but that there was also a fairly copious Gospel literature, presenting materials for future editors and compilers. But we may go yet further. It has often been urged, as against the early date of the Gospels in their present form, that they have left so few traces of themselves in the early history and the early writings of the Church. It has been already shown (Vol. I., pp. xxvii.—xxxi.) that, as far as the Epistles of the New Testament are concerned, those traces are far from few; but it may be admitted that they do not refer, as we might, perhaps, have expected them to refer, to any individual miracles, or parables, or discourses of our Lord. The same holds good of the Apostolic fathers; and it is not till we come to Justin Martyr that we get any such frequency of citation as to make it certain that he had one of our first three Gospels, or another resembling them, in his hands. (See Vol. I., p. xxvii.) Well, be it so; but here we have a work with the same absence of citation, the same vague generalisation in its reference to the outlines only of the Gospel history; and of this book, whatever view may be taken of its date, it is absolutely certain that the writer knew that history in all its fulness. Had the Acts come down to us without the Gospel of St. Luke, its reticence, and vagueness also, might have been urged as against the credibility of the narratives of the Gospels that bear the names of St. Matthew and St. Mark. As it is, it shows that that reticence and vagueness may be compatible with a full and intimate knowledge of the facts so narrated.

(2) *In relation to the Epistles of St. Paul.* Here, as Paley has well put the argument in the opening of his *Horæ Paulinæ*, the case is different. We have a book purporting to be by a contemporary of St. Paul's. We have thirteen or fourteen documents purporting to be Epistles from him. There is not the shadow of a trace in the Epistles that the writer had read the Acts, or even knew of the existence of the book. There is not the shadow of a trace in the Acts of the Apostles that the writer had read the Epistles, or even knew of their existence. He not only does not compile from them nor allude to them, but he does not even record, as might have been expected, the fact that they had been written. He omits facts which we find in them, and which would have been important as materials for his history. Whatever coincidences the two may present are conspicuously undesigned. So far as they do agree and throw light upon each other, they supply a reciprocal testimony each to the trustworthiness of the other.

The coincidences which thus present themselves are dealt with in the Notes in this Commentary on the Acts and the Epistles, and to state them with any fulness here would be to re-write the *Horæ Paulinæ* with numerous additions. It will, however, it is believed, be of some advantage to the student to have at least the more important of these coincidences brought under his notice in such a form as to admit of examination without turning to other books, and the following table has accordingly been drawn up with that view. It has been thought expedient to present them as they occur in the Epistles of St. Paul, and to take those Epistles in their chronological order.

| | | |
|---|---|---|
| 1 Thess. ii. 2; iii. 4 | St. Paul's sufferings at Philippi | Acts xvi. 22, 23. |
| ,, iii. 4 | ,, ,, ,, Thessalonica | ,, xvii. 5. |
| ,, ii. 18; iii. 1, 6, 7 | St. Paul left at Athens alone | ,, xvii. 16. |
| ,, ii. 14 | Sufferings of the Thessalonians from their own countrymen | ,, xvii. 5. |
| ,, i. 9 | Thessalonian converts turning from idols | ,, xvii. 4. |
| ,, ii. 9, 10; iv. 11 | St. Paul's precept and practice in working | ,, xviii. 3. |
| 1 Cor. ii. 1; iv. 19; xvi. 5 | St. Paul's two visits to Corinth | ,, xviii. 1; xx. 2. |
| ,, xv. 32 | Fighting with wild beasts at Ephesus | ,, xix. 29, 30. |
| ,, xvi. 19 | "Aquila and Priscilla salute you much in the Lord" | ,, xviii. 18, 26. |
| ,, xvi. 9 | The "effectual door" opened at Ephesus | ,, xix. 20, 26. |
| | The many adversaries | ,, xix. 9, 28. |
| ,, iv. 17—19 | Timotheus sent to Corinth from Ephesus | ,, xix. 21, 22. |
| ,, xvi. 10, 11 | St. Paul's doubt as to arrival of Timotheus | ,, xix. 22. |
| ,, i. 12; iii. 6 | Work of Apollos at Corinth | ,, xviii. 27, 28. |
| ,, iv. 11, 12 | St. Paul's working for his bread at Ephesus | ,, xx. 34. |
| ,, ix. 20 | ,, becoming to Jews as a Jew | ,, xvi. 3; xviii. 18; xxi. 23—26. |
| ,, i. 14—17 | Baptism of Crispus and Gaius | ,, xviii. 8. |
| ,, xvi. 1 | Collection for the saints in Galatia | ,, xviii. 23. |
| ,, v. 7, 8 | Allusion to the Passover | ,, xix. 22; xx. 3. |
| ,, xvi. 8 | "Tarrying at Ephesus till Pentecost" | (bracketed with above) |

| | | |
|---|---|---|
| 1 Cor. i. 1 | Sosthenes with St. Paul | Acts xviii. 12—17. |
| „ xvi. 6 | St. Paul's wintering at Corinth | „ xx. 3, 6. |
| „ xvi. 5 | „ journey through Macedonia | „ xx. 1. |
| 2 Cor. i. 16; ii. 13 | „ „ „ „ | „ xx. 1. |
| „ xi. 32, 33 | „ escape from Damascus | „ ix. 23—25. |
| „ i. 8 | The trouble that came on him in Asia | „ xix. 29, 30. |
| „ xi. 9 | Supplies from the brethren from Macedonia | „ xviii. 1, 5. |
| „ i. 19 | Silvanus and Timotheus as St. Paul's fellow-workers at Corinth | „ xviii. 5. |
| „ xi. 25 | "Once was I stoned" | „ xiv. 19. |
| „ iii. 1 | Letters of commendation | „ xviii. 27. |
| „ x. 14—16 | Corinth as then the limit of St. Paul's labours | „ xviii. 18. |
| Gal. i. 17, 18 | His visit to St. Peter and James the Lord's brother, after his conversion | „ ix. 28. |
| „ ii. 1 | The journey with Barnabas to Jerusalem | „ xv. 2. |
| „ ii. 13 | Barnabas with St. Paul at Antioch | „ xv. 35—37. |
| „ v. 11 | Persecutions from the Jews | „ xiii. 49; xiv. 1—19; xvii. 4—13; xviii. 12. |
| „ i. 18 | The shortness of the first visit to Jerusalem | „ xxii. 18. |
| „ ii. 9 | The authority of James, the brother of the Lord | „ xii. 17; xv. 13; xxi. 18. |
| Rom. xv. 25, 26 | St. Paul's journey to Jerusalem | „ xx. 6; xxiv. 17. |
| „ xvi. 21—23 | Salutations from Sosipater, Timotheus, and Gaius | „ xx. 4. |
| „ xvi. 3 | Aquila and Priscilla at Corinth and Rome | „ xviii. 2. |
| „ xvi. 27 | Phœbe of Cenchreæ | „ xviii. 18. |
| „ i. 13; xv. 23 | St. Paul's desire to visit Rome | „ xix. 21. |
| „ xv. 19 | The gospel preached in Illyricum | „ xx. 2. |
| „ xv. 30 | Apprehension of coming danger | „ xx. 22, 23. |
| Phil. ii. 19 | Timotheus known to the Philippians | „ xvi. 4; xvii. 14. |
| „ i. 29, 30; ii. 1, 2 | St. Paul's sufferings at Philippi | „ xvi. 22. |
| „ iv. 2, 3 | Euodia, Syntyche, and the other women at Philippi | „ xvi. 13. |
| Eph. vi. 21 | Tychicus as known to the Ephesians | „ xx. 4. |
| „ vi. 19, 20 | St. Paul as an ambassador in a chain | „ xxviii. 16—20. |
| Col. iv. 10 | Mark as sister's son (better, *cousin*) to Barnabas | „ xv. 37—40; xii. 12. |
| | Aristarchus, St. Paul's fellow-prisoner | „ xix. 29; xxvii. 2. |
| 1 Tim. v. 9 | Provision for the maintenance of widows | „ vi. 1. |
| „ i. 13—16 | The persecutor converted | „ viii. 3; ix. 1—10. |
| „ i. 6, 7; iv. 1—4 | State of the Church at Ephesus | „ xx. 29, 30. |
| Titus iii. 13 | Apollos in Crete | „ xviii. 24. |
| 2 Tim. i. 16 | Onesiphorus and St. Paul's chain | „ xxviii. 20. |
| „ iv. 20 | Trophimus left at Miletus | „ xx. 4. |
| „ i. 4, 5 | The mother of Timotheus | „ xvi. 1. |
| „ iii. 15 | His education in the Holy Scriptures | „ xvi. 2. |
| „ iii. 10, 11 | Persecutions at Antioch, Iconium, Lystra | „ xiii., xiv. |
| „ iv. 11 | Mark profitable in ministering | „ xiii. 5. |
| „ iv. 14 | Alexander the coppersmith | „ xix. 33. |

It ought to be stated that the comparison of the Acts and the Pauline Epistles brings to light also some real or apparent difficulties. Of these the most conspicuous are:—

(1) The omission in chap. ix. 19—23 of the journey to Arabia mentioned in Gal. i. 17.

(2) The omission in Gal. ii. 1—10 of any notice of the journey to Jerusalem in chap. xi. 30, or of the decrees of the council of Apostles and elders in chap. xv.

(3) The omission in the Acts of any record of the dispute between St. Peter and St. Paul at Antioch (Gal. ii. 11).

These are examined in detail in the Notes on the several passages connected with them.

This method of inquiry may be extended, with similar results, to the Epistle to the Hebrews, and to the two Epistles of St. Peter. It is in the account of Apollos, in chap. xviii. 24—28, that we get what many critics since Luther's time have looked upon as the only satisfactory explanation of the phenomena presented by the first of these Epistles. Assuming the authorship of Apollos as at least a probable hypothesis, the spiritual condition described in Heb. v. 11, vi. 2, as that of some of those who had been under the teaching of the writer, may be compared with that of the twelve disciples at Ephesus who knew only the baptism of John (chap. xix. 1—7). In the reference to the "saints of Italy" in Heb. xiii. 24—apparently as distinct from Roman Christians—we may, perhaps, see a reference to the Church of Puteoli, the only Italian town, besides Rome, mentioned in the Acts as containing "brethren" (chap. xxviii. 14).

I note, further, a few coincidences of some interest between the Acts of the Apostles and the Epistles of St. Peter:—

| | | |
|---|---|---|
| 1 Pet. i. 11 | The tone in which prophecy is spoken of, as compared with | Acts ii. 16, 17, 30, 31. |
| „ i. 17 | God no respecter of persons | „ x. 34. |
| „ i. 22 | Purity by faith and obedience | „ xv. 9. |
| „ ii. 7 | The stone which the builders rejected | „ iv. 11. |

| | | |
|---|---|---|
| 1 Pet. iv. 16 | The name of Christian | Acts xi. 26; xxvi. 28. |
| „ v. 12 | Mention of Silvanus as accounting for St. Peter's knowledge of St. Paul's Epistles (2 Pet. iii. 15) | „ xv. 32, 40. |
| „ v. 13 | "Marcus my son" | „ xii. 12. |

(3) *In relation to External History.*—It is obvious that the Acts of the Apostles take a wider range, both in space and time, than any other narrative book of the New Testament. They cover a period of more than thirty years. The scene is shifted from Jerusalem to Samaria, Cæsarea, Damascus, Antioch, Cyprus, Asia Minor, Greece, and finally ends in Italy. The writer is constantly brought across some of the events of contemporary history, and the scenes which earlier or later travellers have described. Does he show himself in these respects an accurate observer, faithful in his reports, correct in his language? Does he fall into the blunders which would be natural in a man writing a fictitious narrative a century or so after the events which he professes to relate? For a full answer to these questions the reader is referred to the Notes that follow; but it may be well to indicate briefly some of the more important of these points of contact with the contemporary history of the outer world.

| | |
|---|---|
| Acts v. 37. | Judas of Galilee. |
| Acts vi. 9. | The synagogue of the Libertines. |
| Acts viii. 9. | Simon the sorcerer. |
| Acts viii. 27. | Candace, queen of the Ethiopians. |
| Acts ix. 36. | Dorcas. |
| Acts x. 1. | The centurion of the Italian band. |
| Acts xi. 26. | The name of Christian at Antioch. |
| Acts xi. 28. | The famine under Claudius. |
| Acts xii. 23. | Death of Herod Agrippa I. |
| Acts xiii. 7. | Sergius Paulus of Cyprus. |
| Acts xiv. 11. | Paul and Barnabas taken for Zeus and Hermes. |
| Acts xvi. 12. | Philippi a *colonia*. |
| Acts xvi. 14. | The purple-seller of Thyatira. |
| Acts xvi. 16. | The damsel with a Python spirit. |
| Acts xvi. 22. | The *strategi* of Philippi. |
| Acts xvi. 37. | St. Paul's Roman citizenship. |
| Acts xvii. 6. | The *politarchs* of Thessalonica. |
| Acts xvii. 19. | The court of the Areopagus. |
| Acts xvii. 21. | Character of the Athenians. |
| Acts xvii. 28. | Quotation from Aratus. |
| Acts xviii. 2. | Jews banished from Rome by Claudius. |
| Acts xviii. 12. | Gallio pro-consul of Achaia. |
| Acts xix. 9. | The school of Tyrannus. |
| Acts. xix. 24. | The silver shrines of Artemis. |
| Acts xix. 27—29. | The temple and theatre at Ephesus. |
| Acts xix. 31—35. | The Asiarchs and town-clerk of Ephesus. |
| Acts xix. 38, 39. | The pro-consuls and the lawful assembly. |
| Acts xxi. 38. | The Egyptian rebel. |
| Acts xxii. 28. | St. Paul's Roman citizenship. |
| Acts xxiii. 2. | The high priest Ananias. |
| Acts xxiii. 24. | Felix the governor. |
| Acts xxiv. 24. | Drusilla. |
| Acts xxiv. 27. | Porcius Festus. |
| Acts xxv. 13. | Agrippa and Bernice. |
| Acts xxv. 11. | Appeal to Cæsar. |
| Acts xxvii. | The details of the narrative throughout. |
| Acts xxviii. 7. | The "chief man" of Melita. |
| Acts xxviii. 15. | Appii Forum and the Three Taverns. |

Under this head also it is right to notice that which appears to make against, rather than for, the credibility of the narrative, and I accordingly name the chronological difficulty connected with the name of Theudas in Gamaliel's speech (chap. v. 36).

(4) *Internal Evidence of Credibility.*—The internal consistency of any book is not necessarily evidence of more than the skill of the writer. Every writer of fiction aims more or less at producing the impression of verisimilitude by touches that have the effect of coincidences between one part of the narrative and another; and the art that conceals art will produce, according to the skill of the author, the impression that the coincidences are undesigned. On the other hand, we feel, as we read some stories, that they contain, in the naturalness of their style, the absence of any sensational dove-tailing of incidents, *primâ facie* testimony to their own veracity. And it is submitted to the reader whether instances such as the following may not fairly claim consideration, as coming under the latter category rather than the former.

(1) Hostility of the high priests, as Sadducees, to the preaching of the resurrection (chaps. iv. 1, 2; v. 17).

(2) Barnabas of Cyprus going twice to his own country (chaps. iv. 36; xiii. 4; xv. 39).

(3) The complaints of the Hellenistæ (Grecians), leading to the election of seven men with Greek names (chap. vi. 1—5).

(4) The Cilicians disputing with Stephen (chap. vi. 9). The young man named Saul (chap. vii. 58); afterwards described as of Tarsus (chap. ix. 11).

(5) Philip's arrival at Cæsarea (chap. viii. 40). No further mention of him till we find him again at Cæsarea (chap. xxi. 8).

(6) Mark's return to Jerusalem (chap. xiii. 13) explained by his mother's being there (chap. xii. 12) and the pressure of the famine (chap. xi. 28).

(7) Agabus prophesying the famine (chap. xi. 28); again appearing in the character of a prophet sixteen years later (chap. xxi. 10).

(8) The speech of Lycaonia as accounting for the surprise of Paul and Barnabas at the preparations for sacrifice (chap. xiv. 11—14).

(9) Conversion of Samaritans (chap. viii. 14). Incidental mention of the brethren in Samaria (chap. xv. 3).

(10) Men of Cyprus and Cyrene found the Church at Antioch (chap. xi. 20). Barnabas of Cyprus sent to carry on the work (chap. xi. 22). Lucius of Cyrene among the prophets of the Church (chap. xiii. 1).

(11) Philippi a *colonia* (chap. xvi. 12). Philippians speak of themselves as Romans (chap. xvi. 21).

(12) Trophimus the Ephesian (chap. xxi. 29) recognised by Jews of Asia, *i.e.*, from Ephesus and its neighbourhood.

The list might, it is believed, be easily enlarged, but these will be sufficient to put the student on the track of a method which he can apply almost indefinitely in other instances for himself.*

* It lies on the surface that I am largely indebted in this part of my work to Paley's *Horæ Paulinæ*. I wish also to acknowledge my obligation to Mr. Birks's *Horæ Apostolicæ*.

**VII. Sources of the History.**—It will be assumed here that the use of the first person in parts of the history implies that the writer was then the companion of the Apostle whose labours he records. We have seen, in the *Introduction to St. Luke,* how far the facts that are thus implied brought the writer into contact with persons who could give him trustworthy information as to what he relates in his Gospel; it remains to be seen how far they point to the probable sources of his knowledge as to the events recorded in the Acts.

Acts i.—v. Philip the Evangelist (chap. xxi. 8—10), or Mnason of Cyprus (chap. xxi. 16), or others—and, in particular, the "women" of Luke viii. 2—at Jerusalem.

Acts vi., vii. Philip or St. Paul.

Acts viii. Philip.

Acts ix. St. Paul.

Acts x.—xi. 18. Philip.

Acts xi. 19—30. St. Paul, or, probably, personal knowledge gained at Antioch.

Acts xii. 1—19. John surnamed Mark (Col. iv. 10—14).

Acts xiii. 1—13. St. Paul, or Mark, or Mnason of Cyprus.

Acts xiii. 14—52; xiv. St. Paul; or, possibly, knowledge gained by Luke in person on his journey to Troas, or afterwards from Timotheus.

Acts xv., xvi. 1—7. St. Paul, or, probably, personal knowledge, as staying at Antioch, and, possibly, going up to Jerusalem.

Acts xvi. 8—40. Personal knowledge.

Acts xvii., xviii. Probable communications from the brethren who came from Philippi to Thessalonica (Phil. iv. 16), and again to Corinth (2 Cor. xi. 9). General intercourse between the Romans of Philippi and the Roman Jews at Corinth.

Acts xix. St. Paul; or possibly Aristarchus and Gaius of Macedonia, or Tyrannus.

Acts xx.—xxviii. Personal knowledge.

Looking to the manner in which the Gospel begins with what has the character of a distinct document, so strongly marked by Hebraisms that it could scarcely have been written by a Greek writer, it is probable that the first five chapters of the Acts may, in like manner, have been incorporated from an earlier document, recording, like the later history of Hegesippus, the history of the Church of Jerusalem with a special fulness. It will, at any rate, be clear that at every step in the narrative we are able, in the Acts, as in the Gospel of the same writer, to point with a very high degree of probability to those who here also were "eye-witnesses and ministers of the Word" (Luke i. 2).

**VIII. Its Bearing on the Mission-work, Organisation, and Worship of the Church.**—(1) *Mission-work.* It will not, it is believed, be unprofitable to look at the records of the Acts of the Apostles as presenting the type and pattern for all future labours in the work of evangelising the world. It is obvious that the preaching of the Apostles is something very different from that of those who offer to men's acceptance simply a lofty ideal of virtue or high-toned ethical precepts. The central fact of all their teaching is the resurrection of Christ (chaps. ii. 32, 33; iv. 10; x. 40, 41; xiii. 32—37; xvii. 31; xxvi. 23). Upon that proclamation of a fact in the past they build their assurance that He will come again as the Judge of the living and the dead (chaps. iii. 21; x. 42; xvii. 31); that in the meantime He calls men to repent and believe in Him (chaps. ii. 38; v. 31; x. 43; xiii. 38, 39; xiv. 15; xvii. 30, 31); and that thus they may receive remission of their sins and the gift of the Holy Ghost (chaps. ii. 38; viii. 15; x. 45; xix. 2). They are naturally brought into contact, as they preach this gospel, with men of very different habits of thought, varying in their training, their knowledge, and their culture; and they adapt themselves, as far as lies in their power, to all these variations in their hearers. With the Jews of Jerusalem, Antioch in Pisidia, Corinth, and Rome, they draw their arguments almost exclusively from the correspondence between the acts and death and resurrection of Jesus with what had been written in the Law and Prophets as pointing to the coming Christ (chaps. ii. 14—36; iii. 19—26; vii. 2—53; xiii. 17—41; xxviii. 23). With peasants, such as those at Lystra, they lay their foundation on what we should call the broad lines of a simple natural theology, and appeal to the goodness of God as manifested in the order of nature, in rain from heaven and fruitful seasons (chap. xiv. 15—17). With the Stoics and Epicureans of Athens, St. Paul (he alone, it may be, of the glorious company of the Apostles was fitted for that work) rises to the level of the occasion, and meets the thinkers on their own grounds, appeals to the witness of their own poets, and sets before them what we have ventured to call the outlines of a philosophy at once of worship and of human history (chap. xvii. 22—31).

And it may be noted how carefully in all these cases the preachers abstain from the weapons of terror and of ridicule which men have sometimes used in dealing with the heathen whom they were seeking to convert. There are no statements that the world outside the range of the gospel was sentenced to hopeless condemnation—that the forefathers of those to whom they preached were for ever in the dark prison of Gehenna. They recognised, on the contrary, that in every nation he that feareth God and worketh righteousness is accepted with Him. (See Note on chap. x. 35). They speak of the times of ignorance which God "winked at" (chap. xvii. 30). They are no "blasphemers" even of the worship which they are seeking to supplant (chap. xix. 37). They present the gospel to men's minds as realising at once the conscious prophecies of Israel and the unconscious prophecies of heathenism. They come, it is true, with some weapons in which modern missionaries are wanting. They claim to work signs and wonders as attestations of their divine mission (chaps. iii. 6, 7; v. 15; vi. 8; viii. 13; ix. 34—40; xiv. 10; xix. 12; xxviii. 5—8); but they lay far less stress on these than on the "demonstration of the Spirit"—the prophecy that reveals the secrets of the heart, the conscious experience of the power of that Spirit to give a new peace and a new purity to souls that had been alienated from the life of God through the ignorance that was in them (chaps. ii. 38, 39; xi. 17, 18; Rom. viii. 23—26; 1 Cor. ii. 4).

(2) *Organisation and Worship.* And, it may be noted further, they do not rest satisfied with the conversion of individuals as such, nor with leaving with each believer a book or a rule of life for his own personal guidance. Everywhere they seek to organise a society: the "brethren," the "disciples," the "saints," are formed into a church—*i.e.*, an *ecclesia*, or congregation; and that society receives a distinct and definite constitution. Elders, otherwise known as bishops (chap. xx. 28; Phil. i. 1; Tit. i. 5, 7), are appointed in every city (chaps. xi. 30; xiv. 23; xx. 17), to teach, and preside in

worship, and administer the discipline and laws of the congregation. There are ministers or deacons under them, who assist in baptising, in the subordinate offices of worship, in the relief of the sick and poor, and, if they have special gifts, in preaching the gospel to Jews and heathen, and teaching converts also (chap. vi. 3—6; Phil. i. 1; 1 Tim. iii. 8). The Apostles appoint both elders and deacons, with the consent—and therefore the implied right of veto—of the congregation, and exercise over them an authority analogous to that of the later bishops (chaps. xiv. 23; xx. 17). There is an organisation of the charity of the Church on the basis of systematic almsgiving; and the Apostles, and, in their absence, the bishop-elders of the Church, act, where necessary, with the help of others as representing the laity of the Church, as treasurers and almoners (chaps. iv. 37; v. 2). The disciples meet to break bread, as their Lord had commanded, on the evening of every day; afterwards, as the Church included men of various classes and employments, on that of the first day of the week—probably, *i.e.*, on Saturday evening (chaps. ii. 46; xx. 7); and the history of the institution of what came to be known as the Supper of the Lord formed the centre of the celebration of that feast (1 Cor. xi. 23—26). The feast itself was preceded by a solemn blessing, and closed with a solemn thanksgiving. Psalms, hymns, and unpremeditated bursts of praise, chanted in the power of the Spirit, such as those of the gift of tongues, were the chief elements of the service (chap. iv. 24—30; Eph. v. 19; Col. iii. 16). The right of utterance was not denied to any man (women even seem at first to have been admitted to the same right; chap. xxi. 9; 1 Cor. xi. 5) who possessed the necessary gifts (1 Cor. xiv. 26—33) and was ready to submit them to the control of the presiding elder or Apostle. There were in the unwritten traditions of the Church; in its oral teaching as to our Lord's life and teaching (1 Cor. xi. 23; xv. 1—8); as in its rules of discipline and worship (2 Thess. ii. 15; iii. 6); in the "faithful sayings" which were received as axioms of its faith (1 Tim. i. 15; iv. 9; 2 Tim. ii. 11; Tit. iii. 8), the germs at once of the creeds, the canons, the liturgies, the systematic theology of the future. It is, lastly, instructive and suggestive to note that throughout the history there is no record of any effort to set apart a separate place of worship for the members of the new society. They meet in private houses (chaps. ii. 46; xx. 8; Rom. xvi. 5, 15, 23; 1 Cor. xvi. 19), or in a hired class-room (chap. xix. 9), as opportunities present themselves. There would apparently have been no difficulty in their claiming the privilege which Roman rulers conceded freely to other Jews and proselytes, of erecting a synagogue of their own; but they left this to come in due course afterwards. Their own work was of a different and higher kind. They were anxious rather to found and edify the society which, as built of "living stones," was to be the temple of the living God, than, in the modern sense of the term, to be the builders of churches.

**IX. Its Bearing on the Church History of the Future.**—Nor is the record which we owe to St. Luke less instructive considered as the first volume of the history of Christendom. Fairly considered, while it brings before us the picture of primitive Christianity as a pattern to be followed in its essential features, it is as far as possible from presenting it as a golden age of unalloyed and unapproachable perfection. It tells us of men who were of like passions with ourselves, not free from the bitterness of personal quarrels (chap. xv. 39), or from controversies in which party was arrayed against party on a question on which each held that it was contending for a vital truth (chap. xv. 1—5). It records, as if with an unconscious prevision of future controversies, how that dispute ended in an amicable compromise, each party making concessions, within certain well-defined limits, to its opponents, neither insisting on what an inexorable logic might have looked on as the necessary conclusion from its premisses (chap. xv. 23—30). The writer tends, partly by his natural instincts, partly of deliberate purpose, to dwell on the points of agreement between men rather than on their points of difference; to bring out the good which was to be found in men of different degrees of culture and very varied training. Peter, James, Apollos, Paul, are not for him what they were for so many others—leaders of parties, rivals for allegiance. He is able to recognise in each and all men who are ministers of Christ, fitted for the work of that ministry by the gift of the Holy Ghost. And in striking contrast to the martyrologists and other annalists of the Church who followed him, he avoids what we may call the sensational element of history; does not dwell (with the one marked exception of St. Stephen) on the deaths and sufferings of the disciples; understates the work, the hardships, and the perils of the Apostle who is the chief figure in his history; aims rather at presenting the results of the actual contest between the new and the old societies, now favourable and now quite otherwise, than at representing the two as in irreconcilable enmity. There is, so to speak, a hopefulness and healthiness of tone, which contrasts favourably with that of later writers after the sword of systematic persecution had been unsheathed, or even in some measure with that of the later writings of the New Testament, such as the Epistles of St. Peter and the Apocalypse, and which may fairly be allowed some weight as evidence for the early date of its composition.

## CHRONOLOGICAL TABLE OF APOSTOLIC HISTORY.

It will, it is believed, be helpful to the reader to have before him something like a general survey of the history of the Apostolic Age, indicating, at least approximately, the probable succession of events, and the relation which they bore to what then occupied the minds of men as the prominent facts in the history of the world in which they lived; and with this view the following Table has been compiled. Where the dates are uncertain, and have therefore been variously placed, the doubt is indicated by a note of interrogation (?).

| A.D. | Emperors. | Apostolic History. | Civil Rulers. | High Priests. | Contemporary Events. | A.D. |
|---|---|---|---|---|---|---|
| 28 | Tiberius, from A.D. 14. | The Day of Pentecost, May (?). (Other dates, varying from A.D. 30—33, have been assigned for this.) | Pontius Pilate, Procurator of Judæa from A.D. 26. | Caiaphas from A.D. 25, son-in-law of Annas, or Ananus. | | 28 |
| 29 | | | | | | 29 |
| 30 | | | | | | 30 |

# THE ACTS.

| A.D. | Emperors. | Apostolic History. | Civil Rulers. | High Priests. | Contemporary Events. | A.D. |
|---|---|---|---|---|---|---|
| 31 | | | | | Death of Sejanus. | 31 |
| 32 | | The growth of the Church as described in Acts ii.—v. may be referred to this period, but there are no *data* for going further into detail. | | | Tiberius at Capreæ. New Sibylline books brought under notice of Senate. | 32 |
| 33 | | | | | Drusus, son of Germanicus, starved to death | 33 |
| 34 | | | Vitellius, Prefect of Syria. | | Phœnix reported to have been seen in Egypt. | 34 |
| 35 | | | | | Vitellius in Mesopotamia. | 35 |
| 36 | | Martyrdom of Stephen (?). | | | Philo at Alexandria. | 36 |
| 37 | Caligula. | Peter and John in Samaria. Conversion of Saul. | Herod Agrippa I. | Jonathan, son of Ananus. | Aretas in possession of Damascus. | 37 |
| 38 | | Conversion of Cornelius. Saul at Damascus. | | Theophilus, son of Ananus. | Philo's mission to Rome. | 38 |
| 39 | | Saul at Damascus. | | | Herod Antipas goes to Rome, and is banished to Gaul. Birth of Lucan. | 39 |
| 40 | | Paul at Jerusalem and Tarsus. | Petronius, Prefect of Syria. | | Caligula orders his statue to be set up in the Temple of Jerusalem. Philo at Rome. | 40 |
| 41 | Claudius. | Barnabas sent to Antioch. See of Rome founded by St. Peter (??). | | Simon Cantheras. | Birth of Titus. | 41 |
| 42 | | Paul at Antioch. Disciples called Christians. | | Matthias, son of Ananus. | Herod Agrippa made King of Judæa by Claudius. | 42 |
| 43 | | Paul and Barnabas go to Jerusalem. **The Gospel according to St. Matthew (??).** | | Elionæus, son of Cantharas. | Claudius conquers Britain. | 43 |
| 44 | | Death of James the son of Zebedee. Peter imprisoned. | Cuspius Fadus, Procurator of Judæa. | | Death of Herod Agrippa at Cæsarea. Plautius in Britain. | 44 |
| 45 | | Paul and Barnabas in Cyprus. **Epistle of St. James (?).** | | Joseph, son of Canis. | Apollonius of Tyana in India and Persia. | 45 |
| 46 | | Paul and Barnabas in Pisidia and Lycaonia. | Tiberius Alexander, Procurator of Judæa. | | | 46 |
| 47 | | Paul and Barnabas return to Antioch. | Ventidius Cumanus, Procurator of Judæa. | Ananias, son of Nebedius. | *Ludi sæculares* at Rome. Plautius returns from Britain. | 47 |
| 48 | | | | | Death of Messalina. Claudius under the influence of Narcissus and Pallas. | 48 |
| 49 | | Paul's dispute with Peter (??). | Herod Agrippa II., King of Chalcis. | | Herod Agrippa II. made King of Chalcis. Seneca appointed as Nero's tutor. Jews banished from Rome. | 49 |
| 50 | | Council at Jerusalem. Paul and Barnabas return with Silas to Antioch. | | | Caractacus captive in Rome. Foundation of Cologne by Agrippina. | 50 |
| 51 | | Paul and Silas start on another mission. Paul's dispute with Peter (?). | Felix, Procurator of Judæa. | | Burrus made Prefect of the Prætorian Guards. Astrologers expelled from Italy. | 51 |
| 52 | | Paul at Philippi, Thessalonica, Berœa, Athens, Corinth. | Herod Agrippa II., King of Batanæa and Trachonitis. | | Herod Agrippa II. made King of Batanæa and Trachonitis. | 52 |
| 53 | | Paul at Corinth. **First and Second Epistles to the Thessalonians.** | | | Marriage of Nero with Octavia. | 53 |
| 54 | Nero. | Paul's journey to Ephesus, Cæsarea, Jerusalem, Antioch. Apollos at Ephesus. Dispute with Peter (?). | | | Narcissus put to death by Nero. | 54 |
| 55 | | Apollos at Corinth. Paul in Asia. | | | | 55 |
| 56 | | Tumult at Ephesus (May). **First Epistle to the Corinthians.** Paul in Macedonia. **Epistle to the Galatians. Second Epistle to the Corinthians.** | | | Tumult in Judæa, headed by the Egyptian of Acts xxi. 38. Birth of Trajan. | 56 |
| 57 | | Paul at Corinth. **Epistle to the Romans.** Journey to Jerusalem (April, May). Trial before Felix. | | | Trial of Pomponia Græcina. | 57 |
| 58 | | Paul at Cæsarea. | | | Poppæa Sabina, Nero's mistress. | 58 |
| 59 | | Paul at Cæsarea. | | Ishmael, son of Phabi. | Agrippina, Nero's mother, put to death. | 59 |
| 60 | | Paul at Cæsarea. Appeal to Cæsar. Voyage to Italy. | Porcius Festus, Procurator of Judæa. | | | 60 |
| 61 | | Paul at Melita. Arrives at Rome (April). Lives in his own house. | | Joseph Cabi. | Revolt in Britain, under Boadicea, Queen of the Iceni. Apollonius of Tyana at the Olympic Games. | 61 |
| 62 | | Paul at Rome. **Epistle to the Philippians.** | Albinus, Procurator of Judæa. | Ananus. | Burrus dies, and is succeeded by Tigellinus. Persius dies. Josephus at Rome. | 62 |

# THE ACTS.

| A.D. | Emperors. | Apostolic History. | Civil Rulers. | High Priests. | Contemporary Events. | A.D. |
|---|---|---|---|---|---|---|
| 63 | | Paul at Rome. **Epistles to the Ephesians, Colossians, Philemon.** Release. **First Epistle of St. Peter.** | | Jesus, son of Damnæus. | Earthquakes in Asia Minor. | 63 |
| 64 | | Paul in Spain (?), Asia (?), Nicopolis (?). **First and Second Epistles to Timothy. The Gospel according to St. Luke and Acts of the Apostles (?). Epistle to Titus. Second Epistle of St. Peter.—Jude.** | Gessius Florus, Procurator of Judæa. | | Great fire at Rome. Persecution of Christians. | 64 |
| 65 | | Death of Paul and Peter (?) at Rome. Linus Bishop of Rome (?). | | | Seneca and Lucan put to death by Nero. Death of Poppæa. | 65 |
| 66 | | **Epistle to the Hebrews (?). The Gospel according to St. Matthew (?).** | | | Nero in Greece. Apollonius of Tyana ordered to leave Rome. Martial at Rome. | 66 |
| 67 | | Death of Peter and Paul (?). **The Gospel according to St. Mark. Epistle of St. James (??).** | | | Josephus gains favour with Vespasian after the capture of Jotapata. | 67 |
| 68 | Galba. | St. John in Patmos (?). **The Apocalypse (?).** | | | Vespasian takes Jericho. | 68 |
| 69 | Otho. Vitellius. Vespasian. | Death of James, the Bishop of Jerusalem (?). | | | | 69 |
| 70 | | Simeon Bishop of Jerusalem; Ignatius of Antioch (?). | | | The Capitol rebuilt by Vespasian. Jerusalem taken by Titus (Aug. 31). Josephus released. | 70 |
| 71 | | | | | Temple of Janus closed. Destruction of the Onias Temple in Egypt. Triumph of Titus and Vespasian. | 71 |
| 72 | | | | | | 72 |
| 73 | | | | | | 73 |
| 74 | | | | | Berenice at Rome with Vespasian and Titus. Philosophers banished from Rome. | 74 |
| 75 | | | | | Temple of Peace at Rome dedicated by Vespasian. | 75 |
| 76 | | | | | Coliseum begun. Birth of Hadrian. | 76 |
| 77 | | | | | | 77 |
| 78 | | Cletus Bishop of Rome (?). | | | Britain conquered by Agricola. | 78 |
| 79 | Titus. | | | | Pompeii and Herculaneum destroyed. Death of Pliny the Elder. | 79 |
| 80 | | Epistle of Clement of Rome to the Corinthians (??). | | | Coliseum finished. Pestilence and fire at Rome. Baths of Titus built. | 80 |
| 81 | Domitian. | | | | | 81 |
| 82 | | | | | | 82 |
| 83 | | | | | Domitian banishes all philosophers from Rome. | 83 |
| 84 | | | | | Agricola in Caledonia. | 84 |
| 85 | | | | | | 85 |
| 86 | | | | | Antoninus Pius born. | 86 |
| 87 | | | | | | 87 |
| 88 | | | | | Quintilian at Rome from A.D. 68–88 | 88 |
| 89 | | | | | | 89 |
| 90 | | | | | Philosophers again banished from Rome, Epictetus among them. | 90 |
| 91 | | Clement Bishop of Rome. | | | | 91 |
| 92 | | | | | | 92 |
| 93 | | St. John thrown into boiling oil before the Latin Gate (??). | | | Death of Agricola and Josephus. | 93 |
| 94 | | | | | Juvenal banished. | 94 |
| 95 | | Epistle of Clement (?). **The Apocalypse (??).** Flavius Clemens put to death. Domitilla banished. | | | Grandsons of the brethren of the Lord brought before Domitian. | 95 |
| 96 | Nerva. | **The three Epistles of St. John (?).** | | | | 96 |
| 97 | | **The Gospel according to St. John (?).** | | | Death of Apollonius of Tyana. | 97 |
| 98 | Trajan. | Cerdon Bishop of Alexandria; Ignatius of Antioch; Simon of Jerusalem. | | | Pliny and Plutarch in favour with Trajan. | 98 |
| 99 | | Death of St. John (?). | | | | 99 |
| 100 | | Death of St. John (?). | | | Pliny's Panegyric on Trajan. Martial retires to Spain. | 100 |

# THE ACTS OF THE APOSTLES

CHAPTER I.—(1) The former treatise have I made, O Theophilus, of all that Jesus began both to do and teach, (2) until the day in which he was taken up, after that he through the Holy Ghost had given commandments unto the apostles whom he had chosen: (3) to whom also he shewed himself alive after his passion by many infallible proofs, being seen of them forty days, and speaking of the things pertaining to the kingdom of God: (4) and, being assembled together with *them*,[1] commanded them that they should not

A.D. 33.

1 Or, *eating together with them.*

---

**The Acts of the Apostles.**—See *Introduction* as to the title thus given to the Book.

(1) **The former treatise.**—Literally, *word*, or *discourse;* but the English of the text is, perhaps, a happier equivalent than either. The Greek term had been used by Xenophon (*Anab.* ii. 1; *Cyrop.* viii. 1, 2) as St. Luke uses it, of what we should call the several "Books" or portions of his Histories. The adjective is strictly "first" rather than "former," and the tense of the verb, "I made," rather than "I have made."

**O Theophilus.**—See Note on Luke i. 3. It has been thought that the absence of the words "most excellent" implies that the writer's friendship with Theophilus was now of a more intimate and familiar nature. It is possible, just as a like change of relation has been traced in Shakespeare's dedication of his two poems to the Earl of Southampton, but the inference is, in each case, somewhat precarious.

**That Jesus began both to do and teach.**—The verb "begin" is specially characteristic of St. Luke's Gospel, in which it occurs not less than thirty-one times. Its occurrence at the beginning of the Acts is, accordingly, as far as it goes, an indication of identity of authorship. He sought his materials from those who had been "from the beginning" eye-witnesses and ministers of the word (Luke i. 2).

(2) **Until the day in which he was taken up.**—We notice, as a matter of style, the same periodic structure that we found in the opening of the Gospel, made more conspicuous in the Greek by an arrangement of the words which places "he was taken up" at the close of the sentence. On the word "taken up," see Note on Luke ix. 51.

**That he through the Holy Ghost had given commandments.**—The words admit of two possible meanings—(1) that the work of "commanding" was left to the Holy Spirit, guiding the spirits of the disciples into all the truth; (2) that in His human nature the Lord Jesus, after, as before, His passion, spoke as one who was "filled with the Holy Ghost" (Luke iv. 1), to whom the Father had given the Spirit not by measure (John iii. 34). As the Apostles were still waiting for the promised gift, the latter aspect of the words is, we can scarcely doubt, that which was intended by the writer.

(3) **After his passion.**—Literally, *after He had suffered.* The English somewhat anticipates the later special sense of "passion."

**By many infallible proofs.**—There is no adjective in the Greek answering to "infallible," but the noun is one which was used by writers on rhetoric (*e.g.*, Aristotle, *Rhet.* i. 2) for proofs that carried certainty of conviction with them, as contrasted with those that were only probable or circumstantial. No other New Testament writer uses it.

**Being seen of them forty days.**—St. Luke uses a peculiar and unusual word (it occurs twice in the LXX.: 1 Kings viii. 8, and Tob. xii. 19) for "being seen," perhaps with the wish to imply that the presence was not continuous, and that our Lord was seen only at intervals. This may be noted as the only passage which gives the time between the Resurrection and the Ascension. It had its counterpart in the forty days of the Temptation in the wilderness (Luke iv. 2), as that had had in the earlier histories of Moses (Ex. xxiv. 18; Deut. ix. 9, 18) and Elijah (1 Kings xix. 8). There was a certain symbolic fitness in the time of triumph on earth coinciding with that of special conflict. If we ask what was the character, if one may so speak, of our Lord's risen life between His manifestation to the disciples, the history of the earlier forty days in part suggests the answer. Then, as before, the life was, we may believe, one of solitude and communion with His Father, no longer tried and tempted, as it had then been, by contact with the power of evil—a life of intercession, such as that which uttered itself in the great prayer of John xvii. Where the days and nights were spent we can only reverently conjecture. Analogy suggests the desert places and mountain heights of Galilee (Luke iv. 42, vi. 12). The mention of Bethany in Luke xxiv. 50, and of the Mount of Olives in verse 12, makes it probable that Gethsemane may have been one of the scenes that witnessed the joy of the victory, as it had witnessed before the agony of the conflict.

**The things pertaining to the kingdom of God.**—This implies, it is obvious, much unrecorded teaching. What is recorded points (1) to the true interpretation of the prophecies of the Messiah (Luke xxiv. 27, 44, 45); (2) to the extension of the mission of the disciples to the whole Gentile world, and their admission to the Kingdom by baptism (Matt. xxviii. 19); (3) to the promises of supernatural powers and divine protection (Mark xvi. 15—18); (4) to that of His own perpetual presence with His Church (Matt. xxviii. 20).

(4) **And, being assembled together with them.**—The MSS. present two forms of the participle: one with the meaning given in the English version, the

depart from Jerusalem, but wait for
the promise of the Father, which,[a] *saith
he,* ye have heard of me. (5) For John
truly baptized with water;[b] but ye shall
be baptized with the Holy Ghost not
many days hence. (6) When they there-
fore were come together, they asked of
him, saying, Lord, wilt thou at this time
restore again the kingdom to Israel?
(7) And he said unto them, It is not for
you to know the times or the seasons,
which the Father hath put in his own
power. (8) But ye shall receive power,[1]
after that the Holy Ghost is come upon
you:[c] and ye shall be witnesses unto
me both in Jerusalem, and in all Judæa,
and in Samaria, and unto the uttermost
part of the earth. (9) And when he had
spoken these things,[d] while they beheld,
he was taken up; and a cloud received

a Luke 24. 49.
1 Or, *the power of the Holy Ghost coming upon you.*
b Matt. 3. 11.
c ch. 2. 1.
d Luke 24. 51.

other, but inferior reading, with the sense of "dwelling together with" the disciples. The Vulgate, *convescens,* "eating with," probably rests on a mistaken etymology of the Greek term. The whole verse is in substance a repetition of Luke xxiv. 49, where see Notes.

(5) **John truly baptized with water.**—See Note on Matt. iii. 11. The words threw the disciples back upon their recollection of their first admission to the Kingdom. Some of them, at least, must have remembered also the teaching which had told them of the new birth of water and of the Spirit (John iii. 3—5). Now they were told that their spirits were to be as fully baptised, *i.e.,* plunged, into the power of the Divine Spirit, as their bodies had then been plunged in the waters of the Jordan. And this was to be "not many days hence." The time was left undefined, as a discipline to their faith and patience. They were told that it would not be long, lest faith and patience should fail.

(6) **Lord, wilt thou at this time restore again the kingdom?**—More literally, *art Thou restoring* . . . Before the Passion the disciples had thought that "the kingdom of God should immediately appear" (Luke xix. 11). Then had come the seeming failure of those hopes (Luke xxiv. 21). Now they were revived by the Resurrection, but were still predominantly national. Even the Twelve were thinking, not of a kingdom of God, embracing all mankind, but of a sovereignty restored to Israel.

(7) **It is not for you to know the times or the seasons.**—The combination of the two words is characteristic of St. Luke and St. Paul (1 Thess. v. 1). The answer to the eager question touches the season rather than the nature of the fulfilment of their hopes. They are left to the teaching of the Spirit and of Time to re-mould and purify their expectations of the restoration of Israel. What was needed now was the patience that waits for and accepts that teaching.

**Which the Father hath put in his own power.**—Better, as free from the ambiguity which attaches to the present version, *which the Father appointed by His own authority.*

(8) **But ye shall receive power.**—The use of the same English noun for two different Greek words is misleading, but if "authority" be used in verse 7 then "power" is an adequate rendering here. The consciousness of a new faculty of thought and speech would be to them a proof that the promise of the Kingdom had not failed.

**Ye shall be witnesses unto me.**—The words, which are apparently identical with those of Luke xxiv. 48, strike the key-note of the whole book. Those which follow correspond to the great divisions of the Acts—Jerusalem, chaps. i. and vii.; Judæa, ix. 32, xii. 19; Samaria, viii.; and the rest of the book as opening the wider record of the witness borne "to the uttermost parts of the earth." And this witness was two-fold: (1) of the works, the teachings, and, above all, of the Resurrection of Jesus; (2) of the purpose of the Father as revealed in the Son. The witness was to be, in language which, though technical, is yet the truest expression of the fact, at once historical and dogmatic.

(9) **He was taken up; and a cloud received him . . .**—It is remarkable how little stress is laid in the Gospels on the fact which has always been so prominent in the creeds of Christendom. Neither St. John nor St. Matthew record it. It is barely mentioned with utmost brevity in the verses which close the Gospel of St. Mark, and in which many critics see, indeed, a fragment of apostolic teaching, but not part of the original Gospel. The reasons of this silence are, however, not far to seek. It was because the Ascension was from the first part of the creed of Christendom that the Evangelists said so little. The fact had been taught to every catechumen. They would not embellish it—as, for example, the Assumption of the Virgin was embellished in later legends—by fantastic details. That it was so received is clear. It is implied in our Lord's language, as recorded by St. John, "What and if ye shall see the Son of Man ascend up where He was before?" (John vi. 62), and such words would hardly have been brought before believers at the close of the apostolic age if they had received no fulfilment. It is assumed in the earliest form of the Church's creed, "He was received up into glory," the verb being identical with that which St. Luke employs in St. Peter's speeches (Acts ii. 33; iii. 21), and in St. Paul's epistles (Eph. i. 20; 1 Tim. iii. 16). We may add that there was something like a moral necessity, assuming the Resurrection as a fact, for such a conclusion to our Lord's work on earth. Two other alternatives may, perhaps, be just imagined as possible: He might, like Lazarus, have lived out His restored life to its appointed term, and then died the common death of all men; but in that case where would have been the victory over death, and the witness that He was the Son of Man? He might have lived on an endless life on earth; but in this case, being such as He was, conflict, persecution, and suffering would have come again and again at every stage, and in each instance a miracle would have been needed to save the suffering from passing on to death, or many deaths must have been followed by many resurrections. When we seek, however, to realise the process of the Ascension, we find ourselves in a region of thought in which it is not easy to move freely. With our thoughts of the relations of the earth to space and the surrounding orbs, we find it hard to follow that upward motion, and to ask what was its direction and where it terminated. We cannot get beyond the cloud; but that cloud was the token of the glory of the Eternal Presence, as the Shechinah that of old filled the Temple (1 Kings viii. 10, 11; Isa. vi. 1—4), and it is enough for us to know

him out of their sight. (10) And while
they looked stedfastly toward heaven as
he went up, behold, two men stood by
them in white apparel; (11) which also
said, Ye men of Galilee, why stand ye
gazing up into heaven? this same Jesus,
which is taken up from you into heaven,
shall so come in like manner as ye have
seen him go into heaven. (12) Then re-
turned they unto Jerusalem from the
mount called Olivet, which is from Jeru-
salem a sabbath day's journey. (13) And
when they were come in, they went up
into an upper room, where abode both
Peter, and James, and John, and Andrew,
Philip, and Thomas, Bartholomew, and
Matthew, James *the son* of Alphæus, and
Simon Zelotes, and Judas *the brother* of
James. (14) These all continued with
one accord in prayer and supplication,
with the women, and Mary the mother
of Jesus, and with his brethren.

---

that where God is there also is Christ, in the glory of the Father, retaining still, though under new conditions and laws, the human nature which made Him like unto His brethren.

(10) **Two men stood by them in white apparel.**—Better, *were standing,* the appearance being sudden, and their approach unnoticed. The forms were such as those as had been seen at the portals of the empty sepulchre, bright and fair to look upon, and clad in white garments, like the young priests in the Temple. (See Note on Luke i. 12.)

(11) **Shall so come in like manner as ye have seen him go into heaven.**—So our Lord, following the great prophecy of Dan. vii. 13, had spoken of Himself as "coming in the clouds of heaven" (see Note on Matt. xxvi. 64), in visible majesty and glory. Here, again, men have asked questions which they cannot answer; not only, when shall the end be, but where shall the Judge thus appear? what place shall be the chosen scene of His second Advent? So far as we dare to localise what is left undefined, the words of the angels suggest the same scene, as well as the same manner. Those who do not shrink from taking the words of prophecy in their most literal sense, have seen in Zech. xiv. 4, an intimation that the Valley of Jehoshaphat (= Jehovah judges)—the "valley of decision" —shall witness the great Assize, and that the feet of the Judge shall stand upon the Mount of Olives, from which He had ascended into heaven. This was the current mediæval view, and seems, if we are to localise at all, to be more probable than any other.

(12) **From the mount called Olivet.**— As to the name, see Note on Luke xix. 29. The mention of the distance, and the measure of distance employed are, both of them, remarkable, and suggest the thought that St. Luke's reckoning was a different one from that which Christendom has commonly received, and that the "forty days" expired before the last renewal of our Lord's intercourse with His disciples, and that this ended on the following sabbath—*i.e.*, eight days before the day of Pentecost. On this supposition we get a reason, otherwise wanting, for this manner of stating the distance. Symbolically, too, there seems a fitness in our Lord's entering into His rest, on the great day of rest, which is wanting in our common way of reckoning. On the other hand, it may be noted that it is after St. Luke's manner as in the case of Emmaus (Luke xxiv. 13) to give distances. The "Sabbath day's journey" was reckoned at 2,000 paces, or about six furlongs.

(13) **They went up into an upper room, where abode . . .**—Better, *into the upper room, where they were abiding.* The Greek noun has the article. The room may have been the same as that in which the Paschal Supper had been eaten (Mark xiv. 15). On the other hand, that room seems to have been different from that in which the disciples had lodged during the Paschal week, and to have been chosen specially for the occasion (Luke xxii. 8). The word used is also different in form. So far as we are able to distinguish between the two words, the room of the Paschal Supper was on the first floor, the guest-chamber, used for meals; that in which the disciples now met, on the second floor, or loft, which was used for retirement and prayer. It would seem from Luke xxiv. 53, that they spent the greater part of each day in the Temple, and met together in the evening. The better MSS. give "prayer" only, without "supplication." The prayer thus offered may be thought of as specially directed to the "promise of the Father." Whether it was spoken or silent, unpremeditated or in some set form of words, like the Lord's Prayer, we have no *data* to determine.

**Peter, and James.**—On the lists of the Twelve Apostles see Notes on Matt. x. 2—4. The points to be noticed are—(1) that Andrew stands last in the group of the first four, divided from his brother, thus agreeing with the list in St. Mark (iii. 17); (2) that Philip is in like manner divided from Bartholomew, and Thomas from Matthew; (3) that Zelotes appears here, as in Luke vi. 15, instead of the Cananæan.

(14) **With the women.**—Looking to what we have seen in the Gospels, it is a natural inference that here, too, the "devout women" of Luke viii. 2, 3, were among St. Luke's chief informants. This may, perhaps, account for the variations in the list just noticed. The women were less likely than the disciples to lay stress on what we may call the accurate coupling of the Twelve. The mention of "the women" as a definite body is characteristic of St. Luke as the only Evangelist who names them. (See Notes on Luke viii. 1—3; xxiii. 49.) We may reasonably think of the company as including Mary Magdalene, Salome, Susanna, Joanna, Mary and Martha of Bethany, possibly also the woman that had been a sinner, of Luke vii. 37. Here we lose sight of them, and all that follows is conjectural. It is probable that they continued to share the work and the sufferings of the growing Church at Jerusalem, living together, perhaps at Bethany, in a kind of sisterhood. The persecution headed by Saul was likely to disperse them for a time, and some may well have been among the "women" who suffered in it (chap. viii. 3); but they may have returned when it ceased. St. Luke, when he came to Palestine, would seem to have met with one or more of them.

**Mary the mother of Jesus.**—Brief as the record is, it has the interest of giving the last known fact, as distinct from legend or tradition, in the life of the mother of our Lord. St. John, we know, had taken her to his own home, probably to a private dwelling in Jerusalem (see Note on John xix. 27), and she had now

(15) And in those days Peter stood up
in the midst of the disciples, and said,
(the number of names together were
about an hundred and twenty,) (16) Men
*and* brethren, this scripture must needs
have been fulfilled, which the Holy
Ghost by the mouth of David spake
before concerning Judas,[a] which was
guide to them that took Jesus. (17) For
he was numbered with us, and had ob-
tained part of this ministry. (18) Now
this man purchased a field with the
reward of iniquity;[b] and falling head-
long, he burst asunder in the midst,
and all his bowels gushed out. (19) And
it was known unto all the dwellers at
Jerusalem; insomuch as that field is
called in their proper tongue, Aceldama,
that is to say, The field of blood.
(20) For it is written in the book of
Psalms, Let his habitation be desolate,[c]
and let no man dwell therein: and his

b Matt. 27. 7.

a Ps. 41. 9.

c Ps. 69. 25.

---

come with him to the first meeting of the *Ecclesia*. Here also we trace the influence of the women as St. Luke's informants. They could not have left unnoticed the presence of her who was the centre of their group. The legends of some apocryphal books represent her as staying at Jerusalem with St. John till her death, twenty-two years after the Ascension; while others represent her as going with him to Ephesus and dying there; the Apostles gather around her death-bed; she is buried, and the next day the grave is found emptied, and sweet flowers have grown around it; Mary also had been taken up into heaven. The festival of the Assumption, which owes its origin to this legend, dates from the sixth or seventh century.

**With his brethren.**—The last mention of the "brethren" had shown them as still unbelieving (John vii. 5). Various explanations of their change may be given. (1) They may have been drawn to believe before the Crucifixion by the great miracle of the resurrection of Lazarus. (2) The risen Lord had appeared to James as well as to the Apostles (1 Cor. xv. 7), and that may have fixed him and the other brothers in steadfast faith. (3) If the mother of Jesus was with John, the brethren also were likely to come, in greater or less measure, under the influence of their cousin. It may be noted that the brethren are here emphatically distinguished from the Apostles, and therefore that James the son of Alphæus cannot rightly be identified with James the Lord's brother. (See Note on Matt. xii. 46.)

(15) **The number of names together were about an hundred and twenty.**—The number probably included the Seventy of Luke x. 1, perhaps also Joseph of Arimathæa and Nicodemus, and some of the "five hundred" who had seen their risen Lord in Galilee or elsewhere (1 Cor. xv. 6). The use of "names" may be merely as a synonym for "persons," but it suggests the idea of there having been a list from which St. Luke extracted those that seemed most conspicuous.

(16) **Men and brethren.**—Better, *brethren* only, the word being used as in the LXX. of Gen. xiii. 8. The tone of St. Peter's speech is that of one who felt that his offence had been fully forgiven, and that he was now restored by the charge given him, as in John xxi. 15—17, to his former position as guide and leader of the other disciples. To do that work faithfully was a worthier fruit of repentance than any public confession of his guilt would have been. This, of course, does not exclude—what is in itself probable—that he had previously confessed his fault, either to his special friend St. John, or to the whole company of Apostles and other disciples.

**Which the Holy Ghost by the mouth of David spake . . . .**—We have here, obviously, the firstfruits of the new method of interpretation in which the Apostles had been instructed (Luke xxiv. 27, 45). They had already been taught that the Holy Spirit which their Lord had promised to them had before spoken by the prophets. The recurrence of the same mode of speech in the "holy men of God who spake as they were moved (literally, *borne along*) by the Holy Ghost," in 2 Pet. i. 21, is, as far as it goes, evidence in favour of the genuineness of that Epistle.

**Which was guide to them that took Jesus.**—The actual word "guide" is not found in the Gospel narrative, but it appears as a fact in all four, notably in that of St. John (xviii. 2, 3).

(17) **For he was numbered with us.**—Literally, *he had been numbered*.

**Had obtained part of this ministry.**—Better, *the portion*, or *inheritance*. The Greek has the article, and the noun (*cleros*) is one which afterwards acquired a special half-technical sense in the words, *clerus*, *clericus*, "clerk," "clergy." In 1 Pet. v. 3, as being "lords over the heritage," we find it in a transition sense. (See Note on verse 25.)

(18, 19) **Now this man purchased a field.**—Better, *acquired*, *got possession of*, *a field*, the Greek not necessarily including the idea of buying. On the difficulties presented by a comparison of this account with that in Matt. xxvii. 5—8, see Note on that passage. Here the field bought with Judas's money is spoken of as that which he gained as the reward of his treachery. The details that follow are additions to the briefer statement of St. Matthew, but are obviously not incompatible with it. Nor is there any necessity for assuming, as some have done, that there were two fields known as Aceldama, one that which the priests had bought, and the other that which was the scene of Judas's death. The whole passage must be regarded as a note of the historian, not as part of the speech of St. Peter. It was not likely that he, speaking to disciples, all of whom knew the Aramaic, or popular Hebrew of Palestine, should stop to explain that Aceldama meant "in their proper tongue, The field of blood."

(19) **In their proper tongue.**—Literally, *in their own dialect*. The word is used frequently in the Acts (ii. 6, 8; xxi. 40), but not elsewhere in the New Testament.

(20) **For it is written in the book of Psalms.**—St. Peter's speech is continued after the parenthetical note. His purpose in making the quotation is to show that the disciples should not be staggered by the treachery of Judas, and the seeming failure of their hopes. The Psalms had represented the righteous sufferer as the victim of treachery. They had also spoken of the traitor as receiving a righteous punishment such as had now fallen upon Judas. No strange thing had

bishoprick[1] let another take.[a] (21) Wherefore of these men which have companied with us all the time that the Lord Jesus went in and out among us, (22) beginning from the baptism of John, unto that same day that he was taken up from us, must one be ordained to be a witness with us of his resurrection. (23) And they appointed two, Joseph called Barsabas, who was surnamed Justus, and Matthias. (24) And they prayed, and said, Thou, Lord, which knowest the hearts of all *men*, shew whether of these two thou hast chosen, (25) that he may take part of this ministry and apostleship, from which Judas by transgression fell, that he might go to his own place. (26) And they gave

1 Or, *office*, or, *charge*.
a Ps. 109. 8.

---

happened. What had been of old was typical of what they had heard or known. We need not in this place discuss either the historical occasions of the Psalms cited, or the ethical difficulties presented by their imprecations of evil. Neither comes, so to speak, within the horizon of St. Peter's thoughts. It was enough for him to note the striking parallelism which they presented to what was fresh in his memory, and to believe that it was not accidental.

**His bishoprick let another take.**—Better, as in Ps. cix. 8, *let another take his office*. The Greek word is *episcopè*, which, as meaning an office like that of the *episcopos*, is, of course, in one sense, rightly translated by "bishoprick." The latter term is, however, so surrounded by associations foreign to the apostolic age that it is better to use the more general, and, therefore, neutral, term of the English version of the Psalm. The use of "bishoprick" may be noted as an instance of the tendency of the revisers of 1611 to maintain the use of "bishop" and the like where the office seemed to be placed on a high level (as here and in 1 Pet. ii. 25), while they use "overseer" and "oversight" (as in Acts xx. 28, and 1 Pet. v. 2) where it is identified with the functions of the elders or presbyters of the Church. "Bishoprick" had, however, been used in all previous versions except the Geneva, which gives "charge."

(21) **Wherefore of these men which have companied with us.**—From the retrospective glance at the guilt and punishment of the traitor, Peter passes, as with a practical sagacity, to the one thing that was now needful for the work of the infant Church. They, the Apostles, must present themselves to the people in their symbolic completeness, as sent to the twelve tribes of Israel, and the gap left by the traitor must be filled by one qualified, as they were, to bear witness of what had been said or done by their Lord during His ministry, and, above all, of His resurrection from the dead. That would seem, even in St. Paul's estimate, to have been a condition of apostleship (1 Cor. ix. 1).

**Went in and out . . .**—The phrase was a familiar Hebrew phrase for the whole of a man's life and conduct. (Comp. chap. ix. 28.)

(23) **They appointed.**—It is uncertain whether this was the act of the Apostles, presenting the two men to the choice of the whole body of disciples, or of the community choosing them for ultimate decision by lot.

**Joseph called Barsabas, who was surnamed Justus.**—Some MSS. give the various-reading of "Joses," which was, perhaps, only another form of the same name. Nothing further is known of him. The conditions of the case make it certain that he must have been a disciple almost from the beginning of our Lord's ministry, and that he must have become more or less prominent, and probable therefore, as stated by Eusebius (*Hist.* i. 12), that he was one of the Seventy. The name Barsabas (= son of the oath, or of wisdom) may have been a patronymic, like Barjona, or may have been given, like Barnabas, as denoting character. It appears again in Judas Barsabas of chap. xv. 22, and on the former assumption, the two disciples may have been brothers. The epithet Justus, the just one, is significant, as possibly indicating, as in the case of James the Just, a specially high standard of ascetic holiness. Another with the same surname—Jesus surnamed Justus—meets us as being with St. Paul at Rome as one of "the circumcision" (Col. iv. 11), and another, or possibly the same, at Corinth (chap. xviii. 7). In both cases the use of the Latin instead of the Greek word is noticeable, as indicating some point of contact with the Romans in Judæa or elsewhere.

**Matthias.**—Here, too, probably, the same conditions were fulfilled. The name, like Matthew (see Note on Matt. ix. 9), signified "given by Jehovah," and had become, in various forms, popular, from the fame of Mattathias, the great head of the Maccabean family.

(24) **Thou, Lord, which knowest the hearts of all men.**—Literally, *heart-knower of all men*. The compound word is not found in any Greek version of the Old Testament, but meets us again in chap. xv. 8. The question meets us whether the prayer is addressed to the Lord Jesus, as with a recollection of His insight into the hearts of men (John ii. 24; vi. 64), or to the Father. The prayer of Stephen (chap. vii. 59, 60) shows, on the one hand, that direct prayer to the Son was not foreign to the minds of the disciples; and in John vi. 70, He claims the act of choosing as His own. On the other hand, the analogy of chap. iv. 29, where the Father is entreated to work signs and wonders "through his holy servant Jesus," is in favour of the latter view.

"Whether," as used in the sense of "which of two," may be noted as one of the archaisms of the English version.

(25) **That he may take part of this ministry.**—Better, *the portion*, or *the lot*, so as to give the word (*cleros*, as in verse 17) the same prominence in English as it has in the Greek.

**From which Judas by transgression fell.**—The last three words are as a paraphrase of the one Greek verb. Better, *fell away*.

**That he might go to his own place.**—Literally, as the verb is in the infinitive, *to go* to his own place. The construction is not free from ambiguity, and some interpreters have referred the words to the disciple about to be chosen, "to go to his own place" in the company of the Twelve. If we connect them, as seems most natural, with Judas, we find in them the kind of reserve natural in one that could neither bring himself to cherish hope nor venture to pronounce the condemnation which belonged to the Searcher of hearts. All that had been revealed to him was, that "it had been good for that man if he had not been born" (Mark xiv. 21).

(26) **And they gave forth their lots.**—As interpreted by the prayer of verse 24, and by the word "fell" here, there can be no doubt that the passage

forth their lots; and the lot fell upon Matthias; and he was numbered with the eleven apostles.

A.D. 33.

CHAPTER II.—(1) And when the day of Pentecost was fully come, they were all with one accord in one place.

---

speaks of "lots" and not "votes." The two men were chosen by the disciples as standing, as far as they could see, on the same level. It was left for the Searcher of hearts to show, by the exclusion of human will, which of the two He had chosen. The most usual way of casting lots in such cases was to write each name on a tablet, place them in an urn, and then shake the urn till one came out. A like custom prevailed among the Greeks, as in the well-known story of the stratagem of Cresphontes in the division of territory after the Dorian invasion (Sophocles, *Aias.* 1285; comp. Prov. xvi. 33). The practice was recognised, it may be noted, in the Law (Lev. xvi. 8).

**He was numbered with the eleven apostles.**—The Greek word is not the same as in verse 17, and implies that Matthias was "voted in," the suffrage of the Church unanimously confirming the indication of the divine will which had been given by the lot. It may be that the new Apostle took the place which Judas had left vacant, and was the last of the Twelve.

II.

(1) **When the day of Pentecost was fully come.**—It is natural to assume a purpose in the divine choice of the day on which the disciples were thus to receive the promise of the Father. That choice may have been determined, if one may so speak, either in view of the circumstances of the feast, or of its history and symbolic fitness.

(1) Of all the feasts of the Jewish year, it was that which attracted the largest number of pilgrims from distant lands. The dangers of travel by sea or land in the early spring or late autumn (comp. chap. xxvii. 9) prevented their coming in any large numbers to the Passover or the Feast of Tabernacles. At no other feast would there have been representatives of so many nations. So, it may be noted, it was the Feast of Pentecost that St. Paul went up to keep once and again, during his mission-work in Greece and Asia. (See Notes on chaps. xviii. 21; xx. 16.) So far, then, there was no time on which the gift of the Spirit was likely to produce such direct and immediate results.

(2) Each aspect of the old Feast of Weeks, now known as Pentecost, or the "Fiftieth-day" Feast, presented a symbolic meaning which made it, in greater or less measure, typical of the work now about to be accomplished. It was the "feast of harvest, the feast of the firstfruits;" and so it was meet that it should witness the first great gathering of the fields that were white to harvest (Ex. xxiii. 16). It was one on which, more than on any other, the Israelite was to remember that he had been a bondsman in the land of Egypt, and had been led forth to freedom (Deut. xvi. 12), and on it, accordingly, they were to do no servile work (Lev. xxiii. 31); and it was, therefore, a fit time for the gift of the Spirit, of whom it was emphatically true that "where the Spirit of the Lord is, there is liberty" (2 Cor. iii. 17), and who was to guide the Church into the truth which should make men free indeed (John viii. 32). It was a day on which sacrifices of every kind were offered—burnt offerings, and sin offerings, and meat offerings, and peace offerings—and so represented the consecration of body, soul, and spirit as a spiritual sacrifice (Lev. xxiii. 17—20). As on the Passover the first ripe sheaf of corn was waved before Jehovah as the type of the sacrifice of Christ, of the corn of wheat which is not quickened except it die (Lev. xxiii. 10; John xii. 24), so on Pentecost two wave-loaves of fine flour were to be offered, the type, it may be, under the light now thrown on them, of the Jewish and the Gentile Churches (Lev. xxiii. 17). And these loaves were to be leavened, as a witness that the process of the contact of mind with mind, which—as the prohibition of leaven in the Passover ritual bore witness—is naturally so fruitful in evil, might yet, under a higher influence, become one of unspeakable good: the new life working through the three measures of meal until the whole was leavened. (See Note on Matt. xiii. 33.)

(3) Lastly, the Feast of Pentecost had—traditionally, at least—also a commemorative character. On that day—so it was computed by the later Rabbis, though the Book of Exodus (xix. 1) seems to leave the matter in some uncertainty—the Israelites had encamped round Sinai, and there had been thunders and darkness and voices, and the great Laws had been proclaimed. It was, that is, an epoch-making day in the religious history of Israel. It was fit that it should be chosen for another great epoch-making day, which, seeming at first to be meant for Israel only, was intended ultimately for mankind.

**Was fully come.**—Literally, *was being accomplished.* The word seems chosen to express the fact that the meeting of the disciples was either on the vigil of the Feast-day, or in the early dawn. Assuming the Passover to have occurred on the night of the Last Supper, the Day of Pentecost would fall on the first day of the week, beginning, of course, at the sunset of the Sabbath. So the Churches of East and West have commemorated the day as on the eighth Sunday after Easter. In the Latin nations the name of Pentecost remains scarcely altered. The *Pfingst* of the Germans shows it still surviving in a very contracted form. Some eminent scholars have thought that our *Whitsun*-day represents it after a still more altered form, and that this is a more probable etymology of the word than those which connect it with the *white* garments worn on that day by newly-baptised converts, or with the gift of "*wit*, or wisdom."

**With one accord in one place.**—Probably in the same large upper room as in chap. i. 13. We may reasonably think of the same persons as being present. The hour, we may infer from verse 15, was early in the morning, and probably followed on a night of prayer. It is said, indeed, that devout Jews used to solemnise the vigil of Pentecost by a special thanksgiving to God for giving His Law to Israel; and this may well have been the occasion that brought the disciples together (Schöttgen, *Hor. Hebr. in Acts* ii. 1). It was, in the mystic language of the Rabbis, the night on which the Law, as the Bride, was espoused to Israel, as the Bridegroom. The frequent occurrence of the Greek word for "with one accord" (chaps. i. 14; ii. 46; iv. 24; v. 12) is significant as showing the impression made on the writer by the exceptional unity of the new society. Outside the Acts it is found only in Rom. xv. 16.

(2) And suddenly there came a sound
from heaven as of a rushing mighty
wind, and it filled all the house where
they were sitting. (3) And there ap-
peared unto them cloven tongues like as
of fire, and it sat upon each of them.
(4) And they were all filled with the
Holy Ghost, and began to speak with

---

(2) **And suddenly there came a sound from heaven . . . .**—The description reminds us of the "sound of a trumpet" (Ex. xix. 19; Heb. xii. 19) on Sinai, of the "great and strong wind" that rent the mountains on Horeb (1 Kings xix. 11). Such a wind was now felt and heard, even as the wind, the breath, the Spirit of God, had moved upon the face of the waters, quickening them into life (Gen. i. 2).

**A rushing mighty wind.**—Better, *a mighty breath borne onwards*, so as to connect the English, as the Greek is connected, with St. Peter's words that, "holy men of old spake as they were moved (literally, *borne on*) by the Holy Ghost" (2 Pet. i. 21). The Greek word for "wind" is not that commonly so translated (*anemos*), but one from the same root as the Greek for "Spirit" (*Pnoè* and *Pneuma*—both from *Pneô*, "I breathe"), and rendered "breath" in chap. xvii. 25. It is obviously chosen here as being better fitted than the more common word for the supernatural inbreathing of which they were conscious, and which to many must have recalled the moment when their Lord had "*breathed* on them, and said, Receive ye the Holy Ghost" (John xx. 22). Now, once more, they felt that light yet awful breathing which wrought every nerve to ecstasy; and it filled "the whole house," as if in token of the wide range over which the new spiritual power was to extend its working, even unto the whole Church, which is the House of God (1 Tim. iii. 15), and to the uttermost parts of the earth.

(3) **There appeared unto them cloven tongues like as of fire.**—Better, *and tongues as of fire were seen by them, parted among them.* The word translated "cloven" cannot possibly have that meaning. It is not uncommon (*e.g.*, verse 45; Matt. xxvii. 35; Luke xxii. 17; and John xix. 24), and is always used in the sense of dividing or distributing. What the disciples saw would, perhaps, be best described in modern phrase as a shower of fiery tongues, coming they knew not whence, lighting for a moment on each head, and then vanishing. The verb "it (*sc.*, a tongue of fire) sat upon" is in the tense which expresses momentary, not continuous, action.

(4) **And they were all filled with the Holy Ghost.**—The outward portent was but the sign of a greater spiritual wonder. As yet, though they had been taught to pray for the gift of the Holy Spirit (Luke xi. 13), and, we must believe, had found the answer to their prayer in secret and sacred influences and gradual growth in wisdom, they had never been conscious of its power as "filling" them—pervading the inner depths of personality, stimulating every faculty and feeling to a new intensity of life. Now they felt, in St. Peter's words, as "borne onward" (2 Pet. i. 21), thinking thoughts and speaking words which were not their own, and which they could hardly even control. They had passed into a state which was one of rapturous ecstasy and joy. We must not think of the gift as confined to the Apostles. The context shows that the writer speaks of all who were assembled, not excepting the women, as sharers in it. (Comp. verses 17, 18.)

**And began to speak with other tongues.**—Two facts have to be remembered as we enter upon the discussion of a question which is, beyond all doubt, difficult and mysterious. (1) If we receive Mark xvi. 9—20 as a true record of our Lord's words, the disciples had, a few days or weeks before the Day of Pentecost, heard the promise that they that believed should "speak with new tongues" (see Note on Mark xvi. 17), *i.e.*, with new powers of utterance. (2) When St. Luke wrote his account of the Day of Pentecost, he must have had—partly through his companionship with St. Paul, partly from personal observation—a wide knowledge of the phenomena described as connected with the "tongues" in 1 Cor. xiv. He uses the term in the sense in which St. Paul had used it. We have to read the narrative of the Acts in the light thrown upon it by the treatment in that chapter of the phenomena described by the self-same words as the Pentecost wonder. What, then, are those phenomena? Does the narrative of this chapter bring before us any in addition? (1) The utterance of the "tongue" is presented to us as entirely unconnected with the work of teaching. It is not a means of instruction. It does not edify any beyond the man who speaks (1 Cor. xiv. 4). It is, in this respect, the very antithesis of "prophecy." Men do not, as a rule, understand it, though God does (1 Cor. xiv. 2). Here and there, some mind with a special gift of insight may be able to interpret with clear articulate speech what had been mysterious and dark (1 Cor. xiv. 13). St. Paul desires to subject the exercise of the gift to the condition of the presence of such an interpreter (1 Cor. xiv. 5, 27). (2) The free use of the gift makes him who uses it almost as a barbarian or foreigner to those who listen to him. He may utter prayers, or praises, or benedictions, but what he speaks is as the sound of a trumpet blown uncertainly, of flute or lyre played with unskilled hand, almost, we might say, in the words of our own poet, "like sweet bells jangled, out of tune and harsh" (1 Cor. xiv. 7—9). (3) Those who speak with tongues do well, for the most part, to confine their utterance to the solitude of their own chamber, or to the presence of friends who can share their rapture When they make a more public display of it, it produces results that stand in singular contrast with each other. It is a "sign to them that believe not," *i.e.*, it startles them, attracts their notice, impresses them with the thought that they stand face to face with a superhuman power. On the other hand, the outside world of listeners, common men, or unbelievers, are likely to look on it as indicating madness (1 Cor. xiv. 23). If it was not right or expedient to check the utterance of the tongues altogether, St. Paul at least thought it necessary to prescribe rules for its exercise which naturally tended to throw it into the background as compared with prophecy (1 Cor. xiv. 27, 28). The conclusion from the whole chapter is, accordingly, that the "tongues" were not the power of speaking in a language which had not been learnt by the common ways of learning, but the ecstatic utterance of rapturous devotion. As regards the terms which are used to describe the gift, the English reader must be reminded that the word "unknown" is an interpolation which appears for the first time in the version of 1611. Wiclif, Tyndale, Cranmer, and the Rhemish give no adjective, and the Geneva inserts "strange." It may be noted further that the Greek word for "tongue" had come to be used by Greek writers on Rhetoric

other tongues, as the Spirit gave them utterance. (5) And there were dwelling at Jerusalem Jews, devout men, out of every nation under heaven. (6) Now when

for bold, poetic, unusual terms, such as belonged to epic poetry (Aristot. *Rhet.* iii. 3), not for those which belonged to a foreign language. If they were, as Aristotle calls them, "unknown," it was because they were used in a startlingly figurative sense, so that men were sometimes puzzled by them (Aristot. *Rhet.* iii. 10). We have this sense of the old word (*glossa*) surviving in our *glossary*, a collection of such terms. It is clear (1) that such an use of the word would be natural in writers trained as St. Paul and St. Luke had been in the language of Greek schools; and (2) that it exactly falls in with the conclusion to which the phenomena of the case leads us, apart from the word.

We turn to the history that follows in this chapter, and we find almost identical phenomena. (1) The work of teaching is not done by the gift of tongues, but by the speech of Peter, and that was delivered either in the Aramaic of Palestine, or, more probably, in the Greek, which was the common medium of intercourse for all the Eastern subjects of the Roman empire. In that speech we find the exercise of the higher gift of prophecy, with precisely the same results as those described by St. Paul as following on the use of that gift. (Comp. verse 37 with 1 Cor. xiv. 24, 25.) (2) The utterances of the disciples are described in words which convey the idea of rapturous praise. They speak the "mighty works," or better, as in Luke i. 49, the *great things* of God. Doxologies, benedictions, adoration, in forms that transcended the common lével of speech, and rose, like the Magnificat, into the region of poetry: this is what the word suggests to us. In the wild, half dithyrambic hymn of Clement of Alexandria — the earliest extant Christian hymn outside the New Testament—in part, perhaps, in that of chap. iv. 24—30, and the Apocalyptic hymns (Rev. iv. 8, 11; v. 13; vii. 10), we have the nearest approach to what then came, in the fiery glow of its first utterance, as with the tongues "of men and of angels," from the lips of the disciples. (3) We cannot fail to be struck with the parallelism between the cry of the scoffers here, "These men are full of new wine" (verse 13), and the words, "Will they not say that ye are mad?" which St. Paul puts into the mouth of those who heard the "tongues" (1 Cor. xiv. 23). In both cases there is an intensity of stimulated life, which finds relief in the forms of poetry and in the tones of song, and which to those who listened was as the poet's frenzy. It is not without significance that St. Paul elsewhere contrasts the "being drunk with wine" with "being filled with the Spirit," and immediately passes on, as though that were the natural result, to add "speaking to yourselves in psalms and hymns and spiritual songs" (Eph. v. 18, 19). If we find the old Jewish psalms in the first of these three words, and hymns known and remembered in the second, the natural explanation of the adjective specially alluded to in the third is that the "songs" or "odes" are such as were not merely "spiritual" in the later sense of the word, but were the immediate outflow of the Spirit's working. Every analogy, it will be noticed, by which St. Paul illustrates his meaning in 1 Cor. xiii. 1, xiv. 7, 8, implies musical intonation. We have the sounding brass and the tinkling (or *clanging*) cymbal, the pipe, the harp, the trumpet giving an uncertain sound. It falls in with this view that our Lord Himself compares the new energy of spiritual life which He was about to impart to new wine (Matt. ix. 17), and that the same comparison meets us in the Old Testament in the words in which Elihu describes his inspiration (Job xxxii. 19). The accounts of prophecy in its wider sense, as including song and praise, as well as a direct message to the minds and hearts of men, in the life of Saul, present phenomena that are obviously analogous (1 Sam. x. 10, 11; xix. 20, 24). The brief accounts in chap. x. 46, "speaking with tongues and magnifying God," and chap. xix. 6, where tongues are distinguished from prophecy, present nothing that is not in harmony with this explanation.

In the present case, however, there are exceptional phenomena. We cannot honestly interpret St. Luke's record without assuming either that the disciples spoke in the languages which are named in verses 9—11, or that, speaking in their own Galilean tongue, their words came to the ears of those who listened as spoken in the language with which each was familiar. The first is at once the more natural interpretation of the language used by the historian, and, if we may use such a word of what is in itself supernatural and mysterious, the more conceivable of the two. And it is clear that there was an end to be attained by such an extension of the gift in this case which could not be attained otherwise. The disciples had been present in Jerusalem at many feasts before, at which they had found themselves, as now, surrounded by pilgrims from many distant lands. Then they had worshipped apart by themselves, with no outward means of fellowship with these strangers, and had poured out their praises and blessings in their own Galilean speech, as each group of those pilgrims had done in theirs. Now they found themselves able to burst through the bounds that had thus divided them, and to claim a fellowship with all true worshippers from whatever lands they came. But there is no evidence that that power was permanent. It came and went with the special outpouring of the Spirit, and lasted only while that lasted in its full intensity. (Comp. Notes on chaps. x. 46, xix. 6.) There are no traces of its exercise in any narrative of the work of apostles and evangelists. They did their work in countries where Greek was spoken, even where it was not the native speech of the inhabitants, and so would not need that special knowledge. In the history of chap. xiv. 11, it is at least implied that Paul and Barnabas did not understand the speech of Lycaonia.

(5) **There were dwelling at Jerusalem.**—The phrase is one of frequent occurrence in St. Luke's writings (Luke xiii. 4; Acts i. 19; iv. 16). As a word, it implied a more settled residence than the "sojourning" of Luke xxiv. 18 (see Note), Heb. xi. 9, but was probably sufficiently wide in its range to include the worshippers who had come up to keep the feast.

**Devout men.**—For the meaning of the word see Note on Luke ii. 25. The primary meaning was one of cautious reverence, the temper that handles sacred things devoutly. As such, it was probably used to include proselytes as well as Jews by birth. The words that are added, "from every nation under heaven," reduce the probability to a certainty. It appears again in chap. viii. 2.

(6) **When this was noised abroad . . . .**—Better *When there had been this voice*, or *utterance.* The word for "voice" is never used for rumour or report in the New Testament; always of some utterance—

this was noised abroad,[1] the multitude came together, and were confounded,[2] because that every man heard them speak in his own language. (7) And they were all amazed and marvelled, saying one to another, Behold, are not all these which speak Galilæans? (8) And how hear we every man in our own tongue, wherein we were born? (9) Parthians, and Medes, and Elamites, and the dwellers in Mesopotamia, and in Judæa, and Cappadocia, in Pontus, and Asia, (10) Phrygia, and Pamphylia, in Egypt, and in the parts of Libya about Cyrene, and strangers of Rome, Jews and proselytes, (11) Cretes and Arabians, we do hear them speak in our tongues the wonderful works of God. (12) And they were all amazed, and were in doubt, saying one to another, What

1 Gr. *when this voice was made.*

2 Or, *troubled in mind.*

human (Matt. iii. 3; Gal. iv. 20), angelic (1 Thess. iv. 16; Rev. v. 11), or divine (Matt. iii. 17; xvii. 5). In John iii. 7 (see Note there) we find it used, in the same connection as in this verse, for the "voice" or "utterance" of the Spirit.

**Were confounded.**—The word is peculiar to the Acts (ix. 22; xix. 32). If we were to draw a distinction between two words of cognate meaning with each other and with the Greek, *confused* would, perhaps, be a better rendering than confounded.

**Every man heard them speak.**—The verb is in the imperfect. They went on listening in their amazement as one after another heard the accents of his own language.

**In his own language.**—Another word peculiar to the Acts. (See Note on chap. i. 19.) It stands as an equivalent for the "tongue" in verse 11, but was used for a *dialect*, in the modern sense of the term, as well as for a distinct language.

(7) **They were all amazed and marvelled.**—It will be noted that this is precisely in accordance with what St. Paul describes as the effect of the gift of tongues. They were a "sign" to them that believed not, filling them with wonder, but the work of convincing and converting was left for the gift of prophecy (1 Cor. xiv. 22).

**Are not all these which speak Galilæans?**—This was, of course, antecedently probable, but it is singular that this is the first assertion of the fact as regards the whole company. The traitor had been apparently the only exception (see Note on Matt. x. 4), and he had gone to his own place.

(8) **And how hear we every man in our own tongue?**—We have here, it is obvious, a composite utterance, in which the writer embodies the manifold expressions which came from those who represented the several nationalities that are afterwards enumerated.

(9–11) **Parthians, and Medes, and Elamites . . . .**—The list that follows is characteristic of the trained historian—trained, it may be, as in the school of Strabo (see *Introduction to St. Luke*)—who had carefully inquired what nations were represented at that great Pentecost, who had himself been present, at least, at one later Pentecost (chap. xxi. 15), and knew the kind of crowd that gathered to it. There is a kind of order, as of one taking a mental bird's-eye view of the Roman empire, beginning with the great Parthian kingdom, which was still, as it had been in the days of Crassus, the most formidable of its foes; then the old territory of the Medes which had once been so closely connected with the history of their fathers; then, the name of the Persians having been thrown into the background, the kindred people of Elam (commonly rendered Persia in the LXX.) whom Strabo speaks of as driven to the mountains (xi. 13, § 6); then the great cities of the Tigris and Euphrates, where the "princes of the captivity" still ruled over a large Jewish population; then passing southward and westward to Judæa; then to Cappadocia, in the interior of Asia Minor; then to Pontus, on the northern shore washed by the Euxine; then westward to the Proconsular Province of Asia, of which Ephesus was the capital. From Ephesus the eye travels eastward to the neighbouring province of Phrygia; thence southward to Pamphylia; thence across the Mediterranean to Egypt; westward to Cyrene; northward, re-crossing the Mediterranean, to the great capital of the empire; then, as by an after-thought, to the two regions of Crete and Arabia that had been previously omitted. The absence of some countries that we should have expected to find in the list—Syria, Cilicia, Cyprus, Bithynia, Macedonia, Achaia, Spain—is not easy to explain, but it is, at any rate, an indication that what we have is not an artificial list made up at a later date, but an actual record of those whose presence at the Feast had been ascertained by the historian. Possibly they may have been omitted because Jews and converts coming from them would naturally speak Greek, and there would be no marvel to them in hearing Galileans speaking in that language. The presence of Judæa in the list is almost as unexpected as the absence of the others. That, we think, might have been taken for granted. Some critics have accordingly conjectured that "India" must be the true reading, but without any MS. authority. Possibly, the men of Judæa are named as sharing in the wonder that the Galileans were no longer distinguished by their provincial *patois*. (Comp. Note on Matt. xxvi. 73.)

(10) **Strangers of Rome . . .**—Better, *the Romans who were sojourning there*—*i.e.*, at Jerusalem. The verb is peculiar to St. Luke in the New Testament, and is used by him, as in chap. xvii. 18, of the strangers and visitors of a city.

**Jews and proselytes.**—The words may possibly be applicable to the whole preceding list; but they read more like a note specially emphasising the prominence of the Roman proselytes in that mixed multitude of worshippers. It lies in the nature of the case, that they were proselytes in the full sense of the term, circumcised and keeping the Law. Looking to St. Luke's use of another word ("they that worship God," as in chaps. xvi. 14; xvii. 4, 17) for those whom the Rabbis classed as "proselytes of the gate," it is probable that he used the term in its strictest sense for those who had been received into the covenant of Israel, and who were known in the Rabbinic classification as the "proselytes of righteousness."

(11) **The wonderful works of God.**—Better, *the great things*, or *the majesty, of God.* The word is the same as in Luke i. 49. The word points, as has been said above, distinctly to words of praise and not of teaching.

(12) **They were all amazed, and were in doubt.**—The last word is somewhat stronger in the

meaneth this? (13) Others mocking
said, These men are full of new wine.
(14) But Peter, standing up with the
eleven, lifted up his voice, and said unto
them, Ye men of Judæa, and all *ye* that
dwell at Jerusalem, be this known unto
you, and hearken to my words: (15) for
these are not drunken, as ye suppose,
seeing it is *but* the third hour of the
day. (16) But this is that which was
spoken by the prophet Joel; (17) and it
shall come to pass in the last days,[a]
saith God, I will pour out of my Spirit
upon all flesh: and your sons and your
daughters shall prophesy, and your
young men shall see visions, and your
old men shall dream dreams: (18) and
on my servants and on my handmaidens
I will pour out in those days of my
Spirit; and they shall prophesy:
(19) and I will shew wonders in heaven
above, and signs in the earth beneath;

[a] Isa. 44. 3; Joel 2. 28.

---

Greek: "were much perplexed," as in Luke xxiv. 4. No New Testament writer uses it except St. Luke.

**What meaneth this?**—Better, *What may this mean?* The same phrase occurs in chap. xvii. 18.

(13) **These men are full of new wine.**—Literally, *of sweet drink*—the word "wine" not being used—stronger and more intoxicating than the lighter and thinner wines that were ordinarily drunk. The Greek word was sometimes used, like the Latin *mustum*, for the unfermented grape-juice. Here, however, the context shows that wine, in the strict sense of the word, was intended, and the use of the same word in the LXX. of Job xxxii. 19 confirms this meaning. The word for "new wine" in Matt. ix. 17, Mark ii. 22, is different, but there also (see Notes) fermentation is implied. The words, as has been said above (Note on verse 4), point to a certain appearance of excitement in tone, manner, and words.

(14) **But Peter, standing up with the eleven, . . .**—We are struck at once with the marvellous change that has come over the character of the Apostle. Timidity has become boldness; for the few hasty words recorded in the Gospels we have elaborate discourses. There is a method and insight in the way he deals with the prophecies of the Christ altogether unlike anything that we have seen in him before. If we were reading a fictitious history, we should rightly criticise the author for the want of consistency in his portraiture of the same character in the first and second volumes of his work. As it is, the inconsistency becomes almost an evidence of the truth of the narratives that contain it. The writer of a made-up-history, bent only upon reconciling the followers of Peter and of Paul, would have made the former more prominent in the Gospels or less prominent in the Acts. And the facts which St. Luke narrates are an adequate explanation of the phenomena. In the interval that had passed, Peter's mind had been opened by his Lord's teaching to understand the Scriptures (Luke xxiv. 45), and then he had been endued, by the gift of the Holy Spirit, with power from on high. That which he now speaks is the first utterance of the new gift of prophecy, and followed rightly on the portent of the "tongues" to bring about the work of conversion which they had no power to accomplish. The speech which follows was spoken either in the Aramaic of Palestine, or, more probably, in the Greek, which was common in Galilee, and which would be intelligible to all, or nearly all, of the pilgrims from distant countries.

**And said unto them.**—The verb is not the word commonly so rendered, but that which is translated "utterance," or "to utter," in verse 4. The unusual word was probably repeated here to indicate that what follows was just as much an "utterance" of the Holy Spirit, working on and through the spiritual powers of man, as the marvel of the "tongues" had been.

**Hearken to my words.**—Literally, *give ear to.* The verb is an unusual one, and is found here only in the New Testament. It is used not unfrequently in the LXX., as, *e.g.*, in Gen. iv. 22; Job xxiii. 18.

(15) **Seeing it is but the third hour of the day.**—The appeal is made to the common standard of right feeling. Drunkenness belonged to the night (1 Thess. v. 7). It was a mark of extremest baseness for men to "rise up early in the morning that they may follow strong drink" (Isa. v. 11; comp. also Eccles. x. 16). Were the disciples likely to be drunk at 9 a.m., and that on the morning of the Day of Pentecost, after a night spent in devotion, and when all decent Jews were fasting?

(17) **It shall come to pass in the last days.**—The prophecy of Joel takes its place, with the exception, perhaps, of Hosea, as the oldest of the prophetic books of the Old Testament. The people were suffering from one of the locust-plagues of the East and its consequent famine. The prophet calls them to repentance, and promises this gift of the Spirit as the great blessing of a far-off future. He had been taught that no true knowledge of God comes but through that Spirit. So Elisha prayed that a double portion (*i.e.*, the eldest son's inheritance) of the Spirit which God had given to Elijah might rest upon him (2 Kings ii. 9).

**Your sons and your daughters shall prophesy.**—The Old Testament use of the word, in its wider generic sense, as, *e.g.*, in the case of Saul, 1 Sam. x. 10, xix. 20—24, covered phenomena analogous to the gift of tongues as well as that of prophecy in the New Testament sense. The words imply that women as well as men had been filled with the Spirit, and had spoken with the "tongues."

**Your young men shall see visions.**—The "visions," implying the full activity of spiritual power, are thought of as belonging to the younger prophets. In the calmer state of more advanced age, wisdom came, as in the speech of Elihu, "in a dream, in visions of the night, when deep sleep falleth upon men" (Job xxxiii. 15).

(18) **And on my servants and on my handmaidens . . .**—This was the culminating point of the joyous prediction. Not on priests only, or those who had been trained in the schools of the prophets, but on slaves, male and female, should that gift be poured by Him who was no respecter of persons. The life of Amos, the herdsman of Tekoa, the "gatherer of sycomore fruit" (Amos i. 1; vii. 14), was, perhaps, the earliest example of the gift so bestowed. The apostolic age must have witnessed many. The fisherman of Galilee, who was now speaking, was the forerunner of thousands in whom the teaching of the Spirit has superseded the training of the schools.

(19) **And I will shew wonders in heaven above.**—St. Peter quotes the words of terror that

blood, and fire, and vapour of smoke:
(20) the sun shall be turned into dark-
ness,[a] and the moon into blood, before — a Joel 2. 31.
that great and notable day of the Lord
come: (21) and it shall come to pass,
*that* whosoever shall call on the name
of the Lord shall be saved.[b] (22) Ye men — b Rom. 10. 12.
of Israel, hear these words; Jesus of
Nazareth, a man approved of God
among you by miracles and wonders
and signs, which God did by him in the — c Ps. 16. 8.
midst of you, as ye yourselves also
know: (23) him, being delivered by the
determinate counsel and foreknowledge
of God, ye have taken, and by wicked
hands have crucified and slain:
(24) whom God hath raised up, having
loosed the pains of death: because it
was not possible that he should be
holden of it. (25) For David speaketh con-
cerning him, I foresaw the Lord always
before my face,[c] for he is on my right

---

follow, apparently, for the sake of the promise with which they end in verse 21. But as it was not given to him as yet to know the times and the seasons (chap. i. 7), it may well have been that he looked for the "great and notable day" as about to come in his own time. The imagery is drawn as from one of the great thunder-storms of Palestine. There is the lurid blood-red hue of clouds and sky; there are the fiery flashes, the columns or pillars of smoke-like clouds boiling from the abyss. These, in their turn, were probably thought of as symbols of bloodshed, and fire and smoke, such as are involved in the capture and destruction of a city like Jerusalem.

(20) **The sun shall be turned into darkness.**—Both clauses bring before us the phenomena of an eclipse: the total darkness of the sun, the dusky copper hue of the moon. Signs, of which these were but faint images, had been predicted by our Lord, echoing, as it were, the words of Joel, as among the preludes of His Advent (Matt. xxiv. 29).

**That great and notable day.**—St. Luke follows the LXX. version. The Hebrew gives, as in our version, "the great and terrible day." As seen by the prophet, the day was terrible to the enemies of God; a day of blessing to "the remnant whom the Lord should call" (Joel ii. 32). The Greek word for "notable" (*epiphanès*) lent itself readily to the thought of the great Epiphany or manifestation of Christ as the Judge of all.

(21) **Whosoever shall call on the name of the Lord . . .**—Singularly enough, the precise phrase, to "call upon" God, common as it is in the Old Testament, does not occur in the Gospels. With St. Luke and St. Paul it is, as it were, a favourite word (chaps. vii. 59; ix. 14; Rom. x. 12; 1 Cor. i. 2). Its Greek associations gave to the "invoking" which it expressed almost the force of an appeal from a lower to a higher tribunal. (Comp. chap. xxv. 11, 21, 25.) Here the thought is that that Name of the Eternal, invoked by the prayer of faith, was the one sufficient condition of deliverance in the midst of all the terrors of the coming day of the Lord.

(22) **Jesus of Nazareth.**—We hardly estimate, as we read them, the boldness implied in the utterance of that Name. Barely seven weeks had passed since He who bore it had died the death of a slave and of a robber. The speaker himself had denied all knowledge of Him of whom he now spoke.

**A man approved of God.**—The verb is used in its older English sense, as proved, or *pointed out*, not as we now use the word, as meeting with the approval of God.

**Miracles and wonders and signs.**—Better, *mighty works* . . . The words are three synonyms, expressing different aspects of the same facts, rather than a classification of phenomena. The leading thought, in the first word, is the power displayed in the act; in the second, the marvel of it as a portent; in the third, its character as a token or note of something beyond itself.

(23) **By the determinate counsel and foreknowledge of God.**—The adjective meets us again in St. Peter's speech in chap. x. 42; the word for "foreknowledge" in his Epistle (1 Pet. i. 2), and there only in the New Testament. The coincidence is not without its force as bearing on the genuineness both of the speech and of the letter. It has now become the habit of the Apostle's mind to trace the working of a divine purpose, which men, even when they are most bent on thwarting it, are unconsciously fulfilling. In chap. i. 16, he had seen that purpose in the treachery of Judas; he sees it now in the malignant injustice of priests and people.

**Ye have taken . . . .**—Better, *ye took, and by lawless hands crucified and slew.* Stress is laid on the priests having used the hands of one who was "without law" (1 Cor. ix. 21), a heathen ruler, to inflict the doom which they dared not inflict themselves.

(24) **Whom God hath raised up.**—It is probable enough that some rumours of the Resurrection had found their way among the people, and had been met by the counter-statement of which we read in Matt. xxviii. 11—15; but this was the first public witness, borne by one who was ready to seal his testimony with his blood, to the stupendous fact.

**Having loosed the pains of death.**—The word for "pains" is the same as that for "sorrows" in Matt. xxiv. 8: literally, *travail-pangs.* The phrase was not uncommon in the LXX. version, but was apparently a mistranslation of the Hebrew for "cords," or "bands," of death. If we take the Greek word in its full meaning, the Resurrection is thought of as a new birth as from the womb of the grave.

**Because it was not possible . . . .**—The moral impossibility was, we may say, two-fold. The work of the Son of Man could not have ended in a failure and death which would have given the lie to all that He had asserted of Himself. Its issue could not run counter to the prophecies which had implied with more or less clearness a victory over death. The latter, as the sequel shows, was the thought prominent in St. Peter's mind.

(25) **For David speaketh concerning him.**—More accurately, *in reference to Him—i.e.,* in words which extended to Him. Reading Ps. xvi. without this interpretation, it seems as if it spoke only of the confidence of the writer that he would be himself delivered from the grave and death. Some interpreters confine that confidence to a temporal deliverance; some extend it to the thought of immortality, or even of a

hand, that I should not be moved:
(26) therefore did my heart rejoice, and
my tongue was glad; moreover also my
flesh shall rest in hope: (27) because
thou wilt not leave my soul in hell,
neither wilt thou suffer thine Holy One
to see corruption. (28) Thou hast made
known to me the ways of life; thou
shalt make me full of joy with thy countenance.
(29) Men *and* brethren, let [1] me
freely speak unto you of the patriarch
David,[a] that he is both dead and buried,
and his sepulchre is with us unto this
day. (30) Therefore being a prophet,

1 Or, *I may.*

a 1 Kings 2. 10.

---

resurrection. But Peter had been taught, both by his Lord and by the Spirit, that all such hopes extend beyond themselves—that the ideal of victory after suffering, no less than that of the righteous sufferer, was realised in Christ. The fact of the Resurrection had given a new meaning to prophecies which would not, of themselves, have suggested it, but which were incomplete without it.

**He is on my right hand.**—The Psalmist thought of the Eternal as the warrior thinks of him who, in the conflict of battle, extends his shield over the comrade who is on the left hand, and so guards him from attack. When the Son of Man is said to sit on the right hand of God (Ps. cx. 1; Matt. xxvi. 64) the imagery is different, and brings before us the picture of a king seated on his throne with his heir sitting in the place of honour by his side.

(26) **My tongue was glad.**—The Hebrew gives "my glory," a term which was applied to the mind of man, perhaps also to his faculty of speech (Pss. lvii. 8; lxii. 7), as that by which he excelled all other creatures of God's hand. The LXX. had paraphrased the word by "tongue," and St. Peter, or St. Luke reporting his speech, follows that version.

**Also my flesh shall rest in hope.**—Literally, *shall tabernacle*, or, *dwell as in a tabernacle.* We may, perhaps, trace an echo of the thought in 2 Pet. i. 13, 14.

(27) **Thou wilt not leave my soul in hell.**—Literally, *in Hades.* (See Note on Matt. xi. 23.) As interpreted by St. Peter's words in his Epistle (1 Pet. iii. 19), the words conveyed to his mind the thought which has been embodied in the article of the "Descent into Hell," or *Hades*, in the Apostle's Creed. The death of Christ was an actual death, and while the body was laid in the grave, the soul passed into the world of the dead, the *Sheol* of the Hebrews, the *Hades* of the Greeks, to carry on there the redemptive work which had been begun on earth. (Comp. chap. xiii. 34—37, and Eph. iv. 9.) Here again we have an interesting coincidence with St. Peter's language (1 Pet. iii. 19), as to the work of Christ in preaching to the "spirits in prison."

**Neither wilt thou suffer thine Holy One to see corruption.**—The word for "holy" is different from that commonly so rendered, and conveys the idea of personal piety and godliness rather than consecration. As the Psalmist used the words, we may think of them as expressing the confidence that he himself, as loving, and beloved of, God, would be delivered from destruction, both now and hereafter. St. Peter had learnt to interpret the words as having received a higher fulfilment. Christ was, in this sense, as well as in that expressed by the other word, "the Holy One" of God (Mark i. 24; Luke iv. 34). In Heb. vii. 26; Rev. xv. 4; xvi. 5, this very word is applied to Christ. The Hebrew text of Ps. xvi. 10 presents the various-reading of "the holy ones," as if referring to the "saints that are upon the earth," of verse 3. The LXX., which St. Peter follows, gives the singular, which is indeed essential to his argument, and this is also the reading of the Masoretic text. The Greek word for "corruption" ranges in its meaning from "decay" to "destruction." The Hebrew to which it answers is primarily the "pit" of the grave, and not "corruption," or "wasting away."

(28) **Thou hast made known to me the ways of life.**—The Apostle does not interpret these words, but we can hardly err in thinking that he would have looked on them also as fulfilled in Christ's humanity. To Him also the ways of life had been made known, and so even in *Hades* He was filled with joy (better, perhaps, *gladness*, as in Acts xiv. 17), as being in the Paradise of God (Luke xxiii. 43).

(29) **Let me freely speak.**—Better, *it is lawful for me to speak with freedom.* Those to whom the Apostle spoke could not for a moment dream of asserting that the words quoted had been literally and completely fulfilled in him, and it was therefore natural to look for their fulfilment elsewhere.

**Of the patriarch David.**—The word is used in its primary sense, as meaning the founder of a family or dynasty. In the New Testament it is applied also to Abraham (Heb. vii. 4) and the twelve sons of Jacob (Acts vii. 8). In the Greek version of the Old Testament it is used only of the comparatively subordinate "chief of the fathers" in 1 Chron. ix. 9; xxiv. 31, *et al.*

**His sepulchre is with us unto this day.**—The king was buried in the city which bore his name (1 Kings ii. 10). Josephus relates that vast treasures were buried with him (*Ant.* vii. 15, § 4), and that John Hyrcanus opened one of the chambers of the tomb, and took out three thousand talents to pay the tribute demanded by Antiochus the Pious (*Ant.* xiii. 8, § 4). Herod the Great also opened it and found no money, but gold and silver vessels in abundance. The tradition was that he sought to penetrate into the inner vault, in which the bodies of David and Solomon were resting, and was deterred by a flame that issued from the recess (*Ant.* xvi. 7, § 1). It is difficult to understand how such a treasure could have escaped the plunderer in all the sieges and sacks to which Jerusalem had been exposed; but it is possible that its fame as a holy place may have made it, like the temples at Delphi and Ephesus, a kind of bank of deposit, in which large treasures in coin or plate were left for safety, and many of these, in the common course of things, were never claimed, and gradually accumulated. The monuments now known as the "tombs of the kings" on the north side of the city, though identified by De Sauley with the sepulchres of the house of David, are of the Roman period, and are outside the walls. David and his successors were probably buried in a vault on the eastern hill, in the city of David (1 Kings ii. 10), within the range of the enclosure now known as the *Haram* Area.

(30) **Therefore being a prophet.**—The words "according to the flesh, He would raise up Christ," are wanting in many of the best MSS. Without them

and knowing that God had sworn with
an oath to him,[a] that of the fruit of his
loins, according to the flesh, he would
raise up Christ to sit on his throne;
(31) he seeing this before spake of the
resurrection of Christ, that his soul was
not left in hell,[b] neither his flesh did see
corruption. (32) This Jesus hath God
raised up, whereof we all are witnesses.
(33) Therefore being by the right hand
of God exalted, and having received of
the Father the promise of the Holy
Ghost, he hath shed forth this, which
ye now see and hear. (34) For David is
not ascended into the heavens: but he
saith himself, The LORD said unto my
Lord,[c] Sit thou on my right hand,
(35) until I make thy foes thy footstool.
(36) Therefore let all the house of Israel
know assuredly, that God hath made
that same Jesus, whom ye have cruci-
fied, both Lord and Christ.

(37) Now when they heard *this*, they
were pricked in their heart, and said
unto Peter and to the rest of the
apostles, Men *and* brethren, what shall
we do? (38) Then Peter said unto them,
Repent, and be baptized every one of

a Ps. 132. 11.
c Ps. 110. 1.
b Ps. 16. 10.

---

the sentence, though somewhat incomplete, would run thus: "That God had sworn with an oath *that from his loins one should sit upon his throne.*" The words claim for the Psalmist a prophetic foresight of some kind, without defining its measure or clearness. His thoughts went beyond himself to the realisation of his hopes in a near or far-off future. As with most other prophets, the precise time, even the "manner of time," was hidden from him (1 Pet. i. 11).

**He would raise up Christ.**—The Greek, by using the verb from which comes the word "resurrection," gives to the verb the definite sense of "raising from the dead."

(31) **He seeing this before . . . .**—In the vision of the future which St. Peter thus ascribes to David, the king had been led, as he interprets the words, not only or chiefly to speak out his own hopes, but to utter that which received its fulfilment in the fact of the resurrection. What was conspicuously not true of the historical David was found to be true of the Son of David according to the flesh.

(32) **This Jesus hath God raised up . . .**—From the first the Apostles take up the position which their Lord had assigned them. They are witnesses, and before and above all else, witnesses of the Resurrection.

(33) **Therefore being by the right hand of God.**—The Greek has the dative case without a preposition. The English version takes it, and probably is right in taking it, as the dative of the instrument, the image that underlies the phrase being that the Eternal King stretches forth His hand to raise Him who was in form His Servant to a place beside Him on His right hand; and, on the whole, this seems the best rendering. Not a few scholars, however, render the words "exalted to the right hand of God."

**Having received of the Father.**—The words of St. Peter, obviously independent as they are of the Gospel of St. John, present a striking agreement with our Lord's language as recorded by him (John xiv. 26; xv. 26). The promise throws us back upon these chapters, and also upon chap. i. 4.

**Hath shed forth this.**—Better, *hath poured out.* The verb had not been used in the Gospels of the promise of the Spirit, but is identical with that which was found in the Greek version of Joel's prophecy, as cited in verse 17, "I will *pour out* of My Spirit."

(34) **The Lord said . . . .**—There is, when we remember what had passed but seven weeks before, something very striking in the reproduction by St. Peter of the very words by which our Lord had brought the scribes to confess their ignorance of the true interpretation of the Psalmist's mysterious words (Ps. cx. 1). (See Note on Matt. xxii. 44.) Those who were then silenced are now taught how it was that David's Son was also David's Lord.

(36) **That same Jesus . . . .**—Better, *this Jesus.*

**Both Lord and Christ.**—Some MSS. omit "both." The word "Lord" is used with special reference to the prophetic utterance of the Psalm thus cited. There is a rhetorical force in the very order of the words which the English can scarcely give: "that both Lord and Christ hath God made this Jesus whom ye crucified." The pronoun of the last verb is emphatic, as pointing the contrast between the way in which the Jews of Jerusalem had dealt with Jesus and the recognition which he had received from the Father. The utterance of the word "crucified" at the close, pressing home the guilt of the people on their consciences, may be thought of as, in a special manner, working the result described in the next verse.

(37) **They were pricked in their heart.**—The verb occurs here only in the New Testament, and expresses the sharp, painful emotion which is indicated in "compunction," a word of kindred meaning. A noun derived from it, or possibly from another root, is used in Rom. xi. 8 in the sense of "slumber," apparently as indicating either the unconsciousness that follows upon extreme pain, or simple drowsiness. In "attrition" and "contrition" we have analogous instances of words primarily physical used for spiritual emotions.

(38) **Repent, and be baptized every one of you in the name of Jesus Christ.**—The work of the Apostles is, in one sense, a continuation, in another a development, of that of the Baptist. There is the same indispensable condition of "repentance"—*i.e.* a change of heart and will—the same outward rite as the symbol of purification, the same promise of forgiveness which that change involves. But the baptism is now, as it had not been before, in the name of Jesus Christ, and it is connected more directly with the gift of the Holy Spirit. The question presents itself, Why is the baptism here, and elsewhere in the Acts (x. 48; xix. 5), "in the name of Jesus Christ," while in Matt. xxviii. 19, the Apostles are commanded to baptize in the name of the Father, the Son, and the Holy Spirit? Various explanations have been given. It has been said that baptism in the Name of any one of the Persons of the Trinity, involves the Name of the other Two. It has even been assumed that St. Luke meant the fuller formula when he used the shorter one. But a more satisfactory solution is, perhaps, found in seeing in the words of Matt. xxviii. 19 (see Note there) the formula for the baptism of those who, as Gentiles,

you in the name of Jesus Christ for the remission of sins, and ye shall receive the gift of the Holy Ghost. (39) For the promise is unto you, and to your children, and to all that are afar off, *even* as many as the Lord our God shall call. (40) And with many other words did he testify and exhort, saying, Save yourselves from this untoward generation.

(41) Then they that gladly received his word were baptized: and the same day there were added *unto them* about three thousand souls. (42) And they continued steadfastly in the apostles' doctrine and fellowship, and in breaking

---

had been "without God in the world, not knowing the Father;" while for converts from Judaism, or those who had before been proselytes to Judaism, it was enough that there should be the distinctive profession of their faith in Jesus as the Christ, the Son of God, added on to their previous belief in the Father and the Holy Spirit. In proportion as the main work of the Church of Christ lay among the Gentiles, it was natural that the fuller form should become dominant, and finally be used exclusively. It is interesting here, also, to compare the speech of St. Peter with the stress laid on baptism in his Epistle (1 Pet. iii. 21).

**Ye shall receive the gift of the Holy Ghost.**—The word for "gift" (*dôrea*) is generic, and differs from the more specific "gift" (*charisma*) of 1 Cor. xii. 4, 9, 28. The Apostle does not necessarily promise startling and marvellous powers, but in some way they should all feel that a new Spirit was working in them, and that that Spirit was from God.

(39) **The promise is unto you, and to your children.**—The tendency of sects has always been to claim spiritual gifts and powers as an exclusive privilege limited to a few. It is the essence of St. Peter's appeal that all to whom he speaks can claim the promise as fully as himself. The phrase "those that are afar off," was probably wide enough to cover both the Jews of the Dispersion, to whom the Apostle afterwards wrote (1 Pet. i. 1, 2), and the heathen nations among whom they lived. The use of the phrase in Eph. ii. 13, 17, inclines rather to the latter meaning.

**Even as many as the Lord our God shall call.**—There seems, at first sight, a limitation on the universality of the previous words. And in some sense there is; but it is not more than is involved in the fact that spiritual knowledge and culture are not bestowed on all nations and ages alike. Wherever there is a difference, some possessing a higher knowledge and greater power than others, the Apostle could only see, not chance, or evolution, but the working of a divine purpose, calling some to special privileges, and yet dealing equitably with all.

(40) **With many other words.**—The report breaks off, as if St. Luke's informant had followed closely up to this point and then lost count of the sequence of thought and words.

**Did he testify**—*i.e., continued to testify.*

**Save yourselves.**—Literally, in the passive, *Be ye saved.* They were invited to submit to God's way of salvation, to accept Jesus as their Saviour.

**From this untoward generation.**—Literally, *from this crooked generation,* as the word is rendered in Luke iii. 5; Phil. ii. 15.

(41) **They that gladly received his word were baptized.**—This was, we must remember, no new emotion. Not four years had passed since there had been a like eagerness to rush to the baptism of John. (See Notes on Matt. iii. 5; xi. 12.)

**Three thousand souls.**—The largeness of the number has been urged as rendering it probable that the baptism was by affusion, not immersion. On the other hand, (1) immersion had clearly been practised by John, and was involved in the original meaning of the word, and it is not likely that the rite should have been curtailed of its full proportions at the very outset. (2) The symbolic meaning of the act required immersion in order that it might be clearly manifested, and Rom. vi. 4, and 1 Pet. iii. 21, seem almost of necessity to imply the more complete mode. The swimming-baths of Bethesda and Siloam (see Notes on John v. 7; ix. 7), or the so-called Fountain of the Virgin, near the Temple enclosure, or the bathing-places within the Tower of Antony (Jos. *Wars,* v. 5, § 8), may well have helped to make the process easy. The sequel shows (1) that many converts were made from the Hellenistic Jews who were present at the Feast (chap. vi. 1); and (2) that few, if any, of the converts were of the ruling class (chap. iv. 1). It is obvious that some of these converts may have gone back to the cities whence they came, and may have been the unknown founders of the Church at Damascus, or Alexandria, or Rome itself.

(42) **And they continued steadfastly.**—The one Greek word is expressed by the English verb and adverb. As applied to persons, the New Testament use of the word is characteristic of St. Luke (chaps. ii. 46; vi. 4; viii. 13; x. 7), and peculiar to him and St. Paul (Rom. xii. 12; xiii. 6; Col. iv. 2).

**The apostles' doctrine.**—Four elements of the life of the new society are dwelt on. (1) They grew in knowledge of the truth by attending to the *teaching* of the Apostles. This, and not the thought of a formulated doctrine to which they gave their consent, is clearly the meaning of the word. (See Note on Matt. vii. 28.) (2) They joined in outward acts of fellowship with each other, acts of common worship, acts of mutual kindness and benevolence. The one Greek word diverges afterwards into the sense of what we technically call "communion," as in 1 Cor. x. 16, and that of a "collection" or contribution for the poor (Rom. xv. 26; 2 Cor. ix. 13).

**And in breaking of bread, and in prayers.**—(3) St. Luke uses the phrase, we must remember, in the sense which, when he wrote, it had acquired in St. Paul's hands. It can have no meaning less solemn than the commemorative "breaking of bread," of 1 Cor. x. 16. From the very first what was afterwards known as the Lord's Supper (see Note on 1 Cor. xi. 20) took its place with baptism as a permanent universal element in the Church's life. At first, it would seem, the evening meal of every day was such a supper. Afterwards the two elements that had then been united were developed separately, the social into the *Agapæ,* or Feasts of Love (Jude, verse 12, and—though here there is a various-reading—2 Pet. ii. 13), the other into the Communion, or Eucharistic Sacrifice. (4) Prayer, in like manner, included private as well as public devotions. These may have been the outpouring of the heart's desires: but they may also have been what the disciples had

of bread, and in prayers. (43) And fear
came upon every soul: and many won-
ders and signs were done by the apostles.
(44) And all that believed were together,
and had all things common; (45) and
sold their possessions and goods, and
parted them to all *men*, as every man
had need. (46) And they, continuing
daily with one accord in the temple,
and breaking bread from house to
house,[1] did eat their meat with glad-
ness and singleness of heart, (47) prais-
ing God, and having favour with all
the people. And the Lord added to
the church daily such as should be
saved.

1 Or, *at home.*

---

been taught to pray, as in Matt. vi. 9, Luke xi. 1, as the disciples of John had been taught. The use of the plural seems to indicate recurring times of prayer at fixed hours.

(43) **Fear came upon every soul.**—The Greek text shows a careful distinction of tenses. Fear—*i.e.*, reverential awe—came specially at that season; the "signs and wonders" were wrought continually. (See Note on verse 19.)

(44) **All that believed were together . . . .**—The writer dwells with a manifest delight on this picture of what seemed to him the true ideal of a human society. Here there was a literal fulfilment of his Lord's words (Luke xii. 33), a society founded, not on the law of self-interest and competition, but on sympathy and self-denial. They had all things in common, not by a compulsory abolition of the rights of property (see chap. v. 4), but by the spontaneous energy of love. The gift of the Spirit showed its power, not only in tongues and prophecy, but in the more excellent way of charity. It was well that that inimitable glow of love should manifest itself for a time to be a beacon-light to after ages, even if experience taught the Church in course of time that this generous and general distribution was not the wisest method of accomplishing permanent good, and that here also a discriminate economy, such as St. Paul taught (2 Thess. iii. 10; 1 Tim. iii. 8), was necessary as a safe-guard against abuse. It was, we may perhaps believe, partly in consequence of the rapid exhaustion of its resources thus brought about, that the Church at Jerusalem became dependent for many years upon the bounty of the churches of the Gentiles. (See Note on chap. xi. 29.)

(45) **And sold their possessions and goods.**—The verbs throughout this description are in the imperfect tense, as expressing the constant recurrence of the act. The Greek words for "possessions" and "goods" both mean "property," the former as a thing acquired, the latter as that which belongs to a man for the time being. Custom, however, had introduced a technical distinction, and "possessions" stands for real property, "goods" for personal. So in chap. v. 1, 3, 8, the former word is used interchangeably with that which is translated "field," and in the LXX. of Prov. xxiii. 10, xxxi. 16, is used both for "field" and "vineyard."

**As every man had need.**—The words imply at least the endeavour to discriminate. The money was not given literally to every one who applied for it, and so the way was prepared for more fixed and definite rules.

(46) **Continuing daily with one accord in the temple.**—At first it would have seemed natural that the followers of a Teacher whom the priests had condemned to death, who had once nearly been stoned, and once all but seized in the very courts of the Temple (John viii. 59; x. 31; vii. 45), should keep aloof from the sanctuary that had thus been desecrated. But they remembered that He had claimed it as His Father's house, that His zeal for that house had been as a consuming passion (John ii. 16, 17), and therefore they had attended its worship daily before the Day of Pentecost (Luke xxiv. 53); and it was not less, but infinitely more, precious to them now, as the place where they could meet with God, than it had been in the days of ignorance, before they had known the Christ, and through Him had learnt to know the Father. The apparent strangeness of their being allowed to meet in the Temple is explained partly by the fact that its courts were open to all Israelites who did not disturb its peace, partly by the existence of a moderate half-believing party in the Sanhedrin itself, including Nicodemus, Joseph of Arimathæa, and Gamaliel (chap. v. 35); and by the popularity gained for a time by the holiness and liberal almsgiving of the new community.

**Breaking bread from house to house.**—Better, with the margin, *at home*—*i.e.*, in their own house. The Greek phrase may have a distributive force, but Rom. xvi. 5, 1 Cor. xvi. 19, Col. iv. 14, where the same formula is used, seem to show that that is not the meaning here. They met in the Temple, they met also in what, in the modern sense of the word, would be the "church" of the new society, for the act of worship, above all, for the highest act of worship and of fellowship, for which the Temple was, of course, unsuitable.

**Did eat their meat . . .**—We have again the tense which implies a customary act. The words imply that as yet the solemn breaking of bread was closely connected with their daily life. Anticipating the language of a few years later, the Agapè, or Love-feast, was united with the Eucharistic Communion. The higher sanctified the lower. It was not till love and faith were colder that men were forced to separate them, lest (as in 1 Cor. xi. 20, 21) the lower should desecrate the higher.

**Gladness and singleness of heart.**—This "gladness" is significant. The word was the same as that which had been used by the angel to Zacharias (Luke i. 44) in announcing the birth of the Forerunner. The verb from which the noun was derived had been employed by our Lord when He bade His disciples rejoice and be glad (Matt. v. 12). The literal meaning of the word translated "singleness," which does not occur elsewhere in the New Testament, was the smoothness of a soil without stones. Thence it came to be used for evenness and simplicity, unity of character; thence for that unity showing itself in love; thence, by a further transition, for unalloyed benevolence, showing itself in act.

(47) **Having favour with all the people.**—The new life of the Apostles, in part probably their liberal almsgiving, had revived the early popularity of their Master with the common people. The Sadducean priests were, probably, the only section that looked on them with a malignant fear.

**The Lord added to the church daily such as should be saved.**—Many of the better MSS. omit the words "to the Church," and connect "together,"

CHAPTER III.—(1) Now Peter and
John went up together into the temple
at the hour of prayer, *being* the ninth
*hour.* (2) And a certain man lame from
his mother's womb was carried, whom
they laid daily at the gate of the temple
which is called Beautiful, to ask alms
of them that entered into the temple;
(3) who seeing Peter and John about
to go into the temple asked an alms.
(4) And Peter, fastening his eyes upon
him with John, said, Look on us.

A.D. 33.

---

which in the Greek is the first word in chap. iii. 1, with this verse—*The Lord added together . . .* The verb "added" is in the tense which, like the adverb "daily," implies a continually recurring act. "The Lord" is probably used here, as in verse 39, in its generic Old Testament sense, rather than as definitely applied to Christ. For "such as should be saved"—a meaning which the present participle passive cannot possibly have—read, *those that were in the way of salvation;* literally, *those that were being saved,* as in 1 Cor. i. 18; 2 Cor. ii. 15. The verse takes its place among the few passages in which the translators have, perhaps, been influenced by a Calvinistic bias; Heb. x. 38, "if *any man* draw back," instead of "if *he* draw back," being another. It should, however, be stated in fairness that all the versions from Tyndale onward, including the Rhemish, give the same rendering. Wiclif alone gives nearly the true meaning, "them that were made saaf."

III.

(1) **Now Peter and John went up.**—Better, *were going up.* The union of the two brings the narratives of the Gospels into an interesting connection with the Acts. They were probably about the same age (the idea that Peter was some years older than John rests mainly on the pictures which artists have drawn from their imagination, and has no evidence in Scripture), and had been friends from their youth upward. They had been partners as fishermen on the Sea of Galilee (Luke v. 10). They had been sharers in looking for the consolation of Israel, and had together received the baptism of John (John i. 41). John and Andrew had striven which should be the first to tell Peter that they had found the Christ (John i. 41). The two had been sent together to prepare for the Passover (Luke xxii. 8). John takes Peter into the palace of the high priest (John xviii. 16), and though he must have witnessed his denials is not estranged from him. It is to John that Peter turns for comfort after his fall, and with him he comes to the sepulchre on the morning of the Resurrection (John xx. 6). The eager affection which, now more strongly than ever, bound the two together is seen in Peter's question, "Lord, and what shall this man do?" (John xxi. 21); and now they are again sharers in action and in heart, in teaching and in worship. Passing rivalries there may have been, disputes which was the greatest, prayers for places on the right hand and the left (Matt. xx. 20; Mark x. 35); but the idea maintained by Renan (*Vie de Jésus, Introduction*), that St. John wrote his Gospel to exalt himself at the expense of Peter, must take its place among the *delirantium somnia,* the morbid imaginations, of inventive interpretation. They appear in company again in the mission to Samaria (chap. viii. 14), and in recognising the work that had been done by Paul and Barnabas among the Gentiles (Gal. ii. 9). When it was that they parted never to meet again, we have no record. No account is given as to the interval that had passed since the Day of Pentecost. Presumably the brief notice at the end of chap. ii. was meant to summarise a gradual progress, marked by no striking incidents, which may have gone on for several months. The absence of chronological *data* in the Acts, as a book written by one who in the Gospel appears to lay stress on such matters (Luke iii. 1; vi. 2), is somewhat remarkable. The most natural explanation is that he found the informants who supplied him with his facts somewhat uncertain on these points, and that, as a truthful historian, he would not invent dates.

**At the hour of prayer, being the ninth hour** —*sc.,* 3 P.M., the hour of the evening sacrifice (Jos. *Ant.* xiv. 4, § 3). The traditions of later Judaism had fixed the third, the sixth, and the ninth hours of each day as times for private prayer. Daniel's practice of praying three times a day seems to imply a rule of the same kind, and Ps. lv. 17 ("evening and morning and at noon will I pray") carries the practice up to the time of David. "Seven times a day" was, perhaps, the rule of those who aimed at a life of higher devotion (Ps. cxix. 164). Both practices passed into the usage of the Christian Church certainly as early as the second century, and probably therefore in the first. The *three* hours were observed by many at Alexandria in the time of Clement (*Strom.* vii. p. 722). The seven became the "canonical hours" of Western Christendom, the term first appearing in the Rule of St. Benedict (*ob.* A.D. 542) and being used by Bede (A.D. 701).

(2) **A certain man lame from his mother's womb.**—The careful record of the duration of his suffering is more or less characteristic of St. Luke (chaps. ix. 33; xiv. 8). The minuteness in this narrative suggests the thought that St. Luke's informant may have been the cripple himself.

**Was carried.**—Better, *was being carried.*

**The gate of the temple which is called Beautiful.**—Literally, *door,* though "gate" is used in verse 10. No gate of this name is mentioned by other writers, but it was probably identical either (1) with the gate of Nicanor (so called, according to one tradition, because the hand of the great enemy of Judah had been nailed to it as a trophy), which was the main eastern entrance of the inner court (Stanley's *Jewish Church,* iii. p. 323); or (2) the Susa gate, also on the eastern side, and named in memory of the old historical connection between Judah and Persia, leading into the outer court of the women. The latter was of fine Corinthian brass, so massive that twenty men were required to open or shut it (Jos. *Wars,* v. 5, § 3).

**To ask alms of them that entered into the temple.**—The approaches of the Temple, like those of modern mosques, were commonly thronged with the blind, lame, and other mendicants. (Comp. John ix. 8.) The practice was common at Constantinople in the time of Chrysostom, and has prevailed largely throughout Christendom.

(4) **Peter, fastening his eyes upon him . . .**—See Notes on Luke iv. 20, Acts i. 10, where the same characteristic word is used. The gaze was one which read character in the expression of the man's face, and discerned that he had faith to be healed (verse 16). And he, in his turn, was to look on them that he might read in their pitying looks, not only the wish to heal, but the consciousness of power to carry the wish into effect.

(5) And he gave heed unto them, ex-
pecting to receive something of them.
(6) Then Peter said, Silver and gold
have I none; but such as I have give I
thee: In the name of Jesus Christ of
Nazareth rise up and walk. (7) And he
took him by the right hand, and lifted
*him* up: and immediately his feet and
ancle bones received strength. (8) And
he leaping up stood, and walked, and
entered with them into the temple,
walking, and leaping, and praising God.
(9) And all the people saw him walking
and praising God: (10) and they knew
that it was he which sat for alms at
the Beautiful gate of the temple: and
they were filled with wonder and amaze-
ment at that which had happened unto
him. (11) And as the lame man which
was healed held Peter and John, all
the people ran together unto them in
the porch that is called Solomon's,
greatly wondering.
(12) And when Peter saw *it*, he an-
swered unto the people, Ye men of
Israel, why marvel ye at this? or why
look ye so earnestly on us, as though
by our own power or holiness we had
made this man to walk? (13) The God
of Abraham, and of Isaac, and of Jacob,
the God of our fathers, hath glorified
his Son Jesus; whom ye delivered up,

---

(6) **Silver and gold have I none.**—The narrative of chap. ii. 45 shows that the Apostles were treasurers and stewards of the sums committed to their charge by the generous self-denial of the community. Either, therefore, we must assume that the words meant that they had no silver or gold with them at the time, or that, as almoners, they thought themselves bound to distribute what was thus given them in trust, for the benefit of members of the society of which they were officers and for them only. They, obeying their Lord's commands (Matt. x. 9), had no money that they could call their own to give to those that asked them. But they could give more than money.

**In the name of Jesus Christ of Nazareth ....**—The full trust with which the words were spoken was in part a simple act of faith in their Master's promise (Mark xvi. 18), in part the result of a past experience in the exercise of like powers (Mark vi. 13). And the Name in which they spoke could hardly have been a new name to the cripple. Among the beggars at the Temple-gate there had once been the blind man who received his sight at the pool of Siloam (John ix. 7, 8). The healing of the cripple at Bethesda (John v. 2, 14) could scarcely have been unknown to the sufferer from a like infirmity. What made the call to rise and walk a test of faith was that, but a few weeks before, that Name had been seen on the superscription over the cross on which He who bore it had been condemned to die as one that deceived the people (John vii. 12).

(7) **His feet.**—Better, *his soles*. The precision with which the process is described is characteristic of the medical historian. Both this term and the "ankle bones" employed are more or less technical, as is also the word rendered "received strength," literally, *were consolidated*, the flaccid tissues and muscles being rendered firm and vigorous.

(8) **And he leaping up stood.**—The verb is a compound form of that in the LXX. version of Isa. xxxv. 6—"The lame shall leap as a hart." First there was the upward leap in the new consciousness of power; then the successful effort to stand for the first time in his life; then he "began to walk," and went on step by step; then the two-fold mode of motion, what to others was the normal act of walking, alternating with the leaps of an exuberant joy. And so "he entered with them into the Temple," *i.e.*, into the Court of Women, upon which the Beautiful Gate opened. At this hour, the hour of the evening sacrifice, it would be naturally filled with worshippers.

(10) **They knew.**—Better, *they recognised him that it was he.*

(11) **In the porch that is called Solomon's.**—The porch—or better, *portico* or *cloister*—was outside the Temple, on the eastern side. It consisted, in the Herodian Temple, of a double row of Corinthian columns, about thirty-seven feet high, and received its name as having been in part constructed, when the Temple was rebuilt by Zerubbabel, with the fragments of the older edifice. The people tried to persuade Herod Agrippa the First to pull it down and rebuild it, but he shrank from the risk and cost of such an undertaking (Jos. *Ant.* xx. 9, § 7). It was, like the porticos in all Greek cities, a favourite place of resort, especially as facing the morning sun in winter. (See Note on John x. 23.) The memory of what had then been the result of their Master's teaching must have been fresh in the minds of the two disciples. Then the people had complained of being kept in suspense as to whether Jesus claimed to be the Christ, and, when He spoke of being One with the Father, had taken up stones to stone Him (John x. 31—33). Now they were to hear His name as Holy and Just, as "the Servant of Jehovah," as the very Christ (verses 13, 14, 18).

(12) **Why look ye so earnestly on us?**—The verb is the same as that in verse 4. The pronoun stands emphatically at the beginning of the verse—*Why is it on us that ye gaze?*

**As though by our own .... holiness ....**—Better, *purity*, or *devotion*. The words refer to what may be called the popular theory of miracles, that if a man were devout, *i.e.*, "a worshipper of God," God would hear him (John ix. 31). That theory might be true in itself generally, but the Apostle disclaims it in this special instance. No purity of his own would have availed, but for the Name, *i.e.*, the power, of Jesus of Nazareth.

(13) **The God of Abraham, and of Isaac, and of Jacob.**—Here again we have an echo of our Lord's teaching. That Name had been uttered in the precincts of the Temple, not improbably in the self-same portico, as part of our Lord's constructive proof of the resurrection of the dead (Matt. xxii. 32). Now it was heard again in connection with the witness borne by the Apostles that He Himself had risen. (See also Note on chap. vii. 32.)

**Hath glorified his Son Jesus.**—Better, *Servant.* The word is that used throughout the later chapters of Isaiah for "the servant of Jehovah" (Isa. xlii. 1;

and denied him in the presence of
Pilate, when he was determined to
let *him* go. (14) But ye denied the
Holy One and the Just,[a] and desired
a murderer to be granted unto you;
(15) and killed the Prince[1] of life, whom
God hath raised from the dead; whereof
we are witnesses. (16) And his name
through faith in his name hath made
this man strong, whom ye see and
know: yea, the faith which is by him
hath given him this perfect soundness
in the presence of you all. (17) And
now, brethren, I wot that through
ignorance ye did *it*, as *did* also your
rulers. (18) But those things, which
God before had shewed by the mouth
of all his prophets, that Christ should
suffer, he hath so fulfilled.

(19) Repent ye therefore, and be con-
verted, that your sins may be blotted
out, when the times of refreshing shall

a Matt. 27. 20.

1 Or, *Author.*

---

xlviii. 20; lii. 13; liii. 11). It meets us again in verse 26; iv. 27, 30, and as applied to Christ, is peculiar to the Acts, with the exception of the citation from Isaiah in Matt. xii. 18. It is, therefore, more distinctive than "Son" would have been, and implies the general Messianic interpretation of the prophetic language in which it is so prominent.

**When he was determined.**—Better, *when he had decided;* the word implying, not a purpose only, but a formal act, as in Luke xxiii. 16.

(14) **Ye denied the Holy One and the Just.**—The language, though startlingly new to the hearers, had been partially anticipated. It had been used of the Christ by the demoniacs (Mark i. 24). The best MSS. give St. Peter's confession in John vi. 69 in the form, "Thou art the Holy One of God." Pilate's wife, and Pilate himself, had borne their witness to Jesus as emphatically "Just" (Matt. xxvii. 19, 24). It is interesting to note the recurrence of the word as applied to Christ in the writings of each of the Apostles who were now proclaiming it (1 Pet. iii. 18; 1 John ii. 1), yet more so to think of this as the result of their three years' converse with their Master. To them He was emphatically, above all the sons of men that they had known, the Holy and the Righteous One.

**Desired a murderer to be granted unto you.**—The fact that Barabbas was a murderer as well as a robber is stated by St. Mark (xv. 7) and St. Luke (xxiii. 12) only.

(15) **And killed the Prince of life.**—The word translated "Prince" is applied to Christ here and in chap. v. 31. In Heb. ii. 10 we meet with it in "the *Captain* of their salvation;" in Heb. xii. 2, in "the *Author* and Finisher of our faith." Its primary meaning, like that of prince (*princeps*), is one who takes the lead—who is the originator of that to which the title is attached. The "Prince of life," the "Captain of salvation," is accordingly He who is the source from which life and salvation flow. In the LXX. of the Old Testament it is used for the "chieftains" or "princes" of Moab and the like (Num. xiii. 3; xxiv. 17).

**Whereof we are witnesses.**—St. Peter falls back, as in chap. ii. 32 (where see Note), on this attestation to the one central fact.

(16) **His name through faith in his name.**—We have, in technical language, the efficient cause distinguished from the indispensable condition of its action. The Name did not work as a formula of incantation; it required, on the part both of the worker and the receiver, faith in that which the Name represented, the manifestation of the Father through the Son.

**Hath made this man strong.**—The verb is the same as that which had been used in verse 7 of the "feet and ankle-bones." It was Jesus who had given them that new firmness.

**The faith which is by him.**—The causation of the miracle is carried yet another step backward. The faith which was alike in the healer and in the man healed was itself wrought in each by the power of Christ. The man was first a willing recipient of that faith spiritually, and then was in a state that made him worthy to be a recipient also of the bodily restoration.

**This perfect soundness.**—Literally, *this completeness.* This is the only passage in the New Testament in which the word occurs. The cognate adjective is found in the "whole" of 1 Thess. v. 23; the "complete" of Jas i. 4.

(17) **I wot that through ignorance ye did it.**—The Rhemish is the only version which substitutes "I know" for the now obsolete "I wot." St. Peter's treatment of the relation of "ignorance" to "guilt" is in exact agreement with St. Paul's, both in his judgment of his own past offences (1 Tim. vi. 13) and in that which he passed on the Gentile world (chap. xvii. 30). Men were ignorant where they might have known, if they had not allowed prejudice and passion to overpower the witness borne by reason and conscience. Their ignorance was not invincible, and therefore they needed to repent of what they had done in the times of that ignorance. But because it was ignorance, repentance was not impossible. Even the people and rulers of Israel, though their sin was greater, came within the range of the prayer, offered in the first instance for the Roman soldiers: "Father, forgive them, for they know not what they do." (See Note on Luke xxiii. 34.)

(18) **Those things, which God before had shewed.**—As in chaps. i. 16, ii. 23, we have again an echo of the method of prophetic interpretation which the Apostles had learnt from their Lord.

(19) **Repent ye therefore, and be converted.**—The latter word, though occurring both in the Gospels and Epistles, is yet pre-eminently characteristic of the Acts, in which it occurs eleven times, and, with one exception, always in its higher spiritual sense. The use of the middle voice for "be converted," gives the word the same force as in the "turn yourselves" of the older prophets (Ezek. xiv. 6; xviii. 30, 32).

**That your sins may be blotted out.**—This is the only passage in which the verb is directly connected with sins. The image that underlies the words (as in Col. ii. 14) is that of an indictment which catalogues the sins of the penitent, and which the pardoning love of the Father cancels. The word and the thought are found in Ps. li. 10; Isa. xliii. 25.

**When the times of refreshing shall come.**—Better, "*that so* the times of refreshing may come." The Greek conjunction never has the force of "when." The thought is that again expressed both by St. Peter (2 Pet. iii. 12) and by St. Paul (Rom. xi. 25—27): that

come from the presence of the Lord;
(20) and he shall send Jesus Christ,
which before was preached unto you:
(21) whom the heaven must receive until
the times of restitution of all things,
which God hath spoken by the mouth
of all his holy prophets since the world
began. (22) For Moses truly said unto
the fathers, A prophet shall the Lord
your God raise up unto you of your
brethren,[a] like unto me; him shall ye
hear in all things whatsoever he shall
say unto you. (23) And it shall come to
pass, *that* every soul, which will not
hear that prophet, shall be destroyed
from among the people. (24) Yea, and
all the prophets from Samuel and those
that follow after, as many as have
spoken, have likewise foretold of these
days. (25) Ye are the children of the
prophets, and of the covenant which
God made with our fathers, saying unto
Abraham, And in thy seed shall all
the kindreds of the earth be blessed.[b]

a Deut. 18. 15; ch. 7. 37.

b Gen. 12. 3.

---

the conversion of sinners, especially the conversion of Israel, will have a power to accelerate the fulfilment of God's purposes, and, therefore, the coming of His kingdom in its completeness. The word for "refreshing" is not found elsewhere in the New Testament, but the cognate verb meets us in 2 Tim. i. 16. In the Greek version of Ex. viii. 15, it stands where we have "respite." The "times of refreshing" are distinguished from the "restitution of all things" of verse 21, and would seem to be, as it were, the gracious preludes of that great consummation. The souls of the weary would be quickened as by the fresh breeze of morning; the fire of persecution assuaged as by "a moist whistling wind" (Song of the Three Children, verse 24). Israel, as a nation, did not repent, and therefore hatred and strife went on to the bitter end without refreshment. For every church, or nation, or family, those "times of refreshing" come as the sequel of a true conversion, and prepare the way for a more complete restoration.

(20) **And he shall send Jesus Christ.**—Better, as before, *and that He may send.*

**Which before was preached unto you.**—The better MSS. have, *which was fore-appointed,* or *fore-ordained, for you.*

(21) **Whom the heaven must receive.**—The words have a pregnant force: "must receive and keep."

**Until the times of restitution of all things.**—The "times" seem distinguished from the "seasons" as more permanent. This is the only passage in which the word translated "restitution" is found in the New Testament; nor is it found in the LXX. version of the Old. Etymologically, it conveys the thought of restoration to an earlier and better state, rather than that of simple consummation or completion, which the immediate context seems, in some measure, to suggest. It finds an interesting parallel in the "new heavens and new earth"—involving, as they do, a restoration of all things to their true order—of 2 Pet. iii. 13. It does not necessarily involve, as some have thought, the final salvation of all men, but it does express the idea of a state in which "righteousness," and not "sin," shall have dominion over a redeemed and new-created world; and that idea suggests a wider hope as to the possibilities of growth in wisdom and holiness, or even of repentance and conversion, in the unseen world than that with which Christendom has too often been content. The corresponding verb is found in the words, "Elias truly shall come first, and *restore* all things" (see Note on Matt. xvii. 11); and St. Peter's words may well be looked on as an echo of that teaching, and so as an undesigned coincidence testifying to the truth of St. Matthew's record.

**Which God hath spoken by the mouth of all his holy prophets.**—The relative, if we take the meaning given above, must be referred to the "times," not to "things." The words, compared with 2 Pet. i. 21, are, as it were, the utterance of a profound dogmatic truth. The prophets spake as "they were moved by the Holy Ghost"; but He who spake by them was nothing less than God.

**Since the world began.**—Literally, *from the age—i.e.,* from its earliest point. The words take in the promises to Adam (Gen. iii. 15) and Abraham (Gen. xxii. 18). See Note on Luke i. 70, of which St. Peter's words are as an echo.

(22) **For Moses truly said unto the fathers.**—Better, *For Moses indeed said,* the word being one of the common conjunctions, and not the adverb which means "truthfully." The appeal is made to Moses in his two-fold character as lawgiver and prophet. As the words stand, taken with their context, they seem to point to the appearance of a succession of true prophets as contrasted with the diviners of Deut. xviii. 14; and, even with St. Peter's interpretation before us, we may well admit those prophets as primary and partial fulfilments of them. But the words had naturally fixed the minds of men on the coming of some one great prophet who should excel all others, and we find traces of that expectation in the question put to the Baptist, "Art thou the prophet?" (John i. 21, 25.) None that came between Moses and Jesus had been "like unto the former," as marking a new epoch, the channel of a new revelation, the giver of a new law.

**In all things whatsoever he shall say unto you.**—The words are inserted by St. Peter as a parenthesis in the actual quotation, and suggest the thought of a quotation from memory.

(23) **Shall be destroyed from among the people.**—The original has it, "I will require it of him" (Deut. xviii. 19). The words which St. Peter substitutes are as an echo of a familiar phrase which occurs in Ex. xii. 15, 19; Lev. xvii. 4, 9, *et al.* This, again, looks like a citation freely made.

(24) **All the prophets from Samuel.**—Samuel is named, both as being the founder of the school of the prophets, and so the representative of the "goodly fellowship," and as having uttered one of the earliest of what were regarded as the distinctively Messianic predictions (2 Sam. vii. 13, 14; Heb. i. 5).

(25) **And of the covenant . . . .**—It is a significant indication of the unity of apostolic teaching, which it was St. Luke's aim to bring before his readers, that St. Peter thus refers chiefly to the covenant made with Abraham (Gen. xii. 3), with as full an emphasis as St. Paul does when he had learnt to see that it implicitly involved the calling of the Gentiles into the kingdom of Christ (Gal. iii 8.).

(26) Unto you first God, having raised
up his Son Jesus, sent him to bless you,
in turning away every one of you from
his iniquities.

CHAPTER IV.—(1) And as they spake
unto the people, the priests, and the
captain[1] of the temple, and the Sad-
ducees, came upon them, (2) being
grieved that they taught the people,
and preached through Jesus the resur-
rection from the dead. (3) And they
laid hands on them, and put *them* in
hold unto the next day: for it was now
eventide. (4) Howbeit many of them
which heard the word believed; and
the number of the men was about five
thousand.

(5) And it came to pass on the morrow,
that their rulers, and elders, and scribes,

A.D. 33.

1 Or, *ruler*.

---

(26) **Unto you first . . . .**—Here again we note, even in the very turn of the phrase as well as of the thought, an agreement with St. Paul's formula of the purpose of God being manifested "to the Jew first, and also to the Gentile" (chap. xiii. 46; Rom i. 16; ii. 9, 10). St. Peter does not as yet know the conditions under which the gospel will be preached to the heathen; but his words imply a distinct perception that there was a call to preach to them.

**His Son Jesus.**—Better, as before, *Servant.* (See Note on verse 13.)

**Sent him to bless you.**—The Greek structure gives the present participle where the English has the infinitive, *sent Him as in the act of blessing.* The verb which strictly and commonly expresses a spoken benediction is here used in a secondary sense, as conveying the reality of blessedness. And the blessing is found, not in mere exemption from punishment, not even in pardon and reconciliation, but in a change of heart, in "turning each man from his *wickednesses.*" The plural of the abstract noun implies, as in Mark vii. 22, all the many concrete forms in which man's wickedness could show itself.

IV.

(1) **The priests, and the captain of the temple.**—For the first time in this book, we come across the chief agents in the condemnation passed on our Lord by the Sanhedrin. A few weeks or months had gone by, and they were congratulating themselves on having followed the advice of Caiaphas (John xi. 48). They knew that the body of Jesus had disappeared from the sepulchre, and they industriously circulated the report that the disciples had stolen it (Matt. xxviii. 13—15). They must have heard something of the Day of Pentecost—though there is no evidence of their having been present as spectators or listeners—and of the growth of the new society. Now the two chief members of the company of those disciples were teaching publicly in the very portico of the Temple. What were they to do? The "captain of the Temple" (see Note on Luke xxii. 4) was the head of the band of Levite sentinels whose function it was to keep guard over the sacred precincts. He, as an inspector, made his round by night, visited all the gates, and roused the slumberers. His presence implied that the quiet order of the Temple was supposed to be endangered. In 2 Macc. iii. 4, however, we have a "captain," or "governor of the Temple" of the tribe of Benjamin.

**The Sadducees.** — The higher members of the priesthood, Annas and Caiaphas, were themselves of this sect (chap. v. 17). They had already been foremost in urging the condemnation of Christ in the meetings of the Sanhedrin. The shame of having been put to silence by Him (Matt. xxii. 34) added vindictiveness to the counsels of a calculating policy. Now they found His disciples preaching the truth which they denied, and proclaiming it as attested by the resurrection of Jesus. Throughout the Acts the Sadducees are foremost as persecutors. The Pharisees temporise, like Gamaliel, or profess themselves believers. (Comp. chaps. v. 34; xv. 5; xxiii. 7.)

(2) **Being grieved.**—The verb is one which expresses something like an intensity of trouble and vexation. (Comp. chap. xvi. 18.)

**Preached through Jesus the resurrection from the dead.**—Literally, *preached in Jesus—i.e.,* in this as the crucial instance in which the resurrection of the dead had been made manifest. (Comp. the close union of "Jesus and the resurrection" in chap. xvii. 18.)

(3) **It was now eventide.**—The narrative started, it will be remembered, from 3 P.M. (chap. iii. 1). The "eventide" began at 6 P.M.

**Put them in hold.**—Literally, *in custody.* In chap. v. 18, the word is translated "prison." The old noun survives in our modern word "strong-*hold.*"

(4) **The number of the men was about five thousand.**—Better, *became,* or *was made up to, about five thousand.* It seems probable, though not certain, that St. Luke meant this as a statement of the aggregate number of disciples, not of those who were converted on that day. As in the narrative of the feeding of the five thousand (Matt. xiv. 21), women and children were not included. The number was probably ascertained, as on that occasion, by grouping those who came to baptism and to the breaking of bread by hundreds and by fifties (Mark vi. 40). The connection in which the number is given makes it probable that it represents those who, under the influence of the impression made by the healing of the cripple and by St. Peter's speech, attended the meetings of the Church that evening. The coincidence of the numbers in the two narratives could scarcely fail to lead the disciples to connect the one with the other, and to feel, as they broke the bread and blessed it, that they were also giving men the true bread from heaven.

(5) **And it came to pass on the morrow . . .**—Better, *that there were gathered together the rulers, elders, and scribes in Jerusalem.* The two last words are misplaced in the English version by being transferred to the end of the next verse. The later MSS. give, however, *unto* Jerusalem. The meeting was obviously summoned, like that of Matt. xxvi. 5, to consider what course was necessary in face of the new facts that had presented themselves, and was probably the first formal meeting of the Sanhedrin that had been held since the trial of our Lord. On its constitution, see Notes on Matt. v. 22; xxvi. 57; xxvii. 1. This meeting would, of course, include the Pharisee section of the scribes as well as the Sadducees.

(6) and Annas the high priest, and Cai-
aphas, and John, and Alexander, and as
many as were of the kindred of the high
priest, were gathered together at Jeru-
salem. (7) And when they had set them
in the midst, they asked, By what power,
or by what name, have ye done this?
(8) Then Peter, filled with the Holy
Ghost, said unto them, Ye rulers of the
people, and elders of Israel, (9) if we
this day be examined of the good deed
done to the impotent man, by what
means he is made whole; (10) be it
known unto you all, and to all the
people of Israel, that by the name of
Jesus Christ of Nazareth, whom ye cru-
cified, whom God raised from the dead,
*even* by him doth this man stand here

---

(6) **And Annas the high priest . . .**—These are mentioned by themselves as representing the section that had probably convened the meeting, and came in as if to dominate its proceedings. The order of the first two names is the same as in Luke iii. 2, and as that implied in John xviii. 13, 24. Annas, or Ananus, had been made high priest by Quirinus, the Governor of Syria, filled the office A.D. 7—15, and lived to see five of his sons occupy it after him. At this time, Joseph Caiaphas was the actual high priest (see Note on John xi. 49), having been appointed in A.D. 17. He was deposed A.D. 37. He had married the daughter of Annas; and the latter seems to have exercised a dominant influence, perhaps, as the *Nasi*, the Prince, or President, of the Sanhedrin, during the remainder of his life. If he presided on this occasion, it may explain St. Luke's calling him "the high priest."

**John.**—This may have been the Johanan ben Zaccai, who is reported by Jewish writers to have been at the height of his fame forty years before the destruction of the Temple, and to have been President of the Great Synagogue after its removal to Jamnia. The identification is, at the best, uncertain; but the story told of his death-bed, in itself full of pathos, becomes, on this assumption, singularly interesting. His disciples asked him why he wept: "O light of Israel, . . . . whence these tears?" And he replied: "If I were going to appear before a king of flesh and blood, he is one who to-day is and to-morrow is in the grave; if he were wroth with me, his wrath is not eternal; if he were to cast me into chains, those chains are not for ever; if he slay me, that death is not eternal; I might soothe him with words or appease him with a gift. But they are about to bring me before the King of kings, the Lord, the Holy and Blessed One, who liveth and abideth for ever. And if He is wroth with me, His wrath is eternal; and if He bind, His bonds are eternal; if He slay, it is eternal death; and Him I cannot soothe with words or appease with gifts. And besides all this, there are before me two paths, one to Paradise and the other to Gehenna, and I know not in which they are about to lead me. How can I do aught else but weep?" (*Bab-Beracoth*, fol. 28, in Lightfoot: *Cent.-Chorogr.*, chap. xv.)

**Alexander.**—This name has been identified by many scholars with Alexander, the brother of Philo, the *Alabarch*, or magistrate of Alexandria (Jos. *Ant.* xviii. 8, § 1; xix. 5, § 1). There is, however, not the shadow of any evidence for the identification.

**As many as were of the kindred of the high priest.**—The same phrase is used by Josephus (*Ant.* xv. 3, § 1), and may mean either those who were personally related by ties of blood with the high priest for the time being, or the heads of the four-and-twenty courses of priests. (See Notes on Matt. ii. 4; Luke i. 5.) All these had probably taken part in our Lord's condemnation.

(7) **And when they had set them in the midst.**—The Sanhedrin sat in a semi-circle; the president being in the middle of the arc, the accused standing in the centre.

**They asked.**—Literally, *were asking*. They put the question repeatedly, in many varying forms.

**By what power, or by what name, have ye done this?**—Literally, *By what kind of power, or what kind of name?* apparently in a tone of contempt. They admit the fact that the lame man had been made to walk, as too patent to be denied. (Comp. verse 16.) The question implied a suspicion that it was the effect of magic, or, as in the case of our Lord's casting out devils, by the power of Beelzebub (Luke xi. 15; John viii. 48). There is a touch of scorn in the way in which they speak of the thing itself. They will not as yet call it a "sign," or "wonder," but "have ye done *this?*"

(8) **Then Peter, filled with the Holy Ghost.**—The tense implies an immediate sudden inspiration, giving the wisdom and courage and words which were needed at the time. The promises of Matt. x. 19, 20, Luke xxi. 14, 15, were abundantly fulfilled. The coincidence of names in the juxtaposition of the representatives of the new and the older Israel is striking. On each side there was a John; on each a Cephas, or Caiaphas, the two names possibly coming from the same root, or, at any rate, closely alike in sound. A few weeks back Peter had quailed before the soldiers and servants in the high priest's palace. Now he stands before the Sanhedrin and speaks, in the language of respect, it is true, but also in that of unflinching boldness. We may, perhaps, trace a greater deference in the language of the Galilean fisherman, "Ye rulers of the people," than in the "Men and brethren" of St. Paul (chap. xxiii. 1, 6), who was more familiar with the members of the court, and stood in less awe of them.

(9) **If we this day be examined.**—The word is employed in its technical sense of a judicial interrogation, as in Luke xxiii. 14. It is used by St. Luke and St. Paul (chap. xii. 19; xxiv. 8; 1 Cor. ii. 14, 15; iv. 3, 4), and by them only, in the New Testament.

**Of the good deed.**—Strictly, *the act of beneficence.* There is a manifest emphasis on the word as contrasted with the contemptuous "this thing" of the question. It meets us again in 1 Tim. vi. 2.

**By what means he is made whole.**—Better, *this man.* The pronoun assumes the presence of the man who had been made able to walk. (Comp. John ix. 15.) The verb, as in our Lord's words, "Thy faith hath made thee whole" (Mark x. 52; Luke vii. 50), has a pregnant, underlying meaning, suggesting the thought of a spiritual as well as bodily restoration.

(10) **By the name of Jesus Christ of Nazareth, whom ye crucified.**—The boldness of the declaration was startling. He does not shrink now from confessing the Nazarene as the Messiah. He presses home the fact that, though Pilate had given the formal sentence, it was they who had crucified their King.

before you whole. (11) This is the stone
which was set at nought of you builders,[a]
which is become the head of the corner.
(12) Neither is there salvation in any
other: for there is none other name
under heaven given among men, where-
by we must be saved.

(13) Now when they saw the boldness
of Peter and John, and perceived that
they were unlearned and ignorant men,
they marvelled; and they took know-
ledge of them, that they had been with
Jesus. (14) And beholding the man which
was healed standing with them, they
could say nothing against it. (15) But
when they had commanded them to go
aside out of the council, they conferred
among themselves, (16) saying, What
shall we do to these men? for that
indeed a notable miracle hath been
done by them *is* manifest to all them
that dwell in Jerusalem; and we cannot
deny *it*. (17) But that it spread no
further among the people, let us straitly

[a] Ps. 118. 22; Matt. 21. 42.

---

He proclaims that He has been raised from the dead, and is still as a Power working to heal as when on earth.

(11) **This is the stone which was set at nought of you builders.**—Better, *of you, the builders.* The members of the Council to whom Peter spoke had heard those words (Ps. cxviii. 22) quoted and interpreted before. (See Notes on Matt. xxi. 42—44.) Then they had thought, in their blindness, that they could defy the warning. They, by their calling, the builders of the Church of Israel, did reject the stone which God had chosen to be the chief corner-stone—the stone on which the two walls of Jew and Gentile met and were bonded together (Eph. ii. 20). Here again the Epistles of St. Peter reproduce one of the dominant thoughts of his speeches (1 Pet. ii. 6—8), and give it a wider application. Thirty years after he thus spoke, Christ was still to him as "the head of the corner."

**Set at nought.**—St. Peter does not quote the Psalm, but alludes to it with a free variation of language. The word for "set at nought" is characteristic of St. Luke (Luke xviii. 9; xxiii. 11) and St. Paul (Rom. xiv. 3, 10, *et al.*).

(12) **Neither is there salvation in any other.**—Here the pregnant force of "hath been made whole," in verse 9, comes out; and St. Peter rises to its highest meaning, and proclaims a salvation, not from disease and infirmity of body, but from the great disease of sin. The Greek has the article before "salvation." That of which Peter spoke was *the* salvation which the rulers professed to be looking for.

**Given among men.**—Better, *that has been given.* The words must be taken in the sense which Peter had learnt to attach to the thought of the Name as the symbol of personality and power. To those to whom it had been made known, and who had taken in all that it embodied, the Name of Jesus Christ of Nazareth was the one true source of deliverance and salvation. Speaking for himself and the rulers, Peter rightly says that it is the Name "whereby *we* must be saved." Where it is not so known, it rises to its higher significance as the symbol of a divine energy; and so we may rightly say that the heathen who obtain salvation are saved by the Name of the Lord of whom they have never heard. (Comp. 1 Tim. iv. 13.)

(13) **When they saw the boldness of Peter and John.**—John, so far as we read, had not spoken, but look and bearing, and, perhaps, unrecorded words, showed that he too shared Peter's courage. That "boldness of speech" had been characteristic of his Lord's teaching (Mark viii. 32; John vii. 13). It was now to be the distinctive feature of that of the disciples: here of Peter; in chap. xxviii. 31, 2 Cor. iii. 12, vii. 4, of St. Paul; in 1 John iv. 17, v. 14, of the beloved disciple. It is, perhaps, characteristic that the last named uses it not of boldness of speech towards men, but of confidence in approaching God. The Greek word for "when they saw" implies "considering" as well as beholding; that for "perceived" would be better expressed by *having learnt*, or *having ascertained.* The Greek verb implies, not direct perception, but the grasp with which the mind lays hold of a fact after inquiry. In Acts xxv. 5, it is rightly translated "when I found."

**Unlearned and ignorant.**—The first of the two words means, literally, *unlettered.* Looking to the special meaning of the "letters" or "Scriptures" of the Jews, from which the scribes took their name (*grammateis*, from *grammata*), it would convey, as used here the sense of "not having been educated as a scribe, not having studied the Law and other sacred writings.' It does not occur elsewhere in the New Testament. The second word means literally, *a private person*, one without special office or calling, or the culture which they imply: what in English might be called a "common man." It appears again in 1 Cor. xiv. 16, 23, 24, with the same meaning. Its later history is curious enough to be worth noting. The Vulgate, instead of translating the Greek word, reproduced it, with scarcely an alteration, as *idiota.* It thus passed into modern European languages with the idea of ignorance and incapacity closely attached to it, and so acquired its later sense of "idiot."

**They took knowledge of them, that they had been with Jesus.**—Better, *they began to recognise.* The tense is in the imperfect, implying that one after another of the rulers began to remember the persons of the two Apostles as they had seen them with their Master in the Temple. These two, and these two alone, may have been seen by many of the Council on that early dawn of the day of the Crucifixion in the court-yard of the high priest's palace (John xviii. 15).

(14) **They could say nothing against it.**—Literally, *they had nothing to say against it.*

(16) **What shall we do to these men?**—The question now debated was clearly one that never ought to have been even asked. They were sitting as a Court of Justice, and should have given their verdict for or against the accused according to the evidence. They abandon that office, and begin discussing what policy was most expedient. It was, we may add, characteristic of Caiaphas to do so (John xi. 49, 50).

**A notable miracle.**—Literally, *sign.*

**We cannot deny it.**—The very form of the sentence betrays the will, though there is not the power.

(17) **Let us straitly threaten them.**—The Greek gives literally, *let us threaten them with threats.* The phrase gives the Hebrew idiom for expressing intensity by reduplication, as in "blessing I will bless thee"

threaten them, that they speak hence-
forth to no man in this name. (18) And
they called them, and commanded them
not to speak at all nor teach in the
name of Jesus. (19) But Peter and John
answered and said unto them, Whether
it be right in the sight of God to hearken
unto you more than unto God, judge ye.
(20) For we cannot but speak the things
which we have seen and heard. (21) So
when they had further threatened them,
they let them go, finding nothing how
they might punish them, because of the
people: for all *men* glorified God for
that which was done. (22) For the man
was above forty years old, on whom this
miracle of healing was shewed.

(23) And being let go, they went to
their own company, and reported all
that the chief priests and elders had
said unto them. (24) And when they
heard that, they lifted up their voice to
God with one accord, and said, Lord,
thou *art* God, which hast made heaven,
and earth, and the sea, and all that in
them is: (25) who by the mouth of thy

---

(Gen. xxii. 17), "dying thou shalt die" (Gen. ii. 17, *marg.*), and, as far as it goes, indicates that St. Luke translated from a report of the speech which Caiaphas had delivered in Aramaic. It is a perfectly possible alternative that the High Priest, speaking in Greek, reproduced, as the LXX. often does, the old Hebrew formula.

(18) **Not to speak at all.**—The Greek is even more forcible: *absolutely not to utter* . . . The very name of Jesus was not to pass their lips.

(19) **Whether it be right in the sight of God . . .**—The words assert the right of conscience, recognising a divine authority, to resist a human authority which opposes it. In theory, as the appeal "judge ye" showed even then, the right so claimed is of the nature of an axiom. In practice, the difficulty rises in the question, Is there the divine authority which is claimed? And the only practical answer is to be found in the rule, that men who believe they have the authority are bound to act as if they had it. If the Lord God hath spoken to them, they can but prophesy (Amos iii. 8). In cases such as this, where the question is one of witness to facts, they must not tamper with the truth, if they believe themselves commissioned by God to declare the facts, for fear of offending men. When they pass from facts to doctrines inferred from facts, from doctrines to opinions, from opinions to conjectures, the duty of not saying that which they do not believe remains the same, but there is not the same obligation to proclaim what they thus hold in various stages of assent. There may be cases in which reticence is right as well as politic. And even in regard to facts, the publication—as law recognises in relation to libels—must not be gratuitous. There must be an adequate authority, or an adequate reason for disobedience to the human authority, which is binding until it is superseded by that which is higher than itself. And the *onus probandi* rests on the man who asserts the higher authority. Intensity of conviction may be enough for himself, but it cannot be expected that it will be so for others. In the absence of signs and wonders the question must be discussed on the wide ground of Reason and of Conscience, and the man who refuses to enter into debate on that ground because he is certain he is right is *ipso facto* convicted of an almost insane egotism. The words have clearly no bearing on the "froward retention" of a custom which God has not enjoined and a lawful authority has forbidden.

(20) **We cannot but speak . . .**—The pronoun is emphatic: "we, for our part" . . . The question at issue was one of bearing witness, and that witness they had received a special command to bear (chap. i. 8).

(21) **All men glorified God . . .**—The tense implies continued action. It is specially characteristic of St. Luke thus to note the impression made upon the people by signs and wonders (Luke ii. 20; iv. 15; and in seven other passages).

(22) **The man was above forty years old.**—This precision in noting the duration of disease or infirmity is again characteristic of the writer. Comp. the case of the woman with an issue of blood (Luke viii. 43); of Æneas (chap. ix. 33); of the cripple at Lystra (chap. xiv. 8).

(23) **They went to their own company.**—Literally, *their own people.* The statement implies a recognised place of meeting, where the members of the new society met at fixed times.

**All that the chief priests.**—The word is probably used in its more extended meaning, as including, not only Annas and Caiaphas, but the heads of the four-and-twenty courses (see Note on Matt. ii. 4), and others who were members of the Sanhedrin.

(24) **They lifted up their voice to God with one accord.**—The phrase seems to imply an intonation, or chant, different from that of common speech (chap. xiv. 11; xxii. 22). The joint utterance described may be conceived as the result either (1) of a direct inspiration, suggesting the same words to all who were present; (2) of the people following St. Peter, clause by clause; (3) of the hymn being already familiar to the disciples. On the whole, (2) seems the most probable, the special fitness of the hymn for the occasion being against (3), and (1) involving a miracle of so startling a nature that we can hardly take it for granted without a more definite statement. The recurrence of St. Luke's favourite phrase (see Note on chap. i. 14) should not be passed over.

**Lord.**—The Greek word is not the common one for Lord (*Kyrios*), but *Despotes*, the absolute Master of the Universe. It is a coincidence worth noting that, though but seldom used of God in the New Testament, it occurs again, as used by the two Apostles who take part in it, as in 2 Pet. ii. 1, and Rev. vi. 10. (See Note on Luke ii. 29.) In the Greek version of the Old Testament it is found applied to the Angel of Jehovah in Josh. v. 14, and to Jehovah Himself in Prov. xxix. 25. The hymn has the special interest of being the earliest recorded utterance of the praises of the Christian Church. As such, it is significant that it begins, as so many of the Psalms begin, with setting forth the glory of God as the Creator, and rises from that to the higher redemptive work. More strict, "*the* heaven, *the* earth, and *the* sea," each region of creation being contemplated in its distinctness.

(25) **Who by the mouth of thy servant David . . .**—The older MSS. present many variations of the text. It probably stood originally somewhat in this

servant David hast said, Why did the
heathen rage,[a] and the people imagine
vain things? (26) The kings of the earth
stood up, and the rulers were gathered
together against the Lord, and against
his Christ. (27) For of a truth against
thy holy child Jesus, whom thou hast
anointed, both Herod and Pontius
Pilate, with the Gentiles and the
people of Israel, were gathered together,
(28) for to do whatsoever thy hand and
thy counsel determined before to be
done. (29) And now, Lord, behold their
threatenings: and grant unto thy ser-
vants, that with all boldness they may
speak thy word, (30) by stretching forth
thine hand to heal; and that signs and
wonders may be done by the name of
thy holy child Jesus.
(31) And when they had prayed, the
place was shaken where they were as-
sembled together; and they were all
filled with the Holy Ghost, and they
spake the word of God with boldness.
(32) And the multitude of them that be-
lieved were of one heart and of one soul:
neither said any *of them* that ought of
the things which he possessed was his

[a] Ps. 2. 1.

---

form: "Who through the Holy Ghost, by the mouth of David our father, thy servant," and was simplified by later copyists. In the citation from Ps. ii. we have another lesson from the Apostles' school of prophetic interpretation. The Psalm is not cited in the Gospels. Here what seems to us the most striking verse (verse 7) of it is passed over, and it does not appear as referred to Christ till we find it in Heb. i. 5; v. 5.

**Why did the heathen rage, and the people imagine . . . ?**—Neither noun has the article in the Greek or in the Hebrew. *Why did nations rage and peoples imagine . . . ?* The word for "rage" is primarily applied to animal ferocity, especially to that of untamed horses.

(26) **And against his Christ.**—The question whether the word "Christ" should be used as a proper name, or translated, is commonly answered by accepting the former alternative. Here, perhaps, to maintain the connection with the Psalm and with the verb in the next verse, it would be better to say, "against His Anointed." The "Lord" stands, of course, for the Supreme Deity of the Father.

(27) **Of a truth . . . .**—Many of the better MSS. add the words "in this city."

**Against thy holy child Jesus.**—Better, as before, *Servant.* (See Notes on chap. iii. 13, 36.) The word is the same as that used of David in verse 25.

**Both Herod, and Pontius Pilate.**—The narrative of Herod's share in the proceedings connected with the Passion is, it will be remembered, found only in Luke xxiii. 8—12. So far as the hymn here recorded may be considered as an independent evidence, the two present an undesigned coincidence.

**With the Gentiles, and the people of Israel.**—Even here the nouns are, in the Greek, without an article. The "peoples" (the Greek noun is plural) are rightly defined, looking to the use of the Hebrew word, as those of Israel.

(28) **To do whatsoever thy hand . . . .**—The great problem of the relation of the divine purpose to man's free agency is stated (as before in chaps. i. 16; ii. 23), without any attempt at a philosophical solution. No such solution is indeed possible. If we admit a Divine Will at all, manifesting itself in the government of the world, in the education of mankind, in the salvation of individual souls, we must follow the example of the Apostle, and hold both the facts of which consciousness and experience bear their witness, without seeking for a logical formula of reconciliation. In every fact of history, no less than in the great fact of which St. Peter speaks, the will of each agent is free, and he stands or falls by the part he has taken in it; and yet the outcome of the whole works out some law of evolution, some "increasing purpose," which we recognise as we look back on the course of the events, the actors in which were impelled by their own base or noble aims, their self-interest or their self-devotion. As each man looks back on his own life he traces a sequence visiting him with a righteous retribution, and leading him, whether he obeyed the call, or resisted it, to a higher life, an education no less than a probation. "Man proposes, God disposes." "God works in us, therefore we must work." Aphorisms such as these are the nearest approximation we can make to a practical, though not a theoretical, solution of the great mystery.

(29) **And now, Lord, behold their threatenings.**—The context shows that the prayer of the Church is addressed to the Father. The Apostles, who had shown "boldness of speech" (verse 13), pray, as conscious of their natural weakness, for a yet further bestowal of that gift, as being now more than ever needed, both for themselves and the whole community.

(30) **By stretching forth thine hand to heal.**—There seems something like an intentional assonance in the Greek words which St. Luke uses—*iāsis* (healing) and *Jesus* (pronounced *Iēsus*)—as though he would indicate that the very name of Jesus witnessed to His being the great Healer. A like instance of the *nomen et omen* idea is found in the identification by Tertullian (*Apol.* c. 3) of *Christos* and *Chrestos* (good, or gracious), of which we have, perhaps, a foreshadowing in 1 Pet. ii. 3. (Comp. also chap. ix. 34.)

**Thy holy child Jesus.**—Better, as before, *Servant.* (See Note on chap. iii. 13.)

(31) **The place was shaken . . . .**—The impression on the senses was so far a renewal of the wonder of the Day of Pentecost, but in this instance without the sign of the tongues of fire, which were the symbols of a gift imparted once for all, and, perhaps also, without the special marvel of the utterance of the tongues. The disciples felt the power of the Spirit, the evidence of sense confirming that of inward, spiritual consciousness, and it came in the form for which they had made a special supplication, the power to speak with boldness the word which they were commissioned to speak.

(32) **And the multitude of them that believed.**—Literally, *And the heart and the soul of the multitude of those that believed were one.* Of the two words used to describe the unity of the Church, "heart" represented, as in Hebrew usage, rather the

own; but they had all things common.
(33) And with great power gave the
apostles witness of the resurrection of
the Lord Jesus: and great grace was
upon them all. (34) Neither was there
any among them that lacked: for as
many as were possessors of lands or
houses sold them, and brought the
prices of the things that were sold,
(35) and laid *them* down at the apostles'
feet: and distribution was made unto
every man according as he had need.
(36) And Joses, who by the apostles was
surnamed Barnabas, (which is, being
interpreted, The son of consolation,) a
Levite, *and* of the country of Cyprus,
(37) having land, sold *it*, and brought the
money, and laid *it* at the apostles' feet.

---

intellectual side of character (Mark ii. 6, 8; xi. 23; Luke ii. 35; iii. 15; vi. 45, *et al.*), and "soul," the emotional (Luke ii. 35; xii. 22; John xii. 27, *et al.*). As with most like words, however, they often overlap each other, and are used together to express the totality of character without minute analysis. The description stands parallel with that of chap. ii. 42—47, as though the historian delighted to dwell on the continuance, as long as it lasted, of that ideal of a common life of equality and fraternity after which philosophers had yearned, in which the rights of property, though not abolished, were, by the spontaneous action of its owners, made subservient to the law of love, and benevolence was free and full, without the "nicely calculated less or more" of a later and less happy time. The very form of expression implies that the community of goods was not compulsory. The goods still belonged to men, but they did not speak of them as their own. They had learned, as from our Lord's teaching (Luke xvi. 10—14), to think of themselves, not as possessors, but as stewards.

(33) **With great power gave the apostles witness.**—The Greek verb implies the idea of paying or rendering what was due, as in Matt. xxii. 11. They were doing that which they were bound to do.

**Great grace was upon them.**—The words may stand parallel with Luke ii. 40 as meaning that the *grace* of God was bestowed upon the disciples in full measure, or with chap. ii. 47 as stating that the *favour* of the people towards them still continued. There are no sufficient *data* for deciding the question, and it must be left open. The English versions all give "grace," as if accepting the highest meaning, as do most commentators.

(34) **Neither was there any among them that lacked.**—Better, perhaps, *any one in need.*

**Sold them, and brought the prices.**—Both words imply continuous and repeated action. It is possible that besides the strong impulse of love, they were impressed, by their Lord's warnings of wars and coming troubles, with the instability of earthly possessions. Landed property in Palestine was likely to be a source of anxiety rather than profit. As Jeremiah had shown his faith in the future restoration of his people by purchasing the field at Anathoth (Jer. xxxii. 6—15), so there was, in this sale of their estates, a proof of faith in the future desolation which their Master had foretold (Matt. xxiv. 16—21).

(35) **And laid them down at the apostles' feet.**—The words are a vivid picture of one phase of Eastern life. When gifts or offerings are made to a king, or priest, or teacher, they are not placed in his hands, but at his feet. The Apostles sat, it would seem, in conclave, on their twelve seats, as in the figurative promise of Matt. xix. 28, and the vision of Rev. iv. 4.

(36) **And Joses, who by the apostles was surnamed Barnabas.**—The better MSS. give the name as Joseph. It is possible, as Rabbinic writers often give *Jose* for Joseph, that both were but different forms, like Simon and Simeon, of the same name. The later friendship between the Levite of Cyprus and St. Paul makes it probable that there had been some previous companionship (see Notes on chaps. ix. 27, xi. 25), and it may well have been that he was sent from Cyprus to receive his education in the famous schools of Tarsus, or practised with Saul in early life the craft of tent-making, for which Tarsus was famous, and in which they were afterwards fellow-labourers (1 Cor. ix. 6). As a Levite he had probably taken his place in the ministries of the Temple, and may, therefore, have been among our Lord's actual hearers. His relation Mary, the mother of John surnamed Marcus, was, we know, living at Jerusalem. (See Note on chap. xii. 12; Col. iv. 10.) A tradition, as early as Clement of Alexandria (*Strom.* ii. § 116), makes him one of the Seventy, and this agrees with the prophetic character which we have seen reason to think of as attaching to that body. (See Note on Luke x. 1.) The new name which the Apostles gave him, literally, if we look to its Hebrew etymology, *The son of prophecy*, or, taking St. Luke's translation, *The son of counsel*, implies the possession of a special gift of persuasive utterance, in which the Apostles recognised the work of the Spirit. The Paraclete had endowed him with the gift of *paraclesis*, in the sense in which that word included counsel, comfort, admonition, application of divine truth to the spiritual necessities of men. (See *Excursus G. on St. John's Gospel.*) In chap. xi. 23, we find him *exhorting* the Gentile converts at Antioch, the verb being that from which *paraclesis* is derived. He was, *i.e.*, conspicuous for the gift of prophecy as that gift is described in 1 Cor. xiv. 3. The several stages in his life come before us later. An Epistle bearing his name, and recognised as his by Clement of Alexandria and Origen, is still extant, but its authenticity is, to say the least, questionable. It consists mainly of allegorical interpretations of Old Testament narratives. Some critics have assigned the Epistle to the Hebrews to his authorship, as the expounder of St. Paul's thoughts. It should be noted that a little further on his kinswoman Mary's house is the chief meeting-place of the Church of Jerusalem (chap. xii. 12), and that her son John, surnamed Mark, is mentioned by St. Peter ("Marcus my son," 1 Pet. v. 13) in words which make it almost certain that he was converted by that Apostle.

(37) **Having land, sold it.**—Better, perhaps, *having a farm.* (See Notes on Mark v. 14; vi. 36, 56.) In the original polity of Israel the Levites had cities and land in common, but no private property (Num. xviii. 20, 21; Deut. x. 8, 9, *et al.*), and depended for their support upon the tithes paid by the people. The case of Jeremiah, however (Jer. xxxii. 7—12), shows that there was nothing to hinder priest or Levite from becoming the possessor of land by purchase or inheritance

CHAPTER V.—(1) But a certain man
named Ananias, with Sapphira his wife,
sold a possession, (2) and kept back *part*
of the price, his wife also being privy *to*
*it*, and brought a certain part, and laid
*it* at the apostles' feet. (3) But Peter
said, Ananias, why hath Satan filled
thine heart to lie to[1] the Holy Ghost,
and to keep back *part* of the price of
the land? (4) Whiles it remained, was
it not thine own? and after it was sold,
was it not in thine own power? why
hast thou conceived this thing in thine
heart? thou hast not lied unto men, but

A.D. 33.

1 Or, *to deceive.*

The position of Barnabas's sister Mary shows that she, also, was wealthy, and, though she did not sell her house, she, too, did not call it her own, but gave it up for the public use of the community. The self-chosen poverty of Barnabas led him afterwards to act as St. Paul did in working for his livelihood (1 Cor. ix. 6). It will not be out of place on this first mention of the name of a new disciple to note a few others whose membership of the Church dated probably from this period; Mnason, the "old disciple" of chap. xxi. 16, of Cyprus, and probably, therefore, a friend of Barnabas; Andronicus and Junia (or, more probably, *Junias*, as a man's name), in some sense kinsmen of St. Paul, who were "in Christ" before him (Rom. xvi. 7), and whom we find afterwards at Rome; the seven who in chap. vi. 5 are prominent enough to be chosen as representatives of the Hellenistic members of the Church; Agabus (chap. xi. 28), Judas, and Silas (chap. xv. 32). The last three, however, as being "prophets," may have been among the number of the Seventy; and, possibly, if we follow a fairly early tradition, Stephen and Philip among the Seven. (See Note on Luke x. 1.) We again note the absence of any measure of the interval between the events of this chapter and the history that follows. The picture of the peaceful expansion of the Church's life implies, probably, as in chap. ii. 41—47, one of several months.

V.

(1, 2) **A certain man named Ananias.**—The name meets us again as belonging to the high priest in chap. xxiii. 2, and was the Greek form of the Hebrew Hananiah. It had the same significance as John, or Johanan, "The Lord be gracious." "Sapphira," is either connected with the "sapphire," as a precious stone, or from a Hebrew word signifying "beautiful" or "pleasant." The whole history must be read in connection with the act of Barnabas. He, it seemed, had gained praise and power by his self-sacrifice. Ananias thought that he could get at the same result more cheaply. The act shows a strange mingling of discordant elements. Zeal and faith of some sort had led him to profess himself a believer. Ambition was strong enough to win a partial victory over avarice; avarice was strong enough to triumph over truth. The impulse to sell came from the Spirit of God; it was counteracted by the spirit of evil, and the resulting sin was therefore worse than that of one who lived altogether in the lower, commoner forms of covetousness. It was an attempt to serve God and mammon; to gain the reputation of a saint, without the reality of holiness. The sin of Ananias is, in some aspects, like that of Gehazi (2 Kings v. 20—27), but it was against greater light and intensified by a more profound hypocrisy, and it was therefore visited by a more terrible chastisement. We may well trace in the earnestness with which St. James warns men against the peril of the "double mind"—*i.e.*, the heart divided between the world and God (Jas. i. 8; iv. 8)—the impression made on him by such a history as this.

(2) **And kept back part of the price.**—The mere act of keeping back would not in itself have been sinful. The money was his own, to give the whole or part (verse 4). But the formal act, apparently reproducing that of Barnabas, was an acted lie. The part was offered as if it were the whole. The word for "kept back" is rendered "purloining" in Titus ii. 10, and always carried with it the idea of stealthy and dishonest appropriation. It is used in the LXX. of Josh. vii. 1, as describing the sin of Achan.

(3) **Why hath Satan filled thine heart?**—The narrative is obviously intended to leave the impression that St. Peter's knowledge of the fact came from a supernatural insight. He had that prophetic gift which gave him insight into the hearts of men, and through this outward show of generous devotion he read the baseness and the lie. And that evil he traced to its fountain-head. Like the sin of Judas (John xiii. 2, 27), it had in it a malignant subtlety of evil, which implied the perversion of conscience and will just at the moment when they seemed to be, and, it may be, actually were, on the point of attaining a higher perfection than before. The question "why" implies that resistance to the temptation had been possible. Had he resisted the Tempter, he would have fled from him (Jas. iv. 7).

**To lie to the Holy Ghost.**—The words admit of two tenable interpretations. Ananias may be said to "have lied unto the Holy Ghost," either (1) as lying against Him who dwelt in the Apostles whom he was seeking to deceive; or (2) as against Him who was the Searcher of the secrets of all hearts, his own included, and who was "grieved" (Eph. iv. 31) by this resistance in one who had been called to a higher life. The apparent parallelism of the clause in verse 4 is in favour of (1); but there is in the Greek a distinction, obviously made deliberately, between the structure of the verb in the two sentences. Here it is used with the accusative of the direct object, so that the meaning is "to cheat or deceive the Holy Spirit;" there with the dative, "to speak a lie, not to men, but to God;" and this gives a sense which is at least compatible with (2). The special intensity of the sin consisted in its being against the light and knowledge with which the human spirit had been illumined by the divine. The circumstance that it was also an attempt to deceive those in whom that Spirit dwelt in the fulness of its power comes in afterwards as a secondary aggravation.

(4) **Whiles it remained . . .**—Fresh circumstances are pressed home, as depriving the act of every possible excuse. Ananias had not been bound by any rule of the Church to such a gift. At every stage he was free to act as he thought best; and had he brought part as part, or even brought nothing, he would have been free from any special blame. As it was, the attempt to obtain the reputation of saintliness without the reality of sacrifice, involved him in the guilt at once of sacrilege, though there had been no formal consecration, and of perjury, though there had been no formulated oath.

unto God. (5) And Ananias hearing
these words fell down, and gave up the
ghost: and great fear came on all them
that heard these things. (6) And the
young men arose, wound him up, and
carried *him* out, and buried *him*.
(7) And it was about the space of three
hours after, when his wife, not knowing
what was done, came in. (8) And Peter
answered unto her, Tell me whether ye
sold the land for so much? And she
said, Yea, for so much. (9) Then Peter
said unto her, How is it that ye have
agreed together to tempt the Spirit of
the Lord? behold, the feet of them
which have buried thy husband *are* at
the door, and shall carry thee out.
(10) Then fell she down straightway at
his feet, and yielded up the ghost: and
the young men came in, and found her
dead, and, carrying *her* forth, buried
*her* by her husband. (11) And great fear
came upon all the church, and upon as
many as heard these things.

---

**Thou hast not lied unto men, but unto God.**—The parallelism between this and "lying to the Holy Ghost" in verse 3 has often been used, and perfectly legitimately, as a proof that while the Apostles thought of the Spirit as sent by the Father, and therefore distinct in His personality, they yet did not shrink from speaking of Him as God, and so identifying Him with the Divine Essential Being.

(5) **Ananias hearing these words fell down.**—It is to be noted that St. Peter's words, while they press home the intensity of the guilt, do not contain any formal sentence. In such a case we may rightly trace that union of natural causation and divine purpose which we express in the familiar phrase that speaks of "the visitation of God" as a cause of death. The shame and agony of detection, the horror of conscience not yet dead, were enough to paralyse the powers of life. Retribution is not less a divine act because it comes, through the working of divine laws, as the natural consequence of the sin which draws it down. It was necessary, we may reverently say, that this special form of evil, this worst corruption of the best, should be manifestly condemned on its first appearance by a divine judgment. And we must remember that there is a silence which we may not dare to break as to all but the visible judgment. The dominant apostolic idea of such punishments was that men were delivered to Satan for the destruction of the flesh, that the spirit might be saved in the day of the Lord Jesus (1 Cor. v. 5). St. Peter himself speaks of those who are "judged according to men in the flesh," who yet "live according to God in the spirit" (1 Pet. iv. 6).

(6) **And the young men arose.**—Literally, *the younger men*, implying the existence of a distinct body as contrasted with the "elders" of the Church. So in Luke xx. 26 we find the same word answering in the parallel clause to "him that serveth," and opposed to "elders," where the latter word seems used in a half-official sense rather than of age only. We find here, accordingly, rather than in chap. vi., the germ of the later diaconate as a body of men set apart for the subordinate services of the community. The special work here done by them was afterwards assigned to the *Fossarii*, the sextons, or grave-diggers of the Church.

**Wound him up.**—The word in this sense is found here only in the New Testament. It implies the hurried wrapping in a winding-sheet. It was followed by the immediate interment outside the walls of the city. Custom, resting partly on the necessities of climate, partly on the idea of ceremonial defilement, as caused by contact with a corpse (Num. xix. 11—16), required burial to follow quickly on death, unless there was a more or less elaborate embalmment. In the act itself we note something like a compassionate respect. There is a reverence for humanity, as such, perhaps for the body that had once been the temple of the Spirit (1 Cor. vi. 19), that will not permit men to do as the heathen did, and to inflict dishonour on the lifeless corpse. The narrative implies that the new society had already a burial-place to which they had free right of access. Was it in the Potter's Field that had been bought to bury strangers in? (Matt. xxvii. 7.) Did the body of Ananias rest in the same cemetery with that of Judas? (See Note on Matt. xxvii. 8.)

(7) **And it was about the space of three hours after.**—Literally, *And there was an interval of about three hours.*

(8) **And Peter answered unto her.**—The word does not necessarily imply a previous questioning, but it is probable enough that she came to inquire why her husband had not returned home; perhaps, expecting to find him high in honour. The question asked by Peter gave her an opening for repentance. It had been in her power to save her husband by a word of warning protest. It was now in her power to clear her own conscience by confession. She misses the one opportunity as she had misused the other. The lie which they had agreed upon comes glibly from her lips, and the irrevocable word is spoken.

(9) **To tempt the Spirit of the Lord**—*i.e.*, to try, or *test*, whether the Spirit that dwelt in the Apostles was really a discerner of the secrets of men's hearts. The "Spirit of the Lord" is probably used in its Old Testament sense, as the Spirit of Jehovah. The combination is rare in the New Testament, occurring only in 2 Cor. iii. 17, but is common in the Old, as in Isa. lxi. 1 (quoted in Luke iv. 18); 1 Kings xxii. 24; 2 Kings ii. 16.

**Behold, the feet of them . . .**—In this instance the coming judgment is foretold, and the announcement tended to work out its own completion. Here, to all the shame and agony that had fallen on Ananias, there was now added the bitter thought of her husband's death as in some sense caused by her, inasmuch as she might have prevented the crime that led to it. The prophetic insight given to St. Peter taught him that the messengers, whose footsteps he already heard, had another task of a like nature before them.

(11) **And great fear came upon all the church.**—With the exception of the doubtful reading in chap. ii. 47, this is the first occurrence of the word *ecclesia* since the two instances in which our Lord had used it, as it were, by anticipation. (See Notes on Matt. xvi. 18; xviii. 17.) Its frequent use in the LXX. version for the "assembly," or "congregation," of Israel (Deut. xviii. 16; xxiii. 1; Ps. xxvi. 12; lxviii. 26), its associations with the political life of Greece as applied to the assemblies, every member of which

(12) And by the hands of the apostles
were many signs and wonders wrought
among the people; (and they were all
with one accord in Solomon's porch.
(13) And of the rest durst no man join
himself to them: but the people magnified them.
(14) And believers were the
more added to the Lord, multitudes
both of men and women.) (15) Insomuch that they brought forth the sick
into the streets,[1] and laid *them* on beds
and couches, that at the least the shadow
of Peter passing by might overshadow
some of them. (16) There came also a
multitude *out* of the cities round about
unto Jerusalem, bringing sick folks, and
them which were vexed with unclean
spirits: and they were healed every
one.
(17) Then the high priest rose up, and
all they that were with him, (which is
the sect of the Sadducees,) and were

1 Or, *in every street.*

---

was a full citizen, made it a natural and fitting word for the new society; and the use by our Lord either of the actual Greek word or of the corresponding Aramaic term stamped it with His sanction. Its occurrence here is, perhaps, an indication of the increase of the Hellenistic element among the disciples. The sudden startling death of Ananias and his wife naturally tended to give a new prominence to the society, the rulers of which were seen to be clothed with supernatural powers; and the fear that fell upon all who heard of these things led them in part to draw near with reverence, in part to shrink back in awe.

(12) **Many signs and wonders . . . .**—See Note on chap. ii. 22.

**They were all with one accord in Solomon's porch.**—See Notes on chap. iii. 2; John x. 23. It was, we have seen, at all times a favourite place of resort for teachers. The chronology of this period of the history is still, as before, left somewhat indefinite; but assuming some months to have passed since the Day of Pentecost, what is now related would be in the winter, when, as in John x. 23, that portico, as facing the east and catching the morning sunlight, was more than usually frequented. On "with one accord," see Note on chap. iv. 24.

(13) **Of the rest.**—We are left to conjecture who these were who are contrasted with the Apostles on the one side and with the people on the other. Does it mean that the Apostles stood aloof in an isolated majesty, and so that none of the other disciples dared associate himself with them? or is this St. Luke's way of speaking of the Pharisees and other teachers, who also resorted to the portico, but, as in the days of our Lord's ministry (John vii. 48; xii. 42), had not the courage to attach themselves to those with whom they really sympathised? The latter view seems every way the more probable, and so the passage stands parallel with those which tell us how the people heard our Lord gladly and "came early to hear him" (Luke xxi. 38).

(14) **Added to the Lord.**—Here, probably, the word is used in its definite New Testament sense for the Lord Jesus.

**Both of men and women.**—The mention of the latter forms an introduction to the dissensions connected with the "widows" in chap. vi., and is itself characteristic of St. Luke as a writer who had seen and known the effect of the new Religion in raising women to a higher life, and whose knowledge of its history was in great measure derived from them. (See *Introduction to St. Luke's Gospel.*) So in chap. viii. 3 women are named as prominent among the sufferers in the first general persecution.

(15) **Insomuch that they brought forth the sick . . .**—The tense implies habitual action. For some days or weeks the sick were laid all along the streets—the broad open streets, as distinct from the lanes and alleys (see Note on Matt. vi. 5)—by which the Apostle went to and fro between his home and the Temple.

**That at the least the shadow of Peter . . . .**—It is implied in the next verse that the hope was not disappointed. Assuming that miracles are possible, and that the narratives of the Gospels indicate generally the laws that govern them, there is nothing in the present narrative that is not in harmony with those laws. Christ healed sometimes directly by a word, without contact of any kind (Matt. viii. 13; John iv. 52); sometimes through material *media*—the fringe of His garment (Matt. ix. 20), or the clay smeared over the blind man's eyes (John ix. 5) becoming channels through which the healing virtue passed. All that was wanted was the expectation of an intense faith, as the subjective condition on the one side, the presence of an objective supernatural power on the other, and any medium upon which the imagination might happen to fix itself as a help to faith. So afterwards the "handkerchiefs and aprons" from St. Paul's skin do what the shadow of St. Peter does here (chap. xix. 12). In the use of oil, as in Mark vi. 13, Jas. v. 14, we find a medium employed which had in itself a healing power, with which the prayer of faith was to co-operate.

On the "beds and couches," see Note on Mark ii. 4. The couches were the more portable pallets or mattresses of the poor.

(16) **There came also a multitude.**—Here also the tense points to a continual and daily concourse. The work of expansion is beginning. The "cities round about" may have included Hebron, Bethlehem, Emmaus, and Jericho; perhaps also Lydda and Joppa. (See, however, Notes on chap. ix. 32, 36.) It is obvious here also that we have the summary of what must have occupied, at least, several months.

**Vexed with unclean spirits.**—In this work the Apostles and the Seventy had already experienced the power of the Name of the Lord Jesus (Luke x. 17). Now that they were working in the full power of the Spirit, it was natural that they should do yet greater things (John xiv. 12).

(17) **Then the high priest rose up . . . .**—Probably, as before, Annas or Caiaphas.

**Which is the sect of the Sadducees.**—The fact, of which this is the only distinct record, is of immense importance as throwing light on the course of action taken by the upper class of priests, both during our Lord's ministry and in the history of this book. From the time of the teaching of John v. 25—29, they must have felt that His doctrine was diametrically opposed to theirs. They made one attempt to turn that doctrine, on which, and almost on which alone, He and the Pharisees were in accord, into ridicule, and were baffled (Matt. xxii. 23—33). The raising of Lazarus mingled

filled with indignation,[1] (18) and laid
their hands on the apostles, and put
them in the common prison. (19) But
the angel of the Lord by night opened
the prison doors, and brought them
forth, and said, (20) Go, stand and speak
in the temple to the people all the
words of this life. (21) And when they
heard *that*, they entered into the temple
early in the morning, and taught. But
the high priest came, and they that
were with him, and called the council
together, and all the senate of the
children of Israel, and sent to the
prison to have them brought. (22) But
when the officers came, and found them
not in the prison, they returned, and
told, (23) saying, The prison truly found
we shut with all safety, and the keepers
standing without before the doors: but
when we had opened, we found no man
within. (24) Now when the high priest
and the captain of the temple and the
chief priests heard these things, they
doubted of them whereunto this would
grow. (25) Then came one and told them,
saying, Behold, the men whom ye put
in prison are standing in the temple,
and teaching the people. (26) Then
went the captain with the officers, and
brought them without violence: for
they feared the people, lest they should
have been stoned. (27) And when they
had brought them, they set *them* before
the council: and the high priest asked
them, (28) saying, Did not we straitly

1 Or, *envy*.

a dogmatic antagonism with the counsels of political expediency (John xi. 49—50). The prominence of the Resurrection of Jesus in the teaching of the Apostles now made the Sadducean high priests their most determined opponents. The Pharisees, on the other hand, less exposed now than they had been before to the condemnation passed by our Lord on their unreality and perverted casuistry, were drawing off from those with whom they had for a time coalesced, into a position at first of declared neutrality; then of secret sympathy; then, in many cases, of professed adherence (chap. xv. 5).

**Filled with indignation.**—The word is that elsewhere rendered "zeal," or "envy." Both meanings of the word were probably applicable here. There was "zeal" against the doctrine, "envy" of the popularity of the Apostles.

(18) **Put them in the common prison.**—The word is the same as the "ward" of chap. iv. 3. The addition of the word "common" or "public" perhaps indicates a greater severity of treatment. They were not merely kept in custody, but dealt with as common criminals, compelled to herd with ruffians and robbers and murderers.

(19) **But the angel of the Lord.**—Better, *an angel.* The fact is obviously recorded by St. Luke as supernatural. Those who do not accept that view of it, and yet wish to maintain the general historical character of the narrative, are driven to the hypothesis that the "angel" was some jealous and courageous disciple; and that the Apostle, in the darkness of the night and the excitement of his liberation, ascribed his rescue to the intervention of an angel. Acts xii. 7 may be noted as another instance of a like interposition. It has sometimes been urged, with something of a sneer, what was the use of such a deliverance as this, when the Apostles were again arrested on the very next day. The answer to such a question is not far to seek. (1) The marvellous deliverance was a sign, not without its influence on the subsequent decision of the Council, and on the courage of the two Apostles. (2) It was no small boon for them to be delivered even for a few hours from the vile companionship to which they had been condemned.

(20) **All the words of this life.**—The use of the demonstrative pronoun is significant. The "life in Christ" which the Apostles preach is that eternal life which consists in knowing God (John xvii. 1), and in which the angels are sharers.

(21) **Early in the morning.**—Probably at daybreak, when the worshippers would be going up to the Temple for their early devotions, or, though less probable, at the third hour, the time of the morning sacrifice.

**They that were with him.**—Probably those named in chap. iv. 6, who seem to have acted as a kind of cabinet or committee.

**All the senate . . . .**—Literally the word means, like senate, the assembly of old men, or elders. They are here distinguished from the Sanhedrin, which itself included elders, in the official sense of the word, and were probably a body of assessors—how chosen we do not know—specially qualified by age and experience, called in on special occasions. They may have been identical with the "whole estate of the elders" of chap. xxii. 5.

(24) **The high priest.**—The Received text gives "the priest," but the use of that word as meaning the high priest has no parallel in the New Testament, and the word is omitted by many of the best MSS.

**The captain of the temple.**—The commander of the Levite sentinels. (See Notes on chap. iv. 1; Luke xxii. 52.)

**Whereunto this would grow.**—Literally, *what it might become*, or, possibly, *what it might be.* They do not seem to have recognised at once the supernatural character of what had taken place, and may have conjectured that the Apostles had by some human help effected their escape.

(26) **Without violence . .**—The scene recalls that of John vii. 45. Here, however, the Apostles set the example of unresisting acquiescence, even though the tide of feeling in their favour was so strong that they might have easily raised a tumult in their favour. The signs that had been recently wrought, perhaps also the lavish distribution of alms, the ideal communism of the disciples, were all likely, till counteracted by stronger influences, to secure popular favour.

(28) **Did not we straitly command you . . . ?**—The Greek presents the same Hebrew idiom as in chap. iv. 17, and suggests again that it is a translation of the Aramaic actually spoken.

**Ye have filled Jerusalem with your doctrine.**—Better, *with your teaching*, both to keep up

command you that ye should not teach
in this name?[a] and, behold, ye have
filled Jerusalem with your doctrine,
and intend to bring this man's blood
upon us.
(29) Then Peter and the *other* apostles
answered and said, We ought to obey
God rather than men. (30) The God of
our fathers raised up Jesus, whom ye
slew and hanged on a tree. (31) Him
hath God exalted with his right hand
*to be* a Prince and a Saviour, for to give
repentance to Israel, and forgiveness of
sins. (32) And we are his witnesses of
these things; and *so is* also the Holy
Ghost, whom God hath given to them
that obey him.
(33) When they heard *that,* they were
cut *to the heart,* and took counsel to
slay them. (34) Then stood there up
one in the council, a Pharisee, named
Gamaliel, a doctor of the law, had in

[a] ch. 4. 18.

---

the connection with the previous clause, and because the word is taken, as in Matt. vii. 28, in its wider sense, and not in the modern sense which attaches to "doctrine" as meaning a formulated opinion.

**To bring this man's blood upon us.**—There seems a touch, partly of scorn, partly, it may be, of fear, in the careful avoidance (as before, in "this name") of the name of Jesus. The words that Peter had uttered, in chaps. ii. 36, iii. 13, 14, iv. 10, gave some colour to the conscience-stricken priests for this charge; but it was a strange complaint to come from those who had at least stirred up the people to cry, "His blood be on us and on our children" (Matt. xxvii. 25).

(29) **Then Peter and the other apostles.**—The whole company of the Twelve, it must be remembered, were now the objects of attack, and they all accept Peter as their spokesman.

**We ought to obey God rather than men.**—The words are an assertion of the same general law of duty as that of chap. iv. 19, 20, but the command of the angel in verse 20 had given them a new significance.

(30) **Whom ye slew and hanged on a tree.**—This synonym for crucifying comes from the LXX. version of Deut. xxi. 23, where it is used in a wider sense, including analogous forms of punishment, such as hanging or impaling. It meets us again in Peter's speech to Cornelius (chap. x. 39. Comp. Gal. iii. 13).

(31) **Him hath God exalted.**—It is significant that St. Peter should use a word which, while it does not occur as applied to our Lord in the first three Gospels, meets us as so applied in St. John (iii. 14; xii. 32: "lifted up" in the English version). It had also been used of the righteous sufferer in the LXX. version of Isa. lii. 13, and was afterwards used of the ascended and glorified Christ by St. Paul in Phil. ii. 9.

**A Prince.**—See Note on chap. iii. 15.

**To give repentance.**—We note, as in chap. ii. 38, the essential unity of the teaching of the Apostles with that of the Baptist (Matt. iii. 2). The beginning and the end were the same in each; what was characteristic of the new teaching was a fuller revelation (1) of the way in which forgiveness had been obtained; (2) of the spiritual gifts that followed on forgiveness; and (3) the existence of the society which was to bear its witness of both.

(32) **And so is also the Holy Ghost.**—The signs and wonders, the tongues and the prophecies, the new power and the new love, were all thought of by the Apostles as coming from their Lord; and therefore as an evidence that He had triumphed over death and had ascended into heaven. (Comp. chap. ii. 33.)

(33) **They were cut to the heart.**—The strict meaning of the verb describes the action of a saw, as in Heb. xi. 37. Used figuratively, it seems to imply a more lacerating pain than the "pricked to the heart" of chap. ii. 37, leading not to repentance but to hatred. The persons spoken of are principally the high priest and his Sadducean followers (verse 17).

(34) **A Pharisee, named Gamaliel.**—We are brought into contact here with one of the heroes of Rabbinic history. The part he now played in the opening of the great drama, and not less his position as the instructor of St. Paul, demand attention. We have to think of him as the grandson of the great Hillel the representative of the best school of Pharisaism, the tolerant and large-hearted rival of the narrow and fanatic Shammai, whose precepts—such, *e.g.*, as, Do nothing to another which thou wouldest not that he should do to thee—remind us of the Sermon on the Mount. The fame of Hillel won for him the highest honour of Judaism: the title of Rabban (the *Rabboni* of Mark x. 51; John xx. 16), and the office of President of the Council. For the first time, there seemed likely to be a dynasty of scribes, and the office of chief of the Jewish schools, what we might almost call their Professorship of Theology, was transmitted through four generations. Hillel was succeeded by his son Simeon, whom some have identified with the Simeon of Luke ii. 25 (see Note there), and he by Gamaliel. He, too, was known as the Rabban, and he rose now, with all the weight of years and authority, to counsel moderation. Various motives may have influenced him. He was old enough to remember the wisdom and grace of the child Jesus when, twenty-eight years before, He had sat in the midst of the doctors (Luke ii. 46). He may have welcomed, during our Lord's ministry, the teaching with so much of which Hillel would have sympathised, and been as the scribe who was not far from the kingdom of God (Mark xii. 32—34), rejoicing in the new proof that had been brought forward of the doctrine of the Resurrection. As being himself of the house and lineage of David, he may have sympathised with the claims of One who was welcomed as the Son of David. One who was so prominent as a teacher could not fail to be acquainted with a brother-teacher like Nicodemus, and may well have been influenced by the example of his gradual conversion and the counsels of caution which he had given (John vii. 50, 51). The tone in which he speaks now might almost lead us to class him with the "many" of the chief rulers who secretly believed in Christ, but shrank from confessing Him (John xii. 42, 43). It seems probable that he, like Joseph of Arimathæa, had "not consented to the counsel and deed" of the Sanhedrin which Caiaphas had hastily convened for our Lord's trial, and had contented himself with a policy of absence and expectation. If, as seems probable, Saul of Tarsus was at this time one of his disciples (chap. xxii. 3), the words of warning, though addressed

reputation among all the people, and
commanded to put the apostles forth
a little space; (35) and said unto them,
Ye men of Israel, take heed to yourselves
what ye intend to do as touching
these men. (36) For before these days
rose up Theudas, boasting himself to
be somebody; to whom a number of
men, about four hundred, joined themselves:
who was slain; and all, as
many as obeyed[1] him, were scattered,
and brought to nought. (37) After this
man rose up Judas of Galilee in
the days of the taxing, and drew
away much people after him: he also
perished; and all, *even* as many as
obeyed him, were dispersed. (38) And
now I say unto you, Refrain from these

1 Or, *believed.*

generally to the Council, may well have been intended specially to restrain his fiery and impetuous zeal.

**Commanded to put the apostles forth a little space.** — The practice of thus deliberating in the absence of the accused seems to have been common. (Comp. chap. iv. 15.) The report of the speech that follows may have come to St. Luke from some member of the Council, or, probably enough, from St. Paul himself. The occasional coincidences of language with the writings of that Apostle tend to confirm the antecedent likelihood of the conjecture.

(35) **Ye men of Israel.**—We note the more familiar address of a man in high authority as compared with St. Peter's "Rulers of the people, and elders of Israel" (chap. iv. 8).

**Take heed to yourselves.**—Compare our Lord's use of the same formula (Matt. vi. 1; vii. 15; x. 17), and St. Paul's (1 Tim. i. 4; iv. 13; Tit. i. 14).

(36) **Before these days rose up Theudas.**—An insurrection, headed by a leader of this name, is mentioned by Josephus (*Ant.* xx. 5, § 1). He, however, places it, not "before the taxing"—*i.e.*, circ. A.D. 6—but in the reign of Claudius, and under the procuratorship of Cuspius Fadus, A.D. 44, ten or twelve years after this speech of Gamaliel's. The Theudas of whom he speaks claimed to be a prophet, and promised to lead his followers across the Jordan. Fadus sent a troop of horse against him, and he was taken and beheaded. It has accordingly been inferred by some critics that we have here a blunder so portentous as to prove that the speech was made up long years after its alleged date by a writer ignorant of history, that the whole narrative of this part of the Acts is accordingly untrustworthy, and that the book requires to be sifted throughout, with a suspicious caution. On the other side, it is urged (1) that the circumstances of the two cases are not the same, Josephus speaking of a "very great multitude" as following his Theudas, while Gamaliel distinctly fixes the number of adherents at "about four hundred"; (2) that the name Theudas, whether considered as a form of the Aramaic name *Thaddæus* (see Note on Matt. x. 3), or the Greek *Theodorus*, was common enough to make it probable that there had been more than one rebel of that name; (3) that Josephus mentions no less than three insurrections of this type as occurring shortly after the death of Herod the Great (*Ant.* xvii. 10)—one headed by Judas (a name which appears from Matt. x. 3, Luke vi. 16, to have been interchangeable with Thaddæus or Theudas), the head of a band of robbers who seized upon the fortress of Sepphoris; one by Simon, previously a slave of Herod's, who proclaimed himself king and burnt Herod's palaces at Jericho and elsewhere; one by Athronges and four brothers, each of whom ruled over a band, more or less numerous, of his own—and adds further, that besides these there were numerous pretenders to the name of king, who murdered and robbed at large, and that one of these may well have been identical with the Theudas of whom Gamaliel speaks; (4) that it is hardly conceivable that a writer of St. Luke's culture and general accuracy, writing in the reign of Nero, could have been guilty of such inaccuracy as that imputed to him, still less that such a mistake should have been made by any author writing after Josephus's history was in the hands of men. A writer in the reign of Henry VIII. would hardly have inverted the order of Wat Tyler and Jack Cade. The description given by Gamaliel, *saying that he was some one*—*i.e.*, some great personage—agrees with the sufficiently vague account given by Josephus of the leaders of the revolts on the death of Herod, especially, perhaps, with that of Simon (who may have taken the name of Theudas as an *alias* to conceal his servile origin) of whom he says that "he thought himself more worthy than any other" of kingly power.

(37) **Judas of Galilee.**—In one passage Josephus (*Ant.* xviii. 1) calls him a Gaulonite—*i.e.*, of the country east of Galilee. Had this stood alone, St. Luke might have been charged here also with inaccuracy; but in other passages (*Ant.* xx. 5, § 2; *Wars*, ii. 8, § 1) he is described as a Galilean. On the taxing, in the modern sense of the term, which followed on the census that synchronised with our Lord's nativity, both being conducted under the supervision of Quirinus, see Notes on Luke ii. 1, 2. The insurrection of Judas was by far the most important of the attempts to throw off the yoke of Rome. He was assisted by a Pharisee, named Sadduk, and the absolute independence of Israel was the watchword of his followers. It was unlawful, in any form, to pay tribute to Cæsar. It was lawful to use any weapons in defence of freedom. The war they waged was a religious war; and Josephus, writing long after the movement had collapsed, but giving, obviously, the impressions of his own early manhood, enumerates them as being with the Pharisees, Sadducees, and Essenes, with the first of whom they were very closely allied—one of the four great religious sects of Judaism. Roman procurators and princes, like Archelaus and Antipas, were naturally united against him, and he and his followers came to the end of which Gamaliel speaks. His influence over the excitable population of Galilee was, however, at the time great, and in part survived. One of the Apostles probably derived his name of *Zelotes,* or *Cananite* (see Notes on Matt. x. 4), from having been among the followers of Judas, who were known by that name. His sons, Jacob and Simon, continued to be looked on as leaders after his death, and were crucified under Tiberius Alexander, the successor of Fadus in the procuratorship (Jos. *Ant.* xx. 5, § 2).

(38) **Refrain from these men.**—The advice implies something like a suppressed conviction not bold enough to utter itself. Gamaliel takes his place in the class, at all times numerous, of waiters upon **Providence,**

men, and let them alone: for if this
counsel or this work be of men, it will
come to nought: (39) but if it be of God,
ye cannot overthrow it; lest haply ye
be found even to fight against God.
(40) And to him they agreed: and when
they had called the apostles, and beaten
*them*, they commanded that they should
not speak in the name of Jesus, and let
them go.
(41) And they departed from the pre-
sence of the council, rejoicing that they
were counted worthy to suffer shame
for his name. (42) And daily in the
temple, and in every house, they ceased
not to teach and preach Jesus Christ.

A.D. 33.

CHAPTER VI.—(1) And in those
days, when the number of the disciples
was multiplied, there arose a murmuring

---

who are neutral till a cause is successful, and then come forward with a tardy sympathy, but who, above all, shrink from committing themselves while there seems any possibility of failure. In 1 Thess. ii. 13, St. Paul seems almost to contrast the readiness of his disciples in receiving his gospel, not as "of man," but as "of God," with the timid caution of his Master. As a prudential dilemma, the argument was forcible enough. Resistance was either needless or it was hopeless. If needless, it was a waste of energy; if hopeless, it involved a fatal risk besides that of mere failure. We may legitimately think of the fiery disciple as listening impatiently to this temporising counsel, and as stirred by it to greater vehemence.

**It will come to nought.**—Better, *it will be overthrown*, so as to preserve the emphasis of the repetition of the same verb in the next clause of the dilemma.

(39) **Fighters against God.**—It is interesting to note the recurrence of the same phrase in the reasoning of the Pharisees who took St. Paul's part in chap. xxiii. 9.

(40) **And to him they agreed.**—The Sadducees, after their manner, would probably have preferred a more violent course, but the Pharisees were strong in the Sanhedrin, and the *via media* recommended by Gamaliel was, under such circumstances, likely to command a majority, and was, therefore, apparently accepted without a division.

**And beaten them.**—Here we trace the action of Caiaphas and the priests. They were not content without some punishment being inflicted, and the party of Gamaliel apparently acquiesced in this as a compromise in the hope of averting more violent measures. And this is accordingly to be noted as the first actual experience of persecution falling on the whole company of the Twelve, and not on Peter and John only. They were probably convicted of the minor offence of causing a disturbance in the Temple, though dismissed, as with a verdict of "not" proven," on the graver charge of heresy. The punishment in such a case would probably be the "forty stripes save one," of Deut. xxv. 3 and 2 Cor. xi. 24.

(41) **Rejoicing that they were counted worthy.**—The emotion is probably, in one sense, natural to all who have an intense conviction of the Truth for which they suffer. But in this case there was something more. The Twelve could not fail to remember their Lord's beatitudes; and now, for the first time, felt that they could "rejoice and be exceeding glad" because they were suffering as the prophets had suffered before them (Matt. v. 11, 12). And they were suffering for His Name, or rather, with the best MSS., "for *the* Name"—for that of the Master who had loved them and whom they had learnt to love. We may note, too, in the whole history, the fulfilment of the prediction and the promise of Matt. x. 17—20.

(42) **And daily in the temple.**—Probably, as before, in the Portico of Solomon; the captain of the Temple now acting on the resolution just taken, and letting the movement take its course without interruption.

**And in every house.**—Better, as in chap. ii. 46, *at home:* in their place, or, it may be, places, of meeting.

**To teach and preach Jesus Christ.**—Better, *to teach and to declare the good tidings of Jesus Christ.* The word for "preach" is literally to "evangelise," as in chap. viii. 4, 12, 25; Rom. x. 15, and elsewhere.

As the chief members of the Sanhedrin disappear from the scene at this stage, it may be well to note the later fortunes of those who have been prominent up to this point in the history. (1) Annas lived to see five of his sons fill the office of high priest (Jos. *Ant.* xx. 9, § 1); but his old age was overclouded by the tumults raised by the Zealots under John of Gischala, in the reign of Vespasian, and before he died the sanctuary was occupied by them, and became in very deed a "den of robbers" (Jos. *Wars*, iv. 3, § 7). (2) Joseph, surnamed Caiaphas, his son-in-law, who owed his appointment to Gratus (Jos. *Ant.* xviii. 2, § 2), was deposed by the Proconsul Vitellius, A.D. 36 (Jos. *Ant.* xviii. 4, § 3), and disappears from history. (3) On John and Alexander, see Notes on chap. iv. 6. (4) Gamaliel, who is not mentioned by Josephus, continued to preside over the Sanhedrin under Caligula and Claudius, and is said to have died eighteen years before the destruction of Jerusalem, and to have sanctioned the Anathema, or "Prayer against heretics," drawn up by Samuel the Little (Lightfoot, *Cent. Chorograph*, c. 15). Christian traditions, however, represent him as having been secretly a disciple of Christ (Pseudo-Clement, *Recogn.* i. 65), and to have been baptised by Peter and Paul, with Nicodemus, who is represented as his nephew, and his son Abibas (*Photius Cod.* 171, p. 199). In a legendary story, purporting to come from a priest of Syria, named Lucian, accepted by Augustine, he appears as having buried Stephen and other Christians, and to have been buried himself in the same sepulchre with the Protomartyr and Nicodemus at Caphar-algama (August. *de Civ. Dei* xvii. 8, Serm. 318). Later Rabbis looked on him as the last of the great Teachers or Rabbans, and noted that till his time men had taught the Law standing, while afterwards they sat. The glory of the Law, they said, had departed with Gamaliel.

## VI.

(1) **And in those days, when the number of the disciples was multiplied.**—Better, *were being multiplied*, as by an almost daily increase. The length of the interval between this and the previous chapter is left uncertain. The death of Stephen is fixed by most writers in A.D. 38.

of the Grecians against the Hebrews, because their widows were neglected in the daily ministration.
(2) Then the twelve called the multitude of the disciples *unto them*, and said, It is not reason that we should leave the word of God, and serve tables.
(3) Wherefore, brethren, look ye out among you seven men of honest report, full of the Holy Ghost and wisdom, whom we may appoint over this business.
(4) But we will give ourselves continually to prayer, and to the ministry of the word.

---

**The Grecians.**—The English version always carefully uses this word, and not Greeks, for the Hellenists or Greek-speaking Jews. These were known also as "the dispersion among the Gentiles" (John vii. 35), or generally as "the dispersion," the "sojourners of the dispersion," those that were "scattered abroad" (Jas. i. 1; 1 Pet. i. 1). Many of the converts of the Day of Pentecost must have belonged to this body; so, probably, did Barnabas and the others named in the Note on chap. iv. 37. Now they were becoming a prominent section of the Church, perhaps more numerous than the Hebrews, or Jews of Palestine. They, as their name implies, spoke Greek habitually, and as a rule did not read the older Hebrew or speak the current Aramaic. They read the Septuagint (LXX.) version of the Old Testament. They were commonly more zealous, with the zeal of pilgrims, for the sanctity of the holy places than the Jews of Jerusalem itself, who had been familiar with them from infancy (chap. xxi. 27).

**Because their widows were neglected.**—The words imply something like an organised administration of the common fund: widows and their children being the chief objects of relief. The rules of 1 Tim. v. 3—16, were probably the growth of a more mature experience; and here we have to think of a clamorous crowd of applicants besieging the house at which the Apostles held their meeting at the times appointed for giving relief in money, or, as seems more probable, in kind. The Twelve—singly, or in groups—sat at the table, and gave as they were able. It was like the dole of alms at the gate of a convent. Under such circumstances, jealousies and complaints were all but inevitable. The Twelve were all of them Galileans, and were suspected of favouring the widows of Palestine rather than those of the Dispersion. It was the first sign that the new society was outgrowing its primitive organisation.

(2) **Then the twelve called the multitude of the disciples.**—The Apostles meet the crisis with singular tact and moderation. They do not resent the suspicion; they are not careful to vindicate themselves against it. They remembered, it may be, the precedent presented by the life of Moses (Ex. xviii. 25), and they act, as he had acted, by delegating part of their authority to others. The collective action of the multitude is strikingly in harmony with the Greek ideas attached to the word *Ecclesia*, as the assembly in which every citizen might take his share. Representative government might come as a necessity of later times; as yet, every member of the congregation, every citizen of the new polity, was invited, as having a right to vote.

**It is not reason.**—Literally, *It is not pleasing*, as in chap. xii. 3. The word implies that they had undertaken a burdensome duty, not for their own pleasure, because they liked it, but for the good of the community.

**And serve tables.**—The word was used for the "tables" of money-changers, as in Matt. xxi. 12, John ii. 15, and was, therefore, equally appropriate whether we think of the relief as being given in money or in kind.

(3) **Seven men of honest report.**—The number may have had its origin in the general reverence for the number Seven among the Jews. Possibly, however, the suggestion may have come from the *Libertini*, or Hellenists of Rome, where there was a distinct guild, or *Collegium*, known as the *Septemviri Epulones*, or Seven Stewards (Lucan. i. 602), whose business it was to arrange for the banquets held in honour of the gods, which were more or less analogous to the Christian *agapæ*, on certain set days. (See Smith's *Dict. of Greek and Roman Antiquities*, Art. "Epulones." It is an interesting coincidence that they, too, had been appointed to relieve the Pontifices from a duty which they found too heavy. This view falls in with the inference as to the Roman origin of Stephen which will be found in the Notes on verse 5.

**Full of the Holy Ghost and wisdom.**—The Apostles, it is clear, did not limit their thoughts of the Spirit's working to prophecy and the gift of tongues. Wherever wisdom, and charity, and kindness were requisite, there was need of a supernatural grace, raising men above prejudice and passion. Of these qualities, no less than of the good report, the whole body of believers were to be, in the first instance, the judges, the Apostles reserving to themselves the right of final appointment, and therefore, if necessary, of a veto. It is significant that the word "wisdom" only appears in the Acts in connection with Stephen (here and in verse 10, and in the report of his speech chap. vii. 10, 22). We may, perhaps, think of James, the brother of the Lord, as led by what he now saw and heard to that prayerful seeking after wisdom which is so prominent in his Epistle (Jas. i. 5; iii. 13—17).

(4) **We will give ourselves continually to prayer, and to the ministry of the word.**—Literally, *We will persevere in . . .* These formed the true work of the Apostles, as afterwards of the bishops or elders of the Church. "Prayer" includes the public worship of the Church in all its various developments, as well as private prayer and intercession; the "ministry of the word," all forms of teaching.

It is to be noted that the men thus appointed are never called "deacons" in the New Testament. When they are referred to again it is as "the Seven" (chap. xxi. 8), as though they were a distinct and peculiar body. Their functions were, of course, in some degree, analogous to those of the "deacons" of the Pastoral Epistles and the later organisation of the Church; but these, as we have seen, had their prototypes in the "young men," as contrasted with "elders," in chap. v. 6, 10; and the Seven were probably appointed, so to speak, as *archdeacons*, to superintend and guide them. In some churches, as at Rome, the number of deacons was fixed at seven, in conformity with this precedent (so also at the Council of Neo-Cæsarea, *Can.* 14, A.D. 314), and they were considered, when the bishop came to be distinguished from the elders, as acting more immediately

(5) **And the saying pleased the whole
multitude: and they chose Stephen, a
man full of faith and of the Holy
Ghost, and Philip, and Prochorus, and
Nicanor, and Timon, and Parmenas,
and Nicolas a proselyte of Antioch:**

under the direction of the former, helping him in the details of his office.

(5) **And they chose Stephen.**—The seven who were chosen all bear Greek names, and it is a natural, though not a necessary, inference, that they were all of the Hellenistic section of the Church, either because that section had a majority, or because the Hebrews generously voted for giving them special representatives of their own. The order of names may represent the actual order of election, Stephen obtaining the largest number of votes, and so on. The position occupied by the new teacher is so prominent that we should welcome anything that threw light on his previous training. Unhappily we cannot advance beyond the region of uncertain tradition, or, at best, of probable inference. The coincidences, however, which suggest that inference are not without interest. (1) The name of Stephanus was not a common one, and appears in few inscriptions. Like so many of the names in Rom. xvi., however, it is found in those of the *Columbarium*, or burial-place, of the household of the Empress Livia. The man bearing it is described as a goldsmith (*Aurifaber*), and as *immunis*—*i.e.*, exempted from the religious obligations of his trade-guild. He is a freed-man or *libertinus*. Circumstances, such as the bequest by Herod the Great of his gold plate to Livia (Jos. *Ant.* xvi. 5, § 1; xvii. 8, § 1), indicate an intimate connection between him and the Imperial Court, and make it probable that the goldsmith Stephanus was a Jew. The business was one in which then, as in later ages, Jews conspicuously excelled, and the exemption just mentioned may well have been, as it were, of the nature of a "conscience-clause" in his favour. The name is found also on a tablet in the museum of the *Collegio Romano.* (2) It is obvious that the "strangers of Rome"—the Jews from the capital of the empire—were likely to be among the most prominent of the Hellenists at Jerusalem. It was antecedently probable that the name of one of that body should stand first on the list. (3) When Stephen becomes conspicuous as a teacher, the synagogue which is the most prominent scene of his activity is that of the Libertines, who can be none other than the freed-men or emancipated Jews from Rome. (See Note on verse 9.) (4) Jews from Rome were, we have seen, present on the Day of Pentecost, and some conspicuous converts from among them had been made before Stephen appears on the scene. (See Note on chap. iv. 37.) (5) The very appointment of the Seven has, as we have seen, its origin in the customs of the trade-guilds of Rome, such as that to which the goldsmith Stephanus had belonged. Taking all these facts together, there seems sufficient ground to believe that in the proto-martyr of the Church, whose teaching and whose prayers exercised so marvellous an influence in the history of the Church of Christ, we have one of the earliest representatives of Roman Christianity. A tradition accepted by Epiphanius in the fourth century leads to another conclusion. Stephen and Philip were both, it was said, of the number of the Seventy who were sent shortly after the last Feast of Tabernacles in our Lord's ministry into every city and village where He Himself would come. That mission, as has been said in the Note on Luke x. 1, was in its very form, symbolic of the admission of the Gentile nations to the kingdom of God; and it would seem from Luke ix. 52, xvii. 11, as if, at that time, Samaria had been the chief scene of our Lord's ministry, and therefore of that of the Seventy. In a mission of such a nature, it was not unlikely that Hellenistic Jews should be more or less prominent, and the assumption of some previous connection with Samaria gives an adequate explanation both of Philip's choice of that region as the scene of his work as an Evangelist (chap. viii. 5) and of the general tendency of St. Stephen's speech; perhaps also of one of the real or apparent inaccuracies which criticism has noted as a proof of ignorance either in the speaker or the writer. (See Note on chap. vii. 16.) Admitting the comparative lateness of the tradition mentioned by Epiphanius, it was still antecedently probable that men, who had been brought into prominence by their Lord's special choice, would not be passed over in such an election as that now before us; and if, as suggested in the Note on Luke x. 1, the Seventy were the representatives of the Prophets of the New Testament, then it was natural that men should turn to them when they wanted to find men "full of the Holy Ghost and of wisdom."

**Philip.**—The coincidence of name with that of the Apostle and with two of Herod's sons indicates that the name was as common as that of Stephen was rare. Of his previous history we know nothing, except the tradition that he also had belonged to the Seventy. His long-continued residence at Cæsarea just suggests the probability of an earlier connection with that city. The fact that he had four grown-up daughters when St. Paul came to Cæsarea makes it probable that he was married at the time of his appointment.

**Prochorus, and Nicanor, and Timon, and Parmenas.**—Of these four nothing is known, nor are there any materials even for probable conjecture. The name of Nicanor was memorable as that of the great enemy of Judah, who died in battle fighting against Judas Maccabæus. It appears, later on, as borne by a Jewish friend of Titus and Josephus (*Wars*, v. 6, § 2). That of Timon had been made conspicuous by the philosopher of Phlius and the misanthrope of Athens.

**Nicolas a proselyte of Antioch.**—Next to the first two names on the list, the last is that to which greatest interest attaches. (1) It is the first appearance in the history of the Christian Church of the city which was afterwards to be the mother-church of the Gentiles. (On Antioch and its position, see Note on chap. xi. 19.) Here it will be enough to note that there was a large Jewish population there, and that Herod had gained the favour of the city by building a splendid colonnade along the whole length of its chief street. (2) The name had been made memorable by Nicolaus of Damascus, who wrote a long and elaborate history of his own times, and pleaded for the Jews before Augustus and Agrippa (Jos. *Ant.* xii. 3, § 2; xvi. 2, § 3; 9, § 4). He appeared at Rome again as counsel for Archelaus, and was for many years the confidential friend and adviser of Herod the Great (Jos. *Ant.* xvii. 9, § 6; 11, § 3). Finding, as we do, an adopted son of Herod's at Antioch (chap. xiii. 1), and a proselyte of that city bearing the name of his chosen companion, there seems some ground for assuming a link connecting the three together. (3) In any case Nicolas is memorable as the first person not of

(6) whom they set before the apostles:
and when they had prayed, they laid
*their* hands on them. (7) And the word
of God increased; and the number of
the disciples multiplied in Jerusalem
greatly; and a great company of the
priests were obedient to the faith.
(8) And Stephen, full of faith and power,
did great wonders and miracles among
the people.
(9) Then there arose certain of the
synagogue, which is called *the synagogue*

---

the race of Abraham named as admitted to full membership in the Church. He may have sacrificed to Apollo, or taken part in the licentious festivals of the grove of Daphne. The word "proselyte" is taken in its full sense, as including the acceptance of circumcision and the ceremonial law. He was, in technical language, a proselyte of Righteousness, not of the Gate. Had it been otherwise, his conversion would have anticipated the lesson taught afterwards by that of Cornelius. (4) The name of Nicolas has been identified by an early tradition as the founder of the sect of the Nicolaitanes condemned in Rev. ii. 6. He, it was said, taught men "to misuse the flesh" (Clem. Alex. *Strom.* iii. 4, p. 187; Euseb. *Hist.* iii. 29). Some contended that he meant by this that it was to be subdued by a rigorous asceticism: others, that he held it to be a proof of spiritual progress to yield to sensuous impulses, and yet remain pure. The traditions are not of much value, and another interpretation of the name of the sect is now very generally adopted (see Rev. ii. 6); but the fall of one of the Seven into the error of overstrained rigour, or a reaction from it, is not in itself inconceivable. In the New Testament we never come across his name again.

(6) **When they had prayed, they laid their hands on them.**—This is the first mention of the act in the New Testament. It had had an analogous meaning in the ritual of Israel (Num. xxvii. 23) in acts of blessing (Gen. xlviii. 13, 14) and the transmission of functions. Its primary symbolism would seem to be that of the concentration for the moment of all the spiritual energy of prayer upon him on whom men lay their hands; and so of the bestowal of any office for which spiritual gifts are required. It had been used in the Jewish schools on the admission of a scribe to his office as a teacher. It soon became the customary outward and visible sign of such bestowal (Acts xiii. 3). Instruction as to what it thus meant entered into the primary teaching of all converts (Heb. vi. 2). It was connected with other acts that pre-supposed the communication of a spiritual gift (1 Tim. v. 22). Through well-nigh all changes of polity and dogma and ritual, it has kept its place with Baptism and the Supper of the Lord, among the unchanging witnesses of the Church's universality and permanence, witnessing, as in Confirmation, to the diversity of spiritual gifts, and, as in Ordination, to their connection with every special office and administration in the Church of God.

(7) **The word of God increased.**—The tense indicates gradual and continuous growth. The fact stated implies more than the increase of numbers specified in the next clause. The "word of God" is here the whole doctrine of Christ as preached by the Apostles, and, we must now add, by the Seven who are commonly known as Deacons, and there was, as the sequel shows, at this stage, what we have learnt to call an expansion and development of doctrine.

**A great company of the priests were obedient to the faith.**—The fact is every way significant. No priest is named as a follower of our Lord's. None, up to this time, had been converted by the Apostles. The new fact may fairly be connected with the new teaching of Stephen. And the main feature of that teaching was, as we shall see, an anticipation of what was afterwards proclaimed more clearly by St. Paul and (if we assign the Epistle to the Hebrews to its probable author) by Apollos: that the time for sacrifices had passed away, and that the Law, as a whole, and the ritual of the Temple in particular, were decaying and waxing old, and ready to vanish away (Heb. viii. 13). We might have thought this likely to repel the priests, and to rouse them to a fanatic frenzy. We find that it attracts them as nothing else had attracted. To them, it may well have been, that daily round of a ritual of slaughtered victims and clouds of incense, the cutting-up of the carcases and the carriage of the offal, had become unspeakably wearisome. They felt how profitless it was to their own spiritual life, how little power there was in the blood of bulls and goats to take away sin (Heb. x. 4). Their profession of the new faith did not necessarily involve the immediate abandonment of their official function; but they were drifting to it as to a not far-off result, and were prepared to meet it without misgiving, perhaps with thankfulness, when it became inevitable.

(8) **Stephen, full of faith and power.**—The better MSS. give, "full of *grace* and power."

**Did great wonders and miracles.**—Better, as preserving the familiar combination, *wonders and signs.*

(9) **Certain of the synagogue, which is called the synagogue of the Libertines.**—The structure of the sentence makes it probable that the Libertines, the Cyrenians, and the Alexandrians attended one synagogue, those of Cilicia and Asia another. Each of the names has a special interest of its own. (1) The *Libertini.* These were freed-men, emancipated Roman Jews, with probably some proselytes, descendants of those whom Pompeius had led captive, and who were settled in the trans-Tiberine district of Rome in large numbers, with oratories and synagogues of their own. When Tacitus (*Ann.* ii. 85) describes the expulsion of the Jews under Claudius, he speaks of "four thousand of the freed-men, or *Libertine* class," as banished to Sardinia. From this class, we have seen reason to believe, Stephen himself had sprung. Andronicus and Junias were probably members of this synagogue. (See Note on Rom. xvi. 7.)

**Cyrenians.**—At Cyrene, also, on the north coast of Africa, lying between Egypt and Carthage, there was a large Jewish population. Strabo, quoted by Josephus, describes them as a fourth of the whole (Jos. *Ant.* xiv. 7, § 2). They were conspicuous for the offerings they sent to the Temple, and had appealed to Augustus for protection against the irregular taxes by which the provincial governors sought to intercept their gifts (Jos. *Ant.* xvi. 6, § 5). In Simon of Cyrene we have had a conspicuous member, probably a conspicuous convert, of this community. (See Note on Matt. xxvii. 32.) Later on, clearly as the result of Stephen's teaching, they are prominent in preaching the gospel to the Gentiles of Antioch. We may think

of the Libertines, and Cyrenians, and
Alexandrians, and of them of Cilicia
and of Asia, disputing with Stephen.
(10) And they were not able to resist the
wisdom and the spirit by which he
spake. (11) Then they suborned men,
which said, We have heard him speak
blasphemous words against Moses, and
*against* God. (12) And they stirred up
the people, and the elders, and the
scribes, and came upon *him*, and caught
him, and brought *him* to the council,
(13) and set up false witnesses, which
said, This man ceaseth not to speak
blasphemous words against this holy
place, and the law: (14) for we have
heard him say, that this Jesus of
Nazareth shall destroy this place, and

---

of Simon himself, and his two sons Alexander and Rufus (Mark xv. 21), as probably members of this society.

**Alexandrians.**—Next to Jerusalem and Rome, there was, perhaps, no city in which the Jewish population was so numerous and influential as at Alexandria. Here, too, they had their own quarter, assigned to them by Ptolemy Philadelphus, and were governed, as if they were a free republic, by an ethnarch of their own (Jos. *Ant.* xiv. 7, § 2). They were recognised as citizens by their Roman rulers (*Ibid.* xiv. 10, § 1). From Alexandria had come the Greek version of the Old Testament, known from the legend of the seventy translators who had all been led to a supernatural agreement, as that of the Septuagint, or LXX., which was then in use among all the Hellenistic Jews throughout the empire, and largely read even in Palestine itself. There, at this time, living in fame and honour, was the great teacher Philo, the probable master of Apollos, training him, all unconsciously, to be the preacher of a wisdom higher than his own. The knowledge, or want of knowledge, with which Apollos appears on the scene, knowing only the baptism of John, forbids the assumption that he had been at Jerusalem after the Day of Pentecost (chap. xviii. 25), but echoes of the teaching of Stephen are found in that of the Epistle to the Hebrews, and it is not improbable that thoughts had been carried back to Alexandria by those who had thus been brought under his influence.

**Of them of Cilicia.**—Here we feel at once the interest of the name. The young Jew of Tarsus, the disciple of Gamaliel, could not fail to be among the leading members of this section of the second synagogue, exercising, in the fiery energy of his zeal, a dominant influence even over the others.

**And of Asia.**—The word is taken, as throughout the New Testament, in its later and more restricted sense, as denoting the pro-consular province so called, including the old Lydia and Ionia, and having Ephesus as its capital. Later on in the history, we find Jews of Asia prominent in their zeal for the sacredness of the Temple (chap. xxi. 27).

**Disputing with Stephen.**—The nature of the dispute is not far to seek. The tendency of distance from sacred places which are connected with men's religion, is either to make men sit loose to their associations, and so rise to higher and wider thoughts, or to intensify their reverence. Where pilgrimages are customary, the latter is almost invariably the result. Men measure the sacredness of what they have come to see by the labour and cost which they have borne to see it, and they resent anything that suggests that they have wasted their labour, as tending to sacrilege and impiety. The teaching of Stephen, representing as it did the former alternative, guided and perfected by the teaching of the Spirit, was probably accepted by a few in each community. The others, moved by their pilgrim zeal, were more intolerant of it than the dwellers in Jerusalem, to whom the ritual of the Temple was a part of their every-day life. Those who were most familiar with it, the priests who ministered in its courts, were, as we have seen (verse 7), among the first to welcome the new and wider teaching.

(10) **They were not able.**—Better, *had no strength*; the verb being somewhat more forcible than that commonly translated "to be able."

**To resist the wisdom and the spirit with which he spake.**—It is remarkable that Stephen is the first Christian teacher of whom "wisdom" is thus specially predicted. In the Gospels it is ascribed to our Lord (Matt. xiii. 54; Luke ii. 40, 52); and we read of "the wisdom of Solomon" (Matt. xii. 42). In a writer like St. Luke, it implies something higher even than the "consolation" or "prophecy" from which Barnabas took his name—wider thoughts, a clearer vision of the truth, the development of what had been before latent in hints and parables and dark sayings. The speech that follows in the next chapter, may be accepted as an example, as far as circumstances allowed, of the method and power of his general teaching.

(11) **Blasphemous words against Moses, and against God.**—The words indicate with sufficient clearness the nature of Stephen's teaching. The charge was a false one, but its falsehood was a distortion of the truth, as that against our Lord had been. He was accused of blasphemy in calling Himself the Son of God; making Himself equal with God (Matt. xxvi. 63; John v. 18); threatening to destroy the Temple (Matt. xxvi. 61)—each of the counts in the indictment resting on words that He had actually spoken. And Stephen, in like manner, was charged with offences for which there must have seemed colourable ground. He had taught, we must believe, that the days of the Temple were numbered; that with its fall the form of worship of which it was the representative would pass away; that the Law given by Moses was to make way for the higher revelation in Christ, and the privileges of the elect nation to be merged in the blessings of the universal Church. In this case, accordingly, the antagonism comes, not only or chiefly, as in the previous chapters, from the Sadducean high priests and their followers, but from the whole body of scribes and people. Pharisees and Sadducees, Hebrews and Hellenists, are once more brought into coalition against the new truth.

(13) **Against this holy place.**—The new feature of Stephen's preaching comes into greater prominence.

(14) **This Jesus of Nazareth shall destroy this place.**—The accusation rested in part on the words of John ii. 19, partly on the prediction of Matt. xxiv. 2, which Stephen must have known, and may well have reproduced. It would seem to the accusers a natural inference that He who had uttered the prediction should be the chief agent in its fulfilment.

shall change the customs[1] which Moses delivered us. (15) And all that sat in the council looking stedfastly on him, saw his face as it had been the face of an angel.

CHAPTER VII.—(1) Then said the high priest, Are these things so? (2) And he said, Men, brethren, and fathers, hearken; The God of glory appeared unto our father Abraham, when he was in Mesopotamia, before he dwelt in Charran, (3) and said unto him, Get thee out of thy country,[a] and from thy kindred, and come into the land which I shall shew thee. (4) Then came he out of the land of the Chaldæans, and dwelt in Charran: and from thence,

[1] Or, *rites.*

[a] Gen. 12. 1.

A.D. 33.

**And shall change the customs.**—The words seem to have been used in a half-technical sense as including the whole complex system of the Mosaic law, its ritual, its symbolism, its laws and rules of life, circumcision, the Sabbath, the distinction of clean and unclean meats (chaps. xv. 1; xxi. 21; xxvi. 3; xxviii. 17).

(15) **Looking stedfastly on him.**—St Luke's characteristic word. (See Note on chap. i. 10.)

**Saw his face as it had been the face of an angel.**—We can scarcely be wrong in tracing this description to the impression made at the time on St. Paul, and reported by him to St. Luke. It must be interpreted by the account given of angels as appearing in the form of "young men" (Mark xvi. 5), and so throws some light upon St. Stephen's age, as being, probably, about the same standing as St. Paul, and implies that his face was lighted up as by the radiance of a divine brightness. The phrase seems to have been more or less proverbial. In the expanded version of the Book of Esther, which appears in the LXX., she says to the King, as in reverential awe, "I saw thee, O my lord, as an angel of God" (Esth. v. 2). In 2 Sam. xiv. 17, the words refer to the wisdom of David rather than to anything visible and outward. Here the impression left by St. Luke's narrative is that the face of St. Stephen was illumined at once with the glow of an ardent zeal and the serenity of a higher wisdom.

VII.

(1) **Then said the high priest, Are these things so?**—The question was analogous to that put to our Lord. The accused was called on to plead guilty or not guilty, and had then an opportunity for his defence. On that defence we now enter.

(2) **Men, brethren, and fathers.**—The discourse which follows presents many aspects, each of special interest. (1) It is clearly an unfinished fragment, interrupted by the clamours of the by-standers (verse 51)—the *torso*, as it were, of a great *apologia*. Its very incompleteness, the difficulty of tracing the argument as far as it goes, because we do not see how far it was meant to go, are indirect proofs that we have a true, though not necessarily a verbatim, report. A later writer, composing a speech after the manner of Herodotus and Thucydides, would have made it a much more direct answer to the charges in the indictment. And this, in its turn, supplies a reasonable presumption in favour of other speeches reported by the same author. (2) Looking to the relations between St. Luke and St. Paul, and to the prominence of the latter among the accusers of Stephen, there is a strong probability that the report was derived from him. This is confirmed by some instances of remarkable parallelism between the speech and his later teaching. (Comp. verse 53, Gal. iii. 19; verse 48, Acts xvii. 24). (3) The speech is the first great survey of the history of Israel as a process of divine education—the first development from the lips of a human teacher of principles that had before been latent. As such, it contains the germs which were, in their turn, to be afterwards developed, on the one hand, by St. Paul in the Epistles known to be his, on the other hand by Apollos, or whoever was the author of the Epistle to the Hebrews. (4) The speech is also remarkable as bringing together within a comparatively small compass a considerable number of real or seeming inaccuracies in the details of the history which is commented on. Whether they are real or apparent will be discussed as we deal with each of them. It is obvious that the results thus arrived at will form something like a crucial test of theories which men have formed as to the nature and limits of inspiration. (5) As Stephen was a Hellenistic or Greek-speaking Jew, it is probable that the speech was delivered in Greek, and so far it confirms the inference which has been drawn from the Aramaic words specially recorded in our Lord's teaching—"Ephphatha," "Talitha cumi," and the cry upon the cross—that He habitually used the former language, and that this was the medium of intercourse between the priests and Pilate. (See Notes on Mark v. 41; vii. 34.)

**The God of glory.**—The opening words are an implied answer to the charge of blaspheming God. The name contained an allusive reference to the Shechinah, or cloud of glory, which was the symbol of the Presence of Jehovah. That was the "glory of the Lord." He, in like manner, was the "Lord of glory." (Comp. Jas. ii. 1.)

**Before he dwelt in Charran.**—We come, at the very outset, on one of the difficulties above referred to. Here the call of Abraham is spoken of as *before* he sojourned in Haran, or Charran, west of the Euphrates. In Gen. xii. 1 it is first mentioned *after* Abraham's removal thither. On the other hand, Gen. xv. 7 speaks of God as bringing him "from Ur of the Chaldees"—*i.e.*, from Mesopotamia, or the east of the Euphrates; and this is confirmed by Josh. xxiv. 3, Neh. ix. 7. The language of writers contemporary with Stephen (Philo, *De Abrah.*; Jos. *Ant.* i. 7, § 1) lays stress, as he does, on the first call as well as the second. Here, accordingly, it cannot be said that the statement is at variance with the Old Testament narrative. The word *Mesopotamia* was used by the LXX., and has thence passed into later versions, for the Hebrew *Aram-Naharaim*, "Syria of the two rivers" (Gen. xxiv. 10; Deut. xxiii. 4; Judg. iii. 8), and, less accurately, for Padan-Aram in Gen. xxv. 20; xxviii. 2, 5, 6; where our version retains the Hebrew name.

(4) **From thence, when his father was dead.**—In Gen. xi. 26, 32, Terah, the father of Abraham, is said to have died at the age of 205 years, and after he had reached the age of seventy to have begotten Abram, Nahor, and Haran; while Abraham in Gen. xii. 4 is said to have

when his father was dead, he removed
him into this land, wherein ye now
dwell. (5) And he gave him none in-
heritance in it, no, not *so much as* to set
his foot on: yet he promised that he
would give it to him for a possession,
and to his seed after him, when *as yet*
he had no child. (6) And God spake on
this wise, That his seed should sojourn
in a strange land; and that they should
bring them into bondage, and entreat
*them* evil four hundred years. (7) And
the nation to whom they shall be in
bondage will I judge, said God: and
after that shall they come forth, and
serve me in this place. (8) And he gave
him the covenant of circumcision:[a] and
so *Abraham* begat Isaac,[b] and circum-
cised him the eighth day; and Isaac
*begat* Jacob;[c] and Jacob *begat* the twelve
patriarchs.[d] (9) And the patriarchs,[e]
moved with envy, sold Joseph into

*a* Gen. 17. 9.
*b* Gen. 21. 3.
*c* Gen. 25. 26.
*d* Gen. 29. 31.
*e* Gen. 37. 28.

---

been seventy-five years old when he departed out of Haran. This, *primâ facie*, suggests the conclusion that he lived for sixty years after his son's departure. The explanations sometimes given—(1) that Abraham may have been the youngest, not the eldest son of Terah, placed first in order of honour, not of time, as Shem is among the sons of Noah (Gen. v. 32; vi. 10), though Japheth was the elder (Gen. x. 21); and (2) that the marriage of Abraham's son with the granddaughter of Nahor by the youngest of his eight sons, Bethuel (Gen. xxii. 22), suggests some such difference of age, and that he may therefore have been born when Terah was 130, and so have remained in Haran till his father's death —though probable as an hypothesis, would hardly appear so natural an explanation as that the memory of St. Stephen or of his reporter dwelt upon the broad outlines of the history, and was indifferent to chronological details. It is remarkable that like difficulties present themselves in St. Paul's own survey of the history of Israel. (See Notes on chap. xiii. 20; Gal. iii. 17.) A man speaking for his life, and pleading for the truth with a passionate eagerness, does not commonly carry with him a *memoria technica* of chronological *minutiæ*. This seems, on the whole, a more satisfactory explanation than the assumption that the Apostle, having a clear recollection of the facts as we find them, brought them before his hearers in a form which presented at least the appearance of inaccuracy.

**He removed him.**—The change of subject may be noted as more natural in a speaker than a writer, and as so far confirming the inference that we have probably a *verbatim* report.

(5) **And he gave him none inheritance.**—The apparent exception of the field and cave of Machpelah (Gen. xxiii. 9—17) was not a real one. That was purchased for a special purpose, not given as an inheritance.

(6) **And that they should bring them into bondage . . .**—Here again there is another apparent discrepancy of detail. Taking the common computation, the interval between the covenant with Abraham and that with Moses was 430 years (Gal. iii. 17), of which only 215 are reckoned as spent in Egypt. The Israelites were indeed sojourners in a strange land for the whole 430 years, but the history shows that they were not in bondage nor evil entreated till the Pharaoh arose who knew not Joseph. The chronological difficulty, however, lies in reconciling St. Paul's statement in Gal. iii. 17 with the language of Gen. xv. 13, which gives 400 years as the sojourning in Egypt, and Ex. xii. 40, which gives 430, and with which St. Stephen is in substantial agreement. St. Paul appears to have followed the LXX. reading of Ex. xii. 40, which inserts "in the land of Canaan," and in some MSS. "they and their fathers," and with this the Samaritan Pentateuch agrees. Josephus varies, in some passages (*Ant.* ii. 15, § 2), giving 215 years; in others (*Ant.* ii. 9, § 1; *Wars*, v. 9, § 4), 400. All that can be said is, as before, that chronological accuracy did not affect the argument in either case. It was enough for St. Stephen, as for St. Paul, to accept this or that system of dates, as they had been taught, without inquiring into the grounds on which it rested. Such inquiries were foreign to the Jewish character generally, and above all to that character when possessed by the sense of new and divine realities. Round numbers were enough for them to mark the successive stages of God's dealings with His people.

(7) **And after that shall they come forth.**—The verse combines the promise to Abraham in Gen. xv. 17 with a free rendering of the sign given to Moses (Ex. iii. 12), which referred not to Canaan but to Horeb. What St. Stephen does is to substitute with the natural freedom of a narrative given from memory the words "they shall serve me" for the simpler phrase, "they shall come hither again," of Genesis. The whole context is at variance with the assumption that St Stephen meant the last words of the verse to be taken as applying to the mount of God.

(8) **And he gave him the covenant . . .**—Here we trace an indirect reference to the charge that he had spoken "against the customs." He does not deny the specific charge that he had said that Jesus of Nazareth should change them. He probably had taught that the change was about to come. He does assert (1) that the covenant of circumcision followed on the promise to Abraham, and therefore was not the ground of his election, and so lays the foundation for St. Paul's argument in Gal. iii. 17; (2) that, though part of a provisional, not of a permanent, system, it came from God's appointment, and therefore was to be spoken of with all reverence, and so he clears himself from the charge of blasphemy.

**The twelve patriarchs.**—On the meaning of the word see Note on chap. ii. 29. Here it is applied to the sons of Jacob, as being, each of them, the founder of a *patria*, or family.

(9) **The patriarchs, moved with envy.**—This, interpreted by what follows, is the first step in the long induction which is to show that the elect of God had always been opposed and rejected by those who were for the time the representatives of the nation. Envy had actuated the patriarchs when they sold Joseph; envy had led their descendants to deliver up Jesus (Matt. xxvii. 18). But man's evil will had not frustrated God's gracious purpose. Joseph was made ruler over a kingdom. A greater glory might therefore be in store for Him who had now been rejected by them.

**Sold Joseph into Egypt.**—The objection that Joseph's brethren sold him not into Egypt, but to the Midianites and Ishmaelites (Gen. xxxvii. 25, 28), may

Egypt: but God was with him, (10) and
delivered him out of all his afflictions,
and gave him favour and wisdom in the
sight of Pharaoh king of Egypt;[a] and
he made him governor over Egypt and
all his house. (11) Now there came a
dearth over all the land of Egypt and
Chanaan, and great affliction: and our
fathers found no sustenance. (12) But
when Jacob heard that there was corn
in Egypt,[b] he sent out our fathers first.
(13) And at the second *time* Joseph was
made known to his brethren;[c] and
Joseph's kindred was made known unto
Pharaoh. (14) Then sent Joseph, and
called his father Jacob to *him*, and all
his kindred, threescore and fifteen souls.
(15) So Jacob went down into Egypt,[d]
and died,[e] he, and our fathers, (16) and
were carried over into Sychem, and laid
in the sepulchre that Abraham bought
for a sum of money of the sons of

c Gen. 45. 4.
a Gen. 41. 37.
d Gen. 46. 5.
e Gen. 49. 33.
b Gen. 42. 1.

---

well be dismissed as frivolous. They knew the trade which the Midianite slave-dealers carried on, and where their brother would be taken. So Joseph himself says of them "ye sold me hither" (Gen. xlv. 5).

(11–14) **Now there came a dearth . . .**—So far as we can trace the sequence of thought, there seems the suggested inference that as those who, in the history of Joseph, had persecuted him, came afterwards to be dependent on his bounty, so it might prove to be, in the last parallel which the history of Israel presented. In the coming famine, not of bread, but of sustenance for their spiritual life, they would have to turn to Him of whom they had been, in purpose and in act, the betrayers and murderers.

(14) **Threescore and fifteen souls.**—Seventy is given as the number, including Jacob, Joseph, and his sons, in Gen. xlvi. 27; Ex. i. 5; Deut. x. 22. Here, however, Stephen had the authority of the LXX. of Gen. xlvi. 27, which gives the number at seventy-five, and makes it up by inserting the son and grandson of Manasseh, two sons and a grandson of Ephraim. With them it was probably an editorial correction based upon Num. xxvi. 26—37. Stephen, as a Hellenistic Jew, naturally accepted, without caring to investigate, the number which he found in the Greek version.

(16) **And were carried over into Sychem.**—The words appear to include Jacob, who was buried not at Sychem, but Machpelah (Gen. l. 13). If we limit the verb to the patriarchs, which is in itself a tenable limitation, we are met by the fresh difficulty that the Old Testament contains no record of the burial of any of the Twelve Patriarchs, with the exception of Joseph, whose bones were laid, on the occupation of Canaan, in Shechem (Josh. xxiv. 32); and Josephus states (*Ant.* iv. 8, § 2) that they were buried at Hebron. This, however, only represents, at the best, a local tradition. In the time of Jerome (*Ep.* 86) the tombs of the Twelve Patriarchs were shown at Shechem, and this in its turn witnesses to a Samaritan tradition which continues to the present day (*Palestine Exploration Report*, Dec., 1877), and which Stephen, it may be, followed in preference to that of Judæa. Looking to the probabilities of the case, it was likely that the example set by Joseph would be followed by the other tribes, and that as Shechem was far more prominent than Hebron, as the centre of the civil and religious life of Israel in the time of Joshua, that should have been chosen as the burial-place of his brethren rather than Machpelah. Looking, again, to the fact that one of Stephen's companions, immediately after his death, goes to Samaria as a preacher, and that there are good grounds for believing that both had been previously connected with it (see Note on chap. vi. 5), we may probably trace to this influence his adoption of the Samaritan version of the history. The hated Sychar (Ecclus. l. 26; see Note on John iv. 5) had, from Stephen's point of view, a claim on the reverence of all true Israelites, and his assertion of that claim may well have been one of the causes of the bitterness with which his hearers listened to him.

**That Abraham bought for a sum of money.**—Here we seem to come across a direct contradiction to the narrative of Genesis. The only recorded transaction in which Abraham appears as a buyer, was his purchase of the cave of Machpelah from Ephron the Hittite (Gen. xxiii. 16). The only recorded transaction in which the sons of Emmor, or Hamor, appear as sellers, was in Jacob's purchase of the field at Shechem (Gen. xxxiii. 19; Josh. xxiv. 32). What we have seen above, however, prepares us for there having been a Samaritan tradition carrying the associations of Shechem to a remoter past. And, assuming such a tradition, there are significant facts in the patriarchal history of which it furnishes an explanation. (1) Jacob gives as a special inheritance to Joseph, "one portion" (in the Hebrew, "one *Shechem;*" in the LXX., *Sikima*) above his brethren, which he had taken "out of the hands of the Amorites with his sword and his bow." Of that conquest—as it is clear that the words cannot refer to the massacre connected with the story of Dinah, which Jacob had severely condemned (Gen. xxxiv. 30)—the history contains no record, and to interpret the words as prophetic of future conquests is to strain them to a non-natural interpretation which they will hardly bear. Jacob did not come as an invader, nor had the time for thus taking possession of the whole land as yet arrived. The facts of the case suggest a special right claimed and asserted in regard to this one possession, and that right presupposes a previous purchase by some ancestor of Jacob's—*i.e.*, by Abraham. This being done and the right asserted, to make the portion larger, and perhaps as a measure of conciliation, there followed the subsequent purchase of Gen. xxxiii. 19. (2) Shechem was the earliest settlement of Abraham on his entrance into Canaan, and there he built an altar (Gen. xii. 67). But the feeling of reverence for holy places, always strong in the Hebrew race, as seen, *e.g.*, in the case of David and Araunah, would hardly permit a man of Abraham's wealth and princely nobleness to offer burnt-offerings to the Lord of that which had cost him nothing (2 Sam. xxiv. 24); nor would a devout worshipper be content to see the altar so consecrated in the possession of another, and so exposed to desecration. The building of an altar involved, almost of necessity, as in the case just cited, the purchase of the ground on which it stood. (3) The Samaritans had an immemorial tradition (adopted by Dean Stanley, Ffoulkes, Grove, and others) that the sacrifice of Isaac took place on the mountain of Moriah (Gen. xxii. 2),

Emmor *the father* of Sychem. (17) But
when the time of the promise drew
nigh, which God had sworn to Abraham,
the people grew and multiplied in
Egypt, (18) till another king arose,
which knew not Joseph. (19) The same
dealt subtilly with our kindred, and evil
entreated our fathers, so that they cast
out their young children, to the end
they might not live. (20) In which time
Moses was born,[a] and was exceeding
fair,[1] and nourished up in his father's
house three months:[b] (21) and when
he was cast out, Pharaoh's daughter
took him up, and nourished him for her
own son. (22) And Moses was learned
in all the wisdom of the Egyptians, and
was mighty in words and in deeds.

*a* Ex. 2. 2.
1 Or, *fair to God.*
*b* Heb. 11. 23.

---

or Gerizim, which commands the plain of Moreh (Gen. xii. 6), or Shechem; and, without now discussing the evidence for or against the tradition, it almost involved of necessity the assumption that Abraham had already an altar there, and with it a consecrated field which he could call his own. (4) Another Samaritan tradition, it may be noted, connected Shechem with the sacrifice offered by Melchizedek. This is enough to show the extent of the claims which were made by the Samaritans on behalf of their sacred places, and, taken together with the statement referred to in the previous Note as to the tombs of the Patriarchs, leads us to the conclusion that Stephen, more or less influenced by his recent associations with them, adopted their traditions. This seems, at any rate, the most probable solution of the difficulty which the statement at first sight presents. To do this in Jerusalem, before the very Sanhedrin, the members of which had reviled our Lord as a Samaritan (John viii. 48), required a martyr's boldness, and, claiming as it did, a brotherhood for the hated Samaritans, the hereditary foes of Judah, had, we may believe, much to do with causing the fury that ended in his actual martyrdom. It may be added (1) that the manifest familiarity of St. Luke with Samaria and the Samaritans would dispose him to accept such a tradition without correction (see *Introduction to St. Luke's Gospel*); (2) that the Twelve, some of whom had sojourned for three days at Sychar (John iv. 43), were likely to have become acquainted with it, and to have been ignorant of the Hebron traditions; (3) that the well-known substitution of Gerizim for Ebal in Deut. xxvii. 4, in the Samaritan Pentateuch, not less than their addition of a commandment to build an altar on Gerizim to the ten great laws of Ex. xx., shows a tendency to deal freely with the text and the facts of the Pentateuch, so as to support their own traditions as to their sacred places.

**Of the sons of Emmor the father of Sychem.**—The insertion of the word "father" instead of "son," which would be (as in Matt. x. 3; Luke iii. 23) the natural rendering of the Greek construction, must be looked on as betraying a wish on the part of the translators to meet the difficulty presented by the statement in Gen. xxxiv. 2, that Shechem was the *son* of Hamor the Hivite. It may be noted that it is the only English version that thus tampers with the text—Tyndale giving "at Sychem;" Wiclif, Cranmer, Geneva, and the Rhemish giving "*son* of Sychem." A possible explanation of the apparent discrepancy may be found in the very probable assumption that Shechem may have been a quasi-hereditary name appearing in alternate generations. In this instance, however, textual criticism comes in to cut the knot. Many of the better MSS., including the Vatican and the Sinaitic, give the reading "in Sychem," and so make the name apply to the place and not to a person.

With the exception of verse 43, we have now come to the last of the difficulties, chronological, historical, or numerical, presented by St. Stephen's speech. They have been approached by writers of different schools of thought in ways singularly, sometimes almost painfully, characteristic. On the one hand, there has been something like the eagerness of a partisan mustering all objections and anxious to secure an adverse verdict; on the other, there has been an almost hysterical alarm and indignation that such questions should be ever raised. Here the effort has, at least, been made to deal with each on its own merits, and not to force facts this way or that to meet a foregone conclusion. Should there be errors of transcription, of report, or even of memory in the record of St. Stephen's speech, they need not shake the faith of those who have learnt to take a higher view of inspiration than that which depends upon the registers of genealogies or chronological tables. But it may be well also not to assume too hastily that men of average culture and information would be altogether ignorant of the facts which they narrate, and the sacred writings which have been the object of their continual study. And it may be urged that the appearance of seeming inaccuracies, which a moment's reference to the Book of Genesis would have enabled the writer to correct, is, at any rate, evidence of faithfulness in his report of the speech which he thus reproduces.

(17) **Which God had sworn to Abraham.**—The better MSS. give, *which God promised.*

(18) **Which knew not Joseph.**—The idiom was originally a Hebrew one, for "not remembering, not caring for;" but as the words are quoted from the LXX. they do not affect the question as to the language in which the speech was delivered.

(19) **So that they cast out their young children.**—Literally, *to make their children cast out so that they should not be brought forth alive.* The latter verb is used in the LXX. narrative (Ex. i. 17).

(20) **Exceeding fair.**—Literally, as in the margin, *fair to God.* The adjective is found in the LXX. of Ex. ii. 2, as applied to Moses. The special idiom for expressing pre-eminent excellence is itself essentially Hebrew, the highest goodness being thought of as that which approves itself as good to God; but this also had become familiar to Hellenistic Jews through the LXX. version, as, *e.g.*, in Jonah iii. 3, a city "great to God" = an exceeding great city. St. Paul's "mighty to God" (2 Cor. x. 4) is probably an example of the same idiom. Josephus, following probably some old tradition (*Ant.* i. 9, § 6), describes the beauty of the infant Moses as such that those who met him turned to gaze in admiration.

(22) **Moses was learned in all the wisdom of the Egyptians.**—Better, *was trained,* or *instructed.* There is no direct statement to this effect in the history of the Pentateuch, but it was implied in Moses being brought up as the son of Pharaoh's daughter, and was in harmony with later paraphrases and expansions of the earlier history. The narrative of Josephus (as

(23) And when he was full forty years
old, it came into his heart to visit his
brethren the children of Israel. (24) And
seeing one *of them* suffer wrong,[a] he
defended *him*, and avenged him that was
oppressed, and smote the Egyptian:
(25) for he supposed his brethren would
have understood how that God by his
hand would deliver them: but they
understood not. (26) And the next day
he shewed himself unto them as they
strove,[b] and would have set them at one
again, saying, Sirs, ye are brethren;
why do ye wrong one to another?
(27) But he that did his neighbour
wrong thrust him away, saying, Who
made thee a ruler and a judge over us?
(28) Wilt thou kill me, as thou diddest
the Egyptian yesterday? (29) Then fled
Moses at this saying, and was a stranger
in the land of Madian, where he begat
two sons. (30) And when forty years
were expired, there appeared to him in
the wilderness of mount Sina an angel
of the Lord in a flame of fire in a bush.[c]
(31) When Moses saw *it*, he wondered at
the sight: and as he drew near to
behold *it*, the voice of the Lord came
unto him, (32) *saying*, I *am* the God of
thy fathers, the God of Abraham, and

a Ex. 2. 11.
c Ex. 3. 2.
b Ex. 2. 13.

above) and the references in the New Testament to Jannes and Jambres as the magicians who withstood Moses (2 Tim. iii. 8), and to the dispute of Michael and Satan as to his body (Jude, verse 9), indicate the wide acceptance of some such half-legendary history. The passage is instructive, (1) as an indirect plea on the part of Stephen, like that afterwards made by Clement of Alexandria (*Strom.* i. 5, § 28; vi. 5, § 42) and Justin (*Dial. c. Tryph.* c. 1—4), for the recognition of heathen wisdom as an element in the divine education of mankind; (2) as having contributed to fix the attention of the more cultivated and scholarly of the early Christian critics, such as those named, and Origen, and Jerome, and Augustine, on the teaching of Greek poets and philosophers, and having furnished them with a sanction for such studies.

**Mighty in words and in deeds.**—Josephus (*Ant.* ii. 10), still following the same traditional history, relates that Moses commanded the Egyptian forces in a campaign against the Ethiopians, and protected them against the serpents that infected the country, by transporting large numbers of the ibis that feeds on serpents. The romance was completed by the marriage of Moses with the daughter of the Ethiopian king who had fallen passionately in love with him. This was possibly a development of the brief statement in Num. xii. 1. The language of Moses (Ex. iv. 10), in which he speaks of himself as "not eloquent" and "slow of speech," seems at first inconsistent with "mighty in words," but may fairly be regarded as simply the utterance of a true humility shrinking from the burden of a mighty task.

(23) **It came into his heart.**—The distinct purpose in going out to look after his brethren is stated somewhat more emphatically than in Ex. ii. 11.

(24) **And avenged him.** — The Greek phrase is noticeable as identical with that used by St. Luke (xviii. 7) in reporting the lesson drawn by our Lord from the parable of the Unjust Judge.

(25) **For he supposed his brethren would have understood . . .**—Better, *and he supposed.* The Greek conjunction never has the meaning of "for," and the insertion of that word gives to the act of slaying the Egyptian a deliberate character which, in the narrative of Ex. ii. 11, 12, does not belong to it.

**Would deliver them.**—Literally, *was giving them salvation*, or *deliverance;* the act being itself one of championship and the first step to deliverance.

(26) **Would have set them at one again.**—Literally, *brought them to peace.* The better MSS. give "was bringing them."

**Sirs.**—Literally, *Ye are brethren,* without any word of address. The phrase is the same as "we be brethren" in Gen. xiii. 8.

(27) **Who made thee a ruler and a judge?**—The stress laid on this afterwards, in verse 35, shows that it took its place in the induction which was to show that the whole history of Israel had been marked by the rejection of those who were, at each successive stage, God's ministers and messengers for its good, and that the rejection of Jesus was therefore a presumptive proof that He, too, was sent from God.

(29) **Then fled Moses at this saying.**—The rapid survey of the history passes over the intermediate link of Pharaoh's knowledge of the murder of the Egyptian, and his search for Moses.

(30) **There appeared to him in the wilderness.**—With the exception of the substitution of Sina, or Sinai, for the less familiar Horeb, the fact is stated in nearly the same words as in Ex. iii. 2. The reference to this revelation, besides the bearing it had on the main argument of the speech, was indirectly an answer to the charge that he had spoken "blasphemous words against Moses." Both in the Hebrew and the LXX. the word "angel" is, as here, without the article.

**In a bush.**—The Hebrew word *seneh* is used for a species of thorny acacia, which still grows in the wilderness of Sinai. The Greek word, in the LXX. and here, was used commonly for the bramble, or any prickly shrub.

(31) **The voice of the Lord came unto him.**—The speech agrees with Ex. iii. 4 in ascribing the voice to the Lord, the Eternal, while the visible manifestation was that of the angel of the Lord. It hardly belongs to the interpretation of the speech to discuss the relation between the two statements. Speaking generally, it may be said that all, or nearly all, theophanies, or divine manifestations, in the Old Testament addressed to the sense of sight resolve themselves into angelophanies, all manifestations addressed exclusively to the sense of hearing into revelations by the Son, as the LOGOS, or eternal WORD.

(32) **The God of Abraham.**—It is probable, on the assumption that Stephen had been one of the Seventy disciples of Luke x. 1, that he knew that these words had been cited by the Lord Jesus (Matt. xxii. 32) as witnessing against the unbelief of the Sadducees. In any case, the fact could hardly have been forgotten by the priestly and therefore Sadducean members of the Council, to whom Stephen addressed his defence. They had then been urged as a new proof of immortality,

the God of Isaac, and the God of Jacob.
Then Moses trembled, and durst not
behold. (33) Then said the Lord to him,
Put off thy shoes from thy feet: for the
place where thou standest is holy ground.
(34) I have seen, I have seen the afflic-
tion of my people which is in Egypt,
and I have heard their groaning, and
am come down to deliver them. And
now come, I will send thee into Egypt.
(35) This Moses whom they refused, say-
ing, Who made thee a ruler and a
judge? the same did God send *to be* a
ruler and a deliverer by the hand of the
angel which appeared to him in the
bush. (36) He brought them out, after
that he had shewed wonders and signs
in the land of Egypt,[a] and in the Red
sea, and in the wilderness forty years.[b]
(37) This is that Moses, which said
unto the children of Israel, A prophet
shall the Lord your God raise up unto
you of your brethren,[c] like unto me;[1]
him shall ye hear. (38) This is he, that
was in the church in the wilderness
with the angel which spake to him in
the mount Sina,[d] and *with* our fathers:
who received the lively oracles to give
unto us: (39) to whom our fathers would
not obey, but thrust *him* from them, and
in their hearts turned back again into
Egypt, (40) saying unto Aaron, Make us

*a* Ex. 7. 9.
*b* Ex. 16. 1.
*c* Deut. 18. 15.
1 Or, *as myself.*
*d* Ex. 19. 3.

---

and therefore of the resurrection. They are now connected with the proclamation that He who then spake had himself been raised from the dead and exalted to the right hand of God.

(33, 34) **Then said the Lord to him . . . .**—The words are almost a verbal reproduction of Ex. iii. 5, 7, 8. The citation was in part an implied answer to the charge of disregarding the sanctity of places in which man stands as in the presence of God, partly an implied protest against the narrowing thoughts which limited that sanctity to the Temple of Jerusalem.

(35) **The same did God send to be a ruler and a deliverer.**—Literally, *a ruler and redeemer.* The word is not found elsewhere in the New Testament, but is formed from the noun for "ransom" in Matt. xx. 28, Mark x. 45, and appears to have been chosen to emphasise the parallelism which the speech indicates between Moses and the Christ. In a yet higher sense than Moses, the latter also had been made "a ruler and a redeemer."

(36) **After that he had shewed wonders and signs.**—The two nouns are joined together, as in Deut. vi. 22, Matt. xxiv. 24. The words express different relations, it may be, of the same phenomena, rather than phenomena specifically different;—the first emphasising the wonder which the miracle produces, and therefore answering more strictly to that word; the latter, the fact that the miracle is a token or evidence of something beyond itself. (See also chaps. ii. 22; vi. 8.)

**In the Red sea.**—It may be worth while noting that the familiar name comes to us, not from the Hebrew word, which means, literally, *the Weed Sea,* but from the LXX. version, which Stephen, as a Hellenistic Jew, used, and which gave the word *Erythræan,* or red, which had been used by Greek travellers from Herodotus onward. Why the name was given is an unsolved problem. Some have referred it to the colour of the coast; some to that of the sea-weed, some to an attempt to give an etymological translation of its name as the Sea of Edom (Edom, meaning "red," as in Gen. xxv. 25; xxxvi. 1); some to a supposed connection with an early settlement of Phœnicians, whose name had, with the Greeks, the same significance.

(37) **A prophet shall the Lord your God raise up.**—The parallelism previously suggested is now distinctly proclaimed, and shown to be a fulfilment of the prediction of Deut. xviii. 18. The prediction itself is cited freely, as before. (See Note on chap. iii. 22.) The definite application of the words by St. Peter determined their bearing here. At this point we may reasonably think of the members of the Sanhedrin as catching the drift of his discourse, and showing signs of excitement, the effect of which is, perhaps, traceable in the greater compression of the narrative that follows.

(38) **That was in the church in the wilderness.**—The word *ecclesia* is used, as it had been in the LXX. (Deut. xviii. 16; xxiii. 1; Ps. xxvi. 12), for the "congregation" of Israel. Of the earlier versions. Tyndale, Cranmer, and the Genevan, had given "congregation." Even the Rhemish contented itself with "assembly." The translators of 1611, acting on the instructions which were drawn up for their direction, did not see any reason for making this an exception to the rule, and so gave "church." Assuming that *ecclesia* was so rendered elsewhere, it was, it may be admitted, right, as a matter of consistency, that it should be used here, as presenting the thought, which was emphasised in Stephen's speech, that the society of believers in Christ was like, in character and in its relation to God, to that of Israel. The new *ecclesia* was the development of the old. (See Note on Matt. xvi. 18.)

**The lively oracles.**—The noun was used by the Greeks for the solemn utterances of the Pythian oracles, and thus came to be used by the LXX. in connection with the Urim and Thummim of the high priest (Ex. xxviii. 30), and so for any answer from God (Num. xxiv. 4). In the New Testament it appears again in Rom. iii. 2; Heb. v. 12; 1 Pet. iv. 11.

(39) **To whom our fathers would not obey.**—The historical parallelism is continued. The people rejected Moses then (the same word is used as in verse 27) as they were rejecting Christ now, even after He had shown Himself to be their redeemer from a worse than Egyptian bondage.

**In their hearts turned back again into Egypt.**—The sin was one often repeated, but the history referred to is probably that in Ex. xvi. 3 For a later example see Num. xi. 5.

(40) **Make us gods.**—The speech follows the LXX. and the English version of Ex. xxxii. 4 in giving the plural, but it is probable that the Hebrew, *Elohim,* was used in its ordinary sense as singular in meaning, though plural in form, and that the sin of the Golden Calf was thus a transgression of the Second and not of the First Commandment.

gods to go before us:[a] for *as for* this
Moses, which brought us out of the
land of Egypt, we wot not what is
become of him. (41) And they made a
calf in those days, and offered sacri-
fice unto the idol, and rejoiced in the
works of their own hands. (42) Then
God turned, and gave them up to worship
the host of heaven; as it is written in
the book of the prophets, O ye house of
Israel,[b] have ye offered to me slain beasts
and sacrifices *by the space of* forty years
in the wilderness? (43) Yea, ye took up
the tabernacle of Moloch, and the star
of your god Remphan, figures which ye
made to worship them: and I will carry
you away beyond Babylon. (44) Our
fathers had the tabernacle of witness
in the wilderness, as he had appointed,
speaking unto Moses, that he should
make it according to the fashion that
he had seen.[c] (45) Which also our
fathers that came after brought in
with Jesus into the possession of the
Gentiles, whom God drave out before
the face of our fathers, unto the days

a Ex. 32. 1.

b Amos 5. 25.

c Ex. 25. 40.

(41) **They made a calf.**—The fact is stated in a compound word which is not found in the LXX. version, and which St. Stephen apparently coined for the purpose.

**Rejoiced in the works of their own hands.**—The verb expresses specially the joy of a feast, as in Luke xv. 23, 24, 29; xvi. 19; and is therefore specially appropriate for what is related in Ex. xxxii. 5, 6. The tense "*were rejoicing*" expresses the frequency or continuance of the sin.

(42) **The host of heaven.**—The word includes the host or army of the firmament, sun, moon, and stars, as in 2 Chron. xxxiii. 3, 5; Jer. viii. 2. The sin of Israel was that it worshipped the created host, instead of Jehovah Sabaoth, the "Lord of hosts."

**In the book of the prophets.**—The term is used in conformity with the Rabbinic usage which treated the Twelve Minor Prophets as making up a single book.

**Have ye offered to me . . . ?**—Better, *did ye offer . . . ?* The words are, with one exception, from the LXX. of Amos v. 25, 26. The narrative of the Pentateuch is inconsistent with the statement that no sacrifices were offered to Jehovah during the forty years' wandering; but the question emphasises the thought which Amos desired to press upon the men of his generation, that Jehovah rejected the divided worship offered to them by a people who were all along hankering after, and frequently openly returning to, the worship of Egypt or Chaldæa. Moloch, and not the true God of Abraham, had been their chosen deity.

(43) **Ye took up the tabernacle of Moloch.**—The verb implies the up-lifting of the tabernacle of Moloch, in the same manner as the ark was borne (Ex. xxv. 14; 1 Kings ii. 26), as a sacred ensign in the march of the Israelites. The Hebrew word for "tabernacle" (*Siccuth*) is an unusual one, and may have been used as a proper name; the word rendered "Moloch," being descriptive, *Siccuth your king.* The prohibition of the distinctive rite of Moloch worship in Lev. xviii. 21, xx. 2, is, perhaps, in favour of the common rendering. In spite of this prohibition, however, it reappeared continually under the kings, both of Judah (2 Kings xvi. 3, xxiii. 10; Jer. vii. 31, xxxii. 35) and Israel (2 Kings xvii. 17; Ezek. xxiii. 37).

**And the star of your god Remphan.**—Remphan appears to have been understood by the LXX. translators as an equivalent for the Hebrew "Chiun," which is supposed by many scholars to be identified with the planet Saturn, of which "Ræphan" (the LXX. form of the name) was the Coptic or Egyptian name. There is no adequate proof, however, that the planet was so known, and the Hebrew may bear the meaning of *the pedestal of your images.* As to "star," however, there is no question, and this was enough for Stephen's purpose, as proving the worship of the host of heaven.

**I will carry you away beyond Babylon.**—Both the Hebrew and the LXX. give "Damascus"; and we are left to choose between an intentional variation, to emphasise the actual fulfilment of the words as surpassing what the prophet had foretold, or an inaccuracy naturally incident to a quotation from memory. One section of the speech, that which accumulates proof that Israel, had been all along a rebellious people, seems to end here. The next deals with the charge that Stephen had spoken blasphemous words against the Temple.

(44) **The tabernacle of witness.**—The word was applied by the LXX. to the Tabernacle, as in Num. ix. 15, xvii. 7, as containing the Two Tables of Stone, which were emphatically the testimony of what was God's will as the rule of man's conduct (Ex. xxv. 16, 21; xxxi. 18). It should be noted that the LXX. gives the same rendering for the words which the English version translates as the "tabernacle of the congregation," *e.g.*, in Ex. xxix. 10; xxxiii. 7; Num. xvi. 18, 19.

**As he had appointed, speaking unto Moses.**—The answer to the charge lay in these words. Stephen admitted and asserted the divine sanction that had been given to Tabernacle and Temple. What he denied was that that sanction involved perpetuity. It is not without interest to note in the thought thus implied the germ of Hooker's great argument in the Third Book of his *Ecclesiastical Polity* (c. xi.).

(45) **Brought in with Jesus.**—This is, of course, as in Heb. iv. 8, the "Joshua" of the Old Testament. It would, perhaps, have been better, as a general rule, to have reproduced the Hebrew rather than the Greek form of Old Testament names in the English version of the New. On the other hand, there is, in this instance, something gained in our attention being called to the identity of the two names. It is noticeable that though Stephen was on his trial as a disciple of Jesus of Nazareth, that name does not pass his lips as he speaks in his defence, except in this reference to the great captain of Israel. It is possible that under this reticence, there may have been a half-veiled reference to Him who, also bearing the name that marked Him out as a Saviour, had come, after another fashion, "into the possession of the Gentiles." The word for "possession" is found in verse 5, but not elsewhere in the

of David: (46) who found favour before
God, and desired to find a tabernacle
for the God of Jacob. (47) But Solomon
built him an house.[a] (48) Howbeit
the most High dwelleth not in temples
made with hands;[b] as saith the prophet,
(49) Heaven *is* my throne, and earth *is*
my footstool: what house will ye build
me? saith the Lord: or what *is* the
place of my rest? (50) Hath not my
hand made all these things?

a 1 Chron. 17. 12.

b ch. 17. 24.

(51) Ye stiffnecked and uncircumcised
in heart and ears, ye do always resist the
Holy Ghost: as your fathers *did*, so *do*
ye. (52) Which of the prophets have
not your fathers persecuted? and they
have slain them which shewed before
of the coming of the Just One; of
whom ye have been now the betrayers
and murderers: (53) who have received
the law by the disposition of angels,
and have not kept *it*.

---

New Testament. In the LXX. it is common enough, as in Gen. xlvii. 11; Lev. xxv. 24; Deut. xxxii. 51.

(46) **Who found favour before God.**—Again we trace, though still in the form of a narrative, an indirect answer to the accusation brought against Stephen. He was ready to acknowledge without reserve that the Temple was planned by the man after God's own heart, and built by the wisest of the sons of men. But the question still remained whether it was therefore the symbol of a final and perfect worship, whether it did not bear witness to its own incompleteness.

(48) **Howbeit the most High dwelleth not in temples.**—The sequel shows the impression which these words made on the hearers. Stephen had risen to the truth which, though it had been proclaimed before, had been practically dormant. It broke down the thought of any exclusive holiness in the Temple, and therefore placed its downfall among the chances and changes which might be involved in God's chastisement of the people, and His education of mankind. The inference which we have seen reason to draw as to the probability of some connection, direct or indirect, between Stephen and the Samaritans (see Notes on verse 16 and chap. vi. 5), suggests the thought that we may trace here something like an echo of the teaching of our Lord in His dialogue with the woman of Samaria (John iv. 21—23). It is a fact of singular interest to note how one who now listened to the words as applied to the Temple of the God of Israel, afterwards embraced them in all their fulness, and used them as his text in asserting the truth they embodied as against the Temples of Zeus and Athenê (Acts xvii. 24).

**As saith the prophet.**—The truth which Stephen asserted had been uttered in the very dedication prayer of the Temple (1 Kings viii. 27). The builder of the Temple had himself felt that it was the witness not of a localised but a universal Presence. But he turns to what might seem to his hearers a yet higher authority—to the great prophet (Isa. lxvi. 1, 2), who was preeminently the preacher of glad tidings, and who had closed his mission with the utterance of the truth that, whatever glory and greatness might attach to the Temple in Jerusalem, the prayer of him that was "poor and of a contrite spirit" was equally acceptable wherever it might be offered. The words were full of deep meaning in themselves. They were yet more significant as showing that the thoughts of Stephen had been turned to that great close of a great work, and that he must thus have been led to that wider vision of the future when all nations and tongues should be gathered to see the glory of the Eternal; and the work of Israel, especially of those who, like himself, belonged to the Dispersion, should be to declare His glory to the Gentiles, and when they, too, should be accepted as priests and Levites in the true Temple (Isa. lxvi. 21). Here also we may think of him as anticipating the widest and highest teaching of St. Paul.

(51) **Ye stiffnecked and uncircumcised . . .**—The sudden change of tone from calm argument to vehement indignation cannot be thought of as spontaneous. The excitement of the Sanhedrin, perhaps of the listening crowd also, at this point, would seem to have become uncontrollable. The accused seemed to them to be repeating his offence with defiant boldness, and loud clamours took the place of whispered murmurs. Both the adjectives had been applied to the sins of the older Israel; "stiffnecked" in Ex. xxxiii. 3, 5; xxxiv. 9; "uncircumcised" in Jer. vi. 10. The actual phrase "uncircumcised in heart" had been used by Ezekiel (xliv. 7) of "strangers." It was now applied to those who boasted of their exclusive privileges as Israelites, and it is scarcely possible for us to estimate the sharp incisiveness with which it, or its Aramaic equivalent, must have fallen on the ears of the Sanhedrin. It was to them all, and more than all, that "heretic" and "infidel" have been in the controversies of Christians. Here again, in St. Paul's "circumcision of the heart" (Rom. ii. 29), we have another echo from St. Stephen's speech.

(52) **Which of the prophets have not your fathers persecuted?**—St. Stephen echoes, as it were, our Lord's own words (Matt. v. 12; Luke xiii. 34). Every witness for the truth had in his day had to suffer. The prophet was not only "without honour," but was exposed to shame, treated as an enemy, condemned to death. 1 Thess. ii. 15, perhaps, reproduces the same fact, but more probably refers to the sufferings of the prophets of the Christian Church who were treated as their predecessors had been.

**The coming of the Just One.**—The name does not appear to have been one of the received titles of the expected Messiah, but may have been suggested by Isa. xi. 4, 5. It seems to have been accepted by the Church of Jerusalem, and in 1 John ii. 1, and, perhaps, in Jas. v. 6, we find examples of its application. The recent use of it by Pilate's wife (Matt. xxvii. 19) may have helped to give prominence to it. He who had been condemned as a malefactor was emphatically, above all the sons of men, the "righteous," the "Just One."

**The betrayers and murderers.**—The two words emphasise, the first the act of the Sanhedrin and the people, and secondly, the persistence with which they urged on Pilate the sentence of death, and which made them not merely accessories, but principals in the deed of blood.

(53) **Who have received . . .**—More accurately, *who received.*

**By the disposition of angels.**—Better, *as ordained of angels*; or, more literally, *as ordinances of angels.* The Greek preposition cannot possibly have

(54) When they heard these things,
they were cut to the heart, and they
gnashed on him with *their* teeth.
(55) But he, being full of the Holy
Ghost, looked up stedfastly into heaven,
and saw the glory of God, and Jesus
standing on the right hand of God,
(56) and said, Behold, I see the heavens
opened, and the Son of man standing
on the right hand of God. (57) Then
they cried out with a loud voice, and
stopped their ears, and ran upon him
with one accord, (58) and cast *him* out
of the city, and stoned *him*: and the
witnesses laid down their clothes at a
young man's feet, whose name was

the meaning of "by." The phrase expressed the current Jewish belief that angels were the intermediate agents through whom Israel received the Law; that it was their voice that was heard on Sinai. Here also St. Paul, in speaking of the Law as "ordained by angels" (Gal. iii. 19), reproduced St. Stephen. Comp. also Heb. ii. 2 and Jos. *Ant.* xv. 4, § 3, for like statements. The idea rested mainly on the LXX. version of Deut. xxxiii. 2, "on His right hand were angels with Him" and "the thousands of angels" as connected with Sinai in Ps. lxviii. 17.

(54) **They were cut to the heart.**—Literally, *were sawn through and through.* (See Note on chap. v. 33.) The word describes a keener pang than the "pricked" of chap. ii. 37, producing, not repentance, but the frenzy of furious anger.

**They gnashed on him with their teeth.**—The passage is worth noting as the only example of the literal use of a phrase with which we are so familiar in its figurative application (Matt. viii. 12; xiii. 42, *et al.*). Here it clearly expresses brute passion rather than despair. At this point rage and fury—the fury caused by the consciousness that the stern words are true—had become altogether beyond control. They had passed beyond articulate speech into the inarticulate utterances of animal ferocity.

(55) **Being full of the Holy Ghost.**—There is something suggestive in the fact that this description comes at the close, as at the beginning, of the record of St. Stephen's work (chap. vi. 8). From first to last he had been conspicuous as manifesting the power of the higher life which had, as it were, illumined and transfigured his whole being. The Greek "being full" implies, not a sudden inspiration, but a permanent state.

**And saw the glory of God.**—Stephen had begun with speaking of "the God of glory" (verse 2). He ends with the vision of that glory as belonging to the Son of Man. The fact was inferred partly, we may believe, from the rapt, fixed expression of the martyr's face, partly from the words that followed, interpreting that upward gaze. On the word for "looked up stedfastly," see Note on chap. iii. 4.

(56) **Behold, I see the heavens opened.**—It is manifest that the vision was given to the inward spiritual eye, and not to that of sense. No priest or scribe saw the glory of the opened heavens, and, therefore, the words which declared that Stephen saw them seemed to them but an aggravation of guilt that was already deep. (See Note on Matt. iii. 16.)

**And the Son of man.**—The words call for notice as the only certain instance outside the Gospels of the use of the name which they record to have been constantly used by our Lord in speaking of Himself. (See Note on Matt. viii. 20.) As the speech of Stephen was delivered at least some years before any Gospel was written, and as the whole character of the speech reported, even in its apparent inconsequence and inaccuracy, is against the theory that it was put by the historian into the martyr's lips, its occurrence here is evidence in favour of the Gospel narrative, as showing that the title, which a few years afterwards, for some reason or other, the disciples ceased to use, was at that earlier date familiar. As uttered by Stephen before the Sanhedrin, it had the special emphasis of reminding them of the words which had been spoken by the Son of Man Himself (Matt. xxvi. 64). It was from their point of view a repetition of what they had then condemned as blasphemy. In Rev. i. 14 we have possibly another instance.

**Standing on the right hand of God.**—Our Lord's own language (Matt. xxvi. 64), and that of the Church following it (*e.g.*, Eph. i. 20; Heb. viii. 1), has commonly spoken of Him as *sitting* at the right hand of God. It was not, we may believe, without significance that He was manifested to Stephen's gaze as standing in the attitude of one who rises to help and welcome a follower who had shown himself faithful even unto death.

(57) **Ran upon him with one accord.**—The violence reported presents a singular contrast to the general observance of the forms of a fair trial in our Lord's condemnation. Then, however, we must remember, the Roman procurator was present in Jerusalem. Now all restraint was removed, and fanaticism had full play. That neither office nor age was enough to guard, under such conditions, against shameful outrage has been seen even in the history of Christian assemblies, as, *e.g.*, in that of the Robber Synod of Ephesus in A.D. 449. The caution in 1 Tim. iii. 3, that a bishop should not be a striker, shows how near the danger was even in the apostolic age. The facts in this case seem to imply that the accusers, and perhaps also the excited crowd whom they represented, were present as listening to the speech, as well as the members of the Sanhedrin.

(58) **And stoned him.**—Literally, *were stoning him*, The verb is repeated in verse 59, as if to show that the shower of stones went on even during the martyr's prayers.

**The witnesses laid down their clothes.**—The Law required, as if to impress on witnesses their solemn responsibility, that they should be the first, if the accused were condemned to death, to take part in his execution (Deut. xvii. 7). Our Lord, it will be remembered, had applied the rule in the case of the woman taken in adultery (John viii. 7). The loose, flowing cloak, which was worn as an outer garment, would have impeded the free action of their arms, and had therefore to be laid on one side.

**A young man's feet, whose name was Saul.**—As defined by Philo, on the authority of medical writers, the term thus used extended from twenty-one to twenty-eight years of age. Looking to the prominent position taken by Saul in this matter, and to his description of himself as "Paul the aged," A.D. 64 (Philem. verse 9), it will be safe to assume that he had nearly attained the later limit. It will be convenient on this his first appearance to put together the

Saul. (59) And they stoned Stephen,
calling upon *God*, and saying, Lord
Jesus, receive my spirit. (60) And he
kneeled down, and cried with a loud
voice, Lord, lay not this sin to their
charge. And when he had said this,
he fell asleep.

A.D. 34.

CHAPTER VIII.—(1) And Saul was
consenting unto his death. And at
that time there was a great persecution
against the church which was at
Jerusalem; and they were all scattered
abroad throughout the regions
of Judæa and Samaria, except the

---

chief facts of his life up to this period. He was of the tribe of Benjamin (Phil. iii. 5), and had been named after its great hero-king. His father had obtained, perhaps as a freed-man, after a time of slavery at Rome, the privilege of Roman citizenship (chap. xxii. 28). He had settled at Tarsus. The absence of any reference to him or to the Apostle's mother makes it probable that they were both dead before he appears on the scene. The son of a married sister is found, apparently residing in Jerusalem, in chap. xxiii. 16. At Tarsus the boy would probably receive a two-fold education, instructed at home in the Holy Scriptures daily, and in Greek literature and philosophy in the schools for which the city was famous. Traces of the knowledge thus acquired are found in his quotations from the Cilician poet Aratus (see Note on chap. xvii. 28), Menander (see 1 Cor. xv. 33), Epimenides (see Tit. i. 12), and the Festival Hymn quoted by him at Lystra (see Note on chap. xiv. 17). At twelve he would become a child of the Law (see Note on Luke ii. 42); and showing great devotion to the studies which thus opened on him, was probably dedicated by his parents to the calling of a scribe. This, however, did not involve the abandonment of secular occupation; and after some years spent in Jerusalem, studying under Gamaliel (we may say, with almost absolute certainty, before the commencement of our Lord's ministry), he returned to his native city, and became a "tent-maker" (chap. xviii. 3)—a manufacturer, *i.e.*, of the coarse goats' hair sail-cloth, for which Cilicia was famous. There seems reason to believe that somewhere about this time he became acquainted with Barnabas (see Note on chap. iv. 36), and possibly also with St. Luke (see Note on chaps. xiii. 1, and xvi. 10, and *Introduction to St. Luke's Gospel*). In the interval between the Ascension and the appointment of the Seven Deacons, he came up to Jerusalem. He finds a new sect, as it would seem, added to the three—the Pharisees, Sadducees, Essenes—whom he had known before. In some respects their teaching is such as Hillel, the grandfather of Gamaliel, would have approved. They pray and fast, and give alms. They proclaim a resurrection and a judgment after death. They connect that proclamation with the belief that a teacher of Nazareth, who had died a malefactor's death, was the long-expected Messiah. What is he to think of these startling claims? What were others thinking? Gamaliel, his master, counselled caution and a policy of expectation (chap. v. 35—39); Barnabas, his early friend, had joined the new society (chap. iv. 36); Andronicus and Junias, his kinsmen, had followed the example (Rom. xvi. 7). But Saul had a zeal which was more fiery than theirs. He was a Pharisee after the straitest sect, and the teaching of Stephen, more conspicuously, it would seem, than that of Peter, was a protest against Pharisaism, and told of its coming downfall. He, therefore, could make no truce with that teaching, and burst impatiently from the cautions of his master. For good or for evil, he was at least "thorough," and had the courage of his convictions. Even the face as of an angel and the words of ecstatic joy did but kindle in him the fire of a burning indignation.

(59) **Lord Jesus, receive my spirit.**—The words are memorable as an instance of direct prayer addressed, to use the words of Pliny in reporting what he had learned of the worship of Christians, "to Christ as God" (*Epist.* x. 97). Stephen could not think of Him whom he saw at the right hand of God, but as of One sharing the glory of the Father, hearing and answering prayer. And in the prayer itself we trace an echo of words of which Stephen may well have heard. The Son commended His Spirit to the Father (Luke xxiii. 46); the disciple, in his turn, commends his spirit to the Son. The word "God," in the sentence "calling upon God," it should be noted, is, as the italics show, an insertion to complete the sense.

(60) **Lord, lay not this sin to their charge.**—Here again we cannot help finding proof, not only that the mind of Stephen was after the mind of Christ, but that the narrative of the Crucifixion, as recorded by St. Luke, was, in some measure, known to him. The resemblance to the prayer of Christ, "Father, forgive them, for they know not what they do" (Luke xxiii. 34), could hardly have been accidental. We may well think of the prayer as having for its chief object him who was the foremost of the accusers. The old words of Augustine (*Serm.* 314—318), that we owe the conversion of Saul to the prayers of Stephen, may be accepted as the expression of a great spiritual fact. This prayer, like that which preceded it, was addressed, it will be noted, to the Lord Jesus.

**He fell asleep.**—The thought and the phrase were not altogether new. (Comp. John xi. 11, and Note.) Even a heathen poet had said of one who died the death of the righteous—

> "When good men die, it is not death, but sleep."
> —Callimachus, *Epig.* 10.

VIII.

(1) **And Saul was consenting unto his death.**—The word seems carefully chosen to convey the fact that he did not himself take part in stoning, but contented himself with guiding and directing the murder. He "kept the garments" of the witnesses who flung the stones (chap. xxii. 20). The statement came, we can scarcely doubt, from St. Paul's own lips, and in his use of the same word in the passage just referred to, and in Rom. i. 32, we may see an indication that he had learnt to see that his guilt in so doing was greater, and not less, than that of the actual murderers.

**There was a great persecution against the church.**—It is clear that this involved much suffering, imprisonment, as in verse 3, perhaps the spoiling of men's goods, the being made "a gazing stock by reproaches and afflictions" (Heb. x. 33, 34). In St. James's description of the sufferings of the brethren (Jas. ii. 6, 7), we may see at once the measure of the violence of the persecution, and the prominence in it (though Saul, the Pharisee, was for the time the chief

apostles. (2) And devout men carried
Stephen *to his burial*, and made great
lamentation over him. (3) As for Saul,
he made havock of the church, enter-
ing into every house, and haling men
and women committed *them* to prison.
(4) Therefore they that were scattered
abroad went every where preaching the

---

leader) of the priesthood and the rich Sadducean aristocracy.

**Throughout the regions of Judæa and Samaria.**—Jerusalem was naturally the chief scene of the persecution, and the neighbouring towns, Hebron, and Gaza, and Lydda, and Joppa, became places of refuge. It was probably to this influx of believers in Christ that we may trace the existence of Christian communities in the two latter cities. (See Notes on chap. ix. 32, 36.) The choice of Samaria was, perhaps, suggested by the hatred of that people to the Jews. Those who were fleeing from a persecution set on foot by the priests and rulers of Jerusalem were almost *ipso facto* sure of a welcome in Neapolis and other cities. But the choice of this as a place of refuge indicated that the barriers of the old antipathy were already in part broken down. What seemed the pressure of circumstances was leading indirectly to the fulfilment of our Lord's commands, that the disciples should be witnesses in Samaria as well as in Judæa (chap. i. 8). It seems probable, as already suggested (see Note on chap. vii. 16), that there was some point of contact between the Seven, of whom Stephen was the chief, and that region.

**Except the apostles.**—The sequel of the history suggests two reasons for their remaining. (1) The Twelve had learnt the lesson which their Master had taught them, "that the hireling fleeth because he is an hireling" (John x. 13), and would not desert their post. A tradition is recorded by Clement of Alexandria (*Strom.* vi. 5, § 43) and Eusebius (*Hist.* v. 13), that the Lord had commanded the Apostles to remain for twelve years in Jerusalem lest any should say "We have not heard," and after that date to go forth into the world. (2) The persecution which was now raging seems to have been directed specially against those who taught with Stephen, that the "customs" on which the Pharisees laid so much stress should pass away. The Apostles had not as yet proclaimed that truth; had, perhaps, not as yet been led to it. They were conspicuous as worshippers in the Temple, kept themselves from all that was common and unclean (chap. x. 14), held aloof from fellowship with the Gentiles (chap. x. 28). They may well have been protected by the favour and reverence with which the great body of the people still looked on them, and so have been less exposed than the Seven had been to the violence of the storm. It was probable, in the nature of the case, that the Hellenistic disciples, who had been represented by Stephen, should suffer more than others. It was from them that the next great step in the expansion of the Church in due course came.

(2) **And devout men carried Stephen to his burial.**—It has sometimes been asserted, as *e.g.* by Renan (*Les Apôtres*, p. 145), that these were proselytes. St. Luke, however, always uses a different word to describe that class (comp. chap. xiii. 43, 50; xvi. 14; xvii. 4, 17), and the word used here is applied by him to Simeon (Luke ii. 25), to the multitude of Jews present on the day of Pentecost (chap. ii. 5), to Ananias as devout according to the Law (chap. xxii. 12). This notion must accordingly be rejected as against evidence. On the other hand, had they been members of the Church they would naturally, though perhaps not necessarily, have been described as "brethren" or "disciples." We are left therefore to the conclusion that they were Jews who had been kindled into admiration and half-conviction by the calm heroism of the martyr, and who, without committing themselves to more than that admiration, acted in his case as Nicodemus and Joseph of Arimathæa had acted after the Crucifixion. They would show honour to the memory of the dead, though they had not had the courage to defend the preacher of the truth while he was yet with them. In the legend or tradition as to the death of Stephen, reported and accepted by Augustine (*De Civ: Dei.* xvii. 8; *Serm.* 318, 319; *Tract. in Joann.*, 120), Gamaliel and Nicodemus are named as actually taking part in the entombment, and as afterwards laid in the same sepulchre, on which his name appeared in Aramaic characters as *Chaliel* (= garland), the equivalent in that language of the Greek *Stephanos.* The translation of the martyr's relics to Ancona, Minorca, and to Uzalis, and other towns in Africa, made a deep impression on Augustine, and gave occasion to some of his most eloquent sermons. Oratories were dedicated to his memory, and miraculous cures effected by prayers addressed to him. (See Butler's *Lives of the Saints*, Aug. 3rd.)

**And made great lamentation over him.**—The act was every way significant. Commonly, one who had been stoned to death on the charge of blasphemy would have had no funereal honours. He would have been buried "with the burial of an ass" (Jer. xxii. 19). The public lamentation on the part of men conspicuous for their devout zeal for the Law, was therefore of the nature of a protest, probably on the part of the more moderate section of the Pharisees, such as Joseph, Nicodemus, and Gamaliel, against what would seem to them the unnatural coalition between the Sadducean priesthood and the ultra-zealot section of their own party.

(3) **As for Saul, he made havock of the church.**—The tense in the Greek implies continuous action, and so indicates the severity of the persecution. Further details are given by St. Paul himself. He "persecuted this way unto the death" (chap. xxii. 4). It does not follow, however, that this points to more than the death of Stephen. Both men and women were imprisoned (*ibid*). The fact that the latter class were included among the sufferers, implies that they had been more or less prominent in the activity of the new society. Such may have been the devout women of Luke viii. 2, 3. The victims were punished in every synagogue, most probably with the forty stripes save one (2 Cor. xi. 24) which was the common penalty for minor offences against religious order. They were compelled to blaspheme the "worthy name" of the Master whom they owned as the Christ (chap. xxvi. 11; Jas. ii. 7). They were subject to wanton outrages in addition to judicial severity (1 Tim. i. 13). There was, as the persecutor himself afterwards confessed (chap. xxvi. 11), a kind of insane ferocity in his violence. Even the very word "haling" implies a brutality which might well have been spared.

(4) **They that were scattered abroad.**—These, as has been said above, would in all probability be Stephen's Hellenistic fellow-workers and followers. As

word. (5) Then Philip went down to
the city of Samaria, and preached Christ
unto them. (6) And the people with
one accord gave heed unto those things
which Philip spake, hearing and seeing
the miracles which he did. (7) For un-
clean spirits, crying with loud voice, came
out of many that were possessed *with
them:* and many taken with palsies, and
that were lame, were healed. (8) And
there was great joy in that city. (9) But
there was a certain man, called Simon,
which beforetime in the same city used
sorcery, and bewitched the people of

---

in later ages, the axiom that "the blood of martyrs is the seed of the Church," held true from the beginning. The attempt to stamp out the new faith did but give it a wider scope of action, and urged it on to pass the limits within which it might otherwise have been confined for a much longer period.

**Preaching the word.**—Better, *preaching the glad tidings of the word.*

(5) **Then Philip went down to the city of Samaria.**—More accurately, "*a* city." The sequence of events implies that it was not the Apostle, but his namesake who had been chosen as one of the Seven. As having been conspicuous in the work of "preaching the glad tidings of Christ," he was afterwards known as Philip the Evangelist (chap. xxi. 8). It was natural enough that the identity of name should lead writers who were imperfectly informed to confuse the two, as Polycrates, Bishop of Ephesus, seems to have done in the passage quoted by Eusebius (*Hist.* iii. 31). The "city of Samaria" is described in precisely the same terms as in John iv. 5, where it is identified with Sychar, the Sichem of the Old Testament. (See Note on John iv. 5.) "Samaria," throughout the New Testament (as, *e.g.*, in chap. ix. 31; Luke xvii. 11; John iv. 4, 5), is used for the province, and not for the city to which it had been attached in earlier times. This had been new-named *Sebaste* (the Greek equivalent of Augusta) by Herod the Great in honour of the Emperor, and this had more or less superseded the old name (Jos. *Ant.* xv. 8, § 5). Assuming the identity with Sychar, the narrative of John iv. suggests at once the reason that probably determined Philip's choice. The seed had already been sown, and the fields were white for harvest (John iv. 35). Possibly, as suggested above (Note on chap. vii. 16), there may have been some previous connection with the district. Some of that city had already accepted Jesus as the Christ.

**Preached Christ.**—The verb is not the same as in verse 4, and is the word used for "preaching" or "proclaiming." The tense implies continued action, extending, it may be, over weeks or months. We find in John iv. 25 that the expectation of the Messiah was as strong among the Samaritans as among the Jews, and Philip's work therefore was to proclaim that the long-expected One had come, and that the Resurrection was the crowning proof that He was the Christ the Son of God. The readiness with which the proclamation was accepted shows that in spite of the adverse influence which had come into play since our Lord had taught there, the work then done had not been in vain.

**Hearing and seeing the miracles which he did.**—Better, *the signs*, as being closer, here as elsewhere, to the force of the Greek. It is remarkable that they had believed in the first instance without any other sign than the person and the teaching of the Lord Jesus. Miracles came not as the foundation, but for the strengthening of their faith; perhaps also as a corrective to the adverse influence of which we are so soon to hear.

(7) **For unclean spirits, crying with loud voice.**—The MSS. present several variations in the structure of the sentence, but they do not affect its meaning. The character of the "signs" agrees with those that are recorded in the Gospels. The "great cry," partly, it may be, of agony, partly of exultation at deliverance, agrees with Mark i. 26; Luke iv. 33.

(8) **There was great joy in that city.**—This and the whole narrative may well have been learnt by St. Luke from the lips of Philip himself, when St. Paul and his companions visited the Evangelist at Cæsarea on his way to Jerusalem (chap. xxi. 8), or during the Apostle's two years' imprisonment in that city (chap. xxiv. 27), or, we may add, from St. Paul's report of what he had heard when he travelled through Samaria (chap. xv. 3).

(9) **But there was a certain man, called Simon.**—The man who is thus brought before us in a brief episode, occupies a prominent place in the history and the legends of the Apostolic Church. For the present it will be convenient to deal only with the materials which St. Luke gives us, reserving a fuller account for the close of the narrative. Nothing is told us here as to his earlier history, prior to his arrival in Samaria. The name indicates Jewish or Samaritan origin. He appears as the type of a class but too common at the time, that of Jews trading on the mysterious *prestige* of their race and the credulity of the heathen, claiming supernatural power exercised through charms and incantations. Such afterwards was Elymas at Cyprus (chap. xiii. 6); such were the vagabond Jews exorcists at Ephesus (chap. xix. 13); such was a namesake, Simon of Cyprus (unless, indeed, we have a re-appearance of the same man), who also claimed to be a magician, and who pandered to the vices of Felix, the Procurator of Judæa, by persuading Drusilla (Jos. *Ant.* xx. 7, § 2, see Note on chap. xxiv. 24) to leave her first husband and to marry him. The life of such a man, like that of the Cagliostro fraternity in all ages, was a series of strange adventures, and startling as the statements as to his previous life may seem (see Note on verse 24), they are not in themselves incredible. Apollonius of Tyana is, perhaps, the supreme representative of the charlatanism of the period.

**Used sorcery.**—Literally, *was practising magic.* On the history of the Greek word *magos* and our "magic," as derived from it. see Note on Matt. ii. 1. Our "sorcerer" comes, through the French *sorcier*, from the Latin *sortitor*, a caster of lots (*sortes*) for the purposes of divination. Later legends enter fully into the various forms of sorcery of which Simon made use. (See below.)

**Bewitched the people of Samaria.**—Literally, *threw them into the state of trance or ecstasy; set them beside themselves*, or *out of their wits.* The structure of the sentence shows that the "city" is not identical with Samaria, and that the latter name is used, as elsewhere, for the region.

**Giving out that himself was some great one.**—The next verse defines the nature of the claim

Samaria, giving out that himself was
some great one: (10) to whom they all
gave heed, from the least to the greatest,
saying, This man is the great power of
God. (11) And to him they had regard,
because that of long time he had bewitched them with sorceries. (12) But
when they believed Philip preaching
the things concerning the kingdom of
God, and the name of Jesus Christ, they
were baptized, both men and women.
(13) Then Simon himself believed also:
and when he was baptized, he continued with Philip, and wondered, beholding the miracles and signs which
were done. (14) Now when the apostles
which were at Jerusalem heard that
Samaria had received the word of God,
they sent unto them Peter and John:
(15) who, when they were come down,

---

more clearly. The cry of the people that he was "the great power of God," was, we may well believe, the echo of his own boast. He claimed to be, in some undefined way, an Incarnation of Divine Power. The very name had appeared in our Lord's teaching when He spoke of Himself as sitting on the right hand of "the Power of God," as an equivalent for the Father (Luke xxii. 69).

(10) **To whom they all gave heed, from the least to the greatest.**—The ready acceptance of the claims of the pretender, may, in part, be traced to the impression made by the presence of "the Christ, the Saviour of the world" (John iv. 42). If One had come among them in whom they felt that there was a more than human greatness, why might there not be another manifestation of a like nature? The sorcerer appears as the earliest type of those who were to come with lying signs and wonders so as to deceive, if it were possible, even the elect (Matt. xxiv. 24; 2 Thess. ii. 9).

**This man is the great power of God.**—The better MSS. give, "This is the Power of God that is called great." The word "Powers" was used by the Samaritans of the angels or hosts of God, and they probably recognised Simon as one of these and as of special pre-eminence.

(11) **And to him they had regard.**—The Greek word is the same as in the "gave heed" of the previous verse. The "long time" during which the evil fascination had been exercised, reckoning backwards from the date which we have now reached (A.D. 34), might carry us to a period prior to our Lord's visit to Sychar, in A.D. 30. It is scarcely probable, however, that it was in active operation at that time. And it is likely enough that, finding the people still influenced by the impressions which that visit had left, he wrought on their excited feelings for his own purpose.

(12) **But when they believed Philip . . . .**—The word for preaching is, as in verse 4, "*preaching the glad tidings* of the kingdom of God." The sequel shows that this included baptism as the outward condition of admission to the kingdom. We may infer from the other narrative of Philip's mission-work (verses 31—35) that it also included an outline-history of the passion and death and resurrection of the Prophet whom they had seen among them as fulfilling the great Messianic prophecies.

**They were baptized, both men and women.**—The tense points, not to one great act, but to the continual succession of converts who were thus admitted. We think of the woman of Samaria, of John iv. 7, and wonder whether she was one of them.

(13) **Then Simon himself believed also.**—Endless questions have been raised as to the nature of such a faith, and the effect of such a baptism. It is probable enough that he was impressed by the signs that Philip wrought; that he felt himself in the presence of a Power above his own; that he accepted Philip's statements as to the death and resurrection of the Christ. It was such a faith as that of which St. James speaks (Jas. ii. 14, 19). If we are to use the definite language of theological science, it would be true to say that he had the *fides informis,* faith not preceded by repentance and not perfected by love. And baptism, in such a case, the expressed or implied conditions being absent, brought with it no new birth to a higher life. He remained still "in the gall of bitterness and the bond of iniquity" (verse 23). But even for him it bore its witness of the readiness of God to forgive and to regenerate. The subsequent fulfilment of the conditions which were then absent would have quickened the potential into an actual grace, and no second baptism would have been needed to supplement the shortcomings of the first. Peter calls on him (verse 22) to repent and pray for forgiveness. He does not tell him that he must be baptised again.

**And wondered.**—The verb is the same as that rendered "bewitched" in verses 9 and 11. The tables were turned. The magician yielded to a spell mightier than his own, and was, in his turn, as one beside himself with amazement. The difference between Simon and the believing Samaritans is, in this matter, suggestive. His faith rested on outward miracles. With them the miracles did but serve to confirm a faith which rested on the "prophetic word" as spoken by the Son of Man (John iv. 42).

(14) **When the apostles which were at Jerusalem . . . .**—The tidings came to the Twelve as a proof that the limitation which had at first excluded Samaria from the range of their work as preachers of the kingdom had now passed away (Matt. x. 5), and that the time had now come when they were to be "witnesses" to Christ in Samaria as well as in Judæa (chap. i. 8). Old antipathies of race and worship disappeared, and without hesitation they sent the two who were, in many respects, the chief of the Apostles to sanction the admission of the new converts. The Apostle who in his zeal had once sought to call down the fire of the wrath of God on the village of the Samaritans (Luke ix. 54), was now to bring to them that baptism of the Holy Ghost and of fire (Matt. iii. 11) which spoke not of wrath but of love. That his companion should be Peter, was natural, both from the position which the latter occupied as the leader of the apostolic company and from the friendship by which the two had been throughout their life united.

**The word of God** is characteristically used by St. Luke, as in his Gospel, for the whole sum and substance of the gospel of Christ. (Comp. Luke v. 1; viii. 11, 21.)

(15) **Prayed for them, that they might receive the Holy Ghost.**—The prayer clearly pointed to such a gift of the power of the Spirit as had been bestowed on

prayed for them, that they might receive the Holy Ghost: (16) (for as yet he was fallen upon none of them: only they were baptized in the name of the Lord Jesus.) (17) Then laid they *their* hands on them, and they received the Holy Ghost. (18) And when Simon saw that through laying on of the apostles' hands the Holy Ghost was given, he offered them money, (19) saying, Give me also this power, that on whomsoever I lay hands, he may receive the Holy Ghost. (20) But Peter said unto him, Thy money perish with thee, because thou hast thought that the gift of God may be purchased with money. (21) Thou hast neither part nor lot in this matter: for thy heart is not right in the sight of God. (22) Repent therefore of this thy wickedness, and pray

---

the Day of Pentecost. It assumed that such gifts had been received by the disciples generally at Jerusalem, and that they were distinct from the new birth of water and the Spirit (John iii. 5) which was given through baptism. The Apostles looked on the Samaritans as qualified for that higher gift as well as for admission into the kingdom, and it was given to them, and not to Philip in his subordinate position as an evangelist, to be the channels of communicating it.

(16) **As yet he was fallen upon none of them.**—The same verb is used of the gift of the Spirit in chaps. x. 44, xi. 15, and of Peter's trance in chap. x. 10. It is manifestly used to express an unlooked-for change in a man's normal state of consciousness, the sudden advent of new powers and feelings.

(17) **Then laid they their hands on them.**—The act had already appeared as at once the symbol and the channel of the communication of spiritual gifts and offices in the appointment of the Seven. (See Note on chap. vi. 6.) Historically, the act here recorded has the interest of being the starting-point of what afterwards developed into the rite known as Confirmation. Taking the narrative of the Acts by itself, a question might be raised how far what we read of was normal or exceptional, connected, for a time only, with the bestowal of new and marvellous powers, or powerful, through the whole history of the Church, as a means of grace strengthening the spiritual life after those powers had been withdrawn. In any case it was probable that no hard and fast line marked the disappearance of the special and marvellous forms of spiritual power which were at first manifested in connection with the laying-on of hands, and so the practice had time to become part of the fixed order of the Church. When they ceased altogether we can understand the reluctance of men to give up a rite that had come down from the days of the Apostles. They would feel that the prayer of faith was still mighty to prevail; that the Spirit would still be given in answer to prayer joined with the symbolic act, though no longer in the same form, and would confirm and strengthen the work which had been begun in baptism, and so the primitive laying-on of hands passed into Confirmation, and was accompanied by other symbolic acts, such as anointing. The thought that it is so called because in it adults *confirm* the promises made for them when baptised as infants, is entirely modern, and cannot be traced further back than the sixteenth century.

(18, 19) **When Simon saw that through laying on of the apostles' hands . . . .**—The words imply that the result was something visible and conspicuous. A change was wrought; and men spoke with tongues and prophesied. To the sorcerer, accustomed to charms and incantations, the men who were in possession of this power would seem to be enchanters with a higher knowledge than his own, and he who had purchased many such secrets, after the manner of the time (comp. chap. xix. 19), from previous masters in the magic art, thought that this might be obtained in the same way. The act thus recorded has given its name to a large class of offences in ecclesiastical jurisprudence, and the sin of Simony in all its forms, the act of purchasing spiritual powers and functions, perpetuates the infamy of the magician of Samaria.

(20) **Thy money perish with thee.**—Literally, *Thy money be together with thee, for perdition.* The same word is used as in the "son of perdition" in John xvii. 12 and in Heb. x. 39. The prominence of the word in 2 Pet. ii. 1, 2, 3, iii. 7, 16, is interesting in connection with the question as to the authorship of that Epistle. Another coincidence presents itself in the "gold that perisheth" of 1 Pet. i. 7.

**Because thou hast thought . . . .**—Better, *because thou thoughtest.* The speaker looks at the thought historically, as at the moment when it rose up in the sorcerer's mind. The Greek verb has a transitive not a passive sense, *thou thoughtest to acquire the gift of God by money.* Not so, Peter must have remembered, had he acquired that gift. The very word which he uses is that which our Lord had spoken to him and his brother Apostles, "Freely" (*i.e.,* as a gift) "ye have received" (Matt. x. 8).

(21) **Neither part nor lot.**—A like, though not an identical, combination of the two words meets us in Col. i. 12. On the latter, see Notes on chap. i. 17, 25. It is, perhaps, used here in its secondary sense. Simon had no inheritance in the spiritual gifts nor in the spiritual offices of the Church. The power attached to the apostleship was not a thing for traffic.

**Thy heart is not right in the sight of God.**—"Straight" or "right" is used, as in Matt. iii. 3, Mark i. 3, for "straightforward," not in the secondary sense of "being as it ought to be." The word is not of frequent occurrence in the New Testament, but, like so many of the spoken words of St. Peter, meets us again as coming from his pen (2 Pet. ii. 15).

(22) **Repent therefore of this thy wickedness.**—The stern words of condemnation are, we see, meant to heal, not to slay. Rightly understood, the call to repent in such a case as this, opens the door of hope as wide as the history of the penitent thief. Repentance, and with repentance, forgiveness, were possible, even for the charlatan adventurer who had traded on the credulous superstition of the people, and claimed something like adoration for himself and his mistress.

**Pray God, if perhaps the thought of thine heart . . . .**—The better MSS. give "Lord" instead of "God," either in the Old Testament sense of the word or with special reference to the Lord Jesus. The "if perhaps," in the Greek, as in the English, implies a latent doubt. Did the thought come across the

God, if perhaps the thought of thine heart may be forgiven thee. (23) For I perceive that thou art in the gall of bitterness, and *in* the bond of iniquity. (24) Then answered Simon, and said, Pray ye to the Lord for me, that none of these things which ye have spoken come upon me. (25) And they, when they had testified and preached the word of the Lord, returned to Jerusalem,

---

mind of the Apostle that the sin of Simon came very near that "sin against the Holy Ghost which hath never forgiveness" (Matt. xii. 31)? The use of such words by the chief of the Apostles, after the apparent concession of a plenary power in John xx. 23, are terribly suggestive. He neither forgives nor condemns, but bids the offender turn to the Searcher of hearts and pray for forgiveness. Had he seen repentance, he might have said, "Thy sins are forgiven thee." Had he seen a conscience utterly dead, he might have closed the door of hope. As it is, he stands midway between hope and fear, and, keeping silence, leaves judgment to the Judge.

(23) **In the gall of bitterness, and in the bond of iniquity.**—On "gall," in its literal sense, see Note on Matt. xxvii. 34. This is the only passage in the New Testament in which it is used figuratively. "Bitterness" meets us, as expressing extreme moral depravity, in Rom. iii. 14, Eph. iv. 31, Heb. xii. 15. The latter phrase implies that the iniquity of Simon bound him as with the iron chains of a habit from which he could not free himself.

(24) **Pray ye to the Lord for me.**—There is something eminently characteristic in the sorcerer's words. (1) His conscience reads "between the lines" of St. Peter's address what was not actually found there. That "if perhaps" is to him as the knell of doom. (2) He prays not for deliverance from "the bond of iniquity," but only from the vague terror of a future penalty. (3) He turns, not, as Peter had bidden him, to the Lord who was ready to forgive, but to a human mediator. Peter must pray for him who has not faith to pray for himself.

At this point Simon disappears from the history of the Acts, and this seems accordingly the right place for stating briefly the later traditions as to his history. In those traditions he occupies a far more prominent position than in St. Luke's narrative, and becomes, as it has been said, the "hero of the romance of heresy," as given in the *Homilies* and *Recognitions* of the Pseudo-Clement. Born at Gittom, in Samaria (Justin, *Apol.* i. 26), he received his education at Alexandria, and picked up the language of a mystic Gnosticism from Dositheus (*Hom.* ii. c. 22; *Constt. Apost.* vi. 8). He had for a short time been a disciple of the Baptist (*Hom.* c. 23). He murdered a boy that the soul of his victim might become his familiar spirit, and give him insight into the future (*Hom.* ii. c. 26; *Recogn.* ii. 9). He carried about with him a woman of great beauty, of the name of Luna or Helena, whom he represented as a kind of incarnation of the Wisdom or Thought of God (Justin, *Apol.* i. 6; *Hom.* ii. c. 25; Euseb. *Hist.* ii. 13). He identified himself with the promised Paraclete and the Christ, and took the name of "*He who stands,*" as indicating divine power (*Recogn.* ii. 7). He boasted that he could turn himself and others into the form of brute beasts; that he could cause statues to speak (*Hom.* iv. c. 4; *Recogn.* ii. 9, iii. 6). His life was one of ostentatious luxury. He was accompanied by the two sons of the Syro-Phœnician woman of Mark vii. 26 (*Hom.* i. 19). After the episode related in the Acts, he went down to Cæsarea, and Peter was then sent thither by James, the Bishop of Jerusalem, to confront and hold a disputation with him on various points of doctrine. From Cæsarea he made his way to Tyre and Tripolis, and thence to Rome, and was there worshipped by his followers, so that an altar was seen there by Justin with an inscription, "SIMONI DEO SANCTO" (*Apol.* i. 56). Peter followed him, and in the reign of Claudius the two met, once more face to face, in the imperial city. According to one legend he offered to prove his divinity by flying in the air trusting that the demons whom he employed would support him; but, through the power of the prayers of Peter, he fell down, and had his bones broken, and then committed suicide (*Constt. Apost.* ii. 14; vi. 9). Another represents him as buried alive at his own request, in order that he might show his power by rising on the third day from the dead, and so meeting his death (Irenæus, *Adv. Hær.* vi. 20).

In the midst of all this chaos of fantastic fables, we have, perhaps, one grain of fact in Justin's assertion that he had seen the altar above referred to. An altar was discovered at Rome in 1574, on the island in the Tiber, with the inscription "SEMONI SANCO DEO FIDIO." Archæologists, however, agree in thinking that this was dedicated to the Sabine Hercules, who was known as SEMO SANCUS, and it has been thought by many writers that Justin may have seen this or some like altar, and, in his ignorance of Italian mythology, have imagined that it was consecrated to the Sorcerer of Samaria. His statement is repeated by Tertullian (*Apol.* c. 13) and Irenæus (i. 20). Of the three names in the inscription, Semo (probably connected with *Semen* as the God of Harvest, or as *Semihomo*) appears by itself in the Hymn of the Fratres Arvales, and in connection with Sancus and Fidius (probably connected with *Fides*, and so employed in the formula of asseveration, *medius fidius*) in Ovid, *Fast.* vi. 213; Livy, viii. 20; xxxii. 1.

(25) **And they, when they had testified . . .**—The statement involves a stay of some duration, long enough to found and organise a community of disciples. And this was followed, not by an immediate return to Jerusalem, but, as the Greek tense shows, by one with many halts, at each of which the glad tidings of "the word of the Lord" were proclaimed, and a Church founded. Did the Apostles enter on this journey into the village on which one of them had sought to call down fire from heaven (Luke ix. 54)? Now, at least, he had learnt to know what manner of Spirit claimed him as his own.

The curtain falls at the close of this drama on the Christians of Samaria, and we know but little of their after history. The one glimpse of them which we get is, however, of very special interest. When Paul and Barnabas after their first missionary journey went up to Jerusalem, they passed "through Phenice and Samaria" (chap. xv. 3). St. Paul also had conquered the antagonism that divided the Jew, and, above all, the Pharisee, from the Samaritan. The Samaritans heard with joy of that conversion of the Gentiles which showed that old barriers and walls of partition were broken down. Many, we may believe,

and preached the gospel in many villages of the Samaritans. (26) And the angel of the Lord spake unto Philip, saying, Arise, and go toward the south unto the way that goeth down from Jerusalem unto Gaza, which is desert. (27) And he arose and went: and, behold, a man of Ethiopia, an eunuch of great authority under Candace queen of the Ethiopians, who had the charge of all

---

would elect to take their stand on the ground of the freedom of the gospel rather than on any claim to Jewish descent or the observance of the Jewish Law. Others, however, we know, adhered to that Law with a rigorous tenacity, and left their creed and ritual, their Gerizim worship and their sacred Books, as an inheritance to be handed down from century to century, even to the present day. The whole nation suffered severely in the wars with Rome under Vespasian, and Sychem was taken and destroyed, a new city being built by the emperor on the ruins—a Roman city with Temples dedicated to Roman gods—to which, as perpetuating the name of his house and lineage, he gave the name of *Flavia Neapolis* (=New Town), which survives in the modern *Nablous*. In the early history of the Church there attaches to that city the interest of having been the birthplace of the martyr Justin, and of the heretic Dositheus. In one of the Simon legends, as stated above, the latter appears as the instructor of the sorcerer, but this is probably a distortion of his real history.

(26) **And the angel of the Lord . . .**—Better, *an angel.* The tense of the verbs in the preceding verse, in the better MSS., implies that the events that follow synchronised with the journey of Peter and John through Samaria. The journey which Philip was commanded to take led him by a quicker route across country into the main road from Jerusalem to Gaza. The history of the city so named (appearing at times in the English version—Deut. ii. 23; 1 Kings iv. 24; Jer. xxv. 20—as Azzah) goes even as far back as that of Damascus, in the early records of Israel. It was the southernmost or border-city of the early Canaanites (Gen. x. 19), and was occupied first by the Avim, and then by the Caphtorim (Deut. ii. 23). Joshua was unable to conquer it (Josh. x. 41; xi. 22). The tribe of Judah held it for a short time (Judg. i. 18), but it soon fell into the hands of the Philistines (Judg. iii. 3, xiii. 1), and though attacked by Samson, was held by them during the times of Samuel, Saul, and David (1 Sam. vi. 17; xiv. 52; 2 Sam. xxi. 15). Solomon (1 Kings iv. 24), and later on Hezekiah (2 Kings xviii. 8), attacked it. It resisted Alexander the Great during a siege of five months, and was an important military position, the very key of the country, during the struggles between the Ptolemies and the Seleucidæ, and in the wars of the Maccabees (1 Macc. xi. 61). Its name, it may be noted, meant the "strong."

**Which is desert.**—Literally, as in a separate sentence, *This* (or *It*) *is desert.* There is nothing to show whether this was intended to appear as part of the angel's bidding, or as a parenthetical note added by St. Luke, nor whether the pronoun refers to the "way" or to the "city." If we assume the latter, we may think of it as written after the city had been laid waste during the Jewish war (A.D. 65). On the former hypothesis, it points to a less frequented route than that from Jerusalem through Ramleh to Gaza, which led through Hebron and then through the Southern or *Negeb* country. On the whole, the latter seems most to commend itself, and on this view we may see in it part of the instruction which Philip reported as coming, whether in dream or vision or voice we are not told, from the angel of the Lord. He was to go in faith to the less frequented, less promising route from Jerusalem to Gaza, apparently without passing himself through the Holy City, and so to intercept the traveller whose history was to become so memorable.

(27) **A man of Ethiopia, an eunuch of great authority.**—Literally, *a eunuch, a potentate.* The Ethiopia from which the traveller came was the region so named by the geographers of St. Luke's time in the upper valley of the Nile. Its connection with the Jewish people presents many points of interest. There seems reason to believe that in the time of Manasseh, who (according to the statement in the narrative of Aristeas as to the LXX. translation) formed an alliance with Psammetichus king of Egypt, a considerable body of Jews were sent off to protect the outposts of his kingdom, and it is in reference, probably, to these that Zephaniah speaks of the suppliants of "the daughter of my dispersed beyond the rivers of Ethiopia" (Zeph. iii. 10). Jewish influences had accordingly been at work there for some centuries. They may probably be traced in the piety of the Ethiopian eunuch, Ebed-melech, in the time of Jeremiah (xxxviii. 7—13, xxxix. 16—18). Even at an earlier period the hopes of Israel had looked forward to, perhaps had actually seen, the admission of Ethiopians among the citizens of Zion (Ps. lxxxvii. 4), Ethiopia stretching forth her hands unto God (Ps. lxviii. 31). The fact that the traveller had come as a pilgrim or a proselyte, shows (if, as the narrative implies, the latter) that he was a circumcised "proselyte of righteousness." His baptism was not, like that of Cornelius, the admission of a Gentile as such. The word "eunuch" has been taken by some commentators as meaning only "chamberlain," which is, indeed, the strict etymological sense of the word. Its use in Matt. xix. 12, and indeed in later Greek writers generally, is, however, in favour of the literal sense of the word. The strict letter of Deut. xxiii. 1, forbidding the admission of such persons into the congregation of the Lord, had been already modified (probably on the assumption that the state was not one which they had brought about by their own act) in favour of the sons of the stranger, the eunuchs "who keep my Sabbaths," by Isaiah (lvi. 4); and we may well think of St. Luke, as glad to record a proof that the discipline of the Church of Christ was as liberal on this point as the teaching of the Evangelical prophet. It is interesting to note that the first act of the first Œcumenical Council was to formulate a like rule in dealing with such cases of the kind as then presented themselves (*Conc. Nic. Can.* 1), admitting those who were not self-mutilated even into the ranks of the clergy.

**Under Candace queen of the Ethiopians.**—The quantity of the second syllable is uncertain, but the analogy of Canăce is in favour of its being short. The knowledge of the student of Strabo (Strabo, xvii. p. 820) may, perhaps, be traced in the description. He mentions a Queen of Meroë, in Ethiopia, bearing the name of Candace. The occurrence of the same name in Plin. iv. 35, Dion.-Cass. liv. 5, indicates that it was, like Pharaoh, a dynastic name or title. Eusebius (*Hist.* ii. 1) states that in his time (*circ.* A.D. 430) the region

her treasure, and had come to Jerusa-
lem for to worship, (28) was returning,
and sitting in his chariot read Esaias
the prophet. (29) Then the Spirit said
unto Philip, Go near, and join thyself
to this chariot. (30) And Philip ran
thither to *him*, and heard him read the
prophet Esaias, and said, Understandest
thou what thou readest? (31) And he
said, How can I, except some man
should guide me? And he desired Philip
that he would come up and sit with
him. (32) The place of the scripture
which he read was this, He was led as
a sheep to the slaughter;[a] and like a
lamb dumb before his shearer, so opened
he not his mouth: (33) in his humilia-
tion his judgment was taken away: and

a Isa. 53. 7.

---

was still under the rule of a queen, according to the custom of the country.

**Who had the charge of all her treasure.**—The Greek word for treasure is *Gaza*, a word of Persian origin, which about this time had come into use both among Greek and Latin writers (Cicero, *de Off.* ii. 22). The LXX. translators employ it in Ezra v. 17; vi. 1; vii. 21; Isa. xxxix. 2. Aristotle (*Hist. Plant.* viii. 11) is the first Greek writer in whom we find it naturalised. It is not found elsewhere in the New Testament, but a compound form appears as denoting the treasury of the Temple in Luke xxi. 1. The coincidence between this *Gaza* and the name of the town is at least suggestive of the thought that St. Luke saw in it a *nomen et omen*. The man came from one *Gaza*, and was going to another; and he, like the man in the parable of Matt. xiii. 44, found a *treasure* which he had not looked for, but which came to him as the reward of his diligently seeking.

**Had come to Jerusalem for to worship.**—The act itself, even prior to the eunuch's conversion by Philip, was a fulfilment of the hope of the prophet Zephaniah cited above. Whether of Jewish origin or incorporated as a "proselyte of righteousness," he belonged to "the daughter of the dispersed," and so long a journey by a man in so high a position was in itself a notable event. He came seeking, we must believe, for light and wisdom, and they were given him beyond his expectations.

(28) **Sitting in his chariot read Esaias the prophet.**—After the manner of most Eastern nations, to whom silent reading is almost unknown, the eunuch was reading aloud. Philip heard him, and so gained an opening for conversation. Was the roll of Isaiah a new-found treasure? Had he bought the MS. in Jerusalem, and was he reading the wonderful utterances for the first time? The whole narrative implies that he was reading the LXX. version.

(29) **Join thyself to this chariot.**—The act implied is that of laying hold and, as it were, attaching himself to the chariot in which the eunuch rode.

(30) **Understandest thou what thou readest?**—The Greek play upon the word for understand (*Ginôskein*) and read (*Anaginôskein*) cannot well be produced in English, but is worth noting as parallel to a like play in the well-known saying of the Emperor Julian (*Anegnôn; egnôn; kategnôn*)—"I read; I understood; I condemned."

(31) **How can I, except some man should guide me?**—The words of the inquirer imply, as has been said above, that the prophecy was new to him. It is as though, in turning over, or perhaps unrolling, the MS., this was the passage which, in its strange, touching portraiture of the Man of Sorrows, had riveted his attention, and on which he was consequently dwelling with the prayer that some authorised interpreter would unfold its meaning. The word for "guide" connects itself with the title of "a guide of the blind," which the Rabbis were fond of claiming (Matt. xv. 14; Rom. ii. 19).

(32) **The place of the scripture which he read.**—The word for "place" is apparently used as an equivalent for the Hebrew *Parashah*, or *Haphtarah*, which were technically used for the sections of the Law and Prophets respectively appointed for use as lessons in the synagogue services. It was in common use among the Greek writers, and was adopted by Cicero (*Ep. ad Att.* xiii. 25).

**He was led as a sheep to the slaughter.**—We may venture, taking as our guide the statement in verse 35 that Philip "preached unto him Jesus," to represent to ourselves the method of interpretation which would be given of each clause. In 1 Pet. ii. 23 we find the outlines of such a method. The story of the Passion would be told; the silent patience of the Sufferer; His previous life and work; the proofs which both had given that He was none other than that which He claimed to be—the Christ, the Son of God.

(33) **In his humiliation his judgment was taken away.**—The Hebrew runs, as in the English version of Isa. liii. 8, which fairly represents its natural construction, "He was taken from prison (or *oppression*) and from judgment," *i.e.*, was delivered from His sufferings just when they seemed to culminate. A different meaning has, however, been given to the Hebrew preposition by many scholars, who render the words, "*Through* oppression and [unjust] judgment He was taken away"—*i.e.*, He was the victim of a judicial murder. The LXX., which is here followed, seems to have adopted a different construction, "By His humiliation, by His low estate, His judgment (*i.e.*, the righteous judgment which was His due) was taken away." Here also, however, the word "judgment" has been taken in a different sense, and the words have been interpreted as meaning, "His condemnation was taken away, or cancelled"—*i.e.*, because He humbled Himself He was afterwards exalted. Assuming Philip to have explained the words as they stand in the LXX., the first of these two latter interpretations has most to commend itself. The story of the Passion, the unrighteous sentence passed on the Lord Jesus because He stood before the Council and the Governor as poor and friendless, would be dwelt on as filling in the outlines of the prophetic picture.

**Who shall declare his generation?**—The Hebrew noun may mean, as in Ps. xiv. 5, the men of a given period, or those sharing a common character. The words have, however, been very variously taken: (1) "Who shall declare the number of those who share His life, and are, as it were, sprung from Him"—*i.e.*, Who can count His faithful disciples? (2) "Who shall declare the wickedness of the crooked and perverse generation in which He lived?" (3) "Who, as far as

who shall declare his generation? for
his life is taken from the earth. (34) And
the eunuch answered Philip, and said, I
pray thee, of whom speaketh the prophet
this? of himself, or of some other man?
(35) Then Philip opened his mouth, and
began at the same scripture, and preached
unto him Jesus. (36) And as they went
on *their* way, they came unto a certain
water: and the eunuch said, See, *here is*
water; what doth hinder me to be bap-
tized? (37) And Philip said, If thou
believest with all thine heart, thou
mayest. And he answered and said, I
believe that Jesus Christ is the Son of
God. (38) And he commanded the chariot
to stand still: and they went down both
into the water, both Philip and the
eunuch; and he baptized him. (39) And
when they were come up out of the
water, the Spirit of the Lord caught
away Philip, that the eunuch saw him

---

His generation went, were wise enough to consider?" Assuming, as before, that it was the LXX. that Philip explained, the second of these seems preferable, as corresponding with the frequent use of the word "generation" with condemnatory epithets attached to it both by our Lord Himself (Matt. xii. 39—42; xvi. 4; xvii. 17) and His Apostles (chap. ii. 40; Phil. ii. 15). The sense which some commentators have affixed to it, "Who shall declare His duration?" "Who shall set limits to the life of Him who is One with the Eternal?" or, as others, "Who shall declare the mystery of His mode of birth?"—*i.e.*, of the Incarnation—are, it is believed, untenable as regards the Hebrew, and yet more so as regards the Greek.

**For his life is taken from the earth.**—The Hebrew admits of no other meaning than that the Sufferer was hurried to a violent death. The fact that in being thus taken from the earth the Sufferer was exalted to heaven, though true in itself, cannot be found in the words.

We are not concerned here with a detailed explanation, either of the words that precede, or those that follow, the passage quoted in Isa. liii., but it is difficult to think of Philip as not taking in context as well as text, and unfolding in full, not only the fact of the Passion, but its atoning and redeeming power, as set forth in the prophet's marvellous prediction.

(34) **Of himself, or of some other man?**—Later interpreters, some of them ascribing the whole of the second half of Isaiah's prophecies (chaps. xl.—lxvi.) to a great unknown writer living towards the close of the Babylonian Exile, have given very different answers to the question which the eunuch asked. They have seen in the righteous sufferer of Isa. liii. either the delineation of the character of Jeremiah as the greatest sufferer of all the prophets, or of the righteous few who were sharers in his sufferings. This is not the place to discuss either the authenticity of this part of the writings that bear Isaiah's name, or the primary historical application of this passage. It is enough to remember that here, as with well nigh every other Messianic prophecy cited in the New Testament, there may well have been "springing and germinant accomplishments," and that a primary reference to persons or facts in nearly contemporary history does not exclude a more complete fulfilment in Him who gathered up in Himself all that belonged to the ideal sufferer, as well as to the ideal King, of whom the prophets had spoken, with special reference, we may believe, to the atoning power of His sufferings (Isa. liii. 4—6), and to His silent patience under them (Isa. liii. 7. Comp. 1 Pet. ii. 22—25.)

(35) **Philip opened his mouth.**—The phrase, wherever it occurs in the New Testament, implies something like a set discourse. (Comp. chaps. x. 34; xviii., 14; Matt. v. 2; xiii. 35; 2 Cor. vi. 11). It always means something more than the mere act of speaking.

**And preached unto him Jesus.**—The sequel shows that the teaching must have included, not only an interpretation of the prophecy as fulfilled in Christ, but instruction as to the outward condition of admission to the society of the disciples. The eunuch hears enough to make him eager for the baptism which was to bring with it so great a blessing.

(36) **They came unto a certain water.**—Men have naturally endeavoured to identify the locality. In the time of Jerome, probably in that of Eusebius (*de loc.*), it was fixed at Bethsura, the Bethzur of 2 Chron. xi. 7), about twenty miles from Jerusalem, and two from Hebron. A fountain, now known as *Ain-Edh-Dhirweh* rises near the town, which retains the old name in the slightly altered form of *Beit-Sur*. On the other hand, Robinson is inclined to find the spring in the *Wady-el-Hasey*, between Eleutheropolis and Gaza, not far from the old sites of Lachish and Egln. This agrees better with the mention of Gaza and with the epithet "desert" as attached to the "way."

(37) **And Philip said . . . .**—The verse is a striking illustration of the tendency which showed itself at a very early period to improve the text of Scripture with a view to greater edification. It existed in the time of Irenæus, who quotes it (iii. 12), but is wanting in all the best MSS., including the Sinaitic, and many versions. The motive for the interpolation lies on the surface. The abruptness of the unanswered question, and the absence of the confession of faith which was required in the Church's practice on the baptism of every convert, seemed likely to be stumbling-blocks, and the narrative was completed according to the received type of the prevailing order for baptism. Even with the insertion, the shortness of the confession points to a very early stage of liturgical development, as also does the reference to it in Irenæus.

(38) **They went down both into the water.**—The Greek preposition might mean simply "*unto* the water," but the universality of immersion in the practice of the early Church supports the English version. The eunuch would lay aside his garments, descend chest-deep into the water, and be plunged under it "in the name of the Lord Jesus;" the only formula recognised in the Acts. (See Note on chap. ii. 38.) So it was, in the half-playful language in which many of the Fathers delighted, that "the Ethiopian changed his skin" (Jer. xiii. 23).

(39) **The Spirit of the Lord caught away Philip.**—Human feeling would have naturally led the teacher to continue his work, and to accompany the convert with a view to further instruction; but an impulse

no more: and he went on his way rejoicing. (40) But Philip was found at Azotus: and passing through he preached in all the cities, till he came to Cæsarea.

A.D. 35.

CHAPTER IX.—(1) And Saul, yet breathing out threatenings and slaughter against the disciples of the Lord, went unto the high priest, (2) and desired of him letters to Damascus to the

so strong and irresistible that it was felt to be from the Spirit of the Lord led Philip to an abrupt and immediate departure. He was literally snatched away from his companion. So understood, the history presents a striking parallel to the Spirit hindering St. Paul from going in this or that direction in chap. xvi. 6, 7. Many commentators have, however, taken the words in a yet more literal and material sense, as stating that Philip was caught up into the air and carried out of sight, and compare the cases of Elijah (1 Kings xviii. 12; 2 Kings ii. 11), Ezekiel (iii. 12, 14), and St. Paul (2 Cor. xii. 2, 4). In the last two cases, however, the language of the writer implies a spiritual rather than a bodily transport, and the case of Elijah, in 1 Kings xviii. 12, admits of an explanation like that which has now been offered in the case of Philip. The use of the same verb in 2 Cor. xii. 2, 4, suggests the thought that here also there was a suspension of the normal activity of consciousness. As St. Bernard walked by the Lake of Geneva, and knew not that he was near it, so Philip rushed away, as drawn on he knew not whither, as in a state of ecstasy; and so, in informing St. Luke of what passed (it is obvious that the report must, in the first instance, have come from him), could give no other account of his journeying than that he was "found" at Azotus.

**Went on his way rejoicing.**—A remarkable various-reading runs: "The Holy Spirit fell on the eunuch, and an angel of the Lord caught away Philip;" but it does not appear to be more than a conjectural emendation. Joy at the new-found truth prevailed, we must believe, over any sorrow at the disappearance of the preacher. Eusebius (*Hist.* ii. 1) speaks of him as returning to his native country, and there preaching "the knowledge of the God of the universe and the life-giving abode of the Saviour with men," and so fulfilling the words that "Ethiopia should stretch forth her hands unto God" (Ps. lxviii. 31); but it does not appear that he was acquainted with any historical facts. It is, perhaps, not without significance in connection with this history, that the Ethiopian Church has been throughout its history the most strongly Jewish in its worship and tone of thought of all Christian communities (Stanley, *Eastern Church*, p. 12).

(40) **Philip was found at Azotus.**—The city so named, the Ashdod of the Old Testament, was, like Gaza, one of the cities of the Philistines, about three miles from the sea, and half-way between Gaza and Joppa. Like Gaza its history was chiefly marked by successive sieges: by Tartan, the Assyrian General B.C. 716 (Isa. xx. 1); by Psammetichus, B.C. 630, (Herod. ii. 157); the Maccabees (1 Macc. v. 68; x. 34). It was restored by the Roman general Gabinius in B.C. 55. In remoter times it had been one of the head-quarters of the worship of Dagon (1 Sam. v. 5). The old name lingers in the modern *Esdud*, but the city has sunk into a decayed village. The narrative suggests the thought that here also Philip continued his work as an evangelist. Philistia was, as of old, to be joined with Ethiopia in furnishing the city of God with converts who should be written among the people (Ps. lxxxvii. 4).

**He preached in all the cities.**—The route which Philip would naturally take on this journey led through Lydda and Joppa, and we may probably trace the effect of his labours in the appearance in chap. ix. 32, 36, of organised and apparently flourishing Christian societies in both these towns.

**Till he came to Cæsarea.**—The historical importance of the city, lying on the line of the great road from Tyre to Egypt, dates, as its name shows, from the Roman period. As described by Strabo, it was known only as Strato's Tower, with a landing place for ships. It rose to magnificence, however, under Herod the Great, who built theatres, amphitheatres, and temples, and constructed a harbour as large as the Piræus at Athens. In honour of his imperial patron he named it *Cæsarea Sebaste* (the latter word meaning *Augusta*) (Jos. *Ant.* xvi. 5, § 1). It became, after the deposition of Archelaus, the official residence of the Roman Procurator, and is, as the sequel shows, prominent in the early history of the Church. Tacitus (*Hist.* ii. 79) speaks of it as the chief city—the *caput* of Judæa. It appears from chap. xxi. 8 that Philip took up his abode there and made it the head-quarters of his work as an evangelist. In ecclesiastical history it became famous as the scene for a time of the labours of the great Origen, and as the home of the historian-bishop Eusebius.

IX.

(1) **Yet breathing out threatenings.** — The "yet" implies a considerable interval since the death of Stephen, probably coinciding with the time occupied by the mission-work of Philip in the previous chapter. During this interval the persecution had probably been continuing. The Greek participle, literally, *breathing-in*, is somewhat more emphatic than the English. He lived, as it were, in an atmosphere of threats and slaughter. It was the very air he breathed. Patristic writers and their followers have not unnaturally seen a half-prophetic parallelism between the language of Jacob, "Benjamin shall ravin as a wolf: in the morning he shall devour the prey, and at night he shall divide the spoil" (Gen. xlix. 27), and this description of one who gloried in being of that tribe (Phil. iii. 5), and bore the name of its great hero-king.

**Went unto the high priest.**—It will be remembered that the high priest (whether we suppose Annas or Caiaphas to be meant) was a Sadducee, and that Saul gloried in being a Pharisee of the straitest sect (Acts xxvi. 5). The temper of the persecutor, however, does not shrink from strange companionship, and the coalition which had been formed against our Lord (Matt. xxvi. 3) was renewed against His followers. If, as is probable, the admission of the Samaritans to the new community had become known at Jerusalem, it would naturally tend to intensify their hatred. It would seem to them as if the accursed people were now allied with the Galileans against the Holy Place, and those who were zealous for its honour.

(2) **And desired of him letters to Damascus.**—We learn from 2 Cor. xi. 32, 33, that Damascus was at this time under the government of Aretas, the

synagogues, that if he found any of this
way, whether they were men or women,
he might bring them bound unto Jeru-
salem. (3) And as he journeyed, he
came near Damascus: and suddenly
there shined round about him a light

---

king of Arabia Petræa. How it came to be so, having been previously under Vitellius, the Roman president of Syria (Jos. *Ant.* xiv. 4, § 5), is not clear. It is probable, however, that in the war which Aretas had declared against Herod Antipas, in consequence of the Tetrarch's divorcing his daughter in order that he might marry Herodias (see Notes on Matt. xiv. 3; Luke iii. 14), he had been led, after defeating the Tetrarch (Jos. *Ant.* xviii. 5, § 1), to push his victories further; and, taking advantage of the absence of Vitellius, who had hastened to Rome on hearing of the death of Tiberius (A.D. 37) had seized on Damascus. In this abeyance of the control of the Roman power, Aretas may have desired to conciliate the priestly party at Jerusalem by giving facilities to their action against the sect which they would naturally represent as identified with the Galileans against whom he had been waging war. The Jewish population at Damascus was, at this time, very numerous. Josephus relates that not less than 10,000 were slain in a tumult under Nero (*Wars*, ii. 25), and the narrative of the Acts (verse 14) implies that there were many "disciples of the Lord" among them. Many of these were probably refugees from Jerusalem, and the local synagogues were called upon to enforce the decrees of the Sanhedrin of the Holy City against them. On the position and history of Damascus, see Note on next verse.

**If he found any of this way.**—Literally, *of the way.* We have here the first occurrence of a term which seems to have been used familiarly as a synonym for the disciples of Christ (chaps. xix. 9, 23; xxii. 4; xxiv. 14, 22). It may have originated in the words in which Christ had claimed to be Himself the "Way," as well as the "Truth" and the "Life" (John xiv. 6); or in His language as to the "strait way" that led to eternal life (Matt. vii. 13); or, perhaps, again, in the prophecy of Isaiah (xl. 3) cited by the Baptist (Matt. iii. 3; Mark i. 3), as to preparing "the way of the Lord." Prior to the general acceptance of the term "Christian" (chap. xi. 26) it served as a convenient, neutral designation by which the disciples could describe themselves, and which might be used by others who wished to speak respectfully, or, at least, neutrally, instead of the opprobrious epithet of the "Nazarenes" (chap. xxiv. 5). The history of the term "Methodists," those that follow a distinct "method" or "way" of life, offers a partial but interesting analogue.

**Whether they were men or women.**—The mention of the latter has a special interest. They too were prominent enough to be objects of the persecution. It is probable that those who were most exposed to it would have fled from Jerusalem, and among these we may think of those who had been foremost in their ministry during our Lord's life on earth (Luke viii. 2), and who were with the Apostles at their first meeting after His Ascension (chap. i. 14).

**Might bring them bound unto Jerusalem.**—The mission implied that the offence, as being against the Holy Place and the Law, as involving what would be called, in modern language, sacrilege and heresy, was beyond the jurisdiction of the subordinate tribunals, and must be reserved for that of the Council. (See Notes on Matt. v. 22; x. 17.)

(3) **And as he journeyed.**—The route by which the persecutor and his companions travelled was probably that taken by the Roman road, which extended from Jerusalem to Neapolis (Sychar, or Shechem), thence to Scythopolis, and so by the shores of the Sea of Galilee and Cæsarea Philippi, and thence under the slopes of Hermon, to Damascus. On this supposition Saul would traverse the chief scenes of our Lord's ministry, and be stirred to madness by the progress which the new sect had made in the cities of Samaria. It is, however, possible that he may have taken the road by the Jordan valley by which Galilean pilgrims sometimes travelled in order to avoid Samaria; but the former was beyond all question the most direct and best frequented road.

**He came near Damascus.**—The city has the interest of being one of the oldest in the world. It appears in the history of Abraham (Gen. xiv. 15; xv. 2), and was, traditionally, the scene of the murder of Abel. David placed his garrisons there (2 Sam. viii. 6; 1 Chron. xviii. 6), and, under Rezon, it resisted the power of Solomon (1 Kings xi. 24). Its fair streams, Abana and Pharpar, were, in the eyes of the Syrian leper, better than all the waters of Israel (2 Kings v. 12). It was the centre of the Syrian kingdom in its alliances and wars with those of Israel and Judah (2 Kings xiv. 28; xvi. 9, 10; Amos i. 3, 5). Its trade with Tyre in wares, and wine of Helbon, and white wool is noted by Ezekiel (chap. xxvii. 16, 18). It had been taken by Parmenion for Alexander the Great, and again by Pompeius. It was the birth-place of Nicolaos of Damascus, the historian and rhetorician who is conspicuous as the counsellor of Herod the Great (Jos. *Ant.* xii. 3, § 2; xvi. 2, § 2). At a later period it was the residence of the Ommiyad caliphs, and the centre of the world of Islam. The beauty of its site, the river which the Greeks knew as Chrysorrhoas, the "Golden Stream," its abounding fertility, the gardens of roses, made it, as Lamartine has said, a "predestined capital." Such was the scene which met the bodily eye of the fanatic persecutor. The historian does not care to dwell on its description, and hastens to that which met his inward gaze. Assuming the journey to have been continuous, the approach to Damascus would come on the seventh or eighth day after leaving Jerusalem.

**There shined round about him a light from heaven.**—As in chap. xxvi. 13, "above the brightness of the sun." Three accounts of the event that thus turned the current of the life of Saul of Tarsus meet us in the Acts. (1) This, which gives the writer's report of what he could hardly have heard from any lips but St. Paul's; (2) St. Paul's narrative before the Sanhedrin (chap. xxii. 6—11); (3) that which he gives before Agrippa (chap. xxvi. 13—18). They present, as will be seen, considerable variations, such as were natural in the records of a manifestation which was partial to some, and complete to one only. Those that were with him heard a voice but did not distinguish words (chap. xxii. 9). They saw, as stated here (verse 7), the light, but did not perceive the form of Him who spoke. The phenomena, in this respect, stand parallel to those of the voice from heaven, in which some heard the words, ascribing them to an angel, while others, hearing only the sound, said it thundered (see Note on John xii. 29). It is not possible in such a history to draw a hard and

from heaven: (4) and he fell to the
earth, and heard a voice saying unto
him, Saul, Saul, why persecutest thou
me? (5) And he said, Who art thou,
Lord? And the Lord said, I am Jesus
whom thou persecutest: *it is* hard for

---

fast line between the objective and the subjective. The man himself cannot say whether he is in the body or out of the body (2 Cor. xii. 2, 3). It is enough for him that he sees what others do not see, and hears what they do not hear, while they too hear and see enough to prove both to themselves and to him that something has occurred beyond the range of ordinary phenomena. Nothing in the narrative suggests the thought of a sudden thunderstorm, which has seemed to some writers a probable explanation of the facts. In that case, the gathering gloom, the dark rolling clouds, would have prepared the traveller for the lightning-flash. If this hypothesis be at all entertained—and as it does not necessarily exclude the supernatural element, and presents analogies to the divine manifestations on Sinai (Ex. xix. 16) and Horeb (1 Kings xix. 11, 12), it may be entertained legitimately—we must think of the storm, if we take such a view, as coming with an almost instantaneous quickness, the first flash and crash striking all with terror, while the full revelation of the Christ was made to the consciousness and conscience of the future Apostle.

(4) **Saul, Saul, why persecutest thou me?**—It is remarkable that here only, in the original Greek, and in verse 17, as in the reproduction of the words in chaps. xxii. 27, xxvi. 14, do we find the Hebrew form of the Benjamite name. It is as though he, who gloried in being above all things a Hebrew of the Hebrews, heard himself claimed as such by Him who spoke from heaven, called as Samuel had been called of old (1 Sam. iii. 4—8), and having to decide whether he would resist to the end, or yield, saying with Samuel, "Speak, Lord, for Thy servant heareth." The narrative implies that the persecutor saw the form of the Son of Man as well as heard His voice, and to that visible presence the Apostle afterwards refers as a witness to him of the Resurrection (1 Cor. ix. 1; xv. 8). If we ask as to the manner of the appearance, it is natural to think of it as being such as had met the gaze of Stephen. The martyr's words, "I see the heavens opened, and the Son of Man standing at the right hand of God" (chap. vii. 56), had then seemed to the fiery zeal of the Pharisee as those of a blasphemer. Now he too saw the Son of Man in the glory of the Father stretching forth His hand, not now, as He then had done, to receive the servant who was faithful even unto death, but, in answer to that servant's dying prayer, to transform the persecutor into the likeness of his victim.

(5) **Who art thou, Lord?**—The word "Lord" could not as yet have been used in all the fulness of its meaning. As in many cases in the Gospels, it was the natural utterance of respect and awe (John v. 7; ix. 36; xx. 15), such as would be roused by what the persecutor saw and heard.

**I am Jesus whom thou persecutest.**—Some of the best MSS. give "Jesus of Nazareth"; or better, perhaps, *Jesus the Nazarene*. It is probable, however, that this was inserted from chap. xxii. 18, where it occurs in St. Paul's own narrative. Assuming the words to have been those which he actually heard, they reproduced the very Name which he himself, as the chief accuser of Stephen, had probably uttered in the tone of scorn and hatred (chap. vi. 14)—the very Name which he had been compelling men and women to blaspheme. Now it was revealed to him, or to use his own suggestive mode of speech, "*in* him" (Gal. i. 16), that the Crucified One was in very deed, as the words of Stephen had attested, at the right hand of God, sharing in the glory of the Father. The pronouns are both emphatic, "*I*, in my Love and Might and Glory, I am the Jesus whom *thou*, now prostrate and full of dread, hast been bold enough to persecute." It was not the disciples and brethren alone whom Saul was persecuting. What was done to them the Lord counted as done unto Himself (Matt. x. 40).

**It is hard for thee to kick against the pricks.**—There is a decisive preponderance of MS. authority against the appearance of these words here, and the conclusion of nearly all critics is that they have been inserted in the later MSS. from chap. xxvi. 14. As they occur in the English text, however, and belong to this crisis in St. Paul's life, it will be well to deal with them now. In their outward form they were among the oldest and most familiar of Greek proverbs. The Jew who had been educated in the schools of Tarsus might have read them in Greek poets (Æschylus, *Agam.* 1633; Pindar, *Pyth.* ii. 173; Eurip. *Bacch.* 791), or heard them quoted in familiar speech, or written them in his boyhood. They do not occur in any collection of Hebrew proverbs, but the analogy which they presented was so obvious that the ploughmen of Israel could hardly have failed to draw the same lesson as those of Greece. What they taught was, of course, that to resist a power altogether superior to our own is a profitless and perilous experiment. The goad did but prick more sharply the more the ox struggled against it. Two of the passages cited apply the words directly to the suffering which man is sure to encounter when he resists God, as *e.g.*—

> "With God we may not strive:
> * * * * * * *
> But to bow down the willing neck,
> And bear the yoke, is wise;
> To kick against the pricks will prove
> A perilous emprise."
>
> —Pind. *Pyth.* ii. 173.

We ask what lesson the words brought to the mind of Saul. What were the "pricks" against which he had been "kicking"? The answer is found in what we know of the facts of his life. There had been promptings, misgivings, warnings, which he had resisted and defied. Among the causes of these, we may well reckon the conversion of the friend and companion of his youth (see Note on chap. iv. 36), and the warning counsel of Gamaliel (chap. v. 34—39), and the angel-face of Stephen (chap. vi. 15), and the martyr's dying prayer (chap. vii. 60), and the daily spectacle of those who were ready to go to prison and to death rather than to renounce the name of Jesus. In the frenzy of his zeal he had tried to crush these misgivings, and the effort to do so had brought with it discomfort and disquietude which made him more "exceedingly mad" against the disciples of the Lord. Now he learnt that he had all along, as his master had warned him, been "fighting against God," and that his only safety lay in the surrender of his own passionate resolve to the gracious and loving Will that was seeking to win him for itself. In his later retrospect of this stage of his life he was able, as by a subtle process

thee to kick against the pricks.
(6) And he trembling and astonished said, Lord, what wilt thou have me to do? And the Lord *said* unto him, Arise, and go into the city, and it shall be told thee what thou must do.
(7) And the men which journeyed with him stood speechless, hearing a voice, but seeing no man.
(8) And Saul arose from the earth; and when his eyes were opened, he saw no man: but they led him by the hand, and brought *him* into Damascus.
(9) And he was three days without sight, and neither did eat nor drink.
(10) And there was a certain disciple at Damascus, named Ananias; and to him said the Lord in a vision, Ananias. And he said, Behold, I *am here*, Lord.

---

of self-analysis, to distinguish between the element of ignorance, which made forgiveness possible, and that of a wilful resistance to light and knowledge which made that forgiveness an act of free and undeserved compassion (1 Tim. i. 12, 13).

(6) **And he trembling and astonished . . .**—The words stand, as far as textual authority is concerned, on the same footing as the foregoing, but, for the same reason, will be dealt with here. We note (1) the use of the word "Lord," now, we must believe, with a new meaning, as applied to the Nazarene whom he had before despised. (2) The entire surrender of his own will to that of Him whom he thus recognised as commanding his allegiance. At that moment Christ was formed in him (Gal. i. 16); the new man came to life. He lived in Christ, and Christ in him. "Not I, but Christ that liveth in me" (Gal. ii. 20) was henceforward the axiom of his life.

**Arise, and go into the city.**—In the narrative of chap. xxvi. 16 there appears a fuller manifestation of the divine purpose as made at this time; but there St. Paul, in his rapid survey, is obviously combining, in one brief summary, the whole sum and substance of the teaching that was associated with that great turning-point of his life. We may trace in the command actually given a stage in the divine discipline appointed for his spirit. Silence and submission, and acquiescence in ignorance of the future, and patient expectation, and prayer for light—these were needed before he could be ready for the great work which was to be committed to his charge.

(7) **Hearing a voice, but seeing no man.**—We are told by St. Paul himself (chap. xxii. 9) that they "did *not* hear the voice." What is meant is clearly that they did not hear the words—could attach no meaning to the sounds which for Saul himself had so profound a significance. So, in like manner, they saw the light, but did not see the form. In chap. xxvi. 14, they also are said to have fallen on the ground in terror.

(8) **He saw no man.**—The blindness was that of one who has been dazzled with excess of light (comp. chap. xxii. 11), the natural result of the vision of the supernatural glory, a witness to the man himself that the vision was not a mere play of imagination. Traces of its permanent effect on his powers of sight have been found in his habit of dictating rather than writing letters (see Note on 2 Thess. iii. 17), in the large characters traced by him when he did write (see Note on Gal. vi. 11), in his not recognising the high priest who commanded him to be struck. (See Notes on Acts xxiii. 2—5.) Of the many theories as to the mysterious "thorn in the flesh" (see Note on 2 Cor. xii. 7), there seems most reason for accepting that which connects it with some affection of the eyes, involving, perhaps, attacks of agonising pain. On this assumption, the eager wish of the Galatians, if it had been possible, to have plucked out their own eyes and given them to him, receives a special and interesting significance. (See Note on Gal. iv. 15.) For Saul himself, the blindness may well have had a spiritual significance. He had looked on himself as a "guide of the blind," boasting that he saw clearly (Rom. ii. 19). Now, for a time, till inward and outward light should shine in on him, he had to accept his blindness. The new-born soul had to be as

> "An infant crying for the light,
> And with no language but a cry."

**They led him by the hand, and brought him into Damascus.**—The mission on which Saul had come was already known at Damascus, and his arrival expected with alarm. Now he came, and the mission fell to the ground. The letters to the synagogues were not delivered.

(9) **He was three days without sight.**—It is natural to think of this period of seclusion from the visible world as one of spiritual communion with the invisible, and we can hardly be wrong in referring the visions and revelations of the Lord, the soaring as to the third heaven, and the Paradise of God, of which he speaks fourteen or fifteen years later, to this period. (See Notes on 2 Cor. xii. 1—4.) The conditions of outward life were suspended, and he lived as one fallen into a trance—in the ecstacy of an apocalyptic rapture. (Comp. the analogous phenomena in Ezek. viii. 1—4.)

(10) **A certain disciple at Damascus, named Ananias.**—In chap. xxii. 12 St. Paul speaks of him as a "devout man" (the same word as in chaps. ii. 5; viii. 2) "according to the law," well reported of by all the Jews who dwelt at Damascus. The name was so common that any identification must be in some measure uncertain, but the account which Josephus gives (*Ant.* xx. 2, § 4) of the conversion of Izates, King of Adiabene, to the faith of Israel by a Jewish merchant who bore the name of Ananias, and who taught that it was enough for men to worship the God of Israel without being circumcised, suggests, as probable, the thought that he too was a preacher of the gospel of Christ as St. Paul preached it. The arrival of another teacher, Eleazar of Galilee, who worked on the young king's fears and compelled him to be circumcised, presents a striking parallel to the manner in which the Judaisers followed on the track of St. Paul in Galatia and elsewhere (Gal. ii. 4; iv. 17). The narrative here leaves it uncertain whether this Ananias had been a disciple during our Lord's ministry or had been converted since the Day of Pentecost. In relation to St. Paul the name had a two-fold significance. He had come from one Annas, or Ananias, the Sadducean high priest, he was to be received by another. The meaning of the name—identical with that of Jochanan, Joannes, John, "the Lord is gracious"—was itself an omen and prophecy of pardon.

**To him said the Lord in a vision.**—It is clear from verse 16 that the writer is speaking of the Lord Jesus. The ready acceptance of the command seems

(11) And the Lord *said* unto him, Arise, and go into the street which is called Straight, and enquire in the house of Judas for *one* called Saul, of Tarsus: for, behold, he prayeth, (12) and hath seen in a vision a man named Ananias coming in, and putting *his* hand on him, that he might receive his sight.

(13) Then Ananias answered, Lord, I have heard by many of this man, how much evil he hath done to thy saints at Jerusalem: (14) and here he hath authority from the chief priests to bind all that call on thy name. (15) But the Lord said unto him, Go thy way: for he is a chosen vessel unto me, to bear

---

to imply either personal discipleship or previous visions of the same nature.

(11) **The street which is called Straight.**—A street answering to this description still runs from the Eastern Gate to the palace of the Pacha, and is known locally as the "Street of Bazaars." Somewhat curiously, the house shown by guides as that of Judas is not in it. A piece of ground surrounded by trees, and used as a Christian burial-place, is pointed out as the scene of the Conversion; but this is on the east side of the city, and St. Paul must have approached from the south or south-west.

**Saul, of Tarsus.**—The passage is memorable as the first mention of the Apostle's birth-place. For an account of the city, see Notes on chap. vii. 58 and verse 30.

**Behold, he prayeth.**—The thoughts which the words suggest belong to the preacher rather than the commentator. We can but think of the contrast between the present and the recent past—between the threatening and slaughter which the persecutor breathed out as he drew near to Damascus, and the prayer of humble penitence in which he was now living. Estimating that prayer by that which came as the answer to it, we may think of it as including pardon for the past, light and wisdom for the future, strength to do the work to which he was now called, intercession for those whom he had before persecuted unto the death.

(12) **And hath seen in a vision a man named Ananias.**—The coincidence of the two visions has seemed to some critics, as afterwards in the history of Cornelius, to betray something like the skill of the artistic historian. To those who reject the supernatural altogether, this may, of course, seem a short and easy explanation. To those who have not brought themselves to that point of denial, it will not seem strange that there should be in the work of the highest Designer the same unity of purpose and convergence of varied means which rouse our admiration in works of human skill. For Ananias what he was now told was an implied command that he should fulfil the vision thus reported to him.

(13) **Lord, I have heard by many of this man.**—The words are of interest as showing both the duration and the character of the persecution in which Saul had been the leader. The report of it had spread far and wide. The refugees at Damascus told of the sufferings of the brethren at Jerusalem.

**Thy saints at Jerusalem.**—This is noticeable as the first application of the term "saints" to the disciples. The primary idea of the word was that of men who consecrated themselves, and led, in the strictest sense of the word, a devout life. A term of like import had been taken by the more religious Jews in the time of the Maccabeans. The *Chasidim*, or Saints (the word occurs in Ps. xvi. 3), were those who banded themselves together to resist the inroads of heathenism under Antiochus Epiphanes. They appear in the books of Maccabees under the title of Assideans (1 Macc. ii. 42; vii. 13; 2 Macc. xiv. 6). The more distinctive name of Pharisees (*Separatists*), which came to be attached to the more zealous Chasidim, practically superseded this; and either by the disciples themselves, or by friendly outsiders, the Greek equivalent of the old Hebrew word—and probably, therefore, in Palestine, the Aramaic form of the word itself—was revived to describe the devout members of the new society. The fact that their Master had been conspicuously "the Holy One of God" (the same adjective is used of Him in the quotations from Ps. xvi. 10, in chaps. ii. 27, xiii. 35), made it natural that the term should be extended to His followers, just as He had been spoken of as the "Just One" (chaps. iii. 14; vii. 52); and yet that name was applied, in its Greek form, to James the brother of the Lord, and, in its Latin form of Justus, to the three so named in chaps. i. 23; xviii. 7; Col. iv. 11. It is significant that its first appearance in the New Testament should be as used by the man who was sent to be St. Paul's instructor, and that it should afterwards have been employed so frequently by the Apostle himself (Rom. i. 7; xv. 25; 1 Cor. i. 2; vi. 1, 2; 2 Cor. i. 1; Eph. i. 1; Phil. i. 1, *et al.*). The "devout man according to the Law," may well have been among the *Chasidim* even prior to his conversion to the faith of Christ. The term appears in inscriptions from the Catacombs in the Museum of the *Collegio Romano* at Rome—"N. or M. resteth here with the Saints"; but probably in the later sense, as attached to martyrs and others of distinguished holiness.

(14) **All that call on thy name.**—Here again we have to trace the growth of a new terminology. The description of the disciples of the Lord Jesus as those who called upon or invoked His name, had its origin in the words of Joel cited by St. Peter (chap. ii. 21), and afterwards by St. Paul (Rom. x. 13). It is used again in verse 21, and afterwards in 1 Cor. i. 2; 2 Tim. ii. 22. It may be noted further (1) that the same word is used of calling upon the Father (1 Pet. i. 17), and of calling on Christ (here and chap. vii. 59); and (2) that this also, like the term "saints" discussed in the foregoing Note, passed from Ananias to St. Paul.

(15) **He ir a chosen vessel unto me.**—Literally, *a vessel of election.* The term has nothing directly analogous to it in the Old Testament, but it is Hebrew in its form; the second noun being used as a genitivo of the characteristic attribute, and so equivalent to an intensified adjective. So in Isa. xxii. 7, we have in the LXX. "valleys of election" for the "choicest valleys" of the English version. The term "vessel" is used in the Old Testament of arms (Gen. xxvii. 3), of garments (Deut. xxii. 5), of household goods (Gen. xxxi. 56). In the New Testament its range of meaning is yet wider, as in Matt. xii. 29; Luke viii. 16; John xix. 29; Rom. ix. 22; 2 Cor. iv. 7. Here our word "instrument" or "implement" comes, perhaps, nearest to its meaning. The persecutor had been chosen by the Lord as the "tool" with which He would work out His

my name before the Gentiles, and kings,
and the children of Israel: (16) for I will
shew him how great things he must
suffer for my name's sake. (17) And
Ananias went his way, and entered into
the house; and putting his hands on
him said, Brother Saul, the Lord, *even*
Jesus, that appeared unto thee in the
way as thou camest, hath sent me, that
thou mightest receive thy sight, and be
filled with the Holy Ghost. (18) And
immediately there fell from his eyes as
it had been scales: and he received
sight forthwith, and arose, and was bap-
tized. (19) And when he had received
meat, he was strengthened. Then was

---

gracious will for him and for the Gentiles. In this sense it was used by classical writers of useful and trusty slaves, just as we speak of one man being the "tool" of another. Possibly, however, the words may be interpreted as containing the germ of the parable of the potter's vessel on which St. Paul dwells in Rom. ix. 21—23, and implied that the convert was not only chosen, but moulded, for his future work. The word "election," which occurs here for the first time in the New Testament, and is afterwards so prominent in the teaching of St. Paul (Rom. ix. 11; xi. 5, 7, 8; 1 Thess. i. 4), affords yet another instance of the influence exercised on the Apostle by the thoughts and language of the instructor through whom alone he could have learnt what is here recorded.

**To bear my name before the Gentiles.**—The mission of the Apostle was thus revealed to Ananias in the first instance. He is one who welcomes that expansion of the kingdom on which even the chief of the Apostles would have entered, but for the voice from heaven, with doubt and hesitation (chap. x. 13, 28). He is taught to see in the man of whom he had only heard as the persecutor, one who had been trained and chosen as fitter than all others for the work of that expansion.

**And kings.**—The words find their fulfilment in the speech before Agrippa (chap. xxvi. 12); possibly in one before Nero (2 Tim. i. 16).

(16) **For I will shew him how great things he must suffer . . .**—The words are spoken as by One who knows "what is in man" (John ii. 25), their secret motives, and springs of action. With characters of a lower type, the prospect of what they will have to suffer in any enterprise tends to deter them from embarking on it. With such a one as Saul of Tarsus, now repenting of the sufferings he had inflicted on others, that prospect would be welcome as enabling him, so far as that was possible, if not to atone for the past, at least to manifest fruits worthy of his repentance.

(17) **Putting his hands on him said, Brother Saul.**—The correspondence of the act with the vision spoken of in verse 12, would be the first step in the identification of the visitor. The words would tend to remove all doubt and misgiving. The man who came as the representative of the disciples of Jesus welcomed the persecutor as a "brother." It may be noted that he uses the same Hebrew form of the name as St. Paul had heard in the heavenly vision.

**That thou mightest receive thy sight . . . .**—Better, *regain thy sight*. The narrative clearly implies that here, as in chap. viii. 17, the being "filled with the Holy Ghost" was connected with the laying on of hands as a condition, and it is so far a proof that that gift was not one which attached exclusively to the Apostles. It was, we may well believe, manifested in this instance as in others, by the ecstatic utterance of "the tongues" (comp. chap. xix. 6; 1 Cor. xiv. 18), and by the gift of prophetic insight.

(18) **There fell from his eyes as it had been scales.**—The description suggests the thought that the blindness was caused by an incrustation, caused by acute inflammation, covering the pupil of the eye, or closing up the eye-lids, analogous to the "whiteness," that peeled (or *scaled*) off from the eyes of Tobit (Tob. xi. 13). Like phenomena are mentioned by Hippocrates, and the care with which St. Luke records the fact in this instance, may be noted, with chaps. iii. 7, xxviii. 8, as one of the examples of the technical precision of his calling as a physician.

**Arose, and was baptised.**—It is clear that both Saul and Ananias looked on this as the indispensable condition for admission into the visible society of the kingdom of God. No visions and revelations of the Lord, no intensity of personal conversion, exempted him from it. For him, too, that was the "washing of regeneration" (Tit. iii. 5), the moment of the new birth, of being buried with Christ (Rom. vi. 3, 4). It may be inferred almost as a matter of certainty that it was at the hands of Ananias that he received baptism. The baptism would probably be administered in one or other of the rivers which the history of Naaman had made famous, and so the waters of "Abana and Pharpar, rivers of Damascus" (2 Kings v. 12), were now sanctified no less than those of Jordan for the "mystical washing away of sin."

(19) **And when he had received meat.**—Better, as elsewhere, *food*. The three days' fast had obviously brought about a state of extreme prostration. In St. Paul's account of his conversion in Gal. i. 17, he states that when it pleased God to reveal His Son in him, immediately he "conferred not with flesh, and blood," but went into Arabia and returned again to Damascus. We have, it is obvious, no certain *data* for fixing the time, nor the extent of that journey. St. Luke does not mention it, and his "straightway" balances the "immediately" of St. Paul's account. On the whole, it seems most probable that it was the first step taken by him after he had regained his sight and been baptised. Physically, rest and seclusion would be necessary during the period of convalescence after the great crisis of his conversion. Spiritually, that solitude was needed, we may believe, to prepare him for the continuous labour of the three years that followed. I place the journey to Arabia accordingly, with hardly any hesitation, after the "certain days" of fellowship with the disciples, and his reception at their solemn meeting to break bread in the Supper of the Lord, and before the "preaching Christ" in the synagogues. How far the journey extended we cannot say. "Arabia" was used somewhat vaguely as a geographical term; but the fact that Damascus was at this time occupied by the troops of Aretas, the king of Arabia Petræa, makes it probable that he went to that region. In St. Paul's paronomastic reference to Hagar as a synonym for Mount Sinai in Arabia (Hagar and Sinai both admitting of an etymology which gives "rock" as the meaning of each), we may, perhaps, trace a local knowledge gained during this journey, and draw the inference that he had sought communion with God where Moses and

Saul certain days with the disciples
which were at Damascus. (20) And
straightway he preached Christ in the
synagogues, that he is the Son of God.
(21) But all that heard *him* were amazed,
and said; Is not this he that destroyed
them which called on this name in
Jerusalem, and came hither for that
intent, that he might bring them bound
unto the chief priests? (22) But Saul
increased the more in strength, and
confounded the Jews which dwelt at
Damascus, proving that this is very
Christ.
(23) And after that many days were
fulfilled, the Jews took counsel to kill
him: (24) but their laying await was
known of Saul.[a] And they watched the
gates day and night to kill him.
(25) Then the disciples took him by

A.D. 37.

a 2 Cor. 11. 32.

---

Elijah had found it, on the heights of Sinai and Horeb. (Comp. Gal. iv. 25.) He learnt, it may be, the true meaning and purpose of the Law, as arousing the fear of judgment, amid the terrors of the very rocks from which that Law had first been proclaimed to Israel.

(20) **And straightway he preached Christ in the synagogues.**—The "straightway" as interpreted by the inference drawn in the previous Note, must be taken to refer to the Apostle's first public appearance in the synagogues of Damascus after his return from Arabia. The tense of the verb implies that the work was continued for some length of time. What he had to proclaim was, first, that the Christ was actually and verily the Son of God no less than the Son of David; and, secondly, that Jesus of Nazareth had been shown to be the Christ. The better MSS., however, give the reading, *preached Jesus.* The line of reasoning we may assume to have been identical with that of chap. xiii. 16—41. It is not without interest to remember here also that the Samaritans had a synagogue of their own at Damascus, and that he may thus have preached to them, so following in the footprints of Philip and taking his first step in the great work of breaking down the barriers that divided Israel from the world.

(21) **That destroyed them which called on this name.**—Better, *made havock of them.* It is noticeable that St. Paul uses the same verb as descriptive of his own conduct in Gal. i. 13, where the English version has "wasted." On "them which called on this name," see Note on verse 16.

**And came hither.**—More accurately, *had come hither,* as implying that the purpose of his coming had been abandoned.

(22) **But Saul increased the more in strength.**—The tense implies a continuous growth in power, obviously in the spiritual power which enabled the Apostle to carry on his work. A comparison of dates suggests the connection of this growth with the special vision of 2 Cor. xii. 8, when in answer to his prayer that the infirmity which he describes as "a thorn in his flesh, the minister of Satan to buffet him," he received the comforting assurance from the Lord whom he served—"My strength is made perfect in weakness." It is not without interest that in after years St. Paul once and again uses the same verb of himself—"I can do all things in Christ that *strengthened* me" (Phil. iv. 13). It was Christ who "*enabled* him," or, *made him strong,* for his ministry (1 Tim. i. 12); who "*strengthened* him" in the closing trials of his life (2 Tim. iv. 17). By some commentators the words are connected with the journey to Arabia as following on his first appearance as a preacher in the synagogues; but see Note on the previous verse.

(23) **After that many days were fulfilled.**—We learn from the more definite statement in Gal. i. 18 that these few words cover a period of otherwise unrecorded work, extending over a period of three years. That period must have witnessed the growth of a Christian society at Damascus, with an order of discipline and worship based on the outlines of that at Jerusalem. It follows, however, from the subsequent history that, as yet, Gentile converts were not admitted to the Church as such. The special mission to them came later on (comp. chap. xxii. 21), and it was natural that one, with the intense affection for his brethren according to the flesh which characterised St. Paul (Rom. x. 1), should, till that mission came, have given himself mainly, or even exclusively, to the work of labouring for their conversion. It is probable, however, from the bitter antagonism of the Jews, that his teaching had already pointed to the breaking down of "the middle wall of partition" (Eph. ii. 14), and the passing away of all on which they had prided themselves as being their exclusive privileges. From the first it might almost seem as if Stephen had risen from the dead, and was living again in the spirit and power of his persecutor.

(24) **They watched the gates day and night to kill him.**—A somewhat fuller account of this episode in the Apostle's life is given by him in 2 Cor. xi. 32. There we read that the governor—literally, *ethnarch*—of the city, under Aretas, King of Arabia Petræa, with Petra as his capital, the father of the wife whom Herod Antipas divorced, in order that he might marry Herodias, took an active part in the plot against Paul. On the manner in which Aretas had gained possession of a city which was properly attached to the Roman province of Syria, see Note on verse 2. It is noticeable that there are coins of Damascus bearing the names of Augustus and Tiberius, and again of Nero and his successors, but none of those of Caligula and Claudius, who succeeded Tiberius. Caligula, on his accession, reversed the policy of Tiberius, who had been a friend and supporter of Antipas against Aretas, and it is probable that, as in other instances, he created a new principality, or ethnarchy, in favour of Aretas, to whose predecessors Damascus had belonged (Jos. *Ant.* xiii. 15, § 2). The ethnarch apparently wished to court the favour of the large Jewish population, and, looking on St. Paul as a disturber of the public peace, took measures for his arrest and condemnation. Troops were stationed at each gate of the city in order to prevent his escape.

(25) **Let him down by the wall in a basket.**—The basket is the *spuris* of Matt. xv. 37, where see Note. In 2 Cor. xi. 33 St. Paul describes it by another word (*sarganè*), which gives the idea of a wicker or rope-work hamper. It seems to follow, from the tone in which the Apostle there speaks of this adventure, that it had been made matter of ridicule. It is connected in his thoughts with the "infirmities" (probably with

night, and let *him* down by the wall in
a basket. (26) And when Saul was come
to Jerusalem, he assayed to join himself
to the disciples: but they were all
afraid of him, and believed not that he
was a disciple. (27) But Barnabas took
him, and brought *him* to the apostles,
and declared unto them how he had
seen the Lord in the way, and that he
had spoken to him, and how he had
preached boldly at Damascus in the
name of Jesus. (28) And he was with
them coming in and going out at
Jerusalem. (29) And he spake boldly
in the name of the Lord Jesus, and
disputed against the Grecians: but they
went about to slay him. (30) *Which*
when the brethren knew, they brought
him down to Cæsarea, and sent him
forth to Tarsus. (31) Then had the
churches rest throughout all Judæa and
Galilee and Samaria, and were edified;

---

his smallness of stature) of which he was content to boast. The escape was effected, like that of the spies from the house of Rahab (Josh. ii. 15) and of David from his own house (1 Sam. xix. 11), through an opening or "window" in the town wall. Such a window is still shown in the wall of Damascus as the traditional scene of the escape.

(26) **And when Saul was come to Jerusalem.**—His journey probably took him, as before, through Samaria (see Note on verse 3), and so laid the foundation of the interest in the Samaritan Church, which shows itself later on in the history in chap. xv. 3, when he and Barnabas journeyed "through Phœnice and Samaria."

**He assayed to join himself to the disciples.**—The reader may note the use of the word "assay," which has since been confined to a purely technical meaning, in the wider sense of trying or attempting. The verb for "join" is that which is always used of close and intimate fellowship, such as that of husband and wife, of brothers, and of friends. (Comp. chap. x. 28; Matt. xix. 5; Luke xv. 15; 1 Cor. vi. 16.) He was seeking, in the language of a later time, full communion with the disciples. It was not strange that his motives should be at first suspected. Might he not be coming to "spy out" their weak places, and in time appear again as a persecutor? The difficulty which at first presents itself in understanding how the Church at Jerusalem could have remained ignorant of what Saul had done at Damascus as a preacher of the faith, is adequately explained by the political incidents to which attention has been already drawn. The occupation of the city by Aretas, and his enmity against the Herodian house, may well have stopped the usual intercourse between it and Jerusalem, then under the rule of Agrippa, and so the reports that reached the Apostles would come in uncertain and fluctuating forms, which were not sufficient to lead the disciples to trust in the conversion of the persecutor.

(27) **But Barnabas took him.**—What, we ask, made Barnabas more ready than others, not only to receive the convert himself, but to vouch for his sincerity? The answer is found in the inference that the Levite of Cyprus and the tent-maker had been friends in earlier years. The culture of which Tarsus was the seat, would naturally attract a student from the neighbouring island, and the eagerness of Barnabas to secure Saul's co-operation at a later stage of his work (chap. xi. 25) may fairly be looked on as furnishing a confirmation of the view now suggested. He knew enough of his friend to believe every syllable of what he told him as to the incidents of his conversion.

**Brought him to the apostles.**—In the more definite account in Gal. i. 18, 19, we find that his primary purpose was to exchange thoughts (ἱστορῆσαι = to inquire, the word from which we get our "history") with Peter, and that the only other leading teacher that he saw (we need not now inquire whether he speaks of him as an Apostle or not) was "James, the Lord's brother." It may, perhaps, be inferred from this, either (1) that the other Apostles were absent from Jerusalem at the time, or (2) that the new convert did not attend any public meeting of the Church.

(28) **Coming in and going out.**—The words, like the kindred phrase in chap. i. 21, are used to imply a certain undefined frequency of intercourse. From Gal i. 18 we learn that the whole duration of the visit was not more than fifteen days.

(29) **Disputed against the Grecians.**—It will be remembered that it was as the leader of the Hellenistic Jews of the synagogue named in chap. vi. 9 that Saul had first appeared in the history of the Church. Now, it would seem, he sought to undo the evil that he had then wrought, by preaching to them the faith which he had then opposed, and presenting, we may well believe, the very aspects of the truth that had been most prominent in Stephen's teaching, and which, therefore, now, as then, roused them to a passionate frenzy. Twice, within a few weeks, the Apostle's life was in danger.

(30) **They brought him down to Cæsarea.**—The fact that the brethren at Jerusalem took these measures for the Apostle's safety may be noted as a proof of their friendship. At Cæsarea he would probably, as afterwards in chap. xxi. 8, find Philip, and the friend and the accuser of the proto-martyr met face to face as brethren. In returning to his home at Tarsus, from which he had been absent at the least for four years, and possibly for a much longer period, it would be natural for him to resume his old employment as a tent-maker. (See Note on chap. xviii. 3.) Thence, as from a centre, he did his work as an Evangelist in the regions of Cilicia (Gal. i. 21), where, in chap. xv. 41, we find churches already organised, which had not been founded in what we call the first mission journey of Paul and Barnabas, and must therefore have been planted by the former at an earlier period. Here, for the present, we lose sight of him. It need hardly be said that the Cæsarea here spoken of is that on the sea-coast. Cæsarea Philippi is always distinguished by its special epithet.

(31) **Then had the churches rest.**—The better MSS. have "the Church" in the singular. The tranquility described may have been due, partly to the absence of any leading men among the opponents of the new society; partly, perhaps, to public excitement being diverted to the insane attempt of Caligula to set up his statue in the Temple at Jerusalem—an attempt from which he was only dissuaded by the earnest entreaties of Herod Agrippa, whom he had raised to the

and walking in the fear of the Lord, and in the comfort of the Holy Ghost, were multiplied.
(32) And it came to pass, as Peter passed throughout all *quarters*, he came down also to the saints which dwelt at Lydda.
(33) And there he found a certain man named Æneas, which had

A.D. 33.

dignity of King of Judæa, but who happened at the time to be at Rome, and of Petronius, the *Præses* of Syria. The latter was influenced by great showers of rain falling from a clear sky, after a long drought, in answer to the prayers of Israel (Jos. *Ant.* xviii. 8, § 6). Such prayers, made at a crisis in which believing and unbelieving Jews felt an equal interest, may, probably, have suggested St. James's allusion to the old historical parallel of Elijah (Jas. v. 17).

**Throughout all Judæa and Galilee and Samaria.**—Brief as the notice is, it is every way significant. It is the first intimation since the opening of the apostolic history of the existence, not of disciples only, such as had gathered round our Lord during His personal ministry, but of *organised religious communities*, in the towns and villages of Galilee. We may think of such churches as formed in Capernaum and Tiberias, in Chorazin and the two Bethsaidas, perhaps even in Nazareth. The history is silent as to the agency by which these churches had been founded; but looking to the close relations between St. Luke and St. Philip, and to the probability that the latter made Cæsarea his head-quarters for the work of an Evangelist, we may legitimately think of him as having worked there as he had worked in Samaria. It is not improbable, however, that here also, as in that region, he may have been followed, after he had done his work as an Evangelist, by the Apostles to whom it belonged to confirm and organise. (See Note on chap. viii. 14.) The mention of Samaria in like manner indicates the extent and permanence of the result of Philip's work there, followed up as it had been by the preaching of Peter and John.

**Were edified; and walking . . . .**—The more accurate construction of the sentence gives, *The Church . . . . had peace, being edified and walking in the fear of the Lord, and was multiplied by the counsel of the Holy Ghost.* The passage is noticeable for the appearance of the word "edified," or "built up," in the sense in which St. Paul had used it (1 Cor. viii. 1; xiv. 4), as describing orderly and continuous growth, the superstructure raised wisely upon the right foundation.

**Walking in the fear of the Lord.**—The phrase, so common in the Old Testament, is comparatively rare in the New, being used only by St. Luke here, and in 2 Cor. v. 11, where it is wrongly translated "*the terror* of the Lord." What it describes, as interpreted by its Old Testament use (Job xxviii. 28; Ps. cxi. 10; Prov. i. 7, *et al.*), is the temper of reverential awe; the scrupulous obedience to the commandments of God, which had been described of old as "the beginning" of wisdom.

**The comfort of the Holy Ghost.**—It was natural that the gift of the Spirit who had been promised as the Paraclete, or Advocate (see *Excursus G* on the Gospel of St. John), should be described by the kindred word of *paraclesis*, and equally natural that this connection should re-appear in the two English words of "comfort" and "Comforter." "Comfort" is, however, somewhat too narrow; the Greek word including (see Note on chap. iv. 36) counsel and exhortation, so as to be very nearly equivalent to "prophecy." What is meant here is that the words of counsel which came from the Holy Ghost, speaking through the prophets of the Church, were, then as always, far more than signs and wonders, or human skill of speech, the chief agents in its expansion.

(32) **As Peter passed throughout all quarters.**—The plan of the writer, arranging his materials, leads him from this point of chap. xii. 18 to dwell entirely on the personal work of Peter. So far this section of the book may be described as the Acts of Peter. On the other hand, it is obvious that he only gives those acts as part of his general plan, not caring to follow the Apostle's course, as in a biography, but confining himself to tracing the steps by which he had been led to the part he played in the great work of the conversion of the Gentiles. The "all quarters" may well have included Galilee.

**He came down also to the saints which dwelt at Lydda.**—On the term "saints" see Note on verse 13. Lydda, the Lud of the Old Testament (1 Chron. viii. 12; Ezra ii. 33; Neh. vii. 37; xi. 35), was a town in the rich plain of Sharon, one day's journey from Jerusalem, founded originally by settlers from the tribe of Benjamin, and retaining to the present day its old name as *Ludd.* It is mentioned by Josephus (*Wars*, iii. 3, § 5) as transferred by Demetrius Sotêr, at the request of Judas Maccabeus, to the estate of the Temple at Jerusalem (1 Macc. x. 30, 38; xi. 34). Under the grasping rule of Cassius, the inhabitants were sold as slaves (Jos. *Ant.* xiv. 11, § 2). It had, however, recovered its former prosperity, and appears at this time to have been the seat of a flourishing Christian community. In the wars that preceded the destruction of Jerusalem, it was partially burned by Cestius Gallus A.D. 66 (Jos. *Wars*, ii. 19, § 1), all but fifty of the inhabitants having gone up to the Feast of Tabernacles at Jerusalem, and was again occupied by Vespasian A.D. 68 (Jos. *Wars*, ii. 8, § 1). When it was rebuilt, probably under Hadrian, when Jerusalem received the new name of Ælia Capitolina, it also was renamed as Diospolis (= city of Zeus), and as such was the seat of one of the chief bishoprics of the Syrian Church. It was, at the time when Peter came to it, the seat of a Rabbinic school, scarcely inferior to that of Jabneh, and retained its fame after the scribes of the latter city had migrated to Tiberias. Gamaliel, son of the great Rabbi who was St. Paul's master, and himself honoured with the title of Rabban, presided over it, and was succeeded by the great Tarphon (Lightfoot, *Cent. Chorogr.* c. xvi.). The question which we naturally ask, who had planted the faith of Christ there, carries us once more on the track of Philip the Evangelist. Lying as it did on the road from Azotus to Cæsarea, it would lie in his way on the journey recorded in chap. viii. 40, as he passed "through all the cities;" and we may believe, without much risk of error, that here also he was St. Luke's informant as to what had passed in the Church with which he was so closely connected.

**A certain man named Æneas.**—The Greek name (we note the shortened vowel Ænĕas of the later form of the word), perhaps, implies that he belonged to the Hellenistic section of the Church. Had the fame of Virgil's poem made the name of the Trojan hero

kept his bed eight years, and was sick
of the palsy. (34) And Peter said unto
him, Æneas, Jesus Christ maketh thee
whole: arise, and make thy bed. And
he arose immediately. (35) And all that
dwelt at Lydda and Saron saw him, and
turned to the Lord.

(36) Now there was at Joppa a certain
disciple named Tabitha, which by interpretation is called Dorcas: this woman
was full of good works and almsdeeds
which she did. (37) And it came to pass
in those days, that she was sick, and
died: whom when they had washed, they
laid *her* in an upper chamber. (38) And
forasmuch as Lydda was nigh to Joppa,
and the disciples had heard that Peter
was there, they sent unto him two men,
desiring *him* that he would not delay[1]
to come to them. (39) Then Peter
arose and went with them. When
he was come, they brought him
into the upper chamber: and all
the widows stood by him weeping, and
shewing the coats and garments which
Dorcas made, while she was with them.

1 Or, *be grieved.*

---

known even in the plains of Palestine? In the care with which St. Luke records the circumstances of the case, the eight years of bedridden paralysis, we note a trace of professional exactness, as in chaps. iii. 7; ix. 18; xxviii. 8. The word of "bed," used commonly of the couches of the lower class (see Note on Matt. ii. 4), suggests the thought that poverty also was added to his sufferings.

(34) **Jesus Christ maketh thee whole.**—Better, *Jesus the Christ.* We note the same anxiety to disclaim any personal power or holiness as the cause that wrought the supernatural healing as in chaps. iii. 12; iv. 9, 10. In the assonance of the Greek words (*Iēsus iātai se*) we may, perhaps, trace a desire to impress the thought that the very name of Jesus testified that He was the great Healer. Such a *paronomasia* has its parallel in the later play upon *Christiani* and *Chrestiani* = the good or gracious people (Tertull. *Apol.* c. 3), perhaps also in St. Peter's own language that the Lord is not *Christos* only, but *Chrestos* = gracious (1 Pet. ii. 3). The command seems to imply a reminiscence of the manner in which our Lord had wrought His work of healing in like cases (Matt. ix. 6; John v. 8).

**Make thy bed.**—More accurately, *make*, or, *arrange for thyself.* He was to do at once for himself what for so many years others had done for him.

(35) **All that dwelt at Lydda and Saron.**—The latter name indicates a district rather than a town. The presence of the article with it, and its absence from Lydda, indicates that men spoke of "*the* Saron"—*the* plain—*the* woodlands (so it is rendered by the LXX.: 1 Chron. v. 16; xxvii. 29; Cant. ii. 1; Isa. xxxv. 2)—as we speak of "*the* weald." It lay between the central mountains of Palestine and the Mediterranean, and was proverbial for its beauty and fertility (Isa. xxxiii. 9; lxv. 10).

(36) **There was at Joppa . . . .**—The Hebrew form of the name, *Japho* (pronounced *Yapho*), appears in Josh. xix. 46, but the English version more commonly gives the better-known Joppa, as in 2 Chron. ii. 16; Ezra iii. 7; Jonah i. 3). It was famous in Greek legends as the spot where Andromeda had been bound when she was delivered by Perseus (Strabo, xvi., p. 759; Jos. *Wars*, i. 6, § 2). The town stood on a hill so high that it was said (though this is not in conformity with the fact) that Jerusalem could be seen from its summit. It was the nearest port to that city, and though the harbour was difficult and dangerous of access, was used for the timber that, first under Solomon, and afterwards under Zerubbabel, was brought from Lebanon for the construction of the Temple (1 Kings v. 9; 2 Chron. ii. 16; Ezra iii. 7). In the history of Jonah it appears as a port from which ships sail to Tarshish and Spain (Jonah i. 3). Under the Maccabean rulers the harbour and fortifications were restored (1 Macc. iv. 5, 34). By Augustus it was given to Herod the Great, and afterwards to Archelaus (Jos. *Ant.* xv. 7, § 3; xvii. 11, § 4), and on his deposition, became part of the Roman province of Syria. It was at this time and later on notorious as a nest of pirates. Here also we may, as in the case of Lydda (see Note on verse 32), see the work of Philip as the probable founder of the Church.

**Tabitha, which by interpretation is called Dorcas.**—Both the Hebrew and Greek names mean *Antelope* or *Gazelle.* The fact that she bore both implies some points of connection both with the Hebrew and Hellenistic sections of the Church. The Greek form occurs, in the curious combination of Juno Dorcas, on one of the inscriptions in the *Columbarium* of Livia, now in the Capitoline Museum at Rome, as belonging to an *Ornatrix* of the Empress. Was tho disciple of Joppa in any way connected with the slave, whose very function implied skill in needlework? If, as is probable, the Church at Joppa owed its foundation to Philip (see Note on chap. viii. 40), we may trace in the position which she occupied, in relation to the "widows" of the Church, something of the same prudential wisdom as had been shown in the appointment of the Seven, of whom he had been one.

**Full of good works.**—The form of the expression may be noticed as characteristic of St. Luke, and his favourite formula for conveying the thought of a quality being possessed in the highest degree possible. So we have "full of leprosy" in Luke v. 12, "full of grace" and "full of faith" in Acts vi. 5, 8. (Comp. also chaps. xiii. 10; xix. 28.)

(37) **They laid her in an upper chamber.**—This implies some little delay in the usual rapidity of Eastern funerals. As Lydda was only nine miles from Joppa, the report of Æneas's recovery might well have travelled from the one city to the other, and led to the hope that the power which St. Peter had thus put forth might extend even to the farther work of raising from the dead.

(38) **Desiring him that he would not delay.**—The better MSS. give the message somewhat more dramatically, "*Delay not,*" and "*Be not reluctant* to come." It was, of course, necessary that he should come at once, as interment would have come, as a matter of course, on the following day.

(39) **All the widows stood by him weeping.**—We have apparently the same organisation of charity as that which prevailed in the Church at Jerusalem. The "widows" of the Church were the object of a

(40) But Peter put them all forth, and
kneeled down, and prayed; and turning
*him* to the body said, Tabitha, arise.
And she opened her eyes: and when
she saw Peter, she sat up. (41) And he
gave her *his* hand, and lifted her up,
and when he had called the saints and
widows, presented her alive. (42) And it
was known throughout all Joppa; and
many believed in the Lord. (43) And
it came to pass, that he tarried many
days in Joppa with one Simon a
tanner.

A.D. 41. CHAPTER X.—(1) There was a
certain man in Cæsarea called Cornelius, a centurion of the band called
the Italian *band*, (2) *a* devout *man*, and
one that feared God with all his house,
which gave much alms to the people,

---

special provision. (See Note on chap. vi. 1.) The "coats," were the close-fitting tunics worn next the body, the "garments" the looser outer cloaks that were worn over them. (See Note on Matt. v. 40.) These were now exhibited by those who were mourning over the loss of their benefactress. It is probable that the garments were for the use of men and boys, as well as women, and that the "widows" had been fellow-workers with her in making them. She was, as it were, at the head of a Sisterhood of Mercy.

**Which Dorcas made.**—More accurately, *used to make.*

(40) **Peter put them all forth.**—We may, perhaps, trace in Peter's action his recollection of what our Lord had done in the case of the daughter of Jairus (see Notes on Matt. ix. 23, 24), at which he had been present. The work was one not to be accomplished by the mere utterance of a name, nor as by his "own power or holiness" (chap. iii. 12), but by the power of the prayer of faith, and this called for the silence and solitude of communion with God. Even the very words which were uttered, if he spoke in Aramaic, must have been, with the change of a single letter, the same as the *Talitha cumi* of Mark v. 41. The utterance of the words implied the internal assurance that the prayer had been answered.

(41) **And when he had called the saints.**—See Note on verse 13.

(42) **Many believed in the Lord.**—Here the word is obviously used definitely for the Lord Jesus as the specific object of their faith.

(43) **Many days in Joppa with one Simon a tanner.**—Either as bringing with it, through contact with the carcases and hides of dead beasts, the risks of ceremonial defilement, or being generally a repulsive and noisome business, the occupation was one from which the stricter Jews generally shrunk. The Rabbis held that if a tanner about to marry concealed his occupation from his intended wife, the concealment was of the nature of a fraud that invalidated the contract (Schöttgen, *Hor. Heb., in loc.*). In taking up his abode with one of this calling, Peter must accordingly have been taking one step in advance towards greater freedom. He had learnt, partially at least, the lesson which his Master had taught as to that which alone can bring with it real defilement (Mark vii. 17—23), and was thus being trained for a fuller illumination. We have no *data* for determining the length of time implied in the "many days." In verse 23, as we have seen, the words covered a period of nearly three years.

## X.

(1) **There was a certain man in Cæsarea.**—We enter on a new stage of expansion in the Church's growth, the full details of which St. Luke may have learnt either from Philip the Evangelist during his stay at Cæsarea (chaps. xxi. 8; xxiv. 27) or, possibly, from Cornelius himself. His admission into the Church, even if it were not the first instance of the reception of a Gentile convert as such, became, through its supernatural accompaniments and (in the strict sense of that word) its "prerogative" character, the ruling case on the subject. Whether it were earlier or later than the admission of the Gentiles recorded in chap. xi. 20, we have no adequate *data* for determining. (See Note on that passage.)

Cæsarea was at this time the usual residence of the Roman Procurator of Judæa, and was consequently garrisoned by Roman troops. Greeks, Jews, and Romans, probably also Phœnicians and other traders, were mingled freely in its population.

**Cornelius, a centurion of the band called the Italian band.**—The office was a comparatively subordinate one, the centurion commanding the sixth part of a cohort, the sixtieth part of a legion. The Greek implies that he belonged to the cohort, not that he commanded it. The name Cornelius may indicate a connection with the great Cornelian gens which had been made famous by the Gracchi and by Sylla. The bands, or *cohorts*, stationed at Cæsarea consisted chiefly of auxiliaries levied from the province (Jos. *Wars*, ii. 13, § 6), who were not always to be relied on in times of popular excitement, and this cohort was accordingly distinguished from the others as Italian, *i.e.*, as being at least commanded by Roman officers. A first Italian legion is repeatedly mentioned by Tacitus (*Hist.* i. 59, 64; ii. 100; iii. 22), but this is said by Dion (lv. 24) to have been first raised by Nero; and the term which St. Luke uses for band (*spira*) was, strictly speaking, not used of the legions, the latter term being applied exclusively to Roman troops. In chap. xxvii. 1 we meet with another of these cohorts, also at Cæsarea, known as the Augustan.

(2) **A devout man, and one that feared God with all his house.**—The word for "devout" is not the same as that used in chaps. ii. 5, viii. 2, and Luke ii. 25, and appears to be used by St. Luke, as again in verse 7, for the special type of devotion that belonged to Gentile converts to Judaism. The phrase "those that feared God" is employed distinctly for this class in verses 22 and 35, and again in chap. xiii. 16, 26. There is a special significance in the addition "with all his house." The centurion was not satisfied with having found a higher truth for himself, but sought to impart it to the soldiers and slaves, possibly to those nearer and dearer to him, who came under his influence. (Comp. verse 7.)

**Which gave much alms to the people**—*i.e.*, to the Jews of Cæsarea as distinct from the Gentiles. (Comp. chaps. xxvi. 17, 23; xxviii. 17.)

**And prayed to God alway.**—As the vision that follows may rightly be regarded as an answer to the

and prayed to God alway. (3) He saw
in a vision evidently about the ninth
hour of the day an angel of God
coming in to him, and saying unto
him, Cornelius. (4) And when he
looked on him, he was afraid, and
said, What is it, Lord? And he said
unto him, Thy prayers and thine alms
are come up for a memorial before God.
(5) And now send men to Joppa, and
call for *one* Simon, whose surname is
Peter: (6) he lodgeth with one Simon a
tanner, whose house is by the sea side:
he shall tell thee what thou oughtest to
do. (7) And when the angel which
spake unto Cornelius was departed, he
called two of his household servants,
and a devout soldier of them that waited
on him continually; (8) and when he
had declared all *these* things unto them,
he sent them to Joppa.

(9) On the morrow, as they went on
their journey, and drew nigh unto the
city, Peter went up upon the housetop
to pray about the sixth hour: (10) and
he became very hungry, and would have
eaten: but while they made ready, he
fell into a trance, (11) and saw heaven
opened, and a certain vessel descending
unto him, as it had been a great sheet

---

prayers thus offered, it is natural to infer that Cornelius was seeking for guidance as to the new faith which Philip had brought to Cæsarea, and of which he could scarcely fail to have heard. Was it really a new revelation from God to man? Could he be admitted to the fellowship of the society which confessed Jesus as the Christ without accepting the yoke of circumcision and the ceremonial law from which, as a "proselyte of the gate," he had hitherto kept back?

(3) **In a vision evidently.**—The adverb seems added to distinguish the manifestation from that of a dream like Joseph's in Matt. i. 20, ii. 13, or of a trance like St. Peter's (verse 10) or St. Paul's (chap. xxii. 17).

**About the ninth hour of the day.**—This was, as in chap. iii. 1, one of the three hours of prayer, the hour when the evening sacrifice was offered in the Temple. Cornelius had therefore so far accepted the Jewish rules of devotion, and for him also the Law was "a schoolmaster" bringing him to Christ.

(4) **Are come up for a memorial before God.**—The word so used was emphatically sacrificial and liturgical, as, *e.g.*, in Lev. ii. 2, 9, 16; v. 12; vi. 15; Ecclus. xlv. 16; and elsewhere. The words implied, therefore, that the "prayers and alms" were accepted as a true sacrifice, more acceptable than the blood of bulls and goats. If we ask, in the technical language of a later theology, how they could be accepted when they were offered prior to a clear faith in Christ, and therefore before justification, the answer is that the good works were wrought by the power of God's grace already working in him. He was believing in the Light that lighteth every man, though as yet he did not identify that Light with its manifestation in Jesus as the Christ (John i. 9). He had the faith which from the beginning of the world has justified—the belief that God is, and that He is a rewarder of them that diligently seek Him (Heb. xi. 6).

(5, 6) **Call for one Simon, whose surname is Peter.**—The circumstances of the communication present, it is obvious, a striking parallelism with those attendant on the revelation to Ananias in chap. ix. 10—17. To those who regard both narratives as fictitious, the resemblance will appear as characteristic of St. Luke's style as a writer. Admitting, however, the possibility of a divine guidance being given by a supernatural message, it will not seem strange to us, as has been said already, that it should in each case take the form which made it most effectual, giving directions as to names and places, and yet leaving something open as a test of faith.

(7) **A devout soldier.**—The word implies that the man was, like his superior officer, a convert to the faith of Israel, though not, in the full sense of the word, a proselyte. It is natural to infer the same of the two slaves to whom their master imparted the vision, which to those who were living as heathens would have seemed strange and unintelligible. It is obvious that all such facts are interesting as throwing light on the character of Cornelius, and showing that, to the extent of his power, he sought to lead those over whom he had any influence to the Truth which he had found precious as leading him to a higher life.

(9) **As they went on their journey . . .**—The distance from Cæsarea to Joppa was about thirty Roman miles.

**To pray about the sixth hour.**—As in chap. iii. 1, we again find St. Peter observing the Jewish hours of prayer. The "hunger" mentioned in the next verse implies that up to that time he had partaken of no food, and makes it probable that it was one of the days, the second and fifth in the week, which the Pharisees and other devout Jews observed as fasts. The flat housetop of an Eastern house was commonly used for prayer and meditation (comp. Matt. x. 27; xxiv. 17; Luke xvii. 31), and in a city like Joppa, and a house like that of the tanner, was probably the only place accessible for such a purpose.

(10) **He fell into a trance.**—St. Luke characteristically uses, as in chaps. xi. 5, xxii. 17, the technical term *ekstasis* (whence our English *ecstasy*) for the state which thus supervened. It is obvious that it might in part be the natural consequence of the protracted fast, and the intense prayer, possibly also of exposure under such conditions to the noontide sun. The state was one in which the normal action of the senses was suspended, like that of Balaam in Num. xxiv. 4, or that which St. Paul describes in 2 Cor. xii. 3, "whether in the body or out of the body" he cannot tell, and, as such, it was, in this instance, made the channel for a revelation of the Divine Will conveyed in symbols which were adapted to the conditions out of which it rose.

(11) **A certain vessel descending . . .**—The form of the vision corresponded, as has just been said, with the bodily condition of the Apostle. Its inward meaning may fairly be thought of as corresponding to his prayer. One who looked out from Joppa upon the waters of the Great Sea towards the far-off Isles of the Gentiles, might well seek to know by what process and under what conditions those who dwelt in them would be

knit at the four corners, and let down
to the earth: (12) wherein were all
manner of fourfooted beasts of the
earth, and wild beasts, and creeping
things, and fowls of the air. (13) And
there came a voice to him, Rise, Peter;
kill, and eat. (14) But Peter said, Not
so, Lord; for I have never eaten any
thing that is common or unclean.
(15) And the voice *spake* unto him again
the second time, What God hath
cleansed, *that* call not thou common.
(16) This was done thrice: and the vessel
was received up again into heaven.
(17) Now while Peter doubted in himself
what this vision which he had seen
should mean, behold, the men which
were sent from Cornelius had made
enquiry for Simon's house, and stood
before the gate, (18) and called, and
asked whether Simon, which was surnamed
Peter, were lodged there.
(19) While Peter thought on the vision,
the Spirit said unto him, Behold, three
men seek thee. (20) Arise therefore,
and get thee down, and go with them,
doubting nothing: for I have sent
them. (21) Then Peter went down to
the men which were sent unto him from
Cornelius; and said, Behold, I am he
whom ye seek: what *is* the cause wherefore
ye are come? (22) And they said,
Cornelius the centurion, a just man,
and one that feareth God, and of good

---

brought within the fold of which he was one of the chief appointed shepherds. The place, we may add, could not fail to recall the memory of the great prophet who had taken ship from thence, and who was conspicuous alike as a preacher of a gospel of repentance to the Gentiles, and, in our Lord's own teaching, as a type of the Resurrection (Matt. xii. 40, 41). The Apostle was to be taught, as the prophet had been of old, that the thoughts of God were not as his thoughts (Jon. iv. 10, 11).

**A great sheet knit at the four corners.**—Better, *bound by four ends—i.e.*, those of the ropes by which it seemed to Peter's gaze to be let down from the opened firmament. The Greek word, literally *beginnings*, is used as we use "ends."

(12) **All manner of four-footed beasts . . .** —The classification seems to imply the sheep, the oxen, or the swine that were used as food by the Gentiles, as coming under this head, the deer and goats, and conies and hares under that of "wild beasts." Stress in each case is laid upon there being "all manner" of each class, those that were allowed, and those also that were forbidden by the Jewish law.

(13) **Rise, Peter; kill, and eat.**—In the symbolism of the vision the natural promptings of appetite were confirmed by the divine voice. That which resisted both was the scruple of a hesitating conscience, not yet emancipated from its bondage to a ceremonial and therefore transitory law. It is natural to infer that the spiritual yearnings of Peter's soul were, in like manner, hungering and thirsting after a wider fellowship which should embrace "all manner" of the races that make up mankind, while, on the other hand, he was as yet waiting to be taught that the distinction between Jew and Gentile was done away in Christ.

(14) **Not so, Lord . . .**—The emphatic resistance even to a voice from heaven is strikingly in harmony with the features of St. Peter's character, as portrayed in the Gospels, with the "Be it far from thee, Lord," when he heard of the coming Passion (Luke xvi. 32), with "Thou shalt never wash my feet," in John xiii. 8. He had been taught that that which "goeth into the mouth cannot defile the man" (Mark vii. 15), but he had not taken in that truth in its fulness, either in its literal or symbolic meaning.

**Any thing that is common or unclean.**—"Common" is used, as in Mark vii. 2, in the sense of "defiled" or "impure," that which excludes the idea of consecration to a special service.

(15) **What God hath cleansed, that call not thou common.**—In the framework of the vision, the clean and the unclean beasts stood on the same footing, were let down from heaven in the same sheet. That had purified them from whatever taint had adhered to them under the precepts of the Law. In the interpretation of the vision, all that belongs to humanity had been taken up into heaven; first, when man's nature was assumed by the Eternal Word in the Incarnation (John i. 14), and, secondly, when that nature had been raised in the Ascension to the heaven of heavens, sitting on the right hand of God (chap. vii. 56; Mark xvi. 19).

(16) **This was done thrice.**—The three-fold repetition was at once general and personal in its significance. It was mystically the token of a complete ratification of the truth proclaimed. It reminded him of the three-fold command, "Feed My sheep," and taught him to take a wider range of work in obeying it (John xxi. 15—17).

(17) **While Peter doubted in himself . . . .**—A doubt might well arise whether the teaching of the vision went beyond its immediate scope. The Apostle might have admitted that it abrogated the old distinction between clean and unclean meats, and yet might hesitate to answer the question, "Did it do more than this?"

(19) **The Spirit said unto him, . . . .**—The words seem to imply a state of consciousness intermediate between the "trance" that had passed away and the normal state of every-day life. The "voice" no longer seemed to come from heaven to the outward ear, but was heard as not less divine in the secret recesses of his soul.

(20) **Go with them, doubting nothing.**—The command was specially addressed to the perplexed questionings of the disciple. For a time he was to walk, as it were, blindfold, but trusting in the full assurance of faith in the Hand that was guiding him. As once before (John xiii. 7), he knew not yet what his Lord was doing, but was to know hereafter. He and the messengers from Cornelius were alike acting on the promptings of the Divine Spirit.

(22) **Cornelius the centurion.**—The description seems to imply that the name of the soldier-convert

report among all the nation of the Jews,
was warned from God by an holy angel
to send for thee into his house, and to
hear words of thee. (23) Then called he
them in, and lodged *them.* And on the
morrow Peter went away with them,
and certain brethren from Joppa accom-
panied him. (24) And the morrow after
they entered into Cæsarea. And Cor-
nelius waited for them, and had called
together his kinsmen and near friends.
(25) And as Peter was coming in, Corne-
lius met him, and fell down at his feet,
and worshipped *him.* (26) But Peter
took him up, saying, Stand up; I my-
self also am a man. (27) And as he
talked with him, he went in, and found
many that were come together. (28) And
he said unto them, Ye know how that it
is an unlawful thing for a man that is a
Jew to keep company, or come unto one
of another nation; but God hath shewed
me that I should not call any man
common or unclean. (29) Therefore came
I *unto you* without gainsaying, as soon
as I was sent for: I ask therefore for

---

was not altogether unknown at Joppa. It could not fail to remind Peter of that other centurion whose name is not recorded, who was stationed at Capernaum, and had built the synagogue (Luke vii. 5), and with that recollection there would come back to his memory the words which his Master had spoken in connection with the faith which was greater than he had found in Israel, and which proclaimed that "many should come from east and west and north and south, and sit down with Abraham and Isaac and Jacob in the kingdom of God" (Matt. viii. 11).

**One that feareth God.**—The word was almost a technical one as describing the Gentile converts who stood in the position of "proselytes of the gate." (Comp. verses 2, 35; chap. xiii. 16.)

**Of good report among all the nation of the Jews.**—St. Luke's policy of conciliation, if one may so speak, is traceable in the stress laid on this fact. As in the case of the reception of the Apostle of the Gentiles by Ananias (chap. ix. 10), so in that of Cornelius, all occasion of offence was, as far as possible, guarded against by the attestation given by those who were themselves Jews to the character of those concerned.

(23) **Then called he them in.**—As it was about noon when Peter went up to the house-top to pray, the arrival of the messengers, allowing an adequate interval for the trance and the vision, may be placed at some time in the afternoon.

**Certain brethren from Joppa.**—We learn from chap. xi. 12, that they were six in number. They were obviously taken that "in the mouth of two or three witnesses every word might be established" (Deut. xvii. 6; xix. 15), that they might report to the Church at Joppa what had been done by the Apostle whom they had learnt to reverence.

(24) **His kinsmen and near friends.**—These, we may well believe, were, like the soldiers and slaves under his command, more or less in sympathy with Cornelius. He, at all events, was seeking to bring them also within the range of the new illumination which he was expecting to receive.

(25) **Fell down at his feet, and worshipped him.**—The attitude was the extremest form of Eastern homage. So Jairus had bowed down before Jesus (Matt. ix. 18), so St. John bowed before the angel (Rev. xxii. 8). Peter's answer, in strong contrast with the words and acts, the very ceremonial, of those who claim to be his successors, shows that he looked on it as expressing a homage such as God alone could rightly claim. For man to require or receive it from man was an inversion of the true order. The language of the angel in Rev. xxii. 9—"See thou do it not: for I am thy fellow-servant . . . worship God"—implies the same truth. Both bear their witness, all the more important because not controversial, against any *cultus* of saints or angels that tends to efface the distinction between man and God. We must not pass over the parallelism between St. Peter's words and those of St. Paul at Lystra, "We also are men of like passions with yourselves" (chap. xiv. 15).

(27) **And as he talked with him.**—The word implies a conversation of some length; possibly, as the sequel seems to show, leading to the resolve that each should state separately how they, who had previously been strangers to each other, had thus been brought together.

(28) **Ye know how that it is an unlawful thing.**—St. Peter speaks from the standpoint of traditional Pharisaism rather than from that of the Law itself; but the feeling was widely diffused, and showed itself in forms more or less rigorous wherever Jews and heathens came in contact with each other. The strict Jew would not enter a Gentile's house, nor sit on the same couch, nor eat or drink out of the same vessel. (Comp. Note on Mark vii. 3, 4.) The very dust of a heathen city was defiling. The Hindoo feeling of caste, shrinking from contact with those of a lower grade, driven to madness and mutiny by "greased cartridges," presents the nearest modern analogue.

**God hath shewed me that I should not call any man common or unclean.**—The Apostle had, we find, at last learnt the lesson which the vision had taught him, in all the fulness of its meaning. Humanity as such had been redeemed by the Incarnation and Ascension, and was no longer common or unclean, even in the most outcast heathen. God was willing to receive all men. Sin alone was that which separated men from Him. Impurity was thought of as a moral, not a physical taint, and men were taught to see even in the sinner the potentialities of a higher life. He, too, had been redeemed, and might be justified and sanctified, and to him therefore honour and reverence were due as to one in whom the image of God was not utterly effaced, and might be restored to brightness. It is interesting, in this connection, to note the "Honour all men" of 1 Pet. ii. 17. It is obvious that the pride of class, resting on mere differences of culture, and showing itself in acts and words of contempt, is, from one point of view, even less excusable than that which at least imagined that it rested on a religious basis, while from another, it is less inveterate, and therefore more easily curable.

what intent ye have sent for me?
(30) And Cornelius said, Four days ago I
was fasting until this hour; and at the
ninth hour I prayed in my house, and,
behold, a man stood before me in bright
clothing, (31) and said, Cornelius, thy
prayer is heard, and thine alms are had
in remembrance in the sight of God.
(32) Send therefore to Joppa, and call
hither Simon, whose surname is Peter;
he is lodged in the house of *one* Simon
a tanner by the sea side: who, when he
cometh, shall speak unto thee. (33) Im-
mediately therefore I sent to thee; and
thou hast well done that thou art come.
Now therefore are we all here present
before God, to hear all things that are
commanded thee of God.

(34) Then Peter opened *his* mouth, and
said, Of a truth I perceive that God is
no respecter of persons:[a] (35) but in
every nation he that feareth him, and
worketh righteousness, is accepted with
him. (36) The word which *God* sent

[a] Deut. 10. 17; Rom. 2. 11; 1 Pet. 1. 17.

---

(30) **I was fasting until this hour.**—The hour is not stated, but the facts of the case imply that it could not have been much before noon, and may have been later. Assuming that Cornelius in his fasts observed the usage of devout Jews, we may think of his vision as having been on the second day of the week, and Peter's on the fifth. It is probable, accordingly, that the meeting in the house of Cornelius took place on the Sabbath. Allowing some hours for the conference, of which we have probably but a condensed report, the outpouring of the Spirit, the subsequent baptism, and the meal which must have followed on it, may have coincided with the beginning of the first day of the week.

**In bright clothing.**—The phrase is the same as that used by St. James (chap. ii. 2, 3). The same adjective is employed by St. John to describe the raiment of the angels (Rev. xv. 6), and of the bride of the Lamb (Rev. xix. 8).

(31) **Thy prayer is heard.**—The singular number gives a greater definiteness to the object of the prayer than in verse 4. It must have been, in the nature of the case, a prayer for fuller light and knowledge of the Truth. One who had heard, through Philip's work at Cæsarea, or, it may be, through the brother-officer who had been stationed at Capernaum (Luke vii. 2), of the teaching and the life of Jesus, and of the new society that acknowledged Him as its Head, may well have sought for guidance as to the special conditions of admission to that society. Philip was not as yet authorised to admit one who had not taken on himself the sign of the covenant of Israel. Was that an indispensable condition?

(33) **Thou hast well done.**—The peculiar turn of the phrase, in social usage, made it the expression, not of mere approval, but of heartfelt gratitude. (Comp. St. Paul's use of it in Phil. iv. 14.)

**Now therefore are we all here present.**—The words imply that the circle that had gathered round Cornelius were sharers in his solicitude, ready to comply with whatever might come to them as the command of God, and yet anxiously hoping that it might not impose upon them a burden too heavy to be borne.

(34) **Of a truth I perceive that God is no respecter of persons.**—In regard to all distinctions of social rank, or wealth, or knowledge, Peter had seen in his Master that absence of "respect of persons" which even His enemies acknowledged (Matt. xxii. 16; Luke xx. 21). St. James lays stress on that element of character, within the same limits, as essential to all who seek to be true disciples of the Christ (Jas. ii. 1—7). Both, however, needed to be taught that the same law of an impartial equity had a yet wider application, that the privileges and prerogatives of Israel, whatever blessings they might confer, were not to be set up as a barrier against the admission of other races to an equal fellowship in Christ. God had accepted the centurion. It remained for His servants to accept him also. It is instructive to note that St. Paul reproduces the same thought in nearly the same phrase (Rom. ii. 11).

(35) **In every nation he that feareth him.**—The great truth which Peter thus proclaimed is obviously far-reaching in its range. It applies, not to those only who know the name of Christ and believe on Him when He is preached to them, but to all who in all ages and countries "fear God" according to the measure of their knowledge, and "work righteousness" according to their belief and opportunities. The good works in such a case, are, in their measure and degree, as "fruits of faith, and follow after justification" (Article XII.), justification having been, in such cases, objectively bestowed for the merits of Christ, and subjectively appropriated by the faith which, in the Providence of God, was possible under the conditions of the case. They do not come under the head of "works done before the grace of Christ and the inspiration of His Spirit" (Article XIII.), for Christ is "the true Light that lighteth every man that cometh into the world" (John i. 9), and the Spirit is to every man "the Lord, and giver of life," and the works are done "as God hath willed and commanded them to be done." What such men gain by conversion is a fuller knowledge of the Truth, and therefore a clearer faith, a fuller justification, and a higher blessedness, but as this history distinctly teaches, they are already accepted with God. They are saved, "not by the law or sect which they profess" (Article XVIII.), but, even though they know not the Name whereby they must be saved (chap. iv. 12), by Christ, who is the Saviour of all. The truth which St. Peter thus set forth proclaims at once the equity and the love of the Father, and sweeps away the narrowing dreams which confine the hope of salvation to the circumcised, as did the theology of the Rabbis; or to those who have received the outward ordinance of baptism, as did the theology of Augustine and the Mediæval Church; or, as do some forms of Protestant dogmatism, to those who have heard and believed the story of the Cross of Christ. The language of St. Paul in Rom. x. 9—14 should, however, be compared with this, as showing that the higher knowledge brings with it an incomparably higher blessedness, and that the man first tastes the full meaning of "salvation" when he consciously calls on the Lord by whom he has been saved.

(36) **The word which God sent . . .**—The structure of the sentence, beginning with the object

unto the children of Israel, preaching
peace by Jesus Christ: (he is Lord of
all:)
(37) that word, *I say*, ye know,
which was published throughout all
Judæa, and began from Galilee, after
the baptism which John preached;
(38) how God anointed Jesus of Nazareth
with the Holy Ghost and with power:
who went about doing good, and healing
all that were oppressed of the devil;
for God was with him.
(39) And we are
witnesses of all things which he did
both in the land of the Jews, and in
Jerusalem; whom they slew and hanged
on a tree:
(40) him God raised up the
third day, and shewed him openly;
(41) not to all the people, but unto witnesses chosen before of God, *even* to us,
who did eat and drink with him after
he rose from the dead.
(42) And he
commanded us to preach unto the
people, and to testify that it is he which
was ordained of God *to be* the Judge of
quick and dead.
(43) To him give all

---

and carried on though a series of clauses, is both in the Greek and English somewhat complicated, but it is characteristically like that of St. Peter's speech in chap. ii. 22—24, whether the actual form in which both now appear is due to the speaker or the reporter. It is possible, though the construction is less natural, that "the word which God sent" may look backward to the verb "I perceive" and not to the "ye know" of verse 37.

**Preaching peace.**—Better, as reproducing with the Greek the thought and language of Isa. lii. 7, *preaching glad tidings of peace.*

**He is Lord of all.**—The parenthesis is significant as guarding against the thought which Cornelius might have entertained, that the Jesus of whom he heard as the Christ was only a Prophet and a Teacher. Peter, still holding the truth which had been revealed to him, not by flesh and blood, but by his Father in heaven (Matt. xvi. 17), proclaims that He was none other than the "Lord of all," of all men, and of all things.

(37) **That word, I say, ye know.**—The Greek for "word" differs from that in verse 36, as including more distinctly the subject-matter of the message. In the words "ye know" we may trace the result of the conversation held before the more formal conference. The main facts of the life and ministry of the Christ were already known, either through that conversation, or through the previous opportunities which it had disclosed. The question at issue was the relation in which they stood to those who were now listening.

(38) **How God anointed Jesus of Nazareth.**—In the Greek structure the name stands in apposition with the "word" in the two previous verses—"Jesus of Nazareth, how God anointed him." The word "anointed" is used with distinct reference to the name of Christ in verse 35, and assumes a knowledge of the facts connected with His baptism, as in Matt. iii. 16, Mark i. 10, Luke iii. 21, 22, as the divine witness that that Name belonged of right to Him and to no other.

**Healing all that were oppressed of the devil.**—The words seem to us to refer specially to the works of healing performed on demoniacs, but were probably uttered with a wider range of meaning, all disease being thought of as the work directly or indirectly of the great enemy. So Satan had bound the woman with a spirit of infirmity (Luke xiii. 11). So St. Paul's "thorn in the flesh" was a messenger of Satan to buffet him (2 Cor. xii. 7).

(39) **And we are witnesses of all things.**—The Apostle still keeps before him the main idea of his mission as laid down in the command given by his Lord (chap. i. 8).

**Both in the land of the Jews.**—Speaking as St. Peter did at Cæsarea, and as a Galilean, we must probably take the word in its narrower sense as meaning the inhabitants of Judæa. So taken, the words have the interest of implying the ministry in Judæa, of which the first three Gospels record so little, but which comes out into full prominence in the fourth. (See *Introduction to St. John's Gospel.*)

**Whom they slew and hanged on a tree.**—As in chap. ii. 23, Peter represents the Crucifixion as virtually the act of the rulers and people of Jerusalem, and not of the Roman governor. The mode of death is described as in the Greek of Deut. xxviii. 26 and in Gal. iii. 10, rather than in the more technical language of the Gospels.

(40) **And shewed him openly.**—Literally, *gave him to be manifest.*

(41) **Unto witnesses chosen before.**—Better, *appointed.* The precise word which St. Luke uses occurs nowhere else in the New Testament, but is connected with the word rendered "ordained" in chap. xiv. 23.

**Who did eat and drink with him.**—The three recorded instances of this are found in Luke xxiv. 30, 42; John xxi. 13. This was, of course, the crucial test which showed that the Form on which the disciples had looked was no phantom of the imagination.

(42) **And he commanded us to preach unto the people.** No such command is found in terms in the Gospel narratives of the words of the risen Lord, but it is partly implied in Matt. xxviii. 18—20, and is covered by the general teaching as to the things of the kingdom of God in chap. i. 3. It is interesting to note that St. Peter and St. Paul agree in thus connecting the Resurrection with the assurance that He who had risen was to be the future Judge of all men. (Comp. chap. xvii. 31.)

**Which was ordained.**—More accurately, *which has been ordained.*

(43) **To him give all the prophets witness.**—As in St. Peter's earlier speeches in chap. ii. and iii. so here, we trace the result of our Lord's teaching given in the interval between the Resurrection and Ascension as to the method of prophetic interpretation which discerns, below all temporary and historical references, the under-current of testimony to the kingdom of which Christ was the Head.

**That through his name . . . .**—We can without difficulty represent to ourselves the impression which these words must have made on the anxious listeners. This was the answer to their doubts and perplexities. Not by submitting themselves to the bondage of the Law, not by circumcision and all that it implied, but by the simple act of faith in Christ, and in the power of

the prophets witness,[a] that through his
name whosoever believeth in him shall
receive remission of sins.
(44) While Peter yet spake these words,
the Holy Ghost fell on all them which
heard the word. (45) And they of the
circumcision which believed were astonished, as many as came with Peter,
because that on the Gentiles also was
poured out the gift of the Holy Ghost.
(46) For they heard them speak with
tongues, and magnify God. Then answered Peter, (47) Can any man forbid
water, that these should not be baptized,
which have received the Holy Ghost as
well as we? (48) And he commanded
them to be baptized in the name of
the Lord. Then prayed they him to
tarry certain days.

a Jer. 31. 34; Mic. 7. 18.

A.D. 41.

CHAPTER XI.—(1) And the apostles
and brethren that were in Judæa heard
that the Gentiles had also received the
word of God. (2) And when Peter was
come up to Jerusalem, they that were
of the circumcision contended with him,

---

His Name, *i.e.*, of all the attributes and energies of which the Name was the symbol, they, Gentiles as they were, might receive that remission of sins which conscience, now roused to its full activity, taught them was the indispensable condition of acceptance and of peace. The intensity of that emotion, the satisfaction of all their previous yearnings, placed them subjectively in a spiritual condition which prepared the way for the wonder which the next verse narrates.

(44) **The Holy Ghost fell on all them which heard the word.**—The words imply a sudden thrill of spiritual joy and elevation which showed itself, as it had done on the Day of Pentecost (see Note on chap. ii. 4), in a burst of unpremeditated praise. Now, as then, the "tongues" manifested themselves, not as instruments of teaching, but in "magnifying God." As there is no mention here of the utterance of praise being in any other language than those with which the speakers were familiar, there is no ground for assuming that this feature of the Pentecostal gift was reproduced, and the jubilant ecstatic praise which was the essence of that gift must be thought of as corresponding to the phenomena described in 1 Cor. xiv. 7—9.

(45) **And they of the circumcision which believed . . .**—St. Luke obviously dwells on this as a testimony, beyond suspicion, to the reality of the gift. Those who came with Peter were apparently not sharers at the time in the exultant joy which they were yet compelled to recognise as the Spirit's work. They listened with amazement as they heard the rapturous chant burst from the lips of the as yet unbaptised heathens. Here, accordingly, was one definite fulfilment of Peter's vision. Those who so spake had been, as it were, carried up into heaven, as the four-footed beasts and creeping things had been, and so a proof was given that no man might henceforth call them common or unclean. Peter himself had indeed learnt that lesson so fully (verse 28) as not to need this special attestation, but for those who came with him this evidence was needed and was sufficient.

(47) **Can any man forbid water . . .**—The question was an appeal to the voice of reason. Could the outward sign be refused, when thus the inward and spiritual grace had been so manifestly bestowed? Ordinarily, as in the case of the Samaritans (chap. viii. 15—17), the gift of spiritual powers followed, by the subsequent act of laying on of hands, on the grace given in baptism. Now even that gift had been anticipated, and all that remained was the outward act of incorporation with the society which owned Christ as its Head. While the history thus bore its witness that the gifts of God may flow through other channels than the outward forms which Christ had appointed, it testified no less clearly that no spiritual gifts, however marvellous, superseded the necessity of obedience to the law of Christ which had appointed those outward forms. The exceptional gift was bestowed, in this instance, to remove the scruples which "those of the circumcision" might otherwise have felt as to admitting Gentiles, as such, to baptism; and having served that purpose, as a crucial instance, was never afterwards, so far as we know, repeated under like conditions.

(48) **And he commanded them . . .**—It would seem from this that St. Peter acted on the same general principle as St. Paul (1 Cor. i. 14—17), and left the actual administration of baptism to other hands than his own. Who administered it in this instance we are not told. Possibly there may have been an *ecclesia* already organised at Cæsarea, as the result of Philip's work, and its elders or deacons, or Philip himself, may have acted under Peter's orders. If those who came with him from Joppa had so acted, it would probably we may believe, have been stated.

**Then prayed they him to tarry certain days.**—The days so spent must have included at least one "first day of the week," and both in the solemn breaking of bread, and in the social intercourse of the other days, Peter must have mingled freely with the new converts, eating and drinking with them (chap. xi. 2), without any fear of being thereby defiled. That visit to Cæsarea, St. Luke dwells on as one of the great turning-points in the Apostle's life, attesting his essential agreement with St. Paul. We can well understand how he shrank from marring the effect of that attestation by recording the melancholy inconsistency of his subsequent conduct at Antioch (Gal. ii. 11, 12).

XI.

(1) **And the apostles and brethren that were in Judæa . . .**—The context implies that the tidings travelled, while Peter remained at Cæsarea, first probably to Joppa and Lydda, and afterwards to Jerusalem.

(2) **They that were of the circumcision contended with him.**—The conversion of the Gentiles at Cæsarea had given a new significance to the name of "those of the circumcision." From this time forth they are a distinct section, often a distinct party, in the Church, and here we have the first symptom of the line which they were about to take. They contended with Peter (the tense implies continuous or repeated discussion) because he had eaten with those who were uncircumcised, and therefore, from the Jewish point of view, unclean.

(3) saying, Thou wentest in to men un-
circumcised, and didst eat with them.
(4) But Peter rehearsed *the matter* from
the beginning, and expounded *it* by
order unto them, saying, (5) I was in the
city of Joppa praying: and in a trance
I saw a vision, A certain vessel de-
scend, as it had been a great sheet, let
down from heaven by four corners; and
it came even to me: (6) upon the which
when I had fastened mine eyes, I con-
sidered, and saw fourfooted beasts of
the earth, and wild beasts, and creeping
things, and fowls of the air. (7) And I
heard a voice saying unto me, Arise,
Peter; slay and eat. (8) But I said, Not
so, Lord: for nothing common or un-
clean hath at any time entered into my
mouth. (9) But the voice answered me
again from heaven, What God hath
cleansed, *that* call not thou common.
(10) And this was done three times: and
all were drawn up again into heaven.

*a* ch. 2. 4.

*b* John 1. 26.

(11) And, behold, immediately there were
three men already come unto the house
where I was, sent from Cæsarea unto
me. (12) And the spirit bade me go with
them, nothing doubting. Moreover these
six brethren accompanied me, and we
entered into the man's house: (13) and
he shewed us how he had seen an angel
in his house, which stood and said
unto him, Send men to Joppa, and call
for Simon, whose surname is Peter;
(14) who shall tell thee words, whereby
thou and all thy house shall be saved.
(15) And as I began to speak, the Holy
Ghost fell on them, as on us at the
beginning.[a] (16) Then remembered I the
word of the Lord, how that he said,
John indeed baptized with water;[b] but
ye shall be baptized with the Holy
Ghost. (17) Forasmuch then as God
gave them the like gift as *he did* unto
us, who believed on the Lord Jesus
Christ; what was I, that I could with-

---

(3) **Thou wentest in to men uncircumcised.**—The words cannot well be translated otherwise, but the Greek (literally, *men with a foreskin*) is somewhat more expressive of scorn than the merely negative form of the English. The same word is commonly used by St. Paul where he discusses the relation between circumcision and uncircumcision (Rom. ii. 25, 26; iv. 9, 10; 1 Cor. vii. 18, 19, *et al.*).

(4) **But Peter rehearsed the matter from the beginning.**—Better, perhaps, the word "rehearse" having grown into a different shade of meaning, *began and set forth the matter.* The translators seem to have paraphrased the participle "having begun" somewhat more fully than its actual meaning admits. The almost verbal repetition of the same narrative as that of chap. x. seems, at first sight, inconsistent with our common standard of skill in composition. The probable explanation of it is that St. Luke obtained the first narrative from the disciples whom he met at Cæsarea, and the second from those of Jerusalem, and that the close agreement of the two seemed to him, as indeed it was, a confirmation of the truth of each.

(5) **It came even to me.**—The variations in the narrative are few and of little importance. There is, perhaps, a touch of the vividness of personal recollection in the description of the sheet as coming "even to me," as compared with its being let down "to the earth" in chap. x. 11.

(6) **Upon the which when I had fastened mine eyes, I considered.**—Here again we trace the same kind of vividness as in the previous verse. The Apostle recalls the intense eager gaze with which he had looked on the strange vision.

(10) **All were drawn up again into heaven.**—Once more there is a slight increase of vividness in the word which expresses a rapid upward movement, as compared with "the vessel was received up into heaven," in chap. x. 16.

(12) **The spirit bade me go with them, nothing doubting.**—The Greek verb has a special force as being the same as that for "contended" in verse 2. Peter, guided by the Spirit, raised no debate such as they were raising.

(14) **Whereby thou and all thy house shall be saved.**—The words are not found in the report of the angel's speech in chap. x. 4—6, but may legitimately be thought of as implied in it. The prayer of Cornelius had been for salvation, and when he was told, in answer to that prayer, to send for one who should speak to him, it must have been clear to him that he was to hear of that way of salvation which he had been seeking.

(15) **And as I began to speak . . .**—It is, perhaps, a trait of individual character that the Apostle speaks of what is recorded in chap. x. 34—43 as the mere beginning of what he had meant to say.

**As on us at the beginning.**—The words are spoken, it will be remembered, to apostles and disciples who had been sharers in the Pentecostal gift. St. Peter bears his witness that what he witnessed at Cæsarea was not less manifestly the Spirit's work than what they had then experienced.

(16) **Then remembered I the word of the Lord.**—The special promise referred to was that recorded in chap. i. 5. Then it had seemed to refer only to the disciples, and the Day of Pentecost had appeared to bring a complete fulfilment of it. Now Peter had learnt to see that it had a wider range, that the gift might be bestowed on those who were not of Israel, and who were not called to come outwardly within the covenant of Israel. If the baptism of the Holy Ghost had been thus given to them it implied, as the greater includes the less, that they were admissible to the baptism of water.

(17) **Forasmuch then . . .**—More accurately, *If then.*

**Unto us, who believed on the Lord Jesus Christ.**—The Greek construction gives a somewhat different meaning: *If then God gave to them an equal gift as to us, upon their believing . . .* That condition was sufficient in their case for the greater

stand God? (18) When they heard these
things, they held their peace, and
glorified God, saying, Then hath God
also to the Gentiles granted repentance
unto life.
(19) Now they which were scattered
abroad upon the persecution that arose
about Stephen[a] travelled as far as
Phenice, and Cyprus, and Antioch,
preaching the word to none but unto
the Jews only. (20) And some of them
were men of Cyprus and Cyrene, which,
when they were come to Antioch, spake
unto the Grecians, preaching the Lord

a ch. 8. 1.

gifts, and their admissibility to baptism and to general fellowship followed naturally as a thing of course.

**What was I, that I could withstand God?**—The Greek gives a complex question, *Who was I? Able to withstand God?—i.e.,* How was I, being such a one as I am, able to withstand?

(18) **They held their peace, and glorified God.**—The difference of tenses in the two Greek verbs implies that they first held their peace, and then began a continuous utterance of praise. The fact was obviously one of immense importance in its bearing on the question at issue between St. Paul and the Judaisers, of which St. Luke had seen so much and which he sought, by his narrative, to settle. Not only had the first step in the free admission of the Gentiles been taken by the chief of the Apostles, and under direct guidance from above, but it had received the formal approval of the Apostles and other members of the Church of the Circumcision at Jerusalem. The Judaisers, in opposing St. Paul, were acting against the Church from which they pretended to derive their authority.

(19) **Now they which were scattered abroad.**—A new and important section begins with these words. We are carried back to the date of the persecution of which Stephen was the chief victim.

**The persecution that arose about Stephen.**—The MSS. vary in their reading, some giving the case which would be rendered by "the persecution *in the time of* Stephen;" some, that which answers to the persecution *upon* or *against* or *after* Stephen. The death of the martyr was followed, as chap. viii. 1—4 shows, by a general outburst of fanaticism against the disciples, and this led to a comparatively general flight. It was probable, in the nature of the case, that the Hellenistic or Greek-speaking Jews who had been associated with Stephen would be the chief sufferers. Philip we have traced in Samaria and Cæsarea; others went to Phœnice, *i.e.*, to the cities of Tyre and Sidon and Ptolemais, and were probably the founders of the churches which we find there in chaps. xxi. 4—7, xxvii. 3. In Cyprus (see Note on chap. xiii. 4, for an account of the island) they prepared the way for the work of Barnabas and Paul.

**And Antioch.**—We have here the first direct point of contact between the Church of Christ and the great Syrian capital which was for so many years one of its chief centres. We may, perhaps, think of the proselyte of Antioch (chap. vi. 5) who had been one of Stephen's colleagues as one of those who brought the new faith to his native city. It was, as the sequel shows, a moment of immense importance. Situated on the Orontes, about fifteen miles from the port of Seleucia, the city, founded by Seleucus Nicator, and named after his father Antiochus, had grown in wealth and magnificence till it was one of the "eyes" of Asia. Its men of letters and rhetoricians (among them the poet Archias, in whose behalf Cicero made one of his most memorable orations) had carried its fame to Rome itself, and the Roman Satirist complained that the Syrian Orontes had polluted his native Tiber with the tainted stream of luxury and vice (Juvenal, *Sat.* iii. 62—64). It had a large colony of Jews, and Herod the Great had courted the favour of its inhabitants by building a marble colonnade which ran the whole length of the city. It became the head-quarters of the Prefect or President of Syria, and the new faith was thus brought into more direct contact with the higher forms of Roman life than it had been at Jerusalem or Cæsarea. There also it came into more direct conflict with heathenism in its most tempting and most debasing forms. The groves of Daphne, in the outskirts of the city, were famous for a worship which in its main features resembled that of Aphrodite at Corinth. An annual festival was held, known as the *Maiuma*, at which the harlot-priestesses, stripped of clothing, disported themselves in the waters of a lake. The city was stained with the vices of a reckless and shameless sensuality. It was as one of the strongholds of Satan; and we have to trace, as it were, the stages of the victory which transformed it into the mother-church of the Gentiles.

**Preaching the word to none but unto the Jews only.**—Better, as answering to the singular number in the Greek, *to no one*. This was, of course, to be expected in the work of those who had left Jerusalem before the conversion of Cornelius had ruled the case otherwise. The fact is stated, apparently, in contrast both with the narrative that precedes and the statement that immediately follows.

(20) **And some of them were men of Cyprus and Cyrene.**—Better, *But some*. These were, from the nature of the case, Hellenistic or Greek-speaking Jews. Who they were we can only conjecture. Possibly Lucius of Cyrene, who appears in the list of prophets in chap. xiii. 1; possibly Simon of Cyrene, of whom we have seen reason to think as a disciple of Christ. (See Notes on Matt. xxvii. 32; Mark xv. 21.) The founders of the Church of Antioch, like those of the Church of Rome, must remain unknown.

**Spake unto the Grecians.**—The MSS. present the two readings—*Hellenistæ*, Greek-speaking Jews, and *Hellenes*, Greeks or Gentiles by descent. As far as their authority is concerned, the two stand nearly on the same level, the balance inclining slightly in favour of *Hellenistæ*, which is found in MSS. B and D, while A gives *Hellenes*. The Sinaitic has the almost incomprehensible reading "they spake unto the *Evangelistæ*," which is obviously wrong, but which, so far as it goes, must be thrown into the scale in favour of *Hellenistæ*, as the word which the transcriber had before him, and which he misread or misheard. If we receive that reading, then we must suppose St. Luke to lay stress upon the fact that the preachers of whom he speaks, instead of speaking to the Jews at large, many of whom, being Syrians, would speak Aramaic, addressed themselves specially to the Greek-speaking Jews and proselytes, and were thus following in St. Stephen's footsteps, and indirectly preparing the way for St. Paul—the Hellenistæ being, as a body, the link between the Jews as a race and the Hellenes. On the whole, however, internal evidence seems to turn the scale

Jesus. (21) And the hand of the Lord
was with them: and a great number
believed, and turned unto the Lord.
(22) Then tidings of these things came
unto the ears of the church which
was in Jerusalem: and they sent forth
Barnabas, that he should go as far as
Antioch. (23) Who, when he came, and
had seen the grace of God, was glad,
and exhorted them all, that with pur-
pose of heart they would cleave unto
the Lord. (24) For he was a good man,
A.D. 42. and full of the Holy Ghost and of faith:
and much people was added unto the
A.D. 43. Lord. (25) Then departed Barnabas to
Tarsus, for to seek Saul: (26) and when
he had found him, he brought him unto
Antioch. And it came to pass, that a

---

in favour of the other reading. (1) As the Hellenistæ were "Jews," though not "Hebrews," they would naturally be included in the statement of verse 19, and so there would be no contrast, no new advance, indicated in verse 20 in the statement that the word was spoken to them. (2) The contrast between Jews and Hellenes is, on the other hand, as in chaps. xiv. 1, xviii. 4, a perfectly natural and familiar one, and assuming this to be the true reading, we get a note of progress which otherwise we should miss, there being no record elsewhere of the admission of the Gentiles at Antioch. (3) It does not necessarily follow, however, that the Hellenes who are spoken of had been heathen idolaters up to the time of their conversion. Probably, as in chap. xviii. 4, they were more or less on the same level as Cornelius, proselytes of the gate, attending the services of the synagogue. (4) The question whether this preceded or followed the conversion of Cornelius is one which we have not sufficient *data* for deciding. On the one hand, the brief narrative of verse 19 suggests the thought of an interval as long as that between the death of Stephen and St. Peter's visit to Cæsarea, and it may have been part of the working of God's providence that there should be simultaneous and parallel advances. On the other, the language of those of the circumcision to Peter in verse 3, implies that they had not heard of such a case before; and that of the Apostle himself, in chap. xv. 7, distinctly claims the honour of having been the first (possibly, however, only the first among the disciples at Jerusalem) from whose lips the Gentiles, as such, had heard the word of the gospel. On the whole, therefore, it seems probable that the work went on at Antioch for many months among the Hellenistic and other Jews, and that the men of Cyprus and Cyrene arrived after the case of Cornelius had removed the scruples which had hitherto restrained them from giving full scope to the longings of their heart. We must not forget, however, that there was one to whom the Gospel of the Uncircumcision, the Gospel of Humanity, had been already revealed in its fulness (chap. xx. 21; Gal. i. 11, 12), and we can hardly think of him as waiting, after that revelation, for any decision of the Church of Jerusalem. His action, at any rate, must have been parallel and independent, and may have been known to, and followed by, other missionaries.

**Preaching the Lord Jesus.**—As before, *preaching the glad tidings of the Lord Jesus.*

(22) **They sent forth Barnabas.**—The choice was probably determined, we may believe, by the known sympathies of the Son of Consolation for the work which was going on at Antioch. The friend of Paul, who had been with him when he was at Jerusalem (chap. ix. 27), must have known his hopes and convictions on this matter, and must have welcomed the opening which was thus given him for working in the same direction. The fact that he was himself of the same country would also qualify him for co-operating with the men of Cyprus, who were carrying on that work in Antioch.

(23) **And exhorted them all.**—The tense implies continuous action; and the verb in the Greek is that from which Barnabas took his name as the "Son of Comfort" or "Counsel." (See Note on chap. iv. 36.)

**With purpose of heart.**—The preacher had seen the grace of God, and had rejoiced at it; but he knew, as all true teachers know, that it is possible for man's will to frustrate that grace, and that its co-operation, as manifested in deliberate and firm resolve, was necessary to carry on the good work to its completion. The word for "purpose" meets us again in chap. xxvii. 13.

**They would cleave unto the Lord.**—The noun is probably used in its dominant New Testament sense, as pointing to the Lord Jesus as the new object of the faith and love of those who had turned to Him.

(24) **For he was a good man.**—Words of praise of this kind are comparatively rare in this history, and we may, perhaps, think of them here as expressing St. Luke's personal estimate of the character of the preacher, which he was all the more anxious to place on record because he had to narrate before long the sad contention which separated him from his friend and fellow-worker (chap. xv. 39). The word "good" is probably to be taken as presenting the more winning and persuasive form of holiness, as contrasted with the severer forms of simple justice. (Comp. Rom. v. 7.)

**Full of the Holy Ghost.**—This was implied in his very name as "the Son of Prophecy" (see Note on chap. iv. 31); but it is interesting to note that the words are identical with those in which the historian had previously described Stephen (chap. vi. 5). Barnabas appeared to him to reproduce the mind and character of the martyr.

**Much people.**—Literally, *a great multitude*, implying a large increase upon the work related in verse 21.

(25) **Then departed Barnabas to Tarsus.**—The act is every way significant. It indicates the assurance that Saul would approve of the work which had been going on at Antioch, and the confident belief that he was the right person to direct and organise it. It probably implies also some intercourse with the Apostle, by letter or message, since his departure from Jerusalem. In the absence of any direct record, we can only infer that Saul had remained at Tarsus, carrying on his occupation as a tent-maker (chap. xviii. 3), and preaching the gospel there and in the neighbouring cities of Cilicia (see Note on chap. xv. 41) "to the Jew first and also to the Gentile." It is clear that he must have heard of the grace of God that had been manifested at Antioch with great joy, and accepted the invitation to join in the work there with a ready gladness.

(26) **The disciples were called Christians first in Antioch.**—The term for "were called" is not the word usually so rendered. Better, perhaps

whole year they assembled themselves with the church,[1] and taught much people. And the disciples were called Christians first in Antioch.

(27) And in these days came prophets from Jerusalem unto Antioch. (28) And there stood up one of them named Agabus, and signified by the spirit that there should be great dearth throughout all the world: which came to pass in the days of Claudius Cæsar. (29) Then the disciples, every man according to his ability, determined to send relief unto the brethren which dwelt in Judæa: (30) which also they did, and sent it to the elders by the hands of Barnabas and Saul.

[1] Or, *in the church.*

---

*got the name of Christians.* The Emperor Julian (*Misopog.*, p. 344) notes the tendency to invent nicknames, as a form of satire, as characteristic of the population of Antioch in his time, and the same tone of *persiflage* seems to have prevailed on the first appearance of the new faith. The origin of a name which was afterwards to be so mighty in the history of the world is a subject full of interest. In its form it was essentially Latin, after the pattern of the *Pompeiani, Sullani*, and other party-names; and so far it would seem to have grown out of the contact of the new society with the Romans stationed at Antioch, who, learning that its members acknowledged the *Christos* as their head, gave them the name of *Christiani.* In the Gospels, it is true, however (Matt. xxii. 16, *et al.*), we find the analogous term of *Herodiani*, but there, also, we may legitimately trace the influence of Roman associations. As used in the New Testament, we note (1) that the disciples never use it of themselves. They keep to such terms as the "brethren" (chap. xv. 1), and the "saints" (chap. ix. 13), and "those of the way" (chap. ix. 2). (2) That the hostile Jews use the more scornful term of "Nazarenes" (chap. xxiv. 5). (3) That the term *Christianus* is used as a neutral and sufficiently respectful word by Agrippa in chap. xxvi. 23, and at a somewhat later date, when it had obviously gained a wider currency, as that which brought with it the danger of suffering and persecution (1 Pet. iv. 16). It was natural that a name first given by outsiders should soon be accepted by believers as a title in which to glory. Tradition ascribes its origin to Euodius, the first Bishop of Antioch (Bingham, *Ant.* II. i. § 4), and Ignatius, his successor, uses it frequently, and forms from it the hardly less important word of *Christianismos*, as opposed to *Judaismos* (*Philadelph.* c. 6), and as expressing the whole system of faith and life which we know as "Christianity." It may be worth while to note that another ecclesiastical term, hardly less important in the history of Christendom, seems also to have originated at Antioch, and that we may trace to it the name of *Catholic* as well as *Christian* (Ignatius, *Smyrn.* c. 8). We learn from Tertullian (*Apol.* c. 3) that the name was often wrongly pronounced as *Chrestiani*, and its meaning not understood. Even the name of *Christos* was pronounced and explained as *Chrestos* (= good). The Christians, on their side, accepted the mistake as a *nomen et omen*, an unconscious witness on the part of the heathen that they were good and worthy in their lives, that their Lord was "good and gracious" (1 Pet. ii. 3).

(27) **Came prophets from Jerusalem.**—The mission thus described was obviously a further sanction given by the Church at Jerusalem to the work that Saul and Barnabas were carrying on at Antioch. If we adopt the view suggested in the Note on Luke x. 1, that the Seventy were the representatives of the prophetic order, and were symbolically significant of the conversion of the Gentiles, it will seem probable that those who now came to Antioch belonged to that body, and rejoiced in what they found there as fulfilling the idea of their own commission.

(28) **There stood up one of them named Agabus.**—The same prophet appears again in chap. xxi. 10 as coming down from Jerusalem to Cæsarea. Nothing more is known of him. The prophecy of the "dearth" or "famine" was in part an echo of Matt. xxiv. 7.

**Throughout all the world.**—Literally, *the inhabited earth*, used, as in Luke ii. 1, iv. 5, and elsewhere in the New Testament, for the Roman empire.

**Which came to pass in the days of Claudius Cæsar.**—The reign of Caligula lasted from A.D. 37—41, that of Claudius from A.D. 41—54. The whole reign of the latter emperor was memorable for frequent famines (Suetonius, *Claud.* 28; Tacitus, *Ann.* xii. 43). Josephus (*Ant.* xx. 5) speaks of one as specially affecting Judæa and Syria, under the procuratorship of Cuspius Fadus, A.D. 45. The population of Jerusalem were reduced to great distress, and were chiefly relieved by the bounty of Helena, Queen of Adiabene, who sent in large supplies of corn, figs, and other articles of food. She was herself a proselyte to Judaism, and was the mother of Izates, whose probable conversion to the faith of Christ by Ananias of Damascus is mentioned in the Note on chap. ix. 10. The title of "Cæsar" is omitted in the better MSS.

(29) **Then the disciples, every man according to his ability.**—Literally, *as each man prospered.* It is obviously implied that the collection was made at once, as a provision against the famine, in consequence of the prophecy, before the famine itself came. We may well believe that Saul and Barnabas were active in stirring up the Gentiles to this work of charity. It was the beginning of that collection for the "poor saints at Jerusalem" which was afterwards so prominent in the Apostle's labours (chap. xxiv. 17; Rom. xv. 25, 26; 1 Cor. xvi. 1; 2 Cor. ix. 1—15; Gal. ii. 10), and which he regarded as a bond of union between the Jewish and Gentile sections of the Church. It is probable that the generous devotion and liberality of the converts of Jerusalem in the glow of their first love had left them more exposed than most others to the pressure of poverty, and that when the famine came it found them to a great extent dependent on the help of other churches.

**Determined to send relief.**—The Greek gives the more specific *to send as a ministration*, the half-technical word which St. Paul uses in Rom. xv. 31; 2 Cor. ix. 1.

(30) **And sent it to the elders by the hands of Barnabas and Saul.**—The elders of the Church are here named for the first time, and appear henceforth as a permanent element of its organisation, which in this respect followed the arrangements of the Synagogue. Officers filling like functions were known in the Gentile churches as Episcopi = Bishops, or Superintendents, and where Jews and Gentiles were mingled, the two names were interchangeable, as in chap. xx

A.D. 44.

CHAPTER XII.—(1) Now about that
time Herod the king stretched forth
*his* hands[1] to vex certain of the church.
(2) And he killed James the brother of
John with the sword. (3) And because
he saw it pleased the Jews, he proceeded further to take Peter also.
(Then were the days of unleavened

1 Or, *began.*

17, 18; Titus i. 5, 7. See also Notes on Phil. i. 1; 1 Pet. v. 1, 2. In St. James's Epistle (v. 14), written probably about this time, the "elders" are mentioned as visiting the sick, and anointing them with oil as a means of healing.

It may be noted that this visit to Jerusalem has been identified by some writers with that of which the Apostle speaks in Gal. ii. 1. It will be shown, however, in the Notes on chap. xv. that it is far more likely that he speaks of the journey there narrated. St. Luke would hardly have passed over the facts to which St. Paul refers, had they occurred on this occasion; nor are there any signs that the Pharisaic party had at this time felt strong enough to insist on the circumcision of the Gentile converts. It is probable that the journey would be timed so as to coincide with one of the Jewish festivals, and judging by the analogy of St. Paul's other visits, we may think of this as coinciding with that of Pentecost. (See Notes on chaps. xviii. 21; xx. 16.)

XII.

(1) **Herod the king.**—The previous life of this prince had been full of strange vicissitudes. The son of Aristobulus and Bernice, grandson of Herod the Great, brother of the Herodias who appears in the Gospel history, named after the statesman who was the chief minister of Augustus, he had been sent, after his father had fallen a victim (B.C. 6) to his grandfather's suspicions, to Rome, partly, perhaps, as a hostage, partly to be out of the way of Palestine intrigues. There he had grown up on terms of intimacy with the prince afterwards known as Caligula. On the marriage of Herod Antipas with his sister, he was made the ruler of Tiberias, but soon quarrelled with the Tetrarch and went to Rome, and falling under the displeasure of Tiberius, as having rashly given utterance to a wish for the succession of Caligula, was imprisoned by him and remained in confinement till the death of that emperor. When Caligula came to the throne, he loaded his friend with honours, gave him the tetrarchies first of Philip, and then that of Lysanias (Luke iii. 1), and conferred on him the title of King. Antipas, prompted by Herodias, came to Rome to claim a like honour for himself, but fell under the emperor's displeasure, and was banished to Lugdunum in Gaul, whither his wife accompanied him. His tetrarchy also was conferred on Agrippa. Coins are extant, minted at Cæsarea, and bearing inscriptions in which he is styled the Great King, with the epithets sometimes of Philo-Cæsar, sometimes of Philo-Claudios. At the time when Caligula's insanity took the form of a resolve to place his statue in the Temple at Jerusalem, Agrippa rendered an essential service to his people, by using all his influence to deter the emperor from carrying his purpose into execution, and, backed as he was by Petronius, the Governor of Syria, was at last successful. On the death of Caligula, Claudius, whose claims to the empire he had supported, confirmed him in his kingdom. When he came to Judæa, he presented himself to the people in the character of a devout worshipper, and gained their favour by attaching himself to the companies of Nazarites (as we find St. Paul doing in chap. xxi. 26) when they came to the Temple to offer sacrifices on the completion of their vows (Jos. *Ant.* xix. 7, § 3). It would seem that he found a strong popular excitement against the believers in Christ, caused probably by the new step which had recently been taken in the admission of the Gentiles, and fomented by the Sadducean priesthood, and it seemed to him politic to gain the favour of both priests and people, by making himself the instrument of their jealousy.

(2) **He killed James the brother of John with the sword.**—Had the Apostle been tried by the Sanhedrin on a charge of blasphemy and heresy, the sentence would have been death by stoning. Decapitation showed, as in the case of John the Baptist, that the sentence was pronounced by a civil ruler, adopting Roman modes of punishment, and striking terror by them in proportion as they were hateful to the Jews. The death of James reminds us of his Lord's prediction that he, too, should drink of His cup, and be baptised with His baptism (Matt. xx. 23). The fulfilment of that prophecy was found for one brother in his being the proto-martyr of the apostolic company, as it was found for the other in his being the last survivor of it. What led to his being selected as the first victim we can only conjecture; but the prominent position which he occupies in the Gospels, in company with Peter and John, probably continued, and the natural vehemence indicated in the name of Son of Thunder may have marked him out as among the foremost teachers of the Church. The brevity of St. Luke's record presents a marked contrast to the fulness of later martyrologies. A tradition preserved by Eusebius (*Hist.* ii. 9) as coming from Clement of Alexandria, records that his accuser was converted by beholding his faith and patience, confessed his new faith, and was led to execution in company with the Apostle, who bestowed on him the parting benediction of "Peace be with thee."

(3) **Because he saw it pleased the Jews.**—This was throughout the ruling policy of the Herodian house. The persecution did not spring from any fanatic zeal against the new faith, but simply from motives of political expediency. A somewhat touching incident is recorded, illustrating the king's sensitiveness to popular praise or blame. It was at the Feast of Tabernacles, and the Law was read, and he heard the words of Deut. xvii. 15: "Thou shalt not set a stranger over thee," and he burst into tears at the thought of his own Idumæan descent. The people saw him weeping, and cried out: "Trouble not thyself, Agrippa; thou also art our brother," and the king's heart was comforted (Jost, *Gesch. des Judenthums*, I., p. 420).

**Then were the days of unleavened bread.**—The crowds of Hellenistic and other Jews who were gathered to keep the feast at Jerusalem naturally made this a favourable opportunity for courting the favour of the people. A tradition recorded by St. Jerome states that St. James was beheaded on the 15th of Nisan, *i.e.*, on the same day as that of the Crucifixion. Peter was arrested probably at the same time; but the trial and execution were deferred till the seven days of the feast were over.

bread.) (4) And when he had appre-
hended him, he put *him* in prison, and
delivered *him* to four quaternions of
soldiers to keep him; intending after
Easter to bring him forth to the people.
(5) Peter therefore was kept in prison:
but prayer[1] was made without ceasing
of the church unto God for him.
(6) And when Herod would have brought
him forth, the same night Peter was
sleeping between two soldiers, bound
with two chains: and the keepers be-
fore the door kept the prison. (7) And,
behold, the angel of the Lord came
upon *him*, and a light shined in the
prison: and he smote Peter on the side,
and raised him up, saying, Arise up
quickly. And his chains fell off from
*his* hands. (8) And the angel said unto
him, Gird thyself, and bind on thy
sandals. And so he did. And he saith
unto him, Cast thy garment about thee,
and follow me. (9) And he went out,
and followed him; and wist not that it
was true which was done by the angel;
but thought he saw a vision. (10) When
they were past the first and the second
ward, they came unto the iron gate
that leadeth unto the city; which open-
ed to them of his own accord: and
they went out, and passed on through
one street; and forthwith the angel de-
parted from him. (11) And when Peter
was come to himself, he said, Now I
know of a surety, that the Lord hath
sent his angel, and hath delivered me
out of the hand of Herod, and *from* all
the expectation of the people of the
Jews. (12) And when he had considered
*the thing*, he came to the house of Mary
the mother of John, whose surname was
Mark; where many were gathered

1 *Or, instant and earnest prayer was made.*

(4) **Delivered him to four quaternions of soldiers.**—Agrippa apparently followed the lessons of Roman practice which he had learnt by his own experience. The four quaternions relieved each other at set times, and the prisoner was chained to two of the soldiers of each company, while the others were stationed as sentinels at the door of the dungeon. (Comp. St. Paul's chains in chap. xxviii. 20; Eph. vi. 20.)

**Intending after Easter.**—Better, *after the Passover*, as elsewhere. In this solitary instance the translators have introduced, with a singular infelicity, the term which was definitely appropriate only to the Christian festival which took the place of the Passover.

(5) **Prayer was made without ceasing.**—The adjective is rendered by "fervent" in 1 Pet. iv. 8, and implies, as in the marginal reading, intensity as well as continuity. The words imply that the members of the Church continued, in spite of the persecution, to meet as usual, probably, as in verse 12, in the house of Mary, the mother of Mark.

(6) **Peter was sleeping between two soldiers.**—The picture of the calm repose of the Apostle as of one to whom God had given the sleep of His beloved (Ps. cxxvii. 2), undisturbed by the fear of coming suffering and death, will be felt by most readers to be one of singular interest.

(7) **The angel of the Lord came upon him.**—The phrase is identical with that of Luke ii. 9. The absence of the article in the Greek leaves it open to render it either as "*the* angel" or "*an* angel." The "light" in this instance corresponds to the "glory of the Lord" in that.

**In the prison.**—Literally, *in the dwelling*, or *chamber*. The term appears to be used as an euphemism for "prison."

(8) **Gird thyself, and bind on thy sandals.**—In lying down to sleep the Apostle had naturally laid aside his "cloak," loosened the girdle that bound his tunic, and put off his sandals. As regards the latter we note his continued observance of the rule of Mark vi. 9.

(9) **And wist not that it was true . . .**—The kind of introspective analysis of the Apostle's consciousness suggests the thought that he was himself, possibly through some intermediate channel, St. Luke's informant. As in the activity of somnambulism, the will directed the actions of the body, and yet was only half-conscious of what it did. It may be noted that his experience of the trance and vision narrated in chap. x. would tend to suggest the impression that he was passing through phenomena of a like kind.

(10) **When they were past the first and the second ward.**—It would seem from this that Peter had been placed in the innermost dungeon, and had to pass the two court-yards. Lightfoot supposes the prison to have been between the inner and outer walls of the city, the direction of Peter's movements being from the outer to the inner.

**The iron gate.**—The touch of topographical precision may be noticed as characteristic of St. Luke.

**Passed on through one street.**—The word implies one of the narrow streets or *lanes* of the city. (See Note on Matt. vi. 2.)

(11) **When Peter was come to himself.**—Here again we find the tone of a personal reminiscence. He finds himself at night, free, in the open street. It was no dream. As before (chap. v. 19), his Master had sent His angel to deliver him.

(12) **Mary the mother of John, whose surname was Mark.**—On the probable identity of this Mark with the evangelist of that name, see *Introduction to St. Mark's Gospel.* Here we may note (1) that as being mentioned by St. Peter as his "son" (1 Pet. v. 13) he was probably converted by him; (2) that he was cousin to Barnabas, probably through his mother, and was therefore at least connected with the tribe of Levi (chap. iv. 36), and possibly belonging to it; (3) that the fact that Mary's house was the meeting-place of the Church indicates comparative wealth, as did Barnabas's sale of his estate; (4) that the absence of any mention of Mark's father makes it probable that she was a widow; (5) that the Latin name of *Marcus* indicates some point of contact with Romans or Roman Jews.

**Many were gathered together praying.**—The facts of the case show that the meeting was held

together praying. (13) And as Peter
knocked at the door of the gate, a
damsel came to hearken,[1] named Rhoda.
(14) And when she knew Peter's voice,
she opened not the gate for gladness,
but ran in, and told how Peter stood
before the gate. (15) And they said unto
her, Thou art mad. But she constantly
affirmed that it was even so. Then
said they, It is his angel. (16) But Peter
continued knocking: and when they
had opened *the door*, and saw him, they
were astonished. (17) But he, beckoning
unto them with the hand to hold their
peace, declared unto them how the Lord
had brought him out of the prison.
And he said, Go shew these things unto
James, and to the brethren. And he
departed, and went into another place.
(18) Now as soon as it was day, there
was no small stir among the soldiers,
what was become of Peter. (19) And
when Herod had sought for him, and
found him not, he examined the keepers,
and commanded that *they* should be
put to death. And he went down from
Judæa to Cæsarea, and *there* abode.
(20) And Herod was highly displeased[2]
with them of Tyre and Sidon: but
they came with one accord to him,
and, having made Blastus the king's
chamberlain[3] their friend, desired peace;

1 Or, *to ask who was there.*

2 Or, *bare an hostile mind, intending war.*

3 Gr. *that was over the king's bedchamber.*

---

at night, possibly to avoid persecution, or, it may be, as the sequel of the evening gathering to "break bread."

(13) **A damsel came to hearken, named Rhoda.**—The mention of the name of the slave indicates St. Luke's care in ascertaining details, as far as his opportunities allowed. The office of opening the door to strangers was commonly assigned, as in the case even of the high priest's palace (Matt. xxvi. 69, 71), to a female slave. The name, which means "a rose," is of the same class as Tamar = a palm tree; Deborah = a bee; Margarita = a pearl; Dorcas = an antelope.

(14) **She opened not the gate for gladness.**—The slave, it would seem, had shared the anxiety and borne her part in the prayers of the Church; and the eager desire to tell the good news that their prayers had been answered overpowers her presence of mind. There is something characteristic of the writer in this analysis of a state of consciousness. (See Note on verse 9, and Luke xxiv. 14.)

(15) **It is his angel.**—The language expresses the common belief of the Jews, that every true Israelite had a guardian angel specially assigned to him, who, when he appeared in human form, assumed the likeness of the man whom he protected. It is obvious that the record of the casual utterance of such a belief cannot be taken as an authoritative sanction of it.

(17) **Go shew these things unto James, and to the brethren.**—The James, or Jacob, thus spoken of may have been either James the son of Alphæus or James the brother of the Lord. Many writers have maintained the identity of the person described under these two names; but reasons have been given in the Notes on Matt. x. 3, xii. 47, xiii. 55, for believing that they were two distinct persons, and that the brother of the Lord was therefore not an Apostle. It is obvious that about this time, probably in consequence of the death of his namesake, the son of Zebedee, James the brother of the Lord comes into a fresh prominence. He is named as receiving St. Paul in Gal. i. 19, and as being, with Peter and John, one of the pillars of the Church (Gal. ii. 9). Probably about this time (but see *Introduction to the Epistle of St. James*) he addressed the letter that bears his name to the Twelve Tribes that were scattered abroad. He presides at the Council of Jerusalem in chap. xv. 13, and acted as bishop of the Church at Jerusalem. According to the statement of Hegesippus, a Jewish Christian writer of the second century, preserved by Eusebius (*Hist.* ii. 23), he led the life of a Nazarite in all its rigour, was regarded by the Jews as having a priestly character, wore the linen ephod, and the golden petalon or plate, fitting on the brow of the priests, and as such was admitted to the Holy Place in the Temple. In A.D. 62 or 63 he was tempted by the priestly rulers, especially by the high-priest Ananias, to declare that the Christ was a deceiver, and on proclaiming his faith in Him was thrown from the pinnacle of the Temple, and as he lay on the ground, received a *coup de grace* from a fuller's club. The way in which St. Peter here speaks of him implies that he was, in some way, the head and representative of the Christian community at Jerusalem.

**He departed, and went into another place.**—The act was in accordance with the precept which had been given to the Twelve in Matt. x. 23. What the "other place" was we can only conjecture. Some Romish writers have hazarded the wild guess that he went to Rome, and having founded the Church there, returned to Jerusalem in time for the council in chap. xv. Others have assumed Antioch, which is, perhaps, less improbable; but there are no traces of his presence there till after the council (Gal. ii. 12). Some nearer city, such as Lydda or Joppa, might, however, have been sufficient as a place of refuge, and the absence of the name of the place suggests the inference that it was comparatively unimportant, and that Peter had carried on no conspicuous work there.

(19) **Commanded that they should be put to death.**—Literally, *that they should be led away*—*i.e.*, to execution. The phrase was half-technical, half-euphemistic. Capital punishment was, according to Roman usage, the almost inevitable penalty for allowing a prisoner to escape. So at Philippi, the gaoler, when he thought the prisoners had escaped, was on the point of anticipating the sentence by suicide (chap. xvi. 28). See Note on chap. xxvii. 42.

(20) **Herod was highly displeased with them of Tyre and Sidon.**—Literally, as in the margin, *was in a hostile state of mind;* was, in modern phrase, "contemplating hostilities." The two Phœnician cities were not subject to Agrippa, but were under the control of Rome with a nominal independence.

**Desired peace.**—Literally, *were seeking peace.* They apparently feared that Herod would show his displeasure by prohibiting the export of corn, and oil, and wine, on which the Phœnician cities, with their large population and narrow strips of territory, were dependent for subsistence. Comp. 1 Kings v. 11, and Ezek.

because their country was nourished by the king's *country.* (21) And upon a set day Herod, arrayed in royal apparel, sat upon his throne, and made an oration unto them. (22) And the people gave a shout, *saying, It is* the voice of a god, and not of a man. (23) And immediately the angel of the Lord smote him, because he gave not God the glory: and he was eaten of worms, and gave up the ghost.

(24) But the word of God grew and multiplied. (25) And Barnabas and Saul returned from Jerusalem, when they had fulfilled *their* ministry,[1] and took with them John, whose surname was Mark.

1 Or, *charge,* ch. ii. 29, 30.

A.D. 45.

CHAPTER XIII. — (1) Now there were in the church that was at Antioch certain prophets and teachers; as Barnabas, and Simeon that was called Niger, and Lucius of Cyrene, and Manaen, which had been brought

---

xxvii. 17, as showing the identity of the commercial relations of the two countries at long intervals in their history.

(21) **And upon a set day . . .**—Josephus (*Ant.* xix. 8, § 2) gives an account of the incident that follows substantially agreeing with that here recorded. The scene was the theatre at Cæsarea, which had been built by Herod the Great. Agrippa was celebrating games in honour of the Emperor Claudius, who had succeeded Caligula in A.D. 41, possibly in honour of his return from Britain in A.D. 44. He was arrayed in a robe of silver tissue, such as Caligula had been wont to wear at banquets and games in Rome, which glittered with a dazzling brightness under the rays of the morning sun. His courtiers, taking up the Roman fashion of showing honour to kings and emperors, hailed him as a god, and prayed him, as such, to be propitious to them. The king did not repress the flattery, which fell on the ears of all Jewish by-standers as a fearful blasphemy. He accepted for himself the divine honours which he had dissuaded Caligula from claiming. He looked up, and saw an owl perched on a rope behind him, and recognised in it an omen of evil, fulfilling a prediction which had been made to him by a fellow-prisoner during his confinement at Rome (Jos. *Ant.* xviii. 8). Sharp pain fell on him, and in five days he died.

Comparing St. Luke's narrative with this, it seems probable that the delegates from Tyre and Sidon were among those who raised the cry, "Be thou propitious to us," and that their friend Blastus, knowing the weak point in Herod's character, had instructed them that this was the way to obtain his favour. We feel, as we read the narrative, the contrast between St. Peter's refusal even of Cornelius's attitude of homage, and Agrippa's acceptance of the profane apotheosis of the multitude.

(23) **The angel of the Lord smote him.**—The intervention of the angel is obviously regarded by St. Luke as the only adequate explanation at once of the death of the persecutor and of the escape of his victim, and in the former he recognised not only what has been called the irony of history, or an instance of the law of Nemesis, bringing down the haughty in the very hour of their triumph, but a direct chastisement for an act of impiety.

**Because he gave not God the glory.**—The words probably mean something more than that he did not ascribe to God the praise which was due to Him, and Him only. To "give God the glory" was a phrase always connected with the confession of sin and weakness, as in Josh. vii. 19. (See Note on John ix. 24.)

**He was eaten of worms.**—The specific form of the disease is not named by Josephus, and St. Luke's precision in describing it may fairly be regarded as characteristic of his calling. The form of the disease, probably of the nature of *phtheiriasis*, or the *morbus pedicularis*, from its exceptionally loathsome character, had always been regarded as of the nature of a divine chastisement. The more memorable instances of it recorded in history are those of Pheretime of Cyrene (Herod. iv. 205), Sylla, Antiochus the Great (2 Macc. ix. 2), Herod the Great (Jos. *Ant.* xvii. 8), and Maximinus, among the persecutors of the Church (Euseb. viii. 16; ix. 10, 11; Lactant, *De mort. Persecut.* c. 33). The death of Agrippa took place A.D. 44, in the seventh year of his reign, and at the age of fifty-three.

(24) **But the word of God grew and multiplied.**—The words describe a continuous expansion. The death of the chief persecutor left free scope for the activity of the preachers of the gospel, of which they were not slow to avail themselves.

(25) **When they had fulfilled their ministry.**—The same noun is used as that translated "relief" in chap. xi. 29. We may, perhaps, assign the vision related in chap. xxii. 17—21, to this visit; but see Note there.

**Took with them John, whose surname was Mark.**—The choice is, of course, partly explained by his relationship to Barnabas, but it shows also that he entered heartily into the work of the conversion of the Gentiles; and owing, as he did, his own conversion to Peter, it would naturally be regarded as a proof of that Apostle's interest in it.

XIII.

(1) **Now there were in the church that was at Antioch.**—The fulness of detail in this narrative suggests the inference that the writer was himself at Antioch at this period.

**Certain prophets and teachers.**—The two were not necessarily identical, though the higher gift of prophecy commonly included the lower gift of teaching. The former implies a more direct message from God, coming from the Holy Ghost; the latter a more systematic instruction, in which reason and reflection bore their part.

**Simeon that was called Niger.**—The name seems to indicate the swarth-complexion of Africa; but nothing more is known of him. The epithet was given to him, probably, to distinguish him from the many others of the same name, possibly, in particular, from Simon of Cyrene. (See Note on chap. xi. 20.)

**Lucius of Cyrene.**—Probably one of the company of "men of Cyprus and Cyrene" (chap. xi. 20) who had been among the first evangelists of Antioch. On the ground that Cyrene was famous for its School of Medicine, some writers have identified him with the

up with Herod the tetrarch,[1] and Saul.
(2) As they ministered to the Lord, and
fasted, the Holy Ghost said, Separate
me Barnabas and Saul for the work
whereunto I have called them. (3) And
when they had fasted and prayed, and
laid *their* hands on them, they sent
*them* away.
(4) So they, being sent forth by the
Holy Ghost, departed unto Seleucia;

[1] Or, *Herod's foster-brother.*

---

author of the Acts, but the two names Lucius and Lucas are radically distinct, the latter being contracted for Lucanus.

**Manaen, which had been brought up with Herod the tetrarch.**—Literally, *the foster-brother of Herod.* Here we enter on a name that has historical associations of some interest. In the early youth of Herod the Great, his future greatness had been foretold by an Essene prophet of the name of Menahem or Manaen (Jos. *Ant.* xv. 10, § 5). When the prediction was fulfilled, he sought to show honour to the prophet. The identity of name makes it probable that the man who now meets us was the son, or grandson, of the Essene, and that Herod had had him brought up with Antipas as a mark of his favour. Both Antipas and Archelaus were educated at Rome, and Manaen may therefore have accompanied them thither. By what steps he was led to believe in Jesus as the Christ, we can only conjecture; but it seems probable that the austere type of life, so closely resembling that of the Essenes, which was presented by the Baptist, may have impressed him, as he was living in the court of his early companion, and that, through him, he may have been led on to the higher truth, and, in due time, after the Day of Pentecost, have become a sharer in the prophetic gift. The fact that Herod the Great had adorned the city of Antioch with a long and stately colonnade may, perhaps, have given him a certain degree of influence there.

**And Saul.**—The position of Saul's name at the end of the list seems to indicate that it was copied from one which had been made before he had become the most prominent of the whole company of the prophets.

(2) **As they ministered to the Lord.**—The verb so translated (*leitourgein*) is commonly used, both in the LXX. and in the New Testament, of the ministry of the priests and Levites in the Temple (Luke i. 23; Heb. viii. 6; ix. 21). In Heb. i. 14, the corresponding adjective is used to distinguish the ministry of worship from that of service to man. When St. Paul uses it figuratively of himself (Rom. xv. 16), it is in connection with the idea of a sacrifice or oblation. In later ecclesiastical languag, it was connected specially with the celebration of the Supper of the Lord, and the order for that service was, strictly speaking, *the* "Liturgy" of the Church. It would, perhaps, be too much to say that the word necessarily conveys that meaning here; but it is, at least, probable that a solemn meeting, such as is here described, would end in the "breaking of bread," and that, up to that point, those who were so engaged would naturally be fasting.

**The Holy Ghost said.**—The mode of communication we may believe to have been, as in chap. xx. 23, through the lips of the prophets, speaking as by a sudden burst of simultaneous inspiration. (Comp. 1 Tim. i. 18.)

**Separate me Barnabas and Saul.**—In the Greek a particle follows the imperative, which has no exact equivalent in English (the illative "then" being, perhaps, the nearest), but which seems to indicate that the command given was in answer to a prayer, and that it was to be acted on at once. The verb implies that they were to be set apart for a new work. Up to this time they had been among the prophets and teachers of the Church. Now they were to receive a solemn visible mission, following on the inspired utterances, as those had followed on personal intimations, consecrating them to the work of the Apostleship to the Gentiles.

(3) **And when they had fasted and prayed.**—The repetition of the words that had been used in verse 2 seems to imply that the fast was prolonged till the laying-on of hands had been completed. The new command called for that intensity of spiritual life of which fasting was more or less the normal condition.

**And laid their hands on them.**—See Note on chap. vi. 6. This was, as before, the formal act by which the Church attested its acceptance of the divine mission of those on whom hands were laid, and implored for them the divine blessing.

(4) **Being sent forth by the Holy Ghost.**—The words may be only a summing up of the result of the previous facts, but looking to chap. xvi. 6, 7, it seems more probable that they refer to a fresh revelation, following on what we should call the "ordination" or "consecration" of the Apostles, and guiding them as to the direction of their journey.

**Departed unto Seleucia.**—The town was situated at the mouth of the Orontes, about sixteen miles from Antioch, and served as the port for that city. It had been built by, and named after, Seleucus Nicator.

**Thence they sailed to Cyprus.**—The population of the island was largely Greek, and the name of the chief town at the east end recalled the history or the legend of a colony under Teucer, the son of Telamon, from the Salamis of the Saronic gulf. It owned Aphrodite, or Venus, as its tutelary goddess, Paphos being the chief centre of her worship, which there, as elsewhere, was conspicuous for the licentiousness of the harlot-priestesses of her temple. The copper-mines (the metal *Cuprum* took its name from the island), and its nearness to Syria, had probably attracted a considerable Jewish population, among whom the gospel had been preached by the Evangelists of chap. xi. 19. An interesting inscription—the date of which is, however, uncertain, and may be of the second or third century after Christ—given in M. de Cesnola's *Cyprus* (p. 422), as found at Golgoi in that island, shows a yearning after something higher than the polytheism of Greece:—

THOU, THE ONE GOD,
THE GREATEST, THE MOST GLORIOUS NAME,
HELP US ALL, WE BESEECH THEE.

At the foot of the inscription there is the name HELIOS, the Sun, and we may probably see in it a trace of that adoption of the worship of Mithras, or the sun, as the visible symbol of Deity, which, first becoming known to the Romans in the time of Pompeius, led to the general reception of the *Dies Solis* (=Sunday) as the first day of the Roman week, and which, even in the case of Constantine, mingled with the earlier

and from thence they sailed to Cyprus.
(5) And when they were at Salamis, they preached the word of God in the synagogues of the Jews: and they had also John to *their* minister.
(6) And when they had gone through the isle unto Paphos, they found a certain sorcerer, a false prophet, a Jew, whose name *was* Bar-jesus:
(7) which was with the deputy of the country, Sergius Paulus, a prudent man; who called for Barnabas and Saul, and desired to hear the word of God.
(8) But Elymas the sorcerer (for so is his name by interpretation) withstood them, seeking to turn away the deputy from the faith.
(9) Then Saul,

---

stages of his progress towards the faith of Christ. (See Note on chap. xvii. 23.) The narrative that follows implies that the prudence or discernment which distinguished the proconsul may well have shown itself in such a recognition of the unity of the Godhead; and it is worthy of note that M. de Cesnola (*Cyprus*, p. 425) discovered at Soli, in the same island, another inscription, bearing the name of Paulus the Proconsul, who may, perhaps, be identified with the Sergius Paulus of this narrative.

(5) **When they were at Salamis.**—The city was, as stated above, at the east end of Cyprus. The mention of "synagogues" implies a considerable Jewish population, and to these the Apostles, following the general rule announced in verse 46, naturally, in the first instance, turned.

**They had also John to their minister.**—The noun so rendered is not that commonly used for the "deacons" or "ministers" of the Church, but implies rather the attendance of personal service. It is probable, however, that he was employed in baptising converts, and, where a church was founded, in preparing for the Supper of the Lord. Looking to the afterwork of Mark, it would hardly, perhaps, be too much to say that he was, more than any other disciple, the courier of the Apostolic Church.

(6) **When they had gone through the isle.**—The better MSS. give, *through the whole island.* Paphos lay at its western extremity, and appears to have been the head-quarters of the Roman governor. A local tradition, reported by M. de Cesnola (*Cyprus*, pp. 29, 223), points out a marble column to which St. Paul was bound and scourged by the citizens of Paphos, who are represented as having been among the most wicked of mankind.

**They found a certain sorcerer.**—The word so rendered, *Magos*, is the same as that used for the "wise men" of Matt. ii. 1 (where see Note), but it is obviously used here in the bad sense which had begun to attach to it even in the days of Sophocles, who makes Œdipus revile Tiresias under this name, as practising *magic* arts (*Œd. Rex.* 387), and which we have found in the case of Simon the sorcerer. (See Note on chap. viii. 9.) The man bore two names, one, Bar-jesus, in its form a patronymic, the other Elymas (an Aramaic word, probably connected with the Arabic *Ulema*, or sage), a title describing his claims to wisdom and supernatural powers. We have already met with a character of this type in the sorcerer of Samaria. (See Note on chap. viii. 9.) The lower class of Jews here, as in chap. xix. 14, seem to have been specially addicted to such practices. They traded on the religious prestige of their race, and boasted, in addition to their sacred books, of spells and charms that had come down to them from Solomon.

(7) **Which was with the deputy of the country, Sergius Paulius.**—The translators consistently use the word "deputy" as representing the Greek for "proconsul." It will be remembered that it was applied, under Elizabeth and James, to the governor, known in more recent times as the Viceroy, or Lord-Lieutenant of Ireland, and was therefore a very close approximation to the meaning of the Latin. The provinces of the Roman empire, under the organisation of Augustus, were divided (B.C. 27) into two classes. Those that were looked on as needing direct military control were placed under the emperor as commander of the legions, and were governed by proprætors, or generals; the others were left to the Senate, and were under the rule of proconsuls. Strabo (xiv. *ad fin.*) describes Cyprus as a military or prætorian province, and this has led some to question St. Luke's accuracy. It appears, however, that Augustus, in A.D. 22, re-assigned it to the Senate (Dio. Cass. iv. p. 523). Coins of Cyprus are extant, bearing the date of Claudius, and the name of Cominius Proclus as proconsul (Akerman, *Numismatic Illustrations*, pp. 39—42), and as stated above (Note on verse 4), one has recently been discovered in Cyprus itself, in which that title appears as borne by one of the name of Paulus. Under Hadrian, it appears to have been under a proprætor; under Severus, it was again under a proconsul. Of the proconsul himself we know nothing certain more than is recorded here. The name probably implied a connection with the old Æmilian *gens*, among whom, as in the case of the great conqueror of Macedonia, it was a favourite cognomen. Dr. Lightfoot has, however, pointed out that Pliny, writing *circ.* A.D. 90, names a Sergius Paulus as his chief authority for the facts in Books ii. and xviii. of his *Natural History*, and that among these are two specially connected with Cyprus; and that Galen, writing *circ.* A.D. 150, speaks of one bearing the same name, also a proconsul, as a contemporary of his own, and as distinguished for his love of wisdom. Here, of course, identity is out of the question, but relationship is, at least, probable.

**A prudent man.**—The adjective describes what we should call general intelligence and discernment, as in Matt. xi. 25; Luke x. 21; 1 Cor. i. 19. It was shown in this instance in his at once recognising the higher type of character presented by the Apostles, and desiring to know more of the "word" which they spake to him as a message from God.

(8) **But Elymas the sorcerer.**—See Note on verse 6. The charlatan feared the loss of the influence which he had previously exercised over the mind of the proconsul. His victim was emancipating himself from his bondage and was passing from credulity to faith, and that progress Bar-jesus sought to check.

(9) **Then Saul, (who also is called Paul).**—It is impossible not to connect the mention, and probably the assumption, of the new name with the conversion of the proconsul. It presented many advantages. (1) It was sufficiently like his own name in sound to fall within the general practice which turned Jesus into Jason, Hillel into Pollio, Silas into Silvanus. (2) It was a

(who also *is called* Paul,) filled with
the Holy Ghost, set his eyes on him,
(10) and said, O full of all subtilty
and all mischief, *thou* child of the
devil, *thou* enemy of all righteousness,
wilt thou not cease to pervert the
right ways of the Lord? (11) And now,
behold, the hand of the Lord *is* upon
thee, and thou shalt be blind, not
seeing the sun for a season. And
immediately there fell on him a mist
and a darkness; and he went about
seeking some to lead him by the hand.
(12) Then the deputy, when he saw what
was done, believed, being astonished at
the doctrine of the Lord. (13) Now when
Paul and his company loosed from
Paphos, they came to Perga in Pam-
phylia: and John departing from them
returned to Jerusalem.

(14) But when they departed from
Perga, they came to Antioch in Pisidia,

---

Roman, not a Greek, name, and as such fell in with the ultimate work of the Apostle, already, it may be, contemplated in thought (comp. Rom. xv. 23), of bearing his witness to Christ in the imperial city. (3) It formed a link between him and the illustrious convert whom he had just made. He was, as it were, claiming a brotherhood with him. From this point of view, it is interesting to compare the name of Lucas or Lucanus, as borne both by the evangelist and the poet. (Comp. *Introduction to St. Luke,* Vol. I., p. 237.) Other reasons that have been assigned, as (1) that the Greek word *Saulos* had an opprobrious meaning, as = wanton, or (2) that the meaning of Paulus, as = little, commended itself to the Apostle's humility, may be dismissed as more or less fantastic.

**Filled with the Holy Ghost.**—The tense of the Greek participle implies a sudden access of spiritual power, showing itself at once in insight into character, righteous indignation, and prevision of the divine chastisement.

**Set his eyes on him.**—The word is that already so often noted, as in chap. i. 10, and elsewhere. As applied to St. Paul it may possibly connect itself with the defect of vision which remained as the after-consequence of the brightness seen on the way to Damascus. The Greek word, however, it is right to add, may just as well express the fixed gaze of men of strong powers of sight, as that of those who suffer from some infirmity. (See chaps. i. 10; iii. 4; Luke iv. 20; xxii. 56.)

(10) **Full of all subtilty and all mischief.**—The Greek of the second noun is found here only in the New Testament. Its primary meaning expresses simply "ease in working;" but this passed through the several stages of "versatility," "shiftiness," and "trickery." A kindred word is translated in chap. xviii. 14 as "lewdness."

**Thou child of the devil.**—There is, perhaps, an intentional contrast between the meaning of the name *Bar-jesus* (= son of the Lord who saves) and the character of the man, which led him to oppose righteousness in every form, and to turn "the *straight* paths of God's making" into the crooked ones of man's subtlety. There is a manifest reference to the words in which Isaiah describes the true preparation of the way of the Lord as consisting in making the crooked straight (Isa. xl. 4).

(11) **The hand of the Lord is upon thee.**—The anthromorphic phrase would convey to every Jew the thought of a chastisement which was the direct result of the will of God. (Comp. 1 Kings xviii. 46; Ezek. i. 3; viii. 1.)

**Thou shalt be blind, not seeing the sun for a season.**—The form of the punishment may have been, in part, determined by the Apostle's choice as manifested in prayer. If so, it suggests the thought that he had looked back on his own blindness, the exclusion of the outward light, as being that which had been to him the process by which he was led to the Sun of Righteousness and the Light that lighteth every man, and hoped that it might be so now. (See Note on chap. ix. 8, 9.) In any case, there was a moral fitness in blindness as the penalty of the sin the very essence of which was that the man was fighting against light. That the blindness was to be "for a season" only implies that it was designed to be remedial and not simply retributive.

**There fell on him a mist and a darkness . . .**—Here, as in the "scales" of chap. ix. 13, we seem to trace something of the precision of the trained physician. The first effect of the loss of the power to see was, as in the case of St. Paul, that Elymas, who had selfishly used his knowledge to guide others to his own advantage, now had to seek for others to guide his own steps. The tense of the Greek verb (*he was seeking*) seems to imply that he sought and did not find. He had no friends to help him, and was left to his fate unpitied.

(12) **Being astonished at the doctrine of the Lord.**—The genitive is, probably, that of the object, *the teaching which had the Lord, i.e.,* the Lord Jesus, *as its main theme.*

(13) **Paul and his company.**—Literally, *those about Paul.* The new description is obviously chosen as indicating the new position which from this time the Apostle began to occupy as the leader of the mission.

**Perga.**—The city was at this time the capital of Pamphylia, situated on the river Cestrus, about seven miles from its mouth. The absence of any record of evangelising work there is probably due to the fact that there were no synagogues, and that the Apostles in this mission adhered to the plan of preaching in the first instance to the Jews, and making the synagogue, as it were, their base of operations.

**John departing from them returned to Jerusalem.**—We are left to conjecture the motives of this departure. He may have shrunk from the perils and hardships of the journey into the interior of the country. He may have been drawn by affection for his mother, who lived at Jerusalem. It is clear, in any case, from St. Paul's subsequent conduct (chap. xv. 38), that he looked on the reason as insufficient, while Barnabas saw, at least, enough to admit the plea of extenuating circumstances. The pressure of the famine at Jerusalem may have seemed to him to excuse the desire of the son to minister to the mother's wants.

(14) **They came to Antioch in Pisidia.**—The town was one of the many cities built by Seleucus Nicator, and named after his father, Antiochus. It lay on the slopes of Mount Taurus, which the travellers

and went into the synagogue on the
sabbath day, and sat down. (15) And
after the reading of the law and the
prophets the rulers of the synagogue
sent unto them, saying, *Ye* men *and*
brethren, if ye have any word of
exhortation for the people, say on.
(16) Then Paul stood up, and beckoning
with *his* hand said, Men of Israel,
and ye that fear God, give audience.
(17) The God of this people of Israel
chose our fathers, and exalted the
people when they dwelt as strangers
in the land of Egypt,[a] and with an
high arm brought he them out of it.[b]
(18) And about the time of forty years
suffered[1] he their manners in the wilder-
ness. (19) And when he had destroyed
seven nations in the land of Chanaan,
he divided their land to them by lot.[c]
(20) And after that he gave *unto them*
judges about the space of four hundred

a Ex. 1. 1.

b Ex. 13. 14, 16.

1 Gr. *etropophoresen*, perhaps for *etrophophoresen*, *bore*, or, *fed them, as a nurse beareth*, or, *feedeth her child*, Deut. 1. 31; 2 Mac. 7. 27, according to the LXX., and so Chrysostom.

c Josh. 14. 1.

---

must have crossed, had obtained the "Jus Italicum"—a modified form of Roman citizenship—under Augustus, and had attracted, as the sequel shows, a considerable Jewish population, who had made many proselytes among the Gentiles (verse 42). It lay on the extreme limit of Pisidia, with Phrygia on the west and Lycaonia on the east.

**Went into the synagogue on the sabbath day, and sat down.**—The act implied that they were not listeners only, but teachers. (See Notes on Matt. v. 1; Luke iv. 20.) They sat as in the seat of the Rabbi, and their doing so was an indication, as the sequel shows, that they asked for permission to address the congregation. It will be remembered that the organisation of the synagogue excluded the sacerdotal element altogether, and that lay-preaching, assuming a sufficient training, was an established practice. It need hardly be said that neither elders nor scribes were necessarily of the tribe of Levi.

(15) **After the reading of the law and the prophets.**—The order of the Sabbath lessons was fixed as by a kind of calendar, the Law—*i.e.*, the Pentateuch—being divided into fifty-three or fifty-four *paraschioth*, or sections. These, probably, came into use soon after the return from Babylon. To these were afterwards added special lessons, known technically as the *Haphtaroth*, from the prophets. We are enabled, by two curious coincidences, to fix, with very little uncertainty, the precise Sabbath on which the mission-work at Antioch opened. The opening words of St. Paul refer to Deut. i. 31 (see Note on verse 18) and this was the lesson for the forty-fourth Sabbath in the year, which fell in July or August; the corresponding second lesson from the prophets being Isa. i. 1—27, from which he also quotes. He starts, as was natural, from what the people had just been listening to, as the text of his discourse.

**The rulers of the synagogue sent unto them . . .**—The elders apparently saw strangers taking the position of teachers, probably in the garb of Rabbis, and it belonged to their office to offer such persons an opportunity of addressing the people.

(16) **Beckoning with his hand.**—The gesture was rather that of one who *waves* his hand to command silence and attention than what we commonly describe as beckoning. (Comp. chap. xii. 17.) The graphic touch of description would seem to indicate, as does the full report of the speech, that they came in the first instance from one who had been present. A like touch is found again in connection with St. Paul in chap. xxi. 40. It was, probably, like the "fixing of the eye," in verse 9, just one of the personal characteristics on which the painter-historian loved to dwell. We may assume, as almost certain, that throughout this journey St. Paul used Greek as the common medium of intercourse. The verbal coincidences in verses 17 and 18, already referred to in the Note on verse 15, make it, in this instance, absolutely certain.

**Men of Israel, and ye that fear God.**—The latter phrase denotes, as in chap. x. 2, 22, those who, though in the synagogue, were of heathen origin, and had not become proselytes in the full sense of the term, but were known as the so-called "proselytes of the gate."

**Give audience.**—Literally, *hear ye.* The English phrase may be noted as an example of the use of the word "audience," which has since been applied to the persons who hear, in the old abstract sense of the act of hearing.

(17) **The God of this people of Israel.**—It will be observed that St. Paul, as far as the plan of his discourse is concerned, follows in the footsteps of St. Stephen, and begins by a recapitulation of the main facts of the history of Israel. It was a theme which Israelites were never tired of listening to. It showed that the Apostles recognised it as the history of God's chosen people.

**And exalted the people when they dwelt as strangers.**—Literally, *in their sojourning in the land of Egypt.* The word for "exalt" is found in the Greek of Isa. i. 2, where our version has, "I have nourished and *brought up* children," and may fairly be considered as an echo from the lesson that had just been read. It may be noted that it was only in this sense, as increasing rapidly in population, that Israel could be spoken of as "exalted" in the house of bondage.

(18) **Suffered he their manners.**—The Greek word so rendered differs by a single letter only from one which signifies "to nurse, to carry, as a father carries his child." Many of the better MSS. versions and early writers give the latter reading, and it obviously falls in far better with the conciliatory drift of St. Paul's teaching than one which implied reproach. The word is found in the Greek of Deut. i. 31 ("bare thee, as a man *doth bear* his son"), where also some MSS. give the other word, and suggests the inference, already mentioned, that this chapter, as well as Isa. i., had been read as one of the lessons for the day.

(19) **He divided their land to them by lot.**—Accepting this reading, the reference is to the command given in Num. xxvi. 55, 56, and recorded as carried into effect in Josh. xiv.—xix. The better MSS., however, give a kindred word, which signifies "he gave as an inheritance."

(20) **After that he gave unto them judges . . .**—The statement in the text, assigning 450 years to the period of the judges, and apparently reckoning that period from the distribution of the conquered territory, is at variance with that in 1 Kings vi. 1, which gives

and fifty years,[a] until Samuel the pro-
phet. (21) And afterward they desired
a king:[b] and God gave unto them Saul
the son of Cis, a man of the tribe of
Benjamin, by the space of forty years.
(22) And when he had removed him, he
raised up unto them David to be their
king;[c] to whom also he gave testimony,
and said, I have found David the *son* of
Jesse, a man after mine own heart,
which shall fulfil all my will.[d] (23) Of
this man's seed[e] hath God according to
*his* promise raised unto Israel a Saviour,
Jesus: (24) when John had first preached[f]
before his coming the baptism of re-
pentance to all the people of Israel.
(25) And as John fulfilled his course, he
said, Whom think ye that I am? I am
not *he*.[g] But, behold, there cometh one
after me, whose shoes of *his* feet I
am not worthy to loose. (26) Men *and*
brethren, children of the stock of Abra-
ham, and whosoever among you feareth
God, to you is the word of this salva-
tion sent. (27) For they that dwell at
Jerusalem, and their rulers, because
they knew him not, nor yet the voices
of the prophets which are read every
sabbath day, they have fulfilled *them* in
condemning *him*. (28) And though they
found no cause of death *in him*,[h] yet
desired they Pilate that he should be

a Judg. 3. 9.
b 1 Sam. 8. 5.
g John 1. 20.
c 1 Sam. 16. 13.
d Ps. 89. 20.
e Isa. 11. 1.
f Matt. 3 1.
h Matt. 27. 22.

---

480 years as the period intervening between the Exodus and the building of the temple. The better MSS., however, give a different reading—"He gave their land to them as an inheritance, about 450 years, and after these things he gave unto them judges," the 450 years in this case being referred to the interval between the choice of "our fathers," which may be reckoned from the birth of Isaac (B.C. 1897 according to the received chronology) to the distribution of the conquered country in B.C. 1444. So far as any great discrepancy is concerned, this is a sufficient explanation, but what has been said before as to the general tendency in a discourse of this kind to rest in round numbers, has also to be remembered. (See Note on chap. vii. 6.) Josephus (*Ant.* viii. 3, § 1) gives 592 years from the Exodus to the building of Solomon's Temple. Of this period sixty-five years were occupied by the wanderings in the wilderness and the conquest under Joshua, eighty-four by the reigns of Saul and David and the first four years of Solomon, leaving 443 years for the period of the Judges. This agrees, it will be seen, sufficiently with the Received text in this passage, but leaves the discrepancy with 1 Kings vi. 1 unexplained. There would of course, be nothing strange in St. Paul's following the same traditional chronology as Josephus, even where it differed from that of the present Hebrew text of the Old Testament.

(21) **Saul the son of Cis, a man of the tribe of Benjamin.**—It is natural to think of the Apostle as dwelling on the memory of the hero-king of the tribe to which he himself belonged. (Comp. Phil. iii. 5.) The very fact that he had so recently renounced the name, would bring the associations connected with it more vividly to his recollection.

**Forty years.**—The duration of Saul's reign is not given in the Old Testament, but Ish-bosheth, his youngest son (1 Chron. viii. 33), was forty years old at the time of Saul's death (2 Sam. ii. 10), and Saul himself was a "young man" when chosen as king (1 Sam. ix. 2). A more definite corroboration of St. Paul's statement is given by Josephus (*Ant.* vi. 14, § 9), who states that he reigned eighteen years before Samuel's death and twenty-two after it.

(22) **I have found David the son of Jesse.**—The words that follow are a composite quotation, after the manner of the Rabbis, made up of Ps. lxxxix. 20, and 1 Sam. xiii. 14. The obvious purpose of this opening was, as in the case of St. Stephen's speech, to gain attention by showing that the speaker recognised all the traditional glories of the people. It is possible that we have, as it were, but the *précis* of a fuller statement.

(23) **Raised unto Israel a Saviour, Jesus.**—It is, of course, probable that the names of Jesus and of John were not utterly unknown, even in those remote regions of Pisidia. No Jew could have gone up to keep a feast at Jerusalem for some years past without having heard something of the one or of the other. St. Paul's tone is clearly that of one who assumes that their story is already vaguely known, and who comes to offer knowledge of greater clearness.

(24) **The baptism of repentance.**—See Notes on Matt. iii. 1—12.

(25) **And as John fulfilled his course.**—Better *was fulfilling*, the tense implying continuous action.

**Whom think ye that I am?**—The precise question is not found in the Gospel records of St. John's ministry, but the substance of the answer is implied in Matt. iii. 11; John i. 20, 21.

(26) **Children of the stock of Abraham, and whosoever among you feareth God.**—The two classes are, as before (see Note on verse 16), again pointedly contrasted with each other.

**To you is the word of this salvation sent.**—The demonstrative pronoun implies that the salvation which St. Paul proclaimed rested on the work of Jesus the Saviour (verse 23), and was found in union with Him. (Comp. "this life" in chap. v. 20.)

(27) **For they that dwell at Jerusalem.**—The implied reason of the mission to the Gentiles and more distant Jews is that the offer of salvation had been rejected by those who would naturally have been its first recipients, and who, had they received it, would have been, in their turn, witnesses to those that were "far off," in both the local and spiritual sense of those words.

**The voices of the prophets which are read every sabbath day.**—See Note on verse 15. The Apostle appeals to the synagogue ritual from which the discourse started, as in itself bearing witness, not to the popular notions of a conquering Messiah, but to the true ideal of the chief of sufferers, which had been realised in Jesus.

(28) **And though they found no cause of death in him.**—Technically, the Sanhedrin had condemned our Lord on the charge of blasphemy (Matt. xxvi. 66), but they had been unable to prove the charge by any adequate evidence (Matt. xxvi. 60), and finally

slain. (29) And when they had fulfilled
all that was written of him, they took
*him* down from the tree, and laid *him*
in a sepulchre. (30) But God raised him
from the dead:[a] (31) and he was seen
many days of them which came up with
him from Galilee to Jerusalem, who are
his witnesses unto the people. (32) And
we declare unto you glad tidings, how
that the promise which was made unto
the fathers, (33) God hath fulfilled the
same unto us their children, in that he
hath raised up Jesus again; as it is also
written in the second psalm, Thou art
my Son, this day have I begotten thee.[b]
(34) And as concerning that he raised
him up from the dead, *now* no more to
return to corruption, he said on this
wise, I will give you the sure mercies[1]
of David.[c] (35) Wherefore he saith also
in another *psalm*, Thou shalt not suffer
thine Holy One to see corruption.[d]
(36) For David, after he had served his
own generation by the will of God,[2] fell

b Ps. 2. 7; Heb. 1. 5.

a Matt. 28. 6.

1 Gr. *ta osia, holy,* or, *just things:* which word the LXX. both in the place of Isa. 55. 3, and in many others, use for that which is in the Hebrew, *mercies.*

c Isa. 55. 3.

d Ps. 16. 10.

2 Or, *after he had in his own age served the will of God.*

---

condemned him by extorting words from His own lips. When they came before Pilate they shrank at first from urging that accusation, and contented themselves with stating in general terms that they had condemned Him as a malefactor (John xviii. 30); though afterwards, as if seeking to terrify the wavering governor, they added that by their law He ought to die because He made Himself the Son of God (John xix. 7), and that by making Himself a king He spake against the emperor (John xix. 12).

(29) **When they had fulfilled all that was written of him.**—The words are suggestive of much that lies below the surface. St. Paul, also, had studied in the same school of prophetic interpretation as the writers of the Gospels, and saw as they did, in all the details of the Crucifixion, the fulfilment of that which had been written beforehand, it might be, of other sufferers, but which was to find its highest fulfilment in the Christ.

**They took him down from the tree.**—In the brief summary which St. Paul gives, it was apparently deemed unnecessary to state the fact that our Lord was taken down from the cross and laid in the sepulchre by those who were secretly disciples, like Joseph and Nicodemus. It was enough that they too were among the rulers of the Jews, and that they, in what they did, were acting without any expectation of the Resurrection. On the use of the word "tree" for the cross, see Note on chap. v. 30.

(31) **And he was seen many days.**—The language is that of one who had conversed with the witnesses, and had convinced himself of the truth of their testimony. We find what the Apostle had in his thoughts in a more expanded form in 1 Cor. xv. 3—8.

**Who are his witnesses.**—More accurately, *who are now his witnesses.*

**Unto the people.**—The word is used in its distinctive sense as applied to those who were *the* people of God. (Comp. chap. xxvi. 17, 23.)

(33) **God hath fulfilled the same unto us their children.**—The better MSS. give, with hardly an exception, *unto our children*, and the Received text must be regarded as having been made to obtain what seemed a more natural meaning. St. Paul's language, however, is but an echo of St. Peter's "to us and to our children," in chap. ii. 39.

**As it is also written in the second psalm.**—The various-reading, "in the *first* Psalm," given by some MSS. is interesting, as showing that in some copies of the Old Testament, what is now the first Psalm was treated as a kind of prelude to the whole book, the numeration beginning with what is now the second.

**Thou art my Son, this day have I begotten thee.**—Historically, Psalm ii. appears as a triumph-song, written to celebrate the victory of a king of Israel or Judah—David, or Solomon, or another—over his enemies. The king had been shown by that day of victory to have been the chosen son of God—the day itself was a new begetting, manifesting the sonship. So, in the higher fulfilment which St. Paul finds in Christ, he refers the words, not primarily to the Eternal Generation of the Son of God, "begotten before all worlds," nor to the Incarnation, but to the day of victory over rulers and priests, over principalities and powers, over death and Hades. The Resurrection manifested in the antitype, as the victory had done in the type, a pre-existing sonship; but it was to those who witnessed it, or heard of it, as the ground on which their faith in that sonship rested. Christ was to them the "firstborn of every creature," because He was also "the firstborn from the dead." (See Notes on Col. i. 15, 18.)

(34) **Now no more to return to corruption.**—We note from the turn of the phrase that St. Paul already has the words of Ps. xvi. 10 in his mind, though he has not as yet referred to it.

**I will give you the sure mercies of David.**—The words do not seem in themselves to have the nature of a Messianic prediction. To those, however, whose minds were full to overflowing with the writings of the prophets they would be pregnant with meaning. What were the "sure mercies of David" (Isa. lv. 3) but the "everlasting covenant" of mercy which was to find its fulfilment in One who should be "a leader and commander to the people?" We may well believe that the few words quoted recalled to St. Paul and to his hearers the whole of that wonderful chapter which opens with "Ho, every one that thirsteth, come ye to the waters." The Greek word for "mercies" is the same adjective as that translated "holy" in the next verse, "holiness" being identified with "mercy," and so forms a connecting link with the prophecy cited in the next verse.

(35) **Thou shalt not suffer thine Holy One to see corruption.**—See Notes on the prophecy so cited in chap. ii. 25—31.

(36) **After he had served his own generation.**—Literally, *ministered to his own generation.* There is, perhaps, a suggested contrast between the limits within which the work of service to mankind done by any mere man, however great and powerful, is necessarily confined, and the wide, far-reaching, endless ministry to the whole human family which belongs to the Son of Man.

**By the will of God.**—The words are, perhaps, better connected with the verb that follows. It was by the will (literally, *counsel*) of God that David fell asleep when his life's work was accomplished.

**Fell on sleep.**—It is not without interest to note

on sleep, and was laid unto his fathers,
and saw corruption:[a] (37) but he, whom
God raised again, saw no corruption.
(38) Be it known unto you therefore,
men *and* brethren, that through this
man is preached unto you the forgive-
ness of sins: (39) and by him all that
believe are justified from all things,
from which ye could not be justified
by the law of Moses. (40) Beware there-
fore, lest that come upon you, which is
spoken of in the prophets;[b] (41) Behold,
ye despisers, and wonder, and perish:
for I work a work in your days, a work
which ye shall in no wise believe,
though a man declare it unto you.
(42) And when the Jews were gone out
of the synagogue, the Gentiles besought
that these words might be preached to
them the next sabbath.[1] (43) Now when
the congregation was broken up, many
of the Jews and religious proselytes
followed Paul and Barnabas: who,
speaking to them, persuaded them to
continue in the grace of God.
(44) And the next sabbath day came

[a] 1 Kings 2. 10.

[1] Gr. *in the week between*, or, *in the sabbath between.*

[b] Hab. 1. 5.

---

that St. Paul uses the same word for death as had been used by the historian in the case of Stephen (chap. vii. 36). It agreed with the then current language of mankind that death was as a sleep. It differed from it in thinking of that sleep not as "eternal" (the frequently recurring epithet in Greek and Roman epitaphs), but as the prelude to an awakening.

(38) **Men and brethren.**—Better, *brethren*, simply.

**Is preached . . .**—The force of the Greek tense emphasises the fact that the forgiveness was, at that very moment, in the act of *being proclaimed* or preached.

**Forgiveness of sins.**—This forms the key-note of St. Paul's preaching (here and in chap. xxvi. 18), as it had done of St. Peter's (chaps. ii. 38; v. 31; x. 43), as it had done before of that of the Baptist (Mark i. 4; Luke iii. 3), and of our Lord Himself (Matt. ix. 2, 6; Luke vii. 47; xxiv. 47). It was the ever-recurring burden of the glad tidings which were preached alike by all.

(39) **And by him.**—Literally, *in Him*, as the sphere in which forgiveness was found, rather than as the instrument through whom it came.

**All that believe are justified.**—Literally, with a more individualising touch, *every one that believeth is justified.* The latter verb is not found elsewhere in the Acts. It is interesting to note in this, the first recorded example of St. Paul's teaching, the occurrence of the word which, as time passed on, came to be almost identified with him and with his work. It is clearly used, as interpreted by the "forgiveness of sins" in the context, in its forensic sense, as meaning "acquitted," "declared not guilty." (Comp. Note on Matt. xii. 37.)

**From which ye could not be justified by the law of Moses.**—The words are full of meaning, as the germ of all that was most characteristic in St. Paul's later teaching. The Law, with its high standard of righteousness (Rom. vii. 12), its demand of entire obedience, its sacrifices which bore witness to the burden of sin, yet had no power to liberate conscience from its thraldom (Heb. viii. 1—3), had taught him that its function in the spiritual life of man was to work out the knowledge of sin (Rom. vii. 7), not to emancipate men from it. The sense of freedom from guilt, and therefore of a true life, was to be found, as he had learnt by his own experience, through faith in Christ. "The just by faith shall live" (Hab. ii. 4; Rom. i. 17; Gal. iii. 11).

(40) **Which is spoken of in the prophets.**—This formula of citation seems to have been common, as in chap. vii. 42, in the case of quotations from the Minor Prophets, which were regarded, as it were, as a single volume with this title.

(41) **Behold, ye despisers.**—The quotation is from the LXX. version, the Hebrew giving "Behold, ye among the heathen." So, in the next clause, "wonder, and perish" takes the place of "wonder marvellously." The fact that St. Paul quotes from the prophet (Hab. i. 5) whose teaching (Hab. ii. 4) that "the just by faith shall live" becomes henceforth the axiom of his life, is not without a special interest. The "work" of which the prophet spoke was defined in the following verse as the raising up the Chaldeans, "that bitter and hasty nation," to execute God's judgment. St. Paul may have had in his thoughts the like judgment about to be executed by the Romans, and already known as foretold by Christ (Matt. xxiv. 2—28), or may have thus dimly indicated that which was so closely connected with it—the rejection of Israel, because they, as a nation, had rejected Christ. The sharp tone of warning, as in St. Stephen's speech (see Note on chap. vii. 51), suggests the thought that signs of anger and impatience had already begun to show themselves.

(42) **And when the Jews were gone out of the synagogue.**—The better MSS. give simply, *as they were going out*, the Received text being apparently an explanatory interpretation. The reading, "the Gentiles besought," is an addition of the same character, the better MSS. giving simply, *they besought*, or *were beseeching.* What follows shows, indeed, that some at least of the Jews were led to inquire further. The participle implies that they stopped as they passed out, to request the Apostle to resume his teaching on the following Sabbath. This, and not the marginal reading "in the week between," is the true meaning of the words, though they admit, literally, of the other rendering.

(43) **When the congregation was broken up.**—Better, as keeping to the usual rendering, *the synagogue.* The two preachers withdrew to their inn or lodging, and were followed by many of both classes of their hearers—not, as the Received text of verse 42 implies, by one only. It is probable, looking to St. Paul's language in 1 Cor. ix. 6—which can only refer to their joint life at the Syrian Antioch, or on this journey,—that during the week that followed they worked for their maintenance as tent-makers. (See Note on chap. xviii. 3.) Manufactures of this kind were so common in all the towns lying on or near the Taurus range of mountains, that it would not be difficult for any skilled workman, such as St. Paul, to obtain casual employment.

**Persuaded them.**—The tense implies that they went on throughout the week—probably after their day's labour was over—with this work of persuasion.

(44) **The next sabbath day came almost the whole city together.**—It is clear that the Jewish

almost the whole city together to hear the word of God. (45) But when the Jews saw the multitudes, they were filled with envy, and spake against those things which were spoken by Paul, contradicting and blaspheming. (46) Then Paul and Barnabas waxed bold, and said, It was necessary that the word of God should first have been spoken to you: but seeing ye put it from you, and judge yourselves unworthy of everlasting life, lo, we turn to the Gentiles. (47) For so hath the Lord commanded us, *saying*, I have set thee to be a light of the Gentiles, that thou shouldest be for salvation unto the ends of the earth.[a] (48) And when the Gentiles heard this, they were glad, and glorified the word of the Lord: and as many as were ordained to eternal life believed. (49) And the word of the Lord was published throughout all the region. (50) But the Jews stirred up the devout and honourable women, and the

[a] Isa. 49. 6.

synagogue could not have held such a crowd, and we are led accordingly to the conclusion either that they thronged round portals and windows while the Apostles spoke within, or that the crowd gathered in some open space or piazza in which the synagogue was situated, and were addressed from its entrance. We are left to infer the nature of St. Paul's discourse from what had preceded, and to assume that it was not recorded, either because St. Luke had notes of one discourse and not of the other, or because it went more or less over the same ground, and therefore did not seem to him to require recording.

(45) **They were filled with envy.**—They heard the Apostles speaking to the multitudes, not in the condescending, supercilious tone of those who could just tolerate a wealthy proselyte of the gate, that could purchase their favour, but as finding in every one of them a brother standing on the same level as themselves, as redeemed by Christ, and this practical repudiation of all the exclusive privileges on which they prided themselves was more than they could bear.

**Contradicting and blaspheming.**—The latter word implies reviling words with which the Apostles were assailed, as well as blasphemy in the common meaning of the word.

(46) **It was necessary.**—The preachers recognised the necessity of following what they looked on as the divine plan in the education of mankind, and so they preached "to the Jew first, and also to the Gentile" (Rom. ii. 9, 10). The former were offered, as the fulfilment of the promise made to Abraham, the high privilege of being the channel through which "all families of the earth should be blessed" by the knowledge of Christ (Gen. xxii. 18). When they rejected that offer, it was made, without their intervention, to the Gentiles.

**Judge yourselves unworthy of everlasting life.**—There is a touch of righteous indignation, perhaps something like irony, in the words. The preacher had thought them "worthy" of the highest of all blessings, the life eternal which was in Christ Jesus, but they, in their boastful and envious pride, took what was really a lower estimate of themselves, and showed that they were "unworthy." They passed sentence, *ipso facto*, on themselves.

**Lo, we turn to the Gentiles.**—We have to remember (1) that the words were as an echo of those which the Apostle had heard in his trance in the Temple at Jerusalem (chap. xxii. 21); (2) that they would be heard, on the one hand, by the Gentiles with a joy hitherto unknown, and, on the other, by the Jews as a new cause of irritation.

(47) **I have set thee to be a light to the Gentiles.**—The context of the quotation has to be remembered as showing that St. Paul identified the "Servant of the Lord" in Isa. xlix. 6 with the person of the Christ. (See Note on chap. iv. 27.) The citation is interesting as the first example of the train of thought which led the Apostle to see in the language of the prophets, where others had found only the exaltation of Israel, the divine purpose of love towards the whole heathen world. It is the germ of the argument afterwards more fully developed in Rom. ix. 25; x. 12.

(48) **They were glad, and glorified the word of the Lord.**—Both verbs are in the tense of continued action. The joy was not an evanescent burst of emotion. The "word of the Lord" here is the teaching which had the Lord Jesus as its subject.

**As many as were ordained to eternal life believed.**—Better, *as many as were disposed for*. The words seem to the English reader to support the Calvinistic dogma of divine decrees as determining the belief or unbelief of men, and it is not improbable, looking to the general drift of the theology of the English Church in the early part of the seventeenth century, that the word "ordained" was chosen as expressing that dogma. It runs, with hardly any variation, through all the chief English versions, the Rhemish giving the stronger form "pre-ordinate." The Greek word, however, does not imply more than that they fell in with the divine order which the Jews rejected. They were as soldiers who take the place assigned to them in God's great army. The *quasi*-middle force of the passive form of the verb is seen in the Greek of chap. xx. 13, where a compound form of it is rightly rendered "for so he had appointed," and might have been translated *for so he was disposed.* It lies in the nature of the case that belief was followed by a public profession of faith, but the word "believed" does not, as some have said, involve such a profession.

(49) **Throughout all the region.**—This clearly involves a considerable period of active working. It was not in Antioch only, but in the "region" round about, the border district of the three provinces of Phrygia, Lycaonia, and Galatia, that the new faith was planted. Each town and village in that region presented the spectacle of at least some few men and women who no longer sacrificed to their country's gods, who were no longer content even to worship in the synagogue of the *religio licita* of the Jews, but met in small companies here and there, as the disciples of a new Master.

(50) **The Jews stirred up the devout and honourable women.**—The fact stated brings before us another feature of the relations between Jews and Gentiles at this period. They "compassed sea and land to make one proselyte" (Matt. xxiii. 15). They found it easier to make proselytes of women. Such conversions had their good and their bad sides. In

chief men of the city, and raised persecution against Paul and Barnabas, and expelled them out of their coasts. (51) But they shook off the dust of their feet against them,[a] and came unto Iconium. (52) And the disciples were filled with joy, and with the Holy Ghost.

a Matt. 10. 14.

CHAPTER XIV.—(1) And it came to pass in Iconium, that they went both together into the synagogue of the Jews, and so spake, that a great multitude both of the Jews and also of the Greeks believed. (2) But the unbelieving Jews stirred up the Gentiles, and made their minds evil affected against the brethren. (3) Long time therefore abode they speaking boldly in the Lord, which gave testimony unto the word of his grace, and granted signs and wonders to be done by their hands.

A.D. 45.

---

many cases there was a real longing for a higher and purer life than was found in the infinite debasement of Greek and Roman society, which found its satisfaction in the life and faith of Israel. (See Notes on chap. xvii. 4, 12.) But with many, such as Juvenal speaks of when he describes (*Sat.* vi. 542) the Jewish teacher who gains influence over women—

> "Arcanam Judæa tremens mendicat in aurem
> Interpres legum Solymarum"—
> ["The trembling Jewess whispers in her ear,
> And tells her of the laws of Solymæ,"] *

the change brought with it new elements of superstition and weakness, and absolute submission of conscience to its new directors, and thus the Rabbis were often to the wealthier women of Greek and Roman cities what Jesuit confessors were in France and Italy in the seventeenth and eighteenth centuries. Here we get the darker side of the picture. The Jews stir up the women of the upper class, and they stir up their husbands. The latter were content apparently to acquiesce in their wives accepting the Judaism with which they had become familiar, but resented the intrusion of a new and, in one sense, more exacting doctrine.

**Raised persecution against Paul and Barnabas.**—It lies in the nature of the case that they were not the only sufferers. From the first the Christians of Antioch in Pisidia had to learn the lesson that they must "through much tribulation enter into the kingdom of God" (chap. xiv. 22). The memory of these sufferings came back upon St. Paul's mind, even in the last months of his life, as something never to be forgotten (2 Tim. iii. 11).

(51) **They shook off the dust of their feet against them.**—The act was one of literal obedience to our Lord's commands (see Note on Matt. x. 14), and may fairly be regarded as evidence that that command had come to the knowledge of Paul and Barnabas as well as of the Twelve. It was in itself, however, the language of a natural symbolism which every Jew would understand, a declaration that not the heathen, but the unbelieving and malignant Jews, were those who made the very dust on which they trod common and unclean.

**And came unto Iconium.**—The journey to Iconium is passed over rapidly, and we may infer that it presented no opportunities for mission work. That city lay on the road between Antioch and Derbe at a distance of ninety miles south-east from the former city, and forty north-west from the latter. When the travellers arrived there they found what they probably had not met with on their route—a synagogue, which indicated the presence of a Jewish population, on whom they could begin to work. The city, which from its size and stateliness has been called the Damascus of Lycaonia, was famous in the early Apocryphal Christian writings as the scene of the intercourse between St. Paul and his convert Thekla. In the middle ages it rose to importance as the capital of the Seljukian sultans, and, under the slightly altered name of *Konieh*, is still a flourishing city. By some ancient writers it was assigned to Phrygia, by others to Lycaonia.

(52) **And the disciples were filled with joy and with the Holy Ghost.**—The tense is again that which expresses the continuance of the state. The "joy" expresses what is almost the normal sequence of conversion in the history of the Acts. (See Notes on chap. viii. 8, 39.) The addition of "the Holy Ghost" may imply special gifts like those of tongues and prophecy, but certainly involves a new intensity of spiritual life, of which joy was the natural outcome. As being conspicuous among the Gentile converts, we trace the impression which it then made, in words which St. Paul wrote long years afterwards, "The kingdom of God is not meat and drink, but righteousness and peace, and *joy in the Holy Ghost*" (Rom. xiv. 17).

XIV.

(1) **Both of the Jews and also of the Greeks.**—The latter term is used in its wider sense, as in Mark vii. 26 and elsewhere, as equivalent to Gentile, but it implies that those who were so described spoke and understood Greek. In the former instance these would probably be the "proselytes of the gate" who heard the Apostles in the synagogue.

(2) **The unbelieving Jews stirred up the Gentiles . . .**—It is the distinguishing feature of nearly all the persecutions in the Acts that they originated in the hostility of the Jews. The case of Demetrius furnishes almost the only exception (chap. xix. 24), and even there the Jews apparently fomented the enmity of the Greek craftsmen. So at a considerably later date (A.D. 169) we find them prominent in bringing about the persecution which ended in the death of Polycarp at Smyrna (*Mart. Polyc.* c. 13).

(3) **Long time therefore abode they.**—This can hardly be understood as involving a stay of less than several months, during which, Paul and Barnabas, as before, were working for their livelihood.

**Speaking boldly.**—The "boldness" consisted, as the context shows, in a full declaration of the gospel of the grace of God as contrasted with the narrowing Judaism with which the Greek proselytes had previously been familiar.

**Granted signs and wonders to be done by their hands.**—It will be noted that here also, as so often elsewhere, the miracles that were wrought came as the confirmation of faith, not as its foundation.

* Solymæ, of course, stands for Jerusalem.

A.D. 46.

(4) But the multitude of the city was
divided: and part held with the Jews,
and part with the apostles. (5) And
when there was an assault made both
of the Gentiles, and also of the Jews
with their rulers, to use *them* despite-
fully, and to stone them, (6) they were
ware of *it*, and fled unto Lystra and
Derbe, cities of Lycaonia, and unto the
region that lieth round about: (7) and
there they preached the gospel.

(8) And there sat a certain man at
Lystra, impotent in his feet, being a
cripple from his mother's womb, who
never had walked: (9) the same heard
Paul speak: who stedfastly beholding
him, and perceiving that he had faith
to be healed, (10) said with a loud voice,
Stand upright on thy feet. And he
leaped and walked. (11) And when the
people saw what Paul had done, they
lifted up their voices, saying in the

---

(4) **The multitude of the city was divided.**—The context shows that St. Luke writes of the bulk of the heathen population. No numbers are given, but we may fairly assume that the converts were in a minority, and that they belonged, as a rule, to the lower classes (1 Cor. i. 26, 27), and that the chief men and women of the city, as at the Pisidian Antioch (chap. xiii. 50), were against them. The "rulers" who are named would seem, from the form of punishment selected, to have been those of the Jewish synagogue, and the crime of which the preachers were accused, as in the case of Stephen, to have been blasphemy. (See Notes on chap. vii. 58; John x. 31.)

(5) **To use them despitefully.**—The verb expresses wanton insult and outrage. St. Paul uses the noun derived from it to express the character of his own conduct as a persecutor (1 Tim. i. 13), and must have felt, as afterwards in the actual stoning of verse 19, that he was receiving the just reward of his own deeds.

(6) **And fled unto Lystra and Derbe, cities of Lycaonia.**—Here again, as in chap. xiii. 51, we can scarcely fail to trace a literal obedience to our Lord's commands. (See Note on Matt. x. 23.) The direction of the Apostles' journey now took them into a wilder and less civilised region. The range of the Taurus cut it off from the more cultivated country of Cilicia and Pisidia. It is described as a dreary plain, bare of trees, destitute of fresh water, and with several salt lakes. So Ovid (*Metaph.* viii. 621) speaks of it, as the result of personal observation:

> "Where men once dwelt a marshy lake is seen,
> And coots and bitterns haunt the waters green."

The very name Lycaonia, interpreted traditionally as *Wolf-land* (the local legend derived it from Lycaon, who had been transformed into a wolf), represented but too faithfully the character of the inhabitants. The travellers were also losing the protection which a Roman citizen might claim in a Roman province, Lycaonia, which had been annexed in A.D. 17 to the Roman province of Galatia, having been assigned by Caligula to Antiochus, King of Commagene. So wild a country was hardly likely to attract Jewish settlers; and there is no trace in St. Luke's narrative of the existence of a synagogue in either of the two cities. For the first time, so far as we know, St. Paul had to begin his work by preaching to the heathen. Even the child of a devout Jewish mother had grown up to manhood uncircumcised (see Note on chap. xvi. 3). Of the two towns named, Lystra was about forty miles to the south-east of Iconium, Derbe about twenty miles further to the east. The former, which lies to the north of a lofty conical mountain, the *Kara-dagh* (=Black Mountain) is now known as *Bin-bir-Kilisseh, i.e.,* "the thousand and one churches," from the ruins that abound there. The addition of "the region that lieth round about" suggests the thought that the cities were not large enough to supply a sufficient field of action. The work in the country villages must obviously—even more than in the cities—have been entirely among the Gentiles. Among the converts of this region, and probably of this time, we may note the names of Timotheus of Lystra (see Note on chap. xvi. 1), and Gaius, or Caius, of Derbe (chap. xx. 4).

(8) **Being a cripple from his mother's womb.**—We note, as in chaps. iii. 2, ix. 33, the characteristic care to record the duration of the infirmity which was supernaturally cured.

(9) **Who stedfastly beholding him.**—We note once more the recurrence of the characteristic word and look. (See Note on chap. xiii. 9.)

**Perceiving that he had faith to be healed.**—Here, as so often, as if it were the general, though not the universal, law of miraculous working (see Notes on Mark x. 23), faith is pre-supposed as the condition. It follows from this, no less than from the tense of the verb, "*used to listen* to Paul as he spoke," that he had for some days been among St. Paul's hearers, had heard the gospel of the death and resurrection of Jesus, and had found that such a Saviour met his every need. All this the Apostle read, with that earnest gaze of his, in the man's upward look.

(10) **Stand upright on thy feet.**—What may be called the *modus operandi* of the miracle reminds us of that of the paralytic in Matt. ix. 6, and the cripple at Bethesda in John v. 11, and the lame man in chap. iii. 6. The command, which would have seemed a mockery to one who did not rise beyond the limits of experience, is obeyed by the will that had been inspired by the new power of faith. The natural inference from the special fact recorded in verse 11, is that the command was given in Greek, and therefore that St. Paul had taught in that language.

**And he leaped and walked.**—The two verbs differ in their tense: he leaped, as with a single bound, and then continued walking. (Comp. Note on chap. iii. 8.)

(11) **Saying in the speech of Lycaonia.**—The fact is clearly recorded with a definite purpose, and no explanation seems so natural as that which assumes it to be given as accounting for the passive attitude of the Apostles till what was then said had borne its fruit in acts. It will be admitted by all who are not under the influence of a theory that this serves almost as a crucial instance, showing that the "gift of tongues," which St. Paul possessed so largely (1 Cor. xiv. 18), did not consist in a supernatural knowledge of every provincial *patois* with which he came in contact. (See Note on chap. ii. 4.) It is clear that he might easily

speech of Lycaonia, The gods are come down to us in the likeness of men.
(12) And they called Barnabas, Jupiter; and Paul, Mercurius, because he was the chief speaker.
(13) Then the priest of Jupiter, which was before their city, brought oxen and garlands unto the gates, and would have done sacrifice with the people.
(14) *Which* when the apostles, Barnabas and Paul, heard *of*, they rent their clothes, and ran in among the people, crying out,
(15) and saying, Sirs, why do ye these things? We also are men of like passions with you, and preach unto you that ye should turn from these vanities unto the living God, which made heaven, and earth, and the sea, and all things that are

---

have learnt afterwards, from those who knew both languages, the meaning of what at the time was unintelligible. To suppose, as some have done, that the Apostles, understanding what was said, acquiesced in the preparations for sacrifice in order that they might afterwards make their protest as with a greater dramatic effect, is at variance with the natural impression made by the narrative, and, it need scarcely be said, with any worthy conception of St. Paul's character. The diglottic character of the people, here and in other Asiatic provinces of the empire, would make it perfectly natural that they should speak to one another in their own dialect, while Greek served for their intercourse with strangers. The "speech of Lycaonia" is said to have had affinities with Assyrian.

**The gods are come down to us in the likeness of men.**—Literally, *the gods, made like unto men, are come down to us.* The belief which the words expressed was characteristic of the rude simplicity of the Lycaonians. No such cry would have been possible in the great cities where the confluence of a debased polytheism and philosophical speculation had ended in utter scepticism. And the form which the belief took was in accordance with the old legends of the district. There, according to the *Myth* which Ovid had recently revived and adorned (*Metam.* viii. 625—724), Zeus and Hermes (Jupiter and Mercury) had come in human guise, and been received by Baucis and Philemon (St. Paul's Epistle to Philemon shows that the name lingered in that region), and left tokens of their favour. We find from the poem just referred to that the place where they had dwelt was looked on as a shrine to which devout worshippers made their pilgrimages, and where they left their votive offerings.

(12) **They called Barnabas, Jupiter; and Paul, Mercurius.**—St. Luke gives, as was natural, the Greek forms—Zeus and Hermes. The main reason for the assignment of the two names was that the listeners recognised in St. Paul the gift of eloquence, which was the special attribute of Hermes. Possibly, also, unlike as were the weak bodily presence and the many infirmities of the Apostle to the sculptured grace with which we are familiar as belonging to the sandalled messenger of the gods—young, and beautiful, and agile—there may have been something in the taller stature and more stately presence of Barnabas which impressed them with the sense of a dignity like that of Jupiter. In any case, we must remember that the masterpieces of Greek art were not likely to have found their way to a Lycaonian village, and that the Hermes of Lystra may have borne the same relation to that of Athens and Corinth as the grotesque Madonna of some Italian wayside shrine does to the masterpieces of Raphael. Real idolatry cares little about the æsthetic beauty of the objects of its worship; and the Lycaonians were genuine idolaters.

**The chief speaker.**—Literally, *the ruler of speech*—taking the chief part in it.

(13) **The priest of Jupiter, which was before their city.**—The latter clause probably describes the position of the Temple of Zeus, standing at the entrance of the city, as the shrine of its protecting deity. The identical phrase used by St. Luke is found in Greek inscriptions at Ephesus.

**Brought oxen and garlands unto the gates.**—The garlands were the well-known *vittæ*, so familiar to us in ancient sculptures, commonly made of white wool, sometimes interwoven with leaves and flowers. The priests, attendants, doors, and altars were often decorated in the same way. The "gates" (the form of the Greek implying that they were the folding-doors of a large entrance) were probably those which led into the *atrium*, or court-yard, of the house where the Apostles were dwelling. The whole action is well represented in Raphael's well-known cartoon. Oxen were, in Greek ritual, the right victims for both Zeus and Hermes.

**Would have done sacrifice with the people.**—This would have involved cutting the throats of the oxen, catching the blood in a *patera*, or deep dish, and pouring it upon an altar. There may have been such an altar in the *atrium*, or one may have been improvised for the occasion.

(14) **Which when the apostles, Barnabas and Paul, heard of.**—They were, we may believe, in the house, within the court-yard, and therefore did not see the sacrificial procession; but they heard the noise of the multitude, perhaps also of some sacrificial hymn, and asked what it meant.

**They rent their clothes.**—The act is obviously recorded as that of men who are startled and surprised, and is altogether incompatible with the theory that they knew that they had been taken for deities and were expecting such honours. On the act of rending the clothes, see Note on Matt. xxvi. 65. It was the extremest expression of horror, hardly ever used except in deprecation of spoken or acted blasphemy. How far it would be fully understood by the heathen population of Lystra may be a question, but its very strangeness would startle and arrest them.

(15) **Sirs, why do ye these things?**—It is natural to suppose that the words were spoken in the Greek in which St. Luke records them, and therefore that St. Paul's previous teaching had been in the same language. The metrical structure of the close of the speech (see Note on verse 17) leaves hardly a shadow of doubt on this point.

**We also are men of like passions with you.**—The word, which expresses participation in all the passive conditions of human life, as well as in what are commonly known as "passions," occurs again in Jas. v. 17. There is, it will be noted, a striking parallelism between St. Paul's language here, and that of Peter to Cornelius (chap. x. 26).

**Ye should turn from these vanities.**—The demonstrative pronoun implies a corresponding gesture.

therein:[a] (16) who in times past suffered
all nations to walk in their own ways.[b]
(17) Nevertheless he left not himself
without witness, in that he did good,
and gave us rain from heaven, and
fruitful seasons, filling our hearts with
food and gladness. (18) And with these
sayings scarce restrained they the
people, that they had not done sacrifice
unto them.
(19) And there came thither *certain*
Jews from Antioch and Iconium, who
persuaded the people, and, having stoned
Paul,[c] drew *him* out of the city, supposing
he had been dead. (20) Howbeit,
as the disciples stood round about him,

a Gen. 1. 1; Ps. 146. 6; Rev. 14. 7.
b Ps. 81. 12.
c 2 Cor. 11. 25.

---

The Apostle points to all the pomp and pageantry of the intended sacrifice. The words "vanity" and "vain" were almost the invariable terms used by Jews to describe the emptiness and worthlessness of heathen worship (Eph. iv. 17; 1 Pet. i. 18; and, in the Old Testament, 1 Sam. xii. 21). In contrast with these dead and dumb things, the Apostle calls on them to turn to God, who truly lives and acts, and is the source of all life and power, the Maker of heaven and earth, the Giver of all good gifts, the Judge of all evil deeds. In contrast, alike, with the popular polytheism which assigned heaven, and earth, and sea to different deities, and to the speculative Pantheism which excluded will and purpose from its conception of the Godhead, he proclaims the One God as having every attribute of personal Life and Being.

(16) **Who in times past suffered all nations.**—Better, *all the heathen;* the term used being that which is always employed of the nations outside the covenant of Israel. We have here the first germ of what may be fairly described as St. Paul's philosophy of history. The times of ignorance had been permitted by God, and those who had lived in them would be equitably dealt with, and judged according to their knowledge. The same thought meets us again in the speech at Athens (chap. xvii. 30). In Rom. i., ii., xi., we meet with it, in an expanded form, as a more complete vindication of the righteousness of God. The ignorance and the sins of the Gentile world had been allowed to run their course, as the Law had been allowed to do its partial and imperfect work among the Jews, as parts, if one may so speak, of a great divine drama, leading both to feel the need of redemption, and preparing both for its reception. All were included in unbelief that God might have mercy upon all (Rom. xi. 32).

(17) **He left not himself without witness.**—Here again we have the outline of what is afterwards expanded (Rom. i. 19, 20). In speaking to peasants like those at Lystra, St. Paul naturally dwells most on the witness given through the divine goodness as manifested in nature. In addressing philosophers at Athens and at Rome, he points to the yet fuller witness of consciousness and conscience (chap. xvii. 28; Rom. ii. 14, 15).

**In that he did good.**—Better, as expressing the continuous manifestation of the divine will, "*working* good, *giving* rain, *filling* our hearts . ." The MSS. vary, some giving "us" and "our," and some "you" and "your." The former is more characteristic of the sympathy which led St. Paul to identify himself with Gentile as well as Jew. The "joy of harvest" (Isa. ix. 3) was the common inheritance of each. The latter words in the Greek, from "giving us rain from heaven," are so distinctly rhythmical that they suggest the thought that St. Paul quotes from some hymn of praise which he had heard in a harvest or vintage festival, and which, as with the altar to the Unknown God at Athens, he claims as due to Him whom men ignorantly worshipped. (See Note on chap. xvii. 23.)

(18) **With these sayings scarce restrained they the people.**—On some of those who were thus restrained the effect may well have been that they were roused to a higher life and did turn from "vanities" to the living God. We must, at any rate, think of St. Paul's work at Lystra as lasting long enough to allow time for the foundation of a church there. Among the more conspicuous converts were the devout Jewesses, Lois and her daughter Eunice (more accurately, *Eunike*), and the young Timotheus (2 Tim. i. 5). No mention is made of his father, and Eunice may have been a widow; but the fact that the boy had grown up uncircumcised rather suggests the influence of a living father. (See Note on chap. xvi. 3.)

(19) **There came thither certain Jews from Antioch.**—The context shows that the Pisidian Antioch is meant. The strength of the hostility is shown by the facts, (1) that the Jews of the two cities were acting in concert, and (2) that those of the former had travelled not less than one hundred and thirty miles to hinder the Apostle's work.

**Who persuaded the people.**—The sudden change of feeling is almost as startling as that which transformed the hosannas of the multitudes at Jerusalem into the cry of "Crucify Him!" (Matt. xxi. 9; xxvii. 22.) It is not difficult, however, to understand these vicissitudes of feeling in a barbarous and superstitious people. We find a like sudden change in an opposite direction in the people of Melita (chap. xxviii. 6). If the strangers who were endowed with such mysterious powers were not "gods in the likeness of men," they might be sorcerers, or even demons, in the evil sense of that word. The Jews, ever ready to impute signs and wonders to Beelzebub, the chief of the demons (see Notes on Matt. x. 34, xii. 24), would readily work on this feeling, and terrify the people into the cruel ferocity of panic.

**Having stoned Paul.**—The mode of punishment, as elsewhere, shows that it was planned and executed by Jews. They, apparently, were eager to satisfy themselves that they were inflicting punishment on a blasphemer: stoning him to death, and casting him out to be buried with the burial of an ass. And so, in one sense, as from man's way of looking on such things, the martyr expiated the guilt of the persecutor. The blinding, stunning blows fell on him as they had fallen on Stephen. It was the one instance in St. Paul's life of this form of suffering (2 Cor. xi. 25). The sufferings endured at Lystra stand out, at the close of his life, in the vista of past years with a marvellous distinctness (2 Tim. iii. 11).

(20) **Howbeit, as the disciples stood round about him.**—They, it is obvious, had been powerless to prevent the attack; but they stole out, when all was over, it may be, with the purpose of giving at least a decent interment. We may fairly think of Lois, and Eunice, and Timotheus, as present in that crowd,

he rose up, and came into the city: and the next day he departed with Barnabas to Derbe. (21) And when they had preached the gospel to that city, and had taught many, they returned again to Lystra, and *to* Iconium, and Antioch, (22) confirming the souls of the disciples, *and* exhorting them to continue in the faith, and that we must through much tribulation enter into the kingdom of God. (23) And when they had ordained them elders in every church, and had prayed with fasting, they commended them to the Lord, on whom they believed. (24) And after they had passed throughout Pisidia, they

---

weeping first for sorrow, and then for exceeding joy, to find that the teacher whom they loved was stunned only, and not dead.

**He departed with Barnabas to Derbe.**—The journey was one that must have occupied several hours, and we do well to remember that after the suffering of the previous day, it must have been one of peculiar hardship and fatigue. The city of Derbe was, as has been said, twenty miles to the east of Lystra. It was just within the Cappadocian boundary of Isauria. The exact site has not been identified, but the ruins of an Acropolis have been found not far from the lake *Ak-Ghieul*, which have been supposed to be the remains of Derbe. The whole region was infamous for its brigandage, and there may be a reference to this in the "perils of robbers" of 2 Cor. xi. 26.

(21) **And had taught many.**—Better, *made many disciples*. The word is the same as in Matt. xxviii. 19. Among these we may note Gaius, or Caius, afterwards conspicuous as one of St. Paul's companions (chap. xx. 4). The work done implies a stay of, it may be, some months' duration. During this time the violence of the hostility of the Jews at Antioch and Iconium had probably subsided, and the Apostles could revisit those cities, as they retraced their steps, without any great danger.

(22) **Confirming the souls of the disciples.**—Better, perhaps, *strengthening*, so as to avoid the more definite associations connected with the other term. In chap. xviii. 23, the word is so rendered. It is not the same as that used by later writers for the ecclesiastical rite of Confirmation.

**Exhorting them to continue in the faith.**—The question meets us whether "faith" is used in its subjective sense, the "feeling of trust," or objectively, as including the main substance of what was believed and taught—"a belief or creed." That the latter meaning had become established a few years after St. Luke wrote, we see in 1 Tim. v. 8; Jude verses 3, 20; and on the whole it seems probable that it is so used here.

**And that we must through much tribulation.**—More accurately, *through many tribulations*. The use of the first personal pronoun is suggestive. Is St. Luke generalising what he heard from those who had listened to St. Paul, and giving it in their very words? Was he himself one of those listeners? The two had clearly met before we find them both at Troas; and on the supposition suggested in the last question, the apparently casual use of the pronoun would be analogous to what we find afterwards. (See Note on chap. xvi. 10.) In St. Paul's latest Epistle to the chosen disciple of Lystra we have a touching reproduction of this teaching. He speaks of the afflictions which came on him at Antioch, at Iconium, at Lystra, and adds the general truth that "all that will live godly in Christ Jesus shall suffer persecutions" (2 Tim. iii. 12).

**The kingdom of God.**—We may pause to note the occurrence of the familiar phrase and thought of the Gospels in the earliest recorded teaching of St. Paul. In his Epistles it recurs frequently (Rom. xiv. 17; 1 Cor. iv. 20; vi. 9; Col. iv. 11; 2 Thess. i. 5). For him, too, that which was proclaimed was not a theory or an opinion, but an actual kingdom, of which Jesus the Christ was king.

(23) **And when they had ordained them elders.**—The word for "ordained" occurs in the New Testament here and in 2 Cor. viii. 19, where it is translated "chosen," and certainly seems to imply popular election (election by show of hands), which is, indeed, the natural meaning of the word. In chap. x. 41 a compound form of the verb is translated "chosen of God," and clearly excludes any action but that of the divine will. Used, as it is here, of the act of the two Apostles, not of the Church, the latter meaning seems most in harmony with the context. There may have been, as in chap. vi. 3, a previous election; or the names of those who were to be appointed may have been submitted to the approval of the Church; but the word cannot in itself be held to imply either. On the institution of elders, see Note on chap. xi. 30. It is interesting here to note (1) that Paul and Barnabas, by virtue of the authority which as Apostles they had received, primarily from Christ (Gal. i. 1) and mediately from the Church of Antioch (chap. xiii. 3), exercised the right of appointing, or, in later phrase, ordaining elders. (2) They plant among the Churches of the Gentiles the organisation which we have found in that of Jerusalem, and which was itself based on that of the Synagogue, not on that of the Temple. (3) As this appears as the first appointment, it would seem to follow that the disciples had in the meantime met, and taught, and baptised, and broken bread without them. Organisation of this kind was, *i.e.*, important for the permanence of the life of the Church as such, but not essential to its being, or to the spiritual growth of individual members. (4) It will be remembered that the "elders" so appointed were the same as those who, in the Apostolic Church, were known as "bishops" or "overseers" (*episcopi*), what we call distinctive episcopal functions being reserved for the Apostles, or for their personal representatives (1 Tim. iv. 16; Titus i. 5; see Note on chap. xx. 28).

**Had prayed with fasting.**—See Notes on chap. xiii. 2, 3. It is a legitimate inference, from this recurrence of the act, that Paul and Barnabas recognised it as an established rule or canon of the Church that these two acts should jointly serve as a preparation for the solemn work of appointing men to spiritual functions. Without prayer such an appointment was a mockery, and fasting served to intensify prayer.

**They commended them.**—The word is the same as in chap. xx. 32; Luke xxiii. 46. It implies the confiding trust of one who commits what is very precious to him to the keeping of another. So in 2 Tim. ii. 2 it is used of the *depositum fidei*, the treasure of truth which Timothy was to commit to faithful men. Here it implies an absolute trust in God as ordering all things for His Church and those who love Him.

came to Pamphylia. (25) And when they
had preached the word in Perga, they
went down into Attalia: (26) and thence
sailed to Antioch, from whence they
had been recommended to the grace of
God for the work which they fulfilled.
(27) And when they were come, and
had gathered the church together, they
rehearsed all that God had done with
them, and how he had opened the door
of faith unto the Gentiles. (28) And
there they abode long time with the
disciples.

A.D. 51.

CHAPTER XV.—(1) And certain men
which came down from Judæa taught
the brethren, *and said*, Except ye be
circumcised after the manner of Moses,[a]
ye cannot be saved. (2) When therefore
Paul and Barnabas had no small dissen-
sion and disputation with them, they
determined that Paul and Barnabas,

[a] Gal. 5. 2.

---

(25) **And when they had preached the word in Perga.**—The travellers retrace their steps. There is a coincidence more or less striking in the report of what they did at Perga. In chap. xiii. 13 there is no mention of their having preached in that city. We are simply told that Mark left them there, and that they then went on to Antioch. On their return, accordingly, they did what they had then left undone.

**They went down into Attalia.**—On their first journey they had gone straight from Paphos to Perga up the Cestrus. Now they made a *détour* which led them to the port at the mouth of the Catarrhactes, named after Attalus Philadelphus, King of Pergamus. There is no record of any work done there, and they probably only went to it as the port where they were most likely to find a sailing-vessel that would take them to Antioch. Their ship would naturally pass between Cilicia and Cyprus, enter the Orontes at Seleucia, and sail up to Antioch.

**Whence they had been recommended.**—Better, perhaps, *commended*, the compound form having slightly changed its meaning. The words seem to imply a mental survey on the part of the travellers of all that had passed since they had started on their journey. The "grace of God," to which they had then been commended, had not failed them.

(27) **And when they were come.**—Two years or thereabouts (A.D. 45—48) had passed since their mission. During that interval little probably had been heard of them, and we can picture to ourselves the eagerness with which the *Christiani* of Antioch would gather to listen to their report.

**How he had opened the door of faith unto the Gentiles.**—This is noticeable as the first occurrence, as far as the chronological order of the books of the New Testament is concerned, of a very characteristic phrase. It would seem to have been a favourite metaphor of St. Paul's (comp. 1 Cor. xvi. 1; 2 Cor. ii. 12; Col. iv. 3), and comes in here, probably, as a fragment from his speech. From this point of view it is interesting to note the recurrence of the phrase in Rev. iii. 8, both St. Paul and St. John, representing as they did different sections of the Church (Gal. ii. 9), agreeing in the thought that the door of the Father's house was now opened wider than it had ever been before, and that no man might shut it.

(28) **There they abode long time.**—The words probably cover an interval of more than a year, during which it is reasonable to suppose that the preaching of the two Apostles drew together a large number of Gentile converts.

## XV.

(1) **And certain men which came down from Judæa.**—We enter on the history of the first great controversy in the records of the Christian Church. It might have seemed as if the conversion of Cornelius had been accepted as deciding the question which we now find raised again (chap. xi. 18). It would seem, however, that those who had raised objections to Peter's conduct in that case were not content to accept the conclusion which he drew from it, and it is not difficult to represent to ourselves the train of thought which led them to take a different view. To them it may have seemed the exception that proved the rule. Where signs and wonders came in, they may have been content to accept an uncircumcised convert as a member of the Church, simply on the ground that God had dispensed in such cases with His own law; or they may have urged that though, in such cases, they did not require circumcision as a condition of admission, the continuance in the uncircumcised state after baptism was a wilful transgression, which shut men out from the "salvation" which they were seeking. Circumcision, they may have said, had been given as an "everlasting covenant" (Gen. xvii. 13), and had never been formally abrogated. Who were the new teachers, that they should change what God had thus established? It is clear that they came, claiming to speak in the name of James, the Bishop of Jerusalem, and though he distinctly repudiates having authorised them (verse 24), yet if we suppose, as is probable, that his Epistle was written shortly before the Council, we can easily understand that they might rest their case on the words which he had used in it, that "whosoever shall keep the whole Law, and yet offend in one point, is guilty of all" (Jas. ii. 10). Here, they might say, is a point confessedly in the Law, and even prior to it; and they were not prepared to draw the distinctions which we have learned to draw between the positive and the moral, the transient and the permanent, obligations of that Law. And it is to be noted that they did not merely make circumcision a condition of church communion; they carried their principles to their logical conclusion—as mediæval dogmatism did in the case of baptism—and excluded the uncircumcised from all hope of salvation. (Comp. the account of Ananias and Izates given in the Note on chap. ix. 10.)

(2) **When therefore Paul and Barnabas.**—The two Apostles must obviously have agreed in feeling that the teaching of the Judaisers (it will be convenient to use that term henceforth) involved a direct condemnation of all the work in which they saw the triumph of God's grace. They had proclaimed salvation through faith in Christ. Their converts were now told that they had been teaching a soul-destroying falsehood.

**No small dissension and disputation.**—The first of the two words was that which had been used by classical writers, like Thucydides (iii. 82) and

and certain other of them, should go
up to Jerusalem unto the apostles and
elders about this question. [3] And
being brought on their way by the
church, they passed through Phenice
and Samaria, declaring the conversion
of the Gentiles: and they caused great
joy unto all the brethren. [4] And when
they were come to Jerusalem, they were
received of the church, and *of* the
apostles and elders, and they declared
all things that God had done with them.

A.D. 52.

---

Aristotle (*Polit.* v. 2), to express the greatest evil of all political societies—the spirit of party and of faction. In Mark xv. 7; Luke xxiii. 19, it is used of the "insurrection" in which Barabbas had been the ringleader. That element of evil was now beginning to show itself in the Christian Church.

**They determined that Paul and Barnabas.**—These were naturally chosen as the representatives of the cause of which they had been the chief advocates. The "certain others" are not named, but the prophets of chap. xiii. 1, and the men of Cyprus and Cyrene of chap. xi. 20, were likely enough to have been chosen, and Titus was apparently taken up as an example of the fruits of St. Paul's labours (Gal. i. 3). Looking to the Roman name which this disciple bore, it is not unlikely that he may have been among the first to whom the term *Christian* was applied. (See Note on chap. xi. 26.) The fulness with which the history of the Council is given, suggests the possibility that St. Luke himself may have been present at it. If not, he must have based his report on materials supplied by St. Paul or one of the other delegates from Antioch, possibly Manaen (chap. xiii. 1).

**Should go up to Jerusalem unto the apostles and elders.**—The circumstances of the journey make it all but certain that we may identify it with that of which St. Paul speaks in Gal. ii. 1. The only other visits that can dispute its claim are those of chaps. xi. 30 and xviii. 22; but though the latter view has been taken by some able writers (*e.g.*, Lewin's *St. Paul*, i., p. 302), there are, it is believed, decisive grounds for rejecting both. Against the first there are the facts, (1) that it is not easy to place fourteen years between the visit of chap. ix. 27, and that of chap. xi. 30; (2) the visit of chap. xi. 30 appears in the history as confined to the single object of carrying relief to the suffering poor of the Church at Jerusalem; (3) the question as to enforcing circumcision had not then been raised, after its apparent settlement in the case of Cornelius; (4) had the agreement referred to in Gal. ii. 9 preceded the Council, it would assuredly have been appealed to in the course of the debate at the Council. Against the second there are the facts (1) that the interval would, in that case, have been more than fourteen years; and (2) that it was not likely that the question should have been raised again after the decision of the Council. The only arguments of any weight on the other side are, (1) that the narrative of Acts xv. makes no mention of Titus; and (2) that that of Gal. ii. makes no mention of the Council; but these arguments from omission tell equally against both the other visits. These points will be dealt with as we proceed, and are, in any case, not sufficient to outweigh the evidence in the other scale. The reference of the question to the "Apostles and elders" is in many ways important. (1) As against the dogmatic system of the Church of Rome. On her theory, in its latest forms, the reference should have been to Peter, and to Peter alone, as the unerring guide of the Church into all truth. (2) As a recognition of the authority of the mother-Church of Jerusalem by the daughter-Church of Antioch; and as a precedent for referring local disputes to the decision of a central authority. (3) As showing the confidence which Paul and Barnabas felt that the decision would be in their favour. They could not believe that St. Peter would be false to the lesson which the history of Cornelius had taught him, nor that St. James would recall the definition which he had so recently given of "pure and undefiled religion" (Jas. i. 27). (4) We note that St. Paul ascribes the journey to a "revelation" (Gal. ii. 1). The thought came into his mind as by an inspiration that this, and not prolonged wranglings at Antioch, was the right solution of the problem.

[3] **They passed through Phenice and Samaria.**—The route lay from Seleucia, at the mouth of the Orontes, along the coast of Sidon, Tyre, and, probably, Cæsarea, and then through Samaria. They might have gone to Joppa, and so have avoided the old Canaanite cities and the region of the hated Samaritans. The very journey was, therefore, an assertion of the principles for which they were contending. We note, too, that the facts imply that they found "brethren," *i.e.*, established Christian societies, in both regions. "Tyre and Sidon" had repented and believed, though Chorazin and Bethsaida had hardened themselves in unbelief (Luke xi. 13). The "woman of Canaan," of Mark vii. 26, may, by this time, have eaten not of the "crumbs," but of the "Bread" of Life. Everything points to Philip as the probable Evangelist of this region as well as of Samaria. Paul and Barnabas would accordingly, as they travelled, be setting their seal to his work, claiming fellowship with Canaanites and Samaritans; and wherever they went they were received with joy. Here, at least, they were certain of support; and, on mere grounds of policy, they were strengthening their cause by appearing at Jerusalem as the representatives of such important communities, having the courage of their convictions, and determined, though they might make concessions in things indifferent, not to sacrifice a single principle.

**They caused great joy.**—The tense implies continued action. Wherever they went the tidings of the conversion of the Gentiles were received by the disciples at large with a gladness which presented the strongest possible contrast to the narrowness and bitterness of the Pharisee section of the Church of Jerusalem.

[4] **They were received of the church, and of the apostles and elders.**—The words imply a general gathering of the Church, members of different synagogues coming together, with the elders who presided over them. The position of the Apostles, though in some degree analogous in their relation to the elders to the later office of bishops, was yet in many ways unique. They had no local diocese, but remained at Jerusalem, guiding the progress of the Church at large, as a kind of central council, calling in the "elders," or "presbyters," to consult with them, and submitting the result of their deliberations to the Church at large. The three bodies stood to each other as the *Boulè*, or council, the *Gerusia*, or senate, and the *Ecclesia*, or assembly, in a Greek republic.

(5) But there rose up certain of the sect of the Pharisees which believed, saying, That it was needful to circumcise them, and to command *them* to keep the law of Moses.
(6) And the apostles and elders came together for to consider of this matter.
(7) And when there had been much disputing, Peter rose up, and said unto them, Men *and* brethren, ye know how that a good while ago God made choice among us,[a] that the Gentiles by my mouth should hear the word of the gospel, and believe.
(8) And God, which knoweth the hearts, bare them witness, giving them the Holy Ghost, even as

[a] ch. 10. 20, and 11. 13.

**They declared all things that God had done with them.**—This obviously implied a narrative of considerable length: the history of acts and sufferings, of signs and wonders, of the fruits of the Spirit as seen in the purity, and truth, and love of the Gentile converts. This took place apparently at a preliminary meeting.

(5) **Certain of the sect of the Pharisees which believed.**—This is the first distinct mention of the conversion of any of the Pharisaic party, but there had been a drift in that direction going on for some time, beginning during our Lord's ministry (John xii. 42), and showing itself in the moderate counsels of Gamaliel (chap. v. 38, 39). The position which they occupied was that of accepting Jesus as a teacher sent from God, proved by the Resurrection to be the Christ, and as such the Head of a kingdom which was to present to mankind a restored and glorified Judaism, the Law kept in its completeness, the Temple ritual still maintained, Gentiles admitted only on their confessing their inferiority and accepting the sign of incorporation with the superior race. It appears, from Gal. ii. 1, that here, as in so many later controversies, the general issue was debated on an individual case. Was Titus—a Greek, *i.e.*, a Gentile, whom St. Paul had brought up with him—to be circumcised, or not? Was he to be admitted to communion with the Church, or treated as a heathen? Here, probably, there was no official rank as in the case of Cornelius, no previous transition stage in passing through the synagogue as a proselyte of the gate. He was a Gentile pure and simple, and as such his case was a crucial one. Circumcision, however, did not stand alone. It carried with it every jot and tittle of the Law, the Sabbaths and the feasts, the distinction between clean and unclean meats. It may be noted that the position which Titus occupied in this controversy gave him a special fitness for the work afterwards assigned to him, of contending against the party of the circumcision, with their "Jewish fables" and false standards of purity (Tit. i. 10, 14, 15).

(6) **And the apostles and elders came together.**—The meeting rightly takes its place as the first in the long series of councils, or synods, which mark the course of the Church's history. It bore its witness that the government of the Christian society was not to rest in the autocracy of a single will, but in the deliberative decision of those who, directly or indirectly, having been appointed by the choice, or with the approval, of the people, represented the whole community. Presbyters had an equal voice with the Apostles, whose position was analogous to that of the later bishops. Those whom we should call the laity were present at the deliberations, and, though we have no absolute proof that they took part in them, gave their vote. (Comp. Note on verse 23.) Strictly speaking, it was, in the later ecclesiastical language, a provincial and not an œcumenical synod, called to decide what seemed a question of discipline rather than of doctrine; but the ground on which the question had been argued made it one of world-wide dogmatic importance. If circumcision was necessary, then faith in Christ was insufficient. St. Paul saw and felt this in all its fulness, and therefore would not "give way by subjection, no, not for an hour" (Gal. ii. 5). We have no *data* for estimating the number of the presbyters who were present. Probably they included those of the neighbouring towns and villages of Judæa as well as of Jerusalem, and if so, we may fairly think of some number between fifty and a hundred.

(7) **When there had been much disputing.**—This implies a full discussion, in which the Judaising teachers, probably, though not certainly, presbyters, on the one side, and the advocates of freedom, on the other, took part. Light is thrown on the character of the debate by St. Paul's account of the matter in Gal. ii. 2—10. He did not even then bring out what he held and taught, in its fulness. He shrank from startling and offending the prejudices of his countrymen, and was content to argue that circumcision and the Law were not binding upon the Gentiles, to press the precedent of the case of Cornelius and the analogy of the proselytes of the gate. Privately, in interviews with Peter, James, and John, he had gone further, and had declared his convictions that for Jew and Gentile alike circumcision and the Law were hindrances, and not helps, to the spiritual life, and that faith working by love was everything. And they, as the history of the Council and yet more their Epistles show, accepted his teaching. Of all doctrines as to the development of the Christian Church that which sees in Peter, James, and John the leaders of a Judaising anti-Pauline party is, perhaps, the most baseless and fantastic. The fact that their names were unscrupulously used by that party, both in their lifetime and, as the Pseudo-Clementine *Homilies* and *Recognitions* show, after their death, cannot outweigh their own deliberate words and acts.

**Peter rose up, and said unto them.**—The position of the Apostle is one of authority, but not of primacy. He does not preside, nor even propose, as we should say, a definite canon or resolution. His authority is that of personal and moral influence, that of a *vir pietate gravis*, but nothing more.

**Men and brethren.**—Better, as before, *Brethren* only, and so again in verse 13.

**Ye know how that a good while ago . . .**—Literally, *of ancient days.* Ten or twelve years had passed since the conversion of Cornelius. Where Peter had been in the meantime, and what he had done, we have no record. We can hardly believe, as the Romish theory implies, that he came from the imperial city to attend the Council. It will be noted, as has been said before (see Note on chap. xi. 20), that the Apostle speaks of this as having been the first admission of the Gentiles.

(8) **God which knoweth the hearts.**—We note the recurrence of the epithet as characteristic of St. Peter. (See Note on chap. i. 24.)

*he did* unto us; (9) and put no difference
between us and them, purifying their
hearts by faith.[a] (10) Now therefore
why tempt ye God, to put a yoke upon
the neck of the disciples, which neither
our fathers nor we were able to bear?
(11) But we believe that through the
grace of the Lord Jesus Christ we shall
be saved, even as they.
(12) Then all the multitude kept si-
lence, and gave audience to Barnabas
and Paul, declaring what miracles and
wonders God had wrought among the
Gentiles by them.
(13) And after they had held their
peace, James answered, saying, Men *and*
brethren, hearken unto me: (14) Simeon
hath declared how God at the first did
visit the Gentiles, to take out of them
a people for his name. (15) And to this
agree the words of the prophets; as it
is written, (16) After this I will return,

[a] ch. 10. 43; 1 Cor. 1. 2.

---

(9) **And put no difference between us and them.**—It is obvious that this implies the most entire acceptance of the teaching which St. Paul had privately communicated to the three who were as the pillars of the Church (Gal. ii. 9). In Rom. x. 12 we have almost the very words of St. Peter reproduced.

**Purifying their hearts by faith.**—The addition of these words is very suggestive. It was not only in the "gifts" of the Spirit, the tongues and prophecy, that the Apostle saw the witness which God had borne to the acceptance of the Gentiles, but even more than this, in the new purity growing out of a new faith in God and a new hope. Underlying the words we trace the assertion of a higher ideal of purity than that on which the Pharisees were insisting. They looked on the Gentiles as impure because they did not observe the ceremonial law and the traditions of the elders as to purity. He had learnt to call no man common or unclean (chap. x. 28) and to see that it was in the heart, and not in the flesh, that the work of purifying was to be accomplished. Comp. in connection with the thought suggested in the Note on verse 5, the teaching as to purity in Tit. i. 15.

(10) **Why tempt ye God.**—To tempt God was to make the experiment whether His will, manifested in the acceptance of the Gentiles, or man's will, resenting and resisting it, was the stronger of the two. Nothing but defeat and condemnation could be the issue of such a trial.

**To put a yoke upon the neck of the disciples.**—No words of St. Paul's, in relation to the Law, could be stronger or clearer than these. They reproduced our Lord's own language as to the "heavy burdens" of the Pharisaic traditions (Matt. xxiii. 4) and His own "easy yoke" (Matt. xi. 30). They were echoed by St. Paul when he warned the Galatians not to be entangled again in the yoke of bondage (Gal. v. 1). The words that follow, on the one hand, speak out the experience of the Apostle himself in terms that are hardly less striking than those of St. Paul in Rom. vii. 7, 8, though they deal with the Law in its positive rather than its moral aspects, and contain an implied appeal to the experience of his hearers. Was it worth while to "tempt God" by resisting His teaching in history in order to bring the Gentiles down to the level from which they themselves, Jews as they were, were thankful to have risen?

(11) **We believe that through the grace . . .**—This comes, in what we may well regard as a summary of St. Peter's speech, as the closing argument. The Pharisee might regard the Law as binding, but even he, if he believed in Christ, was compelled to confess that his hope of salvation was found in the work of Christ as the Saviour; and if so, then, as regards that hope, Jew and Gentile were on the same level, and the judgment that men could not be saved without the Law was but the inconsistency of an intolerant dogmatism, insisting on imposing that which was acknowledged to be profitless. It may be noted that this is the last appearance of St. Peter in the Acts, which from this period turns exclusively upon the work of St. Paul. For the subsequent history of the former, see *Introduction* to the Epistles of St. Peter.

(12) **And gave audience to Barnabas and Paul.**—The leaders of the Church had clearly reserved their part in the debate to the last, and the two Apostles of the Gentiles were now called on to repeat more publicly what they had already narrated to the Apostles and elders (verse 4). It was, perhaps, with a special view to the character of their hearers that they laid stress on the "signs and wonders" which had attested God's acceptance of their work (Matt. xii. 38; xvi. 1; 1 Cor. i. 22). Miracles had been wrought among the Gentiles as freely as among the Jews, and those who wrought them, unless they were casting out devils by Beelzebub (and the Judaisers appear to have shrunk from that charge), must have been sent by God (John iii. 2; ix. 31—33).

(13) **James answered.**—The position which James the brother of the Lord (see Notes on chap. xii. 17; and Matt. xii. 46; xii. 55) occupies in the Council is clearly that of pre-eminence, justifying the title of Bishop of Jerusalem, which later writers give him. No one speaks after him; he sums up the whole debate; he proposes the decree which is to be submitted to the Council for approval.

(14) **Simeon hath declared . . .**—The Greek form is *Symeon*, as in 2 Pet. i. 1. The use of the old Hebrew form of the Apostle's name, instead of the more familiar Simon, was natural in the Galilean speaker, and is presumptive evidence in favour of our having a report from notes made at the time.

**Did visit the Gentiles, to take out of them a people.**—The two words present an emphatic contrast. The Jews claimed for themselves the exclusive right to the latter term. They alone were the "people," the rest of mankind were the "nations"—the "heathen." St. James proclaims that out of those heathen nations a people had been taken who were as truly God's people as Israel had ever been. He, too, recognises the change as fully as St. Paul does, when in Rom. ix. 26 he quotes the memorable prophecy of Hosea i. 10. St. James as well as St. Peter had, it is clear, profited by the private teaching referred to in Gal. ii. 2.

(15) **To this agree the words of the prophets.**—On the mode of quoting without naming the prophet see Note on chap. xiii. 40.

(16) **After this I will return.**—It is a fact not without interest that the prophet from whom these words are taken (Amos ix. 11, 12) had been already quoted by

and will build again the tabernacle of
David, which is fallen down;[a] and I will
build again the ruins thereof, and I
will set it up: (17) that the residue of
men might seek after the Lord, and all
the Gentiles, upon whom my name is
called, saith the Lord, who doeth all
these things. (18) Known unto God are
all his works from the beginning of the
world. (19) Wherefore my sentence is,
that we trouble not them, which from
among the Gentiles are turned to God:
(20) but that we write unto them, that
they abstain from pollutions of idols,

[a] Amos 9. 11.

---

Stephen (chap. vii. 42). Those who then listened to him had, we may believe, been led to turn to the writings of Amos, and to find in them meanings which had hitherto been latent. The fact that the inference drawn from the passage mainly turns on a clause in which the LXX. version, which St. James quotes, differs from the Hebrew, shows, beyond the shadow of a doubt, that the discussion must have been conducted in Greek, and not in Hebrew. At first this may appear strange in a council held at Jerusalem, but the trial of Stephen presents a precedent (see Note on chap. vii. 1); and it is obvious that in a debate which chiefly affected the interests of Greeks, and at which many of them, and of the Hellenistic Jews, were likely to be present, the use of that language, both in the debate and the decree in which it resulted, was almost a matter of necessity. Both languages were probably equally familiar to the inhabitants of Jerusalem. (See Note on chap. xxii. 2.) The quotation suggests, perhaps implies, a fuller interpretation than is given in the summary of St. James's speech. It assumes that the "tabernacle of David," which to human eyes had been lying as in ruins, was being rebuilt by Christ, the Son of David, that He was doing the work which, in the prophecy, Jehovah claimed as His.

(17) **That the residue of men . . .**—The Hebrew gives, as in our version, "That they may possess the remnant of Edom and of all the heathen which are called by my name." The LXX. translators either paraphrased the passage, so as to give a wider and more general view of its teaching, or followed a reading in which the Hebrew for "man" (*Adam*) took the place of Edom. It will be seen that the argument of St. James turns upon the Greek rendering. The "name of God" was to be "called" upon by those who were "the residue of men," *i.e.*, all that were outside the pale of Israel. So understood, the words became, of course, a prediction of the conversion of the Gentiles, and to the uncritical habits of the time, accustomed to Targums or Paraphrases of many parts of Scripture, the LXX. was for all but the stricter and more bigoted Hebraists, as authoritative as the original.

(18) **Known unto God are all his works.**—The better MSS. give "all His work"—*i.e.*, the great work of the government and education of mankind. The words are an implicit answer to the charge of innovation. If the work were of God, it could not be so called, for His mercies are everlasting, and the work which He carries on now must be thought of as contemplated and purposed from eternity. The principle has clearly a wider range than that within which St. James applies it. We do well to remember, whenever we are tempted to offer an obstinate resistance to what seems to us a novelty, and which we therefore are ready to condemn, that we ought first to inquire whether the "signs of the times" do not indicate that it is part of the divine plan, working through the ages, that the old order should change and give place to the new.

(19) **Wherefore my sentence is.**—Literally, *Wherefore I judge.* The tone is that of one who speaks with authority, but what follows is not given as a decree, but as a resolution which was submitted to the judgment of the Apostles and elders. (Comp. chap. xvi. 4.)

**That we trouble not them.**—The verb is not found elsewhere in the New Testament, and expresses the idea of "worrying" or "harassing."

**Are turned to God.**—More accurately, *are turning*, as acknowledging that the work was going on at that very moment.

(20) **But that we write unto them.**—The grounds on which the measure thus defined was proposed are not far to seek. (1) It was of the nature of a compromise. The Gentiles could not complain that the burden imposed on them was anything very grievous. The Pharisee section of the Church could not refuse admission to those who fulfilled these conditions, when they had admitted the proselytes of the gate on like conditions to their synagogues, and had so treated them as no longer unclean. (2) The rules on which stress was now laid found a place among the seven precepts traditionally ascribed to Noah, and based upon the commands recorded in Gen. ix. 5. These were held to be binding upon all mankind; while the Law, as such, was binding on Israel only. These, therefore, had been thought sufficient for the proselytes of the gate before, and were urged now as sufficient for the Gentile converts by the teacher who represented the most rigid type of Judaism. (See, once more, the history of Ananias and Izates in the Note on chap. ix. 10.) Special reasons attached, as will be seen, to each precept.

**From pollutions of idols.**—The Greek of the first noun is found only in the LXX. and the New Testament; and perhaps its primary idea is that of "wallowing" in blood and mire, and so incurring pollution. As distinguished from the acts that follow, it indicates any participation, publicly or privately, in idolatrous rites. One who acted on the rule would have to refrain from entering a temple, and to dislodge busts or statues of the gods from his house and gardens. The presence of such things, when they presented themselves on entering a house, was a great stumbling-block to devout Jews, and the Gentile convert who, left to himself, might have been disposed to keep them, though no longer as objects of worship, but as works of art, was required to renounce them. The statues of Zeus and Artemis and Hermes were to be to him henceforth as abominations. In the decree itself, however, we find "things sacrificed to idols" instead of the more general term, and we may accordingly deal here with that question also. So interpreted, the rule brings before us a new phase of the life of the early Christian converts. Under the religion of Greece and Rome, sacrifices were so common that it might fairly be taken for granted that the flesh at any festive meal had been so offered. But a small portion of the flesh was burnt upon the altar, and the rest was cooked for the household meal, or sent to the market for sale. Such meat was, in the eyes of the strict Jews, polluted,

and *from* fornication, and *from* things strangled, and *from* blood. (21) For Moses of old time hath in every city them that preach him, being read in

and the history of Daniel and his companions (Dan. i. 8) was regarded as a precedent to avoiding it. Partly on this ground, partly on that referred to in the next Note but one, the Jew never bought meat in the market, nor of other than a Jewish butcher. He travelled with his *cophinus*, or basket, on his back, and carried his provisions with him. So Juvenal (*Sat.* iii. 14) speaks of—

> "Judæis, quorum cophinus fœnumque supellex."
> ["Basket, and wisp of straw to serve as pillow,—
> That's the Jew's luggage."]

Here, therefore, was a new stumbling-block, and the Gentile was required to avoid this also. It involved many sacrifices, and what would seem privations. The convert had to refuse invitations to birthday, and marriage, and funeral feasts; or, if present, to refuse to eat at them. A man with a sensitive conscience would refuse to partake of what was set before him in a private house or offered for sale in the market, unless he had satisfied himself that it had not so been offered. It was natural that this restriction, which did not rest directly on a moral ground, should give rise to some resistance, and the controversy connected with it assumed many different phases. At Corinth men claimed the right to eat what they chose, and St. Paul conceded the right in the abstract, but urged abstinence on the ground of charity (1 Cor. viii.—x.). At Pergamos and Thyatira, somewhat later in the apostolic age (Rev. ii. 14, 20), the lawfulness of eating things sacrificed to idols was openly maintained in contravention alike of the teaching of St. Paul and of the apostolic decree, and was joined with a like claim to be exempted from the law which forbade illicit sexual intercourse. At Corinth, it would seem from 1 Cor. viii. 10, the assertion of freedom had led men so far as not only to eat of the flesh that had been sacrificed, but actually to sit down to a feast in the idol's temple. (Comp. Rom. ii. 22, as expressing the Jewish feeling.)

**And from fornication.**—We are surprised at first to find, what seems to us, a moral law placed in juxtaposition with two rules which, like those that follow, seem purely positive and ceremonial. We have to remember, however, (1) that the first command was moral also, and that we may fairly recognise something like a practical, though not a formal distinction, by thinking of the first two precepts as grouped together; (2) that the sin named, involving, as it did, the absence of any true sense of self-respecting purity or reverence for womanhood, was the wide-spread evil of the ancient world, against which Israel had from the first been called to bear its witness (Gen. xxxiv. 31; Lev. xix. 29; Deut. xxiii. 17; Prov. vii. 6—27). The increasing laxity of morals throughout the Roman empire, showing itself in the well-known line of Terence—

> "Nihil peccati est adolescentulum scortari,"

had led men to think of it as natural and permissible, bringing with it no sense of wrong or shame (comp. Horace, *Sat.* i. 2, 119), and it might well be that the ethical standard of the Gentile converts was not all at once raised to a true ideal of purity. The old license may have seemed venial, and the disciples may have thought, as Christians have too often thought since, that it did not call for any deep repentance, or exclude them from fellowship with Christ. And yet it was clear that to the Jewish Christian, trained from his childhood to condemn the sin severely, this, too, would legitimately be a very grave stumbling-block in the admission of Gentile converts. How could he feel any assurance that they might not have come from the embraces of a harlot to the Feast of Charity or to the very Supper of the Lord? (Comp. 1 Cor. vi. 15; Rev. ii. 14.) Such a state of things required to be dealt with by a special enactment. The moral command had to be re-enacted, and brought into a new prominence. The Church had to take its first step in purifying the morals of mankind, not only by its general teaching, but by canons and rules of discipline. Stress has often been laid on the fact that in many cases, as in those of the *Hetœræ*, or harlot-priestesses, of Aphrodite at Corinth and Paphos, prostitution was in closest alliance with idolatry, as a reason for the prohibition, and it is, of course, true that in such cases the sin assumed, in the eyes of Jews, an aggravated character. The man identified himself, by his sinful indulgence, with the *cultus* of the woman who was its avowed devotee. We can scarcely think, however, that the sin was forbidden, not on account of its own intrinsic evil, but only or chiefly, with a view to this ulterior and incidental consequence.

**Things strangled.**—Literally, *of that which has been strangled.* The prohibition rested on Gen. ix. 4, and was connected with the symbolic meaning of the blood as representing life, and therefore consecrated to Jehovah. It was repeated in the Law (Lev. iii. 17; vii. 26; Deut. xii. 16; 1 Sam. xiv. 33), and has been maintained with a wonderful tenacity. For this reason, long after sacrifices have ceased, the Jew will still, if possible, only eat what has been killed by a butcher of his own persuasion. Meat so killed, which may be eaten without defilement, is known technically as *Kosher*. Here the moral element falls entirely into the background, and the prohibition has simply the character of a *concordat* to avoid offence. St. Paul and St. Peter were alike persuaded that "there is nothing unclean of itself" (chap. x. 15; Rom. xiv. 14). Practically, the effect of the rule would have been to compel Christians to buy their meat, poultry, &c., from a Jewish butcher or a Christian who followed the Jewish mode of killing, and in some places this must have entailed considerable inconvenience.

**From blood.**—As distinguished from the preceding rule, this forbade the separate use of blood, as with flour and vegetables, or in the black-puddings of modern cookery, as an article of food. Dishes so prepared were common in the *cuisine* both of Greeks and Romans, and here also, therefore, the restriction would have involved a frequent withdrawal from social life, or a conspicuous singularity. On the history of the observance, see Note on verse 28.

(21) **For Moses of old time.**—Literally, *of ancient generations.* The conjunction gives the reason for writing to the Gentiles, and giving them these injunctions. The Jews, who heard the Law in their synagogues every Sabbath, did not need instruction. It might be taken for granted that they would adhere to the rules now specified. So, in verse 23, the encyclical letter is addressed exclusively to "the brethren of the Gentiles."

the synagogues every sabbath day.
(22) Then pleased it the apostles and elders, with the whole church, to send chosen men of their own company to Antioch with Paul and Barnabas; *namely*, Judas surnamed Barsabas, and Silas, chief men among the brethren:
(23) and they wrote *letters* by them after this manner; The apostles and elders and brethren *send* greeting unto the brethren which are of the Gentiles in Antioch and Syria and Cilicia:
(24) Forasmuch as we have heard, that certain which went out from us have troubled you with words, subverting your souls, saying, *Ye must* be circumcised, and

---

(22) **The apostles and elders, with the whole church.**—The latter words are important, as showing the position occupied by the laity. If they concurred in the letter, it must have been submitted to their approval, and the right to approve involves the power to reject and, probably, to modify. It is probable enough, as in the analogous constitution of Greek republics above referred to (see Note on verse 4), that the Ecclesia, or popular assembly, did not possess the power of initiating measures; but their right to vote appears, from this instance, to have been indisputable. (See, however, Note on the next verse.) It does not follow, of course, that what was thus the polity of the apostolic age was necessarily adapted for the Church of all subsequent ages; but the exclusion of the laity from all share in Church synods, though it may be defended as a safeguard against the violence of a barbarous or faithless age, must, at any rate, be admitted to be at variance with primitive and apostolic practice.

**To send chosen men.**—Literally, the participle being active in meaning, *to choose and send men.* This was obviously necessary, to guard against suspicion. Had Paul and Barnabas alone been the bearers of such a letter, it might have been said that they had forged it.

**Judas surnamed Barsabas.**—The same patronymic meets us, it will be remembered, in chap. i. 23, as belonging to "Joseph, called Barsabas, who was surnamed Justus." It is a natural inference that the two were brothers, and therefore that the disciple now mentioned had been among those who were personally followers of our Lord. This would naturally clothe him with a high authority. The fact that he is spoken of in verse 32 as a prophet, makes it probable that he was of the number of the Seventy. (See Note on Luke x. 1.)

**Silas.**—This may have been either a contracted form of Silvanus, as Antipas was of Antipatros, or an Aramaic name, for which Silvanus was adopted as the nearest Greek equivalent. It is probable that he, too, fulfilled the same conditions as his companion. He also was a prophet (verse 32). His later history will be noticed as it comes before us. As the name is connected with the Hebrew for "three," he has by some been identified with the Tertius of Rom. xvi. 22; but it is hardly probable that one who had been known at Corinth as Silvanus (2 Cor. i. 19), should afterwards have changed his name.

**Chief men among the brethren.**—The title thus given is the same as "those that bear rule over you," in Heb. xiii. 17, and implies that they had a position of greater authority than the other elders, as at least *primi inter pares.* This also falls in with the view that they had been disciples of Christ, who, as the number of witnesses diminished, came more and more into prominence.

(23) **And they wrote letters by them.**—Literally, *wrote letters by their hands.* What follows, unless we assume a deliberate fraud, is clearly the transcript of a document—the first in the long list of decrees and canons and encyclical letters which mark the Church's history.

**The apostles and elders and brethren.**—The MSS. present a singular variation of readings, some of the earliest omitting the conjunction and article before the last noun, and giving "the Apostles and elders, brethren." Such a mode of speech, however, is foreign to the usage of the New Testament, and it is probable that this reading originated in a desire to bring the text into harmony with the later practice of the Church, which excluded the laity from all participation in its synods. (See Note on verse 22.)

**Send greeting.**—Literally, *wish joy.* The formula was common in Greek epistles, but is not used in the New Testament, except here and in Jas. i. 1. As it is reasonable to suppose that this letter was written or dictated by him, its occurrence is *primâ facie* evidence of the authorship of the Epistle that bears his name, and which, on the view taken in these Notes, had been already written to the Church of the Circumcision.

**Unto the brethren which are of the Gentiles.**—The letter was therefore addressed to them exclusively (see Note on verse 20), as the Epistle of St. James had probably been previously addressed to the Jews of the "dispersion," and not to the Gentiles.

**In Antioch and Syria and Cilicia.**—The mention of the latter country is important as showing the extent of St. Paul's work there prior to his joining Barnabas at Antioch (chap. xi. 25). There also he had founded churches in which Gentile converts were admitted as such to full communion.

(24) **Certain which went out from us.**—The reference is obviously to the teachers (their names are wisely and charitably suppressed) who had appeared at Antioch, as in verse 1. St. John, who was present at the Council (Gal. ii. 9), and who, though he took no part in the debate, may well have had a share in drawing up the letter, uses a like mode of speech, "They went out from us, but they were not of us" (1 John ii. 19).

**Subverting your souls.**—The Greek verb, literally, *turning upside down,* implies throwing into a state of excitement and agitation. The Gentiles had been "unsettled" by the teaching of the Judaisers.

**And keep the law.**—Assuming the Epistle of St. James to have been already written, there is something almost like a touch of irony in his repeating the phrase of Jas. ii. 10. The teachers who bade the Gentiles keep the Law were reminded in that Epistle that they, in their servile respect of persons, were breaking the Law deliberately in one point, and were therefore guilty of all. Putting the two passages together, they bring St. James before us as speaking in the very accents of St. Paul, "Thou, therefore, which teachest another, teachest thou not thyself?" (Rom. ii. 21.)

**To whom we gave no such commandment.**—The word "such" is a needless interpolation. What

keep the law: to whom we gave no *such* commandment: (25) it seemed good unto us, being assembled with one accord, to send chosen men unto you with our beloved Barnabas and Paul, (26) men that have hazarded their lives for the name of our Lord Jesus Christ. (27) We have sent therefore Judas and Silas, who shall also tell *you* the same things by mouth. (28) For it seemed good to the Holy Ghost, and to us, to lay upon you no greater burden than these necessary things; (29) that ye abstain from meats offered to idols, and from blood, and from things strangled, and from fornication: from which if ye keep your-

---

St. James declares is that the teachers had had no commission of any kind from him. The passage is important as throwing light on the nature of a later claim set up by the same party (Gal. ii. 12).

(25) **Being assembled with one accord.**—Literally, *being of one mind, unanimously.*

**To send chosen men unto you.**—Literally, *to choose men and send them unto you.* The men, are, of course, Barsabas and Silas.

**With our beloved Barnabas and Paul.**—The order in which the names stand is, perhaps, characteristic of the Church of Jerusalem, to whom Barnabas was still the more conspicuous teacher of the two. The way in which the two are named may be taken as illustrating St. Paul's statement that the "pillars" of the Church of Jerusalem gave to him and Barnabas the "right hand of fellowship" (Gal. ii. 9).

(26) **Men that have hazarded their lives.**—It is clear from this that the narrative of the hairbreadth escapes at the Pisidian Antioch (chap. xiii. 50) and Lystra (chap. xiv. 19) must have been laid before the Church. Prominence is given to the fact as likely to secure reverence for those whom many had hitherto regarded with distrust.

(28) **It seemed good to the Holy Ghost, and to us . . .**—The measure was, the Apostles were persuaded, one of wisdom and charity, and they could not ascribe those gifts to any other source than the Spirit who gives a right judgment in all things. The words have since become almost a formula for the decrees of councils and synods, often used most recklessly when those decrees bore most clearly the marks of human policy and passion. Here we may well admit that the claim was founded on a real inspiration, remembering, however, as we do so, that an inspired commandment does not necessarily involve a permanent obligation. (See Note on next verse.)

**To lay upon you no greater burden than these necessary things.**—The words throw light upon the message addressed to the Church of Thyatira, "I will put upon you no other burden" (Rev. ii. 24). Looking to the prominence in the Epistles to the Seven Churches of the two points of fornication and eating things sacrificed to idols, there can scarcely be the shadow of a doubt that we have in those words a distinct reference to the decree of the Council of Jerusalem. The letter does not say why these things were necessary, and the term was probably chosen as covering alike the views of those who held, like the Pharisee Christians, that they were binding on the Church for ever, and those who, like St. Paul, held that they were necessary only for the time, and as a measure of wise expediency.

(29) **From meats offered to idols.**—The specific term takes the place of the more general word which St. James had used. The change, if the two words were not used, as is possible, as altogether equivalent, may be thought of as favouring the Gentiles by narrowing the prohibition to a single point.

**Fare ye well.**—The closing salutation was, like the opening, a Greek and not a Hebrew one. It meets us again in chap. xxiii. 30. Both were naturally used in a letter addressed to Greeks, and intended to be read by them and by Hellenistic Jews. It does not occur, however, in any of the Epistles of the New Testament.

It is natural to ask, at the close of the great encyclical letter, in what relation it really stood to the life of the Apostolic Church. As a *concordat* between the contending parties it was framed, as has been said, with a sagacity that may well be looked on as inspired. But obviously it was not, and from the nature of the case could not be, more than that. The time had not come for proclaiming to the Church of Jerusalem the full width of St. Paul's teaching (Gal. ii. 2), and accordingly, though something may be read between the lines, the decree seems to treat the precepts of Noah as perpetually binding, places moral and positive obligations on the same footing, and leaves the ground on which they are "necessary" an open question. St. Paul, who had accepted it as a satisfactory settlement of the matter in debate, never refers to it, even when he is discussing the chief point with which the decree dealt (1 Cor. viii.—x.). In his narrative of what passed on this occasion (Gal. ii. 1—10) there is no mention of it. The private conference with the three great "pillars" of the Church was for him more than the decree of the synod, and he felt himself able to discuss the whole question again on different grounds, and with a more distinct reference to spiritual and ethical principles. It was wrong to eat things sacrificed to idols, not because the act of so eating in itself brought defilement, but because it might involve a participation in the sin of idolatry in the consciousness of the eater, or wound the conscience of the weaker brother who saw him eat. It was natural that those who lacked his largeness of view should become slaves to the letter of the rules long after the grounds on which they rested had ceased to exist, and so we find that the prohibition of blood was re-enforced in the so-called Apostolic Canons (c. 62), and in the fourth century by the Council of Gangra (c. 2), and in the seventh by that at Constantinople, known as *in Trullo* (c. 67), and continues to be the binding rule of the Greek Church still. In Africa and in Europe, however, truer views prevailed (August. *cont. Faust.* xxxii. 13), and not even the most devout believer in the inspiration of the Apostles, or in the authority of primitive antiquity, would venture to urge that the two last precepts of the four here enjoined were in any degree binding. Hooker (*Eccl. Pol.* iv., xi., § 5) rightly refers to this decree as a crucial instance proving that commands might be divine and yet given only for a season, binding as long as the conditions to which they applied continued, but no longer. It would almost seem, indeed, as if St. Paul felt that the terms of the decree had the effect of placing the sin of impurity on the same level with that of eating things sacrificed to idols, and things strangled, and

selves, ye shall do well. Fare ye well.
(30) So when they were dismissed, they
came to Antioch: and when they had
gathered the multitude together, they
delivered the epistle: (31) *which* when
they had read, they rejoiced for the
consolation.[1] (32) And Judas and Silas,
being prophets also themselves, ex-
horted the brethren with many words,
and confirmed *them.* (33) And after they
had tarried *there* a space, they were let
go in peace from the brethren unto the
apostles. (34) Notwithstanding it pleased
Silas to abide there still. (35) Paul also
and Barnabas continued in Antioch,
teaching and preaching the word of the
Lord, with many others also.
A.D. 53.
(36) And some days after Paul said
unto Barnabas, Let us go again and
visit our brethren in every city where
we have preached the word of the Lord,
*and see* how they do. (37) And Barnabas
determined to take with them John,
whose surname was Mark. (38) But
Paul thought not good to take him with
them, who departed from them from
Pamphylia, and went not with them to
the work. (39) And the contention was
so sharp between them, that they de-
parted asunder one from the other: and

1 Or, *exhortation.*

---

blood, and so tended to keep men from seeing it in its true hatefulness. Those who claimed a right, which in the abstract St. Paul could not deny, to eat of things strangled or offered to idols, thought themselves free to fall back into the old license of the heathen world, and he needed far stronger motives than the canons of the council to restrain them (1 Cor. v. 9, 10; vi. 15—20, and found those motives in the truths that they had been bought with a price, that the will of God was their sanctification, and that their bodies were His temple.

(30) **When they were dismissed, they came to Antioch.**—It is natural, in the absence of anything to the contrary, to infer that they returned, as they had come, through Samaria and Phœnicia, and gladdened the hearts of the disciples there by telling them of the triumph which had been won at Jerusalem for the cause of freedom.

**They delivered the epistle.**—We can picture to ourselves the eager excitement of that moment, the listening crowds, the letter, which as a formal missive would be sealed and tied round with thread, solemnly opened and read out aloud, mortification and murmurs on the one side, clamorous applause on the other, as each sentence repudiated the claims of the Judaisers and confirmed the principles and the work of St. Paul and Barnabas. To the Gentile converts it was, indeed—won, as it had been, after a hard battle—as the great charter of their freedom.

(31) **They rejoiced for the consolation.**—We ought not to forget that the letter was probably read out by one who was himself emphatically "the son of consolation" (chap. iv. 36) in all the manifold aspects of that word, and who now proved himself worthy of the name.

(32) **Judas and Silas, being prophets also themselves.**—See Note on verse 22.

**Exhorted.**—The verb is that from which the Greek for "consolation" was formed, and includes that meaning here. This was the chief end to which the gift of prophecy was directed. The two teachers thus showed that they had not come only as formal representatives of the Church in Jerusalem, but took a personal interest in the work. Their work was the very reverse of those who had previously come from Judæa "subverting the souls of the disciples" (verse 24).

(33) **Unto the apostles.**—The better MSS. have simply, "to those that had sent them," and omit verse 34, which was probably added by a later copyist to explain the fact mentioned in verse 40.

(35) **Preaching the word of the Lord.**—Here, as often elsewhere, *preaching the glad tidings of the word.*

**With many others.**—Among these we may fairly reckon the prophets of chap. xiii. 1. Looking to the later history of the Church of Antioch, it is not improbable that we may think also of the martyr Ignatius, and Euodius, afterwards Bishop of Antioch, as among those who were thus active, though they were not prominent enough, when St. Luke wrote, to be specially named. Ignatius was said to have been, together with Polycarp, a disciple of St. John (*Mart. Ignat.* c. 3), while another tradition represents him as a follower of Peter. It is possible that the dispute between St. Peter and St. Paul, referred to in Gal. ii. 11—13, occurred during this period, but the evidence on the whole tends to connect it with St. Paul's visit to Antioch in chap. xviii. 22, where see Note.

(36) **And some days after Paul said unto Barnabas.**—The commonly received chronology of the Acts makes the interval between the Council of Jerusalem and St. Paul's second missionary journey somewhat more than a year.

**Let us go again.**—The proposal was characteristic of one whose heart was ever full of "the care of all the churches" (2 Cor. xi. 28), ever making mention of them in his prayers night and day (Rom i. 9; Eph. i. 16; Phil. i. 3). We may well believe that it was a desire to know, not only the general condition of the churches, but the spiritual growth of each individual member.

(37) **Barnabas determined.**—The Greek verb is hardly so strong, better, *was minded.* The ties of relationship led the uncle, or cousin, to wish to make another trial of his kinsman's fitness (Col. iv. 10). He saw extenuating circumstances which St. Paul could not recognise, and which half-excused his turning back when he had set his hand to the plough. (See Note on chap. xiii. 13.) To St. Paul one who had so acted, seemed, in our Lord's words, "not fit for the kingdom of God," and needing at least the discipline of rejection for a time, from the higher work for which he had shown himself unworthy.

(39) **And the contention was so sharp between them, that . . .**—Literally, *there was a sharp contention,* (or *paroxysm*), *so that* . . . The warmth of previous affection, of a friendship begun probably in boyhood, and cemented by new hopes, and a great work in which both were sharers, made the breach between the two more painful. At this stage, both Barnabas and Mark

so Barnabas took Mark, and sailed unto
Cyprus; (40) and Paul chose Silas, and
departed, being recommended by the
brethren unto the grace of God. (41) And
he went through Syria and Cilicia, confirming the churches.

CHAPTER XVI.—(1) Then came he
to Derbe and Lystra: and, behold, a
certain disciple was there, named Timotheus,[a] the son of a certain woman, *a Rom. 16. 21.*
which was a Jewess, and believed; but
his father *was* a Greek: (2) which was
well reported of by the brethren that
were at Lystra and Iconium. (3) Him
would Paul have to go forth with him;
and took and circumcised him because *A.D. 53.*
of the Jews which were in those quarters:

disappear from the history of the Acts, but it will be worth while to note the chief facts in the after-history of each. (1) Probably Barnabas and Paul met again in the visit of chap. xviii. 22, unless, indeed, we refer the incidents of Gal. ii. 11—13 to an earlier period, and then there was a yet further cause of division in his yielding to the dissimulation of the Judaising teachers. (2) In writing to the Corinthians (1 Cor. ix. 6) the Apostle names Barnabas as setting the same noble example as himself in labouring with his own hands and accepting nothing from the churches. (3) On the later life of Mark see the *Introduction to St. Mark's Gospel.* Here it will be sufficient to note that the discipline did its work. After labouring with his cousin in Cyprus, he appears to have returned to St. Peter, as his first father in the faith, and to have been with him at Babylon (1 Pet. v. 13). He and St. Paul met during the latter's first imprisonment at Rome (Col. iv. 10; Philem. verse 24), and the Apostle learnt to recognise in him one who was "profitable to him for the ministry" (2 Tim. iv. 11), and whom he wished to have with him at the last.

(40) **Paul chose Silas.**—It is clear from this, even if we reject verse 34 as an interpolation, that Silas had remained when the other delegates from the Church of Jerusalem went back. This in itself was a proof of his interest in the mission-work among the Gentiles, and no one, perhaps, could be found so well fitted to fill the place of Barnabas. He too had the gift of prophetic utterance, and, as we have seen (Note on verse 22), was probably able to speak as one who had followed the Lord Jesus, and could bear witness of the Resurrection.

**Being recommended by the brethren.**—See Note on chap. xiv. 26. This obviously implied a full gathering of the Church and a special service of prayer on the departure of the two Apostles. Silas, as thus sent forth by the Church, might now claim that title no less than Barnabas.

(41) **He went through Syria and Cilicia, confirming the churches.**—Cilicia, it will be remembered, had not been visited on St. Paul's first journey with Barnabas, and the churches must accordingly have been founded at some earlier period, probably during St. Paul's residence at Tarsus before he came to Antioch (chaps. ix. 30; xi. 25).

**Confirming** is, it need hardly be said, used in the general sense of "strengthening," but as the bestowal of spiritual gifts by the laying-on of hands was a chief part of the work so done, it, at least, approximates to the idea of "confirming" in the later and more technical sense of the term.

XVI.

(1) **A certain disciple was there, named Timotheus.**—We read with a special interest the first mention of the name of one who was afterwards so dear to the Apostle, his "true son in the faith" (1 Tim. i. 2). On his probable conversion on St. Paul's first mission in Lystra, see Notes on chap. xiv. 6, 19. We have to think of him as still young; probably, as his youth is spoken of some twelve years later in 1 Tim. iv. 12, not more than eighteen or twenty; but in the six years that had passed since St. Paul's departure he had been conspicuous for his devotion and "unfeigned faith." He had been trained to know the sacred Books of Israel from his childhood (2 Tim. iii. 15); and the fact that he had obtained a good report from the brethren at Iconium as well as Lystra shows that he had been already employed in carrying on intercourse between the two churches. The way in which St. Paul writes to him, and of him, implies a constitution naturally not strong, and, in after life, weakened by a rigorous asceticism (1 Tim. v. 23), emotional even to tears (2 Tim. i. 4), naturally shrinking from hardships and responsibilities, yet facing them in the strength of Christ (1 Cor. xvi. 10). The name Timotheus was not uncommon. It is found in 2 Macc. xii. 21—24, as belonging to a general defeated by Judas Maccabeus, and appears in early Christian inscriptions in the Vatican Museum. Its meaning ("one who honours God") made it a suitable name for the child of a proselyte.

**The son of a certain woman.**—Literally, *of a certain woman, a faithful* (or *believing*) *Jewess.* The adjective is the same as that used by Lydia of herself in verse 15. 2 Tim. i. 4, tells us that her name was Eunikè, and her mother's Lois. They were both devout, and had trained the child in the Law (2 Tim. iii. 15); and this makes it probable that the father was a proselyte of the gate. He naturally thought it sufficient that his child should grow up under the same religious conditions as himself, and they had either thought so, or had yielded to his will.

**His father was a Greek.**—Literally, *of a Greek father.* The adjective is used, as in the New Testament generally, to express the fact that he was a heathen. (See Notes on chap. xi. 20; Mark vii. 26.) It seems, on the whole, probable that he was still living.

(3) **And took and circumcised him.**—The act seems at first inconsistent with St. Paul's conduct as to Titus (Gal. ii. 3), and with his general teaching as to circumcision (Gal. v. 2—6). The circumstances of the two cases were, however, different, and there were adequate reasons here for the course which he adopted. (1) The act was spontaneous, and men may rightly concede as a favour, or as a matter of expediency, what they would be justified in resisting when demanded as a matter of necessity. (2) Titus was a Greek, pure and simple (Gal. ii. 3); but the mixed parentage of Timotheus, according to the received canons of Jewish law, made him inherit from the nobler side, and he was therefore by birth in the same position as an Israelite. (3) By not urging circumcision prior to baptism, or to his admission to that "breaking of bread" which was then, as afterwards, the witness of a full communion with Christ, the

for they knew all that his father was a
Greek. (4) And as they went through
the cities, they delivered them the
decrees for to keep, that were ordained
of the apostles and elders which were
at Jerusalem.[a] (5) And so were the
churches established in the faith, and
increased in number daily. (6) Now
when they had gone throughout
Phrygia and the region of Galatia,
and were forbidden of the Holy Ghost
to preach the word in Asia, (7) after
they were come to Mysia, they assayed
to go into Bithynia: but the

[a] ch. 15. 28.

---

Apostle had shown that he did not look on it as essential to admission into the Christian Church, or continued fellowship with it, and in what he now did he was simply acting on his avowed principle of becoming to the Jews as a Jew (see Notes on chap. xviii. 18; 1 Cor. ix. 20), and guarding against the difficulties which he would have encountered from those whom he sought to win to Christ, had they seen, as one of the travelling company, an Israelite who was ashamed of the seal of the covenant of Abraham. The acceptance of that seal by one who had grown up to manhood without it may be noted as showing that the disciple had imbibed the spirit of his Master. It seems probable, from the youth of Timotheus, that at this period he took the place which had been before filled by Mark, and acted chiefly as an attendant, the "work of an evangelist" coming later (2 Tim. iv. 5).

(4) **They delivered them the decrees.**—The number of copies which the process implies is in itself a sufficient guarantee that that which St. Luke gives is a faithful transcript. The decrees were clearly still regarded by the Gentile converts as being the charter on which they might take their stand in any dispute with the Judaisers, and doubtless helped to determine many who had previously hesitated, to seek admission into the Church.

(6) **When they had gone throughout Phrygia and the region of Galatia.**—In the previous journey St. Paul, when he was at Antioch in Pisidia, was just on the border of the two provinces, but had not travelled through them, Phrygia lying to the west, and Galatia to the north-east. The former name was used with an ethnological rather than a political significance, and did not, at this period, designate a Roman province. It does not possess any special points of interest in connection with St. Paul's work, except as including the churches of the valley of the Lycus, Colossæ, Laodicea, and Thyatira, but the latter was the scene of some of his most important labours. The province, named after the Galatæ, or Gauls, who had poured over Greece and Asia Minor in the third century B.C., as they had done over Italy in the fourth, and to whom it had been assigned by Attalus I., King of Pergamus, had been conquered by the Romans under Manlius (the name appearing a second time in connection with a victory over the Gallic races) in B.C. 189; and under Augustus it had been constituted as a Roman province. The inhabitants spoke a Keltic dialect, like that which the people of the same race spoke in the fourth century after Christ, on the banks of the Moselle, and retained all the distinctive quickness of emotion and liability to sudden change which characterised the Keltic temperament. They had adopted the religion of the Phrygians, who had previously inhabited the region, and that religion consisted mainly in a wild orgiastic worship of the great Earth-goddess Cybele, in whose temples were found the Eunuch-priests, who thus consecrated themselves to her service. (See Note on Gal. v. 12.) The chief seat of this worship was at Pessinus. The incidental reference to this journey in Gal. iv. 13—15, enables us to fill up St. Luke's outline. St. Paul seems to have been detained in Galatia by severe illness, probably by one of the attacks of acute pain in the nerves of the eye in which many writers have seen an explanation of the mysterious "thorn in the flesh" of 2 Cor. xii. 7, which led to his giving a longer time to his missionary work there than he had at first intended. In this illness the Galatians had shown themselves singularly devoted to him. They had received him "as an angel of God, even as Christ Jesus." They had not shrunk from what would seem to have been repulsive in the malady from which he suffered; they would have "plucked out their own eyes," had it been possible, and given them to replace those which were to him the cause of so much suffering. Then they thought it their highest "blessedness" to have had such a one among them. If the memory of that reception made his sorrow all the more bitter when, in after years, they fell away from their first love, it must at the time have been among the most cheering seasons of the Apostle's life.

**Were forbidden of the Holy Ghost to preach the word in Asia.**—It is obviously implied in this that their own plans would have led them to turn their steps to the region from which they were thus turned. The pro-consular province of Asia, with its teeming cities, like Ephesus, Smyrna, and Sardis, its large Jewish population, its great centres of idolatrous worship, was naturally attractive to one who was seeking with all his energy a rapid expansion of the kingdom of his Lord. But in ways which we are not told, by inner promptings, or by visions of the night, or by the inspired utterances of those among their converts who had received the gift of prophecy, as afterwards in chap. xxi. 4, they were led on, step by step, towards the north-western coast, not seeing their way clearly as yet to the next stage of their labours. Their route through the "Galatian region" (the phrase, perhaps, indicates a wider range of country than the Roman province of that name) must have taken them through Pessinus, the great centre of the worship of Cybele, and Ancyra, famous for its goat's-hair manufactures, and for the great historical marble tablets which Augustus had erected there.

(7) **They assayed to go into Bithynia.**—The verse describes very vividly the uncertainty produced day by day by this conflict between human plans and divine direction. Bithynia, lying to the north, had, like Pontus, a considerable Jewish population scattered along its shores, and they were inclined to take that as their next field of labour. They were led on, however, as before, westward and not northward. There is no record of any considerable halt in this stage of their journey, and they probably found few favourable openings in a district which, for great part of the way, presented only unimportant villages. The use of the archaic form "assayed" for "essayed," or "attempted," calls for a word of notice. (Comp. chap. ix. 26.)

**The Spirit suffered them not.**—The better MSS. and versions give the reading, "the Spirit of

Spirit suffered them not. (8) And they
passing by Mysia came down to Troas.
(9) And a vision appeared to Paul in the
night; There stood a man of Macedonia,
and prayed him, saying, Come over into
Macedonia, and help us. (10) And after
he had seen the vision, immediately we
endeavoured to go into Macedonia,
assuredly gathering that the Lord had
called us for to preach the gospel unto
them. (11) Therefore loosing from Troas,
we came with a straight course to
Samothracia, and the next *day* to
Neapolis; (12) and from thence to

---

Jesus," which is of some dogmatic importance, as confirming the doctrine that the Spirit stands in the same relation to the Son as to the Father, and may therefore be spoken of either as the Spirit of God, or of Christ (Rom. viii. 9), or of Jesus.

(8) **Came down to Troas.**—Their travels had at last led them to the coast, and they looked out upon the waters of the Ægean. The town of Alexandria Troas, at this time reckoned as a Roman colony and a free city, recalls to our memories, without entering into vexed questions as to its identity with the site of the older Troy, the great poem which tells us the tale of Ilium. To St. Paul that poem was probably unknown, and had it been otherwise, the associations connected with it would have had no charms for him. The question which must have occupied all his thoughts was, where he was next to proclaim the glad tidings of the Christ, and of forgiveness and peace through Him. That question, we may well believe, expressed itself in prayer, and to that prayer the vision of the next verse was an answer.

(9) **There stood a man of Macedonia.**—The term is probably used in its later sense as applied to the Roman province, which included Macedonia, properly so called, Illyricum, Epirus, and Thessaly, the province of Achaia including, in like manner, the whole of Southern Greece. The vision which St. Paul looked on explained to him all the varied promptings and drawings-back of his journey. This was the door that was to be opened to him. The faith of Christ was to pass from Asia to Europe, and the cry, "Come over and help us," was to him as a call from the whole western world. In view of this, he did not now tarry to preach at Troas. Probably, indeed, as the next verse implies, that work had been already done.

(10) **Immediately we endeavoured . . .**—The natural inference from the sudden appearance of the first person in a narrative previously in the third, is that the author became at this point an actor in the events which he records. (See *Introduction to St. Luke's Gospel.*) The other hypothesis, that he incorporates a narrative written by Silas or Timotheus, is not probable in itself, and would naturally have involved an earlier change in the form of the narrative. Accepting the received view, it seems to follow, as there is no mention of the conversion of the Evangelist, that St. Paul and St. Luke must have been already known to each other, probably either at Tarsus or Antioch, the fulness with which the history of the latter Church is given pointing to it as the scene of their previous intimacy. On this assumption, the narrator must have left Antioch after the Council of Jerusalem, probably after the dispute between Paul and Barnabas, and travelled through the interior of Asia Minor, in part, perhaps, in the track of St. Paul's earlier journey; and so gathered materials for his history till he came to Troas, and there carried on his work as an evangelist. The manner in which St. Luke introduces himself ("the Lord had called *us*") implies, it may be noted, that he too was a preacher of the gospel. There is no record here of any mission-work done by St. Paul; but the language in 2 Cor. ii. 12, and, yet more, the facts of Acts xx. 6, imply the existence of a Christian community. We may look, accordingly, on St. Luke as the founder of the Church of Troas, and place this among the "labours in the gospel" to which St. Paul refers in 2 Cor. viii. 18. The "we endeavoured" (literally, *we sought*) implies an immediate inquiry as to what ship was sailing, bound for any port of Macedonia. Such a call as that which had been given in the vision admitted of no delay. It came from the Lord Jesus, as the sequel of that given in the vision in the Temple (chap. xxii. 17—21), and was, therefore, to be obeyed at once.

(11) **We came with a straight course to Samothracia.**—Their course lay to the north-west, and, probably, after the manner of the navigation of the time, they put into harbour each night; and the historian, with his characteristic love of geographical detail (see *Introduction to St. Luke's Gospel*), notes the main facts of the voyage. The "straight course" implies that they had the wind in their favour. The current, which sets to the south after leaving the Hellespont, and to the east between Samothrace and the mainland, would, of course, be against them. In chap. xx. 6, the voyage from Philippi to Troas takes five days. The name of Samothrace points, probably, to its having been a colony from Samos. In early Greek history it had been one of the chief seats of the worship of the Pelasgic race, and, besides the mysteries of Demeter and Persephone, which it had in common with the rest of Greece, was celebrated for the local *cultus* of the Cabiri, a name of uncertain origin, and applied to the twelve great gods.

**The next day to Neapolis.**—The name (=new town) was naturally common wherever Greek was spoken. It survives in two conspicuous instances—in Naples, and in *Nablous* as the modern name of Sychem. The town now before us was in Thrace, about twelve miles from Philippi, which was the frontier town of Macedonia. It has been identified, on adequate grounds, with the modern *Kavalla*, where a Roman aqueduct, columns, and Greek and Latin inscriptions remain to attest the former importance of the city. Ten or twelve miles to the west are the traces of another harbour at *Eski Kavalla*, which was probably the Palæopolis (=old town) that had been superseded by the new port.

(12) **The chief city of that part of Macedonia.**—More accurately, *a chief* (or *first*) *city of the border-country of Macedonia.* The description is not without difficulty, and has been noted by adverse critics as an instance of St. Luke's inaccuracy. The city of Philippi, rebuilt by the father of Alexander the Great, and bearing his name in lieu of Krenides (=the fountains), was situated on the Gangites, a tributary of the Strymon; but it was not the chief city of any one of the four sub-divisions of the Roman province of Macedonia, that rank being assigned to Amphipolis, Thessalonica, Pella, and Pelagonia. As there is no definite article in the Greek, it

Philippi, which is the chief[1] city of that part of Macedonia, *and* a colony: and we were in that city abiding certain days. (13) And on the sabbath we went out of the city by a river side, where prayer was wont to be made; and we sat down, and spake unto the women which resorted *thither*.

(14) And a certain woman named Lydia, a seller of purple, of the city of Thyatira, which worshipped God, heard *us:* whose heart the Lord opened, that

1 Or, *the first.*

---

is possible that St. Luke simply meant to say it was *a* chief town of the district, the epithet *Prôte* (=first) being often found on the coins of cities which were not capitals. The more probable explanation, however, is that he uses the Greek word translated "part," in the sense of "border-land," as in the LXX. of Ezek. xxxv. 7, Ruth iii. 7, and that it was the *first* city of that frontier district, either as the most important or as being the first to which they came in the route by which they travelled. This was precisely the position of Philippi, which, together with Pella and other towns, had been garrisoned by the Romans as outposts against the neighbouring tribes of Thrace. It had been established as a colony by Augustus after the defeat of Brutus and Cassius, and its full title, as seen on the coins of the city, was Colonia Augusta Julia Philippensis.

**A colony.**—The English reader needs to be reminded that a Roman *colonia* differed from the modern in being essentially a military position. Portions of the conquered territory were commonly assigned to veteran soldiers, and the settlement thus formed was considered politically as an integral part of Rome, all decrees of the emperor or senate being as binding there as in the capital itself. The colonies thus formed were as the "propugnacula imperii" (Cic. *de leg. Agrar.* c. 27), "populi Romani quasi effigies parvæ simulacraque" (Aul. Gell. xvi. 13). Here, then, in the first European city to which St. Paul came, there was something like an earnest of his future victories. Himself a Roman citizen, he was brought into direct contact with Romans. (See Note on verse 21.)

(13) **By a river side, where prayer was wont to be made.**—Better, *where an oratory* (*i.e.*, a place of prayer) *was established.* The word, which was the Greek equivalent for the Hebrew "house of prayer" (Matt. xxi. 13), is used in this sense by Josephus (*Vit.* p. 54), (see Note on Luke vi. 12), and was current among the Jews at Rome. Where they had no synagogue, and in a military station like Philippi there was not likely to be one, the Jews frequented the river-banks, which made ablutions easy, and often succeeded in getting a piece of ground assigned for that purpose outside the walls of the city. Juvenal (*Sat.* iii. 11—13) notes this as one of the instances of the decay of the old faith of Rome:

> "The groves and streams which once were sacred ground
> Are now let out to Jews."

The local meaning is seen in another line from the same writer (*Sat.* iii. 296):

> "Ede, ubi consistas, in quâ te quæro, proseuchâ?"
> ["Say where thou dwell'st, and in what place of prayer
> I am to seek thee?"]

The oratories, or *proseuchæ*, thus formed, were commonly circular, and without a roof. The practice continued in the time of Tertullian, who speaks of the "orationes litorales" of the Jews (*ad Nat.* i. 13). The river, in this instance, was the Gangites. Finding no synagogue in the city, and hearing of the oratory, the company of preachers went out to it to take their part in the Sabbath services, and to preach Christ to any Jews they might find there.

**We sat down, and spake unto the women.**—The fact that there were only women shows the almost entire absence of a Jewish population. Possibly, too, the decree of Claudius, expelling the Jews from Rome (chap. xviii. 2), was enforced, as stated above, in the *colonia*, which was as a part of Rome, and as Jewesses would not be likely to have settled there without their husbands or brothers, it is probable that the women whom St. Paul found assembled were, like Lydia, proselytes who desired to remain faithful to their new faith, even in the absence of any settled provision for their instruction. Women thus placed would naturally welcome the presence of strangers who, probably, wore the garb of a Rabbi, and who showed when they sat down (see Note on chap. xiii. 14) that they were about to preach. We note that here also the narrator speaks of himself as teaching. (See Note on verse 10.)

(14) **Lydia, a seller of purple, of the city of Thyatira.**—The city so named, now known as *Akhissar*, was in the Roman province of Asia, but came within the boundaries of the older kingdom of Lydia, and it is probable that, like so many slaves and women of the *libertinæ* class, she took her name from her country. Afra, Græca, Syra, are familiar examples of like names. "Lydia" occurs, it will be remembered, once and again, in Horace (*Od.* i. 14; iii. 9). Thyatira, one of the cities in the valley of the Lycus, was, like many other towns of Asia Minor, famous for its dyeing works, especially for purple, or crimson, which rivalled the fame of Tyre or Miletus (Strabo, xiii. 4, § 14). Inscriptions found on the spot bear witness to the existence of a guild, or corporation, of purple-sellers, with which Lydia doubtless was connected. In Rev. i. 11, ii. 18, it appears as one of the seven churches to which special epistles were to be sent from their divine Head. It had been founded as a colony, in the modern sense of the term, from Macedonia, as the sequel of the conquest of the Persian monarchy by Alexander the Great, and this may in part explain Lydia's presence at Philippi. The fact that she, and not her husband, is named as the purple-seller, is at least presumptive evidence that she was carrying on the business by herself.

**Which worshipped God.**—She was, *i.e.*, a proselyte (see Note on chap. xiii. 10), and, as the sequel shows, one of the better type, drawn to Judaism, not by superstitious fear, or weak credulity, but by the higher ethical and spiritual teaching which it presented.

**Heard.**—For "heard" read *was listening.*

**Whose heart the Lord opened.**—The scene is one which might well call for the master touches of a great painter. The river flowing calmly by, the preacher sitting and talking familiarly, but earnestly, to the groups of women, one, at least, among them listening with looks and tears that told of deep emotions, and the consciousness of a new life.

**That she attended.**—Better, *to give heed to*, as in chap. viii. 6, and elsewhere.

she attended unto the things which
were spoken of Paul. (15) And when
she was baptized, and her household,
she besought *us*, saying, If ye have
judged me to be faithful to the Lord,
come into my house, and abide *there*.
And she constrained us.

(16) And it came to pass, as we went
to prayer, a certain damsel possessed
with a spirit of divination[1] met us,
which brought her masters much gain
by soothsaying: (17) the same followed
Paul and us, and cried, saying, These
men are the servants of the most high
God, which shew unto us the way of
salvation. (18) And this did she many

1 Or, *of Python*.

---

(15) **And when she was baptized, and her household.**—It does not follow from St. Luke's condensed narrative that all this took place on the same day. The statement that "her household" were baptised has often been urged as evidence that infant baptism was the practice of the apostolic age. It must be admitted, however, that this is to read a great deal between the lines, and the utmost that can be said is that the language of the writer does not exclude infants. The practice itself rests on firmer grounds than a precarious induction from a few ambiguous passages. (See Notes on Matt. xix. 13—15.) In this instance, moreover, there is no evidence that she had children, or even that she was married. The "household" may well have consisted of female slaves and freed-women whom she employed, and who made up her *familia*. It follows, almost as a necessary inference, that many of these also were previously proselytes. For such as these, Judaism had been a "schoolmaster," leading them to Christ. (See Gal. ii. 24.) We may think of Euodias and Syntyche, and the other women who "laboured in the gospel" (Phil. iv. 2, 3), as having been, probably, among them. The names of the first two occur frequently in the inscriptions of the *Columbaria* of this period, now in the Vatican and Lateran Museums, the Borghese Gardens, and elsewhere, as belonging to women of the slave or *libertinæ* class.

**She besought us.**—Up to this time the teachers, four in number, had been, we must believe, living in a lodging and maintaining themselves, as usual, by labour—St. Paul as a tentmaker, St. Luke, probably, as a physician. Now the large-hearted hospitality of Lydia (the offer implies a certain measure of wealth, as, indeed, did her occupation, which required a considerable capital) led her to receive them as her guests. They did not readily abandon the independent position which their former practice secured them, and only yield to the kind "constraint" to which they were exposed.

**If ye have judged.**—The words contain a modest, almost a pathetic, appeal to the fact that the preachers had recognised her faith by admitting her to baptism. If she was fit for that, was she unfit to be their hostess?

(16) **As we went to prayer.**—Better, perhaps, *to the oratory*, or *place of prayer*. (See Note on verse 13.) It should be stated, however, that the Greek noun is used without the article, and that this is so far in favour of the Received rendering. On the other hand, we find the noun *ecclesia*, or *church*, used without the article in 1 Cor. xiv. 4, 19, 35; 3 John 6, and it is, therefore, probable that *proseucha* might be used in the same way, just as we speak of "going to church, or to chapel," without the article. This was probably on the following Sabbath, or possibly after a longer interval, when the mission of the Apostles had become known, and had caused some excitement.

**A certain damsel possessed with a spirit of divination.**—Literally, as in the margin, *a spirit of Python*, or, as some MSS. give it, *a Python spirit*. The Python was the serpent worshipped at Delphi, as the symbol of wisdom, from whom the Pythian priestesses took their name, and from whom Apollo, as succeeding to the oracular power of the serpent, took the same adjective. The fact that St. Luke, who in his Gospel describes like phenomena as coming from *dæmonia*, "evil spirits," "unclean spirits," should here use this exceptional description, seems to imply either that this was the way in which the people of Philippi spoke of the maiden, or else that he recognised in her phenomena identical with those of the priestesses of Delphi, the wild distortions, the shrill cries, the madness of an evil inspiration. After the manner of sibyls, and sorceresses, and clairvoyantes of other times, the girl, whom Augustine describes as a *fœmina ventriloqua*—the phrase probably expressing the peculiar tones characteristic of hysteria—was looked on as having power to divine and predict ("soothsaying," as distinct from "prophesying," exactly expresses the force of the Greek verb), and her wild cries were caught up and received as oracles. Plutarch (*de Defect. Orac.*, p. 737) speaks of the name Python as being applied commonly, in his time, to "ventriloquists" of this type. As she was a slave, her masters traded on her supposed inspiration, and made the girl, whom prayer and quiet might have restored to sanity, give answers to those who sought for oracular guidance in the perplexities of their lives.

(17) **The same followed Paul and us, and cried, saying.**—Better, *kept on crying*. Assuming that the case now before us presented phenomena analogous to those of the cases of demoniac possession we may refer to what has been said in the *Excursus* on that subject appended to St. Matthew's Gospel for general views of the question. Here it will be enough to note the same symptom of a divided consciousness. We lose much of the human interest of the narrative if we merely think of a demon bearing, as in mockery, his witness to the work of Christ, in order that he might thwart that work. That continual cry spoke, we may well believe, of the girl's mind as longing for deliverance, and peace, and calm. She sees in the preachers those whom she recognises as able to deliver her, as unlike as possible to the masters who traded on her maddened misery. And yet the thraldom in which she found herself led her to cries that simply impeded their work. We note, as characteristic, the recurrence of the name of the Most High God, which meets us from the lips of the demoniac in the Gospels. (See Note on Mark v. 7.) As the name which was often in the mouths of exorcists, it became familiar to those who were regarded as subjects for their treatment. As she seems day by day to have gone to the river-side oratory, it is probable that she also had some points of contact with the faith of those who worshipped there, and had listened there to the preaching of the Apostles. Might not she claim a share in "the way of salvation" which was proclaimed to them?

(18) **But Paul, being grieved . .**—It is obvious that the constant repetition of these clamorous cries must

days. But Paul, being grieved, turned
and said to the spirit, I command thee
in the name of Jesus Christ to come out
of her. And he came out the same hour.
(19) And when her masters saw that
the hope of their gains was gone, they
caught Paul and Silas, and drew *them*
into the marketplace [1] unto the rulers,
(20) and brought them to the magis-
trates, saying, These men, being Jews,
do exceedingly trouble our city, (21) and
teach customs, which are not lawful for
us to receive, neither to observe, being
Romans. (22) And the multitude rose
up together against them: and the
magistrates rent off their clothes, and
commanded to beat *them*.[a] (23) And
when they had laid many stripes upon
them, they cast *them* into prison,
charging the jailor to keep them safely:
(24) who, having received such a charge,
thrust them into the inner prison,

a 2 Cor. 11. 25; 1 Thess. 2. 2.

1 Or, *court.*

---

have been a hindrance to the Apostle's work, disturbing him as he talked to the other women at the *proseucha.* Was it not right for him to do as his Master had done with the demoniacs of Gadara (see Notes on Matt. viii. 28—34), and to restore the woman to her true self, by teaching her to distinguish between her longing for deliverance and the wild passions that hindered her from attaining it? And so he spoke, and the evil spirit "came out the same hour." Here the history ends, as far as the damsel was concerned; but we can hardly think that she was left to drift back into ignorance and unbelief. Would not such a one find shelter and comfort at the hands of the women who "laboured" with the Apostle? (Phil. iv. 2.) May we not think of her gratitude as showing itself in the gifts that were sent to the Apostle, upon whom she had unwillingly brought so much suffering? (Phil. iv. 15.)

(19) **That the hope of their gains was gone.**—Better, *of their occupation.* The word for "gains" is the same as that translated "gain" and "craft" in chap. xix. 24, 25. There is something like a prophetic significance in the use, at this stage, of the word which was the key to nearly all the persecutions to which the early believers were exposed. Men could tolerate varieties of worship or the speculations of philosophers: they were roused to madness by that which threatened their business. The use in the Greek of the same verb for "was gone," as had been used in the previous verse for "come out," gives an emphasis which the English does not reproduce. Their business and the spirit of divination "passed away" together.

**Paul and Silas.**—Luke and Timotheus escaped, probably, as less conspicuous.

**Drew them into the marketplace.**—The marketplace, or *Agora,* was, in all Greek cities, the centre of social life. In Philippi, as a *colonia,* reproducing the arrangements of Rome, it would answer to the Forum, where the magistrates habitually sat. What had taken place would naturally cause excitement and attract a crowd.

(20) **The magistrates.**—The Greek word used (*Stratêgi,* literally, *generals*—the name survived in 1750 in the Italian *Stradigo,* used of the prefect of Messina) is used with St. Luke's usual accuracy, for the prætors, or duumviri, who formed the executive of the Roman *colonia.*

**These men, being Jews.**—We must remember that the decree of Claudius (see Note on chap. xviii. 2), banishing the Jews from Rome on account of their disturbing that city, would be known, and probably acted on, at Philippi (see Notes on verses 12, 13), and would give a special force to the accusation. Here, also, there is something specially characteristic of the nature of many of the early persecutions. Christians were exposed, on the one hand, to the relentless enmity of the Jews, and, on the other, they were identified by heathen rulers and mobs with the Jews, and so came in, where the latter were the objects of popular antipathy, for a two-fold measure of suffering.

(21) **And teach customs.**—The word is used as including ritual as well as social habits, and seems to have been specially used of the whole system of Jewish life. (See Notes on chaps. vi. 14; xv. 1; xxi. 21.)

**Being Romans.**—The people of Philippi, as a *colonia,* had a right to claim the title of Roman citizens, which could not have been claimed by those who were merely inhabitants of a Greek city, such as Thessalonica or Corinth. (See Note on verse 12.)

(22) **Commanded to beat them.**—The Greek verb gives the special Roman form of punishment, that of being beaten with the rods of the lictors. This, therefore, takes its place as one of the three instances to which St. Paul refers in 2 Cor. xi. 25. The question naturally occurs, why he did not, on these occasions, claim, as he did afterwards at Jerusalem (chap. xxii. 25), the privileges of a Roman citizen. Some have supposed that the violence of the mob rendered it impossible for his claim to be heard. Others have even questioned the truthfulness of his claim. A more natural supposition is that he would not assert in this instance a right which would only have secured exemption for himself, and left his companion to suffer the ignominious penalty of the law, and that by putting the *strategi* in the wrong, he sought to secure for his disciples afterwards a more tolerant treatment. As far as the first part of this hypothesis is concerned, it may, perhaps, be accepted (see, however, Note on verse 37); but such of the Philippian disciples as belonged to the *colonia,* were already protected from outrages of this kind as Roman citizens. Others, however, of the freed-men class, were still liable to them.

(23) **And when they had laid many stripes upon them.**—The words imply a punishment of more than usual severity, such as would leave their backs lacerated and bleeding. So in 1 Thess. ii. 2, St. Paul speaks of having been "shamefully entreated" at Philippi.

(24) **Thrust them into the inner prison.**—Those who have seen anything of the prisons of the Roman empire, as, *e.g.,* the Mamertine dungeon at Rome itself, can picture to themselves the darkness and foulness of the den into which Paul and his friend were now thrust: the dark cavern-like cell, below the ground, the damp and reeking walls, the companionship of the vilest outcasts. And, as if this were not enough, they were fastened in the "stocks." St. Luke uses the Greek term *xylon,* the same as is used sometimes for the cross (chaps. v. 30; xiii. 29). The technical Latin word was *nervus.* Like the English stocks, it was a wooden frame with five holes, into which head and feet and

and made their feet fast in the stocks.

(25) And at midnight Paul and Silas prayed, and sang praises unto God: and the prisoners heard them. (26) And suddenly there was a great earthquake, so that the foundations of the prison were shaken: and immediately all the doors were opened, and every one's bands were loosed. (27) And the keeper of the prison awaking out of his sleep, and seeing the prison doors open, he drew out his sword, and would have killed himself, supposing that the prisoners had been fled. (28) But Paul cried with a loud voice, saying, Do thyself no harm: for we are all here. (29) Then he called for a light, and sprang in, and came trembling, and fell down before Paul and Silas, (30) and brought them out, and said, Sirs, what must I do to be saved? (31) And they said, Believe on the Lord Jesus Christ, and thou shalt be saved, and thy house.

---

arms were thrust, and the prisoner left in an attitude of "little-ease." Here, however, it would seem, the feet only were fastened, the rest of the body being left lying on the ground. If the Received version of Job xiii. 27, xxxiii. 11, which follows the LXX. and the Vulgate, be correct, the punishment was common at a very early period in the East. (Comp. Jer. xxix. 26.)

(25) **And at midnight Paul and Silas prayed, and sang praises.**—Better, *praying, they were singing hymns*, the Greek expressing one act rather than two. The act was, we may believe, habitual, and they would not intermit it even in the dungeon, and fastened as they were, so that they could not kneel. The hymn may have been one of the prayer-psalms of David, or possibly one of those, of which Pliny speaks in his letters, and which may well have been in use half a century earlier, in which men offered adoration to Christ as God (*Epist.* x. 96). The words of Tertullian to the martyrs of his time may well be quoted: *Nihil crus sentit in nervo quum animus in cœlo est; Etsi corpus detinetur, omnia spiritui patent*—"The leg feels not the stocks when the mind is in heaven. Though the body is held fast, all things lie open in the spirit" (*ad Mart.* c. 2).

**And the prisoners heard them.**—Better, *were listening eagerly*, the kind of listening which men give to a musical performance. Never before, we may be sure, had those outcasts and criminals heard such sounds in such a place. For the most part those vaults echoed only with wild curses and foul jests.

(26) **And suddenly there was a great earthquake.**—Both the region and the time were, it will be remembered, conspicuous for convulsions of this kind. Cities in Asia, such as Sardis, Apamea and Laodicea, and in Campania, suffered severely under Tiberius. (See Note on Matt. xxiv. 7.) St. Luke apparently reads the fact not as in itself miraculous, but as leading to a display of supernatural calmness and courage on the part of the Apostles, and so to the conversion of the gaoler.

**Every one's bands were loosed.**—This seems, at first, beyond the range of the usual effects of an earthquake, but the chains of the prisoners were fastened, we must remember, to rings or staples in the wall, and the effect of a great shock would be to loosen the stones and so make it easy to escape. The fact that the "foundations of the prison were shaken" agrees with what has been said above (Note on verse 24), as to the dungeon into which the prisoners had been thrust.

(27) **He drew out his sword, and would have killed himself.**—We have seen in chap. xii. 19 what was to be expected by a gaoler who, under any circumstances, allowed a prisoner to escape. (See also Note on chap. xxvii. 42.) Here the man sought to anticipate his fate. Suicide was a natural resource under such conditions everywhere, but here there was a local predisposing influence. Philippi, after the great battle in which Brutus and Cassius had been defeated by Antonius, had been conspicuous for the number of those who had thus preferred death to the abandonment of the Republic and the loss of freedom. This act had been looked on as heroic (Plutarch, *Brutus*, c. 52), and was naturally enough contagious.

(28) **Do thyself no harm.**—Few and simple as the words are, they are eminently characteristic of the love and sympathy which burnt in St. Paul's heart. For him the suicide which others would have admired, or, at least, have thought of without horror, would have been the most terrible of all forms of death. He could not bear the thought that even the gaoler who had thrust him into the dungeon, should so perish in his despair.

(29) **Then he called for a light.**—More accurately, *for lights*. As St. Luke does not use, as in chap. xx. 8, the word for "lamps," it is probable that the lights were torches, and that the gaoler, with one in his hand, leapt into the darkness of the subterranean dungeon.

(30) **Sirs, what must I do to be saved?**—The use of "Sirs" differs from that of chap. vii. 26 in having a Greek word, expressive of respect (that used in John xx. 15), corresponding to it. We ask what the gaoler meant by the question. Was he thinking of temporal safety from the earthquake, or from punishment; or had there come upon him, in that suicidal agony, the sense of an inward misery and shame, a "horror of great darkness" from which he sought deliverance? The latter seems every way most probable. It must be remembered that the very circumstances which had brought St. Paul to the prison had pointed him out as "proclaiming the way of salvation" (verse 17). The witness of the demoniac girl was thus not altogether fruitless.

(31) **And they said, Believe on the Lord Jesus Christ.**—The plural pronoun is not without significance. St. Paul was not the only teacher. Silvanus also took part in the work of conversion. The words have naturally become, as it were, the crucial instance—standing nearly on the same level as that of the penitent robber on the cross—of the conditions of salvation. To believe in Christ, with all that this faith involved, was to obtain salvation, *i.e.*, deliverance from sin, and not only from the penalty of sin, in this world and in the world to come. The Greek presents a contrast which is lost in the English. He had called them by the usual title of respect, *Kyrii* (= Sirs, or Lords); they answer that there is one *Kyrios*, the Lord Jesus Christ, who alone can save.

(32) And they spake unto him the word
of the Lord, and to all that were in his
house. (33) And he took them the same
hour of the night, and washed *their*
stripes; and was baptized, he and all
his, straightway. (34) And when he had
brought them into his house, he set
meat before them, and rejoiced, be-
lieving in God with all his house.
(35) And when it was day, the magis-
trates sent the serjeants, saying, Let
those men go. (36) And the keeper of
the prison told this saying to Paul, The
magistrates have sent to let you go:
now therefore depart, and go in peace.
(37) But Paul said unto them, They have
beaten us openly uncondemned, being
Romans, and have cast *us* into prison;
and now do they thrust us out privily?
nay verily; but let them come themselves
and fetch us out. (38) And the serjeants
told these words unto the magistrates:

---

(32) **And they spake unto him the word of the Lord.**—It is clear that belief in the Lord Jesus Christ, unless it were to be a mere formula, repeated as a charm, required an explanation. The very title of Christ; the acts and words that showed that Jesus was the Christ; His life, and death, and resurrection; the truths of forgiveness of sins and communion with Him, and the outward signs which He had appointed as witnesses of those truths; all this must have been included in "the word of the Lord," which was preached to that congregation so strangely assembled, between the hours of midnight and of dawn. Even the Philippian gaoler had to be a catechumen before he was baptised.

(33) **He . . . washed their stripes; and was baptized . . .**—The two-fold washings, that which testified of the repentance of the gaoler and his kindly reverence for his prisoners, and that which they administered to him as the washing of regeneration, are placed in suggestive juxtaposition. He, too, was cleansed from wounds which were worse than those inflicted by the rods of the Roman lictors. No certain answer can be given to the question whether the baptism was by immersion or affusion. A public prison was likely enough to contain a bath or pool of some kind, where the former would be feasible. What has been said above (see Note on verse 15) as to the bearing of these narratives on the question of infant baptism applies here also, with the additional fact that those who are said to have been baptised are obviously identical with those whom St. Paul addressed (the word "all" is used in each case), and must, therefore, have been of an age to receive instruction together with the gaoler himself.

(34) **He set meat before them, and rejoiced.**—Literally, *set a table before them.* The two sufferers may well have needed food. If the tumult had begun, as is probable, as they were going to the *proseucha* for morning prayer, at the third hour of the day (9 A.M.), they had probably been fasting for nearly twenty-four hours. They were not likely to have made a meal when they were thrust into the dungeon. The "joy" of the meal reminds us of that noted as a chief feature of the social life of the disciples at Jerusalem in chap. ii. 46. The new hope, succeeding to the blank despair, brought with it what we may well describe as a new "joy in the Holy Ghost" (Rom. xiv. 17). The absence of the specific term of "breaking bread" excludes the idea of its having been, in the later sense of the term, an eucharistic feast; and St. Paul would probably have hesitated to admit the new convert to the Supper of the Lord without further instruction, such as we find in 1 Cor. x. 15—17, xi. 20—34; but the meal at which the teachers and the disciples, so strangely brought together, now sat down may, at any rate, be thought of as an *agapè* or "feast of charity." (See Note on Jude, verse 12.)

(35) **The magistrates sent the serjeants.**—Literally, *the rod-bearers,* or *lictors.* They would probably be the very officers who had inflicted the stripes. We are not told what led to this sudden change of action. Possibly, as has been suggested, the earthquake had alarmed the *strategi;* more probably they felt that they had acted hastily in ordering the accused to be punished with no regular trial, and without even any inquiry as to their antecedents. They had an uneasy sense of having done wrong, and they wanted to wash their hands of the business as quietly as possible.

(36) **Go in peace.**—The few hours which the gaoler had spent with his new teacher had probably taught him to use the phrase in the fulness of its meaning (see Notes on Luke vii. 50; viii. 48), and not as a mere conventional formula. He naturally looks on the offer —securing, as it did, safety for his new friend—as one that should be accepted.

(37) **They have beaten us openly uncondemned, being Romans.**—By the Lex Porcia (B.C. 247), Roman citizens were exempted from degrading punishment, such as that of scourging. It was the heaviest of all the charges brought by Cicero against Verres, the Governor of Sicily, that he had broken this law: "*Facinus est vinciri civem Romanum, scelus verberari*" (Cic. *in Verr.* v. 57). The words *civis Romanus sum* acted almost like a charm in stopping the violence of provincial magistrates. St. Paul was a citizen by birth (see Note on Acts xxii. 28), his father having probably been wealthy enough to buy the *jus civitatis,* which brought with it commercial as well as personal privileges. It did not necessarily involve residence at Rome, but makes it probable that there were some points of contact with the imperial city.

There is something like a tone of irony in the "being Romans," echoing, as it did, the very words of his accusers (verse 21). He, too, could stand on his rights as a citizen. The judges had not called on the prisoners for their defence, had not even questioned them. Even if they had not been citizens the trial was a flagrant breach of justice, and St. Paul wished to make the *strategi* feel that it was so. Here we note that he seems to couple Silas with himself. It is possible, as the Latin form of his name, Silvanus (2 Cor. i. 19; 1 Thess. i. 1) suggests, that he also was a citizen of Rome, but St. Paul's mode of speech was natural enough, even on the assumption that he only could claim the privilege. We could hardly expect him to say with minute accuracy: "They have beaten *us* uncondemned, and I, for my part, am a Roman citizen."

(38) **They feared, when they heard that they were Romans.**—It is clear that the *strategi* did not

and they feared, when they heard that they were Romans. (39) And they came and besought them, and brought *them* out, and desired *them* to depart out of the city. (40) And they went out of the prison, and entered into *the house of* Lydia:[a] and when they had seen the brethren, they comforted them, and departed.

CHAPTER XVII.—(1) Now when they had passed through Amphipolis and Apollonia, they came to Thessalonica, where was a synagogue of the Jews: (2) and Paul, as his manner was, went in unto them, and three sabbath days reasoned with them out of the scriptures, (3) opening and alleging, that Christ must needs have suffered, and risen again from the dead; and that this Jesus, whom I preach unto you, is Christ. (4) And some of them believed, and consorted with Paul and

a ver. 14.

A.D. 53.

consider their ignorance of St. Paul's citizenship a sufficient defence. They had acted illegally, and the consequence of that illegality went further than they counted on; but they could not, therefore, shake off their responsibility. They were liable to a prosecution, such as that which Cicero, for like offences, instituted against Verres. The tables were turned; the accused had become a possible accuser, and they, instead of hushing the matter up, were compelled to make something like a formal apology. We may well believe that St. Paul's motive in insisting on this, was less the satisfaction of his own honour, than a desire to impress upon the *strategi* that they were not to over-ride or strain the law to gratify the passions of a mob.

(40) **They comforted them, and departed.**—Lydia's house appears to have been the meeting-place of the brethren, as well as the lodging of the Apostle and his party. As the third person is now resumed, we may infer that St. Luke remained at Philippi, Timothy accompanying the other two. It would seem from chap. xx. 2 that the Evangelist made Philippi the centre of his evangelising work for many years. Under the care of the beloved physician, the good work went on, and we may probably trace to his influence, and to Lydia's kindness, the generous help which was sent to St. Paul once and again when he was at Thessalonica (Phil. iv. 15, 16), and, probably, at Corinth also (2 Cor. xi. 9). Long years afterwards he cherished a grateful memory of the men and women who had laboured with him at Philippi. Among these we may think of the Clement, of whom he thus speaks, possibly identical with the Flavius Clemens, who occupies a prominent position among the apostolic fathers, and was traditionally the third Bishop of Rome. (See, however, Note on Phil. iv. 3.)

## XVII.

(1) **Now when they had passed through Amphipolis and Apollonia.**—The two cities were both on the great Roman roads known as the *Via Egnatia.* Amphipolis, formerly known as Ennea Hodoi, or the Nine Ways, was famous in the Peloponnesian War as the scene of the death of Brasidas, and had been made, under the Romans, the capital of *Macedonia prima.* It was thirty-three Roman miles from Philippi and thirty from Apollonia, the latter being thirty-seven from Thessalonica. The site of Apollonia is uncertain, but the name is, perhaps, traceable in the modern village of *Polina,* between the Strymonic and Thermaic Gulfs. A more famous city of the same name, also on the *Via Egnatia,* was situated near Dyrrhacium. It seems clear that the names indicated the stages at which the travellers rested, and that thirty miles a day (a somewhat toilsome journey for those who had so recently been scourged) was, as with most men of ordinary strength, their average rate of travelling. It would seem that there was no Jewish population to present an opening for the gospel at either of these cities, and that St. Paul, therefore, passed on to Thessalonica.

**Thessalonica, where was a synagogue of the Jews.**—The city, which had previously borne the names of Emathia, Halia, and Therma, had been enlarged by Philip of Macedon, and named after his daughter. It was situated on the Thermaic Gulf, and had grown into a commercial port of considerable importance. As such, it had attracted Jews in large numbers. The MSS. differ as to the presence or absence of the Greek article before "synagogue," but, on the whole, it is probable that we should read, "*the* synagogue," that which served for the Jews of the neighbouring cities, who were not numerous enough to have one of their own. The old name survives in the modern *Saloniki,* and there is still a large Jewish population there.

(2) **Paul, as his manner was . . .**—What we read of as occurring in the Pisidian Antioch (chap. xiii. 14, 15), was, we may believe, now reproduced. That he was allowed to preach for three Sabbaths in succession, shows the respect commanded by his character as a Rabbi, and, it may be, by his earnest eloquence. Though he came with the marks of the scourge upon him, he was as fearless as ever, speaking the gospel of God "with much contention," "not in word only, but also in power, and in the Holy Ghost, and in much assurance" (1 Thess. i. 5). And with this boldness there was also a winning gentleness, "even as a nurse cherisheth her children" (1 Thess. ii. 7). And not a few Gentiles "turned from idols to serve the living and true God" (1 Thess. 1. 9).

(3) **Opening and alleging.**—The latter word is used in the sense of bringing forward proofs, and the two words imply an argument from the prophecies of the Messiah, like in kind to that at the Pisidian Antioch. In the intervals between the Sabbaths, the Apostle worked, as usual, for his livelihood, probably, of course, as a tent-maker (2 Thess. iii. 8).

**That Christ must needs have suffered.**—Better, *that the Christ,* as pointing to the expected Messiah, the Anointed of the Lord, whom all Jews were expecting, but whom they were unwilling to recognise in the crucified Jesus. The argument was, therefore, to show that prophecy pointed to a suffering as well as a glorified Messiah, and that both conditions were fulfilled in Jesus.

(4) **And some of them . . .**—Obviously but a few in comparison with the "great multitude" of the Greek proselytes of the gate. The Thessalonian Church was predominantly Gentile, some, apparently, won from idolatry without passing through Judaism

Silas; and of the devout Greeks a great
multitude, and of the chief women not
a few.
(5) But the Jews which believed not,
moved with envy, took unto them cer-
tain lewd fellows of the baser sort, and
gathered a company, and set all the city
on an uproar, and assaulted the house
of Jason, and sought to bring them out
to the people. (6) And when they found
them not, they drew Jason and certain
brethren unto the rulers of the city,
crying, These that have turned the
world upside down are come hither also,
(7) whom Jason hath received: and
these all do contrary to the decrees of
Cæsar, saying that there is another
king, *one* Jesus. (8) And they troubled
the people and the rulers of the city,
when they heard these things. (9) And
when they had taken security of Jason,
and of the other, they let them go.
(10) And the brethren immediately
sent away Paul and Silas by night unto
Berea: who coming *thither* went into
the synagogue of the Jews. (11) These

---

(1 Thess. i. 9). Some good MSS., indeed, express this, by reading, *devout persons and Greeks.*

**Of the chief women not a few.**—These, like the women in the Pisidian Antioch (chap. xiii. 50), had probably come previously under Jewish influence. Here, however, they were attracted by the higher teaching of the Apostles.

(5) **The Jews which believed not.**—The latter words are wanting in many MSS., as "filled with envy" are in others.

**Certain lewd fellows of the baser sort.**—The word "lewd" is used in its older sense, as meaning vile, worthless. At a still earlier stage of its history, as in Chaucer and the Vision of Piers Plowman,

["How thou lernest the people,
The lered and the lewed,"] l. 2100.

it meant simply the layman, or untaught person, as distinct from the scholar. The "baser sort" answers to a Greek word describing the loungers in the *agora*, or market-place, ever ready for the excitement of a tumult—the *sub-rostrani* or *turba forensis* of Latin writers. Men of such a class, retaining its old habits, are found even among the Christian converts in 2 Thess. iii. 11, "working not at all, but busybodies."

**Assaulted the house of Jason.**—The ground of the attack was that he had received the preachers as his guests. The name was locally conspicuous as having belonged to the old hero of the Argonautic expedition, and to the tyrant of Pheræ. It is probable, however, that St. Paul would, in the first instance, take up his abode with a Jew, and that Jason, as in the case of the apostate high priest of 2 Macc. iv. 7, was the Greek equivalent for Joshua or Jesus.

**To bring them out to the people.**—Thessalonica was a free Greek city, and the Jews accordingly in the first instance intended to bring the matter before the popular *ecclesia* or assembly.

(6) **Unto the rulers of the city.**—The Greek term here, *politarchæ*, is a very peculiar one, and occurs nowhere else in the New Testament, nor, indeed, in any classical writer. Aristotle, whose *Politics* well-nigh exhausts the list of all known official titles in Greek cities, does not mention it, although he gives an analogous title (*Politophylakes*) as found at Larissa and elsewhere (*Pol.* v. 6). An inscription on an arch that still spans (or did so till quite lately) one of the streets of the modern city *Saloniki*, shows it to have been a special official title of that city, and St. Luke's use of it may, therefore, be noted as an instance of his accuracy in such matters. The inscription is probably of the date of Vespasian, but it contains some names that are identical with those of the converts in the apostolic history, Sosipater ("Sopater," chap. xx. 4). Gaius (chap. xix. 29), and Secundus (chap. xx. 4). It would seem from the inscription that, as with the Archons of Athens, there were seven magistrates who bore the title.

(7) **These all do contrary to the decrees of Cæsar.**—Thessalonica, though a free city, was yet under the imperial government, and the Jews therefore appeal to the emperor's decree, probably to the edict of Claudius (chap. xviii. 2), as at least showing the drift of the emperor's policy, even though it was not strictly binding except in Rome and the *coloniæ.* This, however, might prove an insufficient weapon of attack, and therefore they add another charge, to which no magistrate throughout the empire could be indifferent. (See Notes on Luke xxiii. 2; John xix. 12.) The preachers were not only bringing in a *relligio illicita*, but were guilty of treason against the majesty of the empire; they said there was "another King." It is clear from the Epistle to the Thessalonians that the Kingdom of Christ, and specially His second coming as King, had been very prominent in the Apostle's teaching (1 Thess. iv. 14; v. 2, 23; 2 Thess. i. 7, 8; ii. 1—12), and this may have furnished materials for the accusation.

(9) **And when they had taken security of Jason.**—The Greek noun, probably used as an equivalent for the Latin *satis accipere*, in common use in legal language, is a technical one (literally, *the sufficient sum*) for the bail which Jason was required to give for the good conduct of his guests, and for their readiness to meet any charge that might be brought against them. It is clear from 1 Thess. i. 6, ii. 14, that St. Paul and Silas were not the only sufferers. The Gentile converts were exposed alike to the violence of their own countrymen and to the malice of the Jews. How anxious he was to visit and comfort them is seen from the fact that he made two attempts to return, before or during his stay at Corinth (1 Thess. ii. 18).

(10) **Sent away Paul and Silas by night unto Berea.**—Timotheus apparently remained behind, partly to help the Thessalonian converts under their present trials, partly to be able to bring word to St. Paul as to their condition. At Berœa Paul and Silas were alone. The city lay to the south of Thessalonica, not far from Pella, on the banks of the Astræus, and still retains its name in the modern *Kara Feria*, or *Verria.* It has now a population of 20,000. Here also there was a Jewish population, but the city was a far less important place commercially than Thessalonica.

(11) **These were more noble than those in Thessalonica.**—The word for "noble" (literally, *well-born*, as in 1 Cor. i. 26) had, like most words

were more noble than those in Thes-
salonica, in that they received the word
with all readiness of mind, and searched
the scriptures daily, whether those
things were so. (12) Therefore many of
them believed; also of honourable
women which were Greeks, and of men,
not a few. (13) But when the Jews of
Thessalonica had knowledge that the
word of God was preached of Paul at
Berea, they came thither also, and stirred
up the people. (14) And then imme-
diately the brethren sent away Paul to
go as it were to the sea: but Silas and
Timotheus abode there still. (15) And
they that conducted Paul brought him
unto Athens: and receiving a com-
mandment unto Silas and Timotheus
for to come to him with all speed, they
departed.

(16) Now while Paul waited for them
at Athens, his spirit was stirred in him,
when he saw the city wholly given to
idolatry.[1] (17) Therefore disputed he in
the synagogue with the Jews, and with
the devout persons, and in the market
daily with them that met with him.
(18) Then certain philosophers of the

[1] Or, *full of idols.*

---

of like origin (such, *e.g.*, as the Latin *ingenuus*), a wide latitude of meaning. Here it stands for the generous, loyal temper which was ideally supposed to characterise those of noble origin. This was the quality which the Apostle and the historian admired in the Berœans. They were not the slaves of prejudice. They were ready to believe in the gospel which St. Paul preached as meeting their spiritual wants; and so they came to the study of the proofs, which the preacher "opened and alleged," with a temper predisposed to faith. On the other hand, they did not accept their own wishes, or the Apostle's assertions, as in themselves sufficient grounds of faith. With a quick and clear intelligence they searched the Scriptures daily to see whether they really did speak of a Christ who should suffer and rise again. The Berœan converts have naturally been regarded, especially among those who urge the duty, or claim the right, of private judgment, as a representative instance of the right relations of Reason and Faith, occupying a middle position between credulity and scepticism, to be reproduced, *mutatis mutandis*, according to the different aspects which each presents in successive ages.

(12) **Therefore many of them believed.**—The narrator dwells with satisfaction on the fact that at Berœa there were many Jewish as well as Gentile converts. Among the latter there were, as at Thessalonica, women of the upper class.

(13) **They came thither also, and stirred up the people.**—To the unbelieving Jews of Thessalonica the conversions at Berœa were simply a cause of offence. It is apparently with reference to this that St. Paul says of them that "they please not God and are contrary to all men, forbidding us to speak to the Gentiles" (1 Thess. ii. 15).

(14) **To go as it were to the sea.**—The English version conveys the impression that the movement was a feint in order to baffle the pursuers. Many of the better MSS., however, give "as far as the sea," and this is probably the meaning even of the reading followed by the Authorised version. The absence of any mention of places between Berœa and Athens, (as, *e.g.*, Amphipolis and Apollonia are mentioned in verse 1), is presumptive evidence that St. Paul actually travelled by sea, and rounding the promontory of Sunium, entered Athens by the Piræus. He had been accompanied so far by some of those who had escorted him from Berœa, but when they too went back, he was, we must remember, for the first time since the commencement of his missionary labours, absolutely alone. His yearning for companionship and counsel is shown in the urgent message sent to Silas and Timotheus to come "with all speed" (literally, *as quickly as possible*). As far as we can gather from 1 Thess. iii. 1—3, Timotheus came by himself to Athens, probably after the scene at the Areopagus, and was sent back at once with words of counsel and comfort to those whom he reported as suffering much tribulation.

(16) **His spirit was stirred in him.**—The verb is the root of the noun from which we get our "paroxysm," and which is translated by "sharp contention" in chap. xv. 39. Athens, glorying now, as it had done in the days of Sophocles (*Œdip. Col.* 1008), in its devotion to the gods, presented to him, even after seeing Tarsus and Antioch, a new aspect. The city was "full of idols;" Hermes-busts at every corner, statues and altars in the *atrium* or court-yard of every house, temples and porticos and colonnades, all presenting what was to him the same repulsive spectacle. He looked on the Theseus and the Ilissus, and the friezes of the Centaurs and Lapithæ on the Parthenon, as we look on them in our museums, but any sense of art-beauty which he may have had (and it was probably, in any case, but weak) was over-powered by his horror that men should bow down and worship what their own hands had made. The beauty of form which we admire in the Apollo or the Aphrodite, the Mercury or the Faun, would be to him, in its unveiled nakedness, a thing to shudder at. He knew too well to what that love of sensuous beauty had led in Greek and Roman life (Rom. i. 24—27), when it had thrown aside what, to a Jew, were not only the natural instincts of purity, but the sanctions of a divine command (Gen. ix. 22).

(17) **And in the market daily.**—To teach in the synagogue, and to gather the devout persons, *i.e.*, the proselytes to whom the Law had been a schoolmaster, leading them to Christ, was after the usual pattern of St. Paul's work. The third mode of action, disputing in the market-place, the *agora*, which in every Greek city was the centre of its life, was a new experiment. He saw, we may believe, others so disputing; teachers of this or that school of philosophy, with listeners round them, debating glibly of the "highest good," and the "chief end" of life, and man's relation to the One and the All. Why should not he take part in the discussion, and lead those who were apparently in earnest in their inquiries to the truth which they were vainly seeking?

(18) **Certain philosophers of the Epicureans, and of the Stoicks.**—The two schools were at this time the great representatives of Greek thought. The former took its name from its founder, Epicurus, who lived a long and tranquil life at Athens, from

Epicureans, and of the Stoicks, encountered him. And some said, What will this babbler[1] say? other some, He seemeth to be a setter forth of strange

1 Or, *base fellow.*

B.C. 342 to 270. As holding their meetings in a garden, which he had left by his will in trust as a place of study for his disciples, they were sometimes known as the School of the Garden, and as such were distinguished from those of the Porch (Diog. Laert. *Epic.* c. 10). His speculations embraced at once a physical and an ethical solution of the problems of the universe. Rejecting, as all thinking men did, the popular Polytheism, which yet they did not dare openly to renounce, he taught that the gods, in their eternal tranquillity, were too far off from man to trouble themselves about his sorrows or his sins. They needed no sacrifices and answered no prayers. The superstition which enslaved the minds of most men was the great evil of the world, the source of its crimes and miseries. The last enemy to be destroyed was with him, as in our own time with Strauss, the belief in an immortality of retribution. A man's first step towards happiness and wisdom was to emancipate himself from its thraldom; the next was to recognise that happiness consisted in the greatest aggregate of pleasurable emotions. Experience taught that what are called pleasures are often more than counterbalanced by the pains that follow, and sensual excesses were therefore to be avoided. Epicurus's own life seems to have been distinguished by generosity, self-control, and general kindliness, and even by piety and patriotism (Diog. Laert. *Epic.* c. 5). But as no law was recognised as written in the heart, and human laws were looked on as mere conventional arrangements, each man was left to form his own estimate of what would give him most pleasure, and most men decided for a life of ease and self-indulgence; sometimes balanced by prudential calculations, sometimes sinking into mere voluptuousness. The poetry of Horace presents, perhaps, the most attractive phase of popular Epicureanism; the sense which has come to be attached to the modern word "Epicure," as applied to one whose life is devoted to the indulgence of the sense of taste, shows to what a depth of degradation it might sink.

In the world of physics, Epicurus has been claimed as anticipating some of the results of modern science. The ideas of creation and control were alike excluded. Matter had existed from eternity, and the infinite atoms of which it was composed had, under the action of attractive and repelling forces as yet unknown, entered into manifold combinations, out of which had issued, as the last stage of the evolution, the world of nature as it now lies before us. The poem of Lucretius, *De Rerum Naturâ*, may be regarded as the grandest utterance of this negative and practically atheistic system, but its real nobleness lies chiefly in its indignant protest against the superstition which had cast its veil of thick darkness over all the nations.

It may be well to give one or two characteristic examples of each of these phases. On the one side we have the ever-recurring advice of the popular poet of society to remember that life is short, and to make the most of it:—

"Quid sit futurum cras, fuge quærere : et,
Quem Fors dierum cunque dabit, lucro
Appone."
["Strive not the morrow's chance to know,
But count whate'er the Fates bestow
As given thee for thy gain"]—Hor. *Od.* i. 9.

"Sapias, vina liques, et spatio brevi
Spem longam reseces. Dum loquimur, fugerit invida
Ætas. Carpe diem, quam minimum credula postero."
["Be wise, and let your wines flow clear,
And as you greet each short-lived year,
Curb hope's delusive play :
E'en as we speak, our life glides by;
Enjoy the moments as they fly,
Nor trust the far-off day."]—*Od.* i. 11.

The student of Scripture will recognise an Epicurean element of this kind in one of the two voices that alternate in the Book of Ecclesiastes, "It is good and comely for one to eat and to drink, and to enjoy the good of all his labour that he taketh under the sun all the days of his life" (Eccles. v. 18. Comp. also Eccles. iii. 19; viii. 15; ix. 7). It appears as the avowed principle of the evil-doers in the Apocryphal Book of Wisdom which, as probably the work of a contemporary writer, represents the impression made by the dominant Horatian phase of Epicureanism on a devout and thoughtful Jew:—

"Our time is a very shadow that passeth away . . . Come on, therefore, let us enjoy the good things that are present . . . Let us crown ourselves with rose-buds before they are withered . . . Let none of us go without his part of our voluptuousness."—*Wisd.* ii. 5–9.

There is a nobler ring, it must be owned, in the bold language in which Lucretius sings the praises of Epicurus:—

"When this our life lay crushed before men's eyes
Beneath the yoke of Faith, who from on high
With horrid aspect frightened mortal hearts,
It was a Greek, himself a mortal too,
Who first had courage to lift up his eyes
And to her face withstand her. Tales of gods,
And thunderbolts from Heaven, with all their threats,
Were impotent to stay him . . . .
. . . . So at last
Faith in its turn lies trampled under foot,
And we through him have triumphed over Heaven."
*De Rer. Nat.* i. 67–80.

We can understand how St. Paul would assert, as against this school of thought, the personality of the living God, as Creator, Ruler, Father; the binding force of the law written in the heart; intuitive morality as against mere utilitarianism; the nobleness of a hero-soul raised above pleasure, and living, not for itself, but for others and for God. And in so teaching them he, in this respect differing from the mere professor of a higher philosophy, would point to the Resurrection and the Judgment as that which should confound the pleasure-seeker by giving him tribulation and anguish, and should assign glory and immortality to the patient worker of righteousness. (Comp. Rom. ii. 7—9.)

The Stoics—who took their name, not from their founder (Zeno, of Citium in Cyprus), but from the *Stoa pœkilè*, the painted porch, at Athens, adorned with frescoes of the battle of Marathon, where Zeno used to teach—presented a higher phase of thought. Josephus (*Vit.* c. 2) compares them with the Pharisees, and their relation to the moral life of heathenism at this time presented many features analogous to those which we find in the influence of that sect in Palestine. They taught that true wisdom consisted in being the master, and not the slave, of circumstances. The things which are not in our power are not things to seek after, nor shrink from, but to be accepted with a calm equanimity. The seeker after wisdom learnt, therefore, to be indifferent alike to pleasure or pain, and aimed at an absolute apathy. The theology of the Stoics was also of a nobler kind than that of

gods: because he preached unto them
Jesus, and the resurrection. (19) And
they took him, and brought him unto
Areopagus,[1] saying, May we know what

[1] Or, *Mars' hill.* It was the highest court in Athens.

Epicurus. They spoke of a divine Mind pervading the universe, and ordering all things by its Providence. They recognised its government in the lives of nations and individual men, and probably reconciled, as the Pharisees did, their acceptance of its decrees with a practical belief in the freedom of the individual will. In the *Manual of Ethics*, by Epictetus, under Nero, and the *Meditations* of Marcus Aurelius, we see how the slave and the emperor stood on common ground. In Seneca, we see how often the Stoics spoke in the accents of Christian ethics. Many of the Stoics were sought after as tutors for the sons of noble families, and occupied a position of influence not unlike that of Jesuit confessors and directors in France in the seventeenth and eighteenth centuries. The main drawbacks were (1) that in aiming at apathy for themselves they shut out sympathy with others as disturbing their tranquillity; (2) that in striving after an ethical perfection in the strength of their own will they anticipated the position of the Pelagians in the history of the Christian Church; and (3) that, as with the Pharisees, the high ideal was often but a mask for selfish and corrupt lives. They, also, were too often "hypocrites," acting a part before the world to which their true character did not correspond. In the language of the satirist—

> "Qui Curios simulant et Bacchanalia vivunt."
> ["They pose as heroes, and as drunkards live."]
> —Juvenal, *Sat.* ii. 3.

It is evident that there would be many points of sympathy between the better representatives of this school and St. Paul, but for them also the message that spoke of Jesus and the Resurrection—of God sending His Son into the world to be first crucified and then raised from the dead—would seem an idle dream, and they would shrink from the thought that they needed pardon and redemption, and could do nothing true and good in their own strength without the grace of God.

**What will this babbler say?**—Better, *What might this babbler mean?* The Greek noun, literally *seed-picker*, was primarily applied to a small bird of the finch tribe. The idle gossips of the *agora* picking up news, and eager to retail it, the chattering parasites of feasts, were likened by the quick wit of Athenian humourists to such a bird as it hopped and chirped. So Zeno himself called one of his disciples, who had more words than wisdom, by the same contemptuous name (Diog. Laert. *Zeno*, c. 19). The philosophers, in their scorn of the stranger who was so ready to discuss great questions with any whom he met, applied the derisive epithet to him.

**He seemeth to be a setter forth of strange gods.**—This was, it will be remembered, the precise charge on which Socrates had been condemned (Xenoph. *Memor.* i. 1, § 1). In his case it rested on his constant reference to the *dæmôn*, the divine monitor who checked and guided him, in whose voice he heard something like the voice of God; but the secret of his condemnation by his countrymen was to be found less in what he actually taught than in the questions with which he vexed their inmost soul, and made them conscious of ignorance or baseness. The questions of St. Paul, as he reasoned "of righteousness, temperance, and judgment to come," were equally disturbing.

**Because he preached unto them Jesus, and the resurrection.**—The verb implies continuous action. This was the ever-recurring theme of his discourses. It is possible that with the strong tendency of the Greek mind to personify all attributes and abstract thoughts, St. Paul's hearers saw in the word *Anastasis* (=Resurrection) the name of a new goddess, representing the idea of immortality, to be worshipped in conjunction with Jesus, and therefore they used the plural and spoke of his bringing in "strange gods." So temples and altars had been dedicated to Concord, and the history of Athens told how Epimenides had bidden them erect two altars to Insolence and Outrage (Cicero, *De Leg.* ii. 11), as the two demons by whom their city was being brought to ruin. What startled them in the Apostle was that he taught not only the immortality of the soul—that had entered into the popular mythical belief, and had been enforced with philosophical arguments by Socrates and Plato—but the resurrection of the body. In 1 Cor. xv. 35 we see the character of the objections raised to this doctrine, and the manner in which St. Paul answered them.

(19) **They took him, and brought him unto Areopagus.**—The name may stand either for the Hill of Mars, simply as a locality, or for the Court which sat there, and was known as the Court of the Areopagus, and which, as the oldest and most revered tribunal in Athens, owing its origin to Athena, and connected with the story of Orestes and the worship of the propitiated *Erinnyes* (the Avengers) as the *Eumenides* (the Gentle Ones), still continued to exercise jurisdiction in all matters connected with the religion of the state, and numbered among its members men of the highest official rank. It had originally consisted only of those who had filled the office of Archon and were over sixty years of age. Its supreme authority had been in some measure limited by Pericles, and it was as the organ of the party who opposed the ideas of freedom and progress of which he was the representative, that Æschylus wrote the tragedy of the *Eumenides*, in which the divine authority of the Court was impressed upon men's minds. Here, however, the narrative that follows presents no trace of a formal trial, and hence it has been questioned whether the Apostle was brought before the *Court* of the Areopagus. Unless, however, there had been some intention of a trial, there seems no reason for their taking him to the Areopagus rather than to the Pnyx or elsewhere; and the mention of a member of the Court as converted by St. Paul's preaching, makes it probable that the Court was actually sitting at the time. The most natural explanation of the apparent difficulty is, that as the charge of bringing in "strange deities" was one which came under the jurisdiction of the Areopagus Court, the crowd who seized on St. Paul hurried him there, not presenting a formal indictment, but calling for a preliminary inquiry, that his speech accordingly, though of the nature of an *apologia*, was not an answer to a distinct accusation, and that having heard it, the Court looked on the matter as calling for no special action, and passed to the order of the day.

**May we know . . . ?**—The form of the question, courteous in semblance, but with a slight touch of sarcasm, is eminently characteristic in itself, and shows also that there was no formal accusation, though the words that followed suggested the thought that there

this new doctrine, whereof thou speak-
est, *is?* (20) For thou bringest certain
strange things to our ears: we would
know therefore what these things mean.
(21) (For all the Athenians and strangers
which were there spent their time in
nothing else, but either to tell, or to
hear some new thing.)

(22) Then Paul stood in the midst of
Mars' hill,[1] and said, *Ye* men of Athens,
I perceive that in all things ye are too
superstitious. (23) For as I passed by,
and beheld your devotions,[2] I found an
altar with this inscription, TO THE
UNKNOWN GOD. Whom therefore
ye ignorantly worship, him declare I

1 Or, *the court of Areopagites.*

2 Or, *gods that ye worship,* 2 Thess. 2. 4.

possibly might be materials for one. What had been said was "strange" enough to require an explanation.

(20) **Thou bringest certain strange things.**—The adjective stands for a Greek participle, *things that startle,* or *leave an impression of strangeness.*

(21) **For all the Athenians and strangers.**—The restless inquisitiveness of the Athenian character had been all along proverbial. In words which St. Luke almost reproduces, Demosthenes (*Philipp.* i., p. 43) had reproached them with idling their time away in the *agora,* asking what news there was of Philip's movements, or the action of their own envoys, when they ought to have been preparing for strenuous action. The "strangers" who were present were probably a motley group—young Romans sent to finish their education, artists, and sight-seers, and philosophers, from every province in the empire.

**Some new thing.**—Literally, *some newer thing;* as we should say, the "very latest news." Theophrastus (c. 8) uses the self-same word in describing the questions of the loquacious prattlers of society, "Is there anything new? . . . Is there anything yet *newer?*"

(22) **Paul stood in the midst of Mars' hill.**—Better, *Areopagus,* as before. The Court sat in the open air on benches forming three sides of a quadrangle. A short flight of sixteen steps, cut in the rock, led from the *agora* to the plateau where the Court held its sittings. If it was actually sitting at the time, the temptation to have recourse to it, if only to cause a sensation and terrify the strange disputant, may well have been irresistible. As the Apostle stood there, he looked from the slight elevation on the temple of the Eumenides below him, that of Theseus to the east, and facing him on the Acropolis, the Parthenon. On the height of that hill stood the colossal bronze statue of Athena as the tutelary goddess of her beloved Athens, below and all around him were statues and altars. The city was "very full of idols."

(23) **I perceive that in all things ye are too superstitious.**—Better, *I observe you as being in all things more fearful of the gods than others.* It is not easy to express the exact force of the Greek adjective. "Superstitious" is, perhaps, too strong on the side of blame; "devout," on the side of praise. The word which the Athenians loved to use of themselves (*theosebês,* a worshipper of God) exactly answers to the latter term. This St. Paul will not use of idolators, and reserves it for those who worship the one living and true God, and he uses a word which, like our "devotee," though not offensive, was neutral with a slight touch of disparagement. The *deisidaimôn* is described at some length in the *Characters* of Theophrastus, the La Bruyere of classical literature (c. xvii.), as one who consults soothsayers, and is a believer in omens, who will give up a journey if he sees a weasel on the road, and goes with his wife and children to be initiated into the Orphic mysteries. Nikias, the Athenian general, ever oppressed with the sense of the jealousy of the gods, and counter-ordering important strategic movements because there was an eclipse of the moon (Thucyd. vii. 50), is a conspicuous instance of the *deisidaimôn* in high places. The Stoic Emperor, Marcus Aurelius (*Meditt.* i. 16), congratulates himself on not being such a *deisidaimôn,* while he gives thanks that he has inherited his mother's devotion (*theosebes*) (i. 2). The opening words would gain, and were perhaps meant to gain, the ears of the philosophers. Here, they would say, is one who, at least, rises, as we do, above the religion of the multitude.

**As I passed by, and beheld your devotions.**—Better, *as I passed by, and was contemplating the objects of your worship.* The English word appears to have been used in its old sense, as meaning what the Greek word means—the object, and not the act, of devotion. So, Wiclif gives "your mawmetis"—*i.e.,* "your idols." Tyndale, Cranmer, and the Geneva version give "the manner how ye worship your gods." The Rhemish follows Wiclif, and gives "your idols."

**I found an altar with this inscription, TO THE UNKNOWN GOD.**—The Greek of the inscription has no article, and might, therefore, be rendered TO AN UNKNOWN GOD, as though it had been consecrated as a votive offering for benefits which the receiver was unable to assign to the true donor among the "gods many and lords many" whom he worshipped. So interpreted, it did not bear its witness directly to any deeper thoughts than those of the popular polytheism, and stands on the same footing as the altars TO UNKNOWN GODS, which are mentioned by Pausanias (i. 1—4) as set up in the harbour and streets of Athens, or to the description which Theophrastus gives (as above) of the *deisidaimôn* as asking the soothsayers, after he has had a disquieting dream, to what god or goddess he ought to pray. Greek usage, however, did not require the use of the article in inscriptions of this nature, and the English translation is quite as legitimate as the other, and clearly gives the sense in which St. Paul understood it. Taking this sense, there come the questions. What thought did the inscription express? To what period did it belong? A story connected with Epimenides of Crete, who, as a prophet of great fame, was invited to Athens at a time when the city was suffering from pestilence, is sometimes referred to as affording a probable explanation of its origin. Diogenes Laertius (*Epimen.* c. 3) relates that he turned sheep loose into the city, and then had them sacrificed, where they stopped, to the god thus pointed out, *i.e.,* to the one whose image or altar was nearest to the spot, and that "altars without a name" were thus to be seen in many parts of Athens; and it has been supposed that this may have been one of these altars, erected where there was no image near enough to warrant a sacrifice to any known deity, and as Epimenides is stated to have offered sacrifices on the Areopagus, that such an altar may have been standing within view as St. Paul spoke. Against this view, however, are the facts (1) that the narrative of Laertius names no such inscription as that of which St. Paul speaks, and

unto you. (24) God, that made the world and all things therein,[a] seeing that he is Lord of heaven and earth, dwelleth not in temples made with

[a] ch. 7. 48.

rather implies that every victim found the god to whom it of right belonged, or else that the altar was left without any inscription; (2) that St. Paul's language implies that he had seen the inscription as he walked through the city, and not that he looked on it as he spoke; and (3) that it is hardly conceivable that such an altar, standing in so conspicuous a place from the time of Epimenides, would have remained unnoticed by a thinker like Socrates. Jerome (on Tit. i. 12) cuts the knot of the difficulty by stating that the inscription actually ran, "To the Gods of Asia and Europe and Africa, to unknown and strange Gods." It is possible that he may have seen an altar with such words upon it, and that he rushed to the conclusion that it was what St. Paul referred to; but it is not likely that the Apostle would have ventured on altering the inscription to suit his argument in the presence of those who could have confuted him on the spot, and his words must be received as indicating what he had actually seen.

A passage in the dialogue of *Philopatris*, ascribed to Lucian, where one of the speakers swears "by the Unknown God of Athens," is interesting; but, as written in the third century after Christ, may be only a reference, not without a sneer, to St. Paul's speech, and cannot be adduced as evidence either as to the existence of such an altar or its meaning. An independent inquiry based upon *data* hitherto not referred to, will, perhaps, lead to more satisfactory conclusions. (1) The verbal adjective means something more than "Unknown." It adds the fact that the Unknown is also the Unknowable. It is the ultimate confession, such as we have heard of late from the lips of some students of science, of man's impotence to solve the problems of the universe. It does not affirm Atheism, but it knows not what the Power is, which yet it feels must be. (2) As such it presents a striking parallel to the inscription which Plutarch (*de Isid. et Osir.*) records as found on the veil of Isis at Sais: "I am all that has been, and all that is, and all that shall be; and no mortal hath lifted my veil." Whether that inscription expressed the older thoughts of Egypt may, perhaps, be questioned. Plutarch gives it in Greek, and this probably indicates a date after the foundation of the monarchy of the Ptolemies (B.C. 367), possibly contemporary with Plutarch (A.D. 46—140). (3) Still more striking, if possible, is the parallelism presented by an altar found at Ostia, and now in the Vatican Museum. It represents what is known as a Mithraic sacrificial group, connected, *i.e.*, with the worship of Mithras, the Sun-god of later Persian mythology, a winged figure sacrificing a bull, with various symbolic emblems, such as a serpent and a scorpion. Underneath appears the inscription (Orelli, *Inscr. Gel.* ii. 5,000)—

SIGNUM INDEPREHENSIBILIS DEI.
[THE SYMBOL OF THE UNDISCOVERABLE GOD.]

It will be admitted that this expresses the same thought as the inscription which St. Paul quotes; that it is the nearest equivalent that Latin can supply for the "Unknown and Unknowable" God. The frequent recurrence of Mithraic groups in nearly all museums, generally without any note of time, but, in the judgment of experts, ranging from the time of Pompeius to that of Diocletian, shows the prevalence of this Sun-worship throughout the Roman world during the early period of the empire. We have found an interesting trace of it in Cyprus. (See Note on chap. xiii. 14.) We may see its surviving influence in the reverence shown by Constantine to the *Dies Solis* in the general observance of that day throughout the empire. Other inscriptions, also in the Vatican Museum, such as SOLI DEO INVICTO (Orelli, i., 1904—14), show its prevalence. Our own Sunday (*Dies Solis*), little as we dream of it, is probably a survival of the Mithraic *cultus*, which at one time seemed not unlikely, as seen from a merely human standpoint, to present a formidable rivalry to the claims of the Church of Christ. It is, at least, a remarkable coincidence that the Twenty-fifth of December was kept as the festival of Mithras long before it was chosen by the Western Church for the Feast of the Nativity. It is true that De Rossi, the great Roman archæologist, in a note to the present writer, gives the probable date of the inscription in question as belonging to the second or third century after Christ; but the Mithraic worship is known to have prevailed widely from a much earlier period, and the church of San Clemente, at Rome, where below the two basilicas have been found the remains of a Christian oratory turned into a Mithraic chapel, presents a memorable instance of the rivalry of the two systems. On the whole, therefore, it seems probable that the altar which St. Paul saw was an earlier example of the feeling represented by the Ostian inscription, and may well have found its expression, with a like characteristic formula, among the many forms of the confluent polytheism of Athens. Plutarch (*Pompeius*) speaks of the worship of Mithras as having been brought into Europe by the Cilician pirates whom Pompeius defeated, and as continuing in his own time.

**Whom therefore ye ignorantly worship.**—Better, as expressing the connection with the inscription, *What therefore ye worship not knowing, that declare I unto you.* The better MSS. give the relative pronoun in the neuter. It was, perhaps, deliberately used, as St. Paul uses the neuter form for "Godhead" in verse 29, and a cognate abstract noun in Rom. i. 20, to express the fact that the Athenians were as yet ignorant of the personality of the living God. That any human teacher should have power and authority to proclaim that "Unknown God," as making Himself known to men, was what neither Epicureans nor Stoics had dreamt of. The verb "declare" is closely connected with the term "setter forth," of verse 18. He does not disclaim that element in the charge against him.

(24) **God that made the world . . .**—The masculine form of the pronoun and participles throughout the sentence presents an emphatic contrast to the neuter pronoun of the previous verse.

**Seeing that he is Lord.**—Better, *He, being Lord.*

**Dwelleth not in temples made with hands.**—We note with special interest the reproduction of the thought which the then persecutor had heard from the lips of the martyr Stephen. (See Note on chap. vii. 48.) As asserted of the Temple at Jerusalem, it had at that time, even though it was quoted from a Jewish prophet, driven the Pharisee Saul into the frenzy of fanaticism. Now, having learnt the lesson as regards that Temple, he proclaims the truth as applicable *à fortiori* to all temples raised by human hands. It is obvious that

hands; (25) neither is worshipped with
men's hands, as though he needed any
thing,[a] seeing he giveth to all life, and
breath, and all things; (26) and hath
made of one blood all nations of men
for to dwell on all the face of the earth,
and hath determined the times before
appointed, and the bounds of their
habitation; (27) that they should seek
the Lord, if haply they might feel after

a Ps. 50. 8.

this truth places the sacredness of Christian churches on a ground entirely different from that which influenced the minds of Jew or Greek in regard to their respective temples. Churches are holy, not because God dwells in them, but because they are set apart for the highest acts of the collective life of the congregation of His people. In those acts men hold communion with God, and so the Church is for them all, and more than all, that the Tabernacle of Meeting (this, as meaning the place where man met God, rather than Tabernacle of the Congregation, being the true rendering of the Hebrew term; comp. Ex. xxix. 42) was to the Israelites of old. Romish theory and practice, in presenting the consecrated wafer in pyx or monstrance, or carrying it in procession, as an object of adoration, revives the old Pagan view which St. Paul disclaims.

(25) **Neither is worshipped with men's hands, as though he needed any thing.**—Literally, *as needing anything in addition.* The previous words had struck at a false theory of temples, this strikes at a false theory of worship. Men have to think of God as the supreme Giver, not as requiring anything at their hands but justice, mercy, and truth. Both Jewish and heathen writers had borne their witness of the same truth: David had said, "Thou desirest not sacrifice; else would I give it" (Ps. li. 16), and the Latin Epicurean poet had written of the Divine nature, that it was—

"Ipsa suis pollens opibus, nihil indiga nostri,
Nec bene promeritis capitur, nec tangitur ira."

["Strong in itself, it needeth nought of ours,
Is neither won by gifts, nor moved by wrath."]
*Lucret.* ii. 649–50.

The passage is found also in some editions in i. 61, 62.

**Life and breath.**—If we can draw a distinction between the two words, the first may be held to mean the higher element of man's life, the latter that which he shares, by virtue of his organisation, with other animals. Stoics and Epicureans would, probably, both of them, so far, accept a teaching which echoed much that was taught in their own schools.

(26) **And hath made of one blood all nations of men.**—Literally, *every nation.* The previous verses had given what we may venture to call St. Paul's Philosophy of Religion. This gives his Philosophy of History. And the position was one which no Greek, above all, no Athenian, was likely to accept. For him the distinction between the Greek and the barbarian was radical and essential. The one was by nature meant to be the slave of the other. (Aristot. *Pol.* i. 2, 6.) In rising above his own prejudices of fancied superiority of race, the Apostle felt that he could attack, as from a vantage-ground, the prejudices of others. He naturally accepted the truth as it was presented to him in the Mosaic history of the Creation; but the truth itself, stated in its fullest form, would remain, even if we were to accept other theories of the origin of species and the history of man. There is a oneness of physical structure, of conditions and modes of life, of possible or actual development, which forbids any one race or nation, Hebrew, Hellenic, Latin, or Teutonic, to assume for itself that it is the cream and flower of humanity.

**Hath determined the times before appointed.**—The better MSS. give simply, "the appointed seasons." Few words, even in St. Paul's teaching, are more pregnant with significance. They justify all that the wise of heart have said as to the "manifold wisdom of God," as seen in history and in the education of mankind. The special gifts of character of each race—Hebrew thought of God, Greek sense of beauty, Roman sense of law, Teutonic truthfulness, Keltic impulsiveness, Negro docility—have all their work to do. All local circumstances of soil and climate that influence character come under the head of the "bounds of men's habitation." All conditions of time—the period at which each race has been called to play its part in the drama of the world's history—come under the head of the "appointed seasons."

(27) **Should seek the Lord, if haply they might feel after him, and find him.**—The word for "feel after" expresses strictly the act of groping in the dark. From the Apostle's point of view, anticipating in part the great *Theodikæa*—the vindication of the ways of God—in the Epistle to the Romans, the whole order of the world's history was planned, as part of the education of mankind, waking longings which it could not satisfy, leading men at once to a consciousness of the holiness of God and of their own sinfulness. The religions of the world were to him as the movements of one who climbs

"Upon the great world's altar stairs,
That slope through darkness up to God;"

who can only say—

"I stretch lame hands of faith, and grope,
And gather dust, and chaff, and call
To what I feel is Lord of all,
And faintly trust the larger hope."

Their ritual in all its manifold variety was but as the inarticulate wailing of childhood—

"An infant crying for the light,
And with no language but a cry."
—Tennyson, *In Memoriam*, liv.

The "if haply" expresses the exact force of the Greek particles, which imply a doubt whether the end had been attained in its completeness. The altar to the Unknown and Unknowable was a witness that they had not been found. "The world by wisdom knew not God" (1 Cor. i. 21). It had not got, in the language of another poet of our own, beyond

"Those obstinate questionings
Of sense and outward things,
Fallings from us, vanishings;"

which are as the

"Blank misgivings of a creature
Moving about in worlds not realised."
—Wordsworth, *Ode on Immortality.*

**Though he be not far from every one of us.**—Better, *and yet He is not far.* The speaker appeals, as he does in Rom. ii. 15, to the witness borne by man's consciousness and conscience. There, in the depths of each man's being, not in temples made with hands, men might find God and hold communion with him. It

him, and find him, though he be not far from every one of us: (28) for in him we live, and move, and have our being; as certain also of your own poets have said, For we are also his offspring. (29) Forasmuch then as we are the offspring of God, we ought not to think that the Godhead is like unto gold,[a] or

a Isa. 40. 18.

---

was natural, in speaking to the peasants of Lystra, to point to the witness of "the rain from heaven and fruitful seasons." (See Note on chap. xiv. 17.) It was as natural, in speaking to men of high culture and introspective analysis, to appeal to that which was within them rather than to that which was without. But it will be noted that he does not confine that witness to the seekers after wisdom. God is not far from "every one of us." St. Paul accepts the truth which St. John afterwards proclaimed, that Christ is the "true Light that lighteth every man that cometh into the world." (See Notes on John i. 9.) The writer of the Book of Deuteronomy (chap. xxx. 11—14) had asserted a like truth when he taught Israel that "the word was not in heaven, or beyond the sea," but "in thy mouth and in thine heart, that thou mayest do it." At this point the Stoics, we may believe, would recognise the affinities which St. Paul's thoughts presented to their own teaching. The Epicureans would be more and more repelled by this attack on the central position of their system.

(28) **For in him we live, and move, and have our being.**—Better, *we live, and are moved, and are.* Each of the verbs used has a definite philosophical significance. The first points to our animal life; the second—from which is derived the Greek word used by ethical writers for passions, such as fear, love, hate, and the like—not, as the English verb suggests, to man's power of bodily motion in space, but to our emotional nature; the third, to that which constitutes our true essential being, the intellect and will of man. What the words express is not merely the Omnipresence of the Deity; they tell us that the power for every act and sensation and thought comes from Him. They set forth what we may venture to call the true element of Pantheism, the sense of a "presence interposed," as in nature, "in the light of setting suns," so yet more in man. As a Latin poet had sung, whose works may have been known to the speaker, the hearers, and the historian:—

> "Deum namque ire per omnes
> Terras que tractusque maris, cœlumque profundum,
> Hinc pecudes, armenta, viros, genus omne ferarum,
> Quemque sibi tenues nascentem arcessere vitas,
> Scilicet hinc reddi deinde ac resoluta referri,
> Omnia; nec morti esse locum sed viva volare
> Sideris in numerum atque alto succedere cælo."
>
> ["God permeates all lands, all tracts of sea,
> And the vast heaven. From Him all flocks and herds,
> And men, and creatures wild, draw, each apart,
> Their subtle life. To Him they all return,
> When once again set free. No place is found
> For death, but all mount up once more on high
> To join the stars in their high firmament."]
>
> —Virg. *Georg.* iv. 221—225.

In the teaching of St. Paul, however, the personality of God is not merged, as in that of the Pantheist, in the thought of the great Soul of the World, but stands forth with awful distinctness in the character of King and Judge. Traces of like thoughts are found in the prophetic vision of a time when God shall be "all in all," (1 Cor. xv. 28), the discords of the world's history harmonised in the eternal peace.

**As certain also of your own poets have said.**—The quotation has a special interest as being taken from a poet who was a countryman of St. Paul's. Aratus, probably of Tarsus (*circ.* B.C. 272), had written a didactic poem under the title of *Phænomena*, comprising the main facts of astronomical and meteorological science as then known. It opens with an invocation to Zeus, which contains the words that St. Paul quotes. Like words are found in a hymn to Zeus by Cleanthes (B.C. 300). Both passages are worth quoting:—

> (1) "From Zeus begin; never let us leave
> His name unloved. With Him, with Zeus, are filled
> All paths we tread, and all the marts of men;
> Filled, too, the sea, and every creek and bay;
> And all in all things need we help of Zeus,
> *For we too are his offspring.*"
>
> —Aratus, *Phænom.* 1–5.

> (2) "Most glorious of immortals, many-named,
> Almighty and for ever, thee, O Zeus,
> Sovran o'er Nature, guiding with thy hand
> All things that are, we greet with praises. Thee
> 'Tis meet that mortals call with one accord,
> *For we thine offspring are*, and we alone
> Of all that live and move upon this earth,
> Receive the gift of imitative speech."
>
> —Cleanthes, *Hymn to Zeus.*

The fact of the quotation would at once quicken the attention of the hearers. They would feel that they had not to deal with an illiterate Jew, like the traders and exorcists who were so common in Greek cities, but with a man of culture like their own, acquainted with the thoughts of some at least of their great poets.

**We are also his offspring.**—We too often think of the quotation only as happily introduced at the time; but the fact that it was quoted shows that it had impressed itself, it may be, long years before, on St. Paul's memory. As a student at Tarsus it had, we may well believe, helped to teach him the meaning of the words of his own Scriptures: "I have nourished and brought up children" (Isa. i. 2). The method of St. Paul's teaching is one from which modern preachers might well learn a lesson. He does not begin by telling men that they have thought too highly of themselves, that they are vile worms, creatures of the dust, children of the devil. The fault which he finds in them is that they have taken too low an estimate of their position. They too had forgotten that they were God's offspring, and had counted themselves, even as the unbelieving Jews had done (chap. xiii. 46) "unworthy of eternal life."

(29) **Forasmuch then as we are the offspring of God.**—One consequence from the thought of sonship is pressed home at once. If we are God's offspring our conception of Him should mount upward from what is highest in ourselves, from our moral and spiritual nature, instead of passing downward to that which, being the creature of our hands, is below us. Substantially asserting the same truth, the tone of St. Paul in speaking of idolatry is very different from that which we find in the older prophets (1 Kings xviii. 27; Ps. cxxxv. 15—18; Isa. xliv. 9—20). He has, as it were, studied the *genesis* of idolatry, and instead of the burning language of scorn, and hatred, and derision, can speak of it, though not with tolerance, yet with pity, to those who are its victims.

**The Godhead.**—The Greek term is neuter, and corresponds to the half-abstract, half-concrete forms of the "Divine Being," the "Deity."

silver, or stone, graven by art and man's
device. (30) And the times of this
ignorance God winked at; but now
commandeth all men every where to
repent: (31) because he hath appointed a
day, in the which he will judge the
world in righteousness by *that* man
whom he hath ordained; *whereof* he
hath given assurance [1] unto all *men*, in
that he hath raised him from the dead.

[1] Or, *offered faith.*

(32) And when they heard of the
resurrection of the dead, some mocked:
and others said, We will hear thee
again of this *matter*. (33) So Paul
departed from among them. (34) How-
beit certain men clave unto him,
and believed: among the which *was*
Dionysius the Areopagite, and a woman
named Damaris, and others with
them.

---

**Gold, or silver, or stone.**—The first word reminds us of the lavish use of gold in the colossal statue of Zeus by Phidias. Silver was less commonly used, but the shrines of Artemis at Ephesus (see Note on chap. xix. 24) supply an instance of it. "Stone" was the term commonly applied to the marble of Pentelicus, which was so lavishly employed in the sculpture and architecture of Athens.

(30) **And the times of this ignorance God winked at.**—Better, perhaps, *overlooked*, the English phrase, though vivid, being somewhat too familiar, and suggesting; strictly taken, not merely tolerance, but connivance and concurrence. The thought is one in which St. Paul manifestly found comfort. He sees in that ignorance a mitigation of the guilt, and therefore of the punishment due to the heathen world. The past history of the world had shown a prætermission of the sins, for which, on the condition of repentance, men were now offered a full remission. (See Note on Rom. iii. 25.) In thus teaching he was reproducing what our Lord had taught as to the servant who "knew not his Lord's will," and should therefore be beaten, but with "few stripes." (See Note on Luke xii. 48.)

**And now commandeth all men every where to repent.**—At this point the feelings of both Stoics and Epicureans would almost inevitably undergo a change. The latter might regret the mistakes he had made in his search after the *maximum* of enjoyment, but a change such as the Greek for "repentance" implied—new aims and purposes, loathing of the past and efforts for the future—was altogether alien to his thoughts. From the Stoics, as measured by Epictetus and Marcus Aurelius, better things might perhaps have been expected, but the doctrine of Necessity, which entered largely into popular Stoicism, blunted their sense of responsibility. They accepted the consequences of their actions with a serene apathy; for the most part, they gave thanks, as the philosophic Emperor did, that they were not as other men, and that the events of their life had led them to an ethical completeness; but the idea of abhorring themselves, and repenting in dust and ashes, had not as yet dawned on the Stoic's thoughts. (*Meditt.* i. 1—16.)

(31) **Because he hath appointed a day.**—Here the speaker would seem, to both sets of hearers, to be falling back into popular superstition. Minos and Rhadamanthus, and Tartarus and the Elysian Fields,—these they had learnt to dismiss, as belonging to the childhood of the individual and of mankind,—

> "Esse aliquid Manes et subterranea regna
> Vix pueri credunt." . . . .
>
> ["Talk of our souls and realms beyond the grave,
> The very boys will laugh and say you rave."]
> —Juvenal, *Sat.* ii. 149.

The Epicurean rejected the idea of a divine government altogether. For the Stoic, to quote a line from Schiller,—

> "Die Welt-geschichte ist das Welt-gericht,"
> ["And the world's story is its judgment day,"]

and he expected no other. The thought of a day of judgment as the consummation of that history, which was so prominent in St. Paul's teaching, was altogether strange to them.

**By that man whom he hath ordained.**—Literally, *by a man.* Who the man was, and what proof there was that he had been raised from the dead, were questions either reserved for a later stage of teaching, or interrupted by the derision of the hearers. Up to this point they had listened attentively, but that the dead should be raised again seemed to them—as to the Sadducean, to the Greeks generally—absolutely incredible (chap. xxvi. 8; 1 Cor. xv. 35).

(32) **Some mocked: and others said, We will hear thee again.**—The word "mocked" implies look and gesture, as well as words, of derision. (See Note on chap. ii. 13.) We may venture to assume that the mockers were found chiefly among the Epicureans, and that the inquirers, perhaps putting off the inquiry to a "more convenient season," were Stoics, who wished to hear more from a teacher with whom they found themselves in sympathy on so many points of contact with their own system. Whether they carried on their inquiry we are not told. The words that follow imply a certain indignation on the part of the Apostle. He would not stay to expose the name or the work of his Lord to the jests of scoffers.

(34) **Certain men clave unto him.**—The word implies practically both companionship and conversion. There was an attractive power in the Apostle's character that drew men unto him.

**Dionysius the Areopagite.**—As the constitution of the Court of the Areopagus required its members to have filled a high magisterial function, such as that of Archon, and to be above sixty, the convert must have been a man of some note. According to a tradition, ascribed by Eusebius (*Hist.* iii. 4, iv. 23) to Dionysius, Bishop of Corinth, he became Bishop of Athens. An elaborate treatise on the Hierarchy of Heaven, Cherubim, Seraphim, Thrones, Dominations, and the like, is extant under his name, but is obviously of much later date, probably of the fourth or fifth century. The legend of the Seven Champions of Christendom has transformed him into the St. Denys of France. A church dedicated to him stands on the Areopagus of modern Athens.

**Damaris.**—Chrysostom says that she was the wife of Dionysius, but this is obviously only a conjecture.

**And others with them.**—The contrast between this and the "great multitude," the "many" at Thessalonica and Berœa, is very significant. Not less striking is the absence of any reference to Athens in St.

CHAPTER XVIII.—(1) After these things Paul departed from Athens, and came to Corinth; (2) and found a certain Jew named Aquila,[a] born in Pontus, lately come from Italy, with his wife Priscilla; (because that Claudius had

A.D. 54.

a Rom. 16. 3.

Paul's Epistles. Of all the cities which he visited, it was that with which he had least sympathy. All that can be said is that he may have included them among "the saints which are in all Achaia" (2 Cor. i. 1) in his prayers and hopes. It would almost seem as if he felt that little was gained by entering into a discussion on the great questions of natural theology; and therefore he came to Corinth, determined to know nothing "but Jesus Christ, and Him crucified" (1 Cor. ii. 2).

XVIII.

(1) **And came to Corinth.**—The journey may have been either by land along the Isthmus of Corinth, or by sea from the Piræus to Cenchreæ. The position of Corinth on the Isthmus, with a harbour on either shore, Cenchreæ on the east, Lechæum on the west, had naturally made it a place of commercial importance at a very early stage of Greek history. With commerce had come luxury and vice, and the verb *Corinthiazein*= to live as the Corinthians, had become proverbial, as early as the time of Aristophanes (*Frag.* 133), for a course of profligacy. The harlot priestesses of the Temple of Aphrodite gave a kind of consecration to the deep-dyed impurity of Greek social life, of which we find traces in 1 Cor. v. 1; vi. 9—19. The Isthmian games, which were celebrated every fourth year, drew crowds of competitors and spectators from all parts of Greece, and obviously furnished the Apostle with the agonistic imagery of 1 Cor. ix. 24—27. Less distinguished for higher culture than Athens, it was yet able (standing to Athens in much the same relation as Venice did to Florence from the 13th to the 16th century) to boast of its artists in stone and metal (Corinthian bronze was proverbial for its excellence), of its rhetoricians and philosophers. On its conquest by the Roman general Mummius (B.C. 146), many of its buildings had been destroyed, and its finest statues had been carried off to Rome; and it was a Roman jest that the general had bound the captains of the ships that carried them, to replace them in case of loss. A century later, Julius Cæsar determined to restore it to its former splendour, and thousands of freed-men were employed in the work of reconstruction. Such was the scene of the Apostle's new labours, less promising, at first sight, than Athens, but, ultimately, far more fruitful in results.

(2) **And found a certain Jew named Aquila, born in Pontus.**—The name presents some interesting associations. Strictly speaking, the Greek form is *Akylas*, but this is undoubtedly the transliterated form of the Latin *Aquila* (= Eagle). The name appears in a yet more altered form in *Onkelos*, the traditional writer of one of the Targums, or Paraphrases of the Law, then current among the Jews. In Aquila, one of the later translators of the Old Testament into Greek, himself also born in Pontus, and possibly (but see Mr. Deutsch's *Remains*, p. 339) identical with Onkelos, we get the Greek form again. In the well-known chief Rabbi of the synagogues of the Jews of London, Dr. Adler, we have it reappearing in a German form (*Adler*=Eagle). The tendency of Jews to take names derived from animals when sojourning in heathen countries, may be noted as not uncommon. Ursulus, Leo, Leopardus, Dorcas, which appear in the early Christian inscriptions in the Vatican and Lateran Museums, present analogous instances. His birth in Pontus indicates that he belonged to the dispersion of the Jews of that province (1 Pet. i. 1) which, as the north-eastern region of Asia Minor, lay between Bithynia and Armenia. Some from that province had been present at Jerusalem on the Day of Pentecost (chap. ii. 9). As the Jews at Rome consisted largely of freed-men, the *libertinum genus* of Latin writers (see Note on the *Libertines* in chap. vi. 9), it is probable that Aquila belonged to that class.

**With his wife Priscilla.**—The name appears in some MSS., both here and elsewhere, in the form of Prisca, of which it is the diminutive. So we have Lucilla from Lucia, Domitilla from Domitia, Atticilla (in an inscription in the Museum of Perugia) from Attica. The name Prisca probably indicates a connection with the *gens* of the *Prisci*, who appear in the earliest stages of Roman history, and supplied a long series of prætors and consuls. The marriage was probably, therefore, an example of the influence gained by educated Jews over the higher class of women at Rome. It was, perhaps, a natural consequence of her higher social position that her name is sometimes placed before Aquila's (verse 18; Rom. xvi. 3; 2 Tim. iv. 19). The fact that she took part in the instruction of Apollos (see Note on verse 26), indicates that she was a woman of more than ordinary culture, a student and interpreter of the Old Testament Scriptures.

The question naturally suggests itself, whether the husband and wife, who were afterwards so prominent in the Apostolic Church, were, at this stage of their career, converted by St. Paul to the faith in Christ. The answer to that question must, it is believed, be a distinct and decisive negative. (1) There is no mention of their listening to St. Paul, and believing, as, *e.g.*, in the case of Lydia (chap. xvi. 14); and it is hardly conceivable that St. Luke, who relates that case so fully, would have omitted a fact of such importance. (2) He joins himself to them, as able to share his thoughts and hopes, even before he begins preaching in the synagogue, as in verse 4. (3) An unbelieving Jew was not likely to have admitted St. Paul into a partnership in his business. The question how and by whom the Church of Christ had been first brought to Rome will be discussed in the next Note.

**Because that Claudius had commanded all Jews to depart from Rome.**—The account of the expulsion is given by Suetonius (*Claudius*, c. 25) in words which are in many ways suggestive—"*Claudius, Judæos, impulsore Chresto, assidue tumultuantes, Româ expulit*" ("Claudius expelled the Jews from Rome on account of their continual tumults, instigated by Chrestus"). The Jews, at this period, were settled mainly in the Transtiberine region of Rome, at the base of the Janiculum, opposite the present *Ghetto*, or Jewry, of the city. They exercised considerable influence over the upper classes, had synagogues and oratories (*proseuchæ*, see Notes on chap. xvi. 13; Luke vi. 12) of their own, were tolerated as possessing a *relligio licita*, had their own cemeteries on the Appian Way. Suddenly there is a change in their relations to the civil power, and the name of Chrestus is connected with it.

commanded all Jews to depart from Rome:) and came unto them. (3) And because he was of the same craft, he abode with them, and wrought: for by their occupation they were tentmakers.

(4) And he reasoned in the synagogue every sabbath, and persuaded the Jews and the Greeks. (5) And when Silas and Timotheus were come from Macedonia, Paul was pressed in the spirit, and

Of the man whom he so mentions, Suetonius tells us nothing further. But we know that the sounds of the Greek "i" and "ē" were hardly distinguishable. Tertullian (*Apol.* c. 3) says that the name of *Christus* was almost invariably pronounced *Chrēstus,* and, as that word signifies "good," "useful," "honest," founds a kind of *argumentum ad hominem* on the prevalent mistake. So in Jewish inscriptions in the Lateran Museum, *Alfius* appears as the equivalent for the Greek form *Alphæus.* The probable explanation of Claudius's decree, accordingly, is that men had come to Rome after the Day of Pentecost proclaiming Jesus as the Christ, that this had been followed by tumults like those of which we read in the Pisidian Antioch (chap. xiii. 50), and Lystra (chap. xiv. 19), and Thessalonica (chap. xvii. 5), and Berœa (chap. xvii. 13), and that as the name of Christus was much in the mouths both of those who received and those who rejected His claim to be the Messiah, the Roman magistrates, like Gallio, careless as to questions about names and words (verse 15), naturally inferred that he was the leader of one of the parties, probably assuming, as at Thessalonica (chap. xvii. 7), that he claimed the title of king after the manner of the pretenders to an earthly throne. If we ask who were the first preachers of the new faith, the answer, though we may be unable to identify individuals, is not far to seek. (1) It was scarcely likely that twenty-three years should have passed since the Day of Pentecost, without bringing to the ears of the Jews of Rome some tidings of what was going on in Palestine. (2) In the list of those who were present at the Pentecostal wonder are strangers of Rome, Jews and proselytes (chap. ii. 10). (3) Among the Hellenistic Jews who disputed with Stephen were *libertini,* or freed-men of Rome, and Stephen himself, we saw reason to believe, belonged to the same class. (See Notes on chap. vi. 5, 9.) (4) Andronicus and Junias (contracted from Junianus, as Lucas from Lucanus), who are among those to whom St. Paul sends messages of affection at Rome, were "in Christ" before him (Rom. xvi. 7). To these, then, and not to St. Peter, we may probably look as among the real founders of the Church of Rome. The facts all indicate that the theology of the disciples of Rome was likely to be based upon the same great principles as that of Stephen, and this explains the readiness with which Aquila and Priscilla received the gospel as St. Paul preached it. It is obvious that many more of those who had been expelled from Rome were likely to have accompanied them from Rome to Corinth, and the long list of names in Rom. xvi. 3—15 probably consists for the most part of those who had thus come within the range of St. Paul's personal acquaintance, and had returned to Rome in the interval. The names in that list are many of them identical with those in the *Columbaria,* or burial-place, on the Appian Way, which contains the names of the men and women of the freed-man class who belonged to the household of the Empress Livia, and make it almost certain that they were of the same class; and that when St. Paul speaks (Phil. iv. 22) of the "saints of Cæsar's household" he is referring to such as these, and not to persons of high official rank. (See Notes on Rom. xvi.) The name of Priscus occurs, it may be added, in a Christian inscription of uncertain date in the Collegio Romano. We need not wonder that Greek should be the medium of intercourse even with these Roman Jews. The inscriptions in the recently discovered Jewish cemetery in the *Vigna Randanini,* at Rome, show a strange blending of the two languages, Greek words appearing sometimes in Latin characters, and Latin words in Greek. Hebrew does not appear, but the symbol of the seven-branched candlestick of the Temple recurs frequently.

(3) **Because he was of the same craft.**—The calling was one which St. Paul had probably learnt and practised in his native city, which was noted then, as now, for the rough goat's-hair fabrics known to the Romans, from the name of the province, as Cilicium (=sack-cloth). The material was one used for the sails of ships and for tents, and on the whole, though some have supposed that leather was used for the latter, it seems more probable that this was the material which St. Paul worked at. It may be added that Pontus, from which Aquila came, was also famous for the same manufacture, the material in each case being furnished by the goats which fed upon the slopes of the Taurus, and the mountain ranges of that province. The fact that St. Paul had learnt this trade is not inconsistent with the comparative opulence suggested by his education both in boyhood at Tarsus and at the feet of Gamaliel in Jerusalem. The Rabbinic proverb, that "He who does not teach his son a trade, teaches him to be a thief," made such instruction almost universal. So the great Hillel was a carpenter. Here, it is clear, he took the course of working for his livelihood, as he had done at Thessalonica, that he might keep himself from the suspicion of self-interest in his work as a teacher (1 Cor. ix. 15—19; 2 Cor. xi. 7—13). Such was the beginning of his labours at Corinth. A new artisan was working for wages, or as a partner, probably the latter, as afterwards with Philemon (Philem. verse 17), in the workshop of the Jew, not as yet known to the outer world as more than a Jew, who had recently arrived in Corinth from Rome.

(4) **He persuaded the Jews and the Greeks.**—It is necessary to remind the reader that the latter word does not mean Greek-speaking Jews, or proselytes in the full sense of the word, but, as elsewhere (see Note on chap. xi. 22), is used for those who were Gentiles by birth, and who, though worshipping in the synagogue, had not accepted circumcision.

(5) **And when Silas and Timotheus were come from Macedonia.**—We learn from 1 Thess. ii. 18, that the latter had come to St. Paul at Athens, but had been almost immediately sent back to Thessalonica to bring further news about the converts, for whose trials the Apostle felt so much sympathy and anxiety. They brought a good report of their faith and love (1 Thess. iii. 6), possibly also fresh proofs of their personal regard, and that of the Philippians, in the form of gifts (2 Cor. xi. 9). This may, however, refer to a later occasion. The First Epistle to the Thessalonians was probably sent back by the brethren who

testified to the Jews *that* Jesus *was*
Christ. (6) And when they opposed
themselves, and blasphemed, he shook
*his* raiment, and said unto them, Your
blood *be* upon your own heads; [a] I *am*
clean: from henceforth I will go unto
the Gentiles.

(7) And he departed thence, and en-
tered into a certain *man's* house, named
Justus, *one* that worshipped God, whose
house joined hard to the synagogue.
(8) And Crispus, [b] the chief ruler of the
synagogue, believed on the Lord with
all his house; and many of the Corin-

a Matt. 10. 14.
b 1 Cor. 1. 14.

---

had accompanied Silas and Timotheus on their journey to Corinth. The reader will note the parallelism (1) between the passage in 1 Thess. iv. 16, 17, which treats of the Second Advent, with the teaching of 1 Cor. xv. 51, 52, and (2) between the few words as to spiritual gifts, in 1 Thess. v. 19—21, with the fuller treatment of the same subject in 1 Cor. xii.—xiv.

**Paul was pressed in the spirit.**—The better MSS. give, "he was constrained *by the Word.*" The words describe something of the same strong emotion as the "paroxysm" of chap. xvii. 16. The Word was within him as a constraining power, compelling him to give utterance to it. His "heart was hot within him, and while he was musing the fire kindled" (Ps. xxxix. 4). Whether there was any connection between the arrival of Silas and Timotheus and this strong feeling is a question which there are no sufficient *data* for answering. It is hardly satisfactory to say, as has been suggested, that they probably brought pecuniary supplies from Macedonia (2 Cor. xi. 9), and that he was therefore relieved from the obligation of working for his livelihood, and able to give himself more entirely to the work of preaching. There is no indication of his giving up tent-making, and 1 Cor. ix. 1 is decidedly against it. A more probable explanation may be found in the strong desire—of which he says, in Rom. xv. 23, that he had cherished it for many years—to see Rome and preach the gospel there. Now he found himself brought into contact with those who had come from Rome, who formed, in fact, part of its population, and the old feeling was stirred to a new intensity.

(6) **And when they opposed themselves, and blasphemed.**—The latter word includes the reviling of which the Apostle himself was the object, as well as blaspheming against God. Assuming what has been suggested in the Note on verse 2, we may think of these disturbances as reproducing what had already taken place at Rome. We may, perhaps, trace an echo of such blasphemies in the words "Anathema be Jesus," of which St. Paul speaks in 1 Cor. xii. 3 as having been uttered as with the vehemence of a simulated inspiration, against which men needed to be warned.

**He shook his raiment.**—On the symbolic significance of the act, see Note on Matt. x. 14. As done by a Jew to Jews no words and no act could so well express the Apostle's indignant protest. It was the last resource of one who found appeals to reason and conscience powerless, and was met by brute violence and clamour.

**Your blood be upon your own heads.**—The phrase and thought were both essentially Hebrew. (See Note on Matt. xxvii. 25.) We can hardly think of the Apostle as using them without a distinct recollection of the language which defined the responsibility of a prophet of the truth in Ezek. iii. 18, 19.

**From henceforth I will go unto the Gentiles.**—The words are almost identical with those in chap. xiii. 46, and are explained by them. It is obvious in each case that the words have a limited and local application. The Apostle did not renounce all future work among the Jews, but gave up preaching to those at Corinth.

(7) **And entered into a certain man's house, named Justus.**—On the name, see Note on chap. i. 23. It may be added here that it occurs also in early Christian inscriptions in the Vatican Museum, in one case at the bottom of a glass cup, in the *Museo Christiano*, in conjunction with the name of Timotheus. In some of the better MSS. the name Titus is prefixed to Justus, and it will be noted that both in chap. i. 23, and Col. iv. 11, the latter is used as an epithet after the names of Joseph and of Jesus. It is found by itself in the Jewish cemetery above referred to. (See Note on verse 1.) It would be rash to infer from this the identity of this Titus Justus with the Titus of Gal. ii. 3, as the disciple left in Crete. The name Titus was, like Caius or Gaius, one of the commonest Roman names, and, if the reading be genuine, we may think of the epithet as added to distinguish the Titus of Corinth from his namesake. On the other hand, to state the evidence on both sides fairly, the Titus who appears in 2 Cor. ii. 12, vii. 14, viii. 16, 23, was obviously very closely connected with the Church of Corinth, and was not unlikely to be sent to Crete to exercise a mission analogous to that which he had been entrusted with at Corinth, and the combination of the names Timotheus and Justus, above referred to, as equally entitled to reverence, is more intelligible if we assume that the latter name belonged to Titus, and that both stood therefore in the same relation to St. Paul as disciples and friends. In any case the Justus who is here named was, like Titus, an uncircumcised Gentile, attending the synagogue as a proselyte of the gate. Up to this time apparently, St. Paul had been lodging in the house of a Jew, in some region of Corinth analogous to the Ghetto of modern Rome, in the hope of conciliating his brethren according to the flesh. Now, in sight of the wild frenzied fanatics, he goes into a house which they would have shrunk from entering, even though it was next door to the synagogue, and though the man who lived in it was a devout worshipper.

(8) **And Crispus, the chief ruler of the synagogue, believed on the Lord.**—The article does not necessarily show that there was only one ruler—commonly, as at the Pisidian Antioch (chap. xiii. 15), there were more—but that this Crispus was thus distinguished from others of the same name. The office was one which gave its holder an honourable position, and, as in inscriptions from the Jewish catacombs now in the Lateran Museum, was recorded on tombstones (*Alfius Archisynagos*) as a personal distinction of which the family of the deceased were proud. In favour of so conspicuous a convert, St. Paul deviated from his usual practice, and baptised Crispus with his own hands (1 Cor. i. 14).

**Many of the Corinthians hearing believed, and were baptized.**—The tense of the two verbs implies a process going on daily for an undefined period. Among the converts we may note Gaius, or Caius, probably a man of higher social position than

thians hearing believed, and were bap-
tized. (9) Then spake the Lord to Paul
in the night by a vision, Be not afraid,
but speak, and hold not thy peace:
(10) for I am with thee, and no man shall
set on thee to hurt thee: for I have
much people in this city. (11) And he
continued [1] *there* a year and six months,
teaching the word of God among them.
(12) And when Gallio was the deputy
of Achaia, the Jews made insurrection
with one accord against Paul, and
brought him to the judgment seat,
(13) saying, This *fellow* persuadeth men

1 Gr. *sat* there.

A.D. 55, ending.

---

others, who made his house the meeting-place of the Church, and at St. Paul's second visit received him as a guest (Rom. xvi. 23), and the household of Stephanas, who, as "the first-fruits of Achaia," must have been among the earliest converts (1 Cor. xvi. 15). These also St. Paul baptised himself (1 Cor. i. 14, 15). Fortunatus and Achaicus, and Chloe, a prominent female convert (1 Cor. i. 11), with Quartus, and Erastus the chamberlain of the city (Rom. xvi. 23), and Epænetus, also among the "first-fruits of Achaia" (Rom. xvi. 5), may also be counted among the disciples made now or soon afterwards.

(9) **Then spake the Lord to Paul.**—We note the recurrence of these visions at each great crisis of the Apostle's life. He had seen the Lord at his conversion (chap. ix. 4—6), he had heard the same voice and seen the same form in his trance in the Temple at Jerusalem (chap. xxii. 17). Now he saw and heard them once more. "In visions of the night, when deep sleep falleth upon men," he passed from the strife of tongues into the presence of the Divine Friend. The words "Be not afraid" imply that he too was subject to fear and depression, and felt keenly the trial of seeming failure and comparative isolation. His converts came chiefly from the slave or freed-man class, and those of a culture like his own, whether Greeks or Jews, were slow to accept his preaching (1 Cor. i. 26, 27). And then, too, he carried, as it were, his life in his hands. The reviling of the Jews might any hour burst into furious violence or deliberate plots of assassination. No wonder that he needed the gracious words, "Be not afraid." The temptation of such a moment of human weakness was to fall back, when words seem fruitless, into the safety of silence, and therefore the command followed, "Speak, and hold not thy peace." We are reminded of the like passing mood of discouragement in one great crisis of Elijah's life (1 Kings xix. 4—14), yet more, perhaps, of its frequent recurrence in Jeremiah (Jer. i. 6—8; xv. 15—21).

(10) **For I am with thee.**—The command was followed by a promise which met the special trial of the time. Men might be against him, but Christ was with him. The general promise given to the Church at large, "Lo! I am with you always" (Matt. xxviii. 20), received a personal application, "I am with *thee;*" and though called to a life of suffering, there was for the time an assurance that the wrath of men should be restrained, and that his work should not be hindered.

**I have much people in this city.**—The words remind us once more of those which Elijah had heard at a moment of like weakness, "Yet have I left me seven thousand men in Israel" (1 Kings xix. 18). Even in the sinful streets of Corinth, among those plunged deepest into its sin (1 Cor. v. 10, 11), there were souls yearning for deliverance, in whom conscience was not dead, and was waiting only for the call to repentance.

(11) **And he continued there a year and six months.**—This obviously gave time not only for founding and organising a Church at Corinth itself, but for work in the neighbouring districts, such as the port of Cenchreæ, where we find in Rom. xvi. 1 a church duly furnished not only with presbyters and deacons, but with a sisterhood of deaconesses. The superscription of 2 Cor. i. 1, "to the Church that is in Corinth and *to all the saints that are in all Achaia,* clearly indicates an extension of evangelising work beyond the limits of the city. The unimpeded progress of this period came to him as an abundant fulfilment of the Lord's promise, and prepared him for the next persecution when it came.

(12) **And when Gallio was the deputy of Achaia.**—"Deputy" stands, as before (see Note on chap. xiii. 7), for "proconsul." Here, also, St. Luke shows his characteristic accuracy in the use of official titles. Achaia, which included the whole of Greece south of the province of Macedonia, had been an imperial province under Tiberius (Tacitus, *Ann.* i. 76), and had been governed by a prætor, but had been recently, in the same year as the expulsion of the Jews from Rome, restored to the senate by Claudius, as no longer needing direct military control (Suetonius, *Claud.* c. 25). Gallio, or to give his full name, M. Annæus Novatus, who had taken the *agnomen* of Gallio on his adoption by the rhetorician of that name, was the brother of L. Annæus Seneca, the tutor of Nero. The philosopher dedicated to him his two treatises on Anger and the Blessed Life, and the kindliness of his nature made him a general favourite. He was everybody's "dulcis Gallio," was praised by his brother for his disinterestedness and calmness of temper, as one "who was loved much even by those who had but little capacity for loving" (Seneca, *Ep.* civ.). On the whole, therefore, we may see in him a very favourable example of what philosophic culture was able to do for a Roman statesman. On the probable connection of the writer of the Acts with his family, see *Introduction to the Gospel of St. Luke.*

**Made insurrection . . . against Paul.**—Better, perhaps, *rose up against,* or *rushed upon;* our word "insurrection" having acquired the special meaning of a revolt of subjects against rulers.

**And brought him to the judgment seat.**—The habit of the Roman governors of provinces was commonly to hold their court in the *agora,* or market-place on certain fixed days (see Note on chap. xix. 38), so that any one might appeal to have his grievance heard. Gallio was now so sitting, and the Jews, having probably preconcerted their plans, took advantage of the opportunity.

(13) **This fellow persuadeth men to worship God contrary to the law.**—It is obvious that in this appeal to the proconsul the Jews must have meant, not the law of Moses, but that of Rome. Their contention was that though Jews had been banished from Rome as a measure of policy, Judaism as such was still a *relligio licita,* tolerated and recognised by the State. Their charge against the Apostle was that he was preaching a new religion, which was not so recognised. The words "this fellow," though they

to worship God contrary to the law.
(14) And when Paul was now about to
open *his* mouth, Gallio said unto the
Jews, If it were a matter of wrong or
wicked lewdness, O *ye* Jews, reason
would that I should bear with you:
(15) but if it be a question of words and
names, and *of* your law, look ye *to it;*
for I will be no judge of such *matters.*
(16) And he drave them from the judg-
ment seat. (17) Then all the Greeks
took Sosthenes, the chief ruler of the
synagogue, and beat *him* before the
judgment seat. And Gallio cared for
none of those things.

(18) And Paul *after this* tarried *there*
yet a good while, and then took his
leave of the brethren, and sailed thence
into Syria, and with him Priscilla and
Aquila; having shorn *his* head in

---

substantive is an interpolation, fairly expresses the contempt implied in the use of the Greek pronoun.

(14) **When Paul was now about to open his mouth.**—The phrase always implies, as has been noticed (see Note on chap. viii. 35), the beginning of a set discourse. St. Paul was about to begin a formal *apologia.* This, however, proved to be unnecessary.

**Gallio said unto the Jews.**—The proconsul could hardly have resided in Achaia for eighteen months without hearing of the new movement. He knew the Jews. He probably knew something of St. Paul. On the assumption already referred to (see Note on verse 12) the knowledge may have been fuller than appears on the surface. In any case, from his standpoint, as philosopher and statesman, it was not a matter for his tribunal. He was not anxious to draw a hard and fast line as to the *relligiones licitæ* recognised by the State.

**A matter of wrong or wicked lewdness.**—Better, *a matter of crime or fraud.* "Lewdness," which to us suggests a special class of crimes, is used as "lewd" had been in chap. xvii. 5. The Greek word is very closely connected with that translated "subtlety" in chap. xiii. 10. Both words were probably used in a strictly forensic sense—the first for acts of open wrong, such as robbery or assault; the second for those in which a fraudulent cunning was the chief element.

**Reason would that I should bear with you.**—The very turn of the phrase expresses an intense impatience. Even in the case supposed, his tolerance would have required an effort. As it was, these Jews were now altogether intolerable.

(15) **But if it be a question of words and names, and of your law.**—The second noun is in the singular number in the Greek. St. Paul was known as a speaker, one who preached the *word* of God, and with that, as distinct from acts, Gallio had nothing to do. The "names" were those which he had probably heard of at Rome, even before he came to Corinth. (See Note on verse 2.) Was a teacher whom both parties spoke of as Jesus the Nazarene entitled also to bear the name of Christos? In the emphasis laid on "your law" (literally, *the law which affects you*), the judge intimates that he sees through their appeal to law. It is Jewish, and not Roman law, which they are seeking to vindicate, and he will not make himself, as Pilate, after a weak protest (John xviii. 3), had done (Gallio may well have known the history), the executioner of an alien code. With a strong emphasis on the pronoun, he ends with, "I, for my part, have no wish to be a judge of these things."

(16) **He drave them from the judgment seat.**—The words imply a magisterial act. The order was given to the lictors to clear the court, and the Jews, who did not immediately retreat were exposed to the ignominy of blows from their rods.

(17) **Then all the Greeks took Sosthenes, the chief ruler of the synagogue.**—The better MSS. omit the word "Greeks," which was probably inserted as an explanatory interpolation by some one who thought it more likely that a ruler of the synagogue should have been assaulted by the Greek bystanders than by those of his own race. Taking the better reading, and assuming the natural construction of the sentence to be "all of them (*sc.*, the Jews) took Sosthenes and beat him," we have to ask for an explanation of conduct which seems so strange. This is probably found in the appearance of the same name in 1 Cor. i. 1, as associated with St. Paul in the Epistle to the Church of Corinth. It is a natural inference that Sosthenes, like his predecessor or partner in office (it does not necessarily follow that he succeeded him) became a convert to the new faith. If so, it is probable that he was already suspected of tendencies in that direction, and when the Jews at Corinth found their plans frustrated, it was natural that they should impute their failure to the lukewarmness or treachery of the man who ought to have carried them to a successful issue. They did not shrink from giving vent to their rage even before the tribunal of the proconsul.

**And Gallio cared for none of those things.**—More accurately, *And Gallio cared nothing for these things.* The words have become almost proverbial for the indifference of mere politicians and men of the world to religious truth. We speak of one who is tolerant because he is sceptical, as a Gallio. It may be questioned, however, whether this was the thought prominent in St. Luke's mind as he thus wrote. What he apparently meant was that the proconsul was clear-sighted enough to pay no regard to the clamours of St. Paul's accusers. If they chose, after failing in their attack on Paul, to quarrel among themselves, what was that to him? "*Laissez faire, laissez aller*" might well be his motto in dealing with such a people. The general impression, however, as to his character is not without its truth. The easy-going gentleness of his character ill fitted him to resist the temptations of Nero's court, and after retiring from Achaia in consequence of an attack of fever (Sen. *Ep.* civ.), he returned to Rome, and, to the distress of Burrhus and his own brother, Seneca, he took part in ministering to the emperor's vices (Dio. lxi. 20). He finally fell under the tyrant's displeasure, and, according to one tradition, was put to death by him. Another represents him as anticipating his fate by suicide; Tacitus, however (*Ann.* xv. 73), only speaks of him as terrified by his brother's death, and supplicating Nero for his own life.

(18) **And Paul after this tarried there yet a good while.**—Literally, *tarried yet many days*, the phrase probably covering a period of some months. The fact is noted as following on Gallio's repression of the

Cenchrea: for he had a vow. (19) And he came to Ephesus, and left them there: but he himself entered into the synagogue, and reasoned with the Jews. (20) When they desired *him* to tarry longer time with them, he consented

---

enmity of the Jews. The Apostle could stay and work on without molestation. The time of his voyage was probably, as in the second journey from Corinth to Jerusalem, after the Passover, and before Pentecost. (See Note on chap. ii. 1.) It was the most favourable time of the year for travelling, and it brought the Apostle into contact with a larger number both of Hellenistic Jews and Hebrews than were found at other times. We can only infer, more or less conjecturally, the motives of his journey. (1) As afterwards, in chap. xx. 3, 4, he may have wished, in carrying out the terms of the compact with the Church of Jerusalem (Gal. ii. 10), to be the bearer of alms collected for the disciples there. By some writers, however, this visit is identified with that of which St. Paul there speaks. (2) The vow which he had taken (see Note below) required a visit to the Temple for its completion. (3) There might be a natural wish to report, as in chap. xv. 4, the results of his ministry among the Gentiles, in what, from the stand-point of Jerusalem, would seem the remoter regions of Macedonia and Achaia.

**Priscilla and Aquila.**—On the priority given to the name of the wife, see Note on verse 2.

**Having shorn his head in Cenchrea: for he had a vow.**—The grammatical structure of the Greek sentence makes it possible to refer the words to Aquila as well as St. Paul, but there is hardly the shadow of a doubt that the latter is meant. (1) If Aquila had taken the vow he too would have to go to Jerusalem instead of remaining at Ephesus. (2) The language of St. James in chap. xxi. 23, 24, implies a conviction, as resting on past experience, that St. Paul would willingly connect himself with those who had such a vow. It remains to inquire (1) as to the nature and conditions of the vow; (2) as to St. Paul's motives in taking it.

(1) There can be no doubt that the "vow" was that of the temporary Nazarite, as described in Num. vi. 1—21. It implied a separation from the world and common life (this was the meaning of the word "Nazarite"), and while under the vow the man who had taken it was to drink no wine or strong drink, and to let no razor pass over his head or face. When the term was completed, he was to shave his head at the door of the Tabernacle, and burn the hair in the fire of the altar. It will be noted that the Nazarites in chap. xxi. 24, who are completing their vow, *shave* their heads. Here a different word ("shorn") is used, which is contrasted with "shaving" in 1 Cor. xi. 6. It was lawful for a man to have his hair cut or cropped during the continuance of the vow, and this apparently was what St. Paul now did. But in this case also the hair so cut off was to be taken to the Temple and burnt there, and this explains the Apostle's eagerness "by all means" (verse 21) to keep the coming feast at Jerusalem.

(2) We cannot exclude from the probable motives the strong feeling of thankfulness for deliverance from danger, following upon fear which, as in nearly all phases of the religious life, has been the chief impulse out of which vows have grown. We have seen the fear, and the promise, and the deliverance, in the record of St. Paul's work at Corinth, and the vow of self-consecration, for a season, to a life of special devotion was the natural result. St. Paul had not learnt to despise or condemn such expressions of devout feeling.

(3) We may add to this motive the principle on which St. Paul acted of being "all things to all men," and, therefore, as a Jew to Jews (1 Cor. ix. 20). A Nazarite vow would testify to all his brethren by blood that he did not despise the Law himself nor teach other Jews to despise it. (See Notes on chap. xxi. 21—24.) Such a vow, involving, as it did, for a time a greater asceticism than that of common life, furnishes a link in the succession of thoughts in 1 Cor. ix. 22—25, between the Apostle's being made "all things to all men" and his "keeping under his body, and bringing it into subjection."

(4) So far we have found reasons for the vow. But taken by itself, the vow would seem to have involved a continuous growth of hair rather than cropping it. How was that act connected with the vow? A probable answer to the question is found in the Apostle's language as to social customs in matters of this kind, in 1 Cor. xi. 14. He condemns long hair as effeminate. But the Nazarite vow led to long hair as its natural consequence, and there was, therefore, the risk that while practising a rigorous austerity, he might seem to outside observers to be adopting an unmanly refinement. At Corinth men would, perhaps, know what his act meant, but in the regions to which he was now going it was wise to guard against the suspicion by a modification of the vow, such as Jewish law allowed.

Cenchreæ was, as has been said, the eastern harbour of Corinth on the Saronic Gulf. Rom. xvi. 1 indicates the existence of an organised Church there. The warm language of gratitude in which St. Paul speaks of Phœbe, the deaconess of the Church there, is best explained by supposing that she had ministered to him as such when he was suffering from bodily pain or infirmity, and this, in its turn, may afford another probable explanation of the vow.

(19) **He came to Ephesus, and left them there.**—The better MSS. give, "They came to Ephesus." What follows seems to imply that he no longer continued to work with them, as at Corinth, but leaving them to establish themselves in their craft, began, under the pressure of his eagerness to reach Jerusalem, an independent course of teaching in the synagogues.

The first mention of Ephesus calls for a short account of its history. It had been one of the early Greek colonies on the western coast of Asia Minor. It fell under the power of Alyattes, King of Lydia, and his successor, Crœsus. It had from the first been celebrated for the worship of Artemis (see Note on chap. xix. 14); and her Temple, with its sacred image, and stately courts, and its hundreds of priests and priestesses of various grades, was visited by pilgrims of all nations. It was one of the cities in which East and West came into close contact with each other, and the religion of Greece assumed there a more Oriental character, and was fruitful in magic, and mysteries, and charms. The Jewish population was sufficiently numerous to have a synagogue, and St. Paul, as usual, appeared in it as a teacher.

(20) **When they desired him to tarry longer time with them.**—This was, obviously, a hopeful sign, the earnest of the fruitful labours that followed. Nowhere, among the churches that he founded, does St. Paul seem to have found so great a receptivity for spiritual truth. While he looked on the Corinthians

not; (21) but bade them farewell, saying,
I must by all means keep this feast that
cometh in Jerusalem: but I will return
again unto you, if God will.[a] And he
sailed from Ephesus. (22) And when he
had landed at Cæsarea, and gone up,
and saluted the church, he went down
to Antioch. (23) And after he had spent
some time *there*, he departed, and went
over *all* the country of Galatia and
Phrygia in order, strengthening all the
disciples.
(24) And a certain Jew named Apollos,[b]
born at Alexandria, an eloquent man,

a 1 Cor. 4. 19; Jas. 4. 15.

b 1 Cor. 1. 12.

---

as being children requiring to be fed with milk (1 Cor. iii. 2), he saw in the Ephesians those to whom he did not shun to declare "the whole counsel of God" (chap. xx. 27), to whom he could, at a later date, appeal as able to measure his knowledge of the mystery of the gospel (Eph. iii. 4).

(21) **I must by all means keep this feast that cometh.**—Literally, *the coming*, or, *the next feast*. This was, probably, as has been said, the Feast of Pentecost. (See Note on verse 18.) If he missed that, there would be no other feast till that of Tabernacles; and then, in October, travelling, whether by sea or land, became dangerous and difficult. (See Note on chap. xxvii. 9.)

**If God will.**—In this resting in the thought of the will of the Father as ordering all things well—even in their use of almost the same formula, to them much more than such a formula as the *Deo volente* has often become in the lips of Christians—we find another point of agreement between St. Paul and St. James (Jas. iv. 15).

(22) **And when he had landed at Cæsarea.**—It is obvious that a great deal is covered by the short record of this verse. In the absence of any *data* in the Acts for settling the question, we may possibly refer to some casualty in this voyage, one of the three shipwrecks of 2 Cor. xi. 25. At Cæsarea, we may believe, he would probably renew his intercourse with Philip the Evangelist. At Jerusalem there would be the usual gathering of the Church, the completion of his Nazarite vow in the Temple, a friendly welcome on the part of St. James and the elders of the Church. Peter was probably at Antioch (Gal. ii. 11), or possibly at Babylon (1 Pet. v. 13). To this visit to Antioch we may probably refer the scene which St. Paul narrates in Gal. ii. 11—14. His long absence from Antioch had left the Judaising party time to gather strength and organise a new attack on the freedom of the Gentiles, and they brought a fresh pressure to bear upon the element of instability which still lingered in St. Peter's character, and he had not been able to resist it. It is, however, possible that the incident may have occurred before Paul and Silas had left Antioch. (See Note on chap. xv. 39, 40.)

(23) **Went over all the country of Galatia and Phrygia in order.**—It is clear from the Epistle to the Galatians that on this visit he found few traces, or none at all, of the work of the Judaisers. The change came afterwards. Some falling away from their first love, some relapse into old national vices, he may have noticed already which called for earnest warning (Gal. v. 21). As he passed through the churches he had founded on his previous journey, he gave the directions for the weekly appropriation of what men could spare from their earnings (the term, a weekly "offertory," though often employed of it, does not represent the facts of the case), to which he refers in 1 Cor. xvi. 2. What churches in Phrygia were visited we are unable to say. A possible construction of Col. ii. 1 might lead us to think of those of the valley of the Lycus, Colossæ, Hierapolis, Laodicea, as having been founded by him, but the more probable interpretation of that passage is, that he included them in the list of those who had not seen his face in the flesh.

(24) **And a certain Jew named Apollos, born at Alexandria.**—The name was probably a contraction of Apollonius or Apollodorus. The facts in the New Testament connected with him show that he occupied a prominent position in the history of the Apostolic Church. Conjectures, more or less probable, indicate a yet more representative character and a wider range of influence. Luther, looking to the obviously Alexandrian character of the Epistle to the Hebrews and to the mystery which shrouds its authorship, and which led Origen to the conclusion that God alone knew who wrote it, hazarded the thought that Apollos was the writer. Later critics have adopted the hypothesis, and have brought it to a closer approximation to certainty by an induction from numerous parallelisms in thought and language between the Epistle and the writings of Philo, who lived between B.C. 20 and A.D. 40 or 50. The present writer has carried the inquiry one step further. Among the ethical books of the LXX. there is one, the Wisdom of Solomon, the authorship of which is also an unsolved problem. It is not named or quoted by any pre-Christian writer, Clement of Rome being the first writer who shows traces of its influence, just as he is the first who reproduces the thoughts of the Epistle to the Hebrews. It has been ascribed to Philo partly on the external evidence of a doubtful passage in the Muratorian Canon, partly on the internal evidence of numerous coincidences with his writings. A careful comparison of the two books shows so close an agreement in style and language between the Wisdom of Solomon and the Epistle to the Hebrews that it is scarcely possible to resist the inference that they must have come from the same pen, and that they represent, therefore, different stages in the spiritual growth of the same man. Those who wish to carry the inquiry further will find the subject discussed at length in two papers, "On the Writings of Apollos," in Vol. I. of the *Expositor*. Without assuming more than the probability of this inference, it is yet obvious that a Jew coming from Alexandria at this time could hardly fail to have come under Philo's influence, and that his mode of interpreting the Scriptures would naturally present many analogies to that of the Alexandrian thinker. To him accordingly may be assigned, without much risk of error, the first introduction of the characteristic idea of Philo that the Unseen Godhead manifests itself in the *Logos*, the Divine *Word*, or *Thought*, as seen in the visible creation, and in the spirit and heart of man (Wisd. ix. 1, 2, 4; xvi. 12; xviii. 15; Heb. iv. 12). It will be remembered that Jews of Alexandria were among those who disputed with Stephen (chap. vi. 9). Some of these may have been more or less persuaded by his preaching, and have carried back to their native city some knowledge, more or less complete, of the new faith.

**An eloquent man.**—The Greek adjective implies learning as well as eloquence. It was applied pre-

*and* mighty in the scriptures, came to Ephesus. (25) This man was instructed in the way of the Lord; and being fervent in the spirit, he spake and taught diligently the things of the Lord, knowing only the baptism of John.
(26) And he began to speak boldly in the synagogue: whom when Aquila and Priscilla had heard, they took him unto *them*, and expounded unto him the way of God more perfectly. (27) And when he was disposed to pass into Achaia, the brethren wrote, exhorting the disciples to receive him: who, when he was

---

eminently to those who wrote history with fulness and insight (Herod. i. 1; ii. 3, 77). The treatment of the history of Israel both in Wisd. x., xi., xviii., and Heb. xi. might well be described by it.

(25) **This man was instructed in the way of the Lord.**—Better, *had been instructed.* The verb is the same as that used in Luke i. 1 (where see Note), and was afterwards used technically in the form of *Catechumen* to describe the status of a convert preparing for baptism. The "way of the Lord" is used in a half-technical sense, as in the phrase "those of the way" (see Note on chap. ix. 2), as equivalent to what, in modern speech, we should describe as the "religion" of Christ.

**And being fervent in the spirit.**—The noun is obviously used, as in the identical phrase in Rom. xii. 11, for the spirit of the man, not for the Holy Spirit of God.

**He spake and taught diligently.**—Better, *he was speaking and teaching accurately.* Both verbs are in the tense which implies continuous action.

**The things of the Lord.**—The better MSS. give, "the things concerning Jesus." We ask in what the teaching, which is thus described as accurate, was yet defective. The position of Apollos at this stage was, it would seem, that of one who knew the facts of our Lord's life, and death, and resurrection, and had learnt, comparing these with Messianic prophecies, to accept Him as the Christ. But his teacher had been one who had not gone beyond the standpoint of the followers of the Baptist, who accepted Jesus as the Christ during His ministry on earth. The Christ was for him the head of a glorified Judaism, retaining all its distinctive features. He had not as yet learnt that "circumcision was nothing" (1 Cor. vii. 19; Gal. v. 6), and that the Temple and all its ordinances were "decaying and waxing old, and ready to vanish away" (Heb. viii. 13).

**Knowing only the baptism of John.**—The words are full of interest, as showing a wider extent in the work of the Baptist, as the forerunner of the Christ, than is indicated in the Gospels. Even at Alexandria, probably among the ascetic communities of the Therapeutæ, whose life was fashioned upon the same model, there were those who had come under his influence.

(26) **Whom when Aquila and Priscilla had heard . . .**—Many of the best MSS. put Priscilla's name first, as in verse 18. The fact mentioned is interesting as showing (1) that Aquila and his wife continued to attend the services of the synagogue, and (2) that Apollos appeared there, as St. Paul had done, in the character of a Rabbi who had a message to deliver, and was therefore allowed, or, it may be, requested (as in chap. xiii. 15), to address the people.

**And expounded unto him the way of God more perfectly.**—Better, as maintaining the right relation of the comparative to the positive adverb of the previous verse, *more accurately.* The prominence given to Priscilla in this instruction implies that she was a woman of more than ordinary culture, a student of the older Scriptures, able, with a prophetic insight, to help even the disciple of Philo to understand them better than he had done before. It follows of necessity that "the way of God" which they "expounded" to him was the gospel as they had learnt it from St. Paul, perhaps as they had learnt it, at an earlier stage, from the lips of Stephen or his followers. (See Note on verse 2.) It would include, to put the matter somewhat technically, the doctrines of salvation by grace, and justification by faith, and the gift of the Spirit, and union with Christ through baptism and the Supper of the Lord. It would seem to follow almost necessarily, as in the case of the twelve disciples in the next chapter (chap. xix. 1—6), that Apollos, who had before known only the baptism of John, was now baptised into "the name of the Lord Jesus."

(27) **And when he was disposed to pass into Achaia.**—In the absence of the name of any city in the province, Corinth naturally suggests itself as the place to which he went. Chap. xix. 1, and the mention of Apollos in 1 Cor. i. 12, turns this into a certainty. He felt, we may believe, that his training in the philosophical thought of Alexandria qualified him to carry on there the work which St. Paul had begun both there and at Athens. One who had written, or even read, the noble utterances of Wisd. i., ii., was well qualified to carry an aggressive warfare into the camp of the Epicureans, while thoughts like those of Wisd. vii., viii., especially viii. 7, with its recognition of the four cardinal virtues of Greek ethics, "temperance and prudence, justice and fortitude," would attract the sympathy of the nobler followers of Zeno.

**The brethren wrote, exhorting the disciples to receive him.**—This is the first instance of what were afterwards known technically as "letters of commendation" (see Note on 2 Cor. iii. 1), written by one church to another in favour of the bearer. The fact that they were given by the Christian community at Ephesus shows how favourable an impression Apollos had made there. It is probable that St. Paul alludes indirectly to these letters in the passage just referred to. The partisans of Apollos had referred to them as one of the points in which he excelled St. Paul. He had come with letters of commendation. He had received them when he left Corinth. The Apostle answers the disparaging taunt in the language of a noble indignation. He needed no such epistle. The church which he had planted was itself an epistle, "known and read of all men" (2 Cor. iii. 3).

**Helped them much which had believed through grace.**—The two last words admit, in the Greek as in the English, of being taken either with "helped" or "believed." The former construction seems preferable. It was through the grace of God, cooperating with the gift of wisdom, that Apollos was able to lead men to a higher stage of thought. It will be noted that this exactly corresponds with the account which St. Paul gives of his relation to the teacher whom some set up against him as a rival: "I have planted;

come, helped them much which had
believed through grace: (28) for he
mightily convinced the Jews, *and that*
publickly, shewing by the scriptures
that Jesus was Christ.

CHAPTER XIX.—(1) And it came to
pass, that, while Apollos was at Corinth,
Paul having passed through the upper

A.D. 56.

coasts came to Ephesus: and finding
certain disciples, (2) he said unto them.
Have ye received the Holy Ghost since
ye believed? And they said unto him,
We have not so much as heard whether
there be any Holy Ghost. (3) And he
said unto them, Unto what then were
ye baptized? And they said, Unto
John's baptism. (4) Then said Paul,

---

Apollos watered." "I have laid the foundation and another buildeth thereon" (1 Cor. iii. 6, 10).

(28) **He mightily convinced the Jews.**—The conclusion to which he led the Jews was the same as that which St. Paul urged on them. The process was, perhaps, somewhat different, as the line of argument in the Epistle to the Hebrews differs from that in the Epistle to the Galatians. To lead men on, after the manner of Philo, into the deeper meanings that lay beneath the letter of Scripture, to deal with them as those who were pressing forwards to the perfection of maturity in spiritual growth (Heb. v. 11—14), instead of treating them as children who must be fed with milk and not with "strong meat" (*i.e.*, solid food), as St. Paul had done (1 Cor. i. 2)—it was natural that this should attract followers to the new preacher, and give him a larger measure of real or apparent success in dealing with the Jews than had attended the labours of St. Paul. As Apollos does not appear again in the Acts, it may be well to bring together what is known as to his after-history. At Corinth, as has been said, his name was used as the watchword of a party, probably that of the philosophising Jews and proselytes, as distinguished from the narrower party of the circumcision that rallied round the name of Cephas (1 Cor. i. 12). Not a word escapes from St. Paul that indicates any doctrinal difference between himself and Apollos, and as the latter had been instructed by St. Paul's friends, Aquila and Priscilla, this was, indeed, hardly probable. It would appear from 1 Cor. xvi. 12, that he returned to Ephesus, probably with letters of commendation from the Church of Corinth (2 Cor. iii. 1). St. Paul's confidence in him is shown by his desire that he should return once more to Corinth with Stephanas and Fortunatus and Achaicus. His own reluctance to be the occasion even of the semblance of schism explains his unwillingness to go (1 Cor. xvi. 12). After this we lose sight of him for some years. These, we may well believe, were well filled up by evangelising labours after the pattern of those which we have seen at Ephesus and Corinth. Towards the close of St. Paul's ministry (A.D. 65) we get our last glimpse of him, in Tit. iii. 13. He is in company with Zenas, the lawyer (see Note on Matt. xxii. 35), one, *i.e.*, who, like himself, had a special reputation for the profounder knowledge of the Law of Moses. St. Paul's feeling towards him is still, as of old, one of affectionate interest, and he desires that Titus will help him in all things. He has been labouring at Crete, and there also has gathered round him a distinct company of disciples, whom St. Paul distinguishes from his own; "Let *our's* also learn to maintain good works" (Tit. iii. 14). After this, probably after St. Paul's death, he wrote—if we accept Luther's conjecture—the Epistle to the Hebrews, addressed, as some have thought, to the Jewish Christians of Palestine, and specially of Cæsarea, but, more probably, as I have been led to believe, to the Christian ascetics, known as Therapeutæ, trained, like himself, in the school of Philo, with whom he had formerly been associated at Alexandria. The mention of disciples of, or from, Italy in Heb. xiii. 24 suggests a connection with some other Italian Christians than those of Rome, probably with those of Puteoli. (See Note on chap. xxviii. 14.)

XIX.

(1) **Paul having passed through the upper coasts.**—This implies a route passing from Galatia and Phrygia through the interior, and coming thence to Ephesus. The "coast," in the modern sense of the term, St. Paul did not even approach.

(2) **Have ye received the Holy Ghost since ye believed?**—Better, as connecting the two facts in the English as in the Greek, *Did ye receive the Holy Ghost when ye believed?*—*i.e.*, on your conversion and baptism. We are left to conjecture what prompted the question. The most natural explanation is that St. Paul noticed in them, as they attended the meetings of the Church, a want of spiritual gifts, perhaps, also, a want of the peace and joy and brightness that showed itself in others. They presented the features of a rigorous asceticism like that of the Therapeutæ—the outward signs of repentance and mortification—but something was manifestly lacking for their spiritual completeness.

**We have not so much as heard whether there be any Holy Ghost.**—The standpoint of the disciples so exactly corresponds to that of Apollos when he arrived at Ephesus, that we may reasonably think of them as having been converted by his preaching. They must, of course, have known the Holy Spirit as a name meeting them in the Sacred Books, as given to the olden prophets, but they did not think of that Spirit as a living and pervading presence, in which they themselves might claim a share. They had been baptised with the baptism of repentance, and were leading a life of fasting, and prayers, and alms, but they had not passed on to "righteousness, and peace, and joy in the Holy Ghost" (Rom. xiv. 17). It lies on the surface that they were Jewish, not Gentile, disciples.

(3) **Unto what then were ye baptized?**—The answer of the disciples had shown (1) an imperfect instruction, falling short of that which catechumens ordinarily received before they were admitted to the new birth by water and the Spirit; (2) an imperfect spiritual experience. Could those who made it have been admitted into the Church of Christ by baptism in His name? The answer to that question showed their precise position. They were practically disciples of the Baptist, believing in Jesus as the Christ, and thinking that this constituted a sufficient qualification for communion with the Church of Christ.

(4) **John verily baptized with the baptism of repentance.**—The words may fairly be regarded as

John verily baptized with the baptism
of repentance,[a] saying unto the people,
that they should believe on him which
should come after him, that is, on
Christ Jesus. (5) When they heard
*this*, they were baptized in the name of
the Lord Jesus. (6) And when Paul had
laid *his* hands upon them, the Holy
Ghost came on them; and they spake
with tongues, and prophesied. (7) And
all the men were about twelve. (8) And
he went into the synagogue, and spake
boldly for the space of three months,
disputing and persuading the things
concerning the kingdom of God. (9) But
when divers were hardened, and believed
not, but spake evil of that way before
the multitude, he departed from them,
and separated the disciples, disputing
daily in the school of one Tyrannus.
(10) And this continued by the space of
two years; so that all they which dwelt

a Matt. 3. 11.

A.D. 57.

---

giving the summary of what was actually a fuller teaching. The distinctive point in it was that the baptism of John was, by his own declaration, simply provisional and preparatory. He taught his disciples to believe in Jesus, and belief implied obedience, and obedience baptism in His name. It is not without significance that the list of elementary doctrines in Heb. vi. 1—4, addressed, we may believe, by Apollos to those who had once been his disciples, includes what those who are now before us might have learnt from him in their spiritual childhood, and that he then passes on to describe the higher state of those who had been "illumined," and had "tasted of the heavenly gift," and been made "partakers of the Holy Ghost" (Heb. vi. 4—6).

(5) **They were baptized in the name of the Lord Jesus.**—On the use of this formula in connection with the baptism of Jewish converts, see Notes on chap. ii. 38; Matt. xxviii. 19.

(6) **They spake with tongues, and prophesied.**—Better, *they were speaking with tongues and prophesying*, the verbs implying continuous action. As to the nature and relation of the two gifts, see Notes on chaps. ii. 4; x. 46. Here all the facts of the case confirm the view which has there been stated. The mere power of speaking foreign languages without learning them, as other men learn, seems a much less adequate result of the new gift than that which we find in the new enthusiasm and intensity of spiritual joy, of which the gift of tongues was the natural expression. It is not without interest to remember that the discussion of the two gifts in 1 Cor. xiv., in which the connection of the "tongues" with jubilant and ecstatic praise is unmistakable (1 Cor. xiv. 14—16), was written not very long after this incident, and while the facts must yet have been fresh in St. Paul's memory. On the "laying on of hands," which was the "outward and visible sign" of the "inward and spiritual grace," see Notes on chap. viii. 14—18, where the laying-on of hands is followed by a gift of the Holy Ghost.

(7) **And all the men were about twelve.**—Better, *The men were in all about twelve.* The whole narrative seems to imply that they were not individual cases, occurring here and there from time to time, but were living together as a kind of ascetic community, attending the meetings of the Church, yet not sharing the fulness of its life.

(8) **Spake boldly for the space of three months.**—We pause for a moment to think of the amount of work of all kinds implied in this short record. The daily labour as a tent-maker went on as before (chap. xx. 34), probably still in partnership with Aquila and Priscilla. The Sabbaths saw him evening and morning in the synagogue preaching, as he had done elsewhere, that Jesus was the Christ, and setting forth the nature of His work and the laws of His kingdom.

(9) **When divers were hardened and believed not.**—Better (the verb implying continuous action), *when some were growing hardened and disobedient.*

**Spake evil of that way before the multitude.**—Better, as before, *of the way*. (See Note on chap. ix. 2.) The unbelieving Jews acted at Ephesus as at Thessalonica, and tried to wreak their hatred against St. Paul by stirring up suspicion among the Gentiles, especially, as before, among those of the lower class, who were always ready for a tumult.

**Disputing daily in the school of one Tyrannus.**—The Greek word for "school" had a somewhat interesting history. Originally meaning "leisure," it was applied to leisure as bestowed on study, then, as here, to the place in which study was pursued; lastly, as in our phrase, "the school of Zeno or Epicurus," as a collective term for the followers of a conspicuous teacher. In this case, it was probably a lecture-room which, as the private property of the owner, was lent or let to the Apostle.

Of the Tyrannus here mentioned nothing more is known with certainty, but the name is connected with one or two interesting coincidences that are more or less suggestive. Like its Latin equivalent, *Rex*, it was not uncommon among the class of slaves or freed-men. It is found in the *Columbarium* of the household of Livia on the Appian Way, and as belonging to one who is described as a *Medicus* or physician. Both names and professions in this class were very commonly hereditary, and the hypothesis that this Tyrannus was also a physician, and that, as such, he may have known St. Luke, or, possibly, may have been among the Jews whom the decree of Claudius (chap. xviii. 2) had driven from Rome, and so shared the faith of Aquila and Priscilla, fits in with and explains the facts recorded. An unconverted teacher of philosophy or rhetoric was not likely to have lent his class-room to a preacher of the new faith. (See also Note on verse 12.)

(10) **So that all they which dwelt in Asia heard the word of the Lord Jesus, both Jews and Greeks.**—Here also there is a gap which can only be partially filled up by inference or conjecture. Ephesus, probably, came to be the centre of St. Paul's activity, from which journeys were made to neighbouring cities; and hence we may legitimately think of the other six churches of Rev. ii. and iii. as owing their origin to him. The growth of the new community among both sections of the population became a conspicuous fact, and began to tell upon the number of pilgrims who brought their offerings to the shrine of Artemis, or carried away memorials from it.

in Asia heard the word of the Lord
Jesus, both Jews and Greeks. (11) And
God wrought special miracles by the
hands of Paul: (12) so that from his body
were brought unto the sick handker-
chiefs or aprons, and the diseases de-
parted from them, and the evil spirits
went out of them.

(13) Then certain of the vagabond
Jews, exorcists, took upon them to call
over them which had evil spirits the
name of the Lord Jesus, saying, We
adjure you by Jesus whom Paul preacheth.
(14) And there were seven sons of *one*
Sceva, a Jew, *and* chief of the priests,
which did so. (15) And the evil spirit
answered and said, Jesus I know, and
Paul I know; but who are ye? (16) And
the man in whom the evil spirit was
leaped on them, and overcame them,
and prevailed against them, so that they
fled out of that house naked and wounded.

A.D. 58.

(11) **And God wrought special miracles by the hands of Paul.**—The Greek phrase is negative: *no common works of power*—not such as one might meet with any day. (See Note on chap. xxviii. 2, where the same phrase recurs.) The noun is that which was technically used by physicians for the healing "powers" or "virtues" of this or that remedy, and is so far, though used freely by other writers, characteristic of St. Luke.

(12) **So that from his body were brought unto the sick handkerchiefs or aprons.**—Both words are, in the original, transliterated from the Latin, the former being *sudaria*, used to wipe off sweat from brow or face; the latter *semicincta*, the short aprons worn by artisans as they worked. We ask how St. Luke, passing over two years of labour in a few words, came to dwell so fully on these special facts. The answer may be found (1) in St. Luke's own habit of mind as a physician, which would lead him to dwell on the various phenomena presented by the supernatural gift of healing; (2) a further explanation may be found in the inference suggested in the Note on verse 9. Such a report of special and extraordinary phenomena was likely enough to be made by a physician like Tyrannus to one of the same calling, and probably of the same faith. The picture suggested is that of devout persons coming to the Apostle as he laboured at his craft, and carrying away with them the very handkerchiefs and aprons that he had used, as precious relics that conveyed the supernatural gift of healing which he exercised. The efficacy of such *media* stands obviously on the same footing as that of the hem of our Lord's garment (see Note on Matt. ix. 20, 21), and the shadow of Peter (see Note on chap. v. 15), and, we may add, of the clay in the healing of the blind (see Note on John ix. 6). The two conditions of the supernatural work of healing were a Divine Power on the one hand, and Faith on the other, and any external medium might serve to strengthen the latter and bring it into contact with the former. Cures more or less analogous, ascribed to the relics of saints, admit, in some measure, of a like explanation. Without pretending to draw a sharp line of demarcation between the natural and supernatural in such cases, it is clear that a strong belief in the possibility of a healing work as likely, or certain, to be accompanied by any special agent, does much to stimulate the activity of the *vis medicatrix Naturæ* which before was passive and inert. It is not unreasonable to see in the works of healing so wrought a special adaptation to the antecedent habits of mind of a population like that of Ephesus. It was something for them to learn that the prayer of faith and the handkerchief that had touched the Apostle's skin had a greater power to heal than the charms in which they had previously trusted.

(13) **Certain of the vagabond Jews, exorcists.**—The men belonged to a lower section of the class of which we have already seen representatives in Simon of Samaria or Elymas of Cyprus. (See Notes on chaps. viii. 9; xiii. 6.) They practised exorcisms as a profession, and went from city to city, pretending with charms and spells to cure those who were looked on as possessed with demons. Many of these were said to have come down from Solomon. In Layard's *Nineveh and Babylon* (c. xxii.) there is an interesting account of several bronze bowls containing such formulæ. To them "the name of the Lord Jesus," which was so often in St. Paul's lips, was just another formula, mightier than the name of the Most High God, or that of the archangels Raphael or Michael, which were used by others.

(14) **Seven sons of one Sceva, a Jew, and chief of the priests.**—Better, *a Jewish chief priest*. The word might mean that he was at the head of one of the twenty-four courses into which the priests of the Temple were divided. (See Notes on Matt. xxi. 15; Luke iii. 2.) It is hardly probable, however, that one in that position would have taken to this disreputable calling, and it seems more likely that the title itself was part of the imposture. He called himself a chief priest, and as such St. Luke, or Tyrannus, described him. The scene is brought vividly before us. The seven exorcists, relying partly, we may believe, in the mystical virtue of their number, stand face to face with a demoniac, frenzied and strong like the Gadarene of Matt. viii. 28; Mark v. 3, 4.

(15) **Jesus I know, and Paul I know . . .**—Better, *Jesus I acknowledge*. The two verbs are different in the Greek, the one implying recognition of authority, the latter, as colloquially used, though originally it had a stronger meaning, a more familiar acquaintance. The possessed man, identifying himself, as the Gadarene did, with the demon, stood in awe of the Name of Jesus, when uttered by a man like St. Paul; but who were these seven pretenders, that they should usurp authority over him?

(16) **And the man in whom the evil spirit was leaped on them.**—The demoniacal possession brought with it, as in the case of the Gadarene, the preternatural strength of frenzy, and the seven impostors (men of that class being commonly more or less cowards) fled in dismay before the violent paroxysms of the man's passionate rage.

**Naked and wounded.**—The first word does not necessarily imply more than that the outer garment, or cloak, was torn off from them, and that they were left with nothing but the short tunic. (See Notes on Matt. v. 40; John xxi. 7.) It may be noted, as an indication of truthfulness, that the narrative stops here. A writer inventing miracles would no doubt have crowned the

(17) And this was known to all the Jews
and Greeks also dwelling at Ephesus;
and fear fell on them all, and the name
of the Lord Jesus was magnified. (18) And
many that believed came, and confessed,
and shewed their deeds. (19) Many of
them also which used curious arts
brought their books together, and
burned them before all *men:* and they
counted the price of them, and found *it*
fifty thousand *pieces* of silver. (20) So
mightily grew the word of God and
prevailed.

A.D. 59.

(21) After these things were ended,

---

story by representing the man who baffled the impostors as healed by the power of the Apostle.

(17) **Fear fell on them all, and the name of the Lord Jesus was magnified.**—The fact thus narrated had shown that the sacred Name stood on quite a different level from that of the other names which exorcists had employed. It was a perilous thing for men to use it rashly, without inward faith in all that the Name implied. Men thought more of it than they had done before, because they saw the punishment that fell on those who had profaned it.

(18) **And many that believed.**—More accurately, *many of those that had believed.* The word is probably used, as in verse 2, for the whole process of conversion, including baptism, confession in this instance following on that rite, instead of preceding it. The words do not definitely state whether the confession was made privately to St. Paul and the other teachers, or publicly in the presence of the congregation; but the latter is, as in the confession made to the Baptist, much the more probable. (See Note on Matt. iii. 6.) The feeling of a vague awe at this contact with the Unseen in some, the special belief in Christ as the Judge of all men in others, roused conscience into intense activity; the sins of their past lives came back upon their memories, and it was a relief to throw off the burden by confessing them.

(19) **Many of them also which used curious arts . . .**—The Greek word expresses the idea of superstitious arts, *overbusy* with the supposed secrets of the invisible world. These arts were almost, so to speak, the *specialité* of Ephesus. Magicians and astrologers swarmed in her streets (comp. the reference to them as analogous to the magicians at the court of Pharaoh in 2 Tim. iii. 8), and there was a brisk trade in the charms, incantations, books of divination, rules for interpreting dreams, and the like, such as have at all times made up the structure of superstition. The so-called "Ephesian spells" (*grammata Ephesia*) were small slips of parchment in silk bags, on which were written strange cabalistical words, of little or of lost meaning. The words themselves are given by Clement of Alexandria (*Strom.* v., c. 46), and he interprets them, though they are so obscure as to baffle the conjectures of philology, as meaning Darkness and Light, the Earth and the Year, the Sun and Truth. They were probably a survival of the old Phrygian *cultus* of the powers of Nature which had existed prior to the introduction of the Greek name of Artemis.

**And burned them before all men.**—This, then, was the result of the two sets of facts recorded in verses 12 and 16. The deep-ingrained superstition of the people was treated, as it were, homœopathically. Charms and names were allowed to be channels of renovation, but were shown to be so by no virtue of their own, but only as being *media* between the Divine power on the one hand and the faith of the receiver on the other; and so the disease was cured. The student of the history of Florence cannot help recalling the analogous scene in that city, when men and women, artists and musicians, brought the things in which they most delighted—pictures, ornaments, costly dresses—and burnt them in the Piazza of St. Mark at the bidding of Savonarola. The tense of the verb implies that the "burning" was continuous, but leaves it uncertain whether it was an oft-repeated act or one that lasted for some hours. In this complete renunciation of the old evil past we may probably see the secret of the capacity for a higher knowledge which St. Paul recognises as belonging to Ephesus more than to most other churches. (See Note on chap. xx. 27.)

**Fifty thousand pieces of silver.**—The coin referred to was the Attic *drachma.* usually estimated at about 8½d. of English money, and the total amount answers, accordingly, to £1,770 17s. 6d., as the equivalent in coin. In its purchasing power, as determined by the prevalent rate of wages (a *denarius* or *drachma* for a day's work), it was probably equivalent to a much larger sum. Such books fetched what might be called "fancy" prices, according to their supposed rareness, or the secrets to which they professed to introduce. Often, it may be, a book was sold as absolutely unique.

(20) **So mightily grew the word of God and prevailed.**—The verbs imply a continuous growth. The better MSS. give, "the word *of the Lord.*"

(21) **Paul purposed in the spirit.**—Better, perhaps, *in spirit.* The Greek word, however, implies a reference to something more than human volition. The spirit which formed the purpose was in communion with the Divine Spirit. (See Notes on chap. xvii. 16; xviii. 5.)

We learn from the First Epistle to the Corinthians what were the chief antecedents of this purpose. There had been intercourse, we may believe, more or less frequent, with the churches of both Macedonia and Achaia during the two years which St. Paul had spent at Ephesus; and there was much to cause anxiety. It had been necessary for him to send a letter, not extant, to warn the Corinthians against their besetting impurity (1 Cor. v. 9). The slaves or freed-men of Chloe had brought tidings of schisms, and incestuous adulteries, and grave disorders in ritual and discipline. (See *Introduction to the First Epistle to the Corinthians.*) These things called for the Apostle's presence. With these was joined another purpose. He wished to revisit Jerusalem, and to appear there as the bearer of a munificent contribution from the Gentile churches to the suffering church of the Hebrews. (See Notes to 1 Cor. xvi. 1; 2 Cor. viii. 1.)

**After I have been there, I must also see Rome.**—This is the first recorded expression of a desire which we learn from Rom. i. 13, xv. 23, had been cherished for many years, possibly from the time when he was first told that he was to be sent far off unto the Gentiles (chap. xxii. 21). It was doubtless strengthened by personal contact with the numerous disciples from that city whom he met at Corinth, some of them dating their conversion from a time anterior to his own (Rom. xvi. 7), and by the report which he heard from them of the faith and constancy of their brethren (Rom. i. 8). His work would not seem to

**Paul purposed in the spirit, when he had passed through Macedonia and Achaia, to go to Jerusalem, saying, After I have been there, I must also see Rome. (22) So he sent into Macedonia two of them that ministered unto him, Timotheus and Erastus; but he himself stayed in Asia for a season. (23) And the same time there arose no small stir about that way. (24) For a certain *man* named Demetrius, a silversmith, which made silver shrines for Diana, brought**

---

him complete until he had borne his witness in the great capital of the empire.

(22) **Timotheus and Erastus.**—Light is thrown on the mission of the former by 1 Cor. iv. 17. He was sent on in advance to warn and exhort, and so to save the Apostle from the necessity of using severity when he himself arrived. St. Paul exhorts the Corinthians (1 Cor. xvi. 10) to receive him with respect, so that he might not feel that his youth detracted from his authority. He was to return to St. Paul, and was accordingly with him when he wrote the Second Epistle to the Corinthians (2 Cor. i. 1). Erastus may fairly be identified with the chamberlain or steward of Corinth of Rom. xvi. 23, and was chosen probably as the companion of Timotheus because his office would carry weight with it. Sosthenes, who was with St. Paul when he wrote the First Epistle to the Corinthians (1 Cor. i. 1), had probably been staying some time at Ephesus, and as having been ruler of the synagogue, was naturally coupled by the Apostle with himself, as a mark of respect and confidence.

(23) **About that way.**—Better, as before, *the way.* (See Note on chap. ix. 2.)

(24) **Demetrius, a silversmith, which made silver shrines for Diana.**—The worship of Artemis (to give the Greek name of the goddess whom the Romans identified with their Diana) had from a very early period been connected with the city of Ephesus. The first temple owed much of its magnificence to Crœsus. This was burnt down, in B.C. 335, by Herostratus, who was impelled by an insane desire thus to secure an immortality of renown. Under Alexander the Great, it was rebuilt with more stateliness than ever, and was looked upon as one of the seven wonders of the world. Its porticos were adorned with paintings and sculptures by the great masters of Greek art, Phidias and Polycletus, Calliphron and Apelles. It had an establishment of priests, attendants, and boys, which reminds us of the organisation of a great cathedral or abbey in Mediæval Europe. Provision was made for the education of the children employed in the temple services, and retiring pensions given to priests and priestesses (reminding us, in the latter instance, of the rule of 1 Tim. v. 9, which it may indeed have suggested) after the age of sixty. Among the former were one class known as *Theologi*, interpreters of the mysteries of the goddess; a name which apparently suggested the application of that title (the Divine, the *Theologus*) to St. John in his character as an apocalyptic seer, as seen in the superscription of the *Revelation*. Large gifts and bequests were made for the maintenance of its fabric and ritual, and the city conferred its highest honours upon those who thus enrolled themselves among its illustrious benefactors. Pilgrims came from all parts of the world to worship or to gaze, and carried away with them memorials in silver or bronze, generally models of the *sacellum*, or sanctuary, in which the image of the goddess stood, and of the image itself. That image, however, was very unlike the sculptured beauty with which Greek and Roman art loved to represent the form of Artemis, and would seem to have been the survival of an older *cultus* of the powers of nature, like the Phrygian worship of Cybele, modified and renamed by the Greek settlers who took the place of the original inhabitants. A four-fold many-breasted female figure, ending, below the breasts, in a square column, with mysterious symbolic ornamentation, in which bees, and ears of corn and flowers were strangely mingled, carved in wood, black with age, and with no form or beauty, this was the centre of the adoration of that never-ceasing stream of worshippers. As we look to the more elaborate reproductions of that type in marble, of which one may be seen in the Vatican Museum, we seem to be gazing on a Hindoo idol rather than on a Greek statue. Its ugliness was, perhaps, the secret of its power. When art clothes idolatry with beauty, man feels at liberty to criticise the artist and his work, and the feeling of reverence becomes gradually weaker. The savage bows before his *fetiche* with a blinder homage than that which Pericles gave to the Jupiter of Phidias. The first real blow to the worship which had lasted for so many ages was given by the two years of St. Paul's work of which we read here. As by the strange irony of history, the next stroke aimed at its magnificence came from the hand of Nero, who robbed it, as he robbed the temples of Delphi, and Pergamus, and Athens, not sparing even villages, of many of its art-treasures for the adornment of his Golden House at Rome (Tacit. *Ann.* xv. 45). Trajan sent its richly-sculptured gates as an offering to a temple at Byzantium. As the Church of Christ advanced, its worship, of course, declined. Priests and priestesses ministered in deserted shrines. When the empire became Christian, the temple of Ephesus, in common with that of Delphi, supplied materials for the church, erected by Justinian, in honour of the Divine Wisdom, which is now the Mosque of St. Sophia. When the Goths devastated Asia Minor, in the reign of Gallienus (A.D. 263), they plundered it with a reckless hand, and the work which they began was completed centuries later by the Turks. The whole city, bearing the name of *Aioslouk*—in which some have traced the words *Hagios Theologos*, as applied to St. John as the patron saint—has fallen into such decay that the very site of the temple was till within the last few years a matter of dispute among archæologists. Mr. George Wood, however, in 1869, commenced a series of excavations which have led to the discoveries of strata corresponding to the foundations of the three temples which had been erected on the same site, enabled him to trace out the ground-plan, and brought to light many inscriptions connected with the temple, one in particular, the trust-deed, so to speak, of a large sum given for its support, from which we learn more than was known before as to its priesthood and their organisation. (See Wood's *Ephesus*, pp. 4—45.)

The word for "shrine" is that which, though translated "temple" in John ii. 19 (where see Note) and elsewhere, is always applied to the inner sanctuary, in which the Divine Presence was supposed to dwell, and therefore, here, to the chapel or shrine in which the

no small gain unto the craftsmen;
(25) whom he called together with the
workmen of like occupation, and said,
Sirs, ye know that by this craft we have
our wealth. (26) Moreover ye see and
hear, that not alone at Ephesus, but
almost throughout all Asia, this Paul
hath persuaded and turned away much
people, saying that they be no gods,
which are made with hands: (27) so that
not only this our craft is in danger to
be set at naught; but also that the
temple of the great goddess Diana should
be despised, and her magnificence should
be destroyed, whom all Asia and the
world worshippeth. (28) And when they
heard *these sayings*, they were full of
wrath, and cried out, saying, Great *is*
Diana of the Ephesians. (29) And the
whole city was filled with confusion:
and having caught Gaius and Aris-
tarchus, men of Macedonia, Paul's com-

---

statue of the goddess stood. It was to the rest of the building what the *Confession* and the *Tribune* are in Italian churches.

(25) **The workmen of like occupation.**—The "craftsmen" of the previous verse represent the higher class of what we call skilled labour. Here we have the unskilled labourers whom they employed. The former were, in a sense, artists, these were artisans.

**Sirs, ye know that by this craft we have our wealth.**—Literally, *Men*, the word used being different from that in chap. xvi. 30. The word for "craft" is the same as that translated "gain" in chap. xvi. 19, where see Note. The opening words of Demetrius bring before us, with an almost *naive* simplicity, the element of vested interests which has at all times played so prominent a part in the resistance to religious and political reforms, and entered largely into the persecutions against which the early preachers of the gospel had to contend. Every city had its temples and priests, its flamens, its oracles or sanctuaries. Sacrifices and feasts created a market for industry which would otherwise have been wanting. In its later development, the Christian Church, employing the services of art, encouraging pilgrimages, organising conventual and collegiate institutions, created a market of another kind, and thus gave rise to new vested interests, which in their turn were obstacles to the work of reformation. At first, however, the absence of the æsthetic element in the aims and life of the Church seemed to threaten those who were occupied in such arts with an entire loss of livelihood, and roused them to a fierce antagonism.

(26) **Not alone at Ephesus, but almost throughout all Asia.**—The language of Demetrius, though, perhaps, betraying the exaggeration of alarm, confirms the statement of verse 10 as to the extent of St. Paul's labours. Pliny, in his Epistle to Trajan (*Epp.* x. 96), uses language, half a century later, which is hardly less strong, speaking of "deserted temples," "worship neglected," "hardly a single purchaser" (*rarissimus emptor*) found for sacrificial victims.

**Saying that they be no gods, which are made with hands.**—The wrath of the mob-leader makes him virtually commit himself to the opposite statement that the idol is the god. Philosophers might speak of symbolism and ideal representations, but this was, and always has been, and will be, the conclusion of popular idolatry.

(27) **Not only this our craft.**—The English word conveys, perhaps, too much the idea of art. *Our business*, or *our interests*, would be a somewhat better equivalent. The Greek word is not the same as that so translated in verse 25.

**The temple of the great goddess Diana.**—The adjective was one specially appropriated to the Artemis of Ephesus, and appears on many of the coins and medals of the city.

**Should be despised.**—Literally, *should come to an exposure—i.e.*, should become a laughing-stock and a by-word. Panic is sometimes clear-sighted in its previsions, and the coppersmith of Ephesus becomes an unconscious prophet of the future.

**And her magnificence should be destroyed.**—The connection between the substantive and the received epithet is closer in the Greek than in the English. The *great* goddess was in danger of being robbed of her attribute of *greatness*.

**Whom all Asia and the world worshippeth.**—Asia is, of course, the proconsular province, and the "world" is used conventionally, as in Luke ii. 1, for the Roman empire. Apuleius uses language almost identical with that of Demetrius, "Diana Ephesia cujus nomen unicum . . totus veneratur orbis."

(28) **They were full of wrath, and cried out.**—Better, *they went on crying out*, the tense implying continued action.

**Great is Diana of the Ephesians.**—The cry was probably the usual chorus of the festivals of Artemis. Stress was now laid on the distinctive adjective, "Great she was, whoever might attack her greatness."

(29) **The whole city was filled with confusion.**—The loud shouts from the quarter in which Demetrius and his workmen met would, of course, attract attention. A rumour would spread through the city that the company of strangers, who had been objects of curiosity and suspicion, were engaged in a conspiracy against the worship which was the pride and glory of their city. It was natural, in such circumstances, that they should flock together to the largest place of public concourse, and drag thither any of that company on whom they might chance to light. We may compare, as an interesting historical parallel, the excitement which was caused at Athens by the mutilation of the Hermæ-busts at the time of the Sicilian Expedition under Alcibiades (Thuc. vi. 27).

**Gaius and Aristarchus.**—The former name represents the Roman "Caius." It was one of the commonest of Latin names, and appears as belonging to four persons in the New Testament: (1) the Macedonian mentioned here; (2) Gaius of Derbe (but see Note on chap. xx. 4); (3) Gaius of Corinth, the host of St. Paul, whom he baptised with his own hands (Rom. xvi. 23; 1 Cor. i. 14); (4) Gaius to whom St. John addressed his third Epistle; (3) and (4), however, may probably be the same. (See *Introduction to the Third Epistle General of John.*) Of Aristarchus we learn, from chap. xx. 4, that he was of Thessalonica. As such he had probably had some previous experience of such violence, and had, we may believe, shown courage in resisting it (1 Thess. ii. 14). He appears as one of St. Paul's companions in

panions in travel, they rushed with one accord into the theatre. (30) And when Paul would have entered in unto the people, the disciples suffered him not. (31) And certain of the chief of Asia, which were his friends, sent unto him, desiring *him* that he would not adventure himself into the theatre. (32) Some therefore cried one thing, and some another: for the assembly was confused; and the more part knew not wherefore they were come together. (33) And they drew Alexander out of the multitude, the Jews putting him forward. And Alexander beckoned with the hand, and would have made his defence unto

---

the journey to Jerusalem (chap. xx. 4), probably as a delegate from the Macedonian churches. He appears, from Col. iv. 10, to have been a Jewish convert, and to have shared the Apostle's imprisonment at Rome, either as himself under arrest, or, more probably, as voluntarily accepting confinement in the Apostle's hired house (chap. xxviii. 30), that he might minister to his necessities. The description given of them, as "Paul's companions in travel" is not without significance as implying a missionary activity beyond the walls of Ephesus, in which they had been sharers.

**They rushed with one accord into the theatre.**—The theatre of Ephesus was, next to the Temple of Artemis, its chief glory. Mr. Wood, the most recent explorer, describes it as capable of holding twenty-five thousand people (*Ephes.* p. 68). It was constructed chiefly for gladiatorial combats with wild beasts and the like, but was also used for dramatic entertainments. The theatre of a Greek city, with its wide open area, was a favourite spot for public meetings of all kinds, just as Hyde Park is with us, or as the Champ de Mars was in the French Revolution. So Vespasian addressed the people in the theatre of Antioch (Tacit. *Hist.* ii. 80; comp. also Apuleius, *Metamorph.*, bk. iii).

(30) **When Paul would have entered in . . .**—We almost see the impetuous zeal which urged the Apostle not to leave his companions to bear the brunt of the attack alone, and the anxious fear which made his friends eager to prevent a step which would probably endanger his own life without helping his friends. He refers probably to this when he speaks of having, as far as man was concerned, "fought with beasts at Ephesus" (1 Cor. xv. 32); not that there was any actual danger of martyrdom in that form, but that the multitude in their fanatic rage presented as formidable an ordeal. So Ignatius (*Ep. ad Rom.* c. 3) speaks of himself as "fighting with wild beasts" (using the same word as St. Paul), and describes the soldiers who kept guard over him in his journey from Antioch to Rome as the "ten leopards" who were his companions.

(31) **And certain of the chiefs of Asia, which were his friends.**—Better, *Asiarchs.* The title was an official one, applied to the presidents of the games, who were selected from the chief cities of the province. The office was an annual one. They were ten in number, and the proconsul nominated one of them as president. Their duties led them now to one city, now to another, according as games or festivals were held, now at Ephesus, now at Colophon, or Smyrna. As connected both with the theatre and with the worship of Artemis, they were probably officially informed of the occasion of the tumult. If, as seems probable from 1 Cor. v. 6—8, that Epistle was written at, or about, the time of the Passover, we may place the tumult at some period in the spring, when the people were keeping or expecting the great festival in honour of Artemis, in the month, named after the goddess, Artemision, spreading over parts of April and May (Boeckh. *Corp. Inscript. Græc.* 2954), and were therefore more than usually open to excited appeals like that of Demetrius. This would also account for the presence of the Asiarchs at Ephesus.

There is something significant in the fact that the Asiarchs were St. Paul's friends. The manliness, tact, and courtesy which tempered his zeal and boldness, seem always to have gained for him the respect of men in authority: Sergius Paulus (chap. xiii. 7), Gallio (chap. xviii. 14—17), Festus and Agrippa (chaps. xxv. 9, xxvi. 28, 32), the centurion Julius (chap. xxvii. 3, 43). The Asiarchs, too, from different motives, took the same course as the disciples. They knew that his appearance would only excite the passions of the crowd, be perilous to himself, and increase the disturbance in the city.

(32) **Some therefore cried one thing, and some another.**—Better, *kept on crying.* The graphic character of the whole narrative makes it almost certain that it must have come from an eye-witness, or possibly from more than one. Aristarchus or Gaius, who travelled to Jerusalem with St. Luke (chap. xx. 4), and were with him also at Rome, may have told him the whole tale of the scene in which they had borne so prominent a part. Possibly, also, following up the hint thrown out in the Note on verse 12, we may think of Tyrannus as having written a report of the tumult to St. Luke. The two conjunctions translated "therefore" (better, *then*) seem to carry the narrative back to what was passing in the theatre, after the parenthetical account of what had been going on between the Apostle, the disciples, and the Asiarchs outside it.

**For the assembly was confused.**—It is not without interest to note that the Greek word for assembly is the *ecclesia,* with which we are so familiar as applied to the Church of Christ. Strictly speaking, as the town-clerk is careful to point out (verse 39), this mob gathering was not an *ecclesia,* but the word had come to be used vaguely.

(33) **And they drew Alexander out of the multitude . . .**—The fact that he was put forward by the Jews indicates, probably, that they were anxious to guard against the suspicion that they were at all identified with St. Paul or his companions. If we identify this Alexander with the "coppersmith" of 2 Tim. iv. 14, who wrought so much evil against the Apostle on his third and last visit to Ephesus, we may assume some trade-connection with Demetrius which would give him influence with the crowd of artisans. His *apologia,* or defence, was obviously made by him as the representative of the Jews. The whole scene is again painted vividly—the vain attempt to gain a hearing by signs and gestures, the fury of the people on recognising his Jewish features and dress, their ready assumption that all Jews were alike in abhorring idols. Perhaps, also, they may have known or suspected that that abhorrence was sometimes accompanied by a readiness to traffic in what had been stolen from the idol's temple. St. Paul's words in Rom. ii. 22 may have had a personal application. The language of the

the people. (34) But when they knew
that he was a Jew, all with one voice
about the space of two hours cried out,
Great *is* Diana of the Ephesians. (35) And
when the townclerk had appeased the
people, he said, *Ye* men of Ephesus,
what man is there that knoweth not
how that the city of the Ephesians is
a worshipper[1] of the great goddess
Diana, and of the *image* which fell down
from Jupiter? (36) Seeing then that
these things cannot be spoken against,
ye ought to be quiet, and to do nothing
rashly. (37) For ye have brought hither
these men, which are neither robbers of
churches, nor yet blasphemers of your
goddess. (38) Wherefore if Demetrius,
and the craftsmen which are with him,
have a matter against any man, the law
is open,[2] and there are deputies: let

[1] Gr. *the temple keeper.*
[2] Or, *the court days are kept.*

town-clerk in verse 37 suggests the same thought. He could point to Aristarchus and Gaius, and say emphatically, "*These* men are not robbers of temples, whatever others may be."

(34) **When they knew that he was a Jew.**—Better, *when they recognised.*

(35) **And when the townclerk had appeased the people . . .**—The Greek word is the same as the "scribe" of the Gospels, and the familiar English expresses his function with adequate correctness. He was the keeper of the records and archives of the city. The title appears in many of the inscriptions in Mr. Wood's volume, often in conjunction with those of the Asiarchs and the proconsul. If, as is probable, his office was a permanent one, he was likely to have more weight with the people than the Asiarchs, who were elected only for a year, and who were not all of Ephesus. The language of the public officer is as characteristic in its grave caution as that of Demetrius had been in its brutal frankness. He, like the Asiarchs, obviously looks on St. Paul and his companions with respect. He has no feeling of fanaticism, and would not willingly be a persecutor. He dares not oppose the multitude, but he will try and soothe them with the loud profession of his attachment to the religion of his country. He was, if we may so speak, the Gamaliel of Ephesus; not without parallels among the princes and statesmen and prelates who have lived in the critical times of political and religious changes, and have endeavoured to hold the balance between contending parties.

**A worshipper of the great goddess Diana.**—The substantive as well as the adjective belonged to the local vocabulary. Its literal meaning is "temple-sweeper," or "sacristan"—one consecrated to the service of the goddess. The Greek word (*neôkoros*) is found on coins and inscriptions of Ephesus as applied to the inhabitants, sometimes in relation to the Emperor, sometimes to the goddess. They looked to her as their guardian and protector. One inscription claims for the city the honour of being the "nurse" of the great goddess (Boeckh. 2954, *ut supra*). She was, as it were, to borrow a phraseology which presents only too painful an analogy, "Our Lady of Ephesus." It is a curious fact that the same month was consecrated to Flora in Rome, and is now the "Mois de Marie" in France and Italy. The omission of the word "goddess" in nearly all the best MSS. is significant. She was, even without that word, emphatically "Artemis the Great." In some of the inscriptions of Ephesus she is described as "the greatest," the "most High."

**The image which fell down from Jupiter.**—The name was often given to old pre-historic images—as, *e.g.*, to that of Athenè Polias at Athens. It may have been merely a legendary way of stating that no one knew what artist had sculptured the image, or when it had been first worshipped. Possibly, however, the word may have had a more literal meaning as applied to a meteoric stone which had been employed by the sculptor, or was worshipped in its original form. The many-breasted image of Artemis described in the Note on verse 24 is, however, reported to have been made of olive-wood. The word *image* is not in the Greek, and one familiar word (*diopĕtes*) was sufficient to express what requires seven in the English paraphrase.

(36) **Seeing then that these things cannot be spoken against . . .**—The language of the town-clerk has the ring of an official acceptance of the established *cultus* rather than of any strong personal devotion. Such language has often been heard from the defenders of institutions which were almost on the verge of ruin.

**Ye ought to be quiet.**—The verb is the same as that of the transitive "appeased" in verse 35. In the exhortation "to do nothing rashly" we hear the voice of a worldly prudence, reminding us partly, as has been said, of Gamaliel, partly of the well-known maxim of Talleyrand, *Surtout, point de zèle.*

(37) **These men, which are neither robbers of churches.**—Better, *robbers of temples.* It was not unusual for the writers of the Elizabethan age to apply the term, which we confine to Christian buildings, to heathen temples. They would speak, *e.g.*, of the "church" of Diana, or the "chapel" of Apollo. The corresponding noun for "robbing temples," or "sacrilege," is found in inscriptions discovered by Mr. Wood (vi. 1, p. 14) among the ruins of the Temple, as denoting a crime to which the severest penalties were attached. The testimony to the general character of St. Paul and his companions, as shown both in word and deed, indicates the quietness and calmness with which they had preached the truth. They persuaded, but they did not ridicule or revile. This was, probably, more than could be said for Alexander and the Jews who put him forward. (See Note on verse 33.)

(38) **The law is open.**—Literally, *the court,* or *forum, days are going on.* The words may either indicate that the proconsul was then actually sitting to hold trials in the *agora* or *forum,* or may be taken as a colloquial idiom for "there are court days coming."

**There are deputies.**—The Greek word is (as in chaps. xiii. 7, xviii. 12) the equivalent for *proconsul.* Strictly speaking, there was only one proconsul in each province, and we must therefore assume either that here also the expression is colloquial, or that the assessors (*consiliarii*) of the proconsul were popularly so described, or that some peculiar combination of circumstances had led to there being two persons at this time at Ephesus clothed with proconsular authority. There are some grounds for adopting the last alternative. Junius Silanus, who was Proconsul of Asia when St. Paul arrived in Ephesus (A.D. 54), had been

them implead one another. (39) But if
ye enquire any thing concerning other
matters, it shall be determined in a
lawful[1] assembly. (40) For we are in
danger to be called in question for
this day's uproar, there being no
cause whereby we may give an account of this concourse. (41) And when
he had thus spoken, he dismissed the
assembly.

A.D. 59.

CHAPTER XX.—(1) And after the
uproar was ceased, Paul called unto *him*
the disciples, and embraced *them*, and
departed for to go into Macedonia.

A.D. 60.

(2) And when he had gone over those

1 Or, *ordinary*.

poisoned by Celer and Helius, the two procurators, at the instigation of Agrippina; and it seems probable that they for a time held a joint proconsular authority.

**Let them implead one another.**—The English word exactly expresses the technical force of the Greek. Demetrius and his followers were to lodge a formal statement of the charge they brought against the accused. They in their turn were to put in a rejoinder, and so joining issue, each side would produce its witnesses.

(39) **It shall be determined in a lawful assembly.**—Better, in *the* lawful assembly. The argument is that, should the alleged grievance be one that called for legislative rather than judicial action, the matter would have to be referred to the regular meeting of the *ecclesia*, which the town-clerk had probably the right to summon. There they could present their *gravamen*, and petition for redress. Here also the inscriptions discovered by Mr. Wood (vi. 6, p. 50) give an interesting illustration of the official phraseology. An image of Athena is to be placed "above the bench where the boys sit," at "every *lawful* (or *regular*) *ecclesia*."

(40) **We are in danger to be called in question.**—The "we" was used to include the rioters. The "called in question" is the same verb as that rendered "implead" in verse 38. There was a risk of which Demetrius and his party had to be reminded, that they might find themselves defendants, and not plaintiffs, in a suit. A riotous "concourse" (the town-clerk uses the most contemptuous word he can find, "this *mob meeting*") taking the law into its own hands was not an offence which the proconsuls were likely to pass over lightly. It would hardly be thought a legitimate excuse that they had got hold of two Jews and wanted to "lynch" them.

An interesting inscription of the date of Trajan, from an aqueduct at Ephesus, gives nearly all the technical terms that occur in the town-clerk's speech, and so far confirms the accuracy of St. Luke's report: "This has been dedicated by the loyal and devoted Council of the Ephesians, and the people that serve the temple (*Neôkoros*), Peducæus Priscinus being *proconsul*, by the decree of Tiberius Claudius Italicus, the *town-clerk* of the people."

XX.

(1) **Paul called unto him the disciples, and embraced them . . .**—The latter verb implies a farewell salutation.

**Departed for to go into Macedonia.**—We are able from the Epistles to the Corinthians to fill up the gap left in the narrative of the Acts. Having sent Timotheus and Erastus to see after the discipline of the Church of Corinth (chap. xix. 17), the Apostle was cheered by the coming of Stephanas and his two companions (1 Cor. xvi. 17), and apparently wrote by them what is now the First Epistle to the Corinthians. A previous Epistle had been sent, probably by Timothy, to which he refers in 1 Cor. iv. 17. When he wrote that Epistle he intended to press on quickly and complete in person the work which it was to begin (1 Cor. iv. 18, 19). He was led, however, to change his purpose, and to take the land journey through Macedonia instead of going by sea to Corinth (2 Cor. i. 16, 17), and so from Corinth to Macedonia, as he had at first intended. He was anxious to know the effect of his letter before he took any further action, and Titus, who probably accompanied the bearers of that letter, was charged to hasten back to Troas with his report. On coming to Troas, however, he did not find him, and after waiting for some time in vain (2 Cor. ii. 12), the anxiety told upon his health. He despaired of life and felt as if the sentence of death was passed on him (2 Cor. i. 8; iv. 10, 11). The mysterious thorn in the flesh "buffeted" him with more severity than ever (2 Cor. xii. 7). He pressed on, however, to Macedonia (2 Cor ii. 13), probably to Philippi, as being the first of the churches he had planted, where he would find loving friends and the "beloved physician," whose services he now needed more than ever. There, or elsewhere in Macedonia, Titus joined him, and brought tidings that partly cheered him, partly roused his indignation. There had been repentance and reformation where he most wished to see them, on the one hand (2 Cor. vi. 6—12); on the other, his enemies said bitter things of him, sneered at his bodily infirmities (2 Cor. x. 10), and compared, to his disparagement, the credentials which Apollos had presented (2 Cor. iii. 1) with his lack of them. The result was that Titus was sent back with the Second Epistle to the Corinthians, accompanied by some other disciple (probably St. Luke, but see Notes on 2 Cor. viii. 18, 19), the Apostle resolving to wait till they had brought matters into better order and had collected what had been laid up in store for the Church of Jerusalem, so that it might be ready for him on his arrival (2 Cor. ix. 5). At or about this time also, to judge from the numerous parallelisms of thought and language between it and the Epistles to the Corinthians on the one hand, and that to the Romans on the other, we must place the date of the Epistle to the Galatians. (See *Introduction* to that Epistle.) Probably after Titus and Luke had left, and before Timotheus had returned—when he was alone, with no one to share the labour of writing, or to give help and counsel—tidings came that the Judaising teachers had been there also, and had been only too successful. How the tidings reached him we do not know, but if the purple-seller of Thyatira was still at Philippi, she might naturally be in receipt of communications from that city, and it was near enough to Galatia to know what was passing there.

(2) **And when he had gone over those parts.**—Here also we can fill up the outline of the narrative from the Epistles. We may take for granted that St. Paul would revisit the churches which he had himself founded at Thessalonica and Berœa, as well as at

parts, and had given them much exhortation, he came into Greece, (3) and *there* abode three months. And when the Jews laid wait for him, as he was about to sail into Syria, he purposed to return through Macedonia. (4) And there accompanied him into Asia Sopater of Berea; and of the Thessalonians, Aristarchus and Secundus; and Gaius of Derbe, and Timotheus; and of Asia,

---

Philippi. The names in verse 4 indicate that delegates were chosen, probably by his direction, for the great journey to Jerusalem, which he now began to contemplate. Rom. xv. 19 indicates a yet wider range of activity. He had taken the great Roman road across Macedonia, and going westward to the shores of the Adriatic, had preached the gospel in Illyricum, where as yet it had not been heard.

**He came into Greece.**—The word Hellas, or Greece, seems used as synonymous with Achaia, the southern province. This may have led to an unrecorded visit to Athens. It certainly brought him to Corinth and Cenchreæ. There, we may hope, he found all his hopes fulfilled. Gaius was there to receive him as a guest, and Erastus was still a faithful friend. There, if not before, he found Timotheus, and he had with him Jason of Thessalonica and Sosipater of Berœa (Rom. xvi. 21—23). In one respect, however, he found a great change, and missed many friends. The decree of Claudius had either been revoked or was no longer acted on. Aquila and Priscilla had gone straight from Ephesus to Rome on hearing that they could do so with safety, and with them the many friends, male and female, most of them of the *libertini* class, whom he had known in Corinth, and whose names fill so large a space in Rom. xvi. The desire which he had felt before (chap. xix. 21) to see Rome was naturally strengthened by their absence. His work in Greece was done, and he felt an impulse, not merely human, drawing him to the further west. A rapid journey to Jerusalem, a short visit there, to show how generous were the gifts which the Gentile Churches sent to the Churches of the Circumcision, and then the desire of his life might be gratified. To preach the gospel in Rome, to pass on from Rome to the Jews at Cordova and other cities in Spain (Rom. xv. 24—28),—that was what he now proposed to himself. How different a path was actually marked out for him the sequel of the story shows.

(3) **When the Jews laid wait for him . . .**—In sailing for Syria, Cenchreæ would naturally be the port of embarkation, and St. Paul's presence there may reasonably be connected with the mention of Phœbe, the deaconess of that church, in Rom. xvi. 1. His intention was, however, frustrated. The malignant Jews of Corinth watched their opportunity. At Cenchreæ, amid the stir and bustle of a port, they might do what they had failed to do before. Here there was no Gallio to curb their fury, and throw the ægis of his tolerant equity over their victim. Their plans were laid, and their victim was to be seized and made away with as he was on the point of embarking. On hearing of the plot, the Apostle had to change his plans, and started with his companions for Macedonia, either travelling by land or taking a ship bound for one of its ports, instead of the one bound for Cæsarea, or Tyre, or Joppa. It is clear that the latter course would have baffled his murderers quite as much as the former.

(4) **And there accompanied him into Asia . . .**—The occurrence of the two names, Timotheus and Sosipater (another form of Sopater) in Rom. xvi. 21 makes it probable that all of those here named were with St. Paul at Corinth. As they were to go with him to Jerusalem, it was indeed natural they should have gone to the city from which he intended to embark. It is not difficult to discover the reason of their accompanying him. He was carrying up a large sum in trust for the churches of Judæa, and he sought to avoid even the suspicion of the malversations which the tongue of slanderers was so ready to impute to him (2 Cor. viii. 20, 21). Representatives were accordingly chosen from the leading churches, who acting, as it were, as auditors of his accounts, would be witnesses that all was right. As regards the individual names, we note as follows: (1) The name of Sopater, or Sosipater, occurs in the inscription on the arch named in the Note on chap. xvii. 8 as belonging to one of the *politarchs* of Thessalonica. (2) Aristarchus had been a fellow-worker with St. Paul at Ephesus, and had been a sufferer in the tumult raised by Demetrius (chap. xix. 29). (3) Of Secundus nothing is known, but the name may be compared with Tertius in Rom. xvi. 22, and Quartus in Rom. xvi. 23, as suggesting the probability that all three were sons of a disciple who had adopted this plan of naming his children. The corresponding name of Primus occurs in an inscription from the Catacombs now in the Lateran Museum, as belonging to an exorcist, and might seem, at first, to supply the missing link; but the inscription is probably of later date. In any case, it is a probable inference that the three belonged to the freed-man or slave class, who had no family names; and the Latin form of their names suggests that they had been originally Roman Jews, an inference confirmed by the fact that both Tertius and Quartus send salutations to their brethren in the imperial city (Rom. xvi. 22, 23). The names Primitivus and Primitiva, which occur both in Christian and Jewish inscriptions in the same Museum, are more or less analogous. (4) Gaius of Derbe. The Greek sentence admits of the description being attached to the name of Timotheus which follows; and the fact that a Caius has already appeared in close connection with Aristarchus makes this construction preferable. On this assumption he, too, came from Thessalonica. (See Note on chap. xix. 29.) (5) Timotheus. (See Note on chap. xvi. 1.) (6) Tychicus. The name, which means "fortunate," the Greek equivalent for Felix, was very common among slaves and freed-men. It is found in an inscription in the Lateran Museum from the Cemetery of Priscilla; and in a non-Christian inscription, giving the names of the household of the Emperor Claudius, in the Vatican Museum, as belonging to an architect. The Tychicus of the Acts would seem to have been a disciple from Ephesus, where men of that calling would naturally find an opening. Such vocations tended naturally, as has been said in the Note on chap. xix. 9, to become hereditary. (7) Trophimus (= "nursling," or "foster-child") was, again, a name of the same class, almost as common as Onesimus (= "profitable"). In a very cursory survey of inscriptions from the *Columbaria* and Catacombs of Rome, I have noted the recurrence of the former four, and of the latter five times Trophimus appears again in chap. xxi. 29, and is described more definitely as an Ephesian. We find him again in contact with St. Paul towards the close of the

Tychicus and Trophimus. (5) These
going before tarried for us at Troas.
(6) And we sailed away from Philippi
after the days of unleavened bread, and
came unto them to Troas in five days;
where we abode seven days. (7) And
upon the first *day* of the week, when
the disciples came together to break
bread,[a] Paul preached unto them, ready
to depart on the morrow; and continued
his speech until midnight. (8) And
there were many lights in the upper

a ch. 2. 46.

Apostle's life, in 2 Tim. iv. 20. That they were seven in number suggests the idea of a reproduction either of the idea of the Seven, who are commonly called Deacons in chap. vi., or of the Roman institution upon which that was probably based. It may be noted here, in addition to what has there been said on the subject, that the well-known pyramidal monument of Caius Cestius, of the time of Augustus, near the Porta Latina at Rome, records that he was one of the *Septemviri Epulonum* there referred to.

We must not forget what the sudden change to the first person plural in the next verse reminds us of, that the name of Luke has to be added to the list of St. Paul's companions. We may, perhaps, assume that he went less as an official delegate from the Church of Philippi than as a friend, and probably, St. Paul's health needing his services, as physician.

(5) **These going before tarried for us at Troas.**—Two motives may be assigned for this arrangement—(1) It enabled St. Paul to keep the Passover with the church at Philippi, starting "after the days of unleavened bread," and that feast was already assuming a new character as the festival of the Resurrection, bringing with it also the commemoration that "Christ our Passover was sacrificed for us" (1 Cor. v. 7, 8); (2) The disciples who went on in advance would announce St. Paul's coming to the church of Troas, and so there would be a full gathering to receive him and listen to him on his arrival.

(6) **And came unto them to Troas in five days.**—The voyage from Troas to Philippi (see Notes on chap. xvi. 11, 12) had taken only three days, but the ship had now to contend against the south-west current that set in from the Dardanelles, and probably also against the Etesian winds blowing from the north-east that prevail in the Archipelago in the spring.

**Where we abode seven days.**—It lies on the surface that the motive for this stay was to keep the Lord's day (the name was probably already current; see Rev. i. 10), and to partake with the Church of what, even before the date of this journey, St. Paul had already spoken of as the Lord's Supper (1 Cor. xi. 20).

(7) **Upon the first day of the week . . .**—This and the counsel given in 1 Cor. xvi. 2, are distinct proofs that the Church had already begun to observe the weekly festival of the Resurrection in place of, or, where the disciples were Jews, in addition to, the weekly Sabbath. It lies in the nature of the case that those who were slaves, or freed-men still in service, under heathen masters could not transfer to it the rigid abstinence from labour which characterised the Jewish Sabbath. And on this day they met together, obviously in the evening after sunset, to "break bread." On the half-technical significance of that phrase, as applied specially to the Lord's Supper, the Communion of the Body and Blood of Christ, see Notes on chap. ii. 46, and 1 Cor. x. 16. Two further questions, however, present themselves—(1) On what evening was the meeting held? (2) How far was a meal such as was known as the *Agapè*, or Feast of Charity, united with the Lord's Supper? In answer to (1), it seems probable that in churches which were so largely organised on the framework of the Jewish synagogue, and contained so many Jews and proselytes who had been familiar with its usages, the Jewish mode of reckoning would still be kept, and that, as the Sabbath ended at sunset, the first day of the week would begin at sunset on what was then or soon afterwards known as Saturday. In this case, the meeting of which we read would be held on what we should call the Saturday evening, and the feast would present some analogies to the prevalent Jewish custom of eating bread and drinking wine at that time in honour of the departed Sabbath (Jost, *Gesch. Judenthums*, i. 180). (2) Looking to St. Paul's directions in 1 Cor. xi. 33, 34, it is probable that the hour of the "breaking bread" became gradually later, so as to allow those who would otherwise have been hungry to take their evening meal at home before they came. The natural result of this arrangement was, as in the instance now before us, to throw the Eucharistic rite forward to midnight, or even later; and, as this was obviously likely to cause both inconvenience and scandal, the next step was to separate it entirely from the *Agapè*, and to celebrate the purely symbolic feast very early in the morning of the first day of the week, while the actual meal came later in the evening of the same day. That this was so in the regions of Troas and Asia we see from Pliny's letter to Trajan (*Epp.* x. 96), in which he describes the Christians as meeting on "a fixed day," for what he calls a *sacramentum* at break of day, and again in the evening to partake of a simple and innocent repast. At Troas we have the connecting-link between the evening communion of the Church of Corinth, and the morning celebration which has been for many centuries the universal practice of the Church.

**Paul preached unto them.**—The fact has a liturgical interest as showing that then, as in the more developed services of the second and third centuries, the sermon, and the lessons from Scripture which it implied, preceded what we now know as the Celebration.

**Ready to depart on the morrow.**—It may perhaps seem to some strange, taking the view maintained in the previous Note, that the Apostle and his companions should thus purpose to travel on a day to which we have transferred so many of the restrictions of the Jewish Sabbath. But it must be remembered (1) that there is no evidence that St. Paul thought of them as so transferred, but rather the contrary (Gal. iv. 10; Col. ii. 16); and (2) that the ship in which his friends had taken their passage was not likely to alter its day of starting to meet their scruples, even had those scruples existed.

(8) **And there were many lights in the upper chamber.**—We learn from verse 9 that it was on the third floor of the house. In the high narrow streets of Eastern towns the upper storey is often chosen for social or devotional purposes, partly as more removed from the noise of the street, partly as giving access to the roof of the house. Such a room in a good-sized house might well hold two or three hundred people. It is a fair inference also that the vividness and

chamber, where they were gathered
together. (9) And there sat in a window
a certain young man named Eutychus,
being fallen into a deep sleep: and as
Paul was long preaching, he sunk down
with sleep, and fell down from the third
loft, and was taken up dead. (10) And
Paul went down, and fell on him, and
embracing *him* said, Trouble not your-
selves; for his life is in him. (11) When
he therefore was come up again, and
had broken bread, and eaten, and talked
a long while, even till break of day, so
he departed. (12) And they brought the
young man alive, and were not a little
comforted.

(13) And we went before to ship, and
sailed unto Assos, there intending to

---

minuteness of the account indicate that we have the narrative of an eye-witness. The *lamps* or *torches* (see Notes on Matt. v. 15; xxv. 3; John v. 35) are probably mentioned, partly as accounting for the sleep of Eutychus by the heat and closeness of the room, partly, perhaps, as an indirect answer to the calumny loudly asserted afterwards (Tertull. *Apol.* c. 8), and probably even then whispered, that at the meetings of the Christians the lamps were extinguished and free scope given for deeds of shameless licence. There is no ground for assuming that the lamps at this early period had any distinctive ritual or symbolic character, though it would be a natural expression of respect that two or more should be placed in front of the Apostle, or other presiding elder, at such a meeting, on either side of the loaf which was to be broken, and the cup which was to be blest. The position of the celebrant (to use a later, but convenient term) may have been, as in the original institution of the Supper, recumbent on the *triclinium*, or couch, which was at this time used by both Greeks and Romans. It is obvious, however, that this would be an inconvenient posture for distribution to a large assembly, and the special mention of "the Lord's table" in 1 Cor x. 21, leads to the conclusion that there was a separate high table (to borrow the familiar language of a college or Inn of Court) at which the celebrant and other ministers sat, their backs to the wall, their faces to the people, and that from that table they distributed the bread and wine, either by taking them, or sending them by the deacons or other ministers, to those who sat in the body of the room, or by giving it to the congregation as they came up to the table in detachments. The later practice of the Church, and the absence of any indication in patristic writings that there was an abrupt change, makes the latter the more probable alternative. The table, so placed, served as a transition stage between the *triclinium* and the altar of the later basilica. The primitive arrangement in which the priest faces the congregation and stands behind the altar, it may be noted, was at first retained in most of the basilicas, and survives to the present day in some of the churches of that type in Rome—as, for example, in that of S. Clemente. This, therefore, and not any eastward or southward position, may claim to be, as has been well said, "at once the most primitive, the most Catholic, the most Protestant" of Eucharistic usages.

(9) **There sat in a window a certain young man named Eutychus . . .**—The name, like those of kindred meaning, such as Felix, Felicia, Felicissimus, Syntyche, Epaphroditus, Fortunatus, Faustus, Felicitas, was sufficiently common, especially among the freed-man class. In one instance, in an inscription in the *Collegio Romano*, the two names of Eutychus and Felicia appear as belonging to husband and wife.

**And was taken up dead.**—What follows is obviously related as a miraculous resuscitation; but it may be questioned, looking to St. Paul's words, "his life is in him," whether more than apparent death is meant. He was to all appearance dead—would have died but for the prayer of the Apostle; but there had been no fracture of limb or skull, and the cause of death, or of the state that looked like death, was the shock given to the brain and nerves by the violence of the fall.

(10) **Paul went down, and fell on him, and embracing him . . .**—The act reminds us of those of Elijah (1 Kings xvii. 21), and Elisha (2 Kings iv. 34). The close contact, the clasp of warm affection, gave a new intensity to the prayer of faith, and, as a current of vitality passed, as it were, from the one body to the other, enabled the Apostle to feel that the heart had not ceased to beat, and to give the calming assurance, "his life is in him." The whole scene is painted, as before, vividly, as by an eye-witness. We have to think of the cries of alarm, the rush of men down the staircase from the third floor with lamps and torches in their hands, the wail of sorrow on finding what looked like death, the undisturbed calmness of the Apostle, sure that his prayer was answered, and returning quietly, leaving the motionless body in the cool night air, to finish the interrupted discourse.

(11) **And had broken bread, and eaten.**—Better, *broken the bread and tasted.* In the early usage of the Lord's Supper the bread was not made, as in the Latin Church, in the form of circular wafers, nor cut up into small cubes, as in most Reformed Churches. The loaf, probably a long roll, was placed before the celebrant, and each piece was broken off as it was given to the communicant. Stress is laid on this practice in 1 Cor. x. 16, and indeed in the very term of "breaking of bread" as a synonym for the Lord's Supper. (See Note on chap. ii. 46.) Whether the next act of "eating" refers to the actual communion (we are obliged to use technical terms for the sake of definiteness), or to a repast, or *Agapè*, we have no adequate *data* for deciding. The use of the same verb, however, in "*tasting* of the heavenly gift," in Heb. vi. 4, suggests the former, and it is probable that the portion of bread and wine thus taken, in the primitive celebration, would be enough to constitute a real refreshment, and to enable the Apostle to continue his discourse.

**Even till break of day.**—The whole service must have lasted some seven or eight hours, sunrise at this time of the year, shortly after the Passover, being between 5 and 6 A.M. The inconvenience of such a protracted service led, as has been stated (see Note on verse 7), to the transfer of the Lord's Supper from the evening of Saturday to the early morning of Sunday, a position which, with some moderate variations, it has retained ever since, till the introduction in recent times of the yet more primitive practice of an evening celebration.

(13) **And sailed unto Assos.**—The port of Assos lay about twenty-four miles to the south of Troas.

take in Paul: for so had he appointed, minding himself to go afoot. (14) And when he met with us at Assos, we took him in. and came to Mitylene. (15) And we sailed thence, and came the next *day* over against Chios; and the next *day* we arrived at Samos, and tarried at Trogyllium; and the next *day* we came to Miletus. (16) For Paul had determined to sail by Ephesus, because he would not spend the time in Asia: for he hasted, if it were possible for him, to be at Jerusalem the day of Pentecost.

(17) And from Miletus he sent to Ephesus, and called the elders of the church. (18) And when they were come to him, he said unto them, Ye know, from the first day that I came into Asia, after what manner I have been with you at all seasons, (19) serving the Lord with all humility of mind, and with many tears, and temptations, which

---

We can only conjecture St. Paul's motives for going thither himself by land while his companions went by sea. In chap. xvi. 8 we find that he had avoided Mysia to press on to Troas; but he may well have extended his labours thither during his two years' sojourn in Asia, and have wished, before he started for Jerusalem, in the full belief that he was never to return to those regions (verse 25), to say a few words of parting counsel. Possibly, also, after the exciting scene at Troas, he may have been glad to have even a couple of days of comparative solitude for meditation and prayer as to the great work that lay before him, before embarking on the ship, with all its motley crew of passengers and sailors.

(14) **We took him in, and came to Mitylene.**—This was the capital of Lesbos, and furnished the island with its modern name of *Mitilini.*

(15) **We sailed thence . . .**—After the usual manner of the Mediterranean navigation of the time, the ship put into harbour, where it was possible, every evening. Each of the stations named—Lesbos, Chios, Samos—has legendary and historical associations of its own, full of interest for the classical student; but these, we may well believe—the revolt of Mitylene in the Peloponnesian War (Thuc. Book iii.), the brilliant tyranny of Polycrates at Samos (Herod. iii. 39—56), even "the blind old man of Scio's rocky isle"—were nothing to the Apostle and his companions. Trogyllium, the last station named before Miletus, was a promontory on the mainland, forming the extremity of the ridge of Mycale, and separated from Samos by a narrow channel of about a mile in width. Miletus, famous for its dyes and woollen manufactures, memorable in its earlier history for the disastrous issue of its revolt against Persia (Herod. v. 28—36), was practically the port of Ephesus, the harbour of which had been gradually choked by the accumulation of silted-up sand.

(16) **For Paul had determined to sail by Ephesus.**—The English phrase is unfortunately ambiguous. What is meant is that he had decided to continue his voyage without going to Ephesus—to pass it by.

**To be at Jerusalem the day of Pentecost.**—The motives for this wish lie on the surface. (1) It was, as has been said in the Note on chap. ii. 1, the Feast that attracted most pilgrims from all parts of the world, and therefore gave most scope for his work as an Apostle, especially for the great task of healing the growing breach between the Jewish and Gentile Christians. (2) It revived the memories and the power of the great day which had been the birthday of the Church's life as a distinct society. (3) St. Paul was contemplating a journey from Syria to Rome after his visit, and that would hardly have been feasible had he waited for the Feast of the Tabernacles. It might have seemed at first as if there was little gained in point of time by sending for the elders to come to him instead of going to them. We must remember, however, that had he taken the journey he would have been exposed to the accidents of travel, perhaps to a fresh riot like that of Demetrius, and might have been detained beyond the day fixed for the departure of the ship. By remaining at Miletus it was in his power to embark at any moment.

(17) **And from Miletus he sent to Ephesus, and called the elders of the church.**—We find, from verse 28, that they were known also as *episcopi* ("bishops," or "overseers"), the two names being interchangeable at this period, and the Apostle standing in relation to those who bore them as the later Bishop did to the elders under him. (See Notes on Phil. i. 1; Tit. i. 5, 6; 1 Pet. v. 1, 2.) The many presbyters represented probably, each of them, a distinct church or congregation. Most, if not all, of these must have been ordained by the Apostle himself. He had found them loyal, faithful, singularly receptive of the truth (verse 20; Eph. iii. 4). He was passing, as he thought, to far-off regions, never to revisit them, and he was naturally anxious to give them parting words of counsel and of warning.

(18) **Ye know, from the first day that I came into Asia . . .**—No discourse recorded in the Acts is so full of living personal interest. St. Luke would naturally be present at the meeting, and able to take notes of the address, and reproduce it almost, if not altogether, word for word. It bears upon the face of it internal marks of genuineness. No writer of a history adorned with fictitious speeches could have written a discourse so essentially Pauline in all its turns and touches of thought and phraseology, in its tenderness and sympathy, its tremulous anxieties, its frank assertions of the fulness of his teaching and the self-denying labours of his life, its sense of the infinite responsibility of the ministerial office for himself and others, its apprehension of coming dangers from without and from within the Church. The words present a striking parallel to the appeal of Samuel to the people in 1 Sam. xii. 3.

(19) **Serving the Lord with all humility of mind . . .**—The participle exactly answers to the epithet of the "servant" or "slave" of Christ which St. Paul so often uses of himself (Rom. i. 1; Gal. i. 10; Phil. i. 1; Tit. i. 1). The "tears," too, are characteristic of the Apostle, whose intense sensitiveness and sympathy had not been hardened into a Stoic apathy, and therefore found vent in a form which the Stoic would have scorned as unmanly. (Comp. verse 31; 2 Cor. ii. 4.) Epictetus (*Enchirid.* c. 2) barely allowed a follower of wisdom to mourn outwardly

befell me by the lying in wait of the
Jews: (20) *and* how I kept back nothing
that was profitable *unto you*, but have
shewed you, and have taught you pub-
lickly, and from house to house, (21) tes-
tifying both to the Jews, and also to the
Greeks, repentance toward God, and
faith toward our Lord Jesus Christ.
(22) And now, behold, I go bound in the
spirit unto Jerusalem, not knowing the
things that shall befall me there:
(23) save that the Holy Ghost witnesseth
in every city, saying that bonds and
afflictions abide me.[1] (24) But none of
these things move me, neither count I
my life dear unto myself, so that I
might finish my course with joy, and
the ministry, which I have received of
the Lord Jesus, to testify the gospel
of the grace of God. (25) And now,

1 Or, *wait for me.*

---

with those who mourned, and added the warning: "Take heed that thou mourn not inwardly."

**Temptations.**—Better, *trials*—the word retaining its dominant meaning of troubles coming from without, rather than allurements to evil from within. The reference to the "lying in wait of the Jews" refers, of course, to something altogether distinct from the Demetrian tumult, and implies unrecorded sufferings. The Apostle's life was never safe, and the air was thick with plots against it.

(20) **How I kept back nothing that was profitable.**—The verb is one which belongs to the vocabulary of sailors, and was used for taking in or reefing sails. He, St. Paul seems to say of himself, had used no such reticence or reserve, but had gone on his course, as it were, before the wind, with all his canvas spread. It must be noted, however, that even here, as in the more limited range of teaching imparted to the Corinthians (1 Cor. iii. 1, 2), he confines his statement to the things that were "profitable." In each case he considered what was required by the capacity of his disciples. That of Ephesus was wider than that of Corinth, and there, accordingly, he was able to set forth "the whole counsel of God" (verse 27).

**Publickly, and from house to house.**—The first word points probably to the teaching in the synagogue and the lecture-room of Tyrannus (chap. xix. 9), the second to the meetings of disciples which were held in private houses, such as that of Aquila and Priscilla (1 Cor. xvi. 19). It may, however, include even more personal and individual counsel.

(21) **Repentance toward God, and faith toward our Lord Jesus Christ.**—These, under all varieties of form, whether speaking to Jews or Gentiles, to philosophers at Athens (chap. xvii. 30) or peasants of Lystra (chap. xiv. 15), formed the substance of his teaching. It is obvious, however, that out of these might be developed a whole system of theology—why repentance was needed, and what it was, and how it should show itself, what was involved in the statement that Jesus was the Christ, and why men should believe in Him, and what works were the proper fruit of faith. All these were questions which had to be answered, before even the most elementary truths could be rightly apprehended.

(22) **And now, behold, I go bound in the spirit.**—The question meets us as before (see Note on chap. xix. 21), whether the words refer to the direct action of the Holy Spirit or to the higher element of St. Paul's own nature, as in 1 Cor. v. 3; 2 Cor. ii. 13. On the whole, the latter seems the more probable, subject, as before, to the reservation that the word is used because it points to that part of his being which was most in communion with the Divine Spirit. (Comp. Rom. viii. 16.) He was going to Jerusalem regardless of results, under a constraint which virtually limited the freedom of his human will. As in 1 Cor. ix. 16, a "necessity" was laid upon him.

(23) **The Holy Ghost witnesseth in every city.**—This can hardly refer to mere internal previsions of the future, but implies, like the analogous phraseology of 1 Tim. iv. 1, predictions uttered by the mouth of prophets, such as that which was afterwards spoken by Agabus (chap. xxi. 11). In every city, Corinth, Berœa, Thessalonica, Philippi, Troas, there had been like utterances, of which, though they are here implied, we have no separate record. There was a general dread as to the results of his journey, which led the disciples who loved him to dissuade him from attempting it. We may trace the influence of such predictions in the anxiety which he himself expresses when he asks for the prayers of his friends at Rome (Rom. xv. 30, 31) that he may be delivered from those that did not believe in Judæa. The words are not without their value as throwing light on the nature and limits of inspiration. The prophets of whom St. Paul speaks were truly inspired, as far as their prevision of the future was concerned, and yet that inspiration did not make them infallible advisers, and the Apostle felt that he was right in acting on those convictions of his own in which he, too, recognised the promptings of the Holy Ghost.

(24) **But none of these things move me . . .**—Literally, *But I take account of nothing, nor do I hold my life . . .* We note the parallelism with Luther's famous declaration, when warned by his friends not to go to Worms, "I will go thither, though there should be devils on every house-top."

**So that I might finish my course with joy.**—The two last words are wanting in many of the best MSS., and were probably inserted as a rhetorical improvement. The passage is grander without them. What St. Paul desired was to finish his course—whether "with joy" or not mattered little. The dominance of the same ruling thought finds utterance once again in his last Epistle (2 Tim. iv. 7).

**The ministry, which I have received of the Lord Jesus.**—We have again to note the parallelism with St. Paul's language elsewhere (2 Cor. iv. 1; v. 18; 1 Tim. i. 12); the words that follow are in apposition with the "ministry," and explain what it consisted in. To bear witness, especially as a living example of its power (1 Tim. i. 12—16), of the good tidings that God was not a harsh Judge, but a gracious Father, willing all men to be saved (1 Tim. ii. 4), that was the truth to the proclamation of which his life was to be devoted. In this there was the central truth of the kingdom of God, of which the next verse speaks.

(25) **I know that ye all . . . shall see my face no more.**—It is clear from these words, as well as from Rom. xv. 23, 24, that at this time St. Paul did not contemplate any further work in the Roman province

behold, I know that ye all, among whom I have gone preaching the kingdom of God, shall see my face no more.
(26) Wherefore I take you to record this day, that I *am* pure from the blood of all *men.* (27) For I have not shunned to declare unto you all the counsel of God.
(28) Take heed therefore unto yourselves, and to all the flock, over the which the Holy Ghost hath made you overseers, to feed the church of God, which he hath purchased with his own blood. (29) For I know this, that after my departing shall grievous wolves enter in among you, not sparing the flock.
(30) Also of your own selves shall men

---

of Asia, or in Greece. It is as clear, if we accept the Pastoral Epistles as genuine, that he did revisit Asia (2 Tim. i. 15), and that that visit included Troas (2 Tim. iv. 13), Miletus (2 Tim. iv. 20), and, in all probability, Ephesus also (1 Tim. i. 3). We need not be startled at this seeming discrepancy. The Apostle expressly disclaims foresight of his own future, and when he says, "I know," he speaks after the manner of men who take the fulfilment of their purpose for granted. In one sense, perhaps, his words were true. When he returned to Asia, and all were turned away from him (2 Tim. i. 15), how many of that company was he likely to have met again?

(26) **I am pure from the blood of all men.**—The image was a familiar one in the Apostle's lips (chap. xviii. 6). It rested on the language of an older prophet (Ezek. iii. 18, 20). He had acted on the teaching of that prophet, and none could require the blood of any man at his hands.

(27) **I have not shunned to declare unto you all the counsel of God.**—The words point to a greater degree of receptivity for Divine truth than had been found elsewhere. So in the Epistle to the Ephesians, which, even on the assumption that it was an encyclical letter, was addressed to them principally, he speaks to them as able to understand his knowledge in the mystery of Christ (Eph. iii. 4), the universality of His redeeming work, the brotherhood of mankind in the common Fatherhood of God. In "I have not shunned" we have the same word and image as in the "kept back" of verse 20.

(28) **Over the which the Holy Ghost hath made you overseers.**—Better, *in which the Holy Ghost set you as watchers.* The word used is the same as that commonly translated *bishops*, but, as used here in connection with the idea of the flock, it requires a word less technically ecclesiastical. It will be noticed that the word is commonly used in the New Testament as associated with this imagery. So in 1 Pet. ii. 25, we have "the Shepherd and *Bishop* of your souls," and the corresponding verb in 1 Pet. v. 2, "feed the flock of God . . . *taking the oversight* thereof." The appointment, as referred to the Holy Ghost, implies, probably, (1) the inward call, the impulse which drew the man to the office; (2) the attestation of that call by the voices of the prophets, as in chap. xiii. 2, 1 Tim. iv. 1; (3) the bestowal of gifts fitting them for the work.

**To feed the church of God, which he hath purchased with his own blood.**—It is clear that the words as they stand in the text are of immense importance, as bearing their witness to the belief of the Apostolic Church at once in the absolute divinity of Christ and in the nature of His redemptive work. The MSS., however, vary in their readings. Some of the best uncials and versions give "God;" others, of almost equal authority, give "Lord;" others, again, combine the two "Lord and God." The fact that elsewhere St. Paul invariably speaks of "the Church of God" (*e.g.*, 1 Cor. i. 2; 2 Cor. i. 1; Gal. i. 13; 1 Thess. ii. 14, *et al.*), and never "the Church of the Lord," may be allowed, from one point of view, some weight as internal evidence in favour of the Received reading; while from another it may be urged that it might have tempted a transcriber to substitute a familiar for an unfamiliar phrase. Accepting that reading, the words not only confirm the great truths of the Church's creed, but give an implicit sanction to the language of theology or devotion, when it applies to the divine nature of our Lord predicates that belong strictly to the human nature which was associated with it. So Ignatius (*Rom.* 6) spoke of "the passion of my God," and Tertullian (*Ad Uxor*, ii. 3) and Clement of Alexandria (*Quis dives*, c. 34) use the very phrase "the blood of God" which this passage suggests, and the Eastern Church at the council of Ephesus gave to the Blessed Virgin the title of *Theotŏkos Deipara*, the mother of the very God. So in the liturgy which bears the name of St. James the brother of the Lord, he is described as *Adelphotheos*, the brother of God, and that name is still current among the Greek Christians of Jerusalem. The general drift of the language of the New Testament writers was, however, in the other direction, and predicated human acts and attributes of the man Christ Jesus, Divine acts and attributes of the eternal Son; and it is obvious that this tends at once to greater accuracy of thought, and is really more reverential than the other.

In the word "purchased" (or, more literally, *acquired for himself*), we recognise the idea, though not the word, of redemption. The same verb is used in 1 Tim. iii. 13. The thought seems to have been one which specially characterised the teaching of St. Paul at Ephesus (Eph. i. 14: "the redemption of the purchased possession"). Comp. also, "ye were bought with a price," in 1 Cor. vi. 20, which, it will be remembered, was written from that city. The same idea is expressed in the "peculiar people" of 1 Pet. ii. 9; literally, *a people for a purchased possession*, and so, as it were, the *peculium*, or personal property of Him who had paid the purchase money.

(29) **After my departing shall grievous wolves enter in among you.**—The figurative language followed naturally on the idea of the flock and of the shepherds who keep watch over it. It lies in the nature of the case that the wolf stands primarily for the open enemies of the flock, the persecutors of all ages. (Comp. John x. 12.) The wolves, however, might come in sheep's clothing (Matt. vii. 15), and so the false prophets, the usurpers of authority, and leaders of parties within the Church, are also included in the term. Here this latter class is distinctly pointed out in the following verse. We find traces of the fulfilment of the prediction in the "turning away" of 2 Tim. i. 15; the "fiery trial" of 1 Pet. i. 7, iv. 12; the suffering "as a Christian" of 1 Pet. iv. 16.

(30) **Of your own selves shall men arise, speaking perverse things.**—The Pastoral Epistles, 2 Peter and Jude, supply but too abundant evidence of

arisė, speaking perverse things, to draw
away disciples after them. (31) There-
fore watch, and remember, that by the
space of three years I ceased not to
warn every one night and day with
tears. (32) And now, brethren, I com-
mend you to God, and to the word of
his grace, which is able to build you up,
and to give you an inheritance among
all them which are sanctified. (33) I
have coveted no man's silver, or gold,
or apparel. (34) Yea, ye yourselves
know, that these hands have ministered
unto my necessities,[a] and to them that
were with me. (35) I have shewed you
all things, how that so labouring ye
ought to support the weak, and to
remember the words of the Lord Jesus,

a 1 Cor. 4. 12; 1 Thess. 2. 9; 2 Thess. 3. 8.

---

the clearness of the Apostle's prevision. Hymenæus and Alexander and Philetus, saying that the resurrection was past already (1 Tim. i. 20; 2 Tim. ii. 17); evil men and seducers becoming worse and worse (2 Tim. iii. 13); resisting the faith, as Jannes and Jambres had resisted Moses (2 Tim. iii. 8); false prophets, bringing in damnable heresies and denying the Lord that bought them (2 Pet. ii. 1); these were part of the rank aftergrowth of the apostolic age, of which St. Paul saw even now the germs. It adds to the pathos of this parting to think that men such as Hymenæus and Philetus may have been actually present, listening to the Apostle's warnings, and warned by him in vain.

**To draw away disciples after them.**—Better, *to draw away the disciples*—those who had previously been disciples of Christ and His Apostles. This was at once the motive and the result of the work of the false teachers. The note of heresy was that it was essentially self-asserting and schismatical.

(31) **Therefore watch . . .**—The word was, as it were, an echo from our Lord's teaching (Matt. xxiv. 42, xxv. 13, *et al.*), which could hardly have been unknown to St. Paul. Here, however, it receives a fresh significance from its connection with the term *episcopi.* They who were the bishops, the overseers, the watchers of the flock, ought, above all others, to set an example of vigilance.

**By the space of three years.**—Strictly speaking, the narrative of the Acts accounts for three months' preaching in the synagogue (chap. xix. 8), two years in the school of Tyrannus (chap. xix. 10), and an undefined period embracing the time immediately before and after the tumult of Demetrius. This would be enough to warrant him describing the time of his ministry, speaking roughly, as extending over three years.

**To warn every one night and day with tears.**—Comp. Note on verse 19.

(32) **And now, brethren, I commend you . . .**—The Greek verb and its derivatives are characteristic of St. Paul's phraseology. Teachers are to "commit" the truth they have received to others (2 Tim. ii. 2), and the truth so committed is the *depositum fidei* which they thus hold, as it were, in trust (2 Tim. i. 14).

**The word of his grace, which is able to build you up . . .**—It can hardly be said that the "word" here is used, as it is by St. John, for the person of Christ as the *Logos.* (See Notes on John i. 14, 16; 1 John i. 1.) There is, however, a quasi-personal character ascribed to it, "able to . . . give an inheritance," which suggests the thought of something more than the written or spoken word. The true explanation is probably to be found in the thought of the "engrafted (or better, *the implanted*) word" of Jas. i. 21, the "word of God, quick and powerful" of Heb. iv. 12; and in so far as this is identical with the "Light that lighteth every man" of John i. 9, we may find in these passages a preparation for the more fully developed teaching of St. John as to the *Logos.* We cannot pass over the word "build" without noting the recurrence of the same thought and word in Eph. ii. 20, 21; iv. 12, 16, 29; Col. ii. 7. The figure was a natural one anywhere (comp. 1 Cor. iii. 10), but it would gain additional vividness from the stately architecture of Ephesus, perhaps also from the presence of one among St. Paul's companions who may have been himself an architect. (See Note on verse 4.)

**An inheritance among all them which are sanctified.**—Here also we find a thought specially characteristic of the teaching of the Epistle to the Ephesians. So we find the "earnest of our inheritance" (Eph. i. 14), the "inheritance in, or among, the saints" (Eph. i. 18), the "inheritance in the kingdom" (Eph. v. 5). The participle is in the perfect tense: *those that have been sanctified,* or *consecrated.* That term was, of course, equivalent to and co-extensive with "the saints," as applied to the whole body of believers. (See Notes on chap. ix. 2; Rom. i. 7; 1 Cor. i. 2; 2 Cor. i. 1.)

(33) **I have coveted no man's silver, or gold, or apparel.**—Comp. the parallel of Samuel's appeal to the people (1 Sam. xii. 3). In each case there was a special reason for what might otherwise seem an uncalled-for boast. Samuel's sons had been guilty of corrupt practices, taking bribes and the like (1 Sam. viii. 3). Among the many calumnies against St. Paul, one was that he used his apostolic ministry "as a cloke of covetousness." (Comp. 2 Cor. vii. 2; xii. 17, 18; 1 Thess. ii. 5.) On "apparel," as constituting a large part of the personal estate of the East, see Notes on Matt. vi. 19; Jas. v. 2.

(34) **These hands have ministered unto my necessities.**—The words clearly cover the whole three years of the Apostle's ministry at Ephesus. The partnership with Aquila and Priscilla (chap. xviii. 3) continued. Philemon was probably a sharer in it (Philem. verse 17). And the Apostle had not been satisfied with working for himself, but ministered also to "those who were with him." His teaching in 2 Thess. iii. 10 makes it improbable that he would have thus laboured to maintain others who were able-bodied in idleness, and the words that immediately follow make it almost certain that we must confine the statement to those who were suffering from infirmity. In 1 Cor. iv. 12, written, it will be remembered, from Ephesus, we have an undesigned coincidence confirming the statement.

(35) **I have shewed you all things.**—The words point to his motive in acting as he did. He sought to teach by example, to *indicate in all things* how others ought to act.

**To support the weak.**—The Greek verb is rightly rendered, but it deserves notice that it is the root of the noun translated "help" in 1 Cor. xii. 28. The word "weak" is to be taken as implying bodily infirmities. (See Note on previous verse.)

**To remember the words of the Lord Jesus.**—The words that follow are not found in any of the four

how he said, It is more blessed to give
than to receive.
(36) And when he had thus spoken, he
kneeled down, and prayed with them all.
(37) And they all wept sore, and fell on
Paul's neck, and kissed him, (38) sor-
rowing most of all for the words which
he spake, that they should see his face
no more. And they accompanied him
unto the ship.

CHAPTER XXI.—(1) And it came to A.D. 60.
pass, that after we were gotten from
them, and had launched, we came with
a straight course unto Coos, and the
*day* following unto Rhodes, and from
thence unto Patara: (2) and finding a
ship sailing over unto Phenicia, we went
aboard, and set forth. (3) Now when
we had discovered Cyprus, we left it
on the left hand, and sailed into Syria,
and landed at Tyre: for there the ship
was to unlade her burden. (4) And
finding disciples, we tarried there seven
days: who said to Paul through the
Spirit, that he should not go up to
Jerusalem. (5) And when we had ac-
complished those days, we departed and

---

Canonical Gospels, nor indeed in any of the Apocryphal. They furnish, accordingly, an example of the wide diffusion of an oral teaching, embodying both the acts and the words of Christ, of which the four Gospels, especially the first three, are but partial representatives. On the other instances of sayings ascribed to our Lord, and probably in many cases rightly ascribed, see the *Introduction to the First Three Gospels* in Vol. I. of this *Commentary*. The injunction to "remember" the words implies that they had often been prominent in the Apostle's teaching.

(36) **He kneeled down, and prayed with them all.**—The historian who has recorded what we may call the "charge" of St. Paul, shrinks, with a natural reverence, from reporting his prayer. Eph. iii. 14—21 will enable the thoughtful reader to represent to himself its substance, perhaps even its very thoughts and words.

(37) **Fell on Paul's neck, and kissed him.**—We note, as before in verse 19, the absence of any suppression of emotion. As David and Jonathan parted of old (1 Sam. xx. 41), so did St. Paul and his fellow-workers part now. In 2 Tim. i. 4 we have a passing reference to another parting scene of perhaps even tenderer emotion. To think that they should see his face no more, that this was their last farewell, made the elders of Ephesus and the other disciples eager, up to the very hour of embarkation, for the last embrace.

XXI.

(1) **After we were gotter from them . . .**—The Greek verb is more emphatic, and might almost be rendered, "When we had *torn ourselves away* from them."

**We came with a straight course unto Coos . . .**—The navigation is, as before (chap. xx. 14, 15), from port to port. It would hardly be within the scope of a Commentary to enter at length into the history of each place. It will be enough to note that Coos was famous both for its wines and its silk fabrics, of fine and almost transparent tissue; that Rhodes, then famous for its Colossus, was one of the largest and most flourishing islands of the Archipelago, and is memorable for us in later history as connected with the history of the Knights Hospitallers of St. John; that Patara was a harbour on the coast of Lycia. For this harbour the ship in which the travellers had left Troas and Miletus was bound, and they had therefore to look out for another. Happily there was no long delay, and they embarked at once on a merchant-ship bound for Phœnicia.

(3) **When we had discovered Cyprus . . .** The use of a technical term here is specially characteristic of St. Luke. Here the meaning is that, as soon as they *sighted* Cyprus, they stood to the southeast, and so had it on their left as they continued their voyage to Syria. At Tyre they had again to change their ship. On the position and history of Tyre, see Note on Matt. xi. 21.

(4) **And finding disciples, we tarried there seven days.**—The word for "finding" implies a previous search. They inquired, when they landed, amid the crowded streets of the still busy port, whether any Christians were to be found there. It will be remembered that St. Paul had passed through that region at least once before. (See Note on chap. xv. 3.) The church had probably been planted by the labours of Philip, as the Evangelist of Cæsarea. It is clear that the believers there were prepared to welcome St. Paul and his companions, and showed a warm interest in their welfare.

The "seven days'" stay, as at Troas (see Note on chap. xx. 6), and afterwards at Puteoli (chap. xxviii. 14), was obviously for the purpose of attending one, or possibly more than one, meeting of the church for the Lord's Supper on the Lord's Day. The utterances through the Spirit implied the exercise of prophetic gifts at such a meeting. It seems, at first, somewhat startling that St. Paul should reject what is described as an inspired counsel; or, if we believe him also to have been guided by the Spirit, that the two inspirations should thus clash. We remember, however, that men received the Spirit "by measure," and the prophets of the churches at Tyre, as elsewhere (chap. xx. 23), though foreseeing the danger to which the Apostle was exposed, might yet be lacking in that higher inspiration which guided the decision of the Apostle, and which he himself defines as the spirit "of power, and of love, and of a sound mind" (2 Tim. i. 7). This is, it is believed, a much more adequate explanation than that which sees in the Apostle's conduct a somewhat self-willed adherence to his own human purpose, and finds a chastisement for that self-will in the long delay and imprisonment that followed on the slighted warnings. He was right, we may boldly say, to go to Jerusalem in spite of consequences. The repeated warnings are, however, an indication of the exceeding bitterness of feeling with which the Judaisers and unbelieving Jews were known to be animated against him.

(5) **We departed, and went our way.**—Literally, *and were going on our way*, the tense bringing before

went our way; and they all brought us
on our way, with wives and children,
till *we were* out of the city: and we
kneeled down on the shore, and prayed.
(6) And when we had taken our leave
one of another, we took ship; and they
returned home again. (7) And when we
had finished *our* course from Tyre, we
came to Ptolemais, and saluted the
brethren, and abode with them one day,
(8) And the next *day* we that were of
Paul's company departed, and came
unto Cæsarea: and we entered into the
house of Philip the evangelist, which
was *one* of the seven;[a] and abode with
him. (9) And the same man had four

a ch. 6. 5.

---

us something like a procession wending its way from the city to the shore.

**We kneeled down on the shore, and prayed.**—The choice of the place was in itself natural enough. It was the spot where the two sets of friends were to part. It was removed from the stir and bustle of the city. We may add that it fell in with the common Jewish practice of using the banks of rivers or the sea-shore as a place of prayer. The beach of Tyre became for the time a *proseuchè*. (See Note on chap. xvi. 13.) It seems implied, from the use of the plural, that in this instance St. Paul was not the only spokesman of the prayers, but that others also (probably St. Luke himself, and the leading members of the Church of Tyre) joined in reciprocal intercession.

(6) **We took ship.**—Literally, *we embarked in the ship*. The article probably, though not necessarily, indicates that they went in the same ship that had brought them, and which, after discharging her cargo at Tyre, was now bound for Cæsarea.

(7) **We came to Ptolemais.**—This city is memorable both for its antiquity and for the varied fortunes of its city. As Accho it appears in Judges i. 31 as one of the old cities of the Canaanites which the Israelites of the tribe of Asher failed to conquer. It was conquered, rebuilt, and re-named by Ptolemy Soter King of Egypt. The old name, however, ultimately revived, or perhaps was never entirely disused; and the natives of the region still speak of it as *Accho*, while to Europeans it is familiar as Acre, or, more fully, St. Jean d'Acre. Here, also, as through all the line of cities along the coast, we find a church already organised, founded probably, as already suggested, by Philip the Evangelist. Here the stay of the travellers was shorter than at Tyre, probably because the ship only put into the harbour for the night. The passengers had time, however, to land and refresh themselves by intercourse with those who were sharers in their faith and hope.

(8) **We that were of Paul's company departed.**—Better, simply, *we departed.* The Greek which answers to the intervening five words is wanting in the best MSS., and seems a needless interpolation, there being no apparent reason for any change in the writer's previous phraseology, or for his distinguishing "Paul's company" from some other person or persons unknown. In some of the MSS. in which it is found, the verb is in the third person: "They that were of Paul's company came . . . ."

**Came unto Cæsarea.**—Comp. chaps. viii. 40; x. 1. This was, it will be remembered, St. Paul's third visit there (chaps. ix. 30; xviii. 22), and we may well believe that he was simply renewing the intercourse of a previous friendship with Philip.

**Philip the evangelist.**—The title given to him is interesting as showing that the work of "serving tables," *i.e.,* of superintending the distribution of alms, had been merged in the higher work of a missionary preacher. (See Note on chap. vi. 3.) He was no longer known, if, indeed, that title had ever been applied to him, as Philip the deacon, but as Philip the evangelist. The office so described is recognised by St. Paul in his enumeration of spiritual gifts and functions, in Eph. iv. 11, as coming next in order of importance to those of apostles and prophets, and before pastors and teachers. It would seem, accordingly, to have been distinct from the "orders," in the later sense, of presbyter or deacon, though capable of being united with either of them. Timotheus was exhorted by St. Paul when he was left at Ephesus, with the authority of a bishop, or, more strictly, of a vicar apostolic, to "do the work of an evangelist," as that to which he had been called (2 Tim. iv. 5). It followed, from the nature of the office, as analogous to that of the missionary of later times, that, though residing mainly at Cæsarea, Philip's labours extended beyond its limits; and we have seen reason to trace his work (see Notes on chaps. viii. 40; xv. 3; xxi. 3, 7) all along the coasts of Palestine and Phœnicia. As far as we know, Philip and St. Luke had not met before, and we can imagine the satisfaction with which the latter, himself, probably, an evangelist in both senses of the word (2 Cor. viii. 18), and already contemplating his work as an historian, would welcome the acquaintance of the former, how he would ask many questions as to the early history of the Church, and learn from him all, or nearly all, that we find in the first eleven chapters of this book.

**Which was one of the seven.**—We note how entirely the Seven of Acts vi. 3 are regarded as a special or distinct body. If the term deacon had ever been applied to them, which is very doubtful, it ceased to be applicable by its wide extension to the subordinate functionaries of the churches throughout the empire.

(9) **The same man had four daughters, virgins, which did prophesy.**—Both elements of the description are full of interest as throwing light on the life of the Apostolic Church. (1) The four daughters were "virgins." The word then, as afterwards, probably indicated, not merely the bare fact that they were as yet unmarried, but that they had devoted themselves, if not by irrevocable vows, yet by a steadfast purpose, to that form of service. In the organisation of women's work in the Church they formed apparently a distinct class, the complement of that of the widows of 1 Tim. v. 10. St. Paul had distinctly sanctioned such a life, as presenting a higher standard of excellence than the duties of domestic life (1 Cor. vii. 8), and on grounds which, in their general character, went beyond the "present distress" of a time of persecution (1 Cor. vii. 26, 34). It was, indeed, a matter on which he had no commandment from the Lord (1 Cor. vii. 25), and in which he was therefore open to the teachings of experience, and these seem to have modified his judgment at a later date, and led him to the conclusion that it was better that the younger "widows" should marry (1 Tim. v. 14), and

daughters, virgins, which did prophesy. (10) And as we tarried *there* many days, there came down from Judæa a certain prophet, named Agabus. (11) And when he was come unto us, he took Paul's girdle, and bound his own hands and feet, and said, Thus saith the Holy Ghost, So shall the Jews at Jerusalem bind the man that owneth this girdle, and shall deliver *him* into the hands of the Gentiles. (12) And when we heard these things, both we, and they of that place, besought him not to go up to Jerusalem. (13) Then Paul answered, What mean ye to weep and to break mine heart? for I am ready not to be bound only, but also to die at Jerusalem for the name of the Lord Jesus. (14) And when he would not be persuaded, we ceased, saying, The will of the Lord be done. (15) And after those days we took up our carriages, and went up to

---

that they should only be received into the list of those who were maintained by the Church in return for their services as "widows," at a more advanced age (1 Tim. v. 9). The order of "virgin," however, continued to exist, and the term *Virgo*, sometimes with *Ancilla Domini* (the handmaid of the Lord; comp. Rom. xvi. 1) added to it, is found in the inscriptions from the catacombs now in the Museums of the Collegio Romano and the Lateran. So Pliny, in his letter to Trajan (*Ep.* x. § 6), speaks of the women who were then called *ministræ* among the Christians, the latter term being probably used as the equivalent for "deaconesses." (2) These virgins "prophesied." The word comprised much more than mere prediction of the future, and included all words that came into the mind of the speaker as an inspiration, and to the hearers as a message from God. (Comp. Notes on chaps. ii. 17; xix. 6; 1 Cor. xiv. 24, 25.) In other words, they preached. We ask when, and where? Did they prophesy in the assemblies of the Church? It is true that St. Paul had forbidden this at Corinth (1 Cor. xiv. 34), and forbade it afterwards at Ephesus (1 Tim. ii. 12); but the very prohibition proves that the practice was common (see also 1 Cor. xi. 5), and it does not follow that St. Paul's rules of discipline as yet obtained in all the churches. It is perfectly possible, however, that they may have confined their ministrations to those of their own sex, and, accompanying their father in his missionary journeys, have gained access to women, both among Jews and Gentiles, and brought them to the knowledge of the Truth. It is obvious that the services of women, acting as deaconesses, would be needed as a matter of decorum in the baptism of female converts.

(10) **As we tarried there many days . . .**—The adjective is in the comparative degree, and implies, accordingly, a longer time than had been intended. Probably the voyage had been quicker than the travellers had expected, and there was therefore time to remain at Cæsarea, and yet to arrive at Jerusalem, as St. Paul purposed, in time for Pentecost (chap xx. 16). There was, at any rate, time for the tidings of his arrival to reach Jerusalem, and for Agabus (see Note on chap. xi. 28) to come down in consequence.

(11) **He took Paul's girdle, and bound his own hands and feet.**—The MSS. vary between "his hands" (St. Paul's) and "his own;" but the latter is by far the best-supported reading. It is interesting to note the revival of the old prophetic manner of predicting by symbolic acts. So Isaiah had walked "naked and barefoot" (Isa. xx. 3, 4); and Jeremiah had gone and left his girdle in a cave on the banks of the Euphrates, and had made bonds and yokes, and had put them on his neck (Jer. xiii. 1—11; xxvii. 2); and Ezekiel had portrayed the siege of Jerusalem on a tile, and had cut the hair from his head and beard (Ezek. iv. 1—3; v. 1—4). Looking to the previous relations between St. Paul and Agabus at Antioch (chap. xi. 27), we may well believe that the latter, foreseeing the danger to which the Apostle would be exposed, came down to Cæsarea, in a spirit of friendly anxiety, to warn him not to come. The feeling which led to the murderous plot of chap. xxiii. 12 could be no secret to a prophet living at Jerusalem.

(12) **Both we, and they of that place . . .**—For the first time the courage even of the Apostle's companions began to fail, and St. Luke admits that he himself had joined in the entreaty. Could not they, who were less known, and therefore in less danger, go up without him, pay over the fund that had been collected among the Gentiles to St. James and the elders, and return to him at Cæsarea? "They of that place" would of course include Philip and his daughters, and possibly, if he were still there, Cornelius and his friends, or, at any rate, those of the latter who were still residing in the city. They besought him, it will be noted, even with tears.

(13) **What mean ye to weep and to break mine heart?**—Better, *What mean ye weeping and breaking . . .?* The intense sensitiveness of St. Paul's nature shows itself in every syllable. It was with no Stoic hardness that he resisted their entreaties. They were positively crushing to him. He adhered to his purpose, but it was as with a broken heart. In spite of this, however, his martyr-like, Luther-like nature carried him forward. Bonds and imprisonment!—these he had heard of when he was yet at Corinth and Ephesus, before he had started on his journey; but what were they to one who was ready to face death? The pronouns are throughout emphatic. "You are breaking *my* heart. *I*, for *my* part, am ready . . ."

(14) **The will of the Lord be done.**—It is, perhaps, too much to see in these words an acceptance of his purpose as being in accordance with the will of the Lord. They were the natural expressions of resignation to what was seen to be inevitable, possibly used as a quotation from the prayer which the Lord had taught the disciples, and which He had used Himself (Luke xxii. 42).

(15) **After those days we took up our carriages . . .**—Better, *we took up our baggage.* The English word now used always of the vehicle that carries, was in common use at the time of the Authorised version, for the things carried—the luggage or *impedimenta* of a traveller. So, in 1 Sam. xvii. 22, David leaves his *carriage* (or, as in the margin, *the vessels from upon him*) in the hand of the "keeper of the *carriage*." So, in Udal's translation of Erasmus's *Paraphrase* of the New Testament (Luke v. 14), the bearers of the paralytic are said to have "taken their

Jerusalem. (16) There went with us
also *certain* of the disciples of Cæsarea,
and brought with them one Mnason of
Cyprus, an old disciple, with whom we
should lodge. (17) And when we were
come to Jerusalem, the brethren received
us gladly. (18) And the *day* following
Paul went in with us unto James; and
all the elders were present. (19) And
when he had saluted them, he declared
particularly what things God had
wrought among the Gentiles by his
ministry. (20) And when they heard *it*,
they glorified the Lord, and said unto
him, Thou seest, brother, how many
thousands of Jews there are which
believe; and they are all zealous of the
law: (21) and they are informed of thee,
that thou teachest all the Jews which
are among the Gentiles to forsake Moses,

---

'heavie carriage' to the house-roof." (Comp. also Judg. xviii. 21; Isa. x. 28; xlvi. 1.)

(16) **One Mnason of Cyprus, an old disciple, with whom we should lodge.**—Better, perhaps, *an early disciple.* The word for "old" refers less to personal age than to his having been a disciple from the beginning of the Church's history. He may accordingly have been among those "men of Cyprus" who came to Antioch, and were among the first to preach the gospel to the Gentiles. (See Note on chap. xi. 20.) We may fairly infer that he was one of those who had been "from the beginning" among the eye-witnesses and ministers of the word to whom St. Luke refers as his informants (Luke i. 2). If so, it is interesting, as showing that our Lord's disciples were not limited to the natives of Galilee and Judæa. It lies on the surface of the narrative that Mnason had a house at Jerusalem in which he could receive St. Paul and his companions. The arrangement seems to have been made as the best course that could be taken to minimise the inevitable danger to which the Apostle was exposing himself. In that house at least he might be sure of personal safety, and the men from Cæsarea would form a kind of escort as he went to and fro in the city.

(17) **The brethren received us gladly.**—This was, perhaps, an informal welcome, given in Mnason's house, by those who came there to receive the expected guests.

(18) **The day following Paul went in with us unto James . . .**—Looking to chap. xx. 16, it seems natural to infer that this was on or near the Day of Pentecost. The city would be crowded with pilgrims. The Church would be holding its solemn festival, not without memories of the great gifts of the Spirit, and prayers for their renewal. The Bishop of Jerusalem—to give him the title which, though apparently not then borne by him, expressed his functions, and was afterwards attached to his name—was there with the elders of the Church. St. Luke is careful to add that they were all there. On their part there was no reluctance to receive the Apostle of the Gentiles into full fellowship.

(19) **He declared particularly . . .**—Better, *one by one*, or, *in detail*, the adverb of the Authorised version having acquired in modern English a slightly different meaning. This must, it is obvious, have implied a narrative of considerable length, including an outline of all that had passed since the visit of chap. xviii. 22, and ending with an account of the contribution which he and his companions had brought with them from well-nigh all the churches of the Gentiles.

(20) **They glorified the Lord.**—The better MSS. give, "they glorified God." The tense implies continued action, and although its meaning would be satisfied by assuming mere ejaculations of wonder and praise, it is, at least, not improbable that there was a more formal thanksgiving.

**How many thousands of Jews there are which believe.**—Literally, *how many myriads—i.e.*, tens of thousands. The numbers seem large if we think of the population of Jerusalem only, but the crowds that came from all quarters to the Feast of Pentecost (see Note on chap. ii. 1) would fully justify the statement. The speaker here is obviously St. James, as the president of the assembly. There is no trace of the presence of any of the Apostles.

**They are all zealous of the law.**—Better, the word being a substantive and not an adjective, *zealots for the law.* The term was an almost technical one for the most rigid class of Pharisees. (See Note on Simon the Canaanite, Matt. x. 4.) So St. Paul describes himself as in this sense a "zealot" (chap. xxii. 3; Gal. i. 14).

(21) **And they are informed of thee . . .**—This, it is clear, was the current version of St. Paul's teaching. How far was it a true representation of its tendencies? As a personal accusation it was, of course, easy to refute it. His rule of adaptation led him to be to the Jews as a Jew (1 Cor. ix. 20). He taught that every man, circumcised or uncircumcised, should accept his position with its attendant obligations (1 Cor. vii. 18—20). He had himself taken the Nazarite vow (chap. xviii. 18), and had circumcised Timotheus (chap. xvi. 3). It was probably false that he had ever taught that Jews "ought not to circumcise their children." But fanaticism is sometimes clear-sighted in its bitterness, and the Judaisers felt that when it was proclaimed that "circumcision was nothing," in its bearing on man's relations to God (1 Cor. vii. 19; Gal. v. 6; vi. 15), it ceased to have a *raison d'être*, and sank to the level of a mere badge of the national exclusiveness, which, in its turn, was assailed by St. Paul's teaching that all middle walls of partition were broken down (Eph. ii. 14), and that Jews and Gentiles were alike one in Christ. If a Jew had asked, Why then should I circumcise my child? it would not have been easy to return a satisfying answer. If it were said, "To avoid giving offence," that was clearly only temporary and local in its application, and the practice would die out as people ceased to be offended. If it were urged that it was a divine command, there was the reply that, as a command, it had been virtually though not formally repealed when the promises and privileges connected with it were withdrawn. It was the seal of a covenant (Rom. iv. 11), and could hardly be looked upon as binding when the covenant itself had been superseded. Few Christians would now hold that a converted Jew was still bound to circumcise, as well as baptise, his children. The writer of the Epistle to the Hebrews did but push St. Paul's teaching to its legitimate conclusions when he said that the "new covenant had

saying that they ought not to circumcise
*their* children, neither to walk after the
customs. (22) What is it therefore? the
multitude must needs come together:
for they will hear that thou art come.
(23) Do therefore this that we say to
thee: We have four men which have a
vow on them; (24) them take, and purify
thyself with them, and be at charges
with them, that they may shave *their*
heads:[a] and all may know that those
things, whereof they were informed con-
cerning thee, are nothing; but *that* thou
thyself also walkest orderly, and keepest
the law. (25) As touching the Gentiles
which believe, we have written *and* con-
cluded that they observe no such thing,[b]
save only that they keep themselves
from *things* offered to idols, and from
blood, and from strangled, and from
fornication. (26) Then Paul took the
men, and the next day purifying himself
with them entered into the temple, to
signify the accomplishment of the days
of purification,[c] until that an offering
should be offered for every one of them.
(27) And when the seven days were
almost ended, the Jews which were of

*a* Num. 6. 18; ch. 18. 18.
*b* ch. 15. 20.
*c* Num. 6. 13.

---

made the first old," and that "that which is decaying and waxing old is ready to vanish away" (Heb. viii. 13).

**That thou teachest all the Jews . . . to forsake Moses.**—Literally, *that thou teachest apostasy from Moses*, the term used, with all its burden of evil import, adding weight to the charge.

**Neither to walk after the customs.**—On the general import of this phrase, as including the "traditions of the elders," as well as the precepts of the Law, see Notes on chaps. vi. 14; xv. 1.

(22) **The multitude must needs come together.**—More accurately, *at all events a crowd must needs come together*. The report of St. Paul's arrival was sure to spread, and those who heard of it would be eager to see how he acted. Would he ostentatiously reproduce in Jerusalem that living as a Greek with Greeks (1 Cor. ix. 22) of which they heard as his manner at Corinth and Ephesus? The advice which followed was intended to allay the suspicion of the timid, and to disappoint the expectations of more determined adversaries.

(23) **We have four men which have a vow on them.**—The advice was eminently characteristic. (1) It came from one who himself lived as bound by the Nazarite vow. "No razor came upon his head, and he drank neither wine nor strong drink" (Hegesippus in Euseb. *Hist.* ii. 23). By connecting himself with such a vow St. Paul would show that he was content in these matters to follow in the footsteps of St. James, that he looked upon the observance of the Nazarite vow, if not as binding, at any rate as right and praiseworthy. (2) It is obvious that St. Paul's conduct on his last visit to Jerusalem had furnished a precedent for the line of action now recommended. He had then come as a Nazarite himself; had in that character burnt the hair which he had cut off at Cenchreæ (see Note on chap. xviii. 18), and had offered the accustomed sacrifices. Why should he not repeat the process now? There was, however, this difficulty: the minimum period of the Nazarite vow was for thirty days, and as St. Paul had not taken the vow previous to the advice, and probably wished to leave Jerusalem soon after the feast was over (chap. xix. 21), it was out of his power to fulfil it now in its completeness. Jewish usage, however, made an intermediate course feasible. A man might attach himself to a Nazarite, or company of Nazarites, join in the final process of purification, which lasted, probably, for seven days (Num. vi. 9), shaving his head, and offering sacrifices with them. This was considered in itself a devout act, especially if the new comer defrayed the cost of the sacrifices. Agrippa I., for instance, had in this way gained credit with the Jews, as showing his reverence for the Law (Jos. *Wars*, ii. 15, § 1). It is clear that the four men were members of the Church of Jerusalem, and the fact is interesting as showing how intensely Jewish that church still was in its observances.

(24) **Purify thyself with them . . .**—This involved sharing their abstinence for the uncompleted term of the vow, and shaving the head at its conclusion.

**Be at charges with them . . .**—Literally, *spend money on them.* This involved payment (1) for the act of shaving the head, for which probably there was a fixed fee to priest or Levite; (2) for the sacrifices which each Nazarite had to offer—*sc.*, two doves or pigeons, a lamb, an ewe lamb, a ram, a basket of unleavened bread, a meat offering and a drink offering (Num. vi. 9—12).

(25) **As touching the Gentiles which believe.**—See Note on chap. xv. 20. St. James, it will be seen, adheres still to the terms of the *concordat* sanctioned at the council of Jerusalem. He has no desire to withdraw any concession that was then made, and the Judaisers who in Galatia and elsewhere were, in his name, urging the necessity of circumcision, were acting without authority. He thinks it fair to call on St. Paul to show that he too adheres to the compact, and has no wish to disparage the "customs" of the Law. St Paul, it will be seen, readily acts upon the suggestion. All promised well; but an interruption came from an unexpected quarter and overturned what seemed so wisely planned in the interests of peace.

(26) **To signify the accomplishment of the days of purification . . .**—The process lasted, as the next verse shows, for seven days, which were probably reckoned from the completion of the thirty days, or other term, of the vow itself. St. Paul, having made himself the representative of the Nazarite company, had to give, in their name, the formal notice to the priests, who were to be ready for the sacrifices when the seven days had expired. Seven days was, it will be noted, the ordinary period for the more solemn purifications (Ex. xxix. 37; Lev. xii. 2; xiii. 6; Num. xii. 14; xix. 14, *et al.*).

(27) **When the seven days were almost ended.**—Literally, *were on the point to be completed.* St. Luke speaks of "*the* seven days" as a definite or known period. They cannot refer, as some have thought, either to the duration of the vow, which was never less than thirty days, or to that of the Feast of Pentecost, which at this time was never extended beyond one, and

Asia, when they saw him in the temple, stirred up all the people, and laid hands on him, (28) crying out, Men of Israel, help: This is the man, that teacheth all *men* every where against the people, and the law, and this place: and further brought Greeks also into the temple, and hath polluted this holy place.
(29) (For they had seen before with him in the city Trophimus an Ephesian, whom they supposed that Paul had brought into the temple.) (30) And all the city was moved, and the people ran together: and they took Paul, and drew him out of the temple: and forthwith the doors were shut. (31) And as they went about to kill him, tidings came unto the chief captain of the band, that all Jerusalem was in an uproar. (32) Who immediately took soldiers and centurions, and ran down unto them: and when they saw the chief captain and the soldiers, they left beating of Paul.
(33) Then the chief captain came near, and took him, and commanded *him* to be bound with two chains; and demanded who he was, and what he had done.
(34) And some cried one thing, some another, among the multitude: and when he could not know the certainty

---

must therefore be understood of the period of special purification which came at the final stage of the fulfilment of the vow.

**The Jews which were of Asia . . .**—Better, *from Asia*—those who had come up to keep the Feast at Jerusalem. They, we may well believe, had been watching the Apostle eagerly as he passed in and out of the courts of the Temple. As it was, they seized him, with all the tokens of his purification still upon him (comp. chap. xxiv. 18), about to offer sacrifices, and raised a cry which was sure to throw the whole city into an uproar. They first reiterate the general charge, and in doing so bring against St. Paul, in almost identical terms, the very accusation which he had brought against Stephen (chap. vi. 11—13), of which they thus make themselves the witnesses. This was backed up by a more specific indictment (verse 28). He had brought Greeks—*i.e.,* uncircumcised Gentiles—into the Holy Place—*i.e.,* beyond the middle wall of partition (Eph. ii. 14) which divided the court that was open to strangers from that which none but Jews might enter (Jos. *Ant.* xv. 11, § 5). The recent excavations of the Palestine Exploration Society (*Report* for 1871, p. 132) have brought to light a slab with an inscription, discovered and deciphered by M. Clermont Ganneau, which illustrates the horror with which the Jews looked on such a profanation. Its contents show that it must have formed part of the low wall just mentioned:—"NO MAN OF ALIEN RACE IS TO ENTER WITHIN THE BALUSTRADE AND FENCE THAT GOES ROUND THE TEMPLE. IF ANY ONE IS TAKEN IN THE ACT, LET HIM KNOW THAT HE HAS HIMSELF TO BLAME FOR THE PENALTY OF DEATH THAT FOLLOWS." This, accordingly, was the punishment which the Jews of Asia were now seeking to bring on St. Paul and on his friends.

(29) **Trophimus an Ephesian.**—See Note on chap. xx. 4. His face was naturally familiar to those who had come from the same city. They had seen the two together in the streets, possibly near the entrance of the Temple, and, hatred adding wings to imagination, had taken for granted that St. Paul had brought his companion within the sacred enclosure.

(30) **The people ran together.**—Better, perhaps, *there was a rush of the people.* St. Luke brings into something like a mental juxtaposition the pictures of the tumult at Ephesus and that at Jerusalem. The Jews of Asia, among whom we may perhaps think of Alexander the coppersmith, working then as afterwards "much evil" against the Apostle Paul (2 Tim. iv. 14), may have taken part in both.

**Forthwith the doors were shut.**—This was obviously the act of the Levite gate-keepers. The Apostle was dragged out, the crowd followed him, and they seized the opportunity to guard the sacred precincts against further profanation.

(31) **The chief captain of the band.**—On the word "band," and its relation to the Latin "cohort," see Notes on chap. x. 1; Matt. xxvii. 27. On the word for "chief captain" (literally, *chiliarch,* or "captain of a thousand men," the cohort being the sixth part of the legion, which consisted of 6,000), see Note on Matt. viii. 29. They were stationed in the tower known as Antonia, built by Herod the Great, and named in honour of the Triumvir, which stood on the north-west side of the Temple area, on a rock, with a turret at each corner, and two flights of stairs leading to the arcades on the northern and western sides of the Temple. The Roman garrison was obviously stationed there to command the crowds of pilgrims, and was likely to be on the alert at a time like the Pentecost Feast. The Procurator Felix, however, was for the time at Cæsarea. The next verse shows that their appearance was sufficient at once to strike some kind of awe into the turbulent mob. Once again the Apostle owed his safety from violence to the interposition of the civil power. (See Notes on chap. xviii. 14—17.) The "beating" would seem to have been rough treatment with the fists rather than any regular punishment.

(33) **Commanded him to be bound with two chains.**—Looking to the usual Roman practices in the treatment of prisoners, we may think of each chain as fastened at one end to the Apostle's arm, and at the other to those of the soldiers who kept guard over him. (See Notes on chaps. xii. 6; xxviii. 16.) So shackled, he was taken before the Chiliarch Lysias for a preliminary inquiry.

(34) **Some cried one thing, some another.**—We note the parallelism with the like confused clamour at Ephesus (chap. xix. 32), which is described in exactly the same terms.

**He commanded him to be carried into the castle.**—The Greek, which literally means *encampment,* is translated "armies" in Heb. xi. 34. By a transition which reminds us of the connection between the words *castrum* and *castellum,* or castle, it came to be applied to a regular structure of stone or brick, such, for example, as the Tower Antonia, described in the Note on verse 31.

for the tumult, he commanded him to be carried into the castle. (35) And when he came upon the stairs, so it was, that he was borne of the soldiers for the violence of the people. (36) For the multitude of the people followed after, crying, Away with him. (37) And as Paul was to be led into the castle, he said unto the chief captain, May I speak unto thee? Who said, Canst thou speak Greek? (38) Art not thou that Egyptian,[a] which before these days madest an uproar, and leddest out into the wilderness four thousand men that were murderers? (39) But Paul said, I am a man *which am* a Jew of Tarsus, *a city* in Cilicia, a citizen of no mean city: and, I beseech thee, suffer me to speak unto the people. (40) And when he had given him licence, Paul stood on the stairs, and beckoned with the hand unto the people. And when there was made a great silence, he spake unto *them* in the Hebrew tongue, saying,

A.D. 60.

a ch. 5. 36.

CHAPTER XXII.—(1) Men, brethren, and fathers, hear ye my defence *which I make* now unto you. (2) (And when they heard that he spake in the Hebrew tongue to them, they kept the more silence: and he saith,) (3) I am verily a man *which am* a Jew, born in

(35) **When he came upon the stairs . . .**—This was one of the flights leading, as has been said, from the tower to the Temple area. Here the violence of the crowd became greater as they were more pressed in, and the soldiers had literally to lift him from his legs and carry him in, while the troops lined the staircase on either side.

(36) **Away with him.**—We remember that the self-same cry had been raised at the time of the Crucifixion (Luke xxiii. 18; John xix. 15), and that it was used now with the same meaning with which it had been used then.

(37) **Canst thou speak Greek?**—The chiliarch apparently expected his prisoner to have spoken Hebrew, *i.e.*, Aramaic, and was surprised to hear Greek; the people expected Greek, and were surprised at Hebrew (chap. xxii. 2). Nothing could better illustrate the familiarity of the population of Jerusalem with both languages.

(38) **Art not thou that Egyptian?**—The Greek has an illative particle which is wanting in the English: *Art not thou then that Egyptian?* This was the inference drawn by the chief captain from the fact that his prisoner spoke in Greek. The Egyptian was a false prophet, who a short time before this, under the procuratorship of Felix, had led 30,000 men (?) to the Mount of Olives, promising them that they should see Jerusalem destroyed (Jos. *Ant.* xx. 8, § 6; *Wars*, ii. 13, § 5). His followers were routed by Felix, but he himself escaped; and the chief captain infers from the tumult raised by a Greek-speaking Jew, that the Egyptian must have reappeared. Probably this was one of the vague reports in the confused clamour of the multitude. The words of the question have, however, been taken, on grammatical grounds, in a different sense: *Thou art not, then, that Egyptian?* as though his speaking Greek had changed the chiliarch's previous impression. Against this, however, there is the fact that an Egyptian Jew, coming from the very land of the Septuagint, would naturally speak Greek, and the inference that St. Paul was not the Egyptian because he knew that language would hardly be intelligible.

**Four thousand men that were murderers.**—Josephus, as has been said, gives a much larger number, but his statistics, in such cases, are never to be relied on. The word for murderer (*sicarii*, literally, *dagger-bearers*) was applied to the cut-throat bands who about this period infested well-nigh every part of Palestine, and who differed from the older robbers in being, like the Thugs in India, more systematically murderous (Jos. *Wars*, ii. 13, § 3). In the siege of Jerusalem, their presence, sometimes in alliance with the more fanatic of the zealots, tended to aggravate all its horrors.

(39) **A citizen of no mean city.**—The boast was quite a legitimate one. In addition to all its fame for culture, the town of Tarsus bore on its coins the word METROPOLIS-AUTONOMOS (Independent).

(40) **Paul stood on the stairs.**—The position was one which raised him above the people, and the characteristic gesture commanded instant attention. And he spoke, not as they expected in the Greek, which belonged to one who fraternised with Gentiles, but in the Hebrew or Aramaic, which he had studied at the feet of Gamaliel. It was a strange scene for that Feast of Pentecost. The face and form of the speaker may have been seen from time to time by some during his passing visits to Jerusalem, but there must have been many who had not heard him take any part in public action since the day when, twenty-five years before, he had kept the garments of those who were stoning Stephen. And now he was there, accused of the self-same crimes, making his defence before a crowd as wild and frenzied as that of which he had then been the leader.

## XXII.

(1) **Men, brethren, and fathers.**—The apparently triple division is really only two-fold—*Brethren and fathers*. (See Note on chap. vii. 2.) It is noticeable that he begins his speech with the self-same formula as Stephen. It was, perhaps, the received formula in addressing an assembly which included the scribes and elders.

(2) **They kept the more silence.**—The opening words had done the work they were meant to do. One who spoke in Hebrew was not likely to blaspheme the sacred Hebrew books. What follows was conceived in the same spirit of conciliation.

(3) **Brought up in this city at the feet of Gamaliel.**—His education may have begun shortly after he became a child of the Law, at the age of twelve. (See Note on Luke ii. 42.) He, too, had sat in the midst of the doctors, hearing and asking questions. The Rabbis sat in a high chair, and their scholars on the ground, and so they were literally at their master's feet.

Tarsus, *a city* in Cilicia,[a] yet brought up
in this city at the feet of Gamaliel, *and*
taught according to the perfect manner
of the law of the fathers, and was zealous
toward God, as ye all are this day.
(4) And I persecuted this way unto the
death, binding and delivering into
prisons both men and women.[b] (5) As
also the high priest doth bear me witness,
and all the estate of the elders:
from whom also I received letters unto
the brethren, and went to Damascus, to
bring them which were there bound
unto Jerusalem, for to be punished.
(6) And it came to pass, that, as I made
my journey, and was come nigh unto
Damascus about noon, suddenly there
shone from heaven a great light round
about me. (7) And I fell unto the
ground, and heard a voice saying unto
me, Saul, Saul, why persecutest thou
me? (8) And I answered, Who art
thou, Lord? And he said unto me, I
am Jesus of Nazareth, whom thou persecutest.
(9) And they that were with
me saw indeed the light, and were
afraid; but they heard not the voice of
him that spake to me. (10) And I said,
What shall I do, Lord? And the Lord
said unto me, Arise, and go into Damascus;
and there it shall be told thee
of all things which are appointed for
thee to do. (11) And when I could not
see for the glory of that light, being led
by the hand of them that were with me,
I came into Damascus. (12) And one
Ananias, a devout man according to the
law, having a good report of all the
Jews which dwelt *there*, (13) came unto
me, and stood, and said unto me,
Brother Saul, receive thy sight. And
the same hour I looked up upon him.
(14) And he said, The God of our fathers
hath chosen thee, that thou shouldest

a ch. 21. 39.

b ch. 8. 3.

---

**Taught according to the perfect manner . .**—The two last words are expressed in the Greek by a single noun, meaning "accuracy," exactness. In the "*most straitest* sect of our religion," of chap. xxvi. 5, we have the corresponding adjective.

**Was zealous toward God.**—The Apostle (see Note on chap. xxi. 20) claims their sympathy as having at one time shared all their dearest convictions. There is, perhaps, a touch of higher enthusiasm in the Apostle's language. He was a zealot for God: they were zealots for the Law.

(4) **And I persecuted this way.**—The speaker obviously uses the current colloquial term (see Notes on chaps. ix. 2 and xix. 23), used by the disciples as indicating that they had found in Christ the way of eternal life; used, it may be, by others with a certain tone of scorn, as of people who had chosen their own way, and must be left to take it.

(5) **As also the high priest doth bear me witness.**—Annas is named as high priest at the time of St. Paul's conversion, acting probably with his son-in-law, Caiaphas, as his coadjutor. (See Notes on Luke iii. 2; John xviii. 13.) At the time which we have now reached, the office was filled by Ananias, son of Nebedæus, who owed his appointment to Herod Agrippa II., then King of Chalcis, to whom Claudius had conceded the privilege of nominating the high priests (Jos. *Ant.* xx. 5, § 2). The official acts of his predecessors would of course be known to the high priest for the time being, and St. Paul can therefore appeal to his knowledge as confirming his own statements.

**All the estate of the elders.**—The word is perhaps used as identical with the Sanhedrin, or Council; perhaps, also, as including the *Gerousia*, or "Senate," of chap. v. 21—a body, possibly of the nature of a permanent committee, or an Upper Chamber, which was apparently represented in the Sanhedrin, and yet had separate rights, and might hold separate meetings of its own.

**I received letters unto the brethren.**—The phrase is interesting, as showing that the Jews used this language of each other, and that it passed from them to the Church of Christ. On the general history of St. Paul's conversion, see Notes on chap. ix. 1—16. Here it will be sufficient to note points that are more or less distinctive. In chap. ix. 2 the letters are said to have been addressed to the "synagogues."

**For to be punished.**—We must remember that the punishments would include imprisonment, scourging, and brutal violence (chaps. ix. 2; xxvi. 10, 11); or, as in the case of Stephen, death by stoning.

(6) **About noon.**—The special note of the hour is not given in chap. ix. 3, and may fairly be taken as characteristic of a personal recollection of the circumstances of the great event.

(7) **Saul, Saul . . .**—We have again, as in chap. ix. 4, the Hebrew form of the name.

(9) **They heard not the voice . . .**—*i.e.*, they did not hear it as a voice uttering articulate words. It was for them as though it thundered. (See Notes on chap. ix. 7, and John xii. 29.)

(11) **And when I could not see for the glory of that light.**—It is again characteristic of a personal recollection that, while the narrative of chap. ix. 8 states only the fact of blindness, St. Paul himself connects it with its cause.

(12) **A devout man according to the law.**—In chap. ix. 10, Ananias is simply described as "a disciple." The special description here was obviously given with a view to conciliate those who were listening to the speech. One, such as Ananias was, was not likely to have connected himself with a profane blasphemer, nor to have received the converted persecutor except on evidence that the change had come from God. St. Paul naturally confines himself to what came within his own experience, and does not dwell on the vision which had been seen by Ananias.

(14) **The God of our fathers . . .**—The report of what was said by Ananias is somewhat fuller than in chap. ix. 17, and gives in outline what had been spoken to him by the Lord. It is obviously implied in chap. ix. 15, 16, that those words were to be reproduced to Saul. We note the recurrence of the same formula

know his will, and see that Just One,
and shouldest hear the voice of his
mouth. (15) For thou shalt be his wit-
ness unto all men of what thou hast
seen and heard. (16) And now why
tarriest thou? arise, and be baptized,
and wash away thy sins, calling on the
name of the Lord. (17) And it came to
pass, that, when I was come again to
Jerusalem, even while I prayed in the
temple, I was in a trance; (18) and saw
him saying unto me, Make haste, and
get thee quickly out of Jerusalem: for
they will not receive thy testimony con-
cerning me. (19) And I said, Lord, they
know that I imprisoned and beat in
every synagogue them that believed on
thee: (20) and when the blood of thy
martyr Stephen was shed,[a] I also was
standing by, and consenting unto his
death, and kept the raiment of them
that slew him. (21) And he said unto
me, Depart: for I will send thee far
hence unto the Gentiles. (22) And they
gave him audience unto this word, and
*then* lifted up their voices, and said,
Away with such a *fellow* from the earth:
for it is not fit that he should live.

a ch. 7. 58.

---

in speaking of God that had been used by Stephen (chap. vii. 32).

**Hath chosen thee.**—The Greek verb is not that commonly rendered by "chosen," and is better translated *fore-appointed.*

**And see that Just One.**—See Note on chap. vii. 52, in reference to the use of this name to designate the Lord Jesus.

(15) **Thou shalt be his witness.**—This mission, identical with that which had been assigned to the Twelve (chap. i. 8), virtually placed the persecutor on a level with them, and was equivalent to his appointment as an Apostle.

(16) **Arise, and be baptized, and wash away thy sins.**—Here, again, we have words which are not in the narrative of chap. ix. They show that for the Apostle that baptism was no formal or ceremonial act, but was joined with repentance, and, faith being presupposed, brought with it the assurance of a real forgiveness. In St. Paul's language as to the "washing" (or, *bath*) of regeneration (Tit. iii. 5) we may trace his continued adherence to the idea which he had thus been taught to embrace on his first admission to the Church of Christ.

**Calling on the name of the Lord.**—The better MSS. give simply, "calling upon His name," *i.e.*, the name of the Just One whom St. Paul had seen. The reading in the Received text probably arose from a wish to adapt the phrase to the language of chap. ii. 21.

(17) **When I was come again to Jerusalem.**—This probably refers to the visit of chap. ix. 26, and Gal. i. 17, 18. The objection that the mission "far hence to the Gentiles" must refer to the subsequent visit of chap. xi. 30, has little or no force. When the Apostle went to Tarsus and preached the gospel to the Greeks at Antioch (chap. xi. 26), there was a sufficient fulfilment of the promise, "I will send thee . . ." What was indicated in the vision was that he was to have another field of work than Jerusalem and the Church of the Circumcision. It may be noted as one of the "visions or revelations of the Lord" referred to in 2 Cor. xii. 1.

**Even while I prayed in the temple.**—Better, *and as I was praying.* The fact is brought forward as showing that then, as now, he had been not a blasphemer of the Temple, but a devout worshipper in it, and so formed an important part of the Apostle's *apologia* to the charge that had been brought against him.

**I was in a trance.**—On the word and the state of consciousness it implies, see Note on chap. x. 10.

(18) **Get thee quickly out of Jerusalem.**—It is obvious that this fits in better with the first hurried visit after St. Paul's conversion than with the second, when he came with Barnabas with alms for the sufferers from the famine. (See Note on chap. xi. 30.)

(19) **Lord, they know that I imprisoned . .**—This was said at the time, and it was repeated now, as with a two-fold bearing. It was partly an extenuation of the unbelief of the people. They were, as he had once been, sinning in ignorance, which, though as yet unconquered, was not invincible. Partly it expressed the hope that they too might listen when they saw him whom they had known as a vehement persecutor preaching the faith which he had once destroyed.

(20) **When the blood of thy martyr Stephen . . . .**—Better, *thy witness.* The English word is, perhaps, a little too definite and technical, and fails to remind us, as the Greek does, that the same word had been used in verse 15 as expressing the office to which St. Paul himself was called. He probably used the Aramaic word *Edh*, of which the Greek *martus* (*witness*, and, in ecclesiastical Greek, *martyr*) was the natural equivalent.

**Consenting unto his death.**—The self-same word is used as in chap. viii. 1, not, we may believe, without the feeling which the speaker had lately expressed in Rom. i. 32, that that state of mind involved a greater guilt than those who had been acting blindly,—almost in what John Huss called the *sancta simplicitas* of devout ignorance—in the passionate heat of fanaticism. The words "unto his death" are wanting in the best MSS., but are obviously implied.

(21) **I will send thee . . .**—It may be noted, in connection with the question discussed in the Note on verse 17, that the words convey the promise of a mission rather than the actual mission itself. The work immediately before him was to depart and wait till the way should be opened to him, and the inward call be confirmed, as in chap. xiii. 2, by an outward and express command.

**Far hence unto the Gentiles.**—The crowd had listened, impatiently, we may believe, up to this point, as the speaker had once listened to St. Stephen. This, that the Christ should be represented as sending His messenger to the Gentiles, and not to Jews, was more than they could bear.

(22) **Away with such a fellow from the earth.**—The scene was ominously like that in which St. Stephen's speech ended. Immediate execution without the formality of a trial—an eager craving for the blood of the blasphemer—this was what their wild cries demanded and expressed. On the words themselves, see Note on chap. xxi. 36.

(23) And as they cried out, and cast off
*their* clothes, and threw dust into the
air, (24) the chief captain commanded
him to be brought into the castle, and
bade that he should be examined by
scourging; that he might know where-
fore they cried so against him. (25) And
as they bound him with thongs, Paul
said unto the centurion that stood by,
Is it lawful for you to scourge a man
that is a Roman, and uncondemned?
(26) When the centurion heard *that*, he
went and told the chief captain, saying,
Take heed what thou doest: for this
man is a Roman. (27) Then the chief
captain came, and said unto him, Tell
me, art thou a Roman? He said, Yea.
(28) And the chief captain answered,
With a great sum obtained I this
freedom. And Paul said, But I was *free*
born. (29) Then straightway they de-
parted from him which should have
examined him:[1] and the chief captain
also was afraid, after he knew that he
was a Roman, and because he had bound
him. (30) On the morrow, because he
would have known the certainty where-
fore he was accused of the Jews, he
loosed him from *his* bands, and com-
manded the chief priests and all their
council to appear, and brought Paul
down, and set him before them.

1 Or, *tortured him.*

---

(23) **Cast off their clothes, and threw dust into the air.**—The latter gesture would seem to have been a natural relief, as with other Oriental nations, to the violence of uncontrolled passion. It may be, however, that the handfuls of dust were aimed at the Apostle as a sign of loathing (comp. Notes on chap. xviii. 6; Matt. x. 14); and if we take the English version, the "casting off" their outer garments looked very much like preparing for the act of stoning, as in chap. vii. 58. The verb may, however, mean only that they "shook their garments," as St. Paul had done in chap. xviii. 6, and so the two gestures might be parts of the same act. On the whole, the latter view seems the more probable.

(24) **Bade that he should be examined by scourging.**—The matter-of-course way in which this is narrated illustrates the ordinary process of Roman provincial administration. The chiliarch had probably only partially understood St. Paul's Aramaic speech, and his first impulse was to have him scourged, so as to elicit from his own lips that which he could not gather from the confused and contradictory clamours of the crowd.

(25) **And as they bound him with thongs.**—The words have sometimes been rendered, "they stretched him forward for the straps"—*i.e.*, put him into the attitude which was required for the use of the scourge; and grammatically the words admit this sense. The Authorised version is, however, it is believed, right. The Greek word for "thong" is always used in the New Testament in connection with the idea of tying (Mark i. 7; Luke iii. 16; John i. 27). It appears here to be expressly distinguished from the "scourges" of verse 24, and in verse 29 we find that St. Paul had actually been bound. He was, *i.e.*, according to Roman custom, stripped to the waist, and tied with leathern thongs, as our Lord had been, to the column or whipping-post which was used within the fortress for this mode of torture. In both instances, it will be noted, the order for the punishment came from a Roman officer.

**Is it lawful for you to scourge a man that is a Roman . . .?**—Stress is laid on both points. It was unlawful to scourge a Roman citizen in any case; it was an aggravation so to torture him, as slaves were tortured, only as a means of inquiry. On the whole question of the rights of Roman citizens, and St. Paul's claim to those rights, see Note on chap. xvi. 37.

(26) **Take heed what thou doest.**—The better MSS. give the words simply as a question: "What art thou about to do?"

(27) **Art thou a Roman?**—The pronoun is emphatic: "*Thou*, the Jew speaking both Greek and Hebrew, art *thou* a citizen of Rome?" The combination of so many more or less discordant elements was so exceptional as to be almost incredible.

(28) **With a great sum obtained I this freedom.**—Better, *this citizenship*, the word expressing, not the transition from bondage to freedom, but from the position of an alien to that of a citizen. Probably the translators used the word in the sense in which we still speak of the "freedom" of a city. The chiliarch was himself, apparently, an alien by birth, and, as was customary at the time, had obtained the citizenship by the payment of a large bribe. As the admission of citizens now rested with the Emperor, as holding the office of Censor, the money had probably been paid to Narcissus, or some other of Claudius' favourite freedmen who carried on a traffic of this kind.

**I was free born.**—The Greek is somewhat more emphatic: *I am one even from birth.* This implies that St. Paul's father or grandfather had received the citizenship; how, we cannot tell. Many of the Jews who were taken to Rome by Pompeius as slaves first obtained their freedom and became *libertini*, and afterwards were admitted on the register as citizens. (See Note on chaps. vi. 9; xvi. 37.) The mention of kinsmen or friends at Rome (Rom. xvi. 7, 11), makes it probable, as has been said, that the Apostle's father may have been among them.

(29) **Which should have examined him.**—The verb had acquired the secondary sense (just as "putting to the question" did in mediæval administration of justice) of examining by torture.

**Because he had bound him.**—The words seem to refer to the second act of binding (verse 25) rather than the first (chap. xxi. 33). The chains fastened to the arms were thought of, as we see afterwards, when St. Paul's citizenship was an acknowledged fact (chap. xxvi. 29; Eph. iii. 1, iv. 1), as not incompatible with the respect due to a Roman citizen. The binding, as slaves were bound, with leathern thongs, was quite another matter.

(30) **Because he would have known the certainty . . .**—Better, *wishing to know the certain fact, namely, why he was accused.* Failing to get the information by the process of torturing the prisoner, the

CHAPTER XXIII.—(1) And Paul,
earnestly beholding the council, said,
Men *and* brethren, I have lived in all
good conscience before God until this
day. (2) And the high priest Ananias
commanded them that stood by him to
smite him on the mouth. (3) Then said
Paul unto him, God shall smite thee,
*thou* whited wall: for sittest thou to
judge me after the law, and commandest
me to be smitten contrary to the law?
(4) And they that stood by said, Revilest
thou God's high priest? (5) Then said
Paul, I wist not, brethren, that he was
the high priest: for it is written, Thou
shalt not speak evil of the ruler of thy
people.[a] (6) But when Paul perceived
that the one part were Sadducees, and
the other Pharisees, he cried out in the
council, Men *and* brethren, I am a

A.D. 60.

a Ex. 22. 28.

---

chiliarch now has recourse to the other alternative of getting a formal declaration from the Sanhedrin, as the chief representative body of the Jews. As yet, it will be remembered, they had taken no official action in the proceedings, and the chief captain had heard only the clamours of the crowd.

XXIII.

(1) **And Paul, earnestly beholding the council.**—We note once more the characteristic word for the eager anxious gaze with which St. Paul scanned the assembly. He had not seen it since he had stood there among Stephen's accusers, a quarter of a century ago. Many changes, of course, had come about in that interval, but some of the faces were probably the same; and at all events the general aspect of the *Gazith*, or Hall of Meeting, on the south side of the Temple, with its circular benches must have remained the same.

**I have lived in all good conscience . . .** —The verb for "I have lived" means literally, *I have used my citizenship*. It had ceased, however, to have this sharply defined meaning (see Note on the kindred substantive in Phil. iii. 20), and had come to be used of the whole course of a man's social conduct. Perhaps *My mode of life has been in all good conscience*, would be the nearest English equivalent. The reference to "conscience" may be noted as eminently characteristic of St. Paul. So we find him saying of himself that he had all his life served God with "a pure conscience" (2 Tim. i. 3); that a "good conscience" is the end of the commandment (1 Tim. i. 5); or, again, recognising the power of conscience even among the heathen (Rom. ii. 15). In the phrase "I know nothing by myself," *i.e.*, "I am conscious of no fault" (see Note on 1 Cor. iv. 4), we have a like reference to its authority. Comp. also chap. xxiv. 16; Rom. xiii. 5; 1 Cor. x. 25. And in all these passages he assigns to conscience its true functions with an exact precision. It is not an infallible guide and requires illumination, and therefore each man needs to pray for light, but it is never right to act against its dictates, and that which is objectively the better course is subjectively the worse, unless the man in his heart believes it to be the better.

(2) **The high priest Ananias.**—See Note on chap. xxii. 5. The son of Nebedæus was conspicuous for his cruelty and injustice, and had been sent to Rome as a prisoner to take his trial before Claudius (A.D. 52). He had been acquitted, or at least released, and had returned to Judæa. To him this assertion of a life so utterly unlike his own seemed almost like a personal insult. He fitted the cap, and raged with a brutal cruelty which reminds us of Jeffreys' treatment of Baxter.

(3) **God shall smite thee, thou whited wall.**—The phrase is interesting as showing either that our Lord, in likening the Pharisees to "whitened sepulchres" (see Notes on Matt. xxiii. 27; Luke xi. 44), had used a proverbial comparison, or else, as seems equally probable, that it had become proverbial among His disciples as having been so used by Him. The whole utterance must be regarded by St. Paul's own confession as the expression of a hasty indignation, recalled after a moment's reflection; but the words so spoken were actually a prophecy, fulfilled some years after by the death of Ananias by the hands of the *sicarii.* (Jos. *Wars*, ii. 17, §§ 2—9).

(5) **I wist not, brethren, that he was the high priest.**—These words admit of three different explanations:—(1) We may take them as stating that St. Paul, either from defective sight (see Notes on chaps. ix. 18; xiv. 9), or because the high priest was not sitting as president of the Sanhedrin, literally did not know who it was that had given the order, and thought it came from one of the subordinate members of the council. (2) That the words were a somewhat ironical protest against the authority of Ananias as having been improperly appointed. (3) That the "I wist not" stands for "I did not consider," and is an apologetic recantation of what had been uttered with a full knowledge that the words had been spoken by the high priest. Of these the first seems by far the most probable. The solemn sneer pointed by words from Scripture suggested by (2) is at variance with St. Paul's character; and (3) puts upon the words a greater strain than they will bear. It is obvious that St. Paul might well think that greater reverence was due to the high priest than to one filling an inferior position in the councils.

**Thou shalt not speak evil of the ruler of thy people.**—The passage (Ex. xxii. 28) is interesting as one of those in which the Hebrew word *Elohim*, commonly translated "God," is used of earthly rulers. St. Paul probably quoted it in Hebrew (see chap. xxii. 2), while St. Luke reproduces it from the LXX. version. It need hardly be said that to act on that law towards the rulers, not of "the people" only, but of the heathen; to see below all the corruptions of human society and the vices of princes, the scheme of a divine order; to recognise that "the powers that be are ordained of God," was throughout the ruling principle of the Apostle's conduct, and, for the most part, of that of the early Christians (Rom. xiii. 1—6; 1 Pet. ii. 13—17). Christianity was a great revolution, but they were not, politically or socially, revolutionists.

(6) **But when Paul perceived that the one part were Sadducees . . .**—We recognise the same parties in the council as there had been twenty-five years before. Whether they sat in groups on different sides, after the manner of the Government and Opposition benches in the House of Commons, or whether St. Paul recognised the faces of individual

Pharisee,[a] the son of a Pharisee: of the hope and resurrection of the dead I am called in question.[b] (7) And when he had so said, there arose a dissension between the Pharisees and the Sadducees: and the multitude was divided. (8) For the Sadducees say that there is no resurrection, neither angel, nor spirit:[c] but the Pharisees confess both. (9) And there arose a great cry: and the scribes *that were* of the Pharisees' part arose, and strove, saying, We find no evil in this man: but if a spirit or an angel hath spoken to him, let us not fight against God. (10) And when there arose a great dissension, the chief captain, fearing lest Paul should have been pulled in pieces of them, commanded the soldiers to go down, and to take him by force from among them, and to bring *him* into the castle. (11) And the night following the Lord stood by him, and said, Be of good cheer, Paul: for as thou hast testified of me in Jerusalem,

a Phil. 3. 5.

b ch. 24. 21.

c Matt. 22. 23.

---

teachers of each sect with whom he had formerly been acquainted, we have no *data* for deciding.

**I am a Pharisee, the son of a Pharisee.**—It is natural, from one point of view, to dwell chiefly on the tact of the Apostle. He seems to be acting, consciously or unconsciously, on the principle *divide et impera*, to win over to his side a party who would otherwise have been his enemies. With this there comes, it may be, a half-doubt whether the policy thus adopted was altogether truthful. Was St. Paul at that time really a Pharisee? Was he not, as following in his Master's footsteps, the sworn foe of Pharisaism? The answer to that question, which obviously ought to be answered and not suppressed, is that all parties have their good and bad sides, and that those whom the rank and file of a party most revile may be the most effective witnesses for the truths on which the existence of the party rests. The true leaders of the Pharisees had given a prominence to the doctrine of the Resurrection which it had never had before. They taught an ethical rather than a sacrificial religion. Many of them had been, like Nicodemus and Joseph of Arimathæa, secret disciples of our Lord. At this very time there were many avowed Pharisees among the members of the Christian Church (chap. xv. 5). St. Paul, therefore, could not be charged with any *suppressio veri* in calling himself a Pharisee. It did not involve even a tacit disclaimer of his faith in Christ. It was rather as though he said, "I am one with you in all that is truest in your creed. I invite you to listen and see whether what I now proclaim to you is not the crown and completion of all your hopes and yearnings. Is not the resurrection of Jesus the one thing needed for a proof of that hope of the resurrection of the dead of which you and your fathers have been witnesses?"

(7) **There arose a dissension between the Pharisees and the Sadducees.**—As a strategic act St. Paul's words had immediately the effect which he desired. They prevented the hasty unanimous vote which might otherwise have united the two parties, as they had been united in the case of Stephen, in the condemnation of the blasphemer. What follows shows that it was not without results as regards the higher aim.

(8) **The Sadducees say that there is no resurrection.**—On the general teaching of the Sadducees, see Note on Matt. xxii. 23. Their denial of the existence of angels and spirits seems at first inconsistent with the known facts that they acknowledged the divine authority of the Pentateuch, which contains so many narratives of angelophanies, and were more severe than others in their administration of the Law. The great body of the higher priestly class were, we know, mere Sadducees (chap. v. 17); and what, on their principles, was the meaning of the Temple ritual? They were, in fact, carried along by one of the great waves of thought which were then passing over the ancient world, and were Epicureans and Materialists without knowing it, just as the Pharisees were, even to the eye of a writer like Josephus (*Life*, c. 3), the counterpart of the Stoics. For them the "angels" of the Pentateuch were not distinct beings, but evanescent manifestations of the divine glory.

(9) **Let us not fight against God.**—If we could receive these words as part of the original text, they would be a singularly characteristic reproduction of the counsel of St. Paul's master (chap. v. 39). They are, however, wanting in many of the best MSS. and versions, and were apparently added to complete the sentence which St. Luke had left in the emphasis of its unfinished abruptness. Possibly its close was drowned in the tumultuous cries of the Sadducees. The line taken by the Pharisees is altogether that of Gamaliel. After twenty-five years they have not got further than the cautious policy of those who halt between two opinions. They give a verdict of "Not Guilty" as to the specific charges brought against St. Paul. They think it possible that he may have received a vision or revelation of some kind. In the word "spirit" they perhaps admit that the form of Jesus may have appeared to him as a spectre from the world of the dead.

(10) **The chief captain, fearing . . .**—We may well believe that the priest who had been rebuked as a "whited wall" would not willingly forego his revenge. He, and the Sadducees generally, would now be able to assume the position of being more devoted defenders of the Law and of the Temple than the Pharisees themselves. The fear of the chiliarch was naturally heightened by his knowledge that he was responsible for the life of a Roman citizen. In the barracks of the fortress, as before, probably in the self-same guard-room as that which had witnessed our Lord's sufferings at the hands of Pilate's soldiers, the prisoner would at least be in safety.

(11) **Be of good cheer, Paul.**—The day had been one of strange excitement, and must have roused many anxieties. Personal fear as to suffering or death he was, more than most men, free from; but was his work to be cut short? Was he to fall a victim to the malice of the Jews? Was the desire, which he had cherished for many years, to preach the gospel in the great capital of the empire (Rom. i. 13; xv. 23) to be frustrated? These questions pressed upon him in the wakeful night that followed the exhausting day; and, with a nature like St. Paul's, such anxieties could not but find expression in his prayers. To those prayers

so must thou bear witness also at Rome.
(12) And when it was day, certain of the
Jews banded together, and bound them-
selves under a curse,[1] saying that they
would neither eat nor drink till they
had killed Paul. (13) And they were
more than forty which had made this
conspiracy. (14) And they came to the
chief priests and elders, and said, We
have bound ourselves under a great
curse, that we will eat nothing until we
have slain Paul. (15) Now therefore ye
with the council signify to the chief
captain that he bring him down unto
you to morrow, as though ye would
enquire something more perfectly con-
cerning him: and we, or ever he come
near, are ready to kill him. (16) And
when Paul's sister's son heard of their
lying in wait, he went and entered into
the castle, and told Paul. (17) Then
Paul called one of the centurions unto
*him*, and said, Bring this young man
unto the chief captain: for he hath a
certain thing to tell him. (18) So he
took him, and brought *him* to the chief
captain, and said, Paul the prisoner
called me unto *him*, and prayed me to
bring this young man unto thee, who
hath something to say unto thee.
(19) Then the chief captain took him by
the hand, and went *with him* aside
privately, and asked *him*, What is that
thou hast to tell me? (20) And he said,
The Jews have agreed to desire thee
that thou wouldest bring down Paul to

1 Or, *with an oath of execration.*

---

the "vision and apocalypse of the Lord" of which we now read was manifestly the answer. To him, tossed on these waves and billows of the soul, as once before to the Twelve tossing on the troubled waters of the Sea of Galilee (Matt. xiv. 27), there came the words, full of comfort and of hope, "Be of good cheer." There might be delay and suffering, and a long trial of patience, but the end was certain; he was to reach the goal of Rome.

(12) **Certain of the Jews banded together . . .**—The casuistry of the more fanatic Jews led them to the conclusion that a blasphemer or apostate was an outlaw, and that, in the absence of any judicial condemnation, private persons might take on themselves the execution of the divine sentence. So, they may have argued, Mattathias, the founder of the Maccabean dynasty, had slain the apostate Jew who offered sacrifice at the altar at Modin (1 Macc. ii. 24); so ten Zealots of Jerusalem had conspired to assassinate Herod the Great because he had built an amphitheatre and held gladiatorial games in the Holy City (Jos. *Ant.* xii. 6, § 2; xv. 8, § 3). It is melancholy but instructive to remember how often the casuistry of Christian theologians has run in the same groove. In this respect the Jesuit teaching, absolving subjects from their allegiance to heretic rulers, and the practical issue of that teaching in the history of the Gunpowder Plot, and of the murders perpetrated by Clement and Ravaillac, present only too painful a parallel. Those who now thus acted were probably of the number of the Zealots, or Sicarii.

**Under a curse.**—Literally, *they placed themselves under an anathema.* This was the Jewish *kherem,* and the person or thing on which it fell was regarded as devoted to the wrath of God. (Comp. Notes on 1 Cor. xvi. 22; Gal. i. 8, 9.) So also in the Old Testament we find that Jericho and all that it contained was a *kherem,* or accursed thing, devoted to destruction (Josh. vii. 1).

(14) **They came to the chief priests and elders.**—It will be remembered that the high priest Ananias had already shown the rough brutality of his nature in his treatment of St. Paul, and was now, we can scarcely doubt, impelled by the spirit of revenge. It lies on the surface that those to whom the conspirators went were the Sadducean party in the Council, not the more moderate and cautious Pharisees.

**We have bound ourselves under a great curse.**—The Greek follows the Hebrew idiom in expressing intensity by the reduplication of the leading word. Literally, *We have anathematised ourselves with an anathema.*

(15) **Now therefore ye with the council . . .**—The plot was necessary, either (1) because the Sanhedrin had lost, under Roman rule, its power to inflict capital punishment (see Notes on chap. vii. 59; John xviii. 31); or (2) because, even if they possessed that power, the chiliarch was not likely to allow its exercise in the case of a Roman citizen; or (3) because the experience of the previous day had shown that the violent party were not likely to obtain a majority in the Council. The plot was, so far, skilfully laid. Even those who had said, "We find no evil in this man," could hardly oppose a proposal for a further investigation.

**We, or ever he come near, are ready to kill him.**—The first word stands in the Greek with a kind of ferocious emphasis "You may safely leave *us* to do our part."

(16) **Paul's sister's son.**—The passage is noteworthy as being the only reference to any of St. Paul's relations in the Acts. The fact that St. Paul lodged with Mnason, as far as it goes, suggests the probability that neither the sister nor the nephew resided permanently in Jerusalem. We do not even know whether they were members of the Christian society, though this may, perhaps, be inferred from the eagerness of the son to save his uncle from the danger which he knew to be imminent. We find that St. Paul had kinsmen at Rome (Rom. xvi. 7, 11). Was this nephew one of them who had come to Jerusalem to keep the feast, and heard the plot talked of (it is difficult to keep a secret in which forty men are sharers) in the caravanserai where he and other pilgrims lodged? We see, from the fact thus stated, that St. Paul, though in custody, was allowed to hold free communication with his friends. This, perhaps, accounts for the fulness with which the whole history is given. The writer of the Acts had come up with the Apostle, and was not likely to desert his friend if he could possibly gain access to him.

(18) **Paul the prisoner . . .**—We may well believe that at the time he little thought how long that name would be used of him, first by others and then by

morrow into the council, as though they
would enquire somewhat of him more
perfectly. (21) But do not thou yield
unto them: for there lie in wait for him
of them more than forty men, which
have bound themselves with an oath,
that they will neither eat nor drink till
they have killed him: and now are they
ready, looking for a promise from thee.
(22) So the chief captain *then* let the
young man depart, and charged *him*,
*See thou* tell no man that thou hast
shewed these things to me. (23) And he
called unto *him* two centurions, saying,
Make ready two hundred soldiers to go
to Cæsarea, and horsemen threescore
and ten, and spearmen two hundred, at
the third hour of the night; (24) and
provide *them* beasts, that they may set
Paul on, and bring *him* safe unto Felix
the governor. (25) And he wrote a letter
after this manner: (26) Claudius Lysias
unto the most excellent governor Felix
*sendeth* greeting. (27) This man was
taken of the Jews, and should have been
killed of them: then came I with an
army, and rescued him, having under-
stood that he was a Roman. (28) And
when I would have known the cause
wherefore they accused him, I brought
him forth into their council: (29) whom
I perceived to be accused of questions
of their law, but to have nothing laid to
his charge worthy of death or of bonds.
(30) And when it was told me how that
the Jews laid wait for the man, I sent
straightway to thee, and gave com-
mandment to his accusers also to say

---

himself, until it became as a title of honour in which he seemed to glory almost more than in that of Apostle. (Comp. Eph. iii. 1; iv. 1; Philem. verses 1, 9.)

(22) **So the chief captain.**—The chiliarch is obviously glad of the intelligence. His sympathies are clearly with St. Paul personally as against the high priest and his followers. He welcomes an opportunity for showing his zeal for the safe-keeping of a Roman citizen, and for making a statement of the whole transaction from his own point of view. With true official caution he treats the communication he has received as confidential, and takes his measures accordingly.

(23) **Spearmen two hundred . . .**—Literally, *right hand graspers.* The word was a strictly technical one, and seems to have been applied to those light-armed troops who carried a light spear or javelin in their right hands, as contrasted with those who carried the old spear, with a heavier shaft, which had to be wielded by both. They are coupled by the military writers of the Byzantine empire with archers and *peltastæ*, or light shield-bearers. The escort seems a large one for a single prisoner, but the tumults of the previous days, and the information just received as to the conspiracy, gave the chiliarch good reason to apprehend a formidable attack.

**At the third hour of the night.**—Assuming that St. Luke uses the Jewish reckoning, this would be about 9 or 10 p.m. It was evidently the object of the chiliarch to place the prisoner beyond the reach of an attack before daybreak. With this view, all, as well as the horsemen, were to be mounted.

(24) **Felix the governor.**—The career of the procurator so named is not without interest as an illustration of the manner in which the Roman empire was at this time governed. In the household of Antonia, the mother of the Emperor Claudius, there were two brothers, first slaves, then freed-men, Antonius Felix and Pallas. The latter became the chosen companion and favourite minister of the emperor, and through his influence Felix obtained the procuratorship of Judæa. There, in the terse epigrammatic language of Tacitus, he governed as one who thought, in his reliance on his brother's power, that he could commit any crime with impunity, and wielded "the power of a tyrant in the temper of a slave" (Tacit. *Ann.* xii. 54; *Hist.* v. 9). His career was infamous alike for lust and cruelty. Another historian, Suetonius (*Claud.* c. 28), describes him as the husband of three queens, whom he had married in succession:—(1) Drusilla, the daughter of Juba, King of Mauritania and Selene, the daughter of Antonius and Cleopatra. (2) Drusilla, the daughter of Agrippa I. and sister of Agrippa II. (See verse 24.) She had left her first husband, Azizus, King of Emesa, to marry Felix (Jos. *Ant.* xx. 7, § 1). Their son, also an Agrippa, died in an eruption of Vesuvius in A.D. 79 (Jos. *Ant.* xx. 7, § 2). The name of the third princess is unknown.

(26) **Claudius Lysias unto the most excellent governor Felix.**—The letter may have been sent unsealed, or a copy of it may have been given to St. Paul or St. Luke after his arrival. What we have obviously purports to be a verbal reproduction of it. We note (1) that the epithet "most excellent" is that which St. Luke uses of Theophilus, to whom he dedicates both the Gospel and the Acts (Luke i. 3; Acts i. 1), and (2) that the formal salutation, "greeting," is the same as that used in the letter of the Council of Jerusalem (chap. xv. 23) and in the Epistle of St. James (Jas. i. 1).

(27) **Then came I with an army.**—Better, *with my troops.* The chief captain ingeniously colours his statement so as to claim credit for having rescued a Roman citizen, though, as a matter of fact, he did not discover that he was a citizen until he was on the point of scourging him without a trial. That fact, of course, is passed over without a word.

(29) **Accused of questions of their law.**—The points which probably presented themselves to the chiliarch's mind as the result of his inquiries were—(1) that the prisoner was accused of transgressing the rules of the Temple; (2) that the question at issue seemed to be whether he had seen a teacher named Jesus risen from the dead; (3) whether that teacher was entitled to the name of Christ.

(30) **Farewell.**—The closing formula, like the opening one, agrees with that used in the letter of the Council of Jerusalem. The "commandment" given to the accusers to go down to Cæsarea was probably given in answer to the high priest's application for another inquiry before the Sanhedrin. We are not told what

before thee what *they had* against him.
Farewell. (31) Then the soldiers, as it
was commanded them, took Paul, and
brought *him* by night to Antipatris.
(32) On the morrow they left the horse-
men to go with him, and returned to
the castle: (33) who, when they came to
Cæsarea, and delivered the epistle to the
governor, presented Paul also before
him. (34) And when the governor had
read *the letter*, he asked of what province
he was. And when he understood that
*he was* of Cilicia; (35) I will hear thee,
said he, when thine accusers are also
come. And he commanded him to be
kept in Herod's judgment hall.

A.D. 60.

CHAPTER XXIV.—(1) And after five
days Ananias the high priest descended
with the elders, and *with* a certain orator
*named* Tertullus, who informed the
governor against Paul. (2) And when
he was called forth, Tertullus began to
accuse *him*, saying, Seeing that by thee
we enjoy great quietness, and that very
worthy deeds are done unto this nation
by thy providence, (3) we accept *it* always,
and in all places, most noble Felix, with

---

became of the vow of the forty conspirators. They doubtless considered themselves absolved from it as soon as they heard of the prisoner's removal, and their fast probably did not last longer than eighteen or twenty hours.

(31) **Antipatris.**—The town, built by Herod the Great, and named after his father, is represented by the modern *Kefr-Saba*, answering to the *Caphar Saba* of Josephus (*Ant.* xvi. 5, § 2). It was about forty-two miles from Jerusalem and twenty-six from Cæsarea. Traces of a Roman road have been discovered between it and Jerusalem, more direct by some miles than the better known route through the pass of Beth-horon. Having started probably at or about midnight, they would reach this town about six or seven A.M. They would then be practically beyond all danger of pursuit or attack, and the foot-soldiers therefore returned, as no longer needed, to their barracks in the Tower Antonia, leaving the horsemen to go on with him.

(34) **He asked of what province he was.**—The question was a natural one for a procurator of Judæa to ask as to any prisoner brought before him. (Comp. Pilate's question in Luke xxiii. 6.) It does not appear why Felix was ready to take cognisance of a matter which apparently, to judge by the precedent set by Pilate, belonged to the jurisdiction of another. Perhaps he had no motive for conciliating the favour of the governor of Cilicia, or thought that the nature of the accusation over-ruled the nationality of the accused.

(35) **I will hear thee.**—The Greek verb expresses the idea of a thorough hearing.

**He commanded him to be kept in Herod's judgment hall.**—The Greek word is *prætorium*, a word somewhat elastic in its application, and ranging from a palace to a barrack. "Judgment hall" hardly gives the meaning here. The building had probably been intended by Herod for use as a royal residence, and was now used by the Roman procurator for himself and his troops. The Apostle had there a second experience of the life of a prætorium. At Rome he does not appear to have been in the prætorium, though the circumstances of his imprisonment brought him into contact with the soldiers who were quartered there. (Comp. Notes on Matt. xxvii. 27; Phil. i. 13.)

XXIV.

(1) **After five days.**—The interval may have just allowed time for messengers to go from Cæsarea to Jerusalem, and for the priests to make their arrangements and engage their advocate. Possibly, however, the five days may start from St. Paul's departure from Jerusalem. and this agrees, on the whole, better with the reckoning of the twelve days from the Apostle's arrival there, in verse 11.

**Descended.**—Better, *came down*, in accordance with the usage of modern English.

**A certain orator named Tertullus.**—Men of this class were to be found in most of the provincial towns of the Roman empire, ready to hold a brief for plaintiff or defendant, and bringing to bear the power of their glib eloquence, as well as their knowledge of Roman laws, on the mind of the judge. There is not the slightest ground for supposing, as some have done, that the proceedings were conducted in Latin, and that while the chief priests were obliged to employ an advocate to speak in that language, St. Paul, who had never learnt it, was able to speak at once by a special inspiration. Proceedings before a procurator of Judæa and the provincials under him were almost of necessity, as in the case of our Lord and Pilate, in Greek. Had St. Paul spoken in Latin, St. Luke, who records when he spoke in Hebrew (chap. xxi. 40), and when in Greek (chap. xxi. 37), was not likely to have passed the fact over; nor is there any evidence, even on that improbable assumption, that St. Paul himself, who was, we know, a Roman citizen, had no previous knowledge of the language. The strained hypothesis breaks down at every point. The name of the orator may be noted as standing half-way between Tertius and Tertullianus.

**Who informed the governor against Paul.**—The word is a technical one, and implies something of the nature of a formal indictment.

(2) **Seeing that by thee we enjoy great quietness.**—The orator had, it would seem, learnt the trick of his class, and begins with propitiating the judge by flattery. The administration of Felix did not present much opening for panegyric, but he had at least taken strong measures to put down the gangs of *sicarii* and brigands by whom Palestine was infested (Jos. *Ant.* xx. 8, § 5; *Wars*, ii. 13, § 2), and Tertullus shows his skill in the emphasis which he lays on "quietness." By a somewhat interesting coincidence, Tacitus (*Ann.* xii. 54), after narrating the disturbances caused by a quarrel between Felix, backed by the Samaritans, and Ventidius Cumanus, who had been appointed as governor of Galilee, ends his statement by relating that Felix was supported by Quadratus, the president of Syria, "et *quies* provinciæ reddita."

**That very worthy deeds . . .**—Better, *reforms*, or *improvements*; the better MSS. giving a word which expresses this meaning, and the others one which

all thankfulness. (4) Notwithstanding,
that I be not further tedious unto thee,
I pray thee that thou wouldest hear us
of thy clemency a few words. (5) For
we have found this man *a* pestilent
*fellow*, and a mover of sedition among
all the Jews throughout the world, and
a ringleader of the sect of the Naza-
renes: (6) who also hath gone about to
profane the temple: whom we took, and
would have judged according to our
law. (7) But the chief captain Lysias
came *upon us*, and with great violence
took *him* away out of our hands, (8) com-
manding his accusers to come unto
thee: by examining of whom thyself
mayest take knowledge of all these
things, whereof we accuse him. (9) And
the Jews also assented, saying that
these things were so. (10) Then Paul,
after that the governor had beckoned
unto him to speak, answered, Forasmuch
as I know that thou hast been of many
years a judge unto this nation, I do the

---

implies it. This, as before, represents one aspect of the procurator's administration. On the other hand, within two years of this time, he was recalled from his province, accused by the Jews at Rome, and only escaped punishment by the intervention of his brother Pallas, then as high in favour with Nero as he had been with Claudius (Jos. *Ant.* xx. 8, § 10).

**By thy providence . . .**—The Greek word had at this time, like the English, a somewhat higher sense than "prudence" or "forethought." Men spoke then, as now, of the "providence" of God, and the tendency to clothe the emperors with quasi-divine attributes led to the appearance of this word—"the providence of Cæsar"—on their coins and on medals struck in their honour. Tertullus, after his manner, goes one step further, and extends the term to the procurator of Judæa.

(4) **That I be not further tedious . . .**—Better, *that I may not detain thee too long.* Here again we note the tact of the sycophant. He speaks as if obliged to restrain himself from the further panegyrics which his feelings would naturally prompt.

**Of thy clemency . . .**—The Greek word expresses the idea of equitable consideration. The epithets of the hired orator stand in striking contrast with the "righteousness, temperance, and judgment to come," of which the Apostle afterwards spoke to the same ruler.

(5) **We have found this man a pestilent fellow.**—The Greek gives the more emphatic substantive, *a pestilence, a plague.* The advocate passes from flattering the judge to invective against the defendant, and lays stress on the fact that he is charged with the very crimes which Felix prided himself on repressing. St. Paul, we may well believe, did not look like a *sicarius*, or brigand, but Tertullus could not have used stronger language had he been caught red-handed in the fact.

**A mover of sedition among all the Jews throughout the world.**—The "world" is, of course, here, as elsewhere, the Roman empire. (See Note on Luke ii. 1.) The language may simply be that of vague invective, but we may perhaps read between the lines some statements gathered, in preparing the case, from the Jews of Thessalonica (chap. xvii. 6) and Ephesus (chap. xxi. 28) who had come to keep the Feast of Pentecost at Jerusalem.

**A ringleader of the sect of the Nazarenes.**—This is the first appearance of the term of reproach as transferred from the Master to the disciples. (Comp. Note on John i. 46.) It has continued to be used by both Jews and Mahometans; and it has been stated (Smith's *Dict. of Bible*, Art. "Nazarene"), that during the Indian Mutiny of 1855 the Mahometan rebels relied on a supposed ancient prophecy that the *Nazarenes* would be expelled from the country after ruling for a hundred years.

(6) **Who also hath gone about to profane the temple.**—Better, *who even attempted to profane.* Here the case was clearly to be supported by the evidence of the Jews of Asia. The charge, we see, was modified from that in chap. xxi. 28. Then they had asserted that he had actually taken Trophimus within the sacred precincts. Now they were contented with accusing him of the attempt.

**Whom we took . . .**—The advocate throughout identifies himself, after the manner of his calling, with his clients; and in his hands the tumult in the Temple becomes a legal arrest by the officers of the Temple, which was to have been followed in due course by a legal trial, as for an offence against the law of Israel, before a religious tribunal.

The words from "according to our law" to "come unto thee" are omitted in many MSS., and may have been either the interpolation of a scribe, or a later addition from the hand of the writer. Assuming them to be part of the speech, they are an endeavour to turn the tables on Lysias by representing him as the real disturber of the peace. All was going on regularly till his uncalled-for intervention.

(8) **By examining of whom . . .**—Literally, *from whom thou shalt be able, by examining him thyself, to know thoroughly . . .* The English construction suggests that the "accusers" are the persons to be examined, but as the Greek relative is in the singular this cannot possibly be the meaning. Tertullus apparently suggests that the judge should interrogate the prisoner—perhaps, by using a technical term, with a well-understood significance, that he should examine him by scourging, or some other mode of torture. Strictly speaking, the "examination" of which Tertullus speaks was a preliminary inquiry, previous to the actual trial, to ascertain whether there were sufficient grounds for further proceedings. It will be observed that he keeps back the fact of St. Paul's being a Roman, and it does not follow that Tertullus knew that Lysias had informed Felix of it. It is possible, however, after all, if we admit the genuineness of verse 7, that the relative pronoun may refer to Lysias and not to the Apostle; and this agrees with the language of Felix in verse 22.

(10) **Forasmuch as I know . . .**—We note at once the difference between St. Paul's frank manliness and the servile flattery of the advocate. He is content to appeal to the experience of the "many years" (really about six, but this was more than the average duration of a procuratorship, and the words might, therefore, be used without exaggeration) during which he had

more cheerfully answer for myself:
(11) because that thou mayest under-
stand, that there are yet but twelve
days since I went up to Jerusalem for
to worship. (12) And they neither found
me in the temple disputing with any
man, neither raising up the people,
neither in the synagogues, nor in the
city: (13) neither can they prove the
things whereof they now accuse me.
(14) But this I confess unto thee, that
after the way which they call heresy, so
worship I the God of my fathers, be-
lieving all things which are written in
the law and in the prophets: (15) and
have hope toward God, which they them-
selves also allow, that there shall be a
resurrection of the dead, both of the
just and unjust. (16) And herein do I
exercise myself, to have always a con-
science void of offence toward God, and
*toward* men. (17) Now after many years
I came to bring alms to my nation, and
offerings. (18) Whereupon certain Jews
from Asia found me purified in the tem-
ple,[a] neither with multitude, nor with
tumult. (19) Who ought to have been
here before thee, and object, if they had
ought against me. (20) Or else let these
same *here* say, if they have found any

a ch 21. 27.

---

held office. Such a man was not likely to attach too much weight to the statements of Tertullus and Ananias. Felix, after having ruled for a short time with a divided authority (see Note on verse 2), had superseded Cumanus in A.D. 52 or 53.

**I do the more cheerfully answer for myself.**—The verb for "answer" is connected with our English "apology" in its older sense of "vindication" or "defence."

(11) **I went up to Jerusalem for to worship.**—This was, by implication, St. Paul's answer to the charge of the attempted profanation. One who had come to worship was not likely to be guilty of the crime alleged against him.

(12) **They neither found me in the temple . . .**—The answer traverses all parts of the indictment. He had not even entered into a discussion in the Temple. He had not even gathered a crowd around him in any part of the city. He challenges the accusers to bring any adequate evidence—*i.e.*, that of two or three witnesses, independent and agreeing—in proof of their charges.

(14) **After the way which they call heresy.**—Better, *which they call a sect.* The Greek noun is the same as in verse 5, and ought, therefore, to be translated by the same English word. As it is, the reader does not see that the "way" had been called a *heresy*. In using the term "the way," St. Paul adopts that which the disciples used of themselves (see Note on chap. ix. 2), and enters an implied protest against the use of any less respectful and more invidious epithet.

**So worship I the God of my fathers.**—Better, perhaps, *so serve I*, the word being different from that in verse 11, and often translated by "serve" elsewhere (chap. vii. 7; Heb. viii. 5). The "service" includes *worship*, but is wider in its range of meaning.

**Believing all things which are written . . .**—This was a denial of the second charge, of being a ringleader of a sect. His faith in all the authoritative standards of Judaism was as firm and full as that of any Pharisee. The question whether that belief did or did not lead to the conviction that Jesus of Nazareth was the Christ, was one of interpretation, with which Felix, at all events, had nothing to do, and which St. Paul, when making a formal *apologia* before a Roman ruler, declines to answer.

(15) **Which they themselves also allow . . .**—We have the same tact, perhaps also the same sympathy, as in chap. xxiii. 6. He identifies himself, on this point, not only with the Pharisees but with the great bulk of the Jewish people.

(16) **And herein do I exercise myself . . .**—The "herein" seems equivalent to "in this belief." Because he held that doctrine of a resurrection as a stern and solemn reality, the one law of his life was to keep his conscience clear from wilful sin. (See Note on chap. xxiii. 1.) The words must have been almost as bitter to Felix as to Ananias; but he has, at all events, the decency to listen in silence.

(17) **Now after many years.**—Four years had passed since the previous visit of chap. xviii. 22. The use of "many" in this instance may be noted as throwing light on verse 10.

**To bring alms to my nation, and offerings.**—The "alms" were, of course, the large sums of money which St. Paul had been collecting, since his last visit, for the disciples (possibly in part, also, for those who were not disciples) at Jerusalem. It is noticeable that this is the only mention in the Acts of that which occupies so prominent a place in the Epistles of this period. (See Rom. xv. 25; 1 Cor. xvi. 1—4; 2 Cor. viii. 1—4.) The manifestly undesigned coincidence between the Acts and the Epistles on this point has naturally often been dwelt on by writers on the evidences which each supplies to the other. The "offerings" were the sacrifices which the Apostle was about to offer on the completion of the Nazarite vow with which he had associated himself. There is, perhaps, a refined courtesy in St. Paul's use of the word "nation" (commonly used only of the heathen) instead of the more usual "people." He avoids the term which would have implied a certain assumption of superiority to the magistrate before whom he stood. (See Notes on Matt. xxv. 32; xxviii. 19.)

(18) **Whereupon certain Jews from Asia . . .**—Literally, *in which things*, or *wherein.* Many of the better MSS. give the relative pronoun in the feminine, as agreeing with "offerings," and indicating that he was, as it were, occupied with them at the very time when the Jews from Asia found him, not profaning the Temple, but purified with all the completeness which the Nazarite vow required.

(19) **Who ought to have been here before thee.**—The originators of the disturbance shrank from the consequences of their actions, and either remained at Jerusalem or else started on their homeward journey as soon as the Feast was over.

(20) **If they have found any evil doing in me . . .**—The better MSS. give, "what evil thing" (or,

evil doing in me, while I stood before
the council, (21) except it be for this one
voice, that I cried standing among them,
Touching the resurrection of the dead I
am called in question by you this day.[a]
(22) And when Felix heard these things,
having more perfect knowledge of *that*
way, he deferred them, and said, When
Lysias the chief captain shall come
down, I will know the uttermost of your
matter. (23) And he commanded a cen-
turion to keep Paul, and to let *him*
have liberty, and that he should forbid
none of his acquaintance to minister or
come unto him. (24) And after certain
days, when Felix came with his wife
Drusilla, which was a Jewess, he sent
for Paul, and heard him concerning
the faith in Christ. (25) And as he
reasoned of righteousness, temperance,

a ch. 23. 6.

*what wrong act*) "they found in me." This, from St. Paul's point of view, was the one instance in which any words of his had been even the occasion of an uproar, and in them he had but proclaimed a belief which he held in common with their best and wisest teachers. So far as the proceedings before the Council were concerned, he had not even entered on the question of the Messiahship or the resurrection of the Lord Jesus.

(22) **Having more perfect knowledge of that way . . .**—Better, *of the way.* (See Note on chap. ix. 2.) The comparative implies a reference to an average standard. Felix was too well-informed to yield any answer to the declamatory statements of Tertullus. He saw that the prisoner was no common *Sicarius*, or leader of sedition. He knew something as to the life of the sect of Nazarenes. That knowledge may well have been acquired either at Jerusalem, which the procurator would naturally visit at the great festivals and other occasions, or at Cæsarea, where, as we know, Philip the Evangelist had, some twenty-five years before, founded a Christian community, which included among its members Cornelius and other Roman soldiers, or even, we may add, in the imperial capital itself. His wife Drusilla, also, the daughter of Herod Agrippa I., may have contributed something to his knowledge.

**I will know the uttermost of your matter.**—Leaving the general attack on the "way" of the Nazarenes, or Christians, Felix proposes to inquire into the actual circumstances of the case brought before him. It is remarkable that this adjournment leads to an indefinite postponement. Possibly the accusers felt that they had fired their last shot in the speech of Tertullus, and, seeing that that had failed, thought that the judge had made up his mind against them, and withdrew from the prosecution. The detention of the prisoner under such circumstances was only too common an incident in the provincial administration of justice in the Roman empire, as it has since been in other corrupt or ill-governed states.

(23) **And he commanded a centurion to keep Paul.**—More accurately, *the centurion*—either the officer in whose custody he had been placed by Lysias, or the one who had the special charge of the prisoners waiting for trial. The favourable impression made on Felix is shown by the unusual leniency with which the prisoner was treated. The attribute of "clemency," on which the orator had complimented Felix, was not altogether dead, but it was shown to the accused and not to the accusers.

(24) **Felix came with his wife Drusilla.**—She was, as has been said (see Note on chap. xxiii. 26), the daughter of the first Herod Agrippa and the sister of the second. In her name, the diminutive of Drusus, and borne also by a sister of Caligula's, we trace the early connection of her father with that emperor. She was but six years of age at the time of her father's death. She had been married at an early age to Azizus, king of Emesa, who had become a proselyte, and accepted circumcision. Felix fell in love with her, and employed the services of a Jewish magician named Simon, whom some writers have identified with the sorcerer of Samaria (see Note on chap. viii. 9), to seduce her from her husband. By her marriage with Felix she had a son named Agrippa, who perished in an eruption of Vesuvius (Jos. *Ant.* xix. 7; xx. 5). It follows from the facts of her life that she could scarcely have been altogether unacquainted with the history of the new society. She must have known of the death of James and the imprisonment of Peter (chap. xii.). She may have connected her father's tragic end at Cæsarea with the part he had taken in persecuting the faith of which one of the chief preachers was now brought before her. It would seem, from her being with her husband at these interviews, that she was eager to learn more of "the faith in Christ." Felix, too, seems to have been willing at first to listen. This new development of his wife's religion, presenting, as it did, a higher aspect than that of the priests and elders of Jerusalem, was for him, at least, an object of more than common interest. The procurator and his wife were apparently in the first stage of an earnest inquiry which might have led to a conversion.

(25) **Righteousness, temperance, and judgment.**—The first word, like our English "justice," includes in Greek ethics the duties which man owes to man. "Temperance" answers to a term with a somewhat wider sense than that which now attaches to the English word, and implies the state in which a man exercises control over all the passions that minister to sensuality, while he yet falls short of a perfect harmony between Reason and Emotion (Aristot. *Eth. Nicom.* vii. 7—10). What has been said of Felix shows how faulty his character was in both these respects. The selection of the unwelcome topics shows how little St. Paul belonged to the class of those who "compassed sea and land to make a proselyte" (Matt. xxiii. 15). It would apparently have been easy to bring about this result with Felix and his wife, had the preacher been content to speak smooth things and prophecy deceits, to put the patch of a ceremonial Judaism on the old garment of a sensual life; but instead of this he presses home the truths which their state needed, and seeks to rouse conscience to something like activity. His own experience (Rom. vii. 7—23; Phil. iii. 7, 8), had taught him that, without this, neither doctrine nor ritual availed to deliver the soul from its bondage to evil, and bring it into the kingdom of God. But he does not confine himself, as a merely ethical teacher might have done, to abstract arguments on the beauty or the utility of "justice" and "temperance." Here, also, his own experience was his guide, and he sought to make the

and judgment to come, Felix trembled,
and answered, Go thy way for this time;
when I have a convenient season, I will
call for thee. (26) He hoped also that
money should have been given him of
Paul, that he might loose him: where-
fore he sent for him the oftener, and
communed with him. (27) But after A.D. 62.
two years Porcius Festus came into
Felix' room: and Felix, willing to shew
the Jews a pleasure, left Paul bound.

CHAPTER XXV. — (1) Now when A.D. 62
Festus was come into the province,
after three days he ascended from
Cæsarea to Jerusalem. (2) Then the
high priest and the chief of the Jews
informed him against Paul, and besought
him, (3) and desired favour against him,
that he would send for him to Jeru-
salem, laying wait in the way to kill
him. (4) But Festus answered, that
Paul should be kept at Cæsarea, and
that he himself would depart shortly
*thither.* (5) Let them therefore, said he,
which among you are able, go down
with *me*, and accuse this man, if there
be any wickedness in him. (6) And

---

guilty pair before whom he stood feel that the warnings of conscience were but the presage of a divine judgment which should render to every man according to his deeds. It will be noted that there is no mention here of the forgiveness of sins, nor of the life of fellowship with Christ. Those truths would have come, in due course, afterwards. As yet they would have been altogether premature. The method of St. Paul's preaching was like that of the Baptist, and of all true teachers.

**Felix trembled, and answered . . .**—Conscience, then, was not dead, but its voice was silenced by the will which would not listen. Felix treats St. Paul as Antipas had treated the Baptist (Mark vi. 20). He does not resent his plainness of speech; he shows a certain measure of respect for him, but he postpones acting "till a more convenient season," and so becomes the type of the millions whose spiritual life is ruined by a like procrastination. Nothing that we know of him gives us any ground for thinking that the "convenient season" ever came.

(26) **He hoped also that money should have been given him of Paul.**—The Greek gives "hoping also," as continuing the previous verse, and so places the fact in more immediate connection with the procurator's conduct. This greed of gain in the very act of administering justice was the root-evil of the weak and wicked character. He had caught at the word "alms" in verse 17. St. Paul, then, was not without resources. He had money himself, or he had wealthy friends; could not something be got out of one or both for the freedom which the prisoner would naturally desire?

**He sent for him the oftener, and communed with him.**—It is not difficult to represent to ourselves the character of these interviews, the suggestive hints—half-promises and half-threats—of the procurator, the steadfast refusal of the prisoner to purchase the freedom which he claimed as a right, his fruitless attempts to bring about a change for the better in his judge's character.

(27) **After two years Porcius Festus came into Felix' room.**—The English states the same fact as the Greek, but inverts the order. Literally, *When a period of two years was accomplished, Felix received Porcius Festus as his successor.* We can, of course, only conjecture how these years were spent. Some writers who maintain the Pauline authorship of the Epistle to the Hebrews have assigned it to this period: others have supposed that the Epistles to the Ephesians, Colossians, and Philemon were written from Cæsarea; but there is no adequate evidence in support of either hypothesis. It is better to confine ourselves to the thought of the Apostle's patient resignation, learning obedience by the things he suffered—of his intercourse with Philip, and other members of the Church of Cæsarea, as comforting and refreshing to him. We may venture, perhaps, to think of St. Luke, who had come with him to Jerusalem, and who sailed with him from Cæsarea, as not far off from him during his imprisonment. Attention has already been called (see *Introduction to St. Luke's Gospel and to the Acts*) to the probable use made by the Evangelist of these opportunities for collecting materials for his two histories.

The change of administration was caused by the complaints which the Jews brought against Felix, and which led Nero to recall him. The influence of his brother Pallas availed, however, to save him from any further punishment. His successor, Festus, who came to the province in A.D. 60, died in his second year of office. Josephus (*Wars*, ii. 14, § 1) speaks of him as suppressing the outrages of the robbers who infested the country, and maintaining the tranquillity of the province. Felix, with characteristic baseness, sought by his latest act to court the favour of the Jews, and left the Apostle in prison as a set-off against the many charges which were brought against him.

**Willing to shew the Jews a pleasure.**—Literally, *to deposit a favour.* The boon conferred was not to be without return. It was, so to speak, an investment in iniquity.

### XXV.

(1) **After three days he ascended . . .**—Better, *he went up.* (See Note on chap. xxiv. 1.)

(2) **Then the high priest and the chief of the Jews . . .**—Some of the best MSS. give the plural, "the chief priests." It is clear that they hoped to take advantage of the newness of Festus to his office. He was likely enough, they thought, to accept their statements and to yield to the pressure of those who had shown themselves powerful enough to bring about his predecessor's recall. And they have not forgotten their old tactics. Once again priests and scribes are ready to avail themselves of the weapon of the assassin. Possibly Festus had heard from Felix or Lysias, or others, of the former plot, and took care to be on his guard against this, and so the conspirators were again baffled.

(5) **Let them . . . which among you are able.**—The adjective is probably used, as in 1 Cor. i. 26, Rev. vi. 15, in the sense of "powerful," "chief," rather than as specifically referring to their being able to accuse the man of whom they had complained. What Festus

when he had tarried among them more than ten days,[1] he went down unto Cæsarea; and the next day sitting on the judgment seat commanded Paul to be brought. (7) And when he was come, the Jews which came down from Jerusalem stood round about, and laid many and grievous complaints against Paul, which they could not prove. (8) While he answered for himself, Neither against the law of the Jews, neither against the temple, nor yet against Cæsar, have I offended any thing at all. (9) But Festus, willing to do the Jews a pleasure, answered Paul, and said, Wilt thou go up to Jerusalem, and there be judged of these things before me? (10) Then said Paul, I stand at Cæsar's judgment seat, where I ought to be judged: to the Jews have I done no wrong, as thou very well knowest. (11) For if I be an offender, or have committed any thing worthy of death, I refuse not to die: but if there be none of these things whereof these accuse me, no man may deliver me unto them. I appeal unto Cæsar. (12) Then Festus, when he had conferred with the council, answered, Hast thou appealed unto Cæsar? unto Cæsar shalt thou go. (13) And after

[1] Or, as some copies read, *no more than eight or ten days.*

---

demanded was that the charges against St. Paul should be supported by the leaders and representatives of the people, and not by a hired rhetorician like Tertullus.

**If there be any wickedness in him.**—The better MSS. give simply, "if there be anything," practically, *i.e.*, anything worth inquiring into.

(7) **Many and grievous complaints.**—These were, we may well believe, of the same nature as those on which Tertullus had harangued. The line of St. Paul's defence indicates the three counts of the indictment. He had broken, it was alleged, the law of Israel, which Rome recognised as the religion of the province, and was therefore subject to the spiritual jurisdiction of the Sanhedrin; he had profaned the Temple; he was a disturber of the peace of the empire, and taught that there was another king than Nero.

(9) **Willing to do the Jews a pleasure.**—See Note on chap. xxiv. 27. The invitation was in itself plausible enough. It practically admitted that there was no evidence on the last head of the accusation of which he, as procurator, need take cognizance. It offered the prisoner a trial before his own national tribunal, with the presence of the procurator as a check upon violence and injustice. It is manifest from St. Paul's answer that this was practically what Festus meant. The proposed trial would, he says, not be before Cæsar's judgment seat, and he, for his part, preferred the secular to the ecclesiastical tribunal.

(10) **I stand at Cæsar's judgment seat.**—The Greek verb is given in a peculiar form, which carries with it the meaning of, *I am standing, and have stood all along* . . . He, as a Roman citizen, claimed the right to be tried by a Roman court, and finding that the procurator had shown a bias which left little hope of a fair trial, exercised the right which attached to his citizenship, and appealed to the highest court of all, that of the emperor himself. This interpretation seems every way more rational than that which paraphrases St. Paul's words thus: "I stand already in mind and purpose before the emperor's court, for God has shown me by a special revelation that I am to preach the gospel at Rome, and my trial there is accordingly part of the divinely ordered course of things which cannot be altered." Whatever influence the promise of chap. xxiii. 11 may have had on the Apostle's conduct, it is scarcely probable that he would have referred to it in this way in giving his reason for appealing to Cæsar.

**As thou very well knowest.**—We have, as in chap. xxiv. 22, the comparative of the adverb. Festus knew this *too well* to need any further proof. He had heard the random charges, and had seen the worthlessness of the evidence.

(11) **No man may deliver me unto them.**—Literally, *no man may give me up to them as a favour.* The words show that he saw through the simulated fairness of the procurator, and did not shrink from showing that he did so.

**I appeal unto Cæsar.**—The history of this right of appeal affords a singular illustration of the manner in which the republic had been transformed into a despotic monarchy. Theoretically the emperor was but the *imperator*, or commander-in-chief of the armies of the state, appointed by the senate, and acting under its direction. Consuls were still elected every year, and went through the shadowy functions of their office. Many of the provinces (see Notes on chaps. xiii. 7; xviii. 12), were directly under the control of the senate, and were accordingly governed by proconsuls. But Augustus had contrived to concentrate in himself all the powers that in the days of the republic had checked and balanced the exercise of individual authority. He was supreme pontiff, and as such regulated the religion of the state; permanent censor, and as such could give or recall the privileges of citizenship at his pleasure. The *Tribunicia potestas*, which had originally been conferred on the tribunes of the *plebs* so that they might protect members of their order who appealed to them against the injustice of patrician magistrates, was attached to his office. As such he became the final Court of Appeal from all subordinate tribunals, and so, by a subtle artifice, what had been intended as a safeguard to freedom became the instrument of a centralised tyranny. With this aspect of the matter St. Paul had, of course, nothing to do. It was enough for him that by this appeal he delivered himself from the injustice of a weak and temporising judge, and made his long-delayed journey to Rome a matter of moral certainty.

(12) **Hast thou appealed unto Cæsar? unto Cæsar shalt thou go.**—There is obviously something like a sneer in the procurator's acceptance of St. Paul's decision. He knew, it may be, better than the Apostle to what kind of judge the latter was appealing, what long delays there would be before the cause was heard, how little chance there was of a righteous judgment at last.

(13) **King Agrippa and Bernice.**—Each of the characters thus brought on the scene has a somewhat memorable history. (1) The former closes the line

certain days king Agrippa and Bernice
came unto Cæsarea to salute Festus.
(14) And when they had been there many
days, Festus declared Paul's cause unto
the king, saying, There is a certain man
left in bonds by Felix: (15) about whom,
when I was at Jerusalem, the chief
priests and the elders of the Jews
informed *me*, desiring *to have* judgment
against him. (16) To whom I answered,
It is not the manner of the Romans to
deliver any man to die, before that he
which is accused have the accusers face
to face, and have licence to answer for
himself concerning the crime laid against
him. (17) Therefore, when they were
come hither, without any delay on the
morrow I sat on the judgment seat, and
commanded the man to be brought
forth. (18) Against whom when the
accusers stood up, they brought none
accusation of such things as I supposed:
(19) but had certain questions against
him of their own superstition, and of
one Jesus, which was dead, whom Paul
affirmed to be alive. (20) And because I

---

of the Herodian house. He was the son of the Agrippa whose tragic end is related in chap. xii. 20—23, and was but seventeen years of age at the time of his father's death, in A.D. 44. He did not succeed to the kingdom of Judæa, which was placed under the government of a procurator; but on the death of his uncle Herod, the king of Chalcis, in A.D. 48, received the sovereignty of that region from Claudius, and with it the superintendence of the Temple and the nomination of the high priests. Four years later he received the tetrarchies that had been governed by his great-uncles Philip and Lysanias (Luke iii. 1), with the title of king. In A.D. 55 Nero increased his kingdom by adding some of the cities of Galilee (Jos. *Ant.* xix. 9, § 1; xx. 1, § 3; 8, § 5). He lived to see the destruction of Jerusalem, and died under Trajan (A.D. 100) at the age of seventy-three. (2) The history of Bernice, or Berenice (the name seems to have been a Macedonian form of Pherenice) reads like a horrible romance, or a page from the chronicles of the Borgias. She was the eldest daughter of Herod Agrippa I., and was married at an early age to her uncle the king of Chalcis. Alliances of this nature were common in the Herodian house, and the Herodias of the Gospels passed from an incestuous marriage to an incestuous adultery. (See Note on Matt. xiv. 1.) On his death Berenice remained for some years a widow, but dark rumours began to spread that her brother Agrippa, who had succeeded to the principality of Chalcis, and who gave her, as in the instance before us, something like queenly honours, was living with her in a yet darker form of incest, and was reproducing in Judæa the vices of which his father's friend, Caligula, had set so terrible an example (Sueton. *Calig.* c. 24). With a view to screening herself against these suspicions she persuaded Polemon, king of Cilicia, to take her as his queen, and to profess himself a convert to Judaism, as Azizus had done for her sister Drusilla (see Note on chap. xxiv. 24), and accept circumcision. The ill-omened marriage did not prosper. The queen's unbridled passions once more gained the mastery. She left her husband, and he got rid at once of her and her religion. Her powers of fascination, however, were still great, and she knew how to profit by them in the hour of her country's ruin. Vespasian was attracted by her queenly dignity, and yet more by the magnificence of her queenly gifts. His son Titus took his place in her long list of lovers. She came as his mistress to Rome, and it was said that he had promised her marriage. This, however, was more than even the senate of the empire could tolerate, and Titus was compelled by the pressure of public opinion to dismiss her, but his grief in doing so was matter of notoriety, "*Dimisit invitus invitam*" (Sueton. *Titus*, c. 7: Tacit. *Hist.* ii. 81; Jos. *Ant.* xx. 7, § 3). The whole story furnished Juvenal with a picture of depravity which stands almost as a pendent to that of Messalina (*Sat.* vi. 155—9).

**To salute Festus.**—This visit was probably, as the word indicates, of the nature of a formal recognition of the new procurator on his arrival in the province.

(14) **Festus declared Paul's cause unto the king.**—The matter seems to have come in, as it were, in the course of conversation. Festus probably thought that Agrippa, who knew all about the Jews and their religion, could throw some light on the peculiar position of his prisoner, who, though a Jew, and professing the utmost reverence for the Law and the Temple, was yet accused and denounced by his compatriots.

(16) **To whom I answered . . .**—The facts of the case are stated with fair accuracy, but there is a certain measure of ostentation in the way in which Festus speaks of "the manner of the Romans." It was, perhaps, natural that a procurator just entering on his term of office, should announce, as with a flourish of trumpets, that he at least was going to be rigidly impartial in his administration of justice. It is fair to state that, as far as we know, his conduct was not inconsistent with his profession.

**To deliver any man . . .**—The use of the same verb as that which St. Paul had used in verse 16 shows that the arrow shot at a venture had hit the mark. Festus is eager to repel the charge. The words "to die" (literally, *unto destruction*) are not found in the best MSS., and seem to have been added by way of explanation. The language of the procurator is strictly official. The accused and the accusers are to stand face to face, and the former is to have an *opening* for his *apologia*, or defence, in answer to the *indictment*.

(19) **Certain questions against him of their own superstition.**—The word is of the same import as that used by St. Paul in chap. xvii. 22 (where see Note), and the use here shows its comparatively neutral character. Festus was speaking to a Jewish king, and would not knowingly have used an offensive term. He falls back, accordingly, upon one which an outsider might use of any local religion which he did not himself accept. What follows shows that he looked on St. Paul as not merely affirming, with other Pharisees, the general doctrine of a resurrection, but as connecting it with the specific witness that Jesus had risen from the dead.

(20) **Because I doubted of such manner of questions.**—Better, *I, being perplexed as to the inquiry about these things.* The word implies more than

doubted of such manner of questions,[1] I asked *him* whether he would go to Jerusalem, and there be judged of these matters. (21) But when Paul had appealed to be reserved unto the hearing [2] of Augustus, I commanded him to be kept till I might send him to Cæsar. (22) Then Agrippa said unto Festus, I would also hear the man myself. To morrow, said he, thou shalt hear him. (23) And on the morrow, when Agrippa was come, and Bernice, with great pomp, and was entered into the place of hearing, with the chief captains, and principal men of the city, at Festus' commandment Paul was brought forth. (24) And Festus said, King Agrippa, and all men which are here present with us, ye see this man, about whom all the multitude of the Jews have dealt with me, both at Jerusalem, and *also* here, crying that he ought not to live any longer. (25) But when I found that he had committed nothing worthy of death, and that he himself hath appealed to Augustus, I have determined to send him. (26) Of whom I have no certain thing to write unto my lord. Wherefore I have brought him forth before you, and specially before thee, O king Agrippa, that, after examination had, I might have somewhat to write. (27) For it seemeth to me unreasonable to send a prisoner, and not withal to signify the crimes *laid* against him.

[1] Or, *I was doubtful how to enquire hereof.*

[2] Or, *judgment.*

A.D. 62.

CHAPTER XXVI.—(1) Then Agrippa said unto Paul, Thou art permitted to speak for thyself. Then Paul stretched forth the hand, and answered for himself: (2) I think myself happy, king Agrippa, because I shall answer for

---

mere doubt, and his perplexity is his justification for bringing the matter before a prince who, being a Jew, might be a better judge of the point at issue.

(21) **Unto the hearing of Augustus.**—The title is the Greek equivalent, as seen in the name Sebaste (= Augusta) given to Samaria, for the epithet which, like our "his majesty," had become a kind of official title of the Roman emperor. It had first been given by the Senate to Octavianus (Sueton. *Aug.* c. 7), and was adopted by his successors. As connected with "augur," it had originally, like *Sebastos*, a religious connotation. The month of August, dedicated to the first emperor as July had been dedicated to Julius, and the names of Augsburg and Sebastopol, are interesting as perpetuating its memory. The word for "hearing" (the same as our medical term *diagnosis*) corresponds rather to our *thorough investigation.*

(22) **I would also hear the man myself.**—Better, *I also was myself wishing*; the phrase implying that the wish was not now formed for the first time.

(23) **When Agrippa was come, and Bernice, with great pomp.**—The description may be noted as probably coming from one who had been an eye-witness of the stately parade, and was able to report with precision all that had passed. The fact was the first fulfilment of the promise that the Apostle was to bear His witness before "kings" as well as rulers (chap. ix. 15). The Greek word for "pomp" (more literally, *show*) is not found elsewhere in the New Testament. There is an almost tragic pathos in the thought, which must have been present to the mind of the historian, and perhaps, also, to that of others, that this display of the pride of state was exhibited in the very city that had witnessed the terrible chastisement of a like display in his father. The vice was inherited: the lesson had not been learnt.

**The chief captains.**—Literally, *chiliarchs*, as in chap. xxi. 31.

(24) **Have dealt with me.**—The general term, "held communication with me," is chosen to cover the proposal of verses 2, 3, as well as the direct accusation of verse 7. It would seem from the addition, "and also here," that the Jews of Cæsarea had also taken part in the proceedings, and that they too had been clamouring for a capital sentence.

(25) **When I found that he had committed nothing worthy of death.**—The words should be noted as an emphatic declaration on the part of Festus that the accusers had failed to sustain their indictment. But a procurator transmitting a case to the supreme court of the emperor was bound to send a formal report as to the matter out of which the appeal arose, and it was on this point that the "perplexed" ruler desired the advice and co-operation of Agrippa.

(26) **To write unto my lord.**—The Greek corresponds to the title of "Dominus," which, though declined by Augustus and Tiberius (Sueton. *Octav.* c. 53; *Tiber.* c. 27), had been assumed by Caligula and Nero. The first of the emperors had rejected it as an "accursed and ill-omened title," and had not allowed it to be used even by his children or grand-children, either seriously or in play. The name "Augustus," with its religious associations, was enough for him.

XXVI.

(1) **Then Paul stretched forth the hand.**—The characteristic attitude reminds us of chap. xxi. 40. Here it acquires a fresh pictorial vividness from the fact that St. Paul now stood before the court as a prisoner, with one arm, probably the left, chained to the soldier who kept guard over him. (Comp. verse 29.)

(2) **I think myself happy, king Agrippa.**—We note the characteristic union of frankness and courtesy. He will not flatter a prince whose character, he must have known, did not deserve praise, but he recognises that it was well for him that he stood before one who was not ignorant of the relations of Sadducees and Pharisees on the great question of the Resurrection, and of the expectations which both parties alike cherished as to the coming of a Messiah, and the belief, which some at least of the latter cherished (chaps. xv. 5; xxi. 20), that their hopes had been fulfilled in Christ.

**Because I shall answer.**—Strictly, *because I am about to make my defence*, or *apologia.*

myself this day before thee touching all
the things whereof I am accused of the
Jews: (3) especially *because I know* thee
to be expert in all customs and ques-
tions which are among the Jews: where-
fore I beseech thee to hear me patiently.
(4) My manner of life from my youth,
which was at the first among mine own
nation at Jerusalem, know all the Jews;
(5) which knew me from the beginning,
if they would testify, that after the
most straitest sect of our religion I lived
a Pharisee. (6) And now I stand and
am judged for the hope of the promise
made of God unto our fathers: (7) unto
which *promise* our twelve tribes, instantly
serving *God* day and night, hope to
come. For which hope's sake, king
Agrippa, I am accused of the Jews.
(8) Why should it be thought a thing
incredible with you, that God should
raise the dead? (9) I verily thought
with myself, that I ought to do many
things contrary to the name of Jesus of
Nazareth. (10) Which thing I also did
in Jerusalem:[a] and many of the saints
did I shut up in prison, having received
authority from the chief priests; and
when they were put to death, I gave my
voice against *them*. (11) And I punished

a ch. 8. 3.

---

(3) **Expert in all customs and questions.**—The former word is used in its half-technical sense, as including all the precepts of the Law of Moses. (See Notes on chaps. vi. 14; xxi. 21.)

(4) **My manner of life from my youth.**—The Apostle refers, of course, to the time when he first came up to Jerusalem to study the Law and the traditions at the feet of Gamaliel. (Comp. his account of the same period in Gal. i. 14; Phil. iii. 5, 6.)

**Know all the Jews.**—The noun seems to be used in its more limited meaning, as including chiefly, if not exclusively, the Jews of Judæa.

(5) **After the most straitest sect.**—Better, *most rigid*, or *most precise*. The Greek does not contain anything answering to the double superlative of the English. The word for "sect" is the same as that used in chap. xxiv. 5, and translated "heresy" in chap. xxiv. 14.

(6) **For the hope of the promise made of God.** The words include the whole expectation of a divine kingdom of which the Christ was to be the head, as well as the specific belief in a resurrection of the dead.

**Unto our fathers.**—Some of the better MSS. have simply, "to the fathers." The Received text is, perhaps, more in harmony with St. Paul's usual manner of identifying himself with those to whom he speaks. He will claim even Agrippa as of the stock of Abraham. (Comp. in this connection the anecdote as to Agrippa I. given in Note on chap. xii. 21.)

(7) **Our twelve tribes.**—The noun is strictly a neuter adjective: *our twelve-tribed nation*. It will be noted that St. Paul, like St. James (Jas. i. 1), assumes the twelve tribes to be all alike sharers in the same hope of Israel, and ignores the legend, so often repeated and revived, that the ten tribes of the northern kingdom of Israel, after they had been carried away by Salmaneser, had wandered far away, and were to be found, under some strange disguise, in far-off regions of the world. The earliest appearance of the fable is in the apocryphal 2 Esdras xiii. 40—46, where they are said to have gone to "a country where never mankind dwelt, that they might there keep the statutes which they never kept in their own land." The Apostle, on the contrary, represents the whole body of the twelve tribes as alike serving God (with the special service of worship) day and night, and speaks as accused because he had announced that the promise of God to their fathers had been fulfilled to them.

(8) **Why should it be thought a thing incredible . . ?**—Some MSS. give a punctuation which alters the structure of the sentence: *What! is it thought a thing incredible . . . ?* The appeal is made to Agrippa as accepting the sacred books of Israel, in which instances of a resurrection were recorded (1 Kings xvii. 17—23; 2 Kings iv. 18—37), and which ought to have hindered him from postulating the incredibility of the truth which St. Paul preached, and which included (1) the doctrine of a general resurrection, and (2) the fact that Christ had risen. The Greek use of the present tense, *that God raiseth the dead*, gives prominence to the first thought rather than the second. Agrippa, as probably allied, as the rest of his kindred had been, with the Sadducean high priests, not a few of whom he had himself nominated, was likely to reject both.

(9) **I verily thought with myself . . .**—The words have a tone of considerate sympathy and hope. He himself had been led from unbelief to faith; he will not despair of a like transition for others, even for Agrippa. (Comp. 1 Tim. i. 12—17.) On the relation of this account of the Apostle's conversion to previous narratives, see Notes on chap. ix. 1—20.

(10) **Many of the saints did I shut up in prison.**—The use of the term as applied to the believers in Christ (see Note on chap. ix. 13) is remarkable as an example of courage. In the presence of Agrippa, St. Paul does not shrink from speaking of them as the "holy ones" of God's people Israel—what the Chasidim, or "devout ones" (the "Assideans" of 1 Macc. vii. 13; 2 Macc. xiv. 6) had been in an earlier generation.

**When they were put to death.**—The history of the Acts records only one instance. Were there other martyrdoms besides that of Stephen, of which we know nothing? or does the Apostle speak in general terms of that single act? On the whole, the former seems the more probable alternative. He was breathing an atmosphere of "slaughter" (chap. ix. 1). On this view, the language of Heb. xii. 4, "ye have not yet resisted unto blood," must be referred to the sufferings of a later time, or, more probably, of a different region. In 1 Thess. ii. 15, Jas. v. 10, we have, perhaps, traces of widely extended sufferings.

**I gave my voice against them.**—Better, *gave my vote*. The words show that St. Paul, though a "young man" (see Note on chap. vii. 58), must have been a member either of the Sanhedrin itself or of some tribunal with delegated authority.

(11) **Compelled them to blaspheme.**—The verb is in the imperfect tense, which may express either continued or incomplete action. It does not follow,

them oft in every synagogue, and compelled *them* to blaspheme; and being exceedingly mad against them, I persecuted *them* even unto strange cities.
(12) Whereupon as I went to Damascus with authority and commission from the chief priests,[a] (13) at midday, O king, I saw in the way a light from heaven, above the brightness of the sun, shining round about me and them which journeyed with me. (14) And when we were all fallen to the earth, I heard a voice speaking unto me, and saying in the Hebrew tongue, Saul, Saul, why persecutest thou me? *it is* hard for thee to kick against the pricks. (15) And I said, Who art thou, Lord? And he said, I am Jesus whom thou persecutest. (16) But

a ch. 9. 2.

rise, and stand upon thy feet: for I have appeared unto thee for this purpose, to make thee a minister and a witness both of these things which thou hast seen, and of those things in the which I will appear unto thee; (17) delivering thee from the people, and *from* the Gentiles, unto whom now I send thee, (18) to open their eyes, *and* to turn *them* from darkness to light, and *from* the power of Satan unto God, that they may receive forgiveness of sins, and inheritance among them which are sanctified by faith that is in me. (19) Whereupon, O king Agrippa, I was not disobedient unto the heavenly vision: (20) but shewed first unto them of Damascus, and at Jerusalem, and throughout all the coasts

---

therefore, that any of the believers yielded to the pressure; and the words may be paraphrased, *I went on trying to compel them.*

**Being exceedingly mad against them.**—The words express, with a wonderful vividness, St. Paul's retrospective analysis of his former state. It was not only that he acted in ignorance (1 Tim. i. 13); he might plead also the temporary insanity of fanaticism.

**Even unto strange cities.**—The words show that the mission to Damascus was not a solitary instance, and the persecution may well have raged in the regions of Samaria and Galilee through which the Apostle passed. (See Note on chap. ix. 3.)

(12) **With authority and commission.**—The former word implies the general power delegated to him, the latter the specific work assigned to him, and for the execution of which he was responsible.

(14) **It is hard for thee to kick against the pricks.**—See Note on chap. ix. 5. Here there is no doubt as to the genuineness of the reading.

(16) **But rise, and stand upon thy feet.**—The report of the words heard by the Apostle is much fuller than in either chap. ix. 11 or chap. xxii. 10, and may fairly be thought of as embodying what followed on the actual words so recorded, the substance of "the visions and revelations of the Lord" (2 Cor. xii. 1), by which, in those days of blindness and ecstasy, the future of his life was marked out for him, and the gospel which he was to preach revealed in its fulness. In such states of consciousness, the man who is in contact with the supernatural life does not take note of the sequence of thoughts with the precision of a short-hand reporter.

**A minister and a witness.**—The first word is the same as that which the Apostle uses of himself in 1 Cor. iv. 1.

(17) **From the Gentiles, unto whom now I send thee.**—The distinct mission to the Gentiles seems, in chap xxii. 21, to be connected with the trance in the Temple, three years after the conversion. Gal. i. 15, 16, however, agrees with what we find here in connecting it with the very time when the Son of God was first "revealed in him." The distinction between "the people," *i.e.*, Israel, as emphatically entitled to that name, and "nations," the "Gentiles," should be noted. (Comp. Note on chap. iv. 25.) The relative "whom" probably refers to the latter of the two nouns rather than to both. In the Greek word for "send" (*apostello*), we find the warrant for St. Paul's claim to be considered an Apostle "not of men, neither by man," but by the direct personal call of the Lord Jesus (Gal. i. 1). The word that had been used of the Twelve (Matt. x. 16) was used also of him; and the pronoun "*I*" is specially emphasised.

(18) **From darkness to light.**—The words gain a fresh interest if we think of them as corresponding with the Apostle's own recovery from blindness. The imagery, though naturally common throughout Scripture, taking its place among the earliest and most widely received of the parables of the spiritual life, was specially characteristic of St. Paul. (Comp. Rom. xiii. 12; 2 Cor. iv. 6; Eph. v. 8—13; Col. i. 12; 1 Thess. v. 5.)

**Among them which are sanctified by faith that is in me.**—Better, *have been sanctified;* the Greek participle being in the perfect. The word, as always, expresses primarily the idea of a completed consecration rather than of a perfected holiness (Heb. ix. 13; x. 10; xiii. 12); but the one thought passes naturally into the other. The last six words may be connected grammatically either with "sanctified" or with "receive." On internal grounds the latter is, perhaps, the best construction. Faith, *i.e.*, is theoretically connected with "forgiveness of sins," as well as with the "inheritance," which implies sanctification.

(19) **I was not disobedient.**—Literally, *I did not become disobedient.* The language of the Apostle is significant in its bearing on the relations of God's grace and man's freedom. Even here, with the "vessel of election" (chap. ix. 15) "constrained" by the love of Christ (2 Cor. v. 14), there was the possibility of disobedience. There was an act of will in passing from the previous state of rebellion to that of obedience.

**The heavenly vision . . .**—The noun is used of Zachariah's vision in the Temple (Luke i. 22), and again by St. Paul, in reference to this and other like manifestations (2 Cor. xii. 1). It is distinctly a "vision," as contrasted with a "dream."

(20) **But shewed . . .**—The verb is in the tense which sums up a long-continued activity, and stands in the Greek after the enumeration of those to whom the

of Judæa, and *then* to the Gentiles, that
they should repent and turn to God, and
do works meet for repentance.
(21) For
these causes the Jews caught me in the
temple, and went about to kill *me.*
(22) Having therefore obtained help of
God, I continue unto this day, witnessing
both to small and great, saying none
other things than those which the
prophets and Moses did say should
come:
(23) that Christ should suffer, *and*
that he should be the first that should
rise from the dead, and should shew
light unto the people, and to the Gentiles.
(24) And as he thus spake for
himself, Festus said with a loud voice,

---

Apostle preached: *But first to them of Damascus . . . and to the Gentiles I went on showing . . .*

**Throughout all the coasts of Judæa, and then to the Gentiles.**—The words refer, in the first instance, to the visit after St. Paul's conversion (see Notes on chap. ix. 29; Gal. i. 17, 18); but the special mention of the Gentiles as following upon "the coasts (*i.e.*, the *region*) of Judæa," points to an evangelising activity in Cilicia prior to the commencement of his work at Antioch.

**That they should repent . . .**—The three stages of the spiritual life are accurately noted: (1) the repentance for past sins, which is more than a regret for their consequences; (2) the "turning to God," which implies faith in Him, as far as He is known, and therefore justification; (3) the doing works meet for repentance (we note the reproduction of the Baptist's phrase; see Note on Matt. iii. 8), which are the elements of a progressive sanctification.

(21) **For these causes . . .**—Better, perhaps, *on account of these things.* With this brief touch, avoiding any elaborate vindication of his own character, St. Paul indicates the real cause of the hostility of the Jews. The one unpardonable sin, in their eyes, was that he taught the Gentiles that they might claim every gift and grace which had once been looked on as the privilege and prerogative of Israel. The historical precedence of the Jew remained (see Notes on chap. xiii. 46; Rom. iii. 1, 2), but in all essential points they were placed on a footing of equality.

(22) **Having therefore obtained help of God.**—The Greek noun for "help" is not used elsewhere in the New Testament. It implies the kind of assistance which one friend or ally gives to another of inferior power. It is found in the Greek of Wisd. xiii. 18. Here the word seems used as being more intelligible to those who are outside the kingdom of God than the more spiritual, more theological, "grace" of which the Apostle habitually spoke.

**Witnessing both to small and great.**—The English version gives the right rendering of the best supported reading. Some MSS., however, have "witnessed to by small and great;" but this, besides the want of authority, and its involving an unusual construction, is at variance with the context. It was true that St. Paul's life was spent in bearing witness that Jesus was Christ. It was not true that he had a good report of all men. The words "small and *great*" were significant as spoken when he was standing before two men like Festus and Agrippa. The phrase may be noted as occurring in chap. viii. 10, and again in Rev. xi. 18; xiii. 16; xix. 5, 18; xx. 12.

**The prophets and Moses.**—The more natural order of "Moses and the prophets" (Luke xvi. 29, 31), and the order of the words in the Greek, *which the prophets said should come, and Moses,* suggests the thought that the sentence would have stopped naturally at "come," and that the name of Moses was added by an instantaneous after-thought to meet the case of those among the hearers who, like the Sadducees, placed the Pentateuch on a higher level of authority than the Prophets.

(23) **That Christ should suffer.**—Literally, *that the Christ was passible—i.e.,* capable of suffering. The great body of the Jews had fixed their thoughts only on the prophetic visions of the glories of the Messiah's kingdom. Even the disciples of Jesus were slow to receive any other thought than that of conquest and triumph. Peter's "Be it far from thee, Lord" (Matt. xvi. 22) expressed the horror with which the thought of a suffering Christ at first struck him. It was not till they were led, after the Crucifixion and the Resurrection, into our Lord's own school of prophetic interpretation (Luke xxiv. 25, 26, 44), and taught to recognise the under-current of types and prophecies that pointed to a righteous Sufferer, as well as to a righteous King, that they were able to receive the truth. So it was that a "Christ crucified" was still "to the Jews a stumbling-block" (1 Cor. i. 23). The speech at Antioch in Pisidia (chap. xiii. 27—35) may be noted as showing the stress which St. Paul laid on this point. The Greek has "if" in both clauses where the English has "that;" but our idiom scarcely admits of its being so translated.

**That he should be the first that should rise from the dead.**—More literally, *that He first by His resurrection from the dead* (strictly, *out of His resurrection) should show light.* It was through the Resurrection only that the hopes of Simeon were fulfilled (Luke ii. 32), and that light shone in on those who had been sitting as in the shadow of death. The "people" are, as almost always when the word is so used, God's people Israel, as distinguished from the heathen.

(24) **Festus said with a loud voice.**—The description may be noted as one of the touches of vividness indicating that the writer relates what he had actually heard. The Roman governor forgot the usual dignity of his office, and burst, apparently, into a loud laugh of scorn.

**Much learning doth make thee mad.**—The Greek gives a neuter plural: *Thy many writings are turning thee to madness.* The word was one which was used by the Jews for the collected body of their sacred writings and traditions, as in the "letters" of John vii. 15 and the "holy Scriptures" of 2 Tim. iii. 15. Festus had probably heard the Law and the Prophets of Israel so described, and knew that St. Paul had with him "books and parchments" (2 Tim. iv. 13), which he was continually studying. That one who had been crucified should rise from the dead and give light to the Gentiles seemed to him the very hallucination of insanity. So have men at all times thought of those who lived after a higher law than their own, whether their faith rested, as in St. Paul's case, on an outward objective fact, or, as in Wisd. v. 4, on a true faith in the Unseen.

Paul, thou art beside thyself; much
learning doth make thee mad. (25) But
he said, I am not mad, most noble
Festus; but speak forth the words of
truth and soberness. (26) For the king
knoweth of these things, before whom
also I speak freely: for I am persuaded
that none of these things are hidden
from him; for this thing was not done
in a corner. (27) King Agrippa, be-
lievest thou the prophets? I know that
thou believest. (28) Then Agrippa said
unto Paul, Almost thou persuadest me
to be a Christian. (29) And Paul said, I
would to God, that not only thou, but
also all that hear me this day, were
both almost, and altogether such as I
am, except these bonds. (30) And when

(25) **I am not mad, most noble Festus.**—There is something characteristic in the union of a calm protest with the courtesy which gives to rulers the honour which is their due. Comp. the use of the same word by Tertullus (chap. xxiv. 3). The painful experience of chap. xxiii. 3 had, we may well believe, taught the Apostle to control his natural impulses, and to keep watch over his lips, so that no unguarded utterance might escape from them.

**The words of truth and soberness.**—The latter word was one of the favourite terms of Greek ethical writers, as having a higher meaning than the "temperance" of chap. xxiv. 25, to express the perfect harmony of impulses and reason (Aristot. *Eth. Nicom.* iii. 10). Here it is contrasted with the "madness" of which Festus had spoken, looking, as he did, on the Apostle as an enthusiastic dreamer. There was doubtless a deep-lying enthusiasm in his character, but it was an enthusiasm which had its root not in madness, but in truth.

(26) **I am persuaded that none of these things are hidden from him.**—The appeal to Agrippa's knowledge is two-fold. He knew that Moses and the prophets had spoken of the great Prophet and Deliverer whom the Jews knew as the Christ. He knew also that for more than a quarter of a century there had been communities of Jews in Judæa and Galilee and Samaria (see Note on chap. ix. 31) resting on the belief that the Christ had come, and that He had suffered and risen from the dead. The congregations of those whom the Jews knew as Nazarenes were as far as possible from being an obscure sect lurking in holes and corners.

(27) **Believest thou the prophets?**—The appeal to Agrippa's knowledge was followed by the assumption of his accepting the ground on which St. Paul invited discussion. He might, of course, dispute St. Paul's interpretation of prophecy, but he could not, as a Jew, in the presence of other Jews, speak of the Law and the Prophets as Festus had spoken of St. Paul's "learning," and so the way might have been opened to that argument from prophecy which, when the Apostle was reasoning with his own countrymen, was (as in chaps. xiii. 16—41; xviii. 2, 3) his favourite method of producing conviction.

(28) **Almost thou persuadest me to be a Christian.**—At the cost of giving up a familiar and impressive text, it must be admitted that the Greek words cannot possibly bear the meaning which is thus put upon them. The words run literally, *In*, or *with, a little thou persuadest me*; and this may be completed by, "with little *speech*," "with little *labour*," or "little *evidence*." So in Eph. iii. 3 we have precisely the same phrase rendered "in few *words*." Agrippa's words, accordingly, are the expression, not of a half-belief, but of a cynical sneer. *Thou art trying to make a Christian of me with very few words, on very slender grounds*, would be the nearest paraphrase of his derisive answer to St. Paul's appeal. It was, it will be seen, evasive as well as derisive; he shrinks from a direct answer to the question that had been put to him. In his use of the Latin term "Christian" (see Note on chap. xi. 26) we may trace, perhaps, the effect of Roman associations. There certainly were Christian communities at Rome at this time (Rom. xvi. *passim*), and they would naturally be described there as they had been at Antioch. It may be noted that, of the prominent English versions, Wiclif gives "in a little thing," Tyndal and Cranmer "somewhat," the Rhemish "a little;" the Geneva agrees with the present version in "almost." The meaning "somewhat," or "a little," is a tenable one, but Eph. iii. 3, as already stated, is in favour of that given above. The phrase was, perhaps, in itself ambiguous, and St. Paul accepts in one sense what had been spoken in another.

(29) **I would to God that not only thou . . .**—It is clear that here also the English "almost" must be abandoned, and that we must take the words *in a little or in a great* (*measure*), or, *with little labour and with great*, as corresponding with what Agrippa had just said. Grammatically the words admit of three possible paraphrases, each of which has found advocates. We may suppose St. Paul to say—(1) "I would pray to God, not as you put it, lightly, but as fully as I can . . . . ;" or (2) "I would pray to God that, whether persuaded with little evidence or much . . . . ;" or (3) "I would pray to God that, both in a little measure and in a great . . . ." The first two of these explanations are open to the objection that they substitute a disjunctive alternative for the natural rendering of the two copulative conjunctions. The last has the advantage of so far taking the words in their natural construction; but, on the other hand, it takes the special phrase, "in a little," in a sense different from that in which we have seen reason to believe that Agrippa had used it. It is, however, perfectly conceivable that, for the purpose of emphasising the strong desire of his heart, St. Paul may have caught up the half-sarcastic phrase, and used it as with a new meaning.

The MSS. present two readings, *in a little and in a great*, and *in a little and in much*; but this scarcely affects the interpretation of the passage.

**Except these bonds.**—The words show, as has been pointed out in the Note on verse 29, that the prisoner was brought into court chained, after the Roman fashion, to the soldier or soldiers who kept guard over him. We cannot read the words without feeling their almost plaintive pathos. "Such as he"—pardoned, at peace with God and man, with a hope stretching beyond the grave, and an actual present participation in the powers of the eternal world—this is what he was desiring for them. If that could be effected, he would be content to remain in his bonds, and to leave them upon their thrones.

(30) **And when he had thus spoken, the king rose up . . .**—The act indicated, as far as it went,

he had thus spoken, the king rose up, and the governor, and Bernice, and they that sat with them:
(31) and when they were gone aside, they talked between themselves, saying, This man doeth nothing worthy of death or of bonds.
(32) Then said Agrippa unto Festus, This man might have been set at liberty, if he had not appealed unto Cæsar.

A.D. 62.

CHAPTER XXVII.—(1) And when it was determined that we should sail into Italy, they delivered Paul and certain other prisoners unto *one* named Julius, a centurion of Augustus' band.
(2) And entering into a ship of Adramyttium, we launched, meaning to sail by the coasts of Asia; *one* Aristarchus, a Macedonian of Thessolonica, being with

---

that the Apostle's words had made a favourable impression. This, they felt, was no common criminal, no fomenter of sedition. The question how he was to be dealt with was one that called for serious consideration; but the result showed that he was treated from this time forward with more respect and courtesy than before.

(31) **This man doeth nothing worthy of death or of bonds.**—St. Luke obviously dwells on the witness thus given to St. Paul's innocence. To us, knowing him as we do, the anxiety to record the witness seems superfluous; but it was not so when the historian wrote. The charge of what we should call lawless and revolutionary tendencies had been too often brought against the Apostle (chap. xvii. 6), and was too current against his followers, to make such a record one that he could willingly pass over.

(32) **This man might have been set at liberty . .**—The decision to which Agrippa came showed the wisdom of the line which St. Paul had taken. The matter could not be hushed up nor got rid of. The authorities could not now free themselves from responsibility for the safe custody of the prisoner, and, by releasing him, expose his life to the conspiracies of the Jews; and thus the Apostle at last gained that safe journey to the imperial city which had for many years been the great desire of his heart.

It is not without interest to note the subsequent relations between Festus and Agrippa, during the short government of the former, as showing a continuance of the same *entente cordiale* as that which we have seen in this chapter. Agrippa took up his abode at Jerusalem in the old palace of the Asmonean, or Maccabean, princes. It commanded a view of the city, and, from a banquet-hall which he had erected, he could look down upon the courts of the Temple and see the priests sacrificing even as he sat at meat. The Jews looked on this as a profanation, and built a wall which blocked up the view both from the king's palace and from the portico where the Roman soldiers used to stand on guard during the festivals. This was regarded by Festus as an insult, and he ordered the wall to be pulled down. The people of Jerusalem, however, obtained leave to send an embassy to Rome. They secured the support of Poppæa, already half a proselyte, after the fashion of the time among the women of the higher class at Rome, and, by the strange irony of history, the Temple of Jehovah was rescued from profanation by the concubine of Nero (Jos. *Ant.* xx. 8, § 11). Agrippa continued to display the taste for building which was the hereditary characteristic of his house. Cæsarea Philippi was enlarged and named Neronias, in honour of the emperor. A vast theatre was erected at Berytus (*Beyrout*) and adorned with statues. The Temple was at last finished, and the 18,000 workmen who were thus thrown out of work were employed in repaving the city with marble. The stateliness of the Temple ritual was enhanced by the permission which the king gave to the Levites of the choir, in spite of the remonstrance of the priests, that they should wear a linen ephod. Once again we note the irony of history. The king who thus had the glory of completing what the founder of his dynasty had begun, bringing both structure and ritual to a perfection never before attained, saw, within ten years, the capture of Jerusalem and the destruction of the Temple (Jos. *Ant.* xx. 8, § 7).

## XXVII.

(1) **Paul and certain other prisoners.**—The Greek for "other" implies that they were prisoners of a different class. It is probable, however, that they also had appealed to the emperor, as there would otherwise be no object in sending them to Rome.

**A centurion of Augustus' band.**—Literally, *of the Sebaste.* On the band or cohort as a subdivision of the Roman legion, see Note on chap. x. 1. Three different explanations have been given of the term translated "Augustus." (1) The cohort may have consisted of soldiers levied in Sebaste (= Augusta) or Samaria. Josephus mentions a squadron of Sebastene cavalry (*Ant.* xx. 6, § 1; xix. 9, § 2), and there may have been a corresponding band of foot-soldiers. (2) Nero about this time had formed a kind of body-guard, consisting of some 3,000 young men of the equestrian order, who accompanied him to games and spectacles, and whose chief business it was to applaud him in his speeches and recitations. To these he gave the name of *Augustani* (Tacit. *Ann.* xiv. 15; Sueton. *Nero*, c. 25), a term of which Sebastene would be the natural Greek equivalent. (3) A certain Julius Priscus appears in Tacit. *Hist.* ii. 92 as appointed by Vitellius to be one of the prefects of the Prætorian cohorts, which, as specially under the emperor's personal command, might naturally be called by his name; and he has been conjecturally identified with the centurion here named. Of these, (2) seems the most probable, but it is not absolutely incompatible with (3). On this assumption, as it is not said that the cohort itself was at Cæsarea, it is possible that he may have accompanied Festus as an escort to his province, and was now returning to Rome.

(2) **Entering into a ship of Adramyttium.**—Better, *embarking in.* Adramyttium was a town on the coast of Mysia, opposite Lesbos. It lay on the Roman road from Assos and Troas to Pergamus, Ephesus, and Miletus. It was a port of considerable importance, and the Gulf of *Adramyti* still retains its name. There would seem to have been but little direct intercourse by sea between Cæsarea and Rome, and the voyage had therefore to be made, now in one ship, now in another. Changes of this kind occurred, it will be remembered, in St. Paul's journey from Philippi to Cæsarea. Possibly it was at first intended that the prisoners should go to Adramyttium, cross to Greece, and then proceed by land. "Asia"

us. (3) And the next *day* we touched
at Sidon. And Julius courteously en-
treated Paul, and gave *him* liberty to go
unto his friends to refresh himself.
(4) And when we had launched from
thence, we sailed under Cyprus, because
the winds were contrary. (5) And when
we had sailed over the sea of Cilicia and
Pamphylia, we came to Myra, *a city* of
Lycia. (6) And there the centurion
found a ship of Alexandria sailing into
Italy; and he put us therein. (7) And
when we had sailed slowly many days,
and scarce were come over against
Cnidus, the wind not suffering us, we
sailed under Crete,[1] over against Sal-
mone; (8) and, hardly passing it, came
unto a place which is called The fair

1 Or, *Candy.*

---

is, of course, the proconsular province so called. Looking to the fact that the "fast," *i.e.*, the Day of Atonement (falling this year on Sept. 24th), was over when St. Paul reached Crete (verse 9), the date of embarkation may be fixed, with much probability, in the middle, or towards the end, of the previous August.

**One Aristarchus, a Macedonian of Thessalonica.**—It is reasonable to infer that Aristarchus, who had come with St. Paul to Jerusalem (chap. xx. 4), had remained in Palestine during the two years of the Apostle's imprisonment, and was now intending to return to his native city. The subsequent alteration of plan (verse 6), however, led to his accompanying him to Rome, and we find him there with St. Paul in Col. iv. 10, sharing his imprisonment.

(3) **And Julius courteously entreated.**—The English fairly expresses the meaning of the Greek adverb, which is literally *philanthropically.* We note, as in other instances, the favourable impression made by St. Paul's conduct on official persons who came in contact with him. (Comp. chaps. xviii. 14; xix. 31, 37.) The "friends" of St. Paul at Sidon were probably Christian disciples who had seen him when he passed through Phœnicia, as in chap. xv. 3, or in other journeys.

**To refresh himself.**—Literally, *to avail himself of their care.* The Greek word suggests the thought of a provision of personal comforts, clothing and the like, for the voyage. After two years' imprisonment we may well believe that such kindly care would be both necessary and acceptable.

(4) **We sailed under Cyprus . . .**—Had the wind been favourable, the ship would naturally have taken the direct course from Sidon to Mysia, leaving Cyprus on the right, as in his previous voyage St, Paul had sailed from Patara to Tyre (chap. xxi. 1). As it was, the wind probably being from the north-west, they made for the channel between Cyprus and Cilicia, and, sailing close under the lee of the long, projecting east coast of the island from Salamis to the promontory of Dinaretium (*Capo Andrea*), were thus sheltered.

(5) **We came to Myra, a city of Lycia.**—The city lay about two miles and a half from the mouth of the river Andriacus. It had been at one time the metropolis of Lycia, and the remains of a theatre and an aqueduct remain to attest its former stateliness.

(6) **A ship of Alexandria sailing into Italy.**—A glance at the map will show that the ship, which was probably one of those engaged in the corn-trade between Egypt and Rome, must have been driven out of its course. This may have been owing to the prevalence of the westerly winds already noticed. The Alexandrian traders, however, as a rule, avoided taking the course along the coast of Africa, through fear of the quicksands of the great Syrtis, and took that between Crete and the Peloponnesus. The presence of this merchant-ship led to a change of plan. It seemed an easier and n[illegible]xpeditious route to go straight to Rome, instead o[illegible]ding at Mysia, and then taking another ship to Macedonia in order to journey by land to the coast of the Adriatic. A local inscription describes Myra as a "horrea," or store-house of corn (Lewin's *St. Paul*, ii. p. 187), and the Alexandrian ship may therefore have gone thither to discharge part of its cargo. It has been assumed, but on insufficient grounds, that Aristarchus here parted from St. Paul, and went on in the Adramyttium ship.

(7) **When we had sailed slowly many days.**—The Etesian gales from the north-west, which prevail in the Archipelago during the latter part of July and the whole of August, were still blowing strongly, and during the "many days" (probably a fortnight or three weeks) the ship had not been able to traverse more than the 120 miles that lay between Myra and Cnidus. To reach the latter place they had probably coasted along Lycia, and gone through the straits between Rhodes and the mainland.

**And scarce were come over against Cnidus.**—Better, *with difficulty.* Cnidus was situated on a neck of land with a harbour on either side, and was apparently a naval station for the ships that were engaged in the corn-trade between Egypt and Greece (Thucyd. viii. 35). Here, as the coast trends away to the north, and they had no longer the shelter of the land, they were exposed to the full force of the Etesian winds. It was useless to attempt to make head against these, and their only alternative was to steer southward, so as to get, if possible, under the lee of the coast of Crete, the modern *Candia.* They succeeded in getting as far as Cape Salmone, the eastern point of the island, and finding here some shelter, went on their way westward under the lee of the coast. The name of Salmone appears in Strabo (x. 4) as Samonion, in Pliny (iv. 12) as Samnonium. In modern Greek it takes the form of *Capo Salomon.*

(8) **And, hardly passing it.**—The Greek adverb is the same as the "scarce" of verse 7, and should be translated as before, *with difficulty.*

**A place which is called The fair havens.**—It was obvious that the ship would have been again exposed, after passing Crete, or even its central promontory, Cape Matala, to the full force of the northwest gales. About two miles to the east of the promontory, however, and therefore sheltered by it, there was tolerably good anchorage, in a harbour known then and now as the Fair Havens (*Limeônes kaloi*).

**Nigh whereunto was the city of Lasea.**—The comparative obscurity of the place has led to a large variety of readings of the name—Lassœa, Alassa, Thalassa, and other forms. Pliny mentions a city in Crete named Lasos, but does not describe its position. The remains of buildings, columns, the walls and foundations of temples have been found about two hours' walk from the Fair Havens, under Cape Leonda, and are locally known as Lasea (Rev. G. Brown, in

havens; nigh whereunto was the city *of*
Lasea. (9) Now when much time was
spent, and when sailing was now dangerous, because the fast was now already
past, Paul admonished *them*, (10) and
said unto them, Sirs, I perceive that
this voyage will be with hurt and much
damage,[1] not only of the lading and
ship, but also of our lives. (11) Nevertheless the centurion believed the master
and the owner of the ship, more than
those things which were spoken by Paul.
(12) And because the haven was not
commodious to winter in, the more part
advised to depart thence also, if by any
means they might attain to Phenice,
*and there* to winter; *which is* an haven
of Crete, and lieth toward the south
west and north west. (13) And when the
south wind blew softly, supposing that
they had obtained *their* purpose, loosing
*thence*, they sailed close by Crete.

1 Or, *injury*.

---

Smith's *Voyage and Shipwreck of St. Paul,* Appendix 3).

(9) **Because the fast was now already past.**—The Fast was the Jewish Day of Atonement, which fell on the tenth of Tisri (in that year, September 24th), the seventh month of the Jewish ecclesiastical year. The sailing season with the Jews was reckoned from the Feast of Pentecost to that of Tabernacles, which fell five days after the Fast. Roman reckoning gave a somewhat wider range, *sc.*, from the sixth day of the Ides of March to the third of the Ides of November. The manner in which St. Luke names the Fast, and not the Feast of Tabernacles, makes it probable that the time to which we are now come was between September 24th and October 1st, when the Etesian winds, which are always of the nature of equinoctial gales, would naturally be most violent. Probably, also, the date may have been fixed on St. Luke's memory by St. Paul's observance of the Fast. He was not likely to leave so memorable a day unregarded, however little he might care to impose its observance upon others. To keep the Feast of Tabernacles on board the ship was, of course, impossible.

(10) **Sirs, I perceive that this voyage will be with hurt.**—The tone is clearly that of a man who speaks more from the foresight gained by observation than from a direct supernatural prediction. St. Paul had had, it will be remembered, the experience of three shipwrecks (2 Cor. xi. 25), and the Epistle to Titus, though probably written later, shows an acquaintance with Crete which suggests that he may have had some knowledge even of the very harbour in which they had found refuge. His advice accordingly was to remain where they were, in comparative safety, in spite of the drawbacks referred to in verse 12. The word for "hurt," which properly means "outrage," is used here in the sense of a violent calamity.

**Not only of the lading.**—The cargo probably consisted chiefly of corn coming from Alexandria to Rome. (Comp. Notes on verses 18 and 38.)

**But also of our lives.**—No lives were actually lost (verse 44), but the Apostle speaks now, as above, from the stand-point of reasonable opinion. When his counsel was rejected he gave himself to prayer, and to that prayer (verse 24) he attributes the preservation of his companions not less than his own.

(11) **Nevertheless the centurion believed the master.**—Better, *the pilot.* The word is the same as that translated "ship-master," in Rev. xviii. 17. The advice was, we may believe, determined by the fact that there was a better harbour but a few miles further on the coast. Could they not press on thither and be safe for the winter? It was natural that the centurion should trust to them as experts rather than to the enthusiastic Rabbi whom he had in charge as prisoner.

(12) **And because the haven was not commodious to winter in . . .**—The anchorage in the Fair Havens, while it gave immediate shelter from the north-west gales, was open to those from other points of the compass, and it was therefore decided by the majority (there would seem to have been something like a vote taken on the question) to press on and face the immediate risk for the sake of the more permanent advantages.

**Phenice . . . which is an haven of Crete, and lieth toward the south west and north west.**—The precise meaning of the phrase is that the harbour looked, as we say, *down* these winds, in the direction *to* which they blew—*i.e.*, that it faced the north-east and south-east, the words used being the names, not of points of the compass, but of the winds which blew from them. The harbour so described has been identified with the modern *Lutro*, on the east of the promontory of *Kavo Muros*, which looks eastward, and so corresponds to the interpretation just given of the words that describe it. The harbour is named by Ptolemy (iii. 17) as Phœnikous, and a city named Phœnix lay a few miles inland. It is still used as a harbour by Greek pirates, and was marked as such in the French admiralty charts of 1738; but, owing to the silting up of the sand, has become unsuitable for larger vessels. An inscription of the time of Nerva, of the nature of a votive tablet to Jupiter and Serapis, found near the spot, records the fact that it was erected by Epictetus, the *tabularius*, or agent, of the fleet to which the ship belonged, with the assistance of Dionysius of Alexandria, the pilot (the same word as that which St. Luke uses) of a ship which had as its sign (the same word as in chap. xxviii. 4) the Isopharia. It is a natural inference from this that the Alexandrian ship (we note the Egyptian element in the dedication to Serapis, and possibly in the connection of the sign with the Pharos, or lighthouse of Alexandria) had anchored, and possibly wintered, at Phœnice, and that the tablet was a thank-offering for its preservation. (See Alford, *Prolegomena.*)

(13) **And when the south wind blew softly.**—There was a change at once in the force and the direction of the wind. With a gentle and favourable breeze from the south, the pilot and the owner thought that all was smooth sailing, and the ship left the Fair Havens and made across the bay, a distance of thirty-four miles, for Phœnice. They still, however, hugged the coast, as afraid to venture too far into the open sea. The Greek adverb *asson*, which is rightly rendered "close" in the Authorised version, has been mistaken, in the Vulgate and some other versions, for the accusative case of *Assos*, as though it were a proper name, and the words have been variously rendered "when they had left Assos," or "when they had made

(14) But not long after there arose[1] against
it a tempestuous wind, called Euro-
clydon. (15) And when the ship was
caught, and could not bear up into the
wind, we let *her* drive. (16) And running
under a certain island which is called
Clauda, we had much work to come by
the boat: (17) which when they had
taken up, they used helps, undergirding
the ship; and, fearing lest they should

1 Or, *beat.*

---

for Assos," or "when they had come in sight of Assos." The island Assos, however, lay far to the north (see Note on chap. xx. 13), and there is no evidence of the existence of any town of that name in Crete. Of the English versions, Wiclif and the Rhemish follow the Vulgate, "when they had removed" (W.), or "parted" (Rh.), "from Assos"; Tyndale and Cranmer, following Luther, "they loosed unto Asson." The Geneva translation was the first to give the true meaning, and is following by the Authorised version. The tense of the Greek verb for "they sailed close," implies that they were in the act of doing this when the storm burst upon them, as in the next verse.

(14) **There arose against it . . .**—The Greek pronoun is in the feminine, and as the noun used for ship is, throughout the narrative, in the neuter, the difference of gender presents a difficulty. Grammatically the pronoun seems to refer to Crete, and if referred to it, the sentence admits of three possible constructions: (1) the wind *drove us against* Crete; or (2), *blew against* Crete; or (3), *drove down on us from* Crete. Of these, (1) and (2) are at variance with the facts of the case, as the gale blew the ship away from Crete to the south, while (3), which is as tenable grammatically, exactly agrees with them. Some translators (*e.g.*, Luther) have, however, referred the pronoun to the noun "purpose,"—"the wind blew against their purpose;" but this gives a less satisfactory sense. Of the English versions Wiclif gives "was against it," leaving the sense ambiguous. Tyndale and Cranmer follow Luther, "there arose against their purpose." The Geneva adopts the first of the above readings, "there arose against Candie," and is followed by the Rhemish, "drove against it."

**A tempestuous wind, called Euroclydon.**—The Greek adjective *typhonic* is perpetuated in the modern "typhoon," as applied to whirlwinds like that now described. The "vortex" of such a wind is indeed its distinguishing feature. The name *Euroclydon*, which is fairly represented by such a word as "wide-wave," or "broad-billow," is not found elsewhere, and, if the reading be genuine, must be looked on as a term which St. Luke reported as actually used by the sailors on board. Some of the best MSS., however, give the form *Euro-aquilo*, which, though a somewhat hybrid word unknown to Greek and Latin writers, fits in, as meaning north-east, or, more strictly, east by north, with all the phenomena described. The earlier English—Wiclif, Tyndale, Cranmer, and the Geneva—all give "north-east," while the Rhemish reproduces the term *Euro-aquilo*, without attempting to translate. A sudden change from south to north, with a great increase of violence, is a common phenomenon in the autumnal storms of the Mediterranean, and in this instance the blast would seem to have rushed down on the ship from the hills of Crete.

(15) **And could not bear up into the wind.**—The Greek verb is literally, "to look into the wind's eye," to *face* the wind. The figure is a sufficiently natural one in all languages; but it perhaps received additional vividness from the fact that a large eye was commonly painted on the prow of Greek vessels. The practice is still not unusual in Mediterranean boats. Assuming the direction of the gale to have been as stated in the previous Note, the ship was now driven in a south-west direction, scudding before the wind.

(16) **And running under a certain island which is called Clauda.**—Some MSS. give the various-reading Cauda, which agrees more closely with the form Gaudos found in Pliny and Suidas. This, in its turn, has passed into the modern *Gozzo.* The island lay about twenty-three miles to the south-west of Crete. Here they got under the lee of the shore, and availed themselves of the temporary shelter to prepare the ship more thoroughly than had been possible before to encounter the fury of the storm. The first step was to get the boat, which hitherto apparently had been towed through the waves, on board the ship. This, as St. Luke says, was a matter of much work (literally, *we were with difficulty able to get hold of the boat*), partly, we may believe, because it was not easy to keep the vessel with her head to the wind, and so avoid the motion which would have impeded the operation, partly, because the boat was probably full of water.

(17) **They used helps, undergirding the ship.**—The word "helps" answers to what we should call "precautions," or "remedial measures." The process described, technically known as "frapping," consisted in carrying a strong cable several times round the ship from stem to stern, so as to keep the planks from starting, and guard against the consequent leakage. The practice has always been a common one. Thucydides (i. 29) mentions the Corcyreans as having recourse to it. The Russian ships taken in the Tagus in 1808 were kept together in this manner in consequence of their age and unsound condition (Arnold, on *Thuc.* i. 29). We have probably an allusion to it in the lines of Horace (*Od.* i. 14).

> "Ac sine funibus,
> Vix durare carinæ,
> Possint imperiosius
> Æquor."
>
> ["And scarcely can our keels keep sound,
> E'en with the ropes that gird them round,
> Against the imperious wave."]

**Fearing lest they should fall into the quicksands.**—Literally, *the Syrtis.* There were two quicksands of this name, the Greater and the Lesser, on the north coast of Africa. The former lay just to the west of Cyrene, the latter further west, and nearer Carthage. St. Luke probably speaks of the Greater. These quicksands were the terror of all Mediterranean sailors (Jos. *Wars*, ii. 16, § 4). A fine description of them is given by the Evangelist's namesake, Lucan, in his *Pharsalia* (ix. 303—310):

> "When Nature gave the world its primal form,
> She left the Syrtes neither sea nor land.
> There neither sinks the shore and welcomes in
> The deep sea's waters, nor the coast can hold
> Its own against the waves, and none can track
> Their way within the uncertain region's bounds.
> The seas are marred with shallows, and the land
> Is broken by the billows, and the surge
> Beats on the shore loud-sounding. Nature leaves
> This spot accursed, and of use to none."

Comp. Milton's *Paradise Lost*, ii. 939:

> "Quenched in a boggy Syrtes, neither sea
> Nor good dry land."

fall into the quicksands, strake sail, and
so were driven. (18) And we being
exceedingly tossed with a tempest, the
next *day* they lightened the ship;
(19) and the third *day* we cast out with
our own hands the tackling of the ship.
(20) And when neither sun nor stars in
many days appeared, and no small
tempest lay on *us*, all hope that we
should be saved was then taken away.
(21) But after long abstinence Paul stood
forth in the midst of them, and said,
Sirs, ye should have hearkened unto me,
and not have loosed from Crete, and to
have gained this harm and loss. (22) And
now I exhort you to be of good cheer:
for there shall be no loss of *any man's*
life among you, but of the ship. (23) For
there stood by me this night the angel
of God, whose I am, and whom I serve,
(24) saying, Fear not, Paul; thou must
be brought before Cæsar: and, lo, God

---

The voyagers knew that the gale was bearing them in that direction, and did not dare to let the ship sail on full before the wind any longer.

**Strake sail.**—The English fails to give the sense of the original. Had they struck sail altogether the ship would simply have drifted in the very direction which they were anxious to avoid. Some sail was absolutely necessary to keep the ship steady. What is meant is that they "lowered the ship's gear," the spars and rigging, and especially, perhaps, the heavy yard and ropes which the ancient ships carried, and which would, in such a gale, make the ship top-heavy.

**And so were driven.**—Better, *thus—i.e.*, in this state, undergirded and with storm-sails set. They aimed at sailing as close as possible to the wind, making for the north-west, so as to avoid the Syrtes.

(18) **The next day they lightened the ship.**—St. Luke uses the technical term for throwing the bulk of the cargo overboard. They effected, in this way, the relief of the ship from the imminent danger of sinking. The act shows that, in spite of the undergirding, leakage was still going on. The cargo, as coming from Alexandria, probably consisted largely of corn; but see Note on verse 38.

(19) **We cast out with our own hands the tackling of the ship.**—The better MSS. give the third person plural, and not the first. If we accept the Received text, the fact that the passengers as well as the crew were pressed into the service indicates the urgency of the peril; but even with the other reading, the words describe the prompt spontaneous action caused by a strong sense of danger. The Greek word for "tackling" (better, perhaps, *furniture*) is wider in its range than the English, and includes the beds and personal luggage and movables of all kinds. Even these the sailors were ready to sacrifice for the chance of safety.

(20) **When neither sun nor stars in many days appeared.**—We have to remember that before the invention of the compass the sun and stars were the only guides of sailors who were out of sight of land. Now the sky was over-cast and this guidance failed. The ship was driving, but whither they knew not.

**All hope that we should be saved was then taken away.**—Better, *finally*, or *at last*. The failure of all hope implies some other cause of fear in addition to the mere violence of the gale, and the successive attempts to lighten the ship make it all but certain that she had sprung a leak, which their efforts were powerless to stop. The want of proper food (see next verse), and the exhaustion of protracted labour, naturally aggravated the feeling of despair.

(21) **After long abstinence . . .**—We find from verses 35—38 that there was still a fair supply of food on board, but, as they could not tell how long it might be before they reached a harbour, the crew, amounting, with passengers, to two hundred and seventy-six men (verse 37), had been naturally put on reduced rations, and the storm, and the sacrifice which they had been obliged to make of all their goods that could be spared probably made cooking all but impossible.

**Paul stood forth in the midst of them.**—The narrative implies that while others had burst into the wailing cries of despair, calling, we may believe, like the sailors in Jonah i. 5, "every man unto his god," the Apostle had passed his hours of darkness in silent communing with God, and now came forward with the assurance that his prayers were heard. With the feeling natural to one whose counsel had been slighted, he reminds them that if they had followed it they would have been spared the harm and loss (the same words are used in the Greek as in verse 10) to which they were now exposed. "Sirs," as in chaps. xiv. 15, xix. 25, answers to the Greek for "men."

**And to have gained this harm and loss.**—Better, *to have been spared*. The English reads as if the words were ironical, but parallel passages from other Greek writers show that to "gain" a harm and loss meant to escape them—to get, as it were, a profit out of them by avoiding them. This, St. Paul says, they would have done had they listened to his advice. The Geneva version adds an explanatory note, "that is, ye should have saved the losse by avoyding the danger." Tyndale and Cranmer take the words as the English reader, for the most part, takes them now, "and have brought unto us this harm and loss."

(22) **And now I exhort you to be of good cheer.**—Look and tone, we may well believe, helped the words. It was something in that scene of misery and dejection to see one man stand forward with a brave, calm confidence.

**For there shall be no loss of any man's life among you.**—The quiet courage of the speaker's tone must at once have struck the listeners, even before they heard the grounds on which that courage rested.

(23) **For there stood by me this night . . .**—With most others of the enthusiastic type of character, visions, real or supposed, of messengers from the unseen world have produced terror and agitation. With St. Paul they are the source of a calm strength and presence of mind which he is able, in his turn, to impress on others.

**Whose I am, and whom I serve.**—The service implied is that of worship rather than labour. The word and thought were eminently characteristic of St. Paul. (Comp. Rom. i. 9; 2 Tim. i. 3.)

(24) **Fear not, Paul.**—The words obviously came as an answer to the prayer, prompted by the fear, not of death or danger in itself, but lest the cherished purpose of his heart should be frustrated when it seemed on

hath given thee all them that sail with
thee. (25) Wherefore, sirs, be of good
cheer: for I believe God, that it shall
be even as it was told me. (26) How-
beit we must be cast upon a certain
island. (27) But when the fourteenth
night was come, as we were driven up
and down in Adria, about midnight the
shipmen deemed that they drew near to
some country; (28) and sounded, and
found *it* twenty fathoms: and when
they had gone a little further, they
sounded again, and found *it* fifteen
fathoms. (29) Then fearing lest we
should have fallen upon rocks, they cast
four anchors out of the stern, and
wished for the day. (30) And as the
shipmen were about to flee out of the
ship, when they had let down the boat
into the sea, under colour as though
they would have cast anchors out of the
foreship, (31) Paul said to the centurion
and to the soldiers, Except these abide
in the ship, ye cannot be saved.
(32) Then the soldiers cut off the ropes
of the boat, and let her fall off.

---

the very verge of attainment. The words that follow imply that his prayer had not been bounded by his own interests, but had included those who were sharing the danger with him. We are reminded, as by the parallelism of contrast, of the words in which Cæsar bade the pilot of his ship not to fear, but to commit himself to the wind, seing that he carried "Cæsar and the fortune of Cæsar" (Plutarch, *de Fortun. Rom.* p. 518).

(26) **We must be cast upon a certain island.**—This had clearly formed part of the special revelation that had been granted to the Apostle. It was more than a conjecture, and the "must" was emphasised as by a prophetic insight into the future.

(27) **When the fourteenth night was come.**—The time is apparently reckoned from their leaving the Fair Havens. (Comp. verses 18, 19, 33.)

**As we were driven up and down in Adria.**—The name was used as including more than the Gulf of Venice, to which the name Adriatic has been confined by more recent geographers. So Ptolemy (iii. 16) speaks of the Adria as washing the south coast of the Peloponnesus and the east coast of Sicily (iii. 4). So Josephus (*Life*, c. 3), narrating his shipwreck, just two years after St. Paul's, on his voyage from Judæa to Puteoli, states that he was picked up by another ship sailing from Cyrene to the same port, "in the middle of Adria." The intersection of the lines of the two vessels would fall, as a glance at the map will show, within the region now mentioned by St. Luke under the same name.

**The shipmen deemed that they drew near to some country.**—Literally, *they suspected*, or *surmised, that a certain country was approaching them.* The sound of breakers, probably the white lines of foam seen through the darkness, gave rise, we may believe, to this impression. The country which they were nearing could hardly be any other than the headland known as the Point of Koura, at the east extremity of St. Paul's Bay, in Malta. To the Apostle the sight and the sound would alike witness that his prediction was on the point of fulfilment.

(28) **Twenty fathoms.**—The Greek noun so rendered was defined as the length of the outstretched arms from hand to hand, including the chest. It was reckoned as equal to four cubits—*i.e.*, to about six feet—and is therefore fairly represented by our "fathom." The soundings here given agree with those that have actually been taken among the breakers off Cape Koura.

(29) **Fearing lest we should have fallen upon rocks.**—Literally, *upon rough places*—the reefs of rock which were indicated by the breakers and by the diminished depth of water.

**They cast four anchors out of the stern.**—It was no unusual thing for a ship to be furnished with this complement of anchors. So Cæsar describes his ships as being secured with four anchors each (*Bell. Civ.* i. 25). In ancient navigation, as in modern, the anchors were commonly cast from the bow. In the battles of the Nile and of Copenhagen, however, Nelson had his ships anchored at the stern, and the fact derives a peculiar interest from the statement that he had been reading Acts xxvii. on the morning of the engagement. The result of this operation was that the ship was no longer in motion, and would be found, when the morning came, with her head to the shore. The tension of hope and fear, the suspense which made men almost cry—

"And if our fate be death, give light, and let us die,"

is vividly brought before us in St. Luke's few words, "they were praying for the day."

(30) **And as the shipmen were about to flee . . .**—The hour of danger called out the natural instinct of self-preservation, to the exclusion of better feelings. It was easy for the sailors to urge that the ship needed anchors fore as well as aft, and, while pretending to be occupied about this, to lower the boat which they had before hoisted on deck (verse 16), and so effect their escape. The boat, it might appear, was necessary to their alleged purpose, as their ostensible aim was not merely to cast anchors from the bow, but to carry them out (as the word which St. Luke uses implies) to the full tether of the cable's length.

(31) **Except these abide in the ship . . .**—We need hardly embarrass ourselves with the question how far the divine promise was dependent on the contingency thus specified. Prompt vigour, and clear discernment of what was needed on the instant, spoke out in the Apostle's words. The assurance that had been graciously given was to be realised, not by the apathy of a blind fatalism, but by man's co-operation. It was obvious that landsmen like the soldiers and the prisoners would be quite unequal to the task of handling a large ship under such critical conditions, and the presence of the sailors was therefore, from a human point of view, essential to the safety of the others. The thoughtful vigilance of St. Paul, even in those hours of darkness, was eminently characteristic.

(32) **Then the soldiers cut off the ropes of the boat.**—The act had to be the work of an instant. The boat was already lowered, the sailors were on the point of leaping into it. We can picture their mortification on finding their selfish plan at once detected and

(33) And while the day was coming on,
Paul besought *them* all to take meat, say-
ing, This day is the fourteenth day that
ye have tarried and continued fasting,
having taken nothing. (34) Wherefore
I pray you to take *some* meat: for this
is for your health: for there shall not
an hair fall from the head of any of you.
(35) And when he had thus spoken, he
took bread, and gave thanks to God in
presence of them all: and when he had
broken *it*, he began to eat. (36) Then
were they all of good cheer, and they also
took *some* meat. (37) And we were in
all in the ship two hundred threescore
and sixteen souls. (38) And when they
had eaten enough, they lightened the
ship, and cast out the wheat into the
sea. (39) And when it was day, they
knew not the land: but they discovered
a certain creek with a shore, into the
which they were minded, if it were pos-
sible, to thrust in the ship. (40) And
when they had taken up the anchors,[1]

[1] *Or, cut the anchors, they left them in the sea, &c.*

---

frustrated. Even in this, however, there was a new element of danger. Men, under such circumstances, were likely to be sullen and unwilling workers.

(33) **Paul besought them all to take meat.**—Better, *to take food;* and so in the next verse. Once again the practical insight of the Apostle—yet more, perhaps, his kindly human sympathy—comes prominently forward. Soldiers and sailors needed something that would draw them together after the incident just narrated. All were liable at once to the despair and the irritability caused by exhaustion.

**That ye have tarried and continued fasting, having taken nothing.**—Better, *that ye continue on the look-out, without a meal, taking no extra food.* The English somewhat exaggerates the force of the Greek. The word for "fasting" is not that which is commonly used in the New Testament to express entire abstinence from food. It was physically impossible that the two hundred and seventy-six who were on board could have gone on for fourteen days without any food at all. Scanty rations had, we must believe, been doled out to those who came for them; but the tension of suspense was so great that they had not sat down to any regular meal. They had taken, as the last word implies, nothing beyond what was absolutely necessary to keep body and soul together. What they wanted physically was food, and morally, the sense of restored companionship; and to this St. Paul's advice led them.

(34) **This is for your health.**—Better, *safety*, or *preservation.* The Greek word is not that commonly translated "health," and the translators seem to have used it in the wider sense which it had in older English. So, for example, in Wiclif's version, "the knowledge of salvation" in Luke i. 77 appears as "the science of health." Wiclif has "health" here also, and is followed by all the chief English versions, except the Geneva, which has "safe-guard." What St. Paul means is that the preservation of his fellow-passengers depended on their keeping up their strength. The gracious assurance that followed was, as before, not independent of their co-operation.

(35) **He took bread, and gave thanks to God.**—The act was a common practice of devout Jews at the beginning and the end of meals. (See Note on Matt. xiv. 9.) To the heathen soldiers and sailors it was probably altogether new, and at such a moment must have been singularly impressive. The act of "breaking bread," though in itself not more than the natural incident of such a meal, must at least have reminded the few Christians who were his companions of the more solemn "breaking of bread" with which they were familiar. (See Note on chap. ii. 46.) For them the meal, if not strictly eucharistic, in the liturgical sense of that term, would be at least as an *Agapè*, or feast of charity.

(36) **Then were they all of good cheer.**—The words present a striking contrast to the despair of verse 20. The hearty cheerfulness (is it too colloquial a phrase to say the "pluck"?) of the Apostle had communicated itself, as by a kind of electric sympathy, to his companions. They looked to him as their friend and leader, and had spirits to eat once more.

(37) **And we were in all in the ship . . .**—The number is given here, either as a fact that had been omitted before, and was not without its interest, or probably because then for the first time, when they were all gathered at their meal, the writer had taken the pains to count them. A man does not commonly count the number of passengers on board a ship until there is some special occasion, and here it comes naturally as explaining the "all" of the previous verse. It was, we may well imagine, a striking spectacle to see the two hundred and seventy-six all under the influence of one brave and faithful spirit.

(38) **And when they had eaten enough . . .**—More accurately, *when they were filled with food.* The words describe a full and hearty meal. The first effect of this was seen in renewed activity for work. In spite of all that had been done before (verses 18, 19), the ship still needed to be lightened. The tense implies a process of some continuance. The "wheat" which they now cast out may have been part of the cargo which had been reserved by way of provisions. As it was clear that they could no longer continue in the ship, this was no longer required, and the one essential point was to keep her floating till they reached the shore.

(39) **They knew not the land.**—It was, of course, probable enough that some at least of the sailors had been at Malta before; but St. Paul's Bay, which we assume to be the point they had now reached, was remote from the Great Harbour, now that of *Valetta*, into which ships commonly sailed, and may therefore well have remained unknown to them.

**A certain creek with a shore.**—Better, *having a beach*, the English word failing to describe why it was that the creek attracted them. The earlier versions have "bank." In Homer and other Greek writers the word is commonly used for a flat, sandy beach.

**To thrust in the ship.**—The word was a quasi-technical one, answering to our "to run the ship aground."

(40) **And when they had taken up the anchors.**—Better, *And when they had cleared away* (or, *cut off*) *the anchors, they let them go into the sea.* It is obvious that nothing would have been gained at such a juncture by encumbering the ship, which they

they committed *themselves* unto the sea, and loosed the rudder bands, and hoised up the mainsail to the wind, and made toward shore. (41) And falling into a place where two seas met, they ran the ship aground; and the forepart stuck fast, and remained unmoveable, but the hinder part was broken with the violence of the waves. (42) And the soldiers' counsel was to kill the prisoners, lest any of them should swim out, and escape. (43) But the centurion, willing to save Paul, kept them from *their* purpose; and commanded that they which could swim should cast *themselves* first *into the sea*, and get to land: (44) and the rest, some on boards, and some on *broken pieces* of the ship. And so it came to pass, that they escaped all safe to land.

A.D. 62.

CHAPTER XXVIII.—(1) And when

---

were anxious to lighten as much as possible, with the weight of the four anchors. The meaning given above is accordingly more in harmony with the facts of the case as well as with the Greek, which does not warrant the insertion of the pronoun in "they committed *themselves.*"

**Loosed the rudder bands.**—This was the necessary sequel to the previous operation. While the ship was anchored the two large paddle-like rudders with which ancient ships were furnished, were lifted up out of the water and lashed with ropes to the ship's side. When the ship was got under way again, and the rudders were wanted, the bands had to be loosed, and the rudders fell into the water.

**And hoised up the mainsail to the wind.**—The Greek term so rendered (*artemôn*) is still found in Italian (*artimone*) and French for the largest sail of a ship. In the structure of ancient ships, however, this was the foresail, not, as with us, the mainsail. The word for wind is strictly the participle, *the* (*breeze*) *that was blowing*. The change of word seems to imply that there was a lull in the fury of the gale.

**Made toward shore.**—More accurately, *were making for the beach*, that which had been described in verse 39.

(41) **And falling into a place where two seas met.**—Better, *But falling*, as in contrast with the attempt described in the previous verse. At the west end of St. Paul's Bay lies the island of Salmonetta. From their place of anchorage the crew could not have seen that it was an island, and in trying to run the ship on the beach they grounded on a mud-bank between the small island and the coast. The waves swept round the island and met on the bank, and the position of the ship was accordingly one of extreme danger, the prow imbedded in the mud, the stern exposed to the billows.

**The hinder part was broken.**—Better, *was being broken up*, the tense expressing continuous action.

(42) **And the soldiers' counsel was to kill the prisoners.**—The vigour of Roman law, which inflicted capital punishment on those who were in charge of prisoners and suffered them to escape (see Notes on chaps. xii. 19; xvi. 27), must be remembered, as explaining the apparently wanton cruelty of the proposal. In putting the prisoners to death the soldiers saw the only chance of escaping death themselves.

(43) **But the centurion, willing to save Paul.**—Better, *wishing*, as expressing a stronger desire than the sense of mere acquiescence which has come to be attached to "willing." The Apostle had, we have seen, from the outset gained the respect of the centurion Julius (verse 1). The courage and thoughtfulness of the night that had just passed was likely to have turned that respect into something like admiration.

**Commanded that they which could swim . . .**—The order which was observed shows that the centurion kept his head clear, and had the power to enforce discipline. It was not the rush of a *sauve qui peut.* The swimmers were to plunge in first so as to get to the beach and be in readiness to help their comrades. St. Paul, who had thrice been shipwrecked, and had once passed a night and day in the open sea (2 Cor. xi. 25), was probably among the former group, and the order itself may well have been suggested by him.

(44) **And the rest, some on boards . . .**—These were probably planks from the decks. The words "broken pieces" are not in the Greek, but fairly express its force. Literally, *on some of the things from the ship.* These might, it is obvious, have been pieces of timber from the bulwarks, loose spars, tables, stools, and the like.

XXVIII.

(1) **Then they knew that the island was called Melita.**—There is no ground for questioning the current belief that this was the modern *Malta.* It was the only island known as *Melita* by the Greeks and Romans. The gale, which had been blowing for fourteen days since the ship left Crete, would drive her in that direction. The local features of St. Paul's Bay agree closely, as has been seen, with the narrative in the Acts. There has from a very early date been a local tradition in favour of the belief. The Bay bears St. Paul's name. A cave is pointed out as having given him shelter. There has, however, been a rival claimant. In the Gulf of Venice, off the coast of Illyria, there is a small island, Meleta (now *Meleda*), which has been identified by some writers with the scene of St. Paul's shipwreck. The view is first mentioned by Constantine Porphyrogenitus, a Greek writer of the tenth century, and was revived in the last century by Padre Georgi, an ecclesiastic of the island. There is, however, not a shadow of evidence in its favour, beyond the similarity (not identity) of name, and the mention of Adria in chap. xxvii. 27. It has been shown, however, that that term was used with far too wide a range to be decisive on such a question; and against the view there are the facts (1) that it would almost have required a miracle to get the ship, with a north-east gale blowing strongly, up to the Illyrian coast of the Gulf of Venice; (2) that a ship would not naturally have wintered on that coast on its way from Alexandria to Puteoli (verse 11); (3) that there has been no local tradition in its favour, as at Malta. The island of Malta was originally a Phœnician colony. It came under the power of Carthage in B.C. 402, and was ceded to Rome in B.C. 242. Its temple, dedicated to Juno, was rich enough

they were escaped, then they knew that
the island was called Melita. (2) And
the barbarous people shewed us no little
kindness: for they kindled a fire, and
received us every one, because of the
present rain, and because of the cold.
(3) And when Paul had gathered a
bundle of sticks, and laid *them* on the
fire, there came a viper out of the heat,
and fastened on his hand. (4) And
when the barbarians saw the *venomous*
beast hang on his hand, they said among
themselves, No doubt this man is a
murderer, whom, though he hath escaped the sea, yet vengeance suffereth
not to live. (5) And he shook off the
beast into the fire, and felt no harm.
(6) Howbeit they looked when he should
have swollen, or fallen down dead suddenly: but after they had looked a great
while, and saw no harm come to him,
they changed their minds, and said that
he was a god. (7) In the same quarters
were possessions of the chief man of the
island, whose name was Publius; who
received us, and lodged us three days

---

to be an object of plunder to Verres, the Prætor of Sicily (Cic. *In Verr.* iv. 46).

(2) **The barbarous people . . .**—It has been urged in favour of *Meleda* that this description is more applicable to the people of that island than to those of Malta, whom Diodorus Siculus (v. 12) describes as "very rich, practising many trades, manufacturing fine clothes, and dwelling in large and splendid houses." It is obvious, however, that St. Luke uses the term, as St. Paul does (Rom. i. 14; 1 Cor. xiv. 11), and as was then common, as applicable to all races that did not speak Greek, and that such a term as "Scythian" (Col. iii. 11) was used to describe what we should call "barbarians" or "savages." For him "barbarian" was like the term "native," which our travellers apply indiscriminately to Fiji Islanders and Cingalese. The language of Malta at the time, if not absolutely Punic, was probably a very bastard Greek. The inscriptions which have been found in the island are, as was natural, in the Greek and Latin, which were used as official languages by their rulers.

**No little kindness.**—Literally, *no common* (or *average*) *philanthropy.* The idiom is the same as that of the "special miracles" of chap. xix. 11.

**And received us . . .**—The word implies both shelter and hospitality. Warmth, above all things, was needful for those who had been chilled and drenched; and for this purpose, probably in some open space, or *atrium*, a large fire was lighted.

**Because of the present rain . . .**—The rain followed naturally on the cessation of the gale. The "cold" shows that the wind was not the Sirocco, which is always accompanied by heat.

(3) **And when Paul had gathered a bundle of sticks . . .**—The act was characteristic of the cheerful energy which had been shown throughout the previous night. The fact thus mentioned has been dwelt on as militating against the identity of Melita and Malta, no wood being now found in the island except at one spot (*Bosquetta*), not near St. Paul's Bay. The Greek word, however, is applied to the dry stalks of herbaceous plants rather than to the branches of trees, and, as such, exactly describes the stout, thorny heather that still grows near the bay. It is clear, however, apart from this, that the people of Malta did not live without fire, and, not having coal, must therefore have had wood of some kind as fuel.

**There came a viper out of the heat.**—There are said to be no venomous serpents now in Malta, and this again has been pressed into the question of the identity of the island. Mr. Lewin, however (*St. Paul,* ii. 208), states that he saw a serpent, near St. Paul's Bay, that looked very like a viper; and even if he were mistaken in this, it would be natural enough that venomous snakes should disappear under the influence of culture, as they have done elsewhere, in the course of 1800 years.

(4) **The venomous beast.**—The adjective, as the italics show, is not in the Greek, and can scarcely be said to be necessary.

**No doubt this man is a murderer.**—They knew, we may believe, that St. Paul was a prisoner. It is hardly conceivable, indeed, that he could have come on shore bound by two chains, or even one, to his keeper, but, looking to the jealous care which the soldiers had shown in the custody of the prisoners (chap. xxvii. 42), it would be natural that they should resume their vigilance over him as soon as they were all safe on shore. And so the natives of Melita, seeing what they did, and ignorant of the prisoner's crime, and with their rough notions of the divine government of the world, rushed to the conclusion that they were looking on an example of God's vengeance against murder. It was in vain that such a criminal had escaped the waves; a more terrible death was waiting for him.

(6) **They looked when he should have swollen . . .**—Better, *and they were expecting that . . .* The verb for "swollen" implies literally "inflammation," and one of the enormous serpents of Africa took its name, Prestes ("the inflamer"), from it. Lucan (ix. 790) describes the effect of its bite—

> "Percussit Prestes, illi ruber igneus ora
> Succendit, tenditque cutem, pereunte figurâ."
> ["The Prestes bit him, and a fiery flush
> Lit up his face, and set the skin a-stretch,
> And all its comely grace had passed away."]

**They changed their minds, and said that he was a god.**—The miraculous escape naturally made an even stronger impression on the minds of the Melitese than what had seemed a supernatural judgment. Their thoughts may have travelled quickly to the attributes of the deities who, like Apollo or Æsculapius, were depicted as subduing serpents. The sudden change of belief may be noted as presenting a kind of inverted parallelism with that which had come over the people of Lystra. (See Notes on chap. xiv. 11, 19.)

(7) **The chief man of the island.**—Literally, *the first man.* The term is found both in Greek and Latin inscriptions, at Malta, of the time of Augustus, as an official title. It probably designated the prefect or governor of the island, as distinct from the procurator. In the time of Cicero (*In Verr.* iv. 18) Melita was

courteously. (8) And it came to pass,
that the father of Publius lay sick of a
fever and of a bloody flux: to whom
Paul entered in, and prayed, and laid
his hands on him, and healed him.
(9) So when this was done, others also,
which had diseases in the island, came,
and were healed: (10) who also honoured
us with many honours; and when we
departed, they laded *us* with such things
as were necessary. (11) And after three
months we departed in a ship of Alexandria,
which had wintered in the isle,
whose sign was Castor and Pollux.
(12) And landing at Syracuse, we tarried
*there* three days. (13) And from thence
we fetched a compass, and came to
Rhegium: and after one day the south

A.D. 63.

included in the "province" of Sicily, and if that arrangement continued, Publius would be the "legate" of the Sicilian proconsul. The Latin name falls in with the supposition of his holding some office of this kind.

**Lodged us three days courteously.**—We can hardly think of the hospitality of Publius as extended to the whole two hundred and seventy-six who had been on board, and the omission of the word "all," which meets us in verse 2, probably indicates a limitation to a chosen few, among whom St. Paul and St. Luke, and, most likely, the centurion Julius, were included. It is implied that after the three days they found a lodging for themselves. The word for "courteously" expresses kindliness of feeling rather than of manner.

(8) **Lay sick of a fever and a bloody flux.**—Literally, *with fevers and dysentery*, both words being used by St. Luke with professional precision. The plural, "fevers," probably indicates the attacks of a recurrent fever, and its combination with dysentery would, according to Hippocrates, who also uses the plural form (*Aph.* vi. 3), make the case more than usually critical. The disease is said to be far from uncommon in Malta.

**Prayed, and laid his hands on him.**—The union of the two acts reminds us of the rule given in Jas. v. 14, 15; and the close sequence of the work of the healing upon the escape from the serpent's bite, of the juxtaposition of the two promises of Mark xvi. 18.

(9) **Others also, which had diseases.**—More accurately, *the others who had infirmities.* The Greek gives the article, and states the fact that there was something like a rush, continuing for some length of time, of all the sick people in the island to profit by the Apostle's power of healing. On the difference between the terms used for diseases, see Note on Matt. iv. 23.

(10) **Who also honoured us with many honours.**—It lies in the nature of the case that the honours took the form of gifts. The very word was, indeed, specially applied, both in Greek and Latin, to the *honorarium*, or fee, paid to the physician, and its use here is accordingly characteristic of St. Luke's calling. (Comp. Ecclus. xxxviii. 1.) In addition to these gifts of courtesy, the things that were wanted for their voyage—clothing, provisions, and the like—were freely supplied at their departure.

**When we departed.**—Better, *as we were setting sail.*

(11) **After three months.**—The date may be approximately fixed. The Fast, falling on the 10th of Tisri, which has been calculated as falling in that year on September 24th, was passed, we are not told how long, when the ship left the Fair Havens (chap. xxvii. 9). Then came the "fourteen days" of chap. xxvii. 27, bringing us to the end of October or beginning of November. Three months from this carries us to the beginning of February. This was earlier than that usually fixed for the general navigation of the Mediterranean (see Note on chap. xxvii. 9), but the officers and the crew of the Alexandrian ship were naturally anxious to take the earliest opportunity for pressing on to their destination. The fact that the latter had wintered in the island is obviously in favour of the identification of Melita with Malta, which lay on the usual line of the voyage from Alexandria to Italy, while Meleda was altogether out of the way.

**Whose sign was Castor and Pollux.**—Literally, *the Dioscuri*, the two sons of Zeus and Leda, who were regarded as the guardian deities of sailors. So Horace (*Od.* i. 3, 2) speaks of the "*fratres Helenæ, lucida sidera*" ("brothers of Helen, beaming stars"), and (*Od.* i. 12, 25) of the "*puerosque Ledæ*" ("the children of Leda"), whose bright star shines propitiously on sailors. In Greek mythology, Zeus had rewarded their brotherly devotion by placing them among the stars as the *Gemini*, which were connected with the month of May in the signs of the Zodiac, and Poseidon (= Neptune) had given them power over the winds and waves that they might assist the shipwrecked. So in the *Helena* of Euripides they appear, in 1550–60, as promising a fair wind and a safe voyage. The figure-heads of the Greek and Roman ships were commonly placed both at the prow and the stern.

(12) **And landing at Syracuse . . .**—The city, famous for the memorable siege during the Peloponnesian war, and at all times taking its place among the most flourishing towns of Sicily, was about eighty or a hundred miles from Malta, and might be reached accordingly in from twenty-four to thirty-six hours. Ships bound from Alexandria to Italy commonly put in there. The stay of three days was probably caused by their waiting for a favourable wind. The fact stated in the next verse implies that it was more or less against them.

(13) **From thence we fetched a compass.**—The phrase, now somewhat obsolete, was formerly in common use for a circuitous route by land or sea from one point to another. (Comp. 2 Sam. v. 33; 2 Kings iii. 9, and—

"For 'tis his custom, like a creeping fool,
To fetch a compass of a mile about,"

in Heywood's *Fair Maid of the Exchange*, ii. 3.) It is found in most of the English versions, but Wiclif gives "we sailed about," and the Rhemish, "compassing by the shore." The latter, however, hardly expresses the fact, which was that the wind being probably from the west, they were compelled to tack so as to stand out from the shore to catch the breeze, instead of coasting.

**Came to Rhegium.**—This town, now *Reggio*, was in Italy, on the southern opening of the Straits of Messina. Ships from Alexandria to Italy commonly touched there, and Suetonius (*Tit.* c. 5) relates that the Emperor Titus, taking the same course as St. Paul, put in there on his way from Judæa to Puteoli, and thence to Rome.

**wind blew, and we came the next day to Puteoli: (14) where we found brethren, and were desired to tarry with them seven days: and so we went toward Rome. (15) And from thence, when the brethren heard of us, they came to meet us as far as Appii forum, and The three taverns: whom when Paul saw, he**

Caligula began the construction of a harbour at Rhegium for the corn-ships of Egypt; but this work, which the Jewish historian notes as the one "great and kingly undertaking" of his reign, was left unfinished (*Ant.* xix. 2, § 5).

**The south wind blew.**—More accurately, *when a breeze from the south had sprung*, the form of the Greek verb implying a change of wind. The south wind was, of course, directly in their favour, and they sailed without danger between the famous rocks of Scylla and the whirlpool of Charybdis.

**We came the next day to Puteoli.**—As the distance was about one hundred and eighty miles, the ship was clearly making good way before the wind. Puteoli (more anciently Dikæarchia, now *Pozzuoli*) lies in a sheltered recess, forming the northern part of the Bay of Naples. It was at this time the chief port of Rome, and was, in particular, the great emporium for the corn ships of Alexandria, upon which the people of Rome largely depended for their food, and the arrival of which was accordingly eagerly welcomed. A pier on twenty-five arches was thrown out into the sea for the protection of the harbour. It may be noted further that but a few months prior to St. Paul's arrival it had been raised to the dignity of a *colonia* (Tac. *Ann.* xiv. 27). It is hardly necessary to describe the well-known beauties of the bay, but the reader may be reminded that as the ship entered it the eye of St. Paul must have rested on the point of Misenum, to the north, behind which was stationed the imperial fleet; on Vesuvius, to the south; on the town of Neapolis (= New-town), now *Naples*, which had taken the place of the old Parthenope; on the islands of Capreæ, Ischia, and Procida.

(14) **Where we found brethren.**—The fact is significant as showing, in the absence of any distinct record, the extent to which the new society had been silently spreading. Who had been the agents in preaching the gospel there we can only conjecture, but a city which was *en rapport*, like Puteoli, with both Alexandria and Rome, may have received it from either. One or two coincidences, however, tend to the former rather than the latter conclusion. We find in Heb. x. 24 a salutation sent from "those of (or, better, *from*) Italy." This would not be a natural way of speaking of Christians of Rome, and we are led, therefore, to think of some other Italian Church. The only such Church, however, of which we read in the New Testament is this of Puteoli, and we naturally infer that the writer of that Epistle refers to it. But the writer was, in the judgment of many critics (see *Introduction to the Epistle to the Hebrews*), none other than Apollos, the eloquent Alexandrian Jew of chap. xviii. 24, and some have been led to think that it was addressed to the Hebrew disciples of the Therapeutæ, or ascetic, class, in the Delta of the Nile. All these facts tend to the conclusion that there was a connection of some kind between Alexandria and some Italian Church, and the theory that that Church was at Puteoli, though not proven, at least combines and explains all the phenomena. We find from Josephus (*Ant.* xvii. 12, § 1) that there was a considerable Jewish element in the population of Puteoli. They had, indeed, spread themselves through the greater part of Italy, and the remains of a Jewish cemetery have been found even near Perugia.

**Were desired to tarry with them seven days.**—As before at Troas (chap. xx. 6) and Tyre (chap. xxi. 4), so here, we can scarcely fail to connect the duration of St. Paul's stay at Puteoli with the wish of the Church there, that he should be with them on one, or, it may be, two Sundays, that so he might break bread with them, and that they might profit by his teaching. The kindness of the centurion is seen once more in the permission which made compliance with the request possible.

**And so we went toward Rome.**—The journey would lead them through Cumæ and Liternum to Sinuessa, a distance of thirty-three miles from Puteoli. Here they would come upon the great Appian Road, which ran from Rome to Brundusium, the modern *Brindisi.* The stages from Sinuessa would probably be Minturnæ, Formiæ, Fundi, and Terracina, making altogether a distance of fifty-seven miles. At this point they would have to choose between two modes of travel, taking the circuitous road round the Pontine Marshes, or going by the more direct line of the canal. Both routes met at Appii Forum, eighteen miles from Terracina. For us well-nigh every stage of the journey is connected with some historical or legendary fact in classical antiquity. We think of the great Appius Claudius, the censor from whom the Via and the Forum took their names; of the passage in the over-crowded canal track-boat, with its brawling sailors, and of the scoundrel inn-keepers, whom Horace has immortalised in the narrative of his journey to Brundusium (*Sat.* i. 5). All this was, we may believe, for the Apostle as though it had not been. Past associations and the incidents of travel, all were for him swallowed up in the thought that he was now on the point of reaching, after long delays, the goal after which he had been striving for so many years (chap. xix. 21; Rom. xv. 23).

(15) **And from thence, when the brethren heard of us . . .**—Better, *the brethren having heard about us.* The seven days at Puteoli had given ample time for the news of the Apostle's arrival to reach the disciples at Rome. Among these "brethren" were many, we may believe, of those whom he had known at Corinth, and to whom he had sent messages of greeting in Rom. xvi.: Aquila and Epænetus, Andronicus and Junias, Herodion, and those of the household of Narcissus. Most of these were Jews by birth, of the *libertini* or freed-man class. All had probably read or heard the Epistle to the Romans. They were yearning, some for the presence of the friend whom they had known seven years before at Corinth, some for a glimpse of one whom, though they had not known him, they had learnt to love. It is clear, from the salutations sent to Aquila and Priscilla and the rest in Rom. xvi., that the decree of Claudius banishing the Jews from Rome had been rescinded or allowed to lapse. The influence of Poppæa, now dominant at Rome, was probably in their favour, and secured their protection. Herself a proselyte to Judaism, after the fashion of her class she would extend her protection to the Jews of Rome, as she did, about the same time, to those of Jerusalem. (See Note on chap. xxvi. 32.)

**They came to meet us.**—The practice of going

thanked God, and took courage. (16) And when we came to Rome, the centurion delivered the prisoners to the captain of the guard: but Paul was suffered to

some miles from the city to meet one whom men delighted to honour was a common one. So the Jews of Rome had gone out to meet the Pseudo-Alexander who claimed to be a son of Herod (Jos. *Ant.* xvii. 12, § 1). So the Romans had poured forth to meet Germanicus (Sueton. *Calig.* c. 4) when he lived, and to do honour to his remains after his death (Tacit. *Ann.* iii. 5). So in earlier days, Cicero had been welcomed on his return from exile, journeying from Brundusium on the self-same Appian Way on which St. Paul was now travelling, senate and people alike going forth to meet him (Cic. *pro Sext.* 63, *in Pison.* 22).

**Appii forum.**—There was an obvious reason for their not going further than this, as they could not tell whether the Apostle and his companions would come by the canal or the road. The town took its name probably from the Appius under whom the road had been made, and was so called as being a centre of local jurisdiction—an assize-town, as it were. So we have Forum Julium (now *Friuli*), Forum Flaminium, &c. Horace (*Sat.* i. 5, l. 4), had condemned the town to a perpetual infamy, as

> "Inde Forum Appi,
> Differtum nautis, cauponibus atque malignis."
> ["With sailors filled, and scoundrel publicans."]

Now, we must believe, on the evening when the two parties met, the wretched little town, notorious for its general vileness, was the scene of a prayer-meeting, thanksgivings and praises pouring forth from rejoicing hearts.

**The three taverns.**—Better, *the Three Tabernæ.* The Latin word has a wider range than the English, and is applied to a booth or shop of any kind, requiring the addition of an adjective such as "*diversoria*" or "*cauponaria*" before it becomes a "tavern" in the modern sense. The Roman itineraries place this town at a distance of ten miles from Appii Forum, and therefore thirty-three from Rome, Aricia forming a kind of half-way stage between the Three Tabernæ and the capital. It is mentioned more than once by Cicero in his letters, and appears to have been on the Via Appia, at a point where a road from Antium fell into it (*Ad Att.* ii. 10). It was accordingly a town of considerable importance. No traces of the name are found now near that position, but it could not have been far from the modern *Cisterna.* The transfer of traffic from the old Via Appia to the new road of the same name (the *Via Appia Nuova*), which takes a more circuitous route from Castella to Terracina, probably deprived it of its importance and led to its decay. A local tradition, indeed, but probably of very late date, finds the name of *Tre Taberne* at a distance of about twelve miles from Rome, on the old Via Appia. Here, it is clear, a second detachment of friends met him, who had either started later than the others or had felt unequal to the additional ten miles.

**He thanked God, and took courage.**—The words imply a previous tendency to anxiety and fear. There had been no possibility of any communication with Rome since he had left Cæsarea, and questions more or less anxious would naturally present themselves. Would he find friends there who would welcome him, or would he have to enter Rome as a criminal, with no escort but that of the soldiers who kept him? Were those Roman disciples to whom he had written so warmly still safe and well, and sound in the faith? Had persecution driven them from their homes, or had the Judaisers perverted their belief? The language of Rom. i. 10—12, shows how prominent they were in his thoughts and prayers. To these questions the arrival of the disciples was a full and satisfying answer, and the Apostle resumed his journey with an eager and buoyant hope.

(16) **And when we came to Rome.**—This journey led them through Aricia (now *La Riccia*), where they would probably either stop for the night or for their noon-tide meal. From that point, as they neared the city, the Appian Road would present more of its characteristic features—the tall milestones, the stately tombs, of which that to Cæcilia Metella, the wife of Crassus, is the most representative example, and which, lining either side, gave to the road the appearance of one long cemetery, and bore their record of the fame or the vanity, the wealth or the virtues, of the dead. As they drew nearer still, St. Paul's companions would point out to him the Grove and the sacred spring in the valley of Egeria, now let to a colony of squatters of his own race.

> "Hic ubi nocturnæ Numa constituebat amicæ,
> Nunc sacri fontis nemus et delubra locantur
> Judæis, quorum cophinus fœnumque supellex."
> ["Here, by the sacred scenes of Numa's love,
> We let on lease the shrines, the stream, the grove,
> To pauper Jews, who bring their scanty store
> Of hay and hamper, and who ask no more."]
> —Juvenal, *Sat.* iii. 12.

He would pass the cemetery of the Jews of Rome, lying on the east of the Appian Way, which within the last few years has been discovered and explored, in the *Vigna Randanini,* and the *Columbaria* (now in the *Vigna Codini*) of the imperial household, with which, as themselves of the *libertini* class, many of his friends and disciples were even then so closely connected. He would see, perhaps, even then, the beginning of the Catacombs, where the Christians, who would not burn their dead like the heathen, and who were excluded from the cemetery of the Jews, laid their dead to sleep in peace, in what was afterwards the Catacomb of St. Callistus. It may be noted here that the earliest inscription on any Jewish burial-place in Italy is one found at Naples, of the time of Claudius (A.D. 44) (Garucci, *Cimitero degli antichi Ebrei,* p. 24; Mommsen, *Inscriptt. Neap. Lat.* 6467), and the earliest Christian inscription with any note of time, of that of Vespasian (De Rossi, *Inscriptt. Christ.* No. 1). It lies in the nature of the case, however, that at first both Jews and Christians were likely to bury their dead without any formal record, and had to wait for quieter times before they could indulge in the luxury of tombstones and epitaphs. Continuing his journey, the Apostle and his companions would come within view of the pyramid of Caius Cestius, would pass under the Arch of Drusus, which still stands outside the Porta di S. Sebastiano, and enter the city by the Porta Capena, or Capuan Gate, proceeding thence to the Palace of the Cæsars, which stood on the Palatine Hill, and looked down, on one side upon the Forum, on the other upon the Circus Maximus.

**Paul was suffered to dwell by himself.**—The centurion, on arriving at the Palace of the Cæsars, would naturally deliver his prisoners to the captain of the division of the Prætorian Guard stationed there as the emperor's body-guard. The favour shown to St. Paul

dwell by himself with a soldier that kept him. (17) And it came to pass, that after three days Paul called the chief of the Jews together: and when they were come together, he said unto them, Men *and* brethren, though I have committed nothing against the people, or customs of our fathers, yet was I delivered prisoner from Jerusalem into the hands of the Romans. (18) Who, when they had examined me, would have let *me* go, because there was no cause of death in me. (19) But when the Jews spake against *it*, I was constrained to appeal unto Cæsar; not that I had ought to accuse my nation of. (20) For this cause therefore have I called for you, to see *you*, and to speak with

may fairly be considered as due to the influence of the centurion Julius, from whom he had, from the first, received so many marks of courtesy. The Prefect of the Prætorium was the natural custodian of prisoners sent from the provinces, and about this time that office was filled by Burrus, the friend and colleague of Seneca. Before and after his time there were two prefects, and the way in which St. Luke speaks of "*the* captain of the guard" may fairly be accepted as a note of time fixing the date of the Apostle's arrival. The Prætorian camp lay to the north-east of the city, outside the Porta Viminalis. The manner in which St. Luke speaks of his "dwelling by himself" implies that he went at once, instead of accepting the hospitality of any friends, into a hired apartment. Tradition points to the vestibule of the Church of Santa Maria, at the junction of the Via Lata and the Corso, as the site of his dwelling; but it has been urged by Dr. Philip, at present working as a missionary in the Ghetto at Rome, in a pamphlet, *On the Ghetto* (Rome, 1874), that this site, forming part of the old Flaminian Way, was then occupied by arches and public buildings, and that it was far more probable that he would fix his quarters near those of his own countrymen. He adds that a local tradition points to No. 2 in the Via Stringhari, just outside the modern Ghetto, as having been St. Paul's dwelling-place, but does not give any documentary evidence as to its nature or the date to which it can be traced back.

**With a soldier that kept him.**—Better, *with the soldier.* The arrangement was technically known as a *custodia libera.* The prisoner, however, was fastened by a chain to the soldier who kept guard over him, and so the Apostle speaks of his "chain" (verse 20), of his being a "prisoner" (Eph. iii. 1; iv. 1), an ambassador in *chains* (Eph. vi. 20), of his "bonds" (Phil. i. 7, 13, 17; Col. iv. 18). It was almost a matter of course that the guard would from time to time be relieved, and so the Apostle's bonds, and the story of his sufferings, and what had brought them on him, would be known throughout the whole Prætorian camp from which the soldiers came. (See Note on Phil. i. 13.)

(17) **After three days Paul called the chief of the Jews together.**—The decree of Claudius had, as has been already stated (see Note on verse 15), been allowed to lapse, and the Jews had settled in their old quarters in the trans-Tiberine region, and in part, perhaps, on the island of the Tiber, and the region on the right bank of the river, now known as the Ghetto, which has been for many centuries the "Jewry" of Rome. Those who are described as the "chief" would naturally include the ruler of the synagogue (the title *Archisynagogus* is found in a Jewish inscription from Capua, now in the Lateran Museum); the *Archontes*, or rulers of the people—perhaps another way of describing the Archisynagogi—(this title is found in the Jewish cemetery at Rome already mentioned; Garucci, *ut supra*, p. 35); the Scribes (the title *Grammateus* is also found, pp. 42, 47, 55, 59); the *Gerousiarchai*, or heads of the Jewish senate, which was allowed, as at Alexandria, a certain measure of independent jurisdiction (pp. 51, 62); the "fathers of the synagogue," perhaps identical with the "rulers" or "elders," perhaps of a slightly higher grade (p. 52); perhaps, also (for this title also is found), the "mothers of the synagogue," occupying, possibly, a position more or less analogous to the widows and deaconesses of the Christian Church (pp. 52, 53);* those who were known as *Nomomatheis*, or students of the Law (p. 57); the wealthier traders; those who, as freedmen, held office of some kind in the imperial court, or, like the Aliturius mentioned by Josephus (*Life*, c. 3), courted the favour of Poppæa, and gained the praise of Nero by acting in his spectacles. To such a mingled crowd, summoned by a special messenger—or, it may be, by a notice read on the Sabbath in the synagogue, or posted on some wall or pillar in the Jewish quarter—after three days spent, partly in settling in his lodging, partly in the delivery of the summons, St. Paul now addressed himself. These he was seeking to win, if possible, for Christ.

(17) **Though I have committed nothing against the people . . .**—We note St. Paul's characteristic tact. He addresses his hearers by the title which they loved, as "*the* people." (See Note on chap. iv. 28.) He speaks with respect of their "customs." (See Notes on chaps. vi. 14; xxi. 21.) He disclaims the thought of treating either with disrespect.

(18) **Who, when they had examined me . . .** It is possible that we have here only the summary of a fuller narrative, and that he gave an outline of the proceedings that had taken place between his first seizure and his appeal to the emperor. What he states, however, was fully warranted by the facts. No Roman magistrate had ever condemned him. Agrippa and Festus had decided that he might have been released (chap. xxvi. 32). He had been constrained to appeal to Cæsar in self-defence, to avoid the danger of being handed over to a prejudiced tribunal or to plots of assassination (chap. xxv. 8—10). But, as it was, he came not, as other appellants so often came, with counter-accusations. On all such matters his lips were sealed, and his motive now was to remove any unfavourable impressions which reports from Judæa might have left on the minds of his hearers.

(20) **For the hope of Israel I am bound with this chain.**—The mention of "chain" in the singular

* Since I wrote the above, I have heard from Dr. A. Edersheim, than whom there is no higher living authority on matters connected with Jewish archæology, that in his judgment the title of "father" or "mother" of the synagogue did not imply any functions, but was assigned as a mark of honour to its oldest members. He rests this belief on the fact that they are found chiefly, or exclusively, in inscriptions which record a very advanced age—such as 80 or 110.

*you:* because that for the hope of Israel
I am bound with this chain. (21) And
they said unto him, We neither received
letters out of Judæa concerning thee,
neither any of the brethren that came
shewed or spake any harm of thee.
(22) But we desire to hear of thee what
thou thinkest: for as concerning this
sect, we know that every where it is
spoken against. (23) And when they had
appointed him a day, there came many
to him into *his* lodging; to whom he
expounded and testified the kingdom of
God, persuading them concerning Jesus,
both out of the law of Moses, and *out of*
the prophets, from morning till evening.
(24) And some believed the things which
were spoken, and some believed not.
(25) And when they agreed not among
themselves, they departed, after that
Paul had spoken one word, Well spake
the Holy Ghost by Esaias the prophet
unto our fathers, (26) saying, Go unto
this people,[a] and say, Hearing ye shall

a Isa. 6. 9; Matt. 13. 14; Mark 4. 12; Luke 8. 10; John 12. 40; Rom. 11. 8.

agrees with the fact stated in verse 30, that he was entrusted to the keeping of a single soldier. There is a certain touch of pathos in this appeal to his sufferings as a prisoner. (Comp. Eph. iii. 1; iv. 1; vi. 20.) The hope for which he suffered was two-fold: (1) the expectation of the Messiah as bringing in a kingdom of heaven, which was cherished by every Israelite; (2) the hope of a resurrection from the dead, which he proclaimed as attested by *the* resurrection which proved (Rom. i. 3, 4) that Jesus was the Christ, the Son of God. (See Notes on chap. xxvi. 6, 7.)

(21) **We neither received letters out of Judæa concerning thee . . .**—It seems strange at first that no tidings should have come from Jerusalem of what had passed there in connection with St. Paul's imprisonment. There was, however, hardly likely to have been time for any letters since his appeal. He had sailed somewhat late in the autumn, immediately after he had made it (chaps. xxv. 13; xxvii. 1), and all communication by sea was suspended during the winter months. And it may be noted further that the Jews do not say that they had heard absolutely nothing about him, but that those who had come had spoken *nothing evil* of him. What they had heard by casual rumour may well have been consistent with St. James's statement that "he walked orderly, and observed the Law" (chap. xxi. 20). It has been urged that the decree of Claudius had suspended the intercourse between the Jews of Rome and those of Jerusalem; but as the former had returned before he wrote the Epistle to the Romans, this is hardly a tenable explanation. It may, however, be taken into account that among the Jews who had returned to Rome would be not a few of those who had known St. Paul at Corinth, and were willing to bear their testimony to his character.

(22) **We desire . . . as concerning this sect . . .**—Better, *we request of thee.* The term is that which had been used by Tertullus when he spoke of the "*sect* of the Nazarenes" (chap. xxiv. 5). The speakers had clearly heard enough of the prisoner to identify him with that sect, but they treat him personally with respect, probably due in part to the favour which the authorities had shown him, and wish for an authoritative exposition of his views. The Christians of Rome had obviously, even if they were Jews, withdrawn from the Jewish quarter, and the residents in that quarter knew of them only by reports. What was the nature of those reports we can only conjecture. They were, as the speakers say, "everywhere spoken against." The darker calumnies which were propagated afterwards—stories of Thyestean (*i.e.*, cannibal) banquets and licentious orgies—may possibly have been even then whispered from ear to ear. In any case the Christians of the empire would be known as abandoning circumcision and other Jewish ordinances, leading a separate life, holding meetings which were more or less secret, worshipping One who had been crucified as a malefactor. They were already, as Tacitus describes them, speaking of their sufferings under Nero, known as holding an *exitiabilis superstitio* ("a detestable superstition"), guilty of *atrocia et pudenda, odio humani generis convicti* ("atrocious and shameful crimes, convicted by the hatred of mankind") (*Ann.* xv. 44), or as Suetonius writes (*Nero,* c. 16), as a *genus hominum superstitionis novæ et maleficæ* ("a race of men holding a new and criminal superstition"). It is conceivable, looking to the early date at which such rumours were current, that even then there may have been caricatures like that which was found among the *graffiti* of the Palace of the Cæsars (now in the Collegio Romano), representing Alexamenos, a Christian convert, worshipping his god, in the form of a crucified human figure with an ass's head. Tertullian (A.D. 160—240) mentions such caricatures as current in his time (*Apol.* c. 16), and the story that the Jews worshipped an ass's head, which we know to have been accepted at this very time (Jos. *cont. Apion.* ii. 7; Tacit *Hist.* v. 4), would naturally be transferred to the Christians, who were regarded as a sect of Jews. In Tertullian's time *Asinarii* ("ass-worshippers") was a common term of abuse for them.

(23) **There came many to him into his lodging.**—The Greek for "many" is a comparative form, implying a larger attendance than might have been looked for. The "lodging" was probably the "hired house," or apartment, of verse 30. (Comp. Philem. verse 22.) The discourse, or, more properly, the discussion, which followed could obviously only be given in outline. The address at Antioch in Pisidia (chap. xiii. 16—42), and the arguments of the Epistles to the Galatians and the Romans enable us to form a general estimate of its probable contents.

(24) **And some believed the things which were spoken.**—Better, as expressing the fact that the verb is the passive form of that translated "persuade," in the previous verse, *some were being persuaded of the things that were spoken.*

(25) **After that Paul had spoken one word.**—The tone of vehement indignation implies a patience almost exhausted by the long contest with prejudice and unbelief. He cannot refrain from reproducing the conviction which he had already expressed in the Epistle to the Romans, that "blindness in part had happened unto Israel," that a remnant only were faithful, and that "the rest were hardened" (Rom. xi. 7—25).

(26) **Go unto this people, and say . . .**—On the passage thus quoted see Notes on Matt. xiii. 14, 15.

hear, and shall not understand; and
seeing ye shall see, and not perceive:
(27) for the heart of this people is waxed
gross, and their ears are dull of hearing,
and their eyes have they closed; lest
they should see with *their* eyes, and
hear with *their* ears, and understand
with *their* heart, and should be con-
verted, and I should heal them. (28) Be
it known therefore unto you, that the
salvation of God is sent unto the Gen-
tiles, and *that* they will hear it. (29) And
when he had said these words, the Jews
departed, and had great reasoning
among themselves. (30) And Paul dwelt
two whole years in his own hired
house, and received all that came in
A.D. 65. unto him, (31) preaching the kingdom
of God, and teaching those things
which concern the Lord Jesus Christ,
with all confidence, no man forbidding
him.

---

Here we are chiefly concerned with the fact that the words had been cited by our Lord as describing the spiritual state of the Jews of Palestine, and that the record of their citation is found in the first three Gospels (Matt. xiii. 13; Mark iv. 12; Luke viii. 10), while St. John (xii. 40) reproduces them as embodying the solution of the apparent failure of our Lord's personal ministry. Looking to the fact that this implies a wide currency given to the prophecy in all reports, oral or written, of our Lord's teaching, and that St. Paul was clearly well acquainted with one collection of our Lord's discourses (chap. xx. 35), we can hardly resist the inference that he now applied them as following in the track of his Master's teaching. What was true of the Jews of Jerusalem was true also of those of Rome. In both there was a wilful blindness and deafness to that which ought to have produced conviction and conversion. (Comp. the language which the Apostle had previously used in Rom. xi. 25.)

(28) **Be it known therefore unto you, that the salvation of God . . .**—The better MSS. give "*this* salvation," the demonstrative adjective having the same force as in "the words of *this* life," in chap. v. 20. The Apostle points, as it were, to that definite method of deliverance (the Greek gives the concrete neuter form, as in Luke ii. 30; iii. 6, and not the feminine abstract) which he had proclaimed to them. The words remind us of those which had been spoken under like circumstances at Antioch in Pisidia (chap. xiii. 46). We can, in some measure, enter into the feelings which filled the Apostle's mind, through what we read in Rom. ix.—xi.,—the bitter pain at the rejection of Israel, relieved by a far-off hope of their restoration, the acceptance of God's ways as unsearchable and past finding out.

(29) **And when he had said these words . . .**—The whole verse is wanting in many of the earliest MSS. and versions. It may have been inserted, either by a transcriber, or by the historian himself in a revised copy, in order to avoid the apparent abruptness of the transition from verse 28 to 30. As far as it goes it confirms the statement of verses 24 and 25, that some of those who had listened were converted.

(30) **And Paul dwelt two whole years . . .**—On the probable incidents of this period, see *Excursus on the Later Years of St. Paul's Life.* The word translated "hired house" (the exact equivalent for the Latin *meritorium*, or *conductum*) means rather a *lodging* (as in verse 23) or *apartment*, and does not imply that he occupied a whole house. The words that follow exactly describe his position. He was a prisoner, and therefore was not allowed to go out to preach in the synagogues, or the "churches" in the houses of this or that disciple, or the open places of the city, but his friends were allowed free access to him, and in this way there was probably a wider and more effectual opening for his personal influence than if he had spoken publicly, and so exposed himself to the risk of an organised antagonism. What seemed at first a hindrance to his work was so ordered, as he afterwards acknowledged, that it fell out "rather unto the furtherance of the gospel" (Phil. i. 12).

(31) **No man forbidding him.**—The fact is interesting as showing the attitude of the Roman empire to the new faith. So far, even under Nero, it was tolerant, and even though the "sect" of the Christians was "everywhere spoken against," a leading teacher of that sect was allowed free room to propagate his views. The rulers of the empire were not as yet alarmed at the thought of the wide-spread secret organisation of the Christian Society, and the influence of Seneca and Burrus may not have been without its share in this policy of toleration. The history closes somewhat abruptly. It may have been the intention of the writer to continue his narrative. It is a natural inference that when he closed it the two years had expired, or were on the point of expiring; that he, who had remained with the Apostle during his imprisonment, started with him on his eastward journey afterwards; and that some incidents to us unknown, hindered him from completing the work which he had begun. It is possible, on the other hand, that Theophilus, as an Italian convert (see *Introduction*), may have known what had passed in Rome during the Apostle's first sojourn there, or subsequently, and that St. Luke did not aim at more than setting before his friend the stages by which St. Paul had been brought to the imperial city.

# EXCURSUS ON NOTES TO THE ACTS

## EXCURSUS ON THE LATER YEARS OF ST. PAUL'S LIFE.

THE date of St. Paul's arrival at Rome may be fixed, with little risk of error, in the spring of A.D. 61. Festus had gone to the province of Judæa, according to the computation of the best chronologists, in the autumn of A.D. 60. He had lost no time in despatching the arrears of business which Felix had left behind him, had inquired at once into the Apostle's case, and, on his appealing to the Emperor, had sent him off. Then came the voyage, the shipwreck, the three winter months at Melita, and, early in the spring, the voyage to Puteoli, and the land journey to Rome. It was the seventh year of Nero's reign, the twenty-fourth of his life. The emperor had already begun to show the baseness and cruelty of his nature. The murder of his mother, Agrippina, by his orders, had been perpetrated in the previous year. False rumours had been circulated as to the manner of her death, but the letter which Nero sent to the Senate, giving his account of it, and which Seneca was suspected of having helped to write, heaped up charges of crimes, old and new, on the memory of the wretched woman, so that it seemed to men almost as an apology for matricide (Tacit. *Ann.* xiv. 4—12).* Even Burrus, hoping still to retain some hold on him, had congratulated him on his deliverance from a great and standing danger (Tacit. *Ann.* xiv. 10). Poppæa, after her fashion, half a proselyte to Judaism (Jos. *Life*, c. 3), was living with the emperor, as his mistress, in his palace on the Palatine Hill. The supreme passion of his life was an insane desire for popular applause. To gain this, descending step by step to lower and lower depths, he drove his chariots in an enclosed circus on the site now occupied by the Vatican. He played on the lyre, and sung his odes at supper. He instituted games known as *Juvenalia* on attaining to the dignity of a beard, and men of the highest rank were compelled to bear their part in representing, in dramas or in tableaux, the foulest and most prurient of the myths of Greece. The emperor and his lyre were conspicuous everywhere (Tacit. *Ann.* xiv. 14). A body-guard of the equestrian order was formed (probably the Augustan band of Acts xxvii. 1), who acted as his *claqueurs*, and led the applause of the multitude. Centurions and tribunes had to attend officially at spectacles which seemed to them to dishonour the Roman name. Even Burrus, "consenting thus far to avoid worse deeds," stood by, praising with his lips and groaning in his soul (Tacit. *Ann.* xiv. 15). By way of showing the extent and variety of his culture, he gave his leisure also to painting and to poetry. He would cap verses or display his skill as an improvisatore among his companions. As if he had not altogether forgotten the teaching of Seneca, he would summon philosophers after a banquet and listen to them as they discussed their theories as to the chief good and true law of duty (*ibid.* c. 16).

With this form of life, entering into various relations with those who were, in greater or less measure, sharers in it, St. Paul was now brought into contact. Strange as it may sound, it presented, in some degree, a more favourable opening for his work than if he had found Rome under a wise and vigorous rule, like Trajan or Aurelius. Poppæa was, as has been said, a proselyte to Judaism, a patroness of Jews. Aliturius, a Jew (a Jew taking his part in the mimes of Nero!), was high in the emperor's favour as an actor. When Josephus came, in the second year of St. Paul's stay in Rome, he found that he had a friend at Court. He obtained the liberation of some priests whom Felix had sent as prisoners to Rome, and returned laden with gifts which Poppæa had presented him (Jos. *Life*, c. 3). The names in Rom. xvi. coinciding, as they do largely, with those in the *Columbaria* of the imperial household on the Appian Way, confirm the natural inference from Phil. iv. 22 as to the presence of Christians, some Gentiles and some of the Circumcision, among the freed-men of the palace.* And St. Paul, we must remember, was in Rome as a Jew, and the favour thus shown to other Jews would naturally be extended to him also. And we have seen that there was no lack of friends: Aquila and Priscilla, and Rufus and his mother, probably the wife of Simon of Cyrene (see Note on Mark xv. 21), and the slaves and freed-men of Narcissus,† and Tryphena, and Tryphosa, and probably Phœbe also. And with these, we may believe on good grounds, there were others. Only four years before (A.D. 57) the conqueror of Britain, Aulus Plautius, brought his wife before a family tribunal as accused of holding "a foreign superstition." She was acquitted by her husband's judgment, but her habits before and after the trial, for forty years (she died A.D. 83), were those of an outward unworldly life and of continual sorrow (Tacit. *Ann.* xiii. 32). The "foreign superstition" may have been only Judaism or some Oriental *cultus*, like that of Isis and Serapis, but the vague way in which it is described suggests the idea of a new religion rather than of one with which men were already familiar, and it does not seem an over-bold inference to rest in the conclusion that she was a Christian.

* May we see a passing reference to Nero's guilt in the mention of "murderers of mothers" in 1 Tim. 1?

* A list of names may be given as common to both lists, or found in other like records:—Amplias, Urbanus, Stachys, Apelles, Aristobulus, Narcissus, Tryphena, Tryphosa, Hermes, Hermas, Patrobas, Philologus, and Nereus (Lightfoot, *Philipp.* pp. 169—176.) To these may be added Tychicus, Trophimus, Onesimus, Dorcas among New Testament names. (Comp. Notes on Acts ix. 36; xx. 4.)

† Narcissus, the freed-man and favourite of Claudius, had been put to death by Nero (A.D. 54), but the household may have continued to be kept by some member of the family. An interesting inscription records the name of *Dikæosyne* (=Righteousness) the wife of T. Claudius Narcissus, who is described as *pientissima et frugalissima* ("most devout, and simple in her life"). The name is not, so far as I know, found elsewhere. Was it taken by one who had learnt from the preachers of the gospel what true righteousness consisted in? (Muratori, *Inscriptt.* 1325; Orelli, 720.) The appearance of new names in the epitaphs of the Roman catacombs, expressing new thoughts and hopes, is singularly suggestive. Elpis (=Hope), Euphrosyne (=Joy), Redempta, Simplicitas, Eusebius (=Devout), Kyriakos (=the Lord's), may be noted as examples.

And connected with Pomponia there were probably two other converts. The names of Claudia and Pudens are coupled together in the salutation of 2 Tim. iv. 21. They are coupled together as husband and wife in the epigrams of Martial. And the Pudens of Martial bears the name of Aulus, and he is married to Claudia, and Claudia is descended from the blue-eyed and fair-haired Britons (*Epig.* xi. 53). Martial, usually so scurrilous in his jests, treats them both with a marked respect. He writes an epithalamium on their union, and, instead of licentious innuendoes, utters his wishes thus:—

"O Concord, bless their couch for evermore,
Be with them in thy snow-white purity,
Let Venus grant, from out her choicest store,
All gifts that suit their married unity;
When he is old may she be fond and true,
And she in age the charms of youth renew."
—*Epig.* iv. 13.

A child is born to them, and he is again ready with his salutations to the father—

"Grant, O ye gods, that she may ever prove
The bliss of mother over girl and boy;
Still gladdened by her pious husband's love,
And in her children find perpetual joy."
—*Epig.* xi. 53.

He jestingly remonstrates with Pudens for objecting to the coarseness of his epigrams—

"You urge me, Pudens, to take pen in hand,
And prune and purge these epigrams of mine;
How much thou lov'st them now I understand,
When thou would'st have each quip a faultless line."
—*Epig.* vii. 11.

He has been ill while Pudens was absent in the north, and has sighed for his presence—

"Yea, all but snatched where flow the gloomy streams,
I saw the clouds that shroud the Elysian plain;
Still for thy face I groaned in weary dreams,
And cold lips 'Pudens, Pudens' cried in vain."
—*Epig.* vi. 58.

The juxtaposition of the two names, and the character thus assigned to those who bore them, justify us, I believe, here also, in spite of some difficulties that have been raised on chronological or other grounds, in identifying them with those whom St. Paul mentions.

The chronological difficulty lies in the fact that Martial, born in Spain, *circ.* A.D. 40, did not come to Rome till A.D. 66, nor collect his epigrams till A.D. 86. It is clear, however, that the former date, the very year after St. Paul's death, is certainly not incompatible with his knowing St. Paul's Claudia and Pudens, and the collected poems may well have ranged over the whole period of his stay in Rome. It is perfectly inconceivable that such a man could have lived in Rome for twenty years without writing epigrams. It may be added that the identification does not assume that Pudens and Claudia were married when St. Paul wrote the Second Epistle to Timothy (A.D. 66), but only that both were then disciples of Christ. If Martial came to Rome in A.D. 66 he might, therefore, have known the young officer before his marriage, and written his congratulatory lines shortly afterwards. The insertion of the name of Linus between Pudens and Claudia is, as far as it goes, against the hypothesis that they were at that period husband and wife.

Another objection has been taken to the identification, on the moral ground that, in some of his epigrams, Martial insinuates that his Pudens shared in the foul immorality of his time. It is not expedient to examine such a question in detail, but it will be found that the incidents to which he alludes (there is literally nothing more than the fact that a young slave of Pudens had cut his hair as a votive offering *) admit, in themselves, of a perfectly innocent interpretation, and that the innuendoes are but the scurril jests of a tainted mind coming into contact with a purity which it cannot comprehend.† They deserve no more attention than the analogous charges which were whispered against St. Paul (see Note on 2 Cor. vii. 2), or those which were brought against Athanasius and Hooker. Such charges are often, indeed, brought against the pure in proportion to their purity.

Further coincidences connect themselves with an inscription discovered in Chichester in A.D. 1723, which runs thus:—

To Neptune and Minerva
This Temple
For the welfare of the Divine (*i.e.*, the Imperial) House,
By the authority of
Tiberius Claudius Cogidubnus
Legate of Augustus (*i.e.*, the Emperor) in Britain,
The Guild of Smiths and those in it
Who minister in sacred things, have
At their own cost dedicated,
The site being given by
Pudens the son of Pudentinus.

Cogidubnus, we learn from Tacitus (*Agricola*, c. xiv.), was king of the Regni, a tribe occupying the modern Sussex, and was the faithful ally of Rome under Claudius, when Aulus Plautius, the husband of Pomponia, was governor of Britain (A.D. 43—52).‡ His daughter, if he had one, would naturally bear the name of Claudia. We find him connected with a Pudens; and it is, to say the least, a highly probable inference that the attachment of the latter to his British bride began during a service in the North prior to that of which Martial speaks, and that she came to Rome under the protection of Pomponia, and, embracing the same faith, was married to her lover.

It may be well to mention another, though less probable, conjecture, that Claudia was the daughter of Caractacus, who had been brought to Rome, with his wife and children, under Claudius, and that Linus was identical with the *Llin* who appears in Welsh hagiography as the son of Caractacus (Lewin, *St. Paul*, ii. 397).

St. Paul's acquaintance with Pudens may have begun through Pomponia; but it is also probable that, through the courteous kindness of the centurion Julius, himself of the Augustan band (see Note on chap. xxvii. 1), he was commended to the favourable notice of Burrus, the Prefect of the Prætorian camp; and that thus, and through the frequent change of soldiers who kept guard over him, his bonds in Christ would become known (as he says) through the whole Prætorian barracks § (Phil. i. 13), and that this may have either originated or strengthened their friendship.

Did the Apostle become acquainted with the great philosophic thinker Seneca, the friend of Burrus, who,

* The cutting of the hair may, indeed, even have been, after St. Paul's example (Acts xviii. 18), the completion of a Nazarite vow.

† It is right, perhaps, to state that Dean Merivale (*St. Paul at Rome*, p. 149) looks on the supposed Christianity of Pomponia as a "hypothesis of the flimsiest character," and rejects the conclusions drawn as to Claudia and Pudens on the strength of objections to which I seem to myself to have given a sufficient answer.

‡ A note is, perhaps, necessary as to the dates thus given. If this, it has been urged, gives the limits of the date of the inscription, then Martial was a boy of ten when Pudens was old enough to be an officer in Britain, and was therefore not likely to have been on the terms of intimacy with him which the epigrams indicate. The date of the inscription, however, may have been considerably later. Cogidubnus was the ally of Rome for many years after the conquest of Caractacus by Ostorius Scapula (Tacit. *Ann.* xii. 14), and even as Tacitus says, "within his own memory." The temple to which the inscription refers may easily therefore have been erected, say, *circ.* A.D. 60—64.

§ The Greek word is *Prætorium*, on which see Note on Matt. xxvii. 27.

though his influence was waning, still endeavoured to reach the mind of Nero by writing ethical treatises for his benefit? We cannot return a decisive answer to that question. Letters were extant in the fourth century, and are mentioned by Jerome as very widely read (*Vir. Illust.* 12), purporting to be a correspondence between Seneca and St. Paul; and though these are certainly apocryphal, the fact of the forgery may well have rested on some tradition of intercourse between the two. The numerous parallelisms of thought and language between the two writers (comp. Lightfoot's *Philippians:* "Excursus on St. Paul and Seneca") may be accidental, but they at least suggest the probability of some communication, direct or indirect. One who saw as clearly as St. Paul did the weak and the strong points of Stoicism, and was necessarily known to Seneca's friend, was not likely to remain altogether outside the range of his acquaintance. If we adopt the suggestion already made (see *Introduction to St. Luke's Gospel*), that there was some previous connection between the Lucas or Lucanus who was St. Paul's companion and the poet who was Seneca's nephew, the probability becomes yet stronger; nor can we quite exclude the probability that Gallio, Seneca's brother, who was now at Rome, and in high favour with the emperor, may have renewed his acquaintance with the Apostle. (See Note on chap. xviii. 17.) The traditional identification of Clement of Rome with the Clement of Phil. iv. 3, presents some serious chronological difficulties which have led Dr. Lightfoot (*Philipp.*, Exc. on iv. 3) to reject it. Apart from this, however, it is in the nature of things probable that those who were appointed to take the oversight of the Church of Rome after the death of the Apostles would be men who had known St. Paul; and we may, therefore, think, with no undue boldness of conjecture, of his knowing Linus, who, indeed, is named in 2 Tim. iv. 21, and who became bishop in A.D. 66, and Cletus, or Anacletus (A.D. 79), and possibly Clement also (A.D. 91).* The full name of this last, Titus Flavius Clemens, indicates that he was probably the first convert of the Flavian imperial house, which in Vespasian and Titus had been brought into close contact with Judaism, and which under Domitian furnished, in Flavius Clemens the Consul and his sister Flavia Domitilla, two illustrious sufferers for the new faith.

Leaving these interesting, even if they are also precarious, inferences, we pass to the more solid ground of the statements in St. Paul's own writings.

A year or more passed, during which he was waiting for his appeal to be heard, and which we cannot fill up with any accurate precision. Timotheus, his true son in the faith, joined him soon after his arrival, or possibly was even one of his companions in the voyage (Phil. i. 1). Mark, the cousin of Barnabas, came to him; Luke, the beloved physician, and Aristarchus remained with him. Linus, whose name appears in the list of Roman bishops as St. Peter's successor, and who was probably even then exercising some pastoral functions, is named as in the same circle of friends with Claudia and Pudens (2 Tim. iv. 21); and Eubulus may well have been another presbyter. A Jew named Jesus, and bearing (probably, as in other cases, as a recognition of character) the surname of Justus, and Demas, were among his fellow-workers (Col. iv. 10—14). Onesiphorus, probably an Ephesian freed-man (the name, like that of Onesimus, indicates his class), found out his lodging, was not ashamed of his chain, and ministered to him diligently there, as he had done, or did afterwards, at Ephesus (2 Tim. i. 16). Onesimus, the runaway slave of Philemon of Colossæ, at one time joined apparently with St. Paul in a partnership, as Aquila and Priscilla had been (Philem. verse 17; Acts xviii. 3), had come to him, had been converted by him, had ministered to him with the loyalty and affection of a son (Philem. verses 10—12). Either with him or about this time came Epaphras, as a messenger from the churches of the valley of the Lycus—Colossæ, Laodicea, and Hierapolis (Col. iv. 12). Tychicus (see Note on chap. xx. 4), the Ephesian, who had gone with him to Jerusalem, or at least to Ephesus, had also found his way to him (Eph. vi. 21; Col. iv. 7). Nor was the Apostle without communications from the Macedonian churches who were so dearly loved by him. Possibly in the "true yoke-fellow" of Phil. iv. 3 we may trace a temporary return of St. Luke to the church with which he had been so closely connected.* If so, his stay was short, and he returned afterwards to Rome, where we find him when the Apostle writes to the Colossians (Col. iv. 14). In the meantime Epaphroditus (the name is that from which Epaphras is contracted, but the difference in the two forms indicates almost certainly difference of persons) had come bearing gifts, probably in money, which were sent by the Philippian converts to their beloved teacher (Phil. iv. 10—17), as they had sent to him some ten years before, when he was at Thessalonica, and afterwards, probably, at Corinth also (2 Cor. xi. 9). Epaphroditus, while at Rome, had been sick nigh unto death† (Phil. ii. 27), and there had been time for a messenger to go from Rome to Philippi reporting his sickness, and bring back tidings of the anxiety of the Church there (Phil. ii. 25—28). It was not in St. Paul's nature to neglect the opportunities which thus presented themselves for reopening communication with the churches from which he had now for some two or three years been parted. The first of these letters of the Imprisonment was in all probability the EPISTLE TO THE PHILIPPIANS.‡ When he wrote it he was exulting in the spread of the gospel. It was becoming known at once in the Prætorian camp, and among the slaves and freed-men of the Palace of the Cæsars (Phil. i. 13; iv. 22). His personal defence was becoming identified with the *apologia* of the gospel (Phil. i. 17). There were, indeed, darker shades in the picture. There were some—probably of the party of the Circumcision, or, as he calls them, as if they were unworthy of the old time-honoured word, of the "concision" (Phil. iii. 2), "dogs," tainted, as the word implies (comp. Deut. xxiii. 18; Rev. xxii. 15), by sharing, as did Aliturius and the other Jews who hung about Poppæa, in the shameless license of the time—who preached Christ, *i.e.*, made his name known, in the spirit of contentious rivalry, and sought to add affliction to the Apostle's bonds. He was hoping, however, to be released shortly, and to revisit his Philippian friends. In the meantime he would send Timotheus, as soon as he saw his way clearly to the probable course of events. He would, at all events, not delay to send Epaphroditus with a letter (Phil. ii. 19—30). Probably about a year

* The succession and dates are given, it must be remembered, as only approximately correct. The *origines* of the Church of Rome are singularly obscure and uncertain.

* The "yoke-fellow" has also been identified with Lydia, but see Note on Phil. iv. 3.

† It is not without interest to note the fact that Rome was visited about this time by a violent epidemic, a catarrh with inflammation of the tonsils. Nero was one of the sufferers; he lost his voice, and sacrifices were offered in the temples for his recovery (Philostr. *Life of Apollonius*, iv. 44).

‡ I follow Dr. Lightfoot in this order of the Epistles of the first imprisonment. Some writers, however, place the Epistle to the Philippians as the last of the four.

passed between this and the next letters, the EPISTLE TO THE EPHESIANS, TO THE COLOSSIANS, and TO PHILEMON. The three were manifestly written at the same time. Tychicus is the bearer both of the letter to the Ephesians, itself probably an encyclical letter to the churches of Asia, and of that to the Colossians. Epaphras, in his turn, is connected with the Epistle to the Colossians and that to Philemon (Col. i. 7; iv. 12), and Timothy also is with St. Paul when he writes these last (Col. i. 1; Philem. verse 1). In the interval that had passed since the letter to the Philippians was despatched, Burrus had fallen a victim to the emperor's suspicions, and had been succeeded by the infamous Tigellinus (Tacit. *Ann.* xiv. 51, 57). The influence of Seneca was waning, and that of Poppæa was more and more in the ascendant (*ibid.* xiv. 52). Octavia was formally repudiated, banished to the island of Pandataria (now *Santa Maria*), and finally murdered (*ibid.* xiv. 63), while the Senate welcomed the birth of Poppæa's child as though it were a gift from heaven (*ibid.* xv. 23). It does not appear, however, that these changes affected St. Paul's condition for the worse. Though he was still the prisoner of the Lord (Eph. iii. 1; iv. 1), an "ambassador in bonds" (Eph. vi. 20), he was not less hopeful than before as to his release, when he sent Tychicus and his companions with their Epistles. He formed the plan of visiting the churches of Colossæ and Laodicea. He wrote to Philemon, as if looking forward to resuming his partnership with him, to prepare him a lodging at the first-named city (Philem. verse 22).

If we accept the PASTORAL EPISTLES as genuine, we are led partly by their style, partly by the difficulty of fitting them into any earlier period of St. Paul's life, partly by the traces they present of a later stage of development both of truth and error, to assign them to a date subsequent to the two years of the imprisonment of chap. xxviii. 30. This leads, in its turn, to the conclusion that he was released from that imprisonment, and started on a fresh journey. How his release was brought about we do not know. His appeal may have come on for hearing, after the long two years' delay, and, in the absence of any "respondents" appearing, personally or by counsel, against it, have been allowed. This seems, at any rate, more probable than the picture drawn by some writers (Conybeare and Howson, *St. Paul*, c. xxvii.; Lewin, ii., p. 380) of a formal trial before the emperor, with priests from the Sanhedrin, and Alexander the coppersmith as prosecutor, Jews from Asia as witnesses, and an advocate like Tertullus to conduct the case against him. A curious synchronism, however, suggests the thought that there may have been wheels within wheels, working to bring about this result. Josephus, the Jewish historian, then in his twenty-seventh year, came to Rome about the close of the second year of St. Paul's confinement. He was shipwrecked on his voyage, picked up by a ship of Cyrene, landed at Puteoli, and made his way to Rome. His main object in coming was, he says, to obtain the release of certain priests who had been sent to Rome by Felix as prisoners, and he accomplished his purpose through the influence of Poppæa, to whom he was introduced by Aliturius, the Jewish actor, already mentioned (Jos. *Life*, c. 3). May we not think it probable that St. Paul reaped the benefit of a general order for the release of Jewish prisoners sent by the Procurator of Palestine obtained through this instrumentality? The reticence of Josephus in regard to the Christian Church, the Gamaliel-like tone in which he speaks (not to dwell on passages of doubtful genuineness) of John the Baptist and of James the Bishop of Jerusalem (*Ant.* xviii. 5, § 2; xx. 9, § 1), his avowed Pharisaism, the tone in which he speaks of Ananias of Damascus (see Note on Acts ix. 10), all make it probable that he would, at least, not be unwilling that the Apostle, "a Pharisee and son of a Pharisee," should share in the freedom which he had obtained for others.

As regards the details of this last journey we are again dependent upon inferences more or less precarious. It is clear that, if he left Rome at all, it must have been before the great fire and the persecution of the Christians which followed on it, and from which a prisoner in St. Paul's position could scarcely have escaped—probably, therefore, about the close of A.D. 63 or the beginning of 64. A vague phrase of Clement of Rome (1 *Ep. ad Cor.* c. 5), stating that he travelled to the "furthest limits of the West," has given rise to wild conjectures. On the one hand, looking to the connection with natives of Britain already traced, and to the fact that the epithet *ultimi* was commonly applied to them, it has been contended that he preached the gospel in this island. A more probable hypothesis is that he started, on his release, to carry into effect his long-intended journey to Spain, to which the epithet "limit of the West" would be nearly as applicable. There, especially at Corduba (now *Cordova*), he would find many Jews, and Luke, as we have seen (*Introduction to St. Luke's Gospel*), had probably earlier points of contact with it. Of such a journey to Spain we find traces in the Muratorian Fragment (see Vol. I., p. xiii.), which speaks of St. Paul as *ab urbe ad Spaniam proficiscentis*, and the language of Jerome, who echoes Clement's phrase, stating that he had been set free that he might preach the gospel *in Occidentis quoque partibus* (*Cat. Script. Illust.* "Paulus"), and of Chrysostom (on 2 Tim. iv.), who says that "after being in Rome he went on for Spain," shows that the tradition was widely accepted. In our own time it has been received even by some critics who do not admit the genuineness of the Pastoral Epistles (Ewald, *Geschichte Israel*, vi. 621, 631; Renan, *L'Antechrist*, p. 106). We have seen reason to fix the liberation of St. Paul in A.D. 63 or 64, *i.e.*, in the tenth or eleventh year of the reign of Nero. The date of his death is fixed by Jerome in the emperor's fourteenth year, *i.e.*, in A.D. 66 or 67. We have, therefore, a period of between two or three years towards which we have only the scanty materials furnished—assuming their genuineness—by the Pastoral Epistles. To these, accordingly we turn. They indicate, as might have been expected, that St. Paul was eager to revisit the Greek and Asiatic churches from which he had so long been separated. Timotheus and Luke, who were with him towards the close of his first imprisonment, were probably his companions in travel. They came—if from Corduba, probably by sea from Gades, and through the Straits of Gibraltar, probably taking Crete on the way (Tit. i. 5)—to Ephesus. The state of things there was altered greatly for the worse. The grievous wolves, some of them in sheep's clothing, had done their worst. Hymenæus, and Philetus, and Alexander were conspicuous as the teachers of heresies that led practically to a denial of the Christian's hope, and the Apostle felt that he had no alternative but to pronounce the sentence which cut them off from Christian fellowship and exposed them to the supernatural chastisements in which lay the only hope of their reformation (1 Tim. i. 20; 2 Tim. ii. 17, 18). Alexander the coppersmith, probably altogether distinct from the heretic of the same name, succeeded in stirring up the passions of men against him (2 Tim. iv. 14), and "wrought him much evil." Everywhere in Asia (the proconsular province of that name) he met averted glances, even, where, as in the case of Phygellus and Hermogenes, he might have expected better things (2 Tim. i. 15). In Onesiphorus, who had ministered so faithfully to him at Rome, alone, or all but alone, had he found the loyal and loving care which had once been general, and he had to think of him as having passed away, with the prayer that "he might find mercy with the Lord in that day" (2 Tim. i. 16, 17; iv. 19). The inspired utterances of the prophets foretold dark and evil times, times at once of apostasy, and heresy, and persecution (1 Tim. iv. 1—4). The churches had lost their first love and their first purity. Their very organisation of charity was becoming the source of great evils, leading some to shift on others the burden of the duties which of right devolved on them, and encouraging a systematic pauperised idleness in others (1 Tim. v. 3—8). The women of the Christian Church, even its deaconesses, widows, virgins, were sinking to the old level of their heathen lives in dress and scandals, in idleness and frivolity (1 Tim. v. 11—13; 2 Tim. iii. 6). It seemed necessary to the Apostle to meet these dangers by asking his true son in the faith—half-shrinking, it would seem, from so grave a responsibility—to remain at Ephesus clothed with a larger measure of authority than before, while he continued his journey and went to Macedonia (1 Tim. i. 3). If we were to receive the note attached in the Authorised version to the FIRST EPISTLE TO TIMOTHY, he passed on from Macedonia to Laodicea, but these foot-notes are of too late a date and too uncertain an authority to be relied on. We must treat them, then, as though they were non-existent, and proceed with our inferences from St. Paul's own words. What his actual movements and plans were we are informed in the EPISTLE TO TITUS. There we learn that either before or after he went to Asia—more probably the former—he had visited Crete. There also the same evils were showing themselves as at Ephesus. Jewish fables and lives "abominable" and "reprobate" were bringing scandal on the name of Christians, and they were aggravated by the proverbial untruthfulness and sensuality of the national character (Tit. i. 5, 12, 16). Apollos, it is true, was there, and with him Zenas, a "lawyer," in the Gospel sense of the term (see Note on Matt. xxii. 35), a Christian teacher, *i.e.*, like Apollos, mighty in the Scriptures, a trained interpreter of the Law of Moses in a Christian sense (Tit. iii. 13); but their influence was confined within the narrow circle of their own immediate followers, and those of whom St. Paul speaks as "ours" (Tit. iii. 14) needed more direct superintendence. For this purpose, Titus (possibly the Justus of Corinth; see Note on Acts xviii. 7), who had once before brought a like special mission to a successful issue (2 Cor. vii. 13, 14; viii. 6, 23), was despatched with a delegated authority which made him what we might fairly call a "vicar apostolic" rather than a bishop. When St. Paul wrote to him he was himself apparently travelling, or intending to travel, in Macedonia, revisiting, we may believe, in accordance with the promise of Phil. ii. 24, the churches of Philippi, Thessalonica and Berœa, and was intending to winter at Nicopolis. It is a natural inference from this, and from the urgency with which he entreats Titus to come to him quickly (Tit. iii. 12), that the Epistle was written in the autumn. The name of Nicopolis (= "the city of victory"), to which, we may believe, he now directed his course, was borne by three cities, one on the borders of Thrace and Macedonia, one in Cilicia, and a third, more conspicuous than the others, on the Bay of Actium, which had been built by Augustus to commemorate his great victory there over the combined fleets of Antonius and Cleopatra. In a previous journey through Macedonia to the Illyrian frontier, probably that of Acts xx. 2 (comp. Rom. xv. 19), he had already laid the foundations of a church in that region of Greece, and may well have been anxious to revisit it.

In the meantime a great change had come over the policy of the imperial court at Rome. Poppæa, with her tendency to protect the Jews, and probably the Christians of "Cæsar's household," who at first passed for a sect of Jews, had died under the brutality of the emperor (A.D. 65),* and the influence of Tigellinus, base, brutal, and cruel, was altogether dominant. The great fire of A.D. 64 had broken out at the foot of the Cœlian and Palatine Hills, after an entertainment which he had given in the gardens of Agrippa, with surroundings of shameless foulness, in honour of the emperor (Tacit. *Ann.* xv. 37—40); and when, after being partially subdued, it renewed its devastations in the Æmilian district of the city, where Tigellinus had large estates, he shared with Nero the odium of having either originated it or at least looked on it with an Epicurean indifference, if not, as the emperor was reported to have done, with a kind of æsthetic complacency. That suspicion had to be stamped out. The Christians of Rome, those especially whose presence in the palace reproved the vices of Tigellinus and his master, were sacrificed as victims to the popular indignation, and the tide of suspicion was turned only too successfully on the strange people who lived in the world but not of it, and talked much of a King who was to come in flaming fire and devour his adversaries (2 Thess. i. 8). The language of Juvenal implies that the better Romans knew that the martyrs whose lurid flames were as torches in the gardens of Nero on those fearful nights were sacrificed to the jealousy and vindictive hatred of the favourite—

> "Dar'st thou to speak of Tigellinus' guilt?
> Thou too shalt flare as they did, whom we saw,
> Standing and burning, throat impaled, in smoke,
> And make wide furrows in the thirsty sand."
> —*Sat.* i. 155.

That of Martial shows that they suffered as Christians, and might have purchased safety by apostasy. He refers to the well-known story of Mucius Scævola thrusting his hand into the fire, which apparently had been dramatised under Nero, and received with much applause—

> "You saw, enacted on the stage of sand,
> How Mucius thrust into the flames his hand;
> Think ye that act true hero's deed to be?
> Dull as Abdera's † dotards then are ye;
> Is it not more, when robe of flame is nigh,
> To say, 'I will not sacrifice,' and die,
> Than with the order 'Burn thy hand,' comply?"
> —*Epig.* x. 25.

The populace, excited, as the Athenians had been by the mutilation of the Hermæ busts, as that of England was by the Fire of London in 1666, rushed upon the members of the "sect everywhere spoken against" with a ferocious eagerness, and beheld their sufferings at first without a shudder. Only in a few, like Juvenal and Tacitus, did a touch of pity mingle with their aversion. All the old calumnies were revived, and the presence of

* It is not without interest to note the fact that the body of Poppæa was embalmed, as if in deference to her known tendencies, after the Jewish manner, and not burnt, after the custom of Rome (Tacit. *Ann.* xvi. 6).

† The town was proverbial for the stupidity of its people. The men of Abdera were as the men of Gotham of our nursery rhyme.

the Christians at Rome was looked on as a reproach to be got rid of with all convenient speed.

Fanaticism is naturally contagious, and though there was no formal organised persecution throughout the empire,* old enmities revived, and the opportunities for acting on them were utilised. The Epistles of St. Peter, written about this time, bear witness to the "fiery trial" that was coming upon all the provinces of Asia Minor (1 Pet. iv. 12), to the fact that men spoke against the disciples of Christ as criminals at large, that the very name of Christian exposed them to persecution (1 Pet. iv. 16). The fact that a medal had been struck at Laodicea, in which the very name of "God" was assigned to Nero, would naturally rouse the horror of all believers, and make them think that the Antichrist had indeed come—the "man of *lawlessness*," who exalteth himself above all that is called God, or that is worshipped.† It only needed that he should follow in the footsteps of Caligula to verify the whole predicted description of one who "sitteth in the Temple of God, showing himself that he is God" (2 Thess. ii. 4). Was not the day of the Lord at hand? Was not a more terrible conflagration than had already been witnessed about to destroy the city on the seven hills, the new "Babylon the Great, the mother of harlots . . . drunken with the blood of the saints, and with the blood of the martyrs of Jesus"? (Rev. xvii. 5, 6.)

It was under these conditions that the warrant was issued, as we must believe, by Tigellinus, for the arrest of St. Paul. It lies in the nature of the case that the charge could not have been the original accusation brought against him by Tertullus (Acts xxiv. 1—8), for that was simply a question of Jewish law, a charge of having profaned the Jewish Temple. But Tigellinus must have known that for two years he had been the central figure among the Christians of Rome—that he was on terms of friendship with officers of the Augustan band and of the Prætorian Guard. True, he had left the city before the fire; but what if he had planned it, or even suggested the idea, and left others to work it out?

It is a reasonable, though not certain, inference, from the facts of the case, that the officers who were in charge of the warrant arrested their prisoner at Nicopolis; and if so, the notes of travel in the SECOND EPISTLE TO TIMOTHY must be referred, as above, to the hasty journey which had led him to that city, and in which he had revisited Corinth, Miletus, and Troas (2 Tim. iv. 13, 20). When he wrote that Epistle, he was, beyond all doubt, at Rome. And he was there not now, as before, in a hired apartment, and with the comparative freedom of a *libera custodia* (see Note on Acts xxviii. 16), but in bonds, as a malefactor and a criminal (2 Tim. ii. 9). The Roman tradition that he was confined in the lower dungeon of the Mamertine prison, dark and damp, with no opening but a hole through which the prisoners were let down, has in it nothing in itself improbable.‡ The persecution that had been raging since his departure had naturally thinned the ranks, and tried the fidelity, of his friends. Aquila and Priscilla had once again been forced to leave Rome, and were now at Ephesus (2 Tim. iv. 9). Demas had forsaken him (2 Tim. iv. 10). Tychicus, still acting as the courier of the Apostolic Church, was the bearer of the Epistle to Timotheus (2 Tim. iv. 12). Crescens had gone to Gaul or to Galatia. Titus, who, we may infer, left Crete, and joined him at Nicopolis, had gone thence, without coming to Italy, to Dalmatia (2 Tim. iv. 10). One friend only, Luke, the beloved physician, probably finding some protection even now in his connection with Seneca and Gallio, was found willing to continue with him (2 Tim. iv. 11). It was probably before Tigellinus, rather than Nero himself, that the Apostle, in the utter loneliness of which he speaks so plaintively, made his first defence against the charge of treason.* Possibly the judge was, for a time, moved by his dauntless innocence; possibly, as when, about the same time, the celebrated impostor, Apollonius, of Tyana, stood before the same judge (Philostr. *Vit. Apollon.* iv. 42—44), he shrank from condemning one who was believed to possess supernatural powers. St. Paul's entreaty that Timothy would bring the books and parchments which he had left at Troas (2 Tim. iv. 13) may imply a delay during which he was waiting for documentary evidence (possibly the "parchments" of 2 Tim. iv. 13), to prove his citizenship. The "cloak" may well have been wanted if he had to spend the winter months in the Mamertine prison. It was after that first hearing (2 Tim. iv. 16), filled with the conviction that the end was near, that the Apostle penned the last words which tell us of his hope and joy at seeing the crown of righteousness at last within his reach (2 Tim. iv. 8).

The confinement of St. Paul probably lasted for several months after this first hearing of his case. Before long, according to traditions which were current in their simplest form in the time of Clement of Rome, and were recognised in their fuller details by Eusebius (*Hist.* ii. 25) in the fourth century, he was joined by the great Apostle of the Circumcision, and the two who, as far as we know, had not met since the memorable dispute at Antioch (Gal. ii. 14), were brought together at last once more in the Mamertine prison. The later Roman fiction of a pontificate of twenty-five years,† the earlier myths in the Clementine *Homilies* and *Recognitions* of a conflict with Simon Magus in the streets of Rome (see Notes on Acts viii. 24), may be dismissed as belonging altogether to the region of the fabulous; but there is nothing improbable in the supposition, either that he had come from the literal to the spiritual Babylon (1 Pet. v. 13) to look after the welfare of the suffering Christians there,‡ or that the wide-spread net of Tigellinus, which

* The inscription found in Spain, and recording the success of Nero in extirpating the new superstition which had spread over the empire ("NERONI CL. CÆS. AUG. PONT. MAX. OB PROVINC. LATRONIBUS ET HIS QUI NOVAM GENER. HUM. SUPERSTITION. INCULCAB. PURGATAM"), is now commonly regarded as spurious (Gruter, *Inscriptt.* p. 238, No. 9).

† For the medal, see Note in Brotier's Tacitus (*Ann.* xv. 74). Even in the Roman senate, however, the title *Divus*, reserved for other emperors as a posthumous apotheosis, had been applied to Nero while he lived (*ibid.*).

‡ Recent excavations by Mr. J. H. Parker have shown that what is now known as the Mamertine prison was probably only part of a much larger building used as a state prison (Macduff's *Footsteps of St. Paul*, p. 76).

* It is hardly probable that St. Paul should have referred in these words to a trial during his former stay at Rome. The whole tone is that of a man writing of what had passed recently. Timotheus would naturally, having been with St. Paul at Rome (Phil. i. 1; Col. i. 1), know the whole history of the first imprisonment.

† The long pontificate of Pius IX. has given a fresh prominence to the traditional "years of St. Peter," and an inscription over the chair of the Apostle in St. Peter's records that it was given to the deceased pontiff, alone among all his successors, to equal those years. The date given in Roman Catholic chronologies to the foundation of the Church of Rome by Peter is A.D. 41.

‡ This view derives a certain support from the Roman tradition that St. Peter dwelt in the house of Pudens, the centurion, and baptised his two daughters, Praxedis and Pudentiana. The absence of any mention of Claudia shows that the tradition was independent of 2 Tim. iv. 21, and of any inference from the *Epigrams* of Martial. Churches dedicated to the two sisters stand near together on the Viminal Hill, and the traditional house of Pudens is below that which bears the name of the latter.

had taken in its meshes St. Paul at Nicopolis and Apollonius at Rome, had caught him also. The story perpetuated by the *Domine, Quo Vadis?* chapel on the Appian Way, that he had endeavoured to effect his escape, and after he had passed the Capuan Gate (now the *Porta San Sebastiano*) had seen the well-remembered form of the Master he had loved, and on asking the question, "Lord, whither goest Thou?" received the answer, "I go to be crucified again," and then returned to the city to face the doom which he was seeking to avoid, has in it, I venture to think, the likelihood which is involved in the fact that it was altogether unlikely that such a story should have been invented at a later age, when the name of the Prince of the Apostles had been identified with the notion of the primacy, if not the infallibility, of his successors. It is at all events, somewhat over-sceptical, in spite of much uncertainty as to dates and details, to reject the tradition that the two Apostles were at last tried and condemned together. For the last time the free-born citizen of Rome was allowed the privileges of his citizenship, and escaped the degradation of the servile punishment of crucifixion. The Galilean Apostle, on the other hand, who had seen the Crucified One, chose, according to a current tradition, to be placed upon the cross head-downwards, unwilling to present himself to the eyes of the disciples as suffering as their Lord had suffered (Euseb. *Hist.* iii. 1). As the story runs, the two Apostles were led out together by the Ostian Gate (now the *Porta San Paolo*), and a small chapel about a mile from the city indicates the spot where they took their last farewell. St. Peter was led, according to one tradition, to the hill of the Janiculum, on the left bank of the Tiber, and a chapel attached to the church of San Pietro in Montorio, was built over the spot where the cross was believed to have been fixed; while his brother Apostle was taken further on the Ostian road to the spot now known as the *Tre Fontane,* from the legend that as the head was struck off by the sword of the executioner it bounded three times from the ground, and that a spring of water sprang up at each spot where it had touched the earth. Both bodies were placed, according to the Roman tradition of the time of Gregory the Great, in the catacombs on the Appian Way, under the modern church of San Sebastiano. Thence that of St. Peter was removed, possibly by the Jewish Christians of Rome, to the site in the Vatican, where the stately temple of Michael Angelo has replaced the old Basilica, the marbles and mosaics of which still remain in the Confession* under the central dome, while that of St. Paul was interred by the pious care of a Gentile convert, Lucina, on the Ostian road, and the Basilica of San Paolo-fuori-le-Mura, built by Theodosius and Valentinian in A.D. 388 on the site of a smaller church erected by Constantine, claims for its Confession the glory of containing his sarcophagus. In the full-blown development of the rival traditions of Roman churches, that of St. John Lateran boasted of possessing the heads of both Apostles, while each of the Churches of St. Paul outside the walls and St. Peter in the Vatican, admitting the claims of its rival, exulted in the thought that it could claim half of the body of each of them.

I have thought it best to lay before the reader as clear and connected a narrative as the imperfect *data* allowed, without entering on the difficult and perplexing questions which have been raised as to the year of the martyrdom of the two Apostles. It is right, however, to state that a very considerable divergency of views prevails on this point, in part connected with the question of the genuineness of the Pastoral Epistles, and that the year has been variously fixed between the limits of A.D. 64 on the one hand, and A.D. 68 on the other. The above has been based on the assumption of the later rather than the earlier date being, at least, approximately true. The Western Church has for many centuries dedicated the 29th and 30th of June (two days being appointed so that due honour might be rendered to each) to the commemoration of the martyrdom of the two Apostles. The calendar of the Reformed Church of England follows that of Rome in assigning June 29th to St. Peter, but contents itself with commemorating the Conversion of St. Paul on January 25th without assigning any day as the anniversary of his death.

What picture, we ask, are we to draw of the man who plays so prominent a part in the history of the Apostolic Church? What was he like? What impression did he make on men at first sight? What when they had learnt to know him? The nearest approximation to an authentic portrait is the medal (an engraving from which may be seen in Lewin's *St. Paul,* ii. p. 411) found in the cemetery of Domitilla, one of the Flavian family, and assigned by archæologists to the close of the first or beginning of the second century. Closely cut hair (comp. Acts xviii. 18), slightly projecting eyes, a high forehead, a nose and mouth that indicate intellectual vigour, moustache, and a beard full rather than long,—this was what the artist gave in his attempt to reproduce a face which he may have seen himself or heard described by others. In stature, it is obvious, he was below the middle height (2 Cor. x. 10). The suffering which he describes as the thorn in the flesh, showed itself in weak eyes, probably in the nervous trembling of one who is constantly liable to severe attacks of pain. (See Notes on 2 Cor. xii. 7.) He went about as one who had the sentence of death on him (2 Cor. i. 9). With this, however, there was great vigour of body. He could travel on foot some thirty miles a day (chap. xvii. 1), or ride on horseback (chap. xxiii. 24), or swim rivers, or keep himself floating for many hours at sea (chap. xxvii. 43). The indomitable energy of the man sustained him under hardships and privations of all kinds. He spoke, not with the rhetorical cadences in which Greek rhetoricians delighted, but with words that went home like an arrow to their mark, and pierced men's hearts (2 Cor. xi. 25). The voice was, perhaps, untuneable, but the words were full of life (1 Cor. xiv. 25; 2 Cor. x. 10). As men saw him in his artisan's dress, living the life of the poor, they might have taken him for what he appeared to be; but when they came to know him they found a culture that surprised them, and a marvellous readiness to adapt himself to different natures. He became "all things to all men;" won the respect of proconsuls, chiliarchs, centurions, of the wild emotional Galatians, of the runaway slave Onesimus. He would listen to any tale of sorrow, and yet a keen sense of humour mingled with his earnestness and tenderness. He did not disdain to mingle an occasional pun (Phil. iv. 2, 18; Philem. verses 10, 11) with serious counsel, nor to paint the weaknesses of silly women and charlatans with a pen that almost reminds us of the caustic sarcasm of Juvenal (1 Tim. v. 11—13; 2 Tim. iii. 6, 7). And yet when the hour of prayer came, sometimes when he was alone, sometimes when in company with others, he would be absorbed as in ecstatic adoration (1 Cor. xiv. 18). Strange mysterious utterances of praise, doxologies,

* The "Confession" is the technical term commonly applied in Italy to the crypt-like shrine which contains the relics of the saint to whom the church is dedicated.

alleluiahs, and the like, in half-musical intonations, would pour forth from his lips. He would seem as one caught up to the third heaven, to the paradise of God (2 Cor. xii. 1—4), and then, again, would speak, as a prophet of the Lord, with thoughts that breathed and words that burnt. And in his prayers there was an almost terrible earnestness. Groans mingled with words, and name after name of churches and beloved disciples passed from his lips, as he laid his intercessions for them before his Father in heaven (Rom. i. 9; viii. 26; 1 Thess. iii. 10). Such are the outlines of the man as he was—very unlike to Raphael's idealised representation of him,—which are given to us indirectly through his own writings, and each reader must fill up those outlines according to his power. The attempt has been made, not without success, by many word-painters and masters of style. Without disparaging other representations of this kind, I venture to lay before the reader two such portraits.

"I dreamed that, with a passionate complaint,
I wished me born amid God's deeds of might,
And envied those who saw the presence bright
Of gifted prophet and strong-hearted saint
Whom my heart loves and fancy strives to paint:
I turned, when straight a stranger met my sight,
Came as my guest, and did awhile unite
His lot with mine, and lived without restraint;
Courteous he was and grave;—so meek in mien,
It seemed untrue, or told a purpose weak;
Yet in the mood, he could with aptness speak,
Or with stern force, or show of feelings keen,
Marking deep craft, methought, or hidden pride:—
Then came a voice—'St. Paul is at thy side!'"
—J. H. Newman, *Lyra Apostolica.*

The other is by a less known author:—

"The third who journeyed with them, weak and worn,
Blear-eyed, dim-visioned, bent and bowed with pain,
We looked upon with wonder.—Not for him
The praise of form heroic, supple limbs,
The glory of the sculptor as he moulds
The locks of Zeus, o'erspreading lofty brows,
Apollo, the far-darter, in the pride
Of manhood's noblest beauty, or the grace
Of sandalled Hermes, messenger of gods:
Not thus he came, but clad in raiment worn,
Of roughest texture, bearing many stains
Of age and travel. In his hand he bore
A staff on which he leant, as one whose limbs
Have lost before their time the strength of youth;
And underneath his arm a strange old book,
Whose mystic letters seemed for him the words
Of wisdom and of truth. And oft he read
In solemn cadence words that thrilled his soul,
And, lighting that worn face with new-born joy,
Bade him go on rejoicing.
So they came;
So entered he our town; but, ere the sun
Had lit the eastern clouds, a fever's chill
Fell on him; parched thirst and darting throbs
Of keenest anguish racked those weary limbs;
His brow seemed circled with a crown of pain;
And oft, pale, breathless, as if life had fled,
He looked like one in ecstasy, who sees
What others see not; to whose ears a voice
Which others hear not, floats from sea or sky:
And broken sounds would murmur from his lips,
Of glory wondrous, sounds ineffable,
The cry of 'Abba, Father,' and the notes
Of some strange solemn chant of other lands
So, stricken, prostrate, pale, the traveller lay,
So stript of all the comeliness of form,
Men might have spurned and loathed him, passing on
To lead their brighter life.—And yet we stayed;
We spurned him not, nor loathed; through all the shrouds
Of poverty and sickness we could see
The hero-soul, the presence as of One
Whom then we knew not. When the pain was sharp,
And furrowed brows betrayed the strife within,
Then was he gentlest. Even to our slaves
He spoke as brothers, winning all their hearts
By that unwonted kindness."

To these ideal portraits we may add such fragmentary notices as are found in ancient writers, and which, from their general consistency, may claim something like the character of a tradition. Thus in the *Philopatris*, ascribed to Lucian (possibly of the second century, but the book is probably spurious and belonging to the fourth), he is described as "bald, and with an aquiline nose;" and in the apocryphal *Acts of Paul and Thecla* (c. i. 7), as "little in stature, bald, crook-legged, vigorous, with knitted brows, slightly aquiline nose, full of grace, appearing now as a man and now as having the face of an angel." Malala, or John of Antioch (in the sixth century), describes him (*Chronograph*, c. x.) as "short, bald, with partly grey hair and beard, a prominent nose, greyish eyes, knitted brows, pale and yet fresh complexion, a well-shaped beard, with a touch of humour, sagacious, self-restrained, pleasant to converse with, gentle, yet filled by the Holy Spirit with an eager enthusiasm. Nicephorus (in the fifteenth century) reproduces the same general type; but the late date makes it impossible for us to look to his account as more than a second-hand portrait. Such as it is, he too speaks of short stature, somewhat bent and stooping; pale and yet comely; bald, and with bright grey eyes; with long and aquiline nose, and a thick beard more or less grizzled (*Hist.* ii. 37).*

Such in outward form, such in manner and character, was the man to whom the Church of Christ owes so much. We are reminded as we read his own account of himself, what others said of him in his lifetime, the traditions that survived after his death, of such a one as Socrates, with his Silenus face, his ecstatic trances, his playful irony and humour, his earnest thought, his deep enthusiasm, his warm affection for the young, his indifference to wealth and ease. There were, of course, distinctive features, rising in part out of differences of race and culture—the difference between the Aryan and the Semitic types of character—in part out of the higher truths which had been revealed to the Apostle and not to the sage; but there is enough in the general features of the life and character of each to help us to understand the words which tell us that "Wisdom in all ages entering into holy souls maketh them friends of God and prophets."

* The two last quotations are taken from Lewin's St. *Paul* ii. p. 412.

THE EPISTLE OF PAUL THE APOSTLE TO THE

# ROMANS

# INTRODUCTION

TO

## THE EPISTLE OF PAUL THE APOSTLE TO THE

# ROMANS

**I. The Epistles of St. Paul generally, and that to the Romans in particular.**—It is a somewhat remarkable fact that so large a part of the documents of Christianity should be taken up with a correspondence. The contents of the Old Testament, heterogeneous as they are, correspond more nearly to what we should expect to find in a sacred volume. A legislation such as that of Moses, songs expressive of deep religious feeling like the Psalms, impassioned addresses like those of the prophets, histories such as the continuous series which trace the fortunes of the Chosen People—all these, we should have thought, were the natural vehicle for a religion. But the composition of the New Testament is something more unique. The foundation of Christianity is laid in a narrative; but the first and greatest development of Christian theology is not embodied in narrative, not in any set and formal treatise, not in liturgies, canons, and works of devotion, but in a collection of letters.

The causes of this peculiarity are not far to seek. Christianity was the first great missionary religion. It was the first to break the bounds of race, and aim at embracing all mankind. But this necessarily involved a change in the mode in which it was presented. The prophet of the Old Testament, if he had anything to communicate, either appeared in person or sent messengers to speak for him by word of mouth. The one exception of any religious significance is the letter of Elijah to Jehoram in 2 Chron. xxi. The narrow limits of Palestine made direct personal communication easy. But the case was different when the Christian Church came to consist of a number of scattered posts, stretching from Mesopotamia in the east to Rome. or even Spain, in the far west. It was only natural that the Apostle by whom the greater number of these communities had been founded should seek to communicate with them by letter. He was enabled to do so by two things: first, the very general diffusion of the Greek language; and, secondly, the remarkable facilities of intercourse afforded at this particular time. The whole world was at peace, and held together by the organised rule of imperial Rome. Piracy had been put down. Commerce flourished to an extraordinary and unprecedented degree. In order to find a parallel to the rapidity and ease of communication along the whole coast of the Mediterranean and the inland districts, intersected as they were with a network of military roads, we should have to come down to the present century. St. Paul was in the habit of travelling surrounded by a group of more intimate disciples, whom, as occasion arose, he despatched to the several churches that he had founded, much as a general sends his *aides-de-camp* to different parts of a battle-field; or, without falling back upon those, he had often opportunities of sending by some chance traveller, such as was probably Phebe, the bearer of the Epistle to the Romans.

The whole of St. Paul's Epistles bear traces of their origin. It is just this occasional character which makes them so peculiarly human. They arose out of actual pressing needs, and they are couched (most of them, at least) in the vivid and fervent language of one who takes a deep and loving interest in the persons to whom he is writing, as well as in the subject that he is writing about. Precept and example, doctrine and practice, theology and ethics, are all mixed and blended together. No religious books present the same variety as the Christian, and that because they are in the closest contact with actual life.

There is, however, as we might naturally expect, a difference in the balance of the two elements—the personal or epistolary element proper on the one hand, and the doctrinal or didactic element on the other. In some of the Epistles the one, in others the other, preponderates. As types of the first class, we might take the First, and still more that noble and unsurpassable Second Epistle to the Corinthians, and the Epistle to the Philippians. At the head of the second class would be placed the Epistles to the Romans and to the Ephesians.

It can hardly be a chance coincidence that precisely in these two Epistles there are certain MSS. which omit the words of address to the particular Church. In the course of the present Commentary the reasons will be stated which have led to the suggestions that the Epistle was at an early period circulated in a double form—one that in which we now have it, and the other, with the personal matter excised, as a general treatise on Christian doctrine. In any case this character in it is marked: it is the most like a theological treatise of any of the New Testament writings.

How are we to account for this? We shall be in a better position to answer such a question when we have considered more particularly the circumstances under which the Epistle was written, the persons to whom it was addressed, and the object for which it was designed.

**II. Time and Place of the Epistle.**—And first, as to the time and place of the Epistle. These are fixed within very definite limits. One set of allusions clearly points to Corinth as the place from which the Apostle is writing. In chap. xvi. 23 he speaks of himself as the guest of one "Gaius," and in 1 Cor. i. 14, he says that he had baptised none of the Corinthian Church "but Crispus and Gaius." The name was a common one; still there would be a *primâ facie* probability in the identification. In the same verse (chap. xvi. 23), the Apostle conveys a salutation from Erastus, "the treasurer" ("chamberlain," Authorised version) "of the city," and in 2 Tim. iv. 20 we are told that Erastus "abode in Corinth," which would be natural if Corinth was his home. These indications are clenched by the commendatory notice in chap. xvi. 1 of Phebe, deaconess of the Church at Cenchrea, to whose care it would seem that the Epistle was entrusted. Cenchrea was the port of Corinth.

From another set of allusions (chap. xv. 25, 26) we gather that at the time at which he was writing, St. Paul was about to go up to Jerusalem, bearing with him the sums collected amongst the comparatively wealthy churches of "Macedonia and Achaia" for the poor Christians at Jerusalem. The order in which the two names are mentioned would quite fall in with the assumption that it was from Achaia—of which province Corinth was the capital—that the Epistle was written; and we should also naturally infer that he had passed through Macedonia on his way to Corinth. We find, besides, the intention expressly declared of extending the journey, after his visit to Jerusalem, to Rome (chap. xv. 23—26). All this tallies exactly with the statement in Acts xix. 21, "After these things were ended (*i.e.*, the success of the Apostle's preaching at Ephesus), Paul purposed in the spirit, when he had passed through Macedonia and Achaia, to go to Jerusalem, saying, 'After I have been there, I must also see Rome.'" Such was his programme; and that it was actually carried out appears from the notices in Acts xx. 1—3, 22, xxi. 15. In the first we find the Apostle spending three months in Greece, in the second he announces at Miletus the destination of his journey for Jerusalem, in the third he actually arrives there. We learn, moreover, incidentally from his speech before Felix, in Acts xxiv. 17, that the object of his visit to Jerusalem was to bring "alms and offerings." And there are repeated allusions to a collection for the same purpose in both the Epistles to the Corinthians. (See 1 Cor. xvi. 3; 2 Cor. viii. 1, 2; ix. 1 *et seq.*)

The Epistle is thus placed, by a remarkable convergence of evidence, in that part of the Apostle's third missionary journey which was spent in Corinth. The journey in question began at Antioch. Thence the Apostle made his way to Ephesus by a detour through Galatia and Phrygia. At Ephesus he stayed in all about three years, and his preaching was attended with a success which roused the heathen population against him. The disturbance that ensued hastened him on his way to Macedonia. Through Macedonia he passed westwards as far as Illyricum (chap. xv. 19), and thence to Greece, where he spent three months.

It was at Corinth, then, during these three months that the Epistle was written. This would be, according to the system of the best chronologists, in the spring of the year A.D. 58. That the time of the year was spring is fixed by the fact that the Apostle had intended to sail for Syria (Acts xx. 3), which he would not have done during the winter season. The navigation of the Mediterranean was held to be unsafe from October to the middle of March. But the Apostle must have left Corinth before the spring was far advanced, as he had time, after passing through Macedonia and coasting along the shore of Asia Minor, to arrive at Jerusalem for the Feast of Pentecost—*i.e.*, our Whitsuntide. We shall not be far wrong if we place the Epistle towards the end of the month of February.

**III. Place of the Epistle in relation to the rest of St. Paul's Epistles.**—Three other Epistles were written during the same journey, the First and Second to the Corinthians, and that to the Galatians. The First Epistle to the Corinthians was written from Ephesus during the spring of the year preceding, A.D. 57. The Second Epistle was written from Macedonia in the autumn of the same year. The Epistle to the Galatians is less clearly dated. It may possibly belong to the earlier part of the three years' residence at Ephesus, and it is assigned to this time and place by the majority of commentators. But when we come to deal with that Epistle reasons will be given for preferring another view, which places it rather between the Second Epistle to the Corinthians and that to the Romans. We should thus have the following order:—

| | | |
|---|---|---|
| 1 Corinthians.. | Ephesus . . . | A.D. 57 Spring. |
| 2 Corinthians.. | Macedonia . . | „ 57 Autumn. |
| Galatians.... | Macedonia, or perhaps more probably Greece | „ 57, 58 Winter. |
| Romans...... | Corinth . . . | „ 58 Early Spring. |

The Epistle to the Romans comes, in any case, last in the group.

Passing to the wider relations of the group to which the Epistle to the Romans belongs, to the rest of the Apostle's writings, we shall see that it comes second of the four larger groups. The order would be this:—

| | | |
|---|---|---|
| A. 1 & 2 Thessalonians | 2nd Missionary journey | A.D. 52 (end), 53 |
| B. 1 & 2 Corinthians, Galatians, Romans | 3rd Missionary journey | „ 57, 58 |
| C. Philippians, Ephesians, Colossians, Philemon (*Epistles of the Imprisonment*) | First Roman Imprisonment | „ 62, 63 |
| D. 1 & 2 Timothy, Titus (*Pastoral Epistles*) | Interval of freedom and Second Roman Imprisonment | „ 66—68 |

**IV. The Roman Church.**—The next point to be determined is the character of the Church to which the Epistle was addressed. And this we may do well to consider from two points of view. First, with reference to what may be learned respecting it from external sources; and, secondly, with reference to the indications supplied by the Epistle itself.

1. At Rome, as elsewhere, Christianity first took root among the Jews. A large colony of this people existed in Rome at the Christian era. The foundation of it had been laid by the captives carried away by Pompey after the taking of Jerusalem in B.C. 63. A number of these were settled in Rome. They attracted the favourable notice first of Julius Cæsar, and then still more of Augustus, who assigned to them a special quarter beyond, *i.e.*, on the right bank of the Tiber, and opposite to the modern Jewish quarter, or Ghetto, which lies between the Capitol and the river. They were allowed the free exercise of their religion, and, as was always the case where they were treated with toleration, rapidly increased in numbers. A Jewish embassy,

which came to Rome after the death of Herod the Great, was able to attach to itself as many as 8,000 Roman Jews, who naturally would represent only the more respectable portion of the male community. This rapid progress received a check under Tiberius, who, in A.D. 19, probably at the instance of Sejanus, obtained a decree of the Senate, sending 4,000 Jews and Egyptians to Sardinia on military service, and forbidding the rest from the practice of their religion on pain of expulsion from Italy. Josephus tells a scandalous story to account for this, but the real reason may, very possibly, have been the fear of secret political machinations under the disguise of religion. In the latter part of his reign Tiberius reversed this policy, and its effects speedily disappeared. Under the next emperor, Caligula, an embassy of Alexandrine Jews, headed by Philo, met with a rough reception, but this would seem to have been more than counterbalanced by the favour extended to Herod Agrippa, who stood high in influence at the Court. This astute politician made use of his position to further the accession of Claudius, and as a reward, not only was restored to the dominions of his grandfather, Herod the Great, but also obtained an extension of privileges for his countrymen throughout the empire. Later in the reign of Claudius disturbances arose among the Jews at Rome which seem to have been connected with the first preaching of Christianity, either through the excitement of the Messianic expectations, or through disputes between the Jews and Christians. Suetonius says that they took place at the instigation "of one Chrestus," which, for the heathen historian, would be a not unnatural misconstruction. The result was a second banishment of the Jews from Rome (Acts xviii. 2). But this again cannot have been really complete, and the Jews who were banished seem in many instances (such as that of Aquila and Prisca) soon to have returned. The effect of the repressive measures might easily be exaggerated. There is abundant evidence to show that, at the time St. Paul was writing, the Jewish community at Rome was numerous and flourishing, and its influence upon Roman society was loudly complained of alike by the philosopher, the satirist, and the historian.

The chronology of the foregoing sketch may be thus exhibited:—

| | |
|---|---|
| Founding of the Jewish community at Rome by prisoners brought from Jerusalem by Pompey ... ... ... | B.C. 63 |
| Favourable position under Julius Cæsar | B.C. 48—44 |
| and Augustus ... ... | B.C. 27—A.D. 14 |
| Embassy to Rome after the death of Herod ... ... ... ... ... | B.C. 4 |
| First decree of banishment under Tiberius | A.D. 19 |
| Philo's embassy to Caligula ... *circa* | „ 40 |
| Second decree of banishment under Claudius ... ... ... ... *circa* | „ 49 |
| Return of Aquila and Prisca to Rome ... | „ 57 |
| Epistle to the Romans ... ... ... | „ 58 |

According to the tradition which is still in vogue among the modern representatives of the Roman Church, Christianity was planted there by St. Peter in the year A.D. 41. St. Peter himself is said to have held the episcopate for twenty-five years. This tradition, however, only dates from the time of Jerome (*ob.* A.D. 420), and is therefore much too late to be of any value. It is contradicted by the whole tenor of St. Paul's Epistle, which could hardly have failed to contain some allusion to the presence of a brother Apostle, especially when we consider the express declaration of St. Paul that he was careful not to "build upon another man's foundation." Besides, a distinct *alibi* can be proved by the comparison of Acts xv. with Gal. ii. 1—9, which shows that, at the time of the Apostolic Council in A.D. 52, not only was Peter at Jerusalem, but Jerusalem had been up to that time his head-quarters. He is still the Apostle of the circumcision, and a pillar of the mother church. At a later period he is found, not at Rome, but at Antioch.

It is more probable that the germs of Christianity were carried back to Rome by the "strangers" (Acts ii. 10) whom we find in Jerusalem at the Feast of Pentecost, *i.e.*, Jews resident in Rome who had come up for the purpose of attending the feast. The rudiments of Christian teaching brought back by these would soon be developed in the constant intercourse which took place between Rome and the provinces. The fact that, in the list of the salutations at the end of the Epistle, so many are mentioned who were not native Romans, but had been already under the personal influence of St. Paul, would readily account for the advanced knowledge of Christianity that the Apostle assumes among them.

2. Turning now more exclusively to the Epistle itself, what are we to gather from it in regard to the Church to which the Apostle is writing? The main question to be decided is the proportion in which the two great constituent elements of the primitive Christian Church were mixed and combined in it. Was the Church at Rome, in a preponderating degree, Jewish or Gentile? The answer to this question usually gives throughout the apostolic times the best clue to the doctrinal bearings and general character of any Christian community.

We find throughout the Epistle an easy interchange of address, first pointed, as it were, towards Gentiles, and then towards Jews. In one place (chap. xi. 13) the Apostle says in so many words, "I speak to you Gentiles." In another place (chap. vii. 1) he says as expressly, "I speak to them that know the law," and in proof that this is not merely an external knowledge, he evidently in chap. iii. 19 is appealing to an authority which he knows that his readers will recognise. "What things soever the law saith, it saith to them that are under the law." Accordingly we find that though the Apostle begins his Epistle by addressing the Romans as a Gentile Church (chap. i. 6, 13), and although the first section of the proof of his great thesis, the universal need and offer of salvation, bears specially upon the Gentiles, he very soon passes from their case to that of the Jews. Chap. ii. contains a direct expostulation with the one, just as chap. i. had contained a condemnation of the other. Nor is it only a rhetorical artifice that in the section chap. ii. 17—24 the Jew is addressed throughout in the second person. The Apostle evidently had actual Jews before his mind. In like manner the long parenthetical discussion of the claims and fall of Israel in chaps. ix.—xi. is clearly intended to be double-edged. It has a two-fold application at once to Jew and Gentile. On the one hand it is intended as an apology for the justice of the divine dealings addressed to the Jew, and on the other hand it contains a warning addressed to the Gentile. If stress is laid upon the calling of the Gentiles, it is to provoke the Jew "to emulation." If stress is laid upon the rejection of the Jews, it is in order that the Gentiles may not "be high minded, but fear."

The whole phenomena of the Epistle, then, point to the conclusion that the Church for which it was destined consisted in almost equal proportions of converts from Judaism and from heathenism; and the easy transitions by which the Apostle turns from the one to the other seem to show that there was no sharp and hard antagonism between them. The Epistle is written as if both might form part of the audience that would hear it read. The Church at Rome was divided as yet by no burning questions. The Apostle did not think it necessary to speak strongly on the subject of circumcision on the one hand, or of laxity and immorality on the other. The differences that existed were of a much milder kind. The "strong" and "weak brethren," whose mutual duties are weighed so judiciously in chap. xiv., are not by any means a synonym for Jew or Gentile, though there would naturally be a tendency in parties to divide according to their origin. The asceticism and observance of days alluded to were not common characteristics of Judaism, but belonged especially to the sect of the Essenes. Nor does it seem that the divisions to which they gave rise extended beyond a greater or less degree of scrupulousness or liberality.

The inferences that we have thus been led to draw receive support from an analysis of a different kind. Much light is thrown upon the composition of the Church by the list of names of the persons selected for salutation in the last chapter of the Epistle. These will be found more fully discussed in the Notes, but in the meantime we may so far sum up the results as to say that they point clearly to a mixture of nationalities. The one name Mary (= Miriam) is exclusively Jewish; Apelles is, if not exclusively, at least typically so. But besides these Aquila and Prisca, Andronicus and Junia (or Junias), and Herodion must have been Jews. As Aristobulus was a Jew, and the Jews generally hung much together, it is probable that the household of Aristobulus would be mostly Jews also. Urban and Ampliatus (the true reading for Amplias) are genuine Latin names. Julia would be a dependent on the imperial household, of what nationality is uncertain. The rest of the names are Greek, which tallies with the fact that the literature of the Roman Church was Greek, and there are other evidences that the Church bore a generally Greek character up to the middle of the second century. A detailed comparison of the names, with those which have come down to us in mortuary and other inscriptions, seems to show that their owners belonged for the most part to the lower section of society—petty tradesmen and officers, or slaves. There is reason to think that the gospel had already found a footing among the slaves and freed-men of the court, who formed a prominent body in the Church some four years later when St. Paul sent greetings to the Philippians "chiefly" from them "of Cæsar's household" (Phil. iv. 20).

We may picture to ourselves the Roman Church as originating in the Jewish synagogues, as gradually attracting converts from the lower orders with which the Jews would come mostly in contact, as thus entering the household of the emperor himself, and, at the time when St. Paul was writing, constantly gaining ground among the Gentile community. As yet, however, the two great divisions of Jew and Gentile exist side by side in amicable relations, and with differences hardly greater than would at this day be found in the opposite views of a body professing the same creed.

**V. General Character of the Epistle to the Romans.**—We have, then, two kinds of *data* which may help us to understand the general character of the Epistle. We know that it was written at the same time as the Epistles to the Corinthians and Galatians, and we know that it was written to a Church composed partly of Jewish and partly of Gentile converts with no very pronounced antagonism between them. In these facts we may seek the explanation of the question that was raised at starting—the question how it was that the Epistle to the Romans comes to be so much of a comprehensive theological treatise.

It was addressed at once to Jews and Gentiles. There was, therefore, nothing to disturb the even balance of the Apostle's teaching. For once, at least, he found himself able to dilate with equal fulness upon both sides of his great theme. His own mind was naturally elevated above controversy. He had worked out a system for himself which, though its main elements were drawn from the Old Testament, yet transcended the narrower limits of Judaism. His philosophy of things was one in which Jew and Gentile alike had their place, and each received justice, but not more than justice. Hitherto his desire to hold the equilibrium between the parties had been thwarted. He wrote to the Corinthians, but his letter had been prompted by an outbreak of Gentile licence, in the face of which it would have been unseasonable to insist on the relaxation of the Mosaic law. He wrote to the Galatians, but then it was with indignation roused by Jewish bigotry. In each case a onesided treatment of Christian doctrine was necessary. It was as necessary as it is for a physician to apply local remedies to a local sore.

In the Roman Church the necessity existed in a much less degree. Nor even if it had existed would the Apostle have felt it as strongly. The character of the Church was only known to him by report. He had not the same vivid personal impressions in respect to it as he had of the churches of Corinth and Galatia.

In these Epistles the strong personal feelings of the Apostle and his vivid realisation of the circumstances with reference to which he is writing, come out in almost every line. "I write not these things to shame you, but as my beloved sons I warn you." "Now some are puffed up, as though I would not come to you. But I will come to you shortly if the Lord will, and will know, not the speech of them that are puffed up, but the power." "I verily, as absent in body, but present in spirit, have judged already, as though I were present, concerning him that hath so done the deed . . . ." "Out of much affliction and anguish of heart I wrote unto you with many tears; not that ye should be grieved, but that ye might know the love which I have more abundantly unto you. But if any have caused grief, he hath not grieved me but in part: that I may not overcharge you all." "Ye are our epistle, written in our hearts, known and read of all men . . . ." "Ye know how through infirmity of the flesh I preached the gospel unto you at the first. And my temptation which was in my flesh ye despised not, nor rejected; but received me as an angel of God, even as Christ Jesus . . . I bear you record, that if it had been possible, ye would have plucked out your own eyes, and have given them to me."

These disturbing influences were wanting in the case of the Romans. If the Epistle loses somewhat in the intensity of its personal appeals, it gains in breadth and comprehensiveness. It is the most abstract of all the Epistles. It is not a special doctrine for special circumstances, but Christian theology in its broadest sense. A double set of reasons combined to produce this. Not only the nature of the Apostle's relation to the Church at Rome and the character of that Church, but also the condition of his own mind at the time of writing. He was writing from Corinth, and just after he had despatched a letter to Galatia. An extreme upon one side balanced an extreme upon the other. Jew and Gentile were present to the mind of the Apostle in equal degree. At last he was able to express his thoughts in their own natural proportions. His mind was in its true philosophical attitude, and the result is the great philosophical Epistle, which was most appropriately addressed to the capital of the civilised world.

**VI. Contents and Analysis of the Epistle.**—The Epistle represents, then, the most mature result of the Apostle's reflection at this period of his life. It gathers up and presents in a connected form the scattered thoughts of the earlier Epistles.

The key to the theology of the apostolic age is its relation to the Messianic expectation among the Jews. The central point in the teaching of the Apostles is the fact that with the coming of Christ was inaugurated the Messianic reign. It was the universal teaching of the Jewish doctors—a teaching fully adopted and endorsed by the Apostles—that this reign was to be characterised by righteousness. But righteousness was just what the whole world, Jew and Gentile alike, had signally failed to obtain. The Mosaic law had indeed held up the ideal of righteousness before those who were subject to it, but it remained an ideal, utterly unfulfilled. Left merely to his own powers, threatened with punishment if he failed, but with no help or encouragement to enable him to succeed, the Jew found in the Law a hard task-master, the only effect of which was to "multiply transgressions"—*i.e.*, to provoke to sin and to increase its guilt. Christianity, on the other hand, does what the Law failed to do; it induces a state of righteousness in the believer, and opens out to him the blessedness and salvation which the Messiah came to bring.

The means by which this state of righteousness is brought about is naturally that by which the believer obtains admission into the Messianic kingdom—in other words, Faith. Righteousness is the Messianic *condition;* Faith is the Messianic *conviction.* But by Faith is meant, not merely an acceptance of the Messiahship of Jesus, but that intense and loving adhesion which such acceptance inspired, and which the life and death of Jesus were eminently qualified to call out. Faith opens out a new road of access to the divine favour. This was no longer to be sought only by the painful and laborious—nay, impossible, way of a fulfilment of the divine commands. The favour of God, and admission into the Messianic kingdom, was promised to all who with a true and heartfelt devotion took the Messiah for their king. Of such it was not asked whether they had actually fulfilled the Law in their own persons; their faith was *imputed to them for righteousness*—*i.e.*, taken in lieu of it, as the condition which would exempt them from the wrath and obtain for them the favour of God.

That which gave to faith this peculiar efficacy was the fact that Jesus, the Messiah, towards whom it was directed, by His sacrificial death had *propitiated* the anger which God could not but feel against sin, and set free the hitherto obstructed current of divine love. Henceforth the anger of God could not rest upon the followers of the Messiah, by virtue of that which the Messiah Himself had done.

But the faith of the Christian was no merely passive principle. Such an ardour of devotion must needs gain strength by its own exercise. It became by degrees a moral lever by which the righteousness, at first imputed, was made more and more real. It placed the believer in so close a relation to Christ as could hardly be described by any word short of *union* itself. And union with One so holy as Christ was could not fail to have the most powerful effect upon him who entered into it. It brought him into a new sphere entirely different from that of the Law. Henceforth the Law was nothing to him. But the end for which the Law existed was accomplished in another way. By union with Christ he became dead to sin. He entered upon a new service and a new state—a state of righteousness, which the indwelling Spirit of Christ (*i.e.*, the closest conceivable influence of the Spirit of Christ upon the soul) enabled him to maintain. The old bondage of the flesh was broken. The lawless appetites and desires engendered by the body were annihilated by the presence of a deeper and stronger emotion, fanned and cherished by the intervention of a power higher than that of man.

Such, at least, was the Christian's ideal, which he was pledged to aim at, even if he failed to reach it. And the presence of the Divine Spirit within him was something more than the guarantee of a moral life here on earth; it was the earnest of an existence still more glorious in the future. The Christian, by his adhesion to Christ, the Messiah, was brought within the range of an order of things in which not he alone, but all creation, was to share, and which was destined to expand into as yet dimly anticipated perfection. As faith is the faculty which the Christian is called upon to exercise in the present, so Hope is that by which he looks forward to the future. He finds the assurance of his ultimate triumph in the unconquerable and inalienable love of Christ.

One objection might naturally be raised to this exposition of the Christian's privileges. What relation did they bear to another set of privileges—the ancient privileges of the chosen people, Israel? At first sight it seemed as if the throwing open of the Messianic kingdom to faith only, and therefore to Gentiles equally with Jews, was a violation of the Old Covenant. To this objection there were several answers. Even if there had been some further act of choice on the part of God, involving a rejection of Israel, His absolute power of choosing one and refusing another was not to be questioned. But really the promise was not made to the whole of Israel, but only to such as should comply with the condition of faith. All Israel did not do this. Nor was all Israel rejected. If a part of Israel was rejected, it was only with the beneficent purpose of bringing in the Gentiles. In the end Israel, too, will be restored.

The privileges of the Christian are naturally connected with his duties, and these, as we should expect, the Apostle insists upon in considerable detail. The two points that seem to have a special reference to the condition of the Roman Christians are :—First, the inculcation of obedience to the civil power. This would seem to allude to the disturbances which had led to the expulsion of the Jews from Rome ("*Judæos assidue tumultuantes Româ expulit,*" Suetonius). The second point is the stress that is laid upon the duty of toleration on the part of the more liberal members of the Church towards those who showed a greater scrupulosity in ceremonial observances, especially those connected with distinctions of meats and drinks. This may, however, have been suggested less by anything that the Apostle knew to have happened in the Church at Rome than by his recent experiences of the Churches of Corinth and Galatia, and the possibility that similar dangers might arise at Rome.

The analysis of the Epistle which follows is intended to give the reader a clearer conception of its contents, and must not always be taken to represent a conscious division of his subject in the Apostle's mind. This is especially the case with the two headings that are printed in italics. The course of his thought happens to lead the Apostle, in the first instance, to deal with the application of the Christian scheme to the individual; and, in the second, to its application to the great question of Jew and Gentile, but this is rather accidentally than because such a distinction entered into his plan. The headings are inserted as helping to bring out a point which really exists, and which is, perhaps, of more importance to the reader who looks upon the Epistle as a theological treatise than it was originally to its author.

A TREATISE ON THE CHRISTIAN SCHEME AS A DIVINELY-APPOINTED MEANS FOR PRODUCING RIGHTEOUSNESS IN MAN, AND SO REALISING THE MESSIANIC REIGN.

**I.—Introduction** (i. 1—15).
*a.* The apostolic salutation (i. 1—7).
*b.* St. Paul and the Roman Church (i. 8—15).

**II.—Doctrinal.**
*a.* THE GREAT THESIS. Righteousness by Faith (i. 16, 17).
Proof—
Righteousness not hitherto attained either by Gentiles (i. 18—32) or by Jews (ii. 1—29).
Parenthetic answer to objections (iii. 1—8).
Confirmatory proof from Scripture (iii. 9—20).

*b.* THE GREAT THESIS REPEATED AND EXPANDED.
Righteousness by faith. The propitiatory death of Christ (iii. 21—26).
(1) This righteousness is open to Jew and Gentile alike, and excludes boasting (iii. 27—31).
(2) Proof from Scripture—
Abraham (iv. 1—5, 9—25).
David (iv. 6—9).
(3) *First Climax.* Blissful effects of righteousness by faith (v. 1—11).
(4) The first and the second Adam (v. 12—19).
Abundance of sin and of grace (v. 20—vi. 1).

*c. The Christian Scheme in its Application to the Individual.*
(1) Progressive righteousness in the Christian.
Death to sin, through union with Christ (vi. 1—14).
(2) The Christian's release (vi. 15—vii. 25).
α. Its true nature (vi. 15—23).
β. Illustration from the marriage bond (vii. 1—6).
γ. The inward struggle and victory (vii. 7—25).
(3) *Second Climax* (viii. 1—39).
α. The flesh and the Spirit (viii. 1—13).
β. The adoption of sons (viii. 14—17).
γ. Creation's yearning (viii. 17—25).
δ. The Spirit's intercession (viii. 26, 27).
ε. Happy career of the Christian (viii. 28—30).
ζ. Triumphant close (viii. 31—39).

*d. The Christian Scheme in its world-wide significance and bearing.*
Israel's rejection (ix., x., xi.).
A saddening thought (ix. 1—5).
α. Justice of the rejection. The promise was not made to all Israel indiscriminately, but confined to the chosen seed (ix. 6—13).
Absoluteness of God's choice, which is not to be questioned by man (ix. 14—23).
β. Cause of the rejection. Self-sought righteousness contrasted with righteousness by faith in Christ (x. 1—13).
The gospel preached and believed (x. 14—21).
γ. Mitigating considerations (xi. 1—36).
(i.) Not *all* Israel fell (xi. 1—10).
(ii.) Special purpose of the fall (xi. 11—24).
The engrafted and original olive branches (xi. 17—26).
(iii.) Prospect of final restoration (xi. 25—29).
*Third Climax.* Beneficent results of seeming severity (xi. 30—32).
Doxology (xi. 33—36).

**III.—Practical and Hortatory.**
*a.* The Christian sacrifice (xii. 1, 2).
*b.* The Christian as a member of the Church (xii. 3—8).
*c.* The Christian in his relation to others (xii. 9—21).
The Christian's vengeance (xii. 19—21).
*d.* Church and State (xiii. 1—7).
*e.* The Christian's one debt; the law of love (xiii. 8—10).
The day approaching (xiii. 11—14).
*f.* Toleration: the strong and the weak (xiv. 1—xv. 3).
*g.* Unity of Jew and Gentile (xv. 4—13).

**IV.—Valedictory.**
*a.* Personal explanations. Motive of the Epistle. Purposed visit to Rome (xv. 14—23).
*b.* Greetings to various persons (xvi. 1—16).
A warning (xvi. 17—20).
Postscript by the Apostle's companions and amanuensis (xvi. 21—23).
Benediction and doxology (xvi. 24—27).

**VII. Style.**—The style of St. Paul's Epistles varies considerably, according to the date at which they were written. A highly-strung and nervous temperament like his would naturally vary with circumstances. His life was excessively wearing. We have only to read a catalogue like that in 2 Cor. xi. 23—28 to see the enormous strain to which he was exposed. The list of bodily hardships and sufferings is almost unparalleled, and his own Epistles show what the "care of all the churches" must have been to him. Hence it is not unnatural that in the later Epistles we should trace a certain loss of vitality. The style is more depressed and formal, and less buoyant and spontaneous. The period at which the Epistle to the Romans was written was, on the contrary, that at which the Apostle's physical power was at the highest. All through the two Epistles to the Corinthians, the Galatians, and the Romans, there is the greatest energy and force of diction. This gains, perhaps, from the fact that all these Epistles were written from dictation. The name of the amanuensis in the case of the Epistle to the Romans, as we gather from chap. xvi. 22, was Tertius. In some of the later Epistles it is possible that the turn of phrase was left more to the amanuensis, but the earlier group of Epistles bears all the appearance of having been taken down just as the Apostle spoke. Hence the broken and disjointed form of some of the sentences, beginning with one construction and ending with another, as in chaps. ii. 5—10, iii. 21—26, v. 12—14, ix. 22—24. A pointed instance would be (if the view taken in this Commentary is correct) chap. vii. 21. Hence, also, the insertion of long parentheses, interrupting the sense, as in chap. ii. 13—15, and of digressions such as chap. iii. 3—8. Hence, lastly, the rapid and vehement cut and thrust of indignant questioning as in chaps. ii. 21—23, ix. 19—21, or of impetuous challenge as in chap. viii. 31—35. The plain and direct style of the Apostle is well exemplified in the practical and hortatory chaps. xii.—xv. On the other hand, the more involved and elaborate style of the later Epistles finds a parallel in the opening and closing paragraphs, chaps. i. 1—7, xvi. 25—27.

VIII.—**External Evidence of the Genuineness of the Epistle.**—It is hardly necessary to collect external evidence to the genuineness of the Epistle, as it bears upon itself the most indisputable marks of originality. As a matter of fact it has not been disputed by any critic of the slightest importance. The external evidences are, however, abundant. Before the first century is out there is a clear allusion to the language of the Epistle in the letter of Clement of Rome to the Corinthians (A.D. 95). This writer entreats the Corinthian Christians to cast off from themselves "*all unrighteousness* and iniquity, *covetousness, strifes, malignities*, and *deceits, whisperings* and *backbitings, hatred of God, pride* and *arrogance*, vain-glory and inhospitality," on the ground that "*they that do* these *things* are hateful to God; and *not only they that do them, but they also that consent to them.*" The words in italics, many of them markedly peculiar, are taken from the passage Rom. i. 29—32. In another place (§ 46) in the same letter occurs the phrase, "We are members of one another," which recalls Rom. xii. 5. Other allusions that have been found in the Epistle are perhaps less certain. In the first quarter of the next century allusions to the Epistle are alleged from the letters of Ignatius and Polycarp. The first of these are, perhaps, themselves of too doubtful authenticity to be claimed very strongly in evidence. The Epistle to Polycarp, itself well guaranteed, presents an exact repetition of the phrase, "we must all stand before the judgment-seat of Christ;" adding, and "each one must give an account of himself." (Comp. Rom. xiv. 10, 12.) The Gnostic writers appealed to the passages "He who raised up Christ from the dead shall also quicken your mortal bodies" (Rom. viii. 11), and "sin reigned from Adam to Moses" (Rom. v. 13, 14), in support of their own peculiar views; but it is somewhat doubtful whether the fragments quoted by Hippolytus in which those allusions occur, are really to be referred to the founders of the respective sects, Basilides (*circ.* A.D. 125) and Valentinus (*circ.* A.D. 140), or to their followers. The date therefore of this evidence is uncertain. So also is that derived from the Epistle to Diognetus which is commonly placed at about A.D. 170. Justin Martyr (*ob.* A.D. 148) seems pretty clearly to have made use of the Epistle, for he quotes precisely the same series of Old Testament passages as is quoted in Rom. iv. 11—17, in the same order, and in the same way—as if they were one connected passage. In the last quarter of the second century, as Christian literature becomes more copious, the references to the Epistle become more express and definite. The letter of the Churches of Vienna and Lyons to that at Rome (A.D. 177) contains an exact verbal coincidence with Rom. viii. 18 ("I reckon that the sufferings of this present time," &c.). In Theophilus of Antioch (A.D. 181) there are unmistakeable paraphrases of Rom. ii. 6—9, and of Rom. xiii. 7, 8. Irenæus, writing about A.D. 185, quotes the Epistle directly by name. "This very construction St. Paul put upon it, writing to the Romans, 'Paul an Apostle of Jesus Christ,' &c.; and again, writing to the Romans concerning Israel, he says, 'whose are the fathers,'" &c. Irenæus also quotes expressly Rom. v. 17. "And in agreement with these St. Paul, too, addressing the Romans, says: 'Much more they who receive abundance of grace and righteousness unto life, shall reign through One, Jesus Christ.'" Besides these there are other long quotations which are the more to be remarked as they show in some cases the presence of readings in the Codex used by Irenæus, which, though supported by other authorities, are certainly false, and therefore show that they have already a long history behind them. There are equally express and direct quotations in Clement of Alexandria (flourished A.D. 185—211), and Tertullian (flourished A.D. 198—210). The Epistle to the Romans is also contained in the Muratorian Fragment on the canon *circ.* A.D. 170. From this point onwards the production of further evidence is superfluous. The main points to notice in what has been given are that the *existence* of the Epistle is proved incontestably by Clement of Rome as early as A.D. 95, and that it was attributed to St. Paul by Irenæus in A.D. 185, or some fifteen years earlier by the Muratorian Fragment.

[Of the many Commentaries on this Epistle most use has been made in the Notes which follow of those of Meyer and Dr. Vaughan. The scholarly tact of the English commentator might, perhaps, have been allowed to correct, even more often than has been the case, the rigorous science of the German. Dr. Vaughan's carefully-assorted references have also been of much service. Special attention has been paid to all that has been written on this Epistle, either directly or incidentally, by Dr. Lightfoot. The Notes themselves are not given to the world with any satisfaction. The writer would have been glad to devote to them more time than the exigencies of publication and the pressure of other work would allow. His most mature thoughts upon the connection between the several parts of the doctrinal teaching of the Epistle will be found in the section of the *Introduction* which deals with this subject, and in the *Excursus* at the end.]

## THE EPISTLE OF PAUL THE APOSTLE TO THE

# ROMANS

Chap. i. 1–7. The apostolic salutation.

CHAPTER I.—(1) Paul, a servant of Jesus Christ, called *to be* an apostle, separated[a] unto the gospel of God, (2) (which he had promised afore by his prophets in the holy scriptures,) (3) concerning his Son Jesus Christ our Lord, which was made of the seed of David according to the flesh; (4) and declared[1] *to be* the Son of God with power, according to the spirit of holiness, by the resurrection from the dead:

A.D. 58 (early in the year).

a Acts 13. 2.

1 Gr. *determined.*

---

(1–7) In writing to the Romans, a Church to which he was personally unknown, and which might be supposed, so far as it was Jewish, to be prejudiced against him, the Apostle delivers with somewhat more than usual solemnity his credentials and commission. A divinely appointed minister of a system of things predicted by the prophets, and culminating in the revelation, divinely ordained and attested, of Jesus Christ, he greets the Roman Christians, themselves also divinely called. Note the repetition of terms signifying "calling," "selection," "determination in the counsels and providence of God;" as if to say: "I and you alike are all members of one grand scheme, which is not of human invention, but determined and ordained of God—the divine clue, as it were, running through the history of the world." A solemn note is thus struck at the very commencement, and in what might have been regarded as the more formal part of the Epistle, by which the readers are prepared for the weighty issues that are to be set before them.

(1) **Servant.**—More strictly, here as elsewhere in the New Testament, *slave;* and yet not wrongly translated "servant," because the compulsory and degrading side of service is not put forward. The idea of "slavery" in the present day has altogether different associations.

**Separated.**—Compare especially Acts xiii. 2 ("Separate me Barnabas and Saul"), where human instruments—the leaders of the Church at Antioch—are employed to carry out the divine will. The reference here is to the historical fact of the selection of St. Paul to be an Apostle; in Gal. i. 15 ("it pleased God, who separated me from my mother's womb"), it is rather to the more distant act of divine predestination.

**Unto the gospel of God.**—Singled out and set apart to convey the message of salvation from God to man. The ambiguous genitive, the gospel of God, seems to mean, "the gospel which proceeds from God," "of which God is the *author;*" not "of which God is the *object.*"

(2) **Which he had promised.**—More correctly, *which He promised before by His prophets in holy writ.* There is a nicety of meaning expressed by the absence of the article before this last phrase. A slight stress is thus thrown upon the epithet "holy." It is not merely "in certain books which go by the name of holy scriptures," but "in certain writings the character of which is holy." They are "holy" as containing the promises referred to in the text, and others like them. It will thus be seen how even this faint shade of meaning works into the general argument. The writings in which the promises are contained, like the promises themselves, their fulfilment, and the consequences which follow from them, all are part of the same exceptional divine scheme.

The prophetic writings describe not only salvation, the *substance* of the gospel, but also the *preaching* of salvation, the gospel itself. (See Isa. xl. 2, "Speak ye comfortably to Jerusalem," and following verses; xlii. 4; lii. 1 *et seq.;* Pss. xix. 4; lxviii. 11, *et al.*)

**Prophets.**—In the wider sense in which the word is used, including not only Samuel (Acts iii. 24), but also Moses and David, and all who are regarded as having prophesied the Messiah.

(3, 4) Who, on the human side—as if to show that the prophecies were really fulfilled in Him—was born of the seed of David, the rightful lineage of the Messiah; who, on the divine side, by virtue of the divine attribute of holiness dwelling in His spirit, was declared to be the Son of God, by that mighty demonstration, the resurrection of the dead.

**According to the flesh.**—The word is here used as equivalent to "in His human nature, in that lower bodily organisation which He shares with us men."

(4) **With power.**—That is, in a transcendent and superhuman manner.

**According to the spirit of holiness.**—In antithesis to "according to the flesh," and therefore coming where we should expect "in His divine nature." And yet there is a difference, the precise shade of which is not easy to define. What are we to understand by the "spirit of holiness"? Are we to regard it as simply convertible with "Holy Spirit"? Not quite. Or are we to look upon it as corresponding to "the flesh," as "spirit" and "flesh" correspond in man? Again, not quite—or not merely. The spirit of Christ is human, for Christ took upon Him our nature in all its parts. It is human; and yet it is in it more especially that the divinity resides. It is in it that the "Godhead dwells bodily," and the presence of the Godhead is seen in the peculiar and exceptional "holiness" by which it is characterised. The "spirit," therefore, or that portion of His being to which St. Paul gives the name, in Christ, is the connecting-link between the human and the divine, and

(5) by whom we have received grace and apostleship, for obedience to the faith[1] among all nations, for his name: (6) among whom are ye also the called of Jesus Christ: (7) to all that be in Rome, beloved of God, called *to be* saints: Grace to you and peace from God our Father, and the Lord Jesus Christ.

1 Or, *to the obedience of faith.*

---

shares alike in both. It is the divine "enshrined" in the human, or the human penetrated and energised by the divine. It is, perhaps, not possible to get beyond metaphorical language such as this. The junction of the human and divine must necessarily evade exact definition, and to carry such definition too far would be to misrepresent the meaning of the Apostle. We may compare with this passage 1 Tim. iii. 16, "God (rather, *Who*) was manifest in the flesh, justified in the Spirit;" or St. Peter's phrase, "Put to death in the flesh, but quickened by the Spirit"—rather, *in the spirit*, as the seat of that divinity by virtue of which He overcame death—(1 Pet. iii. 18).

The particular act in which the Sonship of Christ was most conspicuously ratified and confirmed was His resurrection from the dead. It was ratified by His resurrection, as a manifestation of transcendent and divine power. (Comp. Acts ii. 24 *et seq.*; xvii. 31; Rom. iv. 24.)

It should be observed that this antithesis between the human and divine nature in Christ is not here intended to carry with it any disparagement of the former. Rather the Apostle wishes to bring out the completeness and fulness of the dignity of Christ, as exhibited on both its sides. He is at once the Jewish Messiah (and with the Jewish section of the Church at Rome this fact would carry great weight) and the Son of God.

**By the resurrection from the dead.**—Strictly, *by the resurrection of the dead.* There is a slight distinction to be observed between the two phrases. It is not "by *His* resurrection *from* the dead," but in an abstract and general sense, "by *the* resurrection *of* the dead"—by that resurrection of which Christ was the firstfruits.

(5) Through Him—through Christ the Son—he, Paul, had received his own special endowment and commission to bring over the Gentiles into that state of loyal and dutiful submission which has its root in faith; all which would tend to the glory of His name.

**We have received.**—The Apostle means himself alone, but the plural is used (as frequently in Greek) with delicate tact, so as to avoid an appearance of egotism or assumption.

**Grace and apostleship.**—Grace is here divine favour manifested in various ways, but especially in his conversion. St. Augustine notes that grace is common to the Apostle with all believers—his apostleship is something special and peculiar; yet apostleship is an instance, or case, of grace. Origen distinguishes between the two—"grace for the endurance of labours, apostleship for authority in preaching;" but both terms are perhaps somewhat wider than this. Apostleship includes all those privileges which St. Paul possessed as an Apostle; grace is all those privileges that he possessed as a Christian. At the same time, in either case the meaning tends in the direction of that particular object which is expressed in the next clause. The light in which the Apostle valued most the gifts that had been bestowed upon him, was inasmuch as they enabled him to preach the gospel to the Gentiles.

**For obedience to the faith among all nations.**—Literally, *For* (to produce) *obedience of faith* (the obedience which springs from faith) *among all the Gentiles.*

Faith is not here equivalent to "*the* faith"—a positive body of doctrine received and believed—but, in its strict sense, that active habit and attitude of mind by which the Christian shows his devotion and loyalty to Christ, and his total dependence on Him (Gal. ii. 19).

**For his name.**—*For His name's sake.* "His," *i.e.*, Christ's. The whole of that divine economy of which St. Paul himself forms part, tends to the glory of Christ. The Apostle's call to his office, his special endowment for his ministry, the success of his preaching among the Gentiles, as they proceed from Christ, so also have for their object the extension of His kingdom.

(6) **Among whom are ye also.**—It is, perhaps, best not to put a comma at "also." Among these Gentile churches, to which I am specially commissioned, you Romans too are called to the same obedience of faith, and therefore I have the more right to address you.

**Called of Jesus Christ**—*i.e.*, not "called *by* Jesus Christ," but "called and so belonging to Jesus Christ," "your Master's own elect ones." (Comp. LXX., 1 Kings i. 41, where the words "guests of Adonijah" are in the Greek "called of Adonijah.")

(7) **In Rome.**—It is to be observed that one MS. of some importance, the Codex Boernerianus, omits these words. The same MS., with some others, alters the next phrase, "beloved of God" to "in the love of God," thus substituting for the special address to the Romans a general address to all "who are in the love of God." Traces of a similar reading appear to be found in the two earliest commentators on the Epistle, Origen (*ob.* A.D. 253) and the Ambrosian Hilary (A.D. 366—384). The Codex Boernerianus also omits the words "at Rome" in verse 15, while at the end of the Epistle it interposes a blank space between chaps. xiv. and xv. These peculiarities give some support to the theory that the Epistle to the Romans was circulated, most probably with the sanction of the Apostle himself, in the form of a general treatise, with the personal matter eliminated. This theory will be found more fully discussed in the Notes on the last two chapters.

**Beloved of God.**—Reconciled to God through the death of His Son, and therefore with the barrier that separated you from His love removed.

**Called to be saints.**—Consecrated or set apart by His own special summons, brought within the sphere and range of the holy life.

These epithets, high-sounding as they are, if applied by a modern writer to a modern church would seem to be indiscriminating or conventional, but as coming from St. Paul they have not yet lost their freshness and reality. They correspond to no actual condition of things, but to that ideal condition in which all Christians, by the mere fact of their being Christians, are supposed to be. They are members of the new Messianic kingdom, and share in all its privileges. The Apostle will not let them forget this, but holds it up before them as a mirror to convict them if they are unfaithful.

**Grace . . . and peace.**—May God and Christ look favourably upon you, and may you enjoy, as the

Chap. i. 8—15. St. Paul and the Roman Church.

(8) First, I thank my God through
Jesus Christ for you all,
that your faith is spoken
of throughout the whole
world. (9) For God is my
witness, whom I serve with my spirit[1]
in the gospel of his Son, that without
ceasing I make mention of you always
in my prayers; (10) making request, if by
any means now at length I might have
a prosperous journey by the will of God
to come unto you. (11) For I long to
see you, that I may impart unto you
some spiritual gift, to the end ye may
be established; (12) that is, that I may
be comforted together with you[2] by

1 Or, *in my spirit.*

2 Or, *in you.*

---

result of that favour, the peace and composure of mind which is the proper attribute of the Christian.

The terms "grace" and "peace" nearly correspond to two ordinary forms of Jewish salutation, the first of which has also something of a counterpart among the Greeks and Romans. But here, as elsewhere, the Apostle has given to them a heightened and deepened Christian signification. Grace is the peculiar state of favour with God and Christ, into which the sincere Christian is admitted. Peace is the state of mind resulting from the sense of that favour.

> "The *joy* Thy *favour* gives,
> Let me again obtain."

(8–17) The Apostle congratulates the Romans on the good report of them that he had heard. He had long and earnestly desired to visit them in person. Yes, even in Rome he must preach the gospel—of which he is not ashamed, but proud. It is fraught with nothing less than salvation itself alike to Jew and Gentile. In it is revealed that great plan or scheme of God by which man is made just before Him.

To the modern reader who does not make an effort to enter into the mind of the Apostle, the language of these verses, may seem too high-pitched for the occasion. It is not easy to realise the intensity with which St. Paul felt on what in any degree, however small, affected the spiritual life of those who acknowledged the same Master that he did. He had few of those petty distractions that we have. The whole force of his rich and impressible nature was concentrated upon this one subject; and his expressions reflect the state of tension in which he felt himself to be. Thus it is that they take a solemnity and earnestness to which an ordinary correspondence would not attain.

(8) **I thank my God through Jesus Christ.**—How can the Apostle be said to thank God *through* Jesus Christ? Christ is, as it were, the medium through whom God has been brought into close relation to man. Hence all intercourse between God and man is represented as passing through Him. He is not only the divine *Logos* by whom God is revealed to man, but He is also the Head of humanity by whom the tribute of thanks and praise is offered to God.

**Throughout the whole world.**—A hyperbole, which is the more natural as the Apostle is speaking of Rome, the centre and metropolis of the world as he knew it.

(9) Proof that the Apostle takes this lively interest in the Roman Church conveyed through a solemn adjuration.

**Whom I serve.**—The word for "serve" is strictly used for voluntary service paid to God, especially in the way of sacrifice and outward worship. Here it is somewhat metaphorical: "Whom I serve, not so much with outward acts as with the ritual of the spirit."

**With my spirit.**—"Spirit" is with St. Paul the highest part or faculty in the nature of man. It is the seat of his higher consciousness—the organ by which he communicates with God. "Certainly man is of kin to the beasts by his body; and if he be not of kin to God by his spirit, he is a base and ignoble creature." (Bacon, *Essay on Atheism.*) Of itself the "spirit" of man is neutral. When brought into contact with the Spirit of God, it is capable of a truly religious life; but apart from this influence, it is apt to fall under the dominion of the "flesh"—*i.e.*, of those evil appetites and desires to which man is exposed by his physical organisation.

**In the gospel of his Son.**—The sphere to which the Apostle feels himself called, and in which this heart-worship of his finds its field of operation, is the defence and preaching, &c., of the gospel.

(9–11) It is the constant subject of the Apostle's prayers that he may succeed in making his way to Rome; so anxious is he to open his heart to that Church in personal apostolic intercourse.

(10) **If by any means now at length.**—Note this accumulation of particles, denoting the earnestness of his desire. "All this time I have been longing to come to you, and now at last I hope that it may be put in my power."

(11) **That I may impart unto you some spiritual gift.**—Such gifts as would naturally flow to one Christian (or to many collectively) from the personal presence and warm sympathy of another; in St. Paul's case, heightened in proportion to the wealth and elevation of his own spiritual consciousness and life. His head and his heart alike are full to overflowing, and he longs to disburthen himself and impart some of these riches to the Romans. Inasmuch as he regards all his own religious advancement and experience as the result of the Spirit working within him, he calls the fruits of that advancement and experience "spiritual gifts." All the apostolic gifts—miraculous as well as non-miraculous—would be included in this expression. Indeed, we may believe that the Apostle would hardly draw the distinction that we do between the two kinds. Both alike were in his eyes the direct gift of the Spirit.

**To the end ye may be established.**—That they may grow and be confirmed and strengthened in the faith. As a rule the great outpouring of spiritual gifts was at the first foundation of a church. St. Paul was not the founder of the church at Rome, but he hoped to be able to contribute to its advance and consolidation.

(12) **That is, that I may be comforted.**—A beautiful touch of true courtesy. He is anxious to see them, that he may impart to them some spiritual gift. But no! He hastily draws back and corrects himself. He does not wish it to be implied that it is for him only to impart, and for them only to receive. He will not assume any such air of superiority. In the impulse of the moment, and in the expansiveness

the mutual faith both of you and me.
(13) Now I would not have you ignorant,
brethren, that oftentimes I purposed to
come unto you, (but was let hitherto,)
that I might have some fruit among[1]
you also, even as among other Gentiles.
(14) I am debtor both to the Greeks, and
to the Barbarians; both to the wise,
and to the unwise. (15) So, as much
as in me is, I am ready to preach
the gospel to you that are at Rome
also. (16) For I am not
ashamed of the gospel of
Christ: for it is the power
of God unto salvation to every one that
believeth; to the Jew first, and also

1 Or, *in you.*

Chap. i. 16—17. The great thesis.

---

of his own heart, he had seemed to put it so; but his real meaning was that they should receive mutual comfort and edification.

Strictly, the idea of *mutual* comfort is drawn from the two verses combined, not from this singly. In the last verse the Romans were the subject: "That *ye* may be established." Here St. Paul himself is the subject: "That *I* may be comforted."

**Comforted.**—The Greek word has rather more of the sense of our "encouraged," though the idea of "comfort" is also contained in it. It is a similar word to that which is translated "comforter" in several passages in John xiv., xv., xvi. (where see Notes, and *Excursus to St. John's Gospel*).

**Together with you.**—Literally, *that I may at the same time be comforted among you;* that is, "that I may be comforted at the same time that you are comforted, by my intercourse with you, through that mutual faith which acts and reacts upon each of us." The Apostle looks to obtain benefit from his intercourse with the Roman Christians. He expects that their faith will help to increase his own.

There is a truth underlying the Apostle's courtesy which is not mere compliment. The most advanced Christian will receive something from the humblest. There are very few men whose "spirits are not finely touched" *somewhere;* and St. Paul was conscious that even an Apostle might not be equally strong at every point.

(13) In the previous verses the Apostle has been speaking of his *desire;* here he speaks of his *purpose,* which is one step nearer to the realisation. He had intended to add the Roman Church to the harvest that he was engaged in gathering in.

**Let.**—This is, of course, an archaism for "hindered," "prevented." The Greek is literally, "*and* was prevented hitherto."

It is hardly worth while to speculate, as some commentators have done, on the causes that may have hindered the Apostle from going to Rome. In a life like his there may have been many.

(14, 15) Why is the Apostle so eager to come to them? Because an obligation, a duty, is laid upon him. (Comp. 1 Cor. ix. 16, "necessity is laid upon me.") He must preach the gospel to men of all classes and tongues; Rome itself is no exception.

(14) **To the Greeks, and to the Barbarians.**—The Apostle does not intend to place the Romans any more in the one class than in the other. He merely means "to all mankind, no matter what their nationality or culture." The classification is exhaustive. It must be remembered that the Greeks called all who did not speak their own language "Barbarians," and the Apostle, writing from Greece, adopts their point of view.

**Wise and foolish.**—(Comp. 1 Cor. i. 20, 26—28.) The gospel was at first most readily received by the poor and unlearned. but it did not therefore follow that culture and education were by any means excluded. St. Paul himself was a conspicuous instance to the contrary. And so, in the next century, the Church which began with such leaders as Ignatius and Polycarp, could number among its members before the century was out, Irenæus, and Tertullian, and Clement of Alexandria, and Hippolytus, and Origen—the last, the most learned man of his time.

(15) Accordingly, so far as depends upon his own will, and not upon the external ruling of events by God, the Apostle is ready to preach the gospel, as to the other Gentiles, so also at Rome.

**So, as much as in me is.**—There are three ways of taking this sentence, though the meaning remains in any case the same:—(1) "I (literally, *that which concerns me*) am ready." But it it is doubtful whether this is sanctioned by Greek usage. (2) Still keeping the two phrases separate, As far as concerns me (there is) readiness." (3) Combining them, "The readiness or inclination on my part (literally, *The on-my-part readiness or inclination*) is," &c. Perhaps of these three the last, which looks the most unnatural in English, is the most natural in the Greek.

(16) The Apostle will not be ashamed of his mission, even in the metropolis of the world. He cannot be ashamed of a scheme so beneficent and so grand The gospel that he preaches is that mighty agency which God Himself has set in motion, and the object of which is the salvation of all who put their faith in it, to whatever nation or race they may belong. He has, perhaps, in his mind the reception he had met with in other highly civilised cities. (Comp. Acts xvii. 32.) He had himself once found a "stumbling-block" in the humiliation of the Cross; now, so far from being ashamed of it, it is just that of which he is most proud. The preaching of the Cross is the cardinal point of the whole gospel.

**Of Christ.**—These words are wanting in the oldest MSS., and should be omitted.

**Power of God.**—A powerful agency put forth by God Himself—the lever, as it were, by which He would move the world.

**Unto salvation.**—The object of this gospel is salvation—to open the blessings of the Messianic kingdom to mankind.

**To the Jew first.**—Here again we have another exhaustive division of mankind. "Greek" is intended to cover all who are not "Jews." Before the Apostle was making, what may be called, the secular classification of men, here he makes the religious classification. From his exceptional privileges the Jew was literally placed in a class alone.

It is not quite certain that the word "first" ought not to be omitted. In any case the sense is the same. St. Paul certainly assigns a prerogative position to the

to the Greek. (17) For therein is the righteousness of God revealed from faith to faith: as it is written, The just shall live by faith.[a]

a Hab. 2. 4.

(18) For the wrath of God is revealed from heaven against all ungodliness and unrighteousness of men,

Chap. i. 18, *et seq.* An offending world; natural religion corrupted.

Jews. They have an "advantage" (Rom. iii. 1, 2). To them belong the special privileges of the first dispensation (Rom. ix. 4, 5). They are the original stock of the olive tree, in comparison with which the Gentiles are only as wild branches grafted in (Rom. xi. 17 *et seq.*). It was only right that the salvation promised to their forefathers should be offered first to them, as it is also said expressly in the Fourth Gospel, that "salvation is of the Jews" (John iv. 22).

**First.**—A difficult question of textual criticism is raised here. The word is not found in the Vatican MS. in a citation by Tertullian (*circ.* 200 A.D.), and in the Græco-Latin Codex Boernerianus at Dresden. In all other MSS. and versions it appears. The evidence for the omission is thus small in quantity, though good in quality; and though it shows, in any case, a considerable diffusion in Egypt and Africa as far back as the second century, internal considerations do not tell strongly either way, but it seems a degree more probable that the word was accidentally dropped in some early copy. Of recent editions, it is bracketed by Lachmann, and placed in the margin by Tregelles and Vaughan.

(17) The gospel attains its end, the salvation of the believer, by revealing the righteousness of God, *i.e.*, the plan or process designed by Him for men to become just or righteous in His sight. The essential part on man's side, the beginning and end of that plan, is Faith. For which there was authority in the Old Testament, where it is said, "The just shall live by faith."

**The righteousness of God.**—By this is not meant, as might, perhaps, be supposed, an attribute of the divine nature—as if the essential righteousness of God were first made known through the gospel. St. Paul goes on to show in verses 19, 20, that so much at least of the nature of God might be known without any supernatural revelation. "Of God" means in the present instance "which proceeds from God." And the "righteousness" which thus "proceeds from God" is that condition of righteousness in man into which he enters by his participation in the Messianic kingdom. The whole object of the coming of the Messiah was to make men "righteous" before God. This was done more especially by the death of Christ upon the cross, which, as we learn from chap. iii. 24—26, had the effect of making God "propitious" towards men. The benefit of this act is secured to all who make good their claim to be considered members of the Messianic kingdom by a loyal adhesion to the Messiah. Such persons are treated as if they were "righteous," though the righteousness that is thus attributed to them is not any actual merit of their own, but an ideal condition in which they are placed by God. This is the well-known doctrine of justification by faith. (See *Excursus A: On the Meaning of the word Righteousness in the Epistle to the Romans*, and *Excursus E: On the Doctrine of Justification by Faith and Imputed Righteousness.*)

**Revealed.**—God's purpose of thus justifying men is in process of being revealed or declared in the gospel. It is revealed theoretically in the express statements of the way in which man may be justified. It is revealed practically in the heartfelt acceptance of those statements and the change of life which they involved. To the Romans the moment of revelation was that in which they first heard the gospel. St. Paul wishes them to know the full significance—the philosophy, as it might be called—of that which they had heard.

**From faith to faith.**—It is by faith that man first lays hold on the gospel, and its latest product is a heightened and intensified faith. Apart from faith, the gospel remains null and void for the individual. It is not realised. But when it has been once realised and taken home to the man's self, its tendency is to confirm and strengthen that very faculty by which it was apprehended. It does that for which the disciples prayed when they said, "Lord, increase our faith" (Luke xvii. 5).

**The just shall live by faith.**—The words are part of the consolatory answer which the prophet Habakkuk receives in the stress of the Chaldean invasion. Though his irresistible hosts sweep over the land, the righteous man who puts his trust in God shall live. Perhaps St. Paul intended the words "by faith" to be taken rather with "the just" than as they stand in the English version. "The just by faith," or "The man whose righteousness is based on faith," shall live.

The Apostle uses the word "faith" in his own peculiar and pregnant sense. But this is naturally led up to by the way in which it was used by Habakkuk. The intense personal trust and reliance which the Jew felt in the God of his fathers is directed by the Christian to Christ, and is further developed into an active energy of devotion.

"Faith," as understood by St. Paul, is not merely head-belief, a purely intellectual process such as that of which St. James spoke when he said "the devils also believe and tremble"; neither is it merely "trust," a passive dependence upon an Unseen Power; but it is a further stage of feeling developed out of these, a current of emotion setting strongly in the direction of its object, an ardent and vital apprehension of that object, and a firm and loyal attachment to it. (See *Excursus B: On the Meaning of the word Faith.*)

(18) As a preliminary stage to this revelation of justification and of faith, there is another, which is its opposite—a revelation and disclosure of divine wrath. The proof is seen in the present condition both of the Gentile and Jewish world. And first of the Gentile world, verses 18—32.

**Revealed.**—The revelation of righteousness is, while the Apostle writes, being made in the Person of Christ and in the salvation offered by Him. The revelation of wrath is to be inferred from the actual condition—the degradation doubly degraded—in which sin leaves its votaries.

**From heaven.**—The wrath of God is revealed "from heaven," inasmuch as the state of things in which it is exhibited is the divinely-inflicted penalty for previous guilt. Against that guilt, shown in outrage against all religion and all morality, it is directed.

**Ungodliness and unrighteousness.**—These two words stand respectively for offences against religion and offences against morality.

who hold the truth in unrighteousness;
(19) because that which may be
known of God is manifest in them;[1]
for God hath showed *it* unto them.
(20) For the invisible things of him
from the creation of the world are
clearly seen, being understood by the
things that are made, *even* his eternal
power and Godhead; so that they are[2]
without excuse: (21) because that, when
they knew God, they glorified *him* not
as God, neither were thankful; but
became vain in their imaginations,
and their foolish heart was darkened.
(22) Professing themselves to be wise,
they became fools, (23) and
changed the glory of the
uncorruptible God[a] into an
image made like to corruptible man, and to birds, and four-

Chap. i. 23—26. Idolatry and its moral consequences.

1 Or, *to them.*

a Ps. 106. 20.

2 Or, *that they may be.*

**Who hold the truth in unrighteousness.**—Rather, *who suppress and thwart the truth*—the light of conscience that is in them—*by unrighteousness.* Conscience tells them what is right, but the will, actuated by wicked motives, prevents them from obeying its dictates. "The truth" is their knowledge of right, from whatever source derived, which finds expression in conscience. "Hold" is the word which we find translated "hinder" in 2 Thess. ii. 6, 7—having the force of *to hold down,* or *suppress.*

(19) The Apostle goes on to show how the Gentiles came to have such a knowledge of right, and how they repressed and contravened it.

They had it, because all the knowledge that mankind generally possessed of God they also possessed. So much as could be known without special revelation they knew.

**That which may be known.**—Rather, *that which is* (generally and universally) *known*—the truths of so-called "natural religion."

**Is manifest in them.**—Manifest or imprinted upon their consciences, because God had so imprinted it upon them. The marginal rendering, "to them," is hardly tenable.

(20) For, though there were parts of God's being into which the eye could not penetrate, still they were easily to be inferred from the character of His visible creation, which bore throughout the stamp of Omnipotence and Divinity.

**The invisible things of him.**—His invisible attributes, afterwards explained as "His eternal power and Godhead."

**Are clearly seen . . . by the things that are made.**—There is something of a play upon words here. "The unseen is seen—discerned by the eye of the mind—being inferred or perceived by the help of that which is made," *i.e.,* as we should say, by the phenomena of external nature.

**Even His eternal power and Godhead.**—A summary expression for those attributes which, apart from revelation, were embodied in the idea of God. Of these "power" is the most obvious. St. Paul does not go into the questions that have been raised in recent times as to the other qualities which are to be inferred as existing in the Author of nature; but he sums them up under a name that might be used as well by a Pagan philosopher as by a Christian—the attributes included in the one term "Godhead." *Divinity* would be, perhaps, a more correct translation of the expression. What is meant is "divine *nature,*" rather than "divine *personality.*"

**So that they are without excuse.**—They could not plead ignorance.

(21) They knew enough of God to know that thanks and praise were due to Him; but neither of these did they offer. They put aside the natural instinct of adoration, and fell to speculations, which only led them farther and farther from the truth. The new knowledge of which they went in quest proved to be fiction; the old knowledge that they had was obscured and lost by their folly. Starting with two things—a portion of enlightenment on the one hand, and the natural tendency of the human mind to error on the other, the latter prevailed, and the former became eclipsed.

**But became vain in their imaginations.**—They were frustrated—reached no good and sound result with their speculations.

**Their foolish heart.**—Not the same word as "fools," in the next verse. *Their unintelligent heart;* their heart which, by itself, was endowed with no special faculty of discernment such as to enable them to dispense with the enlightenment from above.

(22, 23) Relying upon their own wisdom, they wandered further and further from true wisdom, falling into the contradiction of supposing that the eternal and immutable Essence of God could be represented by the perishable figures of man, or bird, or quadruped, or insect.

(22) **They became fools.**—They *were made fools.* It is not merely that they expose their real folly, but that folly is itself judicially inflicted by God as a punishment for the first step of declension from Him.

(23) **Into an image made like to.**—*For the likeness of the image of mortal man.* This anthropomorphism applies more especially to the religions of Greece and Rome. Representations of the Deity under the form of beasts were most common in Egypt. "Worship was universally paid to cattle, lions, cats, dogs, weasels, and otters; among the birds, to the sparrow-hawk, the hoopoe, the stork, and the sheldrake; and among fish, to the eel and lepidotus. Besides these, other creatures received local worship. The sheep was worshipped in Sais and the Thebais, but sacrificed and eaten in Lycopolis. The hippopotamus in the district of Papremis, and the crocodile in the greater part of the land, were considered specially sacred; but the latter was chased and eaten in Tentyra and Apollinopolis. The sacred serpent Thermapis which served as head-gear for Isis had holes in all the temples, where it was fed with veal fat." "Among the sacred beasts," says Döllinger, "the first place was given to the divine bulls, of which the Egyptians worshipped four." No doubt the images in Greece and the beasts in Egypt were by some of the people regarded only as *symbols* of the Deity, but it was in all probability only a small minority who were capable of drawing this distinction.

footed beasts, and creeping things. (24)
Wherefore God also gave them up to
uncleanness through the lusts of their
own hearts, to dishonour their own
bodies between themselves: (25) who
changed the truth of God into a lie,
and worshipped and served the crea-
ture more than the Creator, who is
blessed for ever. Amen. (26) For this
cause God gave them up unto vile
affections: for even their women did
change the natural use into that which
is against nature: (27) and likewise
also the men, leaving the natural use
of the woman, burned in their lust one
toward another; men with men work-
ing that which is unseemly, and re-
ceiving in themselves that recompence
of their error which was meet. (28) And
even as they did not like to retain God
in *their* knowledge, God gave them over
to a reprobate mind, to do those things
which are not convenient; (29) being
filled with all unrighteousness, forni-
cation, wickedness, covetousness, mali-
ciousness; full of envy, murder, debate,
deceit, malignity; whisperers, (30) back-
biters, haters of God, despiteful, proud,
boasters, inventors of evil things, dis-
obedient to parents, (31) without under-

---

(24–32) Hence they fell into a still lower depth; for, in anger at their perversion of the truth, God refrained from checking their downward course. He left them to follow their own evil bent. Their idolatry developed into shameless immorality and unnatural crimes. At last the extreme limit was reached. As they voluntarily forsook God, so He forsook them. They ran through the whole catalogue of sins, and the cup of their iniquity was full.

In the passage taken as a whole, three steps or stages are indicated: (1) verses 18—23, idolatry; (2) verses 24—27, unnatural sins allowed by God as the punishment for this idolatry; (3) verses 28—32, a still more complete and radical depravity also regarded as penally inflicted. The first step is taken by the free choice of man, but as the breach gradually widens, the wrath of God is more and more revealed. He interferes less and less to save a sinful world from its fate. It is to be noted that the Apostle speaks in general terms, and the precise proportions of human depravity and of divine judicial impulse are not to be clearly determined.

(25) **Who changed the truth of God into a lie.**—They ceased to worship God as He is—in His own true essential nature, and worshipped false gods instead. The phrase "into a lie," is literally, *with a lie*, the "lie" being regarded as the instrument by which the substitution is made. By "a lie" is meant here "false gods," who are the supreme embodiment of falsehood. (Comp. Isa. xliv. 20; Jer. xiii. 25; xvi. 19, &c.)

The introduction of the doxology in this verse is due to an impulse of reverential feeling. Shocked at the language which he finds himself using, and at the connection in which the most Holy Name has been mentioned, the Apostle turns aside for a moment to testify to his own humble adoration.

(27) **In themselves**—*i.e.*, upon themselves, upon their own persons thus shamefully dishonoured.

**That recompence of their error which was meet.**—The "error" is the turning from God to idols. The "recompence of the error" is seen in these unnatural excesses to which the heathen have been delivered up.

(28) **Even as.**—Rightly translated in the Authorised version: "as" is not here equivalent to "because," but means rather, *just in like proportion as.* The degree of God's punishment corresponded exactly to the degree of man's deflection from God.

**Did not like.**—There is a play upon words here with "reprobate" in the clause following which cannot be retained in English. "As they reprobated the knowledge of God, so He gave them up to a reprobate mind." As they would have nothing to do with Him, so He would have nothing to do with them. "Reprobate" means, properly, tried and found wanting, and therefore cast away as worthless.

**To retain God in their knowledge.**—The word for knowledge here means "exact," "advanced," "thorough knowledge." They refused to hold the true idea of God so as to grow and increase in the knowledge of it.

**Those things which are not convenient.**—That which is unbecoming, disgraceful.

**Fornication.**—This word is wanting in the best MSS. and should be omitted, as also the word "implacable" in verse 31.

**Wickedness, . . . maliciousness.**—These two words appear to be related together, so that the latter expresses rather the vicious disposition—vicious in the special sense, the disposition to do hurt to others—the former rather the active exercise of it. Similar catalogues of sins are given in other of St. Paul's Epistles, as, for example, 2 Cor. xiii. 30; Gal. v. 19 *et seq.*; Eph. v. 3, 4; 1 Tim. i. 9, 10; 2 Tim. iii. 2 *et seq.*

**Murder, debate.**—By "full of murder" the Apostle means "full of murderous thoughts." "Debate" is the spirit of strife and contention generally; not as the English would seem to imply, specially verbal contention.

(29, 30) **Whisperers, backbiters.**—In the Greek the idea of secresy is contained chiefly in the first of these words. "Secret backbiters and slanderers of every kind."

(30) **Haters of God.**—Rather, perhaps, *hated by God.* There seem to be no examples of the active sense. The Apostle apparently throws in one emphatic word summing up the catalogue as far as it has gone; he then resumes with a new class of sins. Hitherto he has spoken chiefly of sins of malice, now he turns to sins of pride.

**Despiteful, proud, boasters.**—The three words correspond to the distinction between act, thought, and word. The first implies distinctly insolence in outward bearing; it is the word translated "injurious" in 1 Tim. i. 13. The second is a strong self-esteem mixed with contempt for others. (See 2 Tim. iii. 2.) The third is used especially of boastfulness or braggadocio in language.

(31) **Without understanding**—*i.e.*, without moral or spiritual understanding; incapable of discriminating between right and wrong, expedient and inexpedient.

standing, covenant breakers, without
natural affection, implacable, unmerci-
ful: (32) who knowing the judgment of
God, that they which commit such
things are worthy of death, not only do
the same, but have pleasure in them[1]
that do them.

Chap. ii. 1—29. The judgment of God admits of no exceptions.

CHAPTER II.—(1) There-
fore thou art inexcusable,
O man, whosoever thou art
that judgest: for wherein thou judgest
another, thou condemnest thyself; for
thou that judgest doest the same things.
(2) But we are sure that the judgment
of God is according to truth against
them which commit such things. (3) And
thinkest thou this, O man, that judgest
them which do such things, and doest
the same, that thou shalt escape the
judgment of God? (4) Or despisest thou
the riches of his goodness and for-
bearance and long-suffering; not know-
ing that the goodness of God leadeth

1 Or, *consent with them.*

A.D. 58.

---

St. Paul prays that the Colossians may possess this faculty (Col. i. 9).

**Without natural affection.**—The affection founded upon natural relationship—*e.g.*, between parent and child, husband and wife, brother and sister. In illustration of this particular expression, we may remember that infanticide and divorce were very common at this period.

(32) **Knowing.**—Again the word for "full or thorough knowledge." With full knowledge of the sentence of eternal death which is in store for them.

They show that it is no mere momentary yielding to the force of temptation or of passion, but a radical perversion of conscience and reason, by the fact that they not only practise such things themselves, but in cold blood commend and applaud those who practise them.

With reference to the truth of the description which is here given of the ancient pagan world, see *Excursus C: On the State of the Heathen World at the Time of St. Paul.*

**Judgment.**—Just decree or sentence.

II.

(1-29) Though such is the guilt of the Gentile, there is no one to judge him, for he who would take upon himself to judge does the very same things himself. And the justice of God has only one standard by which all mankind alike will be judged—truth. Or has he any vain idea that he will escape? Does he count lightly and carelessly upon the long-suffering and forbearance of God? The proper object of that forbearance is to lead him to repentance. But he is hard and impenitent, and therefore all that is in store for him is, not pardon, but wrath. The judgment of God will be according to the strictest laws of justice. It will reward the good and punish the wicked. All the privileges of the Jew will gain for him will be that he should be the first to be either rewarded or punished. Neither Jew nor Gentile will have any advantage. The Gentile cannot plead his freedom from law, for he has a law written in his conscience; the Jew cannot plead his enjoyment of the Law, for he has broken all its provisions. These old ethnological distinctions are quite confused. The real distinction between men is purely spiritual. Jewish birth and its outward sign are nothing. Men will be judged by what they are at heart.

The argument of the chapter is continuous, and does not admit of any real break. Verse 1 is the link of connection with what has gone before; verses 2, 3, 6—13 lay down emphatically the general principles of God's judgment; verses 14—16 apply these to the Gentile; verses 17—24 apply them to the Jew; and verses 25—29 reiterate the conclusion that Jew and Gentile are both as one in the sight of God.

The proposition with which the chapter begins, though general in form, is particular in substance. When the Apostle says, "Whosoever thou art that judgest," he really means the Jews. The Gentiles, being the persons upon whom judgment is supposed to be passed, are excluded, and the class indicated by "whosoever" must therefore be the Jews. At the same time, the proposition is presented in a shape which transcends divisions of race. The special application to the Jew is suggested rather than expressed. This is eminently characteristic of the Apostle's large and comprehensive way of handling history and the phenomena of humanity.

(1) **Therefore.**—The description just given of the state of one section of the human race contains implicitly the condemnation of the other; for it is equally applicable to both.

**Wherein thou judgest another.**—By the very act of sitting in judgment upon your fellow-man, you pass sentence upon yourself. You declare those acts to be criminal of which you are yourself guilty.

The words in the Greek, translated by "judge" and "condemn," are related to each other much the same as the summing up of a judge is related to his verdict. In the first, sentence is in process of being passed, but there is still a possibility of acquittal; in the second, sentence has been definitely given in a sense adverse to the accused. "Another," rather, strictly, *the other, thy fellow*, or *neighbour*.

(2) **We are sure.**—St. Paul assumes that this will be acknowledged as a general principle by his readers, whether Jew or Gentile, as well as by himself. There is still a strong under-current of allusion to the way in which the Jew was apt to fall back upon his privileges. "Do not think that they will save you from standing before precisely the same tribunal as the Gentiles." The Jews, it seems, had an idea that the Gentiles only would be judged, while they would be able to claim admission into the Messianic kingdom as theirs by right of birth.

**According to truth.**—The principle on which God's judgment will proceed will be that of truth or reality, as opposed to appearance, worldly status, formal precedence, &c. It will ask what a man *is*, not to what race he belongs.

(3) **That thou shalt escape.**—Emphatic. "Are *you*—because you are a Jew—to be the only exception to this rule?"

(4, 5) Another alternative is put forward, which has less to do with the distinction of Jew and Gentile, and

thee to repentance? (5) But after thy hardness and impenitent heart treasurest up unto thyself wrath against the day of wrath and revelation of the righteous judgment of God;[a] (6) who will render to every man according to his deeds:[b]

a Jas. 5. 3.
b Ps. 62. 12; Matt. 16. 27; Rev. 22. 12.

in which the Apostle keeps more closely to the general form that his argument has assumed: "Or do you think to take refuge in the goodness, the benevolence and long-suffering of God?" True it is that He is good, and "willeth not the death of a sinner," but His goodness is not absolute and unconditional. Its object is not to interfere with the just punishment of sin, but to lead men to repent of their sins, and so to obtain remission.

(4) **Riches.**—In this metaphorical sense, with reference to the divine attributes, this word is peculiar to and characteristic of St. Paul. It is thus used twelve times in his Epistles, and not besides in the rest of the New Testament, including the Epistle to the Hebrews. This is one of those instances where the evidence of style is important. Of the twelve places where this use occurs, eight are in the Epistles of the Imprisonment, three in the Epistle to the Romans, and one in the Second Epistle to the Corinthians. The later and earlier Epistles are thus linked together. A similar use is not found in the Pastoral Epistles, but it should be remembered that arguments of this kind are more important on the positive side than on the negative. It is an inference of some strength that if a peculiar word or usage is found in two separate books, those books are by the same author, but the absence of such a word or usage goes a very short way towards the opposite negative conclusion if other resemblances on characteristic points are not wanting.

**Forbearance and longsuffering.**—We may compare with this the Sinaitic revelation given in Ex. xxxiv. 6, 7, "The Lord, the Lord God, merciful and gracious, longsuffering." The moral character and relation to His people thus attributed to the Deity was a feature which specially distinguished the religion of the Old Testament from that of the surrounding heathen nations.

We may observe that the fallacy against which the Apostle is protesting in these verses is not yet extinct. The goodness of God—*i.e.*, His disposition to promote the happiness of His creatures—is insisted upon as if it were unconditional, as if it were a disposition to promote their happiness simply and without any reference to what they were in themselves. We do not find that this is the case; but rather the constitution of nature, as well as revelation, tells us that happiness is annexed to certain acts and a certain frame of mind, and that it is withheld from all that is not consonant with this. The bliss of the Christian is reserved for the Christian, and is not showered promiscuously upon all men. Otherwise free-will would have no office, and righteous dealing no reward.

(5) The one condition upon which the goodness of God will come into operation, you directly contravene. Instead of being penitent, you are impenitent, and therefore the load of wrath which you have been accumulating against yourself remains unremoved. It is only waiting for the day of judgment to discharge itself upon you.

**Treasurest.**—The treasuring up of wrath is opposed to that heavenly treasure spoken of in Matt. vi. 20. The guilt of man is accumulated little by little. The punishment will be discharged upon him all at once, in one overwhelming tide.

**Against the day of wrath.**—Strictly, *in the day of wrath*—*i.e.*, wrath to be outpoured upon the day of wrath. "The great and terrible day of the Lord" is a conception running through all the prophetic writings. (Comp. also, in the New Testament, Luke xvii. 30; Acts ii. 20; 1 Cor. i. 8; v. 5; 2 Cor. i. 14; 1 Thess. v. 2, 4; 2 Thess. ii. 2; 2 Pet. iii. 10, 12; Rev. vi. 17; xvi. 14.)

**Revelation.**—There is a double revelation of God's wrath, the one inchoate, the other final. The former revelation, that described in the last chapter, is seen in the depraved condition of the heathen world; the latter revelation is represented as a judgment or trial reserved for the consummation of all things.

(6) **According to his deeds.**—The Apostle here lays down with unmistakable definiteness and precision the doctrine that *works*, what a man has *done*, the moral tenor of his life, will be the standard by which he will be judged at the last day. There can be no question that this is the consistent doctrine of Scripture. (Comp. Matt. xvi. 27; xxv. 31 *et seq.;* 2 Cor. v. 10; Gal. vi. 7 *et seq.;* Eph. vi. 8; Col. iii. 24; Rev. ii. 23; xx. 12; xxii. 12.) How is this to be reconciled with the main theme of the Epistle, the doctrine of justification by *faith?*

We may observe (1) that the theology of St. Paul has two main sides or elements: (*a*) that which is common to all the Jewish schools, developed in direct line from the teaching of the Old Testament, and (*b*) that which is peculiar to himself, or developed from minute and scattered germs in the Old Testament or from the teaching of our Lord. The doctrine of justification by faith belongs to the latter category; that of final recompense in accordance with moral action belongs to the former. Hence we are prepared to find a difference of terminology without any necessary divergence of idea. (2) If we accordingly separate the two doctrines, and look at each in the connection to which it properly belongs, we shall see that they correspond to a difference in the point of view. (*a*) The two great classes into which mankind will be divided at the judgment will be determined by *works*, by the tangible outcome of their lives. No opposition is thought of here between the inward and the outward. Of course such an opposition is possible, but it is not present to the mind of the writer. The rule followed is simply that laid down in Matt. vii. 16, "By their fruits ye shall know them." The nature of his actions, as the expression of his character, will decide whether a man is to be classed among "the good" or among "the wicked." But (*b*) if we isolate the individual, and consider him no longer in relation to other men and to the great classification of mankind, but in his own intimate relations to the Judge and to the judgment, a totally different train of thought is suggested. If the conduct of the believer is to be regarded merely in the light of obedience to law (in other words, as a question of *works*), then he can neither claim nor expect any reward at all. He has broken more commandments than he has kept, and to break the Law, though only on a single point, is to lay himself open to its penalties. In any case, the extent of the reward promised to him far exceeds in proportion the extent of his obedience. It cannot therefore be by

(7) to them who by patient continuance
in well doing seek for glory and honour
and immortality, eternal life: (8) but
unto them that are contentious, and do
not obey the truth, but obey un-
righteousness, indignation and wrath,
(9) tribulation and anguish, upon every
soul of man that doeth evil, of the Jew
first, and also of the Gentile;[1] (10) but
glory, honour, and peace, to every man
that worketh good, to the Jew first, and
also to the Gentile:[2] (11) for there is no

1 Gr. *Greek.*

2 Gr. *Greek.*

---

works, but must be due to a divine act, and that act is conditioned by faith. In consideration, not of any fulfilment of the Law, but that the main tenor and direction of a man's life has been right as proved by his faith in Christ, the grace of God is extended towards him, and makes up that in which he is behind. Though not deserving, in a strict sense, the bliss of the Messianic kingdom, the believer is, nevertheless, admitted to it on account of his faith in the great Head of that kingdom, and his participation through that faith in the Christian scheme. That scheme has been wrought out *objectively, i.e.,* independently of him, but he by a subjective act, in other words, by *faith,* appropriates it to himself. (3) Bearing in mind this difference in the sequence of the thought, the apparent contradiction between the two doctrines is resolved. In the doctrine of final retribution there is no opposition between faith and works, in the doctrine of justification there is no opposition between works and faith. In the former, works may be regarded as the evidence of faith; in the latter, they may be regarded as its natural and necessary outcome. They may, it is true, be set in opposition, as we shall find them later on by St. Paul himself, but that is by a special abstraction of the mind. Works are there regarded as disconnected from faith, though in the nature of things they are rather associated with it. Works may be sincere or they may be hypocritical. They may have an inward foundation in the heart, or they may not. And the Apostle looks at them in both lights, according as the course of his argument requires it. That there is no radical opposition is clearly seen if we refer to the description of the last judgment in the Synoptic Gospels. There can be no question that in those Gospels the doctrine prominently put forward is that of retribution according to works, and yet it is most distinctly laid down that the works so insisted upon are not merely the outward tangible act *apart from* the inward disposition; on the contrary, when such works are pleaded they are expressly disowned (Matt. vii. 23, 24; comp. Matt. xxv. 44); and. on the other hand, we are left to infer that the righteous will have little ostensibly to allege in their own favour (Matt. xxv. 36—39). We are thus led up by easy stages to the Pauline doctrine of justification by faith, even out of the midst of that doctrine of retribution which forms the subject of the section on which we are now commenting.

(7) **To them who.**—Before the words "eternal life," at the end of the verse, we must supply "He will render." The phrase "glory, and honour, and immortality" is practically equivalent to "eternal life." "Those who honestly seek for this life shall find it." The stress is upon the words "by patient continuance in well doing." From the point of view of rhetoric, no doubt exception might be taken to the tautology; but St. Paul was far too much in earnest to attend carefully to the laws of rhetoric, and it is just this spontaneity which is in great part the secret of his power.

**Patient continuance.**—A single word in the Greek, but rightly translated in the Authorised version, *by* (according to, by the rule of) *patience* (persistence or perseverance) *in well doing* (literally, *in good work*). In English we should naturally say, "in good works," but the Greek, here as frequently, by the use of the singular and by the absence of the article, puts the abstract for the concrete, so covering every particular case.

(8) **But unto them . . .**—The scholar will observe that in the original Greek the construction is changed. At the end of verse 7 is an accusative "(he will render) eternal life;" here we have the nominative, "(there shall be) tribulation and anguish."

**That are contentious.**—An error in the Authorised version through a wrong derivation of the word. Strictly, *To those who act in the spirit of a hireling;* hence, according to the secondary meaning of the word, ("to those who act in a spirit of factiousness and self-seeking.") It is, however, quite possible that the mistaken derivation may have been current in St. Paul's time, as it was, no doubt, somewhat later, from Origen downwards. St. Paul, it is true, distinguishes between the proper word for "contention" and that used here (*e.g.,* in 2 Cor. xii. 20; Gal. v. 20), but this would not exclude, it would rather seem to imply, not indeed a formal derivation, but some association of ideas. The shade of meaning will, perhaps, be expressed if we translate by some such word as "factiousness." So in Phil. i. 16 (properly 17, the order of the clauses being reversed), "the one (*the other*) preach Christ of factiousness."

**Indignation and wrath.**—The Greek equivalents for these two words are distinguished as the settled angry feeling from the passionate outbreak of anger.

**The truth.**—Here used in a moral sense, as almost equivalent to "rectitude," "that which is right." There is a tendency towards this meaning in Rom. i. 18, "Who hold down the truth in unrighteousness," though there "the truth" appears to mean rather "natural religion" in general. The ethical sense comes out clearly in John iii. 21, "he that doeth truth," opposed to "he that doeth evil." These phrases, "obey the truth," "obey unrighteousness," in a plainer style, would be simply "do good," "do evil." It may be noted that St. Paul is fond of these quasi-personifications.

(9) **Upon every soul of man.**—The phrase is not quite the same as "upon every man," but more special in character, indicating the part in which the punishment will be felt.

(11) **Respect of persons.**—Regard for the external circumstances of a man as opposed to his internal condition; here, especially, "regard for the circumstances of birth and race." (Comp. Acts x. 34; Gal. ii. 6; Eph. vi. 9; Col. iii. 25; Jas. ii. 1, 9.) It is interesting to observe the phrase appearing in such different quarters. The great result of the Christian revelation was to break down the belief in *race*-religions—the "middle wall of partition," as St. Paul calls it.

The essential equality of Jew and Gentile before God is not affected by the precedence of the former in point of time or order, whether as regards punishment or reward.

respect of persons with God. (12) For as many as have sinned without law shall also perish without law: and as many as have sinned in the law shall be judged by the law; (13) for not the hearers of the law *are* just before God, but the doers of the law shall be justified: (14) (for when the Gentiles, which have not the law, do by nature the things contained in the law, these, having not the law, are a law unto themselves: (15) which shew the work of the law written in their hearts, their conscience also bearing witness,[1] and *their* thoughts the mean while[2] accusing or else excusing one another:) (16) in the day when God shall judge the secrets of men by Jesus Christ according to my

1 *Or, the conscience witnessing with them.*
2 Or, *between themselves.*

(12) Jew and Gentile alike will be judged, each by the method proper to his case; the Jew by the written Law against which he has sinned, the Gentile by the unwritten law of conscience against which he too has sinned. The mere hearing of the Law will bring no exemption to the Jew; and, on the other hand, the Gentile, who, at the dictates of conscience, acts as if he were subject to law, shall have the full benefit that law can give him. In fact, his conscience is to him a law. He undergoes precisely the same conflict of self-condemnation and self-acquittal as one who has a written law to refer to. All this will be done, this strict measure of justice will be applied, at the last great day of judgment.

**In the law.**—Rather, *in law.* Here, as in the phrases which follow, "by law," "the hearers of law," "the doers of law," "the Gentiles which have not law," &c., the article is wrongly inserted by the Authorised version. Its absence shows that the Apostle had in mind, not the particular Mosaic law, but the abstraction of law. "Behind the concrete representation —the Mosaic law itself—St. Paul sees an imperious principle, an overwhelming presence, antagonistic to grace, to liberty, to spirit, and (in some aspects) even to life—abstract law, which, though the Mosaic ordinances are its most signal and complete embodiment, nevertheless is not exhausted therein, but exerts its crushing power over the conscience in diverse manifestations. The one, the concrete and special, is ὁ νόμος; the other, the abstract and universal, is νόμος" (Lightfoot).

(13) **For not the hearers of the law.**—The parenthesis should not be placed here (as usually in the Authorised version), but at the beginning of the next verse. The present verse is explanatory of that which precedes. "Judged, I say, by the Law; for they must not suppose that the mere fact of their being under the Law will exempt them from this judgment. The only exemption will be that which is given to those who have *kept* the Law, and not merely had the privilege of hearing it. And," the argument follows—the Apostle digressing for a moment to pursue this point to its conclusion—"this exemption, may apply quite as much to Gentile as to Jew."

**Hearers of the law.**—Strictly (as above), *hearers of law—i.e.,* those who have a law to which they can listen, and by which they may be guided. (Comp. Acts xiii. 27; xv. 21, "Moses of old time hath in every city them that preach him, being read in the synagogues every sabbath": and for the opposition between hearing and doing, Jas. i. 22, 23, 25.)

(14) A sort of parenthesis begins here. Verse 16 refers back to the main subject of the paragraph, and not to the particular point on which the Apostle digresses in verses 14, 15, the virtual operation of law among the Gentiles as well as Jews.

**By nature.**—Spontaneously; of their own motion; not acting under the coercion of any external rule, but simply by the promptings of their own conscience left to itself.

**The things contained in the law.**—Literally, *the things of the law.* In this one instance the article is used, meaning, however, not "the law of Moses," but "of this law," or "of such law"—*i.e.,* the ideal law spoken of just before.

(15) **Which.**—Rather, *Inasmuch as they.*

**The work of the law.**—The practical effect or realisation of the law—written in their hearts as the original Law was written upon the tables of stone. (Comp. Jer. xxxi. 33; 2 Cor. iii. 3.)

**Also bearing witness.**—Or, *witnessing with them,* as margin. There is a double witness; their actions speak for them externally, and conscience speaks for them internally.

**The mean while.**—Rather, literally, as margin, *between themselves—i.e.,* with mutual interchange, the thoughts of the heart or different motions of conscience sometimes taking the part of advocate, sometimes of accuser.

This seems, on the whole, the best way of taking these two words, though some commentators (among them Meyer) regard this quasi personification of "the thoughts" as too strong a figure of speech, and take "between themselves" as referring to the mutual intercourse of man with man. But in that mutual intercourse it is not the thoughts that accuse or defend, but the tongue. The Apostle is speaking strictly of the private tribunal of conscience.

(16) This verse takes up the main thread of the subject. "God will judge Jew and Gentile alike at the last day." It cannot refer (as some would make it) to what immediately precedes, because there the Apostle is referring to the daily process that goes on whenever doubtful actions are submitted to the law of conscience, here he is speaking expressly of the final judgment held by God and not by man.

**By Jesus Christ.**—As the Son of God is the Mediator of salvation, so also is He the Mediator of judgment. The function of judgment is specially committed to Him. This is the consistent teaching of Scripture. (Comp. John v. 27, "the Father hath given Him authority to execute judgment also, because He is the Son of Man"; Acts xvii. 31, "He hath appointed a day in the which He will judge the world . . by that Man whom He hath ordained"; 1 Cor. iv. 5; 2 Cor. v. 10, *et. al.*)

**According to my gospel.**—How is this to be taken? To what is it that the gospel, as preached by St. Paul, testifies? It may be either to the simple fact that God will judge the secrets of men, or to the particular law or standard by which He will judge them. Probably, on the whole, the former is the preferable explanation. "In the day when, as I teach, God will judge the secrets of men by Jesus Christ."

gospel. (17) Behold, thou art called a
Jew, and restest in the law, and makest
thy boast of God, (18) and knowest *his*
will, and approvest[1] the things that are
more excellent, being instructed out
of the law; (19) and art confident that
thou thyself art a guide of the blind,
a light of them which are in darkness,
(20) an instructor of the foolish, a teacher
of babes, which hast the form of know-
ledge and of the truth in the law.
(21) Thou therefore which teachest an-
other, teachest thou not thyself? thou
that preachest a man should not steal,
dost thou steal? (22) thou that sayest a
man should not commit adultery, dost
thou commit adultery? thou that abhor-
rest idols, dost thou commit sacrilege?
(23) thou that makest thy boast of the
law, through breaking the law dis-
honourest thou God? (24) For the name
of God is blasphemed among the Gentiles
through you, as it is written.[a] (25) For
circumcision verily profiteth, if thou
keep the law: but if thou be a breaker
of the law, thy circumcision is made
uncircumcision. (26) Therefore if the
uncircumcision keep the righteousness
of the law, shall not his uncircumcision
be counted for circumcision? (27) And
shall not uncircumcision which is by
nature, if it fulfil the law, judge thee,

1 Or, *triest the things that differ.*

a Isa. 52. 5; Ezek. 36. 20, 23.

---

(17) **Behold.**—An interesting case of a corrupt reading which has found its way into the Authorised version. For "behold," a decisive consensus of the best MSS. has "but if." The corruption was very obvious and easy. Adopting "but if," the answering clause of the sentence is to be found in the question, "Teachest thou not thyself?" verse 21. The connecting particle "therefore" at the beginning of the same verse is merely resumptive, or, as it is technically called, "epanaleptic."

Turning to the Jew, the Apostle breaks out into indignant and vehement apostrophe, "If you have the name of Jew, and repose upon the Law, and make your boast in God, and do all these other things—why then, while you profess to teach others, do you not teach yourself?" A fine specimen of the natural eloquence which the Apostle derives from intense feeling. The different features of the picture crowd into his mind to point the contrast between what the Jew claimed to be and what he was.

**Restest in.**—Reposest or reliest upon a law. A passive confidence in something external. "In the Law the Jew saw the Magna Charta which gave him his assurance of salvation" (Meyer).

**Makest thy boast of God**—*i.e.*, of a peculiar and exclusive claim to His favour. (Comp. Deut. iv. 7; Ps. cxlvii. 19, 20.)

(18) **His will.**—Literally, *the will*—*i.e.*, "the supreme will."

**Approvest the things that are more excellent.**—Probably rightly given in the Authorised version, though the marginal rendering also is possible, "triest the things that differ"—*i.e.*, "art able to discriminate between good and evil."

**Being instructed.**—With reference to the constant reading of the Law in the synagogue.

(19) **A guide of the blind.**—Comp. Matt. xv. 14, "They be blind leaders of the blind. And if the blind lead the blind," *et seq.*

(20) **The form of knowledge and of the truth.**—As we might say, "the presentation of knowledge and of truth." Here not form as opposed to substance, but as implying substance—"presentation," or "embodiment."

(21) **Therefore.**—See above on verse 17.

(22) **Commit sacrilege.**—Properly, *rob temples*—*i.e.*, idol temples, with a pointed antithesis to that abhorrence of idols on which the Jew prided himself. This is certainly the last offence of which we should have expected the Jews of this date to be guilty, knowing the scrupulousness with which they shunned all contact with idolatry. They may, however, have thought the idol temples fair plunder. At any rate, it is clear that this charge was commonly brought against them. Comp. Acts xix. 37, where the town-clerk of Ephesus specially acquits St. Paul and his companions of "being robbers of temples." Josephus also (*Ant.* iv. 8, § 10) quotes as a precept of the Mosaic legislation, "Let no one blaspheme those gods which other cities esteem such; nor may any one steal what belongs to strange temples; nor take away the gifts that are dedicated to any god."

(23) **Dishonourest thou God?**—This verse has been regarded, not as a question, but as a summary answer to the previous questions, "You, who make all this boast in the Law, by breaking the Law, dishonour God." There is a certain force in this view, but the structure of the clause is so similar to those that have gone before that it seems best, perhaps, upon the whole, to take it in the ordinary way.

(24) **Through you.**—*Because of you.*

**As it is written.**—From the LXX. version of Isa. lii. 5. The sense of the original is that the name of God is dishonoured by the enslavement and oppression of His people. A nearer parallel in sense, though more remote in words, may be found in 2 Sam. xii. 14; Ezek. xxxvi. 22, 23. The Apostle is not careful as to the particular context from which he draws. He knew that he was giving the substance of Scripture, and he takes the aptest words that occur to him at the moment. Translated into our modern modes of thought, the formula "as it is written" at the end of the verse amounts to little more than "in the language of Scripture." The intention, as so frequently with St. Paul, seems, as it were, to be divided between proof and illustration.

(25–29) This section forms a connecting-link with the opening of the next chapter. "The characteristic mark and badge of the Jew has two sides, the one outward and formal, the other inward and real. Its essence consists in the latter, and without this inward circumcision the outward profits nothing. It is not necessary to be born a Jew to possess it." Precisely the same language might be applied to the Christian sacraments, or to the privileges of any particular communion. Privileges they may be, but they depend for their efficacy entirely upon the disposition of the heart which underlies them.

(25) **Is made.**—*Is become,*—*ipso facto,* "is reduced to the case of."

(27) **Judge thee.**—Comp. Matt. xii. 41, 42, "The

who by the letter and circumcision dost
transgress the law? (28) For he is not
a Jew, which is one outwardly; neither
*is that* circumcision, which is outward
in the flesh: (29) but he *is* a Jew, which
is one inwardly; and circumcision *is*
*that* of the heart, in the spirit, *and* not
in the letter; whose praise *is* not of
men, but of God.

CHAPTER III.—(1) What advantage
then hath the Jew? or
what profit *is there* of cir-
cumcision? (2) Much every

Chap. iii. 1—4. The Jew's advantage.

way: chiefly, because that unto them
were committed the oracles of God.
(3) For what if some did not believe?
shall their unbelief make the faith of
God without effect? (4) God forbid:
yea, let God be true, but every man a
liar; as it is written, That thou mightest
be justified in thy sayings,[a] and mightest
overcome when thou art judged. (5) But
if our unrighteousness com-
mend the righteousness of
God, what shall we say?
*Is* God unrighteous who
taketh vengeance? (I speak as a man.)

Chap. iii. 5—8. Digression on doing evil that good may come.

a Ps. 51. 4.

A.D. 58.

---

men of Nineveh shall rise in judgment with this generation, and shall condemn it," *et seq.* The idea is that of "putting to shame by contrast."

**By the letter.**—The preposition here marks the condition or circumstance under which the action is done, and might be paraphrased, "with all the advantages of the written Law and of circumcision."

Here, again, the sentence may not be a question, but an affirmation.

III.

(1–8) Continuing the subject, but with a long digression in verses 3 *et seq.* The Apostle asks, What is the real value of these apparent advantages? He is about to answer the question fully, as he does later in chap. ix. 4, 5; but after stating the first point, he goes off upon a difficulty raised by this, and does not return to complete what he had begun. This, again, is characteristic of his ardent and keenly speculative mind. Problems such as those which he discusses evidently have a fascination for him, and lead him, here as elsewhere, at once to leave the immediate subject before him, and to enter eagerly into the discussion of them. A more lethargic or timid brain would be under no such temptation.

One real and solid advantage on the part of the Jew was that he was made the direct recipient of the divine revelation. This privilege of his is not annulled by the defection of a part of the people. It rests not upon the precarious fidelity of men, but upon the infallible promise of God. Yet is not the ultimate triumph of that promise any excuse for those who have set it at nought. They will be punished just the same, and rightly. Otherwise there could be no judgment at all. The casuistical objection that sin loses its guilt if it redounds to God's glory, or, in other words, that the end justifies the means, carries with it its own condemnation.

(2) **Chiefly.**—In the first place; "secondly," &c., was to follow, but does not, as the Apostle is drawn away to other topics (see above).

**Unto them were committed.**—This is paraphrastic. "Oracle" is the object, and not the subject, of the sentence. "They were entrusted with."

**Oracles.**—A good translation; the Scriptures of the Old Testament as containing a revelation of God.

(3) **For what if.**—What (follows) if, &c. Or we may take the first two words by themselves, and throw the next two clauses together. How stands the case? If some rejected the faith, shall their rejection make void or defeat the faithfulness of God?

The Apostle considers an objection that might be brought against his argument that the divine revelation vouchsafed to them was a special privilege of the Jewish people. It might be said that they had forfeited and cancelled this privilege by their unbelief. He first reduces the objection to its proper limits; it was not *all*, but *some*, who were unbelievers. But granting that there were some who did not believe, this fact would have no power to shake the eternal promises of God.

(4) Impossible! Rather let God be seen to be true though all mankind should be proved false, even as the Psalmist looked upon his own sin as serving to enhance the triumph of God's justice. Speaking of that justice for the moment as if it could be arraigned before the bar of a still higher tribunal, he asserts its absolute and complete acquittal.

**That thou mightest be justified.**—Strictly, *in order that*, here as in the Hebrew of the Psalm. Good is, in some way inscrutable to us, educed out of evil, and this is clearly foreseen by God, and forms part of His design, though so as not to interfere with the free-will of man. Religion assumes that the two things, free-will and omnipotence, are reconcilable, though how they are to be reconciled seems an insoluble problem. The same difficulty attaches to every system but one of blank fatalism and atheism. But the theory of fatalism if logically carried out would simply destroy human society.

Ps. li., in which the quotation occurs, is commonly (in accordance with the heading), though perhaps wrongly, ascribed to David after his sin with Bathsheba. The effect of this sin is to throw out into the strongest relief the justice of the sentence by which it is followed and punished. The original is, "That thou mightest be just in thy speaking; that thou mightest be pure in thy judging." St. Paul adopts the rendering of the LXX., who make the last word passive instead of active, thus making it apply, not to the sentence given by God, but to the imaginary trial to which by a figure of speech that sentence itself is supposed to be submitted.

(5) **But if our unrighteousness.**—A new and profound question suggests itself to the mind of the Apostle, and his keen intellect will not let it go: "If the sin (here the unbelief) of man only tends to vindicate (commends or establishes) the righteousness of God, why should that sin be punished?" The mere

(6) God forbid: for then how shall
God judge the world? (7) For if the
truth of God hath more abounded
through my lie unto his glory; why
yet am I also judged as a sinner?
(8) And not *rather*, (as we be slan-
derously reported, and as some affirm
that we say,) Let us do evil, that
good may come? whose damnation
is just.

(9) What then? are we better *than
they?* No, in no wise: for
we have before proved[1]
both Jews and Gentiles,
that they are all under
sin; (10) as it is written, There is none
righteous, no, not one:[a] (11) there is
none that understandeth, there is none
that seeketh after God. (12) They are all
gone out of the way, they are together

Chap. iii. 9—20. Jew and Gentile alike convicted.

1 Gr. *charged.*

a Ps. 14. 1—3.

---

raising of such a question requires an apology; it is only as a man might speak about man that he dares to utter such a thought. That, too, is an impossible objection, for if it held good there could not be any judgment. No sin would be punishable, for all sin would serve to emphasise the strict veracity of God in His denunciations of it, and therefore would ultimately conduce to His glory. It would thus cease to be sinful, and there would be nothing to hinder us from adopting the principle that is so calumniously attributed to us—that it is lawful to do evil that good may come. A calumny it is, and any such principle with all that appertains to it—*i.e.*, with the whole of the preceding argument,—is justly condemned.

(6) **For then how shall God judge the world?**—St. Paul considers it a sufficient answer merely to propound this question. He and those to whom he was writing all *assumed* that there must be a future judgment.

The way in which Bishop Butler deals with the argument from necessity is very similar to this, substituting only present for future judgment. "It is fact that God does govern even brute creatures by the method of rewards and punishments in the natural course of things. And men are rewarded and punished for their actions—punished for actions mischievous to society as being so, punished for vicious actions as such—by the natural instrumentality of each other under the present conduct of Providence," &c. Hence the necessitarian is in this dilemma: either his opinion is not true, or else it must be capable of being harmonised with these facts. The facts themselves are postulated.

(7) **The truth of God.**—In the first instance His veracity as involved in His threats and promises, and then those other attributes, especially justice, that are intimately connected with this. "Truth" is leaning towards its moral sense. (See Note on chap. ii. 8.)

**My lie.**—The Apostle puts his supposed case in the first person. "Lie," suggested as an antithesis to the word "truth," just used, has also a moral signification. It is the moral deflection that follows upon unbelief.

(8) **And not rather.**—*And* (*why should we*) *not* (*say*), *as some persons slanderously affirm that we say, Let us do evil that good may come.* Some such phrase as "Why should we say" must be supplied; "why" from the previous clause, "say" from that which follows. Or "(Why should we) not (do evil), as some persons slanderously affirm that we say, Let us do evil," &c. The latter, perhaps, is best, as we might then suppose the word for "let us do" repeated precisely in the form in which it stands.

The Apostle does not care to answer this argument in detail; he will not dally with such a perversion of the moral sense, but simply says, "Whose condemnation is just."

What pretext could any one possibly have for attributing such an opinion to St. Paul? The charge was no doubt utterly false as applied to him, but we know that his teaching was made an excuse for Antinomian excesses, which would not unnaturally be fastened upon the Apostle. Or, taking his teaching as it stands, we might well imagine the Jews or the Judaizing party arguing with themselves, "This man openly breaks the Law, and yet he claims to be in the right way, and that all will go well with him; is not this doing evil that good may come? Does he think to win the Messianic kingdom by the breach of the Law, and not by its observance?"

(9—20) Once more the argument returns to the main track, and at last the Apostle asserts distinctly and categorically what he had already proved indirectly, that the Jew is every whit as bad as the Gentile.

(9) **Are we better than they?**—"Can we claim a preference?" The form of the Greek verb is peculiar. It seems upon the whole best to take it as middle for active, which would be apparently unexampled, but is tenable as a question of language, and seems to be compelled by the context. There is no real opposition between the "by no means" of the reply and the "much every way" of verse 2. There the reference was to external advantages, here it is to real and essential worth in the sight of God; as much as to say, "For all our advantages are we really better?"

**Proved.**—Adopt rather the marginal rendering, *For we before charged both Jews and Gentiles with being all under sin.*

The verses are a striking instance of the way in which the Apostle weaves together passages taken from different sources. It also affords an example of the corruptions in the text of the Old Testament to which this practice gave rise. The whole passage as it stands here is found in some manuscripts of the LXX. as part of Ps. xiv., whence it has been copied not only into the Vulgate but also our own Prayer Book, which will be seen to differ from the Bible version.

The quotations have different degrees of appositeness, so far as they may be considered in the modern sense as probative rather than illustrative. The first, from Ps. xiv., is couched in such general terms as to be directly in point; the second and third, from Pss. v. and cxl., are aimed specially against the oppressors of the Psalmist; and so, too, the fourth, from Ps. x., but in a more general and abstract form; that from Isaiah indicates the moral degradation among the prophet's contemporaries that had led to the Captivity; while the last, from Ps. xxxvi., is an expression applied, not to all men, but particularly to the wicked.

(12) **They are together become unprofitable.**—Here the adjective is used to express a state of moral corruption and depravity. "Together" means "altogether;" "the whole mass of mankind, with one consent, has fallen to ruin."

become unprofitable; there is none that
doeth good, no, not one. (13) Their
throat *is* an open sepulchre;[a] with their
tongues they have used deceit; the poison
of asps *is* under their lips;[b] (14) whose
mouth *is* full of cursing and bitterness:[c]
(15) their feet *are* swift to shed blood:[d]
(16) destruction and misery *are* in their
ways: (17) and the way of peace have
they not known: (18) there is no fear of
God before their eyes.[e] (19) Now we
know that what things soever the law
saith, it saith to them who are under
the law: that every mouth may be
stopped, and all the world may become
guilty before God.[1] (20) Therefore by
the deeds of the law there shall no flesh
be justified in his sight: for by the law
*is* the knowledge of sin.

Chap. iii. 21—26. The great thesis repeated.

(21) But now the righteous-
ness of God without the
law is manifested, being
witnessed by the law and the prophets;
(22) even the righteousness of God *which*

a Ps. 5. 9.
b Ps. 140. 3.
1 Or, *subject to the judgment of God.*
c Ps. 10. 7.
d Isa. 59. 7, 8.
e Ps. 36. 1.

---

(13) **Their throat is an open sepulchre**—*i.e.*, their speech is at once corrupt and corrupting. It is compared to a "yawning grave"—not merely to a pit into which a man may fall, but to a sort of pestiferous chasm yawning and ravening, as it were, after its prey.

**They have used deceit.**—Strictly, *they were deceiving;* a continued action brought up to the present time.

**Under their lips.**—As the poison-bag of the serpent is directly under the kind of tooth by which its venom is discharged.

(14) **Bitterness.**—Malignity; from the notion that venom was contained in the gall. (Comp. Acts viii. 23.)

(18) The fear of God, which is properly a subjective feeling, is here projected, as it were, and regarded as an external rule of life.

(19) In order to bring home this testimony of Scripture more directly to the Jews, and to prevent any subterfuge by which they might attempt to shift the reference from themselves on to the Gentiles, the Apostle calls attention to the fact that the Law—*i.e.*, the Old Testament, from which he has been quoting—speaks especially to those to whom it was given.

**Saith . . . saith.** — Different words are here used in the Greek; the first is applicable as much to the matter as to the utterance of that which is spoken, the second refers specially to the outward act by which it is enunciated or promulgated; this is addressed to certain persons.

**Guilty before God.**—Rather, *guilty to God;* the dative expresses the person to whom the penalty is due.

(20) **Therefore.** — Rather, *because.* All mankind alike owe the penalty for their sins. *Because* not even the Law can protect its votaries. It has no power to justify. All it can do is to expose in its true colours the sinfulness of sin.

The proposition is thrown into a general form: not by the works of the (Jewish) Law, but by "works of law"—*i.e.*, by any works done in obedience to any law. Law, in the abstract, as such, is unable to justify. It might perhaps, we gather from later portions of the Epistle, if men could really keep it, but no law can be kept strictly and entirely.

**Knowledge of sin.**—"Full and thorough knowledge."

In the state anterior to law, man is not supposed to know what is sinful and what is not. Conscience, gradually developed, comes in to give him some insight into the distinction, but the full knowledge of right and wrong, in all its details, is reserved for the introduction of positive law. Law has, however, only this enlightening faculty; it holds the mirror up to guilt, but it cannot remove it.

(21—26) This then introduces the solemn enunciation, repeated more fully from chap. i. 16, 17, of the great subject of the Epistle, the declaration of that new scheme by which, through Christ, God had removed the guilt which the Law (whether Jewish or any other) could not remove.

(21—22) Such was the condition of the world up to the coming of Christ. But now, in contrast with the previous state of things, a new system has appeared upon the scene. In this system law is entirely put on one side, though the system itself was anticipated in and is attested by those very writings in which the Law was embodied. Law is now superseded, the great end of the Law, the introduction of righteousness, being accomplished in another way, viz., through faith in Christ, by which a state of righteousness is superinduced upon all believers.

(21) **But now.**—In these latter days. The Apostle conceives of the history of the world as divided into periods; the period of the Gospel succeeds that of the Law, and to it the Apostle and his readers belong. (Comp. for this conception of the gospel, as manifested at a particular epoch of time, chap. xvi. 25, 26; Acts xvii. 30; Gal. iii. 23, 25; iv. 3, 4; Eph. i. 10; ii. 12, 13; Col. i. 21, 26; 1 Tim. ii. 6; 2 Tim. i. 10; Heb. i. 1; 1 Pet. i. 20.)

**The righteousness of God.**—Rather, *a righteousness of God*—*i.e.*, "bestowed by God," "wrought out by Him," as in chap. i. 17. The reference is again, here as there, to the root-conception of righteousness as at once the great object and condition of the Messianic kingdom.

**Without the law.**—In complete independence of any law, though borne witness to by the Law of Moses. The new system is one into which the idea of law does not enter.

**Is manifested.**—Hath been, and continues to be manifested. The initial moment is that of the appearance of Christ upon earth. The scheme which then began is still evolving itself.

**Being witnessed.**—The Apostle does not lose sight of the preparatory function of the older dispensation, and of its radical affinity to the new. (Comp. chap. i. 2; xvi. 26; Luke xviii. 31; xxiv. 27, 44, 46; John v. 39, 46; Acts ii. 25, 31; iii. 22, 24; xvii. 2, 3; xxvi. 22, 23; 1 Pet. i. 10, 11.)

(22) A further definition of the nature of the righteousness so given to the Christian by God; it is a

*is* by faith of Jesus Christ unto all
and upon all them that believe: for
there is no difference: (23) for all
have sinned, and come short of the
glory of God, (24) being justified freely
by his grace through the redemption
that is in Christ Jesus: (25) whom God
hath set forth[1] *to be* a propitiation

[1] Or, *foreordained.*

righteousness that has its root in faith, and is coextensive with faith, being present in every believer.

**By faith of Jesus Christ**—*i.e., by faith which has Christ for its object,* "faith *in* Christ." "Faith" in St. Paul's writings implies an intense attachment and devotion. It has an intellectual basis, necessarily involving a belief in the existence, and in certain attributes, of the Person for whom it is entertained; but it is moral in its operation, a recasting of the whole emotional nature in accordance with this belief, together with a consequent change in character and practice. (See *Excursus B: On the Meaning of the word Faith.*)

**And upon all.**—These words are wanting in the best MSS., and should be omitted.

**For there is no difference.**—The righteousness that God gives is given to *all* that believe, without any distinction of Jew or Gentile; for all equally need it, and it is free equally to all.

(23) **All have sinned and come short.**—Strictly, *all sinned;* the Apostle looking back upon an act done in past time under the old legal dispensation, without immediate reference to the present: he then goes on to say that the result of that act (as distinct from the act itself) continues on into the present. The result is that mankind, in a body, as he now sees them, and before they come within the range of the new Christian system, fall short of, miss, or fail to obtain, the glory of God.

**Glory of God.**—What is this glory? Probably not here, as in chap. viii. 18, 21, the glory which will be inaugurated for the saints at the *Parusià,* or Second Coming of the Messiah—for that is something future—but, rather, something which is capable of being conferred in the present, viz., the glory which comes from the favour and approval of God. This favour and approval Jew and Gentile alike had hitherto failed to obtain, but it was now thrown open to all who became members of the Messianic kingdom. (Comp. for the sense, chap. ii. 29, and for the use of the word, as well as the sense, John xii. 43, "they loved the praise [*glory*] of men more than the praise [*glory*] of God.")

(24) **Being justified.**—We should more naturally say, "but now *are* justified." The construction in the Greek is peculiar, and may be accounted for in one of two ways. Either the phrase "being justified" may be taken as corresponding to "all them that believe" in verse 22, the change of case being an irregularity suggested by the form of the sentence immediately preceding; or the construction may be considered to be regular, and the participle "being justified" would then be dependent upon the last finite verb: "they come short of the glory of God, and *in that very state of destitution* are justified."

**Freely.**—Gratuitously, without exertion or merit on their part. (Comp. Matt. x. 8; Rev. xxi. 6; xxii. 17.)

**By his grace.**—*By His own grace.* The *means* by which justification is wrought out is the death and atonement of Christ; its *ulterior* cause is the grace of God, or free readmission into His favour, which He accords to man.

**Redemption.**—Literally, *ransoming.* The notion of ransom contains in itself the triple idea of a bondage, a deliverance, and the payment of an equivalent as the means of that deliverance. The bondage is the state of sin and of guilt, with the expectation of punishment; the deliverance is the removal of this state, and the opening out, in its stead, of a prospect of eternal happiness and glory; the equivalent paid by Christ is the shedding of His own blood. This last is the pivot upon which the whole idea of redemption turned. It is therefore clear that the redemption of the sinner is an act wrought objectively, and, in the first instance, independently of any change of condition in him, though such a change is involved in the appropriation of the efficacy of that act to himself. It cannot be explained as a purely subjective process wrought in the sinner through the influence of Christ's death. The idea of dying and reviving with Christ, though a distinct aspect of the atonement, cannot be made to cover the whole of it. There is implied, not only a change in the recipient of the atonement, but also a change wrought without his co-operation in the relations between God and man. There is, if it may be so said, in the death of Christ something which determines the will of God, as well as something which acts upon the will of man. And the particular influence which is brought to bear upon the counsels of God is represented under the figure of a ransom or payment of an equivalent. This element is too essentially a part of the metaphor, and is too clearly established by other parallel metaphors, to be explained away; though what the terms "propitiation" and "equivalent" can mean, as applied to God, we do not know, and it perhaps does not become us too curiously to inquire.

The doctrine of the atonement thus stated is not peculiar to St. Paul, and did not originate with him. It is found also in the Synoptic Gospels, Matt xx. 28 (= Mark x. 45), "The Son of Man came to give His life a ransom for many," and in Heb. ix. 15, "And for this cause He is the Mediator of the New Testament, that by means of death, for the redemption (*ransoming*) of the transgressions that were under the first testament, they which are called might receive the promise of eternal inheritance." (Comp. 1 John ii. 2; 1 Pet. i. 18, 19; ii. 24, *et al.*)

(25, 26) The death of Christ had a twofold object or final cause:—(1) It was to be, like the sacrifices of the old covenant, an offering propitiatory to God, and actualised in the believer through faith. (2) It was to demonstrate the righteousness of God by showing that sin would entail punishment, though it might not be punished in the person of the sinner. The apparent absence of any adequate retribution for the sins of past ages made it necessary that by one conspicuous instance it should be shown that this was in no sense due to an ignoring of the true nature of sin. The retributive justice of God was all the time unimpaired. The death of Christ served for its vindication, at the same time that a way to escape from its consequences was opened out through the justification of the believer.

Precisely in what sense the punishment of our sins fell upon Christ, and in what sense the justice of God was vindicated by its so falling, is another point which we are not able to determine. Nothing, we may be sure, can be involved which is in *ultimate* conflict with

through faith in his blood, to declare
his righteousness for the remission[1] of
sins that are past, through the forbear-
ance of God; (26) to declare, *I say*, at
this time his righteousness: that he
might be just, and the justifier of him
which believeth in Jesus.

[1] Or, *passing over.*

(27) Where *is* boasting then? It is
excluded. By what law?
of works? Nay: but by
the law of faith. (28) There-
fore we conclude that a man is justified
by faith without the deeds of the law.
(29) *Is he* the God of the Jews only? *is*

Chap. iii. 27—31. Boasting excluded.

---

morality. At the same time, we see that under the ordinary government of God, the innocent suffer for the guilty, and there may be some sort of transference of this analogy into the transcendental sphere. Both the natural and the supernatural government of God are schemes "imperfectly comprehended." In any case, Christ was innocent, and Christ suffered. On any theory there is a connection between His death and human sin. *What* connection, is a question to which, perhaps, only a partial answer can be given. Some weighty remarks on this subject will be found in Butler's *Analogy of Religion*, Part II., chap. v. (latter part).

(25) **Hath set forth.**—Rather, *set forth, publicly exhibited*, in the single act of the death upon the cross.

**A propitiation.**—The Greek word properly means "that which renders propitious." Here, "that which renders God propitious." In some way, which is not explained at all in this passage, and imperfectly explained elsewhere, the death of Christ did act so as to render God "propitious" towards men. He became more ready to pardon as they became more anxious to be pardoned.

There is a remarkable use of the same Greek word in the LXX. version of the Old Testament to express the *mercy-seat, i.e.*, the lid or covering of the ark which was sprinkled by the high priest with the blood of the victim on the Day of Atonement. Some have thought that there is a reference to this here. Christ is the *mercy-seat* of the New Covenant. It is upon Him, as it were, that the divine grace, drawn forth by His own atoning blood, resides. It would hardly be a conclusive objection to this view that, according to it, Christ would be represented as at once the victim whose blood is sprinkled and the covering of the ark on which it is sprinkled; for a similar double reference certainly occurs in Heb. ix. 11, 12, where Christ is typified at one and the same time both by the victim whose blood is shed and by the high priest by whom it is offered. There seem to be, however, on the whole, reasons for supplying rather the idea of "sacrifice," which is more entirely in keeping with the context, and is especially supported by the two phrases, "whom God hath set forth" (*i.e.*, exhibited *publicly*, whereas the ark was confined to the secrecy of the Holy of Holies), and "in His blood." We should translate, therefore, *a propitiatory* or *expiatory* (*sacrifice*).

**Through faith.**—Faith is the *causa apprehendens* by which the proffered pardon takes effect upon the soul of the believer.

**In his blood.**—On the whole, it seems best not to join these words with "through faith," but to refer them to the main word of the sentence. "Whom God set forth by the shedding of His blood to be a propitiatory offering through faith." It was in the shedding of the blood that the essence of the atonement exhibited upon the cross consisted. No doubt other portions of the life of Christ led up to this one; but this was the culminating act in it, viewed as an atonement.

(26) **To declare.**—The second object of the death of Christ was to remove the misconceptions that might be caused by the apparent condoning of sins committed in times anterior to the Christian revelation. A special word is used to indicate that these sins were not wiped away and dismissed altogether, but rather "passed over" or "overlooked." This was due to the forbearance of God, who, as it were, *suspended* the execution of His vengeance. Now the Apostle shows by the death of Christ that justice that had apparently slept was vindicated.

Thus God appeared in a double character, at once as just or righteous Himself, and as producing a state of righteousness in the believer. Under the Old Testament God had been revealed as *just;* but the justice or righteousness of God was not met by any corresponding righteousness on the part of man, and therefore could only issue in condemnation. Under the New Testament the justice of God remained the same, but it *was* met by a corresponding state of righteousness in the believer: a righteousness, however, not inherent, but superinduced by God Himself through the process of justification by faith. In this way the great Messianic condition of righteousness was fulfilled.

(27—31) A review of the consequences of this process of justification. How does it affect the pretensions of the Jew? It shuts them out by laying stress no longer on works, which were the proper fulfilment of the first law as it stood, but upon faith. Faith is the true medium of justification. And faith belongs as much to Gentile as to Jew. For faith is the appointed means by which all mankind will be justified; and they will all be justified before the same tribunal, whether they be circumcised or not. Still this involves no abrogation of the Law, but rather a confirmation of it.

(27) **It is excluded.**—Strictly, *It was excluded*—at the moment when the law of faith—*i.e.*, the gospel—was brought in.

**By what law?**—Properly, *By what kind of law?* Is this law which gets rid of boasting one which calls for works; or is it one that calls for faith?

**The law of faith.**—Another name for the gospel.

(28) **Therefore . . . .**—There is a remarkable division of some of the best authorities in this verse between "therefore" and "for." The weight of authority seems somewhat in favour of "for," which also makes the best sense. That boasting is excluded is much rather the consequence than the cause of the principle that man is justified by faith. This principle the Apostle regards as sufficiently proved by his previous argument.

**We conclude.**—This conveys too much the idea of an inference; the statement is rather made in the form of an assertion, "we consider," or "we hold." "For we hold that a man (any human being—whether Jew or Greek) is justified by faith, independently of any works prescribed by law."

(29) **Is he not also.**—Insert "or." "Or are we to suppose that God *is the God of* (literally, *belongs to*) the Jews only?"—taking up the point in the last

*he* not also of the Gentiles? Yes, of the Gentiles also: (30) seeing *it is* one God, which shall justify the circumcision by faith, and uncircumcision through faith. (31) Do we then make void the law through faith? God forbid: yea, we establish the law.

A.D. 58.

CHAPTER IV.—(1) What shall we say then that Abraham our father, as pertaining to the flesh, hath found? (2) For if Abraham were justified by works, he hath *whereof* to glory; but not before God. (3) For what saith the scripture? Abraham

Chap. iv. 1—25. Abraham himself justified by faith.

verse, that any man, simply *quâ* man, and without regard to distinction of race, was capable of justification.

(30) **Seeing it is . . .**—With a slight change of reading, *if at least; if, as we are sure is the case.*

The argument is strictly logical. If there is to be any distinction between Jew and Gentile, this can only be upon the assumption either that there are more gods than one by whom they will be justified, or that they will be justified by some different law, in some different way. But neither of these is the case. Therefore it follows that there is no distinction.

**Shall justify.**—The future signifies, "throughout the Christian dispensation"—wherever the Christian system extends.

**By faith.**—*Through faith.* In the one case faith is regarded as the instrument, in the other as the means; but the two expressions come to be almost convertible. In like manner there is no essential difference indicated by the fact that the first noun has not the article, while the second has it. The former is more abstract—the quality of faith in man; the latter more concrete—faith as embodied in the gospel. The two prepositions, "by" and "through," are in English nearly convertible, or differ from each other no more than "instrument" and "means."

(31) **Do we then make void the law.**—In opposition to many commentators it seems right to take this as an isolated statement to be worked out afterwards (chap. vi. 1 *et seq.*) more fully. It cannot, without straining, be connected directly with what follows. The Apostle deals with two objections to his theory of justification by faith: (1) that there ought to be a different rule for the Jew and for the Gentile; (2) that if not, the law is practically abolished. He meets this latter by a contradiction, saying that it is not abolished, but confirmed. This is, however, drawing upon the stock of conclusions in his own mind to which he had come by process of meditation; the detailed proof is reserved.

## IV.

(1—25) The subject of the chapter is an application of the foregoing to the special (and crucial) case of Abraham, with particular reference to two ideas that are continually recurring throughout the last chapter: (1) the supposed superiority of Jew to Gentile (and, *à fortiori*, of the great progenitor of the Jews); (2) the idea of boasting or glorying based upon this superiority. Following out this the Apostle shows how even Abraham's case tells, not against, but for the doctrine of justification by faith. Indeed, Abraham himself came under it. And not only so, but those who act upon this doctrine are spiritually descendants of Abraham. It is entirely a mistake to suppose that they of the circumcision only are Abraham's seed. The true seed of Abraham are those who follow his example of faith. He put faith in the promise, they must put their faith in the fulfilment of the promise.

(1) To come back to the question of chap. iii. 1, repeated in chap. iii. 9, in what did the superiority of Abraham, the great representative of the Jewish race, really consist?

**As pertaining to the flesh.**—The construction of these words appears to be determined by their position in the sentence. According to the best MSS. they are distinctly separated from "hath found" and joined with "our father." They would therefore mean simply "our father according to the flesh," *i.e.*, by natural descent, as in chap. i. 3.

**Hath found.**—*Hath got,* or *gained,* by way of advantage.

(2) We know that he obtained justification. If that justification had been earned by his own works it would then have been something to be proud of; it would be a pride that he might fairly hold both towards men and towards God; for to men he could point to the privileged position that he had gained, and in the sight of God he would be able to plead a certain merit of his own. But he has *not* this merit. His justification was *not* earned, but it was bestowed upon him, not for the sake of his works, but of his faith. This is the express statement of Scripture. And hence it follows that though his privileged position in the sight of men remains, he has nothing to boast of before God.

**But not before God.**—This is an instance of the rapid and eager dialectic of the Apostle. If the whole train of thought had been given it would probably have run much as above, but the greater part of it is suppressed, and the Apostle strikes straight at the one point which he intended to bring into relief. (Whatever there might be before men) there is no boasting before God.

(3) The Apostle gives a proof of this from Scripture. Abraham was not justified by works, and therefore had nothing to boast of in God's sight. He was justified by faith. His righteousness was not real, but imputed. His faith was treated as if it had been equivalent to a righteousness of works. It met with the same acceptance in the sight of God that a righteousness of works would have done. But—the argument goes on—faith carries with it no such idea of merit or debt as works. It is met by a pure act of grace on the part of God.

**Abraham believed God.**—The quotation is taken from Gen. xv. 6, where it appears as a comment upon Abraham's belief in the promise that he should have a numerous posterity. The same passage is elaborately commented upon by Philo and others, so that it would seem to have been a common topic in the Jewish schools. It should be noticed that the word "faith" is not used in quite the same sense in the original and in the application. In Abraham's case it was trust in the fulfilment of the divine promise, in St. Paul's sense it is rather enthusiastic adhesion to a person. This is part of the

believed God,[a] and it was counted
unto him for righteousness. (4) Now
to him that worketh is the reward
not reckoned of grace, but of debt.
(5) But to him that worketh not, but
believeth on him that justifieth the
ungodly, his faith is counted for
righteousness. (6) Even as David also
describeth the blessedness of the man,
unto whom God imputeth righteousness
without works, (7) *saying*, Blessed *are*
they whose iniquities are forgiven,[b] and
whose sins are covered. (8) Blessed *is*
the man to whom the Lord will not
impute sin. (9) *Cometh* this blessedness
then upon the circumcision *only*, or
upon the uncircumcision also? for we
say that faith was reckoned to Abra-
ham for righteousness. (10) How was it
then reckoned? when he was in circum-
cision, or in uncircumcision? Not in
circumcision, but in uncircumcision.
(11) And he received the sign of circum-
cision, a seal of the righteousness of the

a Gen. 15. 6.

b Ps. 32. 1, 2.

---

general enlargement and deepening of the Old Testament terminology by St. Paul. A writer of less profundity (though marked by striking and elevated qualities), the author of the Epistle to the Hebrews, applies the word more strictly. (See Heb. xi. 8 *et seq.*) In Jas. ii. 23 the word has the still thinner meaning of a merely intellectual assent. St Paul quotes the same passage in the same sense as here in Gal. iii. 6. (See *Excursus B: On the Meaning of the word Faith.*)

**It was counted unto him.**—It should be observed that the same words are translated by the Authorised version here, "it was *counted unto* him;" in verse 9, "faith was *reckoned to* Abraham;" in verse 22, "it was *imputed unto* him;" in Gal. iii. 6, "it was *accounted to* him;" in Jas. ii. 23, "it was *imputed to* him." A defect in the translation, which, however, hardly obscures the true meaning.

The sense of imputation is not to be got rid of. It is distinctly a forensic act. The righteousness attributed to Abraham is not an actual righteousness, but something else that is considered and treated as if it were equivalent to such righteousness. It is so treated by God acting as the judge of men. (See *Excursus E: On the Doctrine of Justification by Faith and Imputed Righteousness.*)

(4) This, then (the righteousness attributed to Abraham), was an act of grace on the part of God, and not of merit on the part of man. It therefore carries with it no ground of boasting.

The proposition is put in a general form. Those who base their claim on works have a right to their reward. It is not conceded to them by any sort of imputation, but is their *desert*. On the other hand (verse 5), those who rely only upon faith, even though ungodly themselves, have righteousness imputed to them. This latter was Abraham's case, and not the former. (The specific application to Abraham is not expressed, but implied.)

**The reward.**—Literally, *his wages*. The relation between what he receives and what he does is that of wages for work done. He can claim it, if need be, in a court of law. There is in it no element of grace, or favour, or concession.

(5) **But to him who puts forward no works, but has** *faith* in God, who justifies men, not for their righteousness, but in spite of their sins, &c.

**The ungodly.**—A stronger word is here used than simply "the unrighteous," "the impious," or "ungodly." Their impiety is condoned to them in virtue of their single exercise of faith. It is characteristic of the Apostle not to flinch from the boldest expression, though, as a matter of fact, the two things, faith and positive impiety, would hardly be found together. "The ungodly" clearly belongs to the general form of the proposition, and is not intended to apply to Abraham.

(6–8) A further instance of the nature of the justification which proceeds from faith is supplied by David. From his evidence it will appear that such justification implies, not the absence of sin, but its forgiveness; not its real obliteration, but the forbearance of God to impute it. It is an *amnesty*, not an *acquittal.*

(6) **Even as.**—In strict accordance with this description of the justified state we have another, that of David.

**Describeth the blessedness.**—Rather, *speaks the felicitation, felicitates*, or *pronounces blessed.*

(7) **Forgiven.**—The stress is upon this word; "whose sins are not abolished, but forgiven; not annihilated, but covered up, removed from sight, hidden by the absolving grace of God."

(9–12) What is the bearing of this upon the relation between Jew and Gentile? Is the blessedness of the justified state reserved only for the former? Is it limited to those who are circumcised? On the contrary, the state of justification was attributed to Abraham himself *before* he was circumcised. Justification is the result of faith, not of circumcision. Circumcision is so far from superseding faith that it was only the sign or seal of it.

This, then, is the great test. Those who have it may hope for justification, whether their descent from Abraham is spiritual or literal.

(9) **Cometh this blessedness.**—We shall, perhaps, best see the force of the particles "then" and "for" if we take the sentence out of its interrogative form. "It follows from the language of David that the blessedness thus predicated belongs to the uncircumcised as well as to the circumcised, *for*"—then comes the first premiss of the argument by which this is proved. It was the act of faith which was the cause of Abraham's justification. But both the act of faith and the justification consequent upon it were prior to the institution of the rite of circumcision. The narrative of this institution falls in Gen. xvii., when Abraham was ninety-nine years old, and Ishmael, his son, thirteen (Gen. xvii. 1, 24, 25), while the vision and promise of Gen. xv. apparently came before the birth of Ishmael.

(11) **The sign of circumcision**—*i.e.*, circumcision *as a* sign. The expression is an instance of what is known in Greek as the "genitive of apposition," but it is common in English. Thus we speak of the City *of* London, the County *of* Kent.

Abraham is the father (1) of faithful uncircumcised—

faith which *he had yet* being uncircum-
cised: that he might be the father of
all them that believe, though they be
not circumcised; that righteousness
might be imputed unto them also:
(12) and the father of circumcision to
them who are not of the circumcision
only, but who also walk in the steps of
that faith of our father Abraham, which
*he had* being *yet* uncircumcised. (13) For
the promise, that he should be the heir
of the world, *was* not to Abraham, or
to his seed, through the law, but
through the righteousness of faith.
(14) For if they which are of the law
*be* heirs, faith is made void, and the
promise made of none effect: (15) because
the law worketh wrath: for where
no law is, *there is* no transgression.
(16) Therefore *it is* of faith, that *it might
be* by grace; to the end the promise
might be sure to all the seed; not to
that only which is of the law, but to
that also which is of the faith of Abra-
ham; who is the father of us all, (17) (as
it is written, I have made thee a father
of many nations,[a]) before him whom he
believed, *even* God, who quickeneth the
dead, and calleth those things which be
not as though they were: (18) who
against hope believed in hope, that he
might become the father of many

[a] Gen. 17. 5.

---

he himself being so—and (2) of circumcised, *but only* of faithful circumcised.

**A seal of the righteousness . . .**—The Apostle here puts forth his view of the real import of circumcision. It was not (as so many of his contemporaries supposed) the cause or condition of Israel's privileges so much as the sign or ratification of them. It ratified a state of things already existing when it was instituted. Hence, to those who inherited that state of things (justification by faith) the want of circumcision was no bar.

(12) And on the other hand, the mere performance of the rite was no guarantee for justification, unless it was attended with a faith like Abraham's. Of the two things, faith itself, and circumcision the sign of faith, the first only was essential, and the second was useless without it.

(13) Abraham was the father of *all* who walk in his steps. For this *all* is not limited by the Law any more than it is limited by circumcision. The promise of that world-wide inheritance was not given through the agency of the Law (which at that time did not exist), but as an effect of the righteousness which proceeds from faith.

**Heir of the world.**—This promise was explained by the Jews of the universal sovereignty of the Messiah.

**Through the righteousness of faith.**—As a further consequence of that (imputed) righteousness which proceeds from faith. Three stages are indicated: (1) faith, (2) imputed righteousness, (3) access to the Messianic kingdom with all its privileges.

(14—17) This Messianic kingdom cannot have anything to do with law; for if it had, faith and the promise would cease to have any office. Faith and law cannot co-exist. They are the opposites of each other. The proper effect of law is punishment; for law only exposes sin. Faith, on the other hand, is the real key to the inheritance. It sets in motion grace; and grace, unlike law, excludes no one. It is open alike to the legal and to the spiritual descendants of Abraham; in other words (as the Scripture itself testifies), to all mankind, as the representative of whom Abraham stands before God.

(14) **Is made void.**—Literally, *emptied* of its meaning, becomes an empty name, and the promise is rendered nugatory. There is nothing left for either to do, if the votaries of law, simply as such, are to be the inheritors of the Messianic kingdom.

(15) But in reality the Law is unable to admit them to this. It has an entirely contrary function—namely, to call down punishment upon the offences that it reveals. The Law and faith, therefore, mutually exclude each other, and faith is left to be the sole arbiter of salvation.

**Where no law is.**—Transgression is *ex vi termini* the transgression or breach of law, and therefore has no existence in that age of unconscious morality which precedes the introduction of law.

(16) **Therefore it is of faith.**—The words "it is" have to be supplied. "It" stands for the Messianic inheritance, or, in common phrase, salvation. Faith on man's part is correlative with grace on the part of God, and salvation being thus dependent upon grace is as wide and universal as grace itself. It knows no restriction of law.

**Not to that only which is of the law.**—Not only to that part of the human race which belongs to the dispensation of the Law, but also to that which is in a spiritual sense descended from Abraham by imitating his faith.

(17) **Before him.**—Rather, *in the presence of.* These words are to be connected closely with those which precede the parenthesis: "Who stands as the father of us all in the presence of that God in whom he believed." Abraham is regarded as (so to speak) confronting the Almighty, as he had done when the promise was first given to him.

**Who quickeneth.**—"Who gives life to that which is dead, and issues His fiat to that which is not as though it were." The words have reference, in the first instance, to the dealings of God with Abraham, described in the verses that follow—(1) to the overruling of the laws of nature indicated in verse 19; (2) to the declaration, "So shall thy seed be." There is, however, also an undercurrent of reference to the calling of the Gentiles: "I will call them My people which were not My people, and her beloved which was not beloved."

(18—22) Extended description of the faith of Abraham.

(18) **Who.**—It must be noticed that the relative here refers to Abraham, whereas in the previous verse it referred to God.

nations, according to that which was
spoken, So shall thy seed be.[a] (19) And
being not weak in faith, he considered
not his own body now dead, when he
was about an hundred years old, neither
yet the deadness of Sarah's womb:
(20) he staggered not at the promise
of God through unbelief; but was
strong in faith, giving glory to God;
(21) and being fully persuaded that,
what he had promised, he was able
also to perform. (22) And therefore
it was imputed to him for righteous-
ness. (23) Now it was not written for
his sake alone, that it was imputed
to him; (24) but for us also, to whom
it shall be imputed, if we believe on
him that raised up Jesus our Lord
from the dead; (25) who was delivered
for our offences, and was raised again
for our justification.

a Gen. 15. 5.

A.D. 58.

CHAPTER V.—(1) Therefore being
justified by faith, we have
peace with God through
our Lord Jesus Christ:

Chap. v. 1—11. The effects of justification.

---

**Believed in hope.**—The force of the preposition gives rather to the sentence the meaning of "grounded his faith upon hope"—that internal subjective hope that was strong within him, though there were no objective grounds for hoping.

**That he might become.**—So as by exercise of faith to carry out God's purpose.

(19) **Considered not.**—The negative should, in accordance with the evidence of the best MSS., be omitted. "Who, because he was not weak in faith, considered indeed—took full account of—the natural impediments to the fulfilment of the promise, and yet did not doubt."

(20) **In faith.**—Better, *through* or *by faith*, corresponding to "through unbelief" in the preceding clause. Unbelief did not make him doubt, but faith made him confident and strong.

**Giving glory to God.**—This phrase does not necessarily refer to a verbal ascription of praise, but may be used of anything which tends to God's glory, whether in thought, word, or deed (comp. Josh. vii. 19; Ezra x. 11; Jer. xiii. 16; Luke xvii. 18; John ix. 24; Acts xii. 23); here it seems to be applied to the frank recognition of God's omnipotence involved in Abraham's faith.

(23—25) Application of the foregoing. The history of Abraham is a type of the dispensation of grace; his faith, the imputation of righteousness to him, and his reward, each severally a type of the same things in the Christian. Even in details the resemblance holds. Abraham put faith in a God "who quickeneth the dead," and in like manner the Christian must put faith in God as the Author of a scheme of salvation attested by the resurrection of Christ. The death of Christ was the ground of that scheme, the resurrection of Christ its proof, without which it would not have been brought home to man.

(24) **That raised up.**—It is an association of ideas which leads the Apostle up to this point. The birth of Isaac resembles the resurrection of Christ in that it involved the exercise of Omnipotence, and in that Omnipotence Abraham believed and we are to believe. The Apostle is further led to allude to the Resurrection (though he has not laid so much stress upon it hitherto) because of the place which it held in his theory of the gospel.

(25) **Was delivered**—*i.e., to death*, as in Isa. liii. 12 (LXX. version); Matt. xvii. 22; *et al.*

**For our offences.**—*Because of our offences—i.e.*, in order that He might atone for them.

**For our justification.**—*Because of our justification—i.e.*, that justification might take effect in us.

The death of Christ is the proper cause of justification, or means of atonement, according to St. Paul; the resurrection of Christ is only the mediate or secondary cause of it. The atoning efficacy lay in His death, but the proof of that efficacy—the proof that it was really the Messiah who died—was to be seen in the Resurrection. The Resurrection, therefore, gave the greatest impulse to faith in the atoning efficacy of the death upon the cross, and in this way helped to bring about justification. Comp. especially 1 Cor. xv. 17, "If Christ be not raised, your faith is vain; ye are yet in your sins"—*i.e.*, you have no guarantee that your sins have really been remitted; if the death of Christ had not been followed by His resurrection, the inference would have followed that it was merely the death of an ordinary man, and without any special saving efficacy.

The distinction should be carefully observed between the bearing of these two acts, the death and the resurrection of Christ, on the doctrines of justification and sanctification respectively. For the latter see especially chap. vi. 2 *et seq.*

In looking back over the argument of this fourth chapter, we feel that it is a keen and subtle *argumentum ad hominem*, addressed to Jews, and based upon their own method of interpretation. Its permanent value is derived from its bearing upon the theological system of St. Paul himself—the doctrines of faith, grace, no boasting, the supreme disposing power of God, the saving efficacy of the death of Christ.

## V.

(1—11) A description of the serene and blissful state which the sense of justification brings. Faith brings justification; justification brings (let us see that it *does* bring) peace—peace with God, through the mediation of Jesus. To that mediation it is that the Christian owes his state of grace or acceptance in the present, and his triumphant hope of glory in the future. Nay, the triumph begins now. It begins even with tribulation, for tribulation leads by gradual stages to that tried and approved constancy which is a virtue most nearly allied to hope. Such hope does not deceive. It is grounded upon the consciousness of justifying love assured to us by the wonderful sacrifice of the death of Christ. The one great and difficult step was that which reconciled sinful man to God; the completion of the process of his salvation follows by easy sequence. Knowing this our consciousness just spoken of takes a glow of triumph.

(1) **Being justified.**—The present chapter is thus linked on to the last. Christ was delivered for our

(2) by whom also we have access by
faith into this grace wherein we stand,
and rejoice in hope of the glory of God.
(3) And not only *so*, but we glory in
tribulations also: knowing that tri-
bulation worketh patience; (4) and pa-
tience, experience; and experience,
hope: (5) and hope maketh not ashamed;
because the love of God is shed abroad
in our hearts by the Holy Ghost which
is given unto us. (6) For when we were
yet without strength, in due time[1] Christ

1 Or, *according to the time.*

---

offences, and raised again for our justification. "Being *justified* then," &c. This opening has a wonderful beauty which centres in the Christian idea of peace. After all the gloomy retrospect which fills the preceding chapters, the clouds break, and light steals gently over the scene. Nor is it merely the subsidence of storm, but an ardent and eager hope that now awakens, and looks forward to a glorious future.

**We have.**—A decided preponderance of MSS. authority compels us to read here, "Let us have," though the older reading would seem to make the best sense. A hortatory element is introduced into the passage, which does not seem quite properly or naturally to belong to it. It is just possible that there may have been a very early error of the copyist, afterwards rightly corrected (in the two oldest MSS., Vat. and Sin., the reading of the Authorised version appears as a correction) by conjecture. On the other hand, it is too much always to assume that a writer really used the expression which it seems to us most natural that he should have used. "Let us have" would mean "Let us enter into and possess."

**Peace.**—The state of reconciliation with God, with all that blissful sense of composure and harmony which flows from such a condition. "Peace" is the special legacy bequeathed by Jesus to His disciples (John xiv. 27; xvi. 33); it is also the word used, with deep significance, after miracles of healing, attended with forgiveness (Mark v. 34; Luke vii. 50). Boswell notes a remark of Johnson's upon this word. "He repeated to Mr. Langton, with great energy in the Greek, our Saviour's gracious expression concerning the forgiveness of Mary Magdalene: 'Thy faith hath saved thee; go in peace' (Luke vii. 50). He said, 'The manner of this dismission is exceedingly affecting'" (*Life of Johnson*, ch. 4, under the date 1780). For other illustrations of this supreme and unique phase of the Christian life, we may turn to the hymns of Cowper, especially those stanzas commencing "Sometimes a light surprises," "So shall my walk be close with God," "Fierce passions discompose the mind," "There if Thy Spirit touch the soul"; or to some of the descriptions in the *Pilgrim's Progress.*

(2) **By whom.**—More accurately translated, *through whom also we have had our access* (Ellicott). "Have had" when we first became Christians, and now while we are such.

**Into this grace.**—This state of acceptance and favour with God, the fruit of justification.

**Rejoice.**—The word used elsewhere for "boasting." The Christian *has* his boasting, but it is not based upon his own merits. It is a joyful and triumphant confidence in the future, not only felt, but expressed.

**The glory of God.**—That glory which the "children of the kingdom" shall share with the Messiah Himself when His eternal reign begins.

(3) But much more than this. The Christian's glorying is not confined to the future; it embraces the present as well. It extends even to what would naturally be supposed to be the very opposite of a ground for glorying—to the persecutions that we have to undergo as Christians. (Comp. especially Matt. v. 10, 12, "Blessed are the persecuted;" 2 Cor. xi. 30; xii. 9, 10, "glorying in infirmities;" Acts v. 41, "rejoicing that they were counted worthy to suffer shame;" 1 Pet. iv. 12, 13; "think not the fiery trial strange, but rejoice.") Attention has here been called to Bacon's aphorism, "Prosperity is the blessing of the Old Testament, adversity of the New." This is a very profound side of the Christian revelation.

(3, 4) A climax in which are put forward higher and higher grades of fortitude and constancy.

(4) **Experience.**—"Approvedness," the quality of being tried and approved. The result of patient endurance is to test, confirm, and refine the better elements of faith. Out of this, in its turn, grows hope. Hope began and ends the circle. It is the knowledge of what is in store for him that, in the first instance, nerves the Christian to endure; and that endurance, being prolonged, gives him the steady, calm assurance no longer of the novice but of the veteran.

(5) **Hope maketh not ashamed.**—This Christian hope does not disappoint or deceive. It is quite certain of its object. The issue will prove it to be well founded.

**Because the love of God.**—This hope derives its certainty from the consciousness of justifying love. The believer feeling the love of God (*i.e.*, the love of God for him) shed abroad in his heart, has in this an assurance that God's promises will not be in vain.

**By the Holy Ghost.**—The communication of Himself on the part of God to man is generally regarded as taking place through the agency of the Spirit. (Comp. chap. viii 15, 16; Gal. iv. 6.)

**Which is given.**—Rather, *which was given—i.e.*, when we first believed. (Comp. Acts viii. 15; xix. 2; 2 Cor. i. 22; v. 5; Gal. iv. 6; Eph. i. 13; iv. 30.)

(6–11) Exposition showing how the love of God comes to have this cogency. That love was evidenced in the death of Christ. And consider what that death was. It is rare enough for one man to die for another—even for a good man. Christ died not for good men, but for sinners, and while they were sinners. If then His death had the power to save us from punishment, it is an easy thing to believe that His life will lead us to glory.

(6) **For when we were yet . . .**—The reading at the beginning of this verse is doubtful. The reading of the Vatican MS. is very attractive, "If at least," "If, as we know to be the fact, Christ died," &c. But, unfortunately, this has not much further external support. If we keep the common reading we must either translate "For, moreover," or we may suppose that there is some confusion between two constructions, and the word translated "yet" came to be repeated.

**Without strength.**—Powerless to work out our own salvation.

**In due time.**—Or, *in due season.* So the Authorised version, rightly. Just at the moment when the

died for the ungodly. (7) For scarcely
for a righteous man will one die: yet
peradventure for a good man some
would even dare to die. (8) But God
commendeth his love toward us, in that,
while we were yet sinners, Christ died
for us. (9) Much more then, being now
justified by his blood, we shall be saved
from wrath through him. (10) For if,
when we were enemies, we were recon-
ciled to God by the death of his Son,
much more, being reconciled, we shall be
saved by his life. (11) And not only *so*,
but we also joy in God through our
Lord Jesus Christ, by whom we have
now received the atonement.

(12) Wherefore, as by one man sin
entered into the world,
and death by sin; and
so death passed upon all

Chap. v. 12—21. The first and the second Adam.

forbearance of God (chap. iii. 25) had come to an end, His love interposed, through the death of Christ, to save sinners from their merited destruction.

**For the ungodly.**—The force of the preposition here is "for the benefit of," not "instead of." St. Paul, it is true, holds the doctrine of the vicarious sacrifice of Christ, but this is expressed by such terms as the "propitiation" of chap. iii. 25, or the "offering, and sacrifice for us" of Eph. v. 2, and especially the "ransom for all" of 1 Tim. ii. 6, not by the use of the preposition.

(7–8) What makes the sacrifice of Christ so paradoxical is that it was undergone for *sinners*. Even for a righteous man it is rare enough to find another who will be ready to lay down his life. Yet some such persons there are. The one thing which is most extraordinary in the death of Christ, and which most tends to throw into relief the love of God as displayed in it, is that He died for men as sinners, and at the very moment when they were sinning all around Him.

(7) **Yet peradventure.** — The true reading is, undoubtedly, *for peradventure.*

**For a good man.**—Literally, *for the good* (*man*), *i.e.*, for the good man in question, the righteous man mentioned above. It would be possible to take the phrase "for the good" as neuter rather than masculine, and to understand by it "in a good cause." It would be possible also to give to the word translated "good" the special meaning of "benefactor"—"a man might be found to die for his benefactor." But if this had been intended, it might have been more clearly expressed, and upon the whole it seems best to take the passage as it is taken in the English version. There is a slight distinction in the Greek, as in English, between the words translated "righteous" and "good." To be "righteous" is to direct the will in obedience to an external standard; to be "good" is to have a natural goodness, especially kindness or benevolence of disposition. But this distinction is not insisted upon here. The two words are used almost convertibly.

(8) **Commendeth.** — The English word happily covers the double meaning of the Greek. The same word is used (1) of things in the sense of "prove" or "establish," here and in chap. iii. 5; (2) of persons in the sense of "recommend," in chap. xvi. 1.

**His love.**—Strictly, *His own love.* The love both of God and of Christ is involved in the atonement. Its ultimate cause is the love of God, which is here in question. The love of Christ is evidenced by the fact of His death; the love of God is evidenced by the love of Christ.

**Toward us.**—The question whether these words should be taken as in the English version, "His love to, or toward, us," or whether they should not rather be joined with "commendeth"—"commendeth to us"—is chiefly one of reading, the words being variously placed in the different authorities. The balance of evidence is close, but perhaps the translation may be allowed to remain as it is.

**Sinners.**—There is, of course, a stress upon this word in contrast to "the righteous man," "the good man," of the preceding verse.

(9) **From wrath.** — *From the wrath,* the divine wrath, or the wrath to come.

(10) The interval that separates the state of enmity from the state of reconciliation is a large one, that which separates the state of reconciliation from the state of salvation a small one. And yet there is a difference. Reconciliation is the initial act; the removal of the load of guilt, justification. Salvation is the end of the Christian career, and of the process of sanctification. Justification is regarded as being specially due to the death of Christ. Sanctification is brought about rather by His continued agency as the risen and exalted Saviour. The relations in which the risen Saviour still stands to the individual Christian are more fully worked out in chaps. vi. 4 *et seq.*; viii. 34; 1 Cor. xv. 22 *et seq.*; 2 Cor. iv. 10, 11; Phil. iii. 10.

(11) **And not only so.**—Some such word as "reconciled" must be supplied from the previous verse. "We shall be saved as the sequel of our reconciliation, but we are something more than reconciled. Ours is not merely a passive, but an active state. We exult or glory in God, who, through Christ, has given us this reconciliation."

**Now.**—In this present time, in our present condition. Reconciliation in the present is a foretaste of glory in the future.

(12–21) Contrast between the reign of death introduced by the sin of Adam, and the reign of life introduced by the atonement of Christ.

The sequence is, first sin, then death. Now, the death which passed over mankind had its origin in Adam's sin. Strictly speaking, there could be no individual sin till there was a law to be broken. But in the interval between Adam and Moses, *i.e.*, before the institution of law, death prevailed over the world, which was a proof that there was sin somewhere. The solution is, that the sin in question was not the individual guilt of individual transgressors, but the single transgression of Adam. Here, then, is the contrast. The single sin of the one man, Adam, brought death upon all mankind; the single act of the one Redeemer cleared away many offences—also for all men. Under the old dispensation law entered in to intensify the evil; but, in like manner, under the new, grace has come in to enhance and multiply the benefit. Thus the remedial system and the condemnatory system are co-extensive, the one over against the other, and the first entirely cancels the second.

(12) **Wherefore.**—The train of thought which

men, for that all have sinned: (13) for
until the law sin was in the world: but
sin is not imputed when there is no
law. (14) Nevertheless death reigned from
Adam to Moses, even over them that
had not sinned after the similitude of
Adam's transgression, who is the figure
of him that was to come. (15) But not
as the offence, so also *is* the free gift.
For if through the offence of one many
be dead, much more the grace of God,
and the gift by grace, *which is* by one

---

follows is suggested by the mention which had just been made of atonement, reconciliation. We see here another instance of the Apostle's fondness for transcendental theology, and for the development of the deeper mysteries of God's dealings with man. The rapidity with which ideas of this kind throng into his brain is such as to break the even flow and structure of his sentence.

**As by one man.**—This clause, "As by one man sin and death entered," ought to have been answered by "So by one Man grace and life entered." But a difficulty occurs at the very outset. How can it really be said that sin and death entered by Adam? For sin does not exist without law, and the law did not come in till Moses. And yet we have proof that sin must have been there; for death, its consequence, prevailed all through this period in which law was still wanting. The fact was, the sin which then prevailed, and had such wide and disastrous effects, was Adam's. So that it is strictly legitimate to compare his fall with the act of redemption. It is strictly true to say that by one man sin and death entered into the world, as life and grace entered by another. In either case the consequence was that of one man's act.

**For that all have sinned.**—Rather, *for that*, or *because, all sinned—i.e.*, not by their own individual act, but implicitly in Adam's transgression. They were summed up, and included in him as the head and representative of the race.

(13) So much we can see; so much is simple matter of history, that sin was in the world from Adam downwards. But here comes the difficulty. Sin there was, but why guilt? And why death, the punishment of guilt? The pre-Mosaic man sinned indeed, but could not rightly be condemned for his sin until there was a law to tell him plainly the distinction between right and wrong.

It will be observed that the law of nature (chaps. i. 19, 20; ii. 14, 15) is here left out of consideration. In the places mentioned, St. Paul speaks of the law of nature only as applicable to his contemporaries or to comparatively recent times. He does not throw back its operation into the primitive ages of the world; neither does he pronounce upon the degree of responsibility which men, as moral agents, then incurred. This would fall in with the doctrine that the consciousness of right and wrong was gradually formed. It is not, indeed, to be said that St. Paul exactly anticipated the teachings of the inductive school of moralists, but there is much in their system, or at any rate in the results to which they seem to be coming, that appears to fall into easy and harmonious relations with the teaching of the Apostle.

(14) **After the similitude of Adam's transgression**—*i.e.*, "in direct defiance of divine command." They had not incurred just punishment as Adam had, and yet they died. Why? Because of Adam's sin, the effects of which extended to them all, just in the same way as the effects of the death of Christ extend to all.

**Who is the figure.**—Better, *type*. There is thus hinted at the parallelism which was omitted in verse 12. Adam was the type of Christ, his sin and its effects the type of Christ's death and its effects. No doubt the way in which this point is introduced is, in a mere rhetorical sense, faulty. St. Paul was, however, much above caring for rhetoric. And beside, it must be remembered that he wrote by dictation, and, probably, never revised what the amanuensis had written. This fact has very rightly been insisted on by Dr. Vaughan (Preface to Third Edition, p. xxii.), "We must picture to ourselves in reading this profound Epistle to the Romans a man full of thought, his hands, perhaps, occupied at the moment in stitching at the tent-cloth, dictating one clause at a time to the obscure Tertius beside him, stopping only to give time for the writing, never looking it over, never, perhaps, hearing it read over, at last taking the style into his hand to add the last few words of affectionate benediction."

(15) Now comes the statement of the contrast which extends over the next five verses. The points of difference are thrown into relief by the points of resemblance. These may be, perhaps, best presented by the subjoined scheme:—

| | | |
|---|---|---|
| *Persons of the action.* | One man, Adam. | One Man, Christ. |
| *The action.* | One act of trespass. | One act of obedience. |
| *Character of the action viewed in its relation to the Fall and Salvation of man.* | The great initial trespass or breach of the law of God. | The great accomplished work of grace, or the gift of righteousness. |
| *Persons affected by the action.* | All mankind. | All mankind. |
| *Proximate effect of the action.* | Influx of many transgressions. | Clearing away of many transgressions. |
| *Ulterior effect of the action.* | Death. | Life. |

**The offence.**—Perhaps rather, *trespass*, to bring out the latent antithesis to the *obedience* of Christ. (Ellicott.)

**One . . . many.**—Substitute throughout this passage, "*the* one," "*the* many." By "*the* many," is meant "mankind generally," "all men." Dr. Lightfoot quotes Bentley on the importance of this change: "By this accurate version some hurtful mistakes about partial redemption and absolute reprobation had been happily prevented. Our English readers had then seen what several of the Fathers saw and testified, that *the many*, in an antithesis to *the one*, are equivalent to *all* in verse 12, and comprehend the whole multitude, the entire species of mankind, exclusive only of *the one*." "In other words," Dr. Lightfoot adds, "the benefits of Christ's obedience extend to all men potentially. It is only human self-will which places limits to its operation."

**Much more.**—Because God is much more ready to exercise mercy and love than severity, to pardon than to punish.

**The grace of God, and the gift by grace.**—The grace of God is the moving cause, its result is the gift (of righteousness, verse 17) imputed by His gracious act to the many.

man, Jesus Christ, hath abounded unto
many. (16) And not as *it was* by one
that sinned, *so is* the gift: for the
judgment *was* by one to condemnation,
but the free gift *is* of many offences
unto justification. (17) For if by one
man's offence[1] death reigned by one;
much more they which receive abund-
ance of grace and of the gift of right-
eousness shall reign in life by one, Jesus
Christ. (18) Therefore as by the offence[2]
of one *judgment came* upon all men to
condemnation; even so by the right-
eousness of one[3] *the free gift came*
upon all men unto justification of life.
(19) For as by one man's disobedience
many were made sinners, so by the
obedience of one shall many be made
righteous. (20) Moreover the law en-
tered, that the offence might abound.
But where sin abounded, grace did
much more abound: (21) that as sin
hath reigned unto death, even so
might grace reign through righteous-
ness unto eternal life by Jesus Christ
our Lord.

1 Or, *by one offence.*

2 Or, *by one offence.*

A.D. 58.

3 Or, *by one righteousness.*

CHAPTER VI.—(1) What
shall we say then? Shall
we continue in sin, that

Chap. vi. 1—14. Death to sin by union with Christ.

---

(16) **The judgment was by one.**—The judgment, verdict, or sentence from a single case ends in, or in other words takes the form of, condemnation; whereas, on the other hand, the free gift, starting from or prompted by many sins, ends in, takes the form of, justification. In the former of these cases the verdict is "Guilty," while in the other case it (or, rather, the free act of grace which takes its place) is a verdict of acquittal.

(17) Further confirmation of the contrast between the effect of Adam's sin and the atonement of Christ. The one produced a reign of death, the other shall produce a reign of life.

(18) **Therefore.**—Recapitulating what has just been said.

**The offence of one.**—Rather, *One trespass.*

**Judgment came.**—These words are supplied in the English version, but they are somewhat too much of a paraphrase. It is better to render simply, *the issue was,* which words may also be substituted for the "free gift came," below.

(19) **Many were made sinners.**—*The many,* or mankind collectively, were placed in the position of sinners.

**Obedience.**—This term is chosen in contradistinction to the disobedience of Adam. The obedience of Christ was an element in the atonement. (Comp. Phil. ii. 8, where it is said that he "became obedient unto death;" and Heb. x. 7, "Lo, I come to do thy will, O God," specially in connection with the atonement.) But if we interpret St. Paul by himself, we must not see in it the sole element to the exclusion of the "propitiatory sacrifice" of chap. iii. 25; Eph. i. 7; v. 2; 1 Tim. ii. 6.

(20, 21) The Apostle had already (verses 13, 14) alluded to the intervention of the Law. Now he returns to the topic, and in order to complete his historical view of the origin of sin through Adam, and its atonement through Christ, he considers what was its effect upon the former, and how that effect was met and neutralised by the latter. Mankind had already been led into sin by Adam. The Law came in to make matters still worse. It substituted conscious sin for unconscious, and so heightened its guilt. But all this is more than retrieved by grace.

(20) **Entered.**—A graphic metaphorical expression: "Came in to the side of" the sin already existing; "took its place," as it were, "by the side of" sin, and joined forces with it, thus greatly adding to its extent and power.

**Abound.**—This word should be reserved for the last of the three places in this verse in which it appears in the Authorised version. The original in the other two places is different, and has the force of "Might be multiplied," or "increased"—*i.e.,* made more and made worse.

(21) **Unto death.**—Rather, *in death;* death being, as it were, the domain in which its sovereignty was exercised.

In this last section we seem still to trace the influence of the school of Gamaliel. It appears that the Jewish doctors also attributed universal mortality to the fall of Adam, and regarded his sin as including that of the rest of mankind. (On the whole section, see *Excursus F: On St. Paul's View of the Religious History of Mankind.*)

VI.

(1—5) These considerations might seem to lead to an Antinomian conclusion. If the increase of sin has only led to a larger measure of forgiveness it might be thought well to continue in sin, and so to enhance the measure and glory of forgiving grace. But to the Christian this is impossible. In regard to sin he is, in theory and principle, dead. When he was converted from heathenism and received Christian baptism he gave himself up unreservedly to Christ; he professed adhesion to Christ, and especially to His death; he pledged himself to adopt that death as his own; he entered into fellowship with it in order that he might also enjoy the fellowship of the resurrection of Christ. This fellowship or participation is both physical and ethical.

(1) **Shall we continue in sin?**—Again the Apostle is drawn into one of those subtle casuistical questions that had such a great attraction for him. But he soon returns to the root-ideas of his own system. In previous chapters he had dealt with one of the two great root-ideas, justification by faith; he now passes to the second, union with Christ. The one might be described as the *juridical,* the other as the *mystical,* theory of salvation. The connecting-link which unites them is faith. Faith in Christ, and especially in the death of Christ, is the instrument of justification. Carried a degree further, it involves an actual identification with the Redeemer Himself. This, no doubt, is mystical language. When strictly compared with the facts of the religious consciousness, it must be admitted that all such terms as union, oneness, fellowship, identification, pass into the

grace may abound? (2) God forbid.
How shall we, that are dead to sin,
live any longer therein? (3) Know
ye not, that so many of us as were
baptized into Jesus Christ were bap-
tized into his death? (4) Therefore we
are buried with him by baptism into
death: that like as Christ was raised
up from the dead by the glory of the
Father, even so we also should walk in
newness of life. (5) For if we have been
planted together in the likeness of his

---

domain of metaphor. They are taken to express the highest conceivable degree of attachment and devotion. In this sense they are now consecrated by the use of centuries, and any other phrases substituted for them, though gaining perhaps somewhat in precision, would only seem poor and cold. (See *Excursus G: On the Doctrine of Union with Christ.*)

(2) **That are dead.**—Rather, *that died.* It is well to bear in mind Dr. Lightfoot's remarks on the importance of keeping the strict aorist sense as opposed to that of the perfect (*i.e.*, the single past action as opposed to the prolonged or continued action) in passages such as this. "St. Paul regards this change—from sin to righteousness, from bondage to freedom, from death to life—as summed up in one definite act of the past; potentially to all men in our Lord's passion and resurrection, actually to each individual man when he accepts Christ, is baptised into Christ. Then he is made righteous by being incorporated into Christ's righteousness, he dies once for all to sin, he lives henceforth for ever to God. This is his *ideal.* Practically, we know that the death to sin and the life to righteousness are inchoate, imperfect, gradual, meagrely realised even by the most saintly men in this life; but St. Paul sets the matter in this ideal light to force upon the consciences of his hearers the fact that an entire change came over them when they became Christians—that the knowledge and the grace then vouchsafed to them did not leave them where they were—that they are not, and cannot be, their former selves—and that it is a contradiction of their very being to sin any more. It is the definiteness, the absoluteness of this change, considered as an historical crisis, which forms the central idea of St. Paul's teaching, and which the aorist marks. We cannot, therefore, afford to obscure this idea by disregarding the distinctions of grammar; yet in our English version it is a mere chance whether in such cases the aorist is translated as an aorist" (*On Revision*, p. 85). These remarks will form the best possible commentary upon the passage before us. It may be only well to add that the change between the position of the first Christians and our own involves a certain change in the application of what was originally said with reference to them. Baptism is not now the tremendous crisis that it was then. The ideal of Christian life then assumed is more distinctly an ideal. It has a much less definite hold upon the imagination and the will. But it ought not therefore to be any the less binding upon the Christian. He should work *towards* it, if he cannot work *from* it, in the spirit of Phil. iii. 12—14.

It would be well for the reader to note at once the corrections suggested in the rendering of this verse by Dr. Lightfoot's criticism:—In verse 4, "we *were* buried" for "we are buried;" in verse 6, "the old man *was* crucified" for "is crucified;" in verse 8, "if we *died*" for "if we be dead."

(3) **Know ye not.**—It should be as in the Greek, *Or know ye not.* Do you not admit this principle; or am I to suppose that you are ignorant? &c.

**Were baptized into Jesus Christ**—*i.e.*, "into communion with Him and incorporation in His mystical body" (Ellicott on Gal. iii. 27). "As many of you as have been baptised in Christ have put on Christ." Your baptism signified an intimately close and indissoluble attachment to Christ.

**Were baptized into his death.**—And this attachment had a special relation to His death. It involved a communion or fellowship with His death. This fellowship is ethical, *i.e.*, it implies a moral conduct corresponding to that relation to Christ which it assumes.

Why has baptism this special connection with the *death* of Christ? In the first place, the death of Christ is the central and cardinal fact of the Christian scheme. It is specially related to justification, and justification proceeds from faith, which is ratified in baptism. In the second place, the symbolism of baptism was such as naturally to harmonise with the symbolism of death. It was the final close of one period, and the beginning of another—the complete stripping off of the past and putting on of the "new man."

(4) **We are buried with him.**—Burial, is the consequence of death. It is the seal set upon it, as it were, which shows that no revival is possible. Besides, it is the one step which separates it from resurrection. The idea of "buried with Christ" is therefore introduced, on the one hand, to show that the ethical death with Him was final and decisive, and on the other, to prepare the way for an ethical (as well as physical) resurrection with Him.

**Into death.**—The ideas of physical and moral death and resurrection and life are inextricably blended in the thought of the Apostle.

**By the glory of the Father.**—The resurrection of Christ is more usually and more naturally ascribed to the power or Omnipotence of God. The word "Glory" is here to be taken as standing for the sum of the divine perfections, power being included among them, "the Majesty on High."

**Even so.**—It is to be observed that the mysticism is here resolved into a relation of resemblance. The resurrection of Christ, and the new life of the Christian, are *compared* instead of being identified. The Apostle does not say "being dead with Christ, let us rise with Him;" but, "*as* Christ rose again, *so* we also should walk in newness of life." The mystical expression for this is given in the next verse.

(5) **If we have been planted together.**—"If (so surely as) we have *grown into*—become *conjoined with.*" The metaphor is taken from the parasitic growth of a plant, but applies to *natural* growth, not "*planted* together with," as in the Authorised version. The idea would correspond to the growth of a bud or graft regarded as part of that of the stock in which it is inserted, but without reference to the operation of budding or grafting. It is used here to express the closest intimacy and union.

**In the likeness of his death.**—Not here "His death itself," but "the *likeness* of His death," *i.e.*, an ethical condition corresponding to, or *conformable* to, the death of Christ. If our nature has grown "into conformity with" His death, it will be also conformable to His resurrection.

death, we shall be also *in the likeness*
of *his* resurrection: (6) knowing this,
that our old man is crucified with *him*,
that the body of sin might be destroyed,
that henceforth we should not serve
sin. (7) For he that is dead is freed[1]
from sin. (8) Now if we be dead with
Christ, we believe that we shall also
live with him: (9) knowing that Christ
being raised from the dead dieth no
more; death hath no more dominion
over him. (10) For in that he died, he
died unto sin once: but in that he
liveth, he liveth unto God. (11) Likewise
reckon ye also yourselves to be dead
indeed unto sin, but alive unto God
through Jesus Christ our Lord. (12) Let
not sin therefore reign in your mortal
body, that ye should obey it in the lusts
thereof. (13) Neither yield ye your
members *as* instruments[2] of unright-
eousness unto sin: but yield yourselves
unto God, as those that are alive from
the dead, and your members *as* instru-
ments of righteousness unto God. (14) For
sin shall not have dominion over you:
for ye are not under the law, but under
grace.

Chap. vi. 15—23. True nature of the Christian freedom.

(15) What then? shall
we sin, because we are
not under the law, but
under grace? God forbid.

[2] Gr. *arms*, or, *weapons*.

[1] Gr. *justified*.

This conformity means, of course, dying *to* trespasses and sins, being completely removed from the sphere of their influence, and entering a new sphere corresponding to the glorified life of the Redeemer. The ethical resurrection of the Christian begins (or is ideally supposed to begin, and with the early Christian usually did begin) in baptism, is continued through life, and is completed with his physical resurrection.

(6—11) Further description of this process. The Christian's union with the crucified Christ binds him also to crucify or mortify (ascetically) the sinful desires of his body. Thus he is released from the dominion of those desires. But this is not all. Just as Christ passed from the cross to the resurrection, and overcame death once for all, exchanging for it a life wholly dependent upon God; so, too, His followers must consider themselves cut off irrevocably—as if by death itself—from sin, and living with a new life dedicated and devoted to God, through their participation in the death and life of Jesus Christ their Lord.

(6) **Our old man.**—"Our old self" (Vaughan), as in Eph. iv. 22, 24; Col. iii. 9, 10.

The old self, or that congeries of evil habits acquired in the state of heathenism, was, ideally if not actually, mortified and killed in our baptism. This change was wrought by a power brought to bear upon the will through the contemplation of the crucifixion of Christ. Hence, instead of saying simply "mortified," the Apostle writes rather "crucified," *i.e.* put to death, not in any way, but specially *through the cross.*

**That the body of sin might be destroyed.**—The "body of sin" is the body subject to sin, or that supplies sin with the material on which it works. This substratum of carnal and fleshly desire, the Apostle tells us, is to be ascetically chastened and disciplined until it ceases to be a source of sin.

(7) **Is freed.**—"Absolved," the same word that is used elsewhere for "justified." The dead man is no longer liable to have the charge of sin brought against him. This is the general proposition, the major premise, adduced in proof of what had gone before, viz., the particular proposition that he who is ethically dead is no longer the slave of sin.

(9) **Dieth no more.**—The eternal subsistence of the life of Christ is a guarantee for the permanence and reality of our own life, so far as it is dependent on His. If it were possible that the life of Christ should fail, the whole fabric that the believer's faith builds upon it would fall to the ground.

(10) But it is not possible that the life of Christ should fail. Death has lost all its power over Him. The death which He died, He died to sin. It was the last sacrifice which He made to sin, and one that freed Him from its dominion for ever. He died to it once for all, and His death did not need to be, and could not be, repeated. On the other hand, His life is assured, because it is wholly dependent upon God.

(11) Theoretical application to the readers. They are to regard themselves as dead, *i.e.*, insensible and inaccessible to sin, but living in close allegiance and devotion to God through union with Christ.

(12—14) Practical and hortatory consequence. Therefore expel sin, and refuse to obey its evil promptings. Keep your bodies pure and clean. Let them no longer be weapons in the hands of wickedness; let them rather be weapons with which to fight the battle of righteousness and of God. You have every encouragement to do this. For sin shall no longer play the tyrant over you. The stern and gloomy empire of Law (which only served to heighten the guilt of sin) is over, and in its stead the only power to which you are subject is that of free forgiveness.

(12) **Mortal.**—And therefore at variance with the immortal life just described.

(13) **Instruments.** —Rather, as margin, *arms*, or *weapons* which sin is to wield. The same military metaphor is kept up in verse 23, "the wages of sin" (your pay as soldiers of sin) "is death."

(15—23) *Free* forgiveness! What does that mean? Freedom to sin? Far from it. That were to return into the old slavery. To yield to sin is to be the servant or slave of sin with its consequence—death. On the other hand, obedience and righteousness go together. Happily you have escaped from sin, and taken service with righteousness. Service, I say, using a plain human figure to suit your imperfect and carnal apprehension of spiritual things. Exchange the service of uncleanness for that of righteousness. I appeal to your own experience. You found that sin brought you no pay from your master but death. Now you are started upon a road that leads to sanctification and

(16) Know ye not, that to whom ye yield
yourselves servants to obey, his servants
ye are to whom ye obey; whether of sin
unto death, or of obedience unto right-
eousness? (17) But God be thanked, that
ye were the servants of sin, but ye
have obeyed from the heart that form
of doctrine which was delivered you.[1]
(18) Being then made free from sin, ye
became the servants of righteousness.
(19) I speak after the manner of men
because of the infirmity of your flesh:
for as ye have yielded your members
servants to uncleanness and to iniquity
unto iniquity; even so now yield your
members servants to righteousness unto
holiness. (20) For when ye were the
servants of sin, ye were free from right-
eousness.[2] (21) What fruit had ye then
in those things whereof ye are now
ashamed? for the end of those things
*is* death. (22) But now being made free
from sin, and become servants to God,
ye have your fruit unto holiness, and
the end everlasting life. (23) For the
wages of sin *is* death; but the gift of
God *is* eternal life through Jesus Christ
our Lord.

[2] Gr. *to righteousness.*

[1] Gr. *whereto ye were delivered.*

A.D. 58.

CHAPTER VII.—(1) Know ye not,
brethren, (for I speak to
them that know the law,)
how that the law hath
dominion over a man as long as he liveth?

Chap. vii. 1—6. Release by death.

---

eternal life. This will be given you, not as wages, but as the free gift of God in Christ.

(15) The Apostle returns to a difficulty very similar to that which presented itself at the beginning of the chapter. The answer is couched under a slightly different metaphor. It is no longer death to the one, life to the other, but freedom from the one, service to the other. These are correlative terms. Freedom from sin implies service to God, just as freedom from God means service to sin. The same idea of service and freedom will be found worked out in John viii. 32—34, 36, and in Gal. v. 1.

(16) **Know ye not.**—An apparent tautology, but one which really teaches a deep ethical truth. Don't you know that what you make yourselves that you become? The habit which you form ends by becoming your "second nature."

(17) **Have obeyed.**—Rather, *obeyed.* (See Note on verse 2.) In like manner correct "have yielded" to "yielded" in verse 19.

**That form of doctrine.**—That *pattern of teaching*, or express moral rule of life.

**Delivered you.**—Literally, *to which you were delivered—to the direction of which you were handed over.*

(18) **Ye became the servants.**—Comp. "Whose service is perfect freedom," adopted from St. Augustine.

(19) **I speak after the manner of men.**—I am using a merely human figure of speech, a figure taken from common human relations, and not a high mystical phrase such as I used just now, because of the dulness of your understanding: that form of expression you might not be able to comprehend; this present figure is clear even to a mind that is busy with earthly and carnal things, and has not much faculty for taking in anything beyond.

**Your flesh.**—This corresponds nearly to what is elsewhere called "the carnal mind," a mind alive only to material and sensible things.

**To iniquity unto iniquity.**—Ye yielded up your members to iniquity for the practice of iniquity.

**Unto holiness.**—Rather, *for sanctification; to be made holy.*

(21) **For.**—(You had no fruit) for, &c. Some put the question at "then." "What fruit had ye therefore (omitted in the Authorised version) at that time? Things of which ye are now ashamed; for their end is death." But the construction of the Authorised version is probably best.

(22) **Ye have your fruit.**—You are no longer without fruit. Your fruit is the new Christian life which leads on to sanctification and finally to eternal life.

(23) **The gift of God.**—The natural antithesis would be "wages;" but this would here be inappropriate, and therefore the Apostle substitutes "the free gift." In spite of your sanctification as Christians, still you will not have *earned* eternal life; it is the gift of God's grace.

### VII.

(1—6) The Apostle takes up an idea to which he had alluded in verses 14, 15 of the preceding chapter, "Ye are not under the Law, but under grace;" and as he had worked out the conclusion of the death of the Christian to sin, so now he works out that of his death to the Law. This he does by an illustration borrowed from the marriage-bond. That bond is dissolved by the death of one of the parties to it. And in like manner the death of the Christian with Christ releases him from his obligation to the Law, and opens out to him a new and spiritual service in place of his old subjection to a written code.

(1) **Know ye not.**—Here again insert "or": *Or know ye not,* &c., carrying on the thought from the end of the last chapter. Is not, argues the Apostle, what I say true? Or do I hear the old objection raised again, that the system under which the Christian is living is not one of grace in which eternal life is given freely by God, but the Mosaic law? That would show an ignorance—which in *you* I cannot believe—of the fact that the dominion of the Law ceases with death, of which fact it is easy to take a simple illustration.

**To them that know the law.**—The Roman Church, as we have seen, was composed in about equal proportions of Jewish and of Gentile Christians. The Jews would naturally know the provisions of their own law, while the Gentile Christians would know them sufficiently to be aware of the fact, from their intercourse with Jewish members of their own community, and from hearing the Old Testament read in the synagogues, where their public worship was still conducted. The practice of reading from the Old Testament did not

(2) For the woman which hath an husband is bound by the law to *her* husband so long as he liveth; but if the husband be dead, she is loosed from the law of *her* husband. (3) So then if, while *her* husband liveth, she be married to another man, she shall be called an adulteress; but if her husband be dead, she is free from that law; so that she is no adulteress, though she be married to another man. (4) Wherefore, my brethren, ye also are become dead to the law by the body of Christ; that ye should be married to another, *even* to him who is raised from the dead, that we should bring forth fruit unto God. (5) For when we were in the flesh, the motions[1] of sins, which were by the law, did work in our members to bring forth fruit unto death. (6) But now we are delivered from the law, that being dead[2] wherein we were held; that we should serve in newness of spirit, and not *in* the oldness of the letter.

(7) What shall we say then? *Is* the law sin? God forbid. Nay, I had not known sin, but by the law: for

Chap. vii. 7–25. The inward strife.

1 Gr. *passions.*

2 Or, *being dead to that.*

---

cease on the transition from Jewish to Christian modes of worship; it survives still in the "First Lesson."

(2) **For the woman which hath an husband.**—The illustration is not quite exact. The Law is here represented by the husband, but the Apostle does not mean to say that the Law dies to the Christian, but the Christian to the Law. The proposition must therefore be understood to be stated in a somewhat abstract form. Relations of the kind indicated are terminated *by death* (not necessarily the death of one party to them more than another). The relation of wife and husband ceases absolutely and entirely on both sides, and not merely so much of it as affects the person who dies.

(4) **Are become dead.**—*Were rendered dead*—somewhat stronger than simply "ye died."

**By the body of Christ**—*i.e.*, by the death of the human body of Christ upon the cross. The Christian, as the last chapter has shown, is so united to Christ that whatever has happened to his Master has happened also to him. Christ was put to death upon the cross; *he* therefore has also been put to death with Him. But why put to death *to the Law?* Probably all that is meant is simply that the Christian died, and therefore all the relations contracted before that death came to an end. At the same time he entered upon new relations corresponding to his new and risen state.

The argument can hardly be said to have a logical cogency in a controversial sense. It is not, quite strictly speaking, argument at all, but rather emphatic assertion, with all the weight of apostolic authority, and in a graphic illustrative form. The gist of it all is, "You have done with the Law and assumed a new spiritual life in Christ: see that you make this a reality."

**That we should bring forth fruit unto God.**—This mystical and ethical union with Christ will not be unproductive; it will have for its fruit a life consecrated to God.

(5) The new alliance ought not to be unproductive, for the old alliance was not unproductive. Before that mortification of the flesh which proceeds from our relation to the death of Christ, we bore a fruit generated through our carnal appetites by the Law, and the only being to whose honour and glory they contributed was Death.

The sins committed under the old dispensation are regarded as due to a two-fold agency—on the one hand to the Law (the operation of which is described more particularly in verses 7, 8), and on the other hand to the flesh, which was only too susceptible to any influence that would call out its sinful impulses. Those impulses have now been mortified, as if by a course of asceticism, through union with the death of Christ.

The "body" is regarded by St. Paul as a neutral principle, which is not in itself either good or bad. It is simply the material frame of men, which though itself "of the earth earthy" is capable of becoming a dwelling-place for the Spirit, and being put to holy uses. The "flesh" is the same material frame regarded as the seat of sinful appetites, and with a tendency to obey the lower rather than the higher self. The proper way to overcome this lower self is by that spiritual asceticism which the believer goes through by his appropriation of the death of Christ.

**Motions of sins.**—The same word which is translated in Gal. v. 24, "affections"—those emotions or passions which lead to sin.

**Which were by the law.**—Which the Law served to stimulate and quicken in the manner described below.

**Did work.**—Were active or astir, opposed to that state of torpor or mortification to which they were reduced in the Christian.

**Unto death.**—Death is here personified as the king of that region which sin serves to enrich.

(6) **That being dead.**—Our translators seem to have had a false reading here, which is not found in any MS., but arose from an error of Beza and Erasmus in interpreting a comment of Chrysostom's. The true reading runs thus: "But as it is we were" (not "are") "delivered from the Law, having died to that wherein we were held." In the act of our baptism, which united us to Christ, we obtained a release from our old tyrant, the Law.

**Wherein we were held.**—Oppressed, held in bondage.

**That we should serve.**—Rather, perhaps, *so that we serve;* result, not purpose. Our release from one master implied an engagement to another. Our new state is one in which we serve an active living Spirit; our old state was a bondage to the dead and formal letter.

The "Spirit" is here the Holy Spirit, as the animating principle of the new life, and as opposed to a system which proceeds merely by external precepts and requirements.

(7) **What shall we say then?**—The Apostle had spoken in a manner disparaging to the Law, and which might well give offence to some of his readers. It was necessary to correct this. And so now he proceeds to lay down more precisely in what it was that the Law was defective, and what was its true function and relation to the history and struggles of humanity.

I had not known lust,[1] except the
law had said, Thou shalt not covet.
(8) But sin, taking occasion by the com-
mandment, wrought in me all manner of
concupiscence. For without the law
sin *was* dead. (9) For I was alive with-
out the law once; but when the com-
mandment came, sin revived, and I
died. (10) And the commandment, which
*was ordained* to life, I found *to be* unto
death. (11) For sin, taking occasion by
the commandment, deceived me, and by
it slew *me*. (12) Wherefore the law *is*
holy, and the commandment holy, and
just, and good. (13) Was then that
which is good made death unto me?

[1] Or, *concupiscence*.

---

In what follows the Apostle speaks throughout in the first person. He is really making a general statement which applies to all mankind; but this statement is based upon his own personal experience. Self-analysis is at the bottom of most profound psychology. The Apostle goes back in thought to the time before he had embraced Christianity, and treats his own case as typical. There can be little question that the description which follows to the end of verse 24 is a description of the *unregenerate* state of man. It is one prolonged crisis and conflict, which at last finds its solution in Christ.

**Is the law sin?**—The Law had just been described as stimulating and exciting "the motions of sins." Was this true? Was the Law really immoral? No, that could not be.

**Nay.**—Rather, *howbeit* (Ellicott), *nevertheless.* The Law is not actually immoral, but it is near being made so. It is not itself sin (sinful), but it reveals, and so in a manner incites to, sin.

**I had not known.**—Strictly, *I did not know.* I had no acquaintance with sin except through the Law. Before the introduction of law, acts that are sinful in themselves, objectively viewed, may be done, but they are not sinful with reference to the person who does them. He has no knowledge or consciousness of what sin is until it is revealed to him by law.

**Sin.**—Here a sort of quasi-personification. The principle or power of sin into contact and acquaintance with which the Apostle was brought for the first time by the Law.

**I had not known lust.**—The Apostle introduces an illustration from a special law—the Tenth Commandment. "Lust" is here to be taken in the special sense of covetousness, desire for that which is forbidden. Doubtless there would be many before the giving of the Law who desired their "neighbour's wife, or his manservant, or his maidservant," &c.; but this would not be *coveting*, it would not be desire *of that which was forbidden*, for the simple reason that it was *not* forbidden. Covetousness, then, *as a sin*, the Apostle did not know until he was confronted with the law against it.

(8) **Taking occasion.**—The word in the Greek implies originally a military metaphor: taking as a "base of operations," *i.e.*, an advanced post occupied as the starting-point and rendezvous for further advances. Sin is unable to act upon man without the co-operation of law, without being able to hold up law before him, and so show itself in its true colours.

The words "by the commandment" may either go with "taking occasion" or with "wrought in me." The sense would, in either case, be very much the same, "taking advantage of the commandment," or "wrought in me by the help of the commandment." The first is the construction usually adopted, as in the Authorised version, but there seem to be reasons of some force for preferring the second. The phrase "wrought in me coveting by the commandment" would thus be parallel to "working death in me by that which is good," below.

**Concupiscence.**—Rather, *coveting;* the same word which had been used above. Sin and the Commandment together—Sin, the evil principle in men, acting as the primary cause, and the Commandment as the secondary cause—led their unfortunate victim into all kinds of violation of the Law. This is done in two ways: (1) the perverseness of human nature is such that the mere prohibition of an act suggests the desire to do that which is prohibited; (2) the act, when done, is invested with the character of sin, which hitherto it did not possess. It becomes a distinct breach of law, where previously there had been no law to break. This is what the Apostle means by saying that "without the Law sin was dead." Until there was a written prohibition, Sin (the evil principle) was powerless to produce sinful actions.

(9) **I was alive.**—The state of unconscious morality, uninstructed but as yet uncondemned, may, compared with that state of condemnation, be regarded as a state of "life."

**Revived.**—The English version well represents the meaning of the original, which is not that sin "came to life," but that it "came to life *again.*" Sin is lurking in the heart from the first, but it is dormant until the Commandment comes; then it "revives."

**I died.**—Became subject to the doom of eternal death.

(10) **Which was ordained to.**—"The very commandment which was for life I found to be for death" (Ellicott). The Law was instituted in order that it might give life to those who were under it and who kept it. They did not keep it, and therefore it brought them not life but death.

**(11–13) The cause of this miscarriage lay not with the Law but with Sin. Sin played the tempter, and then made use of the Commandment to condemn and destroy its victims. All this time the Law (*i.e.*, the whole body of precepts) and the Commandment (*i.e.*, the particular precepts included in the Law) remained perfectly good in themselves. They could not be otherwise, having come from the hand of God Himself. Sin was the fatal power. The Law and the Commandment were only passive instruments which it wielded for the destruction of man. But at the same time Sin itself was exposed by them in all its ever-increasing enormity.**

(12) **Wherefore.—This word introduces a conclusion, not from the verse immediately preceding, but from the whole of the last five verses. The Apostle glances back for a moment over the course of his argument.**

(13) **Was then that which is good . . .?—Was it possible that the Law, holy and good as it was, could simply lead miserable men to death and ruin? No, it was not possible. It was not the Law that did this but Sin—acting, it is true, through the instrumentality of**

God forbid. But sin, that it might
appear sin, working death in me by
that which is good; that sin by the
commandment might become exceeding
sinful. (14) For we know that the law
is spiritual: but I am carnal, sold under
sin. (15) For that which I do I allow[1]
not: for what I would, that do I not;
but what I hate, that do I. (16) If then
I do that which I would not, I consent
unto the law that *it is* good. (17) Now
then it is no more I that do it, but sin
that dwelleth in me. (18) For I know
that in me (that is, in my flesh,) dwelleth
no good thing: for to will is present
with me; but *how* to perform that
which is good I find not. (19) For the
good that I would I do not: but the
evil which I would not, that I do.
(20) Now if I do that I would not, it is
no more I that do it, but sin that
dwelleth in me. (21) I find then a law,
that, when I would do good, evil is
present with me. (22) For I delight in
the law of God after the inward man:
(23) But I see another law in my mem-
bers, warring against the law of my
mind, and bringing me into captivity to
the law of sin which is in my members.
(24) O wretched man that I am! who

[1] Gr. *know.*

---

the Law. All this, however, only had for its end to show up Sin for the monster that it really is.

**Sin, that it might appear sin.**—We must supply with this "was made death." Sin, no longer remaining covert and unrecognised, but coming out in its true colours, brought me under the penalty of death.

**By the commandment.**—If the Commandment served to expose the guilt of man, still more did it serve to expose and enhance the guilt of that evil principle by which man was led astray. Such is the deeper philosophy of the whole matter. This short-lived dominion was no triumph for Sin after all. The very law that it took for its stay turned round upon it and condemned it.

(14–25) Further and detailed proof why it was that though the Law appealed to all that was best in man, still he could not obey it.

(14) **For we know.**—There is no need to argue the question. We Christians all *know* that the Law is spiritual. It is divinely given and inspired. On the other hand, man, though capable of communion with God, is dominated by that part of his nature which is the direct opposite of divine, and is entirely earthly and sensual. This sensual part of his nature is the slave—and just as much the slave as if he had been sold in the auction mart—of Sin. (Comp. 1 Kings xxi. 20, 25.)

(15) **That which I do I allow not.**—Rather, *that which I perform I know not.* I act blindly, and without any conscious direction of the will; that higher part of me which should preside over and direct my actions, is kept down by the lower physical nature.

**Which I do.**—St. Paul uses three words for "to do" in this passage, the distinction between which is hard to represent in English. That which is employed here and in verses 17, 20, is the strongest, "*perform*"—deliberate action, thoroughly carried out. The other two words differ, as "do" and "practise," the one referring to single, the other to habitual and repeated actions.

**What I would.**—If my will had free course I should act very differently.

(16) But the fact that I desire to do what is right is itself a witness to the excellence of the Law, which commands that which I desire.

(17) This, then, appears to be the true explanation of the difficulty. There is really a dualism in the soul. I am not to be identified with that lower self which is enthralled by sin.

(18–20) Enthralled it is, and the will is powerless. What I do and what I will are opposite things. It is therefore sin that acts, and not I.

(21) **I find then a law.**—Of the many ways of taking this difficult verse, two seem to stand out as most plausible or possible. In any case "*a* law" should be rather "*the* law." This is taken by the majority of commentators, including Bishop Ellicott, in the sense of "rule," "habitually-repeated fact." "I find this law, or this rule, that when I would do good evil is present with me." Such is my constant and regular experience. The objection to this interpretation is that it gives to the word "law" an entirely different sense from that which it bears in the context, or in any other part of St. Paul's writings. The other view is that which is maintained by Dr. Vaughan. According to this we should have to assume an *anacoluthon.* The Apostle begins the sentence as if he were going to say, "I find therefore the Law (the Mosaic law), when I desire to do good, *unable to help me;*" but he changes somewhat the form of the sentence in the latter portion, and instead of saying "I find the Law unable to help me," he says, "I find that evil is at my side." "To me" is also repeated a second time, in the Greek superfluously, for the sake of greater clearness. Or perhaps a still simpler and better explanation would be that the Apostle had intended in the first instance to say, "I find the Law, when I wish to do good, *putting evil before me,*" and then shrank (as in verse 7) from using so harsh an expression, and softened it by turning the latter half of the sentence into a passive instead of an active form—"I find the Law, when I wish to do good—that evil *is put* before me."

(22) **I delight.**—"I delight in (and with) the Law of God." I sympathise with and approve of it after the inward man, *i.e.*, in the higher part of my being. "The inward man" corresponds nearly, though not quite, to the "law of my mind," in the next verse. It stands rather midway between it and the spirit. The mind is the moral and rational faculties considered as moral and rational. "The inward man" is the higher part of man's nature considered as capable of receiving the divine grace. The "spirit" is the same when actually brought into communion with God.

(23) **Another law.**—A different law. "In my members," *i.e.*, that has its chief seat of activity in my members. This is the law of sin, which is ready to take advantage of every fleshly impulse.

(24) So this intestine struggle goes on unceasingly

shall deliver me from the body of this death?[1] (25) I thank God through Jesus Christ our Lord. So then with the mind I myself serve the law of God; but with the flesh the law of sin.

A.D. 58.

1 Or, *this body of death.*

CHAPTER VIII.—(1) *There is* therefore now no condemnation to them which are in Christ Jesus, who walk not after the flesh, but after the Spirit. (2) For the law of the

Chap. viii. 1–4. The law of the flesh and the law of the Spirit.

---

and reaches no decision, till at last the unhappy man cries out, almost in despair, "Who shall deliver me from the body of this death?" Who, that is, will help me to overcome these fleshly desires, gendered by a corrupt human nature, which are dragging me down to imminent destruction? The body is the cause of sin, and therefore of death. If only it could be released from that, the distracted soul would be at rest and free.

**The body of this death.**—*This body* (the slave of sin and therefore the abode) *of death.* The words are a cry for deliverance from the whole of this mortal nature, in which carnal appetite and sin and death are inextricably mingled. To complete this deliverance the triple resurrection—ethical, spiritual, and physical—is needed.

(25) It *has* been released. It is Jesus our Lord to whom the thanks and praise are due. Though without His intervention there can only be a divided service. The mere human self serves with the mind the law of God, with the flesh the law of sin.

**I myself.**—Apart from and in opposition to the help which I derive from Christ.

The abrupt and pregnant style by which, instead of answering the question, "Where is deliverance to come from?" the Apostle simply returns thanks for the deliverance that has actually been vouchsafed to him, is thoroughly in harmony with the impassioned personal character of the whole passage. These are not abstract questions to be decided in abstract terms, but they are matters of intimate personal experience.

The deliverance wrought by Christ is apparently here that of sanctification rather than of justification. It is from the domination of the body, from the impulses of sense, that the Christian is freed, and that is done when he is crucified to them with Christ.

## VIII.

The Apostle has now again reached a climax in his argument similar to that in the opening of chap. v. His subject is once more the blissful condition of the Christian who has made full use of the means of grace offered to him. This is now worked out at length and in detail. The eighth chapter may, in fact, be described as not only the climax of a particular argument, but also as the climax—the broad extended summit, as it were—of the Epistle. It differs from the first section of chap. v. in this, that while both describe the condition of the regenerate Christian, and both cover the whole range of time from the first admission to the Christian communion down to the ultimate and assured enjoyment of Christian immortality, chap. v. lays stress chiefly on the initial and final moments of this period, whereas chap. viii. emphasises rather the whole intermediate process. In technical language the one turns chiefly upon justification, the other upon sanctification. The connecting-link between the two is the doctrine of Hope. The sense of justification wrought for us by Christ gives rise to hope; the sense of sonship and communion with Christ, carrying with it the assurance of final redemption, also gives rise to hope. It may be said that Faith is also a connecting-link; because faith in the death of Christ is the same apprehensive faculty which later brings home the sense of communion with Christ to the believer. A further link is suggested in the words of chap. v. 5, "Because the love of God is shed abroad in our hearts by the Holy Ghost which is given unto us." There it is the consciousness of justifying love which is so diffused, but the doctrine of the special agency exercised by the Holy Ghost is largely expanded in chap. viii.

This chapter carries us into the inmost circle and heart of Christianity; it treats of that peculiar state of beatitude, of refined and chastened joy for which no form of Secularism is able to provide even the remotest equivalent.

(1–11) A result is thus attained which the law of Moses could not accomplish, but which is accomplished in the gospel. The Christian is entirely freed from the law of sin and death, and from the condemnation that it entails. But he is so upon the condition that this freedom is for him a reality—that it really proceeds from the indwelling Spirit of Christ.

(1) **Therefore.**—The Apostle had already, at the end of the last chapter, "touched the confines" of that state of deliverance and of liberty which he is now going on to describe. The opening of this chapter is, therefore, connected in form with the close of the last. The intervention of Christ puts an end to the struggle waged within the soul. There is *therefore* no condemnation, &c.

**Condemnation.**—The condemnation which in the present and final judgment of God impends over the sinner, is removed by the intervention of Christ, and by the union of the believer with Him. By that union the power and empire of sin are thrown off and destroyed. (Comp. verse 3.) There is a certain play on the word "condemn." By "condemning" the law of sin, Christ *removed* "condemnation" from the sinner. He removed it objectively, or in the nature of things, and this removal is completed subjectively in the individual through that bond of mystical and moral attachment which makes what Christ has done his own act and deed.

**To them which are in Christ Jesus.**—Those "who live and move and have their (spiritual) being" in Christ. To "have the Spirit of Christ" is a converse expression for the same idea. In the one case the believer is regarded as reaching upwards, as it were, through faith, and so incorporating and uniting himself with the Spirit of Christ; in the other case, the Spirit of Christ reaches downwards and infuses itself into the believer. This is the peculiar mysticism of the Apostle.

**Who walk not after the flesh, but after the Spirit.**—These words are wanting in the foremost representatives of every group of authorities (except, perhaps, those which belong to the region of Syria), and must certainly be omitted. They have been brought in here from verse 4.

(2) A statement of the great antithesis, of which the rest of the section is a development, between

Spirit of life in Christ Jesus hath made
me free from the law of sin and death.
(3) For what the law could not do, in
that it was weak through the flesh, God
sending his own Son in the likeness
of sinful flesh, and for sin,[1] condemned
sin in the flesh: (4) that the righteous-
ness of the law might be fulfilled in us,
who walk not after the flesh, but after
the Spirit. (5) For they that
are after the flesh do mind
the things of the flesh; but
they that are after the Spirit
the things of the Spirit.

[1] *Or, by a sacrifice for sin.*

Chap. viii. 5—8. The mind of the flesh and the mind of the Spirit.

the law of the Spirit of life and the law of sin and of death.

**The law of the Spirit of life.**—A phrase defining more fully the mode in which the union with Christ becomes operative in the believer. It begins by imparting to him the Spirit of Christ; this Spirit creates within him a law; and the result of that law is life—that perfect spiritual vitality which includes within itself the pledge of immortality.

**The Spirit.**—That is, the Spirit of Christ, as in verse 9, which is hardly as yet conceived of as a distinct personality, but representing the continued action and influence which the ascended Saviour exercises upon the believer.

**In Christ Jesus.**—These words are best taken with "hath made" (rather, *made,* when it was imparted to me) "me free." The law of the Spirit of life, in Christ (*i.e.,* operating through my union with Christ), made me free from the law of sin and of death.

**From the law of sin and death.**—The direct contrast to the foregoing. Not here the law of Moses, but the power of sin, the corrupt element in our nature, acting upon the soul, and itself erecting a kind of law, saying, "Thou shalt," where the law of God says "Thou shalt not;" and "Thou shalt not," where the law of God says "Thou shalt." The effect of this reign of sin is death—spiritual death—bearing in itself the pledge of eternal death.

(3) How was I freed? Thus. Precisely on that very point where the law of Moses showed its impotence—viz., in the attempt to get rid of sin, which it failed to do because of the counteracting influence of the flesh—precisely on this very point God interposed by sending His Son in a body of flesh similar to that in which sin resides, and as an offering to expiate human sin, and so dethroned and got rid of sin in the flesh which He had assumed. The flesh, the scene of its former triumphs, became now the scene of its defeat and expulsion.

**What the law could not do.**—Literally, *the impossible thing of the Law—i.e.,* "that which was impossible to the Law." The construction is what is called a *nominativus pendens.* The phrase thus inserted at the beginning of the sentence characterises what follows. God did what the Law could not do—viz., condemned sin.

**In that it was weak through the flesh.**—There was one constant impediment in the way of the success of the Law, that it had to be carried out by human agents, beset by human frailty, a frailty naturally consequent upon that physical organisation with which man is endowed. Temptation and sin have their roots in the physical part of human nature, and they were too strong for the purely moral influence of the Law. The Law was limited in its operations by them, and failed to overcome them.

**In the likeness of sinful flesh**—*i.e.,* in the flesh, but not in *sinful* flesh. With a human body which was so far like the physical organisation of the rest of mankind, but yet which was not in Him, as in other men, the seat of sin; at once like and unlike.

**And for sin.**—This is the phrase which is used constantly in the LXX. ("more than fifty times in the Book of Leviticus alone"—Vaughan) for the "sin-offering." The essence of the original sin-offering was that it was accepted by an act of grace on the part of God, instead of the personal punishment of the offender. The exact nature of this "instead" appears to be left an open question in Scripture, and its further definition—if it is to be defined—belongs to the sphere of dogmatics rather than of exegesis. It must only be remembered that St. Paul uses, in regard to the sacrifice of Christ, similar language to that which is used in the Old Testament of this particular class of sacrifice, the sin-offering.

**Condemned sin.**—The meaning of this expression is brought out by the context. It is that which the Law was hindered from doing by the hold which sin had upon the flesh. That hold is made to cease through the participation of the believer in the death of Christ. Sin is, as it were, brought into court, and the cause given against it. It loses all its rights and claims over its victim. It is *dispossessed* as one who is dispossessed of a property.

**In the flesh.**—In that same sphere, the flesh, in which sin had hitherto had the mastery, it now stood condemned and worsted; it was unable to exercise its old sway any longer.

(4) The consequence of this was a great change. Hitherto the Law could not be kept because of the antagonistic influence of the flesh; henceforth it may be kept for the reason that this influence has ceased and that its place is taken by the influence of the Spirit.

**The righteousness.**—The just requirement of the Law, its due and rightful claims.

**Might be fulfilled in us.**—That we might be examples of its fulfilment.

**Who walk not after the flesh.**—Who direct our conduct not as the flesh would guide us, but according to the dictates and guidance of the Spirit—*i.e.,* the indwelling Spirit of Christ, as in verse 2.

(5—8) Further description of the antithesis between flesh and spirit in regard to (1) their object, verse 5; (2) their nature, verses 7, 8; (3) their end, verse 6.

(5) **They that are . . .**—Those who not only walk (direct their conduct) according to the promptings of the flesh, but who are in themselves and in the whole bent of their dispositions the slaves of these promptings.

**Do mind the things of the flesh.**—Their whole mental and moral activity is set upon nothing else but the gratification of these cravings of sense. The phrase "who mind" is not confined to the exercise of the intellect, but includes the affections; in fact it includes all those lesser motives, thoughts, and desires which are

(6) For to be carnally minded[1] *is* death;
but to be spiritually minded[2] *is* life and
peace. (7) Because the carnal mind[3] *is*
enmity against God: for it is not sub-
ject to the law of God, neither indeed
can be. (8) So then they that are in the
flesh cannot please God. (9) But ye are
not in the flesh, but in the
Spirit, if so be that the
Spirit of God dwell in you.
Now if any man have not
the Spirit of Christ, he is none of
his. (10) And if Christ *be* in you, the
body *is* dead because of sin; but the

Chap. viii. 9—13. The quickening power of the Spirit.

Spirit *is* life because of righteousness.
(11) But if the Spirit of him that raised
up Jesus from the dead dwell in you, he
that raised up Christ from the dead
shall also quicken your mortal bodies
by his Spirit[4] that dwelleth in you.
(12) Therefore, brethren, we are debtors,
not to the flesh, to live after the flesh.
(13) For if ye live after the flesh, ye shall
die: but if ye through the Spirit do
mortify the deeds of the body, ye shall
live. (14) For as many as are
led by the Spirit of God,
they are the sons of God.

Chap. viii. 14—17. The adoption of sons.

1 Gr., *the minding of the flesh.*
2 Gr., *the minding of the Spirit.*
3 Gr., *the minding of the flesh.*
4 Or, *because of his Spirit.*

---

involved in carrying out any great principle of action—whether it be selfish and "carnal" or spiritual.

(6) Translate, *For the mind of the flesh is death, but the mind of the Spirit is life and peace.* To think of nothing but the gratification of the senses, is in itself death—that dead condition of the soul which issues in eternal death; and, on the other hand, to have the thoughts and affections governed solely by the Spirit, brings with it that healthful, vital harmony of all the functions of the soul which is a sure pledge and foretaste of a blissful immortality. Death and life are here, as elsewhere, most frequently in St. Paul, neither spiritual death and life alone, nor eternal death and life alone, but both combined. The Apostle does not here draw any distinction between the two things.

(7) The carnal mind is death—because it implies enmity with God, and enmity with God *is* death.

(8) **So then . . .**—Rather, *and.* Neither can it be expected that those who are absorbed in the things of sense should be able to please God.

(9) Such is not your case—if at least the Spirit of God and of Christ dwells in you, as it should in every Christian.

**The Spirit of God . . . the Spirit of Christ.**—It is to be observed that these two terms are used as convertible. The Spirit of Christ is indeed the presence of Christ Himself in the soul. (Comp. John xiv. 16, 18, 20, "I will pray the Father, and He shall give you another Comforter, that He may abide with you for ever. . . . I will not leave you comfortless (*orphans*): I will come to you. . . . At that day ye shall know that I am in My Father, and ye in Me, and I in you.")

**Dwell in you.**—This expression is the complement of the other "to be *in* the Spirit," "to be *in* Christ." It denotes the closest possible contact and influence of spirit upon spirit. No mysticism, however vivid and intense, can really go beyond this without infringing the bounds of personality, and contradicting the direct testimony of consciousness.

(10) The results of the presence of Christ in the soul.

**The body is dead because of sin.**—Here the word is evidently used of physical death. The doom entailed by sin still, indeed, attaches to the body—but only to the body. The body, indeed, must die, but there the hold of sin upon the Christian ends; it cannot touch him farther.

**The Spirit is life because of righteousness.**—But turn to another side of human nature; take it in its highest part and faculty—the spirit. That is full of vitality because it is full of righteousness, first imputed and then real. Life and righteousness are correlative terms, the one involving the other.

(11) And this vitality extends beyond the grave. It will even react upon that material body which had just been spoken of as given over to death. Die it must; but the same Spirit to which the soul owes its life will also reinfuse life into the dead body, just as the body of Christ of Himself was raised from the dead.

**By his Spirit . . .**—The balance of authority is in favour of the reading, "because of His Spirit" (as in margin); the other is an Alexandrian correction. It cannot be thought that God would leave in the grave that body in which His own Spirit has dwelt, *i.e.*, has been with not only in close but permanent contact, though the psychological question was, of course, not present to the mind of the Apostle.

(12—17) These verses form a hortatory application of the foregoing, with further development of the idea to live after and in the Spirit.

(12) **We are debtors.**—*We are under an obligation.* Observe that in the lively sequence of thought the second clause of the antithesis is suppressed, "We are under an obligation, not to the flesh (but to the Spirit)."

(13) **If ye through the Spirit . . .**—If under the influence of the Spirit you reduce to a condition of deadness and atrophy all those practices to which the impulses of your material nature would prompt you.

(14—17) This life in the Spirit implies a special relation to God—that of sons. I say of sons; for when you first received the Holy Ghost it was no spirit of bondage and reign of terror to which you were admitted, but rather the closest filial relation to God. This filial relation is attested by the Divine Spirit endorsing the evidence of our own consciousness, and it includes all that such a relation would naturally include—sonship, heirship, nay, a joint-heirship in the glory of Christ, who is Himself pre-eminently the Son.

This idea of "sonship" is also worked out in the Epistle to the Galatians (iii. 25; iv. 1—7). It is the Christian transformation of the old theocratic idea. The Israelite, *qua* Israelite, had stood in this special relation to God; now it is open to the *spiritual* Israel.

(15) For ye have not received the spirit
of bondage again to fear; but ye
have received the Spirit of adoption,
whereby we cry, Abba, Father. (16) The
Spirit itself beareth witness with our
spirit, that we are the children of God:
(17) And if children, then
heirs; heirs of God, and
joint-heirs with Christ; if
so be that we suffer with *him*, that
we may be also glorified together.
(18) For I reckon that the sufferings
of this present time *are* not worthy
*to be compared* with the glory which
shall be revealed in us. (19) For the
earnest expectation of the creature
waiteth for the manifestation of the
sons of God. (20) For the creature was
made subject to vanity, not willingly,
but by reason of him who hath sub-

Chap. viii. 17—25. Creation's yearning.

---

of whatever race they may be. The idea itself, too, is largely widened and deepened by the additional doctrines of the continued agency of the Spirit and of the Messiahship of Jesus. The sense of sonship is awakened and kept alive by the Spirit; and of all those in whom it is found, the Messiah Himself stands at the head, ensuring for them a share in His own glory.

(15) **Spirit of bondage.**—The Greek corresponds very nearly to what we should naturally understand by the English phrase, "such a spirit as would be found in slaves." The word "spirit" varies much in meaning in these verses. Here it is the "dominant habit or frame of mind;" in the next verse it is used both for the Spirit of God and the spirit of man.

**Again to fear.**—So as to take you back under the old terrorism of the Law. The Law, if it contained promises, was still more essentially a system of threats; for the threats took effect, while the promises remained ineffectual, because the Law could not be fulfilled.

**Spirit of adoption.**—That spirit which is characteristic of those who are taken to be sons, who, like the Christian at his baptism, are admitted into this relation of sonship.

**Whereby we cry.**—The intensity of the Apostle's feeling comes out in this simple definition. Instead of any more formal elaboration of his meaning, he says the Spirit of adoption is that which prompts the impassioned cry, "Abba, Father."

**Abba, Father.**—"Abba" is the Aramaic equivalent for father. The repetition is one of endearment and entreaty, taken from the natural impulse of children to repeat a beloved name in different forms. Comp. Newton's hymn—

> "Jesus, my Shepherd, Husband, Friend,
> My Prophet, Priest, and King," &c.

(16) **The Spirit itself beareth witness.**—What is the nature of this concurrent testimony? It would seem to be something of this kind. The self-consciousness of the believer assures him of his sonship. The relation in which he feels that he stands to God he knows to be that of a son. But, besides this, he is aware of an eternal objective cause for this feeling. That cause is the influence of the Holy Spirit.

This passage makes it clear that the Apostle, in spite of the strongly mystic tone of his language elsewhere, never confuses the human and the divine.

(17) One characteristic of the son is that he is his father's heir. So it is with the Christian. He, too, has an inheritance—an inheritance of glory which he will share with Christ. But he must not be surprised if, before sharing the glory, he also shares the sufferings.

**Suffer with him.**—All who suffer for the sake of the gospel are regarded as suffering with Christ. They "drink of the cup" that He drank of (Matt. xx. 22, 23). (Comp. 2 Cor. i. 5; Phil. iii. 10; Col. i. 24.)

(18—25) The mention of "suffering" and of "glory" recalls the Apostle to a sense of his own position—what he had to go through, and what was the hope that he had to animate and encourage him. A vivid impression of the stormy life of the Apostle at this period is given by Acts xix. 23—41; 2 Cor. vi. 4, 5; xi. 23—28. But he counted it as nothing (Phil. iii. 8) as compared with his triumphant out-look into the future. Here, then, there follows a statement of the nature of the Christian's hope viewed, not only as it affects the individual, but also in its cosmical aspect.

(18) **Revealed in us.**—*Upon us—i.e.*, reaching to us, and illumining and transfiguring us. The Coming of Christ is always thus conceived of as a visible manifestation of glory in those who take part in it.

(19) Nor is ours a merely isolated hope; we have our place—

> "Mid onward sloping motions infinite,
> Making for one sure goal."

The whole creation is looking earnestly and intently for the same manifestation of glory as ourselves.

**Earnest expectation.**—A single word in the Greek, and a very striking one. It means, literally, a straining forward with outstretched head, just as we might imagine the crowds outside a race-course straining over the ropes to catch a sight of the runners; an eager, intent expectation. The same word is used once again in the New Testament (Phil. i. 20).

**Creature.**—Creation, the whole world of nature, animate and inanimate.

**Waiteth for.**—Another strong word, "waits with concentrated longing and expectancy."

**Manifestation.** — Translate rather by the ordinary word, *revelation*, as in the last verse ("glory which shall be *revealed*"). The *Parusia*, or Coming of Christ, is to be accompanied by an appearance of the redeemed in glorified form.

(20) **For the creature.**—The Apostle gives the reason for this earnest expectation in the present state of nature; pointing out what creation *is*. If creation were perfect, and were fulfilling the noblest possible purpose, there would be no cause for looking forward hopefully to the future.

**Was made subject to vanity.**—"Vanity" = "emptiness" or "nothingness." Creation is fulfilling an unworthy instead of a worthy and noble end. (Comp. Gen. iii. 17, 18.) It was made subject to this "not willingly," *i.e.*, by its own act or with its own concurrence, but "by reason of Him who hath subjected the same," *i.e.*, in pursuance of the sovereign purpose and counsel of God. The one thing which takes out

jected *the same* in hope, (21) because the
creature itself also shall be delivered
from the bondage of corruption into the
glorious liberty of the children of God.
(22) For we know that the whole creation[1]
groaneth and travaileth in pain to-
gether until now. (23) And not only
*they*, but ourselves also, which have the
firstfruits of the Spirit, even we our-
selves groan within ourselves, waiting
for the adoption, *to wit*, the redemption
of our body.[a] (24) For we are saved by
hope: but hope that is seen is not
hope: for what a man seeth, why doth
he yet hope for? (25) But if we hope
for that we see not, *then* do we with
patience wait for *it*. (26) Likewise the
Spirit also helpeth our infirmities: for we know not what we should pray for as we ought: but the Spirit itself maketh intercession for us with

a Luke 21. 28.

1 Or, *every creature.*

Chap. viii. 26, 27. The Spirit's intercession.

---

the sting from this impoverished and degraded condition is Hope.

It is needless to say that this is not Darwinism, but it is easily reconcilable with evolution. Indeed, such a theory seems to give it additional force and emphasis. It helps to bring out both the present "vanity" and hope for the future, and to show both as parts of one "increasing purpose" widening through the ages. "Allowing for irregularities and fluctuations, on the whole, higher and higher forms of life have appeared. There has been unquestionably an enormous advance between the times of the Eozoon Canadense and our own. And, further, we have to notice that a new kind of progress, of far greater intrinsic importance than mere physical improvement, has of late appeared. I mean intellectual and moral progress, as it is seen in man. . . . And this progress, I would say, is most important in our argument as to the character of God, for it is full of promise of far better things than this sad world has ever seen. It points most decidedly to a supremacy of the power for good, and a great hope of final happiness for our race." (Rev. S. T. Gibson, *Religion and Science*, p. 34.)

(21) **Because the creature.**—The reason for the hope which survives through the degradation of nature; what creation *is to be.*

**Because.**—Perhaps rather "that," to be joined on to the end of the last verse, "in hope that creation, also," &c. So Meyer and Ellicott.

**Delivered from the bondage of corruption.**—The state of decay and ruin into which the world by nature has fallen, is regarded as a servitude opposed to the state of liberty into which it will be ushered at the Coming of Christ.

**Glorious liberty of the children of God.**—Translate rather, *into the liberty of the glory of the children of God—i.e.*, into the state of liberty or emancipation which will attend the appearance of the Messiah and His redeemed. Their state will be one of liberty, and in that liberty the whole creation hopes to share.

(22) **Groaneth and travaileth.**—In view of the physical evil and misery prevalent in the world, the Apostle attributes a human consciousness of pain to the rest of creation. It groans and travails *together, i.e.*, every member of it in common with its kind. The idea of travailing, as in childbirth, has reference to the future prospect of joyful delivery. (Comp. John xvi. 21.)

**Until now.**—This consciousness of pain and imperfection has been continuous and unbroken (nor will it cease until an end is put to it by the Coming of Christ.)

(23) Nor is it only the rest of creation that groans. We Christians, too, though we possess the firstfruits of the Spirit, nevertheless inwardly groan, sighing for the time when our adoption as the sons of God will be complete, and even our mortal bodies will be transfigured.

**Which have the firstfruits of the Spirit.**—Though we have received the first partial outpouring of the Spirit, as opposed to the plenitude of glory in store for us.

**The adoption.**—The Christian who has received the gift of the Spirit is *already* an adopted child of God. (See verses 15, 16.) But this adoption still has to be ratified and perfected, which will not be until the Coming of Christ.

**The redemption of our body.**—One sign of the imperfect sonship of the Christian is that mortal and corruptible body in which the better and heavenly part of him is imprisoned. That, too, shall be transformed and glorified, and cleared from all the defect of its earthly condition. (Comp. 1 Cor. xv. 49—53; 2 Cor. v. 1 *et seq.*; Phil. iii. 21.)

(24) Why do I say that we "wait for the adoption?" Because hope in the future is of the very essence of the Christian's life. It was by hope that he was saved. Hope, at the time when he first believed, made him realise his salvation, though it is still in the future. This is, indeed, implied in the very nature of hope. Its proper object is that which is future and unseen.

**By hope.**—It is usually faith rather than hope that is represented as the means or instrument of salvation. Nor can it quite rightly be said that hope is *an aspect* of faith, because faith and hope are expressly distinguished and placed as co-ordinate with each other in 1 Cor. xiii. 13: "and now abideth faith, hope, and charity, these three." Hope is rather a secondary cause of salvation, because it sets salvation vividly before the believer, and so makes him strive to obtain it.

It must not, however, be overlooked that the phrase translated "by hope," may be taken, rather to mean "*with*" or "*in* hope." It will then serve to limit the idea of salvation. We were saved, indeed, in an inchoate and imperfect manner, but our full salvation is still a subject for hope, and therefore it is not past but still in the future.

(25) If salvation were something that could be seen, something that could be grasped by sight, then there would be no room for hope. As it is we do *not* see it; we *do* hope for it; and, therefore, we patiently endure the sufferings that lie upon the road to it.

(26, 27) A second reason for the patience of the Christian under suffering. The Spirit helps his weakness and joins in his prayers.

(26) **Likewise.**—While on the one hand the prospect of salvation sustains him, so on the other hand the Divine

groanings which cannot be uttered.
(27) And he that searcheth the hearts
knoweth what *is* the mind of the Spirit,
because[1] he maketh intercession for the
saints according to *the will*
*of* God. (28) And we know
that all things work to-
gether for good to them
that love God, to them who are
the called according to *his* purpose.
(29) For whom he did foreknow, he also
did predestinate *to be* conformed to the
image of his Son, that he might be
the firstborn among many brethren.
(30) Moreover whom he did predestinate,
them he also called: and whom he
called, them he also justified: and whom
he justified, them he also glorified.

Chap. viii. 28—30. The happy career of the Christian.

1 Or, *that.*

---

Spirit interposes to aid him. The one source of encouragement is human (his own human consciousness of the certainty of salvation), the other is divine.

**Infirmities.**—The correct reading is the singular, "infirmity." Without this assistance we might be too weak to endure, but the Spirit helps and strengthens our weakness by inspiring our prayers.

**With groanings which cannot be uttered.**—When the Christian's prayers are too deep and too intense for words, when they are rather a sigh heaved from the heart than any formal utterance, then we may know that they are prompted by the Spirit Himself. It is He who is praying to God for us.

(27) God recognises the voice of His own Spirit, because the prayers that the Spirit prompts are in strict accordance with His will.

**What is the mind of the Spirit.**—What are the thoughts of the Spirit, and therefore what is the echo of those thoughts in the prayers that are offered to Him.

(28—30) These verses contain a third reason for the patience of the Christian. He knows that whatever happens, all things are really working together for good to him.

(28) **All things.**—Persecution and suffering included.

**Work together.**—Contribute.

There is a rather remarkable reading here, found in the Vatican and Alexandrian MSS., and in Origen, inserting "God" as the subject of the verb, and making "all things" the object. "God works all things with," or "co-operates in all things." This reading is very early, if not original.

**To them who are the called.**—Further description of those "who love God." They have also, as in His eternal counsels He had designed it should be, obeyed the call given to them in the preaching of the gospel, and definitely enrolled themselves in the kingdom of the Messiah.

(29, 30) **For whom he did foreknow, he also did predestinate.**—The process already summed up under these two phrases is now resolved more fully and exactly into its parts, with the inference suggested that to those who are under the divine guidance at every step in their career nothing can act but for good. The two phrases indicate two distinct steps. God, in His infinite foreknowledge, knew that certain persons would submit to be conformed to the image of His Son, and He predestined them for this.

When we argue deductively from the omniscience and omnipotence of God, human free-will seems to be obliterated. On the other hand, when we argue deductively from human free-will, the divine foreknowledge and power to determine action seem to be excluded. And yet both truths must be received without detriment to each other. We neither know strictly what God's omnipotence and omniscience are (according to a more exact use of language, we ought to say, perhaps, "perfect power and knowledge"—power and knowledge such as would belong to what we are incapable of conceiving, a perfect Being), nor do we know what human free-will is in itself. It is a necessary postulate if there is to be any synthesis of human life at all; for without it there can be no distinction between good and bad at all. But we do not really know more than that it is that hypothetical faculty in man by virtue of which he is a responsible agent.

**To be conformed . .**—The final cause of the whole of this divine process is that the Christian may be conformed to the image of Christ—that he may be like him not merely in spirit, but also in that glorified body, which is to be the copy of the Redeemer's (Phil. iii. 21), and so be a fit attendant upon Him in His Messianic kingdom.

**Firstborn among many brethren.**—The Messianic kingdom is here conceived of rather as a family. In this family Christ has the rights of primogeniture, but all Christians are His brethren; and the object of His mission and of the great scheme of salvation (in all its stages—foreknowledge, calling, justification, &c.) is to make men *sufficiently like Him to be* His brethren, and so to fill up the number of the Christian family. The word "firstborn" occurs in a similar connection in Col. i. 15, "firstborn of every creature" (or rather, *of all creation*), and in Heb. i. 6, "When he bringeth in the first-begotten (*firstborn*) into the world." It implies two things—(1) priority in point of time, or in other words the pre-existence of the Son as the Divine Word; and (2) supremacy or sovereignty as the Messiah. The Messianic use of the word is based upon Ps. lxxxix. 27, "Also I will make him my firstborn, higher than the kings of the earth."

**Among many brethren.**—Comp. Heb. ii. 11 *et seq.*, "He is not ashamed to call them brethren," &c. There is a stress on "many." The object of the Christian scheme is that Christ may not stand alone in the isolated glory of His pre-existence, but that He may be surrounded by a numerous brotherhood fashioned after His likeness as He is in the likeness of God.

(30) **Predestinate.**—This is the term which seems most to interfere with human free-will. Foreknowledge does not interfere with free-will, because the foreknowledge, though prior in point of time, is posterior in the order of causation to the act of choice. A man does not choose a certain action because it is foreknown, but it is foreknown because he will choose it. Predestination (the word is not inadequately translated) appears to involve a more rigorous necessity. All we can say is that it must not be interpreted in any sense that excludes free-will. Free-will is a postulate on which all the superstructure of morals and religion must rest. The religious mind, looking back over the course by which it has been brought, sees in it predominating the hand of God; but however large the divine element in salvation may be, it must in the end

(31) What shall we then say to these
things? If God *be* for us,
Chap. viii. 31—39. Triumphant close. who *can be* against us?
(32) He that spared not his
own Son, but delivered him
up for us all, how shall he not with him
also freely give us all things? (33) Who
shall lay any thing to the charge of
God's elect? *It is* God that justifieth:
(34) who *is* he that condemneth? *It is*
Christ that died, yea rather, that is
risen again, who is even at the right
hand of God, who also maketh inter-
cession for us: (35) who shall separate
us from the love of Christ? *shall* tribu-
lation, or distress, or persecution, or
famine, or nakedness, or peril, or sword?
(36) As it is written, For thy sake we
a Ps. 44. 22. are killed all the day long;[a] we are
accounted as sheep for the slaughter.
(37) Nay, in all these things we are more
than conquerors through him that loved
us. (38) For I am persuaded, that neither
death, nor life, nor angels, nor princi-

---

be apprehended by faith, which is an act of free-will. And the subsequent actions of which faith is the moving cause, though done under a co-operating divine influence, yet belong to the sphere of human freedom. (See Note on chap. ii. 6.) It should be remembered that St. Paul is not now writing in the calm temper of philosophical analysis, but in an intense access of religious emotion, and therefore he does not stay to put in all the qualifying clauses that philosophy might require. It is well for mankind that he has done so. In all great and creative religious minds the consciousness of free-will has retired into the background.

**Called.**—By presenting to them the gospel, directly or indirectly, through the preaching of Christ and His Apostles.

**Justified.**—In the Pauline sense, as in chap. iii. 24, *et al.*

**Glorified.**—Strictly, the glorifying of the Christian awaits him in the future, but the Apostle regards all these different acts as focussed together as it were on a single point in the past. Glorification is involved in justification.

(31—39) Now follows the sublime and triumphant conclusion from the foregoing—expressed with passionate energy and with the most intense consciousness of the reality of a Christian belief in penetrating and sustaining the mind in all outward trials, however severe.

Erasmus remarks on this, that "Cicero never said anything grander." It is needless to add that, setting aside other considerations, Cicero was not for a moment comparable in spiritual intensity, and therefore in true eloquence, to St. Paul.

(33, 34) **Who shall lay any thing . . . ?**—The punctuation and arrangement of these clauses are somewhat difficult. It seems best on the whole to connect together the two clauses at the end of verse 33, and beginning of verse 34. The whole passage to the end of the chapter will then form a continuous proof of the certainty that all things shall be freely given to the Christian. Nothing can frustrate this: either on the side of *God*, for when He justifies none can condemn; or on the side of *Christ*, whose death, and resurrection, and ascension, and intercession are pledges that nothing can separate us from His love.

What have we to fear? When God pronounces our acquittal there is none who can pronounce our condemnation. Literally, *God is He who justifies, who then can condemn?* And answering to this in the next verse we have, Christ is He that died, &c. This is the two-fold answer to the question, "Who shall come forward to accuse God's elect?" It is a conclusive reply to this to state the relation in which the accused stand to God and to Christ.

**God's elect.**—Christians as such with especial reference to the process which the Apostle has been describing in verses 29, 30.

(34) **It is Christ . . .**—The remainder of this verse is to be closely connected with the opening of the next. "He that died, rose, &c., is Christ: who then shall separate us from His love?" The two questions, "Who is he that condemneth?" and "Who shall separate us?" are really parts of the reply to the main question thrown into an interrogative form. At another moment the sentence would probably have been differently cast, but the Apostle's mind is in an attitude of challenge.

**Yea rather.**—*Yea more.* The pledges that Christ has given us of His love did not end, but only began with His death.

(35) **The love of Christ.**—That is to say, the love which Christ has for us, not that which we have for Christ.

**Shall tribulation?**—Comp. 2 Cor. vi. 4; xi. 23. The Apostle is speaking from his own actual experience.

(36) **For thy sake we are killed.**—The quotation is taken from Ps. xliv. 22, which was apparently written at some period of great national distress, at what precise period the *data* do not enable us to say, but probably not earlier than Josiah. The sufferings of God's people at all times are typical of each other. There is the further reason for the application in the text that the Psalm does not lay stress upon the guilt of the people, but regards their sufferings as undergone in the cause of the theocracy. At the same time, the tone of the Psalmist wants the exulting and triumphant confidence of the Apostle.

(37) **Nay.**—*Yet*, or *But.* So far from being vanquished, we are conquerors: when we are weak then are we strong.

(38) **Neither death, nor life . . .**—The enumeration that follows is intended to include (poetically rather than logically) every possible category of being, especially those unseen powers of evil against which the warfare of the Christian was more particularly directed.

**Nor principalities.**—Comp. Eph. vi. 12, "We wrestle . . . against principalities, against powers;" terms belonging to the Jewish enumeration of angels. The critical evidence is however absolutely decisive in separating "powers" from "principalities" in this instance and placing it after "things present, nor things to come." It would be better therefore to take it in a wider sense: "Agencies of every kind, personal or impersonal."

palities, nor powers, nor things present,
nor things to come, (39) nor height, nor
depth, nor any other creature, shall be
able to separate us from the love of God,
which is in Christ Jesus our Lord.

CHAPTER IX.—(1) I say the truth
in Christ, I lie not, my
conscience also bearing me
witness in the Holy Ghost,
(2) that I have great heavi-

Chap. ix. 1—5. A sad reflection: Israel's privileges and fall.

ness and continual sorrow in my
heart. (3) For I could wish that my-
self were accursed[1] from Christ for
my brethren, my kinsmen according to
the flesh: (4) who are Israelites; to
whom *pertaineth* the adoption, and the
glory, and the covenants, and the giving
of the law, and the service *of God*, and
the promises; (5) whose *are* the fathers,
and of whom as concerning the flesh
Christ *came*, who is over all, God blessed

1 Or, *separated.*

A.D. 58.

---

(39) **Nor height, nor depth.**—No remoteness in space. (Comp. Ps. cxxxix. 8 *et seq.* "If I ascend up into heaven," &c.)

**Any other creature.**—Any other created thing.

**The love of God.**—It is to be observed that for the shorter phrase, "the love of Christ," the Apostle now substitutes the fuller but, as it would seem, equivalent phrase, "the love of God *in* Christ."

IX.

There is a distinct break in the Epistle at this point. The subject of the preceding chapters, the development of the gospel scheme, has been worked up to a climax. We might imagine that at the end of chapter viii. the Epistle was laid aside, and the Apostle now begins upon a new topic, in the discussion of which, however, he still retains the same vein of deep emotion that had characterised his latest utterances. This new topic is the relation of the Christian system just expounded to the chosen people. And here, after a few opening words of patriotic sympathy (verses 1—5), the Apostle discusses: (1) the justice of their rejection (verses 6—29); (2) its causes (verse 30 to chap. x. 21); (3) its compensations and qualifications (chap. xi. 1—32); with a closing doxology (chap. xi. 33—36). The section including these three chapters is complete and rounded in itself.

(1—5) My heart bleeds for Israel, my country, that highly-privileged people. I could fain have changed places with them, and been myself cut off from Christ, if only they might have been saved.

(1) **I say the truth in Christ.**—The meaning of this expression seems to be, "From the bottom of my soul, in the most sacred part of my being, as a Christian man united to Christ, I make this solemn asseveration."

**My conscience.**—Here, as in chap. ii. 15, very much in the modern sense of the word, the introspective faculty which sits in judgment upon actions, and assigns to them their moral qualities of praise or blame. "This conscience of mine being also overshadowed with the Holy Spirit, and therefore incapable of falsehood or self-deception."

(3) **I could wish . . .**—Rather, *I could have wished.* The wish, of course, related to what was really impossible. Still it is a nobly generous impulse, at which some weak minds have been shocked, and out of which others have made sentimental capital. Let us leave it as it is.

**Accursed from Christ.**—Separated from Christ, and devoted to destruction. Does not the intensity of this expression help us to realise one aspect of the Atonement—"being made a curse for us" (Gal. iii. 13)? (The Greek word for "curse" is different, but comes to be nearly equivalent.)

(4) **The adoption.**—They are the theocratic people, the people whom God had, as it were, adopted to Himself, and taken into the special filial relation. (Comp. Hos. xi. 1, "I called my son out of Egypt;" Ex. iv. 22, "Israel is my son, even my firstborn;" *et al.*)

**The glory.**—The Shechinah, or visible symbol of God's presence. (Comp. Ex. xvi. 10; xxiv. 16; xl. 34, 35; 1 Sam. iv. 22; 1 Kings viii. 10, 11; Ezek. i. 28; Heb. ix. 5.)

**The covenants.**—Not the two tables of stone, but the several compacts made by God with Abraham and his descendants (Gen. xii. 1—3, 7; xiii. 14—17; xv. 1—21; xvii. 1—22; xxii. 15—18; xxvi. 2—5, 34; xxviii. 13—15; xxxv. 9—12; xlvi. 3, 4).

**The service of God.**—The temple service and ritual.

**The promises.**—Especially the Messianic promises, a term correlative to the "covenants" above.

(5) **The fathers.**—The patriarchs—Abraham, Isaac, and Jacob.

**Who is over all, God blessed for ever.**—These words are a well-known subject for controversy. Trinitarian and English interpreters, as a rule, take them with the punctuation of the Authorised version, as referring to Christ. Socinian interpreters, with some of the most eminent among the Germans, put a full stop after "came," and make the remainder of the verse a doxology addressed to God, "Blessed for ever be God, who is over all." Both ways are possible. The question is, Which is the most natural and probable? and this is to be considered, putting altogether on one side prepossessions of every kind. We are not to read meaning *into* Scripture, but to elicit meaning *from* it. The balance of the argument stands thus:—(1) The order of the words is somewhat in favour of the application to Christ. If the clause had really been a formal doxology, the ascription of blessing would more naturally have come at the beginning in Greek as in English, "Blessed be God," &c. (2) The context is also somewhat in favour of this application. The break in the form of the sentence becomes rather abrupt on the other hypothesis, and is not to be quite paralleled. Intruded doxologies, caused by a sudden access of pious feeling, are not uncommon in the writings of St. Paul, but they are either worked into the regular order of the sentence, as in chap. i. 25, Gal. i. 5, or else they are formally introduced as in 2 Cor. xi. 31; 1 Tim. i. 17. (3) But on the other hand, to set somewhat decidedly against this application, is the fact that the words used by the Apostle, "Who is over all," and the ascription of blessing in all other places where they occur, are referred, not to Christ, but to God. (Comp. chap. i. 25; 2 Cor. i. 3; xi. 31; Eph. i. 3, iv. 6.) There is, indeed, a doxology addressed to Christ in 2 Tim. iv. 18; it should, however, be remembered

for ever. Amen. (6) Not as though
the word of God hath
taken none effect. For they
*are* not all Israel, which
are of Israel: (7) neither,
because they are the seed of Abra-
ham, *are they* all children: but, In
Isaac shall thy seed be called.[a] (8) That
is, They which are the children of the
flesh, these *are* not the children of God:
but the children of the promise are
counted for the seed. (9) For this *is* the
word of promise, At this time will
I come, and Sarah shall have a
son.[b] (10) And not only *this;* but when
Rebecca also had conceived by one, *even*
by our father Isaac; (11) (for *the children*
being not yet born, neither having done
any good or evil, that the purpose of
God according to election might stand,
not of works, but of him that calleth;)
(12) it was said unto her, The elder[1]
shall serve the younger.[2c] (13) As it is
written, Jacob have I loved,[d] but Esau
have I hated. (14) What shall we say then?
*Is there* unrighteousness with God?

Chap. ix. 6—13. The promise confined to the chosen seed.

*b* Gen. 18. 10.
*a* Gen. 21. 12.
1 Or, *greater.*
2 Or, *lesser.*
*c* Gen. 25. 23.
*d* Mal. 1. 2.

---

that the Pauline origin of that Epistle has been doubted by some, though it is also right to add that these doubts do not appear to have any real validity. The title "God" does not appear to be elsewhere applied to our Lord by St. Paul, though all the attributes of God-head are ascribed to Him: *e.g.*, in Phil. ii. 6 *et seq.*, Col. i. 15 *et seq.* In 1 Tim. iii. 16, which would be an apparent exception, the true reading is, "Who was manifested," and not "God was manifested." On the other hand, St. John certainly makes use of this title, not only in John i. 1, xx. 28, but also in the reading, adopted by many, of John i. 18, "God only begotten" for "Only begotten Son." Weighing the whole of the arguments against each other, the *data* do not seem to be sufficient to warrant a positive and dogmatic conclusion either way. The application to our Lord appears perhaps a little the more probable of the two. More than this cannot be said. Nor is a stronger affirmation warranted by any considerations resting on the division of authorities.

(6–13) Now follows a vindication of the dealings of God in rejecting Israel. And this is divided into three parts. Part 1 extends to the end of verse 13, and the object of it is to clear the way by defining the true limits of the promise. It was not really to *all* Israel that the promise was given, but only to a particular section of Israel.

(6) **Not as though.**—The scholar will observe that there appears to be here a mixture of two constructions, "the case is not such that," and "I do not mean to say that," "I do not intend to say that the case is such as that."

**Taken none effect.** — "Fallen through," or "failed of its accomplishment."

**Of Israel**—*i.e.*, descended from Jacob. (Comp. Gen. xxxii. 28.) The promise of God was indeed given to Israel, but that did not mean roundly all who could claim descent from Jacob without further limitation.

(7) Neither are all the bodily descendants of Abraham also his spiritual descendants. It was expressly stated from the first that the promise was confined to a particular branch of his posterity. The posterity of Abraham, strictly so called, was to be that derived through Isaac. This is very nearly the sense of the original, "In Isaac shall thy seed be called," *i.e.*, in "Isaac shalt thou have posterity, which shall be called thy posterity" — "true and legitimate descendants," thus excluding the seed of Hagar.

(8) **They which are the children.**—The Apostle explains this restriction in a spiritual sense. Mere natural descent gives no claim to membership in the theocracy.

**Of the promise** — *i.e.*, not merely "promised children," but "children born through the miraculous agency of the promise;" the promise is regarded as being possessed of creative power. (Comp. chap. iv. 18—20.)

(9) **This is the word of promise.**—Rather, *this saying is of promise.* The children of promise, I say, for the saying, "At this time will I come," &c., is a matter of promise; it implied a divine and miraculous intervention, and did not come in the ordinary course of nature.

**At this time**—*i.e.*, at the corresponding time of the next year.

(10, 11) Nor was the restriction and special selection confined to the case of Abraham alone. It also appeared when Rebecca bore sons to Isaac. It was indeed *pure* selection. The children themselves had done nothing to make a preference be given to one over the other. There was no merit in the case. The object of the declaration was to ratify the divine electing purpose which had already chosen Jacob to be the inheritor of the Messianic blessings.

Here we have the doctrine of election and predestination stated in a very unqualified and uncompromising form. And it does indeed necessarily follow from one train of thought. However much we lay stress on free-will, still actions are the result of character—the will itself is a part of character; and character is born in us. Of the two elements which go to determine action, outward circumstances, and inward disposition, neither can be said strictly to be made by the man himself. If we follow this train of thought, then it would certainly appear that God, or the chain of natural causes set in motion and directed by God, made him what he is. In other words, he is elected and predetermined to a certain line of conduct. This is the logic of one set of inferences. On the other hand, the logic of the other set of inferences is just as strong —that man is free. There is an opposition irreconcilable to us with our present means of judging. We can only take the one proposition as qualified by the other.

(12) **The elder shall serve the younger.**—The margin gives as an alternative rendering, "the greater shall serve the lesser." The quotation is taken from the LXX., in which there is the same ambiguity.

This ambiguity also appears to exist in the Hebrew, where it is a disputed question whether the words refer to age or to the comparative strength of the two peoples. In either case, it is the nations that should spring from Esau and Jacob that are meant.

(14–18) These verses contain the second part of the vindication. This power of choosing one and refusing

Chap. ix. 14—23. The absoluteness of God's choice.

God forbid. (15) For he saith to Moses,
I will have mercy on
whom I will have mercy,
and I will have compas-
sion on whom I will have
compassion.[a] (16) So then *it is* not
of him that willeth, nor of him that
runneth, but of God that sheweth
mercy. (17) For the scripture saith unto
Pharaoh, Even for this same purpose
have I raised thee up, that I might
shew my power in thee, and that
my name might be declared throughout
all the earth.[b] (18) Therefore hath he
mercy on whom he will *have mercy*, and
whom he will he hardeneth. (19) Thou
wilt say then unto me, Why doth he
yet find fault? For who hath resisted
his will? (20) Nay but, O man, who art
thou that repliest against God?[1] Shall
the thing formed say to him that formed
*it*, Why hast thou made me thus?[c]
(21) Hath not the potter power over the
clay, of the same lump to make one
vessel unto honour, and another unto
dishonour?[d] (22) *What* if God, willing
to shew *his* wrath, and to make his
power known, endured with much long-

a Ex. 33. 19.
1 Or, *answerest again, or, disputest with God?*
c Isa. 45. 9.
d Jer. 18. 6; Wisd. 15. 7.
b Ex. 9. 16.

---

another has always been reserved to Himself by God; as is seen by the examples of Moses and Pharaoh.

(14) **Is there unrighteousness?**—Again, as in chap. iii. 5, the Apostle anticipates a possible objection. Does not this apparently arbitrary choice of one and rejection of another imply injustice in Him who exercises it? The thought is not to be entertained.

(15) **For he saith to Moses.**—In the most characteristic period of the Old Testament the divine favour was promised in this way to Moses and denied to Pharaoh. The original of the first quotation has reference to the special revelation vouchsafed to Moses on Sinai, "I will show grace to whom I will show grace."

(16) **Of him that runneth.**—A metaphor taken from the foot-races as St. Paul may very possibly have seen them practised at Corinth. (Comp. chap. ix. 16; Gal. ii. 2; v. 7; Phil. ii. 16.) The meaning is that the prize does not depend on human will or human effort, but on the grace of God.

(17) The converse proposition is also true, that God also uses the wickedness of men as a means of exhibiting His power and justice.

**Raised thee up.**—Brought into the world and on to the scene of history.

**Show my power.**—By the plagues of Egypt and by the overthrow of Pharaoh and his host in the Red Sea.

(18) Summary conclusion from the above.

**He hardeneth.**—The doctrine of the divine sovereignty is here expressed in its most trenchant and logical form. In Ex. viii. 32, ix. 34, xiii. 15, &c., the hardening of Pharaoh's heart is attributed to his own act. That act may, however, be regarded as a part of the design of Providence. God's decrees include human free-will, without destroying it. But *how* they do this we cannot say.

(19—21) These verses contain the third part of the vindication, which is based upon a possible extension of the objection. Not only might it seem as if this absolute choice and rejection was unjust in itself, but also unjust in its consequences. How can a man be blamed or punished, when his actions are determined for him? The Apostle meets this by a simple but emphatic assertion of the absolute and unquestionable prerogative of God over His creatures.

(20) **Nay but, O man.**—The answer is not so much a solution of the intellectual difficulty, as an appeal to the religious sense to prevent it from being raised. That His dealings should be questioned at all is a breach of the reverence due to God.

(21) **Hath not the potter . . .?**—In strict logic, this verse would supply a confirmation, rather than a refutation, of the original objection. If man is merely as clay in the hands of the potter, it would not be unreasonable to say, "Why doth He yet find fault?" No one would think of blaming a piece of earthenware because it was well or badly made. The argument of the Apostle is not directed to this. He has left the point with which he started in verse 19, and is engaged in proving the position taken up in verse 20. Whatever they may be, God's dealings are not to be canvassed by men. Still, we cannot overlook the fact that there is apparently a flaw in the logic, though, perhaps, only such a flaw as is inseparable from our necessarily imperfect conceptions of this mysterious subject. The two lines of thought—that which proves the divine sovereignty and that which proves human freedom—run parallel to each other, and are apt to collude when drawn together. (See Notes on chaps. viii. 29, 30; ix. 11, 18, above.)

For the imagery of the clay and the potter, compare Isa. lxiv. 8; Jer. xviii. 3—10.

(22—29) These verses supply the concluding section of the vindication. All this scheme of God's dealings, apparently so severe, is really most merciful. To those who really deserved His wrath, He showed longsuffering. While for us who now believe, Gentiles as well as Jews, He had mercy and glory in store. But in both cases the final result was strictly in accordance with prophecy. Hosea had foretold the admission of the Gentiles, Isaiah the exclusion of the greater part of the Jews.

(22) **What if . . .**—The sentence in the original is incomplete. In its full form it would run, "If God willing to show His wrath" . . . (what can man reply?) This latter clause is dropped or lost in the course of the argument. The best and simplest expedient to supply its place is that adopted in the Authorised version, inserting "what" in italics at the beginning: "What if," &c. There is a second suppression later in the sentence. At the end of verse 23 we should have to insert some such clause as "He reserved His glory for them," in order to make the sentence strictly grammatical. These irregularities are due to the Apostle's habit of dictating, and to the lively flow of his thoughts.

suffering the vessels of wrath fitted[1] to
destruction: (23) and that he might
make known the riches of his glory on
the vessels of mercy, which he had afore
prepared unto glory, (24) even
us, whom he hath called,
not of the Jews only,
but also of the Gentiles?
(25) As he saith also in Osee,
I will call them my people, which were
not my people; and her beloved, which
was not beloved.[a] (26) And it shall come
to pass,[b] *that* in the place where it was
said unto them, Ye *are* not my people;
there shall they be called the children
of the living God. (27) Esaias also crieth
concerning Israel, Though the number
of the children of Israel be as the sand
of the sea,[c] a remnant shall be saved:
(28) for he will finish the work,[2] and cut
*it* short in righteousness: because a
short work will the Lord make upon the
earth. (29) And as Esaias said before,
Except the Lord of Sabaoth had left
us a seed,[d] we had been as Sodoma, and
been made like unto Gomorrha. (30) What
shall we say then? That the Gentiles,
which followed not after righteousness,

Chap. ix. 24—33. Exemplified in the different fates of Jew and Gentile.

1 Or, *made up.*

c Isa. 10. 22, 23.

2 Or, *the account.*

d Isa. 1. 9.

a Hos. 2. 23; 1 Pet. 2. 10.

b Hos. 1. 10.

---

**Willing.**—While His will was (ultimately) to execute His wrath and display His sovereign judicial power, nevertheless He bore with evildoers, and gave them time for repentance.

(24) **Even us.**—So far the form of the sentence had been abstract—"vessels of wrath," "vessels of glory." Now the Apostle explains who are meant by these abstract terms. The "vessels of glory" are those who were intended to accept the Christian teaching, whether Jews or Gentiles. The "vessels of wrath" are the unbelieving mass of the people of Israel.

(25) **As he saith also in Osee.**—The original of the prophecy in Hosea relates to the pardon and reconciliation promised to the apostate and idolatrous people of the northern kingdom. It is here typically and prophetically applied to the Gentiles. Those who had ceased to belong to the chosen people, and those who had never belonged to it, were to all intents and purposes in the same position.

**Osee.**—"It may be questioned whether this word should be pronounced as a dissyllable, the double *e* being regarded as an English termination, as in Zebedee, Pharisee, &c., or as a trisyllable, the word being considered as a reproduction of the Greek form of the name." (Lightfoot, *On Revision*, p. 156, n.)

(26) **And it shall come to pass.**—This, too, was originally spoken of the restoration of the northern exiles to the land of Palestine. As applied to the conversion of the Gentiles, it would mean that the lands which had previously been heathen should become Christian. There is some doubt whether the Hebrew of Hosea should not rather be translated, "instead of calling them," for "in her place where it was said unto them." Instead of calling them "Ye are not my people," they will be called "Sons of the living God." So Ewald and Hitzig.

(27) **Crieth.**—With reference to the impassioned utterance of the prophet.

**A remnant.**—Rather, *the remnant*, with an emphasis upon the word. "The remnant, and only the remnant."

**Shall be saved.**—In the original, *shall return*—*i.e.*, as it is explained in the previous verse, "return to God." St. Paul has followed the LXX. in putting the consequences of such conversion for the conversion itself.

(28) **For he will finish.**—Literally, according to the correct reading, *For a sentence, accomplishing and abridging it, will the Lord execute upon the earth*; in other words, "A short and summary sentence will the Lord execute upon the earth." The severity of the sentence is a proof that only a remnant can be saved from it. St. Paul follows the LXX., with but slight deviation. The sense of the Hebrew appears to be somewhat different:—"For though thy people, O Israel, were as the sand of the sea, but a remnant of them shall return: a destruction is decreed overflowing with righteousness—*i.e.*, penal justice. For destruction by a sure decree will Jehovah of Hosts perform in the midst of all the earth." (Cheyne.)

(29) **Said before**—*i.e.*, in an earlier part of his book. The Book of Isaiah was at this time collected in the form in which we have it. In Acts xiii. 33, we find an express reference to the present numbering of the Psalms—"It is also written in the second psalm, Thou art my Son, this day have I begotten thee." (Some authorities read "first," the two psalms being arranged as one, but "second" is probably the true reading.)

**A seed.**—Equivalent to the "remnant" of verse 27. The point of the quotation is, that but for this remnant the rejection of Israel would have been utter and complete.

(30—33) The Apostle has finished with his vindication of the rejection of Israel, and finished also with the course of argument which seemed to bear a strong character of determinism. He now takes up a point of view which is the direct opposite of this, and in explaining the *causes* which led to the rejection of Israel, those which he puts forward are all such as depend for their validity on the freedom of the will. It is needless to say that this is abundantly recognised in other parts of St. Paul's writings, especially in the earnest practical exhortations which he addresses to his readers. This, then, must be taken to qualify the argument that has preceded. The freedom of the will and the absolute sovereignty of God are two propositions which, though apparently contradictory, are both really true at one and the same time. When stated singly, each is apt to appear one-sided. They are reconciled, as it were, beneath the surface, in some way inscrutable to us. Both rest on evidence that in itself is incontrovertible.

The great reason for the rejection of Israel and for the admission of the Gentiles is that the Gentiles did, and that they did not, base their attempts at righteousness upon faith. Righteousness is the middle term which leads to salvation. The Gentiles, without seeking, found; the Jews, seeking in a wrong way, failed to find it.

(30) **Which followed not after righteousness.**—Not having a special revelation, and being inattentive to the law of conscience.

have attained to righteousness, even the
righteousness which is of faith. (31) But
Israel, which followed after the law of
righteousness, hath not attained to the
law of righteousness. (32) Wherefore?
Because *they sought it* not by faith, but
as it were by the works of the law.
For they stumbled at that stumbling-
stone; (33) as it is written, Behold,[a] I
lay in Sion a stumblingstone and rock
of offence: and whosoever believeth on
him shall not be ashamed.[1]

a Isa. 8. 14, & 28. 16; 1 Pet. 2. 6.

1 Or, *confounded.*

CHAPTER X. — (1) Brethren, my
heart's desire and prayer
to God for Israel is, that
they might be saved.
(2) For I bear them record
that they have a zeal of
God, but not according
to knowledge. (3) For
they being ignorant of
God's righteousness, and going about
to establish their own righteousness,
have not submitted themselves unto the

Chap. x. 1—13. The cause of Israel's fall. Self-sought righteousness contrasted with righteousness through faith in Christ.

---

**Attained to righteousness.**—By accepting the offer of Christianity, and especially the Christian doctrine of justification by faith.

(31) Israel, on the other hand, though ostensibly pursuing a law the object of which was righteousness, did not reach such a law. They tried to keep the Law, but failed to keep it, and to bring themselves under its protection. The second "righteousness" is omitted in the best MSS.

(32) **For they stumbled.**—"For," in this clause, should be omitted, and the two clauses thrown together, the words "of the law" also going out—Because (seeking righteousness), not of faith, but as if of works, they stumbled, &c.

**That stumblingstone.** — Christ. When Christianity, with the justification by faith which goes with it, was offered to them, they "were offended," and refused it.

(33) **Behold, I lay in Sion.**—A free combination of Isa. xxviii. 16—"Behold, I lay in Zion for a foundation a stone; . . . he that believeth shall not make haste"—and Isa. viii. 14, "And He shall be . . . for a stone of stumbling and for a rock of offence to both the houses of Israel." In the first of these passages the prophet refers to the foundation-stone of the Temple as a symbol of the divine faithfulness; in the second to God Himself. St. Paul, like the Jewish Rabbis, applied both passages to the Messiah; not wrongly, for they foretold the triumph of the theocracy which was fulfilled in the Messiah. The same two quotations appear in 1 Pet. ii. 6, 7, and with similar variation from the LXX., but they are there kept distinct.

**Shall not be ashamed.**—So, too, the LXX. The Hebrew is, "Shall not make haste."

X.

(1) **My heart's desire.**—Strictly, *the goodwill of my heart.* The earlier portion of this chapter is occupied with a more particular exposition of the cause of Israel's rejection, which has been just alleged. They sought to do a hard thing—to work out a righteousness for themselves—instead of an easy thing—simply to believe in Christ.

This chapter, like the last, is introduced by an expression of the Apostle's own warm affection for his people and his earnest desire for their salvation.

**For Israel.**—The true text is, "for them." "Israel" has been put in the margin as an explanatory gloss, and thence found its way into the text. What made the rejection of Israel so peculiarly pathetic was that they were not a mere godless and irreligious people. On the contrary, they had a sincere zeal for religion, but it was a misdirected and ill-judged zeal.

(2) **A zeal of God, but not according to knowledge.**—It would be difficult to find a more happy description of the state of the Jews at this period. They had "a zeal for God." "The Jew," said Josephus, "knows the Law better than his own name. . . The sacred rules were punctually observed. . . The great feasts were frequented by countless thousands. . . Over and above the requirements of the Law, ascetic religious exercises advocated by the teachers of the Law came into vogue. . . . Even the Hellenised and Alexandrian Jews under Caligula died on the cross and by fire, and the Palestinian prisoners in the last war died by the claws of African lions in the amphitheatre, rather than sin against the Law. What Greek," exclaims Josephus, "would do the like? . . . The Jews also exhibited an ardent zeal for the conversion of the Gentiles to the Law of Moses. The proselytes filled Asia Minor and Syria, and—to the indignation of Tacitus—Italy and Rome." The tenacity of the Jews, and their uncompromising monotheism, were seen in some conspicuous examples. In the early part of his procuratorship, Pilate, seeking to break through their known repugnance to everything that savoured of image-worship, had introduced into Jerusalem ensigns surmounted with silver busts of the emperor. Upon this the people went down in a body to Cæsarea, waited for five days and nights in the market place, bared their necks to the soldiers that Pilate sent in among them, and did not desist until the order for the removal of the ensigns had been given. Later he caused to be hung up in the palace at Jerusalem certain gilded shields bearing a dedicatory inscription to Tiberius. Then, again, the Jews did not rest until, by their complaints addressed directly to the emperor, they had succeeded in getting them taken down. The consternation that was caused by Caligula's order for the erection of his own statue in the Temple is well known. None of the Roman governors dared to carry it into execution; and Caligula himself was slain before it could be accomplished.

Justice must be done to the heroic spirit of the Jews. But it was zeal directed into the most mistaken channels. Their religion was legal and formal to the last degree. Under an outward show of punctilious obedience, it concealed all the inward corruption described by the Apostle in chap. ii. 17—29, the full extent of which was seen in the horrors of the great insurrection and the siege of Jerusalem.

(3) **God's righteousness.**—See chaps. i. 17, iii. 21.

**Their own righteousness.** — A righteousness founded on their own works.

righteousness of God. (4) For Christ *is*
the end of the law for righteousness to
every one that believeth. (5) For Moses
describeth the righteousness which is of
the law, That the man which doeth
those things shall live by them.[a] (6) But
the righteousness which is of faith
speaketh on this wise, Say not in thine
heart, Who shall ascend into heaven?[b]
(that is, to bring Christ down *from
above*:) (7) or, Who shall descend into
the deep? (that is, to bring up Christ
again from the dead.) (8) But what
saith it? The word is nigh thee,[c] *even*
in thy mouth, and in thy heart: that is,
the word of faith, which we preach;
(9) that if thou shalt confess with thy
mouth the Lord Jesus, and shalt believe
in thine heart that God hath raised him
from the dead, thou shalt be saved.
(10) For with the heart man believeth
unto righteousness; and with the mouth
confession is made unto salvation.
(11) For the scripture saith, Whosoever
believeth on him shall not be ashamed.[d]
(12) For there is no difference between
the Jew and the Greek: for the same
Lord over all is rich unto all that call
upon him. (13) For whosoever shall call
upon the name of the Lord shall be saved.[e]
(14) How then shall they call on him
in whom they have not
believed? and how shall
they believe in him of
whom they have not heard? and how
shall they hear without a preacher?

Chap. ix. 14—21. Hearing and believing.

a Lev. 18. 5; Ezek. 20. 11; Gal. 3. 12.
d Isa. 28. 16.
b Deut. 30. 12.
e Joel 2. 32; Acts 2. 21.
c Deut. 30. 14.

(4) **The end of the law.**—"End," in the proper sense of termination or conclusion. Christ is that which brings the functions of the Law to an end by superseding it. "The Law pursues a man until he takes refuge in Christ; then it says, Thou hast found thine asylum; I shall trouble thee no more; now thou art wise; now thou art safe." (Bengel.)

**For righteousness to every one that believeth.**—So that every one who believes may obtain righteousness.

(5) **For Moses describeth.**—The Law required an actual literal fulfilment. Its essence consisted in works. "The man which *doeth* these things shall live."

**By them.**—The true reading is, probably, *in it*—*i.e.*, the righteousness just mentioned. "The man who doeth this righteousness" (according to a more correct text) "shall live in and by it."

(6) **But the righteousness.**—In opposition to this righteousness of works, so laborious and so impracticable, the Apostle adduces another quotation to show that the righteousness which depends on faith is much easier and simpler.

The original of the quotation has, indeed, a quite different application. It referred to that very law which the Apostle is depreciating. Moses had described the *Law* as something quite easy and accessible; but history had shown that, especially in the development in which the Law was known to the Apostle, the words were really much more applicable to his doctrine of a righteousness which was based upon faith. He therefore regards them as spoken allegorically and typically with reference to this.

**The righteousness which is of faith speaketh.**—This faith-righteousness is personified as if it were speaking itself, because the language used is applicable to it.

**That is, to bring Christ down from above.**—The Apostle adds these interpretations so as to give a specially Christian meaning to the words of Moses. All that these had meant was that the Law was not remote either in one direction or in another. The Apostle in the phrase "ascend into heaven" sees at once an allusion to the ascended Saviour, and he interprets it as if it implied that the Christian must ascend up to Him, or, what comes to the same thing, as if He must be brought down to the Christian. In like manner, when mention is made of descending into the abyss, he sees here an allusion to the descent of Christ into Hades. Again, he repudiates the idea that the Christian is compelled to join Him there in literal bodily presence. A far easier and simpler thing is the faith of the gospel. All the Christian has to do is to listen to it when it is preached, and then to confess his own adhesion to it.

(7) **Into the deep.**—In the original, *beyond the sea.* The word which St. Paul uses is found in the LXX. for "the sea," but here means *the abyss of Hades.*

(9) **If thou shalt confess with thy mouth.**—Interesting as containing the earliest formal confession of faith; that in Acts viii. 37 (see Note there) is not genuine.

There is no opposition between the outward confession and the inward act of faith. The one is regarded as the necessary consequence and expression of the other. In the next verse this takes the form of Hebrew parallelism, in which the balanced clauses are regarded as equivalent to each other.

**The Lord Jesus.**—Jesus as Lord.

**Hath raised him from the dead.**—Comp. chap. iv. 25. Though the death of Christ apprehended by faith is more especially the cause of the Christian's salvation, still the Apostle regards the Resurrection as the cardinal point; for without the Resurrection the proof of the Messiahship of Jesus would have been incomplete, and His death would not have had its saving efficacy.

(11) **Whosoever believeth.**—*All* who believe shall be saved, for, &c.

(12) **For the same Lord over all is rich.**—Rather, *for the same Lord* (is Lord) *over all, abounding,* &c. Christ is the Lord alike of Jew and of Gentile. (Comp. Eph. iv. 5.)

(13) **Upon the name of the Lord.**—Originally, as meaning "of Jehovah," but with especial reference to the Messianic Advent. Here, therefore, it is applied to our Lord.

(14—21) Thus there is a distinct order—belief, confession, invocation. But before either the last or the first of these steps is taken the gospel must be preached. The Jew, however, cannot plead that the gospel has not been preached to him. It *has* been preached both to Jew and Gentile. Both Moses and Isaiah had foretold the conversion of the Gentiles, and Isaiah had also foretold the unbelief of the Jews.

(15) And how shall they preach, except
they be sent? as it is written, How
beautiful are the feet of them that
preach the gospel of peace,[a] and bring
glad tidings of good things! (16) But
they have not all obeyed the gospel.
For Esaias saith, Lord,[b] who hath be-
lieved our report? (17) So then faith
*cometh* by hearing, and hearing by the
word of God. (18) But I say, Have they
not heard? Yes verily, their sound
went into all the earth,[c] and their words
unto the ends of the world. (19) But I
say, Did not Israel know? First Moses
saith, I will provoke you to jealousy
by *them that are* no people,[d] *and* by a
foolish nation I will anger you. (20) But
Esaias is very bold, and saith, I was
found of them that sought me not;[e] I
was made manifest unto them that
asked not after me. (21) But to Israel
he saith, All day long I have stretched
forth my hands unto a disobedient and
gainsaying people.[f]

d Deut. 32. 21.

a Isa. 52. 7; Nah. 1. 15.

e Isa. 65. 1.

b Isa. 53. 1; John 12. 38.

f Isa. 65. 2.

A.D. 58.

c Ps. 19. 4.

CHAPTER XI.—(1) I say then, Hath
God cast away his people?
God forbid. For I also
am an Israelite, of the seed
of Abraham, *of* the tribe of

Chap. xi. 1—36. Three trains of reflection on Israel's fall.

(15) The happy consequences of this preaching were already intimated by the prophet Isaiah.

**Preach the gospel of peace.**—These words are omitted in the group of oldest MSS., and should be left out in the text. The whole of the quotation is not given by St. Paul.

(16) Applying this condition of the necessity of preaching to the gospel, we nevertheless see that, as a matter of fact, all did not accept it. Just as Isaiah had said.

The argument does not run quite smoothly. The Apostle has two thoughts in his mind: (1) the necessity that the gospel should be preached before it could be believed; (2) the fact that, although it was preached (and accepted by many among the Gentiles), it was not accepted by the Jews. He begins to introduce this second topic before he has quite done with the first. Verse 17 goes back to and connects logically with verse 15, while verse 16 anticipates verses 19 and 21.

**Our report.**—So Authorised version, rightly. The Greek word means literally, *our hearing.* Here it is, the message preached by us, but heard by those who listened to it.

(17) **So then faith cometh.**—Inference from the prophecy just quoted. Before men can believe, there must be something for them to believe. That something is the word of God, which we preach and they hear. It must be remembered that the word for "report" in verse 16, and for "hearing" in verse 17, is the same, but with a slight difference of meaning. In the first place, both the act of hearer and preacher are involved; in the second place, only the act of the hearer.

**By the word of God.**—We should read here, without doubt, "by the word of *Christ*"—*i.e.*, by the gospel first delivered by Christ and propagated by His ministers.

(18) **Have they not heard?**—The relations of hearing to belief suggest to the Apostle a possible excuse for the Jews, and the excuse he puts forward interrogatively himself: "But, I ask, did they (the Jews) not hear?" Yes, for the gospel was preached to them, as indeed to all mankind.

**Their sound.**—Here, the voice of the preachers; in the original of Ps. xix., the unspoken testimony of the works of nature, and especially the heavenly bodies, to natural religion ("What though no real voice or sound," &c.).

(19) Did not Israel know that the preaching of the gospel would be thus universal, and pass over from them to the Gentiles? Yes, certainly, for Moses had warned them of this.

**First.**—In the order of time and of Scripture.

**I will provoke you.**—In requital for the idolatries of the Jews, Moses prophesied that God would bestow his favour on a Gentile nation, and so provoke their jealousy; and the Apostle sees the fulfilment of this in his own day.

**No people . . . a foolish nation.**—Terms used by the Jews of their Gentile neighbours. They were "no people," because they did not stand in the same recognised relation to God. They were "a foolish nation," because they had not received the same special revelation, but, on the contrary, worshipped stocks and stones.

(20) **Is very bold.**—Comes forward and tells them the naked truth.

**I was found.**—The original of the quotation referred to the apostate Israel; St. Paul here applies it to the Gentiles.

(21) **To Israel.**—With regard to Israel.

**He saith.**—Isaiah, speaking as the mouthpiece of God.

**All day long.**—This quotation is from the next verse to the preceding, and there is no such distinction in the persons to whom it is addressed as the Apostle here draws.

**Gainsaying.**—A people which refused the proffered salvation.

## XI.

The eleventh chapter may be divided into three sections; still dealing with the rejection of Israel, and containing (1) verses 1—10, limitations and qualifications to this; (2) verses 11—24, compensations; (3) verses 25—32, consolations; the whole being closed with a doxology.

(1) **I say then.**—Are we to infer from the language of Isaiah just quoted that God has cast away his people? Far be the thought. The Apostle is himself too closely identified with his countrymen to look upon it with anything but horror.

**I also.**—This appeal to his own descent from Abraham seems to be called forth by the Apostle's patriotic sympathy with his people, and not merely by the thought that he would be included in their rejection. This last explanation, which is that usually given, is less accordant with the generous chivalry of his nature, and does not agree so well with chap. ix. 3.

Chap. xi. 1—10. First reflection: the fall not applicable to all Israel.

Benjamin. (2) God hath not cast away
his people which he fore-
knew. Wot ye not what
the scripture saith of Elias?
how he maketh interces-
sion to God against
Israel, saying, (3) Lord,[a] they have killed
thy prophets, and digged down thine
altars; and I am left alone, and they
seek my life. (4) But what saith the
answer of God unto him? I have
reserved to myself seven thousand men,[b]
who have not bowed the knee to *the
image of* Baal. (5) Even so then at this
present time also there is a remnant
according to the election of grace.
(6) And if by grace, then *is it* no more
of works: otherwise grace is no more
grace. But if *it be* of works, then is it
no more grace: otherwise work is no
more work. (7) What then? Israel
hath not obtained that which he seeketh
for; but the election hath obtained it,
and the rest were blinded[1] (8) (according
as it is written, God[c] hath given them
the spirit of slumber,[2] eyes that they
should not see,[d] and ears that they should
not hear;) unto this day. (9) And
David saith, Let their table be made a
snare,[e] and a trap, and a stumbling-

a 1 Kings 19. 14.
1 Or, *hardened.*
c Isa. 29. 10.
2 Or, *remorse.*
b 1 Kings 19. 18.
d Isa. 6. 9.
e Ps. 69. 22.

---

**Of the tribe of Benjamin.**—And therefore of the purest blood, because the tribes of Judah and Benjamin alone kept up the theocratic continuity of the race after the Exile. (Comp. Phil. iii. 5.)

(2) **Which he foreknew.**—This must not be pressed too far, as implying an absolute indefectibility of the divine favour. God, having in His eternal counsels set His choice upon Israel as His peculiar people, will not readily disown them. Nor is their case really so bad as it may seem. Now, as in the days of Elijah, there are a select few who have not shared in the general depravity.

**Of Elias.**—Literally, *in Elias*—*i.e.*, in the section which contains the history of Elias. So in Mark xii. 26; Luke xx. 37; "in the bush" and "at the bush," mean, in the paragraph relating to the bush.

(3) **I am left alone**—*i.e.*, of the prophets.

(4) **To the image of Baal.**—The name "Baal" is here, as frequently in the LXX., in the feminine gender, and it is to account for this that our translators have inserted the word "image." How the feminine really came to be used is uncertain. Some have thought that the deity was androgynous, others have conjectured that the feminine is used contemptuously. Baal was originally the sun-god. The sun, it may be remembered, is feminine in German and some other languages.

(5, 6) As there was a remnant then, so also is there a remnant now. That there should be so is due not to any human merit on the part of those exempted from the fate of their nation, but to the spontaneous act of the divine grace selecting them from the rest. These two things, "grace" and "works," really exclude each other.

The Apostle reverts somewhat parenthetically, and because his mind is full of the thought, to his idea of chap. ix. 11—16. We have here also a break in the train of argument. After establishing the fact that there *is* this remnant, the Apostle inquires *how* there came to be one. The reason was because the mass of the people trusted to their own works instead of relying upon grace; therefore grace deserted them, and they were left to a judicial blindness.

(6) **And if by grace.**—The true text of this verse differs considerably from that which is translated in the Authorised version, "But if by grace, then is it no more of works, otherwise grace is no more seen to be grace."

The preservation of the remnant cannot be due to grace and works at the same time; it must be due to one or the other.

(7) What is the result? Not only did Israel fail to obtain the salvation which it sought, and which the select few succeeded in obtaining, but it was consigned to a state of complete spiritual apathy and torpor, and its very blessings became a curse and a snare.

**Were blinded.**—An erroneous translation, arising from a confusion of two similar words. The correct rendering, "were hardened," is given in the margin. So, too, "were blinded," in 2 Cor. iii. 14, and "blindness," in verse 25 of this chapter and Eph. iv. 18, should be changed to "were hardened," "hardness." The corresponding words in the Gospels are rightly translated. The term is one used in medicine for the forming of chalkstone, &c.

(8) **The spirit of slumber.**—This phrase, again, has a curious history. Etymologically, the word translated "slumber" would seem to agree better with the marginal rendering, "remorse." It comes from a root meaning to "prick or cut with a sharp instrument." There happens to be another root somewhat similar, but certainly not connected, which means "drowsiness," "slumber." Hence, where the word in the text has been used to render the Hebrew word for "slumber," it has been thought that there was a confusion between the two. It appears, however, from the LXX. usage, that the sense of "slumber" had certainly come to attach to the word here used by St. Paul. From the notion of a sharp wound or blow came to be derived that of the bewilderment or stupefaction consequent upon such a blow, and hence it came to signify stupor in general.

The quotation is a free combination of two passages of the LXX. (Isa. xxix. 10, and Deut. xxix. 4), no doubt put together by the Apostle from memory.

(9) **And David saith.**—It appears highly improbable that this Psalm was really written by David. Nor can the Davidic authorship be argued strongly from this passage, as "David" merely seems to stand for the Book of Psalms, with which his name was traditionally connected.

St. Paul is quoting freely from the LXX. In the original of Ps. lxix. these verses refer to the fate invoked by the psalmist upon his persecutors; here they are applied by St. Paul to the fiat of the Almighty which had been pronounced against the unbelieving people of Israel.

**Let their table . . .**—In the very moment of their feasting, let them be caught in a stratagem of their enemies.

block, and a recompence unto them:
(10) let their eyes be darkened,[a] that they
may not see, and bow down their back
alway. (11) I say then, Have they
stumbled that they should
fall? God forbid: but *rather*
through their fall salvation
*is come* unto the Gentiles,
for to provoke them to jeal-
ousy. (12) Now if the fall of them *be*
the riches of the world, and the diminish-
ing[b] of them the riches of the Gentiles;
how much more their fulness? (13) For
I speak to you Gentiles, inasmuch as I
am the apostle of the Gentiles, I mag-
nify mine office: (14) if by any means I
may provoke to emulation *them which*
*are* my flesh, and might save some of
them. (15) For if the casting away of
them *be* the reconciling of the world,
what *shall* the receiving *of them be*, but
life from the dead? (16) For if the first-
fruit *be* holy, the lump *is* also *holy*: and
if the root *be* holy, so *are* the branches.

Chap. xi. 11—24. Second reflection: special purpose of the fall.

[a] Ps. 69. 23.

[b] Or, *decay*, or, *loss*.

---

**And a trap.**—These words are not found either in the Hebrew or in the LXX., and appear to be added by St. Paul. Translate rather, *Let them be for a chase—i.e.,* instead of feasting, let them be hunted and persecuted.

**And a recompence unto them.**—Similarly the LXX. The Hebrew is, "When they are in peace, let it be a trap" ("that which should have been for their welfare, let it become a trap"—A.V.)—*i.e.,* when they are eating and drinking securely, let them be caught as in a trap; let their security itself deceive them. By "recompence unto them" the Apostle means, Let their prosperity bring upon them retaliation for what they have done—namely, for their rejection of Christ.

(10) **Let their eyes be darkened.**—In the Apostle's sense, "Let them be spiritually blinded, incapable of discerning or receiving the truth, and let their backs be bowed with the yoke of spiritual thraldom!" The Hebrew is, "Let their eyes be darkened, that they see not, and make their loins continually to shake." On which Perowne remarks: "The darkening of the eyes denotes weakness and perplexity, as the enlightening of the eyes denotes renewed vigour and strength. Similarly, the shaking of the loins is expressive of terror and dismay and feebleness."

(11—24) In this section the Apostle goes on to consider further the bearings of the rejection, and here, first (verses 11—16), he considers the more hopeful side of it as regards the Jews themselves; their fall was not to be final, and there was every reason to think that their reconversion would more than make up for their fall; secondly (verses 17—24), he turns to the Gentiles and bids them remember how it was that they came to be inserted like a graft in the true theocratic stem, and warns them not to make use of their new privilege to boast against those who were refused to make way for them.

(11) The Jews did, indeed, stumble at the stumbling-block mentioned in chap. ix. 32—33. Many were offended at Christ. But did their stumbling involve their utter and final ruin? It had a far more beneficent purpose than that. It brought salvation to the Gentiles, and it did this only to react as an incentive upon the Jews.

**For to provoke them to jealousy.**—The reason why salvation had been extended to the Gentiles was to stir up them (the Jews) to emulation. Their privileges had made them negligent and apathetic. The sight of others stepping into those privileges was to rouse them from their apathy

(12) And if the fall of the Jews had such good results, much more might be expected from their reinstatement.

**Diminishing . . . fulness.**—It is, perhaps, difficult to suggest a better translation. The Apostle seems to have in view not only the supersession of the Jews by the Gentiles, but also, under the figure of a defeat in battle, the reduction of their numbers to a small remnant. And, on the other hand, he looks forward to their full and complete restoration, when every Jew shall be a member of the Messianic kingdom, and there shall not be one missing. The full "complement," as it were, of the nation is what is meant by "fulness;" its temporary reduction and degradation is expressed by "diminishing."

(13—16) In this I am speaking to you Gentiles. It is you who will benefit by the restoration of the Jews. And this is the real reason why, as Apostle of the Gentiles, I make the most of my office. I do it in order to incite to emulation my own countrymen, knowing that the effects of their rejection lead us to infer the very happiest effects from their readmission. For their end will be as their beginning was. They began their career as the chosen people of God, and the conclusion of it will be still more glorious.

(13) **For I speak to you Gentiles.**—The connecting particles in this verse must be altered according to an amended reading. "For" should be omitted, a full stop placed after "Gentiles," and "then" inserted after "inasmuch." "I speak to you Gentiles"—spoken with something of a pause. "Inasmuch then" (or, *in so far then*) "as I am the Apostle of the Gentiles, I seek to do honour to my office. But not without an *arrière-pensée.* My motive is at least partly to win over my own countrymen."

(15) **Reconciling of the world.**—The gospel could not be preached to the Gentiles until it had first been offered to and rejected by the Jews. Hence the casting away of the Jews might be said to have caused the reconciling of the rest of the world.

**Life from the dead.**—The reconversion of the Jews will be a signal to inaugurate that reign of eternal life which will be ushered in by the resurrection from the dead.

(16) And we have the strongest reason for believing in this reconversion of the Jews. Their forefathers were the first recipients of the promise, and what they were it is only natural to hope that their descendants will be. When a piece of dough is taken from the lump to make a consecrated cake, the consecration of the part extends over the whole; and the character

Chap. xi. 17—24. The engrafted and the original branches.

(17) And if some of the branches be
broken off, and thou, being
a wild olive tree, wert
graffed in among them, and
with them partakest of the
root and fatness of the olive tree; (18) boast
not against the branches. But if thou
boast, thou bearest not the root, but
the root thee. (19) Thou wilt say then,
The branches were broken off, that I
might be graffed in. (20) Well; because
of unbelief they were broken off, and
thou standest by faith. Be not high-
minded, but fear: (21) for if God spared
not the natural branches, *take heed* lest
he also spare not thee. (22) Behold
therefore the goodness and severity of
God: on them which fell, severity; but
toward thee, goodness, if thou continue
in *his* goodness: otherwise thou also
shalt be cut off. (23) And they also, if
they abide not still in unbelief, shall be
graffed in: for God is able to graff them
in again. (24) For if thou wert cut out
of the olive tree which is wild by nature,
and wert graffed contrary to nature into
a good olive tree: how much more shall
these, which be the natural *branches*, be
graffed into their own olive tree? (25)

Chap. xi. 25—32. Third reflection: Israel's restoration.

For I would not, brethren,
that ye should be ignorant
of this mystery, lest ye
should be wise in your own
conceits; that blindness[1] in part is

[1] Or, *hardness.*

---

which is inherent in the root of a tree shows itself also in the branches. So we may believe that the latter end of Israel will be like its beginning. The consecration that was imparted to it in the founders of the race we may expect to see resumed by their descendants, even though it is for a time interrupted.

**The firstfruit . . . the lump.**—The allusion here is to the custom, described in Num. xv. 19—21, of dedicating a portion of the dough to God. The portion thus taken was to be a "heave-offering"—*i.e.*, it was to be "waved," or "heaved," before the Lord, and was then given to the priest.

(17–24) The admission of the Gentile to the privileges of the Jew is no ground for boasting on his part. It is merely an *admission.* The Gentile is, as it were, a branch grafted into a stem that was none of his planting. Nor is his position absolutely secured to him. It is held conditionally on the tenure of faith. He ought, therefore, anxiously to guard against any failure in faith. For the moment God has turned towards him the gracious side of His providence, as towards the Jew He has turned the severe side. But this relation may easily be reversed, and the Jew received back into the favour which he once enjoyed.

(17) **And.**—Rather, *but.*

**Among them**—*i.e.*, among the branches of the olive-tree generally, both those which are broken off and those which are suffered to remain. This seems on the whole the more probable view; it would be possible to translate the words, *in place of them* (the branches broken off).

**Partakest of the root and fatness.**—The meaning of this is sufficiently obvious as it stands. If, as perhaps is probable, we ought to drop the second "and," reading, "of the root of the fatness," the sense is that the rich flow of sap in which the wild olive partakes does not belong to the wild olive itself, but is all drawn from the root.

The evidence for the omission of the second "and" is that of the Vatican, Sinaitic, and rescript Paris manuscript—a strong combination.

(18) **Thou bearest not the root.**—There can be no boasting, for the privileges which the Gentiles possess are derived, and not original.

(19, 20) It might be possible for the Gentile to claim a special providence in his substitution for the Jew. He should rather be reminded that there is a condition—faith—which is attached to this substitution; this he must be careful to observe, or else he will lose all that he has gained.

(21) **Take heed lest . . .**—The better reading seems to be to omit these words, *neither will He spare thee.*

(22) As Providence had been appealed to, the Apostle states the true Providential aspect of God's rejection of Israel. It had a double side—one of goodness towards the Gentile, one of deserved severity towards the Jew. But, at the same time, the fact that the covenant was made originally with the Jew, and that he was the natural heir to the promises which it contained, is a guarantee for his restoration if he would only dismiss his unbelief.

(25–32) There was a deep meaning underlying the temporary rejection of Israel, of which he has been speaking—a meaning which has hitherto been kept secret, but now to be revealed as a corrective to any possible pride on the part of the Gentiles.

(25) **Mystery.**—The word always means throughout St. Paul's writings something which, though not to be known or fully comprehended by unassisted human reason, has been made known by direct divine revelation. It is therefore not to be taken in this passage in its usual sense, of something hidden and concealed from all except a few, but rather of all such truths as though previously hidden, had been made manifest by the gospel.

It is thus applied to the whole or any part of the Christian system. To the whole, as in chap. xvi. 25; 1 Cor. ii. 7—10; Eph. i. 9; vi. 19; Col. i. 26, 27; ii. 2; 1 Tim. iii. 9, 16. To any part, as (*a*) the admission of the Gentiles, Eph. iii. 3 *et seq.*, and partly here; (*b*) the mystical union of Christ and His Church which is typified in marriage, Eph. v. 32; (*c*) the transformation of the "quick" at the resurrection, 1 Cor. xv. 51; and (*d*) the opposition of Antichrist to the gospel, 2 Thess. ii. 7.

Here the reference is to the whole of the divine purpose as shown in the dealings with Jew and Gentile, and especially in the present exclusion and future

happened to Israel, until the fulness of
the Gentiles be come in. (26) And so all
Israel shall be saved: as it is written,
There shall come out of Sion the Deliverer,[a] and shall turn away ungodliness from Jacob: (27) for this *is* my
covenant unto them, when I shall take
away their sins. (28) As concerning the
gospel, *they are* enemies for your sakes:
but as touching the election, *they are*
beloved for the fathers' sakes. (29) For
the gifts and calling of God *are* without
repentance. (30) For as ye in times past
have not believed[1] God, yet have now
obtained mercy through their unbelief:
(31) even so have these also now not
believed,[2] that through your mercy they
also may obtain mercy. (32) For God
hath concluded[3] them all in unbelief,
that he might have mercy upon all.
(33) O the depth of the riches both of
the wisdom and knowledge of God! how unsearchable *are* his judgments, and his
ways past finding out! (34) For who
hath known the mind of the Lord?[b] or
who hath been his counsellor? (35) or
who hath first given to him, and it shall

Chap. xi. 33—36. Doxology.

2 Or, *obeyed.*

3 Or *shut them all up together.*

a Isa. 28: 9; and 59. 20.

b Isa. 40. 13; 1 Cor. 2. 16; Wisd. 9. 13.

1 Or, *obeyed.*

---

re-admission of the former. This last point the Apostle goes on to prove.

**Blindness.**—Rather, as in the margin, *hardness*, a hardening of the heart so that the gospel could not find entrance into it.

**In part.**—These words qualify "Israel." The hardness extends over some, but not over all. There were Jewish as well as Gentile converts in Rome itself.

**The fulness of the Gentiles.**—As above, *the complete number; the full complement of the Gentiles.*

(26) When this ingathering of the Gentiles is complete, then the turn of Israel will come round again, and the prophecies of their conversion will be fulfilled.

**There shall come . . .**—This prophecy is peculiarly appropriate, as it refers to the exiles who had apostatised in Babylon. Then, as now, a part of the nation had remained true, and those who had not would come back to their obedience.

**Out of Sion.**—There is a curious variation here from the original, which is rather, *to Sion.* The LXX. has "for Sion"—*i.e.*, in the cause of Sion. The Apostle appears to be quoting from memory, and is influenced by a reminiscence of other passages. Zion is the centre and capital of the theocracy, but the Messiah must first take up His abode there before He can issue from it.

(27) The second part of the quotation, "For (rather, *and*), this is my covenant with them," &c., appears to be taken from the LXX. version of Isa. xxvii. 9. The connecting-links between the two are the removing of transgression from Jacob, and the form of the phrase, "This is my covenant with them." ("This is his blessing," Isa. xxvii. 9, LXX.)

(28) The real position of the Jews is this: They have been suffered to fall into a state of estrangement in order to make room for the Gentiles. But this does not abrogate God's original choice of them. They are still His beloved people, for the sake of their forefathers, the patriarchs, if not for their own.

(29) **Without repentance.**—Not to be revoked or withdrawn, not even to be regretted.

(30, 31) **Have not believed . . . unbelief . . . not believed . . .**—Rather, *disobeyed . . disobedience . . disobeyed.*

(31) **Through your mercy**—*i.e.*, through the mercy vouchsafed to you. The sight of the admission of the Gentiles is to act as a stimulus upon the Jews, and so lead to a renewal of their faith and obedience.

(32) Unhappy as the fate of the world might seem, first the Gentiles and then the Jews being consigned to a state of disobedience, this has really had a merciful object in the end. It will lead to a happy and complete reunion, "one flock under one shepherd."

**For God hath concluded them all in unbelief.**—A weighty sentence embracing the whole course of human history, and summing up the divine philosophy of the whole matter. We might almost take these profound words of St. Paul as a motto for the theological side of the theory of evolution. Severe and rigorous as that doctrine may seem, its goal is *perfection*, the absolute harmony of all things working in accordance with the divine will. And if an objection is taken on the ground of the waste of individual life, this may be subject to we know not what beneficent rectifications in a sphere removed from that of the senses. We are able to see only a "part of God's ways," and the drift and tendency of visible things makes it not difficult for us to believe that "all things work together for good," even where the process by which they do so is not to be traced by the human eye.

(33–36) This grand and comprehensive view of the divine purposes makes so deep an impression upon the Apostle that he breaks out into an impassioned ascription of praise, with which the first (doctrinal) portion of the Epistle is brought to a close.

(33) **Riches.**—The two substantives which follow may be taken as dependent upon "riches." This is the construction adopted in the Authorised version, and is expressed by the use of the word "both." Or all three substantives may be independent, *O the depth of the riches, and of the wisdom and knowledge of God!* In either case, "riches" means "inexhaustible resources," implying either that the wisdom and knowledge of God are inexhaustible, or that the materials at their command are inexhaustible. By means of these infinite resources God is able to bring good even out of evil.

**Judgments.**—*Decisions*, such as that by which Israel was excluded and the Gentiles admitted.

(34) **For who hath known the mind of the Lord?**—The two clauses in this verse are illustrative of the wisdom and knowledge of God, just as the next verse is illustrative of His "riches."

(35) The depth of God's knowledge none can penetrate, and the counsels of His wisdom admit of no assessor. The means by which God works are not

be recompensed unto him again? (36) For
of him, and through him, and to him,
*are* all things; to whom *be* glory for ever.
Amen.

CHAPTER XII.—(1) I beseech you
therefore, brethren, by the mercies of
God, that ye present your bodies a
living sacrifice, holy, acceptable unto
God, *which is* your reasonable service.
(2) And be not conformed to this world:
but be ye transformed by the renewing
of your mind, that ye may prove what
*is* that good, and acceptable, and perfect,

A.D. 58.

supplied to Him from without, but proceed from the boundless stores of His omnipotence.

(36) **Of him, and through him, and to him.**—All things proceed from God, all things are made or wrought by Him, and all things exist for His glory, and to carry out His ends. It is a mistake to see in this, as some of the older commentators have done, an allusion to the Trinity. This can hardly be. The subject of the whole verse appears to be God the Father, and the prominent idea is rather the unity of creation corresponding to the unity of the Godhead. The whole system of things issues from and returns to Him, accomplishing in its course His beneficent designs. It is true, however, that the use of the prepositions is such as in more analytical passages would be taken to express the threefold relation (origination, mediate causation, and retrocession) which the doctrine of the Trinity embodies.

XII.

(1) At this point the Apostle turns from the speculative, or doctrinal, portion of his Epistle, and begins a series of practical exhortations to his readers as to their lives as Christians. In the first two verses of the chapter he speaks of this in general terms, but then goes on to give a number of special precepts in no very distinct arrangement or order.

**Therefore.**—We may well believe that the Apostle having brought his argument up to a climax at the close of the last chapter, would make a pause in his dictation, and perhaps not resume it until another sitting. The one prevailing impression left on his mind, both by the argument just ended and by the whole previous portion of the Epistle, is a profound sense of the merciful and benevolent purposes of God, who, out of seeming evil, only educes the highest good. This sense is still strong upon him, and he makes it the link of transition by which the earnest practical exhortations which follow are bound to what precedes. The sequence is as much one of feeling as of ratiocination.

**Your bodies.**—Not merely a periphrasis for "yourselves," but in the strict sense "your bodies," *i.e.*, the very part of you which is apt to be "an occasion of falling." The Apostle takes the two main parts of human nature separately. In this verse he deals with the bodies of men, in the next verse with the "mind," or the intellectual and spiritual faculties.

**A living sacrifice.**—"How is the body to become a sacrifice? Let thine eye look upon no evil thing, and it hath become a sacrifice; let thy tongue speak nothing filthy, and it hath become an offering; let thy hand do no lawless deed, and it hath become a whole burnt offering. But this is not enough, we must do good works also; let the hand do alms, the mouth bless them that despitefully use us, and the ear find leisure evermore for the hearing of Scripture. For sacrifice can be made only of that which is clean; sacrifice is a firstfruit of other actions. Let us, then, from our hands, and feet, and mouth, and all our other members, yield a firstfruit unto God" (St. Chrysostom).

The idea contained in sacrifice is that of dedication. We are to *dedicate* our bodies to God. But there is to be this distinction between the old Jewish sacrifices and the Christian sacrifice: the one was of dead animals, the other of the living man. The worshipper must offer, or present, before God, *himself*, with all his living energies and powers directed consciously to God's service.

**Holy, acceptable unto God.**—The qualification sought for in the Jewish sacrifices was that they were to be unblemished, without spot. In like manner the Christian's sacrifice must be holy and pure in God's sight, otherwise it cannot be acceptable to Him.

**Reasonable service.**—The English phrase is somewhat ambiguous. It might mean "a service *demanded* by reason." Such, however is not the sense of the Greek, but rather "a service *of* the reason," *i.e.*, a service *rendered* by the reason. Just as under the old dispensation the mind expressed its devotion through the ritual of sacrifice, so now under the new dispensation its worship takes the form of a self-dedication; its service consists in holiness of life, temperance, soberness, and chastity.

(2) **Be not conformed . . . but be ye transformed.**—Here the English is somewhat misleading. It would naturally lead us to expect a similar play upon words in the Greek. But it is not so; indeed, there is a clear distinction between the two different words employed. It is the difference between an outward conformity or disguise and a thorough inward assimilation. The Christian is not to copy the fleeting fashions of the present time, but to be wholly transfigured in view of that higher mode of existence, in strict accordance with God's will, that he has chosen.

**This world.**—Not here the same word as that which is used, *e.g.*, in 1 John ii. 15—17, but another, which signifies rather the state of the world as it existed at the Coming of Christ, as opposed to the newly-inaugurated Messianic reign. "To be conformed to this world" is to act as other men do, heathen who know not God; in opposition to this the Apostle exhorts his readers to undergo that total change which will bring them more into accordance with the will of God.

**By the renewing of your mind.**—"The mind" (*i.e.*, the mental faculties, reason, or understanding) is in itself neutral. When informed by an evil principle, it becomes an instrument of evil; when informed by the Spirit, it is an instrument of good. It performs the process of discrimination between good and evil, and so supplies the *data* to conscience. "The mind" here is not strictly identical with what we now mean by "conscience;" it is, as it were, the rational part of conscience, to which the moral quality needs to be superadded. The "*renewed* mind," or the mind acting under the influence of the Spirit, comes very near to "conscience" in the sense in which the word is used by Bishop Butler.

will of God. (3) For I say, through the
grace given unto me, to every man that
is among you, not to think *of himself*
more highly than he ought to think;
but to think soberly,[1] according as God
hath dealt to every man the measure of
faith. (4) For as we have many mem-
bers in one body, and all members have
not the same office: (5) so we, *being*
many, are one body in Christ, and every
one members one of another. (6) Having
then gifts differing according to the
grace that is given to us, whether pro-
phecy, *let us prophesy* according to the
proportion of faith; (7) or ministry, *let*
*us wait* on *our* ministering: or he that

[1] Gr. *to sobriety.*

---

**Prove.**—As elsewhere, "discriminate, and so approve." The double process is included: first, of deciding what the will of God is; and, secondly, of choosing and acting upon it.

**What is that good, and acceptable, and perfect, will of God.**—The "will of God" is here, not the divine attribute of will, but the thing willed by God, the right course of action. Are we to take the adjectives "good, and acceptable, and perfect" (with the Authorised version), as in agreement with this phrase, or are they rather in apposition to it, "that we may prove the will of God, that which is good, and acceptable, and perfect"? Most of the commentators prefer this latter way of taking the passage, but it is not quite clear that the former is impossible, "that good, and acceptable, and perfect thing, or course of action which God wills." "Acceptable," that is to say, to God Himself.

(3) Having thus stated the broad principle which is to govern the conduct of the Christian, the Apostle now goes on to apply it to certain details, and, first, his object is to secure that temper in the members of the Roman Church which will best enable them to act with union and efficiency.

**Through the grace given unto me**—*i.e.*, in virtue of his apostolic authority.

**To every man that is among you.**—A rather more pointed expression than simply "to you all," "to each one of you severally and individually."

**Not to think of himself . . .**—There is a play upon words in this phrase, and those which follow, which is not preserved, and can hardly be preserved, in the English. "Not to be high-minded beyond that which he ought to be minded, but to be minded unto sober-mindedness." Our words, "to be minded," "high-minded," &c., very nearly express the sense of the Greek, which is to have the thoughts and feelings habitually turned in a certain direction. This is brought out with emphatic repetition in the phrase "to be minded unto the being sober-minded," *i.e.*, to keep sobriety of mind constantly in view as the object or ideal towards which all the thoughts and feelings converge.

**According as God hath dealt to every man.**—The standard of action which each Christian ought to propose to himself should be in proportion to the amount of his faith as given to him by God. He who has the strongest faith may assume the highest standard, and offer himself for the highest offices, and so on down the scale. It is, however, essential that the estimate which each man puts upon the strength of his own faith, should be thoroughly single-minded and sincere. nor biassed by self-love. The Apostle assumes that this will be the case.

(4, 5) In the church there must be a graduation, a hierarchy, a division of labour, every one doing that for which he is best fitted, just as in the body one member has one office assigned to it, and another another. All Christians, viewed collectively, make up one body, the unity of which is supplied by their relation to Christ. Viewed individually, they stand to each other in the same sort of relation as the different limbs and organs of the natural body, as foot and hand, or hand and eye.

(4) **Members in one body.**—This figure of the body and the members is worked out more fully in 1 Cor. xii. 12—27.

(5) **In Christ.**—Christ is the unifying principle in the Church, just as the personality or will is the unifying principle in man.

**Every one.**—A somewhat peculiar phrase in the Greek, not found in this form in classical writers, meaning "as individuals."

**Members one of another.**—Strictly speaking, the members are called members in their relation to the body, and not in their relation to each other. We should say, rather, "fellow-members with one another."

(6) **Gifts differing according to the grace.**—The English loses a point here. The word translated "gifts" means specially "gifts of grace," grace standing here for the operation of the Spirit. Different kinds of grace, with different forms of expression, are given to different individuals, and they are to be cherished and used accordingly.

**Prophecy.**—The gift of prophecy is treated at length in 1 Cor. xiv. From the detailed description there given, we gather that it was a kind of powerful and inspired preaching which, unlike the gift of tongues, was strictly within the control of the person who possessed it. What precise relation this bore to the prediction of future events, mentioned in Acts xi. 27, 28; xxi. 10, 11, does not appear.

**According to the proportion of faith.**—It seems best to take this, not as having reference to the objective rule of faith or doctrine, the due proportions of which are to be preserved, but rather of the active faculty of faith present in him who prophesies. It would then be very nearly equivalent to the condition above—"according as God hath dealt to every man the measure of faith." The prophet is to let his utterances be regulated strictly by the degree of faith of which he is conscious in himself. The inward inspiration and the outward deliverance must keep pace, and advance step by step together. Preaching in which this proportion is not observed is sure to become rhetorical and insincere.

(7) **Ministry.**—The word used is the technical term for the discharge of the office of deacon. The institution of this office is described in Acts vi. 1—5. Its object was to provide for the practical business as opposed to the spiritual ministrations of the Church. It included more especially the distribution of alms and the care of the poor, the sick, widows, etc. The functions of the diaconate are called "serving tables" (*i.e.*, in the literal sense, "providing food" for those

teacheth, on teaching; (8) or he that
exhorteth, on exhortation: he that
giveth,[1] *let him do it* with simplicity;[2]
he that ruleth, with diligence; he that
sheweth mercy, with cheerfulness. (9) *Let*
love be without dissimulation. Abhor
that which is evil; cleave to that which
is good. (10) *Be* kindly affectioned one
to another with brotherly love;[3] in
honour preferring one another; (11) not
slothful in business; fervent in spirit;
serving the Lord; (12) rejoicing in hope;
patient in tribulation; continuing in-
stant in prayer; (13) distributing to the
necessity of saints; given to hospitality.
(14) Bless them which persecute you:

3 Or, *in the love of the brethren.*

1 Or, *imparteth.*
2 Or, *liberally.*

who needed it) in Acts vi. 2, 3, and "helps" in 1 Cor. xii. 28.

**Let us wait on . . .**—These words are supplied in the English, "Let us be absorbed in, devoted to, our ministering."

**He that teacheth.**—Comp. 1 Cor. xii. 28; Eph. ix. 11; 1 Tim. v. 17. It would seem from the first of these passages ("thirdly teachers") that teaching was considered as a special office, though not, perhaps, confined to special persons.

(8) **He that exhorteth.**—It will be observed that in the apostolic writings, the one idea of "preaching" is divided into its several branches, "speaking with tongues," "prophesying" (which appears to have had reference to the more recondite portions or relations of the faith), "teaching," "exhortation." This last form of address, corresponding perhaps rather to our word "encouragement," would be especially needed in the troubled circumstances of the early Church.

**He that giveth.**—In this and the following phrases the Apostle passes on from considering the definite functions of the ministry to those which were common to all members of the Church; "giveth" is therefore here to be taken in a wide sense.

**Simplicity.**—With singleness of motive, desiring only God's glory, and to benefit the object for which he gives, and with no secret thought of self-exaltation. He who gives "to be seen of men," or with any selfish motive, exhausts thereby the merit of the act, see Matt. vi. 2 *et seq.*

**He that ruleth.**—He who holds any position of prominence or importance in the Church. The same word is applied to "presbyters" in 1 Thess. v. 12; 1 Tim. v. 17; and to heads of families in 1 Tim. iii. 4, 5, 12.

**He that sheweth mercy, with cheerfulness.**—A happy combination which is an instance of the Apostle's fresh and genuine view of human nature. The kindness of charity is doubled when it is done in a cheerful and kindly way. There is a class of religious minds which is especially apt to forget this. Cheerfulness is not merely a matter of temperament, but to be cultivated as a duty.

(9—21) Now follow to the end of the chapter a number of general exhortations, not addressed to particular persons or classes, but to the Church at large.

(9) **Without dissimulation.**—The same Greek word is translated "unfeigned" in 2 Cor. vi. 6; 1 Tim. i. 5; 2 Tim. i. 5, and "without hypocrisy" in Jas. iii. 17. This last is the most literal rendering, and brings out the resemblance to Matt. xxiii. 13, *et al.*

**Abhor that which is evil.**—This clause seems linked on to the last through the word "without hypocrisy": "Let your love arise from genuine and deep emotion; let the basis of your character be an intense hatred of evil and as strong an adhesion to good." The Apostle does not here enter into the more difficult question as to how those in whom these emotions are naturally weak are to strengthen them. Perhaps no shorter advice is to be given than "become Christians."

(10) **With brotherly love.**—Better translated as in the margin, *In love of the brethren* (fellow Christians) *be kindly affectioned.* The word for "kindly affectioned" is specially used of the family relation, and is, therefore, appropriately applied to the brotherhood of the Christian family.

**Preferring one another.**—Rather, perhaps, *anticipating one another.* The Christian is to take the initiative, and show honour or respect to others without waiting for them to show it to him.

(11) **In business.**—Rather, *in zeal;* the reference is to the spiritual and not to the practical life, as the English reader might suppose.

**Fervent.**—In the literal and etymological sense *boiling* or *seething.* The temperament of the Christian is compared to water bubbling and boiling over the flame.

**In spirit**—*i.e.,* not "in the Holy Spirit," but "in that part of you which is spirit."

**Serving the Lord.**—Some of the extant Græco-Latin codices, and others known to Origen and Jerome, read here by a slight change of vowels "serving the time"; no doubt wrongly, though the expression might be compared with 1 Cor. vii. 29; Eph. v. 16, *et al.*

(12) **In hope.**—The Christian's hope, of which we have had more in chap. viii. 20—25.

**Patient in tribulation.**—This virtue was, of course, specially needed in the troublous times through which the Church was passing. So, again, in the next verse, the "hospitality" of which the Apostle speaks is something more than the ordinary entertainment of friends. The reference is to a state of things in which the Christian was liable to be persecuted and driven from city to city, and often compelled to seek for shelter with those who held the same faith as himself.

(13) **Distributing to the necessity of saints.**—By "saints" is here meant simply "Christians." So, in Eph. i. 1, we find the salutation addressed to the "saints which are at Ephesus." (Comp. Acts ix. 13; xxvi. 10.) The reference is to the well-known poverty of the early Christian communities.

**Necessity.**—Some of the Græco-Latin manuscripts and fathers here read, *memories,* or *commemorations,* by a slight change of letters, "taking part in the commemorations of the saints," as if the allusion was to the later ecclesiastical usage of holding festivals in honour of martyrs. The best manuscripts are wonderfully free from corruptions of this kind, and even inferior manuscripts admit them to a much smaller extent than might have been expected. Other examples would be the insertion of the phrase "and fasting" in Mark ix. 29, and the addition of the doxology to the Lord's prayer in Matt. vi. 13.

(14) **Bless them which persecute you.**—Apparently with allusion to Matt. v. 44. It was probably just about the time that St. Paul was writing this Epistle, or at most a year or two later, that the

bless, and curse not. (15) Rejoice with
them that do rejoice, and weep with
them that weep. (16) *Be* of the same
mind one toward another. Mind not
high things, but condescend to men of
low estate.[1] Be not wise in your own
conceits. (17) Recompense to no man
evil for evil. Provide things honest in
the sight of all men. (18) If it be pos-
sible, as much as lieth in you, live
peaceably with all men. (19) Dearly
beloved, avenge not yourselves, but
*rather* give place unto wrath: for it is
written, Vengeance *is* mine;[a] I will
repay, saith the Lord. (20) Therefore if
thine enemy hunger, feed him;[b] if he
thirst, give him drink: for in so doing
thou shalt heap coals of fire on his head.
(21) Be not overcome of evil, but over-
come evil with good.

a Deut. 32. 35.

b Prov. 25. 21.

1 Or, *be contented with mean things.*

A.D. 58.

CHAPTER XIII.—(1) Let every soul
be subject unto the higher powers. For
there is no power but of God: the powers

---

series of compositions which ultimately took the shape of our present Gospels began. It is not, however, necessary to suppose that St. Paul had actually seen one of these. The record of our Lord's teaching was no doubt at first preserved and circulated in the Church orally, and it would be in this form that St. Paul first became acquainted with the precept to which he here seems to allude. There is, perhaps, another reference to the Sermon on the Mount in I Cor. vii. 10. Such references occur (as we should expect) more frequently in the Epistle of St. James.

(15) **Rejoice with them that do rejoice.**—The feeling of sympathy is perhaps more under the control of the will than might be supposed. It becomes so, however, not so much by isolated efforts as by a conscious direction given to the whole life. The injunction in this verse is one of those that have been perhaps most fully carried out in modern times. It has entered into the social code, and belongs as much to the gentleman as the Christian. The danger, therefore, is that the expression of sympathy should be unreal and insincere. This will be prevented by the presence of the Christian motive.

(16) **Be of the same mind . . .**—In every Christian community there should be that harmony which proceeds from a common object, common hopes, common desires.

**Condescend to men of low estate.**—Probably, on the whole, rightly translated in our version; "Let yourselves be carried on in the stream with those who are beneath yourselves in rank and station; mix with them freely; be ready to lend them a helping hand if ever they need, and do this in a simple and kindly way; do not let any social assumptions keep you at a distance." "Accommodate yourselves," or "condescend"—of course without any conscious idea or appearance of condescension. Another rendering would be "condescend to lowly things," in which case the sense would be nearly equivalent to that of Keble's well-known and beautiful lines—

"The trivial round, the common task,
Will furnish all we ought to ask;
Room to deny ourselves, a road
To bring us daily nearer God."

The scholar will observe that in this way of taking the passage, the Greek word for "condescend" (*sunapagomenoi*) has to be a little forced, or at least is not so expressive and natural as in the other. On the other hand, in the Epistles of a writer like St. Paul, it does not by any means follow that because the word for "high" is neuter that for "low estate" must be neuter too.

**Be not wise in your own conceits.**—Comp. chap. xi. 25, and Prov. iii. 7. Humility is necessary to the Christian not only in his dealings with others, but also to keep his mind open and teachable. He sees his errors, and learns from them.

(17) **Provide things honest . . .**—Let your purposes be such that all men shall recognise their complete integrity. Do not engage in enterprises of a doubtful character, that might bring not only yourselves but the Christian body into ill repute. (Comp. Matt. v. 14—16; 2 Cor. viii. 21.)

(18) The Christian can only be responsible for himself. So far as he is concerned, he is to do his best to maintain peace. The history of St. Paul himself, which is one of almost constant conflict, shows that this would not always be possible.

(19) **Give place unto wrath.**—It seems best to understand this of "the wrath of God" (indicated in the Greek, here as elsewhere, by the use of the article). Stand aside yourself as a mere spectator, and let the wrath of God have free course to accomplish itself as He shall think well. The other most plausible interpretation would be, "Give room to the wrath of your adversary; let it spend itself; resist not evil," etc., as in Matt. v. 39. The sense, "Allow time for your own anger to cool," cannot be got out of the Greek. The view first stated is to be preferred.

**Vengeance is mine; I will repay.**—The form of this quotation, which differs both from the LXX. and from the Hebrew, is precisely similar to that in Heb. x. 30. This should be noted as a point of resemblance between St. Paul and the author of that Epistle, but its strength as an argument for the identity of the two is much diminished by the fact that other marked coincidences are found in the literature of this age, which seem to point to the conclusion that forms of text were current (perhaps confined to a few familiar quotations) of which no direct representations have come down to us.

(20) **Thou shalt heap coals of fire.**—Comp. Ps. xviii. 12, 13, 14, where the phrase "coals of fire" is used of the divine vengeance. So here, but in a strictly metaphorical sense, it means, "Thou shalt take the best and most summary vengeance upon him." There may be the underlying idea of awakening in the adversary the pangs of shame and remorse.

(21) **Be not overcome of evil, but . . .**—A fine sentiment. The infliction of vengeance is not a sign of strength, but of weakness. To repress the desire for revenge is to gain a victory over self, which is not only nobler in itself, but will also be much more effectual. It will disarm the enemy, and turn him into a friend.

## XIII.

(1—7) **Subject unto the higher powers.**—Looking impartially at the passage which follows, it would seem at first sight—and perhaps not only at first sight—that the Apostle distinctly preaches two doctrines, both of which are now discredited, the doctrines of divine right and of passive obedience. The duty of obedience is grounded upon the fact that the power wielded by the magistrate is derived from God, and that duty itself is stated without qualification.

What are we to understand by this? Are we to say, for instance, that Hampden was wrong in refusing the payment of ship-money? Or if he was not wrong—and the verdict of mankind has generally justified his act—what are we to think of the language that is here used by St. Paul?

1. In the first place it should be noticed that though the duty of obedience is here stated without qualification, still the existence of qualifications to it is not therefore denied or excluded. Tribute is to be paid to whom tribute is due. But this still leaves the question open, whether in any particular case tribute is rightfully due or not. There may possibly be a conflict of rights and duties, and the lower may have to yield to the higher. All that is alleged is that, *primâ facie*, the magistrate can claim the obedience of the subject. But supposing the magistrate calls upon the subject to do that which some other authority co-ordinate with that of the magistrate forbids—supposing, for instance, as in the case of Hampden, under a constitutional monarchy, the king commands one thing, and the Parliament another—there is clearly a conflict of obligations, and the decision which accepts the one obligation is not necessarily wrong because it ignores the other. There will always be a certain debatable ground within which opposite duties will seem to clash, and where general principles are no longer of any avail. Here the individual conscience must assume the responsibility of deciding which to obey.

We are not called upon to enter into the casuistry of the subject. It may only be well to add one caution. Any such seemingly direct collision of duties must be at the very lightest a most serious and difficult matter; and though the burden of deciding falls ultimately on the individual, still he must be careful to remember that his particular judgment is subject to that fallibility to which all individual judgments are liable. Where the precept is appealed to, "Render to Cæsar the things that are Cæsar's, and to God the things that are God's," one man will say that the particular point in question comes under the first head, another that it comes under the second. In either case a great responsibility is assumed, and it is especially desirable that the judgment of the individual should be fortified by the consent of others, if possible by the suffrages of the majority of those who are in a position to judge. It is one thing to say that a conflict of duties may arise, and that the higher is to be obeyed. It is another thing to say that in a certain given case such conflict has arisen, and that the duty which commends itself to the individual is the higher of the two. Whatever the decision arrived at, it ought not to be made in a spirit of levity, nor ought it to be supposed that the dictum of the single conscience bears anything like the same validity as the universal principles of morals. And there will be the further drawback, that in such cases the individual usually acts as judge in his own cause, where his conscience is pretty sure to be biassed. There is therefore a very strong *onus probandi* thrown upon the person who takes upon himself to overrule what is in itself a clear obligation.

2. But the question of political obedience cannot be rightly considered without taking into account the relation of Christianity to political life generally, neither can this isolated passage in an Epistle of St. Paul's be considered apart from other teaching upon the same subjects in the rest of the New Testament. Very similar language, it will be remembered, is found in 1 Pet. ii. 13—17. And going back to the fountain-head of Christian doctrine, we find, indeed, no express statements, but several significant facts and some important intimations. When He was arrested by the civil power, and unjustly tried and condemned, our Lord made no resistance. Not only so, but when resistance was made on His behalf, He rebuked the disciple who had drawn the sword for Him. When the didrachma was demanded of Him, which it was customary for the Jew to pay towards the repair and maintenance of the Temple, He, though as Lord of the Temple He claimed exemption, nevertheless, for fear of putting a stumbling-block in the way of others, supplied the sum required by a miracle. On another occasion, when a question was asked as to the legitimacy of the Roman tribute, He replied in words already quoted, "Render to Cæsar the things which are Cæsar's, and to God the things which are God's." And, lastly, when appeal was made to Him to settle a disputed inheritance, He refused, saying to His petitioner, "Man, who made Me a judge or a divider over you?" Here we have really the key to the whole question. So far as His practice was concerned, our Lord pursued a course of simple obedience; into the theory of political or civil obligation He absolutely refused to enter. The answer, "Render to Cæsar," &c., left matters precisely as they stood, for the real question was, "What was Cæsar's, and what was not?" The ambiguity of the reply was intended. It was practically a refusal to reply at all.

The significance of this comes out very strikingly when it is contrasted with the state of feeling and opinion current among the Jews at the same time. With them politics and religion were intimately blended. They carried into the former sphere the fanaticism natural to the latter. Their religious hopes took a political form. The dominion of the Messiah was to be not a spiritual, but a literal dominion, in which they, as a people, were to share.

Clearly, the relations which our Lord assumed towards politics had especial reference to this attitude of the Jews. He wished to disabuse His disciples once and for all of this fatal confusion of two spheres in themselves so distinct. He wished to purify and to spiritualise their conception of the "Kingdom of Heaven," which He came to found. And, lastly, He finally submitted to the civil power, as the instrument divinely employed to inflict upon Him those sufferings which were to be the cause of our redemption. *Vicit patiendo.*

It would seem as if by some intuitive perception the disciples entered into the intention of their Master. Towards the civil power they maintained an attitude of absolute submission. They refused to avail themselves of the elements of fanaticism which existed wherever there were Jews, and at the head of which they might easily have placed themselves. Instead of this, they chose to suffer and die, and their sufferings did what force could never have done—they leavened and Christianised the world.

3. It is an expression of this deliberate policy (if by that name it may be called) which we find in these first seven verses of chap. xiii. At the same time, the Apostle may very well have had a special as well as a general object. The Church at Rome was largely composed of Jews, and these would naturally be imbued with the fanatical spirit of their countrymen. The very mention of the Messiah would tend to fan

that be are ordained[1] of God. (2) Who-
soever therefore resisteth the power,
resisteth the ordinance of God: and
they that resist shall receive to them-
selves damnation. (3) For rulers are
not a terror to good works, but to the
evil. Wilt thou then not be afraid of
the power? do that which is good, and
thou shalt have praise of the same:
(4) for he is the minister of God to thee
for good. But if thou do that which is
evil, be afraid; for he beareth not the
sword in vain: for he is the minister of
God, a revenger to *execute* wrath upon
him that doeth evil. (5) Wherefore *ye*
must needs be subject, not only for

1 Or, *ordered.*

---

their smouldering passions into flame. The Apostle would be aware of this. His informants at Rome may have told him of excitement prevailing among the Jewish portion of the community. His experience in Palestine would tell him to what unscrupulous acts of violence this might lead. And he forestalls the danger by an authoritative and reasoned description of the attitude which the Christian ought to assume.

It does not necessarily follow that precisely the same attitude is incumbent upon the Christian now. In this section of Christian teaching there was something that was temporary and local, and that had reference to conditions that have now passed away. And yet as a *general* principle, the injunctions of the Apostle entirely hold good. The exceptions to this principle are few and far between. And he who would assert the existence of such an exception must count the cost well beforehand.

(1) **Every soul.**—A Hebraism for "every person," though at the same time here, as in chap. ii. 9, there is a slight stress upon the fact that man is a conscious and intelligent being, capable of moral relations, and it is especially with reference to these relations that the phrase is used.

**Higher powers.**—Authorities, *i.e.*, magistrates, the abstract for the concrete.

**There is no power.**—It is strange that the Apostle seems to go almost out of his way to include even usurped and tyrannical power. He is, however, evidently speaking of the magistracy in its abstract or ideal form. It is the magistrate *quâ* magistrate, not *quâ* just or unjust magistrate. In this sense, not only is the human system of society a part of the divinely-appointed order of things, but it partakes more especially in the divine attributes, inasmuch as its object is to reward virtue and to punish vice. It discharges the same functions that God himself discharges, though in a lower scale and degree. Hence Bishop Butler feels himself justified in taking the principles which regulate civil society as an analogy for those which will regulate the ultimate divine disposition of things. "It is necessary to the very being of society that vices destructive of it should be punished as being so—the vices of falsehood, injustice, cruelty—which punishment, therefore, is as natural as society; and so is an instance of a kind of moral government, naturally established, and actually taking place. And, since the certain natural course of things is the conduct of Providence or the government of God, though carried on by the instrumentality of men, the observation here made amounts to this, that mankind find themselves placed by Him in such circumstances as that they are unavoidably accountable for their behaviour, and are often punished and sometimes rewarded under His government in the view of their being mischievous or eminently beneficial to society." In other words, the machinery of civil society is one of the chief and most conspicuous instruments by which God carries out His own moral government of mankind in this present existence. It may be said to be more distinctly and peculiarly derived from Him than other parts of the order of nature, inasmuch as it is the channel used to convey His moral approbation, or the reverse.

**The powers that be.**—Those that we see existing all around us.

(2) **Damnation.**—*Condemnation—i.e.*, the sentence passed upon him by the judge or magistrate as God's representative.

(3) **To good works.**—Literally, *to the good work*, as if it were personified. Human law can only take account of that which is actually done, not of the intention.

In this and the following verse it is clearly the ideal aspect of the magistracy that the Apostle has in view. So Bishop Butler, in the paragraph next to that just quoted, continues: "If it be objected that good actions, and such as are beneficial to society, are often punished, as in the case of persecution and in other cases, and that ill and mischievous actions are often rewarded, it may be answered distinctly: first, that this is in no sort necessary, and consequently not natural, in the sense in which it is necessary and therefore natural, that ill or mischievous actions should be punished; and in the next place, that good actions are never punished considered as beneficial to society, nor ill actions rewarded under the view of their being hurtful to it. So that it stands good . . . that the Author of Nature has as truly directed that vicious actions, considered as mischievous to society, should be punished, and put mankind under a necessity of punishing them, as He has directed and necessitated us to preserve our lives by food." Occasional failures of justice on the part of the executive do not make the strict administration of justice any the less its proper duty and office.

(4) **The sword.**—Not apparently the dagger worn by the Roman emperors, but, in a strict sense, "the sword." "To bear the sword" seems to be a recognised Greek phrase to express the power of the magistrates. It was carried before them in processions, and on other important occasions.

It is clear from this passage that capital punishment is sanctioned by Scripture. At the same time its abolition is not excluded, as the abolition of slavery was not excluded, if the gradual development of Christian principle should seem to demand it. Whether or not capital punishment ought to be abolished, is a question for jurists, publicists, and statesmen. The theologian, as such, has no decision to give either way.

(5) It follows, from this divine authority and title enjoyed by the magistrate, that he ought to be obeyed, not only from fear of the punishment that he is empowered to inflict, but also from the respect due to legitimate power. Of this respect conscience is the natural guardian.

wrath, but also for conscience sake.
(6) For for this cause pay ye tribute also:
for they are God's ministers, attend-
ing continually upon this very thing.
(7) Render therefore to all their dues:
tribute to whom tribute *is due;* custom
to whom custom; fear to whom fear;
honour to whom honour. (8) Owe no
man anything, but to love one another:
for he that loveth another hath fulfilled
the law. (9) For this, Thou shalt not
commit adultery, Thou shalt not kill,
Thou shalt not steal, Thou shalt not
bear false witness, Thou shalt not covet;
and if *there be* any other commandment,
it is briefly comprehended in this saying,
namely, Thou shalt love thy neighbour
as thyself. (10) Love worketh no ill to
his neighbour: therefore love *is* the
fulfilling of the law. (11) And that,
knowing the time, that now *it is* high
time to awake out of sleep: for now *is*

---

(6) **Ministers.**—The words thus translated here and in verse 4 are not the same, but both are words commonly used in the New Testament of a sacred office; that in verse 4 is the original of our word "deacon," that used in this verse is (in another form) the original of our word "liturgy." The choice of such terms harmonises with the conception which is presented in this chapter of the divine origin and character of the state system.

(7) **Tribute.**—Rather, *taxes—i.e.,* taxes upon person or property as opposed to the customs levied upon goods. These were collected by different officers.

**Fear . . . honour.**—There would be one class of officers who could claim respect for their official position, though they had no special means of enforcing it. Another class would have the power of inflicting punishment. This last would necessarily be feared, looked upon with a certain awe and reverence, as well as honoured.

(8) **Owe no man anything.**—The word for "owe" in this verse corresponds to that for "dues" in the last. The transition of the thought is something of this kind. When you have paid all your other debts, taxes, and customs, and reverence, and whatever else you may owe, there will still be one debt unpaid—the universal debt of love. Love must still remain the root and spring of all your actions. No other law is needed besides.

**Another.**—Literally, *the other*—that is to say, his neighbour, the person with whom in any given instance he has to deal.

We naturally compare with this passage Matt. xxii. 39, 40; Gal. v. 14; Jas. ii. 8. It shows how thoroughly the spirit of the Founder of Christianity descended upon His followers, that the same teaching should appear with equal prominence in such opposite quarters. The focussing, as it were, of all morality in this brief compass is one of the great gifts of Christianity to the world. No doubt similar sayings existed before, and that by our Lord Himself was quoted from the Old Testament, but there it was in effect overlaid with ceremonial rules and regulations, and in other moralists it was put forward rather as a philosophical theorem than as a practical basis of morals. In Christianity it is taken as the lever which is to move the world; nor is it possible to find for human life, amid all the intricate mazes of conduct, any other principle that should be at once as simple, as powerful, and as profound.

(9) **Thou shalt not commit adultery.**—It will be seen that in this arrangement the seventh commandment precedes the sixth. The same arrangement is found in Mark x. 19, Luke xviii. 20, and Jas. ii. 11. On the other hand, the ordinary arrangement appears in Matt. xix. 18. There can be no doubt that St. Paul followed an order that was found in the copies of the LXX. that he was in the habit of using. The famous *Codex Vaticanus* still presents the same order in Deut. v. 17. In Ex. xx. 13—15 it places the seventh commandment first, then the eighth, then the sixth.

(10) **Fulfilling of the law.**—The form of the Greek word implies not only that love helps a man to fulfil the law, but that in the fact of the presence of love in his heart the law is actually fulfilled.

The principle here stated is beautifully worked out in 1 Cor. xiii. 4—7.

(11—14) The Apostle now gives a reason for enforcing this and other duties upon his readers. The end of the world itself is near.

St. Paul, like the other Apostles (comp. 1 Pet. iv. 7; Rev. xxii. 20, *et al.*), certainly believed that the *Parusia*, or Second Coming of Christ, was near at hand. This was in strict accordance with Mark xiii. 32, and resulted naturally from the peculiar form of the Jewish Messianic expectation. A great shock had been given to the disciples by the crucifixion of Him whom they thought to be the Messiah, and though they began to recover from this as soon as they were convinced of His resurrection, they yet could not reconcile themselves to it entirely. The humiliation of the cross was still a stumbling-block to them *taken alone*, but, falling back upon another portion of their beliefs, they looked to see it supplemented, and its shameful side cancelled, by a second coming "in power and great glory." Their previous expectations, vague as they were, led them to regard this as part of the one manifestation of the Messiah, and they did not expect to see a long interval of time interposed.

(11) **And that, knowing the time.**—And that there is all the more urgent motive for you to do—this law of love it is the more incumbent on you to practise—because you know what a critical moment it is in which you are living. The word for "time" is different from that used in the next clause, and means a definite and critical season.

**Awake out of sleep.**—A striking metaphor. The true, the genuine Christian life is like the state of a man whose eyes are open and whose faculties are all alert and vigorous. All besides, whatever it be, the state of heathenism or of imperfect and lukewarm Christianity, is like the torpor of sleep.

**Our salvation.**—That blissful participation in His kingdom which the Messiah at His Second Coming should inaugurate for His people. (Comp. chap. viii. 19, 23, "the manifestation of the sons of God," "the redemption of the body;" Luke xxi. 28, "your redemption draweth nigh.")

**When we believed.**—When we first became Christians. Every hour brings the expected end nearer.

our salvation nearer than when we
believed. (12) The night is far spent,
the day is at hand: let us therefore cast
off the works of darkness, and let us put
on the armour of light. (13) Let us
walk honestly,[1] as in the day; not in
rioting and drunkenness, not in chambering and wantonness, not in strife
and envying. (14) But put ye on the
Lord Jesus Christ, and make not
provision for the flesh, to *fulfil* the lusts *thereof.*

A.D. 58.

CHAPTER XIV.—(1) Him that is
weak in the faith, receive ye, *but* not to
doubtful disputations.[2] (2) For one believeth that he may eat all things:
another, who is weak, eateth herbs.
(3) Let not him that eateth despise him
that eateth not; and let not him which

1 Or, *decently.*
2 Or, *not to judge his doubtful thoughts.*

---

(12) **The night.**—The time during which the Messiah is absent from His people is compared to night. He is the sun, whose coming converts it to day.

It is rather strange that here, as in 1 Thess. v. 8, the metaphor of night and day should suggest that of "armour." The warfare in which the Christian is engaged is between the powers of light and of darkness. (Comp. Eph. vi. 12.) And the use of the word "putting off" (stripping oneself as of clothing) supplies a link between the two ideas by suggesting the putting on of a different kind of clothing, the Christian panoply.

(13) **Honestly.**—*Decorously, becomingly,* as men do when their actions are seen.

It is interesting to know that this verse, happening to catch the eye of St. Augustine, had a great effect in leading to his baptism and change of life.

(14) **Put ye on the Lord Jesus Christ.**—A continuation of the metaphor introduced in verse 12. So invest and identify yourselves with the spirit of Christ as to reproduce it in your outward walk and conduct.

**Make not provision for the flesh.**—Take no thought for the flesh, so as to supply a stimulus to its lusts. A life of luxury and self-indulgence is apt to excite those fleshly impulses which the Christian should try rather to mortify. He therefore warns his readers not to give their thoughts to such things.

XIV.

There appears to have been a party in the Church at Rome which had adopted certain ascetic practices over and above the common rule of Christianity. We gather that they abstained altogether from flesh and wine, and that they (or possibly some other persons in the same church) also made a point of observing certain days with peculiar sanctity. When we ask what was the origin and affinities of this party, the answer is not quite obvious. It can hardly have been a branch of the Judaising party, such as it was met with in the Churches of Galatia, for then more stress would have been laid on the duty of circumcision, and their antagonism to St. Paul would probably have been more pronounced. Besides, if they had taken their stand upon the law of Moses, that law only forbade certain meats and drinks, and not all flesh and wine. A more plausible theory would be that which connects the party in question with the scruples mentioned in 1 Cor. viii. 4—13. The avoidance of meat offered to idols might easily be extended so as to cover all meat whatsoever. It would be difficult to ensure the complete absence of such pollution as was involved in the idol sacrifices, and a scrupulous person may have thought that the only safe measure was a total abstinence from animal food. And in like manner, as regards wine, which was liable to be used in heathen libations. The objection to this view is, that there is no allusion to the idol sacrifices, and as the Apostle enters into the subject so minutely in 1 Cor. viii., he might naturally be expected not to pass it over without some allusion here. It seems best, therefore, to regard the practices referred to in the Roman Church as a natural development of ascetic or purist elements within the Church itself. These would be supplied by those who had come over to Christianity from the sect of the Essenes, with the tenets of which sect the allusions in this chapter would quite sufficiently agree. It would appear to have been a further development of the same doctrines which, at a later date, vexed the Church at Colossæ. At Rome, the tendency had hitherto been slight and unaggressive, and the Apostle therefore deals with it mildly; at Colossæ it had become more arrogant and intolerant and therefore, it is rebuked sharply. (See Col. ii. 16—23.)

The whole of this chapter affords a most striking instance of the practical wisdom of St. Paul. It is a *locus classicus* on the two subjects, toleration and asceticism.

(1) **Weak in the faith . . .**—The presence of a single strong master-motive is apt to silence petty scruples. Where the "eye is single"—where all the powers and faculties of the man are concentrated upon one object, and that object the highest that can engage human thought or affection—there will naturally be a certain largeness of view. The opposite of this is to be "weak in the faith." There may be a sincere desire to lead a religious life, and yet the mind is taken up with petty details, each of which is painfully judged by itself, and not by reference to a central principle.

**Receive ye.**—Take to yourselves, stretch out the hand of friendship to him.

**Doubtful disputations.**—The marginal rendering is more exact, "to judge his doubtful thoughts," or "to criticise his scruples." The strong are to deal tenderly with the weak, and not engage them in casuistical discussions.

(2) **Believeth that he may . . .**—Rather, perhaps, *hath confidence to eat all things.* His faith is strong enough to prevent his conscience from becoming uneasy.

(3) **Let not him that eateth.**—The two classes of men are exposed to two opposite faults. The strong *despise* the weak; the weak *judge* the strong. In the one case there is contempt for what is thought to be narrowness and pedantry. In the other case censorious judgments are passed on what is regarded as levity and irreligion. Human nature alters very little.

**God hath received him.**—Strictly, *received him,* admitted him into His Church when he was baptised, and so took him for His own.

eateth not judge him that eateth: for
God hath received him. (4) Who art
thou that judgest another man's ser-
vant? to his own master he standeth or
falleth. Yea, he shall be holden up:
for God is able to make him stand.
(5) One man esteemeth one day above
another: another esteemeth every day
*alike.* Let every man be fully per-
suaded[1] in his own mind. (6) He that
regardeth the day, regardeth *it* unto the
Lord; and he that regardeth not the
day, to the Lord he doth not regard *it.*
He that eateth, eateth to the Lord, for
he giveth God thanks; and he that
eateth not, to the Lord he eateth not,
and giveth God thanks. (7) For none
of us liveth to himself, and no man
dieth to himself. (8) For whether we
live, we live unto the Lord; and whether
we die, we die unto the Lord: whether
we live therefore, or die, we are the
Lord's. (9) For to this end Christ both
died, and rose, and revived, that he
might be Lord both of the dead and
living. (10) But why dost thou judge
thy brother? or why dost thou set at
nought thy brother? for we shall all
stand before the judgment seat of
Christ.[a] (11) For it is written, *As* I live,[b]
saith the Lord, every knee shall bow to
me, and every tongue shall confess to
God. (12) So then every one of us shall
give account of himself to God. (13) Let
us not therefore judge one another any
more: but judge this rather, that no

1 Or, *fully assured.*

a 2 Cor. 5. 10.
b Isa. 45. 23.

---

(4) **Who art thou?**—This is addressed to the weak. The Apostle indignantly challenges his right to judge. That right belongs to another tribunal, before which the conduct of the stronger Christian will not be condemned but approved and upheld.

**He standeth or falleth.**—It seems most in accordance with what precedes to take this of judicial condemnation or approval from the Master whom he serves—*i.e.*, Christ.

**Holden up.**—The same word as that in the clause following, and similar to that in the clause preceding—"Made to stand."

**God is able to make him stand.**—The true reading here is "the Lord"—*i.e.*, Christ; the word is the same as "his Master" above. "Make him stand" seems to be still judicial. "Secure his acquittal," but with reference to his previous course of conduct on which that acquittal is grounded. The trial is not necessarily reserved for the last day, but is rather the judgment which Christ may be supposed at any moment to pass upon His servants. If they can sustain this judgment, it is only because His grace has enabled them so to act as not to be condemned by it.

(5) **One man esteemeth.**—For the observance of days and seasons, compare Gal. iv. 10; Col. ii. 16. From these passages, taken together, it is clear that the observance of special days has no absolute sanction, but is purely a question of religious expediency. That, however, is sufficient ground on which to rest it, and experience seems in favour of some such system as that adopted by our own Church.

(6) **Regardeth.**—Much as we might say, "he who minds the day," or directs his thoughts and feelings to it.

**He that regardeth not the day, to the Lord he doth not regard it.**—This clause is omitted by the best MSS. and editors.

**For he giveth God thanks.**—By the saying of grace at meat, the meal, whatever it may be, is consecrated to God, and he who partakes of it shows that he does so in no irreverent spirit.

(7–9) The larger principle holds good, and therefore much more the smaller. It is not only his food that the Christian consecrates to God (or rather, immediately, to Christ, and through Christ to God), but his whole life, to its very last moments.

(7) **Dieth to himself.**—Even in the act of death the Christian is conscious of his relation to Christ; he dies "*in* the Lord" (Rev. xiv. 13).

(9) **And rose, and revived.**—For these words the best MSS. substitute simply "and lived." The Received text is a gloss upon this. It was through the resurrection that Christ was finally enthroned at His Father's right hand, and that universal dominion was given to Him.

(10–12) Such being our relations to Christ, and such the judgment to which we look forward, there is no room for any human judgment. Censoriousness is thus condemned.

(10) **Judgment seat of Christ.**—The true reading is, *of God.*

(11) **As I live.**—The original has, "I have sworn by Myself," for which St. Paul, quoting from memory, substitutes another common Hebrew formula—"As I live," or, "by my life."

**Shall confess . . .**—The Greek word is capable of two renderings—"confess" and "praise." Most commentators prefer the latter, but it is not quite clear that the English version is wrong. That the word can bear this meaning is, especially in view of Jas. v. 16, unquestionable, and the sense seems to agree better with the next verse.

(13) **Judge this rather.**—The word "judge" forms the connecting-link between what follows and what has gone before. If any judgment is to be formed at all, let it be rather as a principle to guide our own action, and not in the shape of a criticism upon others. This principle, in the case of those who are themselves liberal and large-minded, should be not to put temptation in the way of their weaker brethren.

**Stumblingblock or an occasion to fall.**—The same words that occur in chap. ix. 33. That translated "occasion to fall," is the origin of our word "scandal." It is properly a trap or snare. Both the idea and the word are found in Matt. xviii. 6 (=Mark ix. 42), where it is disguised by the translation "offend," in the sense of "cause to stumble." The same translation appears frequently elsewhere. One of the special characteristics of Christianity is its tenderness for the weak.

man put a stumblingblock or an occasion
to fall in *his* brother's way. (14) I know,
and am persuaded by the Lord Jesus,
that *there is* nothing unclean[1] of itself:
but to him that esteemeth anything to
be unclean,[2] to him *it is* unclean.
(15) But if thy brother be grieved with
*thy* meat, now walkest thou not chari-
tably.[3] Destroy not him with thy
meat,[a] for whom Christ died. (16) Let
not then your good be evil spoken of:
(17) for the kingdom of God is not meat
and drink; but righteousness, and peace,
and joy in the Holy Ghost. (18) For he
that in these things serveth Christ *is*
acceptable to God, and approved of men.
(19) Let us therefore follow after the
things which make for peace, and things

a 1 Cor. 8. 11.

1 Gr. *common.*

2 Gr. *common.*

3 Gr. *according to charity.*

---

(14) **I know, and am persuaded.**—The Apostle clearly identifies himself with the less scrupulous party. For one of his intense penetration and grasp on the realities of things, any other position was impossible. But while these essential features in the Apostle's character find the noblest expression, we cannot but note his attitude of gentle forbearance towards those whose faith is less deep and less robust than his own. This comes out especially in that pathetic and pregnant appeal, "Destroy not him with thy meat, for whom Christ died."

**By the Lord Jesus.**—Rather, *in the Lord Jesus.* A solemn form of asseveration. The Apostle is speaking from the very depths of his Christian consciousness as one who knows that he has himself put on the Spirit of Christ.

**To him that esteemeth.**—This would mean, in philosophical language, that the quality of uncleanness was not an objective property in the thing itself, but a subjective quality in the mind of the person regarding it as such. Still, this subjective quality is for the individual a real one, and should be treated as real. (Comp. Mark vii. 15.)

(15) **But.**—The true reading is undoubtedly *For,* the connection of which is somewhat difficult to trace. It appears to leap over verse 14, and go back to verse 13. We may suppose that the substance of this verse recurs to the Apostle's mind after the parenthetical statement just inserted, and though he does not repeat it in words, he connects on to it the sequence of his thought. "The Christian should not put a stumbling-block in his brother's way. Not, indeed, that there is anything unclean in itself, but relatively to the person who so regards it, it is unclean. [Therefore the Christian should be careful as to what he does.] For to cause distress to another about a mere matter of food is to be uncharitable."

Two stages are noted in the words "grieved" and "destroy." When one man sees another do that which his own conscience condemns, it causes him pain, but when he is further led on from this to do *himself* what his conscience condemns, he is in danger of a worse fate; he is morally ruined and undone. The work of redemption that Christ has wrought for him is cancelled, and all that great and beneficent scheme is hindered of its operation by an act of thoughtlessness or want of consideration on the part of a fellow Christian.

**With thy meat.**—Rather, *because of meat,* on a mere question of meat.

(16) **Your good.**—That blessing of Christian liberty which you enjoy. This is not to be used so as to give rise to reproaches and recriminations which will make a bad impression on the outside world.

(17) **Meat and drink.**—Strictly, *eating and drinking.*

**Righteousness, and peace, and joy in the Holy Ghost.**—By "righteousness and peace" is not here meant imputed righteousness, or justification and reconciliation with God, but rather the moral condition of righteousness in the Christian himself, and concord with his fellow-men. These are crowned in the confirmed Christian by that feeling of subdued and chastened exultation which is wrought in Him by the presence in his heart or constant influence of the Holy Spirit.

It is remarkable how, with all the wide difference in terminology between the writings of St. Paul and the Gospels, they yet come round to the very same point. The "kingdom of God," as here described, is exactly what we should gather from the fuller and more detailed sayings of our Lord. "Not that which goeth into the mouth defileth a man;" "The kingdom of God is within you;" "The kingdom of God cometh not with observation;" "If thine eye be single, thy whole body shall be full of light;" "Blessed are they which do hunger and thirst after righteousness;" "Blessed are the peacemakers;" "Rejoice and be exceeding glad."

It has not been beyond the power of heathen or even Christian philosophers, such, *e.g.,* as Marcus Aurelius, to arrive at the conception of righteousness and peaceableness as duties to be observed and striven after. The peculiarity of Christianity consists in the unity which it gives to these attributes as naturally flowing from a spring of deep religious emotion, and from the finish and perfection which it adds to them by the introduction of that third term, "joy in the Holy Ghost." Many individuals have shown, and still show, with greater or less approximation, what the Christian type should be, but the great and only perfect Exemplar is Jesus Himself, and that less, perhaps, in the later portion of His career, when He was fulfilling that other side of His mission, to "bear the sins of many" as the Saviour of mankind, than in the earlier untroubled phase which finds expression in the Sermon on the Mount. This is in closest contact with the normal life of men.

(18) **In these things.**—The more correct reading is, *in this* (*way*). The meaning, however, is the same.

**Serveth Christ.**—Here the principle of unity which holds together different sides and manifestations of the Christian character is indicated.

**Approved of men.**—So that He will not be "evil spoken of," as the uncompromising legalist or anti-legalist is apt to be.

(19) **Let us therefore follow.**—The best MSS. have the indicative mood, "so then we follow." There is, however, some good support for the Received text, especially in the patristic quotations and versions; and mistakes of this kind were peculiarly liable to be made.

**Edify.**—The word has unfortunately lost its freshness of meaning, but we have no other single equivalent for it in English. It is the "upbuilding," or mutual help and assistance in the spiritual life which Christians receive from their intercourse with each other.

wherewith one may edify another.
(20) For meat destroy not the work of
God. All things indeed *are* pure;[a] but
*it is* evil for that man who eateth with
offence. (21) *It is* good neither to eat
flesh,[b] nor to drink wine, nor *any thing*
whereby thy brother stumbleth, or is
offended, or is made weak. (22) Hast
thou faith? have *it* to thyself before
God. Happy *is* he that condemneth
not himself in that thing which he
alloweth. (23) And he that doubteth
is damned if he eat, because *he eateth*
not of faith: for whatsoever *is* not of
faith is sin.

a Tit. 1. 15.

b 1 Cor. 8. 13.

A.D. 58.

CHAPTER XV.—(1) We then that
are strong ought to bear the infirmities

(20) **Destroy not.**—A different word from that employed in verse 15. It is the correlative and opposite of "edify," and means to "unbuild" or "pull down."

**The work of God.**—The fabric which the grace of God has begun, and which the edification of Christians by each other may help to raise in the soul; the gradual formation of a truly Christian character, both spiritual and moral.

**For that man who eateth with offence.**—It seems, on the whole, best (though the other view is taken) to refer the "eating" here to the strong in faith, and the "offence" to that which his eating causes to the weaker brethren. The force of the preposition is that his eating is *attended* with offence.

(21) **It is good neither to eat flesh.**—These direct, clear, incisive sentences are as characteristic of the style of the Apostle (when he is dealing with moral questions of present urgency, and not with the abstract problems of theology) as the generous impulse which prompts them is of his heart.

**Any thing**—*i.e., to do anything;* all three words have to be supplied.

**Or is offended, or is made weak.**—There is a remarkable division of authority for the omission or retention of these words, the Sinaitic and Alexandrine MSS. with the Paris rescript being on the one side, and the Vatican, with the Græco-Latin Codices, on the other; and the versions pretty nearly divided. Here internal evidence comes in, and decides us to omit the words as most probably a gloss.

(22) **Hast thou faith?**—It is with some reluctance that in deference to the union of the four best MSS. we give up the Received text here, and substitute (by the insertion of the relative) "The faith which thou hast, have to thyself before God," *i.e.,* reserve the exhibition of it to the privacy of your own direct communion with God, and do not display it ostentatiously in public where it may do harm. "It is indeed"—the Apostle continues—"a happy thing to have no self-condemnatory scruples of conscience, but, on the other hand, it is fatal to have scruples and to disregard them."

**In that thing which he alloweth.**—In the acts which he permits himself. He is a happy man who can eat what he pleases, and drink what he pleases, without any qualms of conscience to condemn him while he does so.

(23) **And he that doubteth.** — The one thing which justifies a man in neglecting such nice and punctilious distinctions is a faith so strong that it can afford to make light of them. Where faith is not strong enough for this, and where the conscience deliberately approves one course, and the other course is chosen, this alone stamps the act as wrong. "He who hesitates as to what he ought to do is condemned, or does wrong, if he eats (in opposition to his conscience), for he has not the one faculty which can overrule the decisions of conscience, and give them a different direction."

**Whatsoever is not of faith is sin.**—This is intended as a general principle, but only as a general principle covering this particular kind of case. Where the conscience is in doubt, faith alone can make it right to choose the side against which conscience inclines. Nothing is said about those cases in which conscience is either not appealed to at all, or approves what is done. Hence St. Augustine was wrong in arguing from this passage that even good actions, when done by unbelievers, were of the nature of sin.

## XV.

These concluding chapters present some remarkable phenomena which seem to need a special theory to account for them.

It will be seen that chap. xvi. ends, according to the Received text, with a two-fold benediction and a doxology, one at the end of verse 20, another in verse 24, and the third covering verses 25—27.

Of these, the two benedictions in verses 20 and 24 are alternatives. They are not found in the same group of MSS. at both places, but the MSS. which insert them in the first palce omit them at the second, and *vice versâ.* Weighing the authorities on both sides together, there can be little doubt that the earlier position is the right one—that the doxology ought to stand at chap. xvi. 20 and to be erased in chap. xvi. 24. How it came to be inserted there we shall see presently.

The longer, concluding doxology is also placed where it is by a quite decisive preponderance of authority. At the same time it is also found at the end of chap. xiv. in one important MS., the Codex Laudianus, and in a number of others of lesser value, while the Alexandrine Codex and Porphyrian Palimpsest, with some few others, have it in both places.

It is to be observed also that Marcion, the Gnostic writer, who lived about 140 A.D., had a copy of the Epistle in which these last two chapters were omitted altogether.

How is this series of facts to be accounted for? It is obviously only a rude and reckless logic which infers from them that the whole two chapters are not genuine. The same conclusion has been supported by other arguments, which need not be mentioned in this Commentary. The proof of the genuineness of the chapters is overwhelming.

Other theories have been propounded, which, while assigning the chapters to St. Paul himself, have treated them as either entirely or in part fragments inserted here from some other lost Epistle. For instance, Ewald held that chap. xvi. 3—20 was written by St. Paul from Rome to Ephesus, and M. Renan has recently put forward the view that the main body of the Epistle was sent to different churches with different endings—chaps. i.—xi. with the ending chap. xv. to the Romans;

of the weak, and not to please ourselves.
(2) Let every one of us please *his* neigh-
bour for *his* good to edification. (3) For
even Christ pleased not himself; but, as
it is written, The reproaches of them
that reproached thee fell on me.[a] (4) For
whatsoever things were written afore-
time were written for our learning, that
we through patience and comfort of the
scriptures might have hope. (5) Now
the God of patience and consolation
grant you to be likeminded one toward

[a] Ps. 69. 9.

---

chaps. i.—xiv. with the ending xvi. 1—20 to the Ephesians; chaps. i.—xiv. with the ending xvi. 21—24 to the Thessalonians; and chaps. i.—xiv. with the ending xvi. 25—27 to a fourth unknown church.

This last is an ingenious theory, but, like the rest, does not appear to be tenable when applied in detail.

We will only mention one more theory which has the advantage of being simpler than most, and which seems to account almost if not quite satisfactorily for the complex and peculiar phenomena of the text, while it accords well with the general character of the Epistle. It is this:—

The Epistle was originally written and sent to the Romans in the form in which we have it now, except that it ended at chap. xvi. 23. The portion which was dictated by St. Paul himself really concluded with the benediction given in chap. xvi. 20, but a brief and informal postscript was added by Tertius and his companions.

At some later period of his life, probably during one or other of his two imprisonments, finding the Epistle current in Rome, it occurred to the Apostle that it might with advantage be circulated more widely. Accordingly he struck out the whole of the more personal matter, *i.e.*, chaps. xv. and xvi. And, in order to give somewhat more finish to the composition, he added the elaborate doxology, which now concludes the whole, at the end of chap. xiv. At the same time, at the beginning of the Epistle, he erased the express mention of Rome (chap. i. 7), and left merely the general phrase "To them that are beloved of God"—a change of which some traces are still to be found remaining in the MSS.

There was thus a shorter and a longer recension of the Epistle—the shorter with a formal ending, the longer without. It was the shorter form which happened to fall into the hands of Marcion, who, for reasons of his own, cut off the doxology. Later copyists, observing the ragged edge which was caused by the postscript of Tertius, sought to remedy this by transferring the benediction of verse 20 to verse 24: and others, with more success, by adding to the original Epistle the doxology composed for the shorter recension. The general tendency in the scribes being to add and accumulate rather than to subtract, all three forms have come down to us.

The main arguments in favour of this theory are—(1) the extent to which it accounts for the phenomena of the text; (2) the striking resemblance between the style and diction of the concluding doxology and those of the Epistle to the Ephesians and Pastoral Epistles, which would make it appear as if it had been composed at that later date, rather than when St. Paul originally wrote to the Romans; and (3) the analogy of the Epistle to the Ephesians, which seems to have gone through a somewhat similar process, being circulated in two forms—as a circular or general Epistle, and also as one addressed to a particular Church. The opinion is also growing that the Gospel according to St. Luke received additions, and was issued in an enlarged form during the lifetime of the Evangelist himself.

It would not be well to speak too positively where all is so much a matter of conjecture; but so far as conjecture can carry us, this theory seems, on the whole, the most probable and most likely to represent the real state of the facts. The author of it is Dr. Lightfoot.

(1) **We then that are strong.**—The opening verses of the chapter are intimately connected with the close of the last. Not only ought those who are strong in faith to be careful what they do in the matter of meat and drink, but in all things they should show sympathy and consideration for their weaker brethren. This unbroken continuity in the two chapters would be enough to show that the Epistle cannot originally have ended with chap. xiv.

**Bear the infirmities.**—Take them upon ourselves, act as if they were our own, and, at the same time, by our sympathy relieve the consciences of the weak.

(2) **For his good.**—The object of this tender dealing with others is to be their benefit and growth in spiritual perfection. It is grounded on the example of Christ Himself.

(3) **The reproaches . . . .**—Literally, after the LXX. version of Ps. lxix. 9, one of those Psalms of suffering which, like Isa. liii., afford a type of the sufferings of the Messiah.

**Reproached thee fell on me.**—The insults directed against God Himself fell upon His servants.

(4) **For . . . .**—These words of the Old Testament may rightly be taken as having a bearing upon us, "For," &c.

**Through patience and comfort of the scriptures**—*i.e.*, "by the patience and comfort which the Scriptures afford." The promises and consolations of Scripture support the Christian under his trials, and enable him to endure them not only patiently but cheerfully.

**Might have hope.**—Literally, *the hope*—*i.e.*, the Messianic hope. The promises of Scripture centre in the hope of the future Messianic glory, and the fortitude with which the Christian endures his trials is to be sustained by that hope, and itself reacts upon the hope and makes it held with firmer tenacity.

(5) **Now the God of patience and consolation.**—Such, then, should be the temper of the Roman Christians. The Apostle prays that along with the spirit of steadfast endurance God will also give them that spirit of unanimity which proceeds from singleness of aim. There seems, at first sight, to be little or no connection between the God of "patience and consolation" and the being "likeminded." They are connected, however, through the idea of singleness of purpose. He who is wholly self-dedicated to Christ, and who in the strength of that self-dedication is able to endure persecution, will also have a close bond of union with all who set before themselves the same object.

**Consolation . . . .**—The same word as "comfort" in the previous verse.

**To be likeminded . . . .**—To have the same thoughts, feelings, sentiments, hopes, and aims.

another according to Christ Jesus:[a]
(6) that ye may with one mind *and* one
mouth glorify God, even the Father of
our Lord Jesus Christ. (7) Wherefore
receive ye one another, as Christ also
received us to the glory of God. (8) Now
I say that Jesus Christ was a minister
of the circumcision for the truth of
God, to confirm the promises *made* unto
the fathers: (9) and that the Gentiles
might glorify God for *his* mercy; as it
is written, For this cause I will confess
to thee among the Gentiles,[b] and sing
unto thy name. (10) And again he saith,
Rejoice,[c] ye Gentiles, with his people.
(11) And again, Praise the Lord,[d] all ye
Gentiles; and laud him, all ye people.
(12) And again, Esaias saith, There shall
be a root of Jesse,[e] and he that shall rise
to reign over the Gentiles; in him shall
the Gentiles trust. (13) Now the God of
hope fill you with all joy and peace in
believing, that ye may abound in hope,
through the power of the Holy Ghost.

a 1 Cor. 1. 10.
b Ps. 18. 49.
c Deut. 32. 43.
d Ps. 117. 1.
e Isa. 11. 10.

---

**According to Christ Jesus.**—The conforming to that "spirit of Christ" which it is to be assumed that all who call themselves Christians have put on.

(6) **With one mind and one mouth . . . .**—It is in the heart that the spirit of humanity arises, and with the mouth that it is expressed.

(7) **Received us.**—There is again a division of the best authorities, the Vatican and Claromontane MSS. reading "us," while the Sinaitic, Alexandrine, Paris rescript, and others, read "you." The latter is, perhaps, to be preferred, but with no real difference to the sense. The word "received" is the same as that at the beginning of chap. xiv., the subject of which chapter is still continued, and is now taken up for the last time. The duty of Christians to show cordiality to each other is now based upon the comprehensiveness of the love of Christ, whose mission was directed with the same impartiality towards Jews and Gentiles. To the Jews He came to confirm and fulfil His promises; to the Gentiles He came to bring joys and hopes from which they had been hitherto excluded.

**To the glory of God.**—That God might be glorified by the admission into the Church of Gentiles as well as Jews; a parenthetic remark without direct bearing on the argument.

(8) **Now I say . . . .**—Rather, *For I say.* My doctrine is that Christ came with a two-fold purpose: on the one hand, with a mission to the Jews, the chosen circumcised race, to vindicate to them the truthfulness of God in respect to His promises, by Himself confirming and fulfilling those promises; and, on the other hand, with the object to exhibit the mercy of God in rescuing the Gentiles from their state of condemnation, and giving them cause to glorify God's name.

**Was . . . .**—This is the reading of the Vatican MS. and Paris rescript; the Sinaitic and Alexandrine have, "hath been made."

**For the truth of God**—*i.e.,* to make good the truthfulness of God in keeping His promises.

(9) **For his mercy.**—On account of His mercy. The Jews had their covenant to appeal to, and the attributes of God most clearly brought home to them in Christianity was His veracity in fulfilling the promises contained in this covenant. The Gentiles had no such covenant, and their admission to the blessings of Christianity was an act of pure grace and mercy, which they could only thankfully recognise. The Apostle then proceeds to quote from the Old Testament a succession of passages bearing upon this ultimate reception and triumph of the Gentiles.

**For this cause . . . .**—Ps. xviii., from which this quotation is taken, is assigned by the heading, as most commentators believe, rightly, to David himself, as a review of his past life, and a thanksgiving for his deliverance from his enemies. David is here taken as a type of Christ. He is said to "confess to God among the Gentiles," inasmuch as He is the head of the Gentile Church, in whose name its praises are offered, and by whom they are presented.

**Confess . . . .**—Comp. the Note on chap. xiv. 11. Here the meaning, "praise," is more distinctly brought out. The confession or acknowledgment of mercies is itself an act of praise.

(10) **Rejoice, ye Gentiles, with his people.**—St. Paul here follows the LXX. version, which varies somewhat from the original. The sense of the Hebrew is disputed. That which appears to suit the context best—"Rejoice, O ye nations of His people," *i.e.,* the Jewish tribes—is questioned on the ground of linguistic usage. In place of this, we may either adopt the rendering of the Vulgate—"Ye nations (Gentiles) praise His people," or, "Rejoice, ye nations (Gentiles), who are His people." This, however, hardly seems to fall in with the context so well.

(11) **All ye Gentiles.**—An invitation addressed to the Gentile peoples without restriction, at a time when the monotheistic conception of God as Lord of the whole earth was thoroughly established.

(12) **And again, Esaias saith.**—St. Paul still adheres to the LXX., which here diverges more widely from the Hebrew. The sense of this is rightly given by the Authorised version of Isa. xi. 10—"In that day there shall be a root of Jesse, which shall stand for an ensign of the people; to it shall the Gentiles seek." In either case the passage is Messianic.

**A root of Jesse.**—Strictly, *the root,* or, *root-shoot* of Jesse, as in Prov. v. 5—*i.e.,* the expected descendant of Jesse's line, which, to bring out its intimate connection with the founder of the line, and to distinguish it from all other collateral branches, is identified with the very root, or first shoot, of the line itself.

**Trust.**—The same word as "hope" in the next verse, the introduction of which was probably suggested, through the association of ideas, by the concluding words of the LXX. quotation—"On Him shall the Gentiles place their hopes. Now the God of hope, &c.

(13) **Now the God of hope fill you with all joy and peace . . . . hope.**—Hope, joy, and peace, form a triad which represents the attitude of the Christian in looking towards the future, and so far as that future is reflected on the present. Hope may be taken as including the other two, as it is upon the certainty of the Messianic promises that they all depend, just as it is through the constant energising power of the Holy Ghost that they are kept alive.

(14) And I myself also am persuaded
of you, my brethren, that ye also are
full of goodness, filled with all know-
ledge, able also to admonish one another.
(15) Nevertheless, brethren, I have written
the more boldly unto you in some sort,
as putting you in mind, because of the
grace that is given to me of God,
(16) that I should be the minister of
Jesus Christ to the Gentiles, ministering
the gospel of God, that the offering up
of the Gentiles might be acceptable,
being sanctified by the Holy Ghost.
(17) I have therefore whereof I may
glory through Jesus Christ in those
things which pertain to God. (18) For I
will not dare to speak of any of those
things which Christ hath not wrought

---

(14) **And I myself also.**—From this point onwards the Apostle gives a personal turn to his letter. The greetings at the end are naturally introduced by a few words of explanation as to the way in which the more general exhortations that preceded are to be received by the Roman Christians, and a somewhat longer statement on the part of the Apostle of his own relations to the Church at Rome. This might seem to be the more necessary as the Church was not one of his own founding, and he might seem to be both going out of his way and acting in contradiction to his own principles in writing to them at all.

I write thus to you though you do not really need all these exhortations. Not only do others tell me, but I am convinced myself that you possess all the qualifications which would fit you to teach others instead of receiving instruction yourselves.

**Ye also.**—Rather, *even yourselves*, as you are, and without any stimulus or incitement given to you from without.

**Goodness**—*i.e.*, goodness of disposition, readiness to practise all the Christian virtues, especially those to which the last section had been exhorting.

**Knowledge**—*i.e.*, of the doctrinal aspects of Christianity as they had been set forth in the earlier portion of the Epistle. No doubt the Apostle had really much to teach his readers—he does not say that he had not—but he courteously gives them credit for all they knew.

(15) **Nevertheless, brethren.**—Apologetic. Holding this good opinion of you as I do, I nevertheless presumed somewhat upon my position as an Apostle, and especially as an Apostle of the Gentiles, to write with an earnestness which I should, perhaps, otherwise not have ventured to show.

**Brethren.**—The weight of evidence in the MSS. is against the retention of this word.

**In some sort.**—Literally, *in part*, qualifying the phrase, "I have written more boldly," both in extent and degree. In some passages the Apostle feels that he had gone beyond the modest limits which he might have seemed to mark out for himself by what he had just been saying. He had taken a liberty, but not too great a liberty. He had spoken to them rather pointedly at times, but he had been careful not to go too far. The reference may be supposed to be to exhortations such as those in chaps. xiii. and xiv., and in other parts of the Epistle.

**As putting you in mind.**—Another delicate expression. The Apostle has not been telling them of something that they did not know before, but merely reminding them of what they knew. And he claims the right to do this because of the special grace given to him as an Apostle. The Judaising section in the Church at Rome did not go so far as that in Galatia. It recognised the apostleship of St. Paul, and he knew that he could safely appeal to this recognition.

**Because of the grace.**—Comp. "grace and apostleship" in chap. i. 5. "Grace" is here that special endowment with divine gifts by which the Apostles were distinguished from other Christians.

(16) **Minister . . . ministering.**—These are two different words in the Greek, but allied in their signification. Both refer originally to the liturgical service of the Temple; the first to the whole of the functions both of the priests and Levites, the second to the special function of the priests in the offering of sacrifice. St. Paul is a "minister of Jesus Christ;" *i.e.*, his sacred office was given to him by Christ; it was Christ who appointed and ordained him to it; and his special duty as a priest of the gospel was to see that the Church of the Gentiles, whom it fell to him to present as a sacrifice to God, should be fit for such a sacrifice, made holy by the indwelling Spirit, and therefore acceptable to Him to whom it was offered.

**To the Gentiles.**—Strictly, *in reference to the Gentiles.* The branch, or department of the Christian ministry specially allotted to St. Paul was the evangelisation of the Gentiles.

**Ministering the gospel of God.**—Serving the gospel of God as a priest stands at the altar in the service of the tabernacle. The offering which the priest is thus to present is the Gentile Church.

**The offering up of the Gentiles.**—Not "that which the Gentiles offer," but "the offering which the Gentiles *are*;" the sacrifice which they themselves form and constitute.

**Sanctified by the Holy Ghost.**—Rather, *consecrated in the Holy Ghost.* The sanctifying influence of the Holy Ghost *overshadows*, as it were, the Church, encloses and embraces it on every side.

(17) This is really the title on which I rest my claim. I *can* boast of a specially sacred office and ministry, given to me by Christ, and not merely of my own devising. The sphere of this office is a religious sphere, it relates to "the things pertaining to God."

(18) Nor in basing my claims upon this head do I go at all beyond my own proper province. I will take credit for no man's labours but my own. They have, indeed, been quite signal enough.

**I will not dare to speak.**—I have a certain just and legitimate pride, but I shall not, therefore, presume to boast of successes of which others have been the instrument. *All* successes in the mission field are due ultimately to Christ; for some he has made use of me, for others of other men. I will confine myself to those in which I have been myself directly concerned.

**To make the Gentiles obedient.**—Comp. chap. i. 5, "for obedience to the faith among all nations" (*i.e.*, to bring over all the Gentiles into obedience to the faith; see Note).

by me, to make the Gentiles obedient,
by word and deed, (19) through mighty
signs and wonders, by the power of the
Spirit of God; so that from Jerusalem,
and round about unto Illyricum, I have
fully preached the gospel of Christ.
(20) Yea, so have I strived to preach the
gospel, not where Christ was named,
lest I should build upon another man's
foundation: (21) but as it is written, To
whom he was not spoken of,[a] they shall
see: and they that have not heard shall
understand.
(22) For which cause also I have been
much[1] hindered from coming to you.
(23) But now having no more place in
these parts, and having a great desire
these many years to come unto you;

a Isa. 52. 15.

1 Or, *many ways*, or, *oftentimes*.

**By word and deed.**—This goes with the phrase "wrought by me," and signifies "either by preaching or by miracles."

It will be seen that the structure of this verse is not, in a rhetorical sense, quite elegant. The Apostle uses a negative form of sentence where a positive form would seem to be more appropriate. Instead of saying, "I will confine myself to what Christ *has* wrought by me," he says, "I will *not* speak of what Christ has *not* wrought by me," though the description which follows is that of his own ministry.

(19) **Through mighty signs and wonders.**—Literally, *through the might of signs and wonders—i.e.*, through those extraordinary powers which found their expression in signs and wonders. "Signs and wonders" is the phrase regularly used throughout the New Testament for the Christian miracles: so frequently in the Gospels. (Comp. also 2 Cor. xii. 12; 2 Thess. xi. 9; Heb. xi. 4.) The two words are very similar in meaning. They *de*note the same acts, but they *con*note different aspects in which those acts may be regarded. The word "signs" tends to bring out the symbolical character of the miracle, the spiritual truth of which it was, as it were, the physical expression. In the word "wonders" stress is laid rather upon its character as a portent, a manifestation of supernatural, divine power. That St. Paul himself claimed miraculous powers is a fact that cannot be doubted.

**By the power of the Spirit of God.**—The two clauses at the beginning of this verse correspond roughly to "by word and deed" at the end of the last. "Signs and wonders" are the manifestation of the effectual working of Christ in "deed." The "power of the Spirit of God" is exemplified both in "deed" and in "word."

**So that . . .**—It is to be noticed that the language of the Apostle becomes more and more definite and concrete, till he ends by describing the geographical extent of his own labours.

**Jerusalem.**—The Apostle naturally takes this as the *terminus à quo*, partly because it was at this time the centre and head-quarters of Christianity, and also more especially because it was the extreme point eastwards and southwards of his own public ministry. (His sojourn in "Arabia," which may include the desert of Sinai, appears to have been of a more private character.)

**And round about . . .**—In a sort of rough curve, embracing a large portion of Asia Minor, and finally turning towards the starting-point again in Illyricum.

**Illyricum.**—A Roman province, stretching along the eastern coast of the Adriatic, and forming the northern boundary of Epirus, and the north-western of Macedonia. Whether St. Paul had actually visited Illyricum does not appear from his language in this passage. Illyricum is the *terminus ad quem* of his journeyings, but it may be inclusive, or it may be exclusive. The description would be sufficiently satisfied if he had approached the outskirts of Illyricum during his journey through Macedonia. That journey must be the one recorded in Acts xx. 2. The earlier journey of Acts xvi., xvii. can be traced clearly from place to place, and did not extend far enough inland, while the vague expression which we find in Acts xx. 2, "When he had gone over those parts," affords ample room for the circuit in question. This would place it at the end of the year 57 A.D.

**Fully preached.**—Literally, *fulfilled*. The translation of our version can perhaps hardly be improved, though, at the same time, it seems probable that what is intended is the publication of the gospel to its full geographical extent, and not the subjective sense in the Apostle of his own fulfilment of the duty of preaching the gospel laid upon him.

(20, 21) Throughout all this long missionary career, the Apostle had made it his endeavour not merely to go over old ground where others had been before him, but to seek out new and virgin soil, where he might enter as a pioneer, and convey the good news of the kingdom of heaven for the first time.

(20) **Yea, so have I strived.**—Rather, *but making it my ambition*. The Apostle set it before him as a point of honour, not merely to carry forward a work that others had begun, but to build up the whole edifice from the foundation himself.

**Not where Christ was named.**—Not in places where there were Christians already.

**Another man's foundation.**—Comp. 2 Cor. x. 15, 16; and for the use of the word "foundation" for the first preaching of the gospel, 1 Cor. iii. 10.

(21) **To whom . . .**—From the LXX. of Isa. lii. 15. The original has reference to the servant of Jehovah, first suffering and then glorified, so that *kings* should be dumb with astonishment at the change. Here it is applied to the evangelisation of distant heathen nations.

(22) **For which cause also.**—And just because I was so anxious to preach the gospel in new regions, and to finish what I had begun there, I have been prevented from coming to you sooner.

**Much.**—*These many times; so often.*

(23) **But now having no more place.**—The work had been finished, so far as the Apostle was concerned, in Asia Minor, Macedonia, and Greece. The churches had been founded, and fairly set going; and now he felt it his duty to go on to new fields, his duty in this respect also falling in with his wishes, as it would bring him to Rome.

**Place.**—Room for (new) working. The whole ground had been already occupied.

**Parts.**—A peculiar word from which our word "climate" is derived. The original idea appears to be the *slope* or *inclination* of the earth from the equator

(24) whensoever I take my journey into
Spain, I will come to you: for I trust
to see you in my journey, and to be
brought on my way thitherward by you,
if first I be somewhat filled with your
*company*.[1] (25) But now I go unto Jeru-
salem to minister unto the saints.
(26) For it hath pleased them of Mace-
donia and Achaia to make a certain
contribution for the poor saints which
are at Jerusalem. (27) It hath pleased
them verily; and their debtors they are.
For if the Gentiles have been made
partakers of their spiritual things, their
duty is also to minister unto them in
carnal things. (28) When therefore I
have performed this, and have sealed
to them this fruit, I will come by
you into Spain. (29) And I am sure
that, when I come unto you, I shall
come in the fulness of the blessing
of the gospel of Christ. (30) Now I
beseech you, brethren, for the Lord
Jesus Christ's sake, and for the love
of the Spirit, that ye strive together
with me in *your* prayers to God for
me; (31) that I may be delivered
from them that do not believe[2] in

1 Gr. *with you*, ver. 32.

2 Or, *are disobedient.*

---

towards the pole. Hence a "zone" or "region." The same word occurs in 2 Cor. xi. 10; Gal. i. 21.

(24) **Into Spain.**—In his eagerness to seek out entirely new regions, and to avoid any possibility of crossing the lines of his fellow Apostles, desiring also himself to gather in the "fulness of the Gentiles" so far as lay in his power, he had determined to push on even to Spain. Whether he ever succeeded in carrying out his purpose we cannot say positively, but it is, perhaps, rather more probable than not. A tradition which dates back to the Epistle of Clement of Rome (*circ.* A.D. 95) says that he visited "the extreme limit of the West," a phrase which seems hardly satisfied by being interpreted simply of Rome. The author of the Muratorian Fragment (*circ.* A.D. 170) speaks expressly of a journey to Spain, though his language looks as if it might be an inference from this Epistle. The Acts, it is true, do not carry the Apostle beyond Rome, but the phenomena of the Pastoral Epistles and tradition together seem to justify us in assuming the probability of a later journey or journeys not recorded in that volume, and the argument from silence, as the book in any case stops short of the death of the Apostle, counts for but little. This is just a case in which it cannot be wrong to accept the balance of the argument as it stands. At the same time it is impossible not to feel the grievous blank which lies over the later years of the life of St. Paul, and few things would be more deeply interesting, or would throw more light on the principles of criticism, than the discovery, if only it were possible, of the merest fragment bearing upon it. It is to be feared, however, that there is no reasonable hope of such a discovery being ever made.

**I will come to you . . .**—These words are wanting in the true text, and have to be supplied. The sentence is left unfinished.

**To be brought on my way.**—A graphic description of this "bringing upon the way," is given in the account of the departure of St. Paul after his seven days' sojourn at Tyre, Acts xxi. 5. (Comp. Acts. xx. 36—38.)

**Somewhat filled.**—Another characteristic touch. The Apostle will not allow it to be supposed that he could have *enough* of the society of the Roman Church. He therefore qualifies his expression, "somewhat filled," or "satisfied," "satisfied if only in part."

**If first I be somewhat filled** is practically equivalent to "when I have been filled."

(25) **But now.**—Before very long, I hope to pay you this visit, but for the present I am bound for Jerusalem, in the service of the Church, to convey the alms collected in Macedonia and Achaia for the poorer members of that community. In reference to this contribution, comp. Acts xxiv. 17; 1 Cor. xvi. 1, *et seq.*; 2 Cor. viii. 1, 2; ix. 1, *et seq.*

(26) **The poor saints.**—Literally, *for the poor among the saints.* It cannot, therefore, be inferred from this that the church at Jerusalem consisted entirely of poor. Still from the first it would seem as if persons like Joseph of Arimathæa, and Nicodemus, and Mary the mother of Mark, were exceptions, and we know that the church at Jerusalem suffered severely during the famine in the reign of Claudius. Wealthier churches, such as those of Macedonia and Greece, would naturally be glad to have the opportunity of sending relief to the mother church, from which they might be said to be derived themselves. St. Paul himself proceeds to urge this very argument. From Jerusalem went forth the gospel which had been preached in Greece and Macedonia, and it would be but a small and due return if some of the superfluous wealth of those more favoured regions found its way to Jerusalem.

(27) **It hath pleased them.**—It pleased the Macedonians and Achaians to make their contribution. And, indeed, they owed a debt to the church at Jerusalem which it was their duty, so well as they could, to discharge.

(28) **Sealed to them this fruit.**—Placed in their hands the sum raised by the collection. This will appear at first sight a somewhat stilted expression, but it takes a certain solemnity from the fact that St. Paul seems to regard this journey to Jerusalem as the close of his own apostolic labours in those parts, the dropping of the curtain, as it were, before a new act in his career.

**Will come by you.**—Will pass through your city on my way to Spain.

(29) **I shall come in the fulness.**—I shall bring with me, come furnished with, the fulness of the blessing of Christ. The words "of the gospel" should be omitted. By "the fulness of the blessing of Christ" the Apostle means the full or abundant measure of those spiritual blessings which he, as the Minister and Apostle of Christ, was commissioned to impart to them.

(30) **The love of the Spirit**—*i.e.*, the love inspired in them by the Spirit—flowing from the Spirit.

**Strive together with me.**—Second my own earnest entreaties.

(31) **From them that do not believe.**—This prayer of the Apostle was, perhaps, it may be said, partially granted. He escaped with his life from his

Judæa; and that my service which *I have* for Jerusalem may be accepted of the saints; (32) that I may come unto you with joy by the will of God, and may with you be refreshed.

(33) Now the God of peace *be* with you all. Amen.

A.D. 58.

CHAPTER XVI.—(1) I commend unto you Phebe our sister, which is a

---

unbelieving countrymen (Acts xxiii. 27), but only to be delivered over to the Romans. He was naturally in fear of the party to which he had himself once belonged, and who would regard him as one of the worst of apostates. But it is to be observed that he expresses no apprehension of the Judaising *Christians*, as might have been expected if their antagonism had really been as violent as some would make out.

**My service which I have for Jerusalem.**—*My service or ministration* (*i.e.*, "The gift of which I am the bearer") which is destined for Jerusalem.

**May be accepted.**—It is possible, though we cannot speak at all positively, that there was mingled with the desire of the Apostle to benefit the church at Jerusalem something of a wish to do a graceful and conciliatory act to that Judaising branch of the church from which circumstances tended to estrange him.

(32) The way in which he was received at Jerusalem would make a great difference to the feelings with which the Apostle would arrive in Rome. A favourable reception in Jerusalem would add much to his enjoyment and benefit from intercourse with the Roman Christians.

**With you be refreshed.**—The Greek word is a rare compound, which is found besides in the LXX. version of Isa. xi. 6, "the leopard shall lie down with the kid." The whole phrase ("and may with you be refreshed") is wanting in the Vatican MS.

(33) **Amen.**—The weight of MS. authority is decidedly in favour of retaining this word, though it is omitted by three MSS. of some importance.

It does not, however, follow that the benediction was intended, as some have thought, to close the Epistle. Intercalated benedictions and doxologies are frequent in the writings of St. Paul. (Comp. chaps. ix. 5; xi. 36; Gal. i. 5; Eph. iii. 20, 21, *et al.*)

## XVI.

It has been observed as strange that of all the Epistles of St. Paul, this to the Romans and that to Colossians, contain the greatest number of personal salutations, though these were precisely the two churches that he had never seen up to the date of his writing. A few critics, headed by Baur, have used this as an argument against the genuineness of the portion of the Epistles in question. But reasoning like this may safely be dismissed, as these very portions are just those which it would be most senseless and aimless to forge, even if it were possible on other grounds to think of them as a forgery.

On the other hand, there is some truth in the suggestion that the Apostle might think it invidious to single out individuals for special mention in the churches where he was known, while he would have no hesitation in naming those with whom he happened to be personally acquainted in churches where he was not known.

Besides this, it should be remembered that the Christians at Rome had been recently in a state of dispersion. All Jews by birth had been expelled from Rome by Claudius. It was this fact which had brought Aquila and Priscilla to Corinth and Ephesus, where St. Paul fell in with them, and he would naturally meet with other members of the dispersed church in the same way.

We are apt to underrate the amount of rapid circulation which went on in these early Christian communities. We know from Pagan writers that there was a great tendency all along the shores of the Mediterranean to gravitate towards Rome, and the population thus formed would naturally be a shifting and changing one, loosely attached to their temporary dwelling-place, and with many ties elsewhere. It will be noticed how many of the persons mentioned in the list had some prior connection with St. Paul, quite apart from their relation to the church at Rome. Andronicus, Junias, and Herodion, are described as his "kinsmen." Aquila and Priscilla, and we may add, almost with certainty, Epænetus, he had met in Asia. Of Amplias, Urban, Stachys, Persis, and Rufus, he speaks as if with personal knowledge. If the Received reading were correct ("us" for "you"), Mary would have to be added to this list, and possibly also Apelles.

Analysing these lists of names from another point of view, two further general conclusions appear to be borne out. (1) The church at Rome did not consist to any great extent of native Romans. The only strictly Latin names are Amplias (for Ampliatus), and Urbanus. Julia, in verse 15, merely marks a dependant upon the court. Aquila and Priscilla, Andronicus and Junia (or Junias), Herodion, and probably Rufus, appear to be Jews. The name Apelles, though not confined to Jews, was proverbially common among them. Aristobulus may be the Herodian prince of that name; in which case his household would be likely to be in great part Jews. The rest of the names are Greek. And this would tally with the fact that from the first there seems to have been a large Greek element in the church at Rome, so much so, that out of the twelve first bishops, only three seem to have borne Roman names, while the literature of the church, until some way into the third century, was Greek. (2) The names seem to belong in the main to the middle and lower classes of society. Many are such as are usually assigned to slaves or freed-men. Some are especially frequent in inscriptions relating to the imperial household; and this, taken in connection with the mention of "Cæsar's household" in Phil. iv. 22, may lead to the inference that Christianity had at this early date established itself in the palace of the emperor, though only among the lower order of servants.

(1) **Phebe.**—As the Roman Church is especially exhorted to receive Phebe, it has been inferred that she was one of the party to which St. Paul entrusted his Epistle, if not the actual bearer of it herself.

**Our sister**—*i.e.*, in a spiritual sense—a fellow-Christian.

**Servant.**—Rather, *a deaconess*, keeping the technical term. Deacons were originally appointed to attend to the wants of the poorer members of the Church. This is the first mention of women-deacons, in regard to whom instructions are given to Timothy (1 Tim. iii. 11). The necessity for an order of deaconesses would gradually make itself felt where women were kept in a stricter seclusion, as in Greece and some parts of the East.

servant of the church which is at
Cenchrea: (2) that ye receive her in the
Lord, as becometh saints, and that ye
assist her in whatsoever business she
hath need of you: for she hath been a
succourer of many, and of myself also.
(3) Greet Priscilla and Aquila my helpers
in Christ Jesus: (4) who have for my
life laid down their own necks: unto
whom not only I give thanks, but also
all the churches of the Gentiles.
(5) Likewise *greet* the church that is in
their house. Salute my wellbeloved
Epænetus, who is the firstfruits of
Achaia unto Christ. (6) Greet Mary,
who bestowed much labour on us.
(7) Salute Andronicus and Junia, my
kinsmen, and my fellowprisoners, who
are of note among the apostles, who
also were in Christ before me. (8) Greet
Amplias my beloved in the Lord.
(9) Salute Urbane, our helper in Christ,
and Stachys my beloved. (10) Salute
Apelles approved in Christ. Salute

---

**Cenchrea.**—The port of Corinth, at the head of the Eastern or Saronic Gulf, about nine miles from the city.

(2) **In the Lord.**—With the consciousness that you are performing a Christian act, subject to all those serious obligations implied in the name.

**As becometh saints.**—As Christians ought to receive a fellow-Christian.

**Succourer.**—Patroness or protectress, in the exercise of her office as deaconess.

**Of myself also.**—Perhaps in illness.

(3) **Priscilla.**—The correct reading here is Prisca, of which form Priscilla is the diminutive. It is rather remarkable that the wife should be mentioned first. Perhaps it may be inferred that she was the more active and conspicuous of the two.

Aquila was a Jew of Pontus, whom St. Paul had found with his wife at Corinth (Acts xviii. 1). They had there been converted by him, and afterwards appear in his company at Ephesus (Acts xviii. 18, 26; 1 Cor. xvi. 19). At the time when this Epistle was written they were at Rome, but later they seem to have returned to Ephesus (2 Tim. iv. 19).

The Jew Aquila, who rather more than a century later made a translation of the Old Testament, critically compared with the LXX. in the *Hexapla* of Origen, also came from Pontus.

(4) **Laid down their own necks.**—Whether this expression is to be taken literally or figuratively we do not know, neither can we do more than guess at the event to which it refers. It may have something to do with the tumult at Ephesus, and with that "fighting with beasts" mentioned in 1 Cor. xv. 32.

(5) **The church that is in their house.**—A party of Christians seem to have been in the habit of meeting in the house of Aquila and Priscilla for purposes of worship at Rome, as previously at Ephesus (1 Cor. xvi. 19). Similar instances may be found in Acts xii. 12; Col. iv. 15; Philem. verse 2.

**Salute.**—The same word in the Greek is translated indifferently by "salute" and "greet," an unnecessary caprice.

**Firstfruits of Achaia.**—For "Achaia" we ought certainly to read "Asia"—*i.e.,* the Roman province of Asia, a broad strip of territory including the whole western end of the peninsula of Asia Minor, from the Propontis in the north, to Lycia in the south. Ephesus was the capital, and the seven "churches in Asia" to which St. John wrote in the Apocalypse—Ephesus, Smyrna, Pergamos, Thyatira, Sardis, Philadelphia, Laodicea—were the most central and important of its cities.

By "firstfruits of Asia" is meant one of the first converts won over to Christianity in Asia. (Comp. "firstfruits of Achaia," in 1 Cor. xvi. 15, through the parallelism of which the text of our own passage became corrupted.)

(6) **On us.**—The true reading seems to be, *on you.* The readers would know to what the Apostle referred. It is useless for us to attempt to conjecture.

(7) **Junia.**—Or, possibly, "Junias" (for Junianus), a man's name.

**My kinsmen.**—From the number of persons (six in all, and those not only in Rome but also in Greece and Macedonia) to whom the title is given in this chapter, it would seem as if the word "kinsmen" was to be taken in a wider sense than that which it usually bears. It probably means members of the same nation —Jews like myself.

**Fellow-prisoners.**—It is not at all known to what this refers. The only imprisonment of St. Paul recorded in the Acts after this date would be that at Philippi, but allusions such as those in 2 Cor. vi. 5, and xi. 23, at once show the defectiveness of the narrative, and point to occasions when the persons mentioned might easily have shared imprisonment with him.

**Of note among the apostles.**—An ambiguous expression, which *might* mean, and, judging by the word alone, would perhaps more naturally be taken to mean, "distinguished *as* Apostles themselves." This sense is not to be disregarded as absolutely impossible, for the title "Apostles" does not appear to have been limited to the Twelve. It is decidedly more probable that James, the Lord's brother, who is called an Apostle in Gal. i. 19, and elsewhere, was not identical with James the son of Alphæus. And, however this may be, there can be no question about Barnabas, who is called an Apostle in Acts xiv. 14. St. Paul himself seems to draw a distinction between "the Twelve" and "all the Apostles," in 1 Cor. xv. 7. Still, on the whole, it seems best to suppose that the phrase "of note among the Apostles" means, "highly esteemed by the apostolic circle."

**Were in Christ . . . .**—*i.e.,* became Christians.

(8) **Amplias.**—The three oldest MSS. have "Ampliatus," for which "Amplias" would be in any case a contracted form. The name is a common one, in several instances found in connection with the imperial household.

(9) **Urbane.**—Urbanus, or Urban; the final "e" should not be sounded. Like Ampliatus, a common name found among members of the household.

**Our helper in Christ.**—The "helper," that is, both of St. Paul and of the Roman Church by her efforts in spreading the gospel.

**Stachys.**—A rarer name than the last two; it appears as that of a court physician in the inscriptions of about the date of this Epistle.

(10) **Apelles.**—This name is also found among the dependants of the emperor. Horace, in the well-known

them which are of Aristobulus' *house-*
*hold.* (11) Salute Herodion my kinsman.
Greet them that be of the *household*
of Narcissus, which are in the Lord.
(12) Salute Tryphena and Tryphosa, who
labour in the Lord. Salute the beloved
Persis, which laboured much in the
Lord. (13) Salute Rufus chosen in the
Lord, and his mother and mine.
(14) Salute Asyncritus, Phlegon, Hermas,
Patrobas, Hermes, and the brethren
which are with them. (15) Salute Phi-
lologus, and Julia, Nereus, and his
sister, and Olympas, and all the saints
which are with them. (16) Salute one
another with an holy kiss. The churches
of Christ salute you. (17) Now I be-
seech you, brethren, mark them which
cause divisions and offences contrary to
the doctrine which ye have learned;
and avoid them. (18) For they that are
such serve not our Lord Jesus Christ,
but their own belly; and by good words
and fair speeches deceive the hearts of
the simple. (19) For your obedience is
come abroad unto all *men.* I am glad

---

phrase, "Credat Judæas Apella" (*Ep.* 1, v. 100) takes it as a typical Jewish name.

**Approved in Christ.**—Whose fidelity to Christ has been tried, and has stood the test.

**Aristobulus' household.**—Aristobulus, a grandson of Herod the Great, was educated and lived in a private station at Rome. From the friendly terms on which he stood with the Emperor Claudius, it seems not unlikely that, by a somewhat common custom, his household may have been transferred to the emperor at his death. In that case, his slaves would be designated by a term such as we find in the Greek.

(11) **My kinsman.**—See the Note on verse 7.

**Them that be of the household of Narcissus.**—A phrase similar to that which is translated, "Them which are of Aristobulus' household," above. Narcissus, too, is an historical name. There had been a famous Narcissus, a freed-man and favourite of Claudius, who had been put to death three or four years before this Epistle was written. His household would naturally pass into the hands of the emperor, though still keeping his name. In the case of Aristobulus, the transference would be effected by bequest, in that of Narcissus by confiscation. Many instances of both methods occur in the history and records of the time.

The interpretation here given, and the identification of Aristobulus and Narcissus with the historical bearers of those names, is some way short of certain, but may be said to have some degree of probability.

(12) **Tryphena and Tryphosa.**—Probably sisters or near relatives. They, too, may have been attached to the court.

(13) **Rufus.**—Simon of Cyrene is described in St. Mark's Gospel (xv. 21) as "the father of Alexander and Rufus," and as there is a substantial tradition, favoured by some internal indications, that this Gospel was written at Rome, it is not unlikely that the same Rufus may be meant.

**Chosen in the Lord.**—An eminent Christian.

**His mother and mine.**—His mother, who has also been like a mother to me.

(14) Of the names in this and the next verse, Hermas, Patrobas, Hermes, Philologus, Julia, Nereus (with the corresponding female name Nereis) all occur with more or less frequency in inscriptions relating to the household. Hermas and Hermes are very common. The first is a contraction from several longer forms. Patrobas is contracted from Patrobius. We find that a freed-man of Nero's who bore this name was put to death by Galba; but the person saluted by St. Paul is more likely to have been a dependant of his than the man himself.

Taking the list of names as a whole, and comparing them with the inscriptions, we may—without going so far as to identify individuals, which would be precarious ground—nevertheless, note the general coincidence with the mention of "Cæsar's household" in Phil. iv. 22.

(16) **Salute one another.**—As a mark of brotherly feeling among themselves, St. Paul desires those who are assembled at the reading of his Epistle to greet each other in a Christian way. It is to be their own act and not a salutation coming from him.

**With an holy kiss.**—A common Eastern and Jewish custom specially consecrated in Christianity. (Comp. 1 Cor. xvi. 20; 2 Cor. xiii. 12; 1 Thess. v. 26; 1 Pet. v. 14.)

**The churches of Christ.**—The word "all" should be inserted. As being the Apostle of the Gentiles, and knowing as he did the interest which all would take in the church of the great metropolis, St. Paul feels himself fully justified in speaking for all the churches of his foundation.

(17–20) Here the Epistle would naturally end, but an afterthought occurs to the Apostle. His experience of other churches, especially those at Corinth and in Galatia, suggests to him that he should warn his readers against false teachers, though such had not as yet obtained any great hold among them.

(17) **Cause divisions and offences.**—Set traps in the way of the unwary, so as to entice them into false doctrine and schismatical practices.

(18) **Their own belly.**—Compare the description in Phil. iii. 18, 19, where the Apostle is also denouncing certain persons who made "a god of their belly." It is not, however, quite clear that the class of persons intended is precisely the same. There the Apostle is condemning Antinomian extravagances which professed to be based on his own teaching; here he would seem to have in view some more radical divergence of doctrine, "contrary to" that which they had learned. Selfish indulgence is unfortunately a common goal, to which many diverse ways of error will be found to lead.

**By good words and fair speeches.**—The difference, perhaps, is between "insinuating" or "specious" address, and "fine phrases" in a rhetorical sense.

**Simple.**—Literally, *guileless.* Those who have no evil intentions themselves, and do not readily suspect others of them.

(19) No harm has been done as yet. Still it is well to be upon your guard.

therefore on your behalf: but yet I
would have you wise unto that which
is good, and simple concerning evil.
(20) And the God of peace shall bruise [1]
Satan under your feet shortly. The
grace of our Lord Jesus Christ *be* with
you. Amen. (21) Timotheus my work-
fellow, and Lucius, and Jason, and
Sosipater, my kinsmen, salute you.
(22) I Tertius, who wrote *this* epistle,
salute you in the Lord (23) Gaius mine
host, and of the whole church, saluteth
you. Erastus the chamberlain of the
city saluteth you, and Quartus a
brother. (24) The grace of our Lord
Jesus Christ *be* with you all. Amen.

1 Or, *tread.*

---

**Simple concerning evil.**—This is not at all the same word as that which is translated "simple" above. The first is that freedom from dishonest motives which makes a man an unsuspecting and easy prey for designing persons, and applies rather to natural bent and disposition. The second refers rather to the confirmed habit of one who has come in contact with evil, and is still uncontaminated by it; who has resisted all the plots and schemes that have been laid for him; and whose love for what is good and hatred of evil, has only been strengthened and disciplined. The word for "simple" here means "unmixed," "uncontaminated," "pure and clear."

(20) **The God of peace.**—We can well understand how the Apostle, in the midst of "fightings without and fears within," should look forward with joyous confidence to the time when both for him and his readers all this turmoil and conflict would give way to "peace." The reference seems to be to his near expectation of the Messiah's return, and with it the final victory of the faith. The Romans have not begun to feel the bitterness of divisions as yet; he foresees a time when they will do so, but beyond that he foresees a further time when all will be hushed and quelled, and the Great Adversary himself for ever overthrown.

**Bruise.**—With reference to Gen. iii. 15.

**The grace . . . .**—The more correct reading of the benediction is simply, *The grace of our Lord Jesus be with you,* the other words being omitted. The four principal Græco-Latin Codices omit the benediction here altogether and insert it in verse 24, where it also appears in the Received text, though wanting in MSS. of the best type.

(21–23) The companions of St. Paul add their own greetings to the Roman Church.

(21) **Timotheus.**—Timothy had been sent on in advance from Ephesus (Acts xx. 22). He would seem to have gone on into Greece and to Corinth itself (1 Cor. iv. 17, and xvi. 10). He had thence rejoined St. Paul on his way through Macedonia (2 Cor. i. 1), and he was now with him again in Greece.

In the other Epistles (2 Cor., Phil., Col., 1 and 2 Thess., and Philem.), when Timothy was present with St. Paul at the time of his writing, he is joined with him in the salutation at the outset. Why his name does not appear in the heading of the present letter we can hardly say. Perhaps he happened to be away at the time when it was begun; or, St. Paul may have thought it well that a church which was entirely strange to him, and to which Timothy too was a stranger, should be addressed in his own name alone.

**Lucius.**—This may, perhaps, be the Lucius of Cyrene mentioned in Acts xiii. 1; but the name is too common for anything to be asserted positively.

**Jason.**—A Jason is mentioned as having received St. Paul and his companions on their first visit to Thessalonica, and getting himself into trouble in consequence (Acts xvii. 5—9). It would be some slight argument for this identification if the word "kinsmen" were taken in its narrower sense; there would then be a reason why St. Paul should have found hospitality in the house of Jason.

**Sosipater.**—Possibly "Sopater, the son of Pyrrhus, of Berœa," mentioned in Acts xx. 4 (corrected reading).

(22) **Tertius.**—The Apostle's amanuensis. It was the custom of St. Paul to add a few words of parting benedictory encouragement or admonition in his own handwriting, partly as a mark of his own personal interest in his readers, and partly as a precaution against forgery. (See especially Gal. vi. 11, and 2 Thess. iii. 17.) We have observed in the course of this Commentary how frequently the involved and broken style is to be accounted for by this habit of dictation, and, as it would seem, not very punctilious revision. We have the thoughts and words of the Apostle as they came warm from his own mind.

(23) **Gaius.**—Three persons of this name are mentioned, Gaius of Corinth (1 Cor. i. 14), Gaius, a Macedonian (Acts xix. 29), and Gaius of Derbe in Lycaonia (Acts xx. 4). The Gaius of the Epistle would probably be identical with the first of these. The name was a common one.

**Mine host, and of the whole church.**—St. Paul was now lodging in the house of Gaius, as on his previous visit, first in that of Aquila and then in that of Justus (Acts xviii. 2, 7). It would seem that Gaius lent his house for the meetings of the Church, or it is possible that St. Paul may be alluding, with graceful hyperbole, to the hospitality which he was always ready to exercise.

**Erastus.**—It is not quite easy to identify this Erastus with the one mentioned in Acts xix. 22, 2 Tim. iv. 20, who there appears as a travelling companion of the Apostle. The office of "treasurer" to an important city like Corinth would naturally, we should suppose, involve a fixed residence.

**Chamberlain.**—A better word would seem to be *treasurer.* The officer in question had charge of the revenues of the city. The title appears upon inscriptions.

**A brother.**—Rather, *the brother.* No special predicate seems to be needed, and therefore St. Paul (or Tertius) simply describes him as the Christian of that name.

(24) **The grace of our Lord Jesus Christ.**—This verse is wanting in the oldest group of MSS., and is found chiefly in Græco-Latin Codices and in Antiochene authorities of the fourth and fifth centuries, whose leaning is towards the later text.

If the theory stated in the introduction to chapter xv. is correct, the doxology which follows was added by the Apostle to complete the *shorter* edition of the Epistle, but soon came to be taken as a fitting close to the whole.

Allusion has been made to the resemblance which it presents to the Pastoral Epistles and the Epistle to

(25) Now to him that is of power to
stablish you according to my gospel,
and the preaching of Jesus Christ,
according to the revelation of the
mystery, which was kept secret since
the world began, (26) but now is made
manifest, and by the scriptures of the
prophets, according to the commandment of the everlasting God, made
known to all nations for the obedience
of faith: (27) to God only wise, *be* glory
through Jesus Christ for ever. Amen.

Written to the Romans from Corinthus, *and sent* by Phebe servant of the church at Cenchrea.

---

the Ephesians. This will readily be seen when the parallel expressions are placed side by side.

| | |
|---|---|
| Rom. xvi. 25—27.—"To Him that is of power." | Eph. iii. 20.—"Unto Him that is able" (precisely the same words in the Greek). |
| "According to my gospel." | 2 Tim. ii. 8.—"According to my gospel" (the same phrase is, however, found in Rom. ii. 16). |
| "The preaching of Jesus Christ, according to the revelation of the mystery, which was kept secret since the world began, but now is made manifest, and by the scriptures of the prophets, according to the commandment of the everlasting God, made known to all nations for the obedience of faith." | Eph. iii. 3, 5, 6.—"By revelation He made known unto us the mystery . . . . which in other ages was not made known unto the sons of men, as it is now revealed unto His holy apostles and prophets by the Spirit, that the Gentiles should be," &c. Eph. iii. 9, 10.—"The mystery which from the beginning of the world hath been hid . . . . to the intent that now . . . . might be known." Tit. i. 2, 3.—"Which God . . . . before the world began" (peculiar and identical phrase); "but hath in due times manifested His word through preaching, which is committed unto me according to the commandment" (same word) "of God our Saviour." 2 Tim. i. 9, 10.—"Which was given us . . . . before the world began, but is now made manifest," &c. |
| "To God only wise, be glory, through Jesus Christ for ever" (Greek, "for ever and ever"). "Amen." | 1 Tim. i. 17.—"Now unto the King eternal" (similar to "everlasting God" above), "the only wise God" (but "wise" is a doubtful reading), "be honour and glory for ever and ever. Amen." |

(25) **Stablish**—*i.e.*, to confirm and strengthen in all the elements of a Christian character.

**According to my gospel.**—By those means of grace which the gospel that I preach indicates and enjoins you to use.

**My gospel.**—The gospel preached by me; the gospel preached as I preach it.

**And the preaching of Jesus Christ.**—And in accordance with that preaching, the subject matter of which is Christ. The establishment of the Roman Christians was to take place through those appointed ways and means that are laid down in the gospel, and form the main topic of Christian preaching. All means of grace centre in Christ, and it is only in accordance with the due proclamation of Him that the Christian can hope to become confirmed and strengthened.

**According to the revelation.**—An involved and difficult sentence. The two clauses which began with "according to" are co-ordinate together, and are both dependent upon the word "stablish" above. "May God establish and confirm you in all those ways that the gospel of Christ lays down; that gospel the introduction of which it has been reserved for these latter days to see; a secret long hidden, but now revealed, and corroborated as it is by the prophetic writings, and preached by the Apostles at God's express command; the great instrument of bringing over the Gentiles to the faith."

**Of the mystery.**—The word "mystery" is used elsewhere in the New Testament precisely in the sense which is so clearly defined in this passage of something which up to the time of the Apostles had remained secret, but had then been made known by divine intervention. The "mystery" thus revealed is the same as that described in the two preceding clauses—in one word, Christianity. All through the Old Testament dispensation, the Christian scheme, which was then future, had remained hidden; now, with Christ's coming, the veil has been taken away.

**Since the world began.**—The English phrase here is paraphrastic. Literally, the Greek is *in eternal times—i.e.,* from this present moment, stretching backwards throughout eternity—an emphatic way of saying, "never before." "The Old Testament is the hand of a clock, proceeding silently round the dial—the New Testament is the striking of the hour" (Bengel).

(26) **But now is made manifest.**—The first clause of this verse goes with the last clause of the preceding "mystery," which before was kept secret, but now has been "made manifest." The rest of the verse all hangs together: "this mystery, through the help of the corroboration which it derives from the prophets of the Old Testament, has, by God's command to us, the Apostles, been made known."

**By the scriptures of the prophets.**—Through the help of that appeal to prophecy which we are enabled to make.

**According to the commandment.**—That which had taken place according to the command of God was the making known of the gospel to the Gentiles, as, *e.g.*, when Paul and Barnabas were specially "separated" for the work by the Holy Ghost.

**Made known to all nations.**—The word "to" has a little more stress laid upon it than would appear from the English, "made known so as to reach all nations."

**For the obedience of faith.**—An exact repetition of the phrase in chap. i. 5, "to win over the Gentiles unto the allegiance demanded of them by faith in Christ."

(27) **To God.**—Our English translation has evaded the difficulty of this verse by leaving out two words. The

Greek stands literally thus, "To the only wise God, through Jesus Christ, *to whom* be glory for ever." "To whom," if it refers to God, as it is decidedly more probable that it was intended to refer, is ungrammatical. If it is inserted, the words "To him that is able . . . to God, the only wise," are left without government. This might, indeed, under ordinary circumstances be got over, as such broken constructions are frequent with St. Paul, but it is somewhat different in the last solemn words of an Epistle, and would be especially so if this doxology were composed by itself separately from the rest of the Epistle. There would not then be the usual excuse of haste; and for so short a passage it may be doubted whether the Apostle would even employ an amanuensis. The difficulty is heightened when we ask what is meant by the phrase, "through Jesus Christ." Separated, as it would then be, from the ascription of glory, and joined to "the only wise God," it would seem to be impossible to get any really satisfactory sense out of it. "To God, who through Christ has shown Himself as the alone wise," is maintained, but is surely very forced. Our conclusion then, prior to the evidence, would be that there was a mistake in the reading, and that the words "to whom" had slipped in without warrant. And now we find that a single uncial MS., but that precisely the oldest and best of all the uncials, the *Codex Vaticanus*, with two cursives, omits these words. The suspicion would indeed naturally arise that they had been left out specially on account of their difficulty. But this is a suspicion from which on the whole, the Vatican MS. is peculiarly free. And, on the other hand, it is just as natural to assume that another common cause of corruption has been at work. Doxologies so frequently begin with the relative, "To whom be glory," &c., that the copyist would be liable to fall into the phrase, even in places where it was not originally written. The probabilities of corruption may therefore be taken to balance each other, and it will seem, perhaps, on the whole, the most probable solution that the relative has really slipped in at a very early date, and that the English version as it stands is substantially right. There are some exceptions to the rule that "the more difficult reading is to be preferred," and this is perhaps one.

The subscription in its present form hardly dates back beyond the ninth century. The earliest form of subscription up to the sixth century was simply "To the Romans."

# EXCURSUS ON NOTES TO ROMANS

## EXCURSUS A: ON THE MEANING OF THE WORD "RIGHTEOUSNESS" IN THE EPISTLE TO THE ROMANS.

RIGHTEOUSNESS is necessarily the object of all religions. Religion exists in order to set men right before God, to place them in that relation in which He would have them be, to make them secure of His favour and fit to perform His service.

The conception of "righteousness" entered in a special and peculiar way into the religion of the Jews at the time of our Lord. The word had a clearly-defined sense, which was somewhat narrower than that usually attached to it. It meant, not so much the subjective condition of righteousness—that disposition of the heart and mind which necessarily leads to righteous actions—as the objective fact of acting in accordance with the divine commands. Righteousness was the *fulfilling of the Law*. From what kind of motive the Law was fulfilled the Jew did not stay to inquire. The main point with him was that the Commandments of the Law should be kept, and that having thus fulfilled his share in the compact he could lay claim to the blessings which the divine covenant promised.

As might have been expected, the idea of "righteousness" holding so prominent a place in Jewish teaching generally, held an equally prominent place in that group of ideas which centered in the Messiah. Righteousness was to be the main characteristic of the Messianic reign. This appears distinctly in the *pre-* and *post-*Christian Jewish literature. Thus the Sibylline Books (*circ.* B.C. 140): "For all good order shall come upon men from the starry heaven, and righteous dealing, and with it holy concord, which for mortals excels all things, and love, faith, hospitality. And from them shall flee lawlessness, blame, envy, anger, folly." "And in righteousness, having obtained the law of the Most High, they shall dwell happily in cities and rich fields." The Book of Enoch (B.C. 150—100): "God will be gracious to the righteous, and give him eternal righteousness, and give him dominion, and he shall be in goodness and righteousness, and walk in eternal light. And some shall go down into darkness for ever and ever, and shall no more appear from that day for ever." The Psalms of Solomon (*circ.* B.C. 48): "He shall not suffer unrighteousness to lodge in the midst of them, and there shall not dwell with them any man who knows wickedness." The Book of Jubilees (before A.D. 70): "After this they will turn to me in all righteousness, with all their heart and all their soul, and I will circumcise their heart and the heart of their seed, and will make for them a holy spirit and purify them, that they may no more turn away from me from that day for ever." The Fourth Book of Ezra (perhaps A.D. 80 or 97): "The heart of the inhabitants of the world shall be changed, and turned into another mind. For evil shall be destroyed, and quite extinguished; but faith shall flourish, and corruption be overcome, and truth, which for so long a time was without fruit, shall be displayed."

But the righteousness of the Messianic period was to be as much ceremonial as moral. The Sibyl prophesied that there was to be "a sacred race of pious men, devoted to the counsels and mind of the Most High, who round about it will glorify the temple of the great God with libation and savour of victims, and with sacred hecatombs and sacrifices of well-fed bulls, and perfect rams, and firstlings of the sheep, and purely presenting on a great altar fat flocks of lambs as whole burnt offerings." The Book of Jubilees declares circumcision to be "an everlasting ordinance," and insists upon the obligation of eating the tithe of all produce before the Lord: "It has been established as a law in heaven;" "for this law there is no end of days; that ordinance is written down for ever." The Targum of Isaiah directly connects the Messianic advent with the triumph of the Law: "At that time the Messias of the Lord shall be for joy and for glory, and the doers of the Law for magnificence and for praise;" "they shall look upon the kingdom of their Messiah, . . . . and the doers of the Law of the Lord shall prosper in His good pleasure."

Christianity took the conception of righteousness as it stood in the current Jewish beliefs, but gave to it a profounder significance. Much as the Jews insisted upon righteousness, our Lord insisted upon it still more. The righteousness of the Christian was to surpass that of the Jew, both in its amount and in its nature: "Except your righteousness shall exceed the righteousness of the scribes and Pharisees, ye shall in no case enter into the kingdom of heaven." In exposition of this principle, our Lord proceeds to show by a series of examples how the righteousness, which had hitherto been outward, should become inward, and extend to the inmost thoughts and disposition of the heart. At the same time He proposed Himself as the personal object of the religious life. His invitation was, "Come unto Me;" and His reproach was, "Ye will not come unto Me."

St. Paul arrives at the same result, but in a different way. He, too, took as his starting-point the Jewish conception of righteousness. What impressed him most in it was the impossibility that it could really be carried out. It was impossible to keep the whole law, but to transgress it at all was to transgress it, and so to forfeit the Divine favour. But if righteousness was not to be obtained by the Law, how was it to be obtained? It was to this question that Christianity supplied the great solution through the doctrine of the Messiahship of Jesus. Jesus is the Messiah. With His coming the Messianic reign is begun. But the characteristic of that reign is righteousness. Therefore, by becoming a member of the Messianic kingdom, the Christian enters into a condition of righteousness. This righteousness is, in the first instance, ideal rather than actual. In the language of St. Paul, it is "imputed." It does not necessarily involve a real fulfilment of the Divine Law, but the sincere Christian by virtue of the relation into which he enters with Christ, is treated as if he had fulfilled it. He has recovered his lost state of favour with God.

This is, however, only the beginning of his career. The simple entrance into the Messianic kingdom carries with it so much. But the whole of the Christian's life, as a member of the kingdom, is to be a constantly increasing realisation in his own walk and conduct of the ideal righteousness at first attributed to him. This realisation takes place through the same agency as that by which he first entered into the kingdom—faith. Faith, by intensifying his hold upon Christ, gives him a greater and ever greater power to overcome the impulses of sin and adopt the life of Christ as his own. Hence the Apostle speaks of the righteousness of God being revealed "from faith to faith," meaning that faith ends as well as begins the career of the Christian, and that it is the one faculty that he is called upon to exercise all through.

And yet all the righteousness to which the Christian attains—whether it is as ideal and imputed, or whether it is seen and realised in a course of action consistent with his profession—all this comes to him as a part of his Messianic privileges. He would not have it unless he were a member of the Messianic kingdom. It is not his own making, but he is placed within reach of it by virtue of his participation in the Messianic scheme. Inasmuch, therefore, as that scheme is, in all its parts, a divine act, and the working out of the divine counsel, the righteousness of the Christian is described as a "righteousness *of God*," *i.e.*, a righteousness *proceeding from God*—a state produced by divine intervention, and not by human means. The whole scheme is planned and set in motion by God, man's part consisting in taking to himself what God has prepared for him; and merely to do this involves a life-long effort and a constant call upon the will.

[The references to the Jewish Messianic idea in this Excursus are taken from Prof. Drummond's work, *The Jewish Messiah*, pp. 323—326.]

---

## EXCURSUS B: ON THE MEANING OF THE WORD "FAITH."

Faith is the distinctively Christian faculty. So far as concerns the apprehension by man of the divine scheme of salvation, it is the cardinal point in Christian theology. And that it occupies this place is due more than anything else to the teaching of St. Paul.

If we ask how St. Paul himself arrived at his conception of "faith," the answer would seem to be, From reflection upon certain passages of the Old Testament Scripture, seen in the light of his own religious experience.

There were two passages in which faith was brought into direct connection with ideas that lay at the root of all Jewish theology. In Habakkuk ii. 4, "The just shall live by his faith," faith was associated with life—*i.e.*, salvation. In Gen. xv. 6, the faith of Abraham was said to be "imputed to him for righteousness." Faith was here associated with another idea, the importance of which we have just seen—that of righteousness. There appears to be sufficient evidence to show that this second text was one much discussed in the Jewish schools, both of Alexandria and of Palestine. It is, therefore, very possible that the attention of the Apostle may have been turned to it before his conversion.

But what was the Faith which thus brought with it righteousness and salvation? The answer to this question was furnished to St. Paul by his own religious experience. His own consciousness of a complete revolution wrought within him dated from the time when he accepted Jesus as the Messiah. That one change, he felt, had worked wonders. It placed him in an altogether different relation to his old difficulties. Righteousness was no more impossible to him. If he found a law in his members warring against the law of his mind, he could "thank God through Jesus Christ his Lord." But, apart from this, without any actual righteousness of his own, the mere fact of being assured that he was a member of the Messianic kingdom was enough to give him confidence that righteousness in some sense or other was his. He felt himself bound up with a system of which righteousness was the characteristic. As a member of that system he, too, must be righteous. But that which made him a member of this system was the heartfelt acceptance of the Messiahship of Jesus. And to this acceptance St. Paul gave the name of Faith. Faith, however, was with him, not a single act which began and ended in itself, it was a continued state—an active energy of loyalty and devotion directed towards Jesus as the Messiah.

Faith in the Old Testament had meant "trust," "reliance"—a firm reliance upon God, and confidence in the fulfilment of His promises. When a similar feeling was entertained towards a definite human person, who had exhibited a character in the highest degree winning and attractive, and who had ended a life of self-sacrifice by a nobly and pathetically self-sacrificing death, it was natural that these emotions should develop into something still stronger. Trust became devotion. Passive reliance strengthened into an ardent and energetic service. The strongest feeling that could bind the soldiers of an army to their captain had its place here. Love, veneration, gratitude, devoted loyalty—all were blended into a single feeling, and that feeling was what St. Paul meant by Faith.

As life went on, and the tie which bound the Christian to Christ was tested by experience, faith became stronger and stronger. Its object being personal, it became more and more concentrated on that Person. By degrees it took a different shape. It brought the Christian so closely within the influence of his Master, it led to such an assimilation of his life to his Master's, that something nearer and more intimate had to be found to express the nature of the relation between them. St. Paul speaks of it as if it were an actual union—a oneness, or fellowship, with Christ. But the agency which brings about this union is Faith—the same faith which began with the simple historical affirmation, "Jesus is the Messiah." When once the Messiahship of Jesus was recognised, the rest all followed by natural train and sequence. The last perfection of Christian character is connected with its first initial step, just as the full-blown flower is connected with the germ that first appears above the ground. Its existence is continuous. The forces which give it vitality are the same. And the forces which give vitality to the religious life of the Christian are summed up in the one word, Faith.

## EXCURSUS C: ON THE STATE OF THE HEATHEN WORLD AT THE TIME OF ST. PAUL.

In regard to the terrible description of the state of the heathen world, given at the end of chap. i., two questions may be asked: (1) How far does it correspond with what we gather from other sources? (2) Supposing the picture to be in the main a true one, do the causes and process of corruption appear to have been such as the Apostle describes?

(1) No doubt, if we take the evidence that has come down to us simply as it stands, there is enough to justify the very strongest language. But some considerations, perhaps, may be urged in mitigation of this.

(*a*) Our knowledge of the state of morals in that age is largely derived from the satirists. But it may be said that satire has never been quite a fair index of the average state of things. By the nature of the case it seeks out that which is extravagant and abnormal. It deals with exceptions rather than with the rule. And even where it exposes not so much the vices and follies of an individual as those prevailing over a larger section of society, it still presupposes a higher standard of judgment in the public to which it appeals. It assumes that what it reprehends will be generally held to be reprehensible. It would not be able to hold its ground at all unless it could calculate upon the support of the sounder portion of the community.

(*b*) Accordingly we find that many of the worst forms of corruption are mentioned only to be condemned. It was "burning indignation" which inspired the verse of Juvenal. Historians like Tacitus, moralists like Seneca, Epictetus, and M. Aurelius, lift up their voice to condemn the depravity of the age. Horace, though without being a Puritan himself, complains how the generation to which he belonged had degenerated from their ancestors. Ovid and Martial are obliged to defend themselves against the charge of indecency that was evidently brought against them by some of their contemporaries. Stringent laws were in existence, if seldom enforced, against some of the crimes of which the satires are fullest. And there was a point beyond which the toleration of law and of opinion would not go. Witness the summary punishment that followed upon the discovery of a gross scandal perpetrated in the temple of Isis. The guilty persons were banished, the priests crucified, the temple razed to the ground, and the statue of the goddess flung into the river. It is only fair to state both sides of the question. If the idolatrous worship led to such things, the judgment of mankind was at least not so far perverted that wrong could be done with impunity.

(*c*) Nor was this altogether a hypocritical condemnation. There are some conspicuous exceptions to the general corruption. It may be doubted whether any age can produce examples of a more consistent and earnest pursuit of the highest accessible standard than were afforded by Plutarch, Epictetus, and M. Aurelius. If we estimate them, not so much by the positive value of the morality to which they attained as by the strength of their aim and effort to realise a lofty ideal, these men will not easily be equalled. Again, Cicero, Atticus, the younger Pliny, may be taken as types of the cultivated gentlemen of their day, and they would have had a high place even in our own time. The emperors occupied a position singularly open to temptation, and no less than five of them in succession would have done honour to any throne. The pages of the historian which describe the decline of political and social morals are, nevertheless, lighted up with deeds of heroism and ancient Roman virtue. The women emulated the men. Occasionally, as in the case of the elder Arria, they surpassed them. But many others showed a constancy broken only by death. Descending to lower ranks, the inscriptions tell us not a few touching stories of conjugal fidelity and affection. "She was dearer to me than my life; she died in her twenty-third year, greatly beloved by her friends." "To my dearest wife, with whom I lived for eighteen years, without a complaint." "She never caused me a pang but by her death." "I have done for thee those sad rites which thou shouldest have done for me, and which I know not who will do now." Nor are there wanting in ancient literature touches of domestic felicity which show those times to have been akin to that which is best in our own. We are apt to forget that to a Latin poet is due the original of that familiar scene in the *Cotter's Saturday Night*, and in Gray's *Elegy*—

> "For them no more the blazing hearth shall burn,
> Or busy housewife ply her evening care."

And the Latin version is the finest of the three—the most intense and the most real.

(*d*) Besides these considerations, if we look at certain aspects of modern life—at the court of Charles II. or Louis XV., or at some phenomena among ourselves—the contrast with ancient heathenism may seem less striking.

And yet the darker view of the ancient world is, it is to be feared, on the whole the true one.

It is not by any means the satirist alone from whom the evidence is derived. The Christian apologists in the early centuries accumulate charges which they would not have ventured to publish unless they had been largely supported by facts. The satirists themselves are most damaging when, like Horace, they write with careless ease, evidently taking what they describe as a matter of course. And the evidence thus obtained is confirmed beyond dispute or question by the monumental remains that have come down to us.

It will not be denied that, after all deductions, the standard has been greatly raised. Even Cicero, like Plato and Aristotle before him, accepts much that is now condemned. And even men like Antoninus and Trajan fall short when judged by a Christian standard, especially on the points to which St. Paul is referring.

But it is the condition of the masses that the Apostle has chiefly in view. The elevation of individuals through the gradual development of a purer form of ethics and philosophy, was part of the wide preparation for the gospel which God in His providence had been working. It must not be thought that He had left Himself without witness in the heathen world. The witness was there, and it was listened to by some in every age, while there were more who, under the same divine guidance, were groping their way towards one or another portion of the truth. St. Paul directly contemplates such a class when he speaks of those who "having not the law, are a law unto themselves."

Judging, however, not by these, but by the average condition of mankind, there can be no doubt that modern society in Christian countries does really represent a great improvement upon ancient. And if the exceptions are only too widespread and too glaring, it must be remembered that the success of Christianity, as of every other belief, has always a limit in the free-will of man. The question is *not*, Has Christianity made the world virtuous; but, Does it *tend* to make men virtuous so far as they are Christians? These are two quite distinct things. Instances, such as the Court of Charles II. or of Louis XV., may be quoted as showing how difficult it is for Christianity to take a real root and hold upon men; but they are no proof that, having taken hold, it is ineffectual. Experience proves to us the contrary. Human nature is much the same as ever it was. It is open to the same temptations; it has the same evil tendencies now as ever. In many instances the Christian motive still does not come in to check these tendencies; but where it does come in, it is the strongest restraining force known, and if it should lose its power, there seems none that is at all likely to take its place.

(2) On the second point, the relation of idolatry to immorality and the gradual stages of moral corruption, it may be observed that St. Paul does not regard the question, as has been done in modern times, historically, but ideally. Historically, there may be distinguished a double process. It is hardly to be said that idolatry is a corruption of natural religion. It is rather a stage by which man gradually arrives at natural religion. Anthropomorphism lies on the upward road from fetichism to a pure monotheism. But, on the other hand, it is equally true that idolatry has almost universally had those debasing accompaniments—ever more and more debased—which the Apostle describes. The primitive religions, though of a cruder form intellectually, have been of a purer form morally. The old Roman or Spartan simplicity was not merely a dream of later times. Crude, rude, and coarse it was; but it had not the special and still worse vices of a more advanced civilisation. That which brought to a few select spirits gain, brought to the masses greater loss. And here again it is at the masses that St. Paul is looking. His Rabbinical education probably had not made him acquainted to any great extent with the nobler efforts of philosophy, while the gross material sensualism of the masses was brought vividly and palpably before him. He was writing at this moment from Corinth, a city notorious for the licentiousness of its idol worship, and we cannot wonder that he should see in the abominations by which he was surrounded the worst and latest development of evil.

---

## EXCURSUS D: ON THE PROPITIATORY SACRIFICE OF CHRIST.

The chief "stumbling-block" which had in the first instance prevented St. Paul from becoming a Christian was the death of Christ upon the cross. Like the rest of his countrymen, he could not reconcile himself to the idea of a suffering Messiah. Nor would it seem that he had got over this difficulty at the moment of his conversion. The order of his thoughts was not "The Messiah was to suffer: Jesus suffered, therefore Jesus is the Messiah;" but rather, "Jesus is the Messiah: therefore a suffering Messiah is possible." The vision upon the road to Damascus convinced him once for all of the Messiahship of Jesus; and that great fact being assumed, all his previous difficulties had to be brought into harmony with it.

The question then arose, How was the death of Christ to be interpreted? What could be the significance of the death of the Messiah? As is usually the case with intellectual difficulties, where they are fairly faced and not evaded, the answer to this was found to give a much deeper and clearer insight into a number of collateral questions.

The root idea which supplied the key to these difficulties was that of *sacrifice*. The death of the Messiah was of the nature of a sacrifice.

Our Lord Himself had given an intimation of this. In words, which we know to have been familiar to St. Paul, He had given to His own death a sacrificial meaning. At the last Paschal Feast, when the cup was handed round, He had bidden His disciples drink it, on the ground "This cup is the new testament" (rather, *covenant*) "in My blood." The allusion to the new covenant recalled the ceremony which had inaugurated the old. Upon his return from the mount, Moses offered burnt-offerings and peace-offerings unto the Lord. "And Moses took the blood, and sprinkled it on the people, and said, Behold the blood of the covenant, which the Lord hath made with you concerning all these words" (Ex. xxiv. 8). The first covenant was ratified with the shedding of blood; the second covenant was also to be ratified with the shedding of blood, but in this case not with the blood of calves and of goats, but with nothing less than the blood of the Messiah Himself.

The shedding of blood had a second aspect, to which our Lord had also made allusion. It was the appointed means of making atonement for sin. "The life of the flesh is in the blood: and I have given it to you upon the altar to make an atonement for your souls; for it is the blood that maketh an atonement for the soul" (Lev. xvii. 11). In accordance with this principle of the Mosaic Law, our Lord had spoken of His own life as given to be "a ransom for many" (Mark x. 45), and of His own blood as "shed for many for the remission of sins" (Matt. xxvi. 28).

Here, then, were the main outlines of the doctrine of the significance of the death of Christ already laid down. The Apostle found it easy to adapt them to his own theological system.

He taught that the Coming of Christ was the inauguration of the Messianic reign. The condition of that reign was to be righteousness, and, as he himself taught, all who became members of the Messianic kingdom necessarily entered into a state of righteousness. But from what was this state of righteousness derived? What was it that made the Messiah's presence diffuse righteousness around it? It was the shedding of His cleansing blood. By that blood the new covenant was sealed, a new compact was inaugurated, and once more His followers, the children of the kingdom, became "an holy nation, a peculiar people."

Another train of thought led the Apostle to the same result. He was much addicted to metaphysical speculation, and a difficulty presented itself to his mind founded upon the nature of the divine attributes. The justice of God required the punishment of sin

How then could God still be just if that punishment were remitted? How could these two things—justice and remission—be reconciled? The middle term by which they were reconciled was the propitiatory death of Christ. As under the old Law the death of the victim was accepted instead of the death of the sinner, so in the public exhibition of the death of Christ God had given clear proof that His own attribute of justice remained unimpaired. If the accumulated load of human guilt had brought down no adequate penalty, it was not because the justice of God really slept, but because it was reserving itself for one signal manifestation. That done, its mission was absolved; no further sacrifice was needed either for sins past or for sins future.

The idea of sacrifice borrowed directly from the Levitical legislation is thus too deeply ingrained in the Apostle's system to be got rid of as a merely passing metaphor. In laying the stress upon it that he does, St. Paul is at one with our Lord Himself, with St. Peter and St. John, the "pillar Apostles." Nor can the idea be eliminated from Christian theology without serious loss. The moral and spiritual greatness of St. Paul rests less upon his labours for Christ than upon the spirit in which he underwent them. It was no working out of his own righteousness, no self-complacent survey of his own achievements; it was not the shallow confidence of one who makes light of his own sinfulness because he has never learnt to feel the true character of sin. The attitude of St. Paul is just the opposite of this. He has an almost oppressive consciousness of his own weakness and helplessness. But just where these are felt most deeply the grace of God intervenes. The deliverance is wrought for him by a power outside himself. There is no danger of his boasting, for he acknowledges no merit in his triumph. It is just his very helplessness which brings him relief from above. "Lest I should be exalted above measure through the abundance of the revelations, there was given to me a thorn in the flesh, the messenger of Satan to buffet me, lest I should be exalted above measure. For this thing I besought the Lord thrice, that it might depart from me. And He said unto me, My grace is sufficient for thee: for my strength is made perfect in weakness. Most gladly therefore will I rather glory in my infirmities, that the power of Christ may rest upon me. Therefore I take pleasure in infirmities, in reproaches, in necessities, in persecutions, in distresses for Christ's sake: for when I am weak, then am I strong." This was not said in the first instance quite strictly of the atoning sacrifice, but it represents the habitual attitude of mind of one to whom the sense of that atonement was ever present. "All for me, nothing by me;" "no merit of my own;" "my extremity, God's opportunity," is the language such a one would use. And we cannot but feel that this is really the very loftiest Christian temper. The modern deification of humanity and boasted perfectibility of human nature is shallow and flippant by the side of it. The very paradox marks its grandeur—*When I am weak, then am I strong.*

Nor when we rise to a really elevated and comprehensive view of the dealings of Providence with man do the difficulties in the doctrine of sacrifice appear what they were. If they do not disappear altogether they at least retire into the background. When we accept the lessons taught by the theory of evolution, and prepare ourselves to see the divine action stretching over vast tracts of space and immense periods of time, and leading up through a number of rudimentary forms to some culminating phenomenon, in the light of such broad, general principles the ancient sacrificial rites of Jew and Gentile acquire a new significance. To a dispassionate view no widely diffused institution like this can be called common or unclean. If at certain times and places the forms of sacrifice appear rude, gross, distorted, and even monstrous, this is only what takes place in nature on its way upwards to higher forms of being. In the spiritual world, as in the physical, the rudimentary existences come first, but the philosopher looking back upon them sees in them traces of the divine plan; and he will be ready enough to admit that when the whole of that plan (so far as its extent is concerned) seems to be unrolled before him, there may still be much that he cannot fully grasp and comprehend. "These are parts of His ways, but how little a portion is heard of Him? but the thunder of His power who can understand?"

---

## EXCURSUS E: ON THE DOCTRINE OF JUSTIFICATION BY FAITH AND IMPUTED RIGHTEOUSNESS.

St. Paul treats the case of Abraham as a typical case. The text which spoke of the acceptance that was given to Abraham's faith he takes as laying down a law for all believers. The faith of Abraham was imputed to him for righteousness, and St. Paul elevates this into a general principle. Wherever there is genuine faith, it is "imputed for righteousness."

The metaphor in the word "imputed" is commercial, from the balancing of accounts. Strictly speaking, in order for a man's account to stand right before God, there ought to be placed to his credit "righteousness," or a complete fulfilment of the divine law. But, in the case of the believer, his faith is taken *in lieu of* righteousness. It is treated as an equivalent to it, and has the same effect of setting the account right before God.

Stated in this bare and naked way, in the dry form of a scholastic definition, it is not unnatural that this doctrine should have given rise to some objections. How, it may be asked, can righteousness be imputed? It is of the very essence of righteousness that it should be thoroughly real and genuine. A fictitious righteousness is no righteousness at all.

It may be well to observe in passing that the faith of the Christian is treated as equivalent to righteousness specially in regard to its *effect*. It has the same effect of clearing the account which has to go before the divine tribunal. It is not said that faith takes the place of righteousness in any other way.

When we go back to St. Paul's conception of faith, we shall see that, so far from being the substitute for righteousness in any sense which should seem to diminish the worth of righteousness as an element in the Christian life, it is rather a safeguard and security for it. By faith St. Paul meant an ardent and enthusiastic adhesion to One who was Himself without sin. Faith carried to its full extent involved an assimilation to this ideal character. What better guarantee could possibly be given for a consistently righteous conduct? And the righteousness which springs from faith must needs be as much superior to that which proceeds from the works of the Law as the finest and highest personal devotion is superior to the narrow and mechanical performance of rules. Thus, in the very act of seeming to discard righteousness, the theology of St. Paul really secured a better righteousness than the best of that which was known to the scribes and Pharisees.

---

## EXCURSUS F: ON ST. PAUL'S VIEW OF THE RELIGIOUS HISTORY OF MANKIND.

One striking feature of the Epistle to the Romans is the broad view that it takes of the course of human history. It is, indeed, a philosophy of history considered in its religious aspects; and, as such, it presents much that has but recently found its way into ethical systems.

St. Paul may be said to divide the history of man into four, or, perhaps, rather, three periods. The first is the period prior to all law, when the moral principles are in process of forming and are not yet fully formed. In this stage, though there may be wrong action (*i.e.*, action which is wrong if judged by an objective standard), it does not amount to sin, or carry with it a subjective consciousness of guilt, because it does not involve a breach of law. This would correspond very much to what is now called by moralists the period of "unconscious morality." St. Paul would make, however, just one exception to the absence of positive law, and therefore of sin, in this period. Adam sinned against a positive precept, and that was why his sin entailed a penal consequence—death, which extended also to his descendants, though they had not broken any positive command.

The next great period is that of Law. The Jew was brought under this by the giving of the Mosaic law, the Gentile by the gradual development of the law of nature. Conscience by degrees acquired fixed principles, and the contemplation of the external world brought some knowledge of God. This period had not a hard and fast beginning. With the Gentile it was the result of a gradual process; with the Jew, though the Law was given from Sinai at a definite moment of time, there was still before this a similar process going on to that exemplified in the Gentile. Though not actually under the Law, the patriarch Abraham could not be said to be quite without law. He belonged rather to the margin between the two periods, where the one was passing into the other. In this interval then must be placed the giving of the Promise.

The Law had not its proper and normal effect of producing conformity to the divine will. It was found only to serve to increase and enhance transgressions. The result of the whole period of Law was a general and complete corruption both of Jew and Gentile. This paved the way for the introduction of the Messianic system. The kingdom of the Messiah was founded upon earth; and though the Jews did not take advantage of their privileged position to enroll themselves in it, it was entered largely by the Gentiles. The exclusion of the Jews was, however, not to be final. When they too had been admitted the kingdom would be complete, and the Messiah would return to take it under His direct and personal reign.

The distribution of these periods may be concisely presented in a tabular form:—

### Religious History of the World from the Creation to the Second Coming of the Messiah.

| Jews. | Gentiles. |
|---|---|

Period I.—State of Primitive Innocence, prior to Law (chaps. iv. 15; vii. 7—9).

Broken by the sin of Adam, which entailed death upon his descendants (chap. v. 12), though, strictly speaking, there could be no guilt where there was no law (chap. v. 13, 14).

[*The Promise.*
*Ratified by circumcision* (chap. iv. 11).
*Pre-Messianic privileges of Israel* (chaps. iii. 1, 2; iv. 1, 13; ix. 4, 5).]

Period II.—State of Law.

| Law of Moses. | Law of Nature. |
|---|---|
| Effects of the Law: (1) to enhance guilt by making sin the transgression of positive commandment; (2) to provoke to sin through the perversity of human nature straining after that which is forbidden (chaps. iii. 20; v. 20; vii. 5, 7—11, 13). | Knowledge of God imprinted on conscience, or on the external order of things (chaps. i. 19, 20; ii. 14, 15). This knowledge lost: (1) by self-willed speculations leading to idolatry; (2) idolatry leading to unnatural crimes; (3) these leading to other and yet other sins (chap. i. 21—32). |

Universal wickedness of mankind (chaps. i. 21; iii. 19, 23).

A revelation of divine wrath (chaps. i. 18; xi. 32).

# ROMANS.

THE MESSIANIC ADVENT.

Jews. Gentiles.

Period III.—First stage. A revelation of righteousness proceeding from God (chaps. i. 17; iii. 21—26).

This righteousness is the essential character of the Messianic kingdom obtained for it by the death of Christ whose one righteous act is thus set against the one sin of Adam (chap. v. 15—21).

The Messianic righteousness is offered alike to Jew and Gentile (chaps. i. 16; ii. 28, 29; iii. 29, 30; iv. 11, 12; v. 18; x. 12).

| Jews | Gentiles |
|---|---|
| Attachment to Christ involved release from the Law (chaps. vii. 1—6; viii. 2, 3; x. 4). | [*The Promise fulfilled not to the literal but to the spiritual descendants of Abraham, whether Jew or Gentile* (chap. ix. 6—9).] |

The offer of Messianic righteousness

| Jews | Gentiles |
|---|---|
| Rejected in the main by the Jews (chaps. x. 3, 21; xi. 7). | Accepted by the Gentiles. Object of this, not only the salvation of the Gentiles, but also to provoke the Jews to emulation (chap. xi. 11—16). |
| Final restoration of the Jews (chap. xi. 26—29, 31). | Making up of the full complement of the Gentile Church (chap. xi. 25). |

Universal admission to the divine mercy (chap. xi. 32).

Second stage.—Reappearance of the Messiah, and completion of His kingdom (chap. viii. 18—21).

---

## EXCURSUS G: ON THE DOCTRINE OF UNION WITH CHRIST.

We have seen that faith, or the feeling of personal attachment to the Messiah, when it has had time to deepen and strengthen, attains to such a degree of closeness, and involves so complete an assimilation of the believer to his Lord, that it comes to be called by another name—that of oneness, or fellowship. Looking back over his career, the Apostle saw that the decisive step, to which all this later development was due, had been taken when he first entered the Messianic community. It was then that he assumed that relation to Christ in which all the rest was implicitly contained. But this first decisive step was itself ratified by an outward act. Baptism was the mark of admission to membership in the Messianic kingdom. Baptism and faith went together. The one was the inward apprehension of the Messiahship of Jesus, the other was the outward confession of adhesion to Him. The convert was baptised *into Christ.* Something of the later feeling, which arose from a clearer contemplation of the object of Christian worship and longer experience of the spiritual realities of Christian life, was reflected back upon this phrase. It came to imply something of that mystical communion which was potentially latent in that relation to Christ with the assumption of which it was connected. The believer who was baptised "into Christ," if he was not at once conscious of that closer relation, was sure to become so sooner or later, if his belief was real and vital. That the formula of admission should have somewhat of an ideal character is only in harmony with what all forms are, and ought to be, and with the consistent language of the Apostle himself. Forms for general use should rise to the level of the best of those who can possibly come under them, and not be written down to the level of the worst. They represent standards to be aimed at, rather than measures of what is attained; and even for those who conspicuously fall beneath them, they serve as a stimulus and reminder of better things.

But baptism had also another aspect. It was a mark, not only of the assumption of something new, but of the giving up of something old. At the time when St. Paul wrote it in most cases accompanied conversion. It meant the giving up of heathen or Jewish practices, repentance for past sins, and a more or less complete change of life. It meant, besides, an admission to the Messianic privileges and immunities, including more especially the "righteousness" which was to be the characteristic of the children of the kingdom. This putting off of the old and putting on of the new was symbolised by the immersion in water. The process was one of spiritual cleansing. The conscious effort of the human will, and the divine influences of the Messianic kingdom, both converged upon this one point. Heathenism, Judaism, and the carelessness of life which went with either, were laid aside, and the white robe of Christian righteousness (ideal, or in part actual) was put on.

Now there was another act, the symbolism of which coincided almost exactly with that of baptism. Death is a change from one state to another; it is a putting off of the old and a putting on of the new. But death—a death—the death of Christ—assumed a most important part in that system of things into which the Christian at his baptism entered. It had won for him that "righteousness" which he was to put on; it had removed for him that curse of the Law which he hoped to escape. Was it strange, then, that St. Paul, instead of describing the object of baptism in the usual terms, as a baptism into Christ, should describe it specially as a baptism "into the *death* of Christ?" And having done this, was it strange that he should apply the symbolism of death in the same way in which he would have applied those of cleansing or ablution, and in connection with his teaching as to the union of the Christian with his Saviour? All these three elements enter into the passage on which what has been here said is a comment: "Know ye not that so many of us as were baptised into Jesus Christ were baptised into His death? Therefore, we are buried with Him by baptism into (His) death: that like as Christ was raised up from the dead by the glory of the Father, even so we also should walk in newness of life" (Rom. vi. 3, 4). The conclusion is hortatory and ethical: we are to walk in newness of life. This is based upon the relation of intimate union into which we were brought at our baptism with Christ. But mingled with the argument from the nature of this union, is one based upon the notion which the idea of baptism and of death implied—the necessity of total and complete change. In modern language we should call this a metaphor. In the language of St. Paul it becomes something more than metaphor, through its connection with the mystical doctrine of union—a doctrine which stands side by side with the other great doctrine of the Epistle, that of justification by faith. We have seen how the one passes into the other, and how between them they cover the whole of the Christian career.

It should be observed that the more elaborate teaching of chap. viii. is all an extension of this doctrine of union. The union of the Christian with Christ, as seen from another side, is the indwelling of the Spirit of Christ in the Christian. That indwelling, when fully realised, must needs bring with it holiness of life. It is a testimony to the inclusion of the Christian in the Messianic scheme, and to his close relation to the Messiah. But the Messiah is none other than the Son of God. The Christian, therefore, partakes in His Sonship. He too is a child, if not by birth, yet by adoption; and his filial relation to God assures to him the inheritance of the fulness of the Messianic blessings. It gives to his prayers all that touching tenderness and efficacy of appeal which belongs to the petitions of a child to its father. It establishes a bond of peculiar sympathy within the Godhead itself, so that even its most inarticulate yearnings find an intercessor as well as a response. The terms in which the Apostle expresses the nature of this sympathy and of this intercession, carry us up to those fine relations of the Spirit of God to the spirit of man, and to the Essence of the Godhead, where it is well that definition should cease.

# THE FIRST EPISTLE OF PAUL THE APOSTLE TO THE
# CORINTHIANS

# INTRODUCTION

TO

## THE FIRST EPISTLE OF PAUL THE APOSTLE TO THE

# CORINTHIANS

---

To describe briefly the relation in which St. Paul stood to the Corinthian Church, and the circumstances under which he wrote this Epistle, will, I think, be the best and most efficient help to the ordinary reader.

After a stay at Athens of some few months, St. Paul, towards the end (probably) of the year A.D. 51, left that city for Corinth. At Athens, the centre of philosophic thought and culture, St. Paul had preached Christianity. The wide question of the relation of God's providence to the heathen world in times past—Christ crucified and raised from the dead—all these topics had been dwelt on by the Apostle in a speech which still remains a model of the subtlest rhetorical skill and of the most earnest eloquence. Judged, however, by immediate results, the speech on Mars Hill, and the other addresses at Athens, of which we have no record, but which were probably on the same lines, were not successful. Only a few converts were won for Christ.

The Apostle dwells with no fond recollection on his work here. A single sentence* sums up the results of his labour in a city where the successful planting of the Church would have been of such vast importance: "Howbeit certain men clave unto him, and believed: among the which was Dionysius the Areopagite, and a woman named Damaris, and others with them." There is an undertone of sadness and disappointment in these words of St. Paul's companion and friend, St. Luke.

The Apostle left Athens downcast and thoughtful. The subtle skill, the earnest eloquence, had been employed apparently in vain. The inestimable value which that great exposition of God's dealings with man, as well in the world at large as in the more sacred enclosure of the Christian faith, might have—as we know now it has had—in Christendom, did not present itself to the Apostle's mind as any consolation for the want of practical results at the moment. Athens was a sad memory to St. Paul. He never mentions her name in an Epistle. He sends no words of greeting to any of her children.

From the Piræus—the port of Athens—St. Paul sails for Corinth. It being late in autumn (probably October or November), it is most likely that the Apostle landed at Cenchreæ, a seaport town on the Saronic Bay.† The experience which he had at Athens, and its bearing on the work on which he was now about to enter in the capital of Achaia, were doubtless the uppermost thoughts in the Apostle's mind during this brief journey. He sees that the power of the gospel to win men to Christ lies in the message itself, and not in the method and style of its delivery. He resolves to lay aside the rhetoric and the merely human eloquence, and in the new field of his missionary labours "to know nothing but Jesus Christ, and Him crucified."* This vow he probably made as he landed at Cenchreæ; and when, a year and a half afterwards, he embarked at the same port on his return journey, he could look back with satisfaction and with thanksgiving on the resolution which he had formed, and the glorious results which had followed in Achaia from his preaching.

A journey of nine miles from Cenchreæ brought the Apostle to Corinth, which was situate in the south-west end of the isthmus, and at the northern base of the Acrocorinthus. The two things which in older days had made Corinth famous in Grecian history still rendered her a place of supreme importance. From a military point of view, she might be regarded as the key to the Peloponnesus, and commercially she was the central point of the vast trade which was carried on between Asia and Europe. The storms which so constantly raged on the southern shore of Greece drove the vast tide of commerce through the safer overland route, which lay through Cenchreæ and Lechæum, which latter port was only a mile and a half distant from Corinth. It was at Corinth that, in B.C. 146, the Achaians made their last stand against the Romans, and were finally defeated by Mummius. After this, Achaia became a Roman province, and Corinth for a century remained in the condition of utter desolation to which the sword and fire of the victorious consul had reduced it. Some years before the birth of Christ (B.C. 44) Julius Cæsar restored Corinth, and, under the Emperor Claudius, the direct rule of the province was transferred from the emperor to the senate; and hence we find at the time when St. Paul arrived its government was administered by a pro-consul.† As St. Paul entered Corinth his eyes might for a moment have rested on the grave of Lais amid the cypress grove outside the walls, and the monument of Diogenes which stood by the gate—fit types of the cynical, worldly

---

* Acts xvii. 34.

† I assume that St. Paul went by sea, and not by land, as the words (Acts xviii. 1), "Paul departed from Athens, and came to Corinth," seem to imply a brief and uninterrupted journey. Had he gone by land he would have passed through other towns on the way, some mention of which it would be natural to expect.

* See 1 Cor. ii. 1, 2, and Note there. The word "you," repeated in both these verses, seems emphatic, as if the Apostle meant to bring out a contrast between his former style of teaching among others, and that which he had resolved should be his style of teaching amongst them. The only point on which he had determined when coming to them was, "Jesus Christ, and Him crucified," as the subject-matter of his teaching.

† Acts xviii. 12.

philosophy, and the gross, yet attractive, sensuality with which the society of that day and city were permeated. Within the city, most of the buildings were comparatively modern, "run up" within the last century by the imported population of Roman freed-men; while only here and there, in the stately magnificence of an older style of architecture, stood an occasional edifice which had survived the "fire" that had "tried every man's work" in the great conflagration which had swept away the inferior structures of "wood, hay, stubble" when the conquering troops of Mummius had captured Corinth.* The population of Corinth was composed of many and diverse elements. There were Greeks, who thought, by their delight in a tawdry rhetoric and in a sham and shallow philosophy, to revive the historic glory of a past age. There were a thousand corrupt and shameless priestesses attached to the temple of Aphrodite, which crowned the neighbouring hill. There were the families of the Roman freed-men whom Julius Cæsar had sent to rebuild and recolonise the town. There were traders from Asia and from Italy, and all that nondescript element naturally to be found in a city which was practically a great commercial seaport and the scene, every fourth year, of those Isthmian games which attracted among the athletes the best, and among some of the spectators the worst, of the population of the surrounding provinces. All these, like so many streams of human life, mingled together here, and at this particular juncture were met by the vast returning tide of Jews expelled from Rome by Claudius,† and so formed that turbulent and seething flood of human life on which the barque of Christ's Church was launched at Corinth.

Amongst those who had lately come from Italy were Aquila and Priscilla, his wife. With them the Apostle lodged, joining with them in their occupation of tent-making. Pontus,‡ the native country of Aquila, and Cilicia,§ the native country of St. Paul, were both renowned for the manufacture of the goat's-hair cloth from which the tent-coverings were made. It is probable, however, that an affinity of faith, as well as an identity of occupation, led to the Apostle's intimate association with these friends. If this man and his wife had not been converted to Christianity before this they would scarcely have allowed St. Paul to join himself so intimately with them. The very circumstances of their expulsion from Rome would have embittered them against a Christian. From a remark in Suetonius, we find that the expulsion of the Jews had to do with their riots with Christian converts. Rome cared nothing about the religious opinions of these rival sects; but when their differences led to public riots Rome was then as vigorous and decisive in action as before she had been indifferent.‖ Having left Italy under such circumstances, Aquila and Priscilla would, if unconverted Jews, have certainly not taken a Christian as a partner in their home and work; whereas, if already Christians, and suffering expulsion thus from Rome, they would gladly welcome such a convert as Paul. These considerations are confirmed by the course of events at the outset of St. Paul's

* See St. Paul's recollection of this in the imagery employed in 1 Cor. iii. 10–13.
† Acts xviii. 2.
‡ Acts xvii. 2.
§ Acts xxi. 39.
‖ "Claudius expelled the Jews from Rome on account of their continual tumults instigated by Chrestus." The name Christus, in pronunciation nearly identical with Chrestus, was mixed up in the riots somehow. That was quite sufficient for the authorities to assume that some person of that name was the author of them.

preaching at Corinth. The Apostle first preaches to the Jews and those proselytes (called "Greeks")* who had at least accepted Judaism so far as to attend the synagogue. He is met with opposition and blasphemy by them, and then turns unto the Gentiles, and teaches in a house close by the synagogue, winning many converts to the faith, amongst others, Crispus, the ruler of the synagogue, Gaius, and Stephanas and his household, who received their baptism at the hand of the Apostle himself.† Silas and Timothy joined the Apostle during the earlier part of his sojourn, and probably brought with them some pecuniary help from the Philippians, which was doubly acceptable because of a famine then prevalent and of the Apostle's unflinching determination to take nothing from the Corinthians.‡

Some time in A.D. 53, M. Annæus Novatus, the brother of the philosopher Seneca, arrives at Corinth as pro-consul of Achaia. He was called Gallio, having been adopted into the family of that name. His kindly and loving disposition § gave the Jewish faction some hope that they might make him the unconscious tool by which they would wreak their intensifying rage on St. Paul and his Christian companions. Gallio, with the imperturbable calmness of a Roman governor, refuses to allow himself to be dragged into a religious dispute between two sects. In retaliation for this conduct on the part of the Jews, the Greeks take Sosthenes, who had succeeded Crispus as chief ruler of the synagogue—here, no doubt, the ringleader in the persecution of St. Paul—and beat him. ‖ When the same Sosthenes became a convert it was not strange that he and St. Paul should become firm friends. Both had been active enemies of the faith which they now preached, and the two converted persecutors are joined together in the opening of this Epistle to the Corinthian Church (1 Cor. i. 1). For some considerable time the Apostle remains and teaches at Corinth, and then returns to Syria by Cenchreæ. The vow made on landing there had been kept.¶ Jesus Christ and His crucifixion had been the sole subject and strength of the Apostle's teaching. With what feelings of profound thankfulness must St. Paul, as he sailed from Cenchreæ, have looked back on the work and the success of those intervening months. With Aquila and Priscilla, he arrives at Ephesus, and leaves them there. After a somewhat prolonged tour through Galatia and Phrygia, and a visit to Jerusalem, St. Paul returns to Ephesus, probably in the year A.D. 54. Meanwhile, during the absence of St. Paul on his journey visiting the churches in Galatia and Phrygia, a

* Acts xviii. 4.
† 1 Cor. i. 14–16.
‡ See 2 Cor. xi. 7–12; Phil. iv. 15.
§ Seneca says of Gallio, "He was loved much even by those who had little power to love;" and, "No mortal is so dear to me as Gallio to all men."
‖ In Acts xviii. 17, the words "the Greeks" do not occur in the best MSS., and some commentators conclude that it was the Jewish faction who took Sosthenes and beat him, suspecting him of some leanings towards the faith which he afterwards embraced. I think it more natural to assume that it was the Greek mob who acted thus towards the leader of the defeated faction of the Jews. If it were the Jews writhing under their defeat, surely they would have taken vengeance on some avowed Christian like Paul or Aquila.
¶ Acts xviii. 18. The words here may, as a mere matter of grammar, refer to either Paul or Aquila; but the whole sense of the passage refers them to the former. The fact that Paul goes on to Jerusalem, and Aquila remains at Ephesus, is almost in itself sufficient to indicate Paul as the one having some solemn obligation to fulfil. I have already indicated that in the solemn vow made by the Apostle, and which was carried out apparently according to the law of the Nazarite vow (see Num. vi.), was included a resolve as to his teaching at Corinth. What, if any, other motives for the vow the Apostle could have had, must, of course, be matter of the merest conjecture.

man arrives at Ephesus who is destined to have a remarkable influence in the future on St. Paul's relation with the Corinthian Church. Apollos, a Jew by religion and an Alexandrian by birth, had been brought up in a city where commerce brought together various races, and where philosophy attracted varied schools of thought. Alexandria, famous also as the place where the Greek translation of the Old Testament had been made, became naturally the seat of an intellectual school of scriptural interpretation, as well as the abode of Greek philosophy. Amid such surroundings, Apollos, gifted with natural eloquence, became "mighty in the scriptures," and was "instructed in the way of the Lord," possibly by some of those Alexandrian Jews who, in their disputes with Stephen,* had become acquainted with the elementary principles of Christianity. His imperfect acquaintance with the Christian faith—limited to the tenets of the Baptist †—is supplemented and completed by the instruction which he receives from Aquila and Priscilla, who were attracted by the eloquence and fervour with which he preached in the synagogue at Ephesus his imperfect gospel. The days spent with St. Paul at Corinth were fresh in the memory of these Christians. The incidents of those days were doubtless often recalled in many a conversation with Apollos, and what he hears fires his earnest soul with a desire to preach the gospel in Achaia. To the various churches—including, of course, Corinth—he receives letters of commendation from the Ephesian Christians, and his preaching is attended with great blessing, "helping them much which had believed through grace." His style of teaching was strikingly different from that which St. Paul—in accordance with his vow, "to know nothing but Jesus Christ, and Him crucified,"—had adopted at Corinth. With more intellectual eloquence, and with a wider and more philosophic range of thought, he opened up the deeper spiritual meaning of the Old Testament scriptures, showing from them that Jesus was Christ.‡ The philosophic school of thought in which he had been educated could be traced in the style of his eloquence, which won many converts amongst those classes to whom the simplicity of Paul's preaching had not been acceptable, and who, on that account, had continued to the end his active opponents.

While the eloquent Alexandrian is preaching in Corinth—watering § where Paul had planted, building up where Paul had laid the foundation, giving strong meat to those whom, in their spiritual infancy, Paul had fed with milk, and winning some new converts amongst those whose Jewish and intellectual prejudices had hitherto been invincible—St. Paul rejoins Aquila and Priscilla at Ephesus.‖ This is not the place to dwell upon St. Paul's work at Ephesus (of which a full account is given in Acts xix.), only so far as it directly bears upon his Epistle to Corinth. During his stay at Ephesus he is constantly hearing news of the Corinthians by those whose business necessitated constant journeyings between these two commercial capitals. The Apostle himself also, during the earlier part of his sojourn, pays a brief visit to Corinth, of which we have no record, and of which we should know nothing but for the casual allusion in his Second Epistle that he is coming to them the *third* time.¶ After some two years' residence at Ephesus, the Apostle determines, after some time, to proceed directly by sea to Corinth, and making it his head-quarters, visit the churches in Macedonia, returning after this tour to Corinth again, on his way back to Jerusalem,* from whence, finally, he hoped to visit Rome.† This plan is, however, entirely upset by the course of events which we have now to narrate.

Rumours, more or less vague at first, reach St. Paul of a bad state of affairs in the Corinthian Church. The Corinthian Christians were living in the midst of a heathen society. The religion of heathendom, and the sensual license and indulgence which formed a part of it, pervaded all the social customs and entered into the very fibre of the social life of the country. To define, therefore, the precise position which Christians should assume in relation to the political conditions and the domestic institutions of the heathen was a matter of the utmost delicacy and difficulty. Christian thought and practice perpetually oscillated between the license into which human nature easily transformed the liberty of the gospel, and the rigid rejection of every custom which was tainted with heathen approval. To steady in the line of right that trembling pendulum of vibrating religious thought required all the spiritual skill and all the fine delicacy of touch which were characteristic of the great Apostle of the Gentiles. When the earliest rumours reach him of the unsatisfactory condition of some of the Corinthian Christians, he writes a letter to them, in which he probably mentions his intention of visiting them on his way to Macedonia; and he warns them of the great danger of moral contamination to which they would infallibly be subject if they allowed any of the immoral practices of the heathen to receive any sanction from the Christian Church. Whatever the heathen might think of the lawfulness of sinful indulgence which their own faith surrounded with a distorting moral atmosphere of religious sanction, Christians were to allow no trace of such immorality within the boundaries of the Church. This Epistle has been lost; we can only conjecture its general contents from the circumstances under which it was written, and the reference to it in what is now the First of St. Paul's Epistles to the Corinthians.‡

The Apostle still adheres to his intention of visiting Corinth and Macedonia, and sends Timothy and Erastus to prepare the various churches in Macedonia and Achaia for his coming, and, above all, to set things right at Corinth by, as St. Paul says, "bringing you into remembrance of my ways which be in Christ, as I teach everywhere in every church." §

After the despatch of Timothy and Erastus, more alarming news reaches St. Paul. The household of Chloe ‖—some Christian resident, either at Corinth or Ephesus, evidently well known to the Corinthians—report to the Apostle that the Church is disorganised with sectarian strife, and defiled by sanctioning a marriage between a Christian man and a heathen woman who had been his step-mother, and was now divorced from his father. A letter also arrives ¶ from the Corinthians to St. Paul, which was in part a reply to St. Paul's lost Epistle, and which contained various questions regarding doctrine and practice which

* Acts vi. 9. † Acts xviii. 25. ‡ Acts xviii. 28.
§ 1 Cor. iii. 1, 6, 10. ‖ Acts xix. 1.
¶ I place the unrecorded visit of St. Paul thus early during his residence at Ephesus because it seems to have occurred before the matter treated of in the First Epistle to the Corinthians assumed a serious aspect; otherwise we can scarcely imagine that there should be no allusion in this Epistle to some definite rebuke or instruction for which that visit would have afforded an opportunity.

* 2 Cor. i. 15, 16. † Acts xix. 21. ‡ See 1 Cor. v. 9.
§ 1 Cor. iv. 17. ‖ 1 Cor. i. 11. ¶ 1 Cor. viii. 1.

revealed the disintegrated condition of religious thought and life in Christian Corinth.* The letter was probably brought to Ephesus by Stephanas and his companions, who supplemented the information which it contained by their own knowledge, based upon personal and recent observation. The arrival of this letter, which called for an immediate answer, and the receipt of this intelligence of a state of affairs which required to be dealt with immediately and vigorously, led to a change in the Apostle's plans. He abandons his intention of going direct to Corinth, so as to give time for a change for the better in the state of that Church; and he can no longer, now that he realises the full extent of the evil, leave it to be dealt with by one of Timothy's gentle disposition. He therefore writes this (Second) First Epistle to the Corinthians, and sends with it Titus, who, going direct to Corinth, would reach that city probably before the arrival of Timothy, who would be delayed visiting other churches *en route*. Titus—whom we may call St. Paul's companion in determination, as Timothy was St. Paul's companion in conciliation—was far more competent to meet the difficulties which would present themselves in such a state of affairs as existed then at Corinth. Moreover, Titus was a Gentile, whereas Timothy was half Jewish by birth; and so there would be no danger of the most hostile faction in Corinth—the Jewish—awakening any sympathy for themselves in him. How judicious the selection of Titus was is evident by the success of his mission, which we read of afterwards when he rejoined Paul in Macedonia.†

The Epistle was written and despatched probably about Easter, A.D. 57,‡ and the Apostle's intention is now to remain at Ephesus until after Pentecost, and then proceed, visiting the churches in Macedonia before going to Corinth. This would leave time for this Epistle to have the desired effect, and for St. Paul to meet Titus somewhere—probably at Troas. This Epistle divides itself into two parts. The first Section, extending to chap. vi. 20, deals with the reports which had reached St. Paul as to the condition of the Corinthian Church; and the second Section, which occupies the remainder of the Epistle, is a reply to the letter received from Corinth, including directions for the collection for the saints at Jerusalem and the usual salutations from the brethren.

With characteristic courtesy, the Epistle opens with words of approval and congratulation,§ which show that the writer's subsequent censures arise from no desire to see merely what is bad in the Corinthians, but are forced from him by the serious nature of the evils which have to be checked. Three evils are then rebuked—viz., THE SPIRIT OF FACTION,‖ THE CASE OF PROHIBITED MARRIAGE,¶ THE APPEALS OF CHRISTIANS TO HEATHEN COURTS.* The general principles of the relation of Christianity to heathenism, out of which the advice given under the last two heads has grown, are then solemnly reiterated;† and the first Section of the Epistle closes with these words of earnest warning.

From the second Section of this Epistle we can discover what were the topics concerning which the Corinthians had written to St. Paul. He would doubtless treat of these subjects in the same sequence as they occurred in the letter to which this is the answer. The questions asked were probably these: IS IT RIGHT TO MARRY? The answer to this ‡ is,—that, owing to the exceptional state of circumstances then existing, the unmarried state is better. This advice is, however, to be modified in its practical application in the cases of those who have an irresistible natural desire for marriage and those who have already contracted it.

The second question was: IS IT LAWFUL FOR A CHRISTIAN TO EAT THE FLESH WHICH HAS BEEN ALREADY USED FOR SACRIFICIAL PURPOSES BY THE HEATHEN? To this the answer § is, in general terms, that there is no harm in eating such meat, but that in practice this wide principle of Christian liberty must be limited by regard to the general welfare of others and their tenderness of conscience.

The third inquiry was: WHAT IS THE BECOMING DRESS OF WOMEN IN PUBLIC WORSHIP? This question was rendered necessary by some women pushing the freedom of the faith so far as to appear in public unveiled—a practice which might easily be mistaken by the heathen as the indication of a loose morality. To this the Apostle replies ‖ practically that our Christianity is not to make us transgress the social order and customs of the community in which we live.

The fourth question was; WHAT IS THE PROPER ORDER OF THE CELEBRATION OF THE LORD'S SUPPER? In his answer to this question ¶ the Apostle severely censures the scenes of riot and debauch into which the Love Feasts—with which the Lord's Supper was practically united, though not identical—had fallen, and gives stringent and exact directions as to the means of avoiding such scandal in the future.**

The fifth question was: WHICH IS THE MOST VALUABLE OF SPIRITUAL GIFTS? The discussion of this matter †† involves the condemnation of the extravagant value attached by some to the gift of tongues, and the enunciation of the principle that the value of a gift depends on its utility for the good of the whole Church.

The seventh and last inquiry was: IS THE RESURRECTION OF THE DEAD A VITAL DOCTRINE OF CHRISTIANITY? The reply to this ‡‡ is an elaborate exposition and vindication of the doctrine of the resurrection. The collection for the saints at Jerusalem, information regarding his own change of plans, and some personal matters, occupy the concluding chapter of the Epistle.

After despatching this Epistle, St. Paul is full of

* My reason for thinking that the letter from the Corinthians was in part a reply to St. Paul's lost Epistle is that the Apostle says (1 Cor. v. 9) empatically, "I wrote to you in *the* Epistle,"—*i.e.*, the Epistle to which you refer. They had probably taken exception to his strict injunction, and said in reply. "If we are not to keep company at all with fornicators, then we must go out of the world altogether." His words seem to me to be an answer to some such captious criticism, and not a voluntary modification or explanation of what he had no reason to suppose should be misunderstood. It has been suggested by some commentators that the lost Epistle had been sent by Timothy. But St. Paul seems to assume as certain that the letter has reached them (1 Cor. v. 9), and to be doubtful whether Timothy was there or not (1 Cor. xvi. 10).

† See 2 Cor. ii. 12, 13.

‡ See 1 Cor. v. 7, and Note there, and chap. xvi. 18, showing that it was written before Pentecost, and probably at Passover time.

§ 1 Cor. i. 1—9. ‖ 1 Cor. i. 10—iv. 21. ¶ 1 Cor. v. 1—13.

* 1 Cor. vi. 1—9. † 1 Cor. vi. 5—20. ‡ 1 Cor. vii.

§ 1 Cor. viii. 1—xi. 1.

‖ 1 Cor. xi. 2—16. ¶ 1 Cor. xi. 17—34.

** It seems impossible to us that drunkenness could arise from the abuse of the Eucharistic wine as administered in our own day. A remarkable instance is mentioned in Mrs. Brassey's *Voyage of the "Sunbeam"* (p. 234) of a church which they visited in Tahiti, where cocoa-nut milk was used in the Holy Communion in the place of wine, owing to abuses of the cup which had arisen.

†† 1 Cor. xii. 1—xiv. 40. ‡‡ 1 Cor. xv.

fears lest it may have been written with too much severity, and possibly may have exactly the opposite effect from that which he desired. It may fail to reconcile to him the Church so dear to his heart—it may only widen the breach and embitter opponents. The Apostle leaves Ephesus after Pentecost, but his fears increase. Even an "open door" at Troas* cannot detain him in his restless anxiety. No new love could make up for the posssible loss of the old one at Corinth in that large and tender heart of St. Paul. He passes over into Macedonia—full of care: there are the echoes of tumults at Ephesus behind him—there is the fear of coming disruption with Corinth before him. At last, at Philippi, he meets Titus, who brings him the joyful news that, on the whole, the letter has been successful.† The Corinthian Christians are penitent, the chief offender has been expelled, and there is nothing now to prevent the Apostle taking back into his confidence and love the Church to which he was so warmly attached. A second letter ‡—to express his joy and gratitude, to reiterate his exhortations, and to finally prepare the Corinthians for his coming (which he explains had been delayed from no personal caprice, but for their sakes §)—is written, and the last trace of the cloud which, by separating him from them had cast so terrible a darkness over his own soul, is completely and finally removed.

The authenticity of this Epistle has never been seriously disputed; indeed, to deny it would almost involve a disbelief in the historical existence of the Corinthian Church and in the personality of St. Paul. The earliest fathers refer to it as the recognised letter of the Apostle. Clement of Rome, Polycarp, and Irenæus quote passages from it as St. Paul's writing. All throughout this Epistle we have the heart as well as the intellect of the Apostle displayed to us; the Holy Spirit of God not setting aside, but controlling and guiding those good gifts of which, though we call them "natural," He is the Author and the Giver.

Many of the subjects treated of here were local and personal. The combination of circumstances which give rise to them cannot possibly occur again in Christendom; but the principles on which the Apostle decided these matters are imperishable and of universal obligation. They can guide the Church amid the complex civilisation of the nineteenth century as truly and as clearly as they indicated to her the path of safety in the infancy of the Christian faith.

* 2 Cor. ii. 12.
† 2 Cor. ii. 14.
‡ 2 Corinthians.
§ 2 Cor. i. 23.

The following, among other works, have been consulted in writing the commentary upon this Epistle:—

*The Greek Testament, with a Critically-revised Text, &c.*, by Dean Alford. Vol. II. Rivingtons, 1871.

*The Greek Testament, with Notes*, by Bishop Wordsworth.

*Kritisch-exegetischer Kommentar über das Neue Testament. Göttingen* (English Translation, T. & T. Clark, 1877).

*The Epistles of St. Paul to the Corinthians, with Critical Notes and Dissertations*, by A. P. Stanley, Dean of Westminster. Fourth Edition. John Murray, 1876.

*The Life and Epistles of St. Paul*, by W. J. Conybeare and the Very Rev. J. S. Howson, Dean of Chester. New Edition. Longmans, 1870.

*The Hulsean Lectures for* 1862, by the Very Rev. J. S. Howson. Third Edition. Strahan & Co., 1873.

*The Metaphors of St. Paul*, by the Very Rev. J. S. Howson. Strahan & Co., 1870.

*The Companions of St. Paul*, by the Very Rev. J. S. Howson. Isbister, 1874.

*Expository Lectures on St. Paul's Epistles to the Corinthians*, by the late F. W. Robertson. Smith and Elder, 1870.

*The Life and Epistles of St. Paul*, by Thomas Lewin, M.A. 2 Vols. Third Edition. George Bell & Sons, 1875.

*The Homilies of St. John Chrysostom, Archbishop of Constantinople, on the First Epistle of St. Paul to the Corinthians.* Vols. IV. and V. of the Library of Fathers of the Holy Catholic Church. Parker, 1839.

*The Greek Testament from Cardinal Mai's Edition of the Vatican Bible*, with Notes by Professor Ornsby. J. Duffery, 1865.

G. B. Winer's, *Grammatik des neutestamentlichen Sprachidioms* (English Translation, by Dr. W. F. Moulton. Eighth Edition. T. & T. Clark, 1877).

# THE FIRST EPISTLE OF PAUL THE APOSTLE TO THE
# CORINTHIANS

A.D. 59.

Chap. i. 1—3. Salutation and address.

**CHAPTER I.**—(1) Paul, called *to be*
an apostle of Jesus Christ
through the will of God,
and Sosthenes *our* brother,
(2) unto the church of God which is at
Corinth, to them that are sanctified in
Christ Jesus,[a] called *to be* saints,[b] with
all that in every place call upon the
name of Jesus Christ our Lord, both
their's and our's: (3) Grace *be* unto you,
and peace, from God our Father, and
*from* the Lord Jesus Christ.

Chap. i. 4—9. Introductory commendation.

(4) I thank my God always on your
behalf, for the grace of
God which is given you by
Jesus Christ; (5) that in
every thing ye are enriched by him, in
all utterance, and *in* all knowledge;
(6) even as the testimony of Christ was
confirmed in you: (7) so that ye come
behind in no gift; waiting for the
coming[1] of our Lord Jesus Christ:
(8) who shall also confirm you unto the
end, *that ye may be* blameless in the day

a Acts 15. 9.
b Rom. 1. 7.

1 Gr. *revelation.*

---

(1) **Paul, called to be an apostle.**—Better, *a called Apostle of Jesus Christ.* His apostolic authority, which was questioned by some in Corinth, is thus set out at the commencement of the Epistle.

**And Sosthenes our brother.**—*Sosthenes the brother,* probably the Sosthenes (see Note on verse 16) the chief ruler of the synagogue mentioned in Acts xviii. 17, one of the brethren well known to the Corinthians. From his name being thus joined with that of the Apostle, we may conjecture that he was his amanuensis in writing this Epistle, the salutation only (chap. xvi. 21) having been written by St. Paul's hand.

(2) **Church of God.**—St. Chrysostom remarks how these opening words are a protest against the party-spirit prevailing at Corinth: "The Church of God—not of this or that man."

**Them that are sanctified in Christ Jesus.**—This is not another class of persons, but a description of those who compose "the Church"—who are further described as "called to be saints"—*i.e.,* "holy." The term "saints" is never used by St. Paul with its restricted modern meaning, but is applied to the whole baptised Church. The English word which most nearly expresses the apostolic idea is "Christians"—used in its most comprehensive sense.

**With all that in every place.**—Better translated, *with all that call upon the name of our Lord Jesus Christ in every place, both theirs and ours.* The teaching of the Epistle is thus addressed to the Church at large, which is composed of all who call upon the Lord Jesus, whether it be in Corinth ("our" country—the Apostle identifying himself with his converts) or elsewhere. This idea of the Church, put forward in the very opening of the Epistle, at once directs the reader's mind from the narrow spirit of faction which was exhibiting itself at Corinth. The words of this verse contain a strong testimony to the worship of Christ, not only as being practised in the Apostolic Church, but as being one of the very marks of true union with the Church.

(3) **Grace be unto you, and peace.**—This is the usual style of apostolic greeting (Gal. i. 3; Eph. i. 2), and with these words the address and greeting which open the Epistle conclude.

(4) **I thank my God.**—Expressions of thankfulness (verses 4—9), serving also to secure at the very outset the attention of those to whom the Apostle is writing. He thus shows that he is not blind to, or forgetful of, their good qualities, although this Epistle is specially written to rebuke their present sins; and also that he is not about to utter words of hopeless condemnation, but of wholesome warning. The emphatic use of the singular, *I* thank *my* God, in contrast to the plural in the previous verses, indicates that St. Paul does not join Sosthenes with him as author of the Epistle, but that it is written in his name alone and with his sole authority.

**The grace of God which is given you by Jesus Christ.**—Better, *the grace of God given you in Christ Jesus*—*i.e.,* given to you as being in Christ.

(5) **Ye are enriched.**—Literally, *ye were enriched.* "Utterance" is the power of outward expression of that "knowledge" which dwells within.

(6) **Even as the testimony of Christ.**—The testimony which St. Paul bore to Christ, and from Christ, was confirmed among them by this full bestowal of spiritual gifts.

(7) **So that ye come.**—Not exactly as in the English, "so that ye come behind" (or, *are wanting*) "in no gift," but "the result being that ye come behind *others* in no gift." You have as fully as any others those spiritual gifts which sustain you and enable you to wait for the revelation (*i.e.,* the second visible appearance, which the early Church expected would soon occur) of our Lord Jesus Christ, not with fear, or with impatience, but with a calm trustfulness (Luke xvii. 30; Titus ii. 13).

(8) **Who.**—The use of the words "day of our Lord Jesus Christ," instead of "His day," has been regarded

of our Lord Jesus Christ. (9) God *is*
faithful,[a] by whom ye were called unto
the fellowship of his Son Jesus Christ
our Lord.
(10) Now I beseech you, brethren, by
the name of our Lord
Jesus Christ, that ye all
speak the same thing,
and *that* there be no divisions[1] among
you; but *that* ye be perfectly joined
together in the same mind and in the
same judgment. (11) For it hath been
declared unto me of you, my brethren,
by them *which are of the house* of Chloe,
that there are contentions among you.
(12) Now this I say, that every one of

Chaps. i. 10—c. iv. 20. The Corinthian factions.

1 Gr. *schisms*.

*a* 1 Thess. 5. 24.

---

by some as a sufficient evidence that "who" does not refer to Christ. This by itself would scarcely be so, for there are examples elsewhere of St. Paul using our Lord's name where the possessive pronoun would have seemed more natural (Eph. iv. 12; Col. ii. 11). The general sense of the passage, however, and especially of the following verse, shows that the antecedent to "who" is not "Christ," in verse 7, but "God," in verse 4.

Three distinct periods are referred to in these verses—(1) the time when the grace of God was given them (verse 4); (2) the present time while they wait for the coming of the Lord Jesus, endowed as they are with the qualities described in verses 5—7; and (3) the day of our Lord Jesus Christ, which is still future—if preserved blameless until that, then they are finally and for ever safe; and that they will be so preserved by God the Apostle has no doubt, for the reason stated in the next verse. (See chap. iv. 3.)

(9) **God is faithful.**—The One who called them "unto the communion of His Son" is faithful, and therefore He will complete His work; no trials and sufferings need make them doubt that all will at last be well. The same confidence is expressed in Phil. i. 6, and 1 Thess. v. 24.

(10) **Now I beseech you, brethren.**—With these words the Apostle introduces the topic which is indeed one of the chief reasons of his writing this Epistle (see *Introduction*), viz., the PARTY-SPIRIT existing in the Corinthian Church. The treatment of this subject occupies to chap. iv. verse 20. It is important to remember that the factions rebuked by St. Paul were not sects who separated themselves from the Church, but those who within the Church divided themselves into parties, each calling itself by the name of some Apostle whose teaching and practice were most highly esteemed. The nature and cause of these divisions we shall understand as we consider the Apostle's exhortation to unity, and his rebuke of the spirit which gave rise to them.

**By the name of our Lord Jesus Christ.**—By his previous remark that they had been called unto "the communion" of this Holy Name, the writer has led up to the mention of Christ's name—not in the form of an adjuration, but as reminding them of it. That very name adds strength to his exhortation to "speak the same thing"—*i.e.*, to call themselves by this one name, and not each (as in verse 12) by a different designation, and that there should be no "schisms" among them. The word translated "divisions," signifies literally a "rent," in which sense it occurs in Mark ii. 21 ("*the rent* is made worse"), and is used three times in St. John's Gospel in the sense of schism or difference of opinion (vii. 43; ix. 16; x. 19). See Note on chap. vii. 43, as to the moral application of the word having probably come from Ephesus; and the idea of a tear or rent is carried on in the words, "be perfectly joined together," which in the original signifies the repair of something which was torn, as in Matt. iv. 21 we have the word rendered "*were mending* their nets." The church at Corinth presents to the Apostle's mind the idea of a seamless robe rent and torn into pieces, and he desires its complete and entire restoration by their returning to a united temper of mind and judgment as to word and deed.

(11) **The house of Chloe.**—Who Chloe was we cannot tell. Her name was evidently well known to the Corinthians, and some slaves of her household, probably travelling between Ephesus and Corinth, on their owner's business, had brought to St. Paul the account of the distracted state of the church in their city.

(12) **Now this I say.**—Better, *What I mean is, that,* &c. The following words, "every one of you saith," show how party-spirit pervaded the whole Christian community. It may be well to mention here briefly what we may consider to have been the distinctive characteristics of the factions which called themselves respectively the party of Paul, of Cephas, of Apollos, and of Christ.

1. ST. PAUL places first that section of the Church which called themselves by his name—thus at the outset showing that it is not for the sole purpose of silencing opponents, or from a jealousy of the influence of other teachers, that he writes so strenuously against the disturbances in the Corinthian community. It is the spirit of separation and of faction which he condemns—rebuking it as strongly when it has led to the undue exaltation of his own name, as when it attempted to depreciate his gifts and ministry as compared with those of Apollos or of Cephas. He thus wins at once the attention and confidence of every candid reader. The Pauline party would no doubt have consisted chiefly of those who, were the personal converts of the Apostle. Their esteem for him who had been the means of their conversion, seems to have been carried to excess in the manner in which it displayed itself. This would be increased by the hostility which their opponents' disparagement of the Apostle naturally excited in them. They allowed St. Paul's teaching of the liberty wherewith Christ made them free, to develop in them an unchristian license and a mode of treatment of others essentially illiberal, thus denying by their actions the very principles which they professed to hold dear. They "judged" and "set at nought" (Rom. xiv. 10) brethren who could not take so essentially spiritual a view of Christianity, but who still clung to some of the outward forms of Judaism.

2. APOLLOS was a Jew of Alexandria—"an eloquent man, and mighty in the Scriptures." He came to Ephesus during St. Paul's absence from that city, and taught what he knew of the "things of the Lord." While here, he was instructed further in "the way of God" by Aquila and Priscilla, he having previously only the inadequate knowledge which was possessed by disciples of John (Acts xviii. 24—28). Having preached in parts of Achaia, he came to Corinth. That he came there after St. Paul we may conclude from th Apostle's reference to himself as having "planted," and Apollos having "watered" (chap. iii. 6), and again to himself as having "laid the foundation" (chap. ii. 10). To Corinth Apollos brought with him the arts of the rhetorician, and

you saith, I am of Paul; and I of Apollos;[a] and I of Cephas; and I of Christ.
(13) Is Christ divided? was Paul crucified for you? or were ye baptized in the name of Paul? (14) I thank God that I baptized none of you, but Crispus and Gaius;[b] (15) lest any should say that I had baptized in mine own name. (16) And I baptized also the household

a Acts 18. 24.

b Acts 18. 8; Rom. 16. 23.

the culture of a Greek philosopher; and while preaching Christ crucified, these gifts and knowledge rendered him more acceptable than St. Paul had been, with his studied simplicity of style, to a certain class of intellectual and rationalising hearers in Corinth. When Apollos left, a section of the Church unduly magnified the importance of his gifts and of his manner of teaching. They did so to the depreciation of the simplicity of the gospel. This all led to the development of evils which we shall see more in detail in our examination of verses 18—31 and chap. ii. It ought to be remembered that Apollos was in no sense "the founder of a party." It was the exaggeration and perversion of Apollos' teaching, by some of the converts, that really founded the party. To the end he and Paul remained friends. He was probably with the Apostle while the Epistle was being written, and (chap. xvi. 12) refused, even when St. Paul suggested it, to go so soon again to Corinth, lest his presence should in the least tend to keep that party-spirit alive; and when, ten years (A.D. 67) later, the Apostle writes to Titus, he exhorts him "to bring Apollos on his journey diligently, that nothing be wanting to him" (Titus iii. 13).

3. The third faction in Corinth professed themselves followers of ST. PETER—or, as he was always *called*, "Cephas." This was the name by which our Lord addressed him in Matt. xvi. 18, and by this name (and not by his Greek name, Peter) he would have been spoken of by the Apostles and early Christians. In the New Testament writings he is designated most frequently Peter, as his Greek name would be more intelligible to the larger world for which these writings were intended. This faction of the Corinthian Church still clung to many Jewish ceremonial ideas, from which St. Paul was entirely free. They seem not to have quite passed *through* the cloud. They exalted St. Peter as more worthy of honour than St. Paul, because he had personally been with Christ, and been called "Cephas" (*rock*) by Him. They insinuated that St. Paul's supporting himself was not so dignified as the maintenance of St. Peter and others by the Church, in accordance with their Lord's command (chap. ix. 4—6; 2 Cor. xi. 9, 10); and they unfavourably contrasted St. Paul's celibacy with the married state of St. Peter, and of "the brethren of the Lord" (chap. ix. 5). It is probable that their animosity towards St. Paul was not a little increased by the knowledge that there were certain matters in which he considered St. Peter to be in error, and "withstood him to the face" (Gal. ii. 2). To the detailed difficulties and errors of this section of the Corinthian Church reference is to be found in the chaps. vii.—xi. 1.

4. There was still one other party or faction which dared to arrogate to themselves the name of CHRIST Himself. These over-estimated the importance and value of having seen Christ in the flesh, and despised St. Paul as one who had subsequently joined the Apostolate. Contempt for all human teachers was by them exalted into a virtue. Their greatest sin was that the very name which should have been the common bond of union, the name by the thought and memory of which the Apostle would plead for a restoration of unity, was degraded by them into the exclusive party-badge of a narrow section. We do not find any very definite and detailed allusion to this section in this Epistle, though in the second Epistle a reference to them can be traced in chap. x. 7. There is no need for such at any length. Their condemnation is written in every chapter, the whole of the Epistle is a denunciation of the spirit of faction—of the sin of schism—which in their case reached a climax, inasmuch as they consecrated their sin with the very name of Christ. Such, briefly, were the four schisms which were rending the Corinthian Church. We might call them—1, The Party of Liberty (PAUL); 2, The Intellectual Party (APOLLOS); 3, The Judaizing Party (CEPHAS); 4, The Exclusive Party (who said, "I am of CHRIST").

(12) **I of Christ.**—It has been suggested that this is not the designation of a fourth party in the Church, but an affirmation by the Apostle, "I am of Christ," in contradistinction to those referred to before, who called themselves after the names of men. But in addition to the fact that there is no change in form of expression to indicate a change of sense, we find evident traces of the existence of such a party (chap. ix. 1; 2 Cor. x. 7).

(13) **Is Christ divided?**—Better, *Christ is divided.* Christ, in the communion of the Church, is rent, torn in fragments by you. The mention of the sacred name as a party-cry makes the Apostle burst into that impassioned exclamation. Then there is a momentary pause, and the Apostle goes back from his sudden denunciation of the "Christ" party, to those whom he had originally selected for typical treatment, viz., those who bore his own name, the two streams of thought, as it were, mingling and rushing together; and he asks (with a mind still full of the burning indignation aroused by the mention of the name of union as a symbol of disunion), "Was Paul crucified for you?" "Was your baptism in the name of Paul?" To each of which the answer must of necessity be "No."

Paul being the founder of the Church, these questions apply more forcibly to the others also.

(14) **I thank God.**—"I am thankful to God that it was not so." For if he had baptised a great many, some might have said he had created originally a party in his own name. Crispus (see Acts xviii. 8), a "ruler of the synagogue," Gaius (or Caius, his Roman name), "mine host, and of the whole Church" (Rom. xvi. 23): the evident importance and position of these two, and that they were the first converts, may account for the Apostle having departed from his usual practice in baptising them.

(16) **Stephanas.**—The mention of Stephanas and his household was, from the words preceding, evidently a subsequent correction by the Apostle. He had forgotten them, and was reminded of it possibly by Sosthenes, who was writing from his dictation, and would naturally have known the fact, for Stephanas was the "firstfruits of Achaia" (chap. xvi. 15), and Sosthenes had been chief ruler of the synagogue (Acts xviii. 17) when Paul had been brought before Gallio, deputy of Achaia. Stephanas himself was at Ephesus with St. Paul when this letter was written, and doubtless in daily intercourse both with him and with

of Stephanas: besides, I know not
whether I baptized any other. (17) For
Christ sent me not to baptize, but to
preach the gospel: not with wisdom[a]
of words,[1] lest the cross of Christ should
be made of none effect.
(18) For the preaching of the cross is
to them that perish foolishness; but
unto us which are saved it is the power[b]
of God. (19) For it is written, I will
destroy the wisdom of the wise,[c] and will
bring to nothing the understanding of
the prudent. (20) Where *is* the wise?[d]
where *is* the scribe? where *is* the dis-
puter of this world? hath not God
made foolish the wisdom of this world?
(21) For after that in the wisdom of God
the world by wisdom knew not God,[e] it
pleased God by the foolishness of preach-
ing to save them that believe. (22) For
the Jews require a sign,[f] and the
Greeks seek after wisdom: (23) but
we preach Christ crucified, unto the
Jews a stumblingblock, and unto the
Greeks foolishness; (24) but unto them
which are called, both Jews and
Greeks, Christ the power of God, and
the wisdom of God. (25) Because the
foolishness of God is wiser than men;
and the weakness of God is stronger

e Rom. 1. 20.
a 2 Pet. 1. 16.
1 Or, *speech.*
f Matt. 12. 38.
b Rom. 1. 16.
c Isa. 29. 14.
d Isa. 33. 18.

---

Sosthenes (chap. xvi. 17). Finding how his memory had failed him on this point, the Apostle adds, "And I know not," &c. (*i.e.*, I don't remember) so as to prevent any cavil from hypercritical opponents.

(17) **Not to baptize.**—Preaching was eminently the work of the Apostles. The deacons used to baptise (Acts x. 48). The mention of "the preaching of the glad tidings" affords an opportunity for the Apostle stating in vindication of himself why that, and not philosophy, was the subject of his preaching, "lest the cross of Christ should be made of none effect." Such, and not inability or ignorance, was the grand cause of his simplicity.

(18) **For the preaching.**—In the original the contrast comes out more strongly between this and the previous statement, the same phrase being repeated, thus, "For the *word* of the cross," in contrast to "the wisdom of mere *words*" above. This is the word of real power.

**Them that perish.**—Better, *those that are perishing*, and *us who are being saved*, the former referring to those who have not received the gospel, and the latter to those who have (2 Cor. ii. 15; iv. 3).

**The power of God.**—The cross and all that it represents is the greatest display of the power of God (Acts viii. 10).

(19) **For it is written.**—This is a further explanation of why the word of the gospel, and not the word of merely human wisdom, is "the power of God." The quotation which follows consists of two passages in Isaiah, and is taken from the LXX., one word being altered. We have here "bring to nothing," instead of "I will conceal." Words which originally applied to those who assumed to be the guides of the Jewish race (Isa. xxix. 14), apply with greater force to those who would presume to be Christian leaders.

(20) To the second quotation, which was originally a song of triumph over the enemies of Israel, the Apostle gives a general application.

**The wise.**—The general reference in this word is to those who would exalt human knowledge, while "the scribe" indicates the Jew, and the "disputer" the Greek, who discussed philosophy (Acts vi. 9; ix. 29).

**Of this world.**—These words qualify all three mentioned, and not exclusively "the disputer." "World" (more literally, *age*) does not here mean the physical world, but, in an ethical sense, "this age," in contrast to that which is "to come" (Matt. xii. 32; Mark x. 30). It is employed afterwards (last word of verse 20, and in verse 21) to designate all who are outside the Christian communion, as in the next verse it is contrasted with "them that believe."

(21) **For.**—This is an explanation and evidence of how God made the wisdom of the world to be only "folly."

**After that** (better, *inasmuch as*) is not here a note of time, but of causal relation.

**In the wisdom of God.**—These words can scarcely be taken as an expression of a kind of approval of God's wisdom in so arranging the method of revelation, but rather as referring to God's wisdom evidenced in nature, and in the teachings of lawgivers and prophets. The world by its wisdom did not attain to a knowledge of God in His wisdom displayed in creation (Acts xvii. 26; Rom. i. 19).

**It pleased God.**—The world having thus failed to gain a true knowledge of God in His wisdom, He gave them that knowledge through that very proclamation of "the cross" which those "that perish" call foolishness. The contrast so strikingly put here is between (1) the *failure* of the world by means of its wisdom to know God, in His wisdom displayed to all in His mighty works, and to the Jews in His great teachers; and (2) the *success* of this "folly" of the gospel, as they called it, in saving all who believed it (Rom. i. 16).

(22) **For.**—This is a further unfolding of the fact of the simplicity of the preaching of the Cross. It pandered neither to Jewish-minded persons (not in the Greek "*the* Jews," "*the* Gentiles," but simply "Jews," "Gentiles") who desired visible portents to support the teaching, nor to those of Greek taste who desired an actual and clear philosophic proof of it. (See Matt. xii. 38; Mark viii. 11; Luke xi. 16; John iv. 48.)

(23) **But we preach.**—The gospel of Christ crucified made its way by those very qualities which they regarded as "weakness and folly," vindicating itself as "the power of God," more mighty than any "sign" a Jew might ask for; and "the wisdom of God" surpassing any merely intellectual "wisdom" which a Greek might desire.

(24) **Them which are called.**—St. Paul always speaks of all Christians as "the called," not using that word in the narrower sense to which some modern religious sects have restricted it.

(25) **Because.**—This introduces the reason why Christ, as being crucified, is the power and wisdom of God, viz., because God's folly (as they call it) is wiser, not "than the wisdom of men," as some understand this passage, but than men themselves—embracing in that word all that men can know or hope ever to

than men. (26) For ye see your call-
ing, brethren, how that not many
wise men after the flesh, not many
mighty, not many noble, *are called:*
(27) but God hath chosen the foolish
things of the world to confound the
wise; and God hath chosen the weak
things of the world to confound the
things which are mighty; (28) and base
things of the world, and things which
are despised, hath God chosen, *yea*, and
things which are not, to bring to nought
things that are: (29) that no flesh should
glory in his presence. (30) But of him
are ye in Christ Jesus, who of God is
made unto us wisdom, and righteous-
ness, and sanctification, and redemption:
(31) that, according as it is written, He
that glorieth, let him glory in the Lord.[a]

*a* Jer. 9. 23.

A.D. 59.

CHAPTER II.—(1) And I, brethren,
when I came to you, came not with
excellency of speech or of wisdom,[b] de-
claring unto you the testimony of God.
(2) For I determined not to know any
thing among you, save Jesus Christ,

*b* ch. 1. 17.

---

know; and the weakness of God (as they regard it) is stronger than men.

(26) **For ye see your calling.**—Better, imperative (as in chaps. viii. 9; x. 18; xvi. 10), *For see your calling.* The Apostle directs them to look at the facts regarding their own calling to Christianity, as an illustration of the truth of what he has just written, viz., that though there were, perhaps, a few of high birth and education who were called, and responded to that call, yet that these are "not many." It has been well remarked, "the ancient Christians were, for the greater part, slaves and persons of humble rank; the whole history of the progress of the Church is in fact a gradual triumph of the unlearned over the learned, of the lowly over the great, until the emperor himself cast his crown at the foot of Christ's cross" (Olshausen); or, as an English writer puts it, "Christianity with the irresistible might of its weakness shook the world."

(27) **Foolish things.**—The neuter is used probably for the purpose of generalising, and it expresses the qualities of the men whom God has chosen—"the wise" is masculine in the Greek, showing that it is still of "persons" the Apostle is speaking.

(28) **And things which are not.**—This climax loses somewhat of its force by the insertion of the word "and," which is not in some of the best MSS., and "yea," which is not in any MS. Omitting the word "and," the sentence is not an addition to the things already mentioned, but a general and emphatic summary of all the things which have been already contrasted with their opposites. After the words "hath God chosen" there is a slight pause, and then the Apostle describes all those things which he has declared to be God's choice, as things which "are not"—*i.e.*, do not in men's estimation even exist (Rom. iv. 17; ix. 25; see also Job xxxiv. 19, 24).

(30) **But.**—So far from boasting in His presence, we all owe all to Him. He is the author of the spiritual life of us who are in union with Christ, "who *was* (not "is") made wisdom unto us *from* God." The past tense here refers us back to the fact of the Incarnation; in it Christ became to us God's revelation of Himself, thus giving us a wisdom from the source of all wisdom, which surpasses utterly any wisdom we could have derived from nature or from man. Not only is Christ the source of whatever true wisdom we have, but also (so adds the Apostle) of whatever "righteousness" and "holiness" we have—spiritual gifts, as well as gifts of knowledge, come all from Him—and beyond all that, He is also our redemption, the "ransom" paid for us, by which we are redeemed from the bondage and slavery of sin. (See John viii. 34; Rom. vi. 18, 20; viii. 21. 23; 1 Pet. i. 18, 19.)

(31) **That.**—So that it might be as the prophet wrote, "He that boasteth, let him boast in the Lord." This is not a literal quotation, but only an adaptation and paraphrase from the LXX. of Jer. ix. 23, 24. Our only true boasting before God is that we are in Christ, that all we have we owe entirely to Him; we can only glory in, not ourselves or what we have or are, but in the fact that He is our benefactor. Thus, in St. Chrysostom's quaint words, Paul "always fasteneth them on with nails to the name of Christ."

This concludes St. Paul's general explanation of God's method, and he then turns to his own conduct, to show how entirely it was in harmony with God's plan, which he has just explained and vindicated.

II.

(1) **And I.**—The Apostle now proceeds to show how he personally, in both the matter and manner of his teaching at Corinth, had acted in accordance with those great principles which he has already explained as God's method. "The testimony of God" is St. Paul's testimony concerning God in Christ (chap. i. 6; 2 Tim. i. 8).

(2) **I determined not to know.**—Better, *I did not determine to know.* The only subject of teaching concerning which the Apostle had formed a determined resolve in his mind when coming to Corinth was the preaching Christ and Him as being crucified. We have here a statement of what was ever the subject-matter of apostolic teaching. St. Paul did not dwell on the miraculous in the life of Christ, which would have pandered to the Jewish longing for a "sign"; nor did he put forward elaborate "theories" of the gospel, which would have been a concession to the Greek's longing after "wisdom": but he preached a personal Christ, and especially dwelt on the fact that He had been crucified (chap. i. 17, 23; Gal. vi. 14; Phil. ii. 8). We can scarcely realise now the stumbling-block which the preaching of a crucified Christ must have been to Jews and Greeks, the enormous temptation to keep the cross in the background which the early teachers would naturally have felt, and the sublime and confident faith which must have nerved St. Paul to make it the central fact of all his teaching. For us the cross is illumined with the glories of eighteen centuries of civilisation, and consecrated with the memory of all that is best and noblest in the history of Christendom. To every Jew and to every Gentile it conveyed but one idea, that of the most revolting and most degrading punishment. The remembrance of this fact will enable us to realise how uncompromising was the Apostles' teaching—how it never "accommodated itself" to any existing

and him crucified. (3) And I was with
you in weakness, and in fear, and in
much trembling. (4) And my speech
and my preaching *was* not with enticing[1]
words of man's wisdom,[a] but in demon-
stration of the Spirit and of power:
(5) that your faith should not stand[2] in
the wisdom of men, but in the power of
God.

(6) Howbeit we speak wisdom among
them that are perfect: yet not the
wisdom of this world, nor of the princes
of this world, that come to nought:
(7) but we speak the wisdom of God in a
mystery, *even* the hidden *wisdom*, which
God ordained before the world unto our
glory: (8) which none of the princes of
this world knew:

For had they known *it*, they would
not have crucified the Lord of glory.
(9) But as it is written, Eye hath not
seen, nor ear heard,[b] neither have en-
tered into the heart of man, the things
which God hath prepared for them that

1 Or, *persuasible.*

a 2 Pet. 1. 16.

2 Gr. *be.*

b Isa. 64. 4.

---

desire or prejudice. This surely is no small evidence of the divine origin of the religion of which the Apostles were the heralds!

(3) **And I was with you.**—To show that the real force of his teaching lay in its subject-matter, and not in any power with which he may have proclaimed the gospel, the Apostle now dwells upon his own physical weakness. The "weakness and fear and trembling" of which St. Paul speaks here had in it probably a large element of that self-distrust which so noble and sensitive a nature would feel in the fulfilment of such an exalted mission as the preaching of the Cross. I cannot think, however, the allusion is only to that. There is, I believe, a reference also to what we may call a physical apprehension of danger. The bravest are not those who do not experience any sensation of fear, but rather those who keenly appreciate danger, who have an instinctive shrinking from it, and yet eventually by their moral might conquer this dread. There are traces of this element in St. Paul's character to be found in several places, as, for example, in Acts xviii. 9, when the Lord encourages him when labouring at Corinth with the hopeful words, "Be not afraid;" again in Acts xxiii. 11, when the terrible scene before Ananias had depressed him, the Lord is with him to strengthen him, "Be of good cheer, Paul;" and in Acts xxvii. 24, when the angel of the Lord appears to him amid the storm and shipwreck, "Fear not, Paul."

(4) **And my speech.**—The result which necessarily followed from this weakness and trembling was that neither his "speech" (*i.e.*, the style of his teaching), nor his "preaching" (*i.e.*, the subject-matter of his teaching) were of such a kind as to appeal to the natural tastes of the Corinthians.

**Demonstration of the Spirit.**—The Apostle's demonstration of the truth of the gospel was the result of no human art or skill, but came from the Spirit and power of God, and therefore the Corinthians could glory in no human teacher, but only in the power of God, which was the true source of the success of the gospel amongst them.

(6) **Howbeit we speak wisdom.**—Nevertheless, there is a wisdom in the gospel. The assertion is in the Greek a more striking contrast to verse 4 than appears in the English. In the original (verse 4) the word is "wisdom," and not "*man's* wisdom," as in the English. Thus the statement here is a verbal contradiction of that in verse 4. In using the plural "we," St. Paul implies that he did not stand alone among the Apostles in the method of his teaching.

**Them that are perfect**—*i.e.*, those who are grown up, and not "babes" (chap. iii. 1; see also xiv. 20). The "wisdom" of the gospel is that deep spiritual truth which only those whose spiritual natures have been trained and cultivated were capable of understanding. This "wisdom," however, the Apostle had not taught the Corinthians; he had only taught them the alphabet of Christianity, for they were still but "babes"—they were still only "fleshly" (chap. iii. 3). That the Apostle himself not only grasped the higher truths which he designates the "wisdom" of the gospel, but taught them gladly when there were hearers capable of appreciating them, is evident from many passages in the Epistles to the Romans, Colossians, and Ephesians, where he unfolds the "mysteries" of the gospel. (See Rom. xi. 25; xvi. 25.)

**Yet not.**—Better, *a wisdom, however, not of this world.*

**That come to nought.**—Better, *which are being brought to nought*, the reference here being, not to the inherent transitoriness of human wisdom and teachers, but to the fact that they are being brought to nought by God's rejection of them, and His choice of the "weak" things as the means of spreading the gospel (chap. i. 28).

(7) **In a mystery.**—The writer explains in these words the plan on which his speaking of God's wisdom proceeded, that he dealt with it as the ancient mysteries were dealt with, explaining certain truths only to the initiated, and not to all (chap. iv. 1; Col. i. 26).

**Hidden.**—Heretofore unrevealed, but now made manifest in Christ and by His teachers (Rom. xvi. 25; Eph. iii. 10). And this has been in accordance with what God ordained "before the beginning of time," to our *glory*, as distinct from the humiliation of the world's teaching, which is coming to nought.

(8) **They would not have crucified.**—The conduct of the princes and rulers of this world, alike Jewish and Gentile, illustrates and proves the previous assertion (John viii. 19; xix. 9).

**Lord of glory.**—In striking contrast to the ignominy of the crucifixion.

(9) **As it is written.**—Where do the words which follow occur? They are not to be found as here given anywhere in the Old Testament. It has therefore been suggested (Origen) that they are from some apocryphal book, or some book which has been lost, as is supposed many have been. Chrysostom also suggests that it may be a reference, not to a writing, but to historical facts, as in Matt. ii. 23. None of these explanations would justify the use of that phrase, "it is written," with which these words are introduced, and which in the apostolic writings is confined to quotations from the Old Testament scriptures. It is not used where the words are taken from other sources (see, *e.g.*, Jude, 9, 14). Although the words given here are not to be found in the same sequence in any passage in the Old Testa-

love him. (10) But God hath revealed
*them* unto us by his Spirit:
For the Spirit searcheth all things,
yea, the deep things of God. (11) For
what man knoweth the things of a man,
save the spirit of man which is in him?
even so the things of God knoweth no
man, but the Spirit of God.
(12) Now we have received, not the
spirit of the world, but the spirit which
is of God; that we might know the
things that are freely given to us of
God. (13) Which things also we speak,[a]
not in the words which man's wisdom
teacheth, but which the Holy Ghost
teacheth; comparing spiritual things
with spiritual. (14) But the natural
man receiveth not the things of the
Spirit of God: for they are foolishness
unto him: neither can he know *them*,
because they are spiritually discerned.
(15) But he that is spiritual judgeth[1] all
things,[b] yet he himself is judged[2] of no
man. (16) For who hath known the

a 2 Pet. 1. 16.

1 Or, *discerneth.*

b Prov. 28. 5.
2 Or, *discerned.*

---

ment, still there are phrases scattered through the writings of Isaiah (see Isa. lxiv. 4; lxv. 17; see also lxii. 15 in the LXX.), which would easily be joined together in memory and resemble even verbally the passage as written here by the Apostle. This is not the only place in which St. Paul would seem to thus refer to the Old Testament scriptures (see chap. i. 19, 20) when he is not basing any argument upon a particular sentence in the Scriptures, but merely availing himself of some thoughts or words in the Old Testament as an illustration of some truth which he is enforcing.

(10) **But God hath revealed them unto us.**—Here the emphatic word is "us." The latter part of verses 8 and 9 are parenthetical, and the sense goes back to the beginning of verse 8. "None of the princes of this age know these things, but God hath revealed them unto *us* His apostles and teachers" (Matt. xiii. 11; xvi. 17; 2 Cor. xii. 1). This revelation of spiritual truth is made by the Holy Spirit of God to our spirits (Rom. viii. 16). The Apostle gives two proofs that the Apostles have this knowledge, and that the Holy Spirit is the source of it: 1 (verses 10 and 11), because the Holy Spirit alone is capable of imparting this knowledge; and 2 (verses 12—16), because the Holy Spirit has been given to *us* the Apostles.

**Searcheth all things.**—The word "searcheth" here does not convey the idea of inquiry for the purpose of acquiring knowledge, but rather complete and accurate knowledge itself, as in Rom. viii. 27; see also Ps. cxxxix. 1.

(11) **What man . . .**—Better, *Who of men knoweth the things of a man? but the spirit of the man which is in him knoweth them.*

**The things of God knoweth no man.**—These words cannot be taken as an assertion that man cannot have any knowledge of the things of God; but the Apostle urges that man, as man, cannot know the things of God, but that his knowledge of these things is in virtue of his having the Spirit of God dwelling in him.

(12) **We.**—This must not be confined to the Apostles exclusively. Though referring primarily to them, it includes all the members of the Christian Church as one with its teachers and rulers. The "things freely given us of God" mean all spiritual things.

(13) **Not in the words.**—Not only the gospel truths themselves, but the very form and manner in which those truths are taught is the result of spiritual insight.

**Comparing spiritual things with spiritual.**—Better, *explaining spiritual things in spiritual language;* really only another more pointed form of stating what he has just said. The word translated here "comparing" in our Authorised version is used in the sense of expounding or teaching in the LXX. (Gen. xl. 8, 16; Dan. v. 12), especially of dreams, where the dream is, so to speak, "compared" with the interpretation. So here, the spiritual things are "compared" with the spiritual language in which they are stated. Another meaning—*explaining spiritual things to spiritual men*—has been suggested, but that adopted would seem to be the more simple and natural. This second interpretation, would make these words the introduction to the remark which follows about "the spiritual man," but it involves a use of the word in which it is not found elsewhere in the New Testament.

(14) **But the natural man.**—To understand this and other passages in which St. Paul speaks of "natural" and "spiritual" men, it is important to recollect that our ordinary manner of speaking of man as consisting of "soul and body"—unless "soul" be taken in an untechnical sense to denote the whole immaterial portion—is altogether inaccurate. True psychology regards man as a trinity of natures. (See Note on Matt. x. 28.) In accordance with this, St. Paul speaks of man as consisting of body (*soma*), soul (*psyche*), and spirit (*pneuma*); the *soma* is our physical nature; the *psyche* is our intellectual nature, embracing also our desires and human affections; the *pneuma* is our spiritual nature. Thus in each of us there is a somatical man, a psychical man, and a pneumatical man; and according as any one of those parts of the nature dominates over the other, so is the character of the individual person. One in whom the *soma* is strongest is a "carnal," or "fleshly," man; one in whom the intellect or affections predominate is a "natural," or "psychic," man; and one in whom the spirit rules (which it can do only when enlightened and guided by the Spirit of God, which acts on it) is a "spiritual" man. (See 1 Thess. v. 23.)

**Natural.**—That is, literally, that part of our nature which we call "mind," and hence signifies that man in whom pure intellectual reason and the merely natural affections predominate. Now such a one cannot grasp spiritual truth any more than the physical nature, which is made to discern physical things, can grasp intellectual things. Spiritual truth appeals to the spirit of the man, and therefore is intelligible only to those who are "spiritual," *i.e.*, in whom the *pneuma* is not dormant, but quickened by the Holy *Pneuma.*

(15) **He that is spiritual.**—The spiritual man judges all spiritual truth, but he himself is judged by none who are not spiritual. (See chap. xiv. 29; 1 John iv. 1.)

(16) **For.**—This is the proof that the enlightened spiritual man cannot be judged by any one who is not thus enlightened. "Who (thus uninstructed) can know the mind of the Lord Jesus, that he may instruct Him?"

**But we.**—That is, spiritual men, including the Apostles. The Apostle here identifies Christ with the Spirit, whom he has previously spoken of as the

mind of the Lord,[a] that he may[1] in-
struct him? But we have the mind of
Christ.

CHAPTER III.—(1) And I, brethren,
could not speak unto you as unto spiritual,
but as unto carnal, *even* as unto babes
in Christ. (2) I have fed you with milk,
and not with meat: for hitherto ye
were not able *to bear it*, neither yet now
are ye able. (3) For ye are yet carnal.
For whereas *there is* among you envy-
ing, and strife, and divisions,[2] are ye
not carnal, and walk as men?[3] (4) For
while one saith, I am of Paul; and
another, I *am* of Apollos; are ye not
carnal?

(5) Who then is Paul, and who *is*
Apollos, but ministers by whom ye be-
lieved, even as the Lord gave to every
man? (6) I have planted, Apollos
watered; but God gave the increase.

a Isa. 40. 13; Rom. 11. 34.
1 Gr. *shall.*
2 Or, *factions.*
3 Gr. *according to man?*

A.D. 59.

---

Teacher of spiritual things. He does not mean to assert that the Apostles knew all that the mind of Christ knew, but that all things which they did know were from Him and spiritual (John xv. 15).

III.

(1) **And I.**—Again, as in chap. ii. 6, the Apostle shows how general principles which he has just explained were exemplified in his own conduct. In the closing verses of chap. ii. St. Paul has enunciated the general method of teaching spiritual truth as being dependent upon the receptive powers of those who are being taught. He now proceeds to point out to them that their own character, as being wanting in spirituality, was the real hindrance to his teaching them the higher spiritual truth which may be called "the wisdom" of the gospel.

**As unto carnal.**—Better, *as being carnal.* Our version may seem to imply that the Apostle spoke to them *as if* they were carnal, though they really were not so; but the force of the passage is that they were indeed carnal, and that the Apostle taught them not as if they were such, but as being such. "Carnal" is here the opposite of "spiritual," and does not involve any reference to what we would commonly speak of as carnal sin.

**Babes in Christ.**—This is the opposite of the "full grown" in chap. ii. 6, to whom the "wisdom" could be taught. (See also Col. i. 28, "full grown in Christ.") It may be an interesting indication of the "manliness" of St. Paul's character and his high estimate of it in others, that he constantly uses the words "babe" and "childhood" in a depreciatory sense. (See Rom. ii. 20, Gal. iv. 3, Eph. iv. 14.)

(2) **Milk . . . meat.**—The use of the word "infant" naturally suggests these two images for the higher wisdom and for the simpler truths of the gospel respectively.

**Hitherto ye were not able.**—Better, *for ye were not yet able.* Up to this point the Apostle has been speaking of the condition in which he found the Corinthians when he came first to Corinth, and he proceeds from this to rebuke them for continuing in this condition. He does not blame them for having been "babes" at the outset, but he does in the following passage blame them for not having yet grown up out of infancy.

(2, 3) **Neither yet now are ye able, for ye are yet carnal.**—Better, *but not even now are ye able, for ye are still carnal.* It is for this absence of growth—for their continuing up to this time in the same condition—that the Apostle reproaches them; and he shows that the fault which they find with him for not having given them more advanced teaching really lies at their own door.

(3) **For whereas.**—Better, *For since there is.*

**As men.**—Better, *after the manner of man—i.e.,* after a merely human and not after a spiritually enlightened manner. In Rom. iii. 5, Gal. i. 2, also Rom. xv. 5, the opposite condition is expressed by the same Greek particle used with our Lord's name, "according to Jesus Christ."

(4) **One saith, I am of Paul.**—These and the following words explain exactly what the Apostle means by their being "carnal," and walking after a merely human manner. Only two of the factions—those of Paul and of Apollos—are mentioned as types of the rest. The factious spirit was in each and all the "parties" the same, but the particular difference between the teaching of the higher wisdom and the simpler truths of the gospel was best illustrated by these two.

The selection for rebuke of those who called them selves by the Apostle's own name was, no doubt, intended by him to show that it was no matter of personal jealousy on his part. He specially condemns those who magnified his name. It is for his Master alone that he is jealous.

**Are ye not carnal?**—Better, *are ye not only men?* carrying on the idea expressed in verse 3.

(5) The Apostle now proceeds to explain (verses 5—9) what is the true position and work of Christian ministers. He asserts that all alike—both those who teach the simpler truths, and those who build up upon that primary knowledge—are only instruments in God's hand; and in verses 10—15 (replying to those who sneered at and despised his simple teaching as compared to the higher instruction of Apollos) he points out that though all are only instruments used by God, yet that if there be any difference of honour or utility in the various kinds of work for which God so uses His ministers, the greater work is the planting the seed, or the laying the foundation. There can be only one foundation—it is alike necessary and unvarying—many others may build upon it, with varied material and with different results.

**Who then is Paul, and who is Apollos.**—Better, *What then is Apollos? what is Paul?* and to these abrupt and startling questions the answer is, "Merely those whom Christ used, according as He gave to each his own peculiar powers as the means of your conversion." (Such is the force of the word "believed" here as in Rom. xiii. 11). It is therefore absurd that you should exalt them into heads of parties. They are only instruments—each used as the great Master thought best.

(6) **I have planted, Apollos watered.**—By an image borrowed from the processes of agriculture the Apostle explains the relation in which his teaching stood to that of Apollos—and how all the results were from God. This indication of St. Paul having been the founder, and Apollos the subsequent instructor, of

(7) So then neither is he that planteth
any thing, neither he that watereth;
but God that giveth the increase. (8) Now
he that planteth and he that watereth
are one: and every man shall receive
his own reward according to his own
labour.[a] (9) For we are labourers to-
gether with God: ye are God's hus-
bandry,[1] *ye are* God's building.
(10) According to the grace of God
which is given unto me, as a wise
masterbuilder, I have laid the founda-
tion, and another buildeth thereon.
But let every man take heed how he
buildeth thereupon. (11) For other
foundation can no man lay than that is
laid, which is Jesus Christ. (12) Now if
any man build upon this foundation
gold, silver, precious stones, wood, hay,
stubble; (13) every man's work shall be
made manifest: for the day shall de-
clare it, because it shall be revealed[2]

a Ps. 62. 12; Gal. 6. 5.

1 Or, *tillage.*

2 Gr. *is revealed.*

---

the Corinthian Church, is in complete harmony with what we read of the early history of that Church in Acts xviii. 27 and xix. 1. After St. Paul had been at Corinth (Acts xviii. 1), Apollos, who had been taught by Aquila and Priscilla at Ephesus, came there and "helped them much which had already believed."

(7) **Any thing**—*i.e.*, "anything worth mentioning" (chap. x. 19; Gal. ii. 6 and vi. 3).

(8) **Are one.**—The planter and the waterer are one in that they are both working in the same cause. "But," says the Apostle (not "and," as in our version), "each man shall receive his own reward from God, not from man, according to his labour." There is an individuality as well as a unity in the work of the ministry. This is, however, not a thing to be noticed by men, but it will be recognised by the great Master.

(9) Thrice in this verse the Apostle repeats the name of God with emphasis, to explain and to impress the assertion of the previous verse, that men are to recognise the unity, and God alone the diversity, in the ministerial work and office. "*We* are GOD'S fellow-labourers; *you* are GOD'S field—GOD'S house." The image is thus suddenly altered from agriculture to architecture, as the latter can be more amplified, and will better illustrate the great variety of work of which the Apostle proceeds subsequently to speak. This sudden change of metaphor is a characteristic of St. Paul's style; a similar instance is to be found in 2 Cor. x. 4—8, where the illustration given from architecture is used instead of the military metaphor which is employed in the earlier verses of that passage. See also 1 Cor. ix. 7, and Eph. iii. 17, and Col. ii. 6—7, where there is the introduction of three distinct images in rapid succession in so many sentences. It has been suggested that possibly the use of the word "field," in the Greek "Georgion," was the cause of the Christian name "George" becoming so popular in the Church.

(10) **According to the grace of God.**—The Apostle being about to speak of himself as "a wise masterbuilder," takes care by commencing his statement with these words to show that he is not indulging in self-laudation, but merely pointing out what God had given him the grace to do. (See Rom. i. 5 and xii. 3.)

**Wise**—*i.e.*, skilful or judicious.

**Another buildeth thereon.**—The sequence of the work here is the same as in the planting and watering of the previous illustration. The use of the indefinite word "another" avoids what might be considered the invidiously frequent repetition of the name of Apollos, and also indicates that there were others also who came after Paul, as is evident from chap. iv. 15. (See Rom. xv. 20.)

**But let every man take heed how he buildeth thereupon.**—Better, *But let each one see in what manner he buildeth thereon.* The argument in this and the following verse is that there can be only one foundation in the spiritual building—namely, the personal Jesus Christ. That foundation the Apostle has laid. None can alter it or add to it as a foundation; but there may be an immense variety in the materials with which those who come after the laying of the foundation may build up the superstructure. Therefore their own work and "how" they build (*i.e.*, with what materials), and not the one foundation once for all and unalterably laid, should be the subject of their thought and care.

(12) **Now if any man . . .**—Better, *But if any man.*

**Precious stones.**—Not gems, but grand and costly stones, such as marble. "Hay," dried grass used to fill up chinks in the walls. "Stubble," stalks with the ears of corn cut off, and used for making a roof of thatch.

Many ingenious attempts have been made to apply the imagery of this passage in detail to various doctrines or Christian virtues, but it seems best to regard it as broadly and in outline bringing before the reader the two great ideas of permanent and ephemeral work, and the striking contrast between them. The truth brought forward is primarily, if not exclusively, for teachers. The image is taken from what would have met the eye of a traveller in Ephesus where St. Paul now was, or in Corinth where his letter was to be first read. It is such a contrast as may be seen (though not in precisely the same striking form of difference) in London in our own day. The stately palaces of marble and of granite, with roof and column glittering with gold and silver decorations, and close by these the wretched hovels of the poor and outcast, the walls made of laths of wood, with the interstices stuffed with straw, and a thatched roof above. Then arose before the Apostle's vision the thought of a city being visited by a mighty conflagration, such as desolated Corinth itself in the time of Mummius. The mean structures of perishable wood and straw would be utterly consumed, while, as was actually the case in Corinth, the mighty palaces and temples would stand after the fire had exhausted itself. Thus, says St. Paul, it will be with the work of Christian teachers when the "day of the Lord is revealed in fire." The fire of that day will prove and test the quality of each work.

(13) **Revealed by fire.**—Better, *revealed in fire.* For the general scope of this passage, see verse 12 above. The day of the coming of the Lord is always thus represented as bursting suddenly with a rush of light and blaze of fire upon the earth. (See Mal. iii. 1, 2, 3; iv. 1; 2 Thess. i. 8; ii. 8.)

by fire; and the fire shall try every
man's work of what sort it is. (14) If
any man's work abide which he hath
built thereupon, he shall receive a
reward. (15) If any man's work shall
be burned, he shall suffer loss: but
he himself shall be saved; yet so as
by fire.
(16) Know ye not that ye are the
temple of God,[a] and *that* the Spirit of
God dwelleth in you? (17) If any man
defile[1] the temple of God, him shall
God destroy; for the temple of God is
holy, which *temple* ye are.
(18) Let no man deceive himself. If
any man among you seemeth to be wise
in this world, let him become a fool,
that he may be wise. (19) For the
wisdom of this world is foolishness with
God. For it is written, He taketh the
wise in their own craftiness.[b] (20) And
again, The Lord knoweth the thoughts
of the wise,[c] that they are vain.
(21) Therefore let no man glory in men.
For all things are your's; (22) whether
Paul, or Apollos, or Cephas, or the
world, or life, or death, or things pre-
sent, or things to come; all are your's;
(23) and ye are Christ's; and Christ *is*
God's.

*b* Job 5. 13.
*c* Ps. 94. 11.
*a* ch. 6. 19.
1 Or, *destroy*.

---

(14) This is the general application to Christian teachers of what has gone before. Those who have built well shall have their reward in their work having survived the trial of the fire; those who have built otherwise shall lose everything—their work, which should have remained as their reward, will perish in the fire—and they themselves will be as men who only make good their escape by rushing through a conflagration, leaving all that was theirs to be destroyed. (See Mark ix. 49.)

(15) **So as.**—These words remind us that the whole passage, and especially the reference to fire, is to be regarded as metaphorical, and not to be understood in a literal and physical sense. Forgetting this, Roman divines have evolved from these words the doctrine of purgatory.

(16) **The temple of God.**—From the thought of grand edifices in general the Apostle goes on to the particular case of a building which is not only splendid but "holy"—the temple of God—thus reminding the reader that the rich and valuable metals and stones spoken of previously are to represent spiritual attainments. He introduces the passage with the words "Do ye not know," implying that their conduct was such as could only be pursued by those who were either ignorant or forgetful of the truth of which he now reminds them.

(17) **If any man defile.**—Better, *If any man destroy*—the opposite of "building up," which should be the work of the Christian teacher; the architectural image being still in view.

**Which temple ye are.**—Literally, *the which are ye*, "which" referring rather to holy than to the temple; the argument being that as they are "holy" by the indwelling of God's Spirit, therefore they are the temple of God. As God commanded the punishment of death to be inflicted on whoever defiled the actual Temple (see Ex. xxviii. 43; Lev. xvi. 2), because it was holy unto the Lord, and His presence dwelt there; so they, having the same Spirit in them, were a temple also holy unto the Lord, and God would not leave him unpunished who destroyed or marred this spiritual temple.

(18) Passing from the difference between the work of one teacher and that of another, which has occupied him since verse 5, the Apostle now returns to the subject from which he branched off there (the magnifying of one teacher above another), and proceeds to show (verses 18—21) that merely human wisdom is in itself worthless for spiritual purposes, and, therefore, that the possession of it alone is no reason for the exaltation of the teacher who is endowed with it. For the full meaning of the "wisdom" which the Apostle speaks of here, see chap. i. 20.

**Let him become a fool**—*i.e.*, in the sight of the world, in order that he may become "wise" in the sight of God.

(19) **With God.**—Better, *in the sight of God* (Rom. ii. 13).

**For it is written.**—By two passages, one from Job, and the other from the Psalms, St. Paul proves the truth of his previous assertion regarding God's estimate of mere "worldly wisdom." It may be noticed that with the exception of the reference in Jas. v. 11 to the "proverbial patience" of Job, of which the writer says "ye have *heard*" (not *read*), this is the only allusion to the book of Job or to Job in the New Testament.

(21) **Therefore.**—Not because of what has been mentioned, but introducing what he is about to mention. Let party-spirit cease. Do not degrade yourselves by calling yourselves after the names of any man, for everything is yours—then teachers only exist for you. The enthusiasm of the Apostle, as he speaks of the privileges of Christians, leads him on beyond the bare assertion necessary to the logical conclusion of the argument, and enlarging the idea he dwells, in a few brief and impressive utterances, on the limitless possessions—in life and in death, in the present life and that which is future—which belong to those who are united with Christ. But they must remember that all this is theirs because they "are Christ's." They are possessors because possessed by Him. "His *service* is their perfect *freedom*" as the Collect in the English Prayer Book puts it, or, more strikingly, as it occurs in the Latin version, "Whom to serve, is to reign."

(23) **And Christ is God's.**—Probably these words were added, not only as being the great climax of the gradual ascent up which the Apostle's thoughts and language have gone in the whole passage, but as avoiding any danger of the party who called themselves by the name of Christ, arrogating anything to themselves from the previous words, "Ye are Christ's," if the passage had concluded with them. Christ is God's as being Mediator (as John xiv. 28, and xvii. 3.) There was no danger, in that early age of the Church, of these words being misunderstood (as some have endeavoured to misunderstand them since) as in the least implying a want of absolute identity between the Son, in regard of His Divine Nature, and the Father.

CHAPTER IV.—(1) Let a man so
account of us, as of the ministers of
Christ, and stewards of the mysteries of
God. (2) Moreover it is required in
stewards, that a man be found faithful.
(3) But with me it is a very small thing
that I should be judged of you, or of
man's judgment:[1] yea, I judge not mine
own self. (4) For I know nothing by
myself; yet am I not hereby justified:
but he that judgeth me is the Lord.
(5) Therefore judge nothing before the
time,[a] until the Lord come, who both
will bring to light the hidden things of
darkness, and will make manifest the
counsels of the hearts: and then shall
every man have praise of God.
(6) And these things, brethren, I have
in a figure transferred to myself and *to*
Apollos for your sakes; that ye might
learn in us not to think *of men* above
that which is written, that no one of

A.D. 59.

a Matt. 7. 1; Rom. 2. 1.

1 Gr. *day*.

---

### IV.

(1–5) The first five verses of this chapter contain a further argument against party-spirit as it existed in the Corinthian Church—viz., that God alone can judge of any man's work whether it be worthy, and that God, unlike man, who selects only some *one* for praise, will give to *every* worker his own proper share of approval.

(1) **Man.**—In a generic sense means "every one" (as in chap. xi. 28, and Gal. vi. 1).

**Us**—*i.e.*, Paul himself and Apollos.

**As of the ministers of Christ.**—Better, *as ministers of Christ.* The word used for "ministers" here expresses more strongly the idea of subordination than the word which occurs in chap. iii. 5. It implies not only those who are under one superior, but those who are in a still inferior position—the officer who has to obey orders, as in Matt. v. 25—a "servant" (Matt. xxvi. 58). Though servants, their office is one of great trust; they are "stewards" to whom the owner of the house has entrusted the care of those sacred things—"mysteries"—which heretofore have been hidden, but are now made known to them, his faithful subordinates. It is to be remembered that even the steward in a Greek household was generally a slave.

(2) **Moreover it is required . . .**—Better, *Moreover here* (on earth) *inquiry is made in the case of stewards in order that it may be found that one is faithful.* The word "found" having the force of "discovered," or "proved *to be*" (as in Matt. i. 18; Rom. vii. 10). The argument here is that, as in the case of an earthly steward, inquiry is made into his character as to whether he be trustworthy—so it will be with them who are stewards of the mysteries of God. That inquiry is, of course, made in regard to an earthly steward by his master in whose service he is; and so the Lord alone, whose stewards the Apostles were, shall be the inquirer into *their* faithfulness. If we take verse 2 as it is in our English version, it would seem to imply that on this point of faithfulness the Church might prefer one steward to another. This would be to suggest that to some extent, therefore, party-spirit might exist, which would be contrary to the whole argument from the commencement of the Epistle, and strikingly at variance with the remarks which immediately follow in verse 5. The rendering adopted above is a more literal translation of the best Greek texts, and also perfectly in harmony with the general sense of the passage.

(3) **But with me it is a very small thing . . .**—As, however, the Corinthians had actually "judged" various of their teachers, the Apostle assures them that *their* judgment—or the judgment of the world generally—is to him "a very small matter"—nay, no earthly judgment is of any concern to him. He does not even judge himself as worthy and faithful because he is not conscious of any unfaithfulness; yet that is no justification to him—his only judge is the Lord.

**Man's judgment.**—The literal translation is *man's day.* Some have thought they saw in it a provincialism or a Hebraism. Probably, however, the explanation is that St. Paul lived with the idea of the day of the Lord as the judgment day so constantly before him, that he uses the words as synonymous. (Comp. also chap. iii. 13, "the day shall declare it.")

(4) **For I know nothing by myself.**—The general meaning of this passage is given in the previous Note. The Greek of the words rendered, "I know nothing of myself," is clearly "I am not conscious in myself" of having been unfaithful; the word being almost invariably used in classical Greek in a bad sense. In the English version the word "by" is used in a sense now nearly obsolete. To an English reader the passage at first sight seems to assert that St. Paul of his own power possessed no knowledge. In old English, however, the word "by" meant (not necessarily the instrument *by* which) frequently "in connection with" or "concerning." In this sense it is found in Deut. xxvii. 16; Ezek. xxii. 7. In Foxe's *Book of Martyrs* a woman under examination is accused of having "spoken evil words *by* the queen." It is still common to speak of our place being "by" (*i.e.*, in close contiguity to) another, and a "*bye*-lane" is a passage connected with a thoroughfare. The word "by" does not seem to have had necessarily the meaning of "against" which some have attributed to it; the sense of "concerning" would suit all the passages given above better than "against."

(5) **Before the time.**—This is explained by the following words to be "the day of the Lord." When this arrives the truth will be ascertainable, for God will bring into light all the things at present hidden in the darkness, and will show forth the inner motives of each heart. Then every man (and not only one party leader, as at Corinth) shall have his due and proper praise from God—not from man.

(6) **These things**—*i.e.*, all that he has written about the factions. He only mentioned himself and Apollos (and not the other heads of parties), so that his motive in rebuking this schismatic spirit may not be misunderstood—which possibly it might have been had he written strongly and directly regarding Cephas and his admirers—and that those who read the Epistle might learn a lesson of humility. All that was said in condemnation of the spirit which exalted the Apostle and Apollos into party leaders, would apply with equal or greater force to all others; for they, as the planter and the waterer of the Corinthian vineyard, the layer of the foundation and the builder up of the Corinthian

you be puffed up for one against another.
(7) For who maketh thee to differ *from another?*[1] and what hast thou that thou didst not receive? now if thou didst receive *it*, why dost thou glory, as if thou hadst not received *it?*
(8) Now ye are full, now ye are rich, ye have reigned as kings without us: and I would to God ye did reign, that we also might reign with you.
(9) For I think that God hath set forth us the apostles last, as it were appointed to death: for we are made a spectacle[2] unto the world, and to angels, and to men.
(10) We *are* fools for Christ's sake, but ye *are* wise in Christ; we *are* weak, but ye *are* strong; ye *are* honourable, but we *are* despised.
(11) Even unto this present hour we both hunger, and thirst, and are naked, and are buffeted, and have no certain dwellingplace;
(12) and labour,[a] working with our own hands: being reviled, we bless; being persecuted, we suffer it:
(13) being defamed,[b] we intreat: we

1 Gr. *distinguisheth thee.*

*a* Acts 20. 34; 1 Thess. 2. 9; 2 Thess. 3. 8.

2 Gr. *theatre.*
*b* Matt. 5. 44.

---

spiritual temple, were certainly the two whose exaltation by their followers might have seemed most pardonable.

**That ye might learn in us . . .**—*i.e.*, "by our examples" you should learn not to go beyond what is written in the Scriptures—not to be found in any one particular passage, but in the general tone and scope of the Old Testament writings, which ever ascribe glory to God alone (as found in the passages referred to in chaps. i. 19, 31, iii. 19)—that none of you be puffed up on behalf of one (*i.e.*, Apollos) against another (*i.e.*, Paul), and *vice versâ*. The Apostle here touches on the fact that this exaltation of teachers was really a gratification of their own pride. It was not that they "puffed up" the teacher, but themselves.

(7) **For . . .**—This is the explanation of why such "puffing up" is absurd. Even if one possess some gift or power, he has not attained it by his own excellence or power; it is the free gift of God.

(8) **Now ye are full.**—These three following sentences are ironical. The emphasis is on the word "now." Ye are already (as distinct from us Apostles) full, rich, kings. You act as if you had already attained the crowning point in the Christian course. "Piety is an insatiable thing," says Chrysostom on this passage, "and it argues a childish mind to imagine from just the beginnings that you have attained the whole; and for men who are not even yet in the prelude of a matter to be highminded, as if they had laid hold of the end."

**Without us.**—The Apostle would have his converts be to him as his crown of rejoicing; but they now assume to have "come into the kingdom" without any connection with him who had won them to God.

**And I would to God.**—Here the irony is dropped, and these words are written with intense feeling and humility. The Apostle, reminded, as it were, by the word "reign," that the time will come when the war and controversies of the Church militant shall end, expresses his deep longing for that blessed change. (See chaps. iii. 22 and ix. 23, where similarly the Apostle shows that in rebuking the folly of the Corinthian Church he does not under-estimate their privileges.)

(9) **For . . .**—This introduces the reason why he may well express the devout wish which he has just uttered for the coming of the kingdom of his Lord. The imagery of this passage would be easily understood by the Corinthians, familiar as they were with the arena. The writer, in a few striking phrases, pictures himself and his apostolic brethren forming the "last and most worthless" band brought forth to struggle and die in the great arena, where the whole world, including men and angels, sit, spectators of the fight. There is, perhaps, a slight contrast intended here between the Corinthians sitting by criticising, and the Apostles engaging actually in the struggle against evil—a contrast which is brought out more strikingly in the brief and emphatic sentence forming verse 10.

(10) **We are fools.**—This verse is charged with irony. Our connection with Christ, as His Apostles and preachers, may make us fools; you are, on the contrary, "wise Christians; we are weak Christians, ye strong; ye are glorified, made leaders of factions and churches, we are despised."

(11) **We both hunger.**—From the strong irony of the last verse, the Apostle here passes, in the pathethic and sad description which occupies verses 11—13, to show how intensely true that last word "despised" was, as expressing his own position, not only in time past, but at the very hour of his writing. Here still there is an implied contrast between their condition ("full," "rich," "kings," of verse 8) and that of St. Paul himself.

**Are naked.**—The better reading is, *we are in need of sufficient clothing* (as 2 Cor. xi. 27).

**Are buffeted**—*i.e.*, are treated like slaves, and not like "kings," as you are.

**Have no certain dwellingplace.**—To be without a fixed home was a peculiar sign of want and degradation. (See Matt. viii. 20; x. 23.)

(12) **And labour.**—While at Ephesus, whence this letter was written, the Apostle supported himself by working with Aquila and Priscilla at tent-making. This labour was no recreation or pastime with St. Paul, it was hard and earnest work. (See 1 Thess. ii. 8, 9; 2 Thess. iii. 8.) That this labour was rendered more excessive from the Apostle's characteristic generosity to others, we may conclude from the expression used in his farewell to the Ephesian elders (Acts xx. 17—38), "Ye yourselves know that these hands have ministered unto my necessities, and to them that were with me."

**Being reviled, we bless.**—A striking contrast to the way in which the Corinthians would act under similar circumstances, and yet a literal obedience to the teaching of the Master (Matt. v. 39, 44). Thus the Apostle became in the eyes of the world, "a fool" for Christ's sake.

(13) **The filth of the world.**—The word here used for "filth" occurs only in one other passage in the LXX. Prov. xxi. 18, where it has the idea of an additional expiatory sacrifice. Perhaps the word is used here by the Apostle to include that idea in the sufferings, the description of which here reaches a climax. It is not only that we are the filth and offscouring of all men, but we are so for the sake of others.

are made as the filth of the world, *and*
*are* the offscouring of all things unto
this day.
(14) I write not these things to shame
you, but as my beloved sons I warn *you.*
(15) For though ye have ten thousand
instructors in Christ, yet *have ye* not
many fathers: for in Christ Jesus I
have begotten you through the gospel.
(16) Wherefore I beseech you, be ye
followers of me. (17) For this cause
have I sent unto you Timotheus, who is
my beloved son, and faithful in the
Lord, who shall bring you into remem-
brance of my ways which be in Christ,
as I teach every where in every church.
(18) Now some are puffed up, as though
I would not come to you. (19) But I
will come to you shortly,[a] if the Lord
will,[b] and will know, not the speech of
them which are puffed up, but the
power. (20) For the kingdom of God *is*
not in word, but in power.
(21) What will ye? shall I come unto
you with a rod, or in love, and *in* the
spirit of meekness?

a Acts 19. 21.
b Jas. 4. 15.

---

(14) **I write not these things to shame you.**—Better, *I write these things not as one making you ashamed, but I am warning you as beloved children.* The mingled irony and reproach of the preceding verses here ceases, and from indignant expostulation the writer now turns to make a tender and touching appeal to their better nature and their sympathy. This abrupt and sudden change in style is characteristic of the writings of St. Paul. Similar passages are nowhere to be found in the writings of the other Apostles. The following verses to the end of this chapter soften the severity of this early part of the Epistle by explaining in what spirit he has written, and the right which he has as their "father in the faith" to so address them.

(15) **For.**—The reason why he has a right to address them as a father would his children. They may have had since their conversion a host of instructors, but they could have only one father who begot them in Jesus Christ. That father was Paul. "I have begotten you." *I*, emphatic as opposed to "many." The word rendered "instructors" originally signified the slave who led the child to school, but subsequently had the larger meaning, which we attach to the word pedagogue. (See Gal. iii. 24, 25.) There is a contrast implied between the harsh severity of a pedagogue and the loving tenderness of a father.

(16) **Wherefore.**—Because I stand in this relation I call you to preserve, as it were, in a moral sense, that family likeness which would naturally accompany such a relationship (Gal. iv. 12; Eph. v. 1; Phil. iii. 17).

(17) **For this cause.**—When St. Paul contemplated a visit to the churches in Macedonia and Achaia he sent Timothy and Erastus in advance (Acts xix. 21, 22). It is to this fact allusion is here made—from xvi. 10, we see that the Apostle did not calculate on Timothy's arrival in Corinth until after this letter had reached them. The rumours of the existence of factions in Corinth had reached St. Paul before Timothy had departed, and were the cause of his desire that before himself visiting Corinth Timothy should do so, and bring the Corinthians to a better frame of mind before the Apostle's arrival. After Timothy's departure from Ephesus the Apostle heard from the household of Chloe how very much worse than he had imagined from the previous rumours was the state of affairs at Corinth. It would not do to let such a condition of things continue to grow and intensify until Timothy should arrive there, delayed as he would be in visiting other places in Macedonia and Achaia *en route*. Nor, indeed, would it be safe to leave one of Timothy's nervous (chap. xvi. 10) and gentle temperament (perhaps the result of his having been brought up and educated entirely by women, 2 Tim. i. 5) to deal with such a state of anarchy as the Apostle now knew to exist in Corinth. Further, the letter from Corinth had arrived since Timothy had left, and it required an immediate answer. Such reason, doubtless, influenced St. Paul in sending this letter to Corinth at once so as to anticipate the arrival of Timothy there. That you might return to the dutiful position of sons, I sent you one who is a son—a beloved and a faithful spiritual child—who will not be an addition to the too numerous instructors already at Corinth, but will, by what he says, and by his own example, remind you of my teaching (see 2 Tim. iii. 10), which he fully understands, and which never varies, being the same to every church. The emphatic use of the word "my son" here in reference to Timothy, taken in connection with the clear expression in verse 15 of what was involved in that spiritual relationship, shows that St. Paul had converted Timothy to the faith (Acts xvi. 1). In the Second Epistle to the Corinthians St. Paul speaks of Timothy as his "brother" (2 Cor. i. 1).

(18) **Now some are puffed up.**—Some of those in Corinth who were puffed up were in the habit of saying that the Apostle would not come and visit the Corinthian Church. The moment they heard the announcement that he was sending Timothy, they would naturally say, That is a proof of the truth of our assertion. He is afraid to come himself, so he sends Timothy in his stead. "But," says St. Paul, "I will come to you shortly, God willing"—his intention was to remain at Ephesus until after Pentecost (see chap. xvi. 8)—"and then I shall take cognisance of spiritual power, and not of empty and boastful words; for that kingdom which Christ founded, and which we, his ambassadors, are establishing, does not consist in mere words, but in spiritual might."

(21) **What will ye?**—I give you a choice. I am coming to you as a father in any case. But shall I come as a father comes with a rod (Isa. xi. 4), and going to inflict punishment with it (such is the force of the Greek, "*in* a rod"); or as a father would come when no faults on the child's part need interfere with the perfect and unrestricted outflowing of his gentleness and love. The pathos of these last few words sufficiently indicate what the Apostle would himself prefer. The choice, however, rested with them. His love would be no love, if without any change on their part, it led him to show no displeasure where correction was for their sake absolutely needed. This is a great and striking example of St. Paul having the "mind of God." He treats the Corinthians as God ever treats His children.

Chap. v. 1—13. The case of marriage with a stepmother.

CHAPTER V. — (1) It is reported
commonly *that there is* for-
nication among you, and
such fornication as is not
so much as named among
the Gentiles, that one should have his
father's wife. (2) And ye are puffed up,
and have not rather mourned, that he
that hath done this deed might be
taken away from among you. (3) For I
verily,[a] as absent in body, but present
in spirit, have judged[1] already, as
though I were present, *concerning* him
that hath so done this deed,
(4) In the name of our Lord Jesus
Christ, when ye are gathered together,
and my spirit, with the power of
our Lord Jesus Christ, (5) to deliver
such an one unto Satan for the de-
struction of the flesh,[b] that the spirit
may be saved in the day of the Lord
Jesus.

A.D. 59.

1 Or, *determined.*

b 1 Tim. 1. 20.

a Col. 2. 5.

---

This verse at once concludes this first part of the Epistle, in which the party-spirit and the evils resulting from it in Corinth are treated of, and naturally introduces the second topic to be discussed, viz., the case of incest which had occurred, it being one of the things which would compel the Apostle to visit Corinth, not "in love and in the spirit of meekness," but "with a rod."

V.

An entirely new subject, to which the concluding words of the last chapter form a natural introduction, is now treated of. Intelligence has reached the Apostle, through the members of Chloe's household (chap. i. 11), or through general report, that a member of the Corinthian Church has caused grave scandal by marrying his stepmother. This was aggravated by the fact that her husband, his father, was yet alive (2 Cor. vii. 12). Throughout the Roman empire such a union was regarded with abhorrence, and the toleration of it by the Christian community was calculated seriously to imperil the character of the early Church. Such a state of morals would be promptly seized upon by opponents, as an example of what must result from the "freedom of the gospel." Seeing what enormous interests were thus at stake, and how the success of Christianity itself would be imperilled by such conduct, the Apostle addresses the Corinthians on this topic with an almost startling severity and vehemence.

(1) **It is reported commonly.**—Better, *There is absolutely said to be fornication among you, and such fornication as is not even among the Gentiles.* All the best MSS. omit the word "named." The force of the statement is that the fornication was of such a kind (with a stepmother) as even the Gentile world, immoral as it was, regarded with disgust, and how infinitely worse, then, was it to find such tolerated amongst Christians, whose moral standard ought to be much higher.

**One should have his father's wife.**—The word "have" here used always implies in the New Testament actual marriage. It is, therefore, probable that she had been divorced from his father. The word for "his father's wife" is the Hebrew form of expression for stepmother. St. Chrysostom suggests "he said not his 'stepmother,' but 'his father's wife,' so as to strike much more severely;" but probably St. Paul used the Hebrew phrase instead of the ordinary Greek word for "stepmother," as it was in this phraseology that such a union was forbidden by the law of Moses (Lev. xviii. 8).

(2) **And ye are puffed up.**—Better, *And are ye puffed up ?* &c. We have instances of similar sentences beginning with "and," Luke x. 29. The Apostle cannot mean that they actually gloried in this act of sin, but that their temper of mind was of that kind which he has already described in the earlier chapters, puffing themselves up, one against another, in party rivalry, instead of being united in one common grief by this common cause, which would lead them as one man to remove from among them the person who had done this deed.

(3) **For I verily.**—The Apostle had fully made up his mind that this offender must be removed, and insists on the Corinthians doing it. So that the previous words imply they might as well have done it without waiting for his interference.

**As absent in body.**—Better, omit "as," which is not in the best MSS.

(4, 5) **In the name of our Lord Jesus Christ . . . . and my spirit.**—These two verses contain the apostolic sentence on the offender, and may read thus: "I have already myself decided, in the name of our Lord Jesus, you being gathered together, and my spirit (as in chap. v. 3), in the power of our Lord Jesus, to deliver such a one," &c.

The opening words are probably the form used in all public acts of the Church as a body, and "the power of our Lord Jesus" refers to that continual presence which Christ had promised His Church, and particular power which He had delegated to the Apostles to punish (Matt. xvi. 19; xviii. 18, 20; xxviii. 20). In this sentence we recognise, not merely a formal excommunication from church-fellowship, but a more severe punishment, which could only be inflicted by apostolic authority and power. Satan was regarded as the origin of all physical evil—hence the afflicted woman, in Luke xiii. 16, is spoken of as one "whom Satan hath bound these eighteen years." St. Paul's own bodily suffering is a "messenger of Satan" (2 Cor. xii. 7). The blindness of Elymas (Acts xiii. 8), and the death of Ananias and Sapphira (Acts v. 5), are instances of the infliction of bodily-suffering by the Apostles. The deliverance of an offender unto Satan would therefore mean the expulsion of such a one from the Christian communion, and if that failed the actual infliction of some bodily suffering such as would destroy the flesh (not the body, but the flesh, the source and origin of the evil). Explicit directions for the excommunication by the Church of an offender, are given in chap. vii., but there is no direct instruction to inflict the further punishment spoken of here. It is, indeed, probable that the lesser punishment had the desired effect (see Note on 2 Cor. ii. 6), and we subsequently find St. Paul pleading for the loving re-admission of the offender into all the privileges of Christian communion.

(5) **That the spirit may be saved.**—The object of this punishment was the destruction of the flesh, and the salvation of the man.

(6) Your glorying *is* not good. Know
ye not that a little leaven leaveneth the
whole lump?[a] (7) Purge out therefore
the old leaven, that ye may be a new
lump, as ye are unleavened. For even
Christ our passover is sacrificed[1] for us:
(8) therefore let us keep the feast,[2] not
with old leaven, neither with the leaven
of malice and wickedness; but with the
unleavened *bread* of sincerity and truth.
(9) I wrote unto you in an epistle not
to company with fornicators: (10) yet
not altogether with the fornicators of
this world, or with the covetous, or extortioners,
or with idolaters; for then
must ye needs go out of the world.
(11) But now I have written unto you
not to keep company, if any man that
is called a brother be a fornicator, or
covetous, or an idolater, or a railer, or a
drunkard, or an extortioner; with such
an one no not to eat. (12) For what have
I to do to judge them also that are
without? do not ye judge them that are

a Gal. 5. 9.

1 Or, *is slain.*

2 Or, *holyday.*

---

(6) **Your glorying is not good.**—There is possibly a reference here to some boasting regarding their spiritual state contained in the letter which had reached St. Paul from Corinth, and to which part of this Epistle is a reply. (See chap. vii. 1.) So long as there is that one bad person amongst you it gives a bad character to the whole community, as leaven, though it may not have pervaded the entire lump, still makes it not the unleavened bread which was necessary for the Paschal Feast. This Epistle being written shortly before Pentecost (chap. xvi. 8), it was very likely some time about or soon after Easter, hence the leaven and the Paschal Feast naturally suggest themselves as illustrations. The Apostle passes on rapidly from the mention of the leaven to the whole scene of the feast. As with the most minute and scrupulous care the Jew would remove every atom of leaven when the Paschal lamb was to be eaten, so our Paschal Lamb having been slain, we must take care that no moral leaven remains in the sacred household of the Church while she keeps her perpetual feast of prayer and thanksgiving.

(7) **Purge out therefore the old leaven.**—It is not the offending man who is here spoken of, but it is the spirit in the Church which tolerated the evil, and which is to be purged out of their midst that they may become actually (a new lump) as they are by profession (unleavened).

**Christ our passover is sacrificed for us.**—Better, *Christ our passover is slain;* "for us" is not in the best MSS. The word translated "sacrifice" is generally used in the New Testament in the sense simply of "slaying" or "killing" (Matt. xxii. 4; John x. 10; Acts x. 1, 13; xi. 7); and in the similar expressions regarding our Lord (Rev. v. 6, 12) the word is "wounded."

(8) **Old leaven**—*i.e.*, in their old state generally; and then the Apostle proceeds to particularise. Sincerity and truth are to take the place of malice and wickedness in the continuous life of the Christian. St. Chrysostom well remarks: "He said 'Let us keep the feast' as pointing out that the whole of time is a festival unto Christians, because of the excellence of the good things which have been given."

(9) **I wrote unto you in an epistle.**—These words have given rise to some controversy as to whether the Apostle here refers to some former Epistle addressed to the Corinthian Church, and which has not been preserved, or whether the reference is not to this Epistle itself. It has been suggested by some who adopt the latter view that these words may have been added as an interpolation after the completion of the Epistle, and be intended to intensify the remarks made by the Apostle on this subject in chaps. v. 6—8, and vi. 9—20. Such an interpretation, however, seems rather strained. It is more natural to suppose that the reference is to an Epistle written to the Corinthians, probably from Ephesus, after a visit paid to Corinth of which we have no record, for in 2 Cor. xii. 14, and xiii. 1, we read of a third visit being contemplated, whereas only one previous one is recorded. (See also *Introduction.*) The condition of the Church which caused the Apostle that "heaviness," which he connects with this visit in 2 Cor. ii. 1, would naturally have given rise to an Epistle containing the kind of direction here referred to.

(10) **Yet not altogether with the fornicators of this world.**—This is a limitation and explanation of the command given not to associate with fornicators. It would have been almost impossible for the command to be literally obeyed without the Christian withdrawing altogether from the business of life, so the Apostle explains that it is the fair fame and purity of the Church which he is anxious to preserve. There are so many fornicators, and covetous, and idolaters in this world (*i.e.*, the heathen world) that men *must* meet with them. But the Christian must tolerate no such sins among themselves; they must exclude from the social circle any brother who, bearing the name of Christ, indulges in the vices of the heathen world. The Church is to be the light of the world, and not the recipient of the world's darkness.

(11) **But now I have written unto you . .**—*i.e.*, "But what I meant was" that you were not to associate with a Christian guilty of these things. It may seem strange that the word "idolater" should be included in this category; for in what sense could a "brother" be a worshipper of idols? It is probable that the word "idolater" has involved in it the idea, not merely of worshipping an image, but of the sensuality which accompanied various forms of heathen worship, and of which evidently some of the Corinthian brethren were partakers. (See Eph. v. 5, and Col. iii. 5, where "idolatry" is identified with a vice kindred to lasciviousness.)

(12) **For what have I to do . . ?**—The Apostle in this verse at once explains the grounds of the limitation of his remarks to Christians, and seems to hint also, by the form of expression here, that the Corinthian Church ought to have been able to have understood his remarks as only applicable to themselves and not to the heathen.

**Them also that are without.**—The heathen. It was a common form of expression amongst the Jews to designate the Gentile world (Mark iv. 11).

**Do not ye judge them that are within?**—As the Christian Church could sit in judgment only on its own members, so they should have concluded that only on them had St. Paul passed judgment.

within? (13) But them that are without God judgeth. Therefore put away from among yourselves that wicked person.

CHAPTER VI.—(1) Dare any of you, having a matter against another, go to law before the unjust, and not before the saints? (2) Do ye not know that the saints shall judge the world? and if the world shall be judged by you, are ye unworthy to judge the smallest matters? (3) Know ye not that we shall judge angels? how much more things that pertain to this life? (4) If then ye have judgments of things pertaining to this life, set them to judge who are least esteemed in the church.

Chap. vi. 1—11. The settlement of disputes amongst Christians.

A.D. 59.

(13) **God judgeth.**—In the best MSS. the verb is in the future tense: *God will judge.* He is the judge of the whole earth; we are to leave the heathen world in His hands.

**Therefore put away . . .**—Better omit "therefore." The Apostle in this passage adopts the form of pronouncing sentence on great criminals, with which especially the Jewish converts would be familiar (Deut. xiii. 5; xvii. 7; xxiv. 7).

VI.

(1) **Dare any of you.**—Having rebuked the Corinthian Christians for any attempt to judge those who are outside the Church—*i.e.,* the heathen—St. Paul now insists, on the other hand, on the importance of their not submitting their affairs for decision to the heathen tribunals. Jewish converts would have more easily understood that they should settle disputes among themselves, as the Roman power had, as we learn from Gallio's remarks (Acts xviii. 14, 15), given this liberty to the Jews. The Gentile converts, however, would have been naturally inclined to continue to bring disputes before the tribunals with which they had been so familiar in a proverbially litigious condition of society before their conversion. We can well imagine how detrimental to the best interests of Christianity it would be for the Christian communion, founded as it was on principles of unity and love, to be perpetually, through the hasty temper and weakness of individual members, held up to the scorn of the heathen, as a scene of intestine strife. Repeated lawsuits before heathen judges would have had the further evil effect of practically obliterating the broad line of demarcation which then really existed between the principles of Roman jurisprudence, and the loftier Christian conceptions of self-sacrifice and charity by which the followers of Jesus Christ should, in accordance with His teaching, control their life. These considerations rendered necessary the warnings which the Apostle here commences with the emphatic word "Dare," of which it has been well said (Bengel), "Treason against Christians is denoted by this high-sounding word."

**Unjust . . . . saints.**—These words convey here no essentially moral ideas. They merely signify respectively "heathen" and "members of the Christian Church." These phrases remind us that the state of things when St. Paul wrote this was entirely different from what exists in any Christian country now. The teaching has nothing whatever to do with the adjudication of the courts of a Christian country. The cases to which St. Paul's injunctions would be applicable in the present day would be possible only in a heathen country. If, for example, in India there existed heathen tribunals, it would certainly be wrong, and a source of grave scandal, for native Christians to submit questions between themselves for decision to such courts, instead of bringing them before the legal tribunals established by Christian England. It is not probable that at so early a period there were any regular and recognised tribunals amongst the Christians, and certainly their decisions could scarcely have had any legal force. There is, however, historical evidence of the existence of such in the middle of the second century. The principles here laid down would naturally have led to their establishment. (See chap. v. 4.)

(2) **Do ye not know . . ?**—The knowledge which they possessed of the great future which was in store for the Church of Christ was the strongest argument against the humiliating degradation to which their conduct was subjecting it.

**The saints shall judge the world.**—The Apostle here claims for all Christians the glorious prerogative which Christ had Himself promised to His immediate personal followers (Matt. xix. 28; Luke xxii. 30). Bearing in mind the deep conviction of the early Church that the second personal advent of Christ was near at hand, we may take these words as referring primarily to the conquest of the world by Christianity, which has since been accomplished, though by slower and more spiritual processes than were then anticipated, and indirectly to that final triumph of Christ and His body, the Church, of which every success here on earth is at once the type and the pledge.

**To judge the smallest matters.**—Better, *to pronounce the most trivial judgments,* as compared with the great judgments which you shall pronounce hereafter. The nature of the things which form the subject of those judgments is explained in the following verse.

(3) **We shall judge angels.**—Many conjectures have been made as to the exact significance of the word "angels" here. Some suggest that it must signify bad angels; but this would be an unusual use of the word without any qualifying adjective. It is better, perhaps, to regard the passage as a climax arising out of the Apostle's intense realisation of the unity of Christ and His Church triumphant—a point which seems ever present to the mind of St. Paul when he speaks of the dignity of Christianity. In this sense, redeemed humanity will be superior to, and judges of, the spiritual world. That the words have some such large significance, and are not the expression of a hard and literal fact regarding some members of the angelic host, is, I think, borne out by the subsequent words, where the contrast to "angels" is not "men," but "things" relating to this life.

(4) **If then ye have judgments . . . .**—Better, *If, however, you choose to have judgments to be given on matters of this life.* The last words show that the questions which are alluded to are purely worldly and not spiritual matters. The Apostle subsequently urges that such disputes ought not to arise at all amongst Christians, and that if they do they ought to be settled by the interposition of some mutual friend. Here he says, with something of sarcasm, "The very meanest of those who are to be exalted above angels, and to be

(5) I speak to your shame. Is it so,
that there is not a wise man among
you? no, not one that shall be able to
judge between his brethren? (6) But
brother goeth to law with brother, and
that before the unbelievers. (7) Now
therefore there is utterly a fault among
you, because ye go to law one with
another. Why do ye not rather take
wrong? why do ye not rather *suffer
yourselves to* be defrauded? (8) Nay, ye
do wrong, and defraud, and that *your*
brethren. (9) Know ye not that the
unrighteous shall not inherit the kingdom of God? Be not deceived: neither
fornicators, nor idolaters, nor adulterers,
nor effeminate, nor abusers of themselves with mankind, (10) nor thieves,
nor covetous, nor drunkards, nor revilers, nor extortioners, shall inherit
the kingdom of God. (11) And such
were some of you: but ye are washed,
but ye are sanctified, but ye are justified
in the name of the Lord Jesus, and by
the Spirit of our God.

(12) All things are lawful unto me,

---

judges of spiritual existences, is of sufficient authority to settle such matters as you are bringing before legal tribunals."

(5) **I speak to your shame.**—Better, *I say this to cause you to feel ashamed.* From the latent irony of the previous words, the Apostle turns to ask solemnly whether it be a fact that in the whole Christian community at Corinth, which boasted of their superior wisdom, there is not to be found even one man sufficiently esteemed for his wisdom to be trusted by the brethren with the settlement of their disputes.

**Shall be able to judge . . . .**—Better, *shall be able to arbitrate,* in contrast to the "going to law" of the next verse, the words for these two expressions being different in the original.

(6) **But brother goeth to law with brother.**—"It would almost seem as if it were not so. Your dragging these disputes before tribunals of the heathen would imply that it is not possible to find a Christian friend whom you can trust to settle these trivial disputes." Thus the Apostle answers his question of the previous verse.

(7) **A fault.**—Better, *a falling short* of your privilege and dignity as Christians. It is the same word as is rendered "diminishing" in Rom. xi. 12. The Apostle in this verse goes one step farther, and condemns the Corinthians, not only on the ground of the tribunals to which they resorted being heathen, but further condemns the spirit of litigation itself. He reminds them of how such a temper of mind is the very opposite of that which the Lord Himself had commended to His followers (Matt. v. 40).

(8) **Nay, ye do wrong.**—Better, *No, but you yourselves do wrong.*

(9) **Know ye not that the unrighteous . . ?**—The force of this question comes out more strikingly in the original, where the word rendered "unrighteous" is the same as "ye do wrong" of verse 8. "You do wrong, apparently forgetting that no wrongdoers shall inherit God's kingdom."

**Be not deceived.**—There was great danger of their being led to think lightly of sins which were daily committed by those amongst whom they lived, hence these words of warning with which the sentence opens, as in chap. xv. 33. The mention of gross sensual sins in connection with idolaters points to the fact that they were practically associated in the ritual of the heathen, which, of course, intensified the danger against which the Apostle warns the Corinthians. The prevalence of such scandalous crimes in the heathen world is constantly referred to in the Epistles to Gentile churches (Rom. xiii. 13; Gal. v. 19, 20; 1 Tim. i. 9, 10; Titus i. 12).

(11) **Such were some of you.**—The Greek for "such" is in the neuter, and implies "of such a description were some of you."

**Ye are washed.**—Better, *ye washed them off.* referring to the fact that their baptism was a voluntary act (Acts xxii. 16). The words "sanctified" and "justified" as used here do not point to those definite stages in the Christian course to which they generally refer in theological language. The sanctification is here mentioned before the justification, which is not the actual sequence, and it must not therefore be taken as signifying a gradual progress in holiness. What the Apostle urges is, that as they washed themselves in the waters of baptism, so they, by the power of Christ's name and the Holy Spirit, became holy and righteous, thus putting aside, washing off as it were, that impurity and that unrighteousness which once were theirs, and with which they could not enter into the kingdom.

(12) **All things are lawful unto me.**—This was probably a statement which the Apostle had himself made; at all events, the freedom which it expresses was very dear to him, and it may have been misused by some as an argument for universal license. St. Paul, therefore, boldly repeats it, and proceeds to show that it is a maxim of Christian liberty, which does not refer to matters which are absolutely wrong, and that even in its application to indifferent matters it must be limited, and guarded by other Christian principles. "The eating of things sacrificed to idols (see Note on chap. viii. 4), and the committing fornication," were two subjects of discussion closely connected with heathen worship; and it may seem astonishing to us now that because St. Paul had maintained the right of individual liberty concerning the former, he should perhaps have been quoted as an authority for liberty regarding the latter, yet it is a matter of fact that such a mode of reasoning was not uncommon. They were both regarded as part and parcel of heathen worship, and therefore, as it were, to stand or fall together, as being matters vital or indifferent. (See Acts xv. 29, and Rev. xi. 14, as illustrations of the union of the two for purposes respectively of condemnation and of improper toleration.) We must not regard the use of the singular "me" as being in any sense a limitation of the principle to the Apostle personally. "Paul often speaks in the first person singular, which has the force of a moral maxim, especially in this Epistle (verse 15; vii. 7; viii. 13; x. 23, 29, 30; xiv. 11)" (Bengel). The words refer to all Christians.

**All things are not expedient.**—Better, *all things are not profitable.* The word "expedient" in its highest sense is a proper translation of the Greek

Chap. vi. 12—20. The application of the doctrine of Christian freedom to sensual indulgence condemned.

but all things are not expedient:[1] all
things are lawful for me,
but I will not be brought
under the power of any.
(13) Meats for the belly, and
the belly for meats: but
God shall destroy both it
and them. Now the body
*is* not for fornication, but for the
Lord; and the Lord for the body.
(14) And God hath both raised up the
Lord, and will also raise up us by his
own power. (15) Know ye not that your
bodies are the members of Christ? shall
I then take the members of Christ, and
make *them* the members of an harlot?
God forbid. (16) What? know ye not
that he which is joined to an harlot is
one body? for two, saith he, shall be
one flesh. (17) But he that is joined
unto the Lord is one spirit. (18) Flee
fornication. Every sin that a man
doeth is without the body; but he that
committeth fornication sinneth against

[1] Or, *profitable.*

---

but in modern use it has a somewhat lower and depreciatory meaning generally attached to it.

**All things are lawful for me, but I will not be brought under the power of any.**—There is a verbal contrast in the Greek here which can scarcely be rendered fully in English. The Greek words for "unlawful" and "be brought under the power of" are cognate words. What the Apostle says is, "All things are lawful for me, but I am not the one to allow them therefore to become a law over me." There is such a thing as becoming the very slave of liberty itself. If we sacrifice the power of choice which is implied in the thought of liberty, we cease to be free; we are brought *under* the power of that which should be *in* our power.

(13) **Meats for the belly.**—The Apostle proceeds now to show that the question of eating meats offered to idols does come into that catalogue of indifferent things on which an exercise of Christian freedom is permissible, and that the question of fornication does not. Lawful matters are to be decided upon the highest principle of expediency; but fornication is an unlawful matter, and therefore the question of its expediency does not arise at all. The stomach is adapted to the digestion of food, and food is adapted to it. This is, however, only for this life; both shall be destroyed by death. But the person ("body" being equivalent to "us" in verse 14) of the man is enduring. No food which enters defiles *the man.* Fornication is not a mere transitory gratification; it affects *the man.* The use of the stomach is to receive and digest food, and only the animal organisation is affected by that. It cannot be said that the man is made for fornication. The person of each is made for the Lord; the whole Church is His body; each baptised person is a limb of that body; and the Lord is for the body. He came to earth and died for it, and for each member of it; therefore what affects that body, or any member of that body (*i.e.*, any Christian), cannot be an indifferent matter. Neither shall the man perish, as meats and the belly shall; he is immortal. (See chap. xv. 51, 52.) Such seems to be the argument by which St. Paul maintains liberty to be right regarding meats, and shows that the same principle does not apply to sensual indulgence. It may be put argumentatively thus:

1. Eating meats offered to idols is an "indifferent matter," because—

(*a*) Meats only affect the particular organ designed for them;

(*b*) Meats and that organ shall perish together.

2. Fornication is not an "indifferent matter," because—

(*a*) It affects the man, and he is not designed for the purpose of this indulgence.

(*b*) The man is immortal, and therefore the moral effect of the fornication on his nature does not perish at his death.

*Conclusion.*—Only indifferent matters are to be the subject of Christian liberty; and the decision must be according to the utility of each act. Fornication is not an indifferent matter; therefore it is not so to be decided upon.

(14) **Will also raise up us.**—This phrase is remarkable as one of the few which show that the Apostle, while he in common with the early Church expected the early advent of Christ, did not think that it would necessarily occur in his own lifetime. Here, as ever, the resurrection of the dead, when we shall receive our spiritual body instead of the natural body, is joined with the fact of the resurrection of Christ the firstfruits.

(15) **Shall I then . . . ?**—Having shown the great dignity which attaches to our bodies as immortal members of Christ, the Apostle asks with indignant emphasis, "Shall I take them out from that high and holy membership, and make them members of an harlot?" The double act of taking them away from their glorious union with Christ, and joining them to a base body, is implied in the Greek.

(16) **What?**—As if some one might question and resent the strength of the previous words, and wish them "watered down." "Do you not know that my strong assertion is true? It is not merely my statement; it is to be found in the Old Testament, 'Two shall be one flesh.'" This was originally (Gen. ii. 24) applied to marriage, as showing the intimacy of that sacred union, but here St. Paul applies it to one aspect of a union which, in one respect, was identical with marriage. Of course the other parts of the Apostle's argument do not apply to marriage, the union being a sacred one; two becoming one flesh in marriage is no degradation of a member of Christ—nay, it is a sacred illustration of the complete unity of Christ and His body the Church. (Comp. chap. xi. 29, and Notes there.)

(17) **One spirit.**—The union betwixt Christ and each member of His Church is a spiritual one. This explains the sense in which we are the Lord's body, and intensifies the argument against any degradation of one who shares so holy and intimate a union.

(18) **Flee fornication.**—These last three verses of the chapter contain a solemn exhortation to purity, arising out of the previous argument.

**Without the body.**—The word "body" is still to be understood as used of the whole "human nature," which is spoken of in verse 19 as the temple of the Holy Ghost. Other sins may profane only outer courts

his own body. (19) What? know ye not that your body is the temple of the Holy Ghost *which is* in you,

Which ye have of God, and ye are not your own? (20) For ye are bought with a price: therefore glorify God in your body, and in your spirit, which are God's.

A.D. 59.

CHAPTER VII.—(1) Now concerning the things whereof ye wrote unto me: *It is* good

Chap. vii. 1–18. Marriage.

of the temple; this sin penetrates with its deadly foulness into the very holy of holies—

"It hardens a' within, and petrifies the feelings."

There is a deep significance and profound truth in the solemn words of the Litany, "From fornication, and all other *deadly* sin, good Lord, deliver us."

(19, 20) **What? know ye not . . . ?**—These verses read better rendered thus: *Do you not know that your body is the temple of the Holy Ghost which is in you? Which you have from God, and you are not your own. For you were bought with a price. Glorify God then in your body.*

There are two reasons why we are not our own. (1) The Spirit which has possession of our bodies is not our own, but given us "of God." (2) We have been bought with a price, even the blood of Christ; it is a completed purchase (1 Pet. i. 18, 19). Our bodies not being our own to do as we like with, we have no right to give them over unto sin. The last words of the verse are not a cold logical deduction from the previous argument, but rather an earnest exhortation suggested by the solemn thought of our oneness with Christ, and the price paid by Him to make us His.

The words "and in your spirits," which are in the Authorised version, are not in the older Greek MSS. They were probably added to give a kind of verbal completeness to the exhortation. They only tend, however, to weaken the force of the passage as St. Paul wrote it. The dignity of the body is the subject of the previous passage, and the necessity for its purity the sole theme of the entire argument.

## VII.

**Concerning the things whereof ye wrote unto me.**—Some members of the Church having written to St. Paul to ask his counsel on matters concerning which there existed a difference of opinion at Corinth, the Apostle now proceeds to answer these inquiries, and his reply occupies the remainder of the Epistle (to chap. xvi. 4). The subjects concerning which the Corinthians sought for St. Paul's opinion are treated of in the following order:

I. MARRIAGE, chap. vii.

II. THE EATING OF MEAT OFFERED TO IDOLS, chaps. viii.—xi. 1.

III. THE ATTIRE OF WOMEN IN PUBLIC WORSHIP, chap. xi. 2—16.

IV. THE LORD'S SUPPER, chap. xi. 17—34.

V. SPIRITUAL GIFTS, chaps. xii. 1—xiv. 40.

VI. THE DOCTRINE OF THE RESURRECTION, chap. xv. 1—58.

VII. THE COLLECTION FOR THE POOR IN JUDÆA, chap. xvi. 1—4.

In the consideration of each of these subjects various collateral matters are introduced, and the great principles which guided the Apostle, and which ever should guide the Church and individuals, are set forth. Many of the subjects were of purely local and temporary interest. The particular combination of circumstances which for the moment rendered them important has ceased to exist, and can never arise again; but the principles on which the Apostle based his arguments, and which he enunciates as the ground of his decisions, are eternal. To apply the injunctions of the Apostle in these chapters with a rigid and unyielding literalism to the Church in all ages, is to violate those very principles which guided St. Paul in enunciating them, and to exalt the dead and death-bearing letter at the sacrifice of the living and life-giving spirit of the apostolic teaching. As we proceed with our examination of St. Paul's reply to the Corinthians' letter we shall have little real difficulty in distinguishing between those practical injunctions which were of local and temporary application, and the wider and larger truths which are of universal and lasting obligation; for the Apostle himself is always careful to point out when a command is based upon some particular necessity of the day, and when it arises from some unchanging Christian principle.

The first subject concerning which the Corinthians sought advice was MARRIAGE. From the opening words of St. Paul's reply, "It is good for a man not to marry" (such is the force of the word rendered "touch," Gen. xx. 6; Prov. vi. 29), it would seem that those who wrote for the Apostle's advice were inclined to regard celibacy as preferable to the married state: so much so, indeed, that they had scruples as to whether even those who had been married should not separate (verses 3—5). We may, therefore, conclude that it was probably from the Pauline party that the inquiry came. It would be improbable that those who exalted some other teacher would have written to St. Paul to ask his guidance upon matters of controversy; and the tone of the Apostle's replies on such questions as marriage, and the meats offered to idols (from which we can conjecture the line taken in the letter addressed to him), leads to the same conclusion. It would be natural for the Pauline party unduly to exaggerate the importance of celibacy and to undervalue matrimony. St. Paul's own example, and his strong preference for the unmarried state, would have easily come to be regarded by his followers as matters of moral import, and not of merely temporary advantage and personal predilection. It is likely, also, as we know from other religious controversies, that the opposition of the Petrine party would drive the Pauline party into more extreme views. They would quote the example of their leader as a married man in opposition to the conduct of St. Paul (chap. ix. 5, and Matt. viii. 14).

**Good for a man.**—We must not, on the one hand, force this statement into meaning that it is merely expedient, nor must we, on the other, attach to it so great a moral import as to imply that the opposite is morally wrong (as St. Jerome, "*ergo est malum tangere*"). The English word "good," in its most general sense, accurately conveys the meaning. It is laid down as a proposition that it is in St. Paul's opinion a good thing to remain unmarried. But that general proposition is immediately limited in its application by what follows. St. Chrysostom paraphrases this and the following verse thus: "For if thou inquire what is

for a man not to touch a woman.
(2) Nevertheless, *to avoid* fornication,
let every man have his own wife, and
let every woman have her own hus-
band. (3) Let the husband render
unto the wife due benevolence; and
likewise also the wife unto the hus-
band. (4) The wife hath not power of
her own body, but the husband: and
likewise also the husband hath not
power of his own body, but the wife.
(5) Defraud ye not one the other, except
*it be* with consent for a time, that ye
may give yourselves to fasting and
prayer; and come together again, that
Satan tempt you not for your incon-
tinency. (6) But I speak this by per-
mission, *and* not of commandment.
(7) For I would that all men were even
as I myself. But every man hath his
proper gift of God, one after this manner,
and another after that. (8) I say there-
fore to the unmarried and widows, It is
good for them if they abide even as I.

---

the excellent and greatly superior course, it is better not to have any connection whatever with a woman; but if, what is safe and helpful to thine own infirmity, be connected by marriage."

(2) **To avoid fornication.**—Better, *because of the (prevalent) fornication.* This was so general in Corinth, and so little regarded as sin, that the unmarried were liable to be led into it.

It may at first sight appear as if the Apostle thus put marriage upon very low and merely utilitarian ground: but we must remember that he is here writing with a definite and limited aim, and does not enter into a general discussion of the subject. St. Paul gives a reason why those who wrote to him should marry, and the force of the argument does not extend beyond the immediate object in view. St. Paul's view of the higher aspects of matrimony are fully set forth when he treats of that subject generally (2 Cor. xi. 2; Rom. vii. 4; Eph. v. 25—32).

(3) **Let the husband render unto the wife due benevolence.**—Rather, *Let the husband render unto the wife her due*—such being the reading of the better MSS. In this verse the Apostle answers the scruples of those who already were married and who doubted whether they should continue so.

(4) **Of her own body.**—Bengel notices that these words, "She has not power of her own body," form an elegant paradox, bringing out the equal rights of both.

(5) **Except it be . . . that ye may give yourselves**—*i.e., that ye may have leisure.* Any such separation should be temporary, and with consent of both parties. Even then it must not be from mere caprice, but for some religious purpose, such as a special season of prayer. (See Ex. xix. 15; 1 Sam. xxi. 4.) The alteration in the Greek text of the word "give" into the present tense, so as to make the word "prayer" refer to daily devotions, and not to special and exceptional seasons, and the interpolation of the word "fasting"—not found in the older MSS.—are a striking example of how the ascetic tendencies of a particular ecclesiastical school of thought led to their "amending" the sacred text so as to make it be in harmony with their own views, instead of reverently regarding it as that by which those very views should be corrected.

**And come together again.**—Better (as in the best MSS.), *and be together again.* This is still an explanation of the purpose of the separation, not to be a lasting one, but that we may again return to the state of union. The text here bears further traces of having been altered so as to make it seem that the Apostle meant that the return to matrimonial life should be only to a temporary union, and not to a continuous state of life. The proper reading implies the latter, the word "be" being used as in Acts ii. 44.

**For your incontinency.**—Better, *because of your incontinency;* the reference being, as in verse 2, to the moral condition surrounding them, and to the influence to which a man thus separated would be subject. The Corinthian Christians are here solemnly reminded that this sin, as all sin, is from Satan—because the Corinthians at large did not regard it as sin at all, but even mingled sensuality with worship.

(6) **But I speak this by permission.**—Better, *Now I say this as a permission, and not as a command.* As the passage is given in our English version, it might seem as if the Apostle implied that he had no actual command, but only a permission to write this, which is not at all his meaning. What he does say is, that the foregoing instructions are not to be considered as absolute commands from him, but as general permissive instruction, to be applied by each individual according to circumstances.

It has been much discussed as to what part of the previous passage the word "this" refers. It is perhaps best to take it as referring to the leading thought of the whole passage, which is that marriage is allowable, expressed especially in verse 2.

(7) **For I would that all men were even as I myself.**—Better, *I wish rather that all men were as I myself.* These words do not mean that the Apostle wished that every one was unmarried, but that every one had the same grace of continence which he himself was endowed with, so that they might without risk of sin remain unmarried (see verse 26). Yet, he adds, there are many gifts, and God has given to each man his own gift, so that, though you may not have the particular gift of continence which I have, you have some other. One has one kind of gift; another has another kind.

(8) **I say therefore.**—Better, *Now what I say is,* . . . Widows are here joined with those who have not been married, otherwise discussion might have arisen as to whether the Apostle had intended his advice for them also. It has been curiously conjectured (by Luther amongst others), from the passage where St. Paul recommends widows to "abide even as I," that the Apostle was himself a widower. This, however, requires the word "unmarried" to be restricted to widowers, which is quite inadmissible; and even if such were admissible, the deduction from it that St. Paul was a widower could scarcely be considered logical. The almost universal tradition of the early Church was that St. Paul was never married, and unless we can imagine his having been married, and his wife dead before the stoning of St. Stephen which is scarcely possible (Acts vii. 58), the truth of that tradition is evident. (See Phil. iv. 3.) "Even as I;" that is, unmarried.

(9) But if they cannot contain, let them
marry: for it is better to marry than to
burn.
(10) And unto the married I command,
*yet* not I, but the Lord, Let not the
wife depart from *her* husband: (11) but
and if she depart, let her remain un-
married, or be reconciled to *her* hus-
band: and let not the husband put
away *his* wife.
(12) But to the rest speak I, not the
Lord: If any brother hath a wife that
believeth not, and she be pleased to
dwell with him, let him not put her
away. (13) And the woman which hath
an husband that believeth not, and if

---

(9) **It is better . . .**—Because to be influenced with unlawful desire is a sin, and to marry is no sin.

(10) **And unto the married . . .**—The Apostle has concluded his instruction to the unmarried and widows, and in verses 10 and 11 gives his advice to those married persons who had been troubled with doubts as to whether they ought (if marriage were undesirable) to continue in that state.

**I command, yet not I, but the Lord.**—The contrast which is commenced here, and again brought out in verse 12, is not between commands given by St. Paul as an inspired Apostle, and St. Paul as a private individual. In chap. xiv. 37 the Apostle expressly claims that all his commands as an Apostle should be regarded as "the commandments of the Lord," and in 1 Thess. iv. 15 the Apostle speaks of that knowledge into which he was guided by the Holy Spirit as given "by the word of the Lord." St. Paul must not therefore be regarded as here claiming for some of his instructions apostolic authority, and not claiming it for others. The real point of the contrast is between a subject on which our Lord Himself while on earth gave direct verbal instruction, and another subject on which He now gives His commands through His Apostle St. Paul. Christ had given directions regarding divorce (Matt. v. 31; xix. 3—9; Mark x. 2—12), and the Apostle here has only to reiterate what the Lord had already commanded.

**Let not the wife depart from her husband.**—Better, *Let her not be separated.* The account of our Lord's words given here differs in two respects from the record given of them by St. Matthew (v. 32 and xix. 9), where the reference is, first and more prominently, to the man putting away his wife—not, as here, to the wife separating herself from her husband—and the exception made, "except it be because of fornication," is here omitted. The fact that St. Paul only knew from others what our Lord had said, and that the Evangelists wrote what they had heard themselves, would not sufficiently account for this difference; for surely these very Evangelists, or others who like them had heard the Lord's words, would have been St. Paul's informants. The reason of the variety in the two accounts is to be found, not in inaccurate knowledge on St. Paul's part, which we have no reason to suppose, but in the particular circumstances to which the Apostle was applying the teaching of Christ; and this verbal difference is an instructive indication to us of how the Apostles understood that even in the case of the Lord Himself it was the living spirit of His teaching, and not its merely verbal form, which was of abiding and universal obligation. There was no necessity here to introduce the one exceptional cause of divorce which Christ had allowed, for the subject under consideration is a separation voluntarily made, and not as the result of sin on the part of either husband or wife; so the mention here of that ground of exception would have been inapplicable, and have tended only to confuse.

The other point of difference—viz., the mention here of the woman more prominently as separating from the husband—does not in any way affect the principle of the teaching, and indeed our Lord probably did put the case in both ways. (See Mark x. 12.) It may be also that in the letter to which St. Paul was replying the doubt had been suggested by women, who were—as their sex is often still—more anxiously scrupulous about details of what they conceived to be religious duty; and the question having been asked concerning a woman's duty, the Apostle answers it accordingly, and adds the same instruction for the husband (verse 11).

(11) **But and if she depart.**—Better, *but if she have actually separated.* These words, from "but" to "husband," are a parenthesis, and the concluding words, "and let not the husband put away his wife," are the completion of the Lord's command given in verse 10. The Apostle, in case such a separation should already have taken place, anticipates the difficult question which might then arise by parenthetically remarking that in such a case the woman must not marry again, but ought to be reunited to her former husband.

(12) **But to the rest.**—Up to this point the writer has alluded only to Christians; he has spoken of the duties of unmarried persons, of widows, and of those already married. There still remains one class of marriages concerning which differences of opinion existed—viz., mixed marriages. In a church like Corinth there would have been, no doubt, many cases where one of the partners was a heathen and the other a Christian, arising from the subsequent conversion of only one of the married couple. This subject is treated of in verses 12—16. The words are emphatically, "If any man *have already* a wife," &c. The case of a Christian marrying a heathen is not alluded to. In 2 Cor. vi. 14, the marriage of a Christian to a heathen is forbidden.

**Speak I, not the Lord.**—The Apostle has no word of Christ's to quote on this point, it being one which did not arise during our Lord's life. (See Note on verse 10.)

It is to be noticed that the Apostle, in giving his own apostolic instruction on this point, does not use the word "command," which he applied to our Lord's teaching, but the less authoritative "speak."

**A wife that believeth not.**—That is, a heathen. In some modern religious circles this whole passage has been used (as also 2 Cor. vi. 14) as if by "unbeliever" St. Paul meant a careless Christian, or one who, in modern phraseology, was not "converted." The Apostle is referring under this designation to heathens, and the only case to which his teaching could now or ever apply would be when two heathens had been married, and subsequently only one had embraced the Christian faith. It is to be noticed that both here and in verse 13 the being "pleased to dwell" is put only in reference to the partner who is a heathen, for the Apostle takes for granted that after the instructions he here gives to the Christian partner, no such desire for separation will arise on the part of a Christian.

(13) **Let her not leave him.**—Better, *let her not put him away;* the Greek being the same as is applied

he be pleased to dwell with her, let her
not leave him. (14) For the unbelieving
husband is sanctified by the wife, and
the unbelieving wife is sanctified by the
husband: else were your children unclean; but now are they holy.
(15) But if the unbelieving depart, let
him depart. A brother or a sister is
not under bondage in such *cases:* but
God hath called us to peace.[1] (16) For
what knowest thou, O wife, whether
thou shalt save *thy* husband? or how
knowest thou, O man, whether thou
shalt save *thy* wife? (17) But as God
hath distributed to every man, as the
Lord hath called every one, so let
him walk. And so ordain I in all
churches.

1 Gr. *in peace.*

---

to the husband in verse 12. Under Roman law—and St. Paul was writing to those who were under such law—the wife, as well as the husband, was permitted to obtain a divorce. It is therefore probable that St. Paul uses the stronger term here in reference to the woman's action in the matter, instead of repeating the same word as in verse 10. Some have suggested that the reason St. Paul applies this word to the action of the woman in the matter is that, in the case under consideration, the fact of the wife being a Christian inverts, in St. Paul's opinion, the natural order, and makes her the superior. This is wholly inadmissible, and quite contrary to St. Paul's view of the absolute superiority of the husband. (See chap. xi. 3; Eph. v. 22; 1 Tim. ii. 11.)

(14) **The unbelieving husband is sanctified by the wife.**—Any scruple which a Christian might have felt as to whether matrimonial union with an unbeliever would be defiling is here removed, and the purity of the former teaching justified. In contrast to that other union in which the connection is defiling (chap. vi. 16), the purity of the believing partner in this union, being a lawful one, as it were, entirely overweighs the impurity of the unbeliever, it being not a moral, but a kind of ceremonial impurity. The children of such marriages were considered to be Christian children; and the fruit being holy, so must we regard as holy the tree from which it springs. It must be remembered that the "sanctification" and "holiness" here spoken of is not that inward sanctification which springs from the action of the Holy Spirit in the individual heart, but that consecration which arises from being in the body of Christ, which is the Christian Church (Rom. xi. 16).

(15) **But if the unbelieving depart.**—Supposing, however, the desire for separation arises from the unbelieving partner, how is the Christian partner to act? If the married life, for example, be made intolerable by the unbeliever urging the believer to join in such religious acts as conscience cannot approve, the Apostle's previous commands for continued union do not hold good: a brother or a sister, in such cases, is not bound to insist upon the continuation of the union. "Let the unbeliever, if he so desire, depart."

This permission is in no way contrary to our Lord's permission of divorce on only one ground, for the Apostle has carefully reminded his readers that our Lord's command does not apply to the case of a marriage between a believer and a heathen. In such cases we have no command from Him.

**A brother or a sister.**—That is, a Christian. In such cases, when the unbelieving partner wishes to depart, let him or her do so. The Christian partner is not, under such circumstances, bound by the marriage to continue together. Their doing so might destroy that very peace *in* which (not "*to* peace" as in the English) God has called us.

(16) **For what knowest thou, O wife . . . ?**—This verse has been very generally regarded as a kind of modification of the previous one, as if the Apostle suggested that it might be advisable not to let the unbelieving partner depart from the marriage union when he so desired, in any case where there was even a chance of the believing partner effecting his or her conversion. The true meaning of the passage is, however, precisely the opposite. The Apostle declares that the remote contingency of the unbeliever's conversion is too vague a matter for which to risk the peace which is so essential an element in the Christian life. If the unbelieving partner will depart, do not let any thought as to the possible influence you may exercise over his religious convictions—about which you cannot *know* anything, but only at most vaguely speculate—cause you to insist upon his remaining.

Some historical results, arising from the view that this is a suggestion of the good which may result from such union being continued, are interestingly alluded to by Stanley in his note on this passage:—"This passage, thus interpreted, probably had a direct influence on the marriage of Clotilda with Clovis, and Bertha with Ethelbert, and consequently on the subsequent conversion of the two great kingdoms of France and England to the Christian faith."

(17) **But as God hath distributed . . .**—Regarding verse 16 as a kind of parenthesis, these words follow on from verse 15 as a general principle to be ever borne in mind, as limiting in practice the very broad liberty which the Apostle has given regarding separation in cases of mixed marriages. It is to be noticed that in verse 15 the unbelieving partner is the only one who is spoken of as taking an active part in the separation; the believer is, merely for the sake of peace, to acquiesce in it; he is never to cause or promote a separation, for he is to be guided by the great principle that we are to continue to walk in those social and political relations by which we were bound when God called us. Christianity does not destroy them, but purifies and exalts them, and thus makes them more binding on us than before. According as the Lord has divided to each man his portion in life, and as God has called each man, so in that condition let him continue to walk as a Christian. Let him not try to change it for another. The words "God" and "Lord" have been transposed by later copyists. The order in the English version is different from that in the older MSS. It is important to preserve the accurate reading here, for it speaks of Christ—"the Lord"—as the one who allots to men their natural condition in life, while "God" calls them from heathenism to the Christian faith.

**And so ordain I in all churches.**—This principle was of universal application, and the Apostle lays it down authoritatively for all Churches. The *I* is emphatic, as the writer speaks with apostolic authority. It is noticeable that in some few later MSS. there is an attempt to weaken its force by the substitution of "I teach" for "I appoint or direct." (See chap. xvi. 1.)

Chap. vii. 18—24. Relation of Christianity to various conditions of Life.

(18) Is any man called being circum-
cised? let him not become
uncircumcised. Is any
called in uncircumcision?
let him not be circumcised.
(19) Circumcision is nothing,
and uncircumcision is nothing, but the
keeping of the commandments of God.
(20) Let every man abide in the same
calling wherein he was called.
(21) Art thou called *being* a servant?
care not for it: but if thou mayest be

---

(18) **Is any man called being circumcised?**—Better, *Was any one called having been circumcised?* The previous general rule is now illustrated by, and applied to, two conditions of life—CIRCUMCISION (verses 18—20) and SLAVERY (verses 20—24). If any man was converted after having been circumcised, he was not, as some over-zealous Christians might have been anxious to do, to remove every trace of his external connection with Judaism (Gal. v. 2).

(19) **Circumcision is nothing, and uncircumcision is nothing.**—Often those who regard some ceremony as unimportant magnify the very disregard of it into a necessary virtue. The Apostle carefully guards against that by expressing the nothingness of both circumcision and uncircumcision (Rom. ii. 25; Gal. v. 6; vi. 15). The circumcision of Timothy, and the refusal to circumcise Titus by St. Paul himself, are illustrations at once of the application of the truth here enforced, and of the Apostle's scrupulous adherence to the principles of his own teaching. To have refused to circumcise Timothy would have attached some value to non-circumcision. To have circumcised Titus would have attached some value to circumcision. (See Acts xvi. 3; Gal. ii. 3.)

**But the keeping of the commandments of God** *is everything*, understood. The teaching here is, practically, "To obey is better than sacrifice."

(20) **Let every man abide in the same calling wherein he was called.**—This is an emphatic repetition of the principle on which the previous practical instruction is based. "Calling" must not here be regarded in the modern sense of profession or condition in life; it is nowhere so used in the New Testament, but always signifies God's calling of us. (See Rom. xi. 29; Eph. i. 18.) Continue to be Christians of the kind which God's call to Christianity made you. If you were circumcised—and so God's call into the Christian Church made you a circumcised Christian—continue so; don't do anything which would seem to imply that some other change in addition to your "call" was necessary to complete your admission to the Church.

(21) **Art thou called being a servant?**—Better, *Were you called while a slave? Do not let that make you anxious.* The fact of your being in slavery does not affect the reality of completeness of your conversion; and so you need have no anxiety to try and escape from servitude. In this and the following three verses the subject of SLAVERY is treated of as the second illustration of the general principle laid down in verse 17—viz., that a man's conversion to Christianity should not lead him to change his national or social condition.

**But if thou mayest be made free, use it rather.**—These words may seem to imply that if a slave could obtain his liberty he was to avail himself of the opportunity to do so. Such an interpretation, however, is entirely at variance with the whole drift of the argument, which is, that he is *not* to seek such a change. What the Apostle does say is, that (so far from letting the servitude be a cause of distress to you) if you can even be free, prefer to use it, *i.e.*, your condition as a converted slave. It, as well as any other position in life, can be used to God's glory. Such an interpretation is most in accordance with the construction of the sentence in the original Greek; and it is in perfect harmony, not only with the rest of this passage, but with all St. Paul's teaching and his universal practice on this subject.

It may be well here briefly to notice the attitude which the Apostle of the Gentiles maintains towards the great question of SLAVERY. While there were many points in which ancient slavery under the Greek and Roman Governments was similar to what has existed in modern days, there were also some striking points of difference. The slaves at such a place as Corinth would have been under Roman law, but many of its harsher provisions would doubtless have been practically modified by the traditional leniency of Greek servitude and by general usage. Although a master could sell his slave, punish him, and even put him to death, if he did so unjustly he would himself be liable to certain penalties. The power which a master could exercise over his slave was not so evidently objectionable in an age when parents had almost similar power over their children. Amongst the class called slaves were to be found, not only the commonest class who performed menial offices, but also literary men, doctors, midwives, and artificers, who were constantly employed in work suited to their ability and acquirements. Still, the fact remains that the master could sell his slave as he could sell any other species of property; and such a state of things was calculated greatly to degrade both those who trafficked and those who were trafficked in, and was contrary to those Christian principles which taught the brotherhood of men, and exalted every living soul into the high dignity of having direct communion with its Father.

How, then, are we to account for St. Paul, with his vivid realisation of the brotherhood of men in Christ, and his righteous intolerance of intolerance, never having condemned this servile system, and having here insisted on the duty of a converted slave to remain in servitude; or for his having on one occasion sent back a Christian slave to his Christian master without asking for his freedom, although he counted him his master's "brother"? (See Ep. to Philemon.)

One point which would certainly have weighed with the Apostle in considering this question was his own belief in the near approach of the end of this dispensation. If all existing relations would be overthrown in a few years, even such a relation as was involved in slavery would not be of so great importance as if it had been regarded as a permanent institution.

But there were other grave considerations, of a more positive and imperative nature. If one single word from Christian teaching could have been quoted at Rome as tending to excite the slaves to revolt, it would have set the Roman Power in direct and active hostility to the new faith. Had St. Paul's teaching led (as it probably would, had he urged the cessation of

made free, use *it* rather. (22) For he
that is called in the Lord, *being* a ser-
vant, is the Lord's freeman:[1] likewise
also he that is called, *being* free, is
Christ's servant. (23) Ye are bought with
a price; be not ye the servants of men.
(24) Brethren, let every man, wherein he
is called, therein abide with God.
(25) Now concerning virgins I have no
commandment of the Lord: yet I give
my judgment, as one that hath ob-
tained mercy of the Lord
to be faithful.
(26) I suppose therefore
that this is good for the
present distress,[2] *I say,*
that *it is* good for a man
so to be. (27) Art thou bound unto a
wife? seek not to be loosed? Art thou
loosed from a wife? seek not a wife.

1 Gr. *made free.*

2 Or, *necessity.*

Chap. vii. 25—38. Duty of parents concerning the marriage of their daughters.

---

servitude) to a rising of the slaves—that rising and the Christian Church, which would have been identified with it, would have been crushed together. Rome would not have tolerated a repetition of those servile wars which had, twice in the previous century, deluged Sicily with blood.

Nor would the danger of preaching the abolition of servitude have been confined to that arising from external violence on the part of the Roman Government; it would have been pregnant with danger to the purity of the Church itself. Many might have been led, from wrong motives, to join a communion which would have aided them in securing their social and political freedom.

In these considerations we may find, I think, ample reasons for the position of non-interference which the Apostle maintains in regard to slavery. If men then say that Christianity approved of slavery, we would point them to the fact that it is Christianity that has abolished it. Under a particular and exceptional condition of circumstances, which cannot again arise, St. Paul, for wise reasons, did not interfere with it. To have done so would have been worse than useless. But he taught fearlessly those imperishable principles which led in after ages to its extinction. The object of Christianity —and this St. Paul over and over again insisted on— was not to overturn and destroy existing political and social institutions, but to leaven them with new principles. He did not propose to abolish slavery, but to Christianise it; and when slavery is Christianised it must cease to exist. Christianised slavery is liberty.

(22) **For he that is called in the Lord, being a servant, . . .**—Better, *For he that was converted as a slave is Christ's freedman; and, similarly, the one who was converted as a freeman is Christ's slave.* Therefore, no one need trouble himself as to his mere earthly servitude or freedom. If he be a slave, let him be cheered by remembering that he is a freedman belonging to Christ; and if he be a freeman, let him not despise the state of the one in servitude, realising that he himself is Christ's slave A "freedman," as distinct from a "freeman," was one who had been in bondage but was now free.

(23) **Ye are bought with a price . . .**—Better, *You were bought with a price therefore become not slaves of men.* This carries on the idea of freedmen of the previous verse. With a great price—even the blood of Christ—they have been purchased by Him as freedmen: therefore, do not become slaves of men—do not yield to their views by seeking to change the condition of your calling.

(24) **Brethren, let every man, wherein he is called.**—Better, *was called.* Here we have an earnest reiteration of the principle underlying the previous instruction. Let the converted man abide, as regards his social or political state, as he was; in doing so, he will be with God. They were brought near to God by their conversion, whether free or slave; let them so remain.

(25) **Now concerning virgins . . .**—A new subject is here introduced—viz., the duty of parents regarding their young unmarried daughters. Ought they to give them in marriage? The answer occupies to verse 38. On this subject the Apostle states that he has no actual command from Christ. It was a point to which our Lord had not directly alluded in His teaching, and so the Apostle gives his opinion as one who has obtained mercy to be a faithful instructor. The contrast here is not between Paul inspired by the Lord and Paul not inspired, but, as in verse 12, between Paul quoting the words of Christ and Paul himself instructing as an inspired Apostle.

(26) **I suppose therefore that this is good for the present distress.**—Better, *I think then that it is good because of the impending distress—that it is good for a person to be so—i.e.*, to continue in the state in which he is, married or unmarried, as the case may be.

The construction of this sentence is strikingly characteristic of a writing which has been taken down from dictation. The speaker commences the sentence, and afterwards commences it over again: "I think it is good," &c., and then, "I say I think it is good."

From this verse to the end of verse 35 the Apostle deals again with the general question of marriage, introducing a new element of consideration—"the impending distress"; and at verse 36 he returns to the immediate subject with which he had started in verse 25, viz., duty of parents regarding their young unmarried daughters. The "impending distress" is that foretold by Christ, Matt. xxiv. 8 *et seq.* The Apostle regarded the coming of Christ as no distant event, and in the calamities already threatening the Church, such as the famine in the time of Claudius (Acts xi. 28), and in the gathering persecutions, he heard the first mutterings of the storm which should burst upon the world before the sign of the Son of Man should appear in the heavens.

**It is good for a man.**—It is most important to remember how much stress St. Paul lays upon this point as the ground of his preference for celibacy. As the reason for the preference has ceased to exist, so the advice, so far as it springs from that cause, is no longer of binding obligation (see verses 29—31).

(27) **Art thou bound unto a wife?**—This is an explanation and re-assertion of the previous words "so to be." Being "loosed from a wife" does not mean a separation after marriage. but simply "unmarried."

(28) But and if thou marry, thou hast
not sinned; and if a virgin marry, she
hath not sinned. Nevertheless such
shall have trouble in the flesh: but I
spare you.
(29) But this I say, brethren, the time
*is* short: it remaineth, that both they
that have wives be as though they had
none; (30) and they that weep, as though
they wept not; and they that rejoice,
as though they rejoiced not; and they
that buy, as though they possessed not;
(31) and they that use this world, as
not abusing *it:* for the fashion of this
world passeth away.
(32) But I would have you without care-

(28) **But and if thou marry.**—Better, *If, however, thou hast married.* The teaching here is not for some who will, after this advice, persist in marrying, but the reference is still to those who are actually married, and a further and clearer statement to them that the question is not one of sin, but merely of desirability.

**If a virgin marry.**—In the original it is emphatically "If *the* virgin have married." It is possible that in the letter from Corinth some particular case was referred to in which a Christian parent had scruples as to allowing his daughter to marry, and while dealing, in reply, with the subject generally, the Apostle refers immediately here to the particular case which had given rise to the inquiry. He says that if she have married she will have committed no sin; but that she and those who, like her, have married, will have troubles in the flesh, *i.e.*, earthly troubles. It is not a spiritual question.

**But I spare you.**—This might, at first sight, seem to imply that he does not desire to harass them by any detail of their troubles just referred to; but the true meaning, however, is that the Apostle states his desire in giving this advice is to spare them their troubles. Matrimony will involve you in earthly troubles when the expected distress comes: therefore, in advising you to remain unmarried, my desire is to spare you them.

(29) **But this I say, brethren.**—This does not introduce a reiteration of what he has said already, but commences a solemn and affectionate warning, urging on them earnestly that, whether they applied or did not apply the principle to marriage, still that it is true, and of vast importance in regulating all life,—that men should live as ever expecting the return of the Lord. Let us not for one moment think that this principle was evolved by St. Paul from a mistaken belief that the Second Advent was close at hand. This principle of life was taught by Christ Himself. He warned men against living carelessly because they thought "the Lord delayeth His coming." They were to be ever on the watch, as servants for the unexpected return of their master—as guests for the coming of the bridegroom. It was not the opinion that Christ would soon come which led St. Paul to hold and teach this principle of Christian life. Perhaps it was his intense realisation of this eternal truth which the Lord had taught, his assimilation of it as part of his very being, from which the conviction arose that the Advent was not only in theory always, but, as a matter of fact, then near at hand. Hope and belief mysteriously mingled together in one longing unity of feeling.

It may be asked, if the Apostles were mistaken on this point, may they not have been mistaken about other things also? The best answer to such a question, perhaps, is that this was just *the* one point on which our Lord had said they *should not* be informed, and it is the one point on which they *were not* informed. "Times and seasons" were to be excluded from their knowledge (Acts i. 6).

**The time is short: it remaineth . . .**—Better, *The time that remains is shortened, so that both they that have wives,* &c. (the Greek word for "remain" (*to loipon*) is used frequently by St. Paul in a sort of adverbial way, 2 Cor. xiii. 11; Eph. vi. 10; Phil. iv. 8). The words "so that" do not introduce a series of apostolic exhortations based upon and growing out of the previous statement regarding the brevity of the remaining time, but they express what was God's intention in thus making the time short. St. Paul regards everything as having its place and purpose in the divine economy. If the time were long (and the teaching applies equally—for the principle is the same—to the brevity of life), then, indeed, men might live as having "much goods laid up for many years" (Luke xii. 19); but the time of life is short, that each may keep himself from being the slave of the external conditions and relationships of life. Such is the force of the series of striking contrasts with which the Apostle now illustrates the habit of life which God intended to follow from the shortening of the time.

(31) **Not abusing it.**—We can scarcely find a better word in English than "abusing" by which to render the Greek of this passage. But this word implies, in modern language, an abuse arising from misuse, and not, as in the original here, an abuse arising from over-much use. All the things mentioned in this series by the Apostle are right things; and the warning is against being in bondage to those things which are in themselves right and good, and not against any criminal use of them. Though they are not wrong in themselves, we are not to become slaves of them; we are to renounce them, "so as not to follow nor be led by them."

**For the fashion of this world passeth away.**—Better, *for the outward form of this world is passing away* (the word translated "fashion" occurs only here and in Phil. ii. 8). The allusion is not a merely general reference to the ephemeral nature of things temporal, but arises from the Apostle's conviction that the last days were already commencing, when the outward temporal form of things was being superseded (Rom. viii. 19; Rev. xxi. 1). The word "for" does not introduce a reason for the immediately preceding injunction, but carries us back to the previous statement in verse 29: "the time is short," the intervening series of illustrative exhortations being parenthetical.

(32) **But I would have you.**—These words seem to take up again the form of expression in verse 28. I would spare you trouble; I also wish to have you free from anxious care. That is my reason for so advising you. And here the Apostle returns to the subject immediately under consideration, and shows here what he has been saying bears upon it. This element of anxious care must be borne in mind in considering the desirability or otherwise of marriage.

There are some important variations in the readings of these verses (32, 33, 34) in the Greek MSS. The emendations required in the Greek text, from which the Authorised version is translated, are, I think, as

fulness. He that is unmarried careth
for the things that belong to the Lord,
how he may please the Lord: (33) but
he that is married careth for the things
that are of the world, how he may please
*his* wife. (34) There is difference *also*
between a wife and a virgin. The un-
married woman careth for the things of
the Lord, that she may be holy both in
body and in spirit: but she that is
married careth for the things of the
world, how she may please *her* husband.
(35) And this I speak for your own profit;
not that I may cast a snare upon you,
but for that which is comely, and that
ye may attend upon the Lord without
distraction.
(36) But if any man think that he
behaveth himself uncomely toward his
virgin, if she pass the flower of *her* age,
and need so require, let him do what he
will, he sinneth not: let them marry.
(37) Nevertheless he that standeth sted-
fast in his heart, having no necessity,
but hath power over his own will, and
hath so decreed in his heart that he will
keep his virgin, doeth well. (38) So
then he that giveth *her* in marriage
doeth well; but he that giveth *her* not
in marriage doeth better.

---

follows:—Omit the full-stop after verse 33, connecting it with verse 34 by the insertion of the word "and." Insert "and" in verse 34 before "a wife," and the word "unmarried" after "a wife." The whole passage will then stand thus (rendering the Greek verb as it is in chap. i. 13, "divided," and, not, as in the English version here, "a difference between"): *The unmarried man careth for the things of the Lord, how he may please the Lord. But the married man careth for the things of the world, how he may please his wife, and is divided in his interests* (*i.e.*, distracted). *Also the wife that is unmarried* (*i.e.*, a widow, or divorced), *and the unmarried virgin* (*i.e.*, the maid who is free from any contract of marriage), *cares for the things of the Lord, that she may be holy both in body and spirit. But she that is married careth for the things of the world, how she may please her husband.*

The whole force of the passage is that married persons have, in the fulfilment of their obligations to each other, an additional interest and concern from which the unmarried are free. It must ever be distinctly borne in mind that this advice was given solely under the impression that the end of all earthly things was impending, and that the great trial and desolation was beginning to darken over the world. The Apostle who wrote these words of warning himself expressly condemns those who applied them as involving general moral obligations, and not as suited merely to temporary requirements (1 Tim. iv. 1, 3). He had himself at this time a strong personal inclination for a celibate life; but still he could enjoy and show a preference for the companionship of those who were evidently otherwise minded—he abode and wrought with Aquila and Priscilla his wife, at Corinth (Acts xviii. 3). We can still imagine circumstances arising in individual cases to which the principle enforced by the Apostle would apply. A man might feel it his duty to devote his life to some missionary enterprise, in which marriage would hamper his movements and impede his usefulness. Such an exceptional case would hence only establish the general rule. "It may not be out of place to recall" (writes Stanley, in his *Exposition of St. Paul's View of Celibacy*) "a celebrated instance of a similarly emphatic preference for celibacy on precisely similar grounds—not of abstract right, but of special expediency—in the well-known speech of our great Protestant Queen, when she declared that England was her husband and all Englishmen her children, and that she desired no higher character or fairer remembrance of her to be transmitted to posterity than this inscription engraved upon her tombstone: 'Here lies Elizabeth, who lived and died a maiden queen.'"

(35) **And this I speak for your own profit.**—The reference is to the preceding passage, commencing with verse 32; and the writer explains that these instructions are given, not to please himself, but for (emphatically) *your own* advantage; not to entangle you in a noose, and so take away your liberty, but with a view to comeliness (or, *honesty*, Rom. xiii. 13), and to your waiting upon the Lord without being cumbered with earthly things (as, in Luke x. 40, Martha was "cumbered").

(36) **But if any man think.**—Here the writer turns to the duty of parents, and there is a further explanation to such that the previous expressions are not binding commandments, but apostolic advice. If the case arises that a parent thinks he would be acting unfairly towards his unmarried daughter (*i.e.*, exposing her to temptation) by withholding his permission for her marriage, he ought to do as he feels inclined—*i.e.*, let the lover and his daughter marry.

**Let him do what he will.**—This sentence does not—as it may at first sight in the English appear to do—imply that he may consent or not, and whichever course he adopts he does right. It is implied, in the earlier part of the sentence, that he thinks he ought to give his consent, and therefore that is what he wishes to do. Let him do that which he so wills, says St. Paul, and he need not in doing so fear that he does wrong.

(37) **Nevertheless he that standeth stedfast in his heart.**—The previous verse must not be understood as applying to any other cases than those to which it is strictly limited—viz., those where positive harm is likely to result from the parent withholding his consent. Where no such necessity arises, but the parent has power over his own will (in contrast to the parent whose will must be under the control of the external necessity of the case), and has made this resolution in his heart, the result of which is to keep his daughter with him unmarried, will do well (future tense, see next Note).

(38) **So then . . .**—Better, *So then he that gives his daughter in marriage does well, and* (not "but") *he that giveth her not shall do better.* It is worth noticing how, in the case of the one who gives his daughter in marriage, we have the present tense "does well"—as if the good he did began and ended there; and, in the other case, the future "shall do" (in verse 37 also)

(39) The wife is bound by the law
as long as her husband
liveth; but if her husband
be dead, she is at liberty
to be married to whom she will; only in
the Lord. (40) But she is happier if she
so abide, after my judgment: and I
think also that I have the Spirit of God.

Chap. vii. 39, 40. Marriage of widows.

A.D. 59.

CHAPTER VIII.—(1) Now as touch-
ing things offered unto
idols, we know that we all
have knowledge. (Know-
ledge puffeth up, but
charity edifieth. (2) And
if any man think that he
knoweth any thing, he knoweth nothing

Chap. viii. 1—13. The eating of meat which had been used by the heathen for sacrificial purposes.

---

—the good result of his action continuing while the girl remains with her parent. This passage clearly shows how St. Paul has not been contrasting right and wrong: but comparative degrees of what is expedient.

All throughout this passage the Apostle takes for granted the absolute control of the parent over the child, in accordance with the principles of both Greek and Jewish jurisprudence. Hence, no advice is given to the young maiden herself, but only to her father.

(39, 40) **The wife.**—The question of the re-marriage of widows is here considered. It was probably a matter in which his opinion had been asked, and, in any case, naturally completes the subject of marriage. The widow may be married again if she desire, but "only in the Lord"—*i.e.*, not to a heathen. She, being a Christian, should marry a Christian.

The words "by the law" are not in the best MSS. The opening sentence, asserting the marriage union to be dissoluble only by death, is to guard against any married woman applying these words to herself, they having reference only to widows.

St. Paul explains that she is happier to continue a widow (her case coming under the same considerations as referred to the unmarried in the previous verses).

**I think also that I have the Spirit of God.**—This is no expression of doubt as to whether he had the Spirit of God, but an assurance of his confidence that he, as well as other teachers (who, perhaps, boast more about it), had the Spirit of God to guide him in cases where no direct command has been given by Christ.

VIII.

(1) **Now as touching things offered unto idols.**—A new subject is here introduced, and occupies the whole of this chapter. In Corinth and other cities meat was offered for sale which had been used for sacrificial purposes in the heathen temples, having been sold to the dealers by the priests, who received a large share of the sacrifices for themselves, or by the individuals who offered them, and had more remaining of their own share than they could use themselves. Thus, a Christian might unconsciously eat of meat, either at the house of a friend (see chap. x. 27) or by purchasing it himself in the public shambles, which had been previously brought in contact by sacrificial usage with an idol. There were some in Corinth who felt no scruple on the subject. An idol was nothing in their opinion. It could neither consecrate nor pollute that which was offered in its temple. Such Christians would, to show how completely and effectively their Christianity had dispelled all their previous heathen superstition, buy meat without caring whence it came, partake of a heathen friend's hospitality, regardless of what use the meat had been put to, and even join in a repast held in the outer court of a heathen temple (verse 10), where the meat would almost certainly be what had been saved after the sacrifice. That St. Paul would have done so himself so far as his own personal feelings alone were concerned, we can scarcely doubt. To him, therefore, those who acted upon his authority appealed upon this subject.

There were others at Corinth, however, who felt some scruples upon the subject. There were heathen converts who had not completely got rid of every vestige of the old superstition, or whose conscience would accuse them of not having wholly given up idolatry if they took any part even in its social aspect: for many social acts, as well as purely religious ceremonies, were in the heathen mind included in acts of worship. And there were Jews, the intensity of whose traditional hatred of idolatry could not allow them to regard as "nothing" that against which Jehovah had uttered His most terrible denunciations, and against which He had preserved their race as a living witness.

To both these sections of the Church the conduct of the more liberal party would prove a serious stumbling-block. The argument used by those who asked St. Paul's advice was evidently that the Christians have knowledge enough to feel that an idol is nothing, and that, therefore, there can be no harm in partaking of what has been offered to "nothing." "We know," says St. Paul, in reply, taking up the words of their own letter, "we know that we all have knowledge: we know that an idol is nothing." The last clause of verse 1 and verses 2 and 3 form a parenthesis; and in verse 4 the opening words of verse 1 are repeated, and the line of thought which this parenthesis interrupted is again resumed.

**Knowledge puffeth up, but charity edifieth.**—Those who grounded everything on knowledge are reminded parenthetically that knowledge by itself may have a bad effect, and also (verses 2, 3) that there is an element in the consciousness of our knowledge which destroys the truth and purity of that knowledge itself. Knowledge puffs up the man himself. Love builds up the whole Church. The word "edify" has now only a moral significance. Originally it could be applied to moral conduct only figuratively. The substantive "edifice" has retained its original literal meaning. In Spenser "edify" is used in its literal sense; and in Hakluyt's *Travels* (1553) the "edification" of the castle of Corfu is mentioned. The use made by St. Paul of this figure is of some importance. The word is used only by St. Paul, and once by St. Luke (Acts ix. 31), and the idea which it conveys is not so much the improvement of the individual as the building-up of the whole Christian edifice. We have come to speak of an "edifying discourse" if it helps the individual. St. Paul would have spoken of an "edifying work" if it built up the Church. "We are sometimes too apt to treat Christianity as if it were *monolithic*" (Howson). (See chaps. xii. 19; xiv. 3, 5, 12, 17; Eph. iv. 12—16; 1 Thess. v. 11.) It is worth noting that the word used in the original in Heb. iii. 3, 4, and ix. 11, is quite different from the word employed, here and elsewhere, by St. Paul.

(2) **If any man think that he knoweth any thing . . . .**—There must be a moral as well as a merely intellectual element in knowledge if it is to

yet as he ought to know. (3) But if
any man love God, the same is known
of him.) (4) As concerning therefore
the eating of those things that are
offered in sacrifice unto idols, we know
that an idol *is* nothing in the world,
and that *there is* none other God but
one. (5) For though there be that
are called gods, whether in heaven or
in earth, (as there be gods many, and
lords many,) (6) but to us *there is but*
one God, the Father, of whom *are* all
things,[a] and we in him;[1] and one Lord
Jesus Christ, by whom *are* all things,
and we by him.
(7) Howbeit *there is* not in every man
that knowledge: for some with con-
science of the idol unto this hour eat *it*
as a thing offered unto an idol; and
their conscience being weak is defiled.
(8) But meat commendeth us not to
God: for neither, if we eat, are we
the better;[2] neither, if we eat not, are
we the worse.[3]
(9) But take heed lest by any means
this liberty[4] of your's become a stum-

2 Or, *have we the more.*
3 Or, *have we the less.*
*a* Rom. 11. 36.
1 Or, *for him.*
4 Or, *power.*

---

be true knowledge. Without love to guide us in its use it is not an operative knowledge, and so does not fulfil the true end of knowledge.

It has been suggested (Stanley *in loc*) that "not yet" has here the force of "not in the infirmities of their mortal state;" but such an interpretation introduces altogether a new element of thought, to which there is no antithetical explanation in what follows.

(3) **If any man love God.**—This explains the nature of the love which edifies. Love to God, and therefore love to man, builds up the whole Christian communion. The man gets outside the mere selfish thought of his own indulgence in his liberty. There is the underthought in these words ("the same is known of Him") of the identity between knowing God and being known of Him. The latter is the source of the former. Like water rising to its own level, the love and the knowledge rise as high as their source.

(4) **As concerning therefore the eating of those things.**—See verse 1. The subject resumed after the parenthesis. We have, perhaps, in this repetition of the words a characteristic of a letter written by another from the author's dictation, as was the case with this and other epistles.

**An idol is nothing in the world.**—It is nothing in itself but a piece of wood or metal, and it really represents nothing, for we know that there is "no God but one." The word "other" was inserted in later MSS., probably from a recollection of the words of the first commandment.

(5) **For though there be . . . .**—This is an hypothetic argument. "Be" is the emphatic word of the supposition. Even assuming that there do exist those beings which are called "gods" (we have a right to make such a supposition, for Deut. x. 17, Ps. cv. 2, 3, speaks of "gods and lords" of another kind), the difference between the heathen, "gods many" and the "lords and gods" of whom the Old Testament speaks, is that the former are deities, and the latter only a casual way of speaking of angels and other spiritual subjects and servants of the one God. This is brought out in the following verse.

(6) **But to us.**—Though this be so, yet for us Christians there exists but one God the Father, from whom alone every created thing has come, and for (not "in") whom alone we exist; and one Lord Jesus Christ, through whom all things are created (John i. 3), and we Christians created spiritually by Him. All creation is *of* the Father through the Son. All creation is for the Father and likewise *for* the Son. (See Col. i. 16.) The words "we by Him" must not be regarded as a repetition of part of the thought of the previous sentence; but as the words "by whom are all things" express the fact of physical creation, so the words, "we by Him," attribute our spiritual re-creation as Christians to the same source. (See Gal. vi. 15; Eph. ii. 10.) This sixth verse then sweeps away completely any pantheistic conception which might have been thought to be in the previous words. Even granting, for argument sake, that such gods or lords do exist, we have but one God, one Lord.

(7) **Howbeit there is not in every man that knowledge.**—The Apostle had admitted that in theory all have knowledge which should render the eating of things offered to idols a matter beyond question; but there are some who, as a matter of fact, are not fully grown—have not practically attained that knowledge.

**Some with conscience of the idol unto this hour eat it as a thing offered unto an idol.**—Better, *some, through their familiarity with the idol, even up to this time eat it as offered to an idol.*

The weight of MSS. evidence is in favour of the word "familiarity" instead of the word "conscience," and joins "even up to this time," not with "eat," but with the previous words. Thus the allusion is to heathen converts who, from their previous lifelong belief in the reality of the idol as representing a god, have not been able fully to realise the non-existence of the person thus represented, though they have come to believe that it is not God; and therefore, they regard the meat as offered to some kind of reality, even though it be a demon. (See chap. x. 20, 21.) The Apostle admits that this is a sign of a weak conscience; and the defilement arises from its being weak.

(8) **But meat . . . .**—By showing that the eating is a matter of indifference, the Apostle introduces his reason for yielding to the weakness of another. If the weakness involved a matter of our vital relation to God, then to yield would be wrong. But meat will not (future) affect our relationship to God. The concluding words of this verse are inverted in later MSS., as in the English version, and the better order is: "Neither, if we eat not, do we lose anything in our relation to God; nor, if we eat, do we gain anything in our relation to Him."

(9) **But take heed.**—On this very account, because the matter is one which *is* indifferent, because there is no right or wrong in it, you must look elsewhere for your guide as to how you ought to act. In things which are not indifferent, right or wrong is the sole test of action. In things indifferent you must look for some other guide, and you must regulate your conduct by the effect it may have on others. Your liberty, which arises from the bare fact of the indifferent nature of the thing, may become a stumbling-block to

blingblock to them that are weak.
(10) For if any man see thee which hast
knowledge sit at meat in the idol's
temple, shall not the conscience of him
which is weak be emboldened[1] to eat
those things which are offered to idols;
(11) and through thy knowledge shall the
weak brother perish, for whom Christ
died? (12) But when ye sin so against
the brethren, and wound their weak
conscience, ye sin against Christ.
(13) Wherefore, if meat make my brother
to offend, I will eat no flesh while the
world standeth, lest I make my brother
to offend.

[1] Gr. *edified.*

A.D. 59.

CHAPTER IX.—(1) Am I not an
apostle? am I not free? have I not

---

others, may be the cause of their taking a false step in the Christian course.

(10) **For if any man** (*i.e.*, any of the weak brethren) **see thee which hast knowledge.** — The fact of your being avowedly advanced in the knowledge of the faith will make your example the more dangerous, because more effective.

**Sit at meat in the idol's temple.**—Some went so far as to not only eat, but eat in the precincts of the heathen temple. The Apostle being concerned now only with the point of the eating, does not rebuke this practice here, but he does so fully in chap. x. 14—22. He probably mentions the fact here as an instance in which there could be no salving of his conscience by the heathen convert thinking that it was not certain whence the meat had come.

**Be emboldened.**—Better, *be built up*. The people addressed had probably argued that the force of their example would build up others. Yes, says St. Paul, with irony, it will build him up—to do what, being weak, he cannot do without sin.

(11) **And through thy knowledge shall . . .**—Better, *and by means of thy knowledge the weak one perishes—the brother for whom Christ died.* It is not, as in the English version, a question, but it is the expansion and interpretation of the previous statement. There is a great variety of readings in the MSS., but the weight of evidence is in favour of this reading. Christ *died* for him. The sarcasm passes away in words of solemn and pathetic reproof. You won't give up your liberty for him. You will indulge yourself, and so prevent Christ's death being *his* redemption. A sacrifice of conscience destroys spiritual life.

(12) **When ye sin so.**—When you sin in this way—and he explains further what the sin is: "Striking a blow upon their weak consciences"—you sin against Christ. You wound a member of that body which is His. (See Matt. xxv. 40.)

(13) **Wherefore.**—He states his own solemn determination, arising from the considerations which have just been urged. If a matter of food cause a brother to fall in his Christian course, I will certainly never again eat any kind of flesh, lest I should be the cause of so making him to fall.

It is noticeable that St. Paul in discussing this question makes no reference whatever to the decision of the Council at Jerusalem (see Acts xv. 29), that the Christians should abstain from "meats offered to idols, and from things strangled, and from blood." Probably, the Apostle felt the importance of maintaining his own apostolic authority in a Church where it was questioned by some, and he felt that to base his instruction upon the decision of the Church at Jerusalem might have seemed to imply that he had obtained authority from them, and not directly from the Lord. It was also more in accordance with St. Paul's usual style of instruction to base the smallest details of conduct upon that highest of all principles—our union as Christians with Christ. An appeal to the letter sent from Jerusalem would have been no step in the ascending argument, which reaches its great climax in the 11th and 12th verses, and which, in verse 13, the Apostle enunciates as the guide of his own life.

## IX.

The assertion in the last verse of chap. viii. of his willingness to sacrifice for ever his own right to eat meat, about which he had himself no conscientious scruple, out of a tender regard to the spiritual welfare of others, seems to have reminded the Apostle that another act of self-sacrifice on his part had not only been unappreciated, but made the grounds of an unworthy attempt on the part of some (probably the Jewish Christians) to depreciate and even call in question his apostolic dignity and authority. At Corinth (Acts xviii. 3), and elsewhere (Acts xx. 34, and 1 Thess. iii. 7, 9), the Apostle, instead of depending upon the Church for support, had laboured as a tent-maker. *Cilicium*, a kind of cloth used for tent-coverings, took its name from Cilicia, where the goats out of whose hair it was made were found in abundance; and the manufacture of it was naturally the handicraft which a native of Tarsus in Cilicia would, according to general custom, have learnt in his boyhood. The followers of St. Peter, with maliciously ingenious logic, argued from this practice of St. Paul's that his dignity and authority were thereby proved to be somewhat inferior to that of St. Peter and the Lord's brethren, who were supported by the Christian Church. It is to this subject the Apostle now turns, and the chapter (ix.) is occupied with his reply to their insinuations. If we remember that so long an epistle could not have been written at a single sitting, but probably occupied many days in its composition, such change in subject and style as we have an example of in the last verse of chap. viii. and the first verse of this chapter, will not seem so abrupt and startling as at first sight they may appear. This chapter deals with its subject in a style eminently characteristic of the Apostle. While in the earlier part the style is argumentative, with here and there flashes of sarcasm or of passionate appeal, towards the end it is full of earnest and loving pathos. The subject of the entire chapter is "The vindication of his personal conduct as an Apostle," and this is arranged in the following order:—

I. Verses 1—18. THE ASSERTION OF HIS RIGHTS AS AN APOSTLE, AND HIS VOLUNTARY ABNEGATION OF THEM.

(1) Verses 1—3. The assertion of his apostolic dignity.
(2) Verses 4—14. The assertion of his right to be supported by the Church, and that he did not avail himself of it.

seen Jesus Christ our Lord? are not
Chap. ix. 1—12. The apostolic right of maintenance. ye my work in the Lord?
(2) If I be not an apostle
unto others, yet doubtless
I am to you: for the seal of mine apostle-
ship are ye in the Lord. (3) Mine
answer to them that do examine me is
this, (4) Have we not power to eat and
to drink? (5) Have we not power to
lead about a sister, a wife,[1] as well as

1 Or, *woman.*

---

This right is maintained from the following considerations:—

(*a*) Verses 4—6. The fact that others and their wives are so supported.

(*b*) Verse 7. An appeal to the facts of ordinary life, illustrated by the cases of a soldier, a vine-keeper, and a shepherd.

(*c*) Verses 8—10. A reference to the principles of Jewish law.

(*d*) Verses 11—12. The treatment of other Christian teachers.

(*e*) Verse 13. The support of the Jewish priesthood.

(*f*) Verse 14. The command of Christ Himself.

(3) Verses 15—18. The cause and motive of the Apostle's voluntary abnegation of this right.

II. Verses 19—27. IN OTHER MATTERS AS WELL AS IN THIS, THE APOSTLE WAS INFLUENCED BY A REGARD FOR OTHERS.

(1) Verses 19—22. The various forms which this self-sacrifice assumed for their sakes.

(2) Verses 22—27. The bearing of it on himself personally.

(1) **Am I not an apostle?**—Better, *Am I not free? am I not an Apostle?* such being the order of the words in the better MSS. Thus the thought grows more naturally out of the previous chapter than it seems to do in the English version. He had mentioned his solemn resolve to give up a freedom to which he had a right in regard to eating meat. He had on another occasion, in regard to his right of maintenance by the Church, also voluntarily sacrificed his freedom, and the Jewish party had in consequence denied the existence of the rights, and questioned his apostolic dignity. He asks, with abrupt emphasis, "Was it because I am not free to demand such support? My freedom in this case is as real as in that other case when you questioned it, and to which I shall now refer. Was it because I am not an Apostle?"

**Have I not seen Jesus Christ our Lord?**—To have seen Christ was a necessary qualification for the Apostolate (Acts i. 21). From the manner in which the Apostle here asks the question, and does not answer it, it would seem that although some small minority might, for some party purpose, have at some time questioned it, yet that the fact was generally admitted and universally known that St. Paul did actually see the Lord at the time of his conversion (Acts ix. 4), and on other occasions (Acts xviii. 9; xxii. 17).

**Are not ye my work in the Lord?**—This is a further proof of his Apostleship, and therefore of his right or freedom to have demanded support from the Church. (See chap. iv. 15.)

(2) **If I be not an apostle unto others.**—The allusion here is probably to some who may have arrived at Corinth subsequent to St. Paul's departure, and who, not recognising his Apostleship in relation to themselves, stirred up some of the Corinthians to repudiate it also. So the Apostle says, "Even if I am not an Apostle to these others, I am, at all events, to you; for you are yourselves the very proof and witness—the seal affixed to my appointment to the Apostolate." The repetition of the words "in the Lord" in both these verses expresses the strong conviction, which is characteristic of the Apostle, that the source of all power and of all success is Christ Himself.

(3) **Mine answer . . . .**—The verse refers to what has gone before, and not to what follows. *That* (emphatic) *is my answer to those who examine me as to the truth of my Apostleship.* Both the words "answer" and "examine" are in the Greek the technical terms for a legal defence and examination before a tribunal.

(4) **Have we not power . . . ?**—This follows chap. vi. after the parenthetical argument contained in verses 2, 3. Having established his right to be called an Apostle by the fact that he had seen the Lord, and had been instrumental in their conversion, he now in the same interrogative style asserts his rights as an Apostle. The use of the plural "we" carries on the thought that he is claiming this right as being one of the Apostles—all of whom have, as Apostles, such a right. The form in which the question is asked implies, Surely we have this right. This verse, taken in connection with chap. viii. 9, where the same word in the Greek, "liberty," occurs in connection with eating, shows how this line of thought has grown out of the preceding subject. The question there, however, was that of eating meat offered to idols; the question here is the right to eat and drink (*i.e.*, live) at the expense of the Church (Luke x. 7).

(5) **To lead about a sister, a wife**—*i.e.*, to take with us on our journeys a Christian woman as a wife. Roman divines have interpreted this as referring to "the custom of Christian matrons attending as sisters upon the Apostles." But as the Apostle illustrates his meaning by a reference to Peter, who we know had a wife, such an interpretation is inadmissible. St. Paul, in this verse, carries his statement of apostolic right to support one step further. Not only had he a right to be supported himself, but the support of the married Apostles and their wives by the Church implied the same right on the part of all. A practice which grew out of a misapprehension of the real meaning of this passage, led to grave scandal, and was finally condemned by the first Council of Nicæa (A.D. 325).

**The brethren of the Lord, and Cephas.**—These are mentioned specially, not as distinct from the Apostles (for Cephas, of course, was one), but as examples which would have great weight with the particular Jewish faction to whom this argument was adduced. James was Bishop of Jerusalem (Acts xv. 13; xxi. 18). The other brethren of our Lord were Joses, Simon, and Judas (Matt. xiii. 55). They were not of the twelve Apostles, even after their conversion being mentioned as distinct from the Twelve (Acts i. 14), although James subsequently occupied an apostolic position (Gal. ii. 9). Various and ingenious suggestions have been made as to who these "brethren of the Lord" were; amongst others, that they were cousins, or that they were children of Joseph by a former marriage. These views grew out of a desire to establish the perpetual virginity of Mary. The

other apostles, and *as* the brethren of
the Lord, and Cephas? (6) Or I only
and Barnabas, have not we power to
forbear working? (7) Who goeth a
warfare any time at his own charges?
who planteth a vineyard, and eateth
not of the fruit thereof? or who feedeth
a flock, and eateth not of the milk of
the flock? (8) Say I these things as a
man? or saith not the law the same
also? (9) For it is written in the law
of Moses, Thou shalt not muzzle the
mouth of the ox that treadeth out the
corn.[a] Doth God take care for oxen?
(10) Or saith he *it* altogether for our
sakes? For our sakes, no doubt, *this*
is written: that he that ploweth should
plow in hope; and that he that thresheth
in hope should be partaker of his hope.
(11) If we have sown unto you spiritual

a Deut. 25. 4.

---

natural conclusion from a study of the mention of their names in the Gospels, without preconceived prejudice, would be that Joseph and Mary lived together after the miraculous birth of Christ, and that these were their children. This, too, is supported by the use of the word "*first*-born" in reference to our Lord (Matt. i. 25; Luke ii. 7), and the word "till" (Matt. i. 25), and "before they came together" (Matt. i. 18), and the repeated mention of them as brethren in connection with His mother Mary. (See Note on Matt. xii. 46.)

(6) **Or I only and Barnabas.**—"Or" here does not introduce a question which implies a new right in addition to the rights already claimed, but it completes the argument. Granting the existence of the rights established by the previous questions, the Apostle now says—still preserving the interrogative form—"These things being so, the only way you can possibly do away with this right is by making exceptions of myself and Barnabas." The form in which the question is put shows the impossibility of any such arbitrary exception being made. They as well as the others *had* the right to abstain from working for their living. Barnabas' early association with St. Paul (Acts xi. 30; xii. 25; xv. 38) probably led him to adopt the Apostle's practice of supporting himself, and not being dependent on his fellow-Christians. The word "only" implies that all the other Apostles and brethren of the Lord exercised their right of maintenance by the Church.

(7) **Who goeth a warfare any time at his own charges?**—Three illustrations from human life and business show that the principle which has been adopted in the Christian Church is not exceptional. A soldier receives his pay; the planter of a vineyard eats the fruit of it; and the owner of a flock is supported by selling the milk. The best MSS. omit the word "of" before "fruit." It probably crept into later texts from the occurrence of that word with the "milk"; but a vineyard owner actually eats his fruit, whereas not only would it be strange to speak of "eating" milk, but the owner of flocks would really be sustained chiefly by the sale of the milk and the purchase of food with the money so obtained. He would eat "of" the milk. It is worth noticing that St. Paul never (with the one exception of Acts xx. 28, 29) takes up the image supplied by the Lord Himself of Christ being the Shepherd, and the Church His flock. Even here, where the occurrence of the word "flock" must have suggested it, it is not alluded to. On the other hand, St. Peter's favourite image is that of "the flock." The command, "Feed My flock," would have made it touchingly familiar to him. St. Paul's imagery from nature and country life are on the practical rather than the poetic side; whereas his images from military, political, and social life have the vivid reality which we should expect from one whose life was spent chiefly in towns. It has been observed that St. Paul's vindication falls naturally into three divisions. (1) The argument from induction, verses 1—6; (2) that from analogy, verse 7; (3) that from authority, verse 8.

(8) **Say I these thing as a man?**—He proceeds to show that his appeal is not to a human principle, but to the recognition by men of a principle which is itself divine. The divinely given Law also says these things.

(9) **The ox that treadeth out the corn.**—Better, *the ox while treading out the corn.* In this verse the question of the previous one is answered. The Law does say the same: "For it is written in the Law of Moses," etc. The pointed and emphatic mention of the Law of Moses would give the words great weight with Jewish opponents. On a space of hard ground called a threshing-floor the oxen were driven to and fro over the corn collected there, and thus the separation of the grain from the husk was accomplished.

**Doth God take care for oxen?**—We must not take these and the following words as a denial of the divine regard for the brute creation, which runs through the Mosaic law and is exemplified in Jon. iv. 11, but as an expression of the Apostle's belief as to the ultimate and highest object of God's love. The good which such a provision as the Law achieved for the oxen was nothing compared to the good which it accomplished for man. God did not do this simply as a provision for the ox, but to teach us men humanity—to teach us that it is a divine principle that the labourer should have his reward.

(10) **That he that ploweth should plow in hope.**—There is considerable variation in the MSS. here. The best rendering of the text is, *that the plougher is bound to plough in hope, and the thresher (to thresh) in the hope of having his share.* It has been much discussed whether this passage is to be taken literally as referring to actual ploughing and threshing, or whether we are to give them a spiritual significance. I think it is, perhaps, best to take them literally, as expressing the sanction given by God in the legal provision previously mentioned to the divine principle which unites earthly labour and reward; and the argument, of course, is that this principle applies *à fortiori* to the higher work of a spiritual nature; and this application is brought out clearly in the next verse.

(11) **If we have sown unto you spiritual things.**—The two sentences in this verse contain a striking double antithesis, the "we" and "you" being emphatic, and "spiritual" being opposed to "carnal." The spiritual things are, of course, the things of the Spirit of God, by which their spiritual natures are sustained; the carnal things those which the teachers might expect in return, the ordinary support of their physical nature. The force of the climax will be better realised if we notice that the previous argument proved the right of a labourer to receive a

things,[a] *is it* a great thing if we shall
reap your carnal things? (12) If others
be partakers of *this* power over you, *are*
not we rather?

Chap. ix. 12—27. St. Paul's reason for not availing himself of this right.

Nevertheless we have not used this
power; but suffer all
things, lest we should
hinder the gospel of Christ.
(13) Do ye not know that
they which minister about
holy things live[1] *of the things* of the
temple?[b] and they which wait at the altar
are partakers with the altar. (14) Even so
hath the Lord ordained that they which
preach the gospel should live of the
gospel. (15) But I have used none of
these things: neither have I written
these things, that it should be so done
unto me: for *it were* better for me to
die, than that any man should make
my glorying void.

(16) For though I preach the gospel, I
have nothing to glory of: for necessity
is laid upon me; (yea, woe is unto me,

a Rom. 15. 27.

1 Or, *feed.*

b Deut. 18. 1.

---

remuneration the same in kind as was the quality of his labour. A plougher or a sower would have his reward in a harvest of the same kind as he had sown. That being the principle recognised in civilised life, and sanctioned by the object which the Law of God had in view, the Apostle adds, with a slight touch of sarcasm—Such being an ordinary thing in life, is it a *great* thing for us to have a reward as inferior to our work as carnal things are to spiritual things?

(12) **If others be partakers . . . .**—You do recognise this principle in regard to other teachers, and they actually partake of this right to be supported by you; we, your first teachers, have a stronger right. St. Paul had been literally their "planter" (chap. iii. 6).

**But suffer all things**—*i.e.*, We endure all kinds of hard work and privation rather than use a power which I have demonstrated we possess, and which others actually avail themselves of, lest our doing so might, in a way, hinder the progress of Christ's gospel by giving enemies any even apparent reason for attributing our zeal to unworthy motives.

(13) **Do ye not know.**—The Apostle now turns to appeal to an argument which would have weight with them as Christians. The rights of the ministry to be supported by the Church have already been established by an appeal to ordinary life and to the Jewish law; and the statement has been made that the Apostle having that right, did not, for wise reasons, use it. There is one higher step in the argument. It was not only a principle of Jewish law which Christ might have abrogated, but it was a provision of the Jewish economy which Christ Himself formally perpetuated.

**They which minister . . . .**—Better, *They which minister about the holy things eat from the temple, and they which serve at the altar have their share with the altar.* The first part of this passage refers to the general principle that the priests who were engaged in the Temple services were supported from the various offerings which were brought there, and the second clause more definitely alludes to the particular fact that when a sacrifice was offered on the altar, the sacrificing priests, as well as the altar, had a share of the animal. (See Lev. vi. 16, 26; vii. 6; Num. v.; xviii.; Deut. x. and xviii.) A suggestion that the allusion might be to the custom of the heathen priests is wholly inadmissible, for such would have no force for Christians, and would entirely destroy the sequence of the next verse.

(14) **Even so.**—These words explain why the Apostle again referred to Jewish law, after having in verse 9 already made use of an appeal to the Law as an argument. It is now again referred to only to introduce the crowning argument that Christ Himself perpetuated this law in its application to the Christian ministry. (See Matt. x. 10; Luke x. 7.)

**They which preach the gospel.**—The preaching of the gospel is in the Christian ministry the function which corresponds to the offering of sacrifice in the Jewish priesthood. Bengel well remarks, "If the Mass were a sacrifice, Paul would undoubtedly have accommodated to it the apodosis here."

(15) **But I.**—Again, after the assertion of the right, we have the statement that though he had vindicated the right by the highest and unquestionable authority of Christ Himself, the Apostle had not seen fit to avail himself of it.

**Neither have I written these things.**—Better, *neither am I writing.* The Apostle in these words carefully guards against the possibility of their taking these arguments used here as an indication of any intention on his part to give up now the independent position which he had hitherto assumed.

**It were better for me to die.**—The meaning of these words is evidently that the Apostle would rather die than make void his right to boast or glory in his unremunerated work in the Church—which would be the case if he now or ever condescended to receive, as others did, any support from them. There is, however, a great variety of readings as to the actual mode of expression of this thought. One suggestion is that the words may read thus:—"It were better for me to die than (receive reward from you); no man shall make my ground of boasting void." Another is, "It were better for me to die, rather than any one should make my ground of boasting void." There is great weight in favour of both of these readings. The following have also been suggested as possible readings of the passage:—"It were better for me to die than that my ground of boasting should die; no one shall make it void;" and "It were better for me to die than that my ground of boasting ——; no man shall make it void." In this last case the Apostle pauses in the middle of his impassioned declaration, and leaves the sentence unfinished, as he flings aside the thought that his ground of boasting could be removed, and exclaims earnestly and emphatically, "No man *shall* make it void." Perhaps, on the whole, especially having regard to the character of the writer, this last rendering is most likely to be the true one. In any case, the general drift and meaning of the passage is the same. The Apostle would rather die than lose his ground of boasting, and he boldly asserts his determination to let no one deprive him of it.

(16) **For though I preach the gospel, I have nothing to glory of.**—Better, *For though I preach the gospel, I have no ground of boasting.* St. Paul proceeds now to show how his maintenance by the

if I preach not the gospel!) (17) For if
I do this thing willingly, I have a reward: but if against my will, a dispensation *of the gospel* is committed unto
me. (18) What is my reward then?
*Verily* that, when I preach the gospel, I may make the gospel of Christ without charge, that I abuse not my power in the gospel.

(19) For though I be free from all *men*, yet have I made myself servant unto all, that I might gain the more.
(20) And unto the Jews I became as a Jew, that I might gain the Jews; to them that are under the law, as under the law, that I might gain them that are under the law;
(21) to them that are without law, as without law, (being not without law to God, but under the law to Christ,) that I might gain them that are without law.
(22) To the weak became I as weak, that I might gain the weak: I am made all things to all *men*, that I might by all means save some.

---

Church would deprive him of his right to boast or glory in his work. The mere preaching of the gospel supplies no ground of boasting; it is a necessity; God's woe would await him in the judgment if he did not so. A man can have no ground of boasting in doing that which he *must* do.

(17) **For if I do this thing willingly, I have a reward.**—The previous words, "Yea, woe is unto me if I preach not the gospel," are a parenthesis; and now the writer proves the truth of his assertion—that the necessity of preaching the gospel deprives the mere act itself of any grounds of boasting—by showing that if there were no necessity there would be a ground of boasting. The argument is this:—Suppose it to be otherwise, and that there is no such necessity, then, by voluntarily undertaking it, I have a reward. The undertaking it of my own free will would entitle me to a reward. But if (as is the case) not of my free will, but of necessity, then I am merely a steward—a slave doing his duty (chap. iv. 1; Luke xvii. 7—10).

**A dispensation of the gospel is committed unto me.**—Better, *I am entrusted with a stewardship.*

(18) **What is my reward then?**—It seems better to omit the note of interrogation, and read the whole verse thus:—*What reward then is to be mine, so that* (*i.e.*, which induces me) *in preaching the gospel I make the gospel without charge* (*to my hearers*), *so that I use not my power in the gospel?* The "power" being the right to support maintained in verses 6, 12.

(19) **For.**—The question is here answered. His reward was to gain the greater number of converts—Jews (verse 20), Gentiles (verse 21), weak ones (verse 22). The only reward he sought for or looked for in adopting that course of conduct, for pursuing which they taunted him with selfishness, was, after all, their good.

The word "For," introducing the answer, would seem to imply that the reward must be a greater one. "For" though an Apostle, I became a slave of all that I might gain the greater number. The words "greater number" probably include the two ideas, viz., a greater number than he could have gained had he used his rights as an Apostle, and also a greater number of converts than was gained by any other Apostle.

(20) **And unto the Jews I became as a Jew.**—This and the following verses are a catagorical explanation of the previous statements. They show in detail both how he became the slave of all and the reward he had in view in doing so.

For example, of St. Paul's conformity to Jewish law, see Acts xvi. 3; xviii. 18; xx. 6; xxi. 26.

**To them that are under the law . . . .**—Better, *To them that are under the Law, as under the Law, not being myself under the Law.* These last words are found in all the best MSS., but have been omitted by an oversight of the copyist in the text from which our own translation is made. Those spoken of as "Jews" are, of course, Jews by birth and religion; those "under the Law" are probably proselytes to Judaism. In neither case do they mean Christian converts, for the object of St. Paul's conduct towards those of whom he here speaks was to win them to the Faith of Christ. He himself was no longer "under the Law" being a Christian (Gal. ii. 19).

(21) **To them that are without law**—*i.e.*, the heathen. St. Paul adapted himself to their habits and mode of thought when necessary. He quoted from their literature (Acts xvii. 28); he based an argument on the inscriptions on their altars (Acts xvii. 23); and he did not require them to adopt Jewish ceremonies (Gal. ii. 9, 11). The parenthesis explains in what sense only St. Paul was "without" the Law, so as to prevent the possibility of this statement being used as a justification of lawlessness. As being one with Christ, he was indeed under the law of God as revealed in the person, work, and teaching of the Lord. (See Gal. vi. 2.)

(22) **To the weak.**—We can scarcely take this (as some do) to refer to weak Christians, of whom he has spoken in chap. viii. The whole passage treats of the attitude which the Apostle assumed towards various classes outside the Christian Church, that he might gain them as converts. The words "I became," which have introduced the various classes in verse 20, are here again repeated, and this passage seems to be an explanation and reiteration of what had gone before. "It was to the weak points (not to the strong points) of Jews, proselytes, and Gentiles that I assimilated myself. To the weak ones among all these classes I became weak, that I might gain those weak ones."

**I am made all things to all . . . .**—Better, *I am become all things to all men that I should save at least some.* Although he had thus accommodated himself, so far as was possible, consistently with Christian duty, to the weaknesses of all, he could only hope to win some of them. The natural climax would have been—"I become all things to all men that I might win *all*." But the Apostle's humility could not let him dare to hope for so great a reward as that. All the self-sacrifice he could make was necessary to gain "at all events some," and that would be his ample reward. The word "save" means "win over to Christianity," as in chap. vii. 16, and is used here instead of the previous word "gain," being repeated to prevent any possible perversion of the Apostle's meaning as to "gaining men." His subject was not, as enemies might suggest, to win them to himself—but to Christ.

(23) And this I do for the gospel's
sake, that I might be partaker thereof
with *you.* (24) Know ye not that they
which run in a race run all, but one
receiveth the prize? So run, that ye
may obtain. (25) And every man that
striveth for the mastery is temperate in
all things. Now they *do it* to obtain
a corruptible crown; but we an incor-
ruptible. (26) I therefore so run, not as
uncertainly; so fight I, not as one that
beateth the air: (27) but I keep under
my body, and bring *it* into subjection:
lest that by any means, when I have
preached to others, I myself should be
a castaway.

---

(23) **And this I do . . .**—Better, *And all things I do for the gospel's sake:* such being the reading of the best MSS. Here a new thought is introduced. From them for whom he labours, the Apostle turns for a moment to himself. After all, the highest reward even an Apostle can have is to be a sharer in that common salvation which has been brought to light by the gospel. With argument and illustration, St. Paul had vigorously and unflinchingly maintained the dignity and rights of his office. The pathetic words with which he now concludes show that in defending the dignity of his Apostolate he had not been forgetful of that personal humility which every Christian minister feels more and more deeply in proportion as he realises the greatness of his office.

(24) **Know ye not . . .**—The illustration which follows refers to these Isthmian games (so called from their taking place in the isthmus where Corinth stood) with which his readers would be familiar. These, like the other games of Greece—the Olympian, Pythian, and Nemean—included every form of athletic exercise, and stood on an entirely different footing from anything of the kind in modern times. For the Greek, these contests were great national and religious festivals. None but freemen could enter the lists, and they only after they had satisfied the appointed officers that they had for ten months undergone the necessary preliminary training. For thirty days previous to the contest the candidates had to attend the exercises at the gymnasium, and only after the fulfilment of these conditions were they allowed, when the time arrived, to contend in the sight of assembled Greece. Proclamation was made of the name and country of each competitor by a herald. The victor was crowned with a garland of pine leaves or ivy. The family of the conqueror was honoured by his victory, and when he returned to his native town he would enter it through a breach in the walls, the object of this being to symbolise that for a town which was honoured with such a citizen no walls of defence were needful (Plutarch). Pindar, or some other great poet, would immortalise the victorious hero's name in his verse, and in all future festivals the foremost seats would be occupied by the heroes of former contests.

**So run**—*i.e.,* run in the way referred to, so that you may gain a prize.

(25) **Every man that striveth for the mastery.**—Better, *Every one that enters into the contest.* The Greek word (*agonizomenos*) is identical with the English "agonise." Hence the use in devotional works of the phrase "to agonise in prayer," etc.

**Is temperate in all things.**—He fulfils not only some, but all of the necessary preliminary conditions. He indulges self in no way.

**They do it to obtain a corruptible crown.**—There are two striking points of contrast between the earthly race and the spiritual course. There is but one obtains a reward in the earthly contest; none need fail of it in the heavenly race. That reward in the one case is perishable; in the other it is imperishable. If, then—such is St. Paul's argument—men show such extraordinary devotion and self-sacrifice for a reward which is merely perishable, and which each has only a chance of gaining, what should not be the devotion and self-sacrifice of those for all of whom an imperishable reward is certain!

(26) **I therefore so run.**—The Apostle appeals to his own conduct as an illustration of the lesson which he is teaching, and by means of it reminds the reader that the whole of this chapter has been a vindication of his own self-denial, and that he has a clear and definite object in view.

**So fight I.**—The illustration is changed from running to boxing, both being included in the word used in verse 25, "contending." He has an adversary to contend against, and he strikes him, and does not wildly and impotently strike at him, and so only beat the air.

(27) **But I keep under my body.**—Better, *but I bruise my body.* The word is very strong, and implies to beat the flesh until it becomes black and blue. The only other place the word occurs is in Luke xviii. 5. The body is spoken of as his adversary, or the seat of those lusts and appetites which "war against the mind" (Rom. vii. 23; Gal. v. 17).

**Bring it into subjection.**—Better, *and make it a slave.* The idea is carried on that the body is not only conquered, but led captive. We must remember that the language all throughout this passage is figurative, and the statement here refers, not to the infliction of actual pain on the body, but to the subduing of the appetites and passions which are located in it. The true position of our natural appetites is that they should be entirely our servants, and not our masters; that we "should not follow or be led by them," but that they should follow and be led by us.

**Lest that by any means.**—Better, *lest having been a herald to others, I myself should be rejected.* The image is carried on, and the Apostle says that he has a further motive to live a life of self-denial—viz., that he having acted as a herald, proclaiming the conditions of the contest and the requisite preliminaries for it, should not be found to have himself fulfilled them. It is the same image kept up still of this race, and of the herald who announced the name of the victor, and the fact that he had fulfilled the necessary conditions. It was not the custom for the herald to join in the contest, but the Apostle was himself *both* a runner in the Christian course, and a herald of the conditions of that race to others. Hence, naturally, he speaks of the two characters, which in the actual illustration would be distinct, as united in one when applied spiritually to himself. The word "cast away" conveys a wrong impression. The Greek word signifies one who had not behaved according to the prescribed regulations.

Chap. x. 1—xi. 1. Further warning and direction regarding the eating of meat offered to idols.

A.D. 59.

CHAPTER X.—(1) Moreover, brethren,
I would not that ye should
be ignorant, how that all
our fathers were under the
cloud, and all passed
through the sea; (2) and
were all baptized unto Moses in the
cloud and in the sea; (3) and did all eat
the same spiritual meat; (4) and did all
drink the same spiritual drink: for they
drank of that spiritual Rock that followed [1] them: and that Rock was Christ.
(5) But with many of them God was not
well pleased: for they were overthrown

[1] Or, *went with them.*

---

## X.

(1) **Moreover, brethren, . . . .**—Better, *For I would not, brethren, that you should be ignorant.* From the strong statement of personal self-distrust with which the previous chapter concludes, the Apostle now passes on to show that Jewish history contains solemn examples of the falling-away of those who seemed to stand strong in divine favour and privilege. The same kind of dangers still beset God's people, but they will never be greater than the strength which God will give to bear them. These thoughts are then applied to the immediate subject in hand, viz., the partaking of meat which had been used in the heathen temples. The subject is, as it were, taken up from chap. viii. 13, where an expression of personal willingness to forego a right, led the writer aside to the subject which occupies chap. ix. Uniting chap. xi., 1, with the last verse of this chapter, the general outline of the argument is as follows:—

- Chap. x. 1—11. The history of the Jewish Church contains examples which ought to be warnings against self-confidence.
- Verses 12—14. These thoughts should make the Christians distrustful of themselves, but not hopeless.
- Verses 15—17. The unity of the Christian body with Christ, as expressed and realised in the Holy Communion, renders impossible a communion of the same body with the objects of idolatrous worship.
- Verses 18—22. Any partaking of idolatrous feasts would involve union to such extent as would compromise, just as Israel's partaking of sacrifical offerings involved union with the altar of Jehovah.
- Verse 23—chap. xi. 1. An enunciation of the principles deduced from the foregoing considerations which should guide the Corinthian Christians in their partaking of meat which might have been offered to idols.

**That ye should be ignorant.**—The thought here is not that his readers were at all likely to be ignorant of the mere historical fact which he now recalls, and with which they were doubtless quite familiar, but that they were probably unmindful of the spiritual lessons which are to be learnt from such a grouping of the facts as the Apostle now gives, and of the striking contrast between the enjoyment of great privileges by *all* (five times emphatically repeated) and the apostacy of the greater part of them. The Apostle assumes their familiarity with the facts referred to, and does not feel it needful to mention that of the "all," literally only two (Joshua and Caleb) gained the ultimate approval of Jehovah.

**Our fathers.**—These words need not limit the reference of this teaching to the Jewish Christians only. It would include all Christians by right of spiritual descent.

(2) **Were all baptized unto Moses.**—The weight of evidence is in favour of the middle voice for the verb here used; signifying that they all voluntarily had themselves baptised to Moses. Moses was God's representative under the Law, and so they were baptised unto him in their voluntarily joining with that "Church" of God which marched beneath the shadow of the cloud, and passed through the waters of the sea—as Christians, are baptised unto Jesus Christ,—He being (in a higher sense both in kind and in degree) God's representative in the New Dispensation.

The "cloud" and the "sea" refer to the cloud that overshadowed the Israelites (Ex. xiii. 21, and see Num. xiv. 14), and the passage through the Red Sea (Ex. xiv. 32; Num. xxxv. 8).

(3) **Spiritual meat.**—The manna (Ex. xvi. 13) was not natural food, for it was not produced in the natural way, but it was supplied by the Spirit and power of God. Bread from earth would be natural bread, but this was bread from heaven (John vi. 31). Our Lord (John vi. 50) had already made the Christian Church familiar with the "true bread," of which that food had been the typical forecast.

(4) **That spiritual Rock that followed them.**—There was a Jewish tradition that the Rock—*i.e.,* a fragment broken off from the rock smitten by Moses—followed the Israelites through their journey, and St. Paul, for the purpose of illustration, adopts that account instead of the statement in Num. xx. 11. The emphatic repetition of the word "spiritual" before "drink" and "rock" reminds the reader that it is the spiritual and not the historic aspect of the fact which is present to St. Paul's mind. The traditional account of the Rock was a more complete illustration of the abiding presence of God, which was the point that the Apostle here desires to bring forward.

**And that Rock was Christ.**—As Christ was "God manifest in the flesh" in the New Dispensation, so God manifest in the Rock (the source of sustaining life) was the Christ of the Old Dispensation. The Jews had become familiar with the thought of God as a Rock. (See 1 Sam. ii. 2; Ps. xci. 12; Isa. xxxii. 2.) Though the Jews may have recognised the Rock poetically as God, they knew not that it was, as a manifestation of God's presence, typical of *the* manifestation which was yet to be given in the Incarnation. Such seems to be the force of the statement and of the word "But" which emphatically introduces it. *But* though they thought it only a Rock, or applied the word poetically to Jehovah, that Rock *was* Christ.

(5) **But with many of them.**—Better, *Nevertheless not with the greater part of them was God pleased.* This introduces the point from which the Apostle seeks to draw the great lesson of self-distrust. *All* had *all* these privileges—privileges of a baptism and a spiritual meat and drink which correspond with the sacramental ordinances which are proofs and pledges of all the privileges of us Christians—and yet with the greater part—in fact, with all except two—of

in the wilderness. (6) Now these things
were our examples,[1] to the intent we
should not lust after evil things, as they
also lusted. (7) Neither be ye idolaters,
as *were* some of them; as it is written,
The people sat down to eat and drink,[a]
and rose up to play. (8) Neither let us
commit fornication, as some of them
committed, and fell in one day three
and twenty thousand.[b] (9) Neither let
us tempt Christ, as some of them also
tempted, and were destroyed of ser-
pents.[c] (10) Neither murmur ye, as some
of them also murmured, and were de-
stroyed of the destroyer.[d] (11) Now all
these things happened unto them for

1 Gr. *our figures.*
*b* Num. 25. 9.
*c* Num. 21. 6.
*a* Ex. 32. 6; Ps. 106. 14.
*d* Num. 14. 37.

---

that vast multitude God was not pleased, as is proved by the fact that (Num. xiv. 16) all except Caleb and Joshua perished in the wilderness.

(6) **Now these things were our examples.**—Better, *Now these things were types of us.* "Now" introduces the contrast between the physical Israel and the spiritual Israel, between the physical death which befel the majority of the former, and the spiritual death which, if privileges be neglected or abused, must befal the latter.

**To the intent.**—St. Paul regards everything that has happened in history as having a divine purpose of blessing for others. All this material suffering on their part will not be in vain if it teaches us the spiritual lesson which God would have us learn from it.

**We should not lust after evil things.**—The Apostle now sets forth the causes with which the majority of the Israelities neutralised the great advantages in which all had shared. The lusting after evil things must be taken as applying to their general conduct (evidenced especially in the circumstances mentioned in Num. xi. 4, 18). "As they also" directly connects the sins which the Corinthians were in danger of with the sins which led to the overthrow of the Israelites. The idolatry and eating and drinking and committing fornication all refer to kinds of sin which the Corinthians were liable to commit if they did not keep themselves perfectly distinct from the heathen. (See chap. vi. 12.)

(8) **And fell in one day three and twenty thousand.**—In Num. xxv. 9 the statement is that twenty-four thousand perished. Various and ingenious attempts have been made to reconcile these two accounts of the actual numbers. The explanation most in harmony with the character of the writer, and the utterly unessential nature of the point historically, is, I venture to think, that either the Apostle quoted from memory a fact of no great importance, or else that he referred for his figures to some copy of the LXX., in which the numbers might be specified as here.

(9) **Neither let us tempt Christ.**—Better, *Neither let us tempt the Lord, as some of them tempted, and perished by serpents.* There is much controversy as to whether the word here is "God" or "Christ" or "the Lord," each having a certain amount of MS. support. On the whole, the reading here adopted (the Lord) seems from internal evidence to have been most likely the true reading. It is possible that the word "God" crept into the text, having been put as a marginal explanation to get over the supposed difficulty involved in applying the words which follow, "they also tempted," to Christ. For in what sense could it have been said that the Israelites tempted Christ? There is no reason, however, for connecting "some of them tempted" (the word "also" is not in the original) with the object of the previous clause: and it is noticeable that the second word translated "tempted" is not the same as the first. "Let us not tempt" is in the original an intensified form of the verb which is used in its simple form in "some of them tempted." The reading "Christ" may have come into the text as being an explanation that by the word "Lord" St. Paul meant the Redeemer.

The real meaning of the passage, however, is evident. The Israelites had, by their longing after the things left behind in Egypt, tried God so that God had asserted Himself in visiting them with punishment, and so Christians must be on their guard, with such a warning before them, not to tempt their Lord by hankering after those worldly and physical pleasures from which He by His death has delivered them. (See Num. xxi. 4—6.) Some of the Corinthian Christians seemed by their conduct, as regards eating and drinking and indulging in sensuality, to long for that liberty in reference to things which they had enjoyed before conversion, instead of enjoying these spiritual blessings and feeding on the spiritual sustenance which Christ had provided for them.

**Were destroyed of serpents.**—Better, *and were destroyed by the serpents.* The article before "serpents" indicates that the reference is to a particular and well known fact.

(10) **Neither murmur ye.**—The reference here is to Num. xvi. 41—47, and the historical event alluded to—viz., the murmuring of the Israelites against their God-given leaders, Moses and Aaron—is analogous to the murmuring of the Corinthians against their Apostle, St. Paul. It is noticeable that St. Paul attributes the death of the people to the Destroyer—*i.e.*, God's messenger sent to destroy—while in Numbers they are said to have perished by the "plague." Every pestilence that swept over nations to purify them was a messenger from God. Thus in Ps. lxxviii. 50 God is said to give "their life over to the pestilence," which in Ex. xii. 23 is spoken of as "the destroyer."

(11) **Happened unto them for ensamples.**—Better, *happened unto them typically; and it was written for our admonition.* The verb "happened" is plural, referring to the multiplied occurrences which the Apostle has just mentioned; but "written" is singular, referring to the sacred record in which the historical facts are handed down. The Apostle does not state that the purpose which God had in view in allowing these sins and judgments was that they might serve "for ensamples" for after-generations, as may at first sight seem to be the meaning of the English, but the real point of the passage is—These things which occurred to them are to be looked upon by us, not merely as interesting historical events, but as having a typical significance. Their record remains as a standing warning that great privileges may be enjoyed by many, and used by them to their destruction. The temporal blessings of the Jewish nation foreshadow the greater spiritual blessings of the Christian Church.

**The ends of the world.**—Better, *the ends of the ages* (Matt. xiii. 39).

ensamples[1]: and they are written for
our admonition, upon whom the ends of
the world are come.
(12) Wherefore let him that thinketh
he standeth take heed lest he fall.
(13) There hath no temptation taken
you but such as is common[2] to man:
but God *is* faithful, who will not
suffer you to be tempted above that
ye are able; but will with the temptation
also make a way to escape, that
ye may be able to bear *it*. (14) Wherefore,
my dearly beloved, flee from
idolatry.
(15) I speak as to wise men; judge ye
what I say. (16) The cup of blessing
which we bless, is it not the communion
of the blood of Christ? The bread
which we break, is it not the communion
of the body of Christ? (17) For
we *being* many are one bread, *and* one
body: for we are all partakers of that
one bread.
(18) Behold Israel after the flesh: are

1 Or, *types.*

2 Or, *moderate.*

---

(12) **Wherefore.**—This is the practical conclusion of the whole matter. We are to look back on that strange record of splendid privilege and of terrible fall and learn from it the solemn lesson of self-distrust. Led forth by divinely appointed leaders, overshadowed by the Divine Presence, supported by divinely given food and drink, the vast hosts of Israel had passed from the bondage of Egypt into the glorious liberty of children of the living God; yet amid all those who seemed to stand so secure in their relation to God, but a few fell not. Christians, called forth from a more deadly bondage into a more glorious liberty, are in like peril. Let the one who thinks that he stands secure take great heed, lest he fall. The murmuring against their apostolic teachers, the longing to go so far as they could in indulgence without committing actual sin, were terribly significant indications in the Corinthian Church. When we feel ourselves beginning to dislike those who warn us against sin, and when we find ourselves measuring with minute casuistry what is the smallest distance that we can place between ourselves and some desired object of indulgence without actually sinning, then "let him that thinketh he standeth take heed lest he fall."

(13) **There hath no temptation taken you.**—What is meant by a "temptation common to man" (or rather, *suited to man*) is explained further on as a temptation which one is "able to bear." From the warning and exhortation of the previous verse the Apostle passes on to words of encouragement, "You need not be hopeless or despairing." God permits the temptation by allowing the circumstances which create temptation to arise, but He takes care that no Fate bars the path of retreat. With each temptation he makes a way to escape from it. And that is so, must be so, because God is faithful. The state of salvation to which God has called us would be a delusion if there were an insuperable difficulty to our continuing in it. We have in this verse, perhaps, the most practical and therefore the clearest exposition to be found of the doctrine of free-will in relation to God's overruling power. God makes an open road, but then man himself must *walk* in it. God controls circumstances, but man uses them. That is where *his* responsibility lies.

(14) **Wherefore, my dearly beloved, flee from idolatry.**—These words show that through all the previous argument and warning the writer had in view the particular dangers arising from their contact with the heathen world, and especially the partaking in the sacrificial feasts. Not because they were enemies, but because they are his "beloved" he had written thus to them. Because God is a faithful God—because He makes it possible for you to escape these dangers and sins—*flee* from idolatry. Do not be trying how *near* you can get *to* it, but rather how *far* you can get *from* it.

(15) **I speak as to wise men.**—These words are not hypothetical; they imply the point of view from which the Apostle is now regarding his readers—viz., competent to recognise the force of his argument. Having warned them against any participation in idolatry, even such as would be involved in joining in the sacrificial feasts, as dangerous to themselves, he now proceeds to show that such a participation would be derogatory to, and incompatible with, their union with Christ. The identity and intimacy of that union is first established by a reference to the Holy Communion, in partaking of which both the unity of the Church and its union with Christ are vividly expressed.

(16) **The cup of blessing which we bless.**—In other passages the cup is mentioned after the bread, and not, as here, before it. The order in which they are placed here has been variously accounted for, as arising either (Stanley) from the analogy to the heathen feasts, in which the libation came before the food, or (Meyer) because the Apostle intends to dwell at greater length upon the bread. The use of the plural "we," in reference to both the blessing of the cup and the breaking of the bread, clearly indicates that it was in virtue of his representing the entire company present, and not as individually possessed of some miraculous gift, that the one who presided at a Communion performed the act of consecration. On the whole subject of the Eucharistic feasts in Corinth, see Notes on chap. xi. 17. Communion with the body and blood of Christ is established and asserted in this partaking of the bread and of the cup.

(17) **For we being many are one bread.**—Better, *For it is one bread, and we, the many, are one body, for we all take a portion of that one bread.* This verse explains how "the breaking" of the bread was the significant act which expressed sacramentally the communion of the body of Christ. There is one bread, it is broken into many pieces, and as we all (though each receives only a fragment) partake of the one bread which unbroken consisted of these pieces, we though many individuals are one body, even the Body of Christ with whom, as well as with each other, we have communion in that act.

(18) **Behold Israel after the flesh**—*i.e.*, Israel in its merely human aspect, not the spiritual Israel (Rom. ii. 28; Gal. iv. 29; vi. 16). The sacrifice was divided—a portion offered upon the altar and a portion taken and eaten (Deut. xii. 18; xvi. 11): so whoever ate a

not they which eat of the sacrifices par-
takers of the altar? (19) What say I
then? that the idol is any thing, or that
which is offered in sacrifice to idols is
any thing? (20) But *I say*, that the
things which the Gentiles sacrifice,[a]
they sacrifice to devils, and not to God:
and I would not that ye should have
fellowship with devils. (21) Ye cannot
drink the cup of the Lord, and the cup
of devils: ye cannot be partakers of the
Lord's table, and of the table of devils.
(22) Do we provoke the Lord to jealousy?
are we stronger than he?
(23) All things are lawful for me, but
all things are not expedient: all things
are lawful for me, but all things edify
not. (24) Let no man seek his own, but
every man another's *wealth*.
(25) Whatsoever is sold in the shambles,
*that* eat, asking no question for con-
science sake: (26) for the earth *is* the

[a] Deut. 32. 17; Ps. 106. 37.

---

portion of the same sacrifice was a partaker in common *with* (not "of," as in the English translation) the altar. This is another argument against partaking of the heathen feasts. You cannot do so without connection with the heathen altar. The example of Israel proves that.

(19) **What say I then?**—It might have been argued from the preceding verse that the Apostle admitted the heathen offerings and the idols to which they were offered to be as real as were the offerings and Being to whom the altar was erected by Israel, whereas in chap. viii. 4 he had asserted the contrary.

(20) **But I say.**—Better, *No; but that the things which they sacrifice they sacrifice to devils, and not to God.*

The word "devils" means evil spirits. The heathen world is regarded by the Christian Church as under the dominion of the Evil Spirit and his emissaries (Eph. ii. 2; vi. 12), and in reminding the Corinthians that in Israel an eater of the sacrificial meat became a partaker with the altar of God, the Apostle meant to warn them that they would, if they partook of sacrificial meats offered on an altar of devils, become a sharer with that altar and the beings to whom the altar appertained.

(21, 22) **Ye cannot . . .**—Here follows the special reason why the Apostle desires them not to partake of the wine poured forth in libation to devils, or the table on which meat sacrificed to these devils was spread out as food. Such would deprive them of their participation in the cup of the Lord and the table on which the Lord's Supper was placed. Of course the impossibility was moral, not physical. So the Apostle adds the warning question, Do you in fact do so? Do you do that which is morally impossible, and so provoke the jealousy of our jealous God, who will have no divided allegiance? Surely we are not stronger than He? To such a question there can be but one answer. These words, which are the climax of the argument, are naturally suggested by the passage in Deuteronomy (xxxii. 15—18), which was evidently in the Apostle's mind all through this argument, containing as it does the striking words, "Rock of his salvation." "They sacrifice unto devils and not to God," and "they provoked Him to jealousy."

(23) **All things are lawful for me.**—The Apostle now proceeds to conclude, with some practical direction and advice, the question of the eating of meat offered to idols, from which immediate subject the strong expression of personal feeling in chap. viii. 13 had led him to branch off into the various aspects of collateral matters which have occupied him since, and to which the subject treated of in verses 14—22 of this chapter naturally lead back the thoughts of the writer. He repeats here the great principle of Christian liberty, "All things are lawful for me" (see chap. vi. 12), but insists, as before, that its application must be limited by a regard (1) to the effect which each action has upon ourselves, and (2) its influence on the Church at large. "Does this act tend to my own spiritual profit? Does it tend to build up others?" should be the practical rules of Christian life.

(24) **But every man another's wealth.**—Better, *but each one another's good.* The English word "wealth" has, in process of time, come to bear a limited significance, such as did not originally belong to it. By "wealth" we now mean temporal possessions or advantage; it originally meant "good," including more especially "moral welfare," as in the collect for the Queen in the Prayer Book, "Grant her in health and wealth long to live."

(25) **Whatsoever is sold in the shambles.**—Here is the practical application of the principle laid down. When a Christian sees meat exposed for sale in the public market let him buy it and eat it; he need not ask any question to satisfy his conscience on the subject. Some of the meat which had been used for sacrificial purposes was afterwards sold in the markets. The weaker Christians feared lest if they unconsciously bought and ate some of that meat they would become thereby defiled. The Apostle's view is that when once sent into the public market it becomes simply meat, and its previous use gives it no significance. You buy it as meat, and not as part of a sacrifice. Thus the advice here is not at variance with the previous argument in verses 20, 21. The act which is there condemned as a "partaking of the table of devils" is the eating of sacrificial meat at one of the feasts given in the court of the heathen temple, when the meat was avowedly and significantly a portion of the sacrifice. The words "for conscience sake" have been variously interpreted as meaning, (1) Enter into no inquiry, so that your conscience may not be troubled, as it would be if you learned that the meat had been used for sacrifice; or, (2) Ask no question, lest some weak person's conscience be defiled if they hear that it is sacrificial meat and yet see you eat it. This latter interpretation must be rejected, as the Apostle clearly points out in verse 28 that he has been here speaking of the person's own conscience, and only there proceeds to speak of a brother's conscience.

(26) **The earth is the Lord's . . . .**—All food that earth brings forth or nourishes is God's gift, and therefore good. It was merely when regarded as an actual sacrifice that any meat could be considered that "of devils." This great truth, recognised in the Old Testament as well as in the New, is the reason of the previous statement that conscience need not come into the matter at all.

Lord's,[a] and the fulness thereof. (27) If
any of them that believe not bid you *to*
*a feast*, and ye be disposed to go; what-
soever is set before you, eat, asking no
question for conscience sake. (28) But
if any man say unto you, This is offered
in sacrifice unto idols, eat not for his
sake that shewed it, and for conscience
sake: for the earth *is* the Lord's,[b] and
the fulness thereof: (29) conscience, I
say, not thine own, but of the other:
for why is my liberty judged of another
*man's* conscience? (30) For if I by grace[1]
be a partaker, why am I evil spoken of
for that for which I give thanks?

(31) Whether therefore ye eat, or drink,
or whatsoever ye do, do all to the glory
of God. (32) Give none offence, neither
to the Jews, nor to the Gentiles,[2] nor to
the church of God: (33) even as I please
all *men* in all *things*, not seeking mine
own profit, but the *profit* of many, that
they may be saved.

CHAPTER XI.—(1) Be ye followers
of me, even as I also *am* of Christ.

(2) Now I praise you,
brethren, that ye remem-
ber me in all things, and
keep the ordinances,[3] as I

Chap. xi. 2—16. The duty of women to cover their heads in public.

a Deut. 10. 14; Ps. 24. 1.

2 Gr. *Greeks.*

b Deut. 10. 14; Ps. 24. 1.

A.D. 59.

1 Or, *thanksgiving.*

3 Or, *traditions.*

---

(27) **If any of them that believe not . . . .**—How should a Christian act if a heathen friend invited him to a feast? Should he inquire whether there was any sacrificial meat at the feast, and so avoid eating it? No. The same principle applies here—no question need be asked.

(28) **But if any man . . . .**—If, however, some weak brother present points out that it is sacrificial meat, do not eat for his sake and for conscience sake (see verse 29). Here your personal liberty is to be modified by the principle mentioned in verse 24. If the weak brother see you eat the flesh which he has just informed you was used as a sacrifice, he may be led by your example to eat it himself, though the very fact of his having called your attention to it showed that he thinks it wrong, and so his conscience is defiled.

The word (*hierothuton*) here used (according to the best MSS.) for "offered to an idol" is different from the condemnatory word (*eidolothuton*) elsewhere used; as natural courtesy would lead a Christian at the table of a heathen to use an epithet which would not be offensive to his host. A lesson in controversy—Don't conceal your conscientious convictions, but don't express them in language unnecessarily painful to your opponent.

The repetition of the words "The earth is the Lord's," &c., in this verse is an interpolation not found in the best MSS., and tends to interrupt the thought which is carried on in verse 29.

(29) **Conscience, I say, not thine own, but of the other.**—In the previous verse there is nothing to indicate that the obligation not to eat the meat under such circumstances arises from a consideration of the tenderness of the other's conscience. Here any danger of mistake as to whose conscience is meant is removed. Of course (says St. Paul) I mean *his* conscience, not *yours*. For no other man's scruples are to bind my conscience. While the opinion or weakness of another is never to make my conscience waver from what it knows to be true, it may often be a reason for our sacrificing in act some personal indulgence.

(30) **For if I by grace be a partaker.**—Better, *If I thankfully partake, why am I evil spoken of for that for which I give thanks?* Such a question might be asked by some who object to the restriction on their liberty which the advice just given implies. To the querulous objector the Apostle gives no definitely limited reply. He lays down in the following verses the great principles which should guide all Christian life, and by which therefore every detail of it should be regulated.

(31) **Whether therefore ye eat, or drink, or whatsoever ye do.**—These words embrace all life. The definite acts of eating and drinking are mentioned expressly as they are the subject immediately under consideration. They are, however, to be regulated by the same principle which guides all true life. The modern idea of some acts being religious and some secular is neither here nor elsewhere recognised by St. Paul. No act of life is in itself either religious or secular. The quality of each act depends on the spirit which guides it, and the motive from which it springs. The commonest thing may be done in a high Christian spirit. The greatest deed may spring from a low and selfish motive. A religious act done in a secular spirit is secular. A secular thing done in a religious spirit is religious. This is "the great first principle" of Christian life.

(32) **Give none offence.**—A practical test of whether any course of conduct is to the glory of God. If it cause any human being to offend then it is not to God's glory. Heretofore St. Paul had spoken only of the edification of the Christian Church, and the avoidance of any offence to a Christian brother. Here the sphere of moral obligation is enlarged. Jew and Greek, as well as the Christian Church, are to be objects of our Christian solicitude.

(33) **Even as I please all men . . .**—Better, *even as I in all things am seeking to please all men, not seeking my own profit, but that of the many*—*i.e.*, the whole great mass of men, and not, as the English seems to imply, merely "a great number." This is the same idea as "I am made all things to all men." (See chap. ix. 22.)

With the last verse of this chapter we must connect the first verse of chap. xi., "Become imitators of me, even as I am of Christ." This is the completion of the exhortation. The Apostle refers to his own example, but only to lead his readers up to Christ as the great example of One "who pleased not Himself" (Rom. xv. 3). His own example is valuable inasmuch as it is the example of one who is striving to conform to the image of his Lord. With the mention of the holiest Example and the most sacred Name, the whole of this argument and exhortation reaches its natural climax and conclusion.

XI.

(1) **Be ye followers of me.**—See concluding Note on chap. x.

(2) **Now I praise you.**—A new subject is here introduced, and occupies to verse 16. The exhortation

delivered *them* to you. (3) But I would have you know, that the head of every man is Christ; and the head of the woman *is* the man; and the head of Christ *is* God. (4) Every man praying or prophesying, having *his* head covered, dishonoureth his head. (5) But every woman that prayeth or prophesieth with *her* head uncovered dishonoureth her head: for that is even all one as if she

---

of the previous verse probably recalled to the Apostle's mind that to a certain extent the Corinthians did follow his teaching and example; and had possibly in their letter, to which he was now replying, boasted of their obedience. The rebuke which he is about to administer is, with characteristic courtesy, introduced with words of commendation. While there is a likeness in form in the original in the words "imitators" and "remember," the latter is weaker in its significance. He exhorts them to be "imitators." He praises them only for bearing him in mind in all things to the extent of obeying certain practical directions which he had given them. The word "ordinances," or *traditions*, here refers to matters of Christian discipline (as in Acts xvi. 4; 2 Thess. iii. 6).

(3) **But I would have you know.**—After the general commendation in the previous verse, the reproof for neglecting, or desiring to neglect, his precepts in one particular case, is thus introduced. The subject treated of, viz., the uncovering of their heads by women in assemblies for worship, was of ephemeral moment, and as we all now would regard it, of trivial importance. Every circumstance, however, which could in the least degree cause the principles of Christianity to be perverted or misunderstood by the heathen world was of vital importance in those early days of the Church, and hence we find the Apostle, who most fearlessly taught the principles of Christian liberty, condemning most earnestly every application of those principles which might be detrimental to the best interests of the Christian faith. To feel bound to assert your liberty in every detail of social and political life is to cease to be free—the very liberty becomes a bondage.

**The head of every man is Christ.**—The Apostle does not merely treat of the outward practice on which his advice has been sought, but proceeds to lay down the principles which are opposed to the principle of that absolute and essential equality, which, found its expression and assertion in the practice of women uncovering their heads in public assemblies.

The allusion here is not to Christ as the Head of the whole human race and of all things (as in Eph. i. 22; Col. i. 16; ii. 10), but as the Head of "the Body," the Christian Church: and this thought introduces the general argument regarding the practical subordination of woman, by reminding the Corinthians that though there is in the Church a perfect spiritual equality (as taught in Gal. iii. 28), yet that it is an equality which is of order and not of disorder—that it is an equality which can only be preserved by remembering that each is not an isolated irresponsible atom, but a part of an organic whole. There is a Head to the Church, therefore it is not a machine composed of various parts, but a body consisting of various members. As there is a subordination of the whole body to Christ, so there is in that body a subordination of woman to man. The last clause, "the Head of Christ is God," gives (as is St. Paul's custom, see chaps. iii. 23; viii. 6; xv. 25) completeness to the thought. As the Head of the Church—*i.e.*, as the man Christ Jesus—Christ is subordinate to the Father, and, indeed, perhaps the idea is carried farther into the mystery of the divine nature itself, as consisting of three Persons co-eternal and co-equal, yet being designated with an unvarying sequence as "first," and "second," and "third."

(4) **Every man praying or prophesying.**—The reference here is to public prayer and teaching (the word "prophesying" is used in its less restricted sense). The Apostle probably does not allude to any case in Corinth where a man had actually taken part in a religious meeting with covered head. The Greek practice was for men to have their heads uncovered when joining in religious ceremonies (Grotius *in loc.*). To this practice St. Paul would incline, as being the national custom of the country, and as also being typical of the distinction between the sexes which he has just laid down. The Apostle's teaching on this subject is a remarkable illustration of how completely he had overcome his old Jewish prejudice, and how the whole of his nature had become leavened with the freedom of the gospel—for it was the custom amongst the Jews for the man to pray with covered head, and the face veiled with the *Tallith*, as an expression of his unworthiness to speak face to face with God. It was a profound insight into human nature which enabled the Apostle to realise how an external symbol would infallibly tend to modify doctrine, and how thus the perpetuating of such a custom in the Christian Church might have hindered the full recognition of the great truth of the personal and direct communication of every individual soul with the Father.

**Dishonoureth his head.**—He dishonours his own head inasmuch as it is the part of his body from which Christ has taken His title as "Head of the Body," the Church—and thus he dishonours his Spiritual Head, even Christ.

(5) **But every woman that prayeth . . .** From the hypothetical case of the man praying or preaching with covered head (which was mentioned first for the sake of introducing the antithesis), the Apostle comes now to the actual case of which he has to treat, viz., the woman uncovering her head. At first sight the permission here implied for a woman to pray and teach in public may seem at variance with the teaching in chap. xiv. 34, where she is commanded to observe silence, and the injunction in 1 Tim., ii. 12, that women should not "teach." In these passages, however, it is the public meeting of the whole Church that is spoken of, and in such the women were to be silent—but the meetings spoken of here, though public as distinguished from the private devotions of individuals, were probably only smaller gatherings such as are indicated in Rom. xiv. 5; Col. iv. 5; Philem. verse 2. It has been suggested by some writers that the command in chap. xiv. 34, does forbid the practice which is here assumed to be allowable only for the sake of argument; but surely St. Paul would not have occupied himself and his readers here with the elaborate, and merely forensic discussion of the conditions under which certain functions were to be performed which he was about subsequently to condemn, as not allowable under any restriction whatever?

**Dishonoureth her head.**—Both among Jews and Greeks the long tresses of a woman were her glory

were shaven. (6) For if the woman be not covered, let her also be shorn: but if it be a shame for a woman to be shorn or shaven, let her be covered. (7) For a man indeed ought not to cover *his* head, forasmuch as he is the image and glory of God: but the woman is the glory of the man. (8) For the man is not of the woman; but the woman of the man. (9) Neither was the man created for the woman; but the woman for the man. (10) For this cause ought the woman to

Only in times of mourning (Deut. xxi. 12), or when convicted of shameful sin, was a woman to have her hair cut short.

Here, again, the word "head" must be taken in its double significance. A woman with uncovered head dishonours that head itself by making it thus in the sight of others the type of a shame which is really not hers, and as her head typically is her husband, so she dishonours him also.

(6) **Let her also be shorn.**—The force of this argument depends on the fact that a woman's head being uncovered would be regarded by others as implying the same shame as was indicated by a woman's hair being cut short (*i.e.*, shorn), or altogether removed (*i.e.*, shaven). It is as if the Apostle said—If a woman insists on her right to pray and speak in an assembly with uncovered head, let her carry out this principle to its logical result; let her insist on her right to have her hair cut short, so as to show her equality with man—and what would be thought of her then! No woman with a spark of shame in her would think of doing that. Accordingly you admit that this principle of sexual equality does not apply in all such matters; and it is illogical to argue in favour of any general principle as if it were of universal obligation, when you yourselves admit that it is not applicable in some cases.

(7) **For a man indeed.**—In verses 4—7 the argument against the woman's head being uncovered was based upon (*a*) the woman's relation to man, and (*b*) the man's relation to Christ in the Church. In the three following verses, 7, 8, and 9, the ground of the argument is changed, and the same conclusion is arrived at from a review of (*a*) the woman's relation to man, and (*b*) man's relation to God in the physical Creation. The external form of this argument is the same as that adopted previously. The Apostle first states what the man must not do, and then conversely what the woman must do. The Apostle here takes up the order of creation mentioned in Gen. i. and ii., and the argument runs thus:—Man was made in the image of God, and is the glory of God; but woman is the glory of the man (for woman was made out of man, and also man was not created *for* woman, but woman for—*i.e.*, as a help-meet for—man). Therefore man, as a created being, according to the accepted order of creation, is the direct representative of God, and woman the direct representative of man (and only indirectly and through him of God). The spiritual equality of man and wife does not upset this relationship, and therefore an attempt to destroy the outward expression of it is to be condemned, as it would soon lead to an obliteration of the fact itself.

It is to be remembered all through this passage (and it gives a further emphasis to the allusion to Adam and Eve) that St. Paul is only speaking of married women—it is most unlikely that any case had occurred of an unmarried woman attempting such an outrage upon social feeling and national custom. The Greek women when in public (except those of avowedly bad character) either wore a veil or drew the *peplum*, or shawl, over their heads.

(10) **For this cause ought the woman to have power on her head.**—The two clauses which compose this verse are, perhaps, the two most difficult passages in the New Testament, and, accordingly, have given rise to an almost endless variety of interpretation. What is meant, first, by the woman having "power on her head?"

1. There have been many—some of them most fanciful—suggestions that the word for power (*exousia*) may have crept in instead of some other word by the mistake of some copyist; or that the word used by St. Paul may have been *exiousa*—"When she goes out in public;" or two words (*ex ousias*)—"in accordance with her nature." All explanations, however, which require an alteration in the Greek text of the passage must be set aside, for (1) there is no MS. evidence whatever to support any other reading than the ordinary one, *exousian*; and (2) any alteration of a difficult or unusual word would have been naturally into a word that would simplify the passage—whereas here, if alteration has taken place, it has been to insert a word which has increased the obscurity of a difficult passage.

2. It has been maintained that the word *exousia* here means the sign of power, *i.e.*, a veil, which is the symbol of the husband's power over the wife. The fatal objection to this view, however, is that *exousia* expresses our own power, and not the power exercised by another over us. It is a word frequently used by St. Paul in this sense. (See chaps. viii. 9; ix. 4, 5, 12, 18.) Whatever interpretation, therefore, we put upon this passage, it must be consistent with this word being interpreted as meaning some "power" which the woman herself has, and not some power exercised over her by her husband.

Most commentators have quoted a passage from Diodorus Sic. i. 47, in which the Greek word "kingdom" (*basileia*) is used to signify "crown," as an illustration of the use of the word indicating the thing symbolised for the symbol itself. The parallelism between that use of the word kingdom, and the use here of the word "power," has been very positively denied (Stanley and others), on the ground that the "use of the name of the thing signified for the symbol, though natural when the power spoken of belongs to the person, would be unnatural when applied to the power exercised over that person by some one else." But the parallelism will hold good if we can refer the "power" here to some symbol of a power which belongs to the woman herself.

If we bear in mind the Apostle's constant use of words with a double significance, or rather with both an obvious and a subtly implied meaning, and if we also recall the reference made to a woman's abundance of hair in verses 5, 6, and the further reference to a woman's long hair in verses 14, 15, where the hair of the woman, given her by nature, and the wearing of a veil are used as almost identical thoughts, we may, I think, conclude that the "power" here spoken of is that long hair, which is called in verse 15 her "glory." It is remarkable that Callistratus twice uses this word *exousia* in connection with hair to express its abundance. To the Jews the recollection of Samson's

have power[1] on *her* head because of the
angels. (11) Nevertheless neither is the
man without the woman, neither the
woman without the man, in the Lord.
(12) For as the woman *is* of the man,
even so *is* the man also by the woman;
but all things of God.

(13) Judge in yourselves: is it comely
that a woman pray unto God uncovered?
(14) Doth not even nature itself teach
you, that, if a man have long hair, it is
a shame unto him? (15) But if a woman
have long hair, it is a glory to her: for
*her* hair is given her for a covering.[2]

1 That is, *a covering, in sign that she is under the power of her husband.*

2 Or, *veil.*

history would have given the word "power," when applied to hair, a remarkable significance. To thus turn aside abruptly in the middle of a long passage in which woman's subordination is enforced, and speak suddenly and vividly of her "power," would be eminently Pauline. In the Apostle's writings the thought of inferiority and superiority, of ruler and server, are frequently and almost paradoxically regarded and enforced as identical. To serve because you rule; to be weak because you are in another sense strong, are thoughts strikingly combined again and again in the Epistles of St. Paul. Thus I would imagine him here to suddenly turn aside and say, I have been speaking of your bondage and subordination, you are, because of this, to have a covering (a veil or long hair) on your head as a sign, and yet that very thing which is the symbol of your subjection to man is the sign of your beauty and "power" as a woman.

**Because of the angels.**—Why should a woman have her head covered (either with her natural veil of hair, or with an artificial veil shrouding her face) because of the angels? The same objections which have been already stated to any alteration of the usual Greek text of the earlier clause of this verse apply equally here. The MS. evidence is unanimous in favour of the word "angels," nor can we accept any of the figurative meanings attached to the word angel as "the president" (see Rev. ii. 1), or "messenger," sent by enemies to see what took place contrary to general custom in those assemblies. We must take the word "angel" in its ordinary and general sense.

That the angels were present in assemblies for worship was an idea prevalent among the Jews (Ps. cxxxviii. 1, in the LXX.), and regarded as they were by the Christian as "ministering spirits" (Heb. i. 14), no doubt their presence would be realised in the meetings of Christians.

We have already seen that the Apostle in his argument upon the relation of the sexes to each other (verses 7—9), refers to the first three chapters of Genesis as illustrating and enforcing that relationship. What more natural than that his thoughts should have gone on to chap. vi. of the same book, where is the record of the angels (in the LXX. the word translated "sons of God" is "the angels"—*angeloi*) having been enamoured by the beauty of women, and so having fallen from their high estate. This account of "the fall of the angels" is referred to more than once elsewhere in the New Testament (see Jude verse 1; 2 Pet. ii. 4), and through Rabbinical interpretations would have been familiar to St. Paul's converts. Without at all necessarily expressing his belief in the historic accuracy of this legendary view of the fall of the angels, St. Paul might use it as an argument with those who did believe it (as in the case of the Rock, see chap. x. 4, and Note there). You believe—would be St. Paul's appeal to these women—that once, through seeing the beauty of the daughters of men, the holy angels themselves fell—even that thought ought to make you feel that it is not seemly for you to be without a veil (of which your "power on your head," *i.e.*, your hair, is the type) in those assemblies where the angels are present as God's ministering spirits.

It has been urged (by Meyer and others) that the word "angels," in the New Testament, always signifies *good angels*, and it is in that sense I would regard it here, for the thought surely is, that they are good angels, and should not, therefore, be tempted. I presume the idea was also that the fallen angels were "good" before their fall.

(11) **Nevertheless . . .**—Here follow words of caution, lest the previous express declaration of the subordination of woman to man might be exaggerated or perverted. This very subordination of one sex to the other implies a mutual connection, and not an isolation of each sex. The woman is not independent of, but dependent on the man "in the Lord," *i.e.*, in the Christian economy.

(12) **For as the woman is of the man.**—An appeal to the original act of creation proves the truth of the previous statement of the interdependence of the sexes. If already (verse 7) the fact of woman's having been taken out of man was used as an argument to prove her subordination, there is now coupled with that fact of the origin of woman that other fact of the perpetual birth of man from woman, to show that there is a mutual relation. The first woman was made out of man; therefore woman is dependent on man. Every man has been born of a woman; therefore man is not independent of woman. In the Greek the word rendered "of" represents a finite act—the word rendered "by" a continued process.

**But all things of God.**—Thus, as usual, St. Paul completes the thought by tracing all up to God. The mediate processes of their origin may differ, but the source of their being is common—they, and all beings, and all things, and the sequence of all things come of God. (See chap. viii. 6; Rom. xi. 36; 2 Cor. v. 18.)

(13) **Judge in yourselves.**—In this and the two following verses the Apostle reasons with them—appeals to their own common sense, and to the indications of Nature, as to the evident truth of what he has taught them on this question. Surely you would not think it seemly for a woman (setting aside the question of men and angels altogether) to speak face to face with God in prayer?

(14) **Nature itself.**—This may mean, either "the native inborn sense of what is seemly" as contrasted with revelation; or it may signify the ordinary and evident arrangement of things in creation. Probably the former is the true meaning of the passage which refers to the fact that the heathen who had no direct revelation did (by regarding long hair as a woman's glory) "by nature" the things contained in the Law (Rom. xi. 14).

(15) **But if a woman have long hair, it is a glory to her.**—We should follow the suggestions of Nature. If a woman has naturally long hair, which is given to her as a covering for her head, the covering

(16) But if any man seem to be contentious, we have no such custom, neither the churches of God.

Chap. xi. 17–34. Abuses at the Lord's Supper.

(17) Now in this that I declare *unto you* I praise *you* not, that ye come together not for the better, but for the worse.
(18) For first of all, when ye come together in the church, I hear that there be divisions[1] among you; and

1 Or, *schisms.*

---

of her head can be no shame to her; therefore let her wear a veil. "The will ought to correspond to Nature."

(16) **But if any man seem to be contentious.**—The argument, and the appeal to their own good sense having been completed, the Apostle now adds that if, after all, some one continues to argue the matter captiously, and is not satisfied with the reason given, the answer to such a one must be simply—We, the Apostles and the churches of God, have no such custom as that women should pray and teach with uncovered head. It has been suggested that the word "custom" refers, not to the uncovering the head, but to the "contention" just mentioned. But the former interpretation seems more natural; and the Apostle's object here is, not so much to merely censure the contentious spirit, as to show how such an objector must be dealt with. It is noticeable that the appeal is made to the practice of the churches (plural), not the Church. Thus it is not the authority of the Church as such that is quoted, but it is the uniformity of practice in the several Christian churches that is appealed to. The Church in Corinth has no right to become exceptional.

It may be well to make two general remarks on the scope and bearing of this remarkable passage.

1. As St. Paul taught regarding Slavery (chap. vii. 21) that the object of Christianity was not to suddenly efface existing political arrangements, so he teaches here that Christianity did not seek to obliterate these social distinctions which were universally recognised. We know now how mighty an instrument Christ's Religion has been in elevating the social condition of woman, but this has been accomplished by gradually leavening the world with Christian principle, and not by sudden external revolution. The arguments and illustrations which the Apostle here employs have a more abiding and a wider application than the particular case to which he applied them. They have been written "for our learning" as well as for the instruction of those to whom they were originally addressed. And the lesson which they teach us is, that Christianity did not come to unsex woman, but to raise, dignify, and ennoble her as woman—to abolish for ever her real wrongs, but not to yield to a revolutionary clamour for imaginary rights. Old and New Testament alike emphasise the truth that (as has been quaintly and truly said) "woman was not made from man's head to be his ruler, nor from his feet to be his slave, but from his side to be his equal, and from beneath his strong arm to demand his protection."

2. The influence of St. Paul's instruction as to women not uncovering their heads in public worship has lasted long after the necessity for that particular expression of her relationship to man has passed away. While, in succeeding ages, again and again, some have forgotten the principles of the teaching, which are eternal, the particular application of them, which was only temporary, has been continuously and universally observed. Surely this is an illustration and evidence of the Divine Wisdom which withheld the apostolic writers from, as a rule, laying down minute directions for worship, or dogmatic formulas of faith. Men would, in a servile obedience to rules, have soon and completely forgotten the living principles on which they were based. To this day the universal custom in Christian places of worship, of women being covered and men uncovered, and the increasing revolt against the acknowledgment of the subordination of woman to man, of which that practice was originally the avowed symbol, is a striking proof of how the same spirit, which led Jews of old to be scrupulous in their observance of certain external ordinances, while forgetting the weighter matters of which they were to be the outward expression, was not merely a Jewish but a human weakness.

(17) **Now in this that I declare unto you . . .**—Better, *Now I give you this command, while not praising you that you come together not for the better, but for the worse.* These words lead from the subject which has gone before to another and different abuse of liberty in public assemblies, of which the Apostle is now about to speak. There were evidently three great abuses which had crept into the Church:—1. The discarding by the women of the covering for their heads. This only concerned one sex, and has been treated of in the earlier part of this chapter. The other two affect both sexes. 2. The disorders at the Lord's Supper. 3. The misuse of spiritual gifts. The former of these occupies the remainder of this chapter, while the latter is discussed in chap. xii. 1—30. To render the Greek word "I declare," as in the Authorised version, and so make it refer to what is about to follow, gives a more logical completeness to the passage, but it is scarcely allowable, as the Greek word elsewhere always means a distinct command (chap. vii. 10; 1 Thess. iv. 11; 2 Thess. iii. 6, 10, 12, *et al.*). Others have suggested that St. Paul anticipates in thought the practical direction which occurs in verse 34, and alludes to it here in the words, "This I command you." This view is open to the objections (1) that it completely isolates verse 17 from verse 16, while the Greek evidently intimates a connection between them; (2) that it is unnatural to separate the statement so far from the command to which it refers. It is better to regard these words as given above—forming a sort of intellectual isthmus connecting the two wide fields of thought which the earlier and later portions of the chapter embrace.

**I praise you not.**—This carries the thought back to verse 2, and shows that the commendation expressed there is still the writer's starting-point, or rather the point of departure from which he proceeds to censure.

**That ye come together.**—Although in the English version the word "you" is inserted ("I praise *you* not"), it does not occur in the Greek. The passage is not, "I do not praise you because, &c.," but, "I do not praise your coming together not for the better, but for the worse." These words introduce the new topic which follows.

(18) **For first of all.**—We in vain look for the "secondly," which, in a perfectly systematic treatise, should follow this "first." Some writers maintain that verses 18 and 19 form the first point, and verses 20 to 34 the second. There is, however, no indication of a new subject being introduced with verse 20, but

I partly believe it. (19) For there
must be also heresies[1] among you, that
they which are approved may be made
manifest among you. (20) When ye
come together therefore into one place,
*this* is not to eat[2] the Lord's supper.
(21) For in eating every one taketh
before *other* his own supper: and one
is hungry, and another is drunken.
(22) What? have ye not houses to eat
and to drink in? or despise ye the
church of God, and shame them that
have not?[3] What shall I say to you?
shall I praise you in this? I praise *you*

1 Or, *sects.*
2 Or, *ye cannot eat.*
3 Or, *them that are poor?*

---

the repetition of the words "come together" carries the mind back at once to the "come together" in verse 18, and indicates the continuation of the subject there commenced, and from which the Apostle had, at the mention of the word "divisions," for a moment parenthetically digressed.

It is better to consider the "first point" to be the abuse regarding the Lord's Supper, which is more immediately treated of; and the "second point," the abuse of spiritual gifts, commencing with verse 1 of chap. xii. They are two branches of the one general subject, viz., "Irregularities in religious assemblies," and although the latter is not connected with the former by a definite "secondly," there is a sufficient verbal indication that a second topic is entered upon. It is well to remember in this and similar cases that this is not a treatise, but a letter, and not only a letter, but an answer to a letter, and that if we had a copy of the epistle to which this is a reply, many points of sequence and arrangement, which at present present difficulties, would be as clear to us as they were to those who originally received this Epistle.

**When ye come together in the church.**—The reference here is not to a locality, but to the character of the assembly, as we should say "in church," or, "in parliament." The spirit of faction, which has already, in the earlier part of this Epistle, been dealt with, as pervading Christian society, had invaded the Christian assemblies.

**I partly believe it.**—These words are full of the courtesy and charity so characteristic of the Apostle; and they suggest to us all a lesson regarding our belief of evil reports, even when reaching us on "the very best authority." The general practice is to believe a little more than we are told. St. Paul believed a part only of what he was told.

(19) **For there must be also heresies.**—Better, *For there must be also sects.* There have been many attempts to explain where lies the difference between the "divisions" of the former verse and the "sects" of this verse. From all that we know of the Apostolic Church it is clear that neither of these words can mean sects separated from the Church, but "parties" in the Church. Christ had foretold (Matt. xviii. 7) that "stumbling-blocks," or "scandals," must arise in the Church, and it is possible that our Lord on some occasion spoke of these as "sects" (Justin Martyr attributes the use of this very word to our Lord); and St. Paul, possibly, uses the word here because it was the one traditionally reported as having been used by Christ in some of His unrecorded utterances. Christ has foretold that in the divine economy of permission such divisions will arise. They are allowed because this is a state of continual judgment; and the existence of such "offences" will be God's means of manifesting those who are void of offence, and those who are not.

(20) **When ye come together therefore into one place, this is not to eat the Lord's supper.**—Better, *Therefore, when you assemble in the same place, it is not to eat the supper dedicated to the Lord.* Regarding verse 19 as a parenthesis, the word "therefore" connects this with verse 18. There being divisions among you, it is not possible for you when you assemble as a Church body ("in the same place" being equivalent to "in church" of verse 18) to partake of that supper which is dedicated to the Lord. The whole meal, or "charity-feast" (Jude, verse 12), was distinguished from other meals by being united with the Lord's Supper. To these charity-feasts the Christians brought contributions of food—the rich of their abundance, the poor whatever they could afford—and the food thus provided was partaken of in common by all. The Greek words in this verse for "Lord's Supper" are more general (*kuriakon deipnon*) than those used in verse 27 and in chap. x. 16 and 21 (*kuriou*). The whole meal was dedicated to the Lord by virtue of its union with the sacramental Supper of the Lord.

(21) **For.**—Here follows a description of the conduct and mode of proceeding at this feast, which renders it impossible, as stated in verse 20, for it to be a Lord's Supper. Every one greedily seizes (takes before distribution is made) what he has brought with him, and appropriates it to his own individual use, instead of making it a contribution to the general and common supply. Every one comes to eat *his own supper,* and not the *Lord's Supper.* And the result is that while some poor man, who has not been able to bring enough for himself, remains unfed, some rich man, drinking the wine which he brought, and which he has not shared with others, is drunken. (See Note on verse 34.)

(22) **What? have ye not houses . . ?**—Better, *Surely it is not that you have no houses to eat and drink in?* This cannot be the explanation of their conduct, for they have houses in which they can enjoy their proper meals. Hunger and thirst, which can be satisfied at home, therefore, cannot be the explanation of their conduct at the charity-feasts. The only other alternative explanation, therefore, is that they despise an assembly which is the Church of God; and they put to shame those poor members, who, no doubt, were the majority, who have not houses in which to eat and drink, and have come together in this common assembly of Christians to share in the food which the wealthier members ought to contribute.

The shame which a poor man will feel when the rich come to these feasts bringing supplies for their own private use, and not for general distribution, will arise both from the striking contrast which will come out all the more vividly from his poverty being brought into such direct contact with the wealth of the rich, and from the evident dislike of the rich to partake of a common meal with the poor. Thus those assemblies will, through the misconduct of the wealthier Christians, have precisely the opposite result from that which they were intended to accomplish. It will be an assembly in one place, but not to partake of one supper—even that which is dedicated to the Lord. The Apostle asks indignantly whether such conduct can be included in the catalogue (see verse 17) of those things for which he can praise them, and then in the following verses

not. (23) For I have received of the Lord that which also I delivered unto you, That the Lord Jesus the *same* night in which he was betrayed took bread: (24) and when he had given thanks,[a] he brake *it*, and said, Take, eat: this is my body, which is broken for you: this do in remembrance of me.[1]

[a] Matt. 26. 26; Mark 14. 22; Luke 22. 19.

[1] Or, *for a remembrance.*

---

shows how such conduct cannot be worthy of praise, inasmuch as it is entirely at variance with the solemn and sacred circumstances in which the Lord's Supper originated.

(23) **For I have received of the Lord.**—Better, *For I received from the Lord.* Do these words imply that St. Paul had a direct revelation from Christ of the words and facts which he now recalls, or merely that he knew from the accounts given him by others who had been present, what took place on that memorable and solemn occasion?

The whole structure of the passage seems to imply that what follows had been received by St. Paul directly from Christ, and that he is not appealing to a well-known tradition, in which case he would scarcely have used the singular, "I received," nor to something which he had learnt from the other Apostles, in which case he would not have said "I" emphatically (the word being emphasised by expression in the Greek), nor "from the Lord," for the other Apostles had not received their knowledge of these facts "from the Lord," but from their own observation and hearing. *How* Christ thus communicated these truths to His new Apostle we are not told. The method of communication (whether in a trance, or state of ecstasy, or any other supernatural manner) does not appear to cause either doubt or difficulty to those to whom the Apostle conveyed the information thus miraculously bestowed upon him.

**That which also I delivered unto you.**—The Apostle was not now for the first time communicating these solemn facts to the Corinthians. He had told them all this before, and therefore they were sinning against knowledge when they degraded a feast which they knew to be so solemn to a purpose so unworthy.

There now follows an account of the institution of the Lord's Supper, which, as compared with the accounts given in the Gospel narratives (see Matt. xxvi. 26—29; Mark xiv. 22—25; Luke xxii. 19, 20), possesses some noteworthy features. The Evangelists (St. Matthew and St. Mark) wrote their accounts many years after the occurrence, and recorded what they remembered to have observed and heard. St. Paul writes here, within a very few years at all events of his having received it, an account of what had been directly communicated by the Lord. This was also most probably the first written record of what occurred on that solemn night.

The fact that St. Luke's narrative agrees most closely with St. Paul's, would imply, not as some rationalising critics insinuate, that St. Paul was indebted to St. Luke; but that St. Luke attached high value to an account which his companion had received directly from the glorified Christ. The only differences of any importance between St. Luke's and St. Paul's narrative are—(1) St. Luke writes "given for you;" St. Paul omits the word "given" (see Note on verse 24). (2) St. Luke omits the words "this do ye as oft as ye drink it," after the giving of the cup; but he implies them by stating that the cup was given "in like manner" to the bread, in connection with which he records these words. The suggestion that St. Luke copied his account of the Last Supper from this Epistle is a mere speculation, and in the highest degree improbable. If that Evangelist had used this Epistle in writing his Gospel, is it likely that he would have been content with giving the somewhat scanty account of our Lord's appearances after His resurrection, when he had at hand the much ampler record of the appearance to the 500 brethren and to James, which this Epistle contains? (chap. xv.)

In all the narratives, however, the outlines of the scene are the same. There can be no mistake as to their all being truthful and (as the minor discrepancies prove) honestly independent records of an actual historical scene. It is worthy of remark that in the heated controversies which have raged around the Eucharistic Feast as to its spiritual significance, its evidential value has been frequently lost sight of. If the Betrayal and Crucifixion are not historical facts, how can we account for the existence of the Eucharistic Feast? Here is an Epistle whose authenticity the most searching and ruthless criticism has never disputed. We have evidence of the existence of this feast and its connection with events which occurred only twenty years before. If we bear in mind that the Apostles were Jews, and yet spoke of that wine which they drank as "blood"—that they were lovingly devoted to the person of Christ, and yet spake of that bread which they ate as His "flesh"—can the wildest imagination conceive of that practice having originated with themselves as their most solemn religious rite, and the profoundest expression of their love to their Lord? Could anything but the record given in the Gospel narrative possibly account for such a ceremony holding such a place in a sect composed of Christianised Jews? A dark conspiracy like that of Catiline might have selected the tasting of human blood as the symbol of the conspirators' sanguinary hate of all human order and life; but such a band of men as the early Christians certainly could not of their own thought have made such a choice, and publicly proclaimed it. And if this be true—if Jesus, the night before an ignominious death, instituted this strange and solemn rite, which has been handed down century after century in unbroken continuity—can that foresight as to the future of His Church be assigned to one who was less than what Christendom claims her Lord to be? When Christ died His Apostles gave up all as lost, and went back sorrowfully to their old work as fishermen; Christendom was not an afterthought of the Apostles, but the forethought of the Lord.

**The same night in which he was betrayed.**—These words imply that the history of the Betrayal was familiar, and they also solemnly and touchingly remind the Corinthians of the strange contrast between the events of that night and the scenes in which they indulge now on the same night that they partake of that supper.

(24) **And when he had given thanks . . .**—Better, *and having given thanks, He brake it, and said, "This is My body which is for you."* The insertion of the words, "take, eat," and "broken" is not supported by MS. evidence. The former were probably inserted so as to produce a verbal identity with St. Matthew's account, and the word "broken" possibly as explanatory. At the institution the act of breaking the bread explained sufficiently what was meant. The Master, while in the act of breaking it, said, "This is My body, which is for you."

**This do in remembrance of me**—*i.e.*, all that was done then. Bless the bread, break it, distribute it,

(25) After the same manner also *he took*
the cup, when he had supped, saying,
This cup is the new testament in my
blood: this do ye, as oft as ye drink *it*,
in remembrance of me.
(26) For as often as ye eat this bread,
and drink this cup, ye do shew[1] the
Lord's death till he come. (27) Where-
fore whosoever shall eat this bread, and
drink *this* cup of the Lord, unworthily,
shall be guilty of the body and blood of
the Lord. (28) But let a man examine
himself, and so let him eat of *that* bread,
and drink of *that* cup. (29) For he that
eateth and drinketh unworthily, eateth
and drinketh damnation[2] to himself,

1 Or, *shew ye.*
2 Or, *judgment.*

---

eat it. When I am no longer with you bodily, these acts will make memory grow into realisation of My presence in your midst. If the soft music of those words could reach us now, disentangled from the theological discords of intervening ages, surely they would come to us with some such significance. To those who first heard them they certainly must have implied not that a physical presence was about to be perpetuated, but rather that there was now something for them which would in after ages console them for a physical absence.

(25) **After the same manner also he took the cup, when he had supped.**—We have here an intimation not found in St. Matthew or St. Mark's narrative, that the blessing of the cup took place "after supper," which implies that the blessing of the bread took place earlier in the meal.

**This cup is the new testament.**—Better, *This cup is the new covenant.* The word "new" is peculiar to this and St. Luke's narrative; it does not occur in the best MSS. of St. Matthew and St. Mark. The new covenant of grace between God and Humanity was ratified in the blood of Christ. The cup containing the symbol of that blood is therefore the pledge and witness of that covenant. This was a new covenant in blood (Rom. iii. 25) as contrasted with the old covenant in blood (Ex. xxiv. 8).

**As oft as ye drink.**—This can scarcely be taken as a command to make all occasions of bodily refreshment virtually a eucharist, but must be regarded as referring definitely (as in the following verse) to this particular rite.

(26) **For as often as ye . . .**—The previous verse concluded the account of the institution as conveyed by Christ to St. Paul, and the Apostle himself now again speaks. All this being the true account of the origin of this Supper, as often as you eat this bread and drink this cup (as distinct from other bread and wine) you proclaim the Lord's death until He come. The Greek word for "ye show" is that used for making a public oral proclamation. The passage does not imply, as some have suggested, that the Lord's Supper "was a living sermon or an acted discourse," but, as is still the custom, that when the bread and wine were consecrated to this sacred use, there was an oral declaration made (perhaps in the very words the Apostle here used, verses 22—25) of the facts of the original institution. The imperative form given in the margin of the Authorised version is quite inadmissible.

In the pathetic words "until He come" we may find an expression of the belief, perhaps largely due to the hope, that the Second Advent was not far distant.

(27) **Wherefore whosoever shall eat this bread, and drink this cup of the Lord . . .**—Better, *Wherefore, whosoever eats the bread or drinks the cup of the Lord.* The entire weight of MS. evidence is in favour of the conjunction "or," not "and," which was probably retained in the English version lest the disjunctive "or" might seem to favour the practice of receiving in one kind only. It is, however, clear that if in these early days there was a considerable interval between the receiving the bread and the wine, it would have been quite possible for a partaker to have received one only unworthily, and the Apostle intimates that in either case he is guilty.

Sin was the cause of that body being broken and that blood shed, and therefore the one who unworthily uses the symbols of them becomes a participator in the very guilt of those who crucified that body and shed that blood.

(28—32) There are so many modifications required in these verses of the Greek text from which our translation is taken, so as to bring it into harmony with the best MSS., and so many changes needed in the translation itself, so as to convey more clearly the meaning of the original, that it will be best to give here a consecutive translation of the whole passage. It should read thus:—*But let a man prove himself, and so let him eat of the bread and drink of the cup, for he that eateth and drinketh, eateth and drinketh a judgment to himself if he does not discern the Body—(for this cause many among you are weak and sick, and some sleep)—but if we would discern ourselves we should not be judged; but being judged we are chastened by the Lord, in order that we may not be finally condemned with the world.* There are several words in this sentence which call for remark.

(28) **So let him eat.**—This implies that a man should partake of this sacred feast only after he has carefully examined himself as to the spirit in which he was approaching such holy bread and wine.

(29) **Unworthily.**—This word is not in the best Greek MSS.

**Damnation to himself.**—The Greek word here does not imply final condemnation. On the contrary, it only means such temporal judgments as the sickness and weakness subsequently mentioned, and which are to save the man from sharing the final damnation of the heathen.

**Not discerning the Lord's body.**—The words "the Lord's" are to be omitted, the weight of MS. evidence being altogether against their authenticity. Verse 30 is a parenthesis, and verse 31 re-opens with this same verb. The force of the passage is, "He who eats and drinks without discerning the Body (*i.e.*, the Church) in that assembly, eats and drinks a judgment to himself; for if we would discern ourselves we should not be judged."

There are some important points to be borne in mind regarding this interpretation of the passage. (1) The Greek word, which we render "discerning," "discern," signifies to arrive at a right estimate of the character or quality of a thing. (2) *The* fault which St. Paul was condemning was the practice which the Corinthians had fallen into of regarding these gatherings as opportunities for individual indulgence, and not as Church assemblies. They did not rightly estimate such gatherings as being corporate meetings; they did not rightly estimate themselves as not now isolated individuals, but

not discerning the Lord's body. (30) (For
this cause many *are* weak and sickly
among you, and many sleep.) (31) For
if we would judge ourselves, we should
not be judged. (32) But when we are
judged, we are chastened of the Lord,
that we should not be condemned with
the world. (33) Wherefore, my brethren,
when ye come together to eat, tarry one
for another. (34) And if any man hunger,
let him eat at home; that ye come
not together unto condemnation.[1]
And the rest will I set in order when
I come.

1 Or, *judgment.*

members of the common Body. They ought to discern in these meetings of the Church a body; they ought to discern in themselves parts of a body. Not only is this interpretation, I venture to think, the most accurate and literal interpretation of the Greek, but it is the only view which seems to me to make the passage bear intelligibly on the point which St. Paul is considering, and the real evil which he seeks to counteract. (3) To refer these words directly or indirectly to the question of a physical presence in the Lord's Supper, is to divorce them violently from their surroundings, and to make them allude to some evil for which the explicit and practical remedy commended in verses 33 and 34 would be no remedy at all. Moreover, if the word "body" means the Lord's physical body, surely the word "Lord's" would have been added, and the words, "and the blood," for the non-recognition of the blood would be just as great an offence. (4) St. Paul never uses the word "body" in reference to our Lord's physical body, without some clear indication that such is meant. (See Rom. vii. 4; Phil. iii. 21; Col. i. 22.) On the other hand, the use of the word "Body," or "Body of Christ," meaning the Church, is frequent. We have had it but a few verses before, in reference to this very subject (chap. x. 16). It is also to be found in Rom. xii. 5; Eph. i. 22, 53; v. 23, 30. (In this last passage, "of His flesh and of His bones," are not in the best MSS., and destroy the real force of the "Body," which means "Church.")

(30) **For this cause**—*i.e.*, because you do not regard these feasts, to which the Lord's Supper is joined as gatherings in a common body, but eat and drink to excess, and so gain no spiritual advantage, but actually physical evil, many are weak and sickly.

**And many sleep.**—Better, *and some die.* Even death sometimes resulted from their drunken orgies, either naturally, or by God's direct visitation.

(31) **For.**—This joins verse 31 to verse 30, which see. The change to the first person, courteously identifying himself with them, is characteristic of St. Paul.

(32) **But when we are judged.**—This verse explicitly declares that the condemnation following an unworthy partaking was not final condemnation, but temporal suffering to save them from being condemned with the heathen.

(33, 34) **Wherefore, my brethren.**—To correct the abuses of which he has spoken, and to enable them to escape the judgments which were falling upon them, the Apostle gives them this practical advice. When you come together to this eucharistic feast, do not eagerly eat what you have brought; wait until all have arrived, and then partake in common of this Christian meal. If, however, any man is really hungry, then let him satisfy his hunger at home, and come to this Supper so that he may partake of it not to his judgment.

(34) **The rest**—or, literally, *the remaining matters*—doubtless refers to some other details connected with the charity-feasts.

From the foregoing we gather the following outline of the method of celebration of the Lord's Supper in the Apostolic Church.

It was a common practice amongst the Greeks at this time to hold a feast called *eranos,* to which all contributed, and of which all partook. A similar arrangement soon sprang up in the Christian communities, and were called *agapæ,* or "charity-feasts." At these gatherings was celebrated—probably at first daily, and afterwards weekly—the Lord's Supper. It consisted of two parts—a loaf broken and distributed during the meal, and a cup partaken of by all present after it. This bread and this cup were distinguished from the meal itself by the solemn declaration over them of the fact of the institution (verse 26). The entire feast, however, had a solemnity and sanctity imparted to it by the eucharistic acts which accompanied it; and while this bread and this wine constituted the "Supper of the Lord," the entire "charity-feast" became consecrated by it as a "Lord's Supper" (verse 20), the phrase being similar to "Lord's day" (Rev. i. 10). To it the brethren came, not as individuals, but as members of the body of Christ. This gathering of the Church was His body now on earth; that sacramental bread and wine, the symbols of His body, which had been on earth, and which had been given for them. To the charity-feast the rich brought of their abundance, the poor of their poverty. But once assembled there everything was common. The party spirit which raged outside soon invaded these sacred scenes. The rich members ceased to discern in that gathering "the Body," and to discern themselves as "members of that Body." They regarded themselves as individuals, and the food which they brought as their own. The poor were put to shame; some of them arriving late would remain hungry, while the rich had eaten and drunk to excess. On those who acted thus there fell naturally God's judgments of sickness and of death. To correct this terrible evil and grave scandal, St. Paul recalls to them the solemnity of the act of Holy Communion, what it meant, how it was instituted. He reminds them of how the whole feast was consecrated by having that eucharistic bread and wine united with it, and he commands those who wanted merely to satisfy their natural hunger to do so at home before coming to the "Lord's Supper." The two thoughts of communion with Christ and communion with one another, and of the bread and wine being the medium of the union with Him, and the source of the Christian unity, intersect and interlace each other, like the fine threads of some tapestry which are so skilfully interwoven that you cannot distinguish *them* while you look on the image or scene which they definitely produce. We may with theological subtlety dissever them; but if we do so we shall lose that loving image of the Holy Communion which the Apostle wrought out in his teaching, and on which he and the early Church gazed with tender adoration, and from which they drew the deepest draughts of spiritual life.

**When I come.**—There is no definite indication of an approaching visit in these words. They are quite general, "whenever I come."

A.D. 59.

Chap. xii. 1—31. Spiritual gifts.

CHAPTER XII.—(1) Now concern-
ing spiritual *gifts,* breth-
ren, I would not have you
ignorant. (2) Ye know
that ye were Gentiles, carried away
unto these dumb idols, even as ye were
led. (3) Wherefore I give you to under-
stand, that no man speaking by the
Spirit of God calleth Jesus accursed:[1]
and *that* no man can say that Jesus is
the Lord, but by the Holy Ghost.

(4) Now there are diversities of gifts,
but the same Spirit. (5) And there
are differences of administrations,
but the same Lord. (6) And there
are diversities of operations, but it
is the same God which worketh all
in all.
(7) But the manifestation of the Spirit
is given to every man to profit withal.
(8) For to one is given by the Spirit the
word of wisdom; to another the word

[1] Or, *anathema.*

XII.

(1) **Now concerning spiritual gifts.**—Again the sequence of the topics treated of is probably decided by the subjects contained in the letter from Corinth (see chaps. vii. 1 and viii. 1), and the Apostle replies to inquiries regarding the comparative value and importance of certain spiritual gifts. In this early age the Church was full of the divine energy of spiritual youth. From the indwelling Spirit of God resulted certain marvellous "gifts," some of which ceased with the apostolic age—some of which seem to have lingered for centuries, even to our own day—declaring themselves intermittently in times of profound religious awakening. The party spirit with which the Corinthian Church seems to have been saturated naturally led to diverse views as to the relative importance of certain of these gifts—some were unduly exalted, some unduly depreciated. The truth that these gifts are valuable as evidence of the indwelling Spirit, and so far as they could be useful for the Church, was forgotten. The Apostle reserves for consideration in more detail (see chap. xiii.) the special gift of tongues, which was, perhaps, the gift most exaggerated and most misunderstood at Corinth, and deals in this chapter with the subject of spiritual gifts generally. The subject of the chapter is *The Source, Object, and Value of Spiritual Gifts,* and the chapter may be thus subdivided:—

Verses 1—3. The confession of Christ as Lord is the true evidence of the Spirit.
„ 4—11. The gifts of the Spirit are diverse in character, but the origin is the same.
„ 12—30. The analogy of the human body shows that the spiritual Body (the Church) is not a collection of independent parts, but a living organism consisting of mutually interdependent members.

**I would not have you ignorant.**—Better, *I do not wish you to be ignorant.*

(2) **Ye know that ye were Gentiles.**—Better (according to the weight of MSS. evidence), *Ye know that when ye were Gentiles ye were,* &c. In this and the following verse the Apostle reminds his readers that so far from regarding the marvellous manifestations of the Spirit, such as speaking with tongues and prophesying, as the most wonderful miracles, the greatest miracle of all was their conversion. That blind followers of dumb idols should be transformed into intelligent believers in the living Word was the most striking work of the Spirit. They were now no longer led hither and thither by diverse teachings and diverse gods; they had an unchanging principle of life, and an unerring guide of conduct. The contrast of the present state of Christians with their former state as heathens is a topic of frequent occurrence in St. Paul's writings (Rom. xi. 30; Col. i. 21; iii. 7, &c.).

(3) **Wherefore I give you to understand.**—Better, *Wherefore I make known unto you.* Because such was your condition, and there still seems to linger in your minds some of the ignorance which belonged to such a state, I make known unto you the one great test of your possession of the Holy Spirit. If any man say "Jesus is anathema," that is a proof that he has not that Spirit. If any man say "Jesus is Lord," that is a proof that he has that Spirit.

(4—6) **Now there are diversities of gifts.**—Although conversion is identical in every case, yet afterwards there are spiritual gifts which vary according to individual capacity and character, but they all come from the one Spirit. There are varieties of ministration in which those spiritual gifts are employed, *and* (not "but" in the Greek) the same Lord is served by these varied ministries; there are varieties of operations resulting from these gifts and ministrations, but it is the same God who works them all in all cases. We have here a clear indication of the doctrine of the Holy Trinity—the HOLY SPIRIT, the direct source of spiritual gifts; the SON, the one in whose service these gifts are to be used as ministers; the FATHER, the one supreme origin of all powers thus bestowed in diverse manners by the one Spirit, and for diverse purposes in the ministering to the One Son. Thus, underlying this passage is the vivid realisation of the Trinity in unity, and unity in Trinity of the Divine Nature.

(7) **But the manifestation of the Spirit.**—These gifts which flow from one source are intended to flow towards one object, viz., the benefit of the whole Church. If it were only for a man's own benefit it would cease to be a "manifestation"—it would be sufficient for the person to possess the spirit consciously to himself. But the object of light is to give light to others. The object of the spiritual light is to make manifest to others.

(8) **For to one is given by the Spirit.**—Verses 8—10 illustrate the former statements as to varieties of endowments for the object of the manifestation of the Spirit, still, however, emphasising the unity of their origin, viz., the Holy Spirit. The following division (Meyer's) of the gifts which are here mentioned is, perhaps, the best approach to a classification which can be made. In the Greek the genera (so to speak) are divided by the word *hetero,* the species by *allo,* both words being rendered in the English by the one word "another":—

I. Gifts which have reference to intellectual power.
(1) The word of wisdom.
(2) The word of knowledge.

of knowledge by the same Spirit; (9) to
another faith by the same Spirit; to
another the gifts of healing by the same
Spirit; (10) to another the working of
miracles; to another prophecy; to
another discerning of spirits; to another
*divers* kinds of tongues; to another the
interpretation of tongues: (11) but all
these worketh that one and the selfsame
Spirit, dividing to every man severally
as he will. (12) For as the body is one,
and hath many members, and all the
members of that one body, being many,
are one body: so also *is* Christ. (13) For
by one Spirit are we all baptized into
one body, whether *we be* Jews or Gentiles,[1] whether *we be* bond or free; and
have been all made to drink into one
Spirit. (14) For the body is not one
member, but many. (15) If the foot
shall say, Because I am not the hand,
I am not of the body; is it therefore not
of the body? (16) And if the ear shall
say, Because I am not the eye, I am
not of the body; is it therefore not of
the body? (17) If the whole body *were*
an eye, where *were* the hearing? If the
whole *were* hearing, where *were* the
smelling? (18) But now hath God set
the members every one of them in the
body, as it hath pleased him. (19) And
if they were all one member, where
*were* the body? (20) But now *are they*
many members, yet but one body.

1 Gr. *Greeks.*

II. Gifts which depend upon special energy of faith.
- (1) The faith itself.
- (2) Operating in deeds.
  - (*a*) Healings.
  - (*b*) Miracles.
- (3) Operating in words, as in prophetic utterances.
- (4) Operating in distinguishing true and false spirits.

III. Gifts which relate to tongues.
- (1) Speaking with tongues.
- (2) Interpreting tongues.

The "wisdom" and the "knowledge" differ, in that the former expresses the deep spiritual insight into spiritual truth which some possess, the latter the intellectual appreciation of Christian doctrine, which is not so profound as the former, and which as the man passes into the spiritual state will vanish away (chap. xiii. 8).

(9) **Faith.**—This cannot mean the faith which is necessary to salvation, for that belongs to all Christians; but such faith as is mentioned in Matt. xvii. 20, Luke xvii. 6, the results of such a faith being here enlarged, and not embracing miracles alone, but prophecy and the discerning of spirits. In the Greek "the word of wisdom" is said to be given *by* the Spirit; "the word of knowledge" *according to* the Spirit; and "the faith and gift of healing" *in* the Spirit. By the use of this variety of expression the Apostle probably means to indicate the variety of methods of operation of the Spirit, as well as the diversity of the gifts which He lavishes.

(10) **Prophecy.**—Not in its modern and limited sense of foretelling the future, but forthtelling truth generally.

**Discerning of spirits**—*i.e.*, the power to distinguish between the workings of the Holy Spirit and of evil and misleading spirits (see 1 Tim. iv. 1; 1 John iv. 1). On the gifts of tongues and interpretations of tongues, see chap xiv.

(11) **But all these.**—Again, in striking contrast to the great varieties of gifts, the common source of them all is emphatically repeated. The Corinthians estimated these gifts variously, according to their variety in operation. The Apostle estimates their common value as proceeding from the One Spirit, distributed according to His will. Those who valued men more or less according to the kind of gift they possessed were really, if unconsciously, criticising the giver.

(13) **For.**—Here follows an illustrative proof of the former statement. The human body is composed of many members, and so also is the spiritual body of Christ, which is His Church.

**To drink into one Spirit.**—Better (in accordance with the best MSS.), *to drink one Spirit.* The act of baptism was not only a watering of the convert with the washing of regeneration, but a partaking of one Spirit on his part. It is the same word as is used in chap. iii. 6, Apollos "watered."

(14) **For the body is not one member, but many.**—Here follows a series of suggestions as to the different parts of the body claiming independence of the body itself, which the nature of the case shows to be absurd.

(15) **Is it therefore not of the body?**—Better, *It is not on that account not of the body;* and so omit the note of interrogation in the subsequent passages of these verses also. The illustration is almost the same as that contained in Livy, ii. 32, the fable of the revolt of the limbs against the belly. Pope, in his *Essay on Man* (ix.), employs the same idea thus:—

> "What if the foot, ordain'd the dust to tread,
> Or hand, to toil, aspired to be the head?
> What if the head, the eye, or ear declined
> To serve mere engines to the ruling mind?
> Just as absurd for any part to claim
> To be another in this general frame:
> Just as absurd to mourn the fate or pains
> The great directing MIND OF ALL ordains.
> All are but parts of one stupendous whole,
> Whose body Nature is, and God the soul."

(17) **If the whole body were an eye.**—Here is shown how absurd it would be for the body to be merely one member, and in verse 19 is shown the converse absurdity of the members losing their individuality. There is a corporate body composed of divers members. That is the difference between a dead machine and a living organism.

(20) **But now are they.**—From the *reductio ad absurdum* of the previous verses the Apostle turns to the fact as it is, and proceeds (in verse 21) to state that there is a mutual interdependence in the members of the body. The eye is dependent on the hand, the head upon the feet. Here, no doubt, the illustration is drawn out in this particular direction to rebuke those who

(21) And the eye cannot say unto the hand,
I have no need of thee: nor again the
head to the feet, I have no need of you.
(22) Nay, much more those members of
the body, which seem to be more feeble,
are necessary: (23) and those *members*
of the body, which we think to be less
honourable, upon these we bestow[1]
more abundant honour; and our un-
comely *parts* have more abundant come-
liness.
(24) For our comely *parts* have no need:
but God hath tempered the body to-
gether, having given more abundant
honour to that *part* which lacked:
(25) that there should be no schism[2]
in the body; but *that* the members
should have the same care one for
another. (26) And whether one member
suffer, all the members suffer with it;
or one member be honoured, all the
members rejoice with it. (27) Now ye
are the body of Christ, and members in
particular. (28) And God hath set some
in the church, first apostles, secondarily
prophets, thirdly teachers, after that
miracles, then gifts of healings, helps,
governments, diversities[3] of tongues.
(29) *Are* all apostles? *are* all prophets?
*are* all teachers? *are* all workers[4] of
miracles? (30) Have all the gifts of
healing? do all speak with tongues?
do all interpret? (31) But covet ear-
nestly the best gifts.
And yet shew I unto you a more ex-
cellent way.

CHAPTER XIII.—(1) Though I speak
with the tongues of men and
of angels, and have not

Chap. xiii. Love.

1 Or, *put on.*
3 Or, *kinds.*
4 Or, *powers.*
2 Or, *division.*
A.D. 59.

being themselves possessed of what were considered important spiritual gifts despised the gifts which the Spirit had bestowed on others.

(22) **Which seem to be more feeble.**—The general argument of this and the following verse (without attempting to identify the particular parts of the body referred to) is that the weakest parts of the body are as necessary to the body as the strongest; and those parts which are considered less seemly are more abundantly cared for by being carefully covered with clothes, as distinguished from the face and hands which are uncovered.

(24) **For our comely parts have no need.**—These words (better, *and our comely parts have no need*) conclude the former verse. The words, "But God hath tempered," commence a new sentence, in which the natural practice of covering parts of the body is stated to be in harmony with God's evident intention.

(25) **That there should be no schism.**—The existence of differences of gifts in the Church had been used by the Corinthians to cause schisms, exalting some gifts and depreciating others, when this very variety in the Church ought, as was the intention of variety in the human body, to create a mutual dependence, which would promote unity.

(26) **And whether one member suffer.**—This verse completes the statement of the perfect unity of the members in one body and with one another. They are not only physically joined together, but they are so united as to feel together.

(27) **Now.**—We have here in general terms the application of the foregoing illustration, the detailed application of which follows in verse 28. The Apostles were those selected by our Lord Himself, or afterwards elected by them to join that body. (On prophets and teachers, see verse 10.) The teachers were probably a junior order of instructors. (See Acts xiii. 1; Eph. iv. 11.) The enumeration of the gifts here corresponds with that previously given in verses 9 and 10, with the exception of the mention here of "helps" and "governments," and the omission of "interpretation of tongues" and "discernment of spirit." Possibly, therefore, the words inserted here are only another designation of the same thing. The "helps" being the aid required for those who heard tongues in order to the understanding them, and the "governments" being the due regulation of the acceptance of certain spiritual powers and rejection of others.

(31) **But covet earnestly.**—Better, *But earnestly seek the better gifts.* All this argument is not meant to check ardour and to damp enthusiasm. The Spirit divideth to every man as He wills, but He wills to give to each the best gift that each desires and is capable of receiving. The receptivity which comes with earnest and practical desire is in the case of each individual the determining cause as to what gift the Spirit will give. The last sentence, "And yet show I unto you a more excellent way," ought to form the opening clause of the next chapter. The "more excellent way" is not some gift to be desired to the exclusion of the other gifts, but a more excellent way of striving for those gifts. You are not to strive for any one gift because it is more highly esteemed, or because it is more apparently useful, or because it is more easily attained. That which will consecrate every struggle for attainment and every gift when attained is Love.

XIII.

(1) **Though I speak . . .**—The more excellent way is "Love." Without it all moral and intellectual gifts are valueless. If there be love—the love of God, and the love of our brethren—in our hearts, all will be well. This hymn of praise in honour of love is remarkable, (1) as coming from St. Paul, and not from St. John, from whose pen we might naturally have looked for it; and (2), occurring here in an atmosphere of controversy, preceded and succeeded as it is by close logical argument.

On the first point we may observe what a striking illustration it is of the completeness of St. Paul's character. The clear, vigorous intellect and the masculine energy of the great Apostle are united to a heart full of tenderness. We can almost feel its pulsations, we can almost hear its mighty throbbings, in every line of this poem.

That this passage should be found in the middle of a protracted argument suggests the idea that we have here the result of a sudden and direct inspiration. The

charity, I am become *as* sounding brass,
or a tinkling cymbal. (2) And though
I have *the gift of* prophecy, and under-
stand all mysteries, and all knowledge;
and though I have all faith, so that I
could remove mountains, and have not
charity, I am nothing. (3) And though
I bestow all my goods to feed *the poor,*
and though I give my body to be burned,
and have not charity, it profiteth me
nothing. (4) Charity suffereth long, *and*
is kind; charity envieth not; charity
vaunteth not itself,[1] is not puffed up,
(5) doth not behave itself unseemly, seek-
eth not her own, is not easily provoked,
thinketh no evil; (6) rejoiceth not in

[1] Or, *is not rash.*

Apostle had always been conscious of a mighty power working in him, mastering him, bringing him into captivity to Christ. There suddenly flashes upon him the realisation of what that power is, and he cannot but at once give utterance, in language of surpassing loftiness and glowing with emotion, to the new and profound conviction which has set his whole soul aflame. This chapter is the Baptismal Service of Love. Here it receives its new Christian name. The word (*agapè*) which is used here for love is peculiar to the New Testament (and a few passages in the LXX.). It is not to be found in any heathen writer. The word "charity," which signifies either tolerance or almsgiving, is an insufficient rendering of the original, and destroys the force of the passage, especially in verse 3, where "almsgiving" without love is pronounced worthless. The Latin *caritas* was used as the rendering of *agapè*, probably because the ordinary Latin word *amor* (love) was considered too significant of a mere earthly or fleshly affection; and hence the word "charity" in the English version. Perhaps it was hoped that the word "charity," when planted in such a soil. and with such surroundings, would have grown to have that larger significance to which the original gives expression. If so, the experiment has not succeeded, the word has not become acclimatised to this chapter. The word "love" had better be restored here. The rare purity of its surrounding atmosphere will completely deprive it of any earthly or sensual taint.

This chapter, occupied with the one main thought, divides itself into three parts—

Verses 1—3. The greatest gifts are valueless without LOVE.
„ 4—7. The pre-eminent characteristics of LOVE.
„ 8—13. Gifts are transient; virtues are eternal, and chief of them is LOVE.

**Tongues of men and of angels.**—The gift of tongues (see Notes on chap. xiv.) is placed first as that most over-estimated at Corinth. It is useless without love. It would be impossible to define love, as it is impossible to define life; but the best conception of what St. Paul means by love can be found from the description which he subsequently gave of it. Stanley, contrasting the meaning of the word employed by St. Paul with the various words for love in other literature, remarks: "While the 'love' of the New Testament retains all the fervour of the Hebrew 'aspiration' and 'desire,' and of the 'personal affection' of the Greek, it ranges through as wide a sphere as the comprehensive 'benevolence' of Alexandria. Whilst it retains the religious element that raised the affections of the Hebrew Psalmist to the presence of God, it agrees with the classical and Alexandrian feelings in making its chief object the welfare of man. It is not religion evaporated into benevolence, but benevolence taken up into religion. It is the practical exemplification of the two great characteristics of Christianity, the union of God with man, the union of religion with morality; love to man for the sake of love to God, love to God showing itself in love to man."

**As sounding brass.**—Not a brass trumpet, or instrument of any kind, but simply a piece of metal, which when struck will merely produce noise.

**A tinkling cymbal.**—Better, *a clanging cymbal.* This instrument can produce by itself no intelligible tune. (See Ps. xl. 5.)

(2) **Prophecy.**—The Apostle valued the gift of prophecy—*i.e.*, preaching—more highly than the gift of tongues, which stood first in Corinthian estimation. He therefore naturally selects it as coming into the same condemnation, if unaccompanied by love. All the secrets of God's providence and complete knowledge (see chap. xii. 8), even such a transcendent faith as Christ had spoken of as capable of moving mountains (Matt. xvii. 20), may belong to a man, and without love he is nothing. We must not take these words as implying that the Apostle possessed this vast knowledge and faith personally. The whole argument is put hypothetically—it supposes a man possessed of these qualities.

(3) **Bestow all my goods.**—The Greek word literally means to feed others by giving them morsels of food, and so we have the thought of a charity extensive in its diffusion, as well as complete in its self-sacrifice. The whole of the bestower's property given in charity, and so divided as to reach the largest number.

**I give my body to be burned.**—A still greater proof of devotion to some person or cause, is the sacrifice of life; yet even that may be without love. A strange reading has crept into some MSS.—"that I may boast"—which would make the passage mean that a man gave his body to some torture from a wrong motive, viz., vain-glory. But this would weaken the force of the passage. What renders the self-sacrifice valueless is not a wrong cause, but the absence of love as the motive power. Although burning was not a form of martyrdom at this time, yet such histories as that of the three children in Dan. iii. 19 would make the expression intelligible and forcible.

These words are historically interesting to the English Church. They formed the text from which Dr. Smith preached at the martyrdom of Latimer and Ridley!

(4) **Charity suffereth long.**—Better, *Love is long-suffering.* Here follows a description of love. Descriptions of positive characteristics and negations of evil qualities are now employed by the Apostle in what he would have us believe to be his impossible task of adequately describing true love.

(5) **Thinketh no evil.**—That is, does not dwell upon the evil done to her.

(6) **Rejoiceth not in iniquity.**—The attitude of our mind towards sin is a great test of the truth of our religious feeling.

iniquity, but rejoiceth in the truth;[1]
(7) beareth all things, believeth all things, hopeth all things, endureth all things.
(8) Charity never faileth: but whether *there be* prophecies, they shall fail; whether *there be* tongues, they shall cease; whether *there be* knowledge, it shall vanish away.
(9) For we know in part, and we prophesy in part.
(10) But when that which is perfect is come, then that which is in part shall be done away.
(11) When I was a child, I spake as a child, I understood as a child, I thought[2] as a child: but when I became a man, I put away childish things.
(12) For now we see through a glass, darkly;[3] but then face to face: now I know in part; but then shall I know even as also I am known.
(13) And now abideth faith, hope, charity, these three; but the greatest of these *is* charity.

1 Or, *with the truth.*

2 Or, *reasoned.*

3 Gr. *in a riddle*

---

(7) **Beareth all things.**—The full thought of the original here is that love silently endures whatever it has to suffer.

(8) **Charity never faileth.**—From the positive and negative qualities of love described and enumerated in the preceding passage, the Apostle now turns to contrast the imperishable character of love and other graces with the ephemeral nature of gifts. The Corinthians held an exaggerated estimate of the value of gifts such as tongues and prophecy, and under-valued the graces of faith and love. Now the Apostle shows that they were thereby preferring the things which are for a time to the graces which are for ever. One faction, indeed, exalted to the highest place a gift—that of tongues—which was the most ephemeral of all Christian gifts. On the "tongues," see Note on chap. xiv. 2. "Prophecies," in the plural, intimates the varied gradations of power possessed by the preachers, in some cases including that deep spiritual insight into the realities of the present which enabled the preacher to foretell distant events.

(9) **We know in part.**—Knowledge and preaching are incomplete; therefore, when this dispensation ends, and the complete dispensation is brought in, these imperfect gifts shall cease. Gifts are but the implements of the divine husbandry; graces are the seeds themselves. When the great harvest-time comes, the instruments, however useful, will be cast aside altogether; the seeds will, by the very process of death, be transformed into blossoms and fruits, and in that perfected form remain for ever.

(10) **That which is perfect.**—This verse shows, by the emphatic "then," that the time when the gifts shall cease is the end of this dispensation. The imperfect shall not cease until the perfect is brought in. (See Eph. iv. 11—13.)

(11) **When I was a child.**—The natural childhood and manhood of this life are analogous to the spiritual childhood of this life and the spiritual manhood of the life to come.

**I understood as a child, I thought as a child.**—The first word expresses mere simple apprehension, the second word implies active intellectual exertion. It has been suggested that the three words here used refer back respectively to the gifts previously mentioned. "I spoke" corresponds to the "tongues," "I understood" to the "prophecy," and "I reasoned" to the "knowledge." Without intending any such very definite correspondence of these three expressions, the Apostle probably naturally made the points of analogy correspond in number with what they were intended to illustrate.

**But when I became a man.**—Better, *but now that I have become a man I have given up the ways of a child.* The point brought out is his present state as a man, and not, as the English version might seem to imply, some fixed point of transition in his past history. The contrast he seeks to make clear is between two states of life.

(12) **For now**—*i.e.*, in this earthly life, the "for" connecting the previous statement with that which it illustrates.

**Through a glass, darkly.**—Better, *through a mirror in a dark saying.* The illustration here is from a mirror when the image appears far behind the mirror itself. If we remember the imperfect metal surfaces which formed the mirrors of those days, we can imagine how imperfect and enigmatical (the Greek word is "in an *enigma*") would the image appear; so that the Apostle says, "Like that image which you see when you look at an object in a mirror far off, with blurred and undefined outline, such is our knowledge here and now; but *then* (*i.e.*, when this dispensation is at an end) we shall see as you see a man when you stand before him face to face. (See Num. xii. 7, 8 for a similar thought, but a different illustration of it—"mouth to mouth.") The word for "glass" here is the same as in Jas. i. 23, and must mean a mirror, and not, as some commentators suggest, a pane of transparent stone or horn, such as was then used, for which a quite different word would have been employed.

(13) **And now abideth . . .**—Better, *Thus there abide . . .* The "now" is not here temporal, but logical. It is not "now" (*i.e.*, this present life) contrasted with the future, but it is the conclusion of the whole argument. From all that has been urged in the previous verses it follows that these three graces—faith, hope, love—remain imperishable and immortal. Gifts such as the Corinthian Church rejoiced in shall pass away when the perfect succeeds the imperfect; the graces of faith, hope, love shall remain in the next life, exalted and purified. But even in this trinity of graces there is an order, and love stands first. The contrast is not between love which is imperishable and faith and hope which are perishable, but between ephemeral gifts and enduring graces. It is strange how completely in popular thinking this has been lost sight of, and hence we find such words as these—

> "Faith will vanish into sight,
> Hope be emptied in delight,
> Love in heaven will shine more bright,
> Therefore give us love;"

which express almost the opposite of what the Apostle really wrote.

There need be no difficulty in understanding that "faith," in the sense of trust in Christ as our Saviour, may continue in the heavenly state; indeed, when we see Him face to face, and see actually how great a salvation He hath obtained for us, that faith may be expected to glow with a new and increasing fervour

A.D. 59.

CHAPTER XIV.—(1) Follow after
Chap. xiv. 1—25. The gift of tongues.
charity, and desire spiritual *gifts*, but rather that
ye may prophesy. (2) For
he that speaketh in an *unknown*
tongue speaketh not unto men, but
unto God: for no man understandeth [1]
*him;* howbeit in the spirit he speaketh
mysteries. (3) But he that prophesieth
speaketh unto men *to* edification, and
exhortation, and comfort. (4) He that
speaketh in an *unknown* tongue edifieth

1 Gr. *heareth.*

---

Hope, too, need never cease if that new life is to be progressive. If hope lives by feeding on the present as the promise of the future, surely it will have a more abundant sustenance in that life than in this. Yet love stands supreme; indeed, both faith and hope would perish without her. (See Matt. xxvi. 35; Gal. v. 6.)

XIV.

(1) **Follow after charity.**—Better, *Follow after love.* The preceding chapter is parenthetical, and the Apostle here returns to the subject with which he had been immediately occupied before he branched off into that great Psalm of Love. He has spoken enthusiastically in praise of the superiority of love as the greatest amongst graces, and of all graces as superior to all gifts; but still, though we are to "do this," we are not to leave the other undone. Spiritual gifts are to be "earnestly striven for." As there was a priority in graces, so there is in gifts. To prophesy is the greatest gift; it is so, as we see afterwards, because it makes us useful to our brethren; therefore it is to be striven for rather than any other gift.

(2) **For he that speaketh in an unknown tongue.**—Better, *For he that speaketh in a tongue.* The word "unknown" is not in the original, but it has been inserted in connection with the word "tongue" all through this chapter, so as to make the various passages seem to be consistent with the theory that the gift of tongues was a gift of languages. This is not the place to enter into the question of what particular external manifestation of this gift was evidenced on the Day of Pentecost. (See Acts ii. 1—13.) Still, believing that the gift of tongues here spoken of is identical with the gift of tongues which was first bestowed at Pentecost, I would say that the phenomena described as occurring then must be explained by the fuller and more elaborate account of the nature of the gift which is given to us here. Against the theory that the gift was one of a capacity to speak various languages we have three considerations. (1) The word *dialectos,* which is repeatedly used to express languages (Acts i. 19; ii. 6, 8; xxi. 40; xxii. 2; xxvi. 14), is never used by St. Paul or by the author of the Acts in reference to the utterances of those who possessed the gift of tongues, but the other word, *glossa,* which is, literally, the physical organ of speech—as if the utterances were simply sounds that proceeded from it. (2) There is no trace whatever of this knowledge of languages having been ever used for the purpose of preaching to those who spoke foreign languages. The language of the Lycaonians was evidently not understood by the Apostles when they were addressed in it (see Acts xiv. 11), and they did not speak in it. That the hearers at Pentecost said they heard those who were filled with the Spirit "speak in our own language" would only imply, either that the outpouring on Pentecost had for the moment a miraculous effect, which immediately ceased, or that "all the various elements of Aramaic and Hellenistic speech, latent in the usual language of the time, were quickened, under the power of this gift, into a new life, sometimes intelligible, sometimes unintelligible to those who heard it, but always expressive of the vitality and energy of the Spirit by which it was animated." (3) The description of the gift in this chapter is utterly inconsistent with it being a gift of languages. The gift was the result of a quickened spiritual power by the action of the Holy Ghost (see also Acts ii. 4; x. 44—46; xix. 6); it poured itself forth in wild, impassioned utterances, which were sometimes mistaken for delirium (verse 23); and these were the expressions, not of thoughts, but of feelings, unintelligible always, if uninterpreted, to the listener, and sometimes to the utterer himself.

It is to be observed that very notable spiritual phenomena, not unlike what are recorded here, accompanied many periods of great spiritual revival. The histories of the early work of Wesley and Whitfield, and of Irving—to take examples in England alone—afford some very remarkable illustrations. The general subject of the first part of this chapter (verses 1—25) is the Gift of Tongues, and is thus dealt with:—

I. PROPHECY IS SUPERIOR TO THE GIFT OF TONGUES (verses 2—11)

Because (1) Tongues are the means of communion between the individual and God, whereas prophecy is communion with other men (verses 2, 3).

(2) Tongues do yourself good; prophecy does good to others (verses 4—6).

This truth is illustrated (*a*) by the variety of musical instruments (verse 7); (*b*) by the distinction of musical notes (verses 8, 9); (*c*) by the varieties of human language (verses 10, 11).

II. PRACTICAL APPLICATION OF THE FOREGOING (verses 11—19).

(1) What the aim and object of the Christians should be (verses 12, 13).

(2) His own example (verses 14—19).

III. FURTHER APPEAL TO THEIR INTELLIGENCE AS TO THIS TRUTH (verses 21—25).

(1) The Old Testament teaches the same principle (verses 21, 22).

(2) The gift of prophecy is a means of spreading Christianity, and the gift of tongues is not (verses 23—25).

**In the spirit he speaketh mysteries.**—The utterances come, not from his mind, but from his spirit, stirred by the Holy Spirit; and he speaks mysteries unintelligible to others.

(3) **Edification, and exhortation, and comfort.**—They communed with God by the speaking with tongues; they communed with the brethren by prophecy—building up, stirring up, cheering up, as each required.

(4) **He that speaketh in an unknown tongue.**—Better, *He that speaketh in a tongue.* The introduction of the word "unknown" destroys the whole force of the passage. All tongues—as distinct from languages—were unknown, *i.e.,* unintelligible. The gift of prophecy is superior in usefulness to that of tongues, and therefore to be preferred. The use of the

himself; but he that prophesieth edifieth
the church. (5) I would that ye all
spake with tongues, but rather that ye
prophesied: for greater *is* he that pro-
phesieth than he that speaketh with
tongues, except he interpret, that the
church may receive edifying. (6) Now,
brethren, if I come unto you speaking
with tongues, what shall I profit you,
except I shall speak to you either by
revelation, or by knowledge, or by pro-
phesying, or by doctrine?
(7) And even things without life giving
sound, whether pipe or harp, except
they give a distinction in the sounds,[1]
how shall it be known what is piped or
harped? (8) For if the trumpet give
an uncertain sound, who shall prepare
himself to the battle? (9) So likewise
ye, except ye utter by the tongue words
easy[2] to be understood, how shall it be
known what is spoken? for ye shall
speak into the air. (10) There are, it
may be, so many kinds of voices in the
world, and none of them *is* without sig-
nification. (11) Therefore if I know not
the meaning of the voice, I shall be
unto him that speaketh a barbarian,
and he that speaketh *shall be* a bar-
barian unto me. (12) Even so ye, for-

1 Or, *tunes.*

2 Gr. *significant.*

word "edify," as applied to an individual solely, as distinct from the individual as a part of the whole Church, is unusual with St. Paul (see Note on chap. viii. 1), but is introduced so as to make the antithesis verbally as well as logically more striking.

(5) **I would that ye all spake with tongues.**—To avoid danger of misunderstanding or misrepresentation the Apostle emphatically asserts here that the error which he is combating is the undue exaltation of the gift of tongues to the depreciation of other gifts. The teacher of religious truth to others, who thereby builds up the whole edifice of the body of Christ, is a greater one than he who is himself benefited by being possessed of profound but uncommunicable emotion.

**Except he interpret.**—The gift of interpreting might therefore belong to the same person who had the gift of tongues: and if he had this power of articulating for the benefit of others the emotion which he incoherently expresses in reverie, then the gift of tongues was useful to the Church at large, and so was as valuable as prophecy.

(6) **Now, brethren.**—Transferring these things to himself in an image the Apostle reinforces the preceding teaching. Now (*i.e.*, seeing that these things are so), what profit would I be to come to you speaking in tongues? I have been telling you that you cannot profit others: I ask you, do you think I speaking in tongues could profit you?

**Except I shall speak to you either . . .**—Here is an expansion of the "interpretation of tongues" of the previous verse, and which is the condition on which depends any usefulness of the gift. The "revelation" and the "knowledge" are the internal gifts in the teacher himself which are the sources of his power to communicate "prophecy" (*i.e.*, general exhortation), or "doctrine" (*i.e.*, systematic religious instruction) to his hearers.

(7) **And even things without life.**—The pipe and harp were the best-known instruments, and the principle just laid down of the inutility of sounds unless they be distinctive is illustrated by reference to them. Whether it was a harp or a pipe which was being played you could not know unless each gives a distinct sound of its own. The point here is not, as the English seems to suggest, that there must be a difference in tune, so as know *what* is being piped or harped—*that* illustration comes in in the next verse—but that each instrument has its own peculiar sound.

(8) **For if the trumpet give an uncertain sound.**—Not only has each instrument its own sound, but in each instrument there is a distinction of notes. If a trumpet does not clearly sound the advance when it is intended, or the retreat when it is meant, the trumpet is useless, the soldiers not knowing what to do.

(9) **So likewise ye.**—This is not the application of the foregoing, but the introduction of a third illustration, viz., the varieties of human language. The "tongue" here is simply the actual organ of speech, distinguished in the Greek, by the insertion of the article, from "tongues" which flow from the spiritual gift. If a human being does not use words that those spoken to understand, it is useless; such words pass as sounds into the air and are useless.

(10) **There are, it may be, so many kinds of voices in the world.**—There are a great many voices or languages in the world, and none of them but has a right meaning when spoken rightly and to the right person. No word in any language can be meaningless, but must correspond to some thought—for the thought exists first, and the word is invented as the expression of it.

(11) **Therefore if I know not the meaning of the voice.**—Language is useless unless we know what meaning is attached to each word uttered. The hearer is a foreigner (or *barbarian*), then, in the estimation of the speaker, and the speaker a foreigner in the estimation of the hearer. Thus the truth that sounds of tongues are useless unless they convey definite ideas to the hearers, is illustrated (1) by different instruments of music, (2) by different sounds of an instrument, (3) by different words and languages of living men—in all of which cases the conveyance of distinct ideas is the sign and test of their utility.

(12) **Even so ye.**—Here follows the practical application of the previous teaching and illustration. The "ye" of verse 9 was addressed to them as human beings generally; but here the Apostle returns to the immediate subject in hand, viz., the exaltation of particular spiritual gifts in the Corinthian Church. He passes now from the contrast between prophecy and tongues to give practical instruction (verses 12—19) as to how they should seek to use the gift of tongues. The word for "spiritual gifts" is, in the Greek, literally *spirits,* but is evidently meant to imply the gifts, and especially that one under consideration—the gift of tongues.

**Seek that ye may excel to the edifying of the church.**—Better, *seek, then, to the edifying of the Church, that ye may abound.* The point cannot be that they were to seek to excel in spiritual gifts, that

asmuch as ye are zealous of spiritual[1]
*gifts*, seek that ye may excel to the
edifying of the church. (13) Wherefore
let him that speaketh in an *unknown*
tongue pray that he may interpret.
(14) For if I pray in an *unknown* tongue,
my spirit prayeth, but my understanding
is unfruitful. (15) What is it then? I
will pray with the spirit, and I will
pray with the understanding also: I
will sing with the spirit, and I will sing
with the understanding also. (16) (Else
when thou shalt bless with the spirit,
how shall he that occupieth the room of
the unlearned say Amen at thy giving
of thanks, seeing he understandeth not
what thou sayest? (17) For thou verily
givest thanks well, but the other is not
edified.) (18) I thank my God, I speak
with tongues more than ye all: (19) yet
in the church I had rather speak five
words with my understanding, that *by
my voice* I might teach others also, than
ten thousand words in an *unknown*
tongue.

(20) Brethren, be not children in un-
derstanding: howbeit in malice be ye
children, but in understanding be men.[2]
(21) In the law it is written,[a] With
*men of* other tongues and other lips will
I speak unto this people; and yet for
all that will they not hear me, saith the

1 Gr. *of spirits.*

2 Gr. *perfect*, or, *of a ripe age.*

a Isa. 28. 11.

---

so they might edify the Church, for the next verse explains how the gift is to be sought so that it may edify others; but the force of the passage here is as given above—they are to seek this gift for the benefit of others, and so they will themselves, by serving others, abound yet more and more (chap. viii. 7; 1 Thess. iv. 1).

(13) **In an unknown tongue.**—Better, *in a tongue.* The gift of interpretation would make the gift of tongues useful for the edifying of the Church. This would be an object of unselfish prayer, which God would indeed answer. In the Greek it is suggested that the gift of interpretation is not only to be the object of his prayer, but that it will be the result; and this leads on to the thought in the next verse.

(14) **For if I pray in an unknown tongue.**—Better, *if I pray in a tongue.* Verses 14—19 are expressed in the first person (except verses 16, 17, which are a parenthesis), as enforcing the Apostle's own example. A man praying in a tongue needed the gift of interpretation. The emotions of his spirit, kindled by the Spirit of God, found utterance in a "tongue," the gift of the Spirit of God; but his intellectual faculty grasped no definite idea, and could not, therefore, formulate it into human language; therefore the prayer which is offered merely in a tongue, from the spirit and not from the understanding, is useless as regards others. The Apostle is here speaking of public worship (see verse 16), and not of private devotion; and the word "fruitless" implies the result, or rather the absence of result, as regards others.

(15) **What is it then?**—The Apostle, in answering this question—viz., What, then, is the practical conclusion of the whole matter?—still speaks in the first person, quoting his own conduct and resolution. He will not let his public ministrations as regards prayer and praise evaporate into mere enthusiasm; nor will he, on the other hand, allow a cold intellectual creed to chill and freeze the warm emotions of the spirit.

(16) **Else when thou shalt bless with the spirit.**—In this and the following verse the Apostle speaks in the second person, for they refer, not to his practice, but to that of some in Corinth. Their conduct and its results are introduced parenthetically here, in contrast with what he is laying down as his own earnest desire and practice.

**He that occupieth the room of the unlearned.**—Better, *he that is in the position of a private individual;* as we should say, a "layman"—the one who comes as a private person to the assembly, and does not lead the prayer and thanksgiving. How can he say "Amen" when he does not know what is being said? and he cannot know if you speak in a tongue, without interpreting. It would seem from this verse that from the earliest apostolic times the practice has been for the congregation to join in the thanksgiving by uttering "Amen" (the Hebrew "So be it") at the conclusion.

(17) **For thou verily givest thanks well.**—It is here implied that speaking in a tongue was, as regards an individual, an acceptable mode of worship, and it is the public use of it that all throughout this passage the Apostle is dealing with.

(18, 19) **I thank my God.**—Here the Apostle resumes in the first person, coming back, after the parenthesis, to the continuation of his own desire and example. He does not undervalue that gift the misuse and exaggeration of which he is censuring; he possesses it himself in a remarkable degree; yet in the Church (*i.e.*, in any assembly of Christians for prayer or instruction) he would prefer to speak five words with his mind rather than ten thousand with a tongue only; for the object of such assemblies is not private prayer or private ecstatic communion with God, but the edification of others. The word used for "teach" in this verse is literally our word *catechise.*

(20) **Howbeit in malice be ye children.**—Better, *however in evil be ye infants.* There are three grades spoken of here in the original—infants, children, full-grown men. Their conduct in exalting these "tongues," against which he has been warning them, is a proof that they are yet children in knowledge. They ought to be full-grown; the only thing in which they ought to be children is evil, and in that they cannot be too young, too inexperienced; they should be merely "infants." (A similar thought occurs in chaps. ii. 6; iii. 1; xiii. 10, 11.)

(21, 22) **In the law it is written.**—The preceding teaching is illustrated and enforced by an appeal to Jewish history. The Old Testament as a whole was not infrequently thus designated "the Law." (See John x. 34; xii. 34; xv. 25.) The words are scarcely a quotation, but rather an illustration taken from Isa. xxviii. 9—12. The passage there refers to the refusal of Israel to hearken to Jehovah when He spoke to them with clearness and simplicity, and His judgment on them taking the form of declaring that He would make a foreign people—the Assyrians—be His mouth-

Lord. (22) Wherefore tongues are for a
sign, not to them that believe, but to
them that believe not: but prophesying
*serveth* not for them that believe not,
but for them which believe. (23) If
therefore the whole church be come
together into one place, and all speak
with tongues, and there come in *those*
*that are* unlearned, or unbelievers, will
they not say that ye are mad? (24) But
if all prophesy, and there come in one
that believeth not, or *one* unlearned, he
is convinced of all, he is judged of all:
(25) and thus are the secrets of his heart
made manifest; and so falling down on
*his* face he will worship God, and report
that God is in you of a truth.

Chap. xiv. 26—40. The order of public worship.

(26) How is it then,
brethren? when ye come
together, every one of you
hath a psalm, hath a doctrine, hath a
tongue, hath a revelation, hath an inter-
pretation. Let all things be done unto
edifying. (27) If any man speak in an
*unknown* tongue, *let it be* by two, or at
the most *by* three, and *that* by course;
and let one interpret. (28) But if there
be no interpreter, let him keep silence

---

piece to them in the future, in a language which they knew not. It is as if the Apostle said: Remember there was a time in Jewish history when an unintelligible language was a sign sent by God, and proved unavailing as regards the conversion of Israel. The gift which you so exalt now is equally useless by itself for that same purpose.

(22) **Wherefore tongues are for a sign, not to them that believe.**—This is not an interpretation of the prophecy alluded to in the previous verse, but St. Paul now returns to the gift of "tongues" as existing in the Church, and introduces a thought regarding this gift suggested by the fact mentioned, viz., that in Israel unintelligible tongues, uttered in their hearing, were for a sign to unbelieving Jews. Tongues should not be exalted in estimation above prophecy—inasmuch as the function of the latter is really grander than that of the former. Tongues were useful to arrest the attention of unbelievers, and, if rightly used, to arouse their convictions; but prophecy is in the highest sense useful for believers.

(23) **If therefore.**—Intended, as tongues were, for a "sign," they cease to be thus useful if not properly employed. The report of the strange utterances which take place in the assembled Church may lead some unbeliever to come there: but if there be tongues alone, and they uninterpreted, the stranger will simply think those present are mad. (See Acts ii. 13.) It is not meant here that *all* commence shouting out at the same time, neither is it in the next verse that *all* prophesy simultaneously; but the thought presented is the undue and exclusive cultivation of this gift by all in the Corinthian Church.

(24) **But if all prophesy.**—There is no danger of exaggeration regarding this gift. Each one uttering prophecy, telling forth the gospel truth, and revealing the mind of God, will have a message that will be useful to the unbeliever. As one after another they utter the words of divine truth, they each send something that pierces into his soul. By all of them he is convicted in his own conscience of some sin. He is condemned in his own eyes, a searching light is turned upon his heart. The secrets of his heart are made manifest, and he makes terrible discoveries of his guilt (Heb. iv. 12, 13).

(25) **And thus are the secrets of his heart made manifest.**—Better, *and the secrets of his heart are made manifest*—such being the reading of the best MSS. It is the third result of the prophetic utterances explained in previous Note. His complete conversion is evidenced by his worshipping God and recognising the presence of God in that assembly of Christians: "He will confess that you are not mad, but that God is truly in you, and that He is the true God who is in you" (Bengel). It is to be noticed that though the Apostle speaks in this passage of an "unlearned" person (*i.e.*, a private person, one who has no gift of prophecy or tongues), or an "unbeliever," it is the latter that is most prominently before his mind, and the former only so far as he shared in common with the latter his ignorance and inability to understand.

(26) **How is it then, brethren?**—From a discussion as to the relative value of the gift of tongue and that of prophecy, the Apostle now turns to practical instructions as to the method of their employment in public church assemblies. He first gives directions regarding the tongues (verses 27, 28), then regarding prophecy (verses 29—36), and the concluding verses of this chapter contain a summing up and brief repetition of what has been already laid down. In this verse he introduces the practical application of the truths which he has been enforcing, by the question, "How is it, then?"—*i.e.*, what should follow from all these arguments?—and, instead of answering the question directly, he first recalls the existing state of confusion in their public assemblies, which had rendered necessary the teaching of the previous verses, and which is to be remedied by the practical instructions which now follow.

**When ye come together, every one of you hath . . .**—Better, *when ye are assembling together each one of you hath a psalm, &c.* The uppermost thought in each mind as you are assembling for public worship is the individual gift which he possesses. One had the gift of pouring forth a psalm of praise; another could deliver a doctrinal discourse; another could speak to God in a tongue; another had some deep insight into the spiritual world; another could interpret the tongue. If these varied gifts were employed by each for his own gratification, or even for his own spiritual advancement, they would not be used worthy of the occasion. In public these gifts were to be exercised not by each one for himself, but for the building up of the whole Church.

(27) **If any man speak in an unknown tongue.**—Better, *If any man speak in a tongue.* Here is the practical application of the general rule just laid down to the exercise of the gift of tongues. Those who had that gift were not all to speak together, and so cause confusion; only two, or at the most three, were to speak in each assembly, and each of such group was to speak in turn, one at a time. There was to be with each group one who had the gift of interpretation, and he was to interpret to the listeners.

(28) **But if there be no interpreter.**—But if

in the church; and let him speak to
himself, and to God.
(29) Let the prophets speak two or
three, and let the other judge. (30) If
*any thing* be revealed to another that
sitteth by, let the first hold his peace.
(31) For ye may all prophesy one by one,
that all may learn, and all may be
comforted. (32) And the spirits of the
prophets are subject to the prophets.
(33) For God is not *the author* of con-
fusion,[1] but of peace.
As in all churches of the saints,
(34) let your women keep silence in
the churches: for it is not permitted
unto them to speak; but *they are com-
manded* to be under obedience, as also
saith the law.[a] (35) And if they will
learn any thing, let them ask their
husbands at home: for it is a
shame for women to speak in the
church.
(36) What? came the word of God
out from you? or came it unto you
only? (37) If any man think himself to
be a prophet, or spiritual, let him
acknowledge that the things that I
write unto you are the commandments
of the Lord. (38) But if any man be
ignorant, let him be ignorant.
(39) Wherefore, brethren, covet to
prophesy, and forbid not to speak with

a Gen. 3. 16.

1 Gr. *tumult*, or, *unquietness*.

there be no one with the gift of interpreting, then the speaker with tongues was not to exercise his gift publicly at all; he may only exercise his gift in private with himself and God.

(29) **Let the prophets speak.**—Here follows the application, to those who had the gift of prophecy, of the general principle, Let all be done to edification. Only two or three prophets are to speak in each assembly on each occasion; the others (not "other," as in English version) who had the gift are to sit by silent and judging, *i.e.*, determining whether the utterances were from the Spirit of God. (See chap. xii. 3, and 1 John iv. 1—3.) If, however, while one prophet was standing speaking there came a sudden revelation of truth to some other prophet who was sitting by, the speaker would pause, and the other prophet give utterance to the inspiration which had come to him. The suddenness of the revelation would show that it was a truth needed there and then, and so should find utterance without delay.

(31) **For ye may all prophesy one by one.**—Better, *For it is in your power all to prophesy one by one.* How it is in their power is explained by the following verse. This orderly prophesying will accomplish the instruction and comforting of all; words of instruction will be interspersed with words of comfort, and so the teaching be suited to every condition of mind and soul of those present.

(32) **The spirits of the prophets . . .**—They might have said it was impossible to carry out St. Paul's instructions; that the rushing Spirit of God overcame them—shook them, so that they could not control themselves. To this St. Paul replies (verse 31; see above) that it is not so; that they *can* prophesy one by one; that the spirits of the prophets are under the control of the prophets.

(33) **For God is not the author of confusion.**—Better, *For God is the God, not of confusion, but of peace.* The Church is the Church of God, and should bear on it the moral image of its King: there should be order, therefore, not confusion, in their assemblies.

**As in all churches of the saints.**—It is best to make these words read as the commencement of the next subject, thus:—*As in all the churches of the saints, let the women keep silence in the churches.* At Corinth one evil of neglecting the principles of order just laid down was that women spoke in the public assemblies. This was not the custom in any other churches, therefore the example of other churches was against such a practice.

(34) **But they are commanded to be under obedience.**—Better (as in some of the best MSS.), *but let them be under obedience.* The original precept laid down in Gen. iii. 16 teaches this. "The law" stands for the Old Testament generally.

(35) **If they will learn any thing.**—Better, *if they are desirous to learn anything.* They are not even to ask questions in public assemblies. They are to ask their husbands at home on every point on which they desire special instruction. (See chap. vii.)

(36) **What?**—The church at Corinth had on some of these points acted at variance with the practice of the other churches, and in a manner which assumed an independence of St. Paul's apostolic authority. He therefore asks them, with something of sarcastic indignation, whether they are the source from whence the word of God has come, or whether they think themselves its sole recipients, that they should set themselves above the other churches, and above him?

(37) **If any man think himself . . .**—The best evidence of the possession of these gifts would be that their conduct was the very opposite of what they seemed to think the possession of these gifts should make it. The Apostle asserts positively that what he is now writing to them are the commandments of the Lord. There could be no clearer or more emphatic statement of St. Paul's claim to inspiration.

(38) **But if any man be ignorant.**—There are here two readings in the Greek, for each of which there is strong evidence. The passage may run, either, as in the English, *if any man does not know this, let him not know it:* then the words would mean that a person who could not recognise such an evident and simple truth must be of a perverse mind—his opposition would give the Apostle no further concern. The other reading is, *if any man knows not this, he is himself not known:* this would signify that any man who knows not this truth is not known of God (as in chaps. viii. 2, 3; xiii. 12).

(39) **Wherefore, brethren.**—The practical summing up of the whole matter. Seek earnestly to prophesy, and forbid not to speak with tongues. The phraseology intimates the relative importance of the two gifts in the estimation of the Apostle, which was inverted by those to whom he wrote at Corinth. This ought you to do, but not leave the other undone.

tongues. (40) Let all things be done decently and in order.

CHAPTER XV.—(1) Moreover, brethren, I declare unto you the gospel which I preached unto you, which also ye have received, and wherein ye stand; (2) by which also ye are saved, if ye keep in memory[1] what[2] I preached unto you, unless ye have believed in vain. (3) For I delivered unto you first of all that which I also

Chap. xv. The resurrection.

1 Or, *hold fast.*
2 Gr. *by what speech.*

A.D. 59.

---

(40) **Let all things be done decently.**—The former verse reiterates in a condensed sentence the principles laid down regarding the gifts in the first part of the chapter (verses 1—25). This verse similarly deals with the general principle laid down in the latter part of the chapter regarding the style and order of public worship. The object of all church assemblies is to be the building up of the Body of Christ, which is His Church; and therefore seemliness and ordered regularity are absolutely necessary to this end. Here again, as in so many other instances in this Epistle, while the particular and unique circumstances which called forth the apostolic instructions have for centuries passed away, the writings of St. Paul are of permanent and abiding application, because of the general and eternal principles on which his instructions are based. The strange outbursts of incoherent fanaticism which have occurred from time to time in the after-history of the Church are condemned by the principle with which St. Paul combatted the disorder of the gift of tongues in Corinth; and the practice of the Roman Church, in performing her public services in a tongue not "understanded of the people," is at variance with the principle which in this chapter he reiterates with varied emphasis—that all public utterance of prayer and praise should be such as those present can join in, not only with emotional heart but with clear and understanding intellect.

## XV.

(1) **Moreover, brethren.**—This chapter is throughout occupied with the DOCTRINE OF THE RESURRECTION OF THE DEAD. The occasion which caused the Apostle to dwell at such length and with such emphasis on this subject was the denial of the resurrection by some members of the Corinthian Church. It has been suggested by some writers that what the Apostle had to combat was a false conception of the resurrection—that at Corinth there were probably those who refined away the doctrine of the resurrection into merely a rising from the death of sin into a life of righteousness, something after the manner of Hymenæus and Philetus (2 Tim. ii. 17, 18), who taught that "the resurrection was past already." It seems clear, however, from the emphatic statement in verse 12, and from the general scope and drift of the entire argument, that what the Apostle is here meeting is not a perversion, but a denial of the doctrine. There were many elements in such a mixed body as the Corinthian Church which would have contributed to the growth of this error. Amongst the Jewish converts would be some traces of the Sadducean (Matt. xxii. 23) denial of the resurrection, and in the Gentile section of the Church there would linger the spirit of the Athenians who "mocked when they heard of the resurrection of the dead" (Acts xvii. 32), and of the Epicurean philosophers who said, "Let us eat and drink, for to-morrow we die." From these and from other like sources there had crept into the Church itself a denial of the doctrine of the resurrection. In reading this chapter it is well to remember that the Apostle probably intended it, not only as a reply to these corruptors of the faith, but as supplying those who remained faithful with a confirmation of their own faith, and arguments with which they might meet their opponents. It is always difficult to give a clear, exhaustive analysis of an argument by such a writer as St. Paul. The enthusiasm of his nature leads him to mingle the syllogism of passion with the syllogism of logic; and, as he was not writing himself, but dictating the composition, a word often leads him off from his argument into some splendid outburst of pathetic exhortation, or of prophetic utterance. Still, including such digressions, the general argument of this chapter may be tabulated thus:—

I.—THE DOCTRINE OF THE RESURRECTION (verses 1—34).

Subdivided as follows:

(1) *The resurrection proved by the historical fact of Christ's resurrection* (verses 1—15).
(2) *The resurrection proved by an appeal to the moral consequences involved in a denial of it* (verses 16—28).
(3) *The truth of the resurrection involved in certain existing practices* (verses 29—34).

II.—THE METHOD AND PRINCIPLE OF THE RESURRECTION (verses 35—58).

(1) *Illustration from analogy* (verses 35—44).
(2) *Illustration from our dual descent from Adam and from Christ* (verses 44—49).
(3) *The great change* (verses 50—53).
(4) *A song of triumph* (verses 54—57).
(5) *Concluding exhortation* (verse 58).

**I declare unto you.**—The Apostle opens his historical argument by reminding the Corinthians that this is no new nor unimportant matter. It is the original gospel which he had preached to them, which they received, and in which they stand, and by which they *are being saved* (not "are saved," as in the English).

(2) **If ye keep in memory what I preached unto you.**—Better, *if ye hold fast with what word I preached the gospel to you, unless you believed in vain.* The idea here is not, as implied in the English version, that they were converted, and yet that heretofore no results have followed from their belief; it is the same thought which comes out more fully in verse 17. They are saved by their faith in the gospel as preached by St. Paul, unless (which is impossible) the whole gospel be false, and so their faith in it be vain and useless.

(3) **For I delivered . . .**—Here follows the explanation and illustration of what he meant, in verse 2, by "with what word I preached the gospel." We see here what the subject of apostolic teaching was—not indeed all the gospel that the Apostle taught, but what he considered of the first importance, and therefore put in the forefront of his teaching—viz., the historical fact of Christ's death for our sins,

received, how that Christ died for our sins according to the scriptures; (4) and
that he was buried, and that he rose again the third day according to the scriptures: (5) and that he was seen of
Cephas, then of the twelve: (6) after that,
he was seen of above five hundred brethren at once; of whom the greater part remain unto this present, but some are fallen asleep. (7) After that, he was
seen of James; then of all the apostles.
(8) And last of all he was seen of me also,
as of one born out of due time.[1] (9) For
I am the least of the apostles, that am not meet to be called an apostle, because I persecuted the church of God.
(10) But by the grace of God I am what I am: and his grace which *was bestowed* upon me was not in vain; but I laboured more abundantly than they all: yet not I, but the grace of God which was with
me. (11) Therefore whether *it were* I or
they, so we preach, and so ye believed.
(12) Now if Christ be preached that he

[1] Or, *an abortive.*

---

His burial, His resurrection. This was the first Creed of Christendom.

**For our sins.**—Not only because of, but in behalf of our sins, in order to take them away (Gal. i. 4; 1 Pet. ii. 24; 1 John iii. 5). The fact of the Atonement was not something evolved by the Apostle's own consciousness, but a fact revealed to him by Christ. (See chap. xi. 23, and Note there.)

(4) **And that he rose again.**—Better, *and that He has been raised again.* The burial of our Lord is dwelt upon and emphasised as the proof of the reality of His death. Similarly in the case of Lazarus, his entombment is brought out strongly as showing that it was from no trance, but from death that he arose. (See John xi.)

**According to the scriptures.**—The reiteration with each statement that it was "according to the scriptures," *i.e.*, according to the Old Testament scriptures, the Gospel narratives not yet being in existence—shows how strongly the Apostle dwelt on the unity of the facts of Christ's life and the predictive utterances of the prophets. The death, burial, and resurrection of our Lord were all parts of that providential plan which the deep spiritual insight of God's servants of old illumined by the Holy Spirit had enabled them to foresee. The resurrection was no subsequent invention to try and explain away or mitigate the terrible shock which Christ's death had given to his followers. (See Pss. ii. 7; xvi. 10; xxi. 16; Isa. liii. 9, 10; lv. 3; Hos. vi. 2.)

(5) **That he was seen of Cephas.**—From the indications of sequence here given we may conclude that the appearances here grouped together are arranged in chronological order. We have these appearances:—(1) To Cephas (see Luke xxiv. 34). (2) To the Twelve—the phrase "the Twelve" being used to indicate, not the number of those present, but the group to which they belonged, as Decemviri might be used, or Hebdomadal Council, not to express the exact number but the corporate body—(see Luke xxiv. 36; John xx. 19). This was probably the appearance to the ten Apostles, and is distinguished from a subsequent appearance to "all the Apostles." (3) To above five hundred brethren at once. This must have been in Galilee, for at a later date (see Acts i. 15) the Church at Jerusalem consisted of only one hundred and twenty disciples. (See Matt. xxviii. 16, 17, and Acts i. 15.) (4) To James. This appearance is recorded only here and in the Gospel of the Hebrews, which is quoted by St. Jerome, "But the Lord, when he had given the *sindôn*" (the same word as that for the "linen garment," in Mark xiv. 51) "to the servant of the priest. had a table brought out, and bread on it, which He blessed and gave to James, saying, 'Eat thy bread now, brother, since the Son of Man has risen from the dead;' for James had sworn that he would not eat bread from the hour in which he had drunk the cup of the Lord until he should see Him rising from the dead." (5) To all the Apostles, Thomas being present (John xx. 26). (6) St. Paul himself (Acts ix. 5). To these facts St. Paul appeals. Most of those who saw Him were alive. Their enemies were alive to dispute it if they could. The witnesses had nothing to gain, everything to lose by telling the truth. The evidence was set forth some twenty-five or thirty years after the occurrence of the alleged facts. The Apostle here maintains the truth of an historical fact. He appeals solely to historical proof, and accumulates a mass of historical testimony, such as in any matter of history, if produced so shortly after the occurrence, would be deemed overwhelming.

(6) **Fallen asleep.**—The same word is used of Stephen's death (see Acts vii. 60), so also in verse 18.

(8) **Was seen of me also, as of one born out of due time.**—Better, *Last of all, as to an untimely born one he appeared also to me.* The Apostle here distinctly states that he saw the Lord at the time of his conversion as really as St. Peter and others had seen him, though with touching pathos and strongly marked emphasis he adds that it was not at the same time as the "firstborn" had seen Him, but only as an "untimely born" one.

(9) **For I am the least of the apostles.**—*Paulus Minimus.* Here the mention of his conversion—the thought of what he had been before, what he had become since—leads the Apostle into a digression, occupying this and the next two verses. The two thoughts of his own inherent nothingness and of his greatness by the grace of God are here mingled together in expressions of intense personal feeling. While he was a persecutor he had thought that he was acting *for* the Church of God; he was really persecuting the Church of God. The Christian Church had completely taken the place of the Jewish Church—not merely abolished it, but superseded it.

(10) **But by the grace of God I am what I am.**—This whole verse is full of that maintenance of official dignity as an Apostle and a labourer, and of personal humility, which were characteristic of St. Paul.

(11) **Therefore whether . . .**—Better, *Whether, therefore, it were I or they.* Such (see verses 3, 4) was and is our teaching, such was your belief. It matters not from whom it came, whether from the greatest or least of the Apostles, the gospel was preached, and was accepted by you. These words thus recall the reader from the strong personal feeling shown in the preceding verse to the main argument.

(12) **If Christ be preached that he rose from the dead.**—Better, *is being preached.* It has been

rose from the dead, how say some among
you that there is no resurrection of the
dead? (13) But if there be no resurrec-
tion of the dead, then is Christ not
risen: (14) and if Christ be not risen,
then *is* our preaching vain, and your
faith *is* also vain. (15) Yea, and we are
found false witnesses of God; because
we have testified of God that he raised
up Christ: whom he raised not up, if so
be that the dead rise not. (16) For if
the dead rise not, then is not Christ
raised: (17) and if Christ be not raised,
your faith *is* vain; ye are yet in your
sins. (18) Then they also which are
fallen asleep in Christ are perished.
(19) If in this life only we have hope in
Christ, we are of all men most miserable.
(20) But now is Christ risen from the
dead, *and* become the firstfruits of them
that slept. (21) For since by man *came*
death, by man *came* also the resurrec-
tion of the dead. (22) For as in Adam
all die, even so in Christ shall all be

---

proved as a matter of historical fact that a man has risen from the dead; it is therefore illogical to say that there is no resurrection of the dead.

(14) **If Christ be not risen.**—Better, *but if Christ be not raised;* and so all through this passage.

**Then is our preaching vain, and your faith is also vain.**—The Apostles had preached a risen Christ, their converts had believed in a risen Christ, but now the proposition is, There is no resurrection; therefore Christ is not risen; therefore the preaching and the faith which are based on the delusion that He is risen are both vain and useless. The argument is still purely an appeal to historical evidence supporting an historical fact, and to the consequences involved in denying that fact (see verse 16).

(15) **Yea, and we are found false witnesses.**—Not mistaken witnesses, but witnesses testifying to what they know to be false. This is another result involved in a denial of the doctrine of the resurrection, that the Apostles must be regarded as false witnesses—not deceived, but deceivers. The suppressed part of the argument here is the absurdity of the Apostles being such. There was no motive for them to speak untruth.

**If so be that the dead rise not.**—Better, *if the dead be not raised.*

(16) **For if the dead rise not.**—Better, *if the dead be not raised.* The Apostle has in the previous verse completed the argument as to the historical fact of Christ's resurrection, which proves that the denial of the doctrine of the resurrection cannot be maintained unless it can be shown that the Apostles are wilfully bearing false testimony, and that their preaching, and the faith of those who accepted it, is vain. He now turns to a different line of argument—a *reductio ad absurdum.* He maintains the doctrine of the resurrection by showing the incredible absurdities to which a belief in the contrary must lead. If you do not believe in a resurrection, you must believe—(1) That Christ is not raised, and that your faith, therefore, being false, has no result—that you are still slaves of sin. This you know by personal experience to be false. As well might a living man try to believe that he is a corpse. (2) That all who have fallen asleep in Christ have perished; that is, that the noblest and most unselfish perish like brutes. (3) That God gives men a good hope in Christ, and that it, not being fulfilled here, is never to be fulfilled. In other words, if there be no resurrection, the only alternative is atheism, for otherwise you have to believe that, though there is a God who is wise and just, yet that the purest and greatest life ever lived is no better in the end than the life of a dog; that those who have lived the most unselfish lives have perished like beasts; and that God aroused a hunger and thirst of the purest kind in some souls, only that the hunger should never be satisfied, and the thirst never be quenched.

(20) **But now . . .**—From the hopeless and ghastly conclusion in which the hypothetical propositions of the previous verse would logically land us, the Apostle turns, with the consciousness of truth, to the hopeful faith to which a belief in the resurrection leads. It cannot be so. Now *is* Christ risen from the dead. And that is no isolated fact. As the firstfruits were typical of the whole harvest (Lev. xxiii. 10, 11), so is Christ. He rose, not to the exclusion but to the inclusion of all Humanity. If St. Paul wrote this Epistle about the time of Passover (see *Introduction,* and chaps. v. 6; xvi. 8), the fact that the Paschal Sabbath was immediately followed by the day of offering of firstfruits may have suggested this thought.

(21) **For since by man . . .**—The image of the firstfruits is followed up by an explanation of the unity of Christ and Humanity. The firstfruit must be a sample of the same kind as that which it represents. That condition is fulfilled in the case of the firstfruits of the resurrection.

(22) **As in Adam . . .**—Better, *as in the Adam all die, so in the Christ shall all be made alive.* The first Adam and the second Adam here stand as the heads of Humanity. All that is fleshly in our nature is inherited from the Adam; in every true son of God it is dying daily, and will ultimately die altogether. All that is spiritual in our nature we inherit from the Christ; it is immortal, is rising daily, will ultimately be raised with a spiritual and immortal body. We must remember that the relationship of Christ to Humanity is not to be dated only from the Incarnation. Christ stood in the same federal relation to all who went before as He does to all who have come since. (See the same thought in chap. x. 4, and in Christ's own words, "Before Abraham was, I am.") The results of Christ's death are co-extensive with the results of Adam's fall—they extend to all men; but the individual responsibility rests with each man as to which he will cherish—that which he derives from Christ or that which he derives from Adam—the "offence" of Adam or the "grace" of Christ. The best comment on this passage is, perhaps, the prayer in the Baptismal Office: "O merciful God, grant that the old Adam in this child may be so buried, that the new man may be raised up in him." There seems to be this moral significance in these words of St. Paul, as well as the obvious argument that, as all men die physically, so all shall be raised from the dead; as we have the evidence of death in the death of a man and of all men, so we have the evidence (and not the mere theoretical promise) of a resurrection in the resurrection of the Man Christ Jesus.

made alive. (23) But every man in his
own order: Christ the firstfruits; after-
ward they that are Christ's at his
coming. (24) Then *cometh* the end, when
he shall have delivered up the kingdom
to God, even the Father; when he shall
have put down all rule and all authority
and power. (25) For he must reign,
till he hath put all enemies under his
feet. (26) (The last enemy *that* shall be
destroyed *is* death.) (27) For he hath
put all things under his feet. But when
he saith all things are put under *him*,
*it is* manifest that he is excepted, which
did put all things under him. (28) And
when all things shall be subdued unto
him, then shall the Son also himself be
subject unto him that put all things
under him, that God may be all in all.

(29) Else what shall they do which are
baptized for the dead, if the dead rise
not at all? why are they then baptized

---

(23) **But every man in his own order.**—Or, literally, *in his own troop.* There is to be a sequence in the resurrection of the dead, and St. Paul explains this by the three groups:—(1) Christ Himself, the firstfruits; (2) the faithful in Christ at His coming; (3) all the rest of mankind at the end, when the final judgment takes place. The interval between these latter two, as to its duration, or where or how it will be spent, is not spoken of here. The only point the Apostle has to treat of is the order of the resurrection. (See 1 Thess. iv. 13, 17; Rev. xx.)

(24—28) **When he shall have delivered up the kingdom to God, even the Father.**—The Apostle carries on the thought of a triumph which the use of the word "troop" in the previous verse had commenced or suggested. There rises before the prophetic vision of St. Paul the final triumph of Christ over all evil, over all power, and the Son giving up to the Father (not His humanity, which is "for ever and ever"—Luke i. 32, 33) the kingdom of this world, which in His humanity He conquered for the Father as well as for Himself. He will, the moment He becomes conqueror, sit down with the Father on His throne. Christ laying the spoils of a conquered world at the foot of the throne of the Father, shows, by that supreme act of self-sacrifice, that in His office as Redeemer He came, not to do His own will, but the will of the Father. In this sense the Son Himself, as Redeemer, is "put under Him"—God is all in all. We must clearly remember that the Apostle is here speaking of the Son as Redeemer, and is not penetrating into the deeper mysteries of the relation of the Persons in the Godhead. (See John xvii. 5; Heb. i. 8.)

(24) **All rule and all authority and power.**—Not only hostile rule and authority and power, but all intermediate rule of any sort, good and bad. The direct government by God of all creatures is to be at last attained. All the interventions of authority and power which the fall of man rendered necessary will be needless when the complete triumph of Christ comes in. Thus Humanity, having for ages shared the condition of fallen Adam, will be finally restored to the state of unfallen Adam. Man will see God, and be ruled by God face to face.

(25) **He must reign.**—It is a moral consequence. God must triumph, and so the Son must reign and conquer till that triumph be complete. Some suggest that the force of these words is that He must reign, &c., because it has been prophesied (Ps. cx.); but the more obvious truth is that it was prophesied because it is morally necessary.

(27) **For he hath put all things under his feet.**—Verse 26 is a parenthesis, and the "for" with which this verse commences goes back to verse 25. The connection is, Christ must reign until he has put all enemies under his feet. Christ must triumph, *for* according to the statement in Ps. viii. 6 (see also Ps. cx. 1), God hath put all things under man, and in a higher sense under the Son of Man. (For a similar application of Old Testament statement regarding man to Christ as the Son of Man, see Matt. xxi. 16; Heb. ii. 7.) But when God says that all things are put under Him, He evidently is excepted who did put all things under Him. This leads up logically to the complete triumph of God the Father, expressed in the following verse, which is an expansion of verse 24, on which see Note there.

(28) **That God may be all in all.**—In these words are expressed the complete redemption both of the race and of the individual. It is the great and sublime conclusion to which the moral enthusiasm and the earnest logic of the previous argument has necessarily brought us.

(29) **Else.**—We can well imagine the Apostle pausing, as it were, to take breath after the spendid outburst of mingled rhetoric and logic which we find in verses 23—28; or perhaps even postponing until some other day the further dictation of his Epistle, when he could calmly resume his purely logical argument in favour of the doctrine of the Resurrection. Then there will not appear such a startling or inexplicable abruptness in the words with which this new argument is commenced. "Else"—*i.e.*, if there be no resurrection—*what shall they who are baptised for the dead do? If the dead be not raised at all, why are they then baptised for the dead?* Such is the proper punctuation, and not as in the English version, which joins the clause, "if the dead rise not," with the preceding instead of with the following portion of the verse. Also the word translated "rise," is "are raised." This is an *argumentum ad hominem.* The practice known as baptism for the dead was absurd if there be no resurrection. To practise it and to deny the doctrine of the resurrection was illogical. What shall they do? *i.e.*, What explanation shall they give of their conduct? asks the Apostle. There have been numerous and ingenious conjectures as to the meaning of this passage. The only tenable interpretation is that there existed amongst some of the Christians at Corinth a practice of baptising a living person in the stead of some convert who had died before that sacrament had been administered to him. Such a practice existed amongst the Marcionites in the second century, and still earlier amongst a sect called the Cerinthians. The idea evidently was that whatever benefit flowed from baptism might be thus vicariously secured for the deceased Christian. St. Chrysostom gives the following description of it:—"After a catechumen (*i.e.*, one prepared for baptism, but not actually baptised) was dead, they hid a living man under the bed of the deceased; then coming to the bed of the

for the dead? (30) And why stand we
in jeopardy every hour? (31) I protest
by your[1] rejoicing which I have in Christ
Jesus our Lord, I die daily. (32) If
after the manner of men[2] I have fought
with beasts at Ephesus, what advan-
tageth it me, if the dead rise not? let us
eat and drink; for to morrow we die.
(33) Be not deceived: evil communica-
tions corrupt good manners. (34) Awake

1 Some read, *our.*

2 Or, *to speak after the manner of men.*

---

dead man they spake to him, and asked whether he would receive baptism, and he making no answer, the other replied in his stead, and so they baptised the 'living for the dead.'" Does St. Paul then, by what he here says, sanction the superstitious practice? Certainly not. He carefully separates himself and the Corinthians, to whom he immediately addresses himself, from those who adopted this custom. He no longer uses the first or second person; it is "they" throughout this passage. It is no proof to others; it is simply the *argumentum ad hominem.* Those who do that, and disbelieve a resurrection, refute themselves. This custom possibly sprang up amongst the Jewish converts, who had been accustomed to something similar in their own faith. If a Jew died without having been purified from some ceremonial uncleanness, some living person had the necessary ablution performed on them, and the dead were so accounted clean.

(30) **And why stand we in jeopardy every hour?**—This is the same kind of argument now applied to the Apostles themselves. Their conduct also would be illogical if they did not believe in a resurrection. Notice the strong contrast between "them," in the previous verse, and "we" in this verse.

(31) **I protest by your rejoicing which I have in Christ Jesus.**—Better, *I protest by your boast which I have in Christ Jesus.* His converts are his boasting (2 Cor. ix. 3), and by the fact that they are his in the Lord, he utters the solemn asservation, "I die daily." Such a life as St. Paul's, both as regards the spiritual battles in his own soul and the ceaseless conflict with enemies around him, was indeed a daily dying (2 Cor. xi. 23—28).

(32) **If after the manner of men . . .**—These words imply here, as elsewhere (chap. iii. 3), "merely from a human point of view." What is the advantage or necessity of my incurring daily risks, if I am merely a human being, with a life limited by what we see, and no immortality and resurrection awaiting me?

**I have fought with beasts at Ephesus.**—The question here arises, Are these words to be taken literally or figuratively? Does St. Paul refer to some actual contest in the arena with beasts, or to his conflict with the opponents at Ephesus, whom he thus designates beasts? It is scarcely possible to accept the former interpretation. There is no mention to be found of it in the Acts, and, moreover, his Roman citizenship would have legally protected him against such treatment. We must therefore conclude that the Ephesians themselves are spoken of as "beasts." Both Hebrew and Greek literature would have made such a form of expression familiar to the Apostle and to his readers. In the Psalms (see Ps. xxii. 12, 13, 20, 21) the opponents of God are similarly spoken of. The Cretans are called "evil beasts" by the poet Epimenides, whom St. Paul quotes in Tit. i. 12. Heraclitus calls the Ephesians "beasts"—the same word as St. Paul uses here; and St. Ignatius (*Epis. ad Rom.*) speaks of "fighting with beasts by land and sea," and having been bound to 'ten leopards,' that is a band of soldiers."

Although the Greek verb implies that reference is made, not to general or prolonged opposition, but to some one outburst of rage on the part of his opponents, we must not take it as indicating the scene described in Acts xix. 23—34, which had probably not taken place when this was written; but no doubt the "many adversaries" (chap. xvi. 9) at Ephesus had already availed themselves of some opportunity of venting their rage on the Apostle after the manner of wild beasts. (See *Introduction.*)

**What advantageth it me?**—This sentence is completed with these words, and should be followed by a note of interrogation, thus—"What advantageth it me?" (See next Note.)

**If the dead rise not?**—Better, *if the dead be not raised, let us eat and drink, for to-morrow we die.* If the dead be not raised our conduct is illogical. Consistency then belongs to those who disregard God's call to repentance, and of whom we read in Isa. xxii. 13, that they say, "Let us eat and drink." The reference is directly to this passage in the prophet describing the conduct of abandoned Jews during the siege of Jerusalem; but the words indicate with equal accuracy that school of Epicurean philosophy of which, no doubt, there were many representatives at Corinth. Similar expressions are to be found in many classical writers; but the most remarkable instance of the use of these words is where they occur in an inscription on a statue at Anchiale, a town in Cilicia, which was St. Paul's native province—"Sardanapalus, the son of Anacyndraxes, built Anchiale and Tarsus in one day. Stranger, eat, drink, and play, for all the rest is not worth this." The figure is represented as making a contemptuous motion with its fingers. Saul of Tarsus had probably often seen that statue and inscription.

(33) **Be not deceived.**—The previous words are spoken with sarcasm. *That* is what you must come to if this life be all. The solemn thought then occurs to the Apostle that perhaps these words do only too truly describe the actual state of some of the Corinthians. They had become tainted by the bad moral atmosphere in which they lived and which was impregnated with the teaching of that false philosophy, "Let us eat and drink, for to-morrow we die." "Be not deceived," he adds, solemnly; it is a fact. "Evil communications corrupt good manners." This is a proverb, slightly modified in one word from a line in the *Thais* of Menander. It is impossible to say whether the Apostle was acquainted with the original line in the poem, or not; for in any case he would probably have quoted it in the form in which it was current amongst ordinary people. The force of the proverb is, that even evil words are dangerous. The constant repetition of an immoral maxim may lead to immoral life. Words that seem harmless, because they float lightly like thistledown, may bear in them a seed of evil which may take root and bring forth evil fruit.

(34) **Awake to righteousness, and sin not.**—Literally, *Awake to soberness in a righteous manner.* With this earnest call to arouse from the sleep of indulgence and of death, the Apostle completes this section of the chapter, and the direct proofs of the doctrine of the resurrection. The exhortation is needed, for there are some who call themselves Christians and still have

to righteousness, and sin not; for some have not the knowledge of God: I speak *this* to your shame.

(35) But some *man* will say, How are the dead raised up? and with what body do they come? (36) *Thou* fool, that which thou sowest is not quickened, except it die: (37) and that which thou sowest, thou sowest not that body that shall be, but bare grain, it may chance of wheat, or of some other *grain:* (38) but God giveth it a body as it hath pleased him, and to every seed his own body. (39) All flesh *is* not the same flesh: but *there is* one *kind of* flesh of men, another flesh of beasts, another of fishes, *and* another of birds. (40) *There are* also celestial bodies, and bodies terrestrial: but the glory of the celestial *is* one, and the *glory* of the terrestrial *is* another. (41) *There is* one glory of the sun, and

---

"an ignorance" regarding God. "To their shame" the Apostles speaks this, not only the last words, but the whole preceding argument. It was a shame that to Christians the Apostle should have to vindicate the very fundamental truth of the Faith.

(35) **But some man will say, How are the dead raised up?**—The proof of the truth of the doctrine of the resurrection is concluded in the last verse. The truth of it is, in the early part of this chapter, maintained—(1) by the historical fact of Christ's resurrection; (2) by a *reductio ad absurdum,* showing the consequences logically involved in a denial of it; (3) by an *argumentum ad hominem.* The former two arguments are still those on which we must rest our belief in the doctrine. The latter is, like every argument of that nature, only of force to those to whom it was actually addressed. The Apostle in this verse turns aside to another line of thought. He assumes that his previous arguments are conclusive; there still remain, however, difficulties which will suggest themselves. The difficulty is expressed in two questions, the second being an enlargement of the first —a more definite indication of where the suggested difficulty lies. "How are the dead raised up?"—that is, not by what power? but in what manner? as is further explained by the next question, "In what body do they come?"

(36) **Thou fool.**—Better, *Fool,* or more literally, *Senseless one.* The word in the Greek has not the sense of opprobrium conveyed in the word translated "fool" in Matt. v. 22; xxiii. 17, 19. You who with your own hand sow seed, ask such a question as that! The Apostle now proceeds to show, by the analogies in Nature, how a resurrection of a body is possible, how substantial identity may be preserved under variation of form. The Apostle does not here *prove* anything. Analogy cannot ever be regarded as logically conclusive as an argument. The object of analogy is to show how a difficulty is not insuperable. The doctrine of the resurrection has been logically established. A difficulty is suggested as to how it is possible. Analogy shows that the same difficulty exists in theory in other directions where we actually see it surmounted in fact. It is most important to bear this in mind, as some writers, forgetful of the difference between a logical argument and an illustration from analogy, have regarded some of the Apostle's "arguments" in these verses as inconclusive. The fact of a buried seed rising into flower does not and cannot prove that man will rise; but it does show that the objection suggested in the question, "How are the dead raised up?" is not a practical difficulty.

We have in these verses three illustrations of the preservation of identity under change of form —(1) Seeds growing into flowers and fruit; (2) flesh in the variety of men, beasts, fishes, and birds; (3) heavenly and earthly bodies in infinite variety of form and of glory.

(37, 38) **God giveth it a body.**—Here it is implied that, though the seed grows up, as we say, "in the ordinary course of Nature," it is God who not only has originally established but continually sustains that order. Each seed rises with its own "body;" a corn seed grows up into corn, an acorn into an oak. All through this passage the word "body" is used in a general sense for "organism," so as to keep strictly and vividly before the reader the ultimate truth to illustrate which these analogies are introduced. The points of analogy between the sowing and growth of seed and the life and resurrection of man are *not,* as some writers put it—(1) the seed is sown, and man is buried; (2) the seed rots, and man's body decays; (3) the seed grows up, and man is raised. Such a series of analogies are misleading, for there is no necessity for the body of man to *decay,* but only a necessity for it to die (verses 51, 52). The points of analogy are these:—(1) The seed is sown in the earth, and man is born into the world; (2) the seed dies and decays—man dies; (3) the seed grows through its very decay—man rises through death.

(39) **All flesh is not the same flesh.**—Better, *There is no flesh the same flesh.* All organisms have the same basis; there is a "structural unit" in all animal life; but God gives this a vast variety of form in man, in beast, in fish. The same divine prescience which gives to all flesh here the form suited to its condition and surroundings can give hereafter another form to it suitable to the new conditions and surroundings in which it will then be placed. If we had only seen flesh in the form of an animal, and were told that "flesh" could live in the sea, we might have equally argued, "How, with what body?" but seeing as we do that there is a variety of bodies, we feel no such difficulty.

(40) **There are also celestial bodies, and bodies terrestrial.**—It is held by many that this is a distinct illustration from that which occurs in the next verse, and that the "celestial bodies" here spoken of are the bodies of angels, whose appearances on earth are accompanied (see Matt. xxviii. 3; Acts xii. 7) by a blaze of glory or light. It is better, perhaps, to regard it as a general statement of what is expanded in verse 41. The force of the three analogies introduced in this whole argument is that identity of matter is preserved amid variety of form, and on this point the difference between angelic bodies and human bodies would have no bearing. Between the earthly things and the heavenly things, such as the sun, moon, and stars, there is an identity of substance, but an infinite variety of form and of glory.

(41) **For one star . . .**—Better, *for star differeth*

another glory of the moon, and another glory of the stars: for *one* star differeth from *another* star in glory.
(42) So also *is* the resurrection of the dead. It is sown in corruption; it is raised in incorruption: (43) it is sown in dishonour; it is raised in glory: it is sown in weakness; it is raised in power:
(44) it is sown a natural body; it is raised a spiritual body. There is a natural body, and there is a spiritual body.
(45) And so it is written, The first man Adam was made a living soul; the last Adam *was made* a quickening spirit.
(46) Howbeit that *was* not first which is spiritual, but that which is natural; and afterward that which is spiritual. (47) The first man *is* of the earth, earthy: the second man *is* the Lord from heaven.
(48) As *is* the earthy, such *are* they also that are earthy: and as *is* the heavenly, such *are* they also that are heavenly.
(49) And as we have borne the image of the earthy, we shall also bear the image of the heavenly.

---

*from star in glory.* It is not only that the heavenly bodies differ from earthly, but they differ from each other—sun from moon, moon from stars. And there is a further variety still—even amid the stars themselves there is variety. The word "glory" is naturally used as intimating the aspect in which the difference of the heavenly bodies strikes us, looking at them from earth. The God who is thus not limited to a monotonous form for the substance of which Physical Nature consists, need not be in any difficulty as to some other variety of form for Human Nature beyond that which we see it confined to during its earthly life.

(42) **So also is the resurrection of the dead.**—Here follows the application of these analogies to the subject in hand. As there is in the vegetable growth, in the varieties of animal life, and in the diversities of form assumed by inorganic matter, an identity preserved amid ever-varying form or variety of "body," so a change in the form or glory of our organism which we call our "body" is compatible with the preservation of personal identity. The "it," the personality, remains the same—now in corruption, then in incorruption; now in dishonour, then in glory; now in weakness, then in power.

(44) **It is sown a natural body.**—Here is a further and different application of the three analogies. It is not only that there is a variety of body in these illustrations, but there is also an adaptability. The "body" which a plant has when it is in the form of seed is suited to the condition in which seed is placed; the "body" which it has when grown into a plant is suited to the changed conditions in which a plant exists; the "flesh" in the "body" form of a bird is suited to its sphere of life; the "flesh" in the "body" form of a fish is suited to its condition; and so on. It is not an accidental but a purposely adapted variety. So it will be in the variety of "bodies" for Humanity. A man's organism is sown (*i.e.*, is born into this world) a natural body; it is raised (through and by death) a spiritual body. The body which we have here on earth is suited with a marvellous detail of adaptability to the life, physical and intellectual, amid which we are placed, and of which we form a part. It is, however, a hindrance to the spiritual man in each of us. (See 2 Cor. v.) There will be a time for each when the body will become as perfectly adapted to the spiritual man in each as the human body here is to the natural man—no longer its hindrance, but its help. The "willing spirit" will then never be hampered and thwarted by a "weak flesh;" the body, having become spiritual itself, will be spiritually strong.

**There is a natural body, and there is a spiritual body.**—This emphatic assertion that there are two bodies for man—as really as seed and a blossom are two bodies yet the same plant—is introductory to the further thought introduced in the next verse.

(45) **And so it is written.**—Better, *And so it is written, The first man Adam became a living soul: the last Adam became a quickening spirit.* The quotation which follows here is from Gen. ii. 7, and it is the latter part of that verse which is quoted. The Rabbinical explanation of that passage was—that God breathed into man the breath of life originally, but that man became (not "was made") only a living soul, *i.e.*, one in whom the mere human faculties held sway, and not the spirit. He became this lower thing by his own act of disobedience. Here, then, St. Paul, contrasts the two Adams—the first man and Christ—from whom we derive our natural and our spiritual natures, and our natural and spiritual bodies. The first Adam became, by his disobedience, a mere living soul, and from him we inherit that nature; the second Adam, by his obedience, became a life-giving spirit, and from Him we inherit the spiritual nature in us. The same verb which is expressed in the first clause must be understood in the second clause. The same thought is expressed in Rom. v. 19.

(46) **Howbeit that was not first which is spiritual.**—Here a further thought is introduced. There is not only a variety of bodies—and that variety regulated by adaptability to their state of existence —but there is an ordered sequence in that variety. As the Adam was first from whom we derive the natural body and soul, and the Adam was last from whom comes our spiritual nature, so there will be the like order in regard to our bodies. The natural body first in this life—the spiritual body afterwards in the next life.

(47) **The second man is the Lord from heaven.**—Better, *the second man is from heaven.* The words "the Lord," which occur in the English version, are not in the best Greek MSS. The word which is twice rendered "of" in this verse has the force of "from," "originating from," in the Greek. The first representative man was from the earth, the second representative man was from heaven; and as was the first earthly Adam, so are we in our merely physical condition; and as is the second heavenly Adam, so shall we be in our heavenly state.

(49) **We shall also bear the image of the heavenly.**—Better, *let us bear also the image of the heavenly.* Such is the reading of the best MSS. The words transport the thoughts of the reader to the future glory, and, at the same moment, show a light on present duty. The resurrection life is to be begun in us even

(50) Now this I say, brethren, that
flesh and blood cannot inherit the
kingdom of God; neither doth corrup-
tion inherit incorruption. (51) Behold,
I shew you a mystery; We shall not all
sleep, but we shall all be changed, (52) in
a moment, in the twinkling of an eye,
at the last trump: for the trumpet shall
sound, and the dead shall be raised in-
corruptible, and we shall be changed.
(53) For this corruptible must put on
incorruption, and this mortal *must* put
on immortality. (54) So when this cor-
ruptible shall have put on incorruption,
and this mortal shall have put on im-
mortality, then shall be brought to pass
the saying that is written, Death is
swallowed up in victory. (55) O death,[a]
where *is* thy sting? O grave,[1] where *is*
thy victory? (56) The sting of death *is*
sin; and the strength of sin *is* the law.
(57) But thanks *be* to God, which giveth

a Hos. 13. 14.

1 Or, *hell.*

---

now. "If by any means we can attain to the resurrection of the dead" (2 Cor. iii. 18; Phil. iii. 21).

(50) **Now this I say.**—This is the phrase with which the Apostle is wont to introduce some statement of profound significance. (See chaps. i. 12; vii. 29.) The statement so introduced here is that flesh and blood, being corruption, cannot enter into the heavenly state, which is incorruption. This is still part of the answer to the question, "With what bodies do they come?" but the reply is no longer based upon any analogy. It comes now as a revelation of what he had been taught by the Spirit of God. Flesh and blood are indeed corruption. Blood is everywhere the type of this lower animal life. Blood is the life of the flesh; and so, though Jews might eat the flesh, they might not eat the blood, which is the life thereof (Gen. ix. 4). All offerings which typified the offering up and sacrifice of "self"—the lower sinful self—were sacrifices by shedding of blood, without which was no remission (Heb. ix. 22). When the supreme Sacrifice was made on Calvary the blood was shed—once for all. So when Christ showed His resurrection body to His disciples He did not say, "A spirit hath not flesh and blood, as ye see Me have;" but "A spirit hath not 'flesh and bones,' as ye see Me have." The blood of Christ is never spoken of as existing after His crucifixion. That was the supreme sacrifice of Self to God. The blood—the type of the human self—was poured out for ever. It is to be noticed also that the phrase "of His flesh and of His bones" (not His "blood," which the Eucharistic Feast would have suggested) was evidently in ordinary use, as it was interpolated in Eph. v. 30.

The blood, as the type of our lower nature, is familiar in all popular phraseologies, as when we say, for example, that a "man's blood is up," meaning that his physical nature is asserting itself. One characteristic of the resurrection body, therefore, is that it shall be bloodless.

(51) **Behold, I shew you a mystery.**—It is better to take these words as referring to what follows rather than (as some have done) to the preceding statement. A mystery means something which up to this time has been kept concealed, but is now made manifest (Rom. xi. 25; Eph. iii. 3—5).

**We shall not all sleep, but we shall all be changed.**—There are here a considerable variety of readings in the Greek, but the text from which our English version is taken is probably correct. The Apostle believed that the end of the world might come in the lifetime of some then living. We shall not all, he says, necessarily sleep, but we shall all be changed. The change from the earthly to the spiritual body is absolutely necessary. To some it will come through the ordinary process of death; to those who are alive at Christ's advent it will come suddenly, and in a moment. The dead shall be raised, but we (the living) shall be changed.

(52) **The last trump.**—The trumpet was used to summon an assembly (Ex. xx. 18; Ps. lxxxi. 3; Isa. xviii. 3; xxvii. 13) or to sound a warning. The last trumpet is the one which concludes a series which have already been sounding at intervals in notes of warning to the nations (Ps. xlvii. 5; Isa. xxvii. 13; Jer. li. 27). This verse states with reiterated emphasis that this change shall not be a protracted process, but a sudden and momentary alteration in the condition of our bodies.

(53) **For this corruptible must . . .**—Here again is repeated the truth of verse 50, which shows the absolute necessity for a change in the nature of the resurrection body. There is, however, an additional thought introduced here. Not only must the resurrection body be suited to the condition but also to the duration of the new life. As a spiritual body, it will be adapted to the needs of a spiritual state; and as an immortal and incorruptible body, it will be adapted to a life which is everlasting.

(54) **So when this corruptible shall have put on incorruption.**—The Apostle now transports himself in thought to the time when there shall be the actual accomplishment of that for which there then is this absolute and moral necessity. These words bring before us with vivid power the intensity of the Apostle's own belief in what he is teaching.

**Death is swallowed up in victory.**—These words, originally referring to the Jewish people (Isa. xxv. 8), are naturally applied here to the human race, of which they were the chosen type.

(55) **O death, where is thy sting?**—In the prophet Hosea, where these words originally occur, the passage reads thus—"Where is thy victory, O death? Where is thy sting, O hell?"—the word "hell" referring, not to the place of torment, but to the Hades of departed spirits. This difference between St. Paul's words and those of the prophet has given rise to a variety of readings in the Greek text here. The weight of evidence is in favour of the reading, "Where is thy sting, O death? Where is thy victory, O death?" the word "Hades," or "grave," not being introduced at all. The passage is not a quotation, but the adaptation of the form of a familiar Old Testament phrase.

(56) **The sting of death is sin.**—Death is pictured as a monster, and it is armed with a sting. Its sting is sin. If there were no sin, death would not be capable of inflicting pain, and the strength of sin springs from the fact that it is the violation of God's law. (See this thought fully brought out, Rom. v. 12, and vii. 7.)

(57) **But thanks be to God.**—The future is so certain that the Apostle speaks of it as a subject for present thanksgiving; the victory is one which God gives

us the victory through our Lord Jesus
Christ.
(58) Therefore, my beloved brethren,
be ye stedfast, unmoveable, always
abounding in the work of the Lord,
forasmuch as ye know that your labour
is not in vain in the Lord.

Chap. xvi. Conclusion.

A.D. 59.

CHAPTER XVI.—(1) Now concern-
ing the collection for the
saints, as I have given
order to the churches of Galatia, even
so do ye.
(2) Upon the first *day* of the week let
every one of you lay by him in store, as
*God* hath prospered him, that there be
no gatherings when I come. (3) And
when I come, whomsoever ye shall
approve by *your* letters, them will I
send to bring your liberality[1] unto
Jerusalem. (4) And if it be meet that I
go also, they shall go with me.

1 Gr. *gift.*

---

now through Jesus Christ. His resurrection is the pledge of our resurrection. His death is the power by which we are enabled to conquer that lower self, from whose crucifixion and death we shall rise to the higher incorruptible life of the resurrection day. With this earnest and enthusiastic expression of praise to God the argument concludes. Through arguments historical, moral, philosophical; through explanations from the analogy of Nature, and from the theology of Old and New Testament history, the Apostle has led his readers, vindicating the truth and illustrating the manner of the Resurrection of the Dead. He projects his mind into the future, and, standing in thought with ransomed and raised Humanity after death has been vanquished and the grave been spoiled, he joins in the shout of triumphant praise which shall then ascend to Christ and God.

(58) **Therefore.**—Because all this is so—because there is a life hereafter—let this life here be worthy of it. You might grow weak and faint-hearted if you could think that all your work for God and truth here might be wasted; but it is not so. It cannot be "in vain" if it be "in the Lord." It is very striking and very expressive of the real spirit of the gospel that a chapter which leads us step by step through the calm process of logic, and through glowing passages of resistless eloquence to the sublimest thoughts of immortality, should at last thus close with words of plain and practical duty. Christianity never separates, in precept or in promise, "the life that now is" and "that which is to come."

## XVI.

(1) **Now concerning the collection for the saints.**—This chapter deals briefly with the following subjects:—

Verses 1—4. The collection for the poor at Jerusalem.
„ 5—9. The Apostle's prospective arrangement, as to his journey.
„ 10—18. Commendation of various individuals.
„ 19—20. The salutation of the Church.
„ 21—24. The salutation of Paul himself.

From the fact of a necessity existing for a collection for the poor Christians at Jerusalem, it is clear that the community of goods (see Acts ii. 44) which had at the beginning been established in that Church had not proved successful. Christianity was largely recruited from the lower classes, especially in Jerusalem (Jas. ii. 5), and a common fund would not long have flourished with so few contributors and such a multitude of sharers. Moreover, the many who were shut up in prison had perhaps by this time been released in abject poverty, and would naturally be the subject of anxious solicitation to one who was identical with "persecuting Saul," who "had given his voice against them," and against others now dead. (See Acts xxvi. 10.) It is to be noticed that the Apostle does not speak of them as "the poor," but as "saints." That was the true ground of their claim upon their brethren.

**As I have given order to the churches of Galatia.**—Better, *As I gave order to the churches of Galatia.* The order was definitely given by the Apostle in person when visiting these churches (Acts xviii. 23). It does not occur in his Epistle to that Church. On this passage Bengel's Note is worth quoting—"He proposes the Galatians as an example to the Corinthians, the Corinthians to the Macedonians, and the Corinthians and Macedonians to the Romans (2 Cor. ix. 2; Rom. xv. 26). Great is the power of examples."

(2) **Upon the first day of the week.**—The Greek phrase (as given in the best MSS.) is literally, *on one of the Sabbaths*—that being, after a Hebrew idiom, equivalent to "the day next after the Sabbath." Already the day of the week on which Christ had risen had become noted as a suitable day for distinctively Christian work and Christian worship. It does not yet seem to have been designated by the phrase by which it became subsequently universally known in Christendom—"the Lord's Day;" that name occurs first in Rev. i. 10. This would be a convenient as well as a suitable day for each one to set aside, as he had proposed, something, storing it up until the Apostle's arrival; for this was already the usual day for Christians assembling themselves together (Acts xx. 7). I cannot think with Stanley and others that the Apostle means that each was to lay by "in his own house," and not in some general treasury. The object of this direction is expressly stated to be that the money should all be ready in bulk-sum when the Apostle came, so that his time and that of the Christian community during his visit might not be occupied with this, but with more profitable matters, which result would not have been accomplished if the offering had then to be gathered from each Christian home.

**As God hath prospered him.**—Better, *whatsoever he may be prospered in.* These words do not imply that only in cases of exceptional prosperity was a man to contribute, but every man was to give out of whatever fruits he had from his labour.

(3) **Whomsoever ye shall approve by your letters.**—Better, *whomsoever ye shall approve, them will I send by letters to bring your gifts to Jerusalem.* The Apostle had not made up his mind finally whether he would take the gift himself or send it by messengers, whom he would accredit with letters, to the Church at Jerusalem. He would probably be influenced by the amount collected, and by the urgency, or otherwise, of the needs of those at Jerusalem at the time,

(5) Now I will come unto you, when I
shall pass through Macedonia: for I do
pass through Macedonia. (6) And it may
be that I will abide, yea, and winter with
you, that ye may bring me on my jour-
ney whithersoever I go. (7) For I will
not see you now by the way; but I
trust to tarry a while with you, if the
Lord permit.
(8) But I will tarry at Ephesus until
Pentecost. (9) For a great door and
effectual is opened unto me, and *there*
*are* many adversaries.
(10) Now if Timotheus come, see that
he may be with you without fear: for
he worketh the work of the Lord, as I
also *do*. (11) Let no man therefore de-
spise him: but conduct him forth in
peace, that he may come unto me: for
I look for him with the brethren.
(12) As touching *our* brother Apollos,
I greatly desired him to come unto you

---

The Apostle was, in one sense, the humblest of men; but he valued highly the dignity of his apostolic office, and if but a very small sum were ready for the Church at Jerusalem, he would have felt it to be beneath the dignity of his office, though not of himself, to be the bearer of such an offering. The course finally adopted was that the Apostle went himself, and the selected brethren with him (Acts xxi. 15).

(5) **For I do pass through Macedonia.**—A misrepresentation of these words gives rise to the incorrect statement that this Epistle was written at Philippi, which is to be found in the subscription at the end of this chapter in our English Bible. The Apostle does not here refer to where he is at the moment of writing, but to his intention regarding his journey. He had intended to go first to Corinth (see 2 Cor. i. 15, 16), but he has altered that plan, and says that his intention now is to pass through Macedonia first, and then visit Corinth. Then he says, "For I *do* pass through Macedonia." To this intention the Apostle adheres. (See *Introduction.*)

(6) **And it may be that I will abide . . .**—His former plan had involved but a brief visit to the Church at Corinth, but the arrangement which he now contemplated would permit of a longer stay, and so he adds, with affectionate emphasis, "that *you* may send me on my journey." Whither he would go from Corinth he had not yet determined; and, indeed, it was subsequently determined for him by a conspiracy against him, which was fortunately discovered in time (Acts xx. 3). He remained three months at Corinth, during winter, and, as that brought him to a time of year when a voyage would be safe, he resolved to sail into Syria. The conspiracy of the Jews caused this plan to be abandoned, and a different course, through Troas, &c., adopted. (See Acts xx. 6, 13, 17.) The phrase "that ye may send me on" implies not merely that Corinth should be the starting-point of his journey to Jerusalem, but that he should set out on that journey with the good wishes and blessing of his Corinthian friends (as in Acts xx. 38; xxi. 5).

(7) **For I will not see you now by the way.**—Here again is a reference to his changed intention. (See verse 5.)

(8) **But I will tarry at Ephesus.**—In this and the following verse the Apostle returns to his immediate plans at Ephesus. It was probably now about Easter-time (see verse 7), and the hostility of enemies increases. (See Acts xix. 9—23.) That must be subdued. A door has been opened wide for the effectual spread of the gospel (Acts xix. 20). Of that the Apostle must avail himself. Therefore he will remain where he is until Pentecost. Duty to be done, and danger to be faced in the doing of it, were to such a man as St. Paul sufficient indications as to where he ought to be found.

(10) **Now if Timotheus come . . .**—Timothy and Erastus had been sent (see chap. iv. 17) by St. Paul to remind the Corinthians of his former teaching, and to rebuke and check those evils of which rumours had reached the ears of the Apostle. As, however, they would travel through Macedonia, delaying *en route* at the various churches to prepare them for the visit which St. Paul, according to his then intention, purposed paying them after he had been to Corinth, they possibly might not reach Corinth until after this Epistle, which would be carried thither by a more direct route. The Apostle was evidently anxious to know how Timothy would be received by the Corinthians. He was young in years. He was young also in the faith. He had probably a constitutionally weak and timid nature (see 1 Tim. iii. 15, 23; 2 Tim i. 4), and he was of course officially very subordinate to St. Paul. In a Church, therefore, some of whose members had gone so far as to question, if not actually to repudiate the authority even of the Apostle himself, and to depreciate him as compared with the elder Apostles, there was considerable danger for one like Timothy. By reminding the Corinthians of the work in which Timothy is engaged, and of its identity with his own work, the Apostle anticipates and protests against any insult being offered to Timothy, because of what a great English statesman once called, in reference to himself, "the atrocious crime of being a young man."

(11) **For I look for him with the brethren.**—Timothy and Erastus (Acts xix. 22) had been sent through Macedonia to Corinth some time before this Epsitle was written, but when they had been despatched the full knowledge of the state of affairs at Corinth had not reached St. Paul. Now that he knows how very bad is the condition of the Corinthian Church, and what need it has of vigorous treatment, he sends not only his Epistle, but with it Titus and two other brethren. (See 2 Cor. viii. 18, 22, 23.) In energy and firmness of character Titus was a striking contrast to Timothy, while he equally shared the spirit and confidence of St. Paul. (See *Introduction*, and 2 Cor. vii. and viii.) He therefore was not only a bearer of this Epistle, but one fully competent and willing to deal energetically with the recalcitrant spirit of some sections of the Corinthian Church. The Apostle here expresses the hope that Timothy may join Titus and his party when they take their departure from Corinth.

(12) **As touching our brother Apollos.**—St. Paul, free from the smallest spark of personal jealousy, had wished that Apollos, whose name had been used as the designation of a faction in opposition to the Apostle himself, should go with this letter to Corinth. St. Paul had planted, Apollos had watered

with the brethren: but his will was not
at all to come at this time; but he will
come when he shall have convenient time.
(13) Watch ye, stand fast in the faith,
quit you like men, be strong. (14) Let
all your things be done with charity.
(15) I beseech you, brethren, (ye know
the house of Stephanas, that it is the
firstfruits of Achaia, and *that* they have
addicted themselves to the ministry of
the saints,) (16) that ye submit your-
selves unto such, and to every one that
helpeth with *us*, and laboureth. (17) I
am glad of the coming of Stephanas
and Fortunatus and Achaicus: for that
which was lacking on your part they
have supplied. (18) For they have re-
freshed my spirit and your's: therefore
acknowledge ye them that are such.
(19) The churches of Asia salute you.
Aquila and Priscilla salute you much in
the Lord, with the church that is in
their house. (20) All the brethren greet
you. Greet ye one another with an
holy kiss.

(21) The salutation of *me* Paul
with mine own hand. (22) If any
man love not the Lord Jesus Christ,
let him be Anathema Maran-atha.

---

that Church, and in the absence of the planter, Apollos would have been the most likely and proper person to exercise authority there. The unselfish consideration of St. Paul is equalled by the thoughtful reluctance of Apollos, who fears that his presence might encourage the one faction, and perhaps embitter the other, and he declines, not considering it a "convenient" time to do so. In the thought of these teachers "convenient" meant the good of Christ's Church, and not the ease or comfort of any individual man.

(13, 14) **Watch ye, stand fast.**—These words of stirring exhortation come in here somewhat abruptly. It is possible that they conclude the epistle so far—the Apostle intending to add immediately before sending it, the verses which follow, and which contain messages from, or commendations of their friends who were with him. Living in a profound consciousness of the uncertainty of life, St. Paul might wish not to have such references to friends with him added until the last moment along with his own autograph (see verse 21). The Apostle's mind is full of the hope of beneficial results following from this letter and from the exertions of Titus; yet, after all, everything depends upon the Corinthians themselves. Chrysostom's Note on these words brings out their meaning well. "Now in saying these things, he seems indeed to advise; but he is reprimanding them as indolent. Wherefore he saith, *Watch*, as though they slept; *stand*, as though they were rocking to and fro; *quit you like men*, as though they were playing the coward; *let all your things be done with charity*, as though they were in dissensions. And the first caution refers to the deceivers, viz., *Watch, stand;* the next to those who plot against us, *quit you like men;* the third to those who make parties and endeavour to distract, *let all your things be done with charity*, which thing is the bond of perfection, and the root and the fountain of all blessings."

(15) **The house of Stephanas.**—The Apostle here reminds the Corinthians that the devotion of teachers, and all who serve in the gospel ministry, ought to be rewarded with a return of sympathy and devotion on the part of those whom they serve. There is in the original a characteristic play upon words here which can scarcely be rendered adequately in the English: "Ye know the house of Stephanas, that they have *ordered themselves* to the ministry of the saints, now I exhort you, *order yourselves* to be subject to them." Stephanas (verses 1—16), Fortunatus, and Achaicus had come from Corinth to Ephesus, probably with the letter from the Corinthians (chap. viii. 1), and their presence had cheered the Apostle. They, "faithful amid the faithless," had made up for the want of zeal and love on the part of so many of the Corinthians. The Corinthians might think that these men had told St. Paul much of the evil state of Corinth, and he, therefore, carefully commends them to their consideration as having refreshed, not only his spirit, but "theirs also." They had come on behalf of the whole Church there, not enemies to bear tales, but well-wishing friends to obtain apostolic help and counsel for all. The Apostle did not send his reply back by the same messengers, but by Titus instead, as probably their return to Corinth would have stirred up a good deal of controversy and ill feeling as to what account they had given him verbally of the various parties and their conduct in Corinth.

(19) **The churches of Asia salute you.**—This and the following verse are occupied with the salutations from the churches throughout Asia; from the church in the house of Aquila and Priscilla; and finally, from "all the brethren." Aquila and Priscilla had been the Apostle's friends at Corinth (Acts xviii. 1—3), and he now was with them at Ephesus. (See Rom. xvi. 3—5; 2 Tim. iv. 19.) Probably by "the church in their house" is meant a group of foreigners then resident in Ephesus, and accustomed to meet there for worship, as distinct from those who had been converted in Ephesus.

(20) **An holy kiss.**—The kiss was the ordinary form of affectionate greeting in the East. The Church adopted it; and when thus interchanged between those whose bond of friendship was not earthly, but spiritual, it was designated "the holy kiss." (See Rom. xvi. 16; 1 Thess. v. 26.) The practice was given up in the Latin Church in the thirteenth century, but is still used in the Greek Church on certain great occasions, such as Easter Day.

(21) **The salutation of me Paul with mine own hand.**—It was the Apostle's habit to dictate his Epistles, but to add a few words at the end in his own handwriting. (See 2 Thess. iii. 17.) The concluding verses here are accordingly St. Paul's autograph. The earlier portions had been written by Sosthenes. (See chap. i. 1.)

(22) **If any man love not the Lord Jesus.**—From all the argument and controversy which form the main portion of the Epistle, the Apostle with his own hand brings back the thoughts of the Corinthians to the true test of their Christianity. Do they love the

(23) The grace of our Lord Jesus Christ *be* with you. (24) My love *be* with you all in Christ Jesus. Amen.

The first *epistle* to the Corinthians was written from Philippi by Stephanas, and Fortunatus, and Achaicus, and Timotheus.

---

Lord Jesus? The word here used for love signifies not merely affectionate regard, but personal devotion.

**Let him be Anathema Maran-atha.**—Better *Let him be Anathema. Maranatha.* There is no connection between these two words. *Anathema* signifies "accursed." The absence of love to Christ is condemnation. The word *Maranatha* is a Syriac expression—"the Lord is at hand," or "the Lord is come;" probably the former. The uncertainty of the moment when the Lord may come is the most solemn thought with which to remind them of the importance of being one with Christ. Stanley gives the following interesting Note:—"The name Maronite is sometimes explained by a tradition that the Jews in their expectation of the Messiah were constantly saying, *Maran* (Lord). To which the Christians answered, *Maranatha* (The Lord is come), why do you expect Him? Hence the name, '*Maronite*' is applied to the Jews, especially Spanish Jews and Moors who confessed *Maran*, but not *Maranatha*."

(24) **My love be with you all.**—Like a river which, after rushing, foaming over many a rock and through many a gorge, at last emerges into a broad calm amid sunlit meadows, so this Epistle, after chapters of trenchant logic and fervid rebuke, closes in peaceful words of tenderness and love.

[In reference to the erroneous subscription which follows this Epistle in our English version, see Notes on verses 5, 8, and 10.

For the date of this Epistle, see *Introduction.*]

THE SECOND EPISTLE OF PAUL THE APOSTLE TO THE

# CORINTHIANS

# INTRODUCTION

TO

## THE SECOND EPISTLE OF PAUL THE APOSTLE TO THE

# CORINTHIANS

It is not without some reluctance that I have undertaken to treat of an Epistle which stands in such close connection with that which precedes it that it can scarcely be dealt with by a different hand without some risk of want of unity of treatment.

I have, however, kept on the same main lines of thought and method of interpretation which have been followed in the Commentary on the First Epistle to the Corinthians, and have been glad to find myself on all important points of one mind with the commentator.

Of the genuineness of the Second Epistle to the Corinthians there has never been a moment's doubt, even among critics who allow themselves the widest range in their attacks on the canon of New Testament writings. External evidence is in itself adequate. The Epistle is quoted by Irenæus (*Hær.* iii. 7, § 1), by Athenagoras (*De resurr. mort*), by Clement of Alexandria (*Strom.* iii. 94, iv. 101), and by Tertullian (*De Pudicitiâ*, c. 13). Testimony of this kind is, however, hardly needed. The Epistle speaks for itself. In its intense personality, its peculiarities of style, its manifold coincidences with the Acts and with other Epistles (especially with 1 Corinthians, Romans, and Galatians), its vehement emotions, it may fairly be said to present phenomena beyond the attainment of any later writer wishing to claim for what he wrote the authority of a great name. Pseudonymous authorship is, in this case, simply out of the question.

In order to understand the Epistle we must throw ourselves, as by a mental effort, into the mind and heart of the writer at the moment when he wrote or, more probably, dictated it. Much that is necessary for that purpose has been already said in the Notes to the First Epistle, and it is not necessary to repeat it. Of the sins and disorders of the Corinthians as reported to him by successive informants—the household of Chloe (1 Cor. i. 11), and by Stephanas, Fortunatus, and Achaicus (1 Cor. xvi. 17); of his treatment of the topics then brought before him; of the probable effect of what he wrote upon the several parties in the Corinthian Church, we need not now speak. It will be sufficient to note that he had sent Timotheus before he wrote the First Epistle; that he had then sent the First Epistle by Stephanas, his companion; that when they were gone (or possibly with them *) he despatched Titus to complete the work, perhaps as trusting more to his energy than that of the other messengers. Timotheus had returned to him. It is not certain that he reached Corinth. If he did, he came and left before the Epistle had arrived, and was unable to report what had been its result. His timid and shrinking character probably unfitted him for coping with the many difficulties which presented themselves. (See Note on 1 Cor. iv. 17.) His coming, therefore, however welcome it might be, brought no relief to the Apostle's anxiety. He started from Ephesus, whether before or after the arrival of Timotheus we do not know, and, in pursuance of his plan, went to Troas. But there, too, great as the opportunities for mission-work were (chap. ii. 12), he had no strength or heart to use them. A restless, feverish anxiety devoured him night and day, and he sailed for Macedonia, probably for Philippi. And there, at last, after a time of expectation and anxiety, Titus came to him (chap. vii. 6). His report was evidently more full and satisfactory than that which had been brought by Timotheus. He was able to report, what the latter had not reported—the effect of the First Epistle; and this was, in part, at least, full of comfort. The majority at a meeting of the Church had acted as he had told them to act, in the punishment of the incestuous offender (chap. ii. 6); they had shown generally a desire to clear themselves from the reproach of sensual impurity (chap. vii. 11), and had manifested warm feelings of attachment to the Apostle personally (chap. vii. 7). They had obeyed Titus as the Apostle's delegate, and had made the work which he had undertaken in much anxiety, a labour of love and joy (chap. vii. 13—16). They had taken up the collection for the saints with an eager interest, and had not only accepted the idea, but had begun to act on the suggestion of 1 Cor. xvi. 1, 2, as to the weekly payments, and to the alms-box of the house (chap. ix. 13). So far all was well, and had this been all, the Second Epistle to the Corinthians would probably have been as full of thankfulness, and joy, and comfort, as that to the Philippians. But it was not all. Wisely or unwisely, Titus thought it right to tell him of the words and acts of the two parties in the Church of Corinth, who, at opposite extremes, were agreed in resisting his authority. There were some, the party of license, who needed sharp words of censure, and had given no proof of repentance for the foul evils of their former life (chap xii. 21). There was the Judaising party, claiming to belong to Christ in a sense in which St. Paul did not belong to Him, boasting of their Hebrew descent (chaps. x. 7; xi. 4, 22), arrogating to themselves a special apostolic authority (chap. xi. 5), insolently lording it over their abject followers (chap. xi. 20). And from one or other of these rival parties, probably in some cases from both, there had come—so Titus reported—taunts, sneers, and insinuations against the Apostle's character. He had shown feebleness in his change of plan (chap. i. 17); his personal

* See *Introduction to the First Epistle to the Corinthians.*

appearance, feeble and infirm, did not match the authoritative tone of his letters; his speech had nothing in it to command admiration (chap. x. 10); he threatened supernatural punishments, but he did not dare to put his threats to the proof (chap. xiii. 3). What right had he to claim the authority of an Apostle, when he had never seen the Christ in the flesh? Was it certain that he was a Hebrew, a Jew of the pure blood of Palestine, or even that he was of the seed of Abraham? (chap. xi. 22.) They turned into a reproach the fact that he had worked for his maintenance at Corinth, and yet had received gifts from the Macedonian churches, as though he had been too proud to put himself under obligations to any but his favourites (chap. xi. 2—10). They insinuated that what he would not do directly he meant to do indirectly, through the collection for the poor of Jerusalem (chap. xii. 16). How could they tell that the fund so secured would find its way to those who were ostensibly its objects? Who was this Paul who came without credentials (chap. iii. 1), and expected to be received on the strength of his everlasting self-assertions? (chaps. iii. 1; v. 12; x. 8, 12; xii. 11.) Was there not a touch of madness in his visions and revelations? Could he claim more than the tolerance which men were ready to extend to the insane? (chaps. v. 13; xi. 16—19.)

Conceive all these barbed arrows of sarcasm falling on the ears, and through them piercing the very soul, of a man of singularly sensitive nature, passionately craving for affection, and proportionately feeling the bitterness of loving with no adequate return (chap. xii. 15), and we may form some estimate of the whirl and storm of emotion in which St. Paul began to dictate the Epistle on which we are about to enter. Joy, affection, tenderness, fiery indignation, self-vindication, profound thoughts as to the mysteries of the kingdom of God which flashed upon his soul as he spoke—all these elements were there, craving to find expression. They hindered any formal plan and method in the structure of the Epistle. They led to episodes, and side-glances, and allusive references without number.

It follows from this that an analysis of such an Epistle is not a very easy matter, and that which follows must be received only as an approximately complete one, helping the student to follow the manifold oscillations of thought and feeling.

1.—St. Paul wishes the Corinthians to know his troubles and sufferings before the return of Titus (chap. i. 1—14).

2.—He tells them of his first plan of coming to them, and defends himself against the charge of fickleness in changing it (chaps. i. 15—ii. 1).

3.—He is glad that he did change his plans, for thus there was time for the repentance on the part of the incestuous offender of 1 Cor. v. 1. Such a one now needed sympathy and pardon (chap. ii. 2—11).

4.—He is about to tell them of his meeting with Titus, but the remembrance of the triumphant joy of that moment overpowers him, and fills him with a profound sense of the issues of life and death which hang upon his words (chap. ii. 12—17).

5.—Will this be called the self-assertion of one who has no credentials? His thoughts pass rapidly to the true credentials of effective preaching, and so to the new covenant of which he is the preacher, and so to the contrast between that covenant and the old (chap. iii. 1—18).

6.—The sense of the tremendous responsibility of the work thus committed to him, leads him to dwell on his own fitness and unfitness for it. On the one side there is nothing but infirmity and disease, on the other there is the life of Jesus working in his life (chap. iv. 1—18), and the hope of a life after death, in which all that is spiritual in us now shall find itself emancipated from the flesh and clothed with a new spiritual organism (chap. v. 1—9).

7.—That hope does not, however, exclude the fear of the judgment through which all must pass. At the risk of seeming mad he must dwell on that fear. Only so can he lead men to estimate rightly the preciousness of the message of reconciliation (chap. v. 10—21).

8.—Will those to whom he writes receive that message in vain? He pleads with them by all he has done and suffered for them to give him a place in their affections, above all to give Christ the supreme place in them. Only so can they be indeed God's children (chap. vi. 1—18). They cannot serve Him and the lust-demon, Belial.

9.—His thoughts turn from the party of license, whom he had in view in the previous section, to those who had shown themselves zealous against impurity. Now he can tell these, and such as these, why meeting Titus had given him matter for such warm rejoicing; why he feels that he can trust them (chap. vii. 1—16).

10.—A new topic begins, apparently after a pause. He is about to show that he trusts them, by asking them to let their performance in the matter of the collection for the saints be equal to their readiness of will. He tells them of the arrangements he has made for it, and stirs them up by the example of the Macedonians, by appeals to their own self; by the hope of God's favour (chaps. viii. 1—ix. 15).

11.—As if by the association of contrast, he turns from what he viewed with satisfaction and hope to the sarcasm and insinuations which had caused such acute pain (chap. x. 1—18). He charges his opponents, the Judaising teachers, with intruding into his province, defends himself against some of their special accusations, and challenges them to a comparison of their labours and sufferings with his own (chap. xi. 1—29). Even the infirmities with which they taunted him are for those who understand them rightly, a ground of confidence and strength (chaps. xi. 30—xii. 18).

12.—Having thus defended himself, his thoughts travel on to the time of his projected visit. He looks forward, not without anxiety, to the possibility of having to exercise his apostolic authority in punishing the offenders both of the party of license and that of the Judaisers. But he hopes that that necessity will not arise. His wish and prayer is that they may be restored to completeness without it. The agitation of his own spirit is calmed, and he ends with words of peace and blessing for them (chaps. xii. 19—xiii. 14).

Of the immediate results of the Epistle, and of the after-history of the Church of Corinth, we know but little. Within a few months he paid his promised visit, and was received with hospitality by one of the chief members of the Church (Rom. xvi. 23). Titus and the unnamed brethren of chap. viii. 18, 22, probably Luke and Tychicus, had done their work effectually, and he could tell the Romans to whom he wrote of the collection for the saints which had been made in Achaia as well as in Macedonia (Rom. xv. 26). They apparently had so far gained the confidence of the Corinthians that they did not think it necessary to choose any delegates of their own to watch over the appropriation of the funds collected (Acts xx. 4). The malignant enmity of the Jews, however, had not abated. His life was endangered by a plot to attack him as he was embarking at Cenchreæ, and he had to change his plans and return through Macedonia (Acts xx. 3). After this we lose sight of the Corinthian Church altogether, and the one glimpse which we get, accepting the Pastoral Epistles as genuine, and as coming after St. Paul's first imprisonment at Rome, is that on his return to his former labours, Erastus, who seems to have travelled with him, stopped at the city in which he held a municipal position of authority (Rom. xvi. 23; 2 Tim. iv. 20). The Epistle of Clement of Rome to the Corinthians, written, probably, about A.D. 95—some thirty-five years, therefore, after the date of this Epistle—shows, however, that the character of the Church had not altered, and that the old evils had re-appeared. A few rash and self-confident persons, putting themselves at the head of a factious party, had brought discredit on the Church's name. It was necessary to exhort them once more to submit to their rulers and to follow after peace (Clem. Rom. i. 1), to remind them of the self-denying labours of the two Apostles, Peter and Paul, whose names they professed to honour (i. 2), of the examples of faith and humility presented by Christ Himself and by the saints of the Old Testament (i. 16—18). The old doubts as to the resurrection (1 Cor. xv.) had re-appeared, and Clement, over and above the teaching of Scripture and of the Apostles on this subject, presses on them the analogy of the stories then current as to the death and revival of the Phœnix* (i. 24, 25). The authority of the legitimate pastors of the Church (he names bishops or deacons only, as St. Paul had done in Phil. i. 1) was disputed, and he urges submission, and quotes the Epistle—the first of the two which St. Paul had addressed to them (i. 47)—paraphrasing the section in which he had set forth the excellence of charity (i. 49). The letter was sent by messengers, among whom we find one, Fortunatus, who may have been among the survivors who knew the Apostle's work, and had been the bearer of the Epistle of which Clement has just reminded them. The name, however, like its synonyms, Felix, Eutychus, and the like, was not an uncommon one, and the identification cannot, therefore, be regarded as more than probable.

Somewhat later on, about A.D. 135, the Church of Corinth was visited by Hegesippus, the historian of the Jewish Church, to whom we owe the narrative of the death of James, the Bishop of Jerusalem. He touched at that city on his voyage to Rome, and remained there for several days. He found the Church faithful to the truth under its bishop Primus (Euseb. *Hist.* iv. 22). Dionysius, who succeeded Primus in his episcopate, brought out all that was good in the Church over which he ruled, and extended his activity to the Macedonians, the Athenians, the people of Nicomedia, of Crete, and of the coast of Pontus. He bears his testimony to the liberality of the Church of Corinth in relieving the poverty of other churches, to the traditional liberality which it had, in its turn, experienced at the hand of the Roman churches. The teaching of 2 Cor. viii., ix., had, it would seem, done its work effectually. He records the fact that the Epistle of Clement was read, from time to time, on the Lord's Day. A female disciple, named Chrysophora, apparently of the same type of character as Dorcas and Priscilla, was conspicuous both for her good works and her spiritual discernment (Euseb. *Hist.* iv. 23). With this glimpse into the latest traceable influence of St. Paul's teaching, our survey of the history of the Church of Corinth may well close.

* The elaborate note in Dr. Lightfoot's edition of St. Clement shows that a fresh prominence had recently been given to the phœnix-legend, which may account for the stress thus laid on it. It was said to have re-appeared in Egypt in the reign of Tiberius (A.D. 34—36) (Tacit. *Ann.* vi. 28). In A.D. 47 a live phœnix was actually exhibited in the *comitium* of Rome (Plin. *Nat. Hist.* x. 2). Historians and *savans*, though they might think the particular instance an imposture, accepted the tradition with hardly a question.

## THE SECOND EPISTLE OF PAUL THE APOSTLE TO THE

# CORINTHIANS

Chap. i. 1—7. Thanksgiving to God, as the Giver of all comfort.

A.D. 60

CHAPTER I.—(1) Paul, an apostle
of Jesus Christ by the will
of God, and Timothy *our*
brother, unto the church of
God which is at Corinth,
with all the saints which are in all
Achaia: (2) grace *be* to you and peace
from God our Father, and *from* the Lord
Jesus Christ. (3) Blessed *be* God, even
the Father of our Lord Jesus Christ,
the Father of mercies, and the God of
all comfort; (4) who comforteth us in all
our tribulation, that we may be able to
comfort them which are in any trouble,
by the comfort wherewith we ourselves
are comforted of God. (5) For as the
sufferings of Christ abound in us, so our
consolation also aboundeth by Christ.

---

### I.

(1) **Timothy our brother.**—Literally, *Timothy the brother.* The word is used obviously in its wider sense as meaning a fellow-Christian. The opening words of the Epistle are nearly identical with those of 1 Cor. i. 1. Timotheus, however, takes the place of Sosthenes, having apparently left Corinth before the arrival of the First Epistle, or, possibly, not having reached it. (See *Introduction.*) It is natural to think of him as acting in this instance, as in others where the Apostle joins his name with his own (Phil. i. 1; Col. i. 1), as St. Paul's amanuensis.

**With all the saints.**—On the term "saints," see Note on Acts ix. 13. The term Achaia, which does not occur in the opening of 1 Cor., includes the whole of the Roman province, and was probably used to take in the disciples of Cenchreæ (Rom. xvi. 1) as well as those of Corinth, and possibly also those of Athens.

(2) **Grace be to you.**—See Rom. i. 7; 1 Cor. i. 3.

(3) **Blessed be God . . . the Father of mercies.**—The opening words are spoken out of the fulness of the Apostle's heart. He has had a comfort which he recognises as having come from God. The nature of that comfort, as of the previous sorrow, is hardly stated definitely till we come to chaps. ii. 13; vii. 6, 7. At present the memory of it leads him to something like a doxology, as being the utterance of a more exulting joy than a simple thanksgiving, such as we find in 1 Cor. i. 4; Phil. i. 3; Col. i. 3. The same formula meets us in Eph. i. 3, where also it expresses a jubilant adoration. Two special names of God are added under the influence of the same feeling. He is "the Father of mercies," the genitive being possibly a Hebraism, used in place of the cognate adjective; in which case it is identical with "God, the merciful Father," in Jewish prayers, or with the ever-recurring formula of the Koran, "Allah, the compassionate, the merciful." It seems better, however, to take the words more literally, as stating that God is the *originator* of all mercies, the source from which they flow. So we have the "Father of lights" in Jas. i. 17. The precise phrase does not occur elsewhere in the New Testament; but we have the same noun in "the mercies of God" in Rom. xii. 1.

**The God of all comfort.**—The latter word, of which, taking the books of the New Testament in their chronological order, this is the earliest occurrence, includes the idea of counsel as well as consolation. (See Note on Acts iv. 36.) It is used only by St. Paul, St. Luke, and the writer of the Epistle to the Hebrews, and is pre-eminently characteristic of this Epistle, in which it occurs twelve, or, with the cognate verb, twenty-eight, times.

In the balanced structure of the sentence—the order of "God" and "Father" in the first clause being inverted in the second—we may trace something like an unconscious adoption of the familiar parallelism of Hebrew poetry.

(4) **Who comforteth us.**—For the writer, the name "God of all comfort" was the outcome of a living personal experience. He had felt that ever-continuing comfort flowing into his soul, and he knew that it had not been given to him for his own profit only, but that it might flow forth to others. Heathen poets had asserted one side of the truth. Sophocles had said—

> "They comfort others who themselves have mourned;"
> —*Fragm.*

and Virgil—

> "Not ignorant of ill, I, too, have learnt
> To succour those that suffer."—*Æn.* i. 630.

There was a yet deeper truth in the thought that the power to comfort varies with the measure in which we have been comforted ourselves. Sorrow alone may lead to sympathy, but it falls short of that power to speak a word in season to them that are weary (Isa. l. 4), which is of the very essence of the work of comforting. The words imply that he had passed through a time of tribulation himself. They imply also that he knew of their troubles. (Comp. chap. vii. 7—11.)

(5) **Abound in us.**—Better, *overflow to us.* The sufferings of Christ, as in 1 Pet. iv. 13; v. 1 (the Greek in 1 Pet. i. 11 expresses a different thought), are those which He endured on earth; those which, in His mysterious union with His Church, are thought as passing from Him to every member of His body, that they too may drink of the cup that He drank of. For the thought that in our sufferings, of whatever nature, we share Christ's sufferings, comp. chap. iv. 10;

(6) And whether we be afflicted, *it is* for
your consolation and salvation, which is
effectual[1] in the enduring of the same
sufferings which we also suffer: or
whether we be comforted, *it is* for your
consolation and salvation. (7) And our
hope of you *is* stedfast, knowing, that as
ye are partakers of the sufferings, so *shall
ye be* also of the consolation. (8) For we
would not, brethren, have you ignorant
of our trouble which came to us in Asia,
that we were pressed out of
measure, above strength,
insomuch that we despaired
even of life: (9) but we had
the sentence[2] of death in ourselves,
that we should not trust in ourselves,
but in God which raiseth the dead:
(10) who delivered us from so great a
death, and doth deliver: in whom we

1 Or, *is wrought.*

2 Or, *answer.*

Chap. i. 8–14. The nature of the Apostle's trouble, and his deliverance.

---

Phil. iii. 10; Col. i. 24; 1 Pet. iv. 13. The use of the plural, "*our* tribulations," "overflow to *us*," is dependent partly on the fact that St. Paul has joined Timotheus with himself in his salutation, and partly on the fact that it is his usual way of speaking of himself unless he has distinctly to assert his own individuality.

**So our consolation also aboundeth.**—Better, as before, *overflows.* The consolation which has come to him through Christ, as the channel through whom it flows down from the Father, has, like the suffering, an expansive power, and pours itself out on others.

(6) **And whether we be afflicted . . .**—The better MSS. present some variations in the order of the clauses, some of them giving the words "and our hope of you is steadfast" after "which we also suffer" in this verse. The variation hardly affects the sense in any appreciable degree. That sense is that each stage of the Apostle's experience, that of affliction no less than that of consolation, tended to make others sharers in the latter and not in the former.

**For your consolation and salvation.**—The latter word is added as presenting, in modern phrase, the objective side of the result of which St. Paul speaks, while the former gives prominence to the subjective. There was not only the sense of being comforted: there was also the actual deliverance from all real evil, expressed by the word "salvation." But this deliverance is seen, not in a mere escape from, or avoidance of, sufferings, but in a patient, steadfast endurance of them.

**Which is effectual.**—Better, *which worketh.* The word is the same as in "faith working by love" in Gal. v. 6.

**Which we also suffer.**—What these are has not yet been specifically stated. It is assumed that the sufferings of all Christians have much in common. All have to suffer persecution from without (Acts xiv. 22). All have anxieties, sorrows, disappointments, which bring a keener pain than the ills that threaten the spoiling of goods or even life itself.

(7) **And our hope of you is stedfast.**—Better, *our hope on behalf of you.* The sentence is brought in as a kind of parenthesis connected with the word "enduring." He had not used that word lightly, still less as a tacit reproach, as though they were wanting in endurance. His hope for them, for their salvation in the fullest sense of the word, had never been stronger than it was at that moment.

**So shall ye be also of the consolation.**—Better, *so are ye also.* The verb is not expressed in the Greek, but it is more natural to supply it in the tense which had been used before. The English version practically dilutes the hope by throwing it into a future, which may be near or distant, instead of connecting it with the actual present. The Apostle could not doubt for a moment that they were at that very time sharers in the comfort as well as in the sufferings.

(8) **We would not, brethren, have you ignorant.**—From the generalised language of the previous verses he passes to something more specific. The phrase by which he calls attention to the importance of what he is about to write is characteristic of the Epistles of this period (Rom. i. 13; 1 Cor. x. 1; xii. 1; 1 Thess. iv. 13).

**Our trouble which came to us in Asia.**—The allusion may possibly be to the Demetrius tumult of Acts xix. 24—41, or to some like time of danger, such as that referred to in 1 Cor. xv. 32. On the other hand, however, he would probably, in that case, have spoken of a definitely localised danger, as he does in the last reference as being "in Ephesus." The words "in Asia" suggest a wider range of suffering, such as we find referred to in the speech to the elders at Miletus (Acts xx. 19), and the context leads us to think of bodily illness as well as of perils and anxieties.

**We were pressed out of measure.**—The adverbial phrase is specially characteristic of the Epistles of this period. We find it in the "exceedingly sinful" of Rom. vii. 13; the "more excellent (or, *transcending*) way" of 1 Cor. xii. 31; and again in 2 Cor. iv. 17; Gal. i. 13.

**Insomuch that we despaired even of life.**—The language is obviously more vividly descriptive of the collapse of illness than of any peril such as those referred to in the previous Note. St. Paul could hardly have despaired of life during the tumult of Acts xix.

(9) **We had the sentence of death in ourselves.**—The word translated "sentence" (*apokrima*) does not occur elsewhere in the New Testament, nor indeed in the LXX. Literally, it means *answer,* and was probably a half-technical term, used in medical practice, which St. Paul may have adopted from St. Luke, expressing the "opinion" which a physician formed on his diagnosis of a case submitted to him. The Apostle had found himself in a state in which, so far as he could judge for himself, that opinion would have been against the prospect of recovery. He ceased to trust in himself, *i.e.,* in any remedial measures that he could take for himself. He could only fold his hands and trust in God. Recovery in such a case was a veritable resurrection. It may be noted, however, that a cognate word (*apokrisis*) is frequently used by Hippocrates in the sense of a morbid or virulent secretion, and possibly the word here used may also have had that meaning. In this case, what he says would be equivalent to "We had the symptoms of a fatal disease in us."

(10) **Who delivered us from so great a death.**—Death in itself seems hardly to admit of such a qualifying adjective, but the words appear to have been used to represent the incidents of the death which seemed so near, the bodily anguish, the sense of prostration, almost, one might venture to say, the very presence of the king of terrors. As the word translated "so great" is,

trust that he will yet deliver *us;* (11) ye also helping together by prayer for us, that for the gift *bestowed* upon us by the means of many persons thanks may be given by many on our behalf. (12) For our rejoicing is this, the testimony of our conscience, that in simplicity and godly sincerity, not with fleshly wisdom, but by the grace of God, we have had our conversation in the world, and more

---

strictly speaking, used of quality rather than quantity, we might almost translate it, *so terrible a death.*

**And doth deliver.**—The words are wanting in some of the better MSS., and others give them in the future. They may possibly have been inserted to carry the thought of the deliverance into the present as well as through the past and the future.

**In whom we trust.**—Better, *in whom we have hoped.* The verb is not the same as the "trust" of the preceding verse. The words imply that he was not yet altogether free, as man would judge, from the danger of a relapse. Life was for him, in relation both to bodily infirmities and perils of other kinds, a perpetual series of deliverances.

(11) **Ye also helping together by prayer . . .**—They too to whom he writes can help him as he helps them. Indirectly he asks their prayers for him, but he does so with a refined delicacy of feeling, by assuming that they are already praying, and that their prayers are helpful.

**That for the gift bestowed upon us by the means of many persons.**—The Greek word for "person" (*prosôpon*) is elsewhere throughout the New Testament translated "face" or "countenance," or "person" in the sense of "outward appearance." It has been suggested that that may be its meaning even here: *that thanksgiving may be offered from many upturned faces.* The use of the word *prosopopœia,* however, for "personifying," and of *prosôpon* for the characters in a drama, indicates that the noun was beginning to be used in a different sense, and this must clearly have been well established when it came to be used in theological language for the three "persons" of the Godhead. It is interesting to note, however, as a fact in the history of language, that, if this be its meaning here, it is probably one of the earliest extant instances of its being so used.

The "gift," in this instance, is the deliverance from danger and suffering spoken of in the previous verse. Safety and health deserved the name not less truly than prophecy and the gift of tongues. He assumes, with the same subtle refinement as before, that they will be as ready to give thanks for his recovery or deliverance as they were to pray for it.

(12) **For our rejoicing is this . . . .**—Better, *our boast,* as in Rom. iii. 17; xv. 17; 1 Cor. xv. 31. With the feeling of jubilant thankfulness which has hitherto characterised his language there mingles another of a different character. It had, perhaps, been in the background of his thoughts all along. He had seemed, in 1 Cor. iv. 21, to imply that he was coming to take strong measures against evil-doers ("Shall I come unto you with a rod, or in love?"). In 1 Cor. xvi. 2—8 he had spoken yet more definitely, "I will come unto you, when I shall have passed through Macedonia." And yet he had not come. Titus would seem to have told him what was said of this: "He was fickle, and changeable; said Yes one day, and No another. Perhaps he was afraid to come." He is eager to refute the charge without a formal pleading as in answer to it, and seems to cast about for an opening. He finds it in the words which he had just dictated. He has a right to assume that the Corinthians will pray and give thanks for him, for he can boast that he has never failed, conscience bearing him witness, in transparent sincerity to them.

**The testimony of our conscience.**—The words present an obviously undesigned coincidence with St. Paul's language in Acts xxiii. 1; xxiv. 16, and again with that of Rom. ix. 1. To have nothing on his conscience, to "know nothing by (*i.e., against*) himself" (1 Cor. iv. 4), was the great law of his life. And this was true, as of his whole life in relation to the Corinthians, so especially of the supposed change of purpose with which he had been taunted.

**In simplicity.**—The better MSS. give "holiness" instead of "simplicity." The Greek word for the latter is very characteristic of this Epistle (chap. viii. 2; ix. 11, 13; xi. 3), but then it is used in these passages in quite another sense, as of a single-minded generosity. The word for "holiness" is not a common one, but it appears in Heb. xii. 10. It was, however, the natural correlative of the term "saints" applied to all believers. St. Paul's conscience told him that he had not been false to the *consecrated* character which that term involved.

**Godly sincerity.**—Better, *sincerity which is of God.* It is seldom satisfactory to tone down the bold vigour of the Greek, or perhaps Hebrew, idiom into the tameness of an English adjective. The sincerity which St. Paul claims had come to him as God's gift: he could submit it to God's judgment. The word for "sincerity" (literally, *transparency of character,* or, perhaps, that which bore the test of the strongest light) had been used in 1 Cor. v. 8.

**Not with fleshly wisdom, but by the grace of God.**—Better, *in* or *with* in both clauses. The words indicate the same line of thought as those of 1 Cor. ii. 1—6. Men made invidious comparisons between his plainness of speech and the eloquent wisdom of some other teachers. That kind of "fleshly," *i.e., worldly,* wisdom he disclaims. It was not that, but the favour or the "grace" of God which was the motive-force of his action, the sphere in which he lived and moved.

**We have had our conversation.**—Better, *we conducted ourselves.* The tense of the Greek verb implies a special reference in thought to the time when he had been at Corinth. It is, perhaps, hardly necessary to note that "conversation" means "conduct," but as the first occurrence of the word in the New Testament, it may be well to trace the several stages through which it has passed. On its appearance in English, as in Chaucer, it has its full etymological force as indicating, as it does here, habitual conduct. "Enquire of his *conversation* and of his life before" (*Tale of Melibœus*). So in Wiclif's version of the Bible it is used, as in that of 1611, in Gal. i. 13. In somewhat later writers, *e.g.,* in Sidney and Strype, the sense becomes that of "conduct *with* others," "converse, intercourse," a sense still prominent in the familiar legal term for adultery. In Swift and Cowper it has come to be all but absolutely identified with the intercourse which is carried on by talking. In its fullest sense, the Apostle can say that he had striven to *live* everywhere so as to avoid giving grounds for suspicion. Nowhere had he

abundantly to you-ward. (13) For we
write none other things unto you, than
what ye read or acknowledge; and I
trust ye shall acknowledge even to the
end; (14) as also ye have acknowledged
us in part, that we are your rejoicing,
even as ye also *are* our's in the day of
the Lord Jesus. (15) And in this con-
fidence I was minded to come unto
you before, that ye might
have a second benefit;[1]
(16) and to pass by you into

Chap. i. 15—24. The reasons of the Apostle's change of plan.

Macedonia, and to come again out of
Macedonia unto you, and of you to be
brought on my way toward Judæa.
(17) When I therefore was thus minded,
did I use lightness? or the things that
I purpose, do I purpose according to
the flesh, that with me there should be
yea yea, and nay nay? (18) But *as* God
*is* true, our word[2] toward you was not
yea and nay. (19) For the Son of God,
Jesus Christ, who was preached among
you by us, *even* by me and Silvanus and

[2] Or, *preaching.*

[1] Or, *grace.*

---

been more careful so to live than at Corinth, where men were suspicious in proportion to their own viciousness. (Comp. Notes on chap. vii. 1, 2.)

(13) **For we write none other things . . .**—The Greek presents a play on the two words "read" (*anaginoskein*) and "acknowledge," or "know fully" (*epiginoskein*), which it is impossible to reproduce in English. It is as though he said: "I have no hidden meaning in what I write and you read. What you read you read aright in its plain and simple sense. I hope" (the very hope implies that it had been otherwise) "that the more you know me the more will you so read me and judge me even to the end, the great day when the Lord shall come and all things shall be made plain." (Comp. 1 Cor. iv. 3—5.) Possibly, however, the words "even to the end" may be merely equivalent to "completely." (See Note on John xiii. 1.)

(14) **As also ye have acknowledged.**—The parenthetical clause (better, *ye did acknowledge*) comes in to qualify the fear which had been partly veiled by the hope. They had done him some, though not adequate, justice. The phrase "in part" may be noted as specially characteristic of the Epistles of this period (Rom. xi. 25; xv. 15, 24; 1 Cor. xi. 18; xii. 27; xiii. 9).

**That we are your rejoicing . . .**—Better, *a ground of exultation to you, as you are to us.* The words must be connected with the future rather than the past. "I trust that you will one day recognise that you have as much reason to be proud of me as I have to be proud of you." The word for "rejoicing," "boasting," "glorying," &c., is specially characteristic of this period of St. Paul's life, occurring forty-six times in 1 Corinthians, 2 Corinthians, Galatians, and Romans, and only six times in his other Epistles. The "day of the Lord Jesus," of His great advent to judge the world (comp. Rom. ii. 16), defines the "end" to which the previous verse had pointed.

(15) **And in this confidence.**—What has been said hitherto paves the way for the explanation of his apparent change of purpose which he is anxious to give, though he will not formally plead at the bar of the tribunal of those who accused or suspected him. It was because he trusted that they would judge him rightly that he had done that which had led some to judge him wrongly. His plan had been at first to go straight by sea from Ephesus to Corinth, then to pass on to Macedonia, thence to return to Corinth, and thence set sail for Jerusalem. When he wrote 1 Cor. xvi. 5, 6, he had already modified his plan by deciding to go to Macedonia first. His original scheme had shown his wish to see as much of the Corinthians as possible. They were to have two visits ("a second *favour*"), and not one only. Had he shown less regard, he asks, in the change with which he had been taunted?

(16) **To be brought on my way.**—The change of word is significant. He did not intend merely to go from Corinth to Judæa. He expected the Corinthians to further his intentions, to help him on, to escort him solemnly to the ship in which he was to sail, perhaps to accompany him to Asia. (Comp. the use of the word in Acts xv. 3; xx. 38, "accompanied"; xxi. 5; Rom. xv. 24; 1 Cor. xvi. 6—11.) The wish had been stated in 1 Cor. xvi. 6, but without more than a hint (1 Cor. xvi. 4), that his destination might be Jerusalem.

(17) **Did I use lightness?**—This, then, was the charge which he is anxious to refute. The question meets us, however, When had the Corinthians heard of the plan thus detailed? It had been already abandoned, as we have seen, before the first Epistle was despatched. Had it been communicated in a lost letter (see Note on 1 Cor. v. 9)? or was this what Timotheus, who started before the first letter was written (1 Cor. iv. 17), had been authorised to announce? Either alternative is possible, and there is no evidence to enable us to decide which is most probable.

**Do I purpose according to the flesh . . ?**—The construction is somewhat involved. He may mean: (1) "Do I form my purposes after the flesh" (*i.e.*, from worldly motives), "so as to catch the praise of consistency from those who harp on the rule that 'Yes should be yes, and No, no'?" or (2) "Am I weak and worldly in my purpose, changing my plans, and saying 'Yes' and 'No' in almost the same breath?" On the whole, (2) seems to give the better sense. It is obvious that the words on which he dwells had been used of him by others. Some teacher of the party of the circumcision had, apparently, quoted the rule of the Sermon on the Mount (Matt. v. 37) and of St. James (Jas. v. 12), and had asked, with a sneer, when the First Epistle came and showed that the original plan had been abandoned, whether this was the way in which St. Paul acted on it? The passage has accordingly the interest of being indirectly a reference to our Lord's teaching, showing, like Acts xx. 35, that "the words of the Lord Jesus" were habitually cited as rules of life.

(18) **As God is true.**—Literally, *as God is faithful.* The words were one of St. Paul's usual formulæ of assertion. (Comp. 1 Cor. i. 9; x. 13; 2 Thess. iii. 3.) In other instances it is followed commonly by a statement as to some act or attribute of God. Here it is more of the nature of an oath: "As God is faithful in all His words, so my speech" (the vague term is used to include preaching, writing, personal intercourse) "is true and faithful also." There had been no "Yes" and "No" in the same breath; no saying one thing when he meant another.

(19) **By me and Silvanus and Timotheus.—**

Timotheus, was not yea and nay, but in
him was yea. (20) For all the promises
of God in him *are* yea, and in him Amen,
unto the glory of God by us. (21) Now
he which stablisheth us with you in
Christ, and hath anointed us, *is* God;
(22) who hath also sealed us, and given
the earnest of the Spirit in our hearts.
(23) Moreover I call God for a record upon
my soul, that to spare you I came not
as yet unto Corinth. (24) Not for that
we have dominion over your faith, but
are helpers of your joy: for by faith ye
stand.

---

We note an undesigned coincidence with Acts xviii. 5, where Silas (whose identity with Silvanus is thus proved) is related to have come with Timotheus to join St. Paul at Corinth. The three names are joined together in the same order in 1 Thess. i. 1, and 2 Thess. i. 1.

**Was not yea and nay, but in him was yea.**—From the forensic point of view, this was, of course, hardly an adequate defence against the charge of inconsistency. The argument was, so to speak, one of ethical congruity. It was infinitely unlikely that one who preached Christ, the absolutely True Christ, who enforced every precept with the emphatic "Amen, Amen" (the word occurs thirty-one times in St. Matthew, fourteen times in St. Mark, seven times in St. Luke, and in its reduplicated form twenty-five times in St. John), "Verily, verily," should afterwards be shamelessly untruthful, and use words that paltered with a double sense.

**But in him was yea.**—Better, *but in him Yea has been and still is so,* as His great characterising word.

(20) **All the promises of God . . .**—Literally, *as many as are the promises of God.* Many of the better MSS. give a different reading: "In him is the Yea, wherefore also by him is the Amen to God for glory by our means." The thought in either case is the same. The promises of God have been fulfilled and ratified in Christ. He was, as it were, a living incarnate "Amen" to those promises. Comp. St. John's use of the word Amen as a name of Christ, the "faithful and true witness" (Rev. iii. 14). The words "by us" are determined by the context as referring to the preacher rather than to the hearers of the Word.

(21) **He which stablisheth us with you . . .**—For a moment the thought of an *apology* for his own conduct is merged in the higher thought of the greatness of his mission. The word "stablisheth," or "confirmeth," as in 1 Cor. i. 8, is connected with the previous "Amen" as the emphatic formula of ratification. In the insertion of "with you" we note St. Paul's characteristic anxiety to avoid the appearance of claiming for himself what others might not claim with equal right. He repeats the confident hope which he had expressed in 1 Cor. i. 8.

**In Christ.**—Literally, *into Christ,* as though the result of the "establishing" was an actual incorporation with Him. This seems a truer interpretation than that which paraphrases, "confirms us in believing on Christ."

**And hath anointed us.**—Literally, *and anointed,* as referring to a definite moment in the life of the disciples. The verb follows naturally on the mention of Christ the Anointed One. The time referred to is that when, on baptism or the laying on of hands (Acts viii. 17), they had received the first-fruits of the gift of the Spirit, as in Acts ii. 38; viii. 17; x. 44; xix. 6; the "unction from the Holy One" (1 John ii. 20, 27).

(22) **Who hath also sealed us.**—Better, *who also sealed us.* The thought thus expressed is that the gift of the Spirit, following on baptism or the laying on of hands, is as the seal of the covenant which God makes with His people, attesting its validity. (Comp. Eph. i. 13; iv. 30; and, for the Jewish use of seals, Jer. xxxii. 10.)

**And given the earnest of the Spirit.**—Better, for the same reason as before, *gave.* The Greek word for "earnest" (*arrhabôn*), which occurs here for the first time, and is used only by St. Paul in the New Testament (chap. v. 5; Eph. i. 14), has a somewhat interesting history. Originally a Hebrew word, from a verb meaning "to mix," "to change," "to pledge," and so used, as a cognate noun, with the last of the three senses, it appears simply transliterated in the LXX. of Gen. xxxviii. 17, 18. It would seem to have been in common use among the Canaanite or Phœnician traders, and was carried by them to Greece, to Carthage, to Alexandria, and to Rome. It was used by the Greek orator Isæus, and by Plautus and Terence among the earlier Latin writers. The full form came to be considered somehow as pedantic or vulgar, and was superseded in Roman law by the shortened "arrha," the payment of a small sum given on the completion of a bargain as a pledge that the payer would fulfil the contract; and it has passed into Italian as "arra;" into modern French, as "les arrhes;" into popular Scotch even, as "arles." As applied by St. Paul, it had the force of a condensed parable, such as the people of commercial cities like Corinth and Ephesus would readily understand. They were not to think that their past spiritual experience had any character of finality. It was rather but the pledge of yet greater gifts to come: even of that knowledge of God which is eternal life (John xvii. 3). The same thought is expressed, under a more Hebrew image, in the "*firstfruits* of the Spirit" in Rom. viii. 23. Grammatically, the "earnest of the Spirit" may be taken as an example of the genitive of apposition, "the earnest which *is* the Spirit."

(23) **I call God for a record.**—Better, *I call upon God as a witness against my soul.* The thought seems to come across St. Paul's mind that the Corinthians will require a more specific explanation of his change of plan, and he finds this in what had been in part suggested in 1 Cor. iv. 21. Had he carried out his first purpose, he would have come to punish or chastise. He had been, on this account, reluctant to come. His not coming was an act of leniency.

**I came not as yet.**—Better, *I came no more—i.e.,* not a second time after his first visit. The Greek adverb cannot possibly mean "not yet."

(24) **Not for that we have dominion over your faith.**—Better, *are lording it over.* He has scarcely written, or uttered, the words which imply authority, when the thought comes to him that he may seem to claim too much. He shrinks from "lording it over God's heritage" (1 Pet. v. 3), and half apologises for so strong a word as "sparing." He puts forward, therefore, the other side of his work. He was really seeking, not to domineer, or cause pain, but to be a

A.D. 60.

Chap. ii. 1—5. St. Paul's joy at hearing of the penitence of the sinner of 1 Cor. v.

CHAPTER II.—(1) But I determined this with myself, that I would not come again to you in heaviness. (2) For if I make you sorry, who is he then that maketh me glad, but the same which is made sorry by me? (3) And I wrote this same unto you, lest, when I came, I should have sorrow from them of whom I ought to rejoice; having confidence in you all, that my joy is *the joy* of you all. (4) For out of much affliction and anguish of heart I wrote unto you with many tears; not that ye should be grieved, but that ye might know the love which I have more abundantly unto you. (5) But if any have caused grief, he hath not grieved me, but in part: that I may not overcharge you all. (6) Sufficient to

---

fellow-worker with their "joy and peace in believing" (Rom. xv. 13). He knows that they have a standing-ground, independently of him, in their faith in Christ, and he seeks to confirm that faith.

II.

(1) **But I determined this with myself.**—Better, *I determined for myself.* The chapter division is here obviously wrong, and interrupts the sequence of thought. St. Paul continues his explanation. He did not wish to come again, *i.e.*, to make his second visit to Corinth, in grief, and if he had carried out his first plan that would have been the almost inevitable result. He consulted his own feelings ("*for* myself") as well as theirs.

(2) **Who is he then that maketh me glad?**—The force of the "for," with which the verse opens, lies below the surface. He had wished to avoid a visit that would cause sorrow to himself and others, and events had shown that he was right. But it might be said, perhaps had been said, that he didn't seem to care about giving pain when he wrote, as, *e.g.*, in 1 Cor. iv. 18; v. 2—7; vi. 5—8. "Yes," is his answer; "but then the pain which *I* inflict" (the pronoun is emphatic) "gives to him who suffers it the power of giving me joy, and so works out an ample compensation;" a thought to which he returns in chap. vii. 8. The abruptness of the question and the use of the singular number shows that he has the one great offender, the incestuous adulterer of 1 Cor. v. 1, before his mind's eye. He sees him, as it were, and can point to him as showing how well the course he had taken had answered.

(3) **And I wrote this same unto you.**—Here, again, we have to read between the lines. The pronoun, which does not refer to anything that has been actually said, shows with what definiteness certain passages in his first letter were stamped upon his memory. The question might be asked, "Why had he written so sharply?" And he makes answer to himself that the result had been what he had intended: that his motive in so writing as to give pain had been to avoid giving and receiving pain when he came in person. He wanted his visit to be one of unmixed joy for himself, and if so, it could not fail, looking to their mutual sympathy, to give his disciples joy also.

(4) **Out of much affliction and anguish.**—Men might think that it had cost him little to write sharp words like those which he has in his mind. He remembers well what he felt as he dictated them—the intensity of his feelings, pain that such words should be needed, anxiety as to their issue, the very tears which then, as at other times (Acts xx. 19, 31; 2 Tim. i. 4), were the outflow of strong emotion. Those who were indignant at his stern words should remember, or at least learn to believe this, and so to see in them the strongest proof of his abounding love for them. The heart of St. Paul was in this matter as the heart of Him who said, "As many as I love, I rebuke and chasten" (Rev. iii. 19). The motive in such a case is not to give pain, but to lead those whom we reprove to feel how much we love them. On the word for "anguish," see Note on Luke xxi. 25. Looking to the fact that it is used only by St. Luke and St. Paul in the New Testament, we may, perhaps, see in it another example of medical terminology. The anguish was like that of a tight pressure or constriction of the heart.

(5) **But if any have caused grief.**—The man who had been the chief cause of his sorrow is now prominent in his thoughts. He will not name him. He is, as in 1 Cor. v. 1—5, and here in verse 7, "a man," "such a one." The abrupt introduction of the qualifying clause, "but in part," and the absence of any authoritative punctuation, makes the construction ambiguous. It admits of three possible explanations: (1) "If any have caused grief, it is not *I* alone whom he hath grieved, but in part, to some extent—not to press the charge against *him* too heavily—all of *you.*" They, the members of the Corinthian Church, were really the greatest sufferers from the scandal which brought shame upon it. (2) "If any have caused grief, *he* hath not grieved me, save in part" (*i.e.*, he is not the only offender), "that I may not press the charge against *all of you*—so that I may not treat you as if you were all open to the same condemnation, or had all caused the same sorrow." (3) Combining parts of (1) and (2): "It is not *I* whom he hath grieved, save in part, that I may not lay the blame on all of *you.*" Of these (1) seems the simplest and most natural. In any case, it is important to remember that the position of the pronoun in the Greek, "*me* he hath not grieved," makes it specially emphatic.

(6) **Sufficient to such a man is this punishment.**—Better, perhaps, *this censure,* or *rebuke:* the Greek word *epitimia* being different from those in Matt. xxv. 46, and in Heb. x. 29. It is natural to infer that this was somewhat after the pattern of the course marked out in 1 Cor. v. 3—5. A meeting of the Church had been held, and the man delivered to Satan. Possibly this was followed by some suffering of body, supernaturally inflicted, or coming as the natural consequence (not less divine because natural) of remorse and shame. It was almost certainly followed by excommunication and exclusion from religious and social fellowship. St. Paul had clearly heard what it had been, and thought that it had been enough.

**Which was inflicted of many.**—Actually, *by the majority.* The decision, then, had not been unanimous. The minority may have been either members of the Judaising "Cephas" party, resenting what they would look upon as St. Paul's dictation, and perhaps falling back on the Jewish casuistry, which taught that all the natural relationships of a proselyte were cancelled by his conversion; or the party of license, against whom the Apostle reasons in 1 Cor vi.—viii.,

Chap. ii. 6—11. Directions for the absolution of the offender.

such a man *is* this punishment,[1] which
*was inflicted* of many. (7) So
that contrariwise ye *ought*
rather to forgive *him*, and
comfort *him*, lest perhaps
such a one should be swallowed up with
overmuch sorrow. (8) Wherefore I be-
seech you that ye would confirm *your*
love toward him. (9) For to this end
also did I write, that I might know the
proof of you, whether ye be obedient in
all things. (10) To whom ye forgive any
thing, I *forgive* also: for if I forgave
any thing, to whom I forgave *it*, for
your sakes *forgave I it* in the person[2]
of Christ; (11) lest Satan should get an
advantage of us: for we are not igno-
rant of his devices. (12) Furthermore,
when I came to Troas to *preach* Christ's
gospel, and a door was
opened unto me of the
Lord, (13) I had no rest in

Chap. ii. 12, 13. St. Paul's journey from Troas to Macedonia.

[1] Or, *censure.*

[2] Or, *in the sight.*

---

and who boasted of their freedom. The Passover argument and the form of the sentence in 1 Cor. v. alike suggest the idea that the offender and those who defended him were Jews. On the other hand, see Note on chap. vii. 12.

(7) **Ye ought rather to forgive.**—The indignation which St. Paul had felt has passed, on his hearing of the offender's state, into pity and anxiety. The time had come for words of pardon and comfort and counsel. What if he should be "swallowed up," and sink as in the great deep of sorrow? Suicide, madness, apostasy, seem to float before his mind as but too possible results.

(8) **That ye would confirm your love.**—The word for "confirm" (better, perhaps, *ratify*—comp. Gal. iii. 15) suggests the thought of an act as formal and public as the rebuke had been. The excommunicated man was to be re-admitted to fellowship by a collective act of the Church.

(9) **For to this end also did I write . . .**—The tense of the Greek verb, which may be what is known as the Epistolary aorist, used by the writer of the time at which he writes, would not be decisive as to what is referred to, and the words may mean: "I write to you thus to see whether you are as obedient now as you were before—in one line of action as in the other." If he refers to the First Epistle, it is to intimate that he gave the directions in 1 Cor. v. 3—7, not only for the removal of a scandal and the reformation of the offender who had caused it, but as a test of their obedience. On the whole, the former interpretation seems preferable. It scarcely seems like St. Paul to make the punishment a trial of obedience. There is a characteristic subtle delicacy of thought in his suggesting that, having shown obedience in punishing they should show it also in forgiving.

(10) **To whom ye forgive any thing, I forgive also.**—The procedure of 1 Cor. v. 3—7 is again, obviously, in his mind. Though absent in body, he had made himself a sharer spiritually in that censure. He now, anticipating their compliance with his request, makes himself a sharer in the sentence of absolution.

**For if I forgave any thing.**—Better. *if I have forgiven;* and so in the following clauses. The case is put hypothetically, though he has an actual offender in his thoughts, because he had, in verse 5, all but disclaimed the character of being an aggrieved person. He confines himself, therefore, to saying: "So far as I was aggrieved, I have forgiven; so far as I have forgiven, it is for your sake as a body, not merely for my own and that of the offender."

**In the person of Christ.**—Literally, *in the face of Christ.* (See Note on chap. i. 11.) *In the presence of Christ* is, therefore, a possible rendering. The English version is probably correct, the phrase conveying the same sense as "in the name of our Lord Jesus Christ" in 1 Cor. v. 4, but in a somewhat stronger form. He had forgiven, as though Christ was acting in or by him. The forgiveness would be as authoritative as the censure. It will be noted that he claims in its fulness the authority given to the Apostles of Christ in John xx. 23.

(11) **Lest Satan should get an advantage of us.**—Literally, *lest we should be cheated* (or *outmanœuvred*) *by Satan.* The phraseology is that of one who is, as it were, playing a game against the Tempter, in which the souls of men are at once the counters and the stake. The Apostle's last move in that game had been to "give the sinner over to Satan" with a view to his ultimate deliverance. But what if Satan should outwit him, by tempting the sinner to despair or recklessness? To guard against that danger required, as it were, another move. Stratagem must be met by strategy. The man must be absolved that he may be able to resist the Tempter.

**We are not ignorant of his devices.**—The language comes from a wide and varied experience. St. Paul had been buffeted by a messenger of Satan (chap. xii. 7); had once and again been hindered by him in his work (1 Thess. ii. 18); was ever wrestling, not with flesh and blood, but with principalities and powers (Eph. vi. 12); and so he knew how the Tempter could turn even the rules of an ascetic rigour, or the remorse of a sin-burdened conscience, into an occasion of yet further and more irremediable sin.

(12) **Furthermore, when I came to Troas.**—The article, perhaps, indicates the Troad as a district, rather than the city, just as it does in the case of Saron. (See Note on Acts ix. 35.) The case of the offender had come in as a parenthesis in verses 5—8. He returns to the train of thought which it had interrupted, and continues his narrative of what had passed after he had written the First Epistle. (On Troas, see Notes on Acts xvi. 8.) A Church had probably been founded in that city by St. Luke, but St. Paul's first visit to it had been limited to a few days, and there are no traces of his preaching there. Now he comes "for the gospel's sake." That there was a flourishing Christian community some months later, we find from Acts xx. 6.

**A door was opened unto me.**—Opportunities for mission-work, as we should call them, are thus described in 1 Cor. xvi. 9. There is something of the nature of a coincidence in his using it of two different churches, Ephesus and Troas, within a comparatively short interval.

(13) **I had no rest in my spirit.**—Instead of coming himself straight from Ephesus, as he had at first intended, and had intimated probably in the lost letter of 1 Cor. v. 9, or by Timotheus (1 Cor. iv. 17), or pressing on through Macedonia, as he purposed when he wrote the First Epistle (1 Cor. xvi. 5), he had sent on Titus (himself possibly connected with Corinth: see

my spirit, because I found not Titus my brother: but taking my leave of them, I went from thence into Macedonia. (14) Now thanks *be* unto God, which always causeth us to triumph in Christ, and maketh manifest the savour of his knowledge by us in every place. (15) For we are unto God a sweet savour of Christ, in them that are saved, and in them that perish: (16) to the one *we are* the savour of death unto death; and to the other the savour of life unto life.

Chap. ii. 14—17. The Apostle as an incense-bearer in the triumph of Christ.

Note on Acts xviii. 7) to ascertain what had been the effects of that Epistle on the Corinthian Church. Titus was to return to him at Troas. Not meeting him there, St. Paul, in his eager anxiety to hear something more than Timotheus had been able to tell him, left Troas, in spite of the opening which it presented for his work as a preacher of the gospel, and hastened on into Macedonia. Taking the route that he had taken before, he would probably go to Philippi, where he would find St. Luke; and we may conjecture, without much risk of error, that it was there that he and Titus met.

(14) **Now thanks be unto God.**—The apparent abruptness of this burst of thanksgiving is at first somewhat startling. We have to find its source, not in what the Apostle had written or spoken, but in what was passing through his memory. He had met Titus, and that disciple had been as a courier bringing tidings of a victory. The love of God had won another triumph.

**Causeth us to triumph.**—Better, *who always leads us in His triumph.* There is absolutely no authority for the factitive meaning given to the verb in the English version. In Col. ii. 15, it is translated rightly, "triumphing over them in it." It is obvious, too, that the true rendering gives a much more characteristic thought. It would be unlike St. Paul to speak of himself as the triumphant commander of God's great army. It is altogether like him that he should give God the glory, and own that He, as manifested in Christ, had triumphed, and that Apostle and penitent, the faithful and the rebellious, alike took their place in the procession of that triumph.

The imagery that follows is clearly that of the solemn triumphal procession of a Roman emperor or general. St. Paul, who had not as yet been at Rome, where only such triumphs were celebrated, had, therefore, never seen them, and was writing accordingly from what he had heard from others. Either from the Roman Jews whom he had met at Corinth, many of them slaves or freed-men in the imperial household, or the Roman soldiers and others with whom he came in contact at Philippi, possibly from St. Luke or Clement, he had heard how the conqueror rode along the Via Sacra in his chariot, followed by his troops and prisoners, captive kings and princes, and trophies of victory; how fragrant clouds of incense accompanied his march, rising from fixed altars or wafted from censers; how, at the foot of the Capitoline hill, some of the prisoners, condemned as treacherous or rebellious, were led off to execution, or thrown into the dungeons of the Mamertine prison, while others were pardoned and set free. It is not without interest to remember that when St. Paul wrote, the latest triumph at Rome had been that solemnised at Rome by Claudius in honour of the victory of Ostorius over the Britons in A.D. 51, and commemorated by a triumphal arch, the inscription on which is now to be seen in the court-yard of the Barberini Palace at Rome; that in that triumph Caractacus had figured as a prisoner; and that he and his children, spared by the mercy of the emperor, had passed from the ranks of the "lost" to those of the "saved" (Tacit. *Ann.* xiii. 36). According to a view taken by some writers, Claudia and Linus (2 Tim. iv. 21) were among those children. (See *Excursus on the Later Years of St. Paul's Life*, at the close of the Acts of the Apostles.

**The savour of his knowledge.**—There is obviously a reference to the incense which, as in the above description, was an essential part of the triumph of a Roman general. It is there that St. Paul finds an analogue of his own work. He claims to be, as it were, a *thurifer*, an incense-bearer, in the procession of the conqueror. Words, whether of prayer or praise, thanksgiving or preaching, what were they but as incense-clouds bearing to all around, as they were wafted in the air, the tidings that the Conqueror had come? The "savour of his knowledge" is probably "the knowledge *of Him:*" that which rests in Him as its object.

(15) **We are unto God a sweet savour of Christ.**—If we believe this Epistle to have been written from Philippi, it is interesting to note the recurrence of the same imagery of a "sweet savour" in the Epistle to that Church (Phil. iv. 18). Here the mind of the writer turns to the sterner, sadder side of the Roman triumph. Some who appeared in that triumph were *on their way to deliverance*, some *on their way to perish* (this is the exact rendering of the words translated *saved* and *lost*), and this also has its analogue in the triumph of Christ. He does not shrink from that thought. In his belief in the righteousness and mercy of Christ, he is content to leave the souls of all men to His judgment. He will not the less do his work as incense-bearer, and let the "sweet savour" of the knowledge of God be wafted through the words which it has been given him to utter. All things are for His glory, for His righteousness will be seen to have been working through all.

(16) **To the one we are the savour of death unto death.**—As with other instances of St. Paul's figurative language, we note the workings of a deeply, though unconsciously, poetic imagination. Keeping the image of the triumph in his mind, he thinks of the widely different impression and effect which the odour of the incense would work in the two classes of the prisoners. To some it would seem to be as a breath from Paradise, giving life and health; to others its sweetness would seem sickly and pestilential, coming as from a charnel house, having in it the "savour of death," and leading to death as its issue.

**And who is sufficient for these things?**—The question forced itself on St. Paul's mind as it forces itself on the mind of every true teacher, Who can feel qualified for a work which involves such tremendous issues? If we ask how it was that he did not draw back from it altogether, the answer is found in other words of his: "God has made us able (*sufficient*) ministers of the New Testament" (chap. iii. 6); "our sufficiency is of God" (chap. iii. 5). It is obvious that even here he assumes his sufficiency, and gives in the next verse the ground of the assumption.

And who *is* sufficient for these things?
(17) For we are not as many, which corrupt[1] the word of God: but as of sincerity, but as of God, in the sight of God speak we in Christ.

CHAPTER III.—(1) Do we begin again to commend ourselves? or need we, as some *others*, epistles of commendation to you, or *letters* of commendation from you?
(2) Ye are our epistle written in our hearts, known and read of all men:
(3) *forasmuch as ye are* manifestly declared to be the epistle of Christ ministered by us, written not with ink, but with the Spirit of the living God; not in

1 Or, *deal deceitfully with.*

A.D. 60.

Chap. iii. 1–3. The true letters of commendation.

(17) **For we are not as many, which corrupt the word of God.**—More accurately, *We are not as most, as the greater number.* There is a ring of sadness in the words. Even then the ways of error were manifold, and the way of truth was one. Among Judaisers, and the seekers after Greek wisdom, asserters of license for liberty, questioners of the resurrection: how few were those who preached the true word of God in its purity! The word for "corrupt," formed from a word which signifies "huckster" or "tavern-keeper," implies an adulteration like that which such people commonly practised. We, says St. Paul, play no such tricks of trade with what we preach; we do not meet the tastes of our hearers by prophesying deceits. The very fact that we know the tremendous issues of our work would hinder that. Comp. St. Peter's use of the same figure in "the sincere (the *unadulterated*) milk of the *reason*" (1 Pet. ii. 2). It is doubtful whether the imagery of the triumph is still present to his thoughts. If it were, we may think of the word "corrupt" as connected with the thought of the sweet savour: "Our incense, at any rate, is pure. If it brings death it is through no fault of ours. It is not a poisoned perfume."

**As of sincerity, but as of God.**—The two clauses are half connected, half contrasted. To have said "of sincerity" alone would have been giving too much prominence to what was purely subjective. He could not feel sure that he was sincere unless he knew that his sincerity was given to him by God. (For the word "sincerity," see Note on chap. i. 12.)

III.

(1) **Do we begin again to commend ourselves?**—The MSS. present various readings: "Do we begin again to commend ourselves [Nay, not so], unless we desire [which we do not] letters of commendation;" but the Received text is sufficiently supported, and gives a clearer and simpler meaning. Here, again, we have to read between the lines. Titus has told St. Paul what has been said of him at Corinth. Referring, probably, to what he had said in his First Epistle as to the "wisdom" which he preached (1 Cor. ii. 6), his having "laid the foundation" (1 Cor. iii. 10), his dwelling on his sufferings (1 Cor. iv. 11), his preaching without payment (1 Cor. ix. 15) as a thing he gloried in, they had sneered at him as always "commending himself." They had added that it was no wonder that he did so when he had no authoritative letters of commendation from other churches, such as were brought by other teachers. As soon as the words "We are not as the many" had passed his lips, the thought occurs that the same will be said again. He *hears* it said, as it were, and makes his answer.

**Need we, as some others, epistles of commendation to you?**—We are left to conjecture who are thus referred to. Possibly some of the Apollos party had contrasted the letters which he had brought from Ephesus (Acts xviii. 27) with St. Paul's want of them. Possibly the Judaising teachers who meet us in chap. xi. 13 had come with credentials of this nature from the Church of Jerusalem. The indignant tone in which St. Paul speaks indicates the latter view as the more probable. The "letters of commendation" deserve notice as an important element in the organisation of the early Church. A Christian travelling with such a letter from any Church was certain to find a welcome in any other. They guaranteed at once his soundness in the faith and his personal character, and served to give a reality to the belief in the "communion" of saints, as the necessary sequel to the recognition of a Catholic or universal Church. It is significant of the part they had played in the social victory of the Christian Church that Julian tried to introduce them into the decaying system which he sought to galvanise into an imitative life (Sozomen. *Hist.* v. 16).

(2) **Ye are our epistle written in our hearts.**—This is an answer. They, the Corinthian converts, are written on his heart. In his thoughts and prayers for them he finds his true commendatory letter, and this a letter which is patent to the eyes of all men. In "known and read" we find the familiar play on the two words, *epiginoskein* and *anaginoskein.* (See Note on chap. i. 13.) All who knew St. Paul could read what was there written.

(3) **Forasmuch as ye are manifestly declared.**—The metaphor appears to shift its ground from the subjective to the objective. It is not only as written in his heart, but as seen and known by others, that they (the Corinthians) are as a letter of commendation. They are as a letter which Christ had written as with the finger of God. That letter, he adds, was "ministered by us." He had been, that is, as the *amanuensis* of that letter, but Christ was the real writer.

**Written not with ink.**—Letters were usually written on papyrus, with a reed pen and with a black pigment (*atramentum*) used as ink. (Comp. 2 John, verse 12.) In contrast with this process, he speaks of the Epistle of Christ as written with the "Spirit of the living God." It is noteworthy that the Spirit takes here the place of the older "finger of God" in the history of the two tables of stone in Ex. xxxi. 18. So a like substitution is found in comparing "If I with the finger of God cast out devils," in Luke xi. 20, with "If I by the Spirit of God," in Matt. xii. 28. Traces of the same thought are found in the hymn in the Ordination service, in which the Holy Spirit is addressed as "the finger of God's hand."

**Not in tables of stone.**—The thought of a letter written in the heart by the Spirit of God brings three memorable passages to St. Paul's memory:—(1) the "heart of flesh" of Ezek. xi. 19; xxxvi. 26, 27; (2) the promise that the law should be written in the heart, which was to be the special characteristic of the new covenant (Jer. xxxi. 31—33); and (3) the whole history of the circumstances of the first, or older, covenant; and, from this verse to the end of the chapter, thought

tables of stone, but in fleshy tables
of the heart. (4) And such
trust have we through
Christ to God-ward: (5) not
that we are sufficient of our-
selves to think any thing
as of ourselves; but our sufficiency *is*
of God; (6) who also hath made us
able ministers of the new testa-
ment; not of the letter, but of the
spirit: for the letter killeth, but the
spirit giveth life.[1] (7) But if the minis-

Chap. iii. 4—12. Contrast between the ministry of the letter and that of the spirit.

1 Or, *quickeneth.*

---

follows rapidly on thought in manifold application of the images thus suggested.

**But in fleshy tables of the heart.**—The better MSS. give *in tables* (or, *tablets*), *which are hearts of flesh*, reproducing the words of Ezek. xi. 19. The thought of the letter begins to disappear, and that of a law written on tablets takes its place, as one picture succeeds another in a dissolving view.

(4) **Such trust have we.**—The words carry us back to the expressions of verses 2 and 3, perhaps, also, to the assertion of his own sincerity and sufficiency implied in chap. ii. 16, 17. He has this confidence, but it is through Christ, who strengthens him (Col. i. 11).

(5) **Not that we are sufficient . . .**—He had not used the word "sufficient" of himself, but it was clearly the implied answer to the question, "Who is sufficient for these things?" In the Greek there are two different prepositions for the one "of" in English. "Not as though we are sufficient of ourselves to form any estimate as originating with ourselves," would be a fair paraphrase. The habit of mind which led St. Paul to emphasise the shades of meaning in Greek prepositions to an extent hardly to be expressed in English, and not commonly recognised, it may be, in colloquial Greek, is seen again in Rom. xi. 36.

**Is of God.**—The preposition is the same as in the second of the two previous clauses. The sufficiency flows from God as its source: originates with him.

(6) **Able ministers of the new testament.**—Better, perhaps, as keeping up the stress on the word that had been used in chap. ii. 16, in the English as in the Greek, *sufficient ministers*. The noun is used as carrying out the thought implied in the "ministered by us" in verse 3. In the "new covenant"—new, as implying *freshness* of life and energy—we have a direct reference, both to our Lord's words, as cited in 1 Cor. xi. 25, and given in the Gospel narrative of the Last Supper (see Notes on Matt. xxvi. 28), and to Jer. xxxi. 31. The Greek omits the article before all three words, "of a new covenant, one not of a written letter, but of spirit." The idea of "spirit" comes from Ezek. xi. 19; xxxvi. 26, 27.

**For the letter killeth, but the spirit giveth life.**—The word "letter" (*gramma*) stands, not for what we call the literal meaning of Scripture, as contrasted with one which is allegorical or spiritual, but for the whole written code or law of Judaism. St. Paul does not contrast the literal meaning of that code with the so-called mystical exposition of it (a view which has often led to wild and fantastic interpretations), but speaks of the written code as such. So the plural "the writings, the Scriptures" (*grammata*), are used of the sacred Books of Israel (John v. 47; 2 Tim. iii. 15), and the scribes (*grammateis*) were those who interpreted the writings. The contrast between the "letter" in this sense and the "spirit" is a familiar thought with St. Paul (Rom. ii. 27—29; vii. 6). Of this written code St. Paul says that it "killeth." The statement seems startlingly bold, and he does not here stop to explain its meaning. What he means is, however, stated with sufficient fulness in the three Epistles written about this time (1 Cor. xv. 56; Gal. iii. 10, 21; Rom. vii. 9—11; viii. 2, 3, the references being given in the chronological order of the Epistles). The work of the Law, from St. Paul's view, is to make men conscious of sin. No outward command, even though it come from God, and is "holy, and just, and good" (Rom. vii. 12), can, as such, do more than that. What was wanting was the life-giving power of the Spirit. The word here (as in Rom. ii. 27; vii. 6) appears to hover between the sense of "spirit" as representing any manifestation of the Divine Life that gives life—in which sense the words of Christ are "spirit and life" (John vi. 63), and Christ Himself is a "quickening spirit" (1 Cor. xv. 45, and verse 17 of this chapter)—and the more distinctly personal sense in which St. Paul speaks of "the Spirit," the Holy Spirit, and to which we commonly limit our use of the name of "the Holy Ghost" in His relation to the Father and Son. Of that Spirit St. Paul says that "it quickens:" it can rouse into life not only the slumbering conscience, as the Law had done, but the higher spiritual element in man—can give it strength to will, the healthy energy of new affections, new prayers, new impulses. If we cannot suppose St. Paul to have been acquainted with our Lord's teaching, as recorded in John vi. 63 (where see Note), the coincidence of thought is, at any rate, singularly striking.

(7) **But if the ministration of death, written and engraven in stones, was glorious.**—More accurately, *engraved in a writing* (*i.e.*, in a written formula) *upon stones*. The word for "writing" is the same as the "letter" of the preceding verse, and the whole might, perhaps, be best translated, *if the ministration of death in the letter, engraved upon stones, was glorious*. The English version, by using the two participles, creates a false antithesis between "written" and "engraved," and misses the sequence of thought indicated by the continued use of the word for "letter" or "writing." For "was glorious," more accurately, *came into being with glory*. The thoughts of the Apostle have travelled to the record of the circumstances connected with the giving of the Law as the foundation of the first covenant, and of them he proceeds to speak fully. We can almost picture him to ourselves as taking up his LXX. version of the Law, and reproducing its very words and thoughts.

**So that the children of Israel could not stedfastly behold . . .**—The narrative in Ex. xxxiv. 29—35 records that when Moses came down from the mount with the second tables of stone, "the skin of his face shone," and the "people were afraid to draw nigh unto him." The English version—that "*till* Moses had done speaking with them he put a vail on his face," and that "when he went in before the Lord he took it off until he came out"—suggests the thought that he appeared to the people, after the first manifestation of the unconscious glory, as a veiled prophet. It is doubtful, however, whether this is the natural meaning of the Hebrew, and Ex. xxxiv. 35 repeats the statement that the Israelites saw the glory. The LXX., Vulgate, and most modern versions give, "When he ceased speaking he put a veil on his face." They saw the brightness, they shrank from it in awe, they were not allowed to watch it to the end and gaze on its disap-

tration of death, written *and* engraven
in stones, was glorious, so that the
children of Israel could not stedfastly
behold the face of Moses for the glory of
his countenance; which *glory* was to be
done away: (8) how shall not the minis-
tration of the spirit be rather glorious?
(9) For if the ministration of condemna-
tion *be* glory, much more doth the
ministration of righteousness exceed in
glory. (10) For even that which was
made glorious had no glory in this
respect, by reason of the glory that
excelleth. (11) For if that which is done
away *was* glorious, much more that
which remaineth *is* glorious. (12) Seeing
then that we have such hope, we use
great plainness[1] of speech: (13) and not

1 Or, *boldness.*

pearance. This was the sequence of facts that St. Paul had in his thoughts, and which he certainly found in the LXX.; and it is of this, accordingly, that he speaks. The children of Israel could not bear to look on the glory, even though it was perishing and evanescent. The English rendering, "which glory was to be done away," reads into the participle a gerundial force that does not properly belong to it; and it may be noted that it is the first of the great English versions that does so, the others giving, "which is made void," or "which is done away." It would be better expressed, perhaps, by, *which was in the act of passing away.* The Greek word is the same as that on which our translators have rung so many changes in 1 Cor. xiii. 8—11. It was a favourite word with St. Paul at this period of his life, occurring twenty-two times in 1 Corinthians, 2 Corinthians, Galatians, and Romans, and three times only in his other Epistles.

It may be noted that the Vulgate rendering of Ex. xxxiv. 29, "*ignorabat quod cornuta esset facies ejus*" ("he knew not that his face was horned"), has given rise to the representations of Moses with horns, or rays of light taking the place of horns, as in Michael Angelo's statue in the church of San Pietro in Vincoli at Rome, and pictorial representations generally.

(8) **How shall not the ministration of the spirit be rather glorious?**—Better, *be more in glory.* The ministration of the spirit—that which has spirit for its characteristic attribute, and proceeds from *the* Spirit and imparts it to others—is that which St. Paul claims as his ministry. The glory of the new covenant, must be as much above the glory of the old, as the living, life-giving Spirit is above the dead and death-bringing code which he speaks of as the "letter."

(9) **If the ministration of condemnation be glory . . .**—Many of the better MSS. give the reading, *if there be glory to the ministry of condemnation.* The latter phrase takes the place here of "the ministry of death" in verse 7. The "letter," the "written law," as such, works death, because it brings with it the condemnation which awaits transgressors. It holds out to them the pattern of a righteousness which they have never had, and cannot of themselves attain unto, and passes its sentence on them as transgressors. Contrasted with it is the ministration which has "righteousness" as its object and result, and therefore as its characteristic attribute—the "law of the Spirit of life"—a law written in the heart, working not condemnation, but righteousness and peace and joy (Rom. viii. 1—4).

(10) **For even that which was made glorious had no glory.**—More accurately, St. Paul reproducing the very tense which he found in the LXX. of Ex. xxxiv. 35, *that which had been glorified has not been glorified—i.e.,* has lost its glory.

**In this respect . . .**—The phrase is the same as in chap. ix. 3; 1 Pet. iv. 16. The English expresses it very fairly. "In this point," as compared with the gospel, the Law has lost its glory; it is thrown into the shade by "the glory that excelleth." The imagery seems to bring before us the symbolic meaning of the Transfiguration. Moses and Elijah appear in glory, but the glory of the Son of Man surpasses that of either. (Comp. Notes on Matt. xvi. 1—4.) The word for "excelleth" may be noted as peculiar to St. Paul among the writers of the New Testament.

(11) **For if that which is done away . . .**—The Greek participle is in the present tense, "being done away," or "failing," expressing the same thought as the "decaying and waxing old" of Heb. viii. 13. The contrast between the transient and the permanent is expressed by the same Greek words as in 1 Cor. xiii. 8—11.

**Glorious.**—Literally, *through glory,* seen, as it were, through a medium of glory which surrounded it. The second "in glory" is meant, probably, to express a state of greater permanence.

(12) **Seeing then that we have such hope.**—The "hope" is in substance the same as the "confidence" of verse 4; but the intervening thoughts have carried his mind on to the future as well as the present. He has a hope for them and for himself, which is more than a trust in his own sufficiency.

**We use great plainness of speech.**—The word so rendered expresses strictly the openness which says all, in which there is no reticence or reserve. It stands in contrast with the "corrupting the word" of chap. ii. 17, and answers to the Apostle's claim to have "kept back nothing that was profitable" in Acts xx. 20. We, he practically says, need no veil.

(13) **And not as Moses, which put a vail over his face.**—The Apostle, it must be remembered, has in his thoughts either the LXX. version of Ex. xxxiv. 33, or an interpretation of the Hebrew answering to that version. (See Note on verse 7.) What was the object of this putting on of the veil? The English version of that text suggests that it was to hide the brightness from which they shrank. But the interpretation which St. Paul follows presents a very different view. Moses put the veil over his face that *they might not see the end, the fading away* of that transitory glory. For them it was as though it were permanent and unfading. They did not see—this is St. Paul's way of allegorising the fact stated—that the whole system of the Law, as symbolised by that brightness, had but a fugitive and temporary being.

**Could not stedfastly look to the end of that which is abolished.**—Better, *look on the end of that which was perishing.* Literally, the words state the fact, they could not see how the perishing glory ended. In the interpretation of the parable St. Paul seems to say that what was true of those older Israelites was true also of their descendants. They could not see the true end of the perishing system of the Law, its aim, purport, consummation. There is, perhaps, though most recent commentators have refused to recognise it, a half-allusive reference to the thought expressed in

Chap. iii. 13–18. The veil, once on the face of Moses, now on the heart of Israel, shall one day be withdrawn.

as Moses, *which* put a vail over his face,
that the children of Israel
could not stedfastly look to
the end of that which is
abolished: (14) but their
minds were blinded: for
until this day remaineth
the same vail untaken away in the
reading of the old testament; which
*vail* is done away in Christ. (15) But
even unto this day, when Moses is read,
the vail is upon their heart. (16) Never-
theless when it shall turn to the Lord,
the vail shall be taken away. (17) Now
the Lord is that Spirit: and where the
Spirit of the Lord *is*, there *is* liberty.

---

Rom. x. 4, that "Christ is the *end* of the law for righteousness;" or, in 1 Tim. i. 5, that "the *end* of the commandment is love out of a pure heart." Had their eyes been open, they would have seen in the fading away of the old glory of the decaying "letter" the dawn of a glory that excelled it. And in the thought that this was the true "end" of the Law we find the ground for the Apostle's assertion that he used great plainness of speech. He had no need to veil his face or his meaning, for he had no fear lest the glory of the gospel of which he was a minister should fade away.

(14) **But their minds were blinded.**—The Greek verb expresses strictly the callousness of a nerve that has become insensible, as in Mark vi. 52; viii. 17; Rom. xi. 7. Here, as applied to the faculties of perception, "blinded" is, perhaps, a legitimate rendering.

**Remaineth the same vail untaken away in the reading of the old testament . . .**—The words are better translated: *the same veil remaineth in the reading of the old covenant; the fact not being revealed* (*i.e.*, by the removal of the veil) *that it* (the old covenant) *is being done away in Christ.* The figure is passing through a kind of dissolving change. There is still a veil between the hearers of the Law and its true meaning; but the veil is no longer on the face of the law-giver, but on their hearts; and the reason of this is that, the veil not being withdrawn, they do not see that the glory of the older covenant is done away by the brightness of the new. It is doing violence to the context to refer to the veil the words "is done away," which through the whole passage is applied to the Law itself; and in verse 16 a new and appropriate word is used for the withdrawal of the veil. It is, the Apostle says, because the veil of prejudice and tradition hinders them from seeing the truth that the Jews of his own time still think of the Law as permanent, instead of looking on it as passing through a process of extinction. The "Old Testament" is clearly used, not, as in the modern sense, for the whole volume of the Law—Prophets and Psalms—but specially for the law which was the basis of the covenant. The other, but less adequate, rendering would be, *the veil remaineth . . . unwithdrawn, for it* (the veil) *is abolished in Christ.* If there was any authority for giving an active force to the middle form of the verb, we might translate with a perfectly satisfactory meaning, *the same veil remaineth . . . not revealing the fact that it is being done away in Christ;* but unfortunately there is no such authority. The English, "which veil is done away," fails to give, in any case, the true force of the Greek.

(15) **Even unto this day, when Moses is read . . .**—The mention of Moses is decisive as to the meaning of the "Old Testament," or *covenant*, in the previous verse. When he, as being read, speaks to the people now, St. Paul reasons, there is still a veil between him and them; but it is, to use modern phrase, subjective and not objective—on their heart, and not over his face. It has been suggested that there may be a reference to the *Tallith*, or four-cornered veil which was worn by the Jews in their synagogues when they prayed or listened to the Law, as a symbol of reverence, like that of the seraphim in Isa. vi. 2, who covered their faces with their wings. It is, however, doubtful whether the use of the *Tallith* goes back so far; and even if its antiquity were proved, it has to be remembered that though it covered the head and ears—the symbol, perhaps, of seclusion—it did not cover the face.

(16) **Nevertheless when it shall turn to the Lord.**—Better, *But when it shall turn.* The allegorising process is still carried on. Moses removed the veil when he went into the tabernacle to commune with the Lord (Ex. xxxiv. 35); so, in the interpretation of the parable, the veil shall be taken away when the heart of Israel shall turn, in the might of a real conversion, to the Lord of Israel. The very word for "turn" is taken from the same context: "Moses called them, and Aaron and all the rulers of the congregation *turned* to him" (Ex. xxxiv. 31).

(17) **Now the Lord is that Spirit.**—Better, *the Lord is the Spirit.* The words seem at first inconsistent with the formulated precision of the Church's creeds, distinguishing the persons of the Godhead from each other. We apply the term "Lord," it is true, as a predicate of the Holy Spirit when we speak, as in the Nicene Creed, of the Holy Ghost as "the Lord, and Giver of life," or say, as in the pseudo-Athanasian, that "the Holy Ghost is Lord;" but using the term "the Lord" as the subject of a sentence, those who have been trained in the theology of those creeds would hardly say, "The Lord" (the term commonly applied to the Father in the Old Testament, and to the Son in the New) "is the Spirit." We have, accordingly, to remember that St. Paul did not contemplate the precise language of these later formularies. He had spoken, in verse 16, of Israel's "turning to the Lord;" he had spoken also of his own work as "the ministration of the Spirit" (verse 8). To turn to the Lord—*i.e.*, to the Lord Jesus—was to turn to Him whose essential being, as one with the Father, was Spirit (John iv. 24), who was in one sense, *the* Spirit, the life-giving energy, as contrasted with the letter that killeth. So we may note that the attribute of "quickening," which is here specially connected with the name of the Spirit (verse 6), is in John v. 21 connected also with the names of the Father and the Son. The thoughts of the Apostle move in a region in which the Lord Jesus, not less than the Holy Ghost, is contemplated as Spirit. This gives, it is believed, the true sequence of St. Paul's thoughts. The whole verse may be considered as parenthetical, explaining that the "turning to the Lord" coincides with the "ministration of the Spirit." Another interpretation, inverting the terms, and taking the sentence as "the Spirit is the Lord," is tenable grammatically, and was probably adopted by the framers of the expanded form of the Nicene Creed at the Council of Constantinople (A.D. 380). It is obvious, however, that the difficulty of tracing the sequence of thought becomes much greater on this method of interpretation.

(18) But we all, with open face beholding as in a glass the glory of the Lord, are changed into the same image from glory to glory, *even* as by the Spirit of the Lord.[1]

[1] Or, *of the Lord the Spirit.*

**Where the Spirit of the Lord is, there is liberty.**—The Apostle returns to the more familiar language. To turn to the Lord, who is Spirit, is to turn to *the* Spirit which is His, which dwelt in Him, and which He gives. And he assumes, almost as an axiom of the spiritual life, that the presence of that Spirit gives freedom, as contrasted with the bondage of the letter—freedom from slavish fear, freedom from the guilt and burden of sin, freedom from the tyranny of the Law. Compare the aspect of the same thought in the two Epistles nearly contemporary with this:—the Spirit bearing witness with our spirit that we are the children of God, those children being partakers of a glorious liberty (Rom. viii. 16—21); the connection between walking in the Spirit and being called to liberty (Gal. v. 13—16). The underlying sequence of thought would seem to be something like this: "Israel, after all, with all its seeming greatness and high prerogatives, was in bondage, because it had the letter, not the Spirit; we who have the Spirit can claim our citizenship in the Jerusalem which is above and which is free" (Gal. iv. 24—31).

(18) **But we all, with open face.**—Better, *And we all, with unveiled face.*—The relation of this sentence to the foregoing is one of sequence and not of contrast, and it is obviously important to maintain in the English, as in the Greek, the continuity of allusive thought involved in the use of the same words as in verse 14. "We," says the Apostle, after the parenthesis of verse 17, "are free, and therefore we have no need to cover our faces, as slaves do before the presence of a great king. There is no veil over our hearts, and therefore none over the eyes with which we exercise our faculty of spiritual vision. We are as Moses was when he stood before the Lord with the veil withdrawn." If the *Tallith* were in use at this time in the synagogues of the Jews, there might also be a reference to the contrast between that ceremonial usage and the practice of Christian assemblies. (Comp. 1 Cor. xi 7; but see Note on verse 15.)

**Beholding as in a glass the glory of the Lord.**—The Greek participle which answers to the first five words belongs to a verb derived from the Greek for "mirror" (identical in meaning, though not in form, with that of 1 Cor. xiii. 12). The word is not a common word, and St. Paul obviously had some special reason for choosing it, instead of the more familiar words, "seeing," "beholding," "gazing stedfastly;" and it is accordingly important to ascertain its meaning. There is no doubt that the active voice signifies to "make a reflection in a mirror." There is as little doubt that the middle voice signifies to look at one's self in a mirror. Thus Socrates advised drunkards and the young to "look at themselves in a mirror," that they might learn the disturbing effects of passion (*Diog. Laert.* ii. 33; iii. 39). This meaning, however, is inapplicable here; and the writings of Philo, who in one passage (*de Migr. Abrah.* p. 403) uses it in this sense of the priests who saw their faces in the polished brass of the lavers of purification, supply an instance of its use with a more appropriate meaning. Paraphrasing the prayer of Moses in Ex. xxxiii. 18, he makes him say: "Let me not *behold* Thy form (*idea*) *mirrored* (using the very word which we find here) in any created thing, but in Thee, the very God" (2 *Allegor.* p. 79). And this is obviously the force of the word here. The sequence of thought is, it is believed, this:—St. Paul was about to contrast the veiled vision of Israel with the unveiled gaze of the disciples of Christ; but he remembers what he had said in 1 Cor. xiii. 12 as to the limitation of our present knowledge, and therefore, instead of using the more common word, which would convey the thought of a fuller knowledge, falls back upon the unusual word, which exactly expresses the same thought as that passage had expressed. "We behold the glory of the Lord, of the Jehovah of the Old Testament, but it is not, as yet, face to face, but as mirrored in the person of Christ." The following words, however, show that the word suggested yet another thought to him. When we see the sun as reflected in a polished mirror of brass or silver, the light illumines us: we are, as it were, transfigured by it and reflect its brightness. That this meaning lies in the word itself cannot, it is true, be proved, and it is, perhaps, hardly compatible with the other meaning which we have assigned to it; but it is perfectly conceivable that the word should suggest the fact, and the fact be looked on as a parable.

**Are changed into the same image.**—Literally, *are being transfigured into the same image.* The verb is the same (*metemorphôthè*) as that used in the account of our Lord's transfiguration in Matt. xvii. 2, Mark ix. 2; and it may be noted that it is used of the transformation (a *metamorphosis* more wondrous than any poet had dreamt of) of the Christian into the likeness of Christ in the nearly contemporary passage (Rom. xii. 2). The thought is identical with that of Rom. viii. 29: "Conformed to the likeness" (or *image*) "of His Son." We see God mirrored in Christ, who is "the image of the invisible God" (Col. i. 15), and as we gaze, with our face unveiled, on that mirror, a change comes over us. The image of the old evil Adam-nature (1 Cor. xv. 49) becomes less distinct, and the image of the new man, after the likeness of Christ, takes its place. We "faintly give back what we adore," and man, in his measure and degree, becomes, as he was meant to be at his creation, like Christ, "the image of the invisible God." Human thought has, we may well believe, never pictured what in simple phrase we describe as growth in grace, the stages of progressive sanctification, in the language of a nobler poetry.

**From glory to glory.**—This mode of expressing completeness is characteristic of St. Paul, as in Rom. i. 17, "from faith to faith"; 2 Cor. ii. 16, "of death to death" The thought conveyed is less that of passing from one stage of glory to another than the idea that this transfiguring process, which begins with glory, will find its consummation also in glory. The glory hereafter will be the crown of the glory here. The beatific vision will be possible only for those who have been thus transfigured. "We know that we shall be like Him, for we shall see Him as He is" (1 John iii. 2).

**Even as by the Spirit of the Lord.**—The Greek presents the words in a form which admits of three possible renderings. (1) That of the English version; (2) that in the margin, "as of the Lord the Spirit"; (3) as of the Lord *of* the Spirit. The exceptional order in which the two words stand, which must be thought as adopted with a purpose, is in favour of (2) and (3) rather than of (1), and the fact that the writer had just dictated the words "the Lord is the Spirit" in favour of (2) rather than (3). The form of speech is

A.D. 60.

Chap. iv. 1—6. The gospel is hidden from those whose minds are blinded.

CHAPTER IV.—(1) Therefore seeing we have this ministry, as we have received mercy, we faint not; (2) but have renounced the hidden things of dishonesty,[1] not walking in craftiness, nor handling the word of God deceitfully; but by manifestation of the truth commending ourselves to every man's conscience in the sight of God. (3) But if our gospel be hid, it is hid to them that are lost: (4) in whom the god of this world hath blinded the minds of them which believe not, lest the light of the glorious gospel of Christ, who is the

1 Gr. *shame.*

encompassed with the same difficulties as before, but the leading thought is clear: "The process of transformation originates with the Lord (*i.e.*, with Christ), but it is with Him, not 'after the flesh' as a mere teacher and prophet (chap. v. 16), not as the mere giver of another code of ethics, another 'letter' or writing, but as a spiritual power and presence, working upon our spirits. In the more technical language of developed theology, it is through the Holy Spirit that the Lord, the Christ, makes His presence manifest to our human spirit." (Comp. Notes on John xiv. 22—26.)

### IV.

(1) **Therefore seeing we have this ministry.**—The ministry referred to is that of which such great things have just been said: the ministry of the new covenant, of the Spirit, of righteousness, of glory (chap. iii. 6, 8, 9). Two thoughts rise up in the Apostle's mind in immediate association with this: (1) His own utter unworthiness of it, which finds expression in "as we have received mercy" (comp. 1 Tim. i. 12); and (2) the manifold trials and difficulties in the midst of which it had to be accomplished. The very fact that he has been called to such a work is, however, a source of strength. He cannot faint or show cowardice in discharging it.

(2) **But have renounced the hidden things of dishonesty.**—Better, *the hidden things of shame.* We fail at first to see the connection of the self-vindication which follows with what has gone before, and have once more to go below the surface. He has defended himself against the charge of "fickleness" (chap. i. 17), but another charge, more disturbing still, had also been brought against him. Men had talked, so he had been told, of his "craftiness" (comp. chap. xii. 16), and to that imputation, perhaps also to another covered by the same general term (see Eph. v. 12, and Notes on chap. vii. 1, 2), he now addresses himself. The English word "dishonesty" is used in its older and wider sense. So in Wiclif we have "honest" members of the body in 1 Cor. xii. 23, and in Shakespeare and old English writers generally, and in popular usage even now, "honesty" in a woman is equivalent to chastity. The context shows, however, that St. Paul speaks chiefly not of sensual vices, nor yet of dishonesty in the modern sense of the word, but of subtlety, underhand practices, and the like. Men seem to have tried to fasten his reputation on the two horns of a dilemma. Either his change of plan indicated a discreditable fickleness, or if not that, something more discreditable still.

**Nor handling the word of God deceitfully.**—The word is nearly equivalent to the "corrupting" or "adulterating" of chap. ii. 17. In "commending ourselves" we trace a return to the topic of chap. iii. 1. Yes, he acknowledged that he did "commend himself," but it was by the manifestation of truth as the only means that he adopted; and he appealed not to men's tastes, or prejudices, or humours, but to that in them which was highest—their conscience, their sense of right and wrong; and in doing this he felt that he was speaking and acting in the presence of the great Judge, who is also the searcher of hearts.

(3) **But if our gospel be hid, it is hid to them that are lost.**—Better, in both cases, as keeping the sequence of thought, *has been veiled*, instead of "is hid," and *among them that are perishing.* (See Note on chap. ii. 15.) He cannot close his eyes to the fact that the glorious words of chap. iii. 18 are only partially realised. There are some to whom even the gospel of Christ appears as shrouded by a veil. And these are not, as some have thought, Judaising teachers only or chiefly, but the whole class of those who are at present *on the way to perish*, not knowing God, counting themselves unworthy of eternal life. The force of the present participle, as not excluding the thought of future change, is again to be carefully noted.

(4) **In whom the god of this world . . .**—The word sounds somewhat startling as a description of the devil, but it has parallels in "the prince of this world" (John xiv. 30), "the prince of the power of the air" (Eph. ii. 2). The world which "lieth in wickedness," perhaps *in the evil one* (1 John v. 19), worships the spirit of hate and falsehood and selfishness, and in so doing it practically deifies the devil. And the work of that god of this world is directly in antagonism to that of God. He seeks to lead men back from light to darkness. "*He blinded*" (the Greek tense indicates an act in past time without necessarily including the idea of its continuance in the present) "the minds of the *unbelievers.*" The noun is probably used, as in 1 Cor. vi. 6; vii. 12—15; x. 27; xiv. 22—24, with a special reference to the outside heathen world. Their spiritual state was, St. Paul seems to say, lower than that of Israel. The veil was over the heart of the one; the very organs of spiritual perception were blinded in the other.

**Lest the light of the glorious gospel.**—Better. *to the end that the radiance* (or, *light-giving power*) *of the gospel of the glory of God . . .* The words describe not merely a purpose, but a result. The word for "light" here, and in verse 6, is not the simple noun commonly used, but a secondary form, derived from the verb "to give light" or "illumine." The English version "glorious," though a partial equivalent for the Greek idiom of the genitive of a characteristic attribute, lacks the vigour and emphasis of the original, which expresses the thought that the gospel is not only glorious itself, but shares in the glory of Christ, and has that for its theme and object. But even that gospel may fail of its purpose. The blind cannot see even the brightness of the noon-day sun. The eye of the soul has to receive sight first. So, in the mission to the Gentiles given to the Apostle on his conversion, his first work was "to open their eyes, to turn them from darkness to light" (Acts xxvi. 18).

**Christ, who is the image of God.**—The Greek word is used in the LXX. of Gen. i. 26 for the image of God, after which man was created. So in 1 Cor. xi. 7 man is spoken of as "the image and glory

image of God, should shine unto them.
(5) For we preach not ourselves, but
Christ Jesus the Lord; and ourselves
your servants for Jesus' sake. (6) For
God, who commanded the light to shine
out of darkness, hath shined in our
hearts, to *give* the light of the know-
ledge of the glory of God in the face of
Jesus Christ. (7) But we have this
treasure in earthen vessels, that the
excellency of the power may be of God,
and not of us. (8) *We are* troubled on
every side, yet not dis-
tressed; *we are* perplexed,
but not in despair;[1] (9) per-
secuted, but not forsaken;
cast down, but not de-
stroyed; (10) always bearing
about in the body the dying of the Lord
Jesus, that the life also of Jesus might
be made manifest in our body. (11) For
we which live are alway delivered unto

Chap. iv. 7—11. Contrast between the greatness of the treasure and the frailty of the earthen vessel.

[1] Or *not altogether without help*, or, *means*.

---

of God." (Comp. Col. i. 15; iii. 10.) In Heb. x. 1 it stands as intermediate between the object and the shadow, far plainer than the latter, yet not identical with the former, however adequately representing it.

**Should shine unto them.**—Literally, *should irradiate*, or, *cast its beams upon them.*

(5) **For we preach not ourselves.**—The words, like those about "commending ourselves," imply a reference to something that had been said. He was charged with being egotistic in his preaching, perhaps with special reference to passages like 1 Cor. ii. 1—4; iii. 1—10; iv. 11—18. He indignantly repudiates that charge. "Christ Jesus" had been all along the subject of his preaching. (Comp. 1 Cor. ii. 2.) So far as he had spoken of himself at all, it had been as a minister and servant for their sake (1 Cor. iii. 22, 23; ix. 19).

(6) **For God, who commanded the light to shine out of darkness.**—Better, *For it is God who commanded . . . that hath shined.* The whole verse is in manifest antithesis to verse 4. The god of this world did his work of blinding; the true God called light out of darkness. Here there is obviously a reference to the history of the creation in Gen. i. 3.

**Hath shined.**—The English tense is allowable, but the Greek is literally *shone*, as referring to a definite fact in the past life of the Apostle and other Christians at the very time of their conversion.

**In the face of Jesus Christ.**—Some MSS. give "Christ Jesus," others "Christ." The clause is added as emphasising the fact that the glory of God is for us manifested only in the face (or, possibly, in the *person*, with a somewhat wider sense; see Note on chap. i. 11) of Christ, as it was seen by the Israelites in the face of Moses. The word for "give light" is the same as that rendered "radiance" in verse 4.

(7) **But we have this treasure in earthen vessels.**—The imagery here begins to change. The treasure is "the knowledge of the glory of God" as possessed by the Apostle. It was the practice of Eastern kings, who stored up their treasures of gold and silver, to fill jars of earthenware with coin or bullion (Herod. iii. 103. Comp. also Jer. xxxii. 14). "So," St. Paul says, in a tone of profound humility, "it is with us. In these frail bodies of ours—'earthen vessels'—we have that priceless treasure." The passage is instructive, as showing that the "vessels of wood and of earth" in 2 Tim. ii. 20 are not necessarily identical with those made for dishonour. The words have probably a side glance at the taunts that had been thrown out as to his bodily infirmities. "Be it so," he says; "we admit all that can be said on that score, and it is that men may see that the excellence of the power which we exercise comes from God, and not from ourselves." The words that follow, contrasting sufferings and infirmities in their manifold variety with the way in which they were borne through God's strengthening grace, show this to be the true underlying sequence of thought.

(8) **We are troubled on every side.**—The Greek presents all the clauses in a participial form, in apposition with the "we" with which verse 7 opens. The careful antithesis in each case requires some modification of the English version in order to be at all adequately expressed. *Hemmed-in in everything, yet not straitened for room; perplexed, yet not baffled*; or, as it has been rendered, less literally, but with great vividness, *bewildered, but not benighted.* The imagery in both clauses belongs to the life of the soldier on active service.

(9) **Persecuted, but not forsaken.**—Better, perhaps, as expressing in both terms of the clause the condition of a soldier on the field of battle, *pursued, yet not abandoned.* The next clause is again distinctly military, or, perhaps, agonistic: *stricken down* (as the soldier by some dart or javelin), *yet not perishing.* In the "faint, yet pursuing," of Judg. viii. 4, we have an antithesis of the same kind in a narrative of actual warfare.

(10) **Always bearing about in the body the dying of the Lord Jesus.**—The word for "dying" (again, probably, a distinctly medical term) is literally "*deadness,*" "*the state of a corpse.*" Comp. Rom. iv. 19 for the word itself, and Rom. iv. 19, Col. iii. 5 ("mortify"), Heb. xi. 12 ("as good as dead") for the cognate verb. The word describes, as by a bold hyperbole, the condition of one whose life was one long conflict with disease: "dying daily" (1 Cor. xv. 31); having in himself "the sentence," or, possibly, *the very symptoms*, "of death" (2 Cor. i. 8, 9). He was, as it were, dragging about with him what it was scarcely an exaggeration to call a "living corpse;" and this he describes as "the dying" (or *death-state*) "of the Lord Jesus." The thought implied in these words is not formally defined. What seems implied is that it brought him nearer to the likeness of the Crucified; he was thus made a sharer in the sufferings of Christ, filling up what was lacking in the measure of those sufferings (Col. i. 24), dying as He died, crucified with Him (Gal. ii. 20). It may be noted that Philo (2 *Alleg.* p. 73) uses almost the same word to express the natural frailty and weakness of man's body—"What, then, is our life but the daily carrying about of a corpse?"

**That the life also of Jesus . . .**—The life of Jesus is the life of the new man, "created in righteousness and true holiness" (Eph. iv. 24). It is not that the Apostle is merely looking forward to the resurrection life, when we shall bear the image of the heavenly; he feels that the purpose of his sufferings now is that the higher life may, even in this present state, be manifested in and through them; and accordingly, as if to guard against the possibility of any other interpretation, he changes the phrase in the next verse, and for "our body" substitutes "our mortal flesh."

(11) **We which live are alway delivered unto**

death for Jesus' sake, that the life also
of Jesus might be made manifest in our
mortal flesh. (12) So then
death worketh in us, but
life in you. (13) We having
the same spirit of faith,
according as it is written,
I believed,[a] and therefore
have I spoken; [a] we also believe, and
therefore speak; (14) knowing that he
which raised up the Lord Jesus shall
raise up us also by Jesus, and shall
present *us* with you. (15) For all things
*are* for your sakes, that the abundant
grace might through the thanksgiving
of many redound to the glory of God.
(16) For which cause we faint not; but
though our outward man perish, yet
the inward *man* is renewed day by day.
(17) For our light affliction, which is but

Chap. iv. 12—17. Sufferings and death work out life for the hearers and eternal glory for the preacher.

a Ps. 116. 10.

---

**death.**—Better, *are always being delivered.* The opening clause emphasises the paradox of the statement: "We live, and yet our life is a series of continual deaths. We are delivered as to a daily execution." The words are often interpreted—but, it is believed, wrongly—of the dangers and sufferings caused by persecution. The whole tenor of the Epistle suggests rather (see Note on preceding verse) the thought of the daily struggle with the pain and weakness of disease. It has been urged that the words "for Jesus' sake" determine the sense of the context as referring to the trials of persecution. The position is, however, scarcely tenable. The words, of course, as such, include the idea of such trials; but a man who laboured ceaselessly, as St. Paul laboured, as in a daily struggle with death, and yet went on working for the gospel of Christ, might well describe himself as bearing what he bore "for Jesus' sake."

**In our mortal flesh.**—The reason for the change in the last two words has been given in the Note on the preceding verse. The very "flesh" which, left to itself, is the source of corruption, moral and physical, is by the "excellence of the power of God" made the vehicle of manifesting the divine life. As has been well said: "God exhibits DEATH in the *living* that He may also exhibit LIFE in the *dying*" (Alford).

(12) **So then death worketh in us, but life in you.**—"Life" is here clearly used in its higher spiritual sense, as in the preceding verse. We trace in the words something of the same pathos as in 1 Cor. iv. 8—13, without the irony which is there perceptible. "You," he seems to say, "reap the fruit of my sufferings. The 'dying' is all my own; you know nothing of that conflict with pain and weakness; but the 'life' which is the result of that experience works in you as well as in me, and finds in you the chief sphere of its operation."

(13) **We having the same spirit of faith . . .**—The "spirit of faith" is not definitely the Holy Spirit, but the human spirit in fellowship with the Divine, and therefore characterised by faith. And then, as if pleading that this faith must find utterance, he falls back on the words that are in his mind, almost as an axiom, from Ps. cxvi. 10: "I believed, and therefore I spoke." It will be noted that the context of the words quoted is eminently in harmony with the feelings to which the Apostle has just given expression: "The sorrows of death compassed me; the pains of hell gat hold of me. I found trouble and heaviness . . . I was brought low . . . Thou hast delivered my soul from death" (Ps. cxvi. 3—8). It is as though that Psalm had been his stay and comfort in the midst of his daily conflict with disease.

(14) **Knowing that he which raised up the Lord Jesus . . .**—From his present experience of the triumph of life over death he passes to the future victory of which that triumph was the earnest. It is clear that he speaks here not of any deliverance from danger or disease, but of the resurrection of which he had spoken so fully in 1 Cor. xv. The better MSS. give *with Jesus*, the Received text having apparently originated in a desire to adapt the words to the fact that Christ had already risen. St. Paul's thoughts, however, dwell so continually on his fellowship with Christ that he thinks of the future resurrection of the body, no less than of the spiritual resurrection which he has already experienced (Eph. ii. 6), as not only wrought *by* Him but associated *with* Him; and in this hope of his he includes the Corinthians to whom he writes. It will then be seen, he trusts, that "life" has indeed been "working" in them. The verb "present," as describing the work of Christ, and, we may add, his own work as a minister of Christ, under this aspect, is a favourite one with St. Paul (chap. xi. 2; Eph. v. 27; Col. i. 22).

(15) **For all things are for your sakes.**—We can scarcely doubt that he thinks in his own mind, and intends to remind them, of the glorious words of 1 Cor. iii. 22, 23.

**That the abundant grace might through the thanksgiving of many . . .**—More accurately, *that grace, having abounded by means of the greater part of you, may cause thanksgiving to overflow to the glory of God.* The passage is nearly parallel to chap. i. 11. He takes for granted that the grace which he has received has been given in answer to the prayers, if not of all the Corinthians, yet at least of the majority (comp. the same distinction drawn in chap. ii. 6), and he is sure that it will, in its turn, cause their thanksgiving to be as copious as their prayers. The passage is, however, obscure in its construction, and two other renderings of the Greek are grammatically possible, which is more than can be said of the English version: (1) "that grace having abounded, may, for the sake of the thanksgiving of the greater part of you, redound . . ."; and (2) "that grace having abounded, may, by means of the greater part of you, cause thanksgiving to redound . . ." What has been given above is, it is believed, the closest to St. Paul's meaning.

(16) **For which cause we faint not.**—He returns, after a long digression, to the assertion with which chap. iv. had opened, but in repeating the words he enters once again on the same line of thought, but under a different succession of imagery. The "outward man," the material framework of the body, is undergoing a gradual process of decay, but the "inward man," the higher spiritual life, is "day by day" passing through successive stages of renewal, gaining fresh energies. This verb also, and its derivative "renewal," are specially characteristic of St. Paul. (Comp. Rom. xii. 2; Col. iii. 10; Tit. iii. 5.) The verb in Eph. iv. 23, though not the same, is equivalent in meaning.

(17) **For our light affliction . . .**—More accurately, *the present lightness of our affliction.* This is at once

for a moment, worketh for us a far more exceeding *and* eternal weight of glory; (18) while we look not at the things which are seen, but at the things which are not seen: for the things which are seen *are* temporal; but the things which are not seen *are* eternal.

CHAPTER V.—(1) For we know that if our earthly house of *this* tabernacle

A.D. 60.

were dissolved, we have a building of God, an house not made with hands, eternal in the heavens. (2) For in this we groan, earnestly desiring to be clothed upon with our house which is from heaven: (3) if so be that being clothed we shall not be found naked. (4) For we that are in *this* tabernacle do groan,

Chap. v. 1—8. The desire of the Apostle to be clothed with the spiritual.

more literally in accord with the Greek, and better sustains the balanced antithesis of the clauses.

**A far more exceeding . . .**—The Greek phrase is adverbial rather than adjectival: *worketh for us exceedingly, exceedingly.* After the Hebrew idiom of expressing intensity by the repetition of the same word, (used of this very word "exceedingly" in Gen. vii. 19; xvii. 2), he seeks to accumulate one phrase upon another (literally, *according to excess unto excess*) to express his sense of the immeasurable glory which he has in view.

(18) **While we look not at the things which are seen.**—The "while we look" is, according to the Greek idiom, the condition of what had been stated in the preceding verse. The "look" is that of one who contemplates this or that as the end or goal for which he strives. The "things that are seen" are, of course, all the incidents and circumstances of the present life; the "things that are not seen" (the very phrase of Heb. xi. 1) are the objects of faith, immortality, eternal life, the crown of righteousness, the beatific vision. These things are subject to no time-limits, and endure through all the ages of God's purposes. The others are but for a brief season, and then are as though they had not been. Striking as the words are, they find an echo in the words of a contemporary seeker after wisdom: "These things (the things which most men seek after)," says Seneca (*Ep.* 59), "are but objects of the imagination, and present a show of being but for a time . . . Let us give our minds to the things which are eternal."

V.

(1) **For we know that if our earthly house of this tabernacle were dissolved.**—Better, *be broken up*, as more in harmony with the image of the tent. The words that follow give the secret of his calmness and courage in the midst of sufferings. He looks beyond them. A new train of imagery begins to rise in his mind: linked, perhaps, to that of the preceding chapter by the idea of the tabernacle; in part, perhaps, suggested by his own occupation as a tentmaker. His daily work was to him as a parable, and as his hands were making the temporary shelter for those who were travellers on earth, he thought of the house "not made with hands," eternal in the heavens. The comparison of the body to the house or dwelling-place of the Spirit was, of course, natural, and common enough, and, it may be noted, was common among the Greek medical writers (as, *e.g.*, in Hippocrates, with whom St. Luke must have been familiar). The modification introduced by the idea of the "tent" emphasises the transitory character of the habitation. "What if the tent be broken up?" He, the true inward man, who dwells in the *tent* will find a more permanent, an eternal, home in heaven: a *house* which comes from God. What follows shows that he is thinking of that spiritual body of which he had said such glorious things in 1 Cor. xv. 42—49.

(2) **For in this we groan.**—The "groaning" here, and in verse 4, may, of course, be a strong way of expressing the burden and the weariness of life, but taken in connection with what we have already seen in the Epistle, as pointing to the pressure of disease, we can scarcely fail to find in it the utterance of a personal or special suffering. (See Notes on chap. i. 8, 9.)

**Earnestly desiring to be clothed upon.**—The words have suggested the question whether St. Paul spoke of the "spiritual body" to be received at the resurrection (1 Cor. xv. 42—49), or of some intermediate stage of being, like that represented in the visions which poets have imagined and schoolmen theorised about, in the visions of the world of the dead in the *Odyssey* (Book xi.), in the *Æneid* (Book vi.), in Dante's *Divina Commedia* throughout. The answer to that question is found in the manifest fact that the intermediate state occupied but a subordinate position in St. Paul's thoughts. He would not speak over-confidently as to times and seasons, but his practical belief was that he, and most of those who were then living, would survive till the coming of the Lord (1 Cor. xv. 52; 1 Thess. iv. 15). He did not speculate accordingly about that state, but was content to rest in the belief that when absent from the body he would in some more immediate sense, be present with the Lord. But the longing of his soul was, like that of St. John (Rev. xxii. 20), that the Lord might come quickly—that he might put on the new and glorious body without the pain and struggle of the "dissolution" of the old. In the words "be clothed upon" (literally, the verb being in the middle voice, *to clothe ourselves, to put on*) we have a slight change of imagery. The transition from the thought of a dwelling to that of a garment is, however, as in Ps. civ. 1—3, sufficiently natural. Each shelters the man. Each is separable from the man himself. Each answers in these respects to the body which invests the spirit.

(3) **If so be that being clothed . . .**—The Greek particles express rather more than the English phrase does, the truth of what follows. "If, as I believe . . .," though not a translation, would be a fair paraphrase. The confident expectation thus expressed is that in the resurrection state the spirit will not be "naked," will have, *i.e.*, its appropriate garment, a body—clothing it with the attributes of distinct individuality. To the Greek, Hades was a world of shadows. Of Hades, as an intermediate state, St. Paul does not here speak, but he is sure that, in the state of glory which seemed to him so near, there will be nothing shadowy and unreal. The conviction is identical with that expressed in 1 Cor. xv. 35—49, against those who, admitting the immortality of the spirit, denied the resurrection of the body.

(4) **Being burdened.**—The whole passage is strikingly parallel to Wisd. ix. 15. "The corruptible body presseth down the soul, and the earthly tabernacle weigheth down the mind that museth upon many

being burdened: not for that we
would be unclothed, but clothed upon,
that mortality might be swallowed up
of life. (5) Now he that hath wrought
us for the selfsame thing *is* God, who
also hath given unto us the earnest of
the Spirit. (6) Therefore *we are* always
confident, knowing that, whilst we are
at home in the body, we are absent
from the Lord: (7) (for we walk by
faith, not by sight:) (8) we are con-
fident, *I say*, and willing rather to be
absent from the body, and to be present
with the Lord. (9) Wherefore we la-
bour,[1] that, whether pre-
sent or absent, we may be
accepted of him. (10) For
we must all appear be-
fore the judgment seat of
Christ; that every one may receive the
things *done* in *his* body, according to
that he hath done, whether *it be* good

Chap. v. 9—11. The future judgment as an element in the work of conversion.

[1] Or, *endeavour.*

things." The *Wisdom of Solomon*, which no writer quotes before Clement of Rome, had probably been but recently written (possibly, as I believe, by Apollos), but St. Paul may well have become acquainted with it.

**Not for that we would be unclothed, but clothed upon.**—Better, *Seeing that we do not seek to put off, but to put on a garment.* The thought is that of one who thinks that the Coming of the Lord is near. He wishes, as he expects, to remain till that Coming (comp. 1 Cor. xv. 51; 1 Thess. iv. 15), to let the incorruptible body supervene on the corruptible, to be changed instead of dying. In this way that which is mortal, subject to death, would be swallowed up of life, as death itself is swallowed up in victory. (1 Cor. xv. 54.)

(5) **He that hath wrought us for the selfsame thing.**—Better, *he that wrought us for this very thing.* The "very thing" is the consummation, by whatever stages it may be reached, in which mortality is swallowed up of life. The whole work of God in the past—redemption, the new birth, the gifts and graces of the Spirit—was looking to this as its result. He had given the "earnest of the Spirit" (see Note on chap. i. 22) as a pledge of the future victory of the higher life over the lower. Every gift of spiritual energy not dependent upon the material organism was an assurance that that organism was an impediment to the free action of the Spirit, which would one day be overcome. Our eyes, to take a striking instance, are limits, as well as instruments, to the spirit's powers of perception.

(6) **Therefore we are always confident.**—The Greek construction is participial: *being therefore always confident*; the sentence not being completed, but begun again with the same verb in verse 8. The two verbs for being "at home" and "absent" are not found elsewhere in the New Testament. The latter conveys the special idea of being absent from a man's own home or country. The knowledge of the fact that follows is given as the ground of the Apostle's confidence. It makes him long for the change; not wishing for death, but content to accept it, as it will bring him nearer to his Lord.

(7) **For we walk by faith, not by sight.**—Better, *and not by what we see* (or, *by appearance*). It seems almost sad to alter the wording of a familiar and favourite text, but it must be admitted that the word translated "sight" never means the faculty of seeing, but always the form and fashion of the thing seen. (Comp. Luke iii. 22; ix. 29; John v. 37.) The fact is taken for granted; and it comes as the proof that as we are, we are absent from the Lord. Now we believe in Him without seeing Him; hereafter we shall see Him face to face. Our life and conduct and our "walk" in this world rest on our belief in the Unseen.

(8) **We are confident, I say.**—The sentence begun in verse 6 and half broken off is resumed. The apparent sense is that he prefers death to life, because it brings him to the presence of his Lord. At first, this seems at variance with what he had said in verse 4, as to his not wishing to put off the garment of the present body. Here, however, the expression is not so strong. "We are *content*," he says, "if death comes before the Coming of the Lord, to accept death; for even though it does not bring with it the glory of the resurrection body, it does make us at home with Christ among the souls who wait for the resurrection." If there still seems to us some shadow of inconsistency, we may look upon it as the all but inevitable outcome of the state which he describes in Phil. i. 21—25, as "in a strait between two," and of the form of life in which he now finds himself. The whole passage presents a striking parallelism, and should be compared with this. This is, it is believed, an adequate explanation. Another may, however, be suggested. We find the Apostle speaking of certain "visions and revelations of the Lord," of which he says he knows not whether they are "in the body or out of the body" (chap. xii. 1). May we not think of him as referring here also to a like experience? "We take pleasure," he says, if we adopt this interpretation, wholly or in part, "even here, in that state which takes us, as it were, out of the body, or seems to do so, because it is in that state that our eyes are open to gaze more clearly on the unseen glories of the eternal world." The fact that both verbs are in the tense which indicates a single act, and not a continuous state, is, as far as it goes, in favour of this explanation.

(9) **Wherefore we labour.**—Better, *we strive earnestly after.* The English "labour" is quite inadequate, the Greek expressing the thought of striving, as after some honour or prize. *Our ambition is that . . . we may be accepted* would be, perhaps, the best equivalent. For "accepted of him" read *acceptable*, or better, *well-pleasing to him*: the Greek word implying the quality on which acceptance depends, rather than the act itself.

(10) **For we must all appear.**—Better, *must all be made manifest.* The word is the same as that in 1 Cor. iv. 5 ("shall *make manifest* the counsels of the heart"), and is obviously used with reference to it. It may be noted that it is specially characteristic of this Epistle, in which it occurs nine times. The English version, which can only be ascribed to the unintelligent desire of the translators to vary for the sake of variation, besides being weak in itself, hinders the reader from seeing the reference to 1 Cor. iv. 5, or even the connection with the "made manifest" in the next verse.

**Before the judgment seat of Christ.**—The Greek word shows the influence of Roman associations. In the Gospels the imagery of the last judgment is that of a king sitting on his *throne* (Matt. xxv. 31), and the word is the ever-recurring note of the Apocalypse, in which it occurs forty-nine times. Here the

or bad. (11) Knowing therefore the terror of the Lord, we persuade men; but we are made manifest unto God; and I trust also are made manifest in your consciences. (12) For we commend not ourselves again unto you, but give you occasion to glory on our behalf, that ye may have somewhat to *answer* them which glory in appearance,[1] and not in heart. (13) For whether we

Chap. v. 12—15. St. Paul's defence against the reproach of commending himself and being insane.

1 Gr. *in the face.*

judgment-seat, or *bema*, is the tribunal of the Roman magistrate, raised high above the level of the *basilica*, or hall, at the end of which it stood. (Comp. Matt. xxvii. 19; Acts xii. 21; xviii. 12.) The word was transferred, when basilicas were turned into churches, to the throne of the bishop, and in classical Greek had been used, not for the judge's seat, but for the orator's pulpit.

**That every one may receive the things done in his body.**—It would have seemed almost impossible, but for the perverse ingenuity of the system-builders of theology, to evade the force of this unqualified assertion of the working of the universal law of retribution. No formula of justification by faith, or imputed righteousness, or pardon sealed in the blood of Christ, or priestly absolution, is permitted by St. Paul to mingle with his expectations of that great day, as revealing the secrets of men's hearts, awarding to each man according to his works. "Whatsoever a man soweth, that shall he also reap" (Gal. vi. 7) was to him an eternal, unchanging law. The revelation of all that had been secret, for good or evil; the perfectly equitable measurement of each element of good or evil; the apportionment to each of that which, according to this measurement, each one deserves for the good and evil which he has done: that is the sum and substance of St. Paul's eschatology here and in 1 Cor. iv. 5. At times his language seems to point to a yet fuller manifestation of the divine mercy as following on that of the divine righteousness, as in Rom. v. 17, 18; xi. 32. At times, again, he speaks as if sins were washed away by baptism (1 Cor. vi. 11), or forgiven freely through faith in the atoning blood (Rom. iii. 25; Eph. ii. 13); as though the judgment of the great day was anticipated for all who are in Christ by the absence of an accuser able to sustain his charge (Rom. viii. 3), by the certainty of a sentence of acquittal (Rom. viii. 1). If we ask how we can reconcile these seeming inconsistencies, the answer is, that we are not wise in attempting to reconcile them by any logical formula or ingenious system. Here, as in other truths of the spiritual life—God's foreknowledge and man's free-will, God's election and man's power to frustrate it, God's absolute goodness and the permission of pain and evil—the highest truth is presented to us in phases that seem to issue in contradictory conclusions, and we must be content to accept that result as following from the necessary limitations of human knowledge.

(11) **Knowing therefore the terror of the Lord.**—Better, *the fear of the Lord.* The English word "terror" is unduly strong, and hinders the reader from seeing that what St. Paul speaks of is identical with "the fear of the Lord"—the temper not of slavish dread, but reverential awe, which had been described in the Old Testament as "the beginning of wisdom" (Job xxviii. 28; Ps. cxi. 10). Tyndale's and Cranmer's versions give, "how the Lord is to be feared;" the Rhemish, "fear." "Terror," characteristically enough, makes its first appearance in the Geneva version.

**We persuade men; but we are made manifest unto God.**—The antithesis is singularly indicative of the rapid turn of thought in the Apostle's mind. "*We go on our way of winning men* to Christ." (Comp. the use of the same Greek word in Acts xii. 20, "having made Blastus . . . their friend.") It is singular to note that, in an Epistle probably nearly contemporary with this, St. Paul uses the phrase almost in a bad sense: "Do we now persuade men, or God?" *i.e.*, "Are we seeking to please our friends or God?" (Gal. i. 10.) And here, apparently, the imperfection of the phrase and its liability to misconstruction occurs to him, and he therefore immediately adds, "Yes, we do our work of persuading men" (the case of Felix, in Acts xxiv. 25, may be noted as showing the prominence of "the judgment to come" in St. Paul's method), "but it is all along with the thought that our own lives also have been laid open in their inmost recesses to the sight of God." The word "made manifest" is clearly used in reference to the same word (in the Greek) as is translated "appear" in verse 10.

**And I trust also are made manifest in your consciences.**—The words are an echo of what had already been said in chap. iv. 2. He trusts that in their inmost consciences, in the effect of his preaching there, in the new standard of right and wrong which they now acknowledge—perhaps, also, in the estimate which their illumined judgment passes on his own conduct—he has been made manifest as indeed he is, as he is sure that he will be before the judgment-seat of Christ.

(12) **For we commend not ourselves again unto you.**—The better MSS. omit "For," which may have been inserted for the sake of an apparent sequence of thought. In reality, however, what follows is more intelligible without it. He has scarcely uttered the words that precede this sentence when the poison of the barbed arrow of the sneer to which he had referred in chap. iii. 1 again stings him. He hears his enemies saying, "So he is commending himself again;" and these words are the answer to that taunt. "No," he says, "it is not so, but in appealing to the witness of the work done in your consciences we give you an 'occasion' (or *starting-point*) of a boast which we take for granted that you, the great body of the Church of Corinth, will be ready to make for us."

**That ye may have somewhat to answer.**—The opponents, of whom we are to hear more hereafter (see Notes on chaps. x. 7—18; xi. 12—33), rise up once more in his thoughts. "That such as these should be boasting of *their* work and *their* success!" What did they glory in? *In appearance.* The words may apply to anything external—claims of authority, training, knowledge, and the like. The use of the word, however, in chap. x. 1 seems to imply a more definite meaning. Men contrasted what we should call the dignified "presence" of his rivals with his personal defects, the weakness of his body, the lowness of his stature. "Take your stand," he seems to say, "against that boast, on the work done by us in your consciences."

(13) **For whether we be beside ourselves.**—The recollection of one sneer leads on to another. This also had been said of him, and the intense sensitiveness of his nature made him wince under it. Some there were at Corinth who spoke of his visions and

be beside ourselves, *it is* to God: or whether we be sober, *it is* for your cause. (14) For the love of Christ constraineth us; because we thus judge, that if one died for all, then were all dead: (15) and *that* he died for all, that they which live should not henceforth live unto themselves, but unto him which died for them, and rose again. (16) Wherefore henceforth know we no man after the flesh: yea, though we have known Christ after the flesh, yet

Chap. v. 16—21 Old estimates of man, and even of Christ, swallowed up in the greatness of the ministry of reconciliation.

---

revelations, his speaking with tongues as in ecstasy, his prophecies of future judgment, as so many signs of madness. "He was beside himself." (Comp. Agrippa's words in Acts xxvi. 24, and Note there.) Others, or, perhaps, the same persons, pointed to his tact, becoming all things to all men, perhaps even insinuated that he was making money by his work (chap. ix. 12; xii. 10): "he was shrewd enough when it served his turn." He answers accordingly both the taunts. What people called his "madness"—the ecstasy of adoration, the speaking with tongues (1 Cor. xiv. 18—23)—that lay between himself and God, and a stranger might not intermeddle with it. What people called his "sober-mindedness"—his shrewd common sense, his sagacity—that he practised not for himself, but for his disciples, to win them to Christ, remove difficulties, strengthen them in the faith.

(14) **For the love of Christ constraineth us.**—The Greek, like the English, admits of two interpretations—Christ's love for us, or our love for Christ. St. Paul's uniform use of this and like phrases, however, elsewhere (Rom. v. 5; viii. 35; 1 Cor. xvi. 24; 2 Cor. xiii. 14), is decisive in favour of the former. It was the Apostle's sense of the love that Christ had shown to him and to all men that was acting as a constraining power, directing every act of every spiritual state to the good of others, restraining him from every self-seeking purpose.

**Because we thus judge, that if one died for all.**—Better, as expressing the force of the Greek tense, *Because we formed this judgment.* The form of expression implies that the conviction dated from a given time, *i.e.*, probably, from the hour when, in the new birth of his conversion, he first learnt to know the universality of the love of Christ manifested in His death. Many MSS. omit the "if," but without any real change of meaning. It is obvious that St. Paul assumes the fact, even if it be stated hypothetically. The thought is the same as in the nearly contemporary passage of Rom. v. 15—19, and takes its place among St. Paul's most unqualified assertions of the universality of the atonement effected by Christ's death. The Greek preposition does not in itself imply more than the fact that the death was *on behalf of all;* but this runs up—as we see by comparing Matt. xx. 28, Mark x. 45, with Mark xiv. 24, John xv. 13—into the thought that the death was, in some very real sense, vicarious: *in the place of* the death of all men. The sequence of thought involves that meaning here.

**Then were all dead.**—These strange, mysterious words have received very different interpretations. They cannot be rightly understood without bearing in view what we may call the *mystic* aspect of one phase of St. Paul's teaching. We may, perhaps, clear the way by setting aside untenable expositions. (1) They cannot mean, however true the fact may be in itself, that the death of Christ for all showed that all were previously under a sentence of condemnation and of death, for the verb is in the tense which indicates the momentary act of dying, not the state of death. (2) They cannot mean, for the same reason, that all were, before that sacrifice, "*dead* in trespasses and sins." (3) They can hardly mean that all men, in and through that death, paid vicariously the penalty of death for their past sins, for the context implies that stress is laid not on the satisfaction of the claims of justice, but on personal union with Christ. The real solution of the problem is found in the line of thought of Rom. v. 17—19, 1 Cor. xi. 3, xv. 22, as to the relation of Christ to every member of the human family, in the teaching of Rom. vi. 10, as to the meaning of His death—("He died unto sin once"). "Christ died for all"—this is the Apostle's thought—"as the head and representative of the race." But if so, the race, in its collective unity, died, as He died, to sin, and should live, as He lives, to God. Each member of the race is then only in a true and normal state when he ceases to live for himself and actually lives for Christ. That is the mystic ideal which St. Paul placed before himself and others, and every advance in holiness is, in its measure, an approximation to it.

(15) **Should not henceforth live unto themselves.**—St. Paul was not writing a theological treatise, and the statement was accordingly not meant to be an exhaustive presentment of all the purposes of God in the death of Christ. It was sufficient to give prominence to the thought that one purpose was that men should share at once His death and His life; should live not in selfishness, but in love; not to themselves, but to Him, as He lived to God. (Comp. Rom. vi. 9—11; Eph. ii. 5—7.) Now we see the full force of "the love of Christ constraineth us," and "we love Him because He first loved us." If He died for us, can we, without shame, frustrate the purpose of His death by not living to Him?

(16) **Wherefore henceforth know we no man after the flesh.**—The logical dependence of this sentence on the foregoing lies in the suppressed premiss, that in living not to ourselves, but to Christ, we gain new standards of judgment, new ways of looking at things. To know a man "after the flesh" is to know him by the outward accidents and circumstances of his life: his wealth, rank, culture, knowledge. St. Paul had ceased to judge of men by those standards. With him the one question was whether the man was, by his own act and choice, claiming the place which the death of Christ had secured for him, and living in Him as a new creature. That is the point of view from which he now "knows," or looks on, every man.

**Yea, though we have known Christ after the flesh.**—What, we ask, gave occasion to this strange parenthesis? What did it mean? To what stage of the Apostle's life does it refer? (1) The answer to the first question is probably to be found in once more reading between the lines. There was, we know, a party at Corinth claiming a special relation to Christ (1 Cor. i. 12). They probably did so as having been personal disciples. If they were like those who elsewhere claimed to speak in the name of James (Acts xv. 24; Gal. ii. 12), they were likely to urge his claims as the brother of the Lord. To St. Paul such a way of judging would be to know Christ after the flesh—to

now henceforth know we *him* no more.
(17) Therefore if any man *be* in Christ,
*he is*[1] a new creature: old things are
passed away;[a] behold, all things are
become new. (18) And all things *are*
of God, who hath reconciled us to
himself by Jesus Christ, and hath given
to us the ministry of reconciliation;
(19) to wit, that God was in Christ, re-
conciling the world unto himself, not
imputing their trespasses unto them;
and hath committed unto us[2] the word
of reconciliation. (20) Now then we are
ambassadors for Christ, as though God

1 Or, let him be.

a Isa. 43. 19; Rev. 21. 5.

2 Gr. *put in us.*

---

judge of Him, as of others, by the lower standard of the world. (2) The next question is more difficult. The hypothetical form of the proposition practically implies an admission of its truth. It is hardly conceivable that he refers to the time before his conversion, and means that he too had once seen and known Jesus of Nazareth, judging of Him "after the flesh," by an earthly standard, and therefore had thought that He ought to do many things against him; or that, after the revelation of Christ in him, at the time of his conversion, he had, for a time, known Him after a manner which he now saw to be at least imperfect. The true solution of the problem is probably to be found in the fact that he had once thought, even before he appeared as the persecutor of the Church, of the Christ that was to come as others thought, that his Messianic expectations had been those of an earthly kingdom restored to Israel. Jesus of Nazareth did not fulfil those expectations, and therefore he had opposed His claim to be the Messiah. Now, he says, he had come to take a different view of the work and office of the Christ. (3) It follows, if this interpretation is correct, that he speaks of the period that preceded his conversion, not of an imperfect state of knowledge after it, out of which he had risen by progressive stages of illumination and clearer vision of the truth. Now and from henceforth, he seems to say, we think of Christ not as the King of Israel, but as the Saviour of mankind.

(17) **Therefore if any man be in Christ.**—To be in Christ, in St. Paul's language, is for a man to be united with him by faith and by baptism (Rom. vi. 3, 4), to claim personally what had been secured to him as a member of the race for whom Christ died. In such a case the man is born again (Tit. iii. 5)—there is a new creation; the man, as the result of that work, is a new creature. The old things of his life, Jewish expectations of a Jewish kingdom, chiliastic dreams, heathen philosophies, lower aims, earthly standards—these things, in idea at least, passed away from him at the time when he was united with Christ. We may trace an echo of words of Isaiah's that may have floated in the Apostle's memory: "Remember ye not the former things, neither consider *the things of old.* Behold I make *new* things" (Isa. xliii. 18, 19). The words in italics are in the LXX. the same as those which St. Paul uses here.

(18) **And all things are of God.**—The presence of the article in the Greek indicates that he is speaking, not of the universe at large, but of the new things belonging to the new creation of which he had spoken in the previous verse. The line of thought on which he has now entered raises him for the time above all that is personal and temporary, and leads him to one of his fullest and noblest utterances as to God's redeeming work.

**Who hath reconciled us to himself . . . . and hath given to us the ministry of reconciliation.**—It is worthy of note that this is the first occurrence, in order of time, in St. Paul's Epistles, of this word "reconcile" as describing God's work in Christ, and that so applied it occurs only in this Epistle and in Rom. v. 10, written shortly afterwards. The idea involved is that man had been at enmity and was now atoned (*at-oned*) and brought into concord with God. It will be noted that the work is described as originating with the Father and accomplished by the mediation of the Son. It is obvious that the personal pronoun is used with a different extent in the two clauses: the first embracing, as the context shows, the whole race of mankind; the last limited to those who, like the Apostles, were preachers of the Word. More accurately, the verbs should run: *who reconciled . . . . and gave.* The word translated "reconciliation" is, it should be noted, the same as that rendered "atonement" in Rom. v. 11.

(19) **To wit, that God was in Christ, reconciling the world.**—Better, perhaps, *How that it was God who was reconciling in Christ a world unto Himself.* Both "God" and "world" are, in the Greek, without the article. The English rendering is tenable grammatically, but the position of the words in the original suggests the construction given above. He seems to emphasise the greatness of the redeeming work by pointing at once to its author and its extent. The structure is the same as the "was preaching" of Luke iv. 44. All the English versions, however, from Wiclif downwards, adopt the same construction. Tyndale, Cranmer, and the Geneva version translate, *making agreement between the world and Himself,* instead of "reconciling to Himself." The "world" is, of course, the world of men, the "all" of verse 15.

**Not imputing their trespasses unto them . . .**—The two participial clauses that follow describe the result of the reconciling work. The first is that God no longer charges their transgressions against men: the pronouns being used in the third person plural, as being more individualising than the "world," and more appropriate than would have been the first person, which he had used in verse 18, and which he wanted, in its narrower extension, for the clause which was to follow. The word for "imputing," or *reckoning,* is specially prominent in the Epistles of this period, occurring, though in very varied shades of meaning, eight times in this Epistle and nineteen times in that to the Romans. The difficulty of maintaining a logical coherence of this truth with that of a judgment according to works does not present itself to the Apostle's mind, and need not trouble us. (See Note on verse 10.)

**And hath committed unto us the word of reconciliation.**—Literally, to maintain the participial construction, *placing with* (or *in*) *us the word of reconciliation.* Tyndale gives "atonement" here as in Rom. v. 11.

(20) **Now then we are ambassadors for Christ.**—The preposition "for" implies the same representative character as in verses 14, 15. The preachers of the Word were acting *on behalf of* Christ; they were acting also *in His stead.* The thought or word meets us again in Eph. vi. 20: "I am an ambassador in bonds." The

did beseech *you* by us: we pray *you* in Christ's stead, be ye reconciled to God. (21) For he hath made him *to be* sin for us, who knew no sin; that we might be made the righteousness of God in him.

A.D. 60.

CHAPTER VI.—(1) We then, *as* workers together *with him*, beseech *you* also that ye receive not the grace of God in vain. (2) (For

Chap. vi. 1, 2. The prayer of the Apostle that men would use the accepted time.

earlier versions (Tyndale, Geneva, Cranmer) give "messengers," the Rhemish "legates." "Ambassadors," which may be noted as singularly felicitous, first appears in the version of 1611. The word, derived from the mediæval Latin *ambasciator*, and first becoming popular in the Romance languages, is found in Shakespeare, and appears to have come into prominence through the intercourse with France and Spain in the reign of Elizabeth.

**We pray you in Christ's stead, be ye reconciled to God.**—It will be seen, in this conclusion of the language of St. Paul as to the atonement, how entirely, on the one hand, he recognises the representative and vicarious character of the redeeming work of Christ; how entirely, on the other, he stands aloof from the speculative theories on that work which have sometimes been built upon his teaching. He does not present, as the system-builders of theology have too often done, the picture of the wrath of the Father averted by the compassion of the Son, or satisfied by the infliction upon Him of a penalty which is a quantitative equivalent for that due to the sins of mankind. The whole work, from his point of view, originates in the love of the Father, sending His Son to manifest that love in its highest and noblest form. He does not need to be reconciled to man. He sends His Son, and His Son sends His ministers to entreat them to be reconciled to Him, to accept the pardon which is freely offered. In the background there lies the thought that the death of Christ was in some way, as the highest act of Divine love, connected with the work of reconciliation; but the mode in which it was effective, is, as Butler says (*Analogy*, ii. 5), "mysterious, and left, in part at least, unrevealed," and it is not wise to "endeavour to explain the efficacy of what Christ has done and suffered for us beyond what the Scripture has authorised."

(21) **For he hath made him to be sin for us, who knew no sin.**—The "for" is omitted in many of the best MSS., but there is clearly a sequence of thought such as it expresses. The Greek order of the words is more emphatic: *Him that knew no sin He made sin for us.* The words are, in the first instance, an assertion of the absolute sinlessness of Christ. All other men had an experience of its power, gained by yielding to it. He alone gained this experience by resisting it, and yet suffering its effects. None could "convict Him of sin" (John viii. 46). The "Prince of this world had nothing in Him" (John xiv. 30). (Comp. Heb. vii. 26; 1 Pet. ii. 22.) And then there comes what we may call the paradox of redemption. He, God, made the sinless One to be "sin." The word cannot mean, as has been said sometimes, a "sin offering." That meaning is foreign to the New Testament, and it is questionable whether it is found in the Old, Lev. v. 9 being the nearest approach to it. The train of thought is that God dealt with Christ, not as though He were a sinner, like other men, but as though He were sin itself, absolutely identified with it. So, in Gal. iii. 13, he speaks of Christ as made "a curse for us," and in Rom. viii. 3 as "being made in the likeness of sinful flesh." We have here, it is obvious, the germ of a mysterious thought, out of which forensic theories of the atonement, of various types, might be and have been developed. It is characteristic of St. Paul that he does not so develop it. Christ identified with man's sin: mankind identified with Christ's righteousness—that is the truth, simple and yet unfathomable, in which he is content to rest.

**That we might be made the righteousness of God in him.**—Better, *that we might become.* The "righteousness of God," as in Rom. iii. 21, 22, expresses not simply the righteousness which He gives, nor that which He requires, though neither of these meanings is excluded, but rather that which belongs to Him as His essential attribute. The thought of St. Paul is that, by our identification with Christ—first ideally and objectively, as far as God's action is concerned, and then actually and subjectively, by that act of will which he calls faith—we are made sharers in the divine righteousness. So, under like conditions, St. Peter speaks of believers as "made partakers of the divine nature" (2 Pet. i. 4). In actual experience, of course, this participation is manifested in infinitely varying degrees. St. Paul contemplates it as a single objective fact. The importance of the passage lies in its presenting the truth that the purpose of God in the death of Christ was not only or chiefly that men might escape punishment, but that they might become righteous.

## VI.

(1) **We then, as workers together with him, beseech you . . .**—The thought of the marvel of the atoning love fills the heart of St. Paul with an almost passionate desire to see its purpose realised in those whom he has taught; and so, "as a fellow-worker with Him"—the pronoun may be referred grammatically either to God or Christ, but the general tone of the context, and St. Paul's language elsewhere (1 Cor. xii. 6; Eph. i. 11, 20; Phil. ii. 13), are decisive in favour of the former—he renews his entreaty. The language in which he does so is every way significant. Those to whom he wrote had believed and been baptised, and so they had "received the grace;" but the freedom of the will to choose good or evil remained, and if they chose evil they would frustrate the end which the grace was intended to work out. (Comp. the language of 1 Cor. ix. 27; xv. 10.)

(2) **I have heard thee in a time accepted . . .**—Better, perhaps, *acceptable.* The meaning of the pronoun "He," as referring to God, is determined by the preceding verse. The tense of the Greek is better expressed by, *I heard thee . . . I succoured thee.* As with other citations, it is a natural inference that St. Paul had the context, as well as the words actually cited, in his mind, and it is interesting, accordingly, to remember that context. The words (Isa. xlix. 8) are among those addressed at first to the servant of Jehovah, as "the light of the Gentiles;" then, apparently, in His name, as the Holy One, and in that of Jehovah, to Israel as a nation. In God's dealings with His people through Christ the Apostle saw the true fulfilment of Isaiah's words. Never, in spite of all outward calamities, had there been a time so acceptable, a day so full of deliverance.

**Behold, now is the accepted time . . .**—The word for "accepted" is much stronger than in the

he saith, I have heard thee in a time accepted,[a] and in the day of salvation have I succoured thee: behold, now *is* the accepted time; behold, now *is* the day of salvation.) (3) Giving no offence in any thing, that the ministry be not blamed: (4) but in all *things* approving [1] ourselves as the ministers of God, in much patience, in afflictions, in necessities, in distresses, (5) in stripes, in imprisonments, in tumults,[2] in labours, in watchings, in fastings; (6) by pureness, by knowledge, by longsuffering, by kindness, by the Holy Ghost, by love unfeigned, (7) by the word of truth, by the power of God, by

Chap. vi. 3—10. The contrasts in the life of the minister of Christ.

a Isa. 49. 8.

1 Gr. *commending.*

2 Or, *in tossings to and fro.*

---

previous clause. *Entirely acceptable* is, perhaps, its best equivalent. The solemnity of the words was, it may be, intensified in St. Paul's thoughts by what seemed to him the nearness of the impending judgment. Opportunities, as we should say, were offered which might never again recur. But the prolonged experience of the longsuffering of God has given to the words a yet more profound significance. There is, so to speak, a "now" running through the ages. For each church and nation, for each individual soul, there is a golden present which may never again recur, and in which lie boundless possibilities for the future. The words of the Apostle are, as it were, the transfigured expression of the generalisation of a wide experience which tells us that—

> "There is a tide in the affairs of men
> Which, taken at the flood, leads on to fortune:
> Omitted, all the voyage of their life
> Is bound in shallows and in miseries."
> —Shakespeare, *Julius Cæsar*, iv. 3.

(3) **Giving no offence . . .**—The participial construction is resumed from verse 1, verse 2 being treated as parenthetical. A subtle distinction in the two forms of the Greek negative suggests the thought that he is here giving, as it were, his own estimate of his aim and endeavour in his work. He avoids all occasion of offence, not because he fears censure for himself, but that "the ministry be not blamed."

(4) **But in all things approving ourselves as the ministers of God.**—Better, as keeping up the connection with chaps. iii. 1, and v. 12, *as ministers of God commending ourselves.* He harps, as it were, upon that phrase. Yes, he does commend himself; but how? He looks back on his life of labour and sufferings and challenges comparison. Can others, with their letters of commendation, point to anything like this? The word "ministers" in the Greek is in the nominative case, while the English at least suggests that it is in the objective after the verb. What he means is that he, as the minister of God should do, commends himself by acts and not by words. It is obvious that what follows was likely to expose him to a repetition of the cynical sneer, but of this his generous indignation makes him nobly regardless.

**In much patience . . .**—Better, as elsewhere, *endurance.* The word has a much stronger meaning than our English "patience." (See Notes on Luke viii. 15; xxi. 19.) The general term is naturally followed by a specification of details. It is not, perhaps, easy to specify what he refers to under each head. Possibly he used such words, as we habitually use them, without a formal classification. The root-idea of the first word of the triad is that of being pressed upon; of the second, that of a constraint that leaves no choice of action; of the third, that of being so hemmed in that there is no room to move.

(5) **In stripes . . .**—The list becomes more specific. "Stripes' we have seen at Philippi (Acts xvi. 23), and chap. xi. 23, 24 show that there were other instances. Of "imprisonments," that at Philippi is, so far, the only recorded instance (Acts xvi. 24); but there may well have been others, as in chap. xi. 23. "Tumults" (the same word as in Luke xxi. 9) at Antioch in Pisidia (Acts xiii. 50), Lystra (Acts xiv. 5—19), Thessalonica (Acts xvii. 5), Corinth itself (Acts xviii. 12), and Ephesus (Acts xix. 23—41). "Labours" describe the usual tenor of his life, the daily work of his calling as a tent-maker, as well as that connected with his ministry. "Watchings" and "fastings" are, probably, both of them (comp. chap. xi. 27) to be referred to voluntary acts—nights of vigil and self-imposed abstinence—rather than to privations incidental to his work.

(6) **By pureness . . .**—The word may possibly mean "purity of motive" in its widest sense, but the use of the corresponding adjective in 2 Cor. xi. 2; 1 Tim. v. 22; Titus ii. 3; 1 Pet. iii. 2, and, indeed, its general sense elsewhere, is decisive in favour of "purity from sensual sin"—personal chastity. In the general state of morals throughout the empire, and especially in writing to such a city as Corinth, it was natural to dwell on this aspect of the Christian character. (Comp. 1 Cor. vii. 7.) The "knowledge" is obviously not that of earthly things, but of the mysteries of God (Eph. iii. 4). In "kindness" we trace the consciousness of an effort to reproduce the graciousness which he looked on as a characteristic attribute of God and Christ (Eph. ii. 7; Tit. iii. 4). In the "Holy Ghost" we may see a reference both to spiritual gifts, such as those of tongues and prophecy (1 Cor. xiv. 18, 19), and to the impulses and promptings in which he traced the general guidance of the Spirit (Acts xvi. 6, 7). "Love unfeigned" (*i.e.*, without hypocrisy) presents the same combination as in Rom. xii. 9 ("without dissimulation" in the English version).

(7) **By the word of truth.**—Both words are, in the Greek, without the article, and this throws a slight shade of doubt upon their meaning. With the article, the same combination occurs in Eph. i. 13; 2 Tim. ii. 15; and there can be no doubt that there the sense is objective—"the word which conveys the truth of God to men." Here a subjective meaning, "a word of truthfulness," or "truthful word," as distinct from insincerity of speech, is grammatically possible; but in Jas. i. 18, where precisely the same combination occurs, we have ample warrant for retaining the objective meaning even here.

**By the power of God.**—Here, again, the words hover between a general and a specific sense. As distinguished from the "Holy Ghost" in verse 6, and looking to the general use of the Greek word for "power," it seems natural to refer the word here chiefly, though, perhaps, not exclusively, to the supernatural power given by God for working miracles. (Comp. especially chap. xii. 12; 1 Cor. ii. 5; xii. 10, 28, 29.)

**By the armour of righteousness on the right hand and on the left.**—The thought is found in a more expanded form in Eph. vi. 11—17; 1 Thess. v. 8. Its recurrence in chap. x. 4 shows how familiar it was to

the armour of righteousness on the right hand and on the left, (8) by honour and dishonour, by evil report and good report: as deceivers, and *yet* true; (9) as unknown, and *yet* well known; as dying, and, behold, we live; as chastened, and not killed; (10) as sorrowful, yet alway rejoicing; as poor, yet making many rich; as having nothing, and *yet* possessing all things. (11) O *ye* Corinthians, our mouth is open unto you, our heart is enlarged. (12) Ye are

---

St. Paul's mind. Here it is presented in a more condensed form, but its meaning is sufficiently obvious. The weapon of the right hand is "the sword of the Spirit," aggressive in the conflict with evil (Eph. vi. 17). The armour for the left hand is defensive, the "shield of faith," which is our defence against the fiery darts of the wicked (Eph. vi. 16). This gives, it is believed, a better meaning than the interpretation which translates the Greek word by "instruments," as in Rom. vi. 13, and taking these as meaning opportunities for action, sees in the two adjectives the meaning which sometimes attaches to them in Greek authors, and was derived from the usages of Greek divination, as "favourable" and "unfavourable." It has been urged that the absence of the Greek article before "weapons on the left" is against the distinction which has been drawn above, and therefore that the words refer to the breast-plate which encompasses both sides of the body; but this, though a tenable view grammatically, is somewhat over-subtle. A man dictating a letter under the influence of strong emotion is not always mindful of minute grammatical distinctions, such as that on which this last interpretation rests.

(8) **By honour and dishonour.**—The enumeration of the elements in and by which his ministry is carried on begins to take a more personal character. We trace once more in the words that follow the sensitiveness of a recent experience. He has to do his work, at one time, as through a *glory* which he has not sought; at another time under an ignominy which he has not deserved. Men at one time speak well of him, and at another he falls upon evil and bitter tongues. The very word "deceiver," most galling of all words to one who is conscious of his truthfulness, is recklessly flung at him. Through all these he goes on his work, believing that in them also he may find a way of commending himself as a minister of God.

(9) **As unknown, and yet well known.**—In the absence of fuller information as to what disparaging language had been used in reference to St. Paul, it is not easy to appreciate the precise force of the words thus used. Possibly, he had been spoken of as a man of "unknown" or obscure antecedents, and his answer to that taunt is, as in chap. i. 13, 14, that where he was known at all he was *recognised* as being what indeed he was. He could show even to them, to some of them at least, whether it were not so. In "dying, and, behold, we live" we may trace a reference partly to the "sentence of death" which had, as it were, been passed upon him (chap. i. 9), partly to the malignant exultation with which that fact had been received, or was likely, he thought, to be received by those who hated him. We can picture them as saying, "His course will soon be over; he will not trouble us long;" and his answer to that imagined sneer is that he is still in full energy. What has befallen him has been a chastening and a discipline, but he is not yet, as they fondly thought, "killed" and delivered over unto death.

(10) **As sorrowful, yet alway rejoicing.**—Are we still in the region of the taunts and sneers of which we have found such distinct traces in the previous verses? Did men say of him, as others had said of the saints of God before him, that he was "smitten of God, and afflicted"? Was it with him, as with David, that when he wept, that "was turned to his reproof"? that when he "made sackcloth his garment" he "became a proverb unto them"? (Ps. lxix. 10, 11.) This seems, on the whole, the most probable explanation of the words. His Jewish rivals, or the jesters of Corinth, taunted him with his want of cheerfulness, "He was always in trouble." This, at least, enables us to understand the bitterness of spirit in which St. Paul spoke, and to enter into the full force of his answer: "Yea, but with our sorrow there is also the ever-flowing well-spring of joy—a joy not of the world, but of the Holy Ghost."

**As poor, yet making many rich.**—Better, *as a beggar.* It is not hard to imagine that the outward circumstances of St. Paul's life, his daily toil as a tent-maker, his accepting gifts from the Church of Philippi (chap. xi. 8, 9; Phil. iv. 15), would furnish occasion for some taunting jest. We seem to hear men speaking of him as a "beggar," a "mendicant." "Yes," he answers, "but I am able to make many rich." It is a possible, though perhaps not altogether an adequate, explanation of the words to see in them a reference to the fact that out of his "poverty" he was able to supply the necessities of others (Acts xx. 35). We must, at all events, think of his words as including something more than this, and reminding the Corinthians that he had made many rich with the unsearchable riches of Christ.

**As having nothing, and yet possessing all things.**—The series of paradoxes culminates in this. In language which has found echoes in the thoughts of sages, saints, mystics, he utters the truth that in the absolute surrender of the thought of calling anything its own the soul becomes the heir of the universe. All things are his, as with the certainty of an assured inheritance. The beatitude of the meek, of those who claim nothing, is that they "shall inherit the earth," and so all things are theirs—the forces of nature, and the changes and chances of life—for all are working together for their good. (See Note on Matt. v. 5.)

(11) **O ye Corinthians.**—There was manifestly a pause here as the letter was dictated. The rush of thoughts had reached its highest point. He rests, and feels almost as if some apology were needed for so vehement an outpouring of emotion. And now he writes as if personally pleading with them. Nowhere else in the whole range of his Epistles do we find any parallel to this form of speech—this "O ye Corinthians." He has to tell them that he speaks out of the fulness of his heart, that if his mouth has been opened with an unusual freedom it is because his heart has felt a more than common expansion.

(12) **Ye are not straitened in us.**—The word presents a natural contrast to the expansion, the dilatation, of heart of the previous verse. There was no narrowness in him. In that large heart of his there was room for them and for a thousand others. It had, as it were, an infinite elasticity in its sympathies. The

Chap. vi. 13—17. Warning against intimacy with idolaters.

not straitened in us, but ye are straitened
in your own bowels. (13) Now for a
recompence in the same,
(I speak as unto *my* chil-
dren,) be ye also enlarged.
(14) Be ye not unequally
yoked together with un-
believers: for what fellowship hath
righteousness with unrighteousness?
and what communion hath light with
darkness? (15) And what concord hath
Christ with Belial? or what part hath he
that believeth with an infidel? (16) And
what agreement hath the temple of
God with idols? for ye are the temple
of the living God; as God hath said, I
will dwell in them,[a] and walk in *them*;
and I will be their God, and they shall
be my people. (17) Wherefore come out
from among them,[b] and be ye separate,
saith the Lord, and touch not the
unclean *thing*; and I will receive you,

a Lev. 26. 12.

b Isa. 52. 11.

---

narrowness was found in their own "bowels"—*i.e.*, in their own affections. They would not make room for him in those hearts that were so straitened by passions, and prejudices, and antipathies.

(13) **Now for a recompence in the same.**—Better, perhaps, *as a return*, as expressing the idea of reciprocity. Children should requite the care and love of parents. (Comp. chap. xii. 14.) They, the Corinthians, are his spiritual children. (Comp. 1 Cor. iv. 15.) What does he demand of them, but that they should love him in return for his love? What they needed in their spiritual life was breadth and expansiveness of affection.

(14) **Be ye not unequally yoked together with unbelievers.**—We seem at first to enter, by an abrupt transition, upon a new line of exhortation. The under-current of thought is, however, not difficult to trace. There was a false latitude as well as a true. The baser party at Corinth might think it a matter of indifference whether they married a heathen or a Christian, whether they chose their intimate friends among the worshippers of Aphrodite or of Christ. Against that "enlargement" the Apostle feels bound to protest. The Greek word for "unequally yoked together" is not found elsewhere, and was probably coined by St. Paul to give expression to his thoughts. Its meaning is, however, determined by the use of the cognate noun in Lev. xix. 19 ("Thou shalt not let thy cattle gender with *a diverse kind*"). Cattle were unequally yoked together when ox and ass were drawing the same plough (Deut. xxii. 10). Men and women are so when they have no common bond of faith in God. Another explanation refers the image to the yoke of a balance, or pair of scales, and so sees in the precept a warning against partiality in judgment; but this rests on very slender ground, or rather, no ground at all.

(15) **What concord hath Christ with Belial?**—The passage is remarkable as being the only occurrence of the name in the New Testament, all the more so because it does not appear in the Greek version of the Old. The Hebrew word signifies "vileness, worthlessness;" and the "sons of Belial" (as in Deut. xiii. 13; 1 Sam. ii. 12; xxv. 17) were therefore the worthless and the vile. The English version, following the Vulgate, translates the phrase as though Belial were a proper name, and this has led to the current belief, as shown in Milton's poems, that it was the name of a demon or fallen angel, the representative of impurity—

> "Belial came last, than whom a spirit more lewd,
> Fell not from heaven, or more gross to love
> Vice for itself."—*Paradise Lost*, i. 490.

> "Belial, the dissolutest spirit that fell,
> The sensualest, and, after Asmodai,
> The fleshliest incubus."—*Paradise Regained*, ii. 204.

St. Paul's use of the word would seem to imply that some such belief was floating among the Jews in his time. A strange legend, which possibly had a Jewish origin (it is referred to certain *necromantici*), is found in an obscure and forgotten book (Wierus: *Pseudo-Monarchia Dæmonum*), to the effect that Solomon was led by a certain woman to bow before the image of Belial, who is represented as worshipped by the Babylonians. Of that worship there is no trace in history; and Milton seems to have recognised this—

> "To him no temple stood
> Nor altar smoked."

But if the name had gathered these associations round it, we can understand St. Paul's using it as representing, or, as it were, personifying, the whole system of impure *cultus* that prevailed in the worship of Aphrodite at Corinth.

**With an infidel.**—So many later associations have gathered round the word, that it may be well to remind the reader that it does not mean, as commonly with us, one who has rejected the faith, but simply one who has not as yet received it.

(16) **And what agreement hath the temple of God with idols?**—Here we see clearly the drift of the Apostle's thoughts. His mind travels back to the controversy about things sacrificed to idols. Was there not a risk that what he had said about "width" and "expansion" of feeling would be perverted by those who claimed the right to sit at an idol's feast even in the precincts of the idol's temple (1 Cor. viii. 10)? Against that perversion he thinks it necessary to enter his protest. And the ground of that protest is that they, collectively and individually (1 Cor. iii. 16; vi. 19), are the temples of God, and that there can be no "agreement" between that temple and one dedicated to an idol. The word translated "agreement" expresses like the English, a compact or treaty of alliance. In modern phrase, a *concordat* between the two antagonistic systems was an impossibility.

**I will dwell in them, and walk in them.**—The citation which follows is, like many others in St. Paul's writings, a composite one: Lev. xxvi. 12 giving, "I will walk among you, and will be your God, and ye shall be my people;" and Ex. xxix. 45, "I will dwell among the children of Israel, and will be their God." The implied premiss is that wherever God dwells there is His temple. The word indicates the "sanctuary," or holiest part of the temple. (See Note on John ii. 19.)

(17) **Wherefore come out from among them.**—Another composite quotation follows, beginning with Isa. lii. 11. In their primary historical sense, the words were addressed as to the priests and Levites who were to return from Babylon. They were not to bring back with them any symbol of that "unclean" ritual which they had witnessed there. The local and historical meaning has for the Apostle passed away, and the "unclean thing" is identified with the whole system of heathenism. The close connection of this verse with the great prophecy of the atoning work makes it

(18) and will be a Father unto you,[a] and ye shall be my sons and daughters, saith the Lord Almighty.

[a] Jer. 31. 1.

A.D. 60.

CHAPTER VII.—(1) Having therefore these promises, dearly beloved, let us cleanse ourselves from all filthiness of the flesh and spirit, perfecting holiness in the fear of God. (2) Receive us; we have wronged no man, we have corrupted no man, we have de-

Chap. vii. 1—4. The Apostle's strivings after purity of act and motive.

---

probable that, in writing of that work, St. Paul had remembered, or, perhaps, actually turned to Isa. liii., as it stood in the LXX. version, and so was led on to the verse which almost immediately preceded it. "I will receive you" comes, in lieu of the ending of Isaiah, from the Greek of Ezek. xi. 17; Jer. xxiv. 5.

(18) **And will be a Father unto you . . .**—Again we have, as it were, a mosaic of citations: "I will be a Father . . . ." from 2 Sam. vii. 14; "Sons and daughters" from Isa. xliii. 6; "Saith the Lord Almighty" from the Greek of 2 Sam. vii. 8. It may be noted as not without interest that the Greek word rendered "Almighty" here, and "Omnipotent" in Rev. xix. 6, is commonly used in the LXX. as an equivalent for the Hebrew "Lord of Hosts" or "Lord of Sabaoth."

## VII.

(1) **Having therefore these promises . . . let us cleanse ourselves from all filthiness.**—The thought is identical with that of 1 John iii. 3. In each there is the contrast between the high ideal to which the believer in Christ is called and the infinite debasement into which he may possibly sink. St. John characteristically presents the law of the spiritual life as a generalised fact of experience: "Every man who has the hope actually does purify himself." The word for "filthiness" does not occur elsewhere in the New Testament. In 2 Macc. i. 27, it is used of the "pollution" of idolatry; in the LXX. of Jer. xxiii. 14 (where the English version gives "a horrible thing," and the margin "filthiness") of the sin of Sodom and Gomorrah. The cognate verb is used of sexual impurity in Rev. xiv. 4, and probably with the same sense in Rev. iii. 4, and this is manifestly what St. Paul has in his thoughts here. The two thoughts—idolatry and impurity—were inextricably blended in his mind. He had been warning men against the feasts that were held in the idol's temple. He cannot close his eyes to the "hidden things of shame" that were their constant and inevitable accompaniments. But that contagion of impurity might spread to the inward parts. Mind and conscience might be defiled (Tit. i. 15). The literature of the Empire, as seen in Catullus and Martial and Juvenal, shows only too terribly what St. Paul meant by "filthiness of the spirit." The very element in man by which he is raised above the brute creatures that lead a simply animal or natural life—his imagination, fancy, discernment of analogies—sinks him to an infinite depth below them.

**Perfecting holiness in the fear of God.**—The word for "holiness" involves the idea of consecration, and grows out of the thought that the "saints" of God make up collectively, as in chap. vi. 16, the Temple in which He dwells. As the former clause of the verse presents the negative aspect of purity, abstinence from all that desecrates, this presents the positive, the perfect consecration, and this is wrought out in its completeness, in "the fear of God"—the reverential awe before the thought of God's presence. The word is the same as that mis-translated "terror" in chap. v. 11.

(2) **Receive us; we have wronged no man.**—Better, *Make room for us*; *we wronged no man*: with the same change of tense in the verbs that follow. There is an almost infinite pathos in that entreaty, uttered, we may well believe, as from the very depths of the soul—"Make room for us." The under-current of thought flows on. He had complained of their being straitened in their affections, had entreated that they would enlarge their hearts towards him, as his heart was enlarged towards them. He has travelled on—his thoughts turning now to the party of license, with whom he had pleaded so earnestly in 1 Cor. viii.—x.—to the terribly unutterable contaminations to which they were exposing themselves by their companionship with idolaters. He now, almost, as it were, with sobs, entreats once more: "You can find a place for such as these in your heart. Have you no place for me?" In the words "we wronged no man" we find reference to charges of greed of gain and self-interested motives that had been whispered against him, and to which he refers again in chaps. viii. 20; xii. 18. Perhaps, also, he contrasts himself with others, who "did wrong and defrauded" (1 Cor. vi. 8).

**We have corrupted no man, we have defrauded no man.**—The word for "corrupt" is the same as that translated "defile" in 1 Cor. iii. 17, and is used with manifest reference to sensual impurity in 2 Pet. ii. 12; Jude, verse 10; Rev. xix. 2. The word for "defrauded" is not the same as that in 1 Cor. vi. 8, and though meaning literally "to make a gain," or "seek a gain," had, with its cognate nouns, acquired a darker shade of meaning. The verb is used in obvious connection with impurity in 1 Thess. iv. 3—6, where see Note. The nouns often appear in closest companionship with those which indicate that form of evil (1 Cor. v. 10, 11; Eph. v. 5; 2 Pet. ii. 14; Rom. i. 29; Col. iii. 5). Mere greed of gain is commonly described by another word, which we translate "the love of money" (Luke xvi. 14; 1 Tim. vi. 10; 2 Tim. iii. 2). There seems, then, sufficient reason for connecting this verb also with the same class of sins. It would seem as if the word had colloquially acquired a secondary meaning, and was used of those who sought gain by ministering to the vice of others—who became, as it were, purveyors of impurity. The words, so understood, give us a momentary glimpse into a depth of evil from which we would willingly turn our eyes. But they leave no room for doubt that, in the infinite pruriency of such a city as Corinth, even such things as these had been said of the Apostle in the cynical jests of the paganising party of license. They tolerated such things themselves. They welcomed those who practised them to their friendship (1 Cor. v. 11). They whispered, we may well believe, of private interviews in lonely lodgings, of public gatherings at night of men and women, and of the kiss of peace. They insinuated that, after all, he was even such a one as themselves. So, in like manner, was the fair fame of a disciple of St. Paul's attacked by Martial, not apparently with malignity, but only in the wantonness of jest. (See *Excursus on the Later Years of St. Paul's*

frauded no man.
(3) I speak not *this* to condemn *you:* for I have said before, that ye are in our hearts to die and live with *you.*
(4) Great *is* my boldness of speech toward you, great *is* my glorying of you: I am filled with comfort, I am exceeding joyful in all our tribulation.
(5) For, when we were come into Macedonia, our flesh had no rest, but we were troubled on every side; without *were* fightings, within *were* fears.

Chap. vii. 5—7. His joy at the news brought by Titus.

(6) Nevertheless God, that comforteth those that are cast down, comforted us by the coming of Titus;
(7) and not by his coming only, but by the consolation wherewith he was comforted in you, when he told us your earnest desire, your mourning, your fervent mind toward me; so that I rejoiced the more.
(8) For though I made you sorry with a letter, I do not repent, though I did repent: for I perceive that the same epistle hath made you sorry, though *it*

---

*Life,* at the end of the Acts of the Apostles.) So like charges were levelled at the reputation of Athanasius (Sozomen. *Hist.* ii. 25), and of Hooker (Walton's *Life*). So, generally, it was the ever-recurring calumny of the heathen against the Christians that their *Agapæ*, or Feasts of Love, were scenes of foulest license. It is obvious that there is much in the popular outcry against confession that partakes more or less of the same character. Against charges of this nature St. Paul utters his indignant denial: "No," he virtually says; "you find a place in your affections for those who do such things: can you not find a place also for us who are free from them?" The sense which some have given to the word "corrupt," as referring only to doctrinal corruptions, is manifestly out of the question.

(3) **I speak not this to condemn you.**—Better, *I do not speak as condemning.* There is no "you" in the Greek, and the form of expression seems intentionally vague, as leaving it an open question whether his words might refer to his readers or to others. We trace here a sudden revulsion of feeling. What he had just said seemed to imply that he condemned them for even listening to the calumnies which had been circulated against him, for joining in any measure even of outward friendship with men of evil lives; and then there rushes on his memory the recollection of all the good news which Titus had brought. Indignation and jealous sensitiveness are swallowed up in the overflowing thankfulness to which those tidings had given birth at the time, and which were now renewed.

**I have said before . . .**—He had not used the form of expression before, as far as this letter is concerned, but the fact was implied in what he had said in chap. vi. 11: "Our heart is enlarged." The words that follow are partly an almost proverbial expression for strong attachment, as in Horace (*Odes*, iii. 9): "Tecum vivere amem, tecum obeam libens"—

"With thee I fain would live,
With thee I fain would die;"

partly with a profounder meaning, that, whether in death or life (the order of the words throws us back on "dying, but behold, we live," in chap. vi. 9), his heart and prayers would be with them and for them.

(4) **Great is my boldness of speech.**—The context shows that he is not apologising for bold and plain speaking, but uses the word as implying confidence (1 Tim. iii. 13; Philem. verse 8). He can speak without reticence now, because he is going to express his comfort and joy at what had been reported to him.

**I am exceeding joyful.**—Literally, *I exceedingly abound* (or, *overflow*) *in joy.* The verb is the same as in Rom. v. 20, and answers to the "pressed above measure" which he had used in chap. i. 8, in speaking of his troubles.

(5) **For, when we were come into Macedonia . . .**—His feeling has led him back to the narrative from which he had digressed in chap. ii. 13. He had come from Troas full of anxiety and agitation. He arrived in Macedonia. Much remained the same. His body was still suffering from want of rest, even though his spirit had found relief in the thought that the coming of Titus could not now be far off. (Comp. "our *flesh*" here, with "I had no rest for my *spirit*" in chap. ii. 13.)

**Without were fightings, within were fears.**—We have no knowledge to what the first clause refers. It is natural to think either of dangers and persecutions from the heathen, or, probably, of conflicts with the party of the circumcision, or, as he calls them in Phil. iii., of the "concision," at Philippi. The "fears" manifestly refer to his alarm and anxiety about the effect produced by his first Epistle.

(6) **God, that comforteth those that are cast down.**—The fact of his own experience seems almost to present itself to his thoughts as constituting an attribute of the divine character. In the word for "cast down" (*lowly*) we may, perhaps, trace an allusion to the same word used of him by others as a disparaging epithet. (See Note on chap. x. 1.)

(7) **And not by his coming only.**—There was joy, doubtless, in seeing his true son in the faith (Tit. i. 1) once again, but the great comfort was found in the news which he brought with him. On the part of the majority, at least, of those who had been present when the Epistle was read, there had been all the feelings which he most desired to rouse—longing to see him as he longed to see them (see Rom. i. 11; Phil. i. 8; 1 Thess. iii. 6; 2 Tim. i. 4, for the meaning of the word), their "mourning" (*uttered lamentation*) for having grieved him; their *zeal* (not "towards" him, but) *on his behalf and for him,* as against those who slandered him. All these were elements of comfort, and his sorrow was turned into a yet greater joy than had been caused by the mere arrival of Titus.

(8) **For though I made you sorry with a letter.**—Better, *For even if,* and, as the Greek has the article, *with my letter.* This Titus had told him; and commonly to have caused pain to others would have been a source of grief to him, but he cannot bring himself now to say, *I regret.* (This is, perhaps, better than *repent.* On the words, see Notes on Matt. xxi. 29; xxvii. 3.) He owns, however, that there had been a moment, either on first hearing of their grief or in his previous anxiety, when he had half regretted that he had written so strongly. Now he sees that that grief was but transient, and he trusts that the good wrought by it will be abiding.

Chap. vii. 9—12. The forms in which the Corinthians had manifested their sorrow and repentance.

*were* but for a season. (9) Now I rejoice,
not that ye were made
sorry, but that ye sorrowed
to repentance: for ye were
made sorry after a godly
manner,[1] that ye might re-
ceive damage by us in no-
thing. (10) For godly sorrow
worketh repentance to salvation not to
be repented of: but the sorrow of the
world worketh death. (11) For behold this
selfsame thing, that ye sorrowed after a
godly sort, what carefulness it wrought
in you, yea, *what* clearing of yourselves,
yea, *what* indignation, yea, *what* fear,
yea, *what* vehement desire, yea, *what*
zeal, yea, *what* revenge! In all *things*
ye have approved yourselves to be clear
in this matter. (12) Wherefore, though
I wrote unto you, *I did it* not for his
cause that had done the wrong, nor for
his cause that suffered wrong, but that
our care for you in the sight of God
might appear unto you. (13) Therefore

1 Or, *according to God.*

---

(9) **That ye sorrowed to repentance.**—Here the true word for "repentance" is used in all the fulness of its meaning. (See Notes on Matt. iii. 2, 8.) There is nothing in the Greek corresponding to the variation "ye sorrowed" and "were made sorry," the same word being used in both clauses.

**After a godly manner.**—The English is but a feeble equivalent for the Greek. Literally, *according to God—i.e.* (as may be seen by comparing the sense of the same or like phrases in Rom. viii. 27; Eph. iv. 24; Col. ii. 8), after His will and purpose. "God allowed you," he tells them, "to be grieved in order that you might sustain no loss, as you might have done had we held our peace."

(10) **For godly sorrow.**—Again we note the needless variation which is the easily besetting sin of the English version. Better, as before *the sorrow which is after the will of God.*

**Repentance to salvation not to be repented of.**—Here the English effaces a distinction in the original. (See Note on Matt. xxvii. 3,) Better, *repentance unto salvation, giving no matter for regret.* The adjective, or adjectival phrase, may qualify either "repentance" or "salvation." The latter seems preferable.

**But the sorrow of the world worketh death.**—As contrasted with "salvation," death must be taken in its widest sense. The mere sorrow of the world leads only to remorse and despair, to the death of a broken heart, possibly to suicide; in any case, to the loss of the true eternal life.

(11) **That ye sorrowed after a godly sort.**—Better, as before, *that ye sorrowed after the will of God.* The series of emotional words that follow represent the Apostle's estimate of what he had heard from Titus. There was (1) *earnestness* where there had been indifference to evil, or even approval of it (1 Cor. v. 2); and this was shown (2) in the *vindication* of their conduct which they had sent through Titus, and (3) in their stern "indignation" against the offender; (4) in their "fear," partly of the supernatural chastisement which St. Paul had threatened, partly of the judgment of God, which was against such things; (5) in the *longing* to have him once more among them which mingled with their fear; (6) in their new "zeal" for the law of purity; (7) in their actual *vengeance, i.e.*, their sentence of condemnation passed upon the offender.

**To be clear in this matter.**—Literally, *in the matter*, possibly with exclusive reference to the sin condemned in 1 Cor. v. 1—5, but possibly also, as in 1 Thess. iv. 6, as an euphemistic expression for the sin of impurity generally.

(12) **Wherefore, though I wrote unto you.**—The reference to the man that had suffered wrong implies that the offender in 1 Cor. v. 1 had married his step-mother during his father's life. All other interpretations—such as those which make St. Paul or the community the injured party—are fantastic. But in what sense was the father injured? The union was a marriage, not a mere concubinage or adultery (see Note on 1 Cor. v. 1), and it could not have been so unless the first marriage had been dissolved by a divorce. But if the husband had divorced the wife, then, though the son's marriage may have shocked men as immoral, the father could hardly be said to have suffered a wrong to which he had exposed himself by his own act. The probable explanation is found in supposing that the wife, seduced by her step-son or seducing him, had divorced herself. Wives had this power under Roman law; and it was used with such license under the Empire, that Juvenal speaks of one woman of rank who had—

> "Eight husbands in five autumns. Do you laugh?
> The thing reads well upon an epitaph."—*Sat.* vi. 230.

On this assumption the father had, of course, sustained a very grievous wrong. There is an obvious tone of impatience, almost of annoyance, in the way in which St. Paul speaks of the whole business. It was one of those scandals in which, though it had been necessary to assert the law of purity and enforce the discipline of the Church, he could not bring himself at the time to feel any special interest in either of the parties. Afterwards, when the sinner was repentant, there came, it is true, a new feeling of pity for him, as in chap. ii. 6—8. But when he wrote, it was with a larger aim, to show them how much he cared for his disciples at Corinth, how jealous he was to clear away any stains that affected their reputation as a Church. It is noticeable that no mention is made of the woman's repentance, nor, indeed, of her coming, in any way, under the discipline of the Church. The facts of the case suggest the conclusion that both husband and wife were heathens, and that the son was the only convert of the family. In this case we may fairly assume that she had played the part of temptress, and that his conscience, though weak, had been the more sensitive of the two. On this view the exhortations against being "unequally yoked together" with unbelievers gains a fresh significance. Possibly some idolatrous festival had furnished the first opportunity of sin, and so the fact gave special protest against any attempt to combine the worship of Christ with that of Belial.

(13) **Therefore we were comforted.**—The tense of the Greek verb implies a different structure of the sentence: *Therefore we have been comforted: and upon* (*i.e.*, over and above) *our comfort we rejoiced more exceedingly at the joy of Titus.* That was to

we were comforted in your comfort: yea, and exceedingly the more joyed we for the joy of Titus, because his spirit was refreshed by you all. (14) For if I have boasted any thing to him of you, I am not ashamed; but as we spake all things to you in truth, even so our boasting, which *I made* before Titus, is found a truth. (15) And his inward affection[1] is more abundant toward you, whilst he remembereth the obedience of you all, how with fear and trembling ye received him. (16) I rejoice therefore that I have confidence in you in all *things.*

Chap. vii. 13–16. The affection which Titus felt for the Corinthians.

A.D. 60.

1 Gr. *bowels.*

## CHAPTER VIII.

—(1) Moreover, brethren, we do you to wit of the grace of God bestowed on the churches of Macedonia; (2) how that in a great trial of affliction the abundance of their joy and their deep poverty abounded

Chap. viii. 1–6. The action of the Macedonian churches in regard to the collection for the saints.

---

St. Paul a new source of happiness. The intense sympathy of his nature would have made him share the disappointment of his delegate, and in like manner he now shares his joy. The messenger had shown himself to be his true son in the faith (Tit. i. 1).

**His spirit was refreshed.**—Better, as expressing the permanence of the effect, *has been refreshed.* The term was a favourite one with the writer. Stephanas, and Fortunatus, and Achaicus had "refreshed" his spirit (1 Cor. xvi. 18. Comp. also Philem. verses 7 and 20). The primary idea of the word is, however, rather that of "giving *rest*" to the weary, as in Matt. xi 28; xxvi. 45.

(14) **For if I have boasted any thing to him of you.**—It is obviously implied that he had boasted. He had encouraged Titus, when he sent him, with the assurance that he would find many elements of good mingled with the evil which he was sent to correct. And now St. Paul can add: "*I was not shamed*" (the tense requires this rendering) "when he came back with his report."

**Even so our boasting, which I made before Titus.**—The words "I made" are, as the italics show, not in the Greek. Some of the better MSS. give, indeed, "*your* boasting," and with this reading the sense would be: "As what I said of you to Titus turned out to be true, so I recognise that what you said to him of yourselves, of your zeal and longing (as in verse 11), was spoken truly." The Received reading rests, however, on very good authority, and certainly gives a better sense: "We spoke truly to you of your faults; we spoke truly to Titus of your good qualities."

(15) **His inward affection.**—The margin gives the literal meaning of the Greek, which is used here with the same meaning as in chap. vi. 12. Perhaps "heart," or "feelings," would be the best English equivalent. The recollection of what had passed at Corinth had bound him by ties of closest sympathy with the disciples there.

**With fear and trembling.**—The combination is a favourite one with St. Paul. (Comp. 1 Cor. ii. 3; Eph. vi. 5; Phil. ii. 12.) What it means is that Titus had been received, not, as he feared, with petulant resistance, but with respectful reverence, not without an element of fear.

(16) **I rejoice therefore that I have confidence in you in all things.**—Most of the better MSS. omit "therefore," which may have been inserted for the sake of connecting the verse. "I have confidence in you," though, in one sense, a literal translation of the Greek, fails to give its exact meaning. He does not mean, "I trust you," but "*I am of good cheer,* I take courage *in* you, being what you are." With this expression of thankfulness he leaves the painful subject of which he had been compelled to speak, and passes, probably after a pause of greater or less length, to another.

### VIII.

(1) **Moreover, brethren, we do you to wit . . .**—Better, *we declare,* or *make known to you.* There is no adequate reason for retaining a phrase which is now obsolete. The topic on which the Epistle now touches, and which is carried on through this and the following chapter, was one very dear to the Apostle's heart. (See Note on 1 Cor. xvi. 1.) When he wrote before he had simply given directions as to what the Corinthians were to do. Now he has something to tell them. The churches of Macedonia—Philippi, we must believe, prominent among them—had been true to their old generosity (chap. xi. 8, 9; Phil. iv. 15), and were now showing it, not, as before, in personal kindness to their teacher, but in the truer way of acting as he wished them to act; and he sees in this a means of stirring up his friends at Corinth to an honourable emulation. There is something intensely characteristic in the way in which he opens his statement. He traces the generosity of the Macedonians to its true source. He is going to tell the Corinthians of the "grace of God" that has enabled them to do so much.

(2) **In a great trial of affliction.**—We do not know what is specially referred to, but a community of Christians in a heathen city was always exposed to trials of this kind, and the temper shown before by the rulers at Philippi and the Jews of Thessalonica (Acts xvi. 19, 20; xvii. 5, 6; 1 Thess. ii. 14) makes it almost certain that they would carry on at least a petty persecution with more or less persistency. The "poverty" at Philippi may possibly be connected with the preponderance of women in the Church there, as indicated in Acts xvi. 13. In the absence of the bread-winners of a household, Christian women in a Græco-Roman city would find but scanty means of subsistence. In part, however, the churches were but sharers in a widely-spread distress. Macedonia and Achaia never recovered from the three wars between Cæsar and Pompeius, between the Triumvirs and Brutus and Cassius, and between Augustus and Antonius. Under Tiberius, they petitioned for a diminution of their burdens, and were accordingly transferred for a time from the jurisdiction of the senate to that of the emperor, as involving a less heavy taxation.

**Unto the riches of their liberality.**—The primary meaning of the word, as in chap. i. 12 (where see Note), is simplicity, or singleness of purpose. That singleness, when shown in gifts, leads to "liberality," and so the word had acquired the secondary sense in which it seems here to be used. Tyndale, and Cranmer, however, give "singleness," and the Rhemish

unto the riches of their liberality.
(3) For to *their* power, I bear record,
yea, and beyond *their* power *they were*
willing of themselves; (4) praying us
with much intreaty that we would
receive the gift, and *take upon us* the
fellowship of the ministering to the
saints. (5) And *this they did*, not as we
hoped, but first gave their own selves to
the Lord, and unto us by the will of
God. (6) Insomuch that we desired
Titus, that as he had begun, so he would
also finish in you the same grace also.
(7) Therefore, as ye abound in every
*thing*, *in* faith, and utterance, and
knowledge, and *in* all diligence, and *in*
your love to us, *see* that ye abound in
this grace also. (8) I speak not by
commandment, but by occasion of the forwardness
of others, and to prove
the sincerity of your love.
(9) For ye know the grace
of our Lord Jesus Christ, that, though
he was rich, yet for your sakes he
became poor, that ye through his
poverty might be rich. (10) And herein
I give *my* advice: for this is expedient

Chap. viii. 8—15. Appeal to the good-will and self-respect of the Corinthians.

---

version "simplicity." "Liberality" first appears in that of Geneva.

(3) **They were willing of themselves.**—Literally, *spontaneously.* This was the point of excellence which he wished to indicate as an example to the Corinthians. Those of Macedonia needed no appeal or counsel such as he had given to the Corinthians and to others.

(4) **Praying us with much intreaty . . .**—The words "that we would receive" are not in the Greek, which literally runs: *asking of us the grace* (or *favour*) *and fellowship in the ministry of the saints, i.e.*, asking to be allowed to share in it.

(5) **Not as we hoped . . .**—This means, of course, that they had done what was far beyond his hopes; and here the point lies in the fact that they gave, not their money only, but themselves, their time, thought, energy, primarily to Christ as their Lord, and then to the Apostle as His minister. And this they had done because they allowed the will of God to work upon their will.

(6) **Insomuch that we desired Titus . . .**—The sequence of events seems to have been this: When Titus came to Corinth, he, among other things, after seeing the satisfactory results of the First Epistle in other respects, had begun to take measures for this collection for the poor of Jerusalem. He had been, to a certain extent, successful. Encouraged by the report of that success, St. Paul had now entreated Titus to return to Corinth, and to bring the good work to its completion. "This grace *also*" practically means—this work of liberality, as well as that of repentance and loyal obedience already spoken of in chap. vii.

(7) **Therefore, as ye abound in every thing.**—Literally, *But, as ye abound,* marking the transition from narrative to exhortation. He opens, as was his manner, with words of praise, and dexterously combines the gifts of "utterance and knowledge," which he had acknowledged before (1 Cor. i. 5), with the "earnestness and love" of which he had spoken in this very Epistle (chap. vii. 12).

**And in your love to us.**—Some MSS. give the reading "our love for you," but that in the text has abundant authority, and gives a far better meaning. The English expresses the general meaning, but there is a subtle delicacy in the Greek: "the love which, flowing from you, rests in us as its object." The other reading would convey the sense of "the love which, flowing from us—*i.e.*, from our teaching and influence—now dwells in you, and shows itself in act." In any case, he is praising them for a quality which is actually theirs.

(8) **I speak not by commandment.**—The English, and, indeed, the Greek also, is to some extent ambiguous, and leaves us uncertain whether he disclaims merely the tone of command or the sanction of a divine authority. The former seems the preferable meaning, but ultimately the one runs into the other. He gives no commands in this matter to others because he has received no commandment from the Lord Himself. (Comp. 1 Cor. vii. 6, 12, 25.)

(9) **Ye know the grace of our Lord Jesus Christ.**—The meaning of the word "grace" appears slightly modified by the context. The theological sense of the word, so to speak, falls into the background, and that of an act of liberality becomes prominent.

**That, though he was rich, . . . he became poor.**—Better, *that, being rich* . . . The thought is the same as that expressed in Phil. ii. 6, 7, especially in the words which ought to be translated *He emptied Himself.* He was rich in the ineffable glory of the divine attributes, and these He renounced for a time in the mystery of the Incarnation, and took our nature in all its poverty. This is doubtless the chief thought expressed, but we can scarcely doubt that the words refer also to the outward aspect of our Lord's life. He chose the lot of the poor, almost of the beggar (the Greek word "poor" is so translated, and rightly, in Luke xvi. 20—22), as Francis of Assisi and others have done in seeking to follow in His steps. And this He did that men might by that spectacle of a life of self-surrender be sharers with Him in the eternal wealth of the Spirit, and find their treasure not in earth but heaven. As regards the outward mendicant aspect of our Lord's life, and that of His disciples, see Notes on Matt. x. 10; Luke viii. 1—3; John xii. 6.

(10) **And herein I give my advice.**—We note the same careful distinction between command and counsel which we have seen in 1 Cor. vii. 25.

**Who have begun before . . .**—Better, *who got the start, last year, not only as to the doing, but also as to the willing.* At first, the words seem like an anti-climax, but what is meant is that the Corinthians had been before the Macedonian churches in both those stages. They had formed the purpose of giving, they had begun to lay by and to collect, before their rivals had started. They had, as it were, scored those two points in that game of honourable competition. It was "profitable for them" that he, as a by-stander watching the game, should give them a hint, so that they might not at last be ignominiously defeated. It is not easy to fix the exact limits of time indicated in the "year ago." The First Epistle was written about Easter. Then, after remaining at Ephesus for a while, there came the

for you, who have begun before, not
only to do, but also to be forward[1] a
year ago. (11) Now therefore perform
the doing *of it;* that as *there was* a
readiness to will, so *there may be* a per-
formance also out of that which ye
have. (12) For if there be first a willing
mind, *it is* accepted according to that a
man hath, *and* not according to that he
hath not. (13) For *I mean* not that other
men be eased, and ye burdened: (14) but
by an equality, *that* now at this time
your abundance *may be a supply* for
their want, that their abundance also
may be *a supply* for your want: that
there may be equality: (15) as it is
written, He that *had gathered* much had
nothing over;[a] and he that *had gathered*
little had no lack. (16) But thanks *be*
to God, which put the same earnest
care into the heart of Ti-
tus for you. (17) For indeed
he accepted the exhorta-
tion; but being more for-
ward, of his own accord he
went unto you. (18) And

1 Gr. *willing.*

a Ex. 16. 18.

Chap. viii. 16—24. St. Paul's arrangements for the transmission of the sum collected for the churches of Judæa.

journey to Troas; then that to Macedonia; then the coming of Titus, bringing word that the Corinthians had acted on the command of 1 Cor. xvi. 1. This would bring us to the autumn months; and St. Paul, reckoning, as a Jew would, the year as beginning with Tisri (September or October), might speak of what had taken place in April or May as done "last year," though there had not been an interval of twelve months.

(11) **Now therefore perform the doing.**—Better, *complete the doing:* to "perform the doing" being open, in the modern use of the word, to the charge of tautology. All the English versions, however, have "perform." The three stages are distinctly marked out in St. Paul's mind:—(1) Willing the purpose to give; in this they had shown readiness. (2) Setting about the work of giving; this Titus had reported. (3) Completing the work; this he now urged upon them, so that it might answer to the beginning.

(12) **For if there be first a willing mind.**—This grows "out of that which ye have" in the previous verse. He is expecting a sum large relatively, and not absolutely. The history of the widow's mite, found in the Gospel of his friend St. Luke (Luke xxi. 1—4), was probably not unknown to him as belonging to "the words of the Lord Jesus" which he freely cites (Acts xx. 35). He has, at all events, imbibed the spirit of its teaching from other like words.

(13) **For I mean not that other men be eased.**—The disclaimer is obviously an answer to something that had been said. The "charity begins at home" argument, with which the workers in the cause of missions and other distant works of charity are but too familiar, would seem not to have been unknown in the Church of Corinth.

(14) **But by an equality.**—The meaning of the word is obvious. The Church of Jerusalem was at this time suffering from poverty, and, therefore, St. Paul exhorts the Corinthians to come to its assistance. A time might come in which their relative position would be inverted, and then he would plead not less earnestly that Jerusalem should assist Corinth. It is reading too much between the lines to see in the words the thought which the Apostle expresses elsewhere (Rom. xv. 27), that the equality of which he speaks consisted in the Corinthians giving money and receiving spiritual privileges. But for the fact that controversial ingenuity is "capable of anything," it might have been thought impossible to see in them the doctrine that men are to give to the poor in order that, in their time of need, in the hour of death, and in the day of judgment, they might receive from them a transfer of their superfluous merits. And yet this has actually been done by Roman Catholic commentators—even by such as Estius.

(15) **He that had gathered much.**—The quotation is from one of the readings of the LXX. version of Ex. xvi. 18. The work of love was, in the Apostle's thoughts, like the manna in the wilderness. In the long-run all would be filled, each according to his several necessities.

(16) **Thanks be to God, which put . . .**—Better, *which putteth,* the verb being in the present tense, and referring to what was then passing after Titus's return from Corinth.

**The same earnest care.**—There is no direct comparison, but what he means is the same care as his own. Titus had shown himself a true son of his spiritual father (Tit. i. 1).

(17) **For indeed he accepted the exhortation . . .**—The words have a two-fold purpose:—(1) To show that Titus was authorised by the Apostle, and acting at his request; (2) that he was so eager to go that he did not even need to be requested. The tense, "he went," is what is known as the epistolary aorist. Titus was to start, probably, as the bearer of this letter.

(18) **The brother, whose praise is in the gospel.**—We cannot get beyond probable conjecture in determining who this was. The general current of patristic interpretation (represented, we may add, in the Collect for St. Luke's Day in the Prayer Book of the Church of England, though not in that of the Breviary of the Church of Rome) ran in favour of St. Luke; but this rested on the assumption, for which there is no evidence, and against which there is a strong balance of probabilities, that he was already well known as the writer of a Gospel. (See *Introduction to St. Luke,* Vol. I., p. 239.) Apart from this, however, it may be urged that there is more evidence in favour of this hypothesis than of any other. If the words be interpreted, as they must, as pointing to a preacher of the gospel, we have indications of St. Luke having done this at Antioch, at Troas, and at Philippi. None of the other companions of St. Paul who have been suggested, such as Tychicus or Trophimus, was likely to have so wide-spread a reputation. None was so likely to be with him at the time at Philippi. And it may be noted further—and this, so far as I know, is a point which has not hitherto been dwelt on—that there was no man so fitted to stir up the Corinthians, by his personal character, to a worthy completion of the good work they had begun. We have seen that in his Gospel he dwells emphatically on all parts of our Lord's teaching that point out the danger of riches and the blessedness of a generous almsgiving (see *Introduction to St. Luke,* Vol. I., p. 242); how at Philippi his influence was traceable in the liberal supplies sent to St. Paul at Thessalonica (see Note on Acts xvi. 40, and

we have sent with him the brother,
whose praise *is* in the gospel through-
out all the churches; (19) and not *that*
only, but who was also chosen of the
churches to travel with us with this
grace,[1] which is administered by us to
the glory of the same Lord, and *decla-
ration of* your ready mind: (20) avoiding
this, that no man should blame us in
this abundance which is administered
by us: (21) providing for honest things,
not only in the sight of the Lord, but
also in the sight of men. (22) And we
have sent with them our brother, whom
we have oftentimes proved diligent in
many things, but now much more dili-
gent, upon the great confidence which I
*have*[2] in you. (23) Whether *any do
enquire* of Titus, *he is* my partner and
fellowhelper concerning you: or our
brethren *be enquired of, they are* the
messengers of the churches, *and* the

1 Or, *gift.*
2 Or, he hath.

---

Phil. iv. 15) and at Corinth (see Note on chap. xi. 9). Was not such a man, we may ask, eminently adapted for the mission on which the "brother, whose praise is in the gospel," was now sent? and was not the Apostle likely to choose him above all others for it? For Mark and Gaius, who have also been suggested, there is not a shadow of evidence; and as the latter was of Corinth (Rom. xvi. 23), he was not likely to have been sent thither from Philippi. The tense, "we have sent," is, as before, the epistolary aorist, used of the time at which the letter was being written.

(19) **Who was also chosen of the churches.**—The word, as in Acts xiv. 23, implies a definite appointment, in this case, obviously, by popular election—on the part of the Macedonian churches. This falls in, it need hardly be said, with the facts of the case as indicated by the use of the first person plural in Acts xx. 5, and through the rest of the book.

**With this grace.**—The word is used, as in verses 4, 6, 7, as we familiarly use the word "charity," for the liberality which was the result of the grace.

**To the glory of the same Lord.**—Better, if we keep the Received text, *of the Lord Himself*; but the better MSS. give, *of the Lord*, only. There is no need of inserting the word "declaration of"; *in relation to the glory of the Lord and to your readiness* gives a perfectly intelligible sense.

(20) **Avoiding this, that no man should blame us.**—He gives this as the reason why he wished men thus appointed to travel with him. He desired to guard against the suspicion of those who were too ready to suspect. His companions were to bear witness that the sums which he took up with him from the several churches were what had actually been collected. They were to be, practically, auditors of his accounts. (See Note on Acts xx. 4.) He dwells again, later on in the Epistle (chap. xii. 18, 19), on the same measure of precaution.

**This abundance.**—The word, which primarily signifies "succulence," or juiciness, as used of plants and fruits, does not occur elsewhere in the New Testament. It has rather the look of belonging to St. Luke's medical vocabulary, and is, indeed, used by Hippocrates (*De Gen.* p. 28) of the full habit of body of a youth attaining puberty.

(21) **Providing for honest things . . .**—Many of the best MSS. give: "For we provide for honest things," as though he gave the general principle on which he was now acting in this particular instance. The rule of life is repeated, a few months afterwards, in Rom. xii. 17. The English reader does not recognise the fact, which the Greek reader would see at once, that the words are a quotation from Prov. iii. 4. where the Greek version has: "Write them upon the table of thine heart, and thou shalt find favour. *Provide things honest in the sight of God and man.* The citation is interesting, as showing that even one who was taught by the Spirit, as St. Paul was, could yet find guidance for his daily conduct in a book which seems to many almost to be below the level of the spiritual life. In this case, had the Apostle had only the judgment of God to consider, he could with a pure conscience have taken up the money to Jerusalem by himself. But he had to consider that men were judging him, and might suspect him, and therefore he insisted, as has been said above, on having his accounts audited.

(22) **And we have sent with them our brother.**—Who this second unnamed brother was is again simply matter of conjecture. Of the names connected with St. Paul at this period, that of Tychicus seems to have the greatest balance of probabilities in its favour. He went up with St. Paul to Jerusalem on this very business (Acts xx. 4), and the tone in which the Apostle speaks of him in Eph. vi. 21, Col. iv. 7, exactly agrees with his language here. In 2 Tim. iv. 12, Tit. iii. 12, we have further evidence of his being one of the most trusted of the couriers, or "messengers," of the Apostolic Church. The name of Clement has, however, I think, some claim to consideration. St. Paul refers to him as an active fellow-worker (Phil. iv. 3). He was connected with the Philippians. Assuming his identity with Clement of Rome, this gives him a point of contact with the Church of Corinth, to which Clement addressed his Epistle. On the other hand, the distinction drawn in chap. ix. 4 between these brethren and the Macedonians may seem to exclude Clement, as it has been thought to exclude Aristarchus and Sopater and Secundus. The word translated "diligent" ("earnest" in verse 16) is used by St. Paul only in this passage. It implies what we might almost call the "business-like" side of the Christian type of character, and is therefore employed with special fitness here.

(23) **Whether any do enquire of Titus.**—There is no verb in the Greek, and its insertion is not required for the English. Our common phrase, *As to Titus . . . as to our brethren*, exactly expresses St. Paul's meaning. In the "messengers" of the churches we find in the Greek the word "Apostles" used, as in Phil. ii. 25, and possibly Rom. xvi. 7, in a lower sense (the Greek has no article), for "*delegates* of the churches," as the Twelve and Paul and Barnabas were delegates of Christ. The other epithet—"the glory of Christ"—is an unusual one. To say that they were working only to that glory, though true, seems hardly adequate, and we gain a deeper thought by connecting it with the language of chap. iii. 18. "These messengers," he says, "are like Christ in character: they reflect His glory. You may see that glory in them."

glory of Christ. (24) Wherefore shew
ye to them, and before the churches,
the proof of your love, and of our
boasting on your behalf.

CHAPTER IX.—(1) For as touching
the ministering to the
saints, it is superfluous
for me to write to you:
(2) for I know the for-
wardness of your mind,
for which I boast of you
to them of Macedonia,
that Achaia was ready a

Chap. ix. 1—4. Appeal to the Corinthians to let their conduct answer to the account of them which he had given to the Macedonians.

A.D. 60.

year ago; and your zeal hath pro-
voked very many. (3) Yet have I sent
the brethren, lest our boasting of you
should be in vain in this behalf; that,
as I said, ye may be ready: (4) lest
haply if they of Macedonia come
with me, and find you unprepared,
we (that we say not, ye) should
be ashamed in this same confident
boasting. (5) Therefore I
thought it necessary to
exhort the brethren, that
they would go before unto
you, and make up beforehand your

Chap. ix. 5—9. Exhortation to the spirit of true liberality.

---

(24) **Wherefore shew ye to them.**—In adding "before the churches" (literally, *in the face of the churches*), St. Paul appeals, as he has done throughout the chapter, to that natural love of praise which takes its place as a legitimate, though it may be, and ought to be, a subordinate, motive for the activity of Christian benevolence. They were not to consider only what he and Titus and the two brethren would think of them. The eyes of the churches were upon them. Probably Philippi, Thessalonica, and Berœa are referred to.

**The proof of your love, and of our boasting.**—The "love" to which he appeals is probably their personal regard for him. What the "boast" was he states more fully in chap. ix. 2. With a subtle knowledge of human nature, he attacks them, as it were, on every side. They have to compete with Macedonia; they have to show their love for their teacher; they have to sustain their own reputation.

### IX.

(1) **For as touching . . .**—The division of chapters in the English version, unfortunately, gives the impression of the introduction of a new subject. In reality there is no new topic, and all flows on with unbroken continuity. This is part of the appeal to their self-respect begun in chap. viii. 23, 24. "You will pardon," he practically says, "my words of counsel as to the necessity of prompt action; as to the general duty of that ministration to the saints you have shown that you need no instruction."

(2) **For I know the forwardness of your mind.**—This was the boast to which he had referred in chap. viii. 24. Achaia (*i.e.*, Corinth, and perhaps Cenchreæ also) had been ready *last year.* The urgency of his present appeal indicates a latent misgiving whether he had not unconsciously over-stated the fact, and had mistaken the "will" that had shown itself for an actual readiness to send off the money whenever it was called for. (See Note on verse 3.) The word for "provoke," used here in a good sense, is found in Col. iii. 21, in a bad sense, as "irritating." This was another reason for prompt and generous action. It would be a permanent disgrace to them if, after having been held up as a pattern to others, they afterwards fell short of their excellence.

**Very many.**—Literally, *the greater number.*

(3) **Yet have I sent the brethren . . .**—This, then, was his purpose in the new mission. He wanted the performance not to fall short of the promise. They must be found ready, their money collected. (Comp. 1 Cor. xvi. 2.)

**In this behalf.**—Perhaps, *in this particular,* or, *in this respect,* would be more in harmony with modern English phraseology.

(4) **Lest haply if they of Macedonia . . .**—The Greek for "Macedonians" has no article, and the word is meant to stir up something like an *esprit de corps.* "Surely you Achaians won't allow Macedonians to come and see that you fall short of what I told them about?" It is a probable, but not, as some have thought, a necessary inference, that neither of the two unnamed brethren of chap. viii. 18, 22, were of that province. What he now indicates is, that it is, at all events, probable that when he comes to pay his deferred visit he will be accompanied by Macedonians. If, then, they were still not ready, there would be shame for him; how much more for them!

**In this same confident boasting.**—Literally, *in this confidence of boasting;* but the better MSS. give "in this confidence" only. The word so translated (*hypostasis*), literally, "that which stands under, the base or ground of anything," has the interest of a long subsequent history in metaphysical and theological controversies, of which we find, perhaps, the first trace in Heb. i. 3, where it appears as "person," and Heb. xi. 1, where it is rendered "substance." (See Notes on those passages.) In Heb. iii. 14, it has the same meaning as in this passage.

(5) **Therefore I thought it necessary . . .**—The brethren were to go before St. Paul, so as to get all things ready for his arrival. There were to be no hurried and unsatisfactory collections then.

**Your bounty, whereof ye had notice before.**—Better, *your bounty, announced before.* He is not referring to any notice that he had given, whether in 1 Cor. xvi. 1, 2 or elsewhere, but to the announcement that he himself had made to the churches of Macedonia. The word for "bounty" (*eulogia*) has, like that for "confidence" in the preceding verse, the interest of an ecclesiastical history attaching to it. Literally, it means a "blessing;" then, as in the LXX. of Gen. xxiii. 11, Judg. i. 15, it was used for the "gift," which is the outward token or accompaniment of a blessing. In liturgical language, as connected with the "cup of *blessing,*" it was applied—(1) to the consecrated bread and wine of the Lord's Supper generally; (2) specially to those portions which were reserved to be sent to the sick and other absentees; (3) when that practice fell into disuse, to the unconsecrated remains; and (4) to gifts of bread or cake to friends or the poor, as a residuum of the old distributions at the Agapæ, or Feasts of Charity.

bounty,[1] whereof ye had notice before,[2] that the same might be ready, as *a matter of* bounty, and not as *of* covetousness. (6) But this *I say*, He which soweth sparingly shall reap also sparingly; and he which soweth bountifully shall reap also bountifully. (7) Every man according as he purposeth in his heart, *so let him give;* not grudgingly, or of necessity: for God loveth a cheerful giver. (8) And God *is* able to make all grace abound toward you;[a] that ye, always having all sufficiency in all *things*, may abound to every good work: (9) (as it is written, He hath dispersed abroad;[b] he hath given to the poor: his righteousness remaineth for ever.

1 Gr. *blessing*.

2 Or, *which hath been so much spoken of before*.

a Prov. 11. 25; Rom. 12. 8; Ecclus. 35. 9.

b Ps. 112. 9.

---

**As a matter of bounty, and not as of covetousness.**—The bearing of the last word is not quite obvious. Probably what is meant is this:—"Let your gift be worthy of what you call it, a 'blessing' expressed in act, not the grudging gift of one who, as he gives, is intent on gaining some advantage through his seeming generosity." So understood, it expresses the same thought as Shakespeare's well-known lines:—

> "The quality of mercy is not strained,
>
> It blesseth him that gives and him that takes."

It is possible, however, that the word "covetousness" had been applied tauntingly to St. Paul himself, as always "asking for more," always "having his hand" (as is sometimes said of active organising secretaries in our own time) "in people's pockets," and that this is his answer to that taunt. The use of the corresponding verb in chaps. vii. 2; xii. 17, 18, is strongly in favour of this view. "Don't look on this business," he seems to say, "as a self-interested work of mine. Think of it as, in every sense of the word, a blessing both to givers and receivers."

(6) **He which soweth sparingly . . .**—It is interesting to note the occurrence of this thought in another Epistle of this period (Gal. vi. 7, 8).

**He which soweth bountifully . . .**—Literally, repeating the word before used, *he which soweth in blessings*. The obvious meaning of the passage is that a man "reaps," *i.e.*, gains, the reward of God's favour and inward satisfaction, not according to the quantitative value of the thing given, except so far as that is an indication of character, but according to the spirit and temper in which he has given it.

(7) **Every man according as he purposeth.**—The verb, which does not occur elsewhere in the New Testament, is used in its full ethical significance as indicating, not a passing impulse nor a vague wish, but a deliberate resolve, deciding both on the end and on the means for its attainment (Aristotle, *Eth. Nicom.* iii., c. 2). Such, St. Paul teaches, should be the purpose of the giver—not the outcome of a spent emotion, or a promise half-regretted, but formed with a clear well-defined perception of all attendant circumstances, and therefore neither "grudgingly," as regards amount, nor with reluctance, as giving under pressure.

**God loveth a cheerful giver.**—As in chap. viii. 21, so here, we have a distinct echo from the Book of Proverbs (xxii. 8) as it stands in the Greek version. In that version we find the following: "He that soweth wicked things shall reap evils, and shall complete the penalty of his deed. God blesseth a cheerful man and a giver, and shall complete" (in a good sense) "the incompleteness of his works." It is obvious that this differs much from the Hebrew, which is represented in the English version. and it is interesting as showing that St. Paul used the LXX., and habitually quoted from it, and not from the Hebrew. As coming so soon after the quotation from Prov. iii. 4 in chap. viii. 21, it seems to suggest that the Apostle had recently been studying that book, and that his mind was full of its teaching. As a law of action, it may be noted that the principle has a far wider range of application than that of simple alms-giving. Cheerfulness in visits of sympathy, in the daily offices of kindness, in the life of home, in giving instruction or advice—all come under the head of that which God approves and loves. So the greatest of Greek ethical teachers had refused the title of "liberal" to the man who gave without pleasure in the act of giving. The pain he feels proves that if he could he would rather have the money than do the noble action (Aristotle, *Eth. Nicom.* iv., c. 1).

(8) **God is able to make all grace abound toward you.**—The word "grace" must be taken with somewhat of the same latitude as in chap. viii. 6, 7, 19, including *every form of bounty*, as well as "grace," in its restricted theological sense: the means of giving, as well as cheerfulness in the act. He will bless the increase of those who give cheerfully, that they may have, not indeed the superfluity which ministers to selfish luxury, but the sufficiency with which all true disciples ought to be content. In the word "sufficiency," which occurs only here and in 1 Tim. vi. 6 ("godliness with *contentment*"), we have another instance of St. Paul's accurate use of the terminology of Greek ethical writers. To be independent, *self-sufficing*, was with them the crown of the perfect life; and Aristotle vindicates that quality for happiness as he defines it, as consisting in the activity of the intellect, and thus distinguished from wealth and pleasure, and the other accidents of life which men constantly mistook for it (*Eth. Nicom.* x., c. 7). At the time when St. Paul wrote it was constantly on the lips of Stoics. (Comp. the *Meditations* of Marcus Aurelius, iii. c. 11.)

(9) **As it is written, He hath dispersed abroad.**—The words are quoted from the LXX. version of Ps. cxii. 9. At first it might almost seem as if they were quoted in a different sense from the original, and applied, not to the giver of alms, but to God as the giver of all good, dispersing His bounty and showing His righteousness. There are, however, sufficient grounds for taking them in their true meaning here also. "The good man gives to the poor," the Psalmist had said; "but he is not impoverished by his gifts. His righteousness" (the word is used as it perhaps is in the better text in Matt. vi. 1—but see Note there—in the sense of alms-giving) "continues still and for ever." He can, *i.e.*, go on giving from a constantly replenished store. That this is the meaning is shown by verse 3 of the Psalm: "Wealth and riches shall be in his house, and his righteousness endureth for ever:" the latter clause corresponding to the former, according to the laws of parallelism in Hebrew poetry.

Chap. ix. 10—15. St. Paul's prayers and hopes as to the collection for the saints.

(10) Now he that ministereth seed to
the sower both minister
bread for *your* food,[a] and
multiply your seed sown,
and increase the fruits
of your righteousness ;)
(11) being enriched in every thing to all
bountifulness, which causeth through
us thanksgiving to God. (12) For the
administration of this service not only
supplieth the want of the saints, but
is abundant also by many thanks-
givings unto God; (13) whiles by the
experiment of this ministration they
glorify God for your professed subjec-
tion unto the gospel of Christ, and for
*your* liberal distribution unto them, and
unto all *men;* (14) and by their prayer
for you, which long after you for the
exceeding grace of God in you.
(15) Thanks *be* unto God for his unspeak-
able gift.

[a] Isa. 55. 10.

---

(10) **Now he that ministereth seed to the sower.**—Better, *he that giveth bounteously.* The Greek verb (*epichorêgein*) has a somewhat interesting history. Originally it expressed the act of one who undertook to defray the expenses of the chorus of a Greek theatre. As this was an act of somewhat stately generosity, the verb got a wider range, and was applied to any such act, and was so transferred in like manner by the Apostle, probably, as far as we can trace, for the first time, to the divine bounty. It may be noted that it was not so used by the LXX. translators. The word indeed occurs but once in that version, in Ecclus. xxv. 22 ("if a woman *maintain* her husband"). In its higher sense it becomes a somewhat favourite word with St. Paul (Gal. iii. 5; Col. ii. 19), and is used by St. Peter (2 Pet. i. 5, 11) after he had become acquainted with St. Paul's Epistles, and possibly enriched his vocabulary through them.

The phrase "seed to the sower" occurs, with a different verb, in Isa. lv. 10. In the words that follow, "the fruits of righteousness," there is an obvious reminiscence of Hos. x. 12, and Amos, vi. 12. The phrase occurs again in Phil. i. 11. The construction, according to the better MSS., varies somewhat from that of the Authorised version. *He that bounteously giveth seed to the sower and bread for food* (the beneficence of God thought of, as shown both in seed-time and harvest) *shall give bounteously, and multiply your seed, and increase the produce of your righteousness.* "Righteousness" is taken, as before, as specially presented under the aspect of alms-giving.

(11) **Being enriched in every thing.**—The context points primarily to temporal abundance, but we can scarcely think that the other thought of the spiritual riches that are found in Christ (chap. viii. 9) was absent from the Apostle's mind. On the word for "bountifulness" see Note on chap. viii. 2. The participles are not grammatically connected with the preceding sentence, but the meaning is sufficiently obvious.

**Which causeth through us thanksgiving to God.**—His thoughts are obviously travelling on to the time of his arrival at Jerusalem, to the announcement of the collected gifts of the Gentile churches at a solemn gathering of the Church there, to the thanksgiving which would then be offered.

(12) **For the administration of this service.**—The latter word (*leitourgia*) has, like that for "ministering" in verse 10, an interesting history. In classical Greek it stands for any public service rendered to the State. In the LXX. version it, and its cognate verb and adjective, are used almost exclusively of the ritual and sacrificial services of the Tabernacle and the Temple, as, *e.g.*, in Num. iv. 25; 1 Chron. xi. 13; xxvi. 30; and in this sense it appears in Luke i. 23; Heb. viii. 6; ix. 21; and with the same shade of meaning, used figuratively, in Phil. ii. 17. That meaning survives in the ecclesiastical term "liturgy," applied, as it was at first, exclusively to the service of the celebration of the Lord's Supper. Here, probably, the thought is implied that a large and liberal gift to Christ's poor, and for His sake, is the most acceptable of all forms of "service" in the liturgical sense of that word. So understood it implies the same truth as that stated in Jas. i. 27.

**Not only supplieth the want of the saints.**—Literally, *fills up the things that were lacking.* The wants of the "saints," *i.e.*, the disciples of Jerusalem, were, we must remember, very urgent. They had never quite recovered from the pressure of the famine foretold by Agabus (Acts xi. 28), and the lavish generosity of the first days of the Church (Acts ii. 44, 45; iv. 32) had naturally exhausted its resources.

**But is abundant also by many thanksgivings unto God.**—More accurately, *overflows, by means of many thanksgivings, to God:* the latter noun standing in a closer connection with the verb than the English version suggests. Some of the better MSS. give, *to Christ.*

(13) **Whiles by the experiment of this ministration they glorify God.**—The construction of the Greek sentence is again that of a participle which has no direct grammatical connection with what precedes, but the English version sufficiently expresses the meaning. *Test* would, perhaps, be a better word than "experiment." The word is the same as that rendered, with a needless variation, "experience" in Rom. v. 4, "trial" in 2 Cor. viii. 2, "proof" in 2 Cor. xiii. 3.

**Your professed subjection.**—The English version makes the not unfrequent mistake of merging the genitive in a somewhat weak adjective. Literally, *in your obedience to the confession of faith.* The latter noun is used in this sense in 1 Tim. vi. 12, 13; Heb. iii. 1; iv. 14. The word seems to have acquired a half-technical significance, like that which attaches to "faith" and "religion" used objectively.

**For your liberal distribution.**—The construction is the same as in the previous clause: *for the liberality of your contribution.*

(14) **And by their prayer for you, which long after you.**—The structure of the Greek is again ungrammatical, but the following gives a somewhat more accurate representation: *And while they long after you, in supplication for you, on account of the exceeding grace of God that rests on you.* He seems half lost in his anticipations of what will follow when he hands over the contributions of the Gentiles to the "saints" at Jerusalem. Their utterance of praise and thanksgiving will, he is sure, be followed by a yearning prayer of intercession for their benefactors.

(15) **Thanks be unto God for his unspeakable gift.**—So the section on the collection for the

Chap. x. 1—6. The boldness of the Apostle as warring with no carnal weapons.

A.D. 60.

CHAPTER X.—(1) Now I Paul myself beseech you by the meekness and gentleness of Christ, who in presence[1] *am* base among you, but being absent am bold toward you: (2) but I beseech *you*, that I may not be bold when I am present with that confidence, wherewith I think to be bold against some, which think[2] of us as if we walked according to the flesh. (3) For though we walk in the flesh, we do not war after the flesh: (4) (for the weapons of our warfare *are* not carnal, but mighty through God[3] to the pulling down of strong holds;) (5) casting down imaginations,[4] and every high thing that exalteth itself against the knowledge of God, and bringing into captivity every thought

1 Or, *in outward appearance.*

2 Or, *reckon.*

3 Or, *to God.*

4 Or, *reasonings.*

---

saints comes to its close. We are left to conjecture to what gift the Apostle refers: whether to the love of God as manifested in Christ, or to the spirit of love poured into men's hearts. The use of the word in the Acts (ii. 38; viii. 20; x. 45; xi. 17) is in favour of referring it to the gift of the Holy Ghost; that of Rom. v. 15, 17, to the gift of pardon or righteousness. Probably it did not enter into his thoughts to subject the jubilant utterance of praise to a minute analysis.

At this stage there was manifestly another pause, of greater or less length, in the act of dictating. Fresh thoughts of a different kind are working in his mind, and rousing feelings of a very different kind from those which had been just expressed. At last he again breaks silence and begins anew.

## X.

(1) **Now I Paul myself beseech you.**—His thoughts, as has been said, have travelled back to Corinth. The stinging words which Titus had reported to him (see Note on verse 10) vex his soul. He speaks in the tone of the suppressed indignation which shows itself in a keen incisive irony. The opening formula is one which he reserves as emphasising an exceptionally strong emotion (Gal. v. 2; Eph. iii. 1; Philem. verse 19).

**By the meekness and gentleness of Christ.**—On the precise ethical significance of the former word see Note on Matt. v. 5; on that of the second, on Acts xxiv. 4. The temper described by the latter is that of one who does not press his rights, but acts in the spirit of equitable concession. The use of the formula of adjuration implies (1) that he felt how the opponents of whom he is about to speak were lacking in those two excellencies; (2) that he could appeal to what they knew of the personal character of Jesus as possessing them. This knowledge, it is obvious, must have rested on a general acquaintance with the facts of the Gospel history, like that implied in his treatment of the Lord's Supper in 1 Cor. xi. 23—25; and of the Resurrection in 1 Cor. xv. 1—7; and in his reference to our Lord's teaching in Acts xx. 35.

**Who in presence am base among you.**—Literally, *in person—i.e.*, in personal appearance. Possibly, however, the translators may have used the word "presence" in this sense. So Bacon speaks of "dignity of presence." The fact that "outward appearance" is given in the margin as an alternative reading, suggests, however, that though they changed the word, they meant what Cranmer and the Geneva version had expressed by "when I am present with you." For "base," read *downcast*, or *of low estate.* We have already seen, in chap. vii. 6 a reference to the offensive word.

**But being absent am bold toward you.**—This also was one of the taunts. "It was easy to be bold at a distance; but would he have the courage to face them? Was not his delay in coming a proof that he was shirking that encounter?"

(2) **But I beseech you . . .**—There is, of course, an implied warning, almost a menace, in the entreaty. He would fain be spared the necessity for boldness when he and those of whom he speaks meet face to face; but if the necessity comes it will be the worse for them. They "reckon" him as walking "after the flesh," with low and selfish aims and tortuous arts. (Comp. chap. i. 17; Rom. viii. 12, 13; 1 Cor. i. 26.) He "reckons" that he has daring enough to confront those who take that estimate of him.

(3) **For though we walk in the flesh.**—The phrase is generally used by St. Paul for the simple fact of bodily existence, with all its incidental infirmities and trials, but, commonly, without implying sin, as "*after* the flesh" does (Gal. ii. 20; Phil. i. 22—24; 1 Tim. iii. 16). The thought of participating in the sin of which the body is the occasion is, however, very close to that of sharing its weakness; and the phrase appears with this sense in Rom. viii. 8, 9.

**We do not war after the flesh.**—Strictly, *we are not carrying on our campaign.* See Note on Luke iii. 14, where the same word is used. As so often in St. Paul's style, the word—especially any word like this, connected with the soldier's life—becomes the germ of an elaborate figurative imagery, almost of a parable.

(4) **For the weapons of our warfare . . .**—We learn from the earlier words of 1 Thess. v. 8, yet more from the later ones of Eph. vi. 11—16, what these were—the energies of spiritual powers given by the Eternal Spirit.

**To the pulling down of strong holds.**—The phrase is essentially military, used in the LXX. for the capture and destruction of fortresses (Lam. ii. 2; Prov. xxi. 22); "casting down the strength" (1 Macc. v. 65); "pulled down the fortress" (viii. 10). He speaks as if leading an attack on the strong defences of the powers of evil, possibly thinking of the great system of idolatry and impurity enthroned at Corinth and throughout the Empire, possibly of those of pride and obstinate rebellion in the hearts of his individual opponents. The context favours the latter interpretation. It has been suggested (Stanley, *in loc.*) that the Apostle's language may have been coloured by national memories of the wars against the Cilicians carried on by Pompeius, which ended in the reduction of one hundred and twenty fortresses and the capture of more than 10,000 prisoners.

(5) **Casting down imaginations.**—The participle is in agreement with the "*we* war not" of verse 3. In the Greek word rendered "imaginations," we have the noun derived from the verb rendered "think," or

to the obedience of Christ; (6) and having in a readiness to revenge all disobedience, when your obedience is fulfilled. (7) Do ye look on things after the outward appearance? If any man trust to himself that he is Christ's, let him of himself think this again, that, as he *is* Christ's, even so *are* we Christ's. (8) For though I should boast somewhat more of our authority, which the Lord hath given us for edification, and not for your destruction, I should not be ashamed: (9) that I may not seem as if I would terrify you by letters. (10) For *his* letters, say they, *are* weighty

Chap. x. 7—10. The Apostle's protest against being judged by appearances.

---

*reckon*, in verse 2. It would be better, perhaps, to carry on the continuity by rendering it *thoughts*, or even *reckonings*.

**Every high thing that exalteth itself.**—The noun probably belongs, like "stronghold," to the language of military writers, and indicates one of the rock fortresses, the

> "Tot congesta manu præruptis oppida saxis,"
> ["Towns piled high on rocks precipitous,"]
> —Virgil, *Georg.* i. 156.

which were so conspicuous in all ancient systems of defence.

**Against the knowledge of God.**—The parable and the interpretation are here obviously blended. The thoughts of men resist the knowledge of God as the stronghold of rebels resists the armies of the rightful king.

**Bringing into captivity every thought.**—The verb is used by St. Paul again in Rom. vii. 23; 2 Tim. iii. 6. There can be no doubt that "the obedience of Christ" means "obedience *to* Christ," and it had better, therefore, be so translated.

(6) **And having in a readiness to revenge all disobedience.**—The idiom, *having in a readiness*, is perhaps, somewhat too archaic, and it might be better to render *being ready*, or *holding ourselves ready.* The words that follow imply the thought that those with which the verse opens were somewhat too unqualified. When he spoke of "avenging all disobedience," he was not thinking of those to whom he writes, and whose repentance and obedience had filled him with so much joy (chap. vii. 6—13), but only of the rebellious remnant. He would wait till all had obeyed who were willing to obey. He does not indicate what form of vengeance he thought of taking, but we may think of some such severe discipline as that indicated by "delivering to Satan," in 1 Cor. v. 5; 1 Tim. v. 20, with a view, if it were possible, to their ultimate restoration. (Comp. chap. xiii. 3—10.)

(7) **Do ye look on things after the outward appearance?**—The Greek sentence may be taken either as interrogative, imperative, or indicative. The latter "ye look on things . . . " gives the most satisfactory meaning, as pressing home the charge on which he proceeds to dwell. He has, of course, the party of resistance in his thoughts, but he writes to the whole community, as influenced—some more and some less—by the tendency to attach undue weight to the outward accidents of those who claimed their allegiance rather than to that which was of the essence of all true Apostolic ministry.

**If any man trust to himself that he is Christ's . . .**—There cannot be the shadow of a doubt that the words refer to those whose watchword was "I am of Christ" (see Note on 1 Cor. i. 12), who laid claim to some special connection with Him, either as having been His personal disciples, or, at least, as having seen and known Him. In answer to that claim, with a half-ironical emphasis on "let him *think*," or "let him *reckon*" (comp. verses 2 and 5), he asserts that he is as truly His—*i.e.*, connected with Him, chosen by Him—as they were.

(8) **For though I should boast somewhat more of our authority.**—Literally, *somewhat too much*—perhaps as quoting a word that had been used of him. In referring to his "authority," it scarcely admits of question that he claims—as in 1 Cor. v. 5; 1 Tim. v. 20, and by implication in verse 6—the power to enforce that authority by a supernatural chastisement, as, *e.g.*, in the case of Elymas. He is anxious, however, having used the word "pulling down," or "destruction," to qualify his threat by the assertion that the power had been given him with a view, not "for destruction," but "for edification," or, to express the force of the antithesis more adequately, *for building up*. (Comp. 1 Cor. xiv. 12—26; Eph. iv. 12—16; and Notes on chap. xiii. 10.)

**I should not be ashamed.**—Better, *I shall not be ashamed.* He was quite sure, without any shadow of misgiving, that if he proceeded to the extreme step of delivering his opponents to Satan, the result which he contemplates will follow.

(9) **That I may not seem as if I would terrify you by letters.**—The logical sequence of thought is: "I say this" (*i.e.*, that my sentence of delivery to Satan will not be a hollow form) "in order that I may not seem to frighten you as with a bug-bear." This, it is clear from what follows, had been said. (Comp. the sneer in the next verse.) The use of the plural in this verse and that which follows is in favour of the hypothesis of a lost letter being referred to in 1 Cor. v. 9, but does not absolutely prove it.

(10) **For his letters, say they, are weighty and powerful.**—Allusive references to what had been said of him at Corinth have already appeared frequently. Here, for the first time, we have the very words quoted. The scorn conveyed in them had wounded the Apostle's sensitive nature like a poisoned arrow; and we have here the nearest approach which the New Testament presents to the passionate complaints poured forth by some of the Psalmists of the Old (Pss. lxix., cix.). We note the common element of a burning indignation under the sense of wrong. We note also the absence from the Apostle's feelings of the maledictory element which is so prominent in theirs. The "meekness and gentleness of Christ" had not been without their effect in tempering even the most vehement emotions.

The great majority of MSS. give the verb in the singular: "For his letters, *saith he* . . ." This may be taken, like the French *on dit*, as used impersonally, and possibly this is the meaning which the English version was intended to convey. The context, however, the definite "such a man as that" of the next verse, is obviously decisive. St. Paul has in his thoughts here, and through the rest of the chapter, one conspicuous antagonist,—the head of a clique and cabal of opponents.

and powerful; but *his* bodily presence
*is* weak, and *his* speech contemptible.
(11) Let such an one think this, that,
such as we are in word
by letters when we are absent,
such *will we be* also
in deed when we are present.
(12) For we dare
not make ourselves of the
number, or compare ourselves
with some that commend
themselves: but they measuring
themselves by themselves, and comparing
themselves among themselves,
are not wise.[1] (13) But we will not
boast of things without *our* measure,
but according to the measure of the
rule[2] which God hath distributed to
us, a measure to reach even unto you.
(14) For we stretch not ourselves beyond
*our measure*, as though we reached not
unto you: for we are come as far as

Chap. x. 11–18. Contrast between the boast of the Apostle and that of the rivals who have intruded into his sphere of labour.

1 Or, *understand it not.*

2 Or, *line.*

---

**His bodily presence is weak, and his speech contemptible.**—As with other antithetical epigrams, the sting was found in the tail. It would seem all but incredible that any doubt could ever have been expressed as to the fact that the words point to physical infirmities. They can, indeed, refer to nothing else. For the tradition as to the Apostle's personal appearance, see *Excursus* at the end of the Acts of the Apostles. The "contemptible speech" (literally, *speech of no value; counted as nought*) may refer either to a weak or unmusical voice, or to the absence of the rhetorical artifices, the exordium, divisions, perorations, in which Greek audiences delighted. It may be noted that these words give a fresh significance to a remarkable passage in an Epistle written, in the judgment of many critics, within a few weeks of this. "You," he says to the Galatians (Gal. iv. 13, 14), "though I came to you with that infirmity of the flesh which others sneer at, the chronic trial of my life, you did not contemn" (the self-same verb as that used here) "nor loathe me." There is manifestly a contrast present to his thoughts between the mean insults of his rivals at Corinth and the affection which the Galatians had once manifested, and which made their subsequent alienation all the more painful to him.

(11) **Such will we be also.**—As a verb of some kind must be supplied, it would be better to give the present: *Such are we.* It is not so much a threat of what will happen in a particular instance as a statement of the general consistent character of his life.

(12) **We dare not make ourselves of the number.**—The last five words give the meaning of one Greek verb (*enkrînai*=to insert), the sound of which seems immediately to suggest the cognate verb (*synkrînai*=to compare). It is, of course, hard to convey the half-playful assonance in English. In "some that commend themselves" we note a reference to the charge of self-commending, which he has already noticed four times (chaps. iii. 1; iv. 2; v. 12; vii. 11). Before he had defended himself against the charge; now he retorts it on his opponents. In "we dare" we trace a reference to the charge of cowardice, as in verse 2.

**Measuring themselves by themselves.**—The Greek MSS. present many various readings, some of the best MSS. omitting "are not wise, but," and some giving "not boasting" for "we will not boast;" and the Greek text, on any reading, presents a grammatical difficulty, arising from the fact that the last word may be either the third person plural of a verb in the indicative present, or a participle in the dative case, agreeing with "themselves." It is hardly necessary to discuss here the various possible constructions rising out of the combination of these phenomena. The English version gives, it is believed, substantially the meaning of the original. In the very act of saying, with a touch of irony, that he will not compare himself with the rival teachers, the Apostle virtually does compare himself. And the point he makes is that they instituted no such comparison. They were their own standards of excellence. Each was "*amator sui sine rivali.*" Collectively, they formed what has been described in the language of modern literary history as a "Mutual Admiration Society." Of all such self-admiration—one might almost say, of all such *autolatry*—St. Paul declares, what the experience of all ages attests, that they who practise it "are not wise." They lose, as the Greek verb more definitely expresses it, all power of discernment.

(13) **But we will not boast of things without our measure.**—The words imply, of course, that his opponents were doing this. He refers in it to the *concordat* established between himself and Barnabas, on the one hand, and Peter, James, and John on the other, to which he refers in Gal. ii. 9. He had not transgressed the terms of that *concordat* by thrusting himself upon a Church which had been founded by one of the Apostles of the circumcision. He had gone, step by step, seeking "fresh fields and pastures new," till he had reached Corinth as, at present, the farthest limit of his work. In that apportionment of work, though it was a compact with human teachers, he saw the guidance of God; his opponents, on the other hand, had systematically violated it. They had come to the Church of Antioch, which had been founded by Paul and Barnabas (Acts xv. 1); they had followed in his footsteps in Galatia (see *Introduction to Epistle to the Galatians*); they were now stirring up strife and disloyalty at Corinth. We note as an undesigned coincidence that a few weeks or months later, as in Rom. xv. 19, he had preached the gospel as far as Illyricum, but this was during the time immediately following on the despatch of this Epistle, during which, on his way to Corinth, whence he wrote to Rome, he had "gone over those parts, and given them much exhortation" (Acts xx. 2).

(14) **For we stretch not ourselves . . . as though we reached not unto you.**—Some of the better MSS. omit the negative, and then the sentence must be taken as a question: "Are we over-reaching" (*i.e.*, transgressing boundaries), "as though you were not within the limit assigned to us?"

**For we are come as far as to you also.**—The word for "come" (not the usual verb) is one which almost always in the New Testament, as in classical Greek, carries with it the sense of anticipation, "getting before others." (See Note on Matt. xii. 28.) And this is obviously St. Paul's meaning. "We were the first to come," he says, "as working within our limits; the very fact that we did so come being a proof of it." They (his rivals) came afterwards, and were intruders.

to you also in *preaching* the gospel of
Christ: (15) not boasting of things with-
out *our* measure, *that is*, of other men's
labours; but having hope, when your
faith is increased, that we shall be en-
larged[1] by you according to our rule
abundantly, (16) to preach the gospel in
the *regions* beyond you, *and* not to
boast in another man's line[2] of things
made ready to our hand. (17) But he
that glorieth,[a] let him glory in the Lord.
(18) For not he that commendeth him-
self is approved, but whom the Lord
commendeth.

A.D. 60.

1 Or, *magnified in you.*

3 Or, *you do bear with me.*

2 Or, *rule.*

a Jer. 9. 24; 1 Cor. 1. 31.

CHAPTER XI.—(1) Would to God ye
could bear with me a little
in *my* folly: and indeed
bear[3] with me. (2) For
I am jealous over you
with godly jealousy: for I
have espoused you to one

Chap. xi. 1—6. The anxious jealousy of St. Paul lest his disciples should be perverted.

---

On Corinth, as the then limit of his work, see Note on the preceding verse.

(15) **Not boasting of things without our measure . . .**—The words are not merely defensive. He presses home the charge of intrusion. They, not he, were finding ground for their boasts in other men's labours. The context leads, however, to the conclusion that it was a charge that had been brought against him. They had spoken of him as pushing on from point to point, as with a measureless ambition. Perhaps the fact that he had worked at Antioch, where the gospel had been preached by men of Cyprus and Cyrene (Acts xi. 20), at Troas, where it had been preached by St. Luke (see Notes on chap. ii. 12; Acts xvi. 8), to the Romans whom he found at Corinth, and who, like Aquila and Priscilla, had been already converted (see Notes on Acts xviii. 2), were thought to give a colour to the charge that he was boasting in other men's labours.

**Having hope, when your faith is increased.**—The verb is in the present tense, and should be translated, *as your faith grows.* The words are spoken in the spirit of one—

"Nil actum reputans si quid superesset agendum"

["Who thinks nought done while aught remains to do"]—

who seeks for fresh provinces to annex to the territory of his king. The growth of their faith will give him fresh courage, perhaps also fresh resources. But what does he mean by his "hope that we shall be enlarged according to" (or, perhaps, *in relation to*) "our rule"? The words seem to imply something more than a mere extension of labours, and suggest the probability that in his journey to Jerusalem, with the large and liberal gifts of the Gentile churches, he had an intention, here half-avowed, to endeavour to modify the terms of the *concordat* referred to in Gal. ii. 9, and to get the sanction of the Church of Jerusalem for his mission work at Rome: though there the gospel had been preached by others, and it was, primarily, at least, one of the Churches of the Circumcision. It will be seen that this supposition explains better than any other the apologetic tone of Rom. xv. 20—29. It was his reluctance even to appear to build on another man's foundation that had hitherto kept him from them. He does not intend to appear, when he comes, in the character of the founder of this Church, or even as building the superstructure, but only as a friend, seeking mutual help and counsel. Spain is his goal. He takes Rome as a parenthesis. But he is going to Jerusalem, and he hopes that the difficulty which has hitherto hindered him will be removed.

(16) **To preach the gospel in the regions beyond you.**—It is clear, from Rom. xv. 19—24, that he is thinking (1) of Western Greece, (2) of Rome, (3, and chiefly) of Spain. There, apparently, he could hope to preach the gospel without even the risk of its being said that he was building on another man's foundation.

**And not to boast in another man's line . . .**—The words like those of verse 15, are at once an answer to a charge and a *tu quoque* retort. "Spain! Illyricum!" he seems to say within himself. "Will you say that I am transgressing boundaries and working on another man's lines there? Can you say that you are free from that charge in your work at Corinth?"

(17) **He that glorieth, let him glory in the Lord.**—Better, *He that boasteth,* the English translators having again yielded to their besetting weakness for variation. On the general meaning of the phrase, which has been used before, see Note on 1 Cor. i. 31. Here it has a more special force. "To boast in the Lord" was to boast as in the sight of Christ of that of which the boaster thought as done, not by himself, but by Christ as dwelling in him.

(18) **For not he that commendeth himself is approved.**—Again, as in verse 12 and five earlier passages (see reference there), we trace the impression which the stinging taunt had left on St. Paul's mind. In the word "approved" there is possibly a reference to what had been said in 1 Cor. xi. 19. He had meant something more by it than meeting with men's approval.

## XI.

(1) **Would to God.**—As the words "to God" are not in the Greek, it would be better to treat them as the general expression of a wish: *Would that ye could bear.*

**Ye could bear with me a little in my folly.**—There are two catch-words, as it were, which characterise the section of the Epistle on which we are now entering: one is of "bearing with," or "tolerating," which occurs five times (verses 1, 4, 19, 20), and "folly," which, with its kindred "fool," is repeated not less than eight times (verses 1, 16, 17, 19, 21; chap. xii. 6, 11). It is impossible to resist the inference that here also we have the echo of something which Titus had reported to him as said by his opponents at Corinth. Their words, we must believe, had taken some such form as this: "We really can bear with him no longer; his folly is becoming altogether intolerable."

**And indeed bear with me.**—The words, as the marginal reading indicates, admit of being taken either as imperative or indicative. Either gives an adequate meaning, but the latter, it is believed, is preferable. It is one of the many passages in which we trace the working of conflicting feelings. Indignation prompts him to the wish, "Would that ye could bear." Then he thinks of the loyalty and kindness which he had experienced at their hands, and he adds a qualifying clause to soften the seeming harshness of the words that had just passed from his lips: "And yet (why should I say this? for) ye do indeed habitually bear with me."

(2) **For I am jealous over you . . .**—The word is used with the same sense as in the nearly contemporary

husband, that I may present *you as* a
chaste virgin to Christ. (3) But I fear, lest
by any means, as the serpent beguiled
Eve through his subtilty, so your minds
should be corrupted from the simplicity
that is in Christ. (4) For if he that
cometh preacheth another Jesus, whom
we have not preached, or *if* ye receive
another spirit, which ye have not re-
ceived, or another gospel, which ye have
not accepted, ye might well bear with
*him.* (5) For I suppose I was not a
whit behind the very chiefest apostles.
(6) But though *I be* rude in speech, yet
not in knowledge; but we have been
thoroughly made manifest among you

---

passage of Gal. iv. 17, and the whole passage may be paraphrased thus: "I court your favour with a jealous care, which is not a mere human affection, but after the pattern of that of God." There is probably an implied contrast between the true jealousy which thus worked in his soul and the false jealousy of which he speaks in the passage just referred to.

**For I have espoused you . . .**—The word is not found elsewhere in the New Testament. It appears in this sense in the LXX. version of Prov. xix. 14: "A man's wife is espoused to him from the Lord." Strictly speaking, it is used of the act of the father who gives his daughter in marriage; and this, rather than the claim to act as "the friend of the bridegroom" (see Note on John iii. 29), is probably the idea here. He claims the office as the "father" of the Corinthian Church (1 Cor. iv. 15). The underlying idea of the comparison is that the Church at large, and every separate portion of it, is as the bride of Christ. On the earlier appearances of this thought, see Notes on Matt. xxii. 2; xxv. 1; John iii. 29; and, for its more elaborated forms, on Eph. v. 25—32; Rev. xix. 7—9; xxi. 2, 9). What the Apostle now urges is that it is as natural for him to be jealous for the purity of the Church which owes its birth to him, as it is for a father to be jealous over the chastity of the daughter whom he has betrothed as to a kingly bridegroom.

(3) **But I fear, lest by any means, as the serpent . . .**—An allusive reference to the history of Gen. iii., which meets us again in 1 Tim. iii. 13—15. St. Paul either takes for granted that the disciples at Corinth will recognise the "serpent" as the symbol of the great Tempter, as in Rev. xii. 9; or, without laying stress on that identification, simply compares the work of the rival teachers to that of the serpent. The word for "subtilty" is not that used in the LXX. of Gen. iii. 1. Literally, it expresses the mischievous activity of a man who is *capable de tout*—ready, as we say, for anything.

**Corrupted from the simplicity that is in Christ.**—The Greek for "corrupt" has the same special sense as in chap. vii. 2, as implying something which is incompatible with the idea of purity. The Apostle seeks, as it were, for a chastity of mind as well as of body. Many of the better MSS. give, *from the simplicity* (*i.e.*, singleness of affection) *and chastity*; and some, *chastity and simplicity*.

(4) **For if he that cometh preacheth another Jesus.**—The singular points, like the "any man," "such an one," of chap. x. 7, 11, to an individual teacher who had made himself conspicuously prominent. The words throw light on Gal. i. 7, 8. The false teachers in Galatia and those at Corinth were doing the same thing. In the absence of fuller knowledge of what they taught, it is difficult to define accurately what precise form of error is alluded to. One thing, at least, is clear—that their Jesus was not his Jesus—not the Friend and Brother of mankind who had died for all men, that He might reconcile them to God. Reasoning from probabilities, we may, perhaps, infer that they spoke of Him as the head of a Jewish kingdom, requiring circumcision and all the ordinances of the Law as a condition of admission to it.

**If ye receive another spirit.**—Better, *a different spirit*, as showing that the word is not the same as in the previous clause. The words point, it is clear, to a counterfeit inspiration, perhaps like that of those who had interrupted the praises of the Church with the startling cry, "Anathema to Jesus!" (See Note on 1 Cor. xii. 3.) Such as these were the "false prophets" of 2 Pet. ii. 1; 1 John iv. 3, simulating the phenomena of inspiration, perhaps thought of by the Apostles as really acting under the inspiration of an evil spirit.

**Which ye have not received.**—Better, *did not receive*, as referring definitely to the time of their conversion.

**Another gospel, which ye have not accepted.**—Better, as before, *a different gospel, which ye did not accept*—*i.e.*, different from that which you did accept from me. His gospel, he seems to say, was one of pardon through faith working by love: theirs was based on the old Pharisaic lines of works, ritual, ceremonial and moral precepts, standing in their teaching on the same footing.

**Ye might well bear with him.**—Better, the adverb being emphatic, and intensely ironical, *nobly would ye bear with him.* He means, of course, that they have done much more than tolerate the preachers of the false gospel, and have paid them an extravagant deference. On a like use of irony in our Lord's teaching, see Note on Mark vii. 9.

(5) **For I suppose I was not a whit behind the very chiefest apostles.**—The verb with which the sentence opens is the same as the "I think," "I reckon," which characterises these chapters, and which, being characteristic, ought to be retained. *I reckon I have not fallen short of those apostles-extraordinary.* The whole tone of the passage ought to have made it impossible for any commentator to imagine that the words referred to Peter and James and John as the pillars of the Church of Jerusalem (Gal. ii. 9). Of them he speaks, even in his boldest moments, with respect, even where respect is mingled with reproof. He is glad to remember how they gave to him and Barnabas the right hand of fellowship. He presents himself at Jerusalem a few months after writing these words, and almost submissively follows the counsel which James gives him (Acts xxi. 26). It is, accordingly, simply the insanity of controversy to imagine that these words have any bearing on the question of the primacy of St. Peter. Those whom he holds up to scorn with an almost withering irony, as "apostles-extraordinary" (he coins a word which literally means, "these *extra-special* or *over-extra* apostles"), are the false teachers, claiming to stand in a special relation to Christ, to be His Apostles—perhaps, also, to have a double title to the name, as delegates of the Church of Jerusalem. Of these he speaks more fully in verse 13.

(6) **But though I be rude in speech.**—The word

in all things. (7) Have I committed an offence in abasing myself that ye might be exalted, because I have preached to you the gospel of God freely? (8) I robbed other churches, taking wages *of* *them,* to do you service. (9) And when I was present with you, and wanted, I was chargeable to no man: for that which was lacking to me the brethren which came from Macedonia supplied: and in all *things* I have kept myself from being burdensome unto

Chap. xi. 7—15. St. Paul's defence against the charge of slighting the Corinthians by not receiving their gifts.

---

for "rude" is the same as that translated as "unlearned" in 1 Cor. xiv. 23, 24. This, then, had also been said of him by some at Corinth. It might seem at first as if the contemptuous criticism was likely to have come from the Hellenic or paganising party of culture, who despised the Apostle because he was without the polish and eloquence of the rhetoric in which they delighted. The context, however, makes it clear that the opponents now under the lash are the Judaising teachers, the "apostles-extraordinary." They apparently affected to despise him because he had abandoned, or had never mastered, the subtleties of Rabbinic casuistry, the wild allegories of Rabbinic interpretation. "He talks," we hear them saying, "of others as 'laymen,' or 'unlearned.' What right has he so to speak who is practically but a 'layman' himself? How can a man who is cutting and stitching all day be a 'doctor of the law'? *Ne sutor ultra crepidam.*" Side by side with the recognition of the dignity of labour in some Jewish proverbs (such, *e.g.*, as that the father who did not teach his son to work taught him to be a thief), there was among the later Rabbis something like the feeling of an aristocracy of scholarship. Even the Son of Sirach, after describing the work of the ploughman and the carpenter and the potter, excludes them from the higher life of wisdom. "They shall not be sought for in public counsel . . . they cannot declare justice and judgment; and they shall not be found where parables are spoken" (Ecclus. xxxviii. 33). The word for "rude" was probably used as the equivalent for the Hebrew term by which the Pharisees held up the working classes to contempt as "the people of the earth."

**But we have been throughly made manifest among you in all things.**—The readings vary, some of the better MSS. giving the active form of the verb, *having made (it) manifest in everything among all men.* The apparent awkwardness of having a transitive verb without an object probably led to the substitution of the passive participle.

(7) **Have I committed an offence** (literally, *a sin*) **in abasing myself . . ?**—The rival teachers apparently boasted of their disinterestedness. "They didn't come for what they could get." St. Paul, we know, more than most men, had acted on the law of which they boasted as their special distinction, and in 1 Cor. ix. 1—18, in the discussion on the question of eating things sacrificed to idols, had dwelt with a pardonable fulness on his own conduct in this matter, as an example of foregoing an abstract right for the sake of a greater good. His enemies were compelled to admit this as far as his life at Corinth was concerned; but they had detected what they looked on as a grave inconsistency. He had accepted help from the churches of Macedonia (verse 9), and in this they found ground for a two-fold charge: "He wasn't above taking money from other churches—he was only too proud to take it from that of Corinth;" and this was made matter of personal offence. To take money at all was mean; not to take it from them was contemptuous.

He does not deny the facts. He repeats the irritating epithet, "abasing myself"; he adds the familiar antithesis (Matt. xxiii. 12; Luke i. 52; xiv. 11; xviii. 11), "Yes, but I did it that you might be exalted," perhaps with reference to elevation in spiritual knowledge, perhaps, because the fact that he laboured for them without payment was the greatest proof of disinterested love for them which could be given.

(8) **I robbed other churches, taking wages of them.**—The word for wages—strictly *rations*, or wages in kind, rather than in money—is found in Luke iii. 14; Rom. vi. 23; 1 Cor ix. 7. Its use in the last-named passage had, perhaps, given occasion for a sneer. "He too can take wages when it suits his purpose." From St. Paul's point of view, if what he had received had been wages at all, he had been guilty of an act of spoliation. He had received wages from one employer while he was acting in the service of another.

(9) **I was chargeable to no man.**—There is no doubt that this gives substantially the meaning of the Greek word, but the word is a very peculiar one, and has a history which, as throwing light on the sources of St. Paul's phraseology, and his character as shown in his use of it, is not without interest. The verb (*katanarkaô*) is not found elsewhere in the New Testament, nor in the LXX. versions of the Old, nor, indeed, in any known Greek author, except Hippocrates. Jerome describes it as belonging to the *patois* of Cilicia, which, if true, would be interesting; but he gives no proof of it (*Ep. ad Aglaia*), and the statement must be treated as unproven. The history which we are about to trace, tends, however, to confirm it as a probable conjecture. The root of the verb is found in the noun *narkè*, which is used (1) for "numbness," or "torpor" (a sense found in our "narcotic"), and (2) as the name of a fish of the torpedo genus, causing numbness by its contact with the human body (Aristotle, *Anim. Hist.* vi. 10). The verb derived from the noun is accordingly used by Hippocrates and Galen in the sense of "being benumbed," or causing numbness. (See Foesius, *Lexic. Hippocrat. s.v.* ναρκή.) As used here, it takes its place as a bold figurative expression. To benumb any one, was to exhaust him, to drain him of his vitality by pressing on him, and, as it were, living upon him. St. Paul accordingly means, in using the word, to say, "I didn't drain you of your resources—did not live upon you." An analogous similitude is found in Shakespeare's lines:—

> "That now he was
> The ivy which had hid my princely trunk,
> And suck'd my verdure out on't"
> —*Tempest*, i. 2.

Our modern phrase which speaks of one man as "sponging" on another implies a like metaphor. In the word "parasitic" as applied to plants and animals, we have an inverted transfer of the same idea from the incidents of man's social life to that of lower organisms. As a word belonging, through Hippocrates, to the recognised terminology of physicians, it takes its place in the vocabulary which St. Paul may be

you, and *so* will I keep *myself*. (10) As
the truth of Christ is in me, no man
shall stop me of this boasting[1] in
the regions of Achaia. (11) Wherefore?
because I love you not? God knoweth.
(12) But what I do, that I will do, that I
may cut off occasion from them which
desire occasion; that wherein they
glory, they may be found even as we.
(13) For such *are* false apostles, deceit-
ful workers, transforming themselves
into the apostles of Christ. (14) And
no marvel; for Satan himself is
transformed into an angel of light.

[1] Gr. *this boasting shall not be stopped in me.*

---

supposed to have derived from St. Luke (see *Introduction to St. Luke's Gospel*, Vol. I., p. 239), and which the fame of Tarsus as a medical school may also have made more or less familiar, as Jerome states, in the conversational idioms of Cilicia.

**The brethren which came from Macedonia supplied.**—Not "which came," but *when they came.* The Acts of the Apostles present no record of any such supply, but Phil. iv. 15 presents an interesting and confirmatory coincidence. The Philippians had sent supplies to him twice at Thessalonica, and it was a natural sequel to this that they should send to him also at Corinth. The Apostle may well have accepted what they thus sent, and yet have thought his acceptance perfectly compatible with his boast that he was not preaching at Corinth for the sake of gain (1 Cor. ix. 16—18). He was not to be robbed of whatever credit attached to his working for his own livelihood at Corinth and elsewhere, by any sneers which had that acceptance for their starting-point.

**And so will I keep myself.**—It adds to the interest of this declaration to remember that St. Paul had acted on this principle both at Ephesus, which he had just left (Acts xx. 34), and in the Macedonian churches which he was now visiting (2 Thess. iii. 8). The future tense, obviously points to his resolution to continue to act on the same lines during his promised visit to Corinth.

(10) **As the truth of Christ is in me . .**—The formula is almost, though not quite, of the nature of an oath. He speaks here, as in Rom. ix. 1, in the consciousness that the truth of Christ (the objective sense of the truth revealed in Christ seems almost merged in the subjective sense of the truthfulness that was of the essence of His nature) dwells in him, and that therefore he cannot but speak "the truth, the whole truth, and nothing but the truth."

**No man shall stop me of this boasting.**—Literally, *This boast shall not be stopped for me.* The verb for "stop" means primarily to "hedge round," or "fence." In the New Testament, as in Rom. iii. 19, it is always used of "stopping the mouth." Here, with something like a personification, he says that his boast shall not have its mouth thus sealed.

**In the region of Achaia.**—The word (*klima*) is peculiar to St. Paul among the writers of the New Testament (Rom. xv. 23; Gal. i. 21). Like our word "climate," which is derived from it, it was originally a term of science, and had passed gradually into colloquial usage. He names the province and not the city—probably to include Cenchreæ. There is no evidence of his having preached in any other locality south of the Isthmus of Corinth.

(11) **Because I love you not . .**—This then had been said. Some of the Corinthians were jealous, or affected to be jealous, of the preference shown to the Macedonians in receiving gifts from them. With an emphatic appeal to Him who reads the secrets of men's hearts, he disclaims that imputation.

(12) **That I may cut off occasion from them which desire occasion.**—It lies on the surface that the "occasion," or *opening for attack,* which his opponents had thus desired, was one against which he guarded himself by not taking money. They boasted of their own disinterestedness. They taunted him with his meanness in taking money from the Macedonian churches. The Apostle wishes, therefore, by persisting in his line of conduct, in spite of the appeals of a real or affected jealousy, to place himself on the same level with them, them on the same level with himself. The comparison between them must rest, he says, on other grounds. This seems the only tenable and coherent interpretation; nor is there any force in the objection which has been urged against it, that there is no evidence that the rival teachers did teach gratuitously. If this is a natural inference from St. Paul's language, and there is no evidence to the contrary, that is surely evidence enough. It may be added, however, that there is at least in favour of the interpretation here given, the evidence of antecedent probability. It was likely that those who claimed to be in some special sense followers of Christ, would at least affect to act on the words of Christ, "Freely ye have received, freely give." (See Note on Matt. x. 8.) It was likely that those who, from another point of view, were representatives of the scribes of Judaism, should at least affect to act as the noblest of those scribes had acted, and to teach, not for payment, but for the love of teaching. That it was an affectation, and not a reality, we shall hereafter see reason to believe.

(13) **For such are false apostles . . .**—St. Paul's estimate of the character of his rivals is now given in unsparing language as the reason why he desires to deprive them of any claim which may give them an adventitious superiority to him. In the term "false apostles" we have the explanation of the "apostles-extraordinary" of verse 5. These "*crafty* workers" were carrying on a system of imposture, trying to assume the character of being, in a higher sense than he was, "Apostles of Christ." This again throws light both on the words "if any man trusts that he is Christ's" of chap. x. 7, and on the "I am of Christ" of 1 Cor. i. 12.

(14) **For Satan himself is transformed into an angel of light.**—The present tense of the original excludes the thought that reference is made to any special incident (such as the appearance of Satan among "the sons of God," of Job. i. 6) recorded in the Old Testament, or in tradition. The thought is rather that Satan is ever so transforming himself. If we are to look for any special allusion, we may find a possible explanation in the words "though we, or an angel from heaven," in Gal. i. 8. They suggest the thought, as at least a probable inference, that the Judaising teachers had claimed the authority of an angelic message for the gospel which they preached, and set this against the authority of the angelic visions which St. Luke had recorded in the case of Cornelius (Acts x. 2). It is probable, we may add, that the Christ-party at Corinth,

(15) Therefore *it is* no great thing if his
ministers also be transformed as the
ministers of righteousness; whose end
shall be according to their works.
(16) I say again, Let no man think
me a fool; if otherwise,
yet as a fool receive[1] me,
that I may boast myself a
little. (17) That which I
speak, I speak *it* not after
the Lord, but as it were foolishly,
in this confidence of boasting. (18) See-
ing that many glory after the flesh,
I will glory also. (19) For ye
suffer fools gladly, seeing ye *your-
selves* are wise. (20) For ye suffer,
if a man bring you into bondage,
if a man devour *you*, if a man
take *of you*, if a man exalt him-
self, if a man smite you on the

Chap. xi. 16—21. Ironical defence against the charge of insanity.

1 Or, *suffer*.

---

as distinct from that of Cephas, had affinities with the Jewish sect of the Essenes, and they, we know, were addicted to the worship of angels (Jos. *Wars*, ii. 8, § 6), and made much of revelations conveyed through their ministry. On this supposition St. Paul may, in his allusive way, mean to imply that they were mistaking a satanic for an angelic apparition. Something of the kind is obviously implied in the stress which St. Paul lays on his own visions and revelations in chap. xii. 1.

(15) **If his ministers also be transformed as the ministers of righteousness.**—The words seem to point to one of the special characteristics of the Apostle's rivals. They represented themselves as the preachers of a righteousness which was, they asserted, neglected in St. Paul's teaching. They claimed the authority of one who was known as James the Just, or Righteous, and who had insisted emphatically on the necessity of a righteousness showing itself in act. They presented themselves as a kind of revival of the Chasidim, or righteous ones. (See Note on Acts ix. 13.) It may be noted that the latter developments of the same school, as seen in the Clementine *Homilies* and *Recognitions*, present, in the midst of much that is both false and malignant, an almost ostentatiously high standard of morality.

**Whose end shall be according to their works.**—What the works were is stated, or implied, in verse 20. Here he is content to rest on the eternal law of God's government, that what a man sows that shall he also reap. The abruptness with which the next verse opens indicates that here again there was a pause in the dictation of the letter. After an interval—during which, led by the last words he had spoken, his thoughts had travelled to the contrast between their works, of which they boasted so loudly, and his own—he begins again, half-indignant at the necessity for self-assertion which they have forced upon him, aware that all that had been said of his "insane" habit of "commending himself" was likely to be said again, and yet feeling that he must once for all remind the Corinthians of what he had done and suffered, and then leave them to judge between the rival claims.

(16) **I say again, Let no man think me a fool . . .**—The stinging word is repeated from verse 1. He protests against the justice of the taunt. He pleads that, even if they think him "insane" (this, rather than mere foolishness, is probably the meaning of the word), they will give him the attention which, even in that case, most men would give—which they, at least, were giving to men to whom that term might far more justly be applied.

(17) **I speak it not after the Lord, but as it were foolishly.**—Better, *in foolishness;* as keeping up the emphatic repetition of the same word in the English as in the Greek. From one point of view the distinction drawn is the same as that which we find in 1 Cor. vii. 6, 10, 12. There is, however, a marked difference in the subject-matter of the two cases. There he distinguishes a private opinion from a principle or rule which he feels to be divine. Here he draws the line of demarcation between human feelings and a divine inspiration. It is, of course, easy to raise questions which would be hard, if they were not also frivolous and foolish. Are we to class what he places on the lower side of the boundary-line as inspired or uninspired teaching? If the former, are we not contradicting what he writes as inspired? If the latter, are we not depriving what follows of the authority of an inspired writing? Are we not, in so doing, admitting the principle of recognising a human element mingling with the divine in other parts of Scripture as well as this? The answer to these questions, so far as they need an answer, is best found in taking St. Paul's words in their plain and natural sense, believing that his words have just the authority which he claims for them, and no more. Speaking apart from these questions, there is something almost pathetic in the consciousness which he feels that self-vindication can never, as such, come from the Spirit of God, and that it is, at the best, a pardonable human weakness. It is not wrong, or else his conscience would have forbidden it. It is not the note of the highest or noblest temper, or else he would have felt the Spirit's guidance in it.

(18) **Seeing that many glory after the flesh.**—To glory, or *boast*, after the flesh, as interpreted by chap. v. 16 (where see Note), is to lay stress on things which are the accidents of the spiritual life, not of its true essence—on descent, prerogatives, rank, reputation, and the like. There is a touch half of irony, half of impatience, in the way in which the Apostle says that he too will for once descend to their level and do as they do.

(19) **Ye suffer fools gladly, seeing ye yourselves are wise.**—He falls back into the strain of irony of 1 Cor. iv. 8—10, to which, indeed, the whole passage presents a striking parallelism. He assumes that in their serene, self-complacent wisdom they will be willing to tolerate even those whom they look upon as half-insane. He drives the sarcasm home by urging that they tolerate those who are morally in a far worse condition.

(20) **For ye suffer, if a man bring you into bondage.**—Every word in the sentence clearly points to something that Titus had told him of the action of these rival teachers. They reproduced, in their worst form, the vices of the Pharisaism of Palestine (Matt. xxiii. 4, 14, 25). They enslaved the consciences of men (the same word is used of the same class of men in Gal. ii. 4) by pressing on them an iron code of rules which left no room for the free play of conscience and

face. (21) I speak as concerning re-
proach, as though we
had been weak. How-
beit whereinsoever any is
bold, (I speak foolishly,)
I am bold also. (22) Are
they Hebrews? so *am* I.
Are they Israelites? so *am* I. Are
they the seed of Abraham? so *am* I.
(23) Are they ministers of Christ? (I
speak as a fool) I *am* more; in la-
bours more abundant, in stripes above
measure, in prisons more frequent, in
deaths oft. (24) Of the Jews five

Chap. xi. 21—30. Contrast between his labours and sufferings and those of his rivals.

---

of reason in those over whom they claimed to act as directors.

**If a man devour you.**—The word again reminds us of our Lord's denunciation of the teachers who "devoured widows' houses" (Matt. xxiii. 14).

**If a man take of you . . .**—The words in italics are wrongly supplied, and turn this clause into a feeble repetition of the preceding. Better, *if a man takes you in.* In chap. xii. 16, we have the same construction ("I *caught* you with guile") obviously with this sense.

**If a man smite you on the face.**—This last form of outrage was, as St. Paul was soon to experience (Acts xxiii. 2), not unfamiliar to Jewish priests and scribes, as the most effective way of silencing an opponent. We have an earlier instance of its application in the action of Zedekiah, the son of Chenaanah (1 Kings xxii. 24). That it had found its way into the Christian Church in the apostolic time is seen in St. Paul's rule that a bishop should be no "striker" (1 Tim. iii. 3; Tit. i. 7). It is obvious that he had heard of an instance in which this had actually been done at Corinth and he taunts them with the tameness of their submission. Did he forget, or had he not as yet heard the law of Matt. v. 39; or was he, knowing it, for a time unmindful of it, in this rush of emotion which he himself feels to be simply human, and therefore not inspired?

(21) **I speak as concerning reproach, as though we had been weak.**—Better, *I speak it as a matter of reproach to myself, as though we were weak.* The irony becomes more intense than ever. He has named these acts of outrage, he says, as though by way of self-disparagement. "*We*" (the pronoun is strongly emphasised) "were too infirm to venture on such things." The taunt flung at his bodily infirmities is still present to his thoughts, and he assumes, in the bitterness of his irony, that it was through them he had been kept from like acts of self-asserting authority. Then he resumes his contrast, still dwelling on the offensive words, "folly" or "insanity," which had been used of him: "Yes, but on every ground of daring—I know you will see my insanity again in this—I have as much right to dare as they."

(22) **Are they Hebrews?**—This, then, was one of their boasts. They were Jews of Palestine, speaking Aramaic, reading the Law and Prophets in the original. He, they asserted, or implied, was a Hellenistic Jew (his birth at Tarsus naturally suggesting that thought), content to use the Greek version of the LXX., over which many of the more exclusive Hebrews mourned on an annual fast-day as a national degradation. St. Paul's answer is, that he too was a Hebrew; or, as he puts it in Phil. iii. 5, "a Hebrew born of Hebrews." What he means is obviously that his parents were Jews of Palestine, and that the accident of his birth in Tarsus had not annulled his claim to that nationality. As a matter of fact it made him able to unite things that were commonly looked on as incompatible, and to be both a Hebrew and a Hellenist.

**Are they Israelites? . . .**—The words imply another insinuation. They whispered doubts whether he had any right to call himself an Israelite at all. Had he a drop of Abraham's blood flowing in his veins? Might he not, after all, be but the grandson of a proselyte, upon whom there rested the stigma which, according to a Jewish proverb, was not effaced till the twenty-fourth generation? Did not this account for his heathen sympathies? Strange as the thought may seem to us, the calumny survived, and the later Ebionites asserted (Epiphanius, *Hær.* xxx. 16) that he was a Gentile by birth, who had only accepted circumcision that he might marry the high priest's daughter. The kind of climax which the verse presents points not only to three claims to honour on their part, for in that case the first would include both the second and the third, and the climax would have little meaning, but to successive denials that he possessed any of the three. Jerome, strangely enough (*Cat. Vir. Illust.* c. 5), asserts that St. Paul was a Galilean, born at Gischala; but this, though it may possibly point to a tradition as to the home of his parents, can hardly be allowed to outweigh his own positive statement (Acts xxii. 3).

(23) **Are they ministers of Christ?**—It is obvious that this title was claimed by the rival teachers in some special sense. They were "ministers of Christ" in a nearer and a higher sense than others. This again falls in with all that has been said as to the nature and pretensions of those who said, "I am of Christ." (See Notes on chap. x. 7; 1 Cor. i. 12.)

**I speak as a fool.**—The form of the Greek verb is slightly varied, and means, more emphatically than before, *I speak as one who is insane; I speak deliriously.* In this instance, as before, we must believe that the Apostle is using, in a tone of indignant irony, the very words of insult which had been recklessly flung at him.

**In labours . . .**—All that follows up to verse 28, inclusive, is a proof of his claim to call himself a minister of Christ. The word "labours" is, of course, too vague to admit of more than a general comparison with the picture of his life presented in the Acts of the Apostles. The more specific statements show us that the writer of that book tends to understate rather than exaggerate the labours and sufferings of the Apostle. It tells us, up to this time, only of one imprisonment, at Philippi (Acts xvi. 23), and leaves us to conjecture where and under what circumstances we are to look for the others. In the "deaths oft," we trace an echo of the "sentence of death," the "dying daily" (see Notes on chaps. i. 9, iv. 10); but the words probably include dangers to life of other kinds as well as those arising from bodily disease.

(24) **Of the Jews five times received I forty stripes save one.**—None of these are recorded in the Acts. It is probable that the words refer to the early period of his work in Cilicia, which is implied though not recorded in that book. (See Note on Acts xv. 41). The number of the stripes in Jewish punishments of this kind rested on the rule of Deut. xxv. 3,

times received I forty *stripes* save one.[a]
(25) Thrice was I beaten with rods,
once was I stoned, thrice I suffered
shipwreck, a night and a day I have
been in the deep; (26) *in* journeyings
often, *in* perils of waters, *in* perils of
robbers, *in* perils by *mine own* country-
men, *in* perils by the heathen, *in* perils
in the city, *in* perils in the wilder-
ness, *in* perils in the sea, *in* perils
among false brethren; (27) in weariness
and painfulness, in watchings often, in
hunger and thirst, in fastings often, in
cold and nakedness. (28) Beside those
things that are without, that which
cometh upon me daily, the care of all

[a] Deut. 25. 3.

which fixed forty as the *maximum*. In practice it was thought desirable to stop short of the full number in order to avoid exceeding it. The punishment was inflicted with a leather scourge of three knotted thongs, and with a curiously elaborate distribution: thirteen strokes were given on the breast, thirteen on the right shoulder, and thirteen on the left.

**Thrice was I beaten with rods.**—This, as we see in Acts xvi. 22, 23, was distinctively, though, perhaps, not exclusively, a Roman punishment. The instance at Philippi, as above, is the only one recorded in the Acts. As a Roman citizen he could claim exemption from a punishment which was essentially servile (Acts xvi. 37), and at Jerusalem (Acts xxii. 25) he asserted this claim; but it may well have happened elsewhere, as at Philippi, either that the reckless haste of Roman officials led them to order the punishment without inquiry; or that they disregarded the appeal, and took their chance of impunity; or that there were reasons which led him to prefer enduring the ignominious punishment in silence, without protest.

(25) **Once was I stoned.**—Here the Acts (xiv. 19) give us the solitary instance at Lystra. The accuracy of the Apostle in referring to this form of suffering, where we can compare it with the history, may fairly be urged as evidence of a like accuracy in his other statements.

**Thrice I suffered shipwreck.**—Again we have a picture of unrecorded sufferings, which we must refer either to the period of his life between his departure from Jerusalem (Acts ix. 30) and his arrival at Antioch (Acts xi. 26), or to voyages among the islands of the Ægean Sea during his stay at Corinth or at Ephesus, or to that from Ephesus to Cæsarea in Acts xviii. 22.

**A night and a day I have been in the deep.**—Taken in their natural sense the words probably point to one of the shipwrecks just mentioned, in which, either swimming or with the help of a plank (as in Acts xxvii. 44), he had kept himself floating for nearly a whole day, beginning with the night. They have, however, been referred by some writers to a dungeon-pit, like that into which Jeremiah was cast (Jer. xxxviii. 6), in which the Apostle was either thrown or hid himself after the stoning at Lystra. Bede (*Quæst.* iii. 8) relates, on the authority of Archbishop Theodore of Canterbury—whose evidence, as a native of Tarsus, has here a special interest—that there was such a dungeon known by the name of *Bythos* (the word used here for "deep") in his time at Cyzicus, and, if so, it is probable enough that the same use of the word may have prevailed in other cities. So at Athens there was a dungeon known as the *barathron*—a word used also for a "gulf." On the whole, however, though the conjecture is interesting enough to deserve mention, there seems no adequate reason for adopting it.

(26) **In journeyings often.**—Again we enter on a list of activities and sufferings of which this is the only, or nearly the only, record. Some of them may be referred to journeys (as above) before his arrival at Antioch; some, probably, to that from Antioch to Ephesus through the interior of Asia Minor (Acts xviii. 23; xix. 1); some to excursions from Ephesus. The "perils of waters" (better, *rivers*) point to the swollen torrents that rush down in spring from the mountain heights of the Taurus and other ranges, and render the streams unfordable. "Robbers" infested, then as now, well-nigh every high-road in Syria and Asia Minor, as in the parable of the Good Samaritan (see Note on Luke x. 30), and the story of St. John and the young robber, as reported from Clement of Alexandria by Eusebius (*Hist.* iii. 23). Of the "perils from his own countrymen," we have instances enough up to this time at Damascus (Acts ix. 23), at Jerusalem (Acts ix. 29), at Antioch in Pisidia, Iconium, and Lystra (Acts xiii. 50; xiv. 5—19), at Thessalonica, and at Corinth (Acts xvii. 5—13; xviii. 12). Of "perils from the heathen" we find examples at Philippi (Acts xvi. 20) and Ephesus (Acts xix. 23). City and wilderness (possibly the Arabian desert of Gal. i. 17; possibly the high table-lands of Armenia and Asia Minor) and sea were alike fruitful in dangers. As if with something like a climax he reserves the word "false brethren," such as those of Gal. ii. 4, as the last and worst of his trials.

(27) **In weariness and painfulness . . .**—The same combination meets us in 2 Thess. iii. 8, where the English version has "labour and travail," as Tyndale and Cranmer have in this passage. "Weariness and painfulness" appear first in the Geneva version; *toil and trouble* is, perhaps, the best English equivalent. From the use of the phrase in 2 Thess. iii. 8, it probably refers chiefly to St. Paul's daily labour as a tent-maker. The "watchings" indicate the sleepless nights spent in anxiety, or pain, or prayer. "Hunger and thirst" are named as privations incident to his journeys or his labours. "Fastings," as distinguished from these, can hardly mean anything but times of self-chosen abstinence, of which we have at least two instances in Acts xiii. 2, 3, and which would be natural in St. Paul both as a Pharisee (see Notes on Matt. vi. 16, and Luke xviii. 12) and as a disciple of Christ (see Note on Matt. ix. 15). "Cold and nakedness" seem to speak not only of lonely journeys, thinly clad and thinly shod, on the high passes from Syria into Asia Minor, but also of lodgings without fire, and of threadbare garments. The whole passage reminds us of the narrative given by an old chronicler of the first appearance of the disciples of Francis of Assisi in England, walking with naked and bleeding feet through ice and snow, clothed only with their one friar's cloak, shivering and frost-bitten (Eccleston, *De Adventu Minorum*). He obviously contrasts this picture of his sufferings with what the Corinthians knew of the life of his rivals, who, if they were like their brethren of Judæa, walked in long robes, and loved the uppermost places at feasts (Matt. xxiii. 6). It had become a Jewish proverb that "the disciples of the wise had a right to a goodly house, a fair wife, and a soft couch" (Ursini.

the churches. (29) Who is weak, and I
am not weak? who is offended, and I
burn not? (30) If I must needs glory,
I will glory of the things which con-
cern mine infirmities. (31) The God and
Father of our Lord Jesus
Christ, which is blessed for
evermore, knoweth that I
lie not. (32) In Damascus
the governor under Aretas the king

Chap. xi. 31—33. His escape from Damascus.

---

*Antiqq. Hebr.* c. 5, in Ugolini's *Thesaurus*, vol. xxi.).

(28) **That which cometh upon me daily . . .**—The word so translated primarily signifies a "rush" or "tumult," and is so used in Acts xxiv. 12. Here that meaning is excluded by the fact that perils of that nature had been already specified, and that he now manifestly speaks of something differing in kind as well as in degree. But there is, as our modern phraseology shows, such a thing as a "rush" of business almost as trying as the "ugly rush" of a crowd, and that is manifestly what he means here. The daily visits of inquirers, the confessions of sin-burdened souls, the craving of perplexed consciences for guidance, the reference of quarrels of the household or the church to his arbitration as umpire, the arrival of messengers from distant churches, each with their tidings of good or evil—this is what we have to think of as present to St. Paul's thoughts as the daily routine of his life; and the absence of any conjunction between the two clauses clearly points to the fact that, in his mind, "the care (or *anxiety*) of all the churches" was all but identical with the "rush" of which he had just spoken.

(29) **Who is weak and I am not weak . . .?**—The words obviously spring from a recollection of all that was involved in that "rush" of which he had just spoken. Did any come to him with his tale of body-sickness or soul-sickness, he, in his infinite sympathy, felt as if he shared in it. He claimed no exemption from their infirmities, was reminded by every such tale of his own liability to them. The words that follow have a still stronger significance. The word "offended" (better, *made to stumble—i.e.*, led to fall by a temptation which the man has not resisted) suggests the thought of some grievous sin, as distinct from weakness; and the dominant sense of the word, as in Matt. v. 29, 30; xviii. 8, 9; Mark ix. 42, 43, 45, 47; 1 Cor. viii. 13, is that of the sins to which men are led by the temptations of the senses. The other word—to "burn"—is even more startling in its suggestiveness. It had been used in 1 Cor. vii. 9 of the "burning" of sensual passion, and it is scarcely open to a doubt that the associations thus connected with it mingle with its meaning here. Men came to the Apostle with their tales of shame, and told how they had been tempted and had fallen; and here, too, he, in that illimitable sympathy of his, seemed to have travelled with them on the downward road. He felt himself suffused, as it were, with the burning glow of their shame. He blushed with them and for them, as though the sin had been his own. Simply as a word, it should be added, it is equally applicable to any emotion of intense pain or fiery indignation, and it has been so taken by many interpreters. The view which has been given above seems, however, most in harmony with the Apostle's character.

(30) **If I must needs glory . . .**—The words form a transition to the narratives that follow. The question, "Who is weak and I am not weak?" has suggested the thought of the weakness and infirmity of various kinds with which his enemies reproached him. He will glory—here also with a touch of grave irony—in these and will leave his rivals to find what ground for boasting they can in what they call their strength. He is confident that his weak points are stronger than their strong ones.

(31) **The God and Father of our Lord Jesus Christ.**—The solemn attestation was, we may believe, a natural introduction to what was possibly intended, as the words passed from his lips, to be the beginning of a much fuller narrative than that which was its actual outcome.

**Which is blessed for evermore.**—The Greek has no conjunction, but its force is best given either by *which is, and is blessed for evermore*, or, by an emphasis of punctuation and the insertion of a verb, *which is: blessed is He for evermore.* The Greek participle is not a single predicate of blessedness, such as the English expresses, but is that constantly used in the LXX. version as the equivalent of the Hebrew name for Jehovah: "He that is," the "I AM" of Ex. iii. 13, 14; Jer. xiv. 13; and in a later and probably contemporary work, not translated from the Hebrew, in Wisd. xiii. 1 ("they could not . . . know Him that is"). So Philo, in like manner, speaks of "He that is" as a received name of God. (See also Notes on John viii. 58, 59; Rom. ix. 5.)

(32) **In Damascus the governor under Aretas the king . . .**—The question meets us at the outset whether the fact that follows is brought in as being the first instance of suffering endured for the sake of Christ, and therefore the natural opening to what was intended to have been a long, connected narrative of all such sufferings, or as being connected in some special manner with his "infirmities." On the whole, the evidence—especially the context of verse 30—seems in favour of the latter view, as far, at least, as the selection of the incident is concerned. There was, we can well imagine, an element of the ludicrous—something that gave occasion to jests and sneers—in the way in which the Apostle's escape had been effected. There was, so to speak, something undignified in it. Those who mocked at the stunted growth and weakness of his bodily presence would find good matter for their mirth in this.

On the historical facts connected with this incident, see Notes on Acts ix. 24, 25. The additional details which we learn from St. Paul are—(1) that Damascus was under the immediate control, not of the Governor of Syria, but of a governor or an *ethnarch;* (2) that the ethnarch was appointed, not by the Roman emperor, but by Aretas (the name was hereditary, and was the Greek form of the Arabic *Haret*), the King of the Nabathæan Arabs, who had his capital at Petra, who was the father of the first wife of Herod Antipas (see Note on Matt. xiv. 1); (3) that the ethnarch lent himself to the enmity of the Jews, and stationed troops at each gate of the city to prevent St. Paul's escape. "Ethnarch," it may be noted, was about this time the common title of a subordinate provincial governor. It had been borne by Judas Maccabæus (1 Macc. xiv. 47; xv. 1, 2) and by Archelaus (Jos. *Wars*, ii. 6, § 3).

kept the city of the Damascenes with a garrison, desirous to apprehend me: (33) and through a window in a basket was I let down by the wall, and escaped his hands.

A.D. 60.

CHAPTER XII.—(1) It is not expedient for me doubtless to glory. I will come to visions and revelations of the Lord. (2) I knew a man in Christ above fourteen years ago, (whether in the body, I cannot tell; or whether out of

Chap. xii. 1—6. St. Paul's visions and revelations of the Lord.

---

(33) **Through a window in a basket . . .**—On the mode of escape, see Notes on Acts ix. 24, 25. So the spies escaped from the house of Rahab (Josh. ii. 15), and David from the pursuit of Saul (1 Sam. xix. 12). The word which St. Paul uses for "basket" (*sarganè*) implies, perhaps, a more vivid personal recollection, as meaning specifically a rope-work hamper. St. Luke employs the more general term, *spuris*. (See Note on Matt. xv. 32.)

XII.

(1) **It is not expedient for me doubtless to glory. I will come . . .**—The English "doubtless" corresponds to a Greek illative particle. *To boast, then, is not expedient for me.* The MSS., however, present a considerable variety of readings. The best-authenticated text is probably that which would be represented in English by, *I must needs glory. It is not, indeed, expedient, but I will come . . .* The sequence of thought would seem to be that the Apostle felt constrained by the taunts of his opponents to indulge in what looked like self-assertion in vindication of his own character; that he was conscious, as he did so, that it was not, in the highest sense of the word, expedient for him; and that, under the influence of these mingled feelings, he passed over other topics on which he might have dwelt, and came at once to that which had been made matter of reproach against him.

**Visions and revelations of the Lord.**—It need scarcely be said that the history of the Acts is full of such visions (Acts ix. 4—6; xvi. 9; xviii. 9; xxii. 18; xxiii. 11; xxvii. 23). One other instance is referred to in Gal. ii. 2. There is scarcely any room for doubt that this also had been made matter of reproach against him, and perhaps urged as a proof of the charge of madness. In the Clementine *Homilies*—a kind of controversial romance representing the later views of the Ebionite or Judaising party, in which most recent critics have recognised a thinly-veiled attempt to present the characteristic features of St. Paul under the pretence of an attack on Simon Magus, just as the writer of a political novel in modern times might draw the portraits of his rivals under fictitious names—we find stress laid on the alleged claims of Simon to have had communications from the Lord through visions and dreams and outward revelations; and this claim is contrasted with that of Peter, who had personally followed Christ during his ministry on earth (*Hom.* xvii. 14—20). What was said then, in the form of this elaborate attack, may well have been said before by the more malignant advocates of the same party. The charge of insanity was one easy to make, and of all charges, perhaps, the most difficult to refute by one who gloried in the facts which were alleged as its foundation—who did see visions, and did "speak with tongues" in the ecstasy of adoring rapture (1 Cor. xiv. 18). It may be noted as an instance of St. Luke's fairness that he, ignorant of, or ignoring, the charge of madness that had been brought against St. Paul, does not grudge the Apostle of the Circumcision whatever glory might accrue from a true revelation thus made through the medium of a vision (Acts x. 10, 11).

(2) **I knew a man in Christ above fourteen years ago.**—Better, *I know a man.* The Greek verb, though a perfect tense in form, is invariably used with the force of a present. It is all but impossible to connect the facts that follow with any definite point of time in the Apostle's life as recorded in the Acts. The date of the Epistle may be fixed, without much risk of error, in A.D. 57. Reckoning fourteen years back, we come to A.D. 43, which coincides with the period of unrecorded activity between St. Paul's departure from Jerusalem (Acts ix. 30) and his arrival at Antioch (Acts xi. 26). It would be giving, perhaps, too wide a margin to the words "more than fourteen years ago" to refer the visions and revelations of which he here speaks to those given him at the time of his conversion, in A.D. 37. The trance in the Temple (Acts xxii. 17) on his first visit to Jerusalem may, perhaps, be identified with them; but it seems best, on the whole, to refer them to the commencement of his work at Antioch, when they would have been unspeakably precious, as an encouragement in his arduous work. It may be noted that Gal. ii. 2 specifically refers to one revelation at Antioch, and it may well have been preceded by others. The term "a man in Christ," as a way of speaking of himself, is probably connected with the thought that "if any man be in Christ he is a new creature" (chap. v. 17; Gal. vi. 15). As one who lived and moved and had his being in Christ, he was raised to a higher region of experience than that in which he had lived before. It was in moments such as he describes that he became conscious of that "new creation" with a new and hitherto unknown experience.

**Whether in the body, I cannot tell; or whether out of the body, I cannot tell.**—No words can describe more accurately the phenomena of consciousness in the state of trance or ecstasy. It is dead to the outer world. The body remains, sometimes standing, sometimes recumbent, but, in either case, motionless. The man may well doubt, on his return to the normal condition of his life, whether his spirit has actually passed into unknown regions in a separate and disembodied condition, or whether the body itself has been also a sharer in its experiences of the unseen. We, with our wider knowledge, have no hesitation in accepting the former alternative, or, perhaps, in reducing the whole revelation to an impression on the brain and the phenomena known as cataleptic. St. Paul, however, would naturally turn to such records as those of Ezekiel's journey, in the visions of God, from the banks of Chebar to Jerusalem (Ezek. viii. 3; xi. 1), and find in them the analogue, though, as he admits, not the solution, of his own experience. The lives of many of the great movers in the history of religious thought present, it may be noted, analogous phenomena. Of Epimenides, and Pythagoras, and Socrates, of Mahomet, of Francis of Assisi, and Thomas Aquinas, and Johannes Scotus, of George Fox, and Savonarola, and Swedenborg, it was alike

the body, I cannot tell: God knoweth;)
such an one caught up to the third
heaven. (3) And I knew such a man,
(whether in the body, or out of the
body, I cannot tell: God knoweth;)
(4) how that he was caught up into
paradise, and heard unspeakable words,
which it is not lawful[1] for a man to
utter. (5) Of such an one will I glory:
yet of myself I will not glory, but in
mine infirmities. (6) For though I
would desire to glory, I shall not be a

1 Or, *possible.*

---

true that to pass from time to time into the abnormal state of ecstasy was with them almost the normal order of their lives. (See article "Trance" in Smith's *Dictionary of the Bible*, by the present writer.)

**Such an one caught up to the third heaven.**—Rabbinic speculations on the subject of Heaven present two forms: one which, starting probably from the dual form of the Hebrew word, recognises but two heavens, both visible—the lower region of the clouds and the upper firmament; and a later, which, under the influence of ideas from the further East, spoke of seven. A remarkable legend in the Talmud (*Bereshith Rabba*, 19, fol. 19, col. 3) relates how the Shechinah, or glory-cloud of the Divine Presence, retired step by step from earth, where it had dwelt before the sin of Adam, at every fresh development of evil; into the first heaven at the fall, into the second at the murder of Abel, and so on, till it reached the seventh heaven on Abraham's going down to Egypt, and descended again by successive steps from the birth of Isaac to the time of the Exodus, when it came once more to earth and dwelt in the Tabernacle with Moses. If we assume St. Paul to have accepted any such division, the third heaven would indicate little more than the region of the clouds and sky. It is more probable, however, from the tone in which he speaks, as clearly dwelling on the surpassing excellency of his visions, that he adopts the simpler classification, and thinks of himself as passing beyond the lower sky, beyond the firmament of heaven, into the third or yet higher heaven, where the presence of God was manifested. The seven heavens re-appear naturally in the legends of the Koran (*Sura* lxvii.) and in the speculations of mediæval theology as represented by Dante. We probably hear a far-off echo of the derision with which the announcement was received by the jesting Greeks of Corinth and by St. Paul's personal rivals in the dialogue ascribed to Lucian, and known as the *Philopatris*, in which St. Paul is represented as "the Galilean, bald, with eagle nose, walking through the air to the third heaven."

(3) **And I knew such a man.**—Better, as before, *I know.*

(4) **That he was caught up into paradise.**—The stress laid on this second vision hinders us from thinking of it as identical with the former, either in time or in object-matter. Paradise (see Note on Luke xxiii. 43) was emphatically the dwelling-place of the souls of the righteous, the reproduction in the unseen world of the lost beauty of the Garden of Eden—the "paradise of joy," as the LXX. in Gen. ii. 15 translates the name. There, flowing about the throne of God, was the fountain of the water of life, and the tree of life growing on its banks (Rev. ii. 7; xxii. 1, 2). Speculations on the question whether St. Paul thought of it as nearer or farther from earth than the third heaven are obviously idle and profitless. The nearest approach which we can make to an adequate distinction between the two visions is that the first revealed to his gaze the glory of the Throne of God, with angels and archangels round it, and seraphim and cherubim, —a vision like that of Moses (Ex. xxiv. 10), and Isaiah (Isa. vi. 1—3), and Ezekiel (Ezek. i. 4—28), and St. John (Rev. iv. 2—11)—thoughts like those of Hooker's death-bed (Walton's *Life*)—while the latter brought before his spirit the peace and rest ineffable, even in their intermediate and therefore imperfect state, of the souls who had fallen asleep in Christ and were waiting for their resurrection.

**Unspeakable words, which it is not lawful for a man to utter.**—The first two words present the tone of a paradox—*speech unspeakable*, or *utterances unutterable*. The verb in the second clause hovers between the text, "it is not lawful" and "it is not possible." The hymns which St. John records in Rev. iv. 8, 9, v. 12—14, vii. 12, and xv. 3, may give us some faint approach to what dwelt in St. Paul's memory and yet could not be reproduced. Sounds of ineffable sweetness, bursts of praise and adoration, hallelujahs like the sound of many waters, voices low and sweet as those of children, whispers which were scarcely distinguishable from silence and yet thrilled the soul with a rapturous joy—this we may, perhaps, think of as underlying St. Paul's language. In the mystic ecstatic utterances of the Tongues—themselves needing an interpreter, and helping little to build up those who heard them, though they raised the life of those who spoke with them to a higher level—we may, perhaps, trace some earthly echoes of that heavenly music. (See Notes on Acts ii. 4; 1 Cor. xiv. 2.)

(5) **Of such an one will I glory.**—There is, if we rightly understand it, an almost exquisite sadness in the distinction which is thus drawn by the Apostle between the old self of fourteen years ago, with this abundance of revelations, and the new self of the present, feebler and sadder than the old, worn with cares and sorrows, the daily rush of life and its ever-growing anxieties. Then he saw with open vision; now he walks by faith and not by the thing seen. He can hardly recognise his own identity, and can speak of the man who had then this capacity for the beatific vision as though he were another—almost as if he were dead and gone. The "*non sum qualis eram*" of decay and age presents manifold varieties of form, the soldier recalling the stir and the rush of battle, the poet finding that the vision and the "faculty divine" are no longer entrusted to his keeping, the eloquent orator who had "wielded at will a fierce democracy," complaining of slow speech and of a stammering tongue; but this has a sadness peculiar to itself. Faith, hope, love, peace, righteousness, are still there, but there has passed away a glory from the earth, and the joy of that ecstatic rapture lies in the remote past, never to return on earth.

(6) **For though I would desire to glory . . .**—He had said in the preceding verse that he will glory only in his infirmities. He is about to lay bare to their gaze the greatest of all those infirmities. "If I should boast of that," he says, "I shall not be acting as a madman does" (the thought of insanity is throughout dominant in the words "fool" and "folly"), "for I will confine myself to a simple statement of fact."

fool; for I will say the truth: but *now* I forbear, lest any man should think of me above that which he seeth me *to be*, or *that* he heareth of me. (7) And

(7) **There was given to me a thorn in the flesh.**—The vague mystery with which St. Paul thus surrounds the special form of "infirmity" of which he speaks, has given rise to very different conjectures, which will require to be treated with more or less fulness. It will be well to begin with getting as closely as we can at the idea of the central word. The Greek word for "thorn," then, might better be translated *stake*. It is used, *e.g.*, of stakes thrust into the ground to form a palisade round a grave—

> "And round about they dug a trench full deep,
> And wide and large, and round it fixed their *stakes*."
> —Homer, *Iliad*, vii. 441.

A sharp-pointed stake of this kind was often used as a means of torture in the punishment known as impaling, and the two Greek words for "impaling" and "crucifying" were indeed almost interchangeable (Herod. i. 128; ix. 18). So in Euripides (*Iphig. in Tauris*. 1430)—

> "Say, shall we hurl them down from lofty rock,
> Or fix their bodies on the *stake?*"

It is significant that men like Celsus and Lucian, writing against the faith of Christians, used the term "stake" instead of "cross," as more ignominious, and spoke of Jesus as having been "impaled" instead of "crucified" (Origen, *c. Cels.* ii.; Lucian, *De morte Peregr.*, p. 762). So Chrysostom used the word "impaled" of St. Peter's crucifixion. On the other hand, medical writers, such as Dioscorides and Artemidorus, by whose use of the word, as possibly coming to him through St. Luke, St. Paul was likely to be influenced, apply the term to what we call a "splinter" getting into the flesh and causing acute inflammation (*Diosc.* ii. 29; iv. 176). Dioscorides, it may be noted, was a native of Anazarba in Cilicia, and probably a contemporary of St. Paul's. The word used figuratively, therefore, comes to bring with it the sense of some acute form of suffering, something, to use a word of like history and significance, *excruciating* in its character. So used, it might, as far as the word itself is concerned, be applied to any sharp agony, either of mind or body.

The history of the interpretations which have been given to this mysterious term is not without interest as a psychological study. Men have clearly been influenced, to a large extent, by their subjective tendencies. They have measured the sufferings of St. Paul by their own experience, and thinking that he must have felt as they felt, have seen in his "thorn in the flesh" that which they felt to be their own sharpest trial. Some of these conjectures may be dismissed very briefly. It cannot be, as some have thought, the remembrance of his own guilt in persecuting the disciples of Christ, for that would not have been described as a "thorn *in the flesh*," nor could he well have prayed that it should depart from him. For a like reason, it could not have been, as some Protestant commentators have imagined, any doubt as to the certainty of his own salvation, or of his being included in God's pardoning love. We may safely set aside, again, the view that he refers to his struggle with heathen enemies, like Demetrius, or Judaising rivals, for these had been included in his list of sufferings in chap. xi. 22, 23, and here he is clearly speaking of something generically new. There remain two hypotheses. (1) That he speaks of the conflict with sensual passion; and (2), that he refers to some chronic infirmity of body that brought with it constantly recurring attacks of acute pain. For each of these a strong case may be made out. In favour of (1) it may be urged that the language of St. Paul in not a few places implies the existence of such a struggle with temptation. He sees a law in his members warring against the law of his mind (Rom. vii. 23). Sin wrought in him all manner of concupiscence (Rom. vii. 8). He found it necessary to keep under his body, and bring it into subjection (1 Cor. ix. 27). What has been said as to the question, "Who is offended, and I burn not?" suggests a special sympathy with that form of struggle against evil; and in the "fire-tipt darts of the wicked one" of Eph. vi. 16 (where we have the participle of the same verb), we may, perhaps, trace an allusive reference to impulses of this nature. It is clear that with some temperaments temptations such as this, besides the moral pain which they bring with them, may inflict a bodily suffering little less than excruciating, and the words that speak of the "flesh" as the seat of suffering, and of its being a "messenger of Satan," at least fall in with the view thus presented. Nor is it enough to say, on the other hand, that St. Paul's character made such temptations impossible. The long line of patristic, and mediæval, and modern Romish interpreters who have taken this view, though of little weight as an authority, is, at least, evidence that they knew the bitterness of such temptations, and though their thoughts may have been coloured by the experiences of the monastic life and enforced celibacy, as in the story of the temptations of St. Antony, we may fairly read in their testimony the fact that sensual temptation may assail men who are aiming at a high ascetic standard of holiness. Experience seems, indeed, to show that the ecstatic temperament, with its high-wrought emotional excitement, is more than most others liable to the attacks of this form of evil. So the daily evening hymn of St. Ambrose includes the prayer, "*ne polluantur corpora.*" So Augustine bewails the recurrence in dreams of the old sensuous temptations to which he had yielded in his youth (*Confess.* x. 30); and Jerome is not ashamed to tell the history of such temptations, alternating here also with ecstatic visions of divine glories, to the female friend whom he exhorts to persevere in her vow of chastity (*Epist. ad Eustochium*, c. 7). It may be added that this view falls in with the tone in which St. Paul approaches "the thorn in the flesh" as the crown of all his infirmities. No self-humiliation could go beyond this disclosure of what most men hide. As in the confessions of Augustine and Jerome, just referred to, the last veil is withdrawn, and men are told that the man who has had visions of God is one of like passions with themselves, subject, as they are, to the strongest temptations of his sensuous nature. As in the triumphs of the Emperors of Rome, a slave rode in the same chariot with the conqueror, and bade him ever and anon remember that he also was a man, so here there was a continual reminder that he too might become as others were. If there was any danger of being exalted above measure by the abundance of the revelations, nothing could more easily bring a man down from that ideal height than the consciousness that this was his besetting temptation.

On the other hand, there are some serious considerations that militate against this theory. There is no trace of any sins of this nature in any of St. Paul's

Chap. xii. 7—9. St. Paul's thorn in the flesh, and the answer to his prayer for its removal.

lest I should be exalted above measure through the abundance of the revelations,
there was given to me a thorn in the flesh,[a] the messenger of Satan to buffet me, lest I should be
exalted above measure. (8) For this
thing I besought the Lord thrice, that
it might depart from me. (9) And he
said unto me, My grace is sufficient for
thee: for my strength is made perfect
in weakness. Most gladly therefore will
I rather glory in my infirmities, that
the power of Christ may rest upon
me. (10) Therefore I take pleasure in

a See Ezek. 28 24.

---

retrospects (as in Acts xxii. 3; xxiii. 1; xxvi. 4; Phil. iii. 4, 6) of his state before his conversion. His tone in Rom. vii. 25 is that of one who has fought and overcome in the struggle with "the flesh"; and it is clear from the whole context, that with St. Paul the "fleshly mind" does not necessarily involve sensual sin. The language of 1 Cor. vii. 7 ("I would that all men were even as I myself"), which is the nearest approach to a direct statement on the subject, is scarcely compatible with the thought that, instead of the calmness of habitual self-control, the man who so spoke was all along fighting against impulses which were so strong as to bring with them actual torment. It may be added, as almost decisive, that St. Paul, in writing to the Corinthians, would use language that they could understand, and that there is not a jot or tittle of evidence that the word for "thorn" was ever used by any Greek writer of the sting of sensuous impulse. It was not likely, indeed, that they, accustomed to a licentious indulgence in this matter, would see in such an impulse any cause of pain and anguish. If the Apostle had meant this it would have been necessary for him to express his meaning far more plainly. On the other hand, there is, as we have seen (Notes on chaps. i. 9; iv. 10—12; v. 2—4), abundant evidence that St. Paul did suffer from some acute form of bodily disease. The very word "stake," or "thorn," or "splinter," would suggest to the Corinthian readers of the Epistle the idea of corporeal rather than mental suffering. The "large letter" of his signature (Gal. vi. 11), the characteristic "steadfast gaze" (see Note on Acts xiii. 9), the wish of the Galatians, if it had been possible, to have plucked out their own eyes and given them to him (Gal. iv. 15), all point to brows and eyes as being the seat of suffering. The very word to "buffet" (see Note on Matt. xxvi. 67) suggests the same conclusion. Nor need we be surprised that this infirmity—neuralgia of the head and face, or inflammation of the eyes, perhaps, in some measure, the after consequences of the blindness at Damascus—should be described as "a messenger of Satan." That was, in fact, the dominant Jewish thought as to the causation of disease. The sores and boils of Job (Job ii. 7), the spirit of infirmity of the woman whom Satan had bound (Luke xiii. 16), St. Paul's own reference to Satan as hindering his journeys (1 Thess. ii. 18), his delivering men to Satan for the destruction of their flesh and the salvation of their souls (1 Cor. v. 5; 1 Tim. i. 20), St. Peter's description of our Lord as healing all that are oppressed of the devil (Acts x. 38)—these are enough to prove, that while men referred special forms of suffering of mind and body, chiefly the former, to the agency of demons, they were prepared to recognise the agency of Satan in almost every form of bodily calamity.

On these grounds, then, it is believed the balance turns in favour of the latter of the two hypotheses. A more complete solution of the problem may, perhaps, be found in accepting it as, in some measure, supplemented by the former. I venture to think, however, that all or most of the facts urged on behalf of that view, may legitimately come under the words "lest I should be exalted above measure." The man who is so exalted is in danger of sensual passions. The ecstatic is on the border-land of the orgiastic. He needs a check of some kind. If this were so with St. Paul, as with Luther and Augustine (and the language of Rom. vii. 8 must be admitted to point to some past struggles), what more effective check could there be than the sharp pain of body, crucifying the flesh with the affections and lusts (Gal. v. 24), with which we have seen reason to identify the "thorn" of which St. Paul speaks? One who thus lived as in "the body of this death" could thank God who, even in this way, gave him the victory over the law of sin (Rom. vii. 24). His sufferings were to him, as has been well pointed out by Dean Stanley (in a Note on this verse), what the mysterious agony that used at times to seize on Alfred in the midst of feast and revel, had been to the saintly and heroic king, a discipline working for his perfection.

(8) **For this thing I besought the Lord thrice.**—We are reminded of our Lord's three-fold prayer in Gethsemane (Matt. xxvi. 36; Luke xxii. 42—45). Was St. Paul himself reminded of it? There also the answer to the prayer was not compliance with its petition, but the gift of strength to bear and to endure.

(9) **And he said unto me, My grace is sufficient for thee.**—The words fit in, more or less, with each of the two views that have been discussed above. From one point of view, however, it seems infinitely more in harmony with our thoughts of God, that the prayer to be relieved from pain should be refused, because it was working out a higher perfection than was attainable without it, than that a deaf ear should have been turned to a prayer to be relieved from the temptation to impurity. Such a prayer seems to us to carry with it something like an assurance of its own prevailing power. Some of the better MSS. omit the possessive "My," and with that reading the words take the form of a general axiom affirming that, in the highest sense, "might is perfected in weakness." The last word is the same as that translated "infirmity" in the next clause. The variation, as concealing this, is so far unfortunate.

**Most gladly therefore will I rather glory in my infirmities.**—The word, as has just been said, is the same as the "weakness" in the answer to his prayer. He finds not comfort only, but actual delight, in his consciousness of weakness, because it is balanced by the sense that the might of Christ *dwells in him and around him.* The word for "rest" is literally, as a like word in John i. 14, *to dwell as in a tent,* and suggests the thought that the might of Christ was to him as the Shechinah cloud of glory encompassing him and protecting him.

(10) **Therefore I take pleasure in infirmities.**—The thoughts of the Apostle go back to the sufferings of which he had spoken fully in chap. xi. and elsewhere. One new word is added, "reproaches" (better, *insults*),

infirmities, in reproaches, in necessities, in persecutions, in distresses for Christ's sake: for when I am weak, then am I strong.
(11) I am become a fool in glorying; ye have compelled me: for I ought to have been commended of you: for in nothing am I behind the very chiefest apostles, though I be nothing.
(12) Truly the signs of an apostle were wrought among you in all patience, in signs, and wonders, and mighty deeds.
(13) For what is it wherein ye were inferior to other churches, except *it be* that I myself was not burdensome to you? forgive me this wrong.
(14) Behold, the third time I am ready to come to you; and I will not be burdensome to you: for I seek not your's, but you: for the children ought not to lay up for the parents, but the parents for the children.
(15) And I will very gladly spend and be spent for you[1]; though the more abundantly I love you, the

Chap. xii. 10—13. St. Paul's appeal to the signs of his work as an Apostle.

Chap. xii. 14—21. Announcements of his intended visit, and expression of his feelings of anxiety in connection with it.

1 Gr. *your souls.*

which elsewhere in the New Testament meets us only in Acts xxvii. 10, 21, in the sense of material damage. Here the reference is probably to the taunts and sneers to which we have traced allusions in chaps. i. 17; iii. 1; vii. 8; viii. 2; x. 10; xi. 6, 8, 16. He was able to bear even these with satisfaction when he felt that he was bearing them for the sake of Christ. He had learnt to add another paradox to those of chap. vi. 9, 10, and to feel that the greatest weakness was not only compatible with the highest strength, but might be the very condition of its energy.

(11) **I am become a fool in glorying.**—The two last words are wanting in the better MSS., and the verse opens with a somewhat thrilling abruptness,—*I am become insane—it was you* (emphatic) *who compelled me.* The words are partly ironical — partly speak of an impatient consciousness that what he had been saying would seem to give colour to the opprobrious epithets that had been flung at him. The passage on which we now enter, and of which we may think as begun after a pause, is remarkable for the reproduction, in a compressed form, of most of the topics, each with its characteristic phrase, on which he had before dwelt. The violence of the storm is over, but the sky is not yet clear, and we still hear the mutterings of the receding thunder He remembers once more that he has been called "insane"; that he has been taunted with "commending himself"; that he has been treated as "nothing" in comparison with those "apostles-extraordinary" who were setting themselves up as his rivals. "*I,*" he says, with an emphatic stress on the pronoun, "ought to have had no need for this painful self-assertion. *You* ought to have acknowledged my labour and my love for you."

(12) **Truly the signs of an apostle were wrought among you.**—The passage is remarkable for using the word "signs," first, in the general sense, as "notes" or "tokens," and then more specifically for works of supernatural power. On the special meaning of the three words, "signs," "wonders," "power," see Note on Acts ii. 22. The passage is noticeable as being one of those in which St. Paul distinctly claims a supernatural power for himself, and appeals to its exercise. (Comp. Rom. xv. 19—written, it will be remembered, shortly after this—and 1 Cor. ii. 4.)

**In all patience.**—Better, *in endurance of every kind,* as referring to the hardships and privations specified in chap. xi. 23—28, in the midst of which the work had to be carried on.

(13) **What is it wherein ye were inferior to other churches?**—His mind travels back to the insinuation that he cared less for them than he did for the churches of Macedonia, because he had maintained his independence and had received no gifts from them. If they complained of this, they should, at least, remember that this was the only point of inferiority. They had experienced fully all the advantages that flowed from his special power as an Apostle. For that wrong, so far as it was a wrong, he asks their forgiveness.

**That I myself was not burdensome.**—He uses here, and in the next verse, the same characteristic word for "sponging" on them, which has been commented on in the Note on chap. xi. 9. He obviously dwells on it with a touch of irony, as a word that had been used of him by some of his rivals.

(14) **Behold, the third time I am ready to come to you.**—The visit to Corinth of Acts xviii. 1, followed by a long sojourn, may perhaps be reckoned as the first occasion; then came the projected journey from Ephesus to Corinth and thence to Macedonia (chap. i. 16); now he was preparing for the third journey, announced in 1 Cor. xvi. 5—7, from Macedonia to Corinth. (See, however, the Note on chap. xiii. 1.)

**I seek not your's, but you.**—The words point to the secret motive of the conduct which had annoyed some of the Corinthians. He loved them, as all true friends love, for their own sake, not for anything he might hope to gain from them. He must be sure that he had gained their hearts before he could receive their gifts as poor substitutes for their affections; and therefore he announces beforehand that he meant to persevere in the same line of conduct, working for his own maintenance as before. Rom. xvi. 23 indicates that he so far deviated from his purpose as to accept the hospitality of Gaius of Corinth.

**For the children ought not to lay up for the parents.**—Better, perhaps, *are not bound to lay by.* There is a touch of exquisite delicacy and tenderness, reminding us of like characteristics in the Epistle to Philemon, in this apology for the seeming wrong of which men had complained. He could claim the rights of a father, as in 1 Cor. iv. 15; might he not be allowed to fulfil a father's obligations, and to give to his children rather than receive from them?

(15) **And I will very gladly spend and be spent.**—The pronoun is emphatic, *I, for my part.* The latter verb implies spending to the last farthing. As he sought not *theirs,* but *them,* so he is ready to spend for them not only all that he has, but even, as if to the verge of exhaustion, all that he is. And yet with all this there was the painful consciousness of toiling without adequate return. It seemed to him, in his intense craving for affection, as if their love varied inversely with his own.

less I be loved. (16) But be it so, I
did not burden you: nevertheless, being
crafty, I caught you with guile. (17) Did
I make a gain of you by any of them
whom I sent unto you? (18) I desired
Titus, and with *him* I sent a brother.
Did Titus make a gain of you? walked
we not in the same spirit? *walked we*
not in the same steps? (19) Again, think
ye that we excuse ourselves unto you?
we speak before God in Christ: but *we*
*do* all things, dearly beloved, for your
edifying. (20) For I fear, lest, when I
come, I shall not find you such as I

---

(16) **But be it so, I did not burden you.**—The pronoun is again emphatic. The word for "burden" is not the same as in verses 13, 14, but puts the fact less figuratively. The abruptness of the sentence requires us to trace between the lines the under-currents of unexpressed thoughts. The extreme, almost jealous, sensitiveness of the Apostle's nature leads him to imagine the cynical sneer with which these assertions of disinterested work would be received. "Be it so," he hears them saying; "we admit that he, in his own person, when he was with us, made no demands on our purses; but what are we to think of this 'collection for the saints'? How do we know into whose pockets that money will go? We know him to be *subtle* enough" (the adjective is that from which we get the "subtlety" of chaps. iv. 2, xi. 3) "to take us in somehow: what if the collection be a trap?" There is a specially taunting force in the Greek for "*being* crafty," as taking the fact for granted, and assuming that it would inevitably lead on to some new development of that character in act.

(17) **By any of them whom I sent unto you?**—The English expresses the meaning of the Greek, but does not show, as that does, the vehement agitation which led the writer, as he dictated the letter, to begin the sentence with one construction and finish it with another. *Did any of those I sent . . . did I by this means get more out of you than I ought?* He has in his mind, as far as we know, Timotheus, who had been sent before the First Epistle (1 Cor. iv. 17); Stephanus, Fortunatus and Achaicus, who were the bearers of that Epistle (1 Cor. xvi. 15); and Titus, who was sent, as we have seen, to learn what its effect had been. Had any of these, he asks, been asking for money on his account?

(18) **I desired Titus, and with him I sent a brother.**—Better, *the brother*. The Greek has the article, and he refers definitely to the first of the two unnamed brethren alluded to in chap. viii. 18—22. The Greek idiom of what is known as the "epistolary aorist," hinders the English reader from seeing that St. Paul is referring to what was being done at the time when the letter was written. It would accordingly be better rendered, *I have besought Titus to go; I am sending the brother with him.* The ungenerous suspicions of some of the Corinthians had made him almost morbidly sensitive, and he repeats practically what he had said before (chap. viii. 20, 21), that his motive in sending these delegates was to guard against them. Having stated this, he can appeal to their past knowledge of Titus, as a guarantee for the future. Had he "sponged" on any man, or tried what he could get out of him? Had he not identified himself with the Apostle, both in the general spirit which animated him and in the details of his daily life? It is a natural inference from this that Titus also had worked for his own maintenance and lived in his own lodging. If we may assume the identity of Titus with the Justus into whose house St. Paul went when he left the synagogue at Corinth (see Note on Acts xviii. 7), the appeal to the knowledge which the Corinthians had of him gains a new significance.

(19) **Again, think ye that we excuse ourselves unto you?**—Many of the best MSS. present the reading *palai* (long ago), instead of *palin* (again). In this case the sentence is better taken as an assertion, not as a question—"You are thinking, and have been thinking for a long time, that it is to you that we have been making our defence." The Greek verb for "excuse," is that which is always used of a formal *apologia*, or vindication (Luke xii. 11; xxi. 14; Acts xix. 33; xxiv. 10). St. Paul deprecates the idea that he has any wish to enter on such a vindication. He is anxious to explain his conduct, as in chaps. i. 15—24, viii. 20—24, xi. 7—12, but he does not acknowledge that he stands at the bar before their judgment-seat. He speaks, *i.e.*, in the same tone of independence as in 1 Cor. iv. 3—5. The motive which really prompts him to speak as he has spoken is not the wish to clear himself from aspersions, but "before God in Christ,"—under a profound sense that God is his Judge, and that Christ is, as it were, the sphere in which his thoughts revolve,—he is seeking to "edify," *i.e.*, to build them up in the faith or love of God. He has the same end in view in all this perturbed emotion as in the calm liturgical directions of 1 Cor. xiv. 12—26.

(20) **For I fear, lest, when I come . . .**—Something of the old anxiety which had led him to postpone his visit (chap. i. 23; 1 Cor. iv. 21) comes back upon his spirit. He and some of those Corinthians are likely to meet under very unfavourable conditions, neither of them acceptable to the other, severity meeting with open or masked resistance.

**Lest there be debates . . . .**—The list that follows forms a suggestive parallelism of contrast to that in chap. vii. 11, the ethical imagination of the Apostle, with its keen perception of the shades of human character, dwelling now on the manifold forms of opposition, as before it had dwelt on the manifold fruits of repentance. It will be worth while to attempt to fix the exact significance of each word somewhat more accurately than is done in the Authorised version. "Debates," rather *strifes* or *quarrels*, had in older English a darker shade of meaning than it has now. Men spoke of a "deadly *debate*" between friends. Chapman's *Homer* makes Achilles complain that he has cast his life into "*debates* past end" (*Iliad*, ii. 331). "Envyings" better *jealousies*, another Greek word being appropriated for "envy" in the strict sense. The word, like "jealousy," is capable of a good sense, as in chaps. vii. 11; ix. 2; xi. 2. It is well, perhaps, to notice how closely allied are the qualities which the word expresses, how soon "zeal" (chap. vii. 11; Phil. iii. 6) passes into "jealousy" in a good sense, and that again into "jealousy" in a bad sense. "Wrath." The passion so described is treated by great ethical writers (Aristotle, *Eth. Nicom.* iii. 8) as almost inseparable from true courage. In the New Testament it is always used either of human

would, and *that* I shall be found unto you such as ye would not: lest *there be* debates, envyings, wraths, strifes, backbitings, whisperings, swellings, tumults:
(21) *and* lest, when I come again, my God will humble me among you, and *that* I shall bewail many which have sinned already, and have not repented of the uncleanness and fornication and lasciviousness which they have committed.

A.D. 60.

CHAPTER XIII.—(1) This *is* the third *time* I am coming to you. In the mouth of two or three witnesses shall every word be established.

Chap. xiii. 1—4. Feelings as to his intended visit.

---

wrath in its evil aspects (Luke iv. 28; Acts xix. 28; Heb. xi. 27), or—but only in the Apocalypse, where it occurs in this sense frequently—of the wrath of God (Rev. xiv. 10, 19; xv. 1, 7; xvi. 1, 19). There is, therefore, no need to alter the English here. The three words occur in the same connection in Gal. v. 20, a nearly contemporary Epistle.

**Strifes.**—The Greek word (*erîtheia*) begins with the same three letters as that for "strife," and till a comparatively recent period was supposed to be connected with it, and so to be identical in meaning. It has, however, a very different history, not without interest, even for the English reader. The concrete form of the noun (*erîthos*) meets us in Homer and elsewhere as a day-labourer, as in the description of the shield of Achilles:

> "And there he wrought, a meadow thick with corn,
> And *labourers* reaping, sickles in their hand."
> —*Iliad*, xviii. 550.

The next step in the growth of the word, was the verb "to serve for wages," and this was transferred to those who in matters of state compete for honours and rewards, rather than for their country's good. Aristotle (*Pol.* v. 2, § 6; 3, § 9) enumerates the fact which the word expresses as one of the causes of revolutions, but carefully distinguishes it from "party spirit," or "faction" as being more directly personal. *Rivalries* would, perhaps, be an adequate rendering, but what are known in political life as the *cabals* of cliques or coteries as contrasted with open party-fights exactly correspond to the evils which the Apostle had in his thoughts.

**Backbitings, whisperings.**—The English reads the idea of secret calumny into both words. In the Greek, however, the first expresses "open abuse or invective," as in Jas. iv. 11; 1 Pet. ii. 1, 12. In contrast with this we have the "whispers" of the slanderers, the innuendoes and insinuations of the man who has not the courage for the more open attack. So the "whisperer" is spoken of with special scorn in Ecclus. xxi. 28; xxviii. 13. The word in its primary meaning is used for the low chirp of the swallow, which was, as it were, reproduced in the confidential whispers of the retailer of scandal. (See Note on "babbler" in Acts xvii. 18.)

**Swellings, tumults.**—The first word is found here only in the New Testament, but is formed regularly from the verb "to be puffed up," which is prominent in 1 Cor. iv. 6, 18, 19; v. 2; viii. 1; xiii. 4. It was clearly, in St. Paul's mind, the besetting sin of the Corinthians. As far as we know, the word may have been coined by him, but as connected with the medical idea of *flatus* and inflation, it may not improbably have been one of the technical terms, used figuratively, which he borrowed from St. Luke's vocabulary. It is almost necessary to coin an English word to express it. "Inflated egotisms" is an adequate paraphrase: "puffed-upnesses" would be, perhaps, too bold a coinage. The word for "tumult" has met us before. (See Notes on chap. vi. 5; Luke xxi. 9; 1 Cor. xiv. 33.) *Disorders, confusions*, what figuratively we call the "chaos," into which a public meeting sometimes falls, are what the word expresses, rather than the more open outbreak indicated by "tumult."

(21) **And lest when I come again . .**—The words do not imply more than one previous visit (Acts xviii. 1), but it can scarcely be said that they exclude the supposition of another. (See Note on chap. xiii. 1.)

**My God will humble me among you.**—We lose the force of the Greek verb by not seeing that it reproduces the word which has been so prominent in the Epistle, and which has appeared in chap. vii. 6, as "cast down;" in chap. x. 1 as "base;" in chap. xi. 7 as "abasing." There is something almost plaintive in the tone in which the Apostle speaks of the sin of his disciples as the only real "humiliation" which he has to fear. The readings vary; and one of them may be taken as a question: *Will God humble me again?* There is, however, it is believed, no adequate ground for altering the text.

**That I shall bewail many which have sinned already.**—Literally, *who have sinned beforehand*; leaving it uncertain what time is referred to. He may refer to sins before admission into the Church, of which men had never really repented, or to sins before the time of his writing, or before that of his arrival. On the whole, the first interpretation has most to commend it. He has in his thoughts such persons as those described in 1 Cor. vi. 9, and suspects that some of them have not really renounced the sins which he there names. Of the three forms of evil, the first is generic and the two latter more specific; the last probably indicating the darker forms of evil. It is obvious that the words cannot refer to the incestuous offender who had repented (chap. ii. 7), nor to the Church generally in connection with that offence (chap. vii. 9—11). Probably he had in view the party of license, who maintained the indifference of "eating things sacrificed to idols," and of "fornication," just as, in the previous verse, he had chiefly in view the party of his Judaising opponents.

## XIII.

(1) **This is the third time I am coming to you.**—The words may point either to three actual visits—(1) that of Acts xviii. 1; (2) an unrecorded visit (of which, however, there is no trace), during St. Paul's stay at Ephesus; and (3) that now in contemplation—or (1) to one actual visit, as before; (2) the purposed visit which had been abandoned (see Notes on chap. i. 16); and (3) that which he now has in view. The latter interpretation falls in best with the known facts of the case, and is in entire accordance both with his language in chap. xii. 14, and with his mode of expressing his intentions, as in 1 Cor. xvi. 5.

**In the mouth of two or three witnesses shall every word be established.**—There seems

(2) I told you before, and foretell you,
as if I were present, the second time;
and being absent now I write to them
which heretofore have sinned, and to
all other, that, if I come again, I will
not spare: (3) since ye seek a proof of
Christ speaking in me, which to you-
ward is not weak, but is mighty in you.
(4) For though he was crucified through
weakness, yet he liveth by the power of
God. For we also are weak in him,[1]
but we shall live with him by the power
of God toward you. (5) Examine your-
selves, whether ye be in
the faith; prove your own
selves. Know ye not your
own selves, how that Jesus
Christ is in you, except ye
be reprobates? (6) But I trust that ye
shall know that we are not reprobates.
(7) Now I pray to God that ye do no
evil; not that we should appear ap-
proved, but that ye should do that
which is honest, though we be as

Chap. xiii. 5–14. Closing words of counsel, prayer, and benediction.

[1] Or, *with him.*

---

no adequate reason for not taking these words in their simple and natural meaning. The rule, quoted from Num. xxxv. 30, Deut. xvii. 6, xix. 15, was of the nature of an axiom of Jewish, one might almost say of natural, law. And it had received a fresh prominence from our Lord's reproduction of it in giving directions as for the discipline of the society which He came to found. (See Note on Matt. xviii. 16.) What more natural than that St. Paul should say, "When I come, there will be no more surmises and vague suspicions, but every offence will be dealt with in a vigorous and full inquiry"? There seems something strained, almost fantastic, in the interpretation which, catching at the accidental juxtaposition of "the *third* time" and the "*three* witnesses," assumes that the Apostle personifies his actual or intended visits, and treats them as the witnesses whose testimony was to be decisive. It is a fatal objection to this view that it turns the judge into a prosecutor, and makes him appeal to his own reiteration of his charges as evidence of their truth.

(2) **I told you before, and foretell you . . .**—Better, *I have warned you before* (referring, probably, to the threat of 1 Cor. iv. 13—19, and implied in chap. i. 23). The chief objects of this rigour were to be those whom he had described previously as "having sinned beforehand" (see Note on chap. xii. 21); but he adds that his work as judge will extend to *all the rest* of the offenders. What he has in view is obviously passing a sentence of the nature of an excommunication on the offenders, "delivering them to Satan" (1 Cor. v. 5; 1 Tim. i. 20), with the assured confidence that that sentence would be followed by some sharp bodily suffering. In that case men would have, as he says in the next verse, a crucial *test* whether Christ was speaking in him, and learn that he whom they despised as *infirm* had a reserve-force of spiritual power, showing itself in supernatural effects even in the regions of man's natural life.

(3) **Which to you-ward is not weak.**—There is still a touch of indignant sadness in the tone in which the words are uttered. Men will not be able to cast that reproach of weakness upon Him whose might they will feel all too keenly.

(4) **For though he was crucified through weakness . . .**—The better MSS. give another reading, without the contingent or concessive clause: *For even He was crucified.* St. Paul seems to see in Christ the highest representative instance of the axiomatic law by which he himself had been comforted, that strength is perfected in infirmities. For He too lived encompassed with the infirmities of man's nature, and the possibility of the crucifixion flowed from that fact, as a natural sequel.

**For we also are weak in him, but we shall live with him.**—The thought that underlies the apparently hard saying is that the disciples of Christ share at once in their Lord's weakness and in His strength. "We, too, are weak," the Apostle says; "we have our share in infirmities and sufferings, which are ennobled by the thought that they are ours because we are His; but we know that we shall live in the highest sense, in the activities of the spiritual life, which also we share with Him, and which comes to us by the power of God; and this life will be manifested in the exercise of our spiritual power towards you and for your good." To refer the words "we shall live" to the future life of the resurrection, though the thought is, of course, true in itself, is to miss the special force of the words in relation to the context.

(5) **Examine yourselves, whether ye be in the faith; prove your own selves.**—The position of "yourselves" in the Greek (before the verb in both clauses) shows that that is the word on which stress is emphatically laid, and the thought grows out of what had been said in verse 3: "You seek a test of my power. Apply a test to *yourselves.* Try *yourselves* whether you are living and moving in that faith in Christ which you profess" (the objective and subjective senses of faith melting into one without any formal distinction). "Subject *yourselves* to the scrutiny of your own conscience." The latter word had been used in a like sense in 1 Cor. xi. 28. So far as we can distinguish between it and the Greek for "examine," the one suggests the idea of a special test, the other a general scrutiny.

**How that Jesus Christ is in you, except ye be reprobates?**—On the last word see Notes on Rom. i. 28; 1 Cor. ix. 27. Here its exact meaning is defined by the context as that of failing to pass the scrutiny to which he calls them: "Christ is in you" (the central thought of the Apostle's teaching; Gal. i. 16; Eph. ii. 22; iii. 17; Col. i. 27), "unless the sentence, after an impartial scrutiny by yourselves, or by a judge gifted with spiritual discernment, is that there are no tokens of His presence." The ideas which Calvinistic theology has attached to the word "reprobate" are, it need hardly be said, foreign to the true meaning of the word, both here and elsewhere.

(6) **But I trust . . .**—Better, *But I hope . . .* The "we" that follows is emphatic: "whether *you* fail to pass the test or not, I have a good hope that you will know that *we* do not fail, whether the test be that which you demand (verse 3), or that which I apply to myself as in the sight of God."

(7) **Now I pray to God that ye do no evil.**—The better MSS. give, *we pray.* The words that follow involve a subtle play of thought and feeling on the two forms of the trial or scrutiny of which he has just

reprobates. (8) For we can do nothing
against the truth, but for the truth.
(9) For we are glad, when we are weak,
and ye are strong: and this also we
wish, *even* your perfection. (10) There-
fore I write these things being absent,
lest being present I should use sharp-
ness, according to the power which the
Lord hath given me to edification, and
not to destruction. (11) Finally, brethren,
farewell. Be perfect, be of good comfort,
be of one mind, live in peace; and the
God of love and peace shall be with you.
(12) Greet one another with an holy kiss

---

spoken. "We pray," he says, "that you may be kept from doing evil. Our purpose in that prayer is not that *we* may gain a reputation as successful workers in your eyes or those of others, but that *you* may do that which is nobly good (may advance from a negative to a positive form of holiness), even though the result of that may be that we no longer put our apostolic supernatural powers into play, and so seem to fail in the trial to which you challenge us." This gives, it is believed, the true underlying thought of the words, and, though the paraphrase is somewhat full, it could not well be expressed in a narrower compass.

(8) **For we can do nothing against the truth.**—Better, perhaps, *we are powerless.* Here, again, the meaning lies below the surface. The first impression which the words convey is that he is asserting his own thoroughness as a champion of the truth, so that it was a moral impossibility for him to do anything against it. The true sequence of thought, however, though it does not exclude that meaning, compels us to read much more between the lines. "Yes," he says, "we are content to seem to fail, as regards the exercise of our apostolic power to chastise offenders; for the condition of that power is that it is never exercised against the truth, and therefore if you walk in the truth, there will be no opening for its exercise." The feeling is analogous to that of Rom. ix. 3: "I could wish myself accursed from Christ for my brethren's sake;" perhaps also to that of the Baptist: "He must increase, but I must decrease" (John iii. 30); perhaps, yet again, to that of the patriot dying with the prayer, "May my name be without honour if only my country may be saved."

(9) **For we are glad, when we are weak . . .**—The last words cover many shades of meaning. We may think of the weakness of his bodily presence, of his physical infirmities, of the apparent failure of his supernatural powers because the condition of the Corinthian Church, as walking in faith and truth, presented no opening for their exercise. He can find cause for joy in all these, if only the disciples whom he loves are strong with the strength of God.

**This also we wish, even your perfection.**—Better, *your restoration.* This is the only passage in the New Testament in which the word occurs; but the corresponding verb is found in the "*mending* their nets" of Matt. iv. 21, Mark i. 19, and in the "restore" of Gal. vi. 1. Its proper meaning is to bring back to completeness. This, then, was what the Apostle had been aiming at all along. In his seeming harshness and self-assertion, as in his overflowing tenderness, he was looking forward to their restoration to their first love and their first purity. He would rather threaten than act, even at the cost of the threat appearing an empty vaunt, if only he might be spared the necessity for acting.

(10) **Therefore I write these things being absent . . .**—The words speak of an inner conflict, in which love has triumphed, not without pain, over feelings of bitterness and indignation. The storm has passed, and the sky is again clear. He does not recall what he has written, but he explains and half-apologises for it. It was better to speak with severity than to act. But even had it been necessary to act, as at one time he thought it would be, he wished them to understand that even then his aim would have been, as it was now, to restore them to their true completeness in Christ; not to inflict punishment for the sake of punishing, or as a mere display of power.

(11) **Finally, brethren, farewell.**—The word (literally, *rejoice*) was the natural close of a Greek letter, and is therefore adequately represented by the English "farewell," if only we remember that it was used in all the fulness of its meaning. "Rejoice—let that be our last word to you."

**Be perfect.**—Better, as before, *restore yourselves to completeness; amend yourselves.* In the words "be of good comfort" (better, perhaps, *be comforted,* with the implied thought that the comfort comes through accepting his word of counsel—see Note on Acts iv. 36) we trace an echo of what he had said in the opening of the Epistle, as to the "comfort" which had been given to him (chap. i. 4, 7). *Paraclesis* in its two-fold aspect is, in fact, the key-note of the whole Epistle. Taking the verb and the noun together, the word occurs twenty-eight times in it.

**Be of one mind.**—The phrase was one specially characteristic of St. Paul's teaching (Rom. xv. 6; Phil. ii. 2; iii. 16; iv. 2). His thoughts are apparently travelling back to the schisms over which he had grieved in 1 Cor. i.—iii., and to which he had referred in chap. xii. 20. What he seeks is the restoration of unity of purpose, and with that of inward and outward peace. If these conditions were fulfilled, the "God of love and peace would assuredly be with them," for peace rests ever upon the son of peace (Luke x. 6).

(12) **Greet one another with an holy kiss.**—The tense of the Greek verb indicates that the Apostle is giving directions, not for a normal and, as it were, liturgical usage, but for a single act. In doing so, he repeats what he had said in 1 Cor. xvi. 20. The same injunction appears in Rom. xvi. 16; 1 Thess. v. 26. What he meant was that, as the public reading of the Epistle came to a close, the men who listened should embrace each other and kiss each other's cheeks, in token that all offences were forgotten and forgiven, and that there was nothing but peace and goodwill between them. It was, perhaps, natural, that the counsel should be taken as a rubric, even at the cost of its losing its real significance, and becoming a stereotyped formula. So in the Apostolic Constitutions (possibly of the third century) we find the rubric, "Let the deacons say to all, 'Salute ye one another with a holy kiss:' and let the clergy salute the bishop, the men of the laity salute the men, the women the women." The deacons were to watch that there was no disorder during the act (viii. 57). In the account given by Justin (*Apol.* i. 65) it appears as preceding the oblation of the bread and wine for the Eucharistic Feast, as it did in most of

(13) All the saints salute you. (14) The grace of the Lord Jesus Christ, and the love of God, and the communion of the Holy Ghost, *be* with you all. Amen.

¶ The second *epistle* to the Corinthians was written from Philippi, *a city* of Macedonia, by Titus and Lucas.*

the Eastern liturgies, probably as a symbolic act of obedience to the command of Matt. v. 24. In the Western Church it came after the consecration of the elements and the Lord's Prayer. It was intermitted on Good Friday in the African Church (Tertull. *De Orat.* c. 14) as unsuitable for a day of mourning. It may be noted as the survival of a residuum of the old practice, that when the usage was suppressed by the Western Church, in the thirteenth century, it was replaced by the act of kissing a marble or ivory tablet, on which some sacred subject, such as the Crucifixion, had been carved, which was passed from one to another, and was known as the *osculatorium*, or "kissing instrument."

(13) **All the saints salute you.**—The salutation in the First Epistle came, it will be remembered, from the "brethren" of the Church of Asia. This comes from the "saints" of Philippi. The phrase, familiar as it is, is not without interest, as showing that St. Paul, wherever he might be, informed the Church of one locality when he was writing to another, and so made them feel that they were all members of the great family of God.

(14) **The grace of the Lord Jesus Christ . . .**—It is not without a special significance that the Epistle which has been, almost to the very close, the most agitated and stormy of all that came from St. Paul's pen, should end with a benediction which, as being fuller than any other found in the New Testament, was adopted from a very early period in the liturgies of many Eastern churches, such as Antioch, Cæsarea, and Jerusalem (Palmer, *Origines. Liturg.* i. 251). It may be noted that it did not gain its present position in the Prayer Book of the Church of England till the version of A.D. 1662, not having appeared at all till A.D. 1559, and then only at the close of the Litany.

The order of the names of the three Divine Persons is itself significant. Commonly, the name of the Father precedes that of the Son, as, *e.g.*, in chap. i. 2; Rom. i. 7; 1 Cor. i. 3. Here the order is inverted, as though in the Apostle's thoughts there was no "difference or inequality" between them, the question of priority being determined by the sequence of thought, and not by any essential distinction. To those who trace that sequence here there will seem sufficient reason for the order which we actually find. St. Paul had spoken of the comfort brought to his own soul by the words which he heard in vision from the lips of the Lord Jesus, "My *grace* is sufficient for thee" (chap xii. 9). He had spoken of that *grace* as showing itself in self-abnegation for the sake of man (chap. viii. 9). What more natural than that the first wish of his heart for those who were dear to him should be that that grace might be with them, working on them and assimilating them to itself? But the "favour," or "grace," which thus flowed through Christ was derived from a yet higher source. It was the love of God in Christ reconciling the world unto Himself (chap. v. 18—20), the love of the Eternal Father that was thus manifested in the "grace" of the Son. Could he separate those divine acts from that of Him whom he knew at once as the Spirit of God and the Spirit of Christ? (Rom. viii. 9—14; 1 Cor. ii. 11; vi. 11; Gal. iv. 6.) Was it not through their participation, their fellowship in that Spirit (the phrase meets us again in Phil. ii. 1) shedding down the love of God in their hearts (Rom. v. 5) that the grace of Christ and the love of the Father were translated from the region of abstract thoughts or mere empty words into the realities of a living experience?

And so the Epistle ends, not, we may imagine, if we may once picture to ourselves the actual *genesis* of the letter, without a certain sense of relief and of repose. It had been a hard and difficult task to dictate it. The act of dictation had been broken by the pauses of strong emotion or physical exhaustion. The Apostle had had to say things that went against the grain, of which he could not feel absolutely sure that they were the right things to say. (See Note on chap. xi. 17.) And now all is done. He can look forward to coming to the Corinthian Church, not with a rod, but in love and in the spirit of meekness (1 Cor. iv. 21). What the actual result of that visit was we do not know in detail, but there are at least no traces of disappointment in the tone of the Epistle to the Romans, which was written during that visit. He has been welcomed with a generous hospitality (Rom. xvi. 23). He has not been disappointed in the collection for the saints (Rom. xv. 26) either in Macedonia or Achaia. If we trace a reminiscence of past conflicts in the warning against those who cause divisions (Rom. xvi. 18), it is rather with the calmness of one who looks back on a past danger than with the bitterness of the actual struggle.

* The note, added by some unknown transcriber, though having no shadow of authority, is, probably, in this instance, as has been shown in the Notes on chap. viii. 16—22, a legitimate inference from the *data* furnished by the Epistle.

THE EPISTLE OF PAUL THE APOSTLE TO THE

# GALATIANS

# INTRODUCTION

TO

## THE EPISTLE OF PAUL THE APOSTLE TO THE

# GALATIANS

I. **Galatia.**—The name Galatia is used in two senses. In ordinary speech it was used to designate that portion of Asia Minor lying chiefly between the rivers Sangarius and Halys, which was inhabited by the tribe of Galatæ, or Galli. This warlike people had been invited over from Europe by Nicomedes king of Bithynia, who repaid their services by a grant of land. Issuing forth from thence, they had been for a time the terror and the scourge of Asia Minor, but they had been at last driven back and confined within the territory originally assigned to them. These events took place in the latter half of the third century B.C. Their power was broken by the Romans in B.C. 189, and though for another century and a half they retained a nominal independence, in B.C. 25 they were formally annexed to the empire of Rome.

Just before this final annexation, during the reign of the last king, Amyntas, the kingdom of Galatia had been considerably enlarged. Amyntas had ranged himself on the winning side in the great civil wars, and he had received as his reward Pisidia, Isauria, parts of Lycaonia and Phrygia, and Cilicia Trachæa. On his death the greater part of these dominions, with the exception of Cilicia Trachæa, became a single Roman province, which, for administrative purposes, was also known by the name Galatia.

To which of these two Galatias did St. Paul address his Epistle? Was it to the narrower Galatia—Galatia proper—or to the wider Galatia—the Roman province? There are some temptations to adopt the second of these views. In that case we should have a graphic account of the founding of the Galatian churches—for such they would be—in Acts xiii., xiv. At Antioch in Pisidia, which we are expressly told formed part of the kingdom of Amyntas, the Apostle had preached with a success which had called down violent opposition. Iconium, to which he retreated, appears not to have been given to Amyntas, and whether it formed part of the Roman province at this time is uncertain. There is, however, no doubt as to Lystra—where the two Apostles were received so enthusiastically—and Derbe. On the hypothesis that the Galatia of the Epistle is the Roman province, the scenes of this first missionary journey would be directly associated with it. On the contrary assumption, no details whatever as to the founding of the Galatian churches have come down to us.

In spite of this, and in spite of some other points in which the history may seem to be simplified by assigning to Galatia the wider signification, a balance of considerations seems to prevent us from doing so. There can be no question that St. Luke, in the Acts, wherever he speaks of Galatia, uses the word in its narrower and proper sense, and though this would not be in itself decisive as to the usage of St. Paul, still it is impossible to think that in impassioned passages like Gal. iii. 1, "O foolish Galatians, who hath bewitched you," &c., the Apostle is using only an official title. We shall be safe in assuming that he was really writing to the descendants of the Gallic invaders, and that he addresses them by the name by which they were familiarly known.

II. **The Galatians.**—It does not, however, follow from what has just been said that the Christian converts were taken solely or even chiefly from the native Galatians. They did but give a name to the country; three other nationalities went to make up its population. First came the Greeks, who were so numerous as to give to their adopted home the second name of Gallogræcia. Then, beneath the upper layer of conquering Galatians, there lay a large substratum of the older inhabitants, the conquered Phrygians; and by the side of both—brought partly by colonisation and partly by purposes of trade—were considerable numbers of Jews. Of the disturbing presence of this latter element the Epistle itself gives us ample evidence.

Still, the predominant body, and that which gave its most distinctive characteristics to the Church, were the genuine Galatians themselves. A question similar to that as to the boundaries of Galatia has been raised in regard to these. To what race did they belong? A large section of the ablest German commentators until quite recently were disposed to claim them as Teutons, the main ground for this being that Jerome, in the fourth century, observed a resemblance between the language spoken in Galatia and that of the Treveri, who bequeathed their name to the modern district of Treves, and who are said to have been German. This point, however, is itself perhaps more than doubtful, and as to the Galatæ there is abundant evidence, besides their name, to show that they were Celts, and not Teutons. This was the universal opinion of antiquity, to which even Jerome, notwithstanding his statement about the language, was no exception; and it is confirmed by a philological analysis of the names both of persons and of places in Galatia that have come down to us. The theory of the Teutonic origin of the Galatians is now given up, not only in England, but in Germany.

The Galatians, then, were Celts, and we are not surprised to find in them the Celtic qualities. They came of the race which "shook all empires, but founded none." Their great failing was in stability. Quick to receive impressions, they were quick to lose them; at one moment ardently attached, at the next violently opposed. This is precisely what St. Paul complains of. He gives a striking picture of the enthusiasm with which he had been received on his first visit. He himself was stricken down with sickness, but that did not damp the ardour of his converts. They would even have "plucked out their eyes," and given them to him. But in a short space of time all this was gone. They had now made common cause with his adversaries. They had forsaken his teaching and repudiated his authority.

The cause of the evil lay in the intrigues of certain Judaisers. And the consideration of the question in debate between them and St. Paul opens out a new subject for discussion.

**III. Contents and Doctrinal Character of the Epistle.**—The controversy that divided, and could not but divide, the infant Church, came to a head most conspicuously in Galatia. Was the Jewish Law to be binding upon Christians? It was only natural that many should be found to say that it was. Christianity had sprung out of Judaism. The first and most obvious article in the Christian creed—the Messiahship of Jesus—was one that might easily be accepted, and yet all the prejudices in favour of the Jewish Law be retained. It was only a deeper and prolonged reflection that could show the fundamental antagonism between the Jewish view of things and the Christian. St. Paul saw this, but there were many who were not so clear-sighted. The main body of the Church at Jerusalem held tenaciously to the Jewish practices. The old Pharisaic passion for making proselytes still clung to them. And emissaries from this Church had found their way—as they easily might, through the chain of Jewish posts scattered over Asia Minor—as far north as Galatia.

These emissaries pursued the same tactics as they had pursued elsewhere. They called in question the Apostle's authority. They claimed to act from a superior commission themselves. They disparaged his teaching of personal faith in Jesus. They knew nothing of such faith. They acknowledged Jesus as the Messiah, and with that they were content. They still looked for salvation, as they had done hitherto, from the literal performance of the Mosaic Law, and they forced this view upon the Galatians. They insisted specially on the rite of circumcision. They would not allow the Gentile converts to escape it. They proclaimed it as the only avenue to the covenant relation with God. And no sooner had the convert submitted to circumcision than they proceeded to lay upon him an oppressive burden of ritualistic ceremonies. He was to keep a multitude of seasons, "days, and months, and times, and years." If he was to enjoy the Messianic privileges he must be righteous. But to be righteous was to perform scrupulously the precepts of the Mosaic Law, and in the attempt to do this the convert's whole powers and energies were consumed. The Messiahship of Jesus was something secondary and subordinate. The Judaisers accepted it so far as it seemed to hold out to them a prospect of advantage, but otherwise it remained a mere passive belief. The key to life and conduct was still sought in the fulfilment of the Mosaic Law.

With such a position as this the Apostle could not but be directly at issue. To him the Messiahship of Jesus (including, as it did, His eternal Sonship) formed the very root and centre of his whole religious being. Faith—or the ardent conviction of this Messiahship in its completest sense—was the one great motive power which he recognised. And the state in which the Christian was placed by faith was itself—apart from any laborious system of legal observances—an attainment of righteousness. The Messianic system was everything. The Law henceforth was nothing. By his relation to the Messiah the Christian obtained all of which he had need. Sin stood between him and the favour of God, but the Messiah had died to remove the curse entailed by sin; and by his adhesion to the Messiah the Christian at once stepped into the enjoyment of all the blessings and immunities which the Messianic reign conferred. It was not that he was released from the obligations of morality (as represented by the Law), but morality was absorbed in religion. One who stood in the relation that the Christian did to Christ could not but lead a holy life; but the holy life was a consequence—a natural, easy, necessary consequence—of this relation, not something to be worked out by the man's unaided efforts, independently of any such relation. The command, "Be ye holy as I am holy," remained, but there intervened the motive and stimulus afforded by the death and exaltation of Christ. "Be ye holy, because ye are bought with a price; because ye are Christ's, and your life is hid with Christ in God."

The Law then no longer held that primary position which it had occupied under the old covenant. It had fulfilled its functions, which were preparatory and not final. Its object had been to deepen the sense of sin, to define unmistakably the line which separated it from righteousness, and so to prepare the way for that new Messianic system in which the power of sin was not ignored but overcome, and overcome by lifting the believer as it were bodily into a higher sphere. He was taken out of a sphere of human effort and ritual observance, and raised into a sphere in which he was surrounded by divine influences, and in which all that he had to do was to realise practically what had already been accomplished for him ideally. In that sphere the centre and life-giving agency was Christ, and the means by which Christ was to be apprehended was Faith. So that Christ and Faith were the watchwords of the Apostle, just as the Law and Circumcision were the watchwords of the Jews.

Thus the line that the Apostle takes in this Epistle was clearly marked out for him. Against the attacks upon his apostolic authority he defended himself by claiming that, although he was a late comer in point of time, this did not imply any real inferiority. His was not an authority derived at second-hand. On the contrary, he owed his calling and commission directly to God Himself. The proof was to be seen both in the circumstances of his conversion and also in the fact that, though he had once or twice been brought into apparent contact with the elder Apostles, his teaching was entirely independent of them, and was already fully formed when he had at last an opportunity of consulting them about it. And in practice, not only was he recognised by them as an equal, but even Peter submitted to a rebuke from him. On the other hand, upon the great dogmatic question, St. Paul meets his opponents by an emphatic statement of his own position. Christianity is not something accessory to the Law, but supersedes it. Righteousness is to be sought not by legal observances, but by faith. The old system was carnal, material, an affair of externals. The new system is a spiritual renewal by spiritual forces. Not that there is any real contradiction between the new and the old. For the very type and pattern of the old dispensation—Abraham himself—obtained the righteousness that was imputed to him not by works, but by faith. Thus, the true descendant of Abraham is he who puts faith in Christ. It was to Christ that the promise related, in Christ that the whole divine scheme of redemption and regeneration centred. The Law could not interfere with it, for the Law came after the Promise, by which it was guaranteed. The function of the Law was something temporary and transient. It was, as it were, a state of tutelage for mankind. The full admission to the privileges of the divine patrimony was reserved for those who became personal followers of the Messiah. He was the Son of God, and those who cast in their lot wholly with Him were admitted to a share in His sonship. To go back to the old stage of ritual observance was pure retrogression. It was an unnatural exchange—a state of drudgery for a state of freedom. It was a reversal of the old patriarchal story—a preferring of Hagar and Ishmael for Isaac, the child of promise. The Apostle cannot think that the Galatians will do this. He exhorts them earnestly to hold fast to their liberty, to hold fast to Christ, not to give up their high privilege of seeking righteousness by faith, and accepting it through grace, for any useless ordinance like circumcision. Yet the liberty of the Christian is far from meaning license. License proceeds from giving way to the impulses of the flesh, but these impulses the Christian has got rid of. His relation to Christ has brought him under the dominion of the Spirit of Christ. He is spiritual, not carnal; and to be spiritual implies, or should imply, every grace and every virtue. The Galatians should be gentle and charitable to offenders. They should be liberal in their alms. The Epistle concludes with a repeated warning against the Judaising intruders. Their motives are low and interested. They wish to pass off themselves and their converts as Jews, and to escape persecution as Christians. But to do so they must give up the very essentials of Christianity.

The Epistle is not constructed upon any artificial system of divisions, but the subject-matter falls naturally into three main sections, each consisting of two of our present chapters, with a short preface and conclusion, the last in the Apostle's own handwriting. The first section contains the defence of his apostolic authority and independence in a review of his own career for the first seventeen years from his conversion. This leads him to speak of the dispute with St. Peter at Antioch, and the doctrinal questions involved in that dispute lead up to the second or doctrinal section, in which his own main tenet of righteousness by faith is contrasted with the teaching of the Judaisers and established out of the Old Testament. This occupies chaps. iii. and iv. The last section, is, as usual with St. Paul, hortatory, and consists of an application of the principles just laid down to practice, with such cautions as they may seem to need, and one or two special points which his experience in the Church at Corinth and the news brought to him from Galatia appear to have suggested.

The following may be taken as a tabular outline of the Epistle*:—

**I.—Introductory Address** (chap. i. 1—10).
- *a.* The apostolic salutation (chap. i. 1—5).
- *b.* The Galatians' defection (chap. i. 6—10).

**II.—Personal Apologia: an Autobiographical Retrospect** (chaps. i. 11—ii. 21).

The Apostle's teaching derived from God and not man (chap. i. 11, 12), as proved by the circumstances of—
- (1) His education (chap. i. 13, 14).
- (2) His conversion (chap. i. 15—17).
- (3) His intercourse with the other Apostles whether at (*a*) his first visit to Jerusalem (chap. i. 18—24), or (*b*) his later visit (chap. ii. 1—10).
- (4) His conduct in the controversy with Peter at Antioch (chap. ii. 11—14);
  The subject of which controversy was the supersession of the Law by Christ (chap. ii. 15—21).

**III.—Dogmatic Apologia: Inferiority of Judaism, or Legal Christianity, to the Doctrine of Faith** (chaps. iii. 1—iv. 31).
- (*a*) The Galatians bewitched into retrogression from a spiritual system to a carnal system (chap. iii. 1—5).
- (*b*) Abraham himself a witness to the efficacy of faith (chap. iii. 6—9).
- (*c*) Faith in Christ alone removes the curse which the Law entailed (chap. iii. 10—14).
- (*d*) The validity of the Promise unaffected by the Law (chap. iii. 15—18).
- (*e*) Special pædagogic function of the Law, which must needs give way to the larger scope of Christianity (chap. iii. 19—29).
- (*f*) The Law a state of tutelage (chap. iv. 1—7).
- (*g*) Meanness and barrenness of mere ritualism (chap. iv. 8—11).
- (*h*) The past zeal of the Galatians contrasted with their present coldness (chap. iv. 12—20).
- (*i*) The allegory of Isaac and Ishmael (chap. iv. 21—31).

**IV.—Hortatory Application of the Foregoing** (chaps. v. 1—vi. 10).
- (*a*) Christian liberty excludes Judaism (chap. v. 1—6).
- (*b*) The Judaising intruders (chap. v. 7—12).
- (*c*) Liberty not license, but love (chap. v. 13—15).
- (*d*) The works of the flesh and of the Spirit (chap. v. 16—26).
- (*e*) The duty of sympathy (chap. vi. 1—5).
- (*f*) The duty of liberality (chap. vi. 6—10).

**V.—Autograph Conclusion** (chap. vi. 11—18).
- (*a*) The Judaisers' motive (chap. vi. 12, 13).
- (*b*) The Apostle's motive (chap. vi. 14, 15).
- (*c*) His parting benediction, and claim to be freed from further annoyance (chap. vi. 16—18).

* Figures are used where the subdivisions are continuous steps in the same argument, letters where they are distinct arguments.

The subject of the Epistle to the Galatians might be summarily described as the same as that to the Romans—the doctrine of justification by faith—*i.e.*, the state of righteousness entered by means of faith. For a further discussion of the group of ideas involved in this the reader may be referred to the *Excursus* on Romans.

**IV. Date of the Epistle.**—Mention has just been made of the Epistle to the Romans, and the resemblance between these two Epistles forms an important element in the consideration of the next question with which we have to deal—the question as to the date of the Epistle, and the place from which it was written.

On this point two views are current. It is agreed that the Epistle was written on St. Paul's third great missionary journey. It is agreed that it belongs to the group which includes 1 and 2 Corinthians and Romans. The difference is as to the place which it occupies in this group. A large majority of commentators suppose it to have been the first of the four Epistles, and date it from Ephesus at some time during the Apostle's lengthened stay there, *i.e.*, at some time during the three years A.D. 54—57. The other view is that the Epistle was written after the two Epistles to the Corinthians, but before the Epistle to the Romans, *i.e.*, at the end of the year 57 or beginning of 58, from Macedonia or Greece. This view has until recently not had many supporters, but it has lately found a strong advocate in Dr. Lightfoot.

Practically there is a single main argument on each side. In favour of the earlier date, the one point that can be pressed is the expression used in chap. i. 6: "I marvel that ye are *so soon* removed from Him that called you, into another gospel." The conversion of the Galatians appears to have taken place in A.D. 51. St. Paul paid them a second visit in A.D. 54. In the autumn of that year his three years' stay at Ephesus began. And it is argued that the expression "soon" will not allow us to go beyond these three years. "Soon," however, is a relative term. It may mean any interval from a few minutes to one or more centuries. The context must decide. A change, which in the natural course of things would take a protracted length of time to accomplish, might be described as taking place "soon" if it was brought about in a space of time conspicuously shorter than might have been expected. But for the conversion of a whole community to Christianity, and for their second conversion to another form of Christianity wholly distinct from the first, we should surely expect a long and protracted period. Under such circumstances a period of six or seven years might very well be called "soon." To this argument, then, it does not seem that very much, or indeed any, weight can be attached.

The one chief argument upon the other side is the very close and remarkable similarity, both in ideas and language, between the Epistles to Galatians and the Romans, and, in somewhat lower degree, 2 Corinthians. Any one may observe in himself a tendency to use similar words, and to fall into similar trains of thought at particular periods. This is especially the case with strong thinkers who take a firm grip of ideas, but are possessed of less facility and command of words in which to express them. Such was St. Paul. And accordingly we find that the evidence of style as a help to determine the chronological relations of the different Epistles is peculiarly clear and distinct. But in the doctrinal portions of Romans and Galatians we have a resemblance so marked—the same main thesis, supported by the same arguments, the same Scripture proofs (Lev. xviii. 5; Ps. cxliii. 2; Hab. ii. 4), the same example, Abraham, thrown into relief by the same contrast, that of the Law, developed to the same consequences and couched throughout in language of striking similarity—that we seem to be precluded from supposing any interval between them sufficient to allow of a break in the Apostle's mind. And considering the throng of events and emotions through which the Apostle was now passing; observing further that the three Epistles, 2 Corinthians, Galatians, and Romans, in this order, form a climax as to the distinctness with which the ideas expressed in them are elaborated, it would seem that the Epistle with which we are dealing should be placed between the other two; that is to say, we should assign it to the end of the year 57, or beginning of 58, and the place of its composition would probably be Macedonia or Greece.

The course, then, of the history will be this: St. Paul first visited Galatia on the occasion of his second missionary journey soon after the memorable conference at Jerusalem, and probably about the year A.D. 51. His intention had been to pass from Lycaonia due west into the Roman province of Asia. From this, however, he was prevented, as St. Luke informs us, by some supernatural intimation. Accordingly he turned northwards through Phrygia, and so entered Galatia. Here he seems to have been detained by illness (Gal. iv. 13, 14). He took the opportunity to preach, and his preaching was so successful that the Church in Galatia was definitely founded. This work accomplished, he left for Mysia, and thence passed on to Troas and Macedonia, where the better known portion of the second missionary journey begins. After the conclusion of this journey St. Paul, in starting upon his third missionary journey, again directed his course to Galatia. This time the historian mentions "the country of Galatia and Phrygia" in a different order from that in which they had occurred before. We should conclude, therefore, that St. Paul made his way straight from Antioch; and as no mention is made this time of the churches of Lycaonia, it would seem probable that he took the direct Roman road skirting Cappadocia. On his arrival in Galatia we read that he went through it "in order, strengthening the disciples" (Acts xviii. 23). We should gather from some indications in the Epistle (chaps. iv. 16; v. 21) that he had found it necessary to administer rather severe reproof to his converts. Already there were signs of false teaching in the Church. The Apostle's Judaising opponents had obtained an entrance, and he was obliged to speak of them in language of strong condemnation (Gal. i. 9). But the warning was in vain. This second visit had taken place in the autumn of A.D. 54, and from the end of that year till the autumn of A.D. 57, during which he was settled at Ephesus, disquieting rumours continued to be brought to him of the increasing defection of his converts, and the increasing influence of the Judaising party. Matters went on from bad to worse; and at last, apparently upon his way through Macedonia to Greece, the Apostle received such news as determined him to write at once. The Epistle bears marks of having been written under the influence of a strong and fresh impression; and Dr. Lightfoot, with his usual delicate acumen, infers from the greeting, "from all the brethren that are with me" (chap. i. 2), that it was probably written *en voyage*, and not from any of the larger churches of Macedonia, or, as might have been otherwise thought natural, Corinth. At all events, it would seem that we should be keeping most closely to the canons of probability if we assign the Epistle to the winter months of the years 57—58.

**V. Genuineness of the Epistle.**—No doubt of any real importance has been or can be cast upon the genuineness of the Epistle. It is one of those fervid outbursts of impassioned thought and feeling which are too rare and too strongly individual to be imitated. The internal evidence, therefore, alone would be sufficient, but the external evidence is also considerable. It is true that nothing conclusive is found in the apostolic fathers. The clearest allusion would seem to be in the Epistle of Polycarp to the Philippians, cap. 5: "Knowing, then, that *God is not mocked*" (a peculiar and striking word) "we ought to walk in His commandment and His glory" (comp. Gal. vi. 7); and again, in chap. iii., with perhaps a somewhat more direct reference, "who (St. Paul) also in his absence wrote unto you Epistles that you might be able to be built up unto the faith given you, *which is the mother of us all.*" (Comp. Gal. iv. 26.) It is noticeable that though Justin Martyr does not name the Epistle, and, indeed, nowhere directly quotes from St. Paul, yet in two consecutive chapters he makes use of two passages of the Old Testament (Deut. xxi. 23, and xxvii. 26), which are also quoted in close connection by St. Paul, and that these passages are given with precisely the same variations both from the Septuagint and the Hebrew. There is also a clear quotation in Athenagoras (*circ.* 177 A.D.). But, until we get towards the end of the second century, the best evidence is not so much that of orthodox writers as of heretics. Marcion, who flourished A.D. 140, laid great stress upon this Epistle, which he placed first of the ten which he recognised as St. Paul's. The Ophites and Valentinians, in writings belonging to this century, quoted largely from it. Celsus (*circ.* 178) speaks of the saying, Gal. vi. 14, "The world is crucified unto me, and I unto the world," as commonly heard amongst Christians. The author of the Clementine *Homilies* (which may be probably, though not certainly, placed about 160 A.D.) grounds upon St. Paul's account of the dispute at Antioch an attack upon the Apostle himself; and the Epistle furnishes other material for accusation. As we draw near the last quarter of the century the evidence for this, as for most other books of the New Testament, becomes ample. The Muratorian Canon (*circ.* 170 A.D.) places the Epistle in the second place, next to 1 and 2 Corinthians. The Syriac and the Old Latin translations (the second of which was certainly, and the first probably, made before this time), both contain it. Irenæus, Clement of Alexandria, and Tertullian, quote the Epistle frequently, and as a work of St. Paul's. And, what is of still more importance, the text, as it appears in quotations by these writers, as well as in the versions, and even so far back as Marcion, already bears marks of corruption, showing that it had been for some time in existence, and that it had passed through a lengthened process of corruption. But to prove the genuineness of the Epistle to the Galatians is superfluous. It is rather interesting to collect the evidence as a specimen of the kind of evidence that, in the case of a work of acknowledged genuineness, is forthcoming.

[The English commentator upon the Epistle to the Galatians has no excuse beyond the calibre of his own powers, if his treatment of the subject is inadequate. He has before him two commentaries in his own language, Dr. Lightfoot's and Bishop Ellicott's, which, in their kind, cannot easily be surpassed. It is needless to say that these, along with Meyer, have been taken as the basis of the present edition. Wieseler, Alford, and Wordsworth being occasionally consulted.]

# THE EPISTLE OF PAUL THE APOSTLE TO THE

# GALATIANS

CHAPTER I.—(1) Paul, an apostle, (not of men, neither by man, but by Jesus Christ, and God the Father, who raised him from the dead;) (2) and all the brethren which are with me, unto the churches

Chap. i. 1–5. The salutation.

A.D. 58.

I.

(1–5) It is no self-constituted teacher by whom the Galatians are addressed, but an Apostle who, like the chosen Twelve, had received his commission, not from any human source or through any human agency, but directly from God and Christ. As such, he and his companions that are with him give Christian greeting to the Galatian churches, invoking upon them the highest of spiritual blessings from God, the common Father of all believers, and that Redeemer whose saving work they denied and, by their relapse into the ways of the world around them, practically frustrated.

St. Paul had a two-fold object in writing to the Galatians. They had disparaged his authority, and they had fallen back from the true spiritual view of Christianity—in which all was due to the divine grace and love manifested in the death of Christ—to a system of Jewish ceremonialism. And at the very outset of his Epistle, in the salutation itself, the Apostle meets them on both these points. On the one hand, he asserts the divine basis of the authority which he himself claimed; and on the other, he takes occasion to state emphatically the redeeming work of Christ, and its object to free mankind from those evil surroundings into the grasp of which the Galatians seemed again to be falling.

(1) **An apostle.**—This title is evidently to be taken here in its strictest sense, as St. Paul is insisting upon his equality in every respect with the Twelve. The word was also capable of a less exclusive use, in which the Apostle would seem to be distinguished from the Twelve (1 Cor. xv. 5, 7). In this sense Barnabas and James the Lord's brother, possibly also Andronicus and Junias in Rom. xvi. 7, were called "Apostles."

**Not of men, neither by man.**—Two distinct prepositions are used:—"not of" (*i.e., from*) "men," in the sense of the ultimate source from which authority is derived; "neither by" (or, *through*) "man," with reference to the channel or agency by which it is conveyed. Thus we speak of the Queen as the "fount" of honour, though honour may be conferred by the ministry acting in her name. The kind of honour which St. Paul held (his Apostleship) was such as could be derived only from God; nor was any human instrumentality made use of in conferring it upon him. His appointment to the Apostolate is connected by St. Paul directly with the supernatural appearance which met him upon the way to Damascus. The part played by Ananias was too subordinate to introduce a human element into it; and the subsequent "separation" of Paul and Barnabas for the mission to the Gentiles, though the act of the Church at Antioch, was dictated by the Holy Ghost, and was rather the assignment of a special sphere than the conferring of a new office and new powers.

**By Jesus Christ.**—The preposition here, as in the last clause, is that which is usually taken to express the idea of mediate agency. It represents the channel down which the stream flows, not the fountain-head from which it springs. Hence it is applied appropriately to Christ as the *Logos*, or Word, through whom God the Father communicates with men as the divine agent in the work of creation, redemption, revelation. (See John i. 3; 1 Cor. viii. 6; Heb. i. 2, *et al.*) It is also applied to men as the instruments for carrying out the divine purposes. The intervention of Jesus Christ took place in the vision through which, from a persecutor, St. Paul became a "chosen vessel" for the propagation of the gospel.

**And God the Father**—*i.e., and by* (or, *through*) *God the Father;* the same preposition governing the whole clause. We should naturally have expected the other preposition ("of," or "from"), which signifies source, and not this, which signifies instrumentality; and it would have been more usual with the Apostle to say, "*from* God," and "*by*, or *through*, Christ." But God is at once the remote and the mediate, or efficient, cause of all that is done in carrying out His own designs. "Of him, and through him, and to him are all things" (Rom. xi. 36).

**The Father.**—This is to be taken in the sense in which our Lord Himself spoke of God as "*My* Father," with reference to the peculiar and unique character of His own sonship—the Father, *i.e.*, of *Christ*, not of all *Christians*, and still less, as the phrase is sometimes used, of all *men*. This appears from the context. The title is evidently given for the sake of contradistinction; and it is noticeable that at this very early date the same phrase is chosen as that which bore so prominent a place in the later creeds and the theology of which they were the expression.

**Who raised him from the dead.**—Comp. Rom. i. 4: "Declared to be the Son of God with power . . . by the resurrection from the dead." The resurrection is the act which the Apostle regards as completing the divine exaltation of Christ. It is this exaltation, therefore, which seems to be in his mind. He had derived his own authority directly from God and Christ as sharers of the same divine majesty. It was not the man Jesus by whom it had been conferred upon him, but the risen and ascended Saviour, who, by the fact of his resurrection, was "declared to be the Son of God with power." So that the commission of the Apostle was, in all respects, divine and not human.

(2) **All the brethren which are with me**—*i.e.,*

of Galatia: (3) grace *be* to you and peace from God the Father, and *from* our Lord Jesus Christ, (4) who gave himself for our sins, that he might deliver us

all his travelling companions. We are unable to say exactly who these were, the more so as we do not know with any certainty the place from which St. Paul was writing. He may have had in his company most of those who are mentioned in Acts xx. 4 as accompanying him back into Asia: Sopater, son of Pyrrhus (according to an amended reading); Aristarchus and Secundus, of Thessalonica; Gaius, of Derbe; Tychicus and Trophimus, of Asia; in any case, probably Timothy, and perhaps Titus.

It was usual with St. Paul to join with his own name that of one or other of his companions in the address of his Epistles. Thus, in the First Epistle to the Corinthians he associates with himself Sosthenes; in the Second Epistle to Corinth, and in those to the Philippians and Colossians, Timothy and Silvanus. In writing to the Galatians, St. Paul includes all his companions in his greeting, hardly with the view of fortifying himself with their authority, for he is ready enough to take the whole defence of his own cause upon himself, but, perhaps, not altogether without the idea that he is possessed of their sympathy.

**The churches of Galatia.**—See the *Introduction* to this Epistle.

This opening salutation is intentionally abrupt and bare. Usually it was the Apostle's custom to begin with words of commendation. He praises all that he can find to praise even in a Church that had offended so seriously as the Corinthians. (See 1 Cor. i. 2, 4—7.) But the errors of the Galatians, he feels, go more to the root of things. The Corinthians had failed in the practical application of Christian principles; the Galatians (so far as they listened to their Judaising teachers) could hardly be said to have Christian principles at all. The Apostle is angry with them with a righteous indignation, and his anger is seen in the naked severity of this address.

(3) **Grace . . . and peace.**—See Note on Rom. i. 7.

**God the Father.**—We may see by this verse how the title "Father," originally used in the present formula to distinguish between the Divine Persons, came gradually to contract a wider signification. God is, through Christ, the Father of all who by their relation to Christ are admitted into the position of "sons" (Rom. viii. 14—17; Gal. iv. 5—7). Hence, where no special limitation is imposed by the context, this secondary sense may be taken as included.

**And from our Lord Jesus Christ.**—Strictly, it would be more in accordance with the theology of St. Paul to say that grace and peace were given *from* the Father, *by*, or *through*, the Son. Here the one preposition *from* is used to cover both cases, just as *by* had been used in verse 1. It is equally correct to use the word "from" with reference to a mediate and to the ultimate stage in the act of procession. Water may be drawn not only from the fountain-head, but also from the running stream.

(4) **Who gave himself.**—Surrendered Himself, of His own free act and will, to those who sought His death. The phrase has a parallel in Tit. ii. 14, and appears in its full and complete form in the Gospel saying (Matt. xx. 28; Mark x. 45): "The Son of Man came to give His life a ransom for many"; and in 1 Tim. ii. 6: "Who gave Himself a ransom" (the word is here a compound, which brings out more strongly the sense of vicariousness) "for all."

**For our sins.**—In the Greek there are three prepositions, which can only be translated by the single word "for" in English. The first has for its primary sense "concerning," or "relating to"; it merely marks a connection or relation between two facts. The second has rather the sense "in behalf of," "in the interests of." The third means strictly "in place of." The first, as might be expected, is naturally used in respect of *things;* the second and third of *persons.* The death of Christ was a sacrifice *for sins, i.e.,* the sins of mankind stood in a distinct relation to it, which was really that of cause. The sins of mankind it was which set the whole scheme of redemption in motion, and to take away those sins was its main object. The death of Christ was a sacrifice *for sinners.* It was a sacrifice wrought in their behalf, for their benefit. It was also a sacrifice wrought *in their stead.* Christ suffered in order that they might not suffer. He gave His life "a ransom *for* (*i.e., in place of*) many." The first of these meanings is represented in Greek by the preposition *peri,* the second by *huper,* the third by *anti.* The distinction, however, is not quite strictly kept up. We not unfrequently find the death of Christ described as a sacrifice for (*on behalf of*) sins. This would correspond rather to our phrase "for the sake of." The object was to do away with sins. They were, as it were, the final cause of the atonement.

It is somewhat doubtful which of the first two prepositions is to be read here. By far the majority of MSS. have *peri,* but the famous Codex Vaticanus, and one of the corrections of the Sinaitic MS., have *huper.* The two prepositions are not unfrequently confused in the MSS., and the probability in this case is that the numerical majority is right. It will then be simply stated in the text that the sins of men and the sacrifice of Christ have a relation to each other. If there had been no sin there would have been no redemption.

**Deliver us.**—The deliverance present to the mind of the Apostle appears to be rather (in technical language) that of sanctification than that of justification. The object of redemption is regarded for the moment as being to deliver men from sin, and not so much to deliver them from guilt, the consequence of sin. The Atonement has really both objects, but it is the first that the Apostle has in view in this passage.

**This present evil world.**—The reading of the three oldest and best MSS. tends rather to emphasise the word "evil"—"this present world, with all its evils." A question is raised as to the word translated "present," which might probably mean "impending;" but the Authorised version is probably right. "This present world" is strictly *this present age.* The Jews divided the history of the world into two great periods —the times antecedent to the coming of the Messiah, and the period of the Messianic reign. The end of the first and the beginning of the second were to be especially attended with troubles; and it was just in this transition period—the close of the older dispensation of things—in which the Apostles regarded themselves as living. The iniquities of the Pagan society around them would naturally give them an intense longing for release; but the release which they seek is moral and spiritual. They do not so much pray that they may be "taken out of the world" as that they may be "kept from the evil." This the Christian scheme, duly accepted and followed, would do. The Atonement frees

from this present evil world, according
to the will of God and our Father:
(5) to whom *be* glory for ever and ever.
Amen.
(6) I marvel that ye are so soon re-
moved from him that called you into
the grace of Christ unto
another gospel: (7) which
is not another; but there
be some that trouble you, and would

Chap. i. 6—10. The Galatians' defection.

---

men from guilt, but its efficacy does not cease there; it sets going a train of motives which hold back the Christian from sin, and constrain him to use his best endeavours after a holy life. The Galatians had lost sight of the power of the Atonement to do this, and had fallen back upon the notion of a legal righteousness, through the vain attempt to keep the commandments of the Law.

**According to the will.**—The scheme of redemption was willed by God, and therefore all that was done, either on the part of man or of his Redeemer, was a carrying out of His will.

**Of God and our Father.**—Or, as it might be, *of our God and Father.* It was the fatherly love of God for His creature, man, that set the work of redemption in motion; hence, in reference to the work of redemption, He is spoken of as "*our* Father"—*i.e.*, the Father of mankind.

(5) **Glory.**—Perhaps, properly, *the glory*—*i.e.*, the divine glory: that pre-eminent glory with which no other can compare.

If this is the case, then it would be better to supply "is" than "be." His own peculiar glory *does* belong to God, and therefore the Christian ascribes it to Him as that which is already His; he does not pray for it as something unfulfilled, as, *e.g.*, he prays for the coming of God's kingdom.

In the insertion of this brief doxology the mind of the Apostle obeys an involuntary impulse of reverential awe. For a similar ascription in the same parenthetic form, comp. Rom. ix. 5.

**For ever and ever.**—Literally, *for ages of ages,* a Hebraising expression for infinite time. Commonly, time was divided only into two great world-periods; but the second is, as it were, multiplied indefinitely—"for all possible ages."

(6–10) The Apostle is surprised at their rapid defection. The doctrine to which they had at first given in their adhesion was a doctrine of salvation by grace: they now imagined that they were only hearing a different version of the same truths. A different version? How was that possible? There could not be any second gospel, nor was there really anything of the kind. It was not a new gospel, but only a factious perversion of the *old.* Those who do this—no matter who they be—are accursed. That, at least, is plain speaking, and no one can accuse it of time-serving.

The Apostle had ended his address to the Galatians abruptly, and now he plunges abruptly, and without more preface, into the midst of his charges against them. He cannot understand their sudden apostasy.

(6) **Removed.**—The Greek word is one regularly used for a "deserter," "turn-coat," or "apostate," either in war, politics, or religion. The tense is strictly present: "You are now, at this moment, in the act of falling away."

**Him that called you.**—The call of the Christian is attributed by St. Paul to God the Father; so even in Rom. i. 6. The Christian, having been *called* by God, *belongs to* Christ. The part taken by Christ in the calling of the Christian is rather a mediate agency, such as is expressed in the next phrase.

**Into the grace of Christ.**—Rather, *by the grace of Christ.* The grace (*i.e.*, the free love) of Christ becomes the instrument of the divine calling, inasmuch as it is through the preaching of that free love and free gift that the unbeliever is at first attracted and won over to the faith. The "grace of Christ" is His voluntary self-surrender to humiliation and death, from no other prompting than His own love for sinful men.

(6, 7) **Unto another gospel: which is not another.**—It is to be regretted that the English language hardly admits the fine shade of distinction which exists here in the Greek. The Greek has two words for "another:" one (the first of those which is here used) implying a difference in kind, the other implying mere numerical addition.

Another gospel do I call it? That would seem to concede its right to be called a gospel at all. It might be supposed to be some alternative theory, existing side by side with that which you originally heard; but this cannot be. This "other gospel" is not a second gospel; for there cannot be two gospels. The inference, therefore, to be drawn is that it is not a gospel in any sense of the word. This, then, may be dismissed. It is no true gospel, but only mischievous and factious meddling on the part of certain false teachers.

(7) **But there be some.**—The force of the Greek conjunction is, rather, *except that,* as the word "only" is used idiomatically in English. So far from being a second gospel, it is really no gospel, "*only* there are some . . . ," *i.e.*, the only sense in which there can be any mention of a second gospel is that there are some who pervert the old gospel. The existence of this party is the only excuse for the name. And it is a mere excuse. They do not deserve any such dignity. They really lay themselves under the curse of God.

**That trouble you.**—The Judaising party, with its restless factiousness and bigotry, causing schisms and divisions in the Church.

**Pervert.**—The Greek is even still stronger—*reverse,* or *change to its very opposite.* This they did by substituting a doctrine of righteousness by works—self-justification before God by performing the precepts of the Mosaic law—for the doctrine of reconciliation with God through the free forgiveness which He has promised to faith in Christ.

**The gospel of Christ.**—Where combinations of this kind occur, the question naturally suggests itself: What is the relation of the two words to each other? For instance, in the present case, is it "the gospel taught by Christ," or the "gospel *concerning* Christ?" The following rule has been proposed:—In such phrases as the "gospel of salvation," the "gospel of the kingdom," the genitive is that of the object—"of" is equivalent to "concerning." In the phrase "the gospel of God" it represents rather the cause or authorship: "the gospel of which God *is the Author.*" In the present phrase, "the gospel of Christ," it may be either

pervert the gospel of Christ. (8) But
though we, or an angel from heaven,
preach any other gospel unto you than
that which we have preached unto you,
let him be accursed. (9) As we said
before, so say I now again, If any *man*
preach any other gospel unto you than
that ye have received, let him be
accursed. (10) For do I now persuade
men, or God? or do I seek to please
men? for if I yet pleased men, I should
not be the servant of Christ.
(11) But I certify you, brethren, that
the gospel which was preached of

---

one or the other, according to the context. We must not, however, narrow too much the Apostle's use of language. A somewhat vague and ambiguous term sometimes best expresses the fulness of his meaning. In English we might use the phrase "Christ's gospel" to include at once "the gospel which *proceeds from* Christ," and "the gospel which *relates to* Christ," all, in fact, which makes it in any sense *belong to* Him and bear His name.

(8) **Though.**—The Greek is, strictly, *even though*, marking an extreme and improbable supposition.

**We.**—It seems, perhaps, too much to say, in the face of 2 Thess. ii. 2 ("by letter as from us"), that St. Paul never used the plural in speaking of himself alone. Still there may, both there and here, be some thought of associating his more immediate companions ("the brethren which are with me," verse 2) with himself, the more so as he knew them to be entirely at one with him in doctrine.

**Than that.**—The Greek has here, not a conjunction, but a preposition, the precise sense of which is ambiguous. It may mean "besides," "in addition," or it may mean "contrary to." The first of these senses has met with the most favour from Protestant, the second from Roman Catholic commentators, as, on the one hand, it seemed to exclude, and on the other to admit, the appeal to tradition. Looking at it strictly in connection with the context, the sense "contrary" seems best, because the gospel taught by the Judaising teachers was "another," in the sense of being *different from* that of St. Paul. It was a fundamental opposition of principles, not merely the addition of certain new doctrines to the old.

**Accursed.**—See 1 Cor. xvi. 22. The original Greek word is retained in the translation, *Let him be Anathema.* The word exists in two forms, with a long *e* and a short *e* respectively; and whereas its original meaning was simply that of being "devoted to God," the form with the long vowel came by gradual usage to be reserved for the good side of this: "devoted, in the sense of consecration;" while the form with the short vowel was in like manner reserved for the bad sense: "devoted to the curse of God." Attempts have been made to weaken its significance in this passage by restricting it to "excommunication by the Church;" but this, though a later ecclesiastical use of the word, was not current at such an early date.

In considering the dogmatic application, it is right to bear in mind the nature of the heretical doctrines which it was the Apostle's object to denounce. They made no profession to be deduced from his own, but were in radical and avowed opposition to them. Still, there is room to believe that if the Apostle could have reviewed his own words at a calmer moment he might have said of himself: "I spake as a man."

(9) **As we said before.**—Probably, upon his last (*i.e.*, his second) visit, at the beginning of this, his third, great missionary journey (Acts xviii. 23). The germs of the apostasy in the Galatian Church would be already visible.

(10) You may take this vehemence of language as my answer to another charge that has been brought against me. I am accused of seeking popularity with men. Well, here at least is plainness of speech. If I seek to win favour with any one it is not with men, but God. The two things are really incompatible. If I were a favourite with men I should be no true servant of Christ.

St. Paul naturally laid himself open to the charge of men-pleasing by the flexibility and largeness of his character. The trifles about which others quarrelled he could look upon with indifference, and his ready power of sympathy led him to enter as much as possible into the point of view of others: "To the Jews he became as a Jew," &c. But where a question of principle was at stake he knew how to take his stand, and he let the Galatians see it in the very unequivocal language he is now using.

(10) **Now.**—*In speaking thus.*

**Persuade.**—*Conciliate, seek to win favour with,* or *to make friends of.*

**For.**—This word is omitted by all the best MSS. and editors. It is characteristic of the Apostle, especially in animated passages like the present, to omit the connecting particles which are so common in Greek. He has a simple answer to give to the accusation of time-serving, and he states it roundly: "If my present conduct was really that of a man-pleaser I should be something very different from what I am."

**Yet.**—*Still; at this late period of my career.* The Apostle has cut himself adrift from the current of his age too thoroughly and too long for him to be still floating with the tide.

(11, *et seq.*) The Apostle now enters at length upon his personal defence against his opponents. He does this by means of an historical retrospect of his career, proving by an exhaustive process the thesis with which he starts that the doctrine taught by him comes from a divine source, and possesses the divine sanction. My doctrine is not human, but divine; it could not be otherwise. For (*a*) I did not learn it in my youth—very much the contrary (verses 13—14); (*b*) I did not learn it at my conversion, for I went straight into the desert to wrestle with God in solitude (verses 15—17); (*c*) I did not learn it at my first visit to Jerusalem, for then I saw only Peter and James, and them but for a short time (verses 18—24); (*d*) I did not learn it at my later visit, for then I dealt with the other Apostles on equal terms, and was fully and freely acknowledged by them as the Apostle of the Gentiles (chap. ii. 1—10); (*e*) Nay, I openly rebuked Peter for seeming to withdraw the support he had accorded to me (chap. ii. 11—14); (*f*) the law is dead, and the life which the Christian has he draws solely from Christ (chap. ii. 15—21).

(11) **But.**—There is a nearly even balance of MSS. authority between this word and *For.* In any case we

me is not after man. (12) For I
neither received it of man
neither was I taught *it*,
but by the revelation of
Jesus Christ. (13) For ye
have heard of my conver-
sation in time past in the
Jews' religion, how that beyond mea-
sure I persecuted the church of God,
and wasted it: (14) and profited in
the Jews' religion above many my
equals[1] in mine own nation, being more
exceedingly zealous of the traditions of
my fathers. (15) But when it pleased
God, who separated me
from my mother's womb,

Chaps. i. 11—ii 21. Autobiographical retrospect.

Chap i. 13, 14 Education.

Chap. i. 15, 16. Conversion.

1 Gr. *equals in years.*

should in English naturally omit the conjunction, though a translation must represent it.

**Certify.**—The word which is thus translated is the same as that which is translated "declare" in 1 Cor. xv. 1; "give you to understand," in 1 Cor. xii. 3; and "do you to wit," in 2 Cor. viii. 1. It is used to introduce a statement made with emphasis and solemnity.

**After man.**—Perhaps the best way to express the force of this phrase would be by the adjective, "Is not human." Literally it is, *is not according to the standard of man*—to be judged by human measure, and therefore human in all respects, in its nature and origin.

(12) **For I neither received it.** — The first "neither" in this verse does not answer to the second, but qualifies the pronoun "I." The connection in the thought is perhaps something of this kind: "The gospel is not human as it comes to *you*; neither was it human as it first came to *me*."

**Taught.**—There is an antithesis between this word and "revelation" in the next clause. "I did not receive my doctrine from man by a process of teaching and learning, but from Christ Himself by direct revelation."

**By the revelation.**—It is better to omit the article: "by," or "through the medium of," revelation. What was this revelation, and when was it given? The context shows that it must have been at some time either at or near the Apostle's conversion. This would be sufficient to exclude the later revelation of 2 Cor. xii. 1. But can it be the vision on the way to Damascus itself alone? At first sight it would seem as if this was too brief, and its object too special, to include the kind of "sum of Christian doctrine" of which the Apostle is speaking. But this at least contained the two main points—the Messiahship of Jesus, and faith in Jesus, from which all the rest of the Apostle's teaching flowed naturally and logically. When once it was felt that the death of Christ upon the cross was not that of a criminal, but of the Son of God, the rest all seemed to follow. Putting this together with the sense, which we may well believe had been growing upon him, of the inefficacy of the Law, we can easily see how the idea would arise of a sacrifice superseding the Law, and in the relegation of the Law to this very secondary position the main barrier between Jew and Gentile would be removed. St. Paul himself, by laying stress upon his retreat to the deserts of Arabia, evidently implies that the gospel, as taught by him in its complete form, was the result of gradual development and prolonged reflection; but whether this is to be regarded as implicitly contained in the first revelation, or whether we are to suppose that there were successive revelations, of which there is no record in the Acts, cannot be positively determined.

**Of Jesus Christ**—*i.e.*, given *by* Jesus Christ; of which Jesus Christ is the *Author.*

(13, 14) Proof that the doctrine of the Apostle is derived from God and not from man, in that it could not be accounted for by his antecedents and education, all of which told *against*, rather than *for*, a Christian belief of any kind.

(13) **Ye have heard.**—Rather, *ye heard.* It was indeed notorious; but the Apostle may be referring to the fact that he himself usually (see Acts xxii. 3—21; xxvi. 4—20; 1 Cor. xv. 8—10) brought his own career and experiences into his preaching, so that they may have heard it from his own lips.

**My conversation . . . in the Jews' religion.**—How I behaved in the days of my Judaism. The phrase "Jews' religion" (literally, *Judaism*) is not used with any sense of disparagement.

**Wasted it.**—The same word is translated "destroyed" in Acts ix. 21: "Is not this he that destroyed them which called on this name?"

(14) **Profited.**—Made progress. The kind of progress would correspond to the width of the term "Judaism," with which it is connected, and would imply, not merely proficiency in theological knowledge, but also increase in zeal and strictness of ritualistic observance.

**My equals.**—Strictly, *my equals in age.* St. Paul is thinking of his contemporaries among the young men who came up, ardent like himself, to study the Law at the feet of Gamaliel or some other eminent Rabbi. He looks back upon them much as some English political or religious leader might look back upon his contemporaries at the university, and might point to his zealous advocacy of a cause that he has long since given over.

**Traditions.**—The "traditions of the elders" mentioned in Matt. xv. 2, Mark vii. 3, by which the commandment of God "was made of none effect" (Matt. xv. 6); the oral or unwritten law, which had gradually grown up by the side of the Pentateuch, and was afterwards embodied in the Mishnah.

(15) In pursuance of his main argument, the Apostle lays stress upon the fact that his very conversion and mission to the Gentiles had been first predestinated in the divine counsels, and afterwards carried out through divine interposition: it was throughout the work of God, and not of man.

**Pleased.**—The word specially used of the free will and pleasure of God, determined absolutely by itself, and by no external cause.

**God.**—The word should be printed in italics. It is wanting in the true text, but is left to be supplied by the reader.

**Separated me.**—Set me apart, marked me off from the rest of mankind, for this special object (*i.e.*, the Apostleship of the Gentiles). (Comp. Rom. i. 1, and Note there.)

**From my mother's womb.**—A comparison of other passages where this phrase is used seems to make it clear that the sense is rather "from the moment of my birth" than "from before my birth." (See

and called *me* by his grace, (16) to reveal
his Son in me, that I might preach him
among the heathen; immediately I
conferred not with flesh and blood:

(17) neither went I up to Jerusalem to
them which were apostles
before me; but I went
into Arabia, and returned

Chap. i. 17. Retreat into Arabia.

Ps. xxii. 10; Isa. xlix. 1, 5; Matt. xix. 12; Acts iii. 2; xiv. 8.) From the moment that he became a living and conscious human being he was marked out in the purpose of God for his future mission.

**Called me.**—The call is identical with the conversion of the Apostle through the vision which appeared to him on the way to Damascus. As the Apostle was conscious of having done nothing to deserve so great a mark of the divine favour, it is set down entirely to an act of grace.

(16) **To reveal his Son in me.**—That is, probably, *in my mind*, or *consciousness.* Before the Apostle could preach Christ to the Gentiles he needed to have first that intense inward conviction which was wrought in him during that sustained mental struggle which followed upon his conversion. It is possible that "in me" might be equivalent to "through me, as an organ or instrument"; but the sense above given, "in my heart and soul," seems more likely.

**That I might preach him.**—The one process was preparatory to the other. Having once obtained a firm inward apprehension of Christ as the Messiah and Saviour, the Apostle then comes forward to preach Him among the heathen. But that firm inward apprehension was not to be attained all at once, and it was in seeking this that "the Spirit drove him" into the wilderness of Arabia. First comes the instantaneous flash of the idea upon his soul ("to reveal his Son in me"); then the prolonged conflict and meditation, in which it gets thoroughly consolidated, and adjusted, and worked into his being (during the retirement into Arabia); lastly, the public appearance as a preacher to the heathen upon the return to Damascus.

**Immediately.**—This brings out the promptness and decision of the Apostle's action. The moment that the idea of Jesus as the Saviour was presented to his mind he sought no human aid to help him to work out the conception, but went at once into the desert.

**Conferred not.**—A substantially correct translation, though not quite exact. The Greek word contains the idea of taking counsel in personal interview, much as we now use the word "apply" in the phrase to "apply to a person."

**With flesh and blood**—*i.e.*, with man, with especial reference to human frailty and fallibility. Compare, for a like contrast between human and divine revelation, the commendation of St. Peter in Matt. xvi. 17: "Flesh and blood hath not revealed it unto thee, but my Father which is in heaven."

(17) **Went I up.**—The usual phrase is to go up to "Jerusalem," from the fact that Jerusalem stood upon high ground, and was approached from all sides by an ascent. Here, however, the reading is doubtful between "went up" and "went away," each of which is supported by nearly equally good authority. In so close a balance of the authorities the less common phrase is, perhaps, more likely to have been the original reading, though there is an almost equal probability that it may have slipped in from the second "went" (really the same word, "went away"), a little further on in the verse.

**Unto Arabia.**—The question, what part of Arabia St. Paul retired into can only be one of speculation. There is nothing in the context to show at all decisively. The boundary of Arabia at this period was not exactly defined. By some writers it was made to include Damascus itself. It is therefore possible that by "Arabia" may have been meant the desert in the neighbourhood of the city. This would be the most obvious supposition. But, on the other hand, there would be a certain appropriateness if we could imagine, as we are certainly permitted to do, that the scene of his sojourn may have been the region of Mount Sinai itself. The place where the Law was first given may have seen its renewal in his mind—not destroyed, but fulfilled in the new law of love. Like Moses, and like Elijah, the great minister of the new dispensation may have here received strength for his work. And if this was the case, we can the more readily understand the typical allusion to Mount Sinai later in the Epistle. Such arguments may have some slight weight, but the real locality must remain uncertain.

As to the *time* of the Apostle's withdrawal, and its duration, little can be said beyond the fact that it must have come within the three years that intervened between his conversion and the first visit to Jerusalem. When we compare this account with the narrative of the Acts, it is not clear how they are to be reconciled. St. Paul says, that after his conversion, "immediately (*eutheōs*) he conferred not with flesh and blood . . . but went unto Arabia." St. Luke says, after recording the same event, "Then was Saul certain days with the disciples which were at Damascus. And straightway (*eutheōs*) he preached Christ (or, according to a more correct reading, *Jesus*) in the synagogues, that He is the Son of God" (Acts ix. 19, 20). There does not seem room here to insert the retreat into Arabia. It would indeed come in more naturally among the "many days," mentioned in a later verse, which were terminated by the plot of the Jews against the life of the Apostle and his final escape from Damascus. There would still, however, be some apparent collision between "conferring not with flesh and blood" and "spending certain days with the disciples" at Damascus. The discrepancy is only such as we might expect to find between two perfectly independent narratives, one of which was compiled from secondary sources, and is, besides, very brief and summary in its form. We are obliged, by the Apostle's own words, to believe that his withdrawal into Arabia took place "immediately" after his conversion; and as it would not take a very long time to attract the attention or excite the animosity of the Jews at Damascus, it seems natural to suppose that this period of silent seclusion occupied the larger half of the whole period of three years.

The patristic commentators seem to have held, for the most part, to the belief that the object of his visit to Arabia was to preach to the heathen there; but the whole context of the Epistle shows that it was rather for solitary meditation and communion with God.

**Damascus.**—We gather from 2 Cor. xi. 32 that Damascus was at this time in the possession, or in some manner, at least, under the rule, of Aretas, the Arabian king. How this can have been is an obscure and difficult question. (See Note on that passage.) It may have been seized by him, and held for a time, during his war with Herod Antipas and the Romans at the end of the reign of Tiberius, in A.D. 36—37;

again unto Damascus. (18) Then after
Chap. i. 18—24. First visit to Jerusalem. three years I went[1] up to
Jerusalem to see Peter, and
abode with him fifteen days.
(19) But other of the apostles saw I none,
save James the Lord's brother. (20) Now
the things which I write unto you,
behold, before God, I lie not. (21) After-
wards I came into the regions of Syria
and Cilicia; (22) and was unknown by

[1] Or, *returned*.

or it may possibly have been placed in his hands by Caligula on the disgrace of his rival, Antipas; or "the ethnarch under Aretas the king" may have been an officer subordinate to the Romans, and charged with a sort of consulship over the Arabians in Damascus. The first theory does not seem quite probable in the face of a power so strong as that of Rome; the second is a pure hypothesis, with no support from any contemporary writer; and the third hardly seems to satisfy the conditions of the problem. In any case, the most probable date of these events would be soon after the death of Tiberius in A.D. 37.

(18–24) Nor did that consultation with the elder Apostles, which had hitherto been impossible, take place when, at last, after the lapse of three years, the Apostle did go up to Jerusalem. He saw indeed Peter and James, but for so short a time that he could have learnt nothing essential from them. To the rest of the churches of Judæa he was known only by report; and they were too rejoiced at his conversion to show any jealousy of him.

(18) **After three years.**—This date is probably to be reckoned from the great turning-point in the Apostle's career—his conversion. It need not necessarily mean three full years, just as the three days during which our Lord lay in the grave were not three full days. It may have been only one whole year and parts of two others; but the phrase may equally well cover three whole years. This ambiguity shows the difficulty of constructing any precise system of chronology.

**To see.**—The word used is a somewhat peculiar one, and is applied specially to sight-seeing—in the first instance of things and places, but secondarily also of persons. It would be used only of something notable. St. Paul's object was to make the personal acquaintance of St. Peter as the head of the Christian community, not to seek instruction from him.

**Peter.**—The true reading here is undoubtedly *Cephas.* There is a natural tendency in the MSS. to substitute the more common name for the less common. St. Paul seems to have used the two names indifferently.

Roman Catholic commentators argue from this passage, not without reason, that St. Peter must at this time have taken the lead in the Church.

**Fifteen days.**—Only a small portion of this time can have been actually spent in the company of St. Peter, as we gather from the Acts that much of it must have been occupied by public disputations with the Greek-speaking Jews. (See Acts ix. 28, 29.)

(19) **Other of the apostles.**—From the form of this phrase it would appear that James, the Lord's brother, was considered to be an Apostle. In what sense he was an Apostle will depend very much upon who he was (see the next Note). If he was a cousin of our Lord, and identical with James the son of Alphæus, then he was one of the original Twelve. If he was not the son of Alphæus, but either the son of Joseph alone or of Joseph and Mary, then the title must be given to him in the wider sense in which it is applied to Paul and Barnabas.

**The Lord's brother.**—What relationship is indicated by this? The question has been already dealt with in the Notes on the Gospels. (See Notes on Matt. xii. 46; xiii. 55; John vii. 3, 5.) The present writer has nothing to add, except to express his entire agreement with what has been there said, and his firm conviction that the theory which identifies the "brethren of the Lord" with His *cousins*, the sons of Clopas, is untenable. A full account of the James who is here mentioned will be found in the *Introduction* to the Epistle which goes by his name.

(20) A solemn asseveration of the truth of these statements as to the extent of the Apostle's relation with the elder disciples.

(21) **Afterwards I came into the regions of Syria and Cilicia.**—We gather from the parallel narrative in Acts ix. 30; xi. 25, 26, that the course which the Apostle followed was this:—He was first conveyed secretly by the disciples to the sea-port Cæsarea Stratonis; there he took ship and sailed for Tarsus. Here he was found, somewhat later, by Barnabas, and taken to Antioch, where he remained a year. It would thus appear that the order in which the two names, Syria and Cilicia, occur does not represent the order in which the two provinces were visited. The Apostle, reviewing his past career at a distance of time, and with a certain special object in view, which is not affected by the geographical direction of his movements, speaks in this general way. It hardly seems necessary to suppose an unrecorded visit to Syria on the way to Tarsus, though that, of course, is possible. Still more gratuitous is the supposition that there is any contradiction between the historical narrative and our Epistle, for such generalities of expression are what most persons may constantly detect themselves in using. The accuracy of the pedant neither belongs to St. Paul's Epistles nor to real life.

**Regions.**—The Greek word here is the same as that which is translated "parts" in Rom. xv. 23, where see the Note.

(22) **Was unknown by face.**—The Greek is a shade stronger: *I continued unknown.* If in Jerusalem itself the Apostle had not had time to receive instruction from any one, still less was this the case with the other Christian communities of Judæa. To these he was not known even by sight. At the same time, so far were they from manifesting any opposition to his teaching, that their one thought was joy to hear of his conversion.

**The churches of Judæa.**—Judæa is here distinguished from Jerusalem. The phrase is noticeable as pointing to the spread and early organisation of the Church at a date removed by not more than ten years from our Lord's ascension.

**Which were in Christ.**—This is added in order to distinguish the Christian from the Jewish communities. It means, however, something more than merely "Christian." The various sections of the Christian Church not only professed a common creed, and were called by a common name, but they stood in the same direct and personal relation to Christ as their Head.

face unto the churches of Judæa which
were in Christ: (23) but they had heard
only, That he which persecuted us in
times past now preacheth the faith
which once he destroyed. (24) And they
glorified God in me.

CHAPTER II.—(1) Then fourteen
years after I went up again to Jeru-
salem with Barnabas, and
took Titus with *me* also.
(2) And I went up by revelation, and
communicated unto them that gospel
which I preach among the Gentiles, but
privately[1] to them which were of repu-
tation, lest by any means I should run,

Chap. ii. 1–10. Later visit.

1 Or, *severally*.

A.D. 58.

---

It was His presence diffused among them which gave them unity.

(23) **Had heard.**—Rather, *were hearing.*

**The faith.**—Not quite, as yet, "the body of Christian doctrine," which was in process of forming rather than already formed, but the one cardinal doctrine of faith in Christ. (Comp. Rom. i. 5, and Note there.)

(24) **They glorified God in me.**—This verse represents the proper attitude of Christian hero-worship. An eminent Christian is like a "city set on a hill." But the admiration which he attracts does not rest in him; it is made the occasion for giving praise to God.

II.

(1–10) The argument proceeds, still taking the shape of vivid personal retrospect:—The next visit at which I had any communication with the elder Apostles was after an interval of fourteen years. That, too, only served to bring out at once the independence and the soundness of my teaching. I spoke on the subject freely to the whole Church, and besides I had private conferences with the leaders; but no alteration was made either in my teaching or in my practice. One crucial instance was that of Titus, my companion, who, Gentile as he was, was not compelled to be circumcised, though his circumcision was urged upon me, not by the free motion of the Apostles themselves, but to silence the malicious rumours set on foot by certain Judaising spies who had found their way into our midst. To these Barnabas and I did not give way for a moment. And the upshot of the matter was that my mission was fully recognised by the leading Apostles, and that we agreed to go different ways—they to the Jews, we to the Gentiles—with the one condition, which I needed no prompting to accept, that we should not forget the poor.

Thoughts and arguments crowd in upon the Apostle with great vehemence. His amanuensis cannot take them down fast enough. Sentences are begun and not rightly ended, and much of the sense is left to be supplied by conjecture. The general drift of the passage is sufficiently plain, but there is much uncertainty about the details. This will appear in the Notes which follow.

(1) **Fourteen years after.**—From what date is this fourteen years to be reckoned? The phrase "I went up *again*" seems to be decisive in favour of reckoning it from the visit to Jerusalem just mentioned. We should therefore have to add the three years of chap. i. 18, in order to reach the date of the Apostle's conversion .The relation of the present narrative to that in the Acts will be more fully discussed in an excursus. (See *Excursus A: On the Visits of St. Paul to Jerusalem.*)

In the meantime, it may be assumed that there appear to be sufficient reasons for identifying the visit to Jerusalem here described with that recorded in Acts xv., commonly known as the Council of Jerusalem, which is placed by the best chronologists about A.D. 50 or 51.

**And took Titus with me also.**—In the corresponding passage (Acts xv. 2) we are told that "certain others" were sent with Paul and Barnabas. St. Paul mentions especially Titus because of the part which he subsequently played in the history of the Council, and because of the importance of this for his present argument.

(2) **By revelation.**—Revelations seem to have been vouchsafed to the Apostle in various ways—most frequently in dreams or nocturnal visions (Acts xvi. 9; xviii. 9; xxiii. 11; xxvii. 23), but also in a state of trance (Acts xxii. 17), and through other undefined modes of intimation (Acts xvi. 6, 7; xx. 22, 23). By what particular form of revelation he was guided in this instance does not appear. It would seem that this inward spiritual guidance granted privately to the Apostle coincided with a formal commission from the Church at Antioch (Acts xv. 2), which, as the external and apparent side of the transaction, is naturally related by the historian, while it is just as naturally omitted by the Apostle, whose thoughts are directed rather to his own personal conduct and motives.

**Communicated unto them**—*i.e.*, the Church at Jerusalem. A distinction appears to be drawn between what the Apostle said in his public intercourse with the Church and the more detailed conference or conferences into which he entered privately with the Apostles.

**Which I preach.**—The present tense is noticeable. The gospel which the Apostle had been preaching up to the time of the Council of Jerusalem was the same as that which he still preached at the time of his writing to the Galatians. It had undergone no change in its essential features, especially in the one doctrine which he was most anxious to impress upon the Galatians—the doctrine of justification by faith.

**Privately to them which were of reputation.**—Better, more simply, *to them of repute.* The present tense is again used, the Apostle hinting, not only at the position which the Judaic Apostles held at the time of the Council, but also at the way in which their authority was appealed to by the Judaising partisans in Galatia. There is a slight shade of irony in the expression. It is not so much "those which *were* of reputation" in the gathering at Jerusalem as "those who *are still* held to be the only authorities *now.*"

Who are meant by "them of repute" appears more distinctly from verse 9, where James, Peter, and John are mentioned by name.

**Lest by any means.**—The Apostle did not really want confidence in his own teaching. And yet he was aware that it rested solely upon his own individual conviction, and upon the interpretation that he had put upon the intimation to him of the divine will. There was, therefore, still a certain element of uncertainty and room for confirmation, which the Apostle desired to receive. His character hits the happy mean between confidence in his cause (self-confidence, or self-reliance, as it would be called if dealing with a lower sphere), without which no great mission can be accomplished,

or had run, in vain. (3) But neither
Titus, who was with me, being a Greek,
was compelled to be circumcised: (4) and
that because of false brethren unawares
brought in, who came in privily to spy
out our liberty which we have in Christ
Jesus, that they might bring us into
bondage: (5) to whom we gave place by
subjection, no, not for an hour; that
the truth of the gospel might continue
with you. (6) But of these who seemed
to be somewhat, (whatsoever they were,

and opinionatedness or obstinacy. He, therefore, wished to "make assurance doubly sure," and it is this confirmed and ratified certainty which animates his whole language in writing to the Galatians. Something of it, perhaps, is reflected back upon his account of the earlier stages in the process through which his opinions had gone, given in the last chapter.

**I should run, or had run.**—St. Paul here introduces his favourite metaphor from the foot-races, such as he might see in the Isthmian games at Corinth. Comp. especially, for a similar reference to his own career, Phil. ii. 16; 2 Tim. iv. 7.)

(3) **But neither Titus . . .**—This and the two following verses are parenthetical. The result of the private conference with the Judaic Apostles is not given till verse 7; but without waiting for this, the Apostle turns aside to give one emphatic piece of evidence that his practice in regard to the Gentile converts was not interfered with. The question of principle was raised in the case of Titus, and there he stood his ground, in spite of the pressure that was put upon him.

In addition to its bearing upon the main argument, there is probably a special reason for this mention of the case of Titus. At the beginning of his second missionary journey, on taking with him his youthful convert Timothy, St. Paul made so much of a concession to Jewish prejudices as to have him circumcised (Acts xvi. 3). We shall see later that this gave rise to a charge of inconsistency, which the Judaising party in Galatia were not slow to make use of. (See chap. v. 11, and Notes there.) There was indeed some real inconsistency, but not more than any one who is engaged in the struggles of active life will constantly find himself drawn into. The meeting at Jerusalem was a crisis in the history of the Church. The question of principle was at stake. Concession herein would have been ruinous and fatal, and the Apostle stood firm. On the other hand, the circumcision of Timothy was merely a practical compromise to smooth the way for the preaching of the gospel in new regions. The Apostle was too wise to incur needless opposition, which would bar the way to essential truths on a point which, though in some of its aspects involving principle, was yet in others of quite minor importance. Besides, there is this to be noticed, that whereas Titus was by descent wholly a Gentile, Timothy was, on his mother's side, a Jew.

Turning to the phraseology of the passage, we may observe that the opening clause would be better translated, *But not even was Titus . . . compelled to be circumcised.* "Not even" refers to the prominence which Titus assumed as being associated with St. Paul in his ministry. This was a special reason for insisting upon his circumcision; and yet he was not circumcised.

**Being a Greek.**—Rather, *a Gentile.* It is observed that the Peshito version translated the word here rendered "Greek" by "Aramæan" or "Syrian." All idea of pure Hellenic descent has dropped out of it.

(4) **And that because of . . .**—The sense is here, in any case, broken and imperfect. It seems, on the whole, best to supply the missing clause thus: "But (or, *though*) on account of false brethren . . . [I was urged to have him circumcised]." The leaders of the Church at Jerusalem took the ground, not of insisting upon circumcision as a necessity, but rather advising it as a matter of policy, to allay the ill feeling excited against St. Paul by designing men, traitors in the camp, who, though Christians in name, were Jews at heart. Many commentators, however, adopt the rendering of the Authorised version: "And that because of false (or rather, *the false*) brethren," understanding that he was not compelled to be circumcised. The reason why Titus was not circumcised was the evidently interested and treacherous motives of the Judaising partisans who clamoured for it.

**Unawares brought in, who came in privily.**—These two words correspond to each other in the Greek, and bring out in a graphic and forcible way the insidious and designing character of the party most violently opposed to St. Paul. Professing to be Christians, they were really Jews of the narrowest sort, who only entered into the Church to spy into and restrict its liberties.

**Which we have in Christ Jesus.**—The Christian Church is the Messianic kingdom, which derives all its attributes directly from its Head. If it is free, Christ has won for it its freedom, by relieving it from the burden of the Law, by abolishing race distinctions, and offering all the Messianic privileges to those who through faith are united to Him.

**Bring us into bondage.**—The "bondage" is, in the first instance, that of the Mosaic law, and through it the personal domination of the Jewish partisans.

(5) **To whom**—*i.e.*, to the Jewish agitators, though probably not so much in their own persons as through the Apostles who advocated concession to their views.

**We gave place.**—St. Paul himself, with Barnabas and Titus.

**By subjection.**—By yielding to them the submission which they claimed of us.

**No, not for an hour.**—It is strange that the negative here and the relative at the beginning of the verse are wanting in some Latin authorities, including Irenæus and (partially, at least) Tertullian. This, however, is only interesting as pointing to a very early corruption of the text, and not for any bearing that it has on the exegesis of the passage.

**The truth of the gospel.**—The gospel in its true form, with all the liberty which its essential doctrine of justification by faith involves, not mutilated or restricted by any false conditions.

**Might continue with you.**—The words used in the Greek are expressive of undiminished continuance: "Might reach to you and persist among you in its full extent."

(6) The Apostle returns from his digression on the case of Titus to give the result of his experience with the elder Apostles, in continuation of verse 3. "I did indeed hold conference with them privately; but with all their advantages, real or assumed, I learnt nothing from them that I did not already know, and they ended

it maketh no matter to me: God accepteth no man's person:) for they who seemed *to be somewhat* in conference added nothing to me: (7) but contrariwise, when they saw that the gospel of the uncircumcision was committed unto me, as *the gospel* of the circumcision *was* unto Peter; (8) (for he that wrought effectually in Peter to the apostleship of the circumcision, the same was mighty in me toward the Gentiles:) (9) and when James, Cephas, and John, who seemed to be pillars, perceived the grace that was given unto me, they gave to me and Barnabas the right hands of fellowship; that we *should go* unto the heathen, and they unto the circumcision. (10) Only *they would* that

---

by recognising the independence and validity of my mission."

**But of these who seemed to be somewhat.**—Translate rather, *But from those who are reputed to be somewhat.* The phrase corresponds to "them which are of reputation" in verse 2; and here, as there, it is important to keep the present tense. It is not only "those who *were* of authority at the Council," but "those who *are* the great authorities with you Galatians now." The Apostle speaks with a certain amount of irony. "From these very great authorities, these persons of such especial reputation [I got nothing]."

**Whatsoever they were.**—We shall, perhaps, not be wrong in keeping to the Authorised version, though some of the best commentators translate rather, *What they* (once) *were*, with a stress on "were," and referring to the advantage which they possessed over St. Paul in having "known Christ after the flesh" through their early call to the Apostleship.

**God accepteth no man's person.**—This phrase is a curious instance of a Greek expression framed after the analogy of the Hebrew, and yet in the process contracting a different signification, through the influence of the idiomatic use of one of the Greek expressions involved. "To accept the face" in the Old Testament is used in a good sense of "showing favour" to any one, but without any imputation of partiality. "To accept the face" (or *person*) in the New Testament always carries with it the idea of partiality; the word for "face" being idiomatically used for "a mask," and hence coming to mean "the outward, assumed, accidental characteristics of a man" as opposed to his real and inward character. (Comp. Matt. xxii. 16; Luke xx. 21; Acts x. 34; Rom. ii. 11; Eph. vi. 9; Col. iii. 25; Jas. ii. 1, 9; Jude, verse 16.) The meaning here is that even if the elder Apostles had "seen with their eyes," and "looked upon and handled the Word of Life" (1 John i. 1), God would not regard the advantages implied in this more than any other external advantage of birth, position, natural gifts, &c.

**For they who seemed to be somewhat.**—The same phrase as in verse 2: *they who were of reputation.* There is here another break in the regular construction of the sentence. The Apostle begins as if he were going to finish differently: "From those who are reputed to be somewhat . . . I received nothing in the conference which I had with them;" but he suddenly changes his point of view: "From those who are reputed to be somewhat" (sentence left unfinished) "to me, I say, these reputable persons added nothing."

**In conference added nothing.**—"Added in conference" is all one word in the Greek, and corresponds to "communicated" in verse 2. The idea of "adding" (*i.e.*, imparting fresh knowledge) seems, however, to be derived rather from the context than from the form of the Greek compound, as our translators apparently supposed.

(7—9) So far from contributing anything *new* to my stock of doctrine, they were content to confirm and ratify what I taught already.

(7) **Gospel of the uncircumcision**—*i.e.*, a gospel for the uncircumcised. The elder Apostles recognised St. Paul because they saw that his teaching was fundamentally the same as their own. At the same time, the success of St. Paul among the Gentiles proved that his mission to them had the divine sanction, just as the success of St. Peter among the Jews specially marked him out as the "Apostle of the circumcision."

(8) **He that wrought effectually in Peter . . . the same was mighty in me.**—This is an instance of that capriciousness in our translators which was due to their free poetic handling and superabundant command of words. "Wrought effectually" and "was mighty" are the same word in the Greek, and there does not seem to be any sufficient reason why the translation should be altered. "In Peter" and "in me" would be better translated *for Peter* and *for me. He that wrought effectually for Peter to the apostleship of the circumcision, the same wrought effectually for me towards the Gentiles.*

(9) **James, Cephas, and John.**—In some few MSS. and patristic quotations the reading is *Peter and James and John.* This doubtless arose from the tendency to exalt St. Peter, though the reading (which is found in Tertullian and Origen, and therefore must run up into the second century) is too early to be directly connected with the pretensions of the Papacy. The way in which St. Paul speaks respectively of St. Peter and St. James is in strict accordance with the historical situation. When he is speaking of the general work of the Church (as in the last two verses) St. Peter is mentioned prominently; when the reference is to a public act of the Church of Jerusalem the precedence is given to St. James.

**Who seemed to be pillars.**—Rather, *who are held* (same word as *reputed* above) *to be pillars.* The metaphor is a natural one, and is found not unfrequently in classical writers. It was in common use among the Jews as a designation for the great Rabbinical teachers.

**Right hands of fellowship.**—The giving of the right hand is a symbol of friendship. Instances occur, both in the East and West (comp. Xen. *Anab.* ii. 4, 1; Tac. *Hist.* i. 54, ii. 8), in which images of clasped right hands were sent in suing for alliance.

(10) **The poor**—*i.e.*, at Jerusalem and in Judæa. St. Paul had already been the means of bringing contributions from the wealthier churches of Antioch to Jerusalem (Acts xi. 29, 30). This seems to have been gracefully received, not only as an act of charity, but as a recognition of the claims of the mother Church. The Apostles expressed a hope that the same good feeling might continue, to which St. Paul willingly assented. That he did not forget his promise appears

we should remember the poor; the
same which I also was forward to do.
(11) But when Peter was come to Antioch,
I withstood him to the face, because he was to be blamed.

Chap. ii. 11—14. Controversy at Antioch.

(12) For before
that certain came from James, he did
eat with the Gentiles: but when they
were come, he withdrew and separated
himself, fearing them which were of the
circumcision. (13) And the other Jews
dissembled likewise with him; insomuch
that Barnabas also was carried away
with their dissimulation. (14) But when

---

from Acts xxiv. 17; Rom. xv. 26, 27; 1 Cor. xvi. 3; 2 Cor. viii. 1, 2; ix. 1 *et seq.* (See Notes on Rom. xv. 25—27.)

(11—14) The next phase in this question was at Antioch. On his coming thither Peter was guilty of a great inconsistency. He began by eating freely with the Gentile converts, but the arrival of a party of the stricter Jews from Jerusalem was enough to make him alter his practice. He gradually withdrew and held aloof, and a number of others, including even Barnabas, followed his example. This conduct of his I openly reproved, asking him why it was that at one moment he himself did not hesitate to adopt the custom of the Gentiles, while at another he insisted upon their conforming to those of the Jews.

(11) **When Peter . . .**—The true reading here is undoubtedly *Cephas.* The visit alluded to probably took place soon after the return of Paul and Barnabas, in the interval described in Acts xv. 35, shortly before the separation of these two Apostles and the departure of St. Paul on his second missionary journey.

**Because he was to be blamed.**—The Greek here is simply, *because he was condemned.* The act carried with it its own condemnation.

The blame thus imputed to St. Peter was a subject of much controversy in antiquity. It was made a ground of accusation against both Apostles. The Ebionites—as represented in the well known heretical work, the Clementine *Homilies*—charged St. Paul with hostility to the faith, asserting that by calling Peter "condemned" he was really accusing "God who revealed Christ in him." On the other hand, Marcion, the Gnostic, saw in the incident a proof of the antagonism between Judaism and Christianity (as he understood it), represented by their several champions. The heathen critic Porphyry attacked both Apostles alike, the one for error, the other for forwardness in rebuking that error, and points to the whole scene as one of ecclesiastical wrangling.

The unfortunate result of these criticisms was that they led to attempts, on the part of the orthodox writers, to explain away the simple meaning of the narrative. Clement of Alexandria maintained that the Cephas here mentioned was not the Apostle St. Peter, but an inferior person, one of the seventy disciples. A more popular theory was that which was started by Origen, elaborated by Chrysostom, and defended with great vehemence by Jerome in a controversy with Augustine. This theory was that the two Apostles had arranged the scene beforehand between themselves, and acted it out for the edification of the Judaisers. St. Paul was to represent the view sanctioned by the Church, and St. Peter was to give an eminent example of submission. This view, though it held its ground for two centuries, was finally put down by the straightforwardness and good sense of St. Augustine.

The true explanation of the incident is to be found in the character of St. Peter—at once generously impulsive and timidly sensitive to the opinion of others. An inconsistency very similar to this appears in his ardent confession, followed by the betrayal of his Master (Mark xiv. 29, 66 *et seq.*). It had been seen at an earlier date in his attempt to walk upon the water (Matt. xiv. 28—33); and is, indeed, one of the features in his character most conspicuous in the Gospels. A little more attention to this would have saved many doctrinaire objections to the narrative of the Acts, where the inconsistency, which is really one of character, is treated as if it stood in the way of the objective truth of the events.

(12) **Certain came from James.**—The expression used leaves it an open question whether the persons intended brought, or claimed to bring, any sort of official authorisation from St. James (comp. Acts xv. 24), or whether they merely belonged to the Church of Jerusalem, in which, if St. James was not actually bishop, he at least exercised a sort of presidential jurisdiction.

**He did eat with the Gentiles.**—By eating with Gentiles a Jew contracted Levitical defilement. St. Peter had been accused of this before, on account of his intercourse with Cornelius. (Comp. Acts xi. 3.) He had not, however, stability and firmness enough to treat the question of principle as settled for him then once for all, and he yielded to a repetition of the old remonstrances. Our Lord Himself had braved Jewish opinion on this point. (Comp. Luke xv. 2.)

**When they were come.**—The reading of the oldest MSS. here is "when *he* came," of which it seems impossible to make any satisfactory sense. It may have been a slip of the pen, either in the original or in some very early copy. Other instances of mistakes in the oldest MSS. would be—Mark iv. 21, "*under* a candlestick," instead of "*on* a candlestick;" John i. 15, "he *who* said," for "he *of whom I* said;" and a Greek form in Phil. ii. 1.

**Withdrew and separated himself.**—The Greek expression brings out the timid and gradual withdrawal, ending in complete separation.

**Them which were of the circumcision.**—This appears to mean, not merely "those who advocated circumcision," but "those who were made converts from a state of circumcision"—*i.e.,* from Judaism.

(13) **The other Jews . . .**—*i.e.,* converts from Judaism, as distinct from Gentile converts, in the Church at Antioch.

**Dissembled.**—The "dissimulation," or "hypocrisy" (the literal sense of the Greek word), consisted in suppressing their real convictions, and acting as if from a set of convictions different from their real ones.

**Barnabas also.**—Rather, *even Barnabas,* my own familiar friend, and so recently my ally in pleading the cause of the Gentiles. The beginning of the breach which soon afterwards led to the definite separation of the two Apostles would seem to be traceable here.

(14) **Walked not uprightly.**—This is a single word in the Greek, and found here alone in the New Testament. It means, literally, "to walk on straight

I saw that they walked not uprightly
according to the truth of the gospel, I
said unto Peter before *them* all, If thou,
being a Jew, livest after the manner of
Gentiles, and not as do the Jews, why
compellest thou the Gentiles to live as
do the Jews? (15) We *who are* Jews by
nature, and not sinners of
the Gentiles, (16) knowing
that a man is not justified
by the works of the law, but by the
faith of Jesus Christ, even we have

Chap. ii. 15—21. The Law abandoned for Christ.

---

feet"—*i.e.*, erect and straightforwardly, as opposed to "shuffling."

**Unto Peter before them all.**—The true reading is again *Cephas*. The Apostle lays stress upon the publicity of his remonstrance, as showing that in his controversy with the Apostles of the circumcision he did something more than hold his own.

**Being a Jew.**—"Being" is here emphatic, and means, "with all the antecedents of a Jew." It is implied that a different rule must be applied to the Gentiles, with totally different antecedents.

**Livest after the manner of Gentiles**—*i.e.*, in the matter of eating promiscuously with those whom the Law (or rather, the Pharisaic tradition) forbids you to eat with.

**Why.**—The great preponderance of MSS. is here in favour of the reading *how*—*i.e.*, how does it come about that?

**Compellest.**—Do what you can to compel.

(15—21) The section which follows is, in form at least, still a continuation of the rebuke addressed to St. Peter; but the Apostle soon drifts away from this, and begins imperceptibly a comment upon his own words, which is addressed directly to the Galatians. We are thus led, without any real break, from the historical and personal to the doctrinal portion of the Epistle. It is impossible to say exactly where the speech at Antioch ends and where the comment upon it begins; the Apostle glides from one to the other without any conscious division in his own mind. A similar mingling of narrative and comment is found in St. John's Gospel: compare, *e.g.*, John iii. 14—21, 31—36, the first of which sections formally belongs to the discourse with Nicodemus, and the second to the reply of John the Baptist, though it is clear that much after comment of the Evangelist's is interwoven with them. If we are to draw a dividing line at all in the section before us, it might be said that verses 15 and 16 were still most nearly a paraphrase of the words actually addressed to St. Peter; while from verse 17 onwards the Apostle is giving the rein more freely to his own reflections. The sequence of the thought seems to be somewhat as follows:—

We belong by our birth to a privileged people. We are not of Gentile descent, and therefore abandoned to our sins. And yet, with all our privileges, we found that we could get no justification whatever from the Law; and this sent us to Christ. We thus abdicated our privileged position; we put ourselves on the same level as the Gentiles, and became (in the eye of the Law) sinners like them. Sinners? Must we then admit that all Christ has done for us is to make us *sinners?* Far be so irreverent a thought. Our sin consists not in quitting the Law, but in returning to that which has once been abandoned. The function of the Law was preparatory and transitional. The Law itself taught me to expect its own abrogation. It was a stage on the way to Christ. To Him have I given in a complete adhesion. In His death I am severed from ancient ties. In His death I ceased to have any life of my own. All the life I have, man as I am, I owe to Christ, my Saviour. Thus I accept and do not reject and frustrate the gift so freely offered me: whereas, by going back to the Law for justification, I should be practically declaring the death of Christ useless and unprofitable.

(15) **Who are.**—It will be seen that these words are in italics, and have to be supplied in the Greek. The Received text, which is followed in our version, also omits a connecting particle, found in the best MSS., at the beginning of verse 16. Restoring this, a better way of taking the whole passage appears to be to supply only the word "are" in the present verse, and make the next mark a certain opposition to it: "We are (indeed) by birth Jews . . . but" (or, *and yet*), "knowing as we did that the Law cannot justify any one, we believed on Christ." The first clause is concessive: "We grant you that we were born Jews, and not Gentiles: members of the chosen race, and not sinners." The next clause explains why it was that, with all these privileges, the Christian, though thus born a Jew, transferred his allegiance from the Law to Christ. The reason was that the Law failed in the one great object—to justify us or obtain our acquittal in the sight of God.

**By nature**—*i.e.*, by birth. The privileges of the Jew belonged to all Jews alike, simply by the mere fact that they were Jews.

**Sinners.**—The word was almost a synonym for "heathen" in the mouth of a strict Jew. Hence there is a slight irony in its use by St. Paul. "I grant you that from our lofty position we can look down upon those poor Gentiles, sinners by virtue of mere descent."

**Of the Gentiles.**—"Of" in the sense of natural descent: "Of Gentile parentage (and therefore) sinners."

(16) **Is not justified.**—Here the Apostle introduces, for the first time in the Epistle, the word which plays so prominent a part in the Epistle to the Romans—"pronounced just or righteous"—free from guilt, and therefore from punishment—in the sight of God. This condition could not be produced by works done in obedience to the Law.

**But.**—The sense of the Greek is not clearly brought out by the Authorised version. A more strict translation would be *except*, which is made to refer only to the word "justified," and not to the previous negation of works, as the cause of justification. "A man is not justified by works (nor is he justified at all), *except* by faith in Christ."

**By the faith of Jesus Christ.**—The preposition "by" occurs five times in this verse. In every case except the present it is represented by the same word in Greek. There is, however, no substantial difference of meaning; the only difference is that in the other cases stress is laid rather upon the *cause*, here rather upon the *means*. "Faith *of* Jesus Christ" means, as we are more accustomed to say, "faith *in* Jesus Christ."

**Even we.**—Rather, *we too*. Jews as we are, in spite of all our privileges.

**Have believed.**—Rather, *believed*. This was the

believed in Jesus Christ, that we might be justified by the faith of Christ, and not by the works of the law: for by the works of the law shall no flesh be justified.
(17) But if, while we seek to be justified by Christ, we ourselves also are found sinners, *is* therefore Christ the minister of sin? God forbid.
(18) For if I build again the things which I destroyed, I make myself a trans-

---

great motive of our conversion. We found that the Law could not justify us and that Christ could.

**By the works of the law shall no flesh be justified.**—This is a quotation for which no exact equivalent is to be found in the Old Testament. The nearest appears to be Ps. cxliii. 2: "In thy sight shall no man living be justified." This, as written under the dispensation of the Law, naturally applied to that dispensation, so that the Apostle was justified in adding "by the works of the Law." The same quotation, in the same words, is made in Rom. iii. 20.

The inability of the Law to justify comes out in two ways. (1) The only way in which the Law could justify was through a complete obedience to its provisions. But it was impossible to render a *complete* obedience to it: and to offend in one point was "to be guilty of all;" so that practically, as a matter of fact, no one was justified by it. (2) Nor did it *help* men to justify themselves. It was something dead and lifeless—a mere written letter, possessing none of those "means of grace" which are offered by Christianity. Christ Himself, through faith in Him, is the great means.

(17) We sought justification in Christ. But if, with all our seeking, something more was needed: viz., a rigid performance of the Law—that Law which we had abandoned—then there was still something wanting to our justification. We were sinners on a par with the Gentiles, and all that Christianity seemed to have done for us was to lead us deeper into sin. A profane thought!

**By Christ.**—Strictly, *in Christ*—*i.e.*, by the relation into which we are brought with Him. The reference is here, however, not exactly to the mystical union with Christ, which is regarded by the Apostle rather in connection with sanctification (the actual growth in holiness) than with justification (the judicial absolution from guilt). In the present instance the Apostle is speaking of justification; and when he says that "we are justified in Christ," he means practically through faith in Him, or through that circle of forces within which we are brought by faith.

**We ourselves also.**—We who were by our birth Jews, as well as the Gentiles.

**Are found.**—Strictly, *were found*—*i.e.*, at a time subsequent to our embracing Christianity, if the only *result* of our Christianity was that we were still sinners.

**Sinners.**—Sinners actually, through our positive transgressions, and sinners theoretically or judicially (in the eyes of God), through the fact that we have lost the old Jewish justification through the fulfilment of the Law; while, according to this Judaising theory which St. Paul is combating, our new Christian justification is insufficient.

**Is therefore Christ the minister of sin?**—Our English version is probably right in making this a question. It is put ironically, and as a sort of *reductio ad absurdum* of the Judaising position. The Judaisers maintained the necessity of a strict fulfilment of the Mosaic law. They, however, still called themselves Christians; and here St. Paul had a hold upon them. "You call yourselves Christians," he says, "and yet you insist upon the Mosaic law. You say that a man cannot be justified without it: it follows that we, who have exchanged the service of the Law for the service of Christ, are not justified. In other words, our relation to Christ has made us, not better, but worse—a thought which no Christian can entertain."

No doubt St. Paul used some such argument as this in his controversy with St. Peter at Antioch, but it would probably be stated in a simpler and less speculative form: "If you still fall back upon the separatist Jewish observances, what is the good of being a Christian?" Here, in writing to the Galatians, the Apostle paraphrases what he had said in language more suited to a theological treatise and to the natural speculative bias of his own mind.

**God forbid.**—The Judaising theory was quite sufficiently condemned by showing the consequences to which it would lead. It makes Christ Himself a minister of sin—a suggestion which the Apostle puts away with pious horror.

(18) But Christ is not a minister of sin. The thought is not to be tolerated. For, on the contrary, the sin is seen, not in leaving the Law for Christ, but in going back from Christ to the Law. The sin is seen doubly: for on one theory—the theory that the Law is valid—it was wrong to give it up; while on the other theory, that Christianity has taken its place, it is still more wrong to restore the fabric that has once been broken down.

**For.**—The connection is with the words immediately preceding: "God forbid that Christ should be the minister of sin." The idea is absurd as well as profane. *For*, instead of the Pauline Christian (who follows Christianity to its logical results) being the sinner, it is really the Judaising Christian who stands self-condemned—*i.e.*, in returning to what he has forsaken.

**If I build again.**—The first person is used out of delicate consideration for his opponents. The Apostle is going to put a supposed case, which really represents what they were doing; but in order to soften the directness of the reference he takes it, as it were, upon himself.

St. Paul is fond of metaphors taken from building. Comp. Rom. xv. 20 (building upon another man's foundation), 1 Cor. iii. 10—14 (Christ the foundation), Eph. ii. 20—22 (the Church built on the foundation of Apostles and prophets), and the words "edify" and "edification" wherever they occur. The idea of "pulling down" or "destroying" is also frequently met with. So in Rom. xiv. 20 ("for meat destroy not the work of God," the same word as here used, in opposition to "edify," immediately before); 2 Cor. v. 1 ("if our earthly house of this tabernacle were dissolved"—pulled down or destroyed); 2 Cor. x. 4 ("mighty to the pulling down of strongholds")—a different word in the Greek, but similar in meaning.

We may compare with the whole verse the well-known saying, "Burn what you have adored, and adore what you have burned."

gressor. (19) For I through the law am dead to the law, that I might live unto God. (20) I am crucified with Christ: nevertheless I live; yet not I, but Christ liveth in me: and the life which I now live in the flesh I live by the faith of

**The things which I destroyed**—*i.e.*, the Mosaic law, the binding obligation of which had been done away in Christ.

**Make myself.**—*Show*, or *prove myself to be*: the same word as that translated "commend" in Rom. iii. 5, v. 8.

**A transgressor.**—Hitherto the Apostle had kept up a sort of studied ambiguity in his use of the words "sin," "sinner." The Jews called the Gentiles "sinners," simply from the fact of their being Gentiles. The Pauline Christian placed himself on the same footing with the Gentiles, so far as the Law was concerned, and therefore he, too, in the same phraseology, was a sinner. But now the Apostle uses a word that could not be mistaken. A sinner the Christian might be, in the Judaising sense of the word, but the Judaiser himself was the real sinner: it was he who offended against the immutable principles of right and wrong.

(19) In the last verse the Apostle had been putting a supposed case, but by a not unnatural process of thought he gradually takes the "I" rather more in earnest, and appeals directly to his own personal experience. The "I" of verse 18 is really St. Peter or the Judaisers; the "I" of this verse is St. Paul himself. The object of his appeal is to make good his assertion that to restore the dethroned Law to its old position is positively sinful.

Once having done with the Law I had done with it for ever. The Law itself had prepared me for this. It was a stage which I could not but pass through, but which was in its very nature temporary. It carried with it the sentence of its own dissolution.

**For . . .**—This assigns the reason for the use of the word "transgressor" in the verse before. It is a transgression to rebuild the demolished fabric of the Law, because the true Christian has done with the Law once for all.

**Through the law am dead to the law.**—In what sense can this be said? The Apostle himself had got rid of his obligations to the Law—not, however, by simply evading them from the first, but by passing through a period of subjection to them. The road to freedom from the Law lay through the Law. The Law, on its prophetic side, pointed to Christ. The Law, on its moral side, held up an ideal to which its votaries could not attain. It did not help them to attain to it. It bore the stamp of its own insufficiency. Men broke its precepts, and its weakness seemed to lead up to a dispensation that should supersede its own. St. Paul would not have become a Christian if he had not first sat at the feet of Gamaliel. If we could trace the whole under-current of silent, and perhaps only half-conscious, preparation, which led to the Apostle's conversion, we should see how large a part was played in it by the sense, gradually wrought in him, of the Law's insufficiency. Thus the negative side was given by his own private meditation; the positive side, faith in Christ, was given by the vision on the road to Damascus.

**That I might live unto God.**—We might not unnaturally expect here "unto Christ," instead of "unto God." But the Christian lives unto Christ *in order that* he may live unto God. The ultimate object of the Christian scheme is that he may be presented righteous before God. By the Law he could not obtain this righteousness. It is obtained in Christ.

(20) In the last verse the Apostle had spoken of himself as "dead to the Law, and living unto God." The prominent idea in the first half of this clause had been the release from that burdensome ceremonial which the Judaising party wished to bind upon Christian consciences. By a natural transition, the Apostle's thought had passed from what the Law could not do to what Christianity could do.

The Law could not make men righteous before God. In Christ they were made righteous. How? Here, too, there was death. The Christian died with Christ to something else besides the Law. With his eye fixed upon the cross, he died a spiritual death and rose to a new spiritual life. The "old man" in him, the self-seeking and sinful element in his nature, is slain, and for it is substituted a life of such close and intimate communion with Christ that it seems as if Christ Himself were dwelling in the soul. Living upon the earth in a body of human flesh, as he is, he is animated by an intense faith in the Saviour who has given him such proofs of self-sacrificing love.

Here we come upon the same vein of mysticism that is developed in Rom. vi. One main way of conceiving of the specially Christian life is through the idea of union with Christ. This idea, when ultimately pressed to precise logical definition, must necessarily contain a certain element of metaphor. Consciousness, rigorously examined, tells us that even in the most exalted souls there is no such thing as an *actual* union of the human and divine. At the same time, there is possible to man an influence from above so penetrating and so powerful that it would seem as if the figure of union could alone adequately express it. Nor ought this to be questioned or denied because the more common order of minds do not find themselves capable of it. (See the Notes on Rom. vi., and *Excursus G* to that Epistle.)

**I am crucified . . .**—The idea is something more than that of merely "dying with Christ"—*i.e.*, imitating the death of Christ after a spiritual manner: it involves, besides, a special reference to the cross. It is through the power of the cross, through contemplating the cross and all that is associated with it, that the Christian is enabled to mortify the promptings of sin within him, and reduce them to a state of passiveness like that of death.

**Nevertheless I live.**—This death unto sin, death upon one side of my nature, does not hinder me from having life upon another side. The fact is that I live in a truer sense than ever before.

**Yet not I.**—It is, however, no longer the old natural man in me that lives: it is not that part of the human personality which has its root in matter, and is "of the earth, earthy," but that part which is re-formed by the Spirit of Christ.

**Now.**—In my present condition as a Christian, opposed to the old condition prior to the conversion.

**In the flesh.**—In this bodily human frame; man though I be. The Christian is outwardly the same as other men; it is his inner life which is "hid with Christ in God."

the Son of God, who loved me, and
gave himself for me. (21) I do not
frustrate the grace of God: for if right-
eousness *come* by the law, then Christ is
dead in vain.

A.D. 58.

CHAPTER III.—(1) O foolish Gala-
tians, who hath bewitched
you, that ye should not
obey the truth, before whose
eyes Jesus Christ hath been evidently

Chap. iii. 1. The evil eye of Judaism.

**By the faith.**—The article is better omitted: *by faith.* The Apostle does not quite go so far as to say that faith is the cause of his physical life, though we may see, by other passages, that he is at least prepared to look upon faith as the great pledge, and even cause, of the physical resurrection. Here he is speaking of faith rather as the element or atmosphere in which the Christian lives. He is, as it were, *steeped* in faith.

**Of the Son of God**—*i.e.,* faith of which the Son of God is the object; faith *in* the Son of God.

There is a curious variation of reading here. Some ancient authorities (including the Codex Vaticanus) instead of "faith in the Son of God," have "faith in God and Christ." This might appear to have some internal probability, as the less obvious expression of the two; but it may be perhaps explained satisfactorily in another way. On the whole, it seems best to abide by the Received text, which is that of the majority of MSS.

**Who loved me.**—Christ died for the whole world, but each individual Christian has a right to appropriate His death to himself. The death of Christ was prompted by love, not for the abstraction humanity, but for men as individuals.

(21) In thus attaching himself devotedly to Christ, the Christian escapes the charge of refusing and thwarting the free gift of justification which God has offered to him in His Son. He has made his choice of Christ, and not of the Law. On the other hand, if he had chosen the Law, and gone to it, and not to Christ, in his search for righteousness, he would have practically declared the death of Christ to be a useless and unnecessary sacrifice.

**Frustrate.**—An exactly literal translation of the Greek word, which means "to render nugatory or ineffectual." The grace of God goes forth with a certain mission to perform; but the Judaising party, by still clinging to the Law, prevented it from taking effect, and made it "return void" unto its Giver.

**If righteousness come by the law.**—What all men seek is justification in the sight of God. This is given to the just or righteous. But there were two ways of becoming thus just or righteous. The Law professed to make righteous those who complied with its provisions. But this was only a profession, for no one could really keep the Law. The Christian, therefore, rightly falls back upon faith in Christ, which brings him both an imputed righteousness, and also, in part, at least, a real righteousness. A deep and genuine faith in Christ is allowed to atone for the many unavoidable breaches of the Law, and that faith by degrees operates a real and vital change in the character and life of the man.

**Then Christ is dead in vain.**—If the Law had been enough to give actual righteousness to its votaries, and with righteousness the judicial declaration of freedom from guilt, then there would have been nothing for Christ to die for. His death would have had no object and been of no benefit to mankind.

III.

(1—5) Whence this strange relapse? It is not as if you were ignorant of better things. The crucified Saviour, the one great object of faith, has been preached before you in a way too plain to be mistaken. It has been written, as it were, in large characters before your eyes. It could only be some kind of evil enchantment or fascination that has prevented you from looking upon it. You have given up Christ and gone back to the Law. Yet, let me ask you—and surely no other proof is needed—all this outpouring of spiritual gifts that you have enjoyed since you became Christian, to what do you owe it? Is that due to the Law and works, or is it due to Christ and faith in Him? The one system is spiritual, the other is carnal and material. Will you begin with what is high and descend to what is low? Will you by such a declension practically admit that all the persecutions that you underwent were undergone in a mistaken cause? (I can hardly believe it.) At this present moment the gift of spiritual grace and miraculous power still in some measure continues, and where it is seen, is it not in clear connection—not with legal observances—but with faith in Christ?

In the last section of the last chapter the Apostle had been gradually working away from the historical retrospect with which he had begun to the doctrinal polemic in which he is about to engage, and now he addresses the Galatians with impassioned directness and earnestness, upbraiding them with their shameful apostasy.

(1) **Foolish.**—The same word as that which is used in Luke xxiv. 25, "O ye fools and slow of heart," and in Rom. i. 14, "wise and foolish," 1 Tim. vi. 9, and Tit. iii. 3, but not the same as that which is used in Matt. vii. 26; xxiii. 17; Luke xi. 40; Rom. i. 22; 1 Cor. i. 20; iv. 10; 2 Cor. xi. 19, &c. The combination, "fools and slow of heart," helps to bring out its meaning. "Slow of heart" refers to deadness of the moral affections; "fools" and "foolish" to the absence or undisciplined condition of the reasoning faculty. The Gauls of Galatia were a people intellectually shallow and frivolous. A little reason and reflection would have kept them from so gross an inconsistency.

**Bewitched you.**—The Greek word for this is probably connected in origin with the Latin word from which is derived our own "fascinate," and the idea prominent in both is that which is embodied in the popular superstition of the evil eye. This superstition lingers still, especially in some southern countries, such as Italy and Spain. In Italy it is well known under the names "jettatura," "occhio cattivo." In Spain its existence has been graphically illustrated by a picture of the late J. Phillip, R.A., now in the museum at Stirling.

The metaphor here is strikingly in harmony with that which follows. The cross of Christ has been "evidently set forth" (*i.e.,* posted up in large and bold characters) before the Galatians, but some evil fascination (that of their Judaising teachers) has drawn away their eyes from looking upon it, and held them fixed upon

set forth, crucified among you? (2) This
Chap. iii. 2—5. Retrogression. only would I learn of you,
Received ye the Spirit by
the works of the law, or by the hearing
of faith? (3) Are ye so foolish? having
begun in the Spirit, are ye now made
perfect by the flesh? (4) Have ye suf-
fered so many [1] things in vain? if *it be*
yet in vain. (5) He therefore that minis-
tereth to you the Spirit, and worketh

1 Or, *so great.*

another object (legal observances), as baneful as the cross was salutary.

**That ye should not obey the truth.**—These words are omitted by the best MSS. and by all recent editors. They were, without doubt, originally a gloss, put in to explain more fully the single word "bewitched." As an explanation they are sufficiently right, but they certainly did not form part of the text as it left the hands of St. Paul.

**Evidently set forth.**—This hardly brings out the full force of the metaphor, which is that of a picture or writing conspicuously and publicly exhibited.

**Crucified.**—This word is emphatic: "Jesus Christ, and Him crucified."

**Among you.**—If these words are to be retained in the text they must, of course, be taken, not with "crucified," but with "evidently set forth." They will then be a repetition, intended to enhance the force of the phrase "before whose eyes"—"before whose eyes and in whose very midst Jesus Christ was set forth crucified." But the probability is that the words ought to be omitted altogether, as they are wanting in the four most ancient MSS., as well as in a majority of the oldest versions.

(2) **This only.**—The Apostle considers a single argument enough. He will only place the present conduct of the Galatians in contrast with their past, and ask how they can possibly reconcile the two.

**Received ye the Spirit.**—The reference is to those spiritual gifts, described more fully in 1 Cor. xii., xiv.—the gift of prophecy, the gift of tongues, the interpretation of tongues, the discerning of spirits, gifts of healing, &c.—which attended the first preaching of the gospel, and were poured out upon the first converts in a manner and degree since unknown. The Galatians, it seems, had had a share in this outpouring, like the other churches, though their fickleness prevented them from reaping the full benefit from it. But a spiritual effect, such as this outpouring was, could only have a spiritual cause; it could not come from a mechanical performance of legal obligations.

**By the works of the law.**—By works done in obedience to the Law. There is a certain emphasis on both words, for the main point in the contrast which the Apostle is drawing is between the Law, on the one hand, and faith, on the other. Still, faith is as much opposed to works (*i.e.*, a spirit of literal and mechanical obedience) as it is to Law, and excludes both at once. It is to be noted, however, that the works here meant are those done, in a Judaising sense, as themselves the direct means of salvation—not Christian works, the natural product and outcome of faith.

**By the hearing of faith.**—These words correspond very nearly to a phrase which we should perhaps use more naturally: *by the preaching of faith—i.e.*, by that preaching or hearing (hearing on the part of the recipients, preaching on that of the missionary Apostles) which has for its subject faith. What the Apostle had taught the Galatians on his first coming among them was not any system of laborious observances, but the duty of faith. They at first responded to his teaching: and in answer to their enthusiastic impulse of adhesion to Christ the gifts of the Spirit were abundantly shed upon them. Now all this had ceased. For the use of the word translated "hearing," see the Note on Rom. x. 16.

(3) **Foolish.**—See the Note on verse 1.

**Having begun in the Spirit.**—Begun your career as Christians in a manner so entirely spiritual—with the spiritual act of faith on your part, and with an answering gift of spiritual graces and powers.

**Made perfect by the flesh.**—Do you wish to finish and complete the career thus auspiciously begun under a system of things entirely different—a system carnal and material, narrow, slavish, and literal—the Law in place of the Gospel? By "the flesh" is here meant the Law, which, though described as spiritual in Rom. vii. 14, and though it really was spiritual in view of its origin, in another aspect—as imposing a system of literal obedience upon its adherents—was carnal, "earthly," rigid, petty, and low. It had none of that sublime expansiveness and aspiration which belongs to faith. It was a grievous reversing of the whole order of progress—to begin with faith, and, instead of completing with faith that which faith had begun, to fall back upon a condition of things which was shared with the Christian by the unemancipated Jew.

(4) **Suffered so many things.**—The Galatians, like other churches, were subjected to much persecution when first they embraced Christianity. The persecutors were probably their own Jewish countrymen, whose jealousy and rage they had braved in the name of the gospel as preached by St. Paul. Now they were abandoning that very gospel for the principles of those by whom they had been persecuted. Conduct could not be more fickle and "foolish."

**If it be yet in vain.**—*If it be indeed in vain.* The Apostle cannot quite bring himself to believe that it is, and he puts in this delicate qualification parenthetically, to show the Galatians that, much as appearances may be against them, he will not give up the hope that a lingering spark of their first joyous conviction, in the strength of which they had undergone persecution, yet remained.

(5) The appeal by which the Apostle sought to check the defection of his thoughtless converts was not only an appeal to their past experience, when first they listened to his own preaching, but also to their present experience of facts that they saw actually going on among them. The first great outpouring of the Spirit, both in its miraculous and non-miraculous forms, though checked, had not entirely ceased; and the Galatians might thus see, simply by looking around them, that the channel which God chose for conveying His gifts was not that upon which the Judaisers insisted—the Law—but rather the preaching of faith. Where the faith implanted by the Apostle's preaching still showed signs of vital growth, there the gifts of the Spirit were seen in connection with it; but not amongst the Judaisers and their party.

**Therefore.**—This word takes up again the question which had been started in verse 2, but brings it down, as it were, to the present time. The opposition between

miracles among you, *doeth he it* by the
works of the law, or by the hearing of
faith? (6) Even as Abraham believed
God, and it was accounted[1]
to him for righteousness.
(7) Know ye therefore that
they which are of faith, the same are
the children of Abraham. (8) And the
scripture, foreseeing that God would
justify the heathen through faith,
preached before the gospel unto Abra-
ham, *saying*, In thee shall all nations

Chap. iii. 6—9. Abraham's faith.

[1] Or, *imputed.*

---

the effects of faith, on the one hand, and works, on the other, was conspicuous when the Galatians were first converted; it is as conspicuous still. The argument is the same, whichever standpoint is assumed.

**Ministereth.**—The notion contained in this word is not only that of "supply," but of "*liberal* supply." At Athens it was the custom for wealthy citizens to bear the cost of bringing out the chorus—which was practically equivalent to putting a play upon the stage—at the great public feasts. The word translated "ministereth" was the technical term for this. The same word is used in 2 Cor. ix. 10; Col. ii. 19; 2 Pet. i. 5, 11. In three out of the four places it is rendered by the same word "minister;" in 2 Pet. i. 5 it appears in the phrase "*add* to your faith virtue" (rather, *furnish forth in your faith virtue—i.e.*, "let your faith prompt you to abundant acts of virtue"). "He that ministereth" is, of course, God.

**Worketh miracles among you.**—The Greek means not so much "causes miracles to be wrought in your midst" as "implants in you miraculous powers." The power to work miracles is regarded as a special faculty bestowed by God upon individual Christians. The means by which they become receptive of it is that enthusiastic condition aroused in them by faith. Mere formal obedience to a written law had no such efficacy.

(6—14) These prolific results are due to faith, and not to the Law; just as it was faith which won for Abraham that imputed righteousness. Faith was the cause, blessing the consequence, which extends to all the spiritual descendants of Abraham. The Scripture distinctly foresaw this when it declared that the heathen too (*i.e.*, those who believe from among the heathen) should be blessed in Abraham. The effects of the Law are just the opposite of this. Where faith brings a blessing the Law brought a curse. The Law never made any man accepted as righteous. This is a privilege reserved for faith. The Law demands a literal fulfilment, which is impossible. Hence the Law entailed a curse, which Christ has removed by taking it upon Himself. Thus the blessing promised to Abraham, and the outpouring of the Spirit included in it, have been opened out to Gentiles as well as Jews, and indeed to all who give in their adhesion to Christ by faith.

(6) **Even as.**—The argument is here very condensed. Ideas lie close together in the Apostle's mind which are some distance apart in ours. He asks whether, in bestowing the gifts of the Spirit upon the Christian Church, God made use of the medium of the Law or of faith. The answer he assumes to be faith; and his thoughts fly at once to that crucial instance of faith—the faith of Abraham.

**Abraham believed God . . .**—Quoted from the LXX. version of Gen. xv. 6. The same quotation is made, in the same words and with the same object, in Rom. iv. 3, where see the Note. Comp. also the *Excursus E* to that Epistle, on "Imputed Righteousness."

(7) The main point of the Apostle's argument in the present passage is the superiority of faith over the Law. He has, however, also in view the ulterior consequences of that superiority. Unlike the Law, faith is open to all Gentiles as well as Jews. The promise, therefore, being annexed to faith, contained the death-blow of all those exclusive privileges which the Judaising party in Galatia claimed for themselves, and of all those burdensome regulations which they were for imposing upon the Galatian Christians. This, too, the Apostle brings out by showing that the believers in Christ, whatever their nationality, are the true spiritual descendants of Abraham.

**Know ye.**—The verb here may either be in the indicative or in the imperative: "know ye," or "ye know." Perhaps, on the whole, the imperative, as in the Authorised version, is best.

**They which are of faith.**—Those whose principles of action are derived from faith; those whose master-motive is faith.

**Children of Abraham.**—This idea of a spiritual descent from Abraham is found also in Rom. iv. 11, 12, 16; ix. 6—8.

(8) The universalism of the promise is accounted for by the fact that it is rested upon faith and not on works—thus showing a distinct prevision of a time when the whole world should be invited to claim a share in it by the exercise of faith.

**The scripture.**—Here, with a more decided personification than usual, the Scripture is said to foresee what God, by whom Scripture is inspired, foresaw.

**Foreseeing.**—It appears to have been a rather common formula among the Jews to say "What *saw* the Scripture?" (*i.e.*, What had the Scripture in sight, or in view?) for "What did it mean?" Here the metaphor falls in naturally with the personification.

**Would justify.**—Literally, *justifies.* The use of the present tense implies that the justification of the Gentiles is regarded as forming part of the eternal purpose of God, to whom the future and the present are one.

**The heathen.**—It is to be noticed that the same word is translated indifferently by "heathen" (as here, and also in 2 Cor. xi. 26; Gal. i. 16; ii. 9), "nations" (as in the second clause of this verse, and frequently elsewhere), and "Gentiles" (as in chaps. ii. 2, 8, 12, 14, 15; iii. 14 of this Epistle, and most commonly in other places where it occurs).

**Preached before the gospel.**—For this translation we might substitute, *announced the glad tidings beforehand.* The Authorised version, however, hardly involves an anachronism, as the promise is regarded as *anticipating* the gospel, inasmuch as it already contained the doctrine of justification by faith, in which the essence of the gospel consisted.

**In thee.**—The righteousness which was imputed to Abraham his spiritual descendants also could claim by virtue of their descent from him. What applied to him applied (potentially and prophetically) to them. In

be blessed.[a] (9) So then they which be
of faith are blessed with faithful Abra-
ham. (10) For as many as are of the
works of the law are under
the curse: for it is written,
Cursed *is* every one that
continueth not in all things which are
written in the book of the law to do
them.[b] (11) But that no man is justified
by the law in the sight of God, *it is*
evident: for, The just shall live by
faith.[c] (12) And the law is not of faith:

Chap. iii. 10—12. The curse of the Law.

a Gen. 12. 3.

b Deut. 27. 26.

c Hab. 2. 4; Rom. 1. 17.

like manner it is said, in Heb. vii. 9, that "Levi paid tithes in Abraham."

The quotation is a combination of Gen. xii. 3 ("In thee shall all families of the earth be blessed") and Gen. xviii. 18 ("All the nations of the earth shall be blessed in him.")

**Be blessed.**—With the bliss of the Messianic kingdom.

(9) **They which be of faith.**—The same phrase as in verse 7 above.

**With faithful Abraham**—*i.e.*, in company with Abraham. The same idea is presented in two different forms. Abraham's spiritual descendants are blessed "*in* him;" they are also blessed "*with* him." He is the head of a great company, in which they all are included.

(10) In this and the following verses the action of the Law is contrasted with that of faith, and the necessity of faith and the system of things to which faith belongs brought out into strong relief. The antithesis is: faith—blessing; law—curse. The "curse" was the penalty which the Law itself imposed upon all who failed to keep it. None really kept it, and therefore none escaped this curse.

**As many as are of the works of the law.**—An expression corresponding to "they which are of faith" in verses 7 and 9. The meaning is, "Those who take their character from works done in obedience to law—the cast of whose lives is determined by the principle of legal obedience.

**Under the curse.**—Strictly, *are under a curse;* subject to a curse.

**For it is written.**—The Apostle proceeds to quote the clause in the Law by which this curse was entailed. The quotation is from Deut. xxvii. 26, where it forms the conclusion of the series of curses to be pronounced from Mount Ebal. The Hebrew text is, "Cursed be he that confirmeth not the words of this law to do them." The word "all" is inserted in the Authorised version, probably from this passage. The Hebrew has also simply "he that" for "every one who;" so that the absolute and sweeping nature of the condemnation would seem to be much less marked in the original. It is not, however, clear that this character was first given to it by St. Paul. "Every one" is found in the Peshito Syriac, which *may* have been influenced by the language of St. Paul; "in *all* things" is found in the Samaritan Pentateuch, which certainly was not so influenced. The quotation is made by Justin (*Trypho*, § 95) in precisely the same words as by St. Paul. Justin, however, is not improbably quoting through the medium of this Epistle. (See *Introduction.*)

(11, 12) The Law could not bring a blessing. It could not justify. For the condition of justification is faith; and the Law has nothing to do with faith. Its standpoint was entirely different—that of works.

(11) **In the sight of God.**—Standing as a prisoner before His tribunal.

**The just shall live by faith.**—The stress is on the word "faith." It is *faith* (not law) which gives life. In St. Paul's application of the passage, the word "just" must be taken in what is technically termed a slightly proleptic sense. A man is not just *before* the exercise of faith, but he *becomes* just *by* the exercise of it; and, in another aspect, the state of righteousness upon which he then enters is also a state of life. Strictly speaking, the order is—faith, justification, life. It would be possible to take the Greek in such a way as to bring out this more distinctly: "The just by faith" (*i.e.*, he whose righteousness is based on faith) "shall live." Some good commentators take the passage thus, but a balance of considerations seems, on the whole, to be in favour of the sense adopted in the Authorised version.

The quotation is from Hab. ii. 4, where it refers to the preservation of the righteous Israelite amidst the general ruin caused by the Chaldean invasion. Though the wicked and proud shall be destroyed, the righteous man shall live "by his faith." There is some division of opinion amongst commentators as to whether the word translated "faith" means, in the original, faith in the active sense or faith in the passive sense—"fidelity," "faithfulness," or "trust in God." The sense in which the word is used by St Paul is most nearly related to the latter. It has the full-developed Christian meaning, which begins in belief, includes trust, and passes on to become an active energy of devotion. (Comp. the Note and *Excursus* on Rom. i. 17, where the same quotation is made.)

(12) **The law is not of faith.**—The ruling principle of the Law is not faith, but something else—works.

**The man that doeth them.**—By "them" is meant the "statutes" and "judgments" mentioned immediately before in the verse (Lev. xviii. 5) from which the quotation is taken. Just as the stress was upon "faith" in the last verse, so here it falls on the word "doeth:" it is a matter of *works.*

**Shall live.**—The idea of life receives an enlargement, corresponding to the fuller revelation of immortality in the New Testament as compared with the Old. In the Old Testament, "life is an existence upon earth, shortened by no judgment, reposing upon God, and delighting itself in God." On the other hand, "death is the sudden and dreadful end, the destruction of this existence through a judgment of some special kind" (Schultz, *Theology of the Old Testament*, ii. 163). Such a judgment would be the Chaldean invasion; and when the prophet Habakkuk says that the "just shall live," he means that he should be saved from this calamity, and still continue to enjoy the divine favour and protection. The promise in Leviticus declares that he who keeps the Law shall be preserved from all judgments of this kind. With St. Paul, as in the Old Testament, the root idea is that of drawing support and sustenance from God; but with him this is not confined to the present life, or extended beyond the grave only in some dim and shadowy way: it begins in time and stretches on into eternity.

**In them.**—His life shall spring out of them and

but, The man that doeth them shall live in them.[a] (13) Christ hath redeemed us from the curse of the law, being made a curse for us: for it is written, Cursed *is* every one that hangeth on a tree:[b] (14) that the blessing of Abraham might come on the Gentiles through Jesus Christ; that we might receive the promise of the Spirit through faith.

Chap. iii. 13, 14. Removed by faith in Christ.

a Lev. 18. 5.
b Deut. 21. 23.

---

be nourished by them, just as a tree strikes its roots *into* the earth.

(13, 14) The Law brought a curse, but the Christian is delivered from that curse. How? Christ has taken it upon Himself. The Crucifixion brought Him under the curse of the Law. At the same time, it abolished the dominion of the Law, and threw open the Messianic blessedness to Gentiles as well as Jews: in other words, to all who gave in their adhesion to the Messiah *by faith*.

(13) **Christ hath redeemed us.**—Better, *Christ redeemed us*. The opening of this verse without any connecting particle lends sharpness and emphasis to the contrast. The Law brought a curse. There it stopped short. That was all it could do. The first thing that Christianity does is to undo this result of the Law by deliverance from the curse.

This deliverance is represented under the form of a *ransom*. Christ "bought off" the human race from the penalty of its sins, the price paid being His death. Comp. 1 Cor. vi. 20; vii. 23, "Ye are (were) bought with a price;" 2 Pet. ii. 1, "The Lord that bought them;" Rev. v. 9, "Thou wast slain and hast redeemed (bought) us to God by thy blood;" Rev. xiv. 4, "These were redeemed (bought) from among men." The word used in these passages, as well as in that before us, is the general word for "buying." But that the "buying" intended is that more definitely conveyed by the idea of "ransom" appears from the use of the special word for ransom in Matt. xx. 28 (=Mark x. 45), "The Son of Man came to give His life a ransom for many;" 1 Tim. ii. 6, "Who gave Himself a ransom for all." The word commonly translated "redemption" (Rom. iii. 24; 1 Cor. i. 30; Eph. i. 7, 14; iv. 30; Col. i. 14; Heb. ix. 15) also contains the same special idea of "a ransoming."

**Us.**—In the first instance, "the Jews," but not to be confined too strictly to them. The Apostle is writing to a Gentile (though Judaising) Church, and he does not wish to exclude any of his readers. Though the Gentiles do not come directly under "the curse of the Law," they came under God's condemnation. From this they were released, and the blessings of the theocracy hitherto annexed to the Law were thrown open to them by the death of Christ.

**From the curse of the law.**—From that curse which the Law pronounced upon all who failed to keep its precepts.

**Being made a curse.**—Being treated as if He were accursed. Comp. 2 Cor. v. 21, "For he hath made Him to be sin for us who knew no sin"—*i.e.*, treated as sinful One who was not sinful. The idea is somewhat strengthened by the use of the substantive for the adjective. The curse identifies itself with its object: seizes, as it were, upon the person of its victim.

**For us**—*i.e.*, "on our behalf," "for our sakes," not "in our stead." It is impossible to escape the conclusion that St. Paul, like the rest of the Apostles, regarded the sufferings of Christ as undergone *in our stead*. The idea is, indeed, distinctly expressed in this very passage; but it must be gathered from the context, not from the use of the preposition. The preposition which means "instead" is found in Matt. xx. 28; 1 Tim. ii. 6. (See Note on chap. i. 4.)

**As it is written.**—The way in which the curse of the Law fell upon Christ was through His death. The ignominious death by which He died was one to which the curse of God specially attached. The Law expressly declared that that criminal who died upon the cross or gibbet was an object of the divine wrath. Christ died as such a criminal, and so came under the curse.

It is to be observed, in considering the doctrinal bearings of this passage, that the curse which fell upon Christ was *not* the same curse as that described above as the consequence of human guilt in failing to keep the requirements of the Law. It is not the accumulated penalty for the whole mass of human disobedience, but rather an incidental defilement, contracted by an involuntary breach of a particular ceremonial precept. The death of Christ involved a curse because the manner of it was by suspension from a cross. Nothing more than this is said. Christ, the sinless One, died for sinful men. If He had not died they must have died. And His death acted (in some inscrutable way) so as to propitiate the wrath of God. But it is not said that the actual load of human guilt was laid upon Him. It is not said that His death was the actual punishment of that guilt. The death of Christ removed the necessity for the punishment of men, but it could not be regarded as a punishment in relation to Christ Himself. In this respect it would seem as if the symbolism of the scapegoat (which is sometimes adduced in explanation of the present passage) was imperfectly applicable. In the case of the scapegoat, the high priest was to lay his hands upon his head, and to "confess over him all the iniquities of the children of Israel, and all their transgressions in all their sins, putting them upon the head of the goat;" and the goat was to "bear upon him all their iniquities unto a land not inhabited" (Lev. xvi. 21, 22). No such process as this really took place in the case of our Lord; nor is it applied to Him even in 1 Pet. ii. 24, otherwise than in vague and general metaphor. The literal application derives no countenance from the present passage, but is rather contradicted by it. It expressly distinguishes between the curse which fell upon Christ and the curse which was due to the sins of men, though the incurrence of the one led to the abrogation of the other.

**Cursed is every one that hangeth on a tree.**—From Deut. xxi. 23. The Hebrew and LXX. insert "of God"—"He that is hanged is cursed of God"—which St. Paul instinctively omits. The reference in the original is to the exposure of the body upon a stake or gibbet after death.

(14) The abolition of the Law, consummated upon the cross, involved the doing away of all the old restrictions which confined the Messianic inheritance to the Jews. Henceforth this inheritance, and the promised outpouring of the Spirit which was to accompany it, was open equally to the Gentiles. The one condition now

(15) Brethren, I speak after the manner
of men; Though *it be* but
a man's covenant,[1] yet *if*
*it be* confirmed, no man
disannulleth, or addeth thereto. (16) Now
to Abraham and his seed were the
promises made. He saith not, And to
seeds, as of many; but as of one, And

Chap. iii. 15—18. The promise irrevocable.

1 Or, *testament.*

---

was faith, and that intimate relation to the Messiah which faith implied.

**The blessing of Abraham.**—That is, the blessing pronounced upon Abraham and to be fulfilled in his seed.

**Through Jesus Christ.**—Through the relation into which they enter with Christ by embracing Christianity.

**We.**—The Apostle and his readers, whether Jews or Gentiles.

**Receive the promise of the Spirit.**—A special outpouring of the Spirit was to be one of the characteristics of the great Messianic manifestation. (Comp. Joel ii. 28, 29; Acts ii. 16—21.) The promise is said to be "received" by the generation on which it is fulfilled, not by that to which it is given. The same phrase occurs in Acts ii. 33; Heb. ix. 15.

(15—18) To take an illustration from purely human relations. A covenant once ratified is binding. It cannot be treated as if it did not exist, neither can fresh clauses be added to it. Now the covenant and promise made to Abraham (by the terms in which it was made) could point to no one but the Messiah. That covenant remained unaffected by the Law, which was four hundred and thirty years subsequent to it in point of date. Law and promise are two totally different and mutually exclusive things. But the covenant with Abraham was given by promise. The Law, therefore, had nothing to do with it.

(15) **I speak after the manner of men.**—The figure that I am going to use is one taken from the ordinary civil relations between man and man, and therefore, it is left to be inferred, supplies an *à fortiori* argument in things relating to God, for men may change and break the most solemn engagements; God is absolutely faithful and unchangeable. The phrase translated "I speak after the manner of men" is found in the same, or a very similar form, in Rom. iii. 5; vi. 19; 1 Cor. ix. 8, where see the Notes.

**Though it be but a man's covenant.**—This is well rendered in the Authorised version. A covenant, even though it is only between two men—though it is regulated by the provisions only of human law—does not admit of alteration or addition after it has once been signed and sealed; much more a covenant which depends on God.

**Covenant.**—The word thus translated is that which gave its name to the "Old and New Testaments," where a more correct rendering would be the "Old and New *Covenants*." The word has both senses. It meant originally a "disposition" or "settlement," and hence came, on the one hand, to be confined to a "testamentary disposition," while, on the other hand, it was taken to mean a settlement arrived at by agreement between two parties. The first sense is that most commonly found in classical writers; the second is used almost entirely in the LXX. and New Testament. The one exception is in Heb. ix. 15—17, where the idea of "covenant" glides into that of "testament," the argument rather turning upon the double meaning of the word.

**Addeth thereto.**—Adds new clauses or conditions. Such new clauses could only be added by a second covenant. The reason why the Apostle introduces this point is that the Law might be supposed to restrict the bearings of the promise. It might be thought to add certain new and limiting conditions, without compliance with which the blessings of the promise could not be obtained. This was the position of the Judaising party, against which St. Paul is arguing.

(16) A parenthetical explanation of the true object of the promise. That promise was shown by its wording to have reference to the Messiah. It did not speak of "seeds," but of "seed"—not of "descendants," but of "descendant." And the Messiah is, *par excellence*, the "descendant" of Abraham.

The object of this parenthesis is to prove a point which the Judaising opponents of the Apostle would not contest—viz., that the fulfilment of the promise to Abraham was reserved for that Messianic dispensation to which they themselves belonged. The Law therefore *intervened* between the promise and its fulfilment, but, inasmuch as it was itself *later* than the promise, could not alter the terms of its fulfilment. If the promise had been fulfilled *before* the giving of the Law, and if the Messianic dispensation to which the Apostle and his readers belonged was *not* a fulfilment of the promise, then the Law might have had something to do with it: the restrictions of the Law might have come in to limit and contract the promise: the Gentiles might have been saddled with the obligations of the Jews. But it was not so.

**To Abraham and his seed were the promises made.**—It was expressly stated that the promises were given "to Abraham and his seed." The exact terms are worth noting.

The quotation appears to be made from Gen. xiii. 15, or Gen. xvii. 8. The word "promise" is put in the plural because the promise to Abraham was several times repeated—to Abraham first, and, after him, to the other patriarchs. The object of the promise, as recorded in the Book of Genesis, was, in the first instance, the possession of the land of Canaan; but St. Paul here, as elsewhere, gives it a spiritual application.

**He saith not.**—The "he" is not expressed. We must supply either "God" or the promise given by God—"it says," as in quotations from an authoritative document.

**And to seeds, as of many; but as of one.**—The argument of the Apostle turns upon the use, both in the Hebrew and in the LXX., of a singular instead of a plural noun. Both in the Hebrew and in the LXX., however, the noun, though singular, is collective. It meant, in the first instance at least, not any one individual, but the posterity of Abraham as a whole. The Apostle refers it to Christ and the "spiritual Israel" (*i.e.*, the Church, of which He is the Head), on the same principle on which, throughout the New Testament, the history of the chosen people under the old covenant is taken as a type of the Christian dispensation. We may compare Matt. ii. 15, where an allusion to the exodus of Israel from Egypt is treated as a type of the return of the Holy Family from their flight into Egypt. Such passages are not to be

to thy seed, which is Christ. (17) And
this I say, *that* the covenant, that was
confirmed before of God in Christ, the
law, which was four hundred and thirty
years after, cannot disannul, that it
should make the promise of none effect.
(18) For if the inheritance *be* of the law,
*it is* no more of promise; but God gave
*it* to Abraham by promise. (19) Where-
fore then *serveth* the law?
It was added because of
transgressions, till the seed
should come to whom the promise was
made; *and it was* ordained by angels in

Chap. iii. 19—24. Temporary function of the Law.

---

regarded as *arguments* possessing a permanent logical validity (which would be to apply the rigid canons of Western logic to a case for which they are unsuitable), but rather as marked illustrations of the organic unity which the apostolic writers recognised in the pre-Christian and Christian dispensations. Not only had both the same Author, and formed part of the same scheme, but they were actually the counterparts one of the other. The events which characterised the earlier dispensation had their analogies—sometimes spiritual, sometimes literal—in the later.

(17) The fulfilment of the promise is thus to be seen in the Messianic dispensation now begun. The Law, which was given four hundred and thirty years *after* the promise, had no power to cancel it.

This verse contains the direct inference from the argument stated in verse 15. When a document has been sealed, no subsequent addition can affect it. The Law was subsequent to the promise; therefore the Law cannot affect it.

**And this I say.**—Now, what I mean to say is this; the inference that I intend to draw is this.

**Confirmed before of God**—*i.e.*, confirmed by God before the giving of the Law.

**In Christ.**—These words are omitted in the group of oldest MSS., and should certainly be struck out. If retained, the translation should be: *unto Christ*—*i.e.*, "with a view to Christ," to find its fulfilment in Christ.

**Four hundred and thirty years after.**—The giving of the Law from Mount Sinai is thus placed four hundred and thirty years after the giving of the promise to Abraham. This would include the two periods of the sojourn of the patriarchs in Canaan and the sojourn in Egypt. According to another system of chronology, the sojourn in Egypt alone occupied four hundred and thirty—or, in round numbers, four hundred—years. Thus, in Gen. xv. 13, Abraham is warned that his seed is to be a stranger in a land that is not theirs, and to be afflicted "four hundred years." In Ex. xii. 40 it is expressly stated that "the sojourning of the children of Israel, who dwelt in Egypt, was four hundred and thirty years." In Acts vii. 6 the prophecy of Gen. xv. 13 is quoted: the people were to be "entreated evil four hundred years." It is noticeable, however, that in Ex. xii. 40, which is the least ambiguous of the three passages, the LXX. and Samaritan Pentateuch add, "and in the land of Canaan," so as to make the four hundred and thirty years cover the whole of the two periods, in agreement with the present passage. It has been thought that an examination of the genealogy of Levi favours the same reckoning. It would seem, however, that there were two systems of chronology really current. Josephus adopts both in different parts of his writings (comp. *Ant.* ii. 15, § 2, with *Ant.* ii. 9, § 1; *Wars*, v. 9, § 4), and both are represented in other writers of the period, or not very much later. It is possible that the shorter reckoning may have arisen from difficulties observed in the longer, though it may be questioned whether it does not raise greater difficulties itself.

(18) The fulfilment of the promise is unaffected by the Law. For it is not dependent upon the Law, or upon the Law and the promise combined (the Law *modifying* the promise), but upon the promise alone. The Law does not come in at all. Law and promise—in other words, contract and free gift—are incompatible ideas. But the land of Canaan was promised to Abraham as a free gift, and as a free gift the spiritual Canaan is thrown open to his spiritual descendants.

**The inheritance.**—In the first instance, the temporal inheritance of the land of Canaan; but here understood of the spiritual blessings of the Messianic kingdom.

**Gave it.**—In the original a strong word: *God hath freely given it.* There is an antithesis to the idea of "covenant" or "contract," in which both parties have to perform a part. The promise was given by God to Abraham freely, gratuitously, unfettered by any engagement on his side by the non-fulfilment of which it might be made void.

(19, 20) If such was *not* the function of the Law—if it had *no* power to modify the promise—what was its true function? It was a sort of measure of police. Its object was to deal with transgressions. It was also a temporary measure, of force only until it should be superseded by the coming of the Messiah. Unlike the promise, too, it was a contract. It was given by a mediator—that is, a person acting between two parties. Two parties were involved, with rigid conditions binding them both. On the other hand, the promise was given unconditionally by the sole act of God.

In stating the true function of the Law, the Apostle brings out its inferiority to the promise in four respects. (1) It dealt with sins, not with holiness; (2) it was temporary and transitory; (3) it was given, not directly, but indirectly, through the double mediation of the angels and of Moses; (4) it was conditional, and not like the promise, unconditional. It depended upon the fallible action of man, and not only upon the infallible word of God.

(19) **Wherefore then serveth the law?**—Literally, *What then is the Law?* What is its object or function? If it did not affect the promise, what did it do? The Apostle proceeds to answer this question.

**It was added.**—It was not a part of the original scheme, but came in as a sort of marginal addition. It was, as it were, a parenthesis in the design of Providence. The direct line of God's dealings with man ran through the promise and its fulfilment. The Law came in by the way.

**Because of transgressions.**—It has been usual to give to this one of two opposite interpretations, to make it mean (1) to check or put down transgressions; (2) to

the hand of a mediator. (20) Now a
mediator is not *a mediator* of one, but
God is one. (21) *Is* the law then against
the promises of God? God forbid: for
if there had been a law given which
could have given life, verily righteousness
should have been by the law.
(22) But the scripture hath concluded all
under sin, that the promise by faith of
Jesus Christ might be given to them
that believe. (23) But before faith came,
we were kept under the law, shut up
unto the faith which should afterwards
be revealed. (24) Wherefore the law was

---

multiply and increase transgressions, as in Rom. v. 20. The expression seems wide enough to cover both ideas. The Law was given "*because of transgressions:*" *i.e.*, it *had its object in* transgressions. Its original purpose was to make them known, and by imposing a penalty to check them; its real effect was to provoke and enhance them. The expression "because of transgressions" leaves it ambiguous which of these points is meant, or rather, it includes them all.

**Till the seed should come to whom the promise was made.**—By "the seed" is meant, as above, in verse 16, Christ, the Messiah. The promise is said to have *been made* to Him in whom it is fulfilled, just as, in verse 14, Christians are said to "receive the promise"—*i.e.*, the fulfilment of the promise "of the Spirit."

**Ordained by angels.**—The idea of angels having had a share in the giving of the Law appears in Deut. xxxiii. 2: "The Lord came from Sinai . . . He shined forth from mount Paran, and He came with ten thousands of saints." For "saints" the LXX. substitutes, in the next verse, "angels." Similar allusions are found at the end of St. Stephen's speech (Acts vii. 53): "Who have received the law by the disposition (as ordinances) of angels, and have not kept it;" and in Heb. ii. 2: "If the word spoken by (*through*) angels was stedfast." In this last instance, as in the present passage, the ministration of angels employed in it is quoted as showing the inferiority of the Law to the Gospel. In St. Stephen's speech and in Josephus (*Ant.* xv. 5, 3) the same ministration is appealed to as enhancing the dignity of the Law. The different point of view is natural enough, according as the subject is regarded from the side of man or from the side of God.

**In the hand of a mediator.**—Through the instrumentality of a third person, distinct from the contracting parties—*i.e.*, in this case, Moses. The term "mediator" was commonly applied to Moses in the Rabbinical writings, and appears to be hinted at in Heb. viii. 6, where our Lord is spoken of as "a mediator of a better covenant." Many of the fathers, following Origen, took the mediator here to be Christ, and were thus thrown out in their interpretation of the whole passage.

(20) The mention of the word "mediator" implies a contract to which there are at least two parties. But where there is a contract there must be also conditions, and if these conditions are not observed the whole falls to the ground. Such was the Law. The Law was not kept, and therefore the blessings annexed to it were forfeited. On the other hand, the promise depends upon God alone. He gave it, and He will assuredly keep it, no matter what man may do. God alone is concerned in it.

This passage is a conspicuous instance of the advance which has been made in New Testament exegesis. It is said to have received as many as 250 or 300 (according to another estimate, even 430) interpretations, but at the present moment there is a tendency to acquiesce in that given above, which, it is hoped, will be thought satisfactory.

**Now a mediator is not a mediator of one.**—The very idea of a mediator involves two parties at least. The Law had a mediator, therefore the Law involves two parties. In other words, it is a contract.

**But God is one.**—On the other hand, God, the giver of the promise, stands alone: therefore the promise is *not* a contract; and, resting on God, it is indefeasible.

(21–24) If the Law was thus inferior to the promise, does it therefore follow that it is contrary to it? By no means. The Law could not indeed give life; it could not justify, or place in a state of righteousness. Its real result was rather to place all men in a state of sin. But by so doing it prepared the way for the fulfilment of the promise in all who put faith in Christ. The Law was a close and strict, yet salutary, discipline to make us fit for faith in Christ.

(21) **The promises.**—Here, as in verse 16, the plural, because the promise to Abraham was several times repeated, and afterwards ratified to his descendants.

**For if . . .**—The argument which follows begins with a concession. Though the Law was no substitute for the promise, it yet directly led up to it.

**Given life.**—This is practically equivalent to "justified," or "made righteous." He who is justified has life—both true spiritual life in the present and eternal life in the future. That the Law could not justify had been shown in verse 11 and in Rom. iii. 20.

(22) **The scripture.**—Slightly personified.

**Hath concluded.**—The same peculiar word occurs in Rom. xi. 32, with a similar sense. It means to "shut up," "hem in," "prevent from straying either to the right hand or to the left," as a shepherd shuts up his flock in the fold.

**All.**—This is put in the neuter gender, but only to give a more complete universality to the statement. What is meant is "all mankind."

**The promise by faith of Jesus Christ.**—The promise which originates in faith in Christ, which derives its fulfilment from faith, is due to faith.

(23) **Before faith came.**—Before faith awoke into exercise, began to exist, or the preaching of Christ as its object.

**We were kept.**—Better, *we were kept in ward,* so as to bring out more clearly the force of the metaphor which runs through the verse. The Law was a kind of prison-house, in which we were kept shut up. It was a custody from which we were not permitted to escape—a stern guardian that we were made to obey.

**Unto the faith . . .**—With a view to the dispensation of faith which was in store for us. The object of this state of guardianship was to fit us for the dispensation of faith looming in the future.

(24) **The law was our schoolmaster.**—Not quite

our schoolmaster *to bring us* unto Christ,
that we might be justified by faith.
(25) But after that faith is come, we are
no longer under a school-
master. (26) For ye are all
the children of God by
faith in Christ Jesus. (27)
For as many of you as have been bap-
tized into Christ have put on Christ.
(28) There is neither Jew nor Greek,
there is neither bond nor free, there is
neither male nor female: for ye are all
one in Christ Jesus. (29) And if ye *be*
Christ's, then are ye Abraham's seed,
and heirs according to the promise.

Chap. iii. 25—29. The Law superseded by faith.

A.D. 58.

CHAPTER IV.—(1) Now I say, *That*
the heir, as long as he
is a child, differeth nothing
from a servant, though he

Chap. iv. 1—7. State of tutelage.

---

a satisfactory translation; yet it is difficult to suggest a better. The Greek word is that from which is derived the English "pedagogue." Originally it meant the slave who was placed in charge of a child, and whose duty it was to conduct it to school. The idea is that of moral rather than of intellectual discipline. The care of the "pedagogue" ceased where that of the schoolmaster began, but it was he who had more especially to form the character of the child. Horace notes as a peculiar advantage of his own that his father himself had taken the place of pedagogue to him (*Sat.* l. vi., 81, 82).

**To bring us unto Christ.**—The words "to bring us," it will be seen, are supplied. They may be retained, provided that the metaphor is not pressed to the extent of supposing that Christ represents the schoolmaster proper to whom the child is led by the pedagogue slave. The work of Christ as a *Teacher* is not what the Apostle has in mind. It is rather a higher kind of guardianship, which is to succeed that of the Law, and to which the Law *hands over* its pupil. Once brought within the guardianship of Christ, and so made a member of the Messianic kingdom, the Christian is *justified by faith*, he receives an amnesty for his past sins, and is accounted righteous before God. (See Epistle to the Romans, *Excursus E: On the Doctrine of Justification by Faith and Imputed Righteousness*.)

(25—29) But now the Law has been exchanged for the dispensation of faith. Henceforth the old state of pupilage is at an end. We are no longer like children, but adult members of the divine family—*sons* of God. We have entered into this relation by faith in Christ. For to be baptised into Christ is to enter into the closest possible relation to Him. It is to be identified with Him entirely. Nor is any excluded. The old barriers of race, status, and even sex, are done away. Through their relation to Christ, all Christians, as it were, unite to form a single man. They are a body animated by a single personality and will. And their relation to Christ stamps them as the true descendants of Abraham. In them is the promise of the Messianic blessing fulfilled.

(26) **Children of God.**—The translation "children" here is unfortunate, as the point to be brought out is that the Christian is no longer in the condition of "children," but in that of grown-up "*sons.*" The pre-Messianic period bears to the Messianic period the same relation that a childhood or minority bears to full age. The Christian, as such, has the privileges of an adult son in his Father's house. He is released from pupilage, and has received his freedom.

(27 **For.**—This introduces the reason why the Christian stands to God in the relation of an adult son. He is so by virtue of his relation to Christ.

**Baptized into Christ.**—To be baptised "*into* Christ" is something more than merely "to be baptised *in the name of* Christ." It implies the contracting of a very close and intimate relation, the nature of which is expressed in the phrase which follows.

**Have put on Christ.**—The metaphor has been thought to be taken from the putting on of the white baptismal robes. It is, however, commonly used in the LXX., where it means "to adopt," or "take to oneself." The Christian, at his baptism, thus "took to himself" Christ, and sought to grow into full unison and union with Him.

(28) This verse continues the proof that *all* Christians are, in the fullest sense, "sons of God." Verse 27 showed *why* this was so; the present verse shows that there are no exceptions, no inequalities. All Christians alike, no matter what their race, status, or sex, stand on the same footing of sonship before God. There is a unity or solidarity in the Christian body. What is true of one is true of all.

**Greek.**—The spread of the Greek race through the conquests of Alexander, their ubiquitous presence, and the use of the Greek language as a universal medium of communication, led to the name "Greek" being applied to all who were not Jews. "Jew and Greek" is intended to be an exhaustive division of the human race, just as "bond or free," "male and female."

This verse marks the immense stride made by Christianity in sweeping away the artificial distinctions which had been the bane of the ancient world, and prevented any true feeling of brotherhood springing up in it. Christianity, at one stroke, established the brotherhood and abolished the distinctions.

**One.**—The word "one" is masculine—"one man," "a single person"—as explained in the paraphrase above.

(29) Conclusion of the whole argument. The followers of the Messiah are the true seed of Abraham. The kingdom of the Messiah, which they possess, is the promised inheritance.

## IV.

(1—31) The present chapter continues the argument of the last. St. Paul had been reproaching the Galatians with their relapse. They had fallen back from a spiritual system to a material system; from a system that brought blessing to a system that brought a curse; from faith and the promise to the Law; from the freedom of the adult man to the constraint and discipline of the minor. Now the idea of constraint and freedom is taken up and carried out further. It is treated

be lord of all; (2) but is under tutors and governors until the time appointed of the father. (3) Even so we, when we were children, were in bondage under the elements[1] of the world: (4) but when the fulness of the time was come, God

1 Or, *rudiments.*

directly in the first seven and last eleven verses, and forms the link of transition to the next chapter, the opening key-note of which is "freedom." The middle portion of chap. iv. is somewhat of a personal digression, the object of which, however, is really to support this view of the opposition between the Apostle and the Judaising party as one between liberty on the one hand and slavery on the other. In the first section (verses 8—11) the Apostle expresses his surprise that the Galatians could descend from the height they had reached to anything so poor, so narrow, and so enslaving. A rush of personal feeling comes over him, and he goes on to remind them of the warm and eager welcome that they had given him when he first came among them, and of the contrast between their Judaising troublers and himself. His old feelings return, and his heart goes out towards them. On this tide of emotion the concluding arguments of the chapter are carried home.

(1—7) A further description, continued from the last chapter, of the state of wardship, with its restraints and servitude, compared with that Christian freedom—the freedom of sons—to which the Galatians had been admitted through their adoption into the Messianic family by adhesion to Christ.

It may be observed that the allusions to the condition of minors are not in strict accordance either with Jewish or Roman law. It has been suggested that they have reference to a special code current in Galatia. It is, however, far more probable that the Apostle is referring exclusively to neither, but has in his mind a sort of abstraction of the law of minority, such as would present itself to one who had not himself had a legal education.

(1) **Now I say.**—This phrase introduces a further and fuller explanation of what is involved in the state of nonage, as compared with that of adult freedom.

**A child**—*i.e.*, an infant, a minor; though the term is not technically chosen.

**Differeth nothing from a servant.**—Both the child and the slave were incapable of any valid act in a legal sense; the guardian was as entirely the representative of the one as the master of the other. Both the child and the slave were subject to the same restraint, discipline, correction.

**Though he be lord of all.**—Strictly speaking, the inference from this would be that the father was dead. This, however, is a point that does not really enter into the Apostle's thoughts. The illustration does not hold good in *all* particulars, but in the *chief* particulars—viz., the state of constraint and subordination in which the minor is placed so long as he is a minor.

(2) **Under tutors and governors.**—The distinction between these two terms is that between guardians of the person and stewards of the property. It would be better to translate, *guardians and stewards.*

**Until the time appointed of the father.**—From this it would appear that the length of the minority was determined by the father. This, however, was not the case either in Greek or Roman law; and the suggestion that the father may have had larger powers in Galatia than elsewhere, though supported by some remote indications, seems to be one of those subtleties in which learning sometimes overreaches itself; it being unlikely that the short sojourn of the Apostle in Galatia would have been enough to make him acquainted with the technicalities of the Galatian code. It is more probable that the application of the analogy has here come in to modify the statement of the analogy itself. The minority of the human race *is* fixed by the heavenly Father, though the earthly father, in disposing of his children, has to conform to another law than his own will.

(3) **We.**—That is, in the first instance, and specially, the Jews; but the Gentiles are also included. The Apostle is speaking from the point of view of the Christians: "all who are now Christians, whatever their antecedents." Before the coming of Christ both Jews and Gentiles had been subject to law; and what the Apostle says of the law of Moses applies more faintly to the law of conscience and of nature.

**Elements of the world.**—The word translated "elements" is peculiar. The simpler word from whence it is derived means "a row." Hence the derivative is applied to the letters of the alphabet, because they were arranged in rows. Thus it came to mean the "elements" or "rudiments" of learning, and then "elements" of any kind. The older commentators on this passage, for the most part, took it in the special sense of "the elements of nature," "the heavenly bodies," either as the objects of Gentile worship or as marking the times of the Jewish festivals. There is, however, little doubt that the other sense is best: "the elements (or *rudiments,* as in the margin) of religious teaching." These are called "the elements of *the world,*" because they were mundane and material; they included no clear recognition of spiritual things. The earlier forms of Gentile and even of Jewish religion were much bound up with *the senses;* the most important element in them was that of ritual. The same phrase, in the same sense, occurs twice in the Epistle to the Colossians (Col. ii. 8, 20).

(4) **The fulness of the time.**—That which was predetermined in the counsels of God as the right and proper time when the whole course of previous preparation both for Jew and Gentile was complete. Here we have a very clear expression of the conception of religion as progressive, divided into periods, and finding its culmination in Christianity. The phrase "fulness of the time" corresponds to "the time appointed of the father" in verse 2.

**Sent forth**—*i.e.*, from Himself; from that station which is described in John i. 1: "The Word was *with* God." The pre-existence of the Son is distinctly recognised by St. Paul.

**Made of a woman.**—Perhaps better translated, *born of a woman.* There is no allusion here to the miraculous conception. The phrase "born of a woman" was of common use. Comp. Matt. xi. 11: "Among them that are born of women there hath not risen a greater than John the Baptist." So here the expression is intended to bring out, not the divinity, but the true humanity of Christ.

**Made under the law.**—*Born under law—i.e.,* born into a state of things where the whole world was subject to law—born under the legal dispensation, though Himself destined to put an end to that dispensation.

sent forth his Son, made of a woman,
made under the law, (5) to redeem them
that were under the law, that we might
receive the adoption of sons. (6) And
because ye are sons, God hath sent
forth the Spirit of his Son into your
hearts, crying, Abba, Father. (7) Where-
fore thou art no more a servant, but
a son; and if a son, then an heir of God
through Christ. (8) Howbeit then, when
ye knew not God, ye did
service unto them which
by nature are no gods.
(9) But now, after that ye have known
God, or rather are known of God, how
turn ye again[1] to the weak and beggarly
elements,[2] whereunto ye desire again to
be in bondage? (10) Ye observe days,

Chap. iv. 8—11. The Galatians' relapse.

1 Or, *back.*

2 Or, *rudiments.*

---

(5) **To redeem them that were under the law.**—To redeem, or ransom, at the price of His death, both Jew and Gentile at once from the condemnation under which the law, to which they were severally subject, placed them, and also from the bondage and constraint which its severe discipline involved.

**That we might receive the adoption of sons.**—Redemption is followed by adoption. The admission of the believer into the Messianic kingdom, with its immunities from sin and from law, implies an admission into the Messianic family, of which God is the Father and Christ the Eldest Son, "first born amongst many brethren."

(6) It is because you are sons that you are able to address your Heavenly Father in such genuine accents of filial emotion. It is not ye that speak, but the Spirit of Christ which has been given to you in virtue of your adoption. He prompts your prayers.

This verse should be read in connection with Rom. viii. 15, 16, to which it forms a close parallel.

**Because.**—It is, perhaps, on the whole, best to retain this translation. The conjunction may, however, possibly mean "in proof that."

**Abba, Father.**—A reduplication of loving entreaty. (See Note on Rom. viii. 15.) For similar instances of a Greek word being repeated in Aramaic, or an Aramaic word in Greek, we may compare Rev. ix. 11: "The angel of the bottomless pit, whose name in the Hebrew tongue is Abaddon, but in the Greek tongue hath his name Apollyon;" Rev. xii. 9: "That old serpent, called the Devil, and Satan." The Aramaic "Abba" appears in our word "abbot."

(7) Thus, by your redemption, adoption, and the gift of the Spirit, it is distinctly proved that the old state of servitude and minority is past. You have entered upon the full privileges of the adult son. And the son is also called to the Messianic inheritance.

**Thou.**—The singular is used in order to individualise the expression and bring it home pointedly to each of the readers.

**No more.**—Since the coming of Christ, and your own acceptance of Christianity.

**If a son, then an heir . . .**—The Roman law (which the Apostle seems to be following) treated *all* the sons as heirs, and provided for an equal division of the property between them.

**Of God through Christ.**—The true reading here appears to be, *through God*—a somewhat unusual expression. The Christian is admitted as an heir, not through any merits of his own, but through the process of redemption and adoption wrought for him by God.

(8—11) The results of the foregoing argument are now turned against the Galatians. In their old heathen state they had been in bondage to gods that were no gods. From this bondage they had been delivered. They had been raised to a true knowledge of God, and received a Father's recognition from Him. How then could they possibly think of returning to a system of mere ceremonialism. All this painful observance of times and seasons could only make the Apostle think that his labours on their behalf had been thrown away.

(8) **Them which by nature are no gods.**—The gods of the heathen are called by St. Paul "devils." (See 1 Cor. x. 20: "The things which the Gentiles sacrifice they sacrifice to devils, and not to God.")

(9) **Known God.**—The word for "known" is different from that so translated in the verse above. It brings out more distinctly the process of obtaining knowledge, especially with reference to a state of previous ignorance. *Having come to know God.*

**Or rather are known of God.**—In speaking of the Galatians as "coming to know" God, it might seem as if too much stress was laid on the human side of the process, and therefore, by way of correction, the Apostle presents also the divine side. Any true and saving knowledge of God has for its converse the "being known *of* God"—*i.e.*, recognition by God and acceptance by Him, such as is involved in the admission of the believer into the Messianic kingdom.

**Again.**—In the Greek a double phrase, for the sake of emphasis, *over again from the very beginning*, as a child might be said to go back to his alphabet.

**Weak and beggarly elements.**—"Elements" is used here, in the same sense as in verse 3, of that elementary religious knowledge afforded in different degrees to Jew and Gentile before the coming of Christ. These are called "weak" because they were insufficient to enable man to work out his own salvation. (Comp. St. Paul's account of the inward struggle, and of the helpless condition to which man is reduced by it, in Rom. vii. 7—24.) They are called "beggarly," or "poor," because, unlike the gospel, they were accompanied by no outpouring of spiritual gifts and graces. The legal system was barren and dry; the gospel dispensation was rich with all the abundance and profusion of the Messianic time (Joel ii. 19; iii. 18; Amos ix. 13, 14; Isa. lv. 1; lxv. 21—25; John vii. 37, 38, *et al.*)

(10) **Ye observe.**—A compound word, signifying not only "to observe," but "to observe *scrupulously*." The word is used by Josephus in his paraphrase of the fourth commandment: "Remember the sabbath day to *keep* it holy" (*Ant.* iii. 5, § 5).

**Days**—*i.e.*, in the first instance and especially, the Jewish sabbaths; but other fasts or festivals which occupied a single day may be included.

**Months.**—The description mounts in an ascending scale—days, months, seasons, years. The "months,"

and months, and times, and years.
(11) I am afraid of you, lest I have
bestowed upon you labour in vain.
(12) Brethren, I beseech you, be as I
*am;* for I *am* as ye *are:* ye have not
injured me at all. (13) Ye know how
through infirmity of the
flesh I preached the gospel
unto you at the first.
(14) And my temptation which was in my

Chap. iv. 12—20. Their past zeal and present coldness.

however, mean really "the first day of the month," the "new moon." (See Lev. xxiii. 24; Num. xxviii. 11; Ps. lxxxi. 3.)

**Times.**—*Seasons:* such as the Passover, Pentecost, and the Feast of Tabernacles.

**Years.**—Such as the sabbatical year and the year of jubilee. The Apostle is giving a list which is intended to be exhaustive of all Jewish observances, so that it would not necessarily follow that the Galatians had actually kept the year of jubilee, or even that it was kept literally by the Jews at this time.

As to the bearing of this passage on the general question of the observance of seasons, it is to be noticed that the reference is here to the adoption by the Galatians of the *Jewish* seasons as a mark of the extent to which they were prepared to take on themselves the burden of the Mosaic law. It does not necessarily follow that the observance of Christian seasons is condemned. At the same time, it is quite clear that St. Paul places all such matters under the head of "elements" or "rudiments." They belong to the lowest section of Christian practice, and the more advanced a Christian is the less he needs to be bound by them. This, again, is qualified by the consideration that it is dangerous for any one individual to assume his own advanced condition, and to think himself able to dispense with the safeguards which his brother-Christians require. It is safest to follow the general rule of the Church, so long as it is done *intelligently*—*i.e.*, with a consciousness of the reason and expediency of what is done, and not in a spirit of mere mechanical routine. The comparison between the literal and the spiritual observance of seasons, and the superiority of the latter as the more excellent way, is well brought out by Origen in some comments upon this passage: "If it be objected to us on this subject that we are accustomed to observe certain days—as, for example, the Lord's Day, the Preparation, the Passover, or Pentecost—I have to answer that, to the perfect Christian—who is ever in his thoughts, words, and deeds serving his natural Lord, God the Word—all his days are the Lord's, and he is always keeping the Lord's Day. He, also, who is unceasingly preparing himself for the true life, and abstaining from the pleasures of this life which lead astray so many, such a one is always keeping the Preparation Day. Again, he who considers that 'Christ our Passover was sacrificed for us,' and that it is his duty to keep the feast by eating of the flesh of the Word, never ceases to keep the Paschal Feast. And, finally, he who can truly say: 'We are risen with Christ,' and 'He hath exalted us, and made us sit with Him in heavenly places in Christ,' is always living in the season of Pentecost . . . But the majority of those who are accounted believers are not of this advanced class; but from being either unable or unwilling to keep every day in this manner, they require some sensible memorial to prevent spiritual things from passing away altogether from their minds" (*Against Celsus*, viii. 22, 23).

(12—16) Let me beg of you: cast off the bondage of Judaism as I have done, just as I gave up its privileges to place myself on a level with you. I have no complaint to make against you. You remember the illness which detained me among you, and led me first to preach to you the gospel. You received me kindly and warmly enough *then*, though my bodily infirmities might well have tempted you to despise me. You treated me as if I had been a messenger direct from heaven. You thought yourselves "blest" by my teaching. You would have done anything for me; you would have given me even your eyes. What has become of all this now? Why do you consider yourselves "blest" no more? Why do you treat me as an enemy, merely for telling you the truth?

(12) **Be as I am.**—Use the same Christian freedom that I use.

**For I am as ye are.**—I lay no stress on my pure Jewish descent. I claim no privileges because I was circumcised the eighth day. I do not count myself holier than you because I belonged to the strictest of all sects, the Pharisees. I stripped myself of all this, and became a Gentile among Gentiles.

**Ye have not injured me at all.**—*Ye did me no wrong.* There is a transition of subject at this clause. The Apostle goes back in thought to his first visit to Galatia. He had no complaint to make of the Galatians then. They did him no injury, showed him no unkindness, but, on the contrary, received him gladly.

(13) **Through infirmity of the flesh.**—Rather, *because* (or, *on account*) *of infirmity of flesh*—*i.e.*, some bodily weakness or ill-health. We should gather from this that St. Paul was detained in Galatia accidentally by illness, and that this led to his preaching the gospel there.

**At the first.**—*The first time;* on my first visit. This would be the one mentioned in Acts xvi. 6, in distinction from that referred to in Acts xviii. 23. (See *Introduction.*)

(14) **My temptation which was in my flesh.**—The true reading is here, *your temptation in my flesh*—*i.e.*, my bodily infirmities, which might have been a temptation to you to reject me. St. Paul seems to have suffered from grievous bodily infirmity, which he elsewhere (2 Cor. xii. 7) describes as a "thorn (or rather, *stake*) in the flesh." The effects of this were seen in his personal appearance, which his enemies described as "mean" (2 Cor. x. 10); and he himself felt it as a corrective against any tendency to spiritual pride (2 Cor. xii. 7). An attack of this malady came upon him during his visit to Galatia, and it was with health shattered by this that he first preached the gospel to the Galatians. Still, to their credit, they took no notice of it, and gave him the warmest possible reception. As to the nature of the malady referred to, see Notes on 2 Cor. xii.

**Despised not, nor rejected.**—The second of these two words is stronger than would appear from the English version. It is used of the expression of physical disgust: *ye despised not, nor loathed.* The Apostle says that the Galatians did not despise "their temptation," meaning "the thing (malady) which they were tempted to despise."

flesh ye despised not, nor rejected; but received me as an angel of God, *even* as Christ Jesus.
(15) Where is then[1] the blessedness ye spake of? for I bear you record, that, if *it had been* possible, ye would have plucked out your own eyes, and have given them to me.
(16) Am I therefore become your enemy, because I tell you the truth?
(17) They zealously affect you, *but* not well; yea, they would exclude you, that ye might affect them.
(18) But *it is* good to be zealously affected always in *a* good *thing,* and not only when I am present with you.
(19) My little children, of whom I travail in birth again until Christ be formed in

[1] Or, *What was then.*

**Even as Christ Jesus.**—You showed to the ambassador of Christ as much enthusiasm, as deep and ardent an affection, as you could have shown to Christ Himself.

(15) **Where.**—The reading of the Received text is "What," which, however, must be taken as if it were equivalent to "where," the reading which has the strongest attestation.

**The blessedness ye spake of.**—The Greek is a single word: *your felicitation of yourselves; your boast of blessedness;* or (as we should say) *your boasted blessedness.* What has become of all those loud assertions in which you were once heard declaring yourselves "blest" in the presence of the Apostle?

**For.**—You did declare yourselves blest; for, &c.

**Ye would have plucked out your own eyes.**—The word "own" should be struck out, and the emphasis laid on "eyes." The inference which has been drawn from this passage, that St. Paul suffered from an affection of the eyes, hardly seems to hold good. The "eyes" may be mentioned only as something peculiarly dear and precious. Comp. the Old Testament phrase, "to keep as the apple of an eye" (Deut. xxxii. 10; Ps. xvii. 8; Prov. vii. 2).

(16) **Your enemy.**—"The enemy" was the name by which St. Paul was commonly referred to by the party hostile to him in the next century. It is quite possible that the phrase "your enemy" ought to be placed, as it were, in inverted commas, and attributed to the Judaising sectaries—"your enemy," as these false teachers call me.

**Because I tell you the truth.**—It would seem that something had happened upon St. Paul's second visit to Galatia (the visit recorded in Acts xviii. 23) which had caused a change in their feelings towards him. His plain speaking had given offence.

(17–20) All this eagerness to court your favour springs from an interested motive: they wish to make a sect of you, in which they shall be masters and courted in their turn. Not but that it is a good thing for teachers and taught—you and I—to seek favour with each other, so long as it is done disinterestedly, and that, too, when I am absent as well as when I am present. My heart yearns towards you. I cannot forget that you owe your life, as Christians, to me. Now, once more, it seems as if all that long travail has to be gone over again. You must be re-fashioned in the likeness of Christ, as the infant is fashioned in the form of man. Would that I could be with you and speak in a different tone, for how to deal with you I do not know.

(17) **They zealously affect you.**—"Zealously affect" is a single word in the Greek, and means "to show zeal towards," "to court," "to curry favour with," "to canvass eagerly, so as to win over to their side." The subject of this verse is the Judaising teachers.

**They would exclude you.**—They desire to separate you from the rest of the Gentile churches, and to make a sect by itself, in which they themselves may bear rule. All the other Gentile churches had accepted the freer teaching of St. Paul; the Judaising party wished to make of Galatia an isolated centre of Judaism. They did this with personal motives, "not well"—*i.e.,* from honest and honourable motives—but with a view to secure their own ascendancy.

**That ye might affect them.**—The same word as "zealously affect" above and in the next verse. They expect to have all this zeal on their part returned to them in kind. With them it is the proselytizing zeal of the faction leader; from you they expect the deferential zeal of devoted followers.

(18) **It is good to be zealously affected always in a good thing.**—A disinterested zeal between teachers and taught is indeed good in itself. The Apostle does not wish to dissuade the Galatians from that. He would be only too glad to see such a mutual interchange himself—in his absence as well as in his presence. It seems a mistake to refer this either to the Galatians alone or to St. Paul alone. The proposition is stated in a general form, so as to cover both. It is right to be zealously affected *always.* Their eager zeal should not have its ebbs and flows, but should subsist constantly, whether those between whom it is felt are present together or not.

**In a good thing.**—This expression corresponds to "but not well" in the last verse, and means *honestly, disinterestedly,* with a view to the spread of the gospel, and not to personal ascendancy.

(19) **My little children.**—The form is a diminutive, not found elsewhere in the writings of St. Paul, though common in St. John. It is used to heighten the tenderness of the appeal. The simple form, however, "my children," is found in some of the best MSS., and perhaps should be adopted. St. Paul regards as his spiritual children all who first received the gospel from him.

**Of whom I travail in birth again.**—The struggle which ends in the definite winning over of his converts to Christ, the Apostle compares to the process of birth by which "a man is born into the world." In the case of the Galatians, after their relapse, this struggle has all to be gone through again.

**Until Christ be formed in you.**—Just as the formless embryo by degrees takes the shape of man, so the unformed Christian by degrees takes the likeness of Christ. As he grows in grace that likeness becomes more and more defined, till at last the Christian reaches the "stature of the fulness of Christ" (Eph. iv. 13). There is some question as to the punctuation of this verse: whether it should be divided from the last by a full stop, and from the next by a comma, as is usually done; or from the last by a comma, and from the next by a full-stop. It is a nice question of scholarship, in which the weight or preponderance of authority seems, perhaps, rather to incline to the usual view, though some good commentators take the other side. It has

you, (20) I desire to be present with you
now, and to change my voice; for I
stand in doubt of you.[1]
(21) Tell me, ye that desire to be
Chap. iv. 21–31. Allegory of Isaac and Ishmael. under the law, do ye not
hear the law? (22) For it
is written, that Abraham
had two sons, the one by a bondmaid,
the other by a freewoman. (23) But he
*who was* of the bondwoman was born
after the flesh; but he of the freewoman
*was* by promise. (24) Which things
are an allegory: for these are the two
covenants; the one from the mount

[1] Or, *I am perplexed about you.*

---

been thought best not to alter the punctuation of the English text, though without a clear conviction that it is right.

(20) **I desire.**—The Greek is not quite so definite: "I could indeed wish."

**Change my voice.**—Rather, *change my tone;* speak in terms less severe.

**I stand in doubt of you.**—Rather, as in the margin, *I am perplexed about you—i.e.,* I do not know what to say to you—how I ought to deal with you so as to win you back from this defection. If the Apostle had been present, so as to see what effect his words were having, he would know what line to take. As it is, in writing to them he is at a loss, and fears to make matters worse instead of better.

(21—31) The next eleven verses contain an elaborate argument from the history of the two sons of Abraham, as types of the two covenants, in further proof that freedom is the essential character of the Christian dispensation.

We have seen that St. Paul applies the history of the natural Israel allegorically to the spiritual Israel; and not only does he do this with reference to the history of the formed theocracy, but he goes back to its origin in the time of the patriarchs, and traces there the first beginnings of the separation between the Law and the promise. The same history had been already allegorically treated by Philo. The treatment of it by St. Paul is, however, quite different, and in keeping with the line of argument followed in the context.

The points of parallelism, which are drawn out in much detail, may be exhibited thus:—

| *Jewish Church.* | *Christian Church.* |
|---|---|
| The bondwoman, Hagar. | The freewoman, Sarah. |
| Son of the bondwoman, Ishmael. | Son of the freewoman, Isaac. |
| Natural birth (the flesh). | Supernatural birth (the promise). |
| Mount Sinai. } | { Mount Zion. |
| The Law. } | { The Promise. |
| The earthly Jerusalem. | The heavenly Jerusalem. |
| Enslaved. | Free. |
| Fruitful. | Barren. |
| Small offspring. | Large offspring. |
| Persecuting. | Persecuted. |
| Expulsion. | Inheritance. |
| *The Jewish Church is enslaved.* | *The Christian Church is free.* |

(21) **Ye that desire to be under the law.**—A direct appeal to those who were inclined to give way to the Judaising party.

**Do ye not hear the law?**—"Hear" is probably to be taken in the sense of "give heed to," "listen to with attention," as in Matt. x. 14; xiii. 9, 13; Luke xvi. 29, 31. Some have thought that it merely refers to the practice of reading a lesson from the Old Testament, which was adopted into the Christian Church from the synagogue.

(22) **For.**—This particle would naturally not be expressed in English. It was a reason for the question which had been asked just before: "For the Law *does* supply a case in point."

**The one by a bondmaid.**—Hagar, it seems from Gen. xvi. 1, was an Egyptian. The word for "bondmaid" was not confined to this sense in earlier Greek, but was used for any young girl.

(23) **But.**—Both were alike in being children of Abraham; they were unlike in that one was born naturally, the other by divine instrumentality.

**Was born.**—Strictly, *is born—i.e.,* is stated to have been born, was born *as we still read.*

**After the flesh**—*i.e.,* in the regular course of nature.

**By promise.**—The birth of Isaac is regarded as due to the direct agency of the promise. The promise itself is conceived of as possessing a creative power. The birth of Isaac was the result of a miraculous intervention. (See Gen. xviii. 10.)

(24) **Which things are an allegory.**—Literally, *Which things are allegorised—i.e.,* spoken in double sense,—

"Where more is meant than meets the ear."

The allegorical sense does not exclude the literal sense. but is added to it. In like manner St. Paul speaks of the events which happened to the Israelites in their wanderings in the wilderness as happening "for our ensamples," or, more correctly, "by way of types or figures" (1 Cor. x. 11): though elsewhere a distinction is drawn between "type" and "allegory," the first implying that the narrative on which it is based is true, the second that it is fictitious. St. Paul does not use the word here in this strict sense. The justification for the allegorical treatment of the patriarchal history may be expressed in the words of Calvin: "As the house of Abraham was at that time the true Church, so there can be no doubt that the chief and most memorable events which happened in it are so many types for us." At the same time, the argumentative force of the passage evidently rests upon the apostolic assertion of Christian liberty, not upon the logical cogency of the inference from the details of the type to the thing typified.

**These are the two covenants.**—"These," *i.e.,*

Sinai, which gendereth to bondage,
which is Agar. (25) For this Agar is
mount Sinai in Arabia, and answereth
to[1] Jerusalem which now is, and is in
bondage with her children. (26) But
Jerusalem which is above is free, which
is the mother of us all. (27) For it is
written,[a] Rejoice, *thou* barren that bearest
not; break forth and cry, thou that
travailest not: for the desolate hath
many more children than she which
hath an husband. (28) Now we, brethren,
as Isaac was, are the children of pro-
mise. (29) But as then he that was

a Isa. 54. 1.

1 Or, *is in the same rank with.*

---

these women, Hagar and Sarah. "Are," in the sense of "stand for," "typically represent," as in the interpretation of the parable of the tares: "The enemy that sowed them *is* the devil; the harvest *is* the end of the world" (Matt. xiii. 39); or, in the words of the institution of the Lord's Supper: "this *is* my body . . . this *is* my blood" (Matt. xxvi. 26, 28), where the meaning is really as little doubtful as here. "The two covenants" should be simply "two covenants." *What* covenants the Apostle goes on to explain. So, too, "the one" in the next clause should be rather *one.*

**Which gendereth to bondage.**—Rather, *bringing forth children unto bondage—i.e.,* unto a state of bondage, so that from the moment they are born they are subject to bondage. The progeny of Hagar is a nation of bondsmen, like the Jews under the old covenant.

(25) **For this Agar is mount Sinai in Arabia.**—This clause will be, perhaps, best dealt with in an excursus, of which we will at present merely summarise the result by saying that the true (or, rather, most probable) reading appears to be: *Now this Agar is Mount Sinai in Arabia;* and the sense: "By the word Hagar is meant Mount Sinai in Arabia." There appears to be sufficient evidence to show that Hagar may be regarded as the Arabic name for Sinai, so that there would be a special reason for identifying Hagar allegorically with the old covenant. For a fuller discussion see *Excursus B* (p. 467).

**Answereth to Jerusalem which now is.**—The word for "answereth" is a technical term in philosophy, applied to the parallel columns containing such antithetical pairs as good—evil; one—many; finite—infinite, &c. Here it will be illustrated by the parallel arrangement of the different points of the allegory given above. "Answereth to" will thus mean "stands in the same column with." Hagar, Sinai, the old covenant, the Jewish nation, or the earthly Jerusalem, all stand upon the same side of the antithesis. They are arranged one above another, or, in other words, *they rank in the same line,* which is the primitive meaning of the word.

**Jerusalem which now is.**—*The present Jerusalem—i.e.,* the Jewish people still subject to the Law. It is opposed to "Jerusalem which is above," as the pre-Messianic to the Messianic system.

**And is in bondage with her children.**—The true reading is, *for she is in bondage with her children.* Jerusalem is, as it were, personified, so that "with her children" means "all who are dependent upon her"—the Jewish system and all who belong to it.

(26) **Jerusalem which is above.**—The ideal or heavenly Jerusalem. (Comp. Heb. xii. 22, "Ye are come to . . . the heavenly Jerusalem;" Rev. xxi. 2, "the holy city, new Jerusalem." This "new" or "heavenly" Jerusalem is the seat or centre of the glorified Messianic kingdom, just as the old Jerusalem had been the centre of the earthly theocracy. The conception of the "heavenly Jerusalem" among the Jews, like the rest of their Messianic beliefs, took a materialistic form. It was to be a real but gorgeous city suspended in mid-air, "three parasangs" ($11\frac{1}{4}$ miles) above the earthly city. Sometimes it is regarded as the exact copy of its earthly counterpart, and at other times as forming a perfect square. (Comp. Rev. xxi. 16.) No such materialistic notions attach to the idea as presented by St. Paul. "Jerusalem which is above" is to him a spiritual city, of which the Christian is a member here and now. It is part of the Messianic kingdom, to the whole of which the Apostle gave an ideal character. He could not but do so, seeing that the kingdom began with the coming of its King, though there was no earthly and visible realisation of it. The Christian "conversation" (or, rather, *commonwealth,* the constitution that he was under) was "in heaven," while he himself was upon earth. (See Phil. iii. 20.)

**Which is the mother of us all.**—The true reading is, undoubtedly, *which is our mother,* omitting "all." The heavenly Jerusalem was the metropolis of Christianity, just as the earthly Jerusalem was the metropolis of Judaism.

(27) **Rejoice, thou barren.**—The quotation is from Isa. liv. 1. It has reference, in the first instance, to the restoration of the exiled Jews to Jerusalem and to the coming greatness of the newly-settled city. Though at present it is desolate and in ruins, it shall become greater and more populous than ever it had been in its best days before. The revived theocracy under Zerubbabel is naturally taken as a type of the final theocratic reign of the Messiah. The representation of the theocracy under the figure of marriage is common, both in the prophetic writings and in St. Paul.

**Thou barren that bearest not.**—This was originally spoken of the revived condition of Jerusalem, in which for a long time no children had been born. Here it is applied to the despised and persecuted condition of the early Church.

**Break forth**—*i.e.,* into singing. The phrase is expressed in full in the Authorised version of Isa. liv. 1.

**The desolate . . . . she which hath an husband.**—In the original, Jerusalem after the exile, opposed to Jerusalem in the time of its prosperity under David and Solomon; in the typical application, Sarah, who had long been barren, as opposed to Hagar, whose marriage had been fruitful; in the anti-typical application, the new dispensation, Christianity, with its small beginnings, as opposed to the old dispensation, with its material possessions and privileges.

(28) **We.**—The better reading appears to be *Ye.*

**Children of promise.**—Children born in accomplishment of the promise. (See Rom. ix. 8, and Note.)

(29) **Persecuted.**—The expression used in Gen. xxi. 9 is translated in our version "mocking." It seems doubtful whether the Hebrew can really mean more than "playing." The Jewish traditions added that Ishmael took out the child Isaac and "shot at him with arrows under pretence of sport." The Arab tribes, Ishmael's descendants, had always been a thorn in the side of their Israelite neighbours.

**Him that was born after the Spirit.**—A miracu-

born after the flesh persecuted him *that*
*was born* after the Spirit, even so *it is*
now. (30) Nevertheless what saith the
scripture? Cast out the bondwoman
and her son:[a] for the son of the bond-
woman shall not be heir with the son
of the freewoman. (31) So then, breth-
ren, we are not children of the bond-
woman, but of the free.

a Gen. 21. 10.

CHAPTER V.—(1) Stand fast there-
fore in the liberty wherewith Christ
hath made us free, and be
not entangled again with
the yoke of bondage.
(2) Behold, I Paul say unto you, that
if ye be circumcised, Christ
shall profit you nothing.
(3) For I testify again to
every man that is circumcised, that he is
a debtor to do the whole law. (4) Christ
is become of no effect unto you, whoso-

A.D. 58.

Chap. v. 1. Christian liberty.

Chap. v. 2—6. Excludes Judaism.

---

lous agency intervened in the birth of Isaac, and the Christian Church was inaugurated and inspired by the same agency—that of the Spirit. The Messianic reign was realised through the Spirit; and their participation in this reign made all Christians true and spiritual descendants of Abraham.

**Even so it is now.**—This seems to have especial reference to the behaviour of the Judaising party in Galatia, but would also apply to the relations between Jews and Christians generally.

(30) **What saith the scripture?**—In Gen. xxi. 10 the words are put into the mouth of Sarah, but they are afterwards endorsed by the divine command.

**The son of the bondwoman shall not be heir.**—A bold declaration of the incompatibility of Judaism with Christianity, by which the Apostle clinches his argument against the practices which the Galatian Judaisers were trying to introduce. This is followed by an emphatic assertion of the point on which the whole gist of the previous allegory consists—that the essential character of the Christian Church is freedom. The practical conclusion is given in the opening verse of the next chapter, which should be taken in close connection with the end of this.

V.

(1) **Stand fast therefore.**—The external evidence is very strong in favour of a different reading: *With* (or, perhaps, *For*) *liberty did Christ make us free. Stand fast, then, and be not entangled,* &c. There seems to be no sufficient reason why this should not be adopted.

**In the liberty.**—The best grammarians seem agreed to take this rather in the sense, *for liberty;* otherwise it would be tempting to explain it as an instance of the Hebraising construction which we find in John iii. 29: "Rejoice with joy" (Authorised version "rejoice greatly"). It would then mean: "with a system, or state, of freedom Christ freed us;" in other words: "placed us in a state of freedom, so that we are free."

**The yoke of bondage**—*i.e.,* the Judaising restraints and restrictions.

(2—6) There can be no compromise between Christianity and Judaism. If you accept the one you must give up the other. Circumcision is a pledge or engagement to live by the rule of the Law. That rule must be taken as a whole. You are committed to the practice of the whole Law, and in that way alone you must seek for justification. Our position is something quite different. We hope to be admitted into a state of righteousness through the action of the Spirit on God's side, and through faith on our own. The Christian owes the righteousness attributed to him, not to circumcision, but to a life of which faith is the motive and love the law.

The whole tenor of the Epistle shows that the Apostle viewed the attempts of the Judaising party with indignation; and at this point his language takes a more than usually stern and imperative tone. He speaks with the full weight of his apostolic authority, and warns the Galatians that no half-measures will avail, but that they must decide, once for all, either to give up Judaism or Christ.

This is one of the passages which have been insisted on as proving a direct antagonism between St. Paul and the other Apostles; but any one who enters into the thought of the Apostle, and follows the course of his impassioned reasoning, will see how unnecessary any such assumption is. Nothing is more in accordance with human nature than that the same man should at one time agree to the amicable compromise of Acts xv., and at another, some years later, with the field all to himself, and only his own converts to deal with, should allow freer scope to his own convictions. He is speaking with feelings highly roused, and with less regard to considerations of policy. Besides, the march of events had been rapid, and the principles of policy themselves would naturally change.

(2) **Behold, I Paul.**—The strong personality of the Apostle asserts itself; instead of going into an elaborate proof, he speaks with dogmatic authority, as though his bare word were enough.

**Shall profit you nothing.**—"Profit," *i.e.,* in the way of justification, as producing that state of righteousness in the sight of God by virtue of which the believer is released from wrath and received into the divine favour. The Apostle says that if this state of justification is sought through circumcision, it cannot be sought through Christ at the same time.

(3) **For I testify again.**—Translate rather, *Nay, I protest again,* introducing a further argument. He who allows himself to be circumcised thereby commits himself wholly to the Law, just as, it might be said, he who is baptised commits himself wholly to Christ. The act of circumcision placed a man under the legal system, just as the act of baptism placed him under the Christian system. From that time forward he could not choose one part and refuse another, but was bound alike by all.

**He is a debtor.**—He is under an obligation.

(4) **Christ is become of no effect unto you.**—Literally, *Ye were* (or, more idiomatically, *are*) *abolished, made nothing, from Christ;* a condensed form of expression for, *Ye are made nothing* (unchristianised), *and cut off from Christ.* Your relations to Christ are cancelled, and you are Christians no longer.

**Are justified.**—Strictly, *seek to be justified.*

ever of you are justified by the law; ye
are fallen from grace. (5) For we
through the Spirit wait for the hope of
righteousness by faith. (6) For in Jesus
Christ neither circumcision availeth any
thing, nor uncircumcision; but faith
which worketh by love. (7) Ye did run
well; who did hinder you[1]
that ye should not obey
the truth? (8) This per-

Chap. v. 7—12. The Judaising Intruders.

suasion *cometh* not of him that calleth
you. (9) A little leaven leaveneth the
whole lump. (10) I have confidence in
you through the Lord, that ye will be
none otherwise minded: but he that
troubleth you shall bear his judgment,
whosoever he be. (11) And I, brethren,
if I yet preach circumcision, why
do I yet suffer persecution? then is
the offence of the cross ceased.

1 Or, *who did drive you back.*

---

**Ye are fallen from grace.**—The Christian is justified by an act of grace, or free, unearned favour, on the part of God. He who seeks for justification in any other way loses this grace. Grace is not here a state or disposition in the believer, but a divine act or relation.

(5) **Through the Spirit.**—Through the operation of the Spirit. It is the Spirit which makes faith effectual and righteousness real. The righteousness which comes by the Law is entirely human or "carnal," the product of a man's own efforts. The righteousness which is by faith is the gift of God, and that gift is communicated through the Spirit.

**Wait for.**—The Greek word means "to wait earnestly or eagerly," as in Rom. viii. 19, 23, 25, *et seq.*

**The hope of righteousness.**—The righteousness which is the object of our hopes; the hoped-for, promised righteousness. More often the Apostle speaks of the state of righteousness as conferred upon the Christian at his baptism. This is, however, only a sort of ideal or potential righteousness; it is a state inherent in that kingdom of which the Christian then becomes a member, not a state inherent in the Christian himself. This ideal or potential righteousness becomes real and actual only at the end of the Christian's career, when it is finally confirmed to him. Looking forward to this point, it is an object of hope.

(6) **In Jesus Christ.**—When the Christian has entered into those close relations with Christ which his Christianity assumes.

**Availeth any thing.**—As "shall profit" in verse 2; avail in the way of justification.

**Faith which worketh by love.**—Faith in Christ, the devoted attachment to Christ, is the great motive power, the source or mainspring of action; and the law by which that action is regulated is the law of love. (Comp. verses 13, 14 below, and Rom. xiii. 8—10.) Faith makes a man seek to do the will of Christ; love tells him what that will is. It is clear that the faith thus described by St. Paul does not stop short in a mere head notion, and so is in no conflict with the teaching of St. James. (See Jas. ii. 14—26.)

(7—12) All was going well at first. What sudden intruder has stopped your path and led you astray? Certainly it is not God, to whom you owe your calling, that has persuaded you to such a course. You tell me that not many have fallen away. But those few are enough to infect the whole. Not that I wish to implicate all in the sin of some. Most of you I can trust to be true to me. The author of your troubles, whoever he is, shall not escape. God shall judge him. Do you turn round on me and say that I, too, have preached circumcision? The persecutions that I have to undergo from the Jews are proof that I preach it no longer. If I *do* preach circumcision, then the other stumbling-blocks in the way of my teaching are removed. I have no need to lay stress upon a crucified Messiah. The advocates of circumcision may carry their self-mutilation a step further if they please.

This section is very abrupt in style. The thought bounds from subject to subject, not stopping to insert links of connection. At the end of the passage there is a vein of severe irony.

(7) **Ye did run well.**—Again, as in chap. ii. 2, a metaphor from foot racing. The Galatians had made a good start, but suddenly changed their course.

**Who did hinder you?**—The metaphor here is not quite the same, but is somewhat akin to that just used. The original meaning of the word translated "hinder" is to "break up a road," as an army before the advance of hostile forces.

**The truth**—*i.e.*, the doctrine taught by St. Paul in opposition to the Judaising tenets which had been introduced into the Galatian Church.

(8) **This persuasion . . .**—He who *calls* the Galatians is here, as elsewhere, God; and certainly, the Apostle says, it can have been by no intimation or guidance from Him that they were led to accept such perverted teaching.

(9) **A little leaven . . .**—A pregnant expression, which leaves a good deal to the reader to supply. The proverb is true which says that *a little leaven leavens the whole mass of dough.* And so, in your case, the malcontents may be few, but they will soon ruin the whole Church. It seems decidedly more in accordance with the context to take the "little leaven" as referring rather to *a few seceders* than to *a little bad doctrine.*

(10) **I have confidence in you through the Lord.**—Literally, *I have confidence with regard to you in the Lord*—*i.e.*, such confidence as a Christian teacher ought to have in Christian scholars. This has reference to the main body of the Church; an exception is immediately made as to the disaffected party, and especially their leader.

**That ye will be none otherwise minded**—*i.e.*, no otherwise than I would have you be.

**Shall bear his judgment.**—"Judgment" is here not equivalent to "condemnation." He shall be "put upon his trial," "shall bear the sentence that shall be passed on him"—viz., by God.

**Whosoever he be.**—The Apostle does not fix upon any one particular person as the cause of the troubles in the Galatian Church, but he says that, whoever he may be, God will judge him.

(11) **And I, brethren.**—Rather, *But I, brethren.* Another abrupt transition. We should naturally infer from this passage that St. Paul had at one time seemed to preach, or at least to *permit*, circumcision. Thus, in the Acts, we should gather, from the account of the conference at Jerusalem in chap. xv., that he did not

(12) I would they were even cut off
which trouble you.
(13) For, brethren, ye have been called
unto liberty; only *use* not liberty for
an occasion to the flesh, but by love
serve one another. (14) For all the law
is fulfilled in one word,
*even* in this; Thou shalt love
thy neighbour as thyself.[a]
(15) But if ye bite and devour one another,

Chap. v. 13—15. Liberty, not license, but love.

a Lev. 19. 18; Matt. 22. 39.

---

insist strongly upon this point, and on taking Timothy with him upon his second missionary journey—the very journey in which he first visited Galatia—his first step was to have him circumcised. It was only natural that the progress of time and of events should deepen the Apostle's conviction of the radical antagonism between the ceremonial Judaism and Christianity. This he is now stating in the most emphatic manner, and he feels that he is open to a charge of something like inconsistency. The Galatians might say that he preached circumcision himself. His answer is, that if he really preached circumcision he would not be so persecuted by the Judaising party. And he has also a further answer, which is conveyed in an ironical form: "If I *do* preach circumcision, and if I have ceased to lay stress on that one great stumbling-block, the cross of Christ, I may assume that there are no more hindrances in the way of my teaching." Circumcision is taken as occupying, in the Judaising system, the same place that the cross of Christ occupied in that of St. Paul. The two things are alternatives. If one is taught there is no need for the other.

**Ceased.**—*Done away;* the same word as that which is translated "become of no effect" in verse 4.

(12) **I would they were even cut off.**—The Authorised version is undoubtedly wrong here. The words may mean "cut themselves off," *i.e.*, from your communion, but it seems far best to take the words, with all the ancient Greek interpreters and a large majority of modern commentators, including Dr. Lightfoot and Bishop Wordsworth, as referring to an extension of the rite of circumcision, such as the Galatians might see frequently practised by the priests of Cybele, whose worship had one of its most imporant centres in their country—*I would they would even make themselves eunuchs.* Let them carry their self-mutilation still further, and not stop at circumcision.

The expression is in several ways surprising as coming from St. Paul. We should remember, in some mitigation of it, the fact just alluded to, that the Galatians were themselves familiar with this particular form of self-mutilation; and familiar with it, no doubt, in discourse as well as in act. Christianity, while it has had the effect of putting a stop to such horrible practices, has also banished them even from thought and word. It is less, perhaps, a matter of wonder that we should have to appeal to the difference in standard between the Apostle's times and our own, than that we have to appeal to it so seldom. Still, at the best, words like these must be allowed to come some way short of the "meekness and gentleness of Christ." We may compare with them, as well for the particular expression as for the general vehemence of language, Phil. iii. 2: "Beware of dogs, beware of evil workers, beware of concision" (with a play on "circumcision"). The Apostle himself would have been the last to claim that he had "already attained, either were already perfect." A highly nervous and excitable constitution such as his, shattered by bodily hardships and mental strain, could not but at times impair his power of self-control. It is to be noticed, however, that his indignation, if it sometimes carries him somewhat too far, is always roused in a worthy cause. Such momentary ebullitions as these are among the very few flaws in a truly noble and generous character, and are themselves in great part due to the ardour which makes it so noble.

**Which trouble you.**—A different word from that which is similarly translated in verse 10. Its meaning is stronger: "to uproot and overthrow."

(13—15) The Judaisers would deserve such a fate; for they are undoing the whole object with which you were called. You were called, not to legal bondage, but to *freedom.* This caution only is needed: Do not make freedom a pretext for self-indulgence. One servitude you may submit to—the service of love. So doing, you will fulfil the Law without being legalists. He who loves his neighbour as himself will need no other rule. On the other hand, dissensions will be fatal, not to one party only, but to all who take part in them.

(13) **For.**—This connecting particle supplies the reason for the Apostle's severe treatment of the Judaisers.

**An occasion to the flesh.**—Do not, under the name "liberty," give way to sensual excesses. This was the especial danger of the Gentile churches, such as Corinth, from which, as we have seen, the Apostle may have been writing. Galatia, too, was a Gentile church; and though it was for the present subject rather to Judaising influences, the character of the people was fickle, and St. Paul may have thought it well to hint a caution in this direction.

**Serve.**—There is a stress upon this word. The Apostle had been dissuading the Galatians from submitting to other forms of servitude. This one he will permit them.

(14) This verse is another of the marked points of contact between this Epistle and that to the Romans. The theme of it is worked out at length in Rom. xiii. 8—10.

**Thy neighbour.**—In the original command this appears to mean "thy fellow Israelite." Our Lord, in the parable of the Good Samaritan, had given it a wider signification, and in the same wider sense it is used here.

(16—26) To follow the guidance of the Spirit is to obtain a double release: on the one hand, from the evil appetites and passions of the flesh or of sense—which is the direct antithesis to the Spirit—and on the other hand, from the dominion of the Law. It is easy to tell which has the upper hand—the flesh or the Spirit. The flesh is known by a long catalogue of sins, the Spirit by a like catalogue of Christian graces, the mere mention of which is enough to show that the Law has no power over them. Those who belong to Christ have got rid of the flesh, with all its impulses, by their union with a crucified Saviour. All the Christian has to do is to act really by the rule of the Spirit, without self-parade or quarrelling.

take heed that ye be not consumed one
of another. (16) *This* I say then, Walk
in the Spirit, and ye shall
not fulfil[1] the lust of the
flesh. (17) For the flesh
lusteth against the Spirit,
and the Spirit against the flesh: and
these are contrary the one to the other:
so that ye cannot do the things that ye
would. (18) But if ye be led of the
Spirit, ye are not under the law. (19) Now
the works of the flesh are manifest,
which are *these;* Adultery, fornication,
uncleanness, lasciviousness, (20) idolatry,
witchcraft, hatred, variance, emula-
tions, wrath, strife, seditions, heresies,
(21) envyings, murders, drunkenness, re-
vellings, and such like: of the which I

Chap. v. 16—26. Works of the flesh and of the Spirit.

[1] Or, *fulfil not.*

---

(16) **Walk.**—Conduct yourselves: a metaphor very common in the writings of St. Paul, but not peculiar to them. It occurs three times in the Gospels, once in the Acts, thirty-three times in St. Paul's Epistles, once in the Hebrews, ten times in the Epistles of St. John, and once in the Apocalypse.

**In the Spirit.**—Rather, *by the Spirit—i.e.,* by the rule of the Spirit, as the Spirit directs. "The Spirit" is here undoubtedly the Holy Spirit—the Spirit of God, not the spirit in man.

(17) **For the flesh . . .**—In this verse we have brought out most distinctly the antithesis between the flesh and the Spirit, which is one of the root ideas in the psychology of St. Paul. It does not amount to dualism, for the body, as such, is not regarded as evil. There is nothing to show that St. Paul considered matter *in itself* evil. But the body *becomes the seat* of evil; from it arise those carnal impulses which are the origin of sin. And it is the body, looked at in this light, which is designated as "the flesh." The flesh is the body, as animated by an evil principle. It thus becomes opposed to the good principle: whether the good principle in itself—the Spirit of God, or that organ in which the good principle resides—the spirit in man.

**So that ye cannot do the things that ye would.**—The opposition between the flesh and the Spirit, each pulling a different way, prevents the will from acting freely. For a full comment on this, see Rom. vii. 15—23, 25.

(18) **Ye are not under the law.**—Strictly, *Ye are not under law*—law in the abstract. The flesh and law are correlative terms: to be free from the one is to be free from the other. The flesh represents unaided human nature, and law is the standard which this unaided human nature strives, but strives in vain, to fulfil. By the intervention of the Spirit, the law is fulfilled at the same time that its domination is abolished and human nature ceases to be unaided. In its highest part it is brought into direct contact with the divine nature, and the whole tenor of its actions changes accordingly.

(19) **Now the works of the flesh are manifest.**—It needs no elaborate disquisition to show what is meant by fulfilling the lust of the flesh. The effects which the flesh produces are plain and obvious enough. The catalogue which follows is not drawn up on any exact scientific principle, but divides itself roughly under four heads: (1) sins of sensuality; (2) sins of superstition; (3) sins of temper; (4) excesses.

It has been said that all our sinfulness may be resolved "into two elementary instincts: the instinct of self-preservation and the reproductive instinct." The third class of sins—sins of temper—would be referred to the first of the heads; sins of sensuality and excess—the one immediately, the other more remotely—to the second. The sins of superstition mentioned are of a more secondary character, and arise out of intellectual errors.

**Adultery.**—This word is omitted in the best MSS.

**Uncleanness, lasciviousness.** — The first of these words signifies any kind of impurity, secret or open; the second flagrant breaches of public decency.

(20) **Idolatry.** — When the Christian is warned against idolatry, it is not, of course, *systematic* idolatry that is meant, but that occasional compliance with idolatrous customs—taking part in the idol feasts, or eating of things offered to idols—which he might easily be led into by his intercourse with his heathen neighbours.

**Witchcraft.**—*Sorcery,* or *magic.* It would seem that practices of this kind were especially common in Asia Minor. In Acts xix. 19 we read that at Ephesus, "many of them which used curious arts brought their books together and burned them before all men;" and there is other evidence to the same effect.

**Variance.**—*Strife,* or *contention.*

**Emulations.**—Singular and plural are somewhat strangely mixed throughout the list. There is a division of authorities as to the reading in the case of this word. It seems probable, upon the whole, that the singular is right—*emulation,* or *jealousy.* "Wrath," on the other hand, should be *wraths—i.e.,* ebullitions or outbreaks of wrath. (See the Note on Rom. ii. 8.)

**Strife.** — This appears to be a mistake in the Authorised version. The word was supposed to be connected with that translated "variance" above, and the two words received the same translation indifferently. The word *ereis,* which is here translated "variance," is rendered by "strife" in Rom. xiii. 13, 1 Cor. iii. 3, Phil. i. 15, 1 Tim. vi. 4; on the other hand, the word *eritheia* is rendered by "strife" here and in 2 Cor. xii. 20, Phil. ii. 3, Jas. iii. 14—16. It is rendered by "contention" in Rom. ii. 8 ("them that are contentious") and Phil. i. 16. The true derivation of this latter word is, however, something quite different: it is to be sought in a word meaning "a day-labourer." Hence we get the senses—(1) labour for hire; (2) interested canvassing for office; (3) a spirit of factious partisanship; factiousness. (This word, too, is really in the plural.)

**Seditions, heresies.**—Rather, *divisions, parties.* The Authorised version has too special and technical a sound, as if the first related to factions in the State, and the second in the Church. This is not really so. The two words are distinguished from each other, as the lighter and more aggravated forms of division: the first, divisions; the second, divisions organised into parties.

(21) **Murders.**—There is considerable doubt as to whether this word ought to stand in the text. It is wanting in the two oldest MSS. and in some other good authorities. Internal considerations may be made to tell either for its omission or for its retention.

**I tell you before.**—*I foretell* (or, *forewarn*) *you;* I tell you before the event proves my words to be true —*i.e.,* before the day of judgment.

tell you before, as I have also told *you*
in time past, that they which do such
things shall not inherit the kingdom of
God. (22) But the fruit of the Spirit is
love, joy, peace, longsuffering, gentle-
ness, goodness, faith, (23) meekness,
temperance: against such there is no
law. (24) And they that are Christ's
have crucified the flesh with the affec-
tions[1] and lusts. (25) If we live in the

[1] Or, *passions.*

---

**As I have also told you in time past.**—*As I also told you before.* The idea is the same as that in the last phrase. In the Greek all that corresponds to "in time past" is the use of the past tense. The occasion appears to have been on St. Paul's last or second visit to Galatia.

**The kingdom of God.**—The Messianic kingdom; so called frequently in the Gospels (especially the second and third), and also by St. Paul in 1 Cor. vi. 9, 10; xv. 50.

(22) **The fruit of the Spirit.**—There does not seem to be any essential difference between this term and that used above: "the *works* of the flesh." The fruit of the Spirit is that which naturally grows out of the operation of the Spirit, in which it naturally results. The expression "fruit" is, however, generally used by St. Paul in a good sense.

The list which follows brings out in a striking manner the peculiar finish and perfection which belongs to the Christian morality. It will be seen at a glance how it differs from any form of pagan or philosophic ethics. At the head of the list is "love," which Christianity takes as its moving principle—not being, perhaps, alone in this, but alone in the systematic consistency with which it is carried out. Next comes "joy," a peculiarly Christian grace, which has a much deeper root than mere natural cheerfulness of temper, and is rather the unfailing brightness and equanimity which proceeds from calm and settled principles animated by the Divine Spirit itself. It may be questioned whether "peace" is here the tranquillity which is shed abroad in the heart by the sense of reconciliation with God, or rather, from the context that follows, peaceableness towards men. The remainder of the list, it will be seen, is made up of those delicate and fragile forms of virtue which the ordinary course of society is least likely to foster. Patriotism, courage, generosity, prudence, fortitude, are virtues that would be produced by the regular action of natural selection left to itself. "Long-suffering," "gentleness," "goodness," "faith," "meekness," "temperance," need a more spiritual process for their development.

**Gentleness, goodness.**—Perhaps, rather, *kindness, goodness.* The difference between the two Greek words and the ideas which they denote would appear to be somewhat similar to the difference between these two words in English. The second would represent a rather more positive tendency of disposition than the first.

**Faith.**—Rather, perhaps, *faithfulness;* not here in the sense peculiar to St. Paul, in which faith is the primary Christian virtue, but rather (as the context shows) "faithfulness," or "trustworthiness" in dealing with men, along with, perhaps, that frank and unsuspicious temper which St. Paul ascribes specially to charity (1 Cor. xiii. 7).

(23) **Meekness, temperance.**—"Meekness" is something more than "mildness," which has been suggested as an alternative translation. "Mildness" would represent that side of the virtue which is turned towards men; but it has also another side, which is turned towards God—a gentle submissiveness to the divine will. By "temperance" is meant, in a general sense, "self-control"—a firm control over the passions.

**Against such**—*i.e.,* "against such *things;*" not, as it was understood by many of the older commentators, "against such *men.*"

**There is no law.**—For such things law has no condemnation, and therefore they are removed beyond the sphere of law. This is the first and obvious meaning; it may be noticed, however, that these delicate Christian graces are above law as well as beyond. The ruder legal system of commands, sanctioned by punishment, would have no power to produce them; they can only grow in a more genial and softer soil, under the direct influence of the Spirit.

(24) But such things are just what the Christian would do. He will have nothing to make him act differently. He will not need to be taught peaceableness, goodness, or self-control, for the impulses which run counter to these are dead within him: they were killed at the moment when he gave himself up wholly to a crucified Saviour.

**And.**—Better, *How,* or *But;* introducing a summary conclusion from what has gone before, applying it to the Christian.

**They that are Christ's.**—The reading of the oldest MSS. is, *they that are of Christ Jesus.* The Messianic character of the Christian scheme is put forward prominently: "they that belong to Jesus, the Messiah."

**Have crucified the flesh.**—Strictly, *crucified:* viz., in their baptism. A full comment on this expression is afforded by Rom. vi. 2—14, where see Notes. The relation into which the Christian is brought with Christ is such as to neutralise and deaden all the sensual impulses within him; and inasmuch as the central point in that relation is the crucifixion: inasmuch, further, as crucifixion is death, and the Christian is bound to make the death of his Master his own, so far as relates to sin, he is said not merely to "kill" but to "crucify" the flesh, with its evil appetites and passions.

**Affections and lusts.**—Passions and desires. "Affections" are passive—susceptibility to evil impressions; "lusts" active—desire for that which is forbidden.

(25) **If we live in the Spirit.**—It seems, on the whole, best to translate: *If we live by the Spirit;* if we derive our life from the Spirit; if it is by the action of the Spirit that our moral activity as Christians is kept alive. At the same time, another way of taking the words is possible: *If we live to the Spirit,* following the analogy of Rom. xiv. 8: "Whether we live, we live *unto* the Lord," &c.

**Let us also walk in the Spirit**—*i.e., by the rule* of the Spirit, as the Spirit dictates (comp. verse 16, and the Note). The life which the Spirit quickens needs human co-operation, an active effort on the part of the Christian, to realise it completely in practice. St. Paul first sets before his readers what God has done for them, and then uses this as an argument and stimulus to renewed efforts on their own part.

Spirit, let us also walk in the Spirit.
(26) Let us not be desirous of vain glory, provoking one another, envying one another.

CHAPTER VI.—(1) Brethren, if[1] a man be overtaken in a fault, ye which are spiritual, restore such an one in the spirit of meekness; considering thyself, lest thou also be tempted.
(2) Bear ye one another's burdens, and so fulfil the law of Christ.
(3) For if a man think himself to be something, when he is nothing, he deceiveth himself.
(4) But let every man prove his own work, and then shall he have rejoicing in himself alone, and not in

Chap. vi. 1—5. The duty of sympathy.

A.D. 58.

1 Or, *although.*

---

(26) **Let us not be.**—Strictly, *Let us not become.* When he left the Galatian Church St. Paul was satisfied with their condition, but he fears that they will change. The warning that he addresses to them exactly hits the weak points in the national character—fickleness, vanity, and a quarrelsome disposition.

VI.

(1—5) Be charitable to the fallen, for you, too, may fall yourselves. Sympathise with each other. Indulge in no delusions as to your own superiority. Look each to his own work, and see that that is sound. He will find enough to do without entering into idle comparisons with others.

Verses 2 and 3 are a sort of repetition, with some expansion, of verse 1. Deal considerately and kindly with the fallen, *for* you may fall. Bear each other's burdens, *for* to claim any superiority to them is mere delusion.

It has been acutely suggested that the Apostle's tone in this passage has been affected by the recent occurrence at Corinth, where he had to warn the Corinthians against over-severity (see 2 Cor. ii. 6—8).

(1) **Brethren.**—The unfortunate conventional use of this word rather tends to weaken our sense of the delicacy and earnestness of this appeal.

**If a man be overtaken.**—*If a man be even surprised,* or *detected;* not only *caught,* but *caught red-handed,* in the very act, before he can escape. A special expression is used in order to aggravate the circumstances of the detection. No matter what these circumstances may be, one who is truly spiritual will still deal gently with the offender.

**Ye which are spiritual.**—This has reference to what had been said in the last chapter (verses 16—25). St. Paul assumes that all Christians are animated by the Spirit of God. If, while claiming to be better than others, and to condescend towards them, they were not so animated, their presumption would be seen in all the more glaring light.

**Restore.**—A good translation. The idea is that of correcting with no feeling of resentment or thought of punishment, but with a single eye to the amendment of the offender. The same word is used for "*mending* their nets" in Matt. iv. 21; Mark i. 19. It is also found as a medical term for setting dislocated limbs.

**In the spirit of meekness.**—"Spirit" here has reference to "ye that are spiritual" in the clause before. It does not mean exactly "the Holy Spirit," but "such a state of mind as is produced by the operation of the Spirit." One characteristic of a truly spiritual state is "meekness." (Comp. chap. v. 23, where "meekness" is mentioned expressly as one of the "fruits of the Spirit.")

**Considering thyself.**—In other words, "Do unto others as ye would they should do unto you." You, too, are liable to fall, and then you would be glad of the same gentle restoration.

(2) **Bear ye one another's burdens.**—Take them upon yourselves by kindly sympathy. Our Lord Himself was said to "bear" the physical infirmities of those whom He healed. (Matt. viii. 17: "He bare our sicknesses.")

**So fulfil.**—The reading here is somewhat doubtful, and the balance of authorities interesting. On the one hand, for the Received text adopted in our version is a large majority of the MSS.; on the other hand, the reading, *ye shall fulfil,* is found in the Vatican and two good Græco-Latin* MSS., but has besides *an almost unanimous support* from the versions. As several of these were composed at a very early date, and as they necessarily represent a wide geographical dispersion; as, further, the MS. authority for the reading —though small in quantity is good in quality—also representing the evidence of widely separated regions; and as, finally, the internal evidence or probabilities of corruption are also in favour of the same reading, it would seem, on the whole, to have the greater claim to acceptance. The meaning is that by showing sympathy to others in their distress, of whatever kind that distress may be—whether physical, mental, or moral—the Christian will best fulfil that "new commandment" bequeathed to him by his Master, the "law of love." (See John xiii. 34; 1 John iii. 23.)

(3) **He deceiveth himself.**—A peculiar word, perhaps coined by St. Paul: *puts himself under an hallucination;* persuades himself of the existence of that which has no reality.

(4, 5) The best antidote for such false estimates of self is severe self-criticism. Let a man judge his own work, not by comparison with others, but by the ideal standard, then he will see what it is worth and how much he has to boast of. His boasting will be at least real, and not based upon any delusive comparisons. He must stand or fall by himself. He must bear the weight of his own virtues and his own sins. By them he will be judged, and not by any fancied superiority or inferiority to others. For the thought, compare 2 Cor. x. 12—14.

(4) **Prove.**—*Test,* or *examine,* by reference to an objective standard. The word is used specially of the assaying of metals.

**Rejoicing in himself alone, and not in another.**—Rather, *he shall have his ground of boasting with reference to himself alone, and not with reference to his neighbour.* He will judge his own actions by the standard properly applicable to them, and will find as much ground for boasting as this will

* Practically, these two MSS. can only count as one, as both seem to have been copied from the same original.

another. (5) For every man shall bear
his own burden. (6) Let him that is
Chap. vi. 6—10. And liberality. taught in the word com-
municate unto him that
teacheth in all good things. (7) Be not
deceived; God is not mocked: for what-
soever a man soweth, that shall he also
reap. (8) For he that soweth to his
flesh shall of the flesh reap corruption;
but he that soweth to the Spirit shall
of the Spirit reap life everlasting.
(9) And let us not be weary in well
doing: for in due season we shall reap,
if we faint not. (10) As we have there-
fore opportunity, let us do good unto
all *men*, especially unto them who are
of the household of faith. (11) Ye see
how large a letter I have written unto

---

give him, and no more. His standard will be absolute and not relative, and the amount of his boasting will be proportioned accordingly. He will not seek to excuse himself by dwelling upon his neighbour's weaknesses.

(5) **Every man shall bear his own burden.**—The word for "burden" here is different from that which had been used above, though its meaning is very much the same. The distinction would be sufficiently represented if we were to translate in the one case *burden*, in the other *load*. The context, however, is quite different. In verse 2 the Christian is bidden to "bear the burdens" of others, in the sense of sympathising with them in their troubles. Here he is told that he must "bear his own load," in the sense that he must answer directly to God for his own actions. His responsibility cannot be shifted on to others. It will make him no better that there are others worse than himself.

(6—10) Special exhortation to liberality in the support of teachers, grounded upon the fact that we shall all receive, in the harvest at the end of the world, according as we have sown during the time of our probation here. The self-indulgent will find the flesh that he has indulged fall to dissolution, and there will be an end. On the other hand, he who in all his actions has sought the approval of the Spirit shall be rewarded with everlasting life. The same rule holds good for every kind of beneficence. Let us do what good we can, whenever an opportunity is given us, especially towards our fellow Christians.

(6) **Him that is taught in the word.**—He who receives instruction in the truths of the gospel. Even at this early date there seems to have been a more or less organised system of instruction in the Church. Teaching was regarded as a separate function, though those who took part in it do not seem as yet to have formed a separate class. See Acts xiii. 1; Rom. xii. 7; 1 Cor. xii. 28, 29; Eph. iv. 11; Jas. iii. 1 ("masters" should be rather "teachers"). The teacher was dependent on the alms of his scholars.

**Communicate . . . in all good things.**—Let him impart or share with his teacher in all those temporal goods with which God has blessed him. The teacher would not receive any settled and regular payment, but the scholar would make him presents—many of them, probably, in kind—so as to relieve him from the care of providing for his own livelihood, and so give him more leisure for his work of teaching.

(7) **Be not deceived; God is not mocked.**—It is all very well for you to make large professions to which you do not act up. These may deceive others, but do not let them deceive yourselves. Do not think that God will allow you thus to mock Him.

It might seem, perhaps, as if the language of this warning was almost too solemn for the occasion (an exhortation to liberality towards teachers), but the Apostle has in his mind the wider scope that he is going to give to his treatment of the subject. In this—and indeed in all this—"with what measure ye meet, it shall be measured to you again."

**Whatsoever a man soweth that shall he also reap.**—Compare especially 2 Cor. ix. 6: "This I say, He which soweth sparingly shall reap also sparingly; and he which soweth bountifully shall reap also bountifully," where the same metaphor is used in reference to the same thing—liberality in almsgiving.

(8) **He that soweth to his flesh.**—The seed sown is a man's actions here on earth. If the object of those actions is merely self-indulgence, they are, as it were, sown in a field the owner of which is the flesh (*i.e.*, the lower, carnal self). The flesh alone benefits by them, and for it alone are they garnered up.

**Shall of the flesh reap corruption.**—If such has been a man's conduct, he must look to the flesh for his reward, and all the reward it can give him will be a share in its own corruption. The flesh perishes, and so shall the fruit of his actions perish, and "leave not a wrack behind."

**He that soweth to the Spirit . . .**—On the other hand, where all the actions are like seed deposited in the field of which the owner and lord is the Spirit, that same Spirit will reward them in the world to come with the gift of everlasting life.

(9) **And.**—Rather, *But.* There is something of a stress on "well-doing," which continues the idea of "sowing to the Spirit" in the verse before: "But in well-doing, &c."

**Be weary.**—Rather, *let us not be faint-hearted; lose heart.*

(10) **As we have therefore opportunity.**—"Therefore" is emphatic, and should come first. It introduces a summary conclusion from the preceding argument. *Therefore* (or, *so then*), *as we have opportunity;* wherever an opportunity offers.

**Them who are of the household of faith.**—It would seem, on the whole, that this translation might stand. It is true that the Greek word, meaning originally a "member of a household," came to mean simply "acquainted with," or "belonging to," the idea of a "household" being dropped; still, in view more especially of Eph. ii. 19—"Fellow citizens with the saints, and of the household of God"—where there seems to be a play upon the words "city" and "house," it would appear as if it ought in the present phrase to be retained. The Church is represented as a household in 1 Tim. iii. 15; Heb. iii. 6; 1 Pet. ii. 5; iv. 17.

(11—18) Concluding section of the Epistle, written in the Apostle's own hand. These Judaising teachers only wish to have you circumcised as a matter of outside show, in order to disguise their own professed Christianity from their fellow Jews, and so escape persecution. They show that they really care nothing for circumcision, for they freely break the rest of the Law to which they affect to give in their adhesion. Their

you with mine own hand. (12) As many as desire to make a fair shew in the flesh, they constrain you to be circumcised; only lest they should suffer persecution for the cross of Christ.

Chap. vi. 11—18. Autograph conclusion.

Chap. vi. 12, 13. A repeated warning.

(13) For neither they themselves who are circumcised keep the law; but desire to have you circumcised, that they may glory in your flesh. (14) But God forbid that I should glory, save in the cross of our Lord Jesus Christ, by whom [1] the

Chap. vi. 14—16. The true gospel.

1 Or, *whereby*.

---

true object is to make capital out of their influence over you, to boast publicly of your submission to the rite. I, too, will boast, but of something very different. My boast is in the cross of Christ. When I attached myself to the crucified Messiah, from that moment the world became nothing to me. Circumcision and uncircumcision matter not. The essential point is that total change which such a relation implies. On all who take this for their rule I can invoke a blessing, for they are the true Israel. Enough. I have a right to claim exemption from these attacks. The scars that I bear upon me are marks of the place I hold in my Master's service.

(11) **Ye see.**—Rather, *See.* The Apostle calls the attention of his readers to the handwriting of these concluding paragraphs.

**How large a letter.**—Rather, *in what large letters: i.e.*, characters. The exact significance of these words is somewhat enigmatic, and can only be matter of conjecture. Two points, however, are clear:—(1) The latter part of the Greek phrase means "in" or "with" letters—*i.e.*, characters of hand-writing—and not "a letter," "an epistle," as it is taken in the Authorised version; (2) The former half of the phrase means "how large," strictly in respect of size. The Apostle, for some reason or other, points out that the characters in which he is writing are larger than usual. What is his reason? It is hard to say. Some have thought that the reference was to the "shapelessness" of the letters, whether as due to the fact that the Apostle himself was not accustomed to the manual work of writing, or possibly to physical weakness from the hardships that he had undergone. The idea of "shapelessness," however, is not necessarily included in that of size. It seems, on the whole, most probable that the size of the characters express the emphasis and authority with which the Apostle is writing. He adds to the Epistle—which had so far been written by an amanuensis—a few bold incisive strokes in his own hand, trenchantly exposing the motives of the Judaising faction, and re-asserting his own position.

**I have written.**—Must this be so taken: *I have written?* or may it be idiomatically translated: *I write?* In other words, does it refer to the whole previous portion of the Epistle, or only to these concluding paragraphs? The question turns upon a nice point of Greek scholarship, on which such authorities as Bishop Ellicott and Dr. Lightfoot take different sides. It will only be possible in a Commentary like this to express a general conclusion, without going into the arguments on which it is based. That conclusion would be that the Greek may, quite fairly and tenably, be translated: *I write;* and that being so, considerations of exegesis would seem to tell somewhat decidedly in the same direction. The whole character of this concluding section is very much what we should expect if St. Paul followed his usual custom of taking the pen from the amanuensis to write it, and its brief weighty summarising style would correspond well with the "large letters" in which he says that it was written. If this description is to be applied to the whole Epistle, it must remain a riddle to which there is no clue.

**With mine own hand.**—It was the Apostle's custom to make use of an amanuensis, and only to add a few final words in proof of the genuineness of the writing. (See especially 2 Thess. iii. 17; and comp. also Rom. xvi. 22; 1 Cor. xvi. 21; Col. iv. 18.)

(12) **To make a fair shew in the flesh.**—To obtain a reputation for religiousness in externals, like the hypocrites, who "love to pray standing in the synagogues and in the corners of the streets, that they may be seen of men" (Matt. vi. 5). The object of the Judaisers was by this means to keep in with their countrymen, the Jews, and even to gain favour amongst them by seeming to win over proselytes to the Mosaic law.

**Only lest they should suffer persecution for the cross of Christ.**—What aroused the antagonism of the Jews against the Christians was evidently not so much the confession of the Messiahship of Jesus as the declared abolition of the Law of Moses. By suppressing this side of Christian teaching, the Judaisers could easily obtain toleration for their other tenets. If, on the other hand, they were to emphasise it, the full weight of persecution would fall upon them—its ostensible ground being the doctrine of a crucified Messiah. Accordingly, they persuaded as many of the Galatians as they could to accept circumcision, and made the most of this propagandist zeal to their Jewish neighbours.

(13) Their insincerity is shown by the fact that they are not really careful to observe the Law. What they do is only to serve as a blind, that they may be able to point to your mutilated flesh as the visible sign of their success in gaining proselytes.

**They themselves who are circumcised.**—The expression in the Greek includes, not only those who were circumcised themselves, but also those who were for circumcising others.

**Glory in your flesh.**—Make a boast of getting this rite performed upon your bodies.

(14) **God forbid that I should glory.**—There is a stress upon the pronoun "I," which, in the Greek, stands first, in emphatic contrast to the party who had been the subjects of the last verse. They make their boast in a mere external; but for me—far be it from me to make my boast in anything but the cross of Christ.

**The cross of our Lord Jesus Christ**—*i.e.*, "in the death and passion which Christ underwent for me." The Apostle is aware that in this he is putting forward a startling paradox. The cross of Christ was "to the Jews a stumbling-block." They attached to it only ideas of ignominy and shame, and yet it is precisely this of which the Apostle is most proud. He is proud of it

world is crucified unto me, and I unto
the world. (15) For in Christ Jesus
neither circumcision availeth any thing,
nor uncircumcision, but a new creature.
(16) And as many as walk according to
this rule, peace *be* on them, and mercy,
and upon the Israel of God. (17) From
henceforth let no man trouble me:
for I bear in my body the
marks of the Lord Jesus.
(18) Brethren, the grace of
our Lord Jesus Christ *be* with your
spirit. Amen.

Chap. vi. 17. Christ's branding mark.

¶ Unto the Galatians written from Rome.

---

as the ground of his salvation, and therefore as the cardinal object of all his hopes and aims.

**By whom.**—It seems better, on the whole, to adopt the marginal rendering: *whereby.* The antecedent is thus not Christ, but more especially the *cross* of Christ. It is the intense contemplation of a *crucified* Saviour through which the Christian dies to the world.

**The world.**—By this is meant here the world of sense, the sphere of outward and sensible things, at once with its manifold temptations to sin and with its inadequate methods of escaping from them—mere external rites, such as circumcision.

(15) **In Christ Jesus.**—These words are omitted by the Vatican MS. and by the best editors. They would seem to have come in from the parallel passage in chap. v. 6.

**Neither circumcision . . .**—We have had almost the same words in chap. v. 6 and in 1 Cor. vii. 19. It is interesting to note the different ways in which the sentence is completed:—

Circumcision is nothing, and uncircumcision is nothing, but {
Faith which worketh by love (chap. v. 6).
A new creature (chap. vi. 15).
Keeping the commandments of God (1 Cor. vii. 19).
}

The first is an analytical statement of the process which takes place in the Christian; the second is the state resulting from that process; the last is the visible sign and expression of the presence of that state.

**A new creature.**—The Greek may mean either the "act of new creation" or the "person newly created." The Authorised version apparently takes it in the latter sense, which perhaps is to be preferred.

(16) **According to this rule.**—The word for "rule" is the same that afterwards received a special application in the phrase, "Canon of Scripture." It meant originally a carpenter's rule, or the line that a carpenter works by—hence, a rule or standard; and, from that, the list of books coming up to a certain standard—not (as might be thought) which themselves supplied a standard.

The Apostle confines his benediction to those who hold the fundamental truths of Christianity—*i.e.*, here more especially, the doctrine of justification by faith and the spiritual view of Christianity connected with it, as opposed to the merely external and mechanical system of the Judaisers.

**And upon the Israel of God.**—The benediction is addressed, not to two distinct sets of persons ("those who walk by this rule" *and* "the Israel of God"), but to the same set of persons described in different ways. "And" is therefore equivalent to "namely:" *Yea, upon the Israel of God.* By the "Israel of God" is here meant the "spiritual Israel;" not converts from Judaism alone, but all who prove their real affinity to Abraham by a faith like Abraham's. (Comp. chap. iii. 7—9, 14, 29; Rom. iv. 11, 12; ix. 6—8.)

(17) The Apostle has done. He will not dally with these vexatious attacks upon himself and his authority any more. He dismisses them with an appeal which ought to be final. He points to the scars of wounds which he had received in his Master's service. The branding-irons of Christ, he says, have imprinted these upon me. They show that I, like the slaves of a heathen temple, am devoted and consecrated to His service. They are my credentials, and I shall produce no others. My assailants must leave me in peace.

**The marks.**—The *stigmata,* or marks inflicted with branding-irons, such as those which show that a slave is attached to a particular temple or to the service of some particular deity. Branding was applied in some other cases, but especially to temple slaves. Those with which the Galatians were most familiar would be engaged in the worship of Cybele.

There does not seem to be evidence to connect this passage directly with the incident of the "stigmata" in the life of St. Francis of Assisi, but it would seem very probable that the use of the word, which was left untranslated in the Latin versions, suggested, whether by a more or by a less distant association, the idea which took so strong a hold upon his mind that in a moment of extreme spiritual tension the actual marks of the Passion seemed to imprint themselves upon his body.

**Of the Lord Jesus.**—The true text is simply, "of Jesus."

(18) **With your spirit.**—The grace of God works especially on the "spirit," or highest part, of man.

[The subscription, as it stands in our Bibles, appears for the first time in MSS. dating from about the beginning of the ninth century, though before this the Epistle had been described as written from Rome by Theodoret, Euthalius, and Jerome. We have seen that the choice really lies between Ephesus and Macedonia, or Corinth, and that the probability seems to be somewhat in favour of the latter.]

# EXCURSUS ON NOTES TO GALATIANS

## EXCURSUS A: ON THE VISITS OF ST. PAUL TO JERUSALEM.

THE parallel accounts of the intercourse of St. Paul with the Church at Jerusalem, given in this Epistle and in the Acts of the Apostles, have been a double source of difficulty. To writers who have accepted the general truthfulness of both narratives, they have seemed hard to harmonise and arrange in due chronological sequence; and, on the other hand, to those who were already prepared to cast a doubt upon the veracity of the historical work, the autobiographical notices in the Epistle have furnished a means of attack of which they have very unsparingly availed themselves.

The critic who wishes to look at things as they really are, without prejudice and without captiousness, will certainly confess that all is not perfectly smooth or plain, and that the two narratives do not fit into each other at once with exact precision; but he will none the less vehemently repudiate the exaggerated conclusions which have been drawn from the differences which exist—conclusions which, while professing to be based upon the application to the Bible of the same principles that would be made use of in judging any other book, are such as in fact are totally inapplicable both to books and to real life. It is not too much to say that, if the principles carried out, *e.g.*, by F. C. Baur in his famous criticism of these narratives were applied with equal thoroughness elsewhere, history would not exist, or would simply become a field for the exercise of the imagination, and common affairs would be reduced to a dead-lock of universal scepticism. The standard by which these writers have judged of what is historical and what is not, is a standard which exists only in the pedantry of the study or the lecture-room, and which is least of all applicable here, where our ignorance of all the surrounding circumstances is so large, and the whole body of direct evidence so very small.

We shall proceed to place the two narratives side by side, pointing out as well as we can what are the real and what are only apparent differences between them. At the same time it must be fully acknowledged that, however sincere the motives with which any particular statement of the case is made, there will still be a certain room for honest diversity of opinion. One mind will lean to a greater and another to a less amount of stringency, though it is hard to believe that any properly-trained and soundly-balanced judgment will fall into the extravagances to which the criticism of this unfortunate chapter of history has been subject.

In estimating the apparent divergencies of the two writers, the position and object of each should be borne in mind. St. Paul is writing with the most intimate acquaintance with the inner course of events, but at the same time with a definite and limited object in view—to vindicate his own independence. He is writing under the pressure of controversy which served sharply to accentuate the points of difference between himself and all who were in any way mixed up with the Judaising party. On the other hand, St. Luke was writing at a greater distance of time, from information which in this part of his narrative he was obliged to take at second-hand, and that from persons who were themselves only acquainted with so much of the events as had passed in public. He may have had a wish not to give too much relief to the oppositions which still threatened the peace of the Church, but there is nothing to show that this went so far as to distort his representation of the facts.

We shall assume the view which is current amongst a large majority of the best and most trustworthy critics as to the order of the visits, and we shall confine ourselves to considering the relation between the two narratives.

The first visit, then, with which we have to deal will be that recorded in Acts ix. 26—30, Gal. i. 18—24, which we place in parallel columns.

| ACTS ix. 26—30. | GAL. i. 18—24. |
|---|---|
| When Saul was come to Jerusalem, he assayed to join himself to the disciples: but they were all afraid of him, and believed not that he was a disciple. But Barnabas took him, and brought *him* to the apostles, and declared unto them how he had seen the Lord in the way, and that he had spoken to him, and how he had preached boldly at Damascus in the name of Jesus. And he was with them coming in and going out at Jerusalem. And he spake boldly in the name of the Lord Jesus, and disputed against the Grecians [*Hellenists, or Greek-speaking Jews*]: but they went about to slay him. *Which* when the brethren knew, they brought him down to Cæsarea, and sent him forth to Tarsus. | Then after three years I went up to Jerusalem to see Peter [*Cephas*], and abode with him fifteen days. But other of the apostles saw I none, save James the Lord's brother. Now the things which I write unto you, behold, before God, I lie not. Afterwards I came into the regions of Syria and Cilicia; and was unknown by face unto the churches of Judæa which were in Christ: but they had heard only, That he which persecuted us in times past now preacheth the faith which once he destroyed. And they glorified God in me. |

The narratives here do not really clash, though they are presented from different sides. St. Paul says nothing about his introduction to the Church at Jerusalem by Barnabas, because that had no bearing upon his argument; neither does he speak of his public preaching at Jerusalem, for that, too, was not to the point. There would be ample time for this preaching during the fifteen days that he was residing in the house of St. Peter; and as he would be seen coming in and going out of this house—sometimes, no doubt, in company with St. Peter, and once or twice, perhaps, also in company with St. James—it would be very natural that St. Luke's informants and St. Luke, wishing to show how entirely the former persecutor was now reconciled to the Church, should speak of him as "coming in and going out" with the Apostles. St. Paul himself hints at the impression which this great change made upon the churches of Judæa collectively, though he was brought directly in contact only with the Church at Jerusalem. There is nothing to surprise us in the fact that St. Paul saw only two of the Apostles: the rest may have been absent upon some mission, or there may have been other causes, about which it would be vain to speculate. It would, perhaps, be possible to derive from St. Luke's narrative an exaggerated idea of the extent to which the Apostle preached in public; but there, too, it is to be noticed that the preaching is described as confined to a particular, not very large, section of the Jewish community; and St. Luke relates nothing that would carry him beyond the walls of Jerusalem. The question whether St. Paul went direct from Cæsarea to Tarsus, or landed upon the coast of Syria on the way, will be found discussed in the Notes to Gal. i. 21.

The second visit to Jerusalem is mentioned only in the Acts. After recounting the success of the Apostle's preaching at Antioch, and the great famine of the reign of Claudius, the historian proceeds to give an account of the collection that was made for the suffering churches of Judæa.

| Acts xi. 29, 30; xii. 25. | |
|---|---|
| Then the disciples, every man according to his ability, determined to send relief unto the brethren which dwelt in Judæa: which also they did, and sent it to the elders by the hands of Barnabas and Saul. [*Here follows an account of the imprisonment and deliverance of St. Peter, and of the death of Herod.*] And Barnabas and Saul returned from Jerusalem, when they had fulfilled *their* ministry, and took with them John, whose surname was Mark. | |

The only question that occurs to us here is, Why is this visit omitted by St. Paul? Nor is the answer far to seek. If St. Paul had been giving a professed list of his visits to Jerusalem, it might have seemed strange. But he is not giving such a list. His object is to explain the extent of his communications with the elder Apostles. But on this occasion there is every reason to think that he had no such communication. From the order of the narrative in the Acts we should infer that St. Paul arrived at Jerusalem during the confusion which was caused by Herod's persecution. St. Peter was in prison; the Elder James had just been slain; James, the Lord's brother was in hiding (Acts xii. 17). No sooner was St. Peter delivered than he too went into hiding again (Acts xii. 17—19). In the Church assembled at the house of Mary, none of the prominent members seem to have been present. And that Paul and Barnabas came to this house, we have an incidental proof in the fact that they took back with them John Mark, the son of the lady to whom it belonged. We should gather from the Acts that all they did was simply to fulfil their commission, by depositing the sums of which they were the bearers, in trustworthy hands, and return. But if so, there was no reason why St. Paul should allude to this visit in his argument with the Galatians. It had taken place nearly fourteen years before the date at which he was writing; and though it is not necessary to suppose that he had exactly forgotten it, still there was nothing to recall it to him, and it was not present to his mind. This is quite sufficient to explain the expression with which he introduces his account of his next, really his *third*, visit. He does not use a precise expression, "I went up *a second time,*" but simply, "I went up *again.*"

This third visit is the most important. That both accounts relate to the same visit cannot be doubted, though there is, at the first blush, a considerable difference between them.

| Acts xv. 1—31. | Gal. ii. 1—11. |
|---|---|
| And certain men which came down from Judæa taught the brethren, *and said,* Except ye be circumcised after the manner of Moses, ye cannot be saved. When therefore Paul and Barnabas had no small dissension and disputation with them, they determined that Paul and Barnabas, and certain other of them, should go up to Jerusalem unto the apostles and elders about this question . . . And when they were come to Jerusalem, they were received of the church, and *of* the apostles and elders, and they declared all things that God had done with them. But there rose up certain of the sect of the Pharisees which believed, saying, That it was needful to circumcise them, and to command *them* to keep the law of Moses. And the apostles and elders came together for to consider of this matter. And when there had been much disputing, Peter rose up, and said unto them, Men *and* brethren, ye know how that a good while ago God made choice among us, that the Gentiles by my mouth should hear the word of the gospel, and believe . . . Now therefore why tempt ye God, to put a yoke upon the neck of the disciples, which neither | Then fourteen years after I went up again to Jerusalem with Barnabas, and took Titus with *me* also. And I went up by revelation, and communicated unto them that gospel which I preach among the Gentiles, but privately to them which were of reputation, lest by any means I should run, or had run, in vain. But neither Titus, who was with me, being a Greek, was compelled to be circumcised: and that because of false brethren unawares brought in, who came in privily to spy out our liberty which we have in Christ Jesus, that they might bring us into bondage: to whom we gave place by subjection, no, not for an hour; that the truth of the gospel might continue with you. But of these who seemed to be somewhat, (whatsoever they were, it maketh no matter to me: God accepteth no man's person:) for they who seemed *to be somewhat* in conference added nothing to me: but contrariwise, when they saw that the gospel of the uncircumcision was committed unto me, as *the gospel* of the circumcision *was* unto Peter; (for he that wrought effectually in Peter to the apostleship of the circumcision, the same was mighty in me toward the Gentiles:) |

our fathers nor we were able to bear? But we believe that through the grace of the Lord Jesus Christ we shall be saved, even as they. Then all the multitude kept silence, and gave audience to Barnabas and Paul, declaring what miracles and wonders God had wrought among the Gentiles by them. And after they had held their peace, James answered, saying, Men *and* brethren, hearken unto me: Simeon hath declared how God at the first did visit the Gentiles, to take out of them a people for his name. And to this agree the words of the prophets; . . . Wherefore my sentence is, that we trouble not them, which from among the Gentiles are turned to God: but that we write unto them, that they abstain from pollutions of idols, and *from* fornication, and *from* things strangled, and *from* blood.

[*To the same effect the letter is written, and sent by the hands of Judas Barsabas, and Silas, who returned to Antioch with Paul and Barnabas, as a delegation from the Church of Jerusalem.*]

and when James, Cephas, and John, who seemed to be pillars, perceived the grace that was given unto me, they gave to me and Barnabas the right hands of fellowship; that we *should go* unto the heathen, and they unto the circumcision. Only *they would* that we should remember the poor; the same which I also was forward to do. But when Peter [*Cephas*] was come to Antioch, I withstood him to the face, because he was to be blamed, &c.

In one respect the narrative of St. Paul is strikingly supplemented by that of St. Luke. It tells us who were the "false brethren unawares brought in." They were "certain of the sect of Pharisees which believed," *i.e.*, Pharisees who called themselves Christians, though without forsaking their peculiar tenets, and wishing to impose them upon the Church. The true opposition to St. Paul came from these. Both in the Epistle and in the work of the historian it is they who are put forward prominently. And it is a gross exaggeration, nay, a distortion of the facts, to represent the opposition as proceeding from the Judæan Apostles. These appear rather as mediators, standing by birth and antecedents upon the one side, but yielding to the reasonableness of the case so far as to make large concessions upon the other.

It is noticeable, too, as another minute coincidence between the two accounts, that in both stress is laid upon the *success* of the Gentile Apostle's preaching as a proof that he enjoyed the divine favour. In the Acts Paul and Barnabas defend themselves by "declaring what miracles and wonders God had wrought among the Gentiles by them;" and in the Galatians the Judæan Apostles are described as giving to St. Paul and Barnabas the right hands of fellowship because they "perceived the grace given to him," and because they saw that the same Power who enabled Peter to preach to the Jews "was mighty in him toward the Gentiles."

These two quite "undesigned" coincidences are a strong confirmation of the narratives in which they are found. But the differences must also be noticed. (1) In the Epistle St. Paul speaks of himself as going up "by revelation"—*i.e.*, in accordance with some private intimation of the divine will. In the Acts it is determined for him that he should go as the deputy of the Church at Antioch. But the two things do not exclude each other: they rather represent the different aspects of the same event as it would appear when looked at from without and when looked at from within. A precisely similar difference may be observed in Acts ix. 29, 30, compared with Acts xxii. 17 *et seq.* In the one passage *the disciples* are said to have "brought down" St. Paul to Cæsarea, for fear the Jews should slay him. In the other passage St. Paul himself, relating the same incident, says that, while praying in the Temple, he "fell into a trance," and heard a voice bidding him "make haste and get quickly out of Jerusalem," because his testimony would not be received. In like manner a double cause—the prompting of the Holy Spirit and the act of the Church at Antioch—is assigned to the same event in Acts xiii. 2—4. Discrepancies like these in two independent narratives are common and natural enough. (2) Nothing is said about the incident of Titus in the Acts. But Titus is included amongst the "others" of Acts xv. 2 ("Paul and Barnabas and certain other of them"); and the incident is sufficiently pointed to in verse 5, where the Pharisaic converts insist on the circumcision of the Gentile converts. Nor if it had been entirely omitted need this cause any surprise. St. Luke knew only so much of what happened at the Council as his informants themselves knew or were able to tell him. (3) In the Acts we have described to us a great public meeting: the Epistle seems to speak rather of private conferences. But a public meeting on a matter of this kind, so far from excluding would naturally pre-suppose private conferences. We have recently had a conspicuous instance of this in the conduct so discreetly pursued at the Congress which resulted in the Treaty of Berlin. And a public meeting is both indicated by the Greek of the phrase "communicated unto them" (Gal. ii. 2; see the Commentary *ad loc.*), and falls in naturally with the account of the dismissal of the two Apostles in verse 9. So far the differences are of no importance, and are perfectly compatible with the complete truth of both accounts; but the one that remains is rather more substantial. (4) St. Paul makes no mention of the so-called "apostolic decree." The exhortation to "remember the poor" is all that he retains of the letter enjoining the Gentile Christians to "abstain from meats offered to idols, and from things strangled, and from fornication." Nor is the decree appealed to —as it might have been here to the Galatians—as a proof that circumcision was not held to be obligatory even by the mother Church; while some of these provisions—*e.g.*, the abstinence from meat offered to idols —are left entirely unnoticed in the discussion of the subject in the Epistles to the Corinthians and Romans. A partial answer to the questions raised by this remarkable silence may be found in the fact that the letter was addressed, in the first instance, to the churches of a particular district—Antioch, Syria, and Cilicia—which was in comparatively close communion with Judæa. It would not follow that the decree would be binding on other Gentile churches. A partial answer, again, is supplied by the Apostle's natural independence of character. The argument from authority is the last that he would use; and if he had been more inclined to use it, the authority of the Church of Jerusalem was too often set in opposition to his own for it to be safe for him to have recourse to it as if to a higher court of appeal. These considerations may go some way, and yet we feel that the answer is still incomplete. If we knew the whole circumstances, there would probably be something more to be said. We do not know them, and therefore we must be content to remain in ignorance. But to take this ignorance as a ground for discrediting the history of the Acts is wanton in the extreme, and wholly unwarranted by anything that we see in the events that pass under our eyes or in the general relation of testimony to fact. Discrepancies greater than any that appear here may be observed in the accounts of events separated from their record by but a small interval of time, and attested by numerous witnesses: how much more, then, are they to be expected where two writers are looking back, one at a distance of seven or eight, the other, perhaps, of thirty years; where the one is writing a continuous history, and the other an apology for himself against a special and definite charge; and where they, and they two alone, supply all the information we possess as to the event itself, while all around it is little more than darkness visible!

So shallow and so slight is the foundation on which has been built that house of cards which forms one of the most imposing structures of modern negative criticism! To say that it has collapsed already would not be true, as men of learning and ability are still found to support it; but to say that it is doomed to collapse would be a prophecy based upon all the laws which distinguish between what is solid and permanent and what is fictitious and unreal.

## EXCURSUS B: ON THE PASSAGE (chap. iv. 25), "FOR THIS AGAR IS MOUNT SINAI IN ARABIA."

The words "For this Agar is Mount Sinai in Arabia" present difficulties which seem to need a somewhat longer and more technical discussion than could properly be given to them in the body of the Commentary, and it has seemed the more desirable to devote to them a short *excursus*, as the view taken is one that, in this instance, diverges from that adopted by more than one of the best authorities, and conspicuously by Dr. Lightfoot.

The first question is one of reading. The words appear in no less than four different forms. Two of these, however, may be set aside at once. For the two that remain the authorities are nearly equally balanced. The simple reading "For Sinai is a mountain in Arabia" has in its favour the Sinaitic MS.; the Codex Ephraem; the Codex Augiensis, in the library of Trinity College, Cambridge; and another Dresden MS., which usually agrees with it, and seems to have been derived from the same copy; a good—perhaps the best—cursive; quotations in Origen and Epiphanius; and the Latin authorities generally. The other reading, "Now this Agar is Mount Sinai in Arabia," is supported by the Vatican, Alexandrine, and Claromontane MSS., and by a fourth MS., now at Paris, which bears to the Claromontane a somewhat similar relation to that which the Dresden Codex bears to the Augiensis; a good cursive (somewhat inferior to that on the other side); and the Memphitic version. Balancing these authorities, the preponderance would seem—if we may venture to say so, where Dr. Lightfoot thinks differently—to be with the longer reading last mentioned. It is true that the list on the other side is more copious, and represents a wider diffusion of text; but, taking the two groups together, we believe that the second represents the older and purer form of text, and that its readings will be verified in the greater number of instances. It is indeed just that very group, headed by the Codex Sinaiticus, which comes in to mark the first stage of corruption—one of the very first and earliest forms of corruption, it is true, and one that is most nearly allied to the true text, but still a corruption and deviation from the original.

But if the external evidence bears in this direction, internal evidence would seem to confirm it. No doubt internal evidence is a treacherous and double-edged weapon, and it is very often as easy to turn it to one side as to the other. It has been quoted here in support of the shorter reading, and something, perhaps, is to be said for that view. Still, the simpler and more obvious considerations (which should be chiefly looked to) seem to tell rather decidedly the other way. The longer reading is much the more difficult; but it is one of the chief canons of internal evidence that the more difficult reading is to be preferred. It is also easy to see in the form of the Greek phrase what would induce an ignorant scribe to change, and by changing to simplify it. Or even failing this, there is never anything very forced in the hypothesis of an omission which is always one of the most natural of accidents.

The reading of the Received text (with the slight change of "now" instead of "for") would seem, then, upon the whole, to be the more probable; and the next question would be, Assuming this reading, what sense is to be placed upon it? There is an Arabic word corresponding very nearly (though not quite) in sound to "Hagar," with the meaning "stone." Hence Chrysostom, in his exposition of this Epistle, assumes that St. Paul is playing upon this similarity of sound. He says that Sinai "is so called (or *translated*) in the native tongue" of the Arabs, and he speaks of the mountain as "bearing the same name with the bondmaid." This statement of Chrysostom does not appear to have received much independent corroboration, though one traveller (Harant), in the sixteenth century, makes the same assertion. Still, even if Sinai were *not* called in a special sense "*the* stone" or "rock," the identity of the Arabic word for "rock" *might possibly* have suggested to St. Paul a play on words so very much in his style. "The very word Hagar," we may imagine him arguing, "itself the name for 'rock,' suggests the propriety of the analogy which I am applying. It points to the parallel between the stern and relentless legislation of Sinai and the history of Hagar the bondwoman and her son, who persecuted the child of promise." The literary methods of the present day are different, and such an explanation will seem far-fetched. It may be thought a conclusive argument against it that, whether St. Paul himself knew the Arabic signification of "Hagar" or not, he could not expect a Celtic people like the Galatians to know it. But even this argument is less conclusive when applied to one who is so fond of following the course of his own thought as St. Paul. And yet it must be admitted that there are too many elements of uncertainty for the explanation to be pressed at all strongly: it must remain a possibility—not more. On the other hand, even if it should break down, it would not necessarily follow that the reading would have to be abandoned—it would only lose something of its point. We should then have simply an assertion where otherwise there would be also an argument. "This Hagar—the Hagar of which I am speaking—stands for Mount Sinai which is in Arabia, the country of Hagar. The scene of the Mosaic legislation was part of the domains of the Ishmaelites, the children of Hagar, so that the two may very well be compared." This interpretation has the authority of Theodore of Mopsuestia and Theodoret, and it is, perhaps, the safest to fall back upon. At the same time there may be something of the additional point which Chrysostom and those who have followed him in modern times have supposed.